THIRTY YEARS' WAR

Treaty of Augsburg

Spanish Armada defeated

Grotius publishes first book on international law

Treaty of Westphalia

| 1555 | 1588 | 1618 | 1625 | 1648 | 1651 | 1661 |

Tokugawa Era of premodern Japan begins

Manchu dynasty founded in China

Hobbes publishes *Leviathan*

Louis XIV begins to govern

Marx's *Communist Manifesto*

Great Britain acquires Hong Kong

Most of Latin America independent

Napoleon defeated

Napoleon emperor

World population 1 billion

French Revolution

American Revolution

Rousseau's *Social Contract*

| 1848 | 1842 | 1824 | 1815 | 1804 | 1800 | 1789 | 1776 | 1762 |

Era of modern European imperialism in Africa and Asia begins

Shaka establishes modern Zulu nation in southern Africa

Popular nationalism begins/Divine Right challenged

BIPOLAR ERA

U.S.–USSR Peaceful Coexistence

India and Pakistan independent

Cold War

Containment

Israel independent

NATO established

Chinese Communists take power

Vietnam independent and split into North and South

Ghana independent

European Common Market formed

World population 3 billion

| 1947 | 1948 | 1949 | 1953 | 1954 | 1957 | 1958 | 1960 | 1961 | 1962 |

Stalin dies

Beginning of African independence

Bay of Pigs

Cuban Missile Crisis

BIPOLAR SYSTEM DECLINES

Berlin Wall opened

Gorbachev in power

Reagan in power

Soviets invade Afghanistan

Mao dies

U.S. out of Vietnam

South Vietnam falls to North

New international economic order proposed

SALT I

Nixon visits China

First man on the Moon

U.S. enters war in Vietnam

| 1989 | 1987 | 1985 | 1981 | 1979 | 1976 | 1975 | 1974 | 1972 | 1969 | 1964 |

Tiananmen Square massacre

World population 5 billion

Soviet reforms begin

Chinese reforms begin

First personal minicomputer (Altier 8800) advertised

World population 4 billion

For Michael and Michelle Rourke

He is the half part of a blessed man,
Left to be finished by such as she,
And she a fair divided excellence,
Whose fullness of perfection lies in him.

Shakespeare, King John

J ohn T. Rourke, Ph.D., is a professor and head of the Department of Political Science at The University of Connecticut. He is a coauthor with Mark A. Boyer of *World Politics: International Politics on the World Stage, Brief,* Third Edition (McGraw-Hill/Dushkin, 2000); the author of *Presidential Wars and American Democracy: Rally 'Round the Chief* (Paragon House, 1993); a coauthor of *Direct Democracy and International Politics: Deciding International Issues through Referendums* (Lynne Rienner, 1992); the editor of *Taking Sides: Clashing Views on Controversial Issues in American Foreign Policy* (McGraw-Hill/Dushkin, 2000) and *Taking Sides: Clashing Views on Controversial Issues in World Politics,* Ninth Edition (McGraw-Hill/Dushkin, 2000), the author of *Making Foreign Policy: United States, Soviet Union, China* (Brooks/Cole, 1990), *Congress and the Presidency in U.S. Foreign Policymaking* (Westview, 1985), and numerous articles and papers. He enjoys teaching introductory classes, and he does so each semester at the university's Storrs and Hartford campuses. His regard for the students has molded his approach of conveying scholarship in a language and within a frame of reference that undergraduates can appreciate. Rourke believes, as the theme of this book reflects, that politics affect us all, and we can affect politics. Rourke practices what he propounds; he is involved in the university's internship program, advises one of its political clubs, has served as a staff member of Connecticut's legislature, and has been involved in political campaigns on the local, state, and national levels.

International Politics on the World Stage

Eighth Edition

John T. Rourke
University of Connecticut

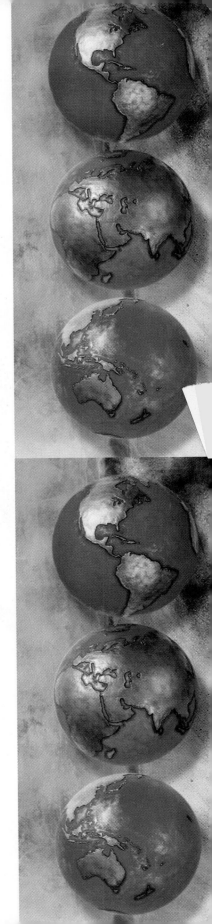

McGraw-Hill/Dushkin

A Division of The McGraw-Hill Companies

Book Team
Vice President and Publisher   *Jeffrey L. Hahn*
List Manager   *Theodore Knight*
Developmental Editor   *Ava Suntoke*
Director of Production   *Brenda S. Filley*
Director of Technology   *Jonathan Stowe*
Art Editor   *Pamela Carley*
Designer   *Charles Vitelli*
Typesetting Supervisor   *Juliana Arbo*
Typesetting   *Marie Lazauskas*
Proofreaders   *Robin N. Charney, Diane Barker*
Graphics   *Laura Levine, Tom Goddard, Eldis N. Lima, Michael Campbell*
Permissions Editor   *Rose Gleich*

McGraw-Hill/Dushkin

A Division of The **McGraw-Hill** Companies

Cover © 2000 TSM/Jean-Luc De Zorzi
Cover Design *Lara Johnson*

The credit section for this book begins on page 613 and is considered an extension of the copyright page.

Library of Congress Catalog Card Number 136005

ISBN 0-07-242836-8

Printed in the United States of America
10 9 8 7 6 5 4 3 2

http://www.mhhe.com/

PREFACE

This Edition: Changes and Organization   As a result of this text's view that our lives are inescapably affected by world politics, *International Politics on the World Stage*, Eighth Edition, stresses the impact that world events and international interdependence have on your students' lives. In addition to highlighting the effect that the world has on them, this approach points out to students the connection between the events of current history and the theories of international politics that have been conceived and refined by political scientists.

Each time I revise this text I think to myself, "The world will settle down and the next edition will be easier." Wrong! This edition proved to be a major challenge and effort. You will see that there is a continued emphasis on being current in order to engage the students without being journalistic. The end of the Yeltsin years and the beginning of the Putin presidency in Russia; the rejection of the Comprehensive Test Ban Treaty by the U.S. Senate; the advent of the euro as the currency of the European Union; the failure at the second Camp David meeting on the Middle East to repeat the success of the first meeting in 1979; the violence in Sierra Leone and East Timor; and other recent events are all extensively detailed. It is also important to be as current as possible with the massive amount of changing data that details economic performance and capacity, weapons levels and transfers, and other statistical aspects of world politics. I have used original sources for my data when possible so that students will have the most recent information available.

The organizational scheme reflecting this text's view that the world is at a juncture brings to mind Robert Frost's poem, "Two Roads Diverged in a Wood." One road is the traditional way of sovereign states pursuing their self-interests in an often inequitable and conflict-filled world. The alternative, less-traveled-by path is the way of cooperation in a system in which states are less sovereign and international organizations play a wider and more authoritative role.

The text begins with an introduction to the importance of world politics to students and to the methods, theories, and purposes of political science (chapter 1), the evolution of and current instability in the world political system (chapter 2), and the three levels of analysis that need to be studied simultaneously—the system, state, and individual levels (chapters 3, 4, and 5). Then, beginning with chapter 6, the two roads theme organizes the remaining chapters of this edition, with usually alternating discussions of national conflict and international cooperation in successive chapters. In this way, equal attention can be given to the two roads without losing sight of the fact that they lead in divergent directions.

The substantial changes in this edition make it reflect more accurately the changing nature of world politics. The more I study the subject, the more I am impressed with the idea that the world is a primitive political society. As such, it is a political system that is marked by little organization, frequent violence, and a limited sense of global responsibility. It is a world of conflict. But there is also a world of cooperation, a countertheme, based on a still-limited desire among states and their people to work together globally as they begin to realize that their fates are inextricably entwined with one another and with the political, economic, social, and environmental future of our planet.

Data and Graphics   Many new tables, figures, photographs, maps, and other graphics have been added, for the first time in full color, to emphasize, expand, and give visual life to ideas. Full-color maps with geographical, historical, and statistical information, which students should find especially relevant to the text's discussion, are placed throughout the text. Also, significant revisions have been made to both the instructor's manual and to the extensive testbank, which are available from the publisher in both printed and computerized versions. These are further explained in the paragraph on Supplements on the next page.

Research, Citations, Bibliography, and Suggested Readings   One of the aims of this text is to bring together a representative sampling of the latest research in international relations. Scholarly articles, so often ignored in survey texts, are particularly emphasized. This research is documented by extensive references using the "in-text" style and by a significant bibliography. In addition to recognizing my intellectual debt to a host of scholars, the references and bibliography also serve as a reading list for students, as explained to them in the "To the Students" section of this preface. As such, references are often meant to serve as suggestions for further reading and do not necessarily mean that the cited author(s) propounded what is being said at the point of reference. Using this approach instead of the end-of-chapter placement gives inquisitive students immediate thoughts for additional reading.

For those instructors whose organization differs from mine, care has been given to the table of contents and to the index in order to facilitate integrating the text with your syllabus. You will find, for example, that:

> **Economics** is discussed in chapter 1 (how it affects students), 9 (as a basis of power), 14 (general global conditions), 15 (national economic competition), 16 (international economic cooperation), and 18 (sustainable development). **Arms and force** are addressed in all or in parts of chapters 1, 12, and 13. **Moral and humanitarian issues** are taken up extensively in chapters 11 and 17 and also form an important part of the discussions of national interest, coercion, and economic challenges in, respectively, chapters 6, 12, and 16 and 17.

The organization of the text flows from this conception of the world as a primitive, but developing, political system. The text not only analyzes world division and conflict but also focuses on cooperation both as a goal and in practice.

The Parts   Part I, which includes chapters 1 through 5, discusses how to study international politics. Students will read in chapter 1 that there are realists and idealists and will, I hope, be prompted to think about where they, their professors, and others with whom they may discuss politics stand on the realist-idealist scale. Although I began as a realist, I find myself less sure of my own wisdom on this point as time goes by. In fact, I have become convinced that substantial changes have to be made in the way international politics is conducted. Perhaps "realism with a nagging idealist conscience" would be an apt description of this text's orientation.

Part I also addresses levels of analysis. As students will soon discover, academics disagree about the proper focus of study. Three levels (system, state, and individual) are presented here. The text primarily utilizes state-level analysis (how countries make foreign policy) as discussed in chapter 4, but, here again, my views have evolved and changed since the first edition. The more I learn, the more I have become impressed with the role of system-level analysis (how the nature of the world system influences politics); there are two full chapters on this subject. Chapter 2 outlines the evolution of the world political system, and chapter 3 discusses system-level theory. Both of these chapters pay particular attention to the profound system change that is now occurring. Since it is unwise to ignore the human factor in international politics, that level is explored in chapter 5.

Part II, which includes chapters 6 and 7, deals with two divergent political orientations. The traditional orientation is nationalism. The alternative orientation is made up of transnational ideas, identifications, and processes.

Part III, consisting of chapters 8 and 9, examines the alternative ways that the world can be organized politically. In this part, I alternate between national and international approaches, with discussions of the state in chapter 8 and international organizations in chapter 9.

Part IV, which includes chapters 10 and 11, explores divergent approaches to the conduct of world politics. Chapter 10 covers the traditional approach, national diplomacy; chapter 11 examines the alternative road of international law and morality.

Part V, consisting of chapters 12 and 13, introduces two approaches to physical security in the world political system: national security (chapter 12) and international security and other alternative approaches (chapter 13).

Part VI, chapters 14 through 16, describes in detail global economic conditions and trends (chapter 14), then turns to a chapter on national economic competition (chapter 15) and contrasts that with international economic cooperation (chapter 16).

Part VII looks into current conditions and ways to preserve and enhance human rights and dignity (chapter 17) and the environment (chapter 18).

Supplements   There are several supplements that have been created to assist both instructors and students in the use of this text. The instructor's manual *Teaching and Testing from International Politics on the World Stage* outlines and discusses the text's objectives, contains several analytical exercises, and gives several other teaching supports, in addition to providing approximately 1,800 multiple-choice and essay questions organized by chapter and degree of difficulty. These examination questions are also available on MicroTest III computer disk. The text Web site may be found at www.dushkin.com/rourke/. It features additional study and assessment tools, some of which are interactive, to enhance the classroom and learning experience of students. The Web site also provides links to other sources. PowerPoint slides for each chapter are available and offer the instructor an easy-to-use and effective visual aid in the classroom.

PowerWeb This is a new online feature. It offers online current course-specific articles by leading authorities in the field, daily news updates, weekly updates by content experts, interactive exercises, research links, and student study tips. The package is available free to students with a new copy of the text, at http://www.dushkin.com/rourke.

TO THE STUDENT

The world, familiar to us and unknown.

Shakespeare, *Henry V*

The world is changing at breathtaking speed! That reality is one of the most important things for you to understand about international politics. Yet I have found that most undergraduate students, having been born into this era of warp-speed change, consider it normal. It is not. Recorded history dates back over 30 centuries. A great deal of what we will discuss in this text has happened in the last century, even within your lifetime. But truly understanding this rate of change—maybe *feeling* the rate of change is a better way to put it—is hard without perspective.

As a way of trying to convey the dramatic pace of change, I will introduce you to Mohammed El-Wasimy of Egypt and Elizabeth "Ma Pampo" Israel of Dominica. These amazing individuals are thought to have been born in 1875, have lived in three different centuries, and turned 125 during the first year of the new millennium. Among other things, they give us a sense of how quickly the world is changing.

When they were born, Ulysses Grant was president of the United States. Queen Victoria ruled the British Empire, which included both Egypt and Dominica. There was an emperor in China, an Ottoman Empire ruled by a sultan, a czar in Russia, a kaiser in Germany, and an emperor in Austria-Hungary who ruled much of Central Europe. Most of Africa and Asia were still colonies of European powers. There were less than 1.5 billion people in the world; only birds (and insects and bats) could use wings to fly, and the world's most ferocious weapons were the Gatling gun and the fairly short-range artillery piece.

The communist revolution in Russia occurred when the two modern Methuselahs were 44; the Soviet Union disappeared when they were 116. For me, communism and the cold war were the totality of my historical experience; for Mohammed El-Wasimy and Ma Pampo Israel they were mere interludes.

If you think about events, trends, and technology in this way—in terms of what one person has seen and experienced—you can begin to grasp how fast they are moving. When the two centenarians were born, people were basically earthbound. El-Wasimy and Israel were 28 when the first airplane flew, 69 when the first jet plane took off, 89 when Soviet cosmonaut Yuri Gagarin became the first human in space, and 94 when Neil Armstrong stepped onto the Moon's surface. There are many other things to consider. The two very senior citizens are more than twice as old as atomic weapons; the world's population has quadrupled during their lives; the two are older than three-quarters of the countries that exist today. Radios, televisions, computers, and some of the other technological innovations that affect us so profoundly now did not exist when El-Wasimy and Israel were born.

One of the strong themes in this book is the challenges that face the world and the alternative approaches to addressing those challenges. Use the two seemingly ancient people to help you think about these issues. If, for example, it took all of human history—tens of thousands of years—to reach a world population of less than 1.5 billion in 1880, and if, during their lives, we have added another 4.5 billion people, then how much time do we have to get the world population under control? If you live as long as El-Wasimy and Israel have (and you might, given modern medical technology), then what will the world population be when you are 125 years old?

In this sense of contemplating the future by pondering the past, thinking about El-Wasimy and Israel is really more about tomorrow than about yesterday or even today. When I talk about them, my thoughts are on our twenty-first century more than on their nineteenth and twentieth centuries.

Using this Text   The text that follows is my attempt to introduce you to the complex and compelling study of international politics. Prefaces are often given scant attention, but they can be a valuable learning tool for you. They let you in on the author's conceptions, the mental pictures of a text. What is the author's approach? What are the author's orientations and biases? Does the text have one or more basic themes? How is the text organized? In this preface I have addressed these issues. I hope you'll read it.

In writing this text I have tried to use straightforward prose and have assumed that students who take this course know little about international politics. To help you further, I have included an outline at the beginning of each chapter. Before you read the chapter, pay attention to its outline. It is axiomatic that if you know where you are going, you will find it a lot easier to get there! Additionally, I have written a numbered summary at the end of each chapter to help you quickly review the scope of the chapter. This, of course, is no substitute for carefully studying the chapter.

There are many figures, tables, maps, and photographs in this book. Pay close attention to them. You will find that they graphically represent many of the ideas presented in the text and will help you understand them. But if you really want to know all about something, you will have to read a lot more than just this book and to involve yourself in more than just the course for which it has been assigned. To make it easier for you to do this, I have chosen an "in-text" reference system that gives you citations as you read. Thus (Hobbes, 2000;171) refers to page 171 of the book or article written by (in this case, Professor Heidi) Hobbes in 2000, which is listed alphabetically in the references and bibliography. References to more journalistic sources, such as newspapers, are dealt with through footnotes. You may notice that the older notes have page references, while the newer ones do not. That is because the sources of these periodicals are increasingly on the Internet, where page numbers are not available. I do list the specific URL for these citations, but the address will have usually disappeared within a few days.

I have also noted studies that helped me think about and organize various topics and those that might be informative to you. I encourage you to utilize the references and bibliography to advance your knowledge beyond the boundaries of this text. You will find a list of the abbreviations that I have used throughout the book on pages 583–584. Explanations for terms set in **boldface** will be found in the glossary at the end of the text.

Some note should be made of this book's title, *International Politics on the World Stage*, and the Shakespearean quotations that begin each chapter and are used from time to time to highlight a point. The idea behind this motif is to convey some of the sweep and complexity of the world drama. No one who has ever read William Shakespeare can dismiss his masterpieces as easily understood or inconsequential. The events on the world stage are similar—complex, full of drama, sometimes hopeful, often tragic, and always riveting. But you, the reader, would be mistaken to assume that the play analogy means that, as a member of the audience, you can be content to sit back and watch the plot unfold. Quite the contrary, part of what makes the world drama so compelling is that the audience is seated on stage and is part of, as well as witness to, the action that is unfolding. And that is one reason why I have also quoted more recent world players. Shakespeare's plays are of the past; the world drama is ongoing. Furthermore, as in an improvisational play, you in the audience can become involved, and, given the consequences of a potentially tragic rather than a happy ending, you ought to become involved. If there is anything that this text proposes, it is that each of us is intimately affected by international politics and that we all have a responsibility and an ability to become shapers of the script. As we shall see, our play has alternative scripts, and what the next scene brings depends in part on us. There is wisdom, then, in Shakespeare's advice in *All's Well that Ends Well* that, "Our remedies oft in ourselves do lie."

I am sincerely interested in getting feedback from the faculty members and students who use this text. My pretensions to perfection have long since been dashed, and your recommendations for additions, deletions, and changes in future editions will be appreciated and seriously considered. People do write me, and I write or call them back! You are encouraged to join this correspondence by writing to me in care of McGraw-Hill/Dushkin, Sluice Dock, Guilford, Connecticut, 06437. This book, just like the world, can be made better, but its improvement depends heavily on whether or not you are concerned enough to think and act.

John T. Rourke

ACKNOWLEDGMENTS

Over the first seven editions of this text, I have been glad not only to thank my faculty colleagues from around the country who have reviewed the last edition, but to list as well all those who contributed through their comments to earlier editions. Alas, sheer space constraints no longer permit this. Still, I gratefully acknowledge those who contributed so much to the first seven editions. Also, beginning the list of reviewers anew, I wish to thank those faculty members from around the country who have taken the time to give their suggestions for this, the eighth edition. I have tried to make adjustments wherever possible. Some contributors have pointed out specific concerns about matters of fact or interpretation, and a number of corrections have been made. On a larger scale, comments on the ever-changing staging and script of world drama leads me to constantly revise the structure of the book and the balance of its coverage in ways great and small. For these contributions, I would like to thank the following for their perspicacity:

E. Donald Briggs
University of Windsor

Jose A. da Cruz
Ozarks Technical Community College

Paul Haber
University of Montana

Donald L. Hafner
Boston College

Kent J. Kille
Ohio State University

Joe Mac McKenzie
San Diego Mesa College

Charles McCloy
Trident Technical College

Chaldeans Mensah
Grant MacEwan College

John R. Queen
Glendale Community College

Donald Roy
Ferris State University

Karrin Scapple
Southwest Missouri State University

Jaroslav Tir
University of Illinois at Urbana-Champaign

Primo Vanicelli
University of Massachusetts, Boston

I also owe a debt to each author listed in the bibliography of this and the previous editions. The work that these scholars have done on specific subjects provides the intellectual building blocks that are a significant part of the final structure of this, or any worthwhile, introductory textbook. This text is also evolutionary, and I want to continue to express my appreciation to all those who read and commented on the previous editions. Additionally, I also want to thank the colleagues who called, wrote, or e-mailed me or have taken the time at International Studies Association meetings or other conferences to give me the benefit of their views. I have even, on occasion, taken off my name tag and helped the staff at the publisher's booth at professional meetings. The comments I have received in this anonymity have been sometimes encouraging, sometimes humbling, but always helpful.

Best of all, I have received many good suggestions from students. My own students have had to both read the text and listen to me, and their often obviously candid comments have helped the generations of students who will follow. My favorite was a sophomore who did not do well on his first exam and came to my office to lay blame on that blankety-blank textbook. As we talked, he made some interesting observations. It was also clear that he had not connected the author's name on the front of the book with his professor. You can image how surprised, not to mention disconcerted, he was when it finally dawned on him that he was grumping about the book to its author!

I owe special thanks to Kimberly Weir of the University of Connecticut, who served as a research and editorial assistant during the preparation of this edition. Kimberly has proven to have an extraordinary ability to not only comment on my handling of the big substantive topics but to also ferret out the smallest substantive and technical errors that bedevil all authors. For this attention to detail she has frequently earned one of my most laudatory margin comments, "good eye." Kimberly is also responsible for revising the instructor's manual, *Teaching and Testing from International Politics on the World Stage*. She shouldered the task of preparing, revising, and updating the test items for the eighth edition of the instructor's guide, as well as adding to the list of readings for each chapter in the text.

Then there is the staff of McGraw-Hill/Dushkin. They have encouraged me and supported me. Ava Suntoke is my editor, and I am delighted with her expertise and patience. Robin Charney's proofreading, and her amazing eye for technical detail and substantive consistency, added to the process of ensuring accuracy. I also want to thank the McGraw-Hill/Dushkin typesetters, Juliana Arbo and Marie Lazauskas, for their diligence and for not threatening my life through innumerable changes.

One of the things I like best about this edition is "its look." Pamela Carley has assembled photographs and editorial cartoons that bring powerful visual life to the concepts I express in words. Charles Vitelli not only performed the difficult, but crucial, task of arranging text and illustrations; he drew the original cartoons in this book. He and his able associates (Michael Campbell, Tom Goddard, and Eldis Lima) took my raw mental images and turned them into wonderful representations of the issues being discussed in the text. In the same area, Laura Levine did an extraordinary job with the exacting art of creating the text's many tables, figures, and maps, and Lara Johnson designed this edition's striking cover. I owe a great debt to those who have created such a visually attractive, educationally effective package for my words. Thanks are also due to Alice and Will Thiede of Carto-Graphics in Eau Claire, Wisconsin, for their standard of excellence in producing the maps that appear in the textbook. Another feature of this text is the accompanying Web site with supplementary material and exercises. For this I thank Jonathan Stowe, Marcuss Oslander, and Chris Santos.

Finally, anyone who has written will recognize that it is an intensely personal, as well as professional, experience. I am fortunate to have people around me who understand when I am seemingly glued to my computer for long periods of time and who sometimes insist that I shut it off. My son and friend John Michael helps me endure the ups and downs of the New York Giants and UConn athletic teams, shares the frustrations of fishing, and occasionally tries to interpret X-generation culture for me.

To all of you:

I can no other answer make but thanks, thanks, and ever thanks.

Shakespeare, *Twelfth Night*

Visit the Web site and PowerWeb site of

International Politics on the World Stage, Eighth Edition

http://www.dushkin.com/rourke/

Contents In Brief

CONTENTS

 MAPS:

 PART I: APPROACHES TO WORLD POLITICS

PART V: PURSUING PEACE

PART VI: PURSUING PROSPERITY

CHAPTER 1

THINKING AND CARING ABOUT WORLD POLITICS

An honest tale speeds best being plainly told.

Shakespeare, Richard III

Be not too tame neither, but let your own discretion be your tutor:
suit the action to the word, the word to the action.

Shakespeare, Hamlet

We will have to repent in this generation not merely for the vitriolic words and
actions of the bad people, but for the appalling silence of the good people.

Martin Luther King Jr., "Letter from Birmingham Jail"

We must be more than an audience, more even than actors. We must be authors
of the history of our age.

U.S. secretary of state Madeleine K. Albright, Senate confirmation hearings, 1997

CHAPTER OBJECTIVES

After completing this chapter, you should be able to:

- Explain the interconnection of all the actors in the international system and the effects that events taking place in one country have on other countries.
- Describe some of the effects of world politics on individuals.
- Describe how the world is interconnected economically.
- Analyze how world politics affects the way countries distribute their economic resources.
- Consider how global problems and challenges, such as population increases, pollution, and resource depletion, affect individuals and their living space.
- Discuss the role of political cooperation as a response to environmental degradation.
- Consider how individuals can make a difference in world politics.
- Summarize realist beliefs and assess their impact on the world political system.
- Understand the tenets and goals of idealism as a present and future force in world politics.
- Identify the analytical orientations of political scientists.
- Identify the goals and research methods of political scientists.
- Understand the three levels of analysis used in the study of world politics.

"All the world's a stage, and all the men and women merely players," William Shakespeare (1564–1616) wrote in *As You Like It*. The Bard of Avon was a wise political commentator as well as a literary giant (Alulis & Sullivan, 1996). Shakespeare's lines are used here because they help convey the drama of world politics. The characters are different, of course, with Canada, China, Germany, Japan, Russia, and the United States replacing those of his time and imagination. Beyond that, though, there are remarkable parallels between international relations and the master's plays. Both are cosmic and complex. The characters are sometimes heroic; at other times they are petty. The action is always dramatic and often tragic. As with any good play, the audience was drawn into the action at The Globe, the London theater where Shakespeare staged his works. Similarly, the global theater of international politics draws us in. Indeed, we are seated on the stage, no matter how remote the action may seem or how much we may want to ignore it. Like it or not, we and the world are stuck with each other. The progress of the play, whether it continues its long run or closes early, is something we will all enjoy or endure.

Another quotation from Shakespeare—this time from *Macbeth*—is also worth pondering. Macbeth despairs that life "struts and frets his hour upon the stage" in a tale "full of sound and fury." Again the playwright hits the mark! The global drama has a cast of national actors (countries) that are often at odds with one another. It is true that many examples of cooperation and humanity can be found in them. But they are also full of ambition, self-serving righteousness, and greed, and it is a rare day when some of the countries are not in open conflict. And even when they are not threatening one another, they are forever calculating what is good for themselves and taking action based on their national interests.

THE IMPORTANCE OF STUDYING WORLD POLITICS

The last line from Macbeth's soliloquy is where this text and Shakespeare part company. The Bard pessimistically pronounces the action of life as "signifying nothing." That thought has a certain fatalistic appeal that allows us to ignore our responsibility. "What the hell," we can say, "why bother with a complicated subject about faraway places that have little to do with me?"

Many people take this "why bother" approach and normally pay little or no attention to world events and issues. A study of the political views of Americans found that only 20 percent of them say they follow foreign news.[1] While it is true that this lack of attention for global events is evident in virtually all countries, Americans' lack of information is particularly startling for a relatively well-educated populace with easy access to an impressive array of broadcast, print, and other news sources. One survey asked four factual questions of people in eight countries, as detailed in Figure 1.1. The result after averaging the percentage of correct responses to the four questions is that Germans scored more than twice as well as Americans, and the percentage of correct responses by Americans was higher than only those from Mexico (where only about 60 percent of children get as far as high school). With regard to the specific questions, the average German answered all four correctly; most French and Italians could answer three; a majority of the British and Canadians got two questions right; the average Spaniard could correctly answer just one question; and the average American and Mexican were unable to answer any of the four correctly.

Is this widespread lack of information about or interest in world events justifiable? The answer is no! This text does not often try to tell you what to think or do. But one message *is* stressed here: The world drama is important and deserves our careful attention. We are more than mere observers. We are all on the stage along with

MAP
World Countries, pp. 28–29

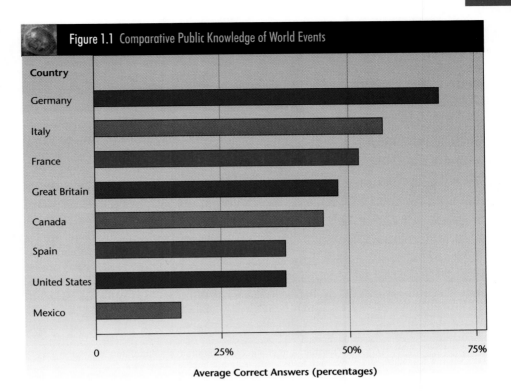

Figure 1.1 Comparative Public Knowledge of World Events

Average Correct Answers (percentages)

Data source: *Time*, March 28, 1994, p. 22.

How much people know about world politics varies greatly from country to country. This figure shows the average percentage of correct answers given by people in different countries to four relatively easy questions about who was fighting in the Balkans, what group Israel was trying to achieve peace with, the name of the president of Russia; and the name of the UN secretary-general. Most Germans could correctly answer each of the four questions: most Americans could answer none of them correctly.

everybody else, and, whether we like it or not, we are all caught up in the tidal ebb and flow of global events.

This does not mean, though, that you are stuck with the world as it exists or as it is evolving. The Irish literary lion, Oscar Wilde (1854–1900), once observed wryly that "the world is a stage, but the play is badly cast." If you agree, do not stand idly by. You can play an active part; you can make a difference! The script is not set. It is an improvisational play with lots of room for ad-libbing and even for changing the story line. We do not have to accept playing the role of a walk-on with no lines. We can speak up if we so wish and join the action if we try. Capturing center stage is difficult, and even the great have not held it for long, but we can all play a part. The important message of this text is that your efforts to become knowledgeable about the world and to try to shape its course to your liking are worthwhile because international politics does matter. It plays an important role in your life, and you should be concerned. To understand that further, let us turn to a number of ways, some dramatic, some mundane, in which international politics affects your economic life, your living space, and, potentially, your very existence. Then we will turn to the pivotal question: Can we make a difference?

WORLD POLITICS AND YOUR POCKETBOOK

World politics affects the personal economic conditions of each of us. The impact of international economics on individuals continues to expand as world industrial and financial structures become increasingly intertwined. Trade wins and loses jobs. We are dependent on foreign sources for vital resources. That reality was brought sharply into

The theme of this book is the great drama of international politics on the world stage. You cannot choose to be apart from the action, because in the global theater, unlike most theaters, we are all seated on the stage and there is no exit and no intermission during our lifetimes. It is therefore wise to join the action, to become a player, and to try to improve the story line in the ongoing improvisational play to take a direction you favor.

focus in early 2000 as the prices of gasoline, heating oil, and other petroleum products skyrocketed. Gasoline prices, for example, increased as much as 70 percent in the United States, which, beyond the immediate costs, threatened to cause higher prices for many products due to the higher energy costs to manufacture and transport them. The rise and fall of inflation is also influenced by foreign economic tides, as is the domestic allocation of our own resources. People in one country invest in and even own companies in other countries. The ties between national and international affairs are so close that many social scientists now use the term **intermestic** to symbolize the merger of *inter*national and d*omestic* concerns. To illustrate the increasingly ubiquitous connections between your own personal economic well-being and world politics, we will briefly explore three aspects of that relationship: how international trade affects your job, how the flow of international capital helps determine your economic well-being and your personal wealth, and how defense spending impacts your job and taxes.

International Trade and Your Job

There is a steadily increasing likelihood that international trade and your job are related. Exports create jobs. The United States is the world's largest exporter, providing other countries with $958.5 billion worth of U.S. goods and services in 1999. Creating these exports employed some 16 million Americans, about 13 percent of the total U.S. workforce. Employment in many other countries is even more reliant on exports. For example, about 25 percent of Canadian workers depend on exports for their jobs.

While exports create jobs, other jobs are lost to imports. The clothes, toys, electronics, and many other items that Americans buy were once produced extensively in the United States by American workers. Now most of these items are produced overseas by workers whose wages are substantially lower.

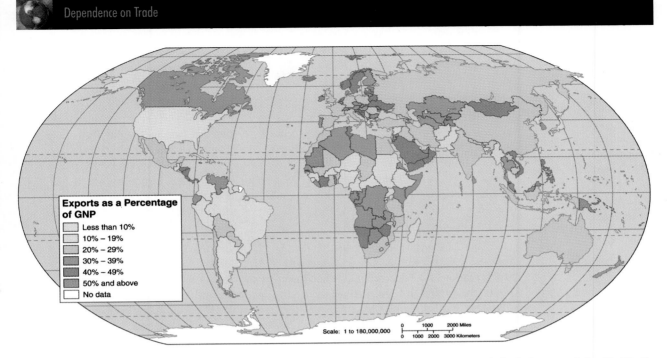

Dependence on Trade

Exports as a Percentage of GNP
- Less than 10%
- 10% – 19%
- 20% – 29%
- 30% – 39%
- 40% – 49%
- 50% and above
- No data

Scale: 1 to 180,000,000

All countries, even the most economically powerful ones, are becoming increasingly dependent on trade for their economic health. Whether you are American or Zimbabwean, there is a good chance that your job, the price you pay for the goods you buy, and other factors in your economic well-being are dependent on global trade.

Jobs are also lost to service imports. Experienced computer programmers in India command a monthly salary about one-fourth the salary paid to American programmers. India's software exports grew from $225 million in 1992 to $2.6 billion in 1999, and now more than 125,000 Indians create computer programs, mostly for the U.S. market. This work is sometimes done over links established between programmers' computers in India and servers in the United States and elsewhere.

Lost jobs are a serious matter, but before you cry "Buy American!" and demand barriers to exclude foreign goods, it is important to realize that your standard of living is improved by inexpensive foreign products. The United States annually imports over $56 billion worth of clothes and footwear. What Americans pay for these shirts, sneakers, and other items of apparel would be much higher if they were made by American workers earning American wages and bore the label, "Made in the U.S.A."

The Flow of International Capital and Your Economic Well-Being

The global flow of international finance affects you in more ways than you probably imagine. Investment capital is one aspect of this flow. Many familiar U.S. companies that provide jobs for Americans are owned by foreign investors, and the product and marketing decisions that they make have a wide impact. For example, the textbooks that are available to American college students are, in part, produced by foreign corporations, which have bought up American publishing companies in a quest to capture the $23 billion U.S. book market, including the $3 billion in textbook sales. Among the largest academic presses, the British media conglomerate Pearson P.L.C. recently acquired Simon & Schuster (the owner of Prentice Hall and other academic imprints), and St. Martin's is a subsidiary of Holtzbrinck of Germany. Reference book giants Encyclopedia Britannica and Merriam-Webster are both controlled by Switzerland's Safra Group. In some cases, companies are facing economic difficulty, and they and the jobs they provide are saved by the infusion of foreign capital. In other cases, the inflow of foreign investment capital creates jobs for Americans. This is true, for example, for American workers who make Nissan automobiles in Tennessee, Hondas in Ohio, Toyotas in Kentucky, and Mitsubishis in Illinois.

International financial markets are yet another connection between your pocketbook and the global economy. The percentage of American families owning individual stocks or mutual fund shares, either directly or through personal or pension-related mutual funds holdings, jumped from 32 in 1989 to 49 in 1998. Another indicator is that in 1997, stock holdings made up 28 percent of the assets owned by Americans. Furthermore, 60 percent of all mutual fund shares are owned by households with earnings under $75,000. Such statistics mean that the stock and bond markets are no longer the concern of just the rich.

There are a number of ways this data is related to the world economy. One way is that the companies that make up the Standard & Poor's 500, a key index of the U.S. stock market, do 40 percent of their business overseas. When the world economy is good, the profits they earn result in part in dividends and capital gains for American investors and for the pension funds of American workers. Additionally, institutions also invest heavily in stocks and bonds in other countries. Sometimes, such as with retirement earnings, individuals may be directly affected. Other times, you may be indirectly affected. To cite just one example, your college or university, especially if private, may invest part of its endowment in foreign securities. How they do will affect areas such as scholarship aid and tuition.

Defense Spending and Your Economic Circumstances

The budget of your national government and the taxes it raises to fund the budget are yet another way that world politics affects you economically. At the very least, you pay taxes to support your country's involvement in world affairs. In FY1999 the U.S. government spent $1.7 trillion (that's right, trillion, not billion). Spending on general foreign affairs (such as foreign aid) was minor, accounting for only $17 billion, about 1 percent of the budget. Defense spending was considerably more important. It amounted to $261 billion, approximately 15.4 percent of the U.S. budget. This equals about $1,000 per American for national defense.

The more of a country's wealth that is devoted to military spending, the less is available for private use and for domestic government spending. Table 1.1 compares countries by a number of defense spending criteria. As you can see, some countries devote huge sums to defense; others spend little. Countries also vary widely in their defense expenditures compared to such economic measures as their **gross domestic product** (GDP: a measure of all goods and services produced within a country).

One way to think about defense spending and to relate it to yourself is to compare defense spending with federal spending on higher education. With about 5 percent of the world's population, the United States accounts for 37 percent of the world's military spending. Some people question the need to spend more than a quarter trillion dollars a year with no hostile, extraordinarily powerful opponent facing the country. Yet, the government has now built twenty-one B-2 bombers at a cost of over $2.1 billion each, and has begun to develop the next generation of fighter aircraft, which may eventually cost $1 trillion to deploy.

Did You Know That:
Tourists provide considerable revenue for Americans. During 1998, 47 million foreign visitors spent over $74 billion in the United States, more than twice as much as in any other country and 17 percent of the world total.

Table 1.1 Comparative Military Expenditures

Country	Total (US$ Billions)	As Percentage of Budget	As Percentage of GNP	Per Capita (US$)
Canada	7.1	5.9	1.2	229
China	12.6	18.0	5.7	10
India	10.0	23.8	2.7	10
Israel	8.7	15.0	9.5	1,513
Japan	42.9	6.0	0.9	339
Mexico	6.0	4.9	1.3	60
Nigeria	0.2	1.4	0.7	2
Russia	40.1	57.1	5.8	274
Sweden	4.9	3.9	2.2	467
United States	267.2	15.5	3.4	980
World	884	10.2	2.6	145

Data sources: CIA (2000); Center for Defense Information; *World Almanac* (2000). Defense spending figures tend to be less reliable than most economic data. The data for China is especially controversial, with some estimates of China's real military expenditures as high as $40 billion.

The range of government spending on defense as an overall amount, as a percentage of a country's budget or of its gross national product, and as a per capita expenditure varies widely. Whatever the exact figures, defense spending affects your economic conditions in a number of ways, such as jobs, taxes, and budget choices.

Although there is no one-to-one relationship between reduced defense spending and increased higher education spending, it is worth thinking about what would be possible if some defense spending were reallocated to higher education. In 1999 about 14 million students were enrolled in U.S. colleges. The annual cost of room, board, and tuition at the average four-year private college was $18,745; at the average public college it was $7,788. If, for example, the Pentagon deleted just one B-2 bomber (a saving of $2.1 billion), that money would be enough to give an all-expenses-paid scholarship at the average private college to 112,030 students or at the average state university to 269,646 students.

Such concerns are not confined to the United States. Some 40,000 German students protested in Bonn over what they considered to be gross underfunding of higher education. A particular point of ire was the $13 billion that Germany had committed to develop the joint European warplane, the Eurofighter. "For a billion marks, 6.5 Eurofighters or 6,481 smart students—which do we need more in the future?" one protest placard read.[2]

Yet the reallocation of defense spending that might bring economic relief to some people, such as college students, would harm the economic circumstances of other people. Many national economies, industries, and workers are heavily dependent on defense spending. Defense spending in the United States declined from about 6.4 percent of the GDP in 1985 to 3.7 percent in 1999. Many jobs have been lost. In the late 1980s there were some 8 million people employed in military uniform, as civilian employees of the Department of Defense, or as defense industry workers. This combined uniformed and civilian U.S. workforce has now declined by 38 percent, or about 3 million wage earners. The lost jobs have created tremendous pressure from negatively affected individuals, communities, and businesses to maintain defense spending. As former assistant secretary of defense Lawrence J. Korb has commented, to

Did You Know That:

Even limited military operations are very costly. Recent U.S. interventions and their costs are:

Grenada	1983	$76 million
Panama	1989	$164 million
Persian Gulf	1990	$61 billion
Somalia	1992	$675 million*
Haiti	1994	$427 million
Bosnia	1996	$1.3 billion*
Kosovo	1999	$5.2 billion*

*first year of multiyear operation

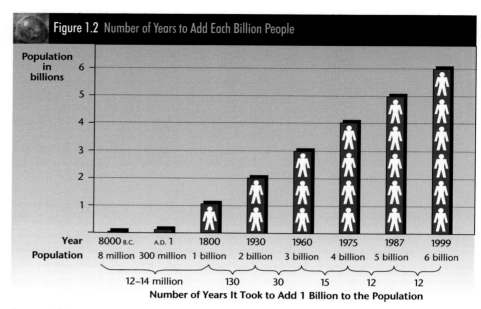

Figure 1.2 Number of Years to Add Each Billion People

Year	8000 B.C.	A.D. 1	1800	1930	1960	1975	1987	1999
Population	8 million	300 million	1 billion	2 billion	3 billion	4 billion	5 billion	6 billion

12–14 million   130   30   15   12   12

Number of Years It Took to Add 1 Billion to the Population

Data sources: U.S. Census Bureau at http://www.census.gov/ipc/www/worldhis.html; United Nations Population Fund (1998)

The world population is growing at an alarming rate. In October 1999 it passed the 6 billion mark and is expanding at a rate of about 210,728 people a day, 8,764 an hour, 146 a minute, 2.4 a second. You can go to a "world population clock" at http:// metalab.unc.edu/lunarbin/worldpop and enter the day you were born to see how much the world population has grown in the intervening years.

some degree, "Both the administration and Congress... view defense as a federal jobs program."[3]

WORLD POLITICS AND YOUR LIVING SPACE

International politics can affect far more than your pocketbook. It can determine the quality of the air you breathe, the water you drink, and many other aspects of the globe you inhabit.

The growth of the world's population and its pressure on resources threaten to change the quality of life as we know it. It took 100,000 years of human existence for the world population to reach 6 billion, a dubious mark that the UN calculates occurred on October 12, 1999. The increase of 77 million people in 1999 alone is the equivalent of a new U.S. population every 3.5 years or a new Canadian population every 147 days. The UN Population Fund (UNFPA) predicts that by 2050 the population will have exploded to 9 billion people, a fifty percent increase in only half a century. Figure 1.2 depicts the population explosion.

Americans and Canadians will not be immune to this avalanche of humanity. The burning of fossil fuels to warm and propel this mass and to supply it with material goods creates emissions of over 6 billion tons a year of carbon dioxide and other gases that, most scientists worry, are causing global warming. The decade of the 1990s was the warmest in recorded history, with 1998, at an average of 62.46 degrees Fahrenheit, the warmest year since records were first kept in 1856. The last year of the century, 1999, fell just short of that mark, but was still the fifth highest ever recorded. These global climate changes are clearly evident in the United States. During the three-month winter of December 1999–February 2000, temperatures in the continental 48 states set new records for warmth for the third year in a row. The average temperature of 38.4 degrees Fahrenheit marked the warmest winter in 105 years.

MAP
Population Growth,
pp. 524–525

Warmer temperatures may be welcome to some, but the ramifications are worrisome. Among other things, many scientists claim that the warming is melting the polar ice caps, thereby raising sea levels and threatening to flood coastal areas of the world. There are some Pacific island countries that worry about virtually disappearing under the rising seas. Scientists project that global warming will also increase the frequency and intensity of torrential rainfall, hurricanes and other windstorms, and other forms of violent weather. The annual World Disasters Report issued by the International Red Cross in March 2000 said that during the six previous years, the number of people who needed aid after natural disasters like floods and earthquakes had risen, from fewer than 500,000 a year to more than 5.5 million. A significant majority of them were victims of weather-related catastrophes, including the El Niño/La Niña conditions that originate in the Pacific. This phenomenon, with a range of damaging climatic effects, including torrential rains in some areas and droughts in others, is due to global warming. Among its other effects in the last few years have been torrential rains and horrendous flooding in Central and South America, which cost billions of dollars in damage and killed thousands, and, conversely, one of the worst droughts in 50 years in Southeast Asia, with resulting widespread forest fires, crop failures, and other damage.

The chemicals we spew into the air also cause disease. Among other things, they attack the Earth's ozone layer, which helps shield the Earth from the Sun's deadly ultraviolet rays. Higher exposure to ultraviolet rays increases your risk of developing melanoma, the deadliest form of skin cancer, whenever you enjoy yourself at the beach or are otherwise outdoors. It is well established that the ozone layer has thinned considerably during recent decades. Concomitantly, the rate of new melanoma cases has grown dramatically from 1,168 of every 100,000 Americans to 3,650. This 213 percent increase means that 47,700 Americans were diagnosed with melanoma in 1999, and a projected 9,600 of these victims will die of the disease.

Changes in the environment are one concern that the world must solve collectively. Global warming is thought to be related to the growing intensity and frequency of the El Niño/La Niña phenomena, in which abnormally warm/cool waters in the mid-Pacific Ocean bring torrential rains to some areas and droughts to others. The impact of this drastic weather is evident in this picture. A man in Venezuela is digging out his car after it was covered in a mud slide, which resulted from one of the severe storms that inundated the U.S. and Latin American west coasts in 1999.

Some scientists even believe that pollution is threatening the ability of humans to reproduce. Chemicals categorized as PCBs (polychlorinated biphenyls), which are used to make pesticides, plastic, and other products, find their way into human food through fish and even through breast milk. Studies of male alligators in waters with high concentrations of the PCBs found reptiles that have "feminized hormones and half-male, half-female genitals" and are sterile.[4] Other studies have found that the sperm count of males in many countries in Europe and elsewhere has plunged, in some cases by more than 50 percent over the last half century. Such studies are not yet conclusive and the findings have been criticized by other scientists, but the evidence has led one analyst to warn that "nature is sending a very strong signal that something is amiss."[5]

There are numerous other proven or suspected deleterious environmental trends that are despoiling our living space. The United Nations Environment Programme (UNEP) reports that in addition to the perils already mentioned, erosion destroys 25 billion tons of topsoil each year, 900 million urban dwellers breathe dangerous levels of sulfur dioxide, and 25 percent of the Earth's animal and plant species may become

Cindy Marie Beaudoin arrived at the University of Connecticut as a first-year student in September 1990. Just a month earlier, Iraq had invaded Kuwait. Cindy enrolled in the usual liberal arts courses, facing the terrors of college calculus and chemistry. On November 17, her life turned a corner. Cindy was also Specialist Beaudoin, a soldier in the 142nd Medical Company of the Connecticut National Guard. Her company was called up to active duty. Specialist Beaudoin, at age 19, was on her way to the war that waited in the Persian Gulf. Cindy withdrew from classes rather than opt to make up the work when she returned. "I probably won't remember half the stuff I've learned when I get back," she explained.[1]

On Sunday, January 13, 1991, just four days before the war began, her unit left for Saudi Arabia. The 142nd moved forward behind advancing combat units when the ground war began on February 24.

1972–1991

Specialist Beaudoin penned a two-line stanza on her helmet that read: "Look at this place that we have found. No one knows where we are bound."

Four days later, Iraq's army had been routed, and President Bush declared a cease-fire. The war was not over yet for Specialist Beaudoin. The 142nd's journey had taken it north from Saudi Arabia into Iraq and then east just across the border into Kuwait. There, at about 3:00 P.M. on February 28, an explosion rocked the 142nd's convoy. "God-damn," trooper Beaudoin shouted as she tumbled from her truck; "They're firing at us." A moment later she realized that she had been hit. The cause of the blast is still uncertain. It hardly matters. Cindy Beaudoin's leg was gone; shrapnel had torn her abdomen. Three hours later she was in a medivac helicopter headed for the rear. It wasn't soon enough; Cindy died during the flight. There is, in war and death, a grim equality.

extinct by the year 2020. "The environment is worse now than 20 years ago," declared UNEP head Mustafa K. Tolba. "Time is running out. Critical thresholds may already have been breached."[6]

It is true that most environmental problems have not been caused by world politics. It is also true, however, that we humans are unlikely to be able to stem, much less reverse, the degradation of the biosphere without global cooperation. That has begun, but only slowly and somewhat uncertainly, as detailed in chapter 18.

WORLD POLITICS AND YOUR LIFE

Plants and animals may be joined by humans on the endangered species list. International politics now has the potential of extinguishing most or all of the human race. Unlike most of history, when the vast majority of war deaths were soldiers, civilian casualties in the twentieth century have risen drastically as civilians have increasingly become a target of military operations. Nearly as many civilians as soldiers were killed during World War II. Now more civilians than soldiers are killed. According to the UN, civilians comprised 75 percent of everyone killed during wars in the 1980s and 90 percent of all war deaths during the 1990s. Most tragically, these casualties included 2 million children, who died from wounds and other war-related causes. In a nuclear war or act of nuclear terrorism, military casualties would be a mere footnote to the overall death toll.

The possibility of war is a special concern for college-age adults because they are of prime military age. An examination of the ages of U.S. Marines killed during the Vietnam War shows that of those who died, 84 percent were aged 18 to 22. Some soldiers killed in war are volunteers, but not all are. Many countries have a draft to staff their military services. The United States abandoned the draft in the early 1970s, but draft registration is still required of all military-age males.

It is also the case that military combat is a matter that increasingly affects women directly as well as men. In the United States and elsewhere, the types of combat units in

World politics can affect your life if you join or are drafted into your country's military forces. This possibility increasingly includes women, such as this real-life "G.I. Jane."

which women are allowed to serve are expanding. Either by volunteering or by being required to go, many more women may fight and die in future wars.

Such an idea is not farfetched. American women now serve as combat pilots and as officers on warships. Women in some other countries are also pressing their government for equal access to all military units. The Supreme Court of Israel, for instance, ruled in favor of a woman who contested the military's refusal to allow her and other women to become combat pilots. Public attitudes are moving slowly toward accepting the idea of women in combat. A poll of Americans just before the war against Iraq asked, "If there is ground fighting in the war, do you think women members of the armed forces there should participate in combat, or not?" Of respondents, 47 percent said yes, 41 percent said no, and 12 percent were unsure.[7]

Even if they are not allowed into ground combat units, women are serving in military roles that bring more of them ever closer to the fighting. Thirty-five thousand women served in the Persian Gulf during the war against Iraq in 1991. Thirteen of them were killed in action, accounting for 9 percent of U.S. battle deaths. It may be a statistical anomaly because of the relatively low casualty rate during the war, but it is worth noting that women experienced a higher per capita death rate in the war zone than did men. Of every 10,000 troops of their gender, 3.7 women died, compared to 2.6 men. The story of one of those women, Cindy Beaudoin, is told in the accompanying box.

Don't be surprised, then, if you, female or male, someday find yourself directly involved in world politics by way of the draft and an all-expenses paid government trip to some exotic corner of the world. You can try to ignore world politics, but it may not ignore you.

World politics, then, does count. We are all involved economically and environmentally. Furthermore, it can threaten our very lives. Wars have continued and will continue to happen. Young men—and probably young women—have been and will be drafted. Some will die—perhaps you. In the worst possible circumstance, nuclear war, it will not matter whether you were drafted or not.

CAN WE MAKE A DIFFERENCE?

The next logical question is: Can I make a difference? The answer is: Yes, you can make a difference! It is true that we cannot all be president or secretary of state, but we can take action and we can make our views known. Furthermore, as the box on the next page, Making a Difference, illustrates, there are many roles that you can play to help shape the world more to your liking.

Direct action, such as protests, is one way to influence policy. Students, for example, have often been important agents of political change through direct action. The sum of millions of individual actions—ranging from burning draft cards, to massive demonstrations in front of the White House, to students protesting and even dying on U.S. campuses—helped end American involvement in Vietnam. Consumer boycotts can also play a part. Individuals have made a difference by refusing to eat tuna fish that does not bear the "dolphin safe" label. Even more recently, students on many U.S. college campuses have participated in protests and brought consumer pressure to bear on clothing and footwear companies that sell products manufactured in so-called sweatshops in Asia and elsewhere. These manufacturers pay little, require long hours, and have poor safety records. Adding to the pressure, colleges began to follow the lead of their students. The

(continued on page 13)

MAKING A DIFFERENCE

Presidents, foreign ministers, and other leaders are not the only ones who affect world politics. They are in the best position to do so, but so can you. Each of the people here is a private citizen who has made a difference by being more than a member of the audience, content to merely watch international politics on the world stage.

Lori Wallach helped lead the massive anti–World Trade Organization protests in Seattle in December 1999. A Harvard Law School graduate, she is director of Public Citizen's Global Trade Watch and believes that current WTO trade rules do not sufficiently protect the environment or workers. She argues that the current system "ain't working, it's one choice, it's not inevitable, it was the wrong choice, it can be transformed into something that works."[1] Whether you agree or disagree with Wallach, you have to admire her conviction and effort.

Mike McCaskey, the chairman of the Chicago Bears football team, believes that conflict should be confined to the playing field. A former Peace Corps volunteer in Ethiopia in the 1960s, McCaskey is heading up a group of other Peace Corps veterans from East Africa who are working the region to promote peace between Ethiopia and Eritrea, which have had sporadic fighting along their mutual border since 1998. As youths, the presidents of both countries were taught by Peace Corps volunteers.

Jody Williams of Putney, Vermont, is the head of the American chapter of the International Campaign to Ban Landmines. For this effort, she and the overall campaign received the Nobel Peace Prize in 1997. President Clinton, who opposed the ban, declined to call and congratulate her. "If he calls me, he knows I am going to say, 'What's your problem?'" she explained.[2]

Trick-or-Treaters are kids who care. Since 1950, kids dressed in ghost, witch, and other Halloween disguises and rattling orange and black milk cartons have raised tens of millions of dollars for the United Nations Children's Fund, popularly known as UNICEF. On Halloween night 1998 alone, these children improved the lives of other children by raising over $3 million.

Rigoberta Menchú, a Guatemalan of Mayan descent, has campaigned for the rights of indigenous people around the world. These efforts brought Menchú the 1992 Nobel Peace Prize. The prize ci-

You don't have to be a president to affect world politics. Lori Wallach isn't one, but as an organizer of the growing movement against unregulated globalization, she has captured the attention of many presidents.

tation, which came on the 500th anniversary year of the arrival of Columbus in the Western Hemisphere, read, "Today, Rigoberta Menchú stands out as a vivid symbol of peace and reconciliation across ethnic, cultural, and social dividing lines, in her own country, on the American continent, and in the world."[3]

My Lai heroes, three U.S. soldiers—Hugh Thompson, Lawrence Colburn, and Glen Andreotta—were honored in 1998, 30 years after the event, for intervening to stop the massacre of innocent villagers by other U.S. troops in My Lai, South Vietnam. At a ceremony at the Vietnam Memorial in Washington, D.C., the Soldiers Medal, the country's highest award for heroism not involving an enemy, was presented to Thompson, Colburn, and, posthumously, to Andreotta, who died in combat three weeks after he and his comrades engaged in an armed confrontation with their murderous fellow soldiers. Thompson accepted the award on behalf of the vast majority of U.S. soldiers "who served their country with honor on the battlefield in Southeast Asia. This is a very important day for us."[4] It certainly was.

University of Notre Dame, for one, announced in April 2000 that it will ban the manufacture of its licensed products in 13 countries that have unfair labor standards. As a result of these efforts, Nike and other companies have joined the Fair Labor Association (FLA), a coalition organization of human rights groups, manufacturers, and activists at over 130 universities and colleges, who work together to help protect the rights of factory workers worldwide.

Voting for candidates is another way to affect policy. Elected leaders do not always follow their campaign promises, but, in a broad sense, who gets elected does influence policy. It made a difference in Israeli foreign policy and, potentially in global politics, when in 1999 liberal candidate Ehud Barak defeated and replaced conservative prime minister Benjamin Netanyahu. Also in 1999, changes in Russian foreign relations quickly occurred when Russia's president, Boris Yeltsin, resigned on December 31 and was replaced by Vladimir Putin (who was subsequently elected to a four-year term in March 2000). Putin has shown some signs of being less cooperative than was Yeltsin with the United States and Western Europe. He has also intensified the military campaign against breakaway Chechnya, and the brutality of that campaign has created friction with the United States and other countries. The U.S. presidential election in 2000 was waged primarily on domestic issues, but there were still important foreign policy differences between candidates Al Gore and George W. Bush. For example, Bush, compared to Gore, favored higher defense spending, was less supportive of the Kyoto Treaty on global warming gases, was more favorable to building a ballistic missile defense system, and was more apt to view China as a rival. The simultaneous congressional elections also made a difference. Americans who voted helped decide which course to follow.

Direct voting on international questions is also possible in some countries (Setala, 1999; Rourke, Hiskes, & Zirakzadeh, 1992). During the 1990s, East Timorese, Croatians, Ukrainians, and several other nationalities voted to declare independence from the countries of which they had been a part. Also during the decade, and taking an opposite view, Puerto Ricans rejected independence (or statehood), and citizens of Quebec also voted against autonomy (Conley, 1997). The Swiss voted by referendum to

Protesting is one of the many ways that you and other individuals can influence world politics. The college students in this photograph are outside a Disney store in New York City protesting against that company for selling clothing and other Disney logo items that were allegedly manufactured in sweatshops in less developed countries. These factories pay very low wages and have poor working conditions.

join the World Bank and the International Monetary Fund, but they have rejected proposals to join the UN. Citizens in Austria, Finland, and Sweden voted in favor of joining the European Union; voters in Norway rejected membership. Hungarians voted to join the North Atlantic Treaty Organization (NATO). Finally, expressing your opinion orally, or in writing, or even having your opinion sampled in a poll, can have an impact. Public opinion polls are widely published, and political leaders in many countries keep a weather eye on public attitudes.

The point is that you count—by voting, protesting, joining issue-oriented groups, donating money to causes you support, or even by having your thoughts recorded in a political poll. Few individual actions are dramatic, and by themselves few significantly change world politics, but the sum of many smaller actions can and does make a difference. Do not consider politics a spectator sport. It is more important than that. Treat politics as a participant—even a contact—sport.

THE WORLD TOMORROW: TWO ROADS DIVERGE

The imperative to be active is particularly important as the world begins a new millennium. It is not too strong to argue that we have arrived at a crucial junction in the paths by which we organize and conduct our global politics. Contemplation of that junction brings to mind Robert Frost and his famous poem, "The Road Not Taken" (1916). Frost concluded his poem with the thought that

> I shall be telling this with a sigh
> Somewhere ages and ages hence:
> Two roads diverged in a wood, and I—
> I took the one less traveled by,
> And that has made all the difference.

Like the works of Shakespeare, Frost's lines are timeless and challenge the reader's intellect and emotions. We can build on Frost's imagery of two roads, one the traditional, "more traveled-by" road, the other an alternative, "less traveled-by" road, to discuss two possible paths for the future. The traditional road is a continuation of the path that world politics has mostly followed for at least five centuries. This route has been characterized by self-interested states struggling to secure their self-interests in a largely anarchistic international system.

The alternative direction entails significant changes in the way that politics is organized and conducted. Those who favor the alternative path argue that states need to abandon the pursuit of short-term self-interest and take a more cooperative, globalist approach. From this perspective, the advent of nuclear weapons, the deterioration of the global environment, and other looming problems create worries that, time is running out, unless the world finds a new way to govern itself.

Some of those who advocate this road see, and even favor, a decline in the central role played by states in the international system. These analysts also see, and often favor, a rise of global institutions, such as the UN, and regional organizations, such as the European Union (EU), as authoritative actors capable of constraining individual countries. At its extreme, this process would lead to regional governments or even to a global government, as discussed in chapter 9. Such ideas are not new, but they represent the road less traveled by in world politics.

Frost leaves his reader with the thought that choosing the less familiar road "made all the difference." What is unknown is whether Frost's "sigh" was one of contentment or regret. Frost wisely left that to the reader's imagination and judgment. Similarly, a major challenge that this text presents to you is deciding which road you think the world should travel by.

REALISM AND IDEALISM: SOME TRAVEL NOTES ON TWO ROADS

To help you begin to make your choice, the following section describes and contrasts the two paths and discusses those who advocate each direction. Those who favor adhering to the traditional road are often associated with the philosophical approach to politics called realism. Those who favor charting a new course along the alternative road are frequently identified with the philosophical approach to politics called idealism.

Before we detail these two approaches, some comments on the terms are appropriate. First, realism and idealism are not absolutely dichotomous. Rather, the terms characterize two ends of a spectrum of attitudes. In between the extremes, there are multitudinous views about the nature of politics and about what that portends for the future. One reflection of this complexity is that political scientists use disparate terms to describe the ideas. The traditional path is variously associated with words such as realist (realism, realpolitik), balance of power, national (nationalist), conservative, and state-centered (state-centric, state-based). The alternative approach is associated with such words as idealism (idealist), globalism, (new) world order, liberal, liberal institutionalism, and internationalist. You will also find the prefix "neo" sometimes attached to some of these words (as in neorealism or neoliberalism) to designate recent variations on the more classic concepts (Beer & Harriman, 1996).

Furthermore, there are a number of orientations that some political scientists have toward their subject that, depending on the theorist, either combine elements of realism and idealism or are rooted in realism or idealism. *Feminism* and *political economy* are two such orientations that deserve particular mention. They vary from general realism and idealism in part because they have different assumptions about what is important and, therefore, focus on different things. "Most contemporary feminist scholarship," one scholar notes, "takes gender—which embodies relationships of power inequality—as its central category of analysis" (Tickner, 1997:614). For economic theorists the unit of analysis is wealth (Burch & Denemark, 1997). Each of these two theoretical orientations is important and multifaceted, and each deservedly receives extended attention later in this text.

Second, do not get fooled by the connotations of realism and idealism. The terms are used here because they are the common names for their schools of thought in international relations theory. But the sobriquets are flawed. "Realists" are not necessarily those who see things as they "really" are. Nor are "idealists" a bunch of fuzzy-headed dreamers. As you will see, perhaps a better name for realists would be "pessimists." Conversely, "optimists" is probably a more enlightening, if not more precise, label for idealists. The point is not to prejudge books by covers or theories by labels.

Third, it is possible to consider realism and idealism from three perspectives: descriptive, predictive, and prescriptive. The *descriptive approach* is concerned with "what is." Political scientists who follow this approach use empirical evidence to determine the degree to which realism or idealism influences policy (Fozouni, 1995; Griffiths, 1995). The *predictive approach* tries to estimate "what will be." If one's theory is valid, then it should be possible not only to explain what has occurred, but also to predict what is likely to occur.

The *prescriptive approach* to realism and idealism asks the normative question, "What ought to be?" As you will see, a great deal of this book is organized to contrast descriptive analysis of the two—traditional (realist) and alternative (idealist)—roads. The discussion of security, for example, is divided into two chapters: traditional national security and its alternative, international security. Beyond this empirical analysis, there is a more important conundrum: Which road should we take: realism or idealism?

There are occasional junctions in the course of international events when the world has the opportunity to make fundamental decisions about the future. We are now at such a fork in the road. The cold war has ended, and the new world order is yet to be determined. The paths suggested by realists and idealists are very different. The realist path is more familiar; the idealist path is less traveled by. Which one we choose could make all the difference.

To help decide this question, the following sections compare realism and idealism according to their respective views about the fundamental nature of politics, the roles of power and justice in the conduct of political affairs, and the prospects for international competition and cooperation (Sterling-Folker, 1997; Rosenau & Durfee, 1995).

THE NATURE OF POLITICS: REALISM AND IDEALISM

The disagreement between **realists** and **idealists** about the nature of politics is perhaps the most fundamental division in all of political discourse. The two schools of thought disagree over the very nature of *Homo politicus* (political humankind), and their respective views govern their approaches to domestic as well as to international politics. At root, realists are pessimists about human nature; idealists are optimists about human nature. The following sections will explore various schools of thought about the nature of politics (Beitz, 1999; Osiander, 1998; Rose, 1998; Schmidt, 1998).

Realism and the Nature of Politics

Realism portrays politics in somber hues (Spegele, 1996). Realists believe that political struggle among humans is probably inevitable because people have an inherent dark side. Many realists would trace their intellectual heritage to such political philosophers as Thomas Hobbes (1588–1679). He believed that humans possess an inherent urge to dominate, an *animus dominandi*. Hobbes argued in *Leviathan* (1651) that "if any two men desire the same thing, which nevertheless they cannot both enjoy, they become enemies and... endeavor to destroy or subdue one another." Taking the same point of view, one leading realist scholar, Hans Morgenthau, wrote that an "ubiquity of evil in human actions" inevitably turns "churches into political organizations... revolutions into dictatorships... and love of country into imperialism" (Zakaria, 1993:22).

Morgenthau represents what might be called the classic realist school. Joining the realist camp more recently is the neorealist school of thought (Schweller & Priess, 1997). Neorealists focus on the anarchic nature of a world system based on competition among sovereign states, rather than on human nature, as the factor that shapes world politics. As one neorealist puts it, the international system based on sovereign actors (states), which answer to no higher authority, is "anarchic, with no overarching authority providing security and order." The result of such a self-help system is that "each state must rely on its own resources to survive and flourish." But because "there is no authoritative, impartial method of settling these disputes—i.e. no world government—states are their own judges, juries, and hangmen, and often resort to force to achieve their security interests" (Zakaria, 1993:22).

Idealism and the Nature of Politics

Idealists reject the notion that all or most humans are inherently political predators. Instead, idealists are prone to believe that humans and their countries are capable of achieving more cooperative, less conflictive relations. In this sense, idealists might trace their intellectual lineage to political philosophers such as Jean-Jacques Rousseau (1712–1778). He argued in *The Social Contract* (1762) that humans had joined together in civil societies because they "reached the point at which the obstacles [to bettering their existence were] greater than the resources at the disposal of each individual." Having come to that point, Rousseau reasoned, people realized that their "primitive condition can then subsist no longer; and the human race would perish unless it changed its manner of existence." Like Rousseau, contemporary idealists not only believe that in the past people joined together in civil societies to better their existence; they are confident that now and in the future people can join together to build a cooperative and peaceful global society (Moravcsik, 1997).

There is also a neoidealist (often called neoliberal) school of thought (Mansbach, 1996). *Neoidealists,* like neorealists, ascribe much of world conflict to the same cause: the anarchic world system based on competition among sovereign states (Legro & Moravcsik, 1999). It is reasonable to ask, "If neoidealists and neorealists both focus on the impact of the system on political relations, what is the difference between the two?" The answer is that while neorealists and neoidealists may agree that the anarchistic nature of the system is the cause of most international conflict, they disagree about what can be accomplished (Jervis, 1999).

Like all idealists, neoidealists believe that humans can cooperate in order to achieve mutual benefits. Therefore, since neoidealists also hold that the anarchic system hinders cooperation, they further believe that the best path to cooperation is through building effective international organizations. This prescription is why neoidealists are often also called liberal institutionalists. Typically, two theorists of this school contend that "when states can jointly benefit from cooperation,… we expect governments to attempt to construct" international organizations to facilitate cooperation. The two scholars go on to argue that, in turn, international organizations add to the growth of cooperation by providing various benefits to member-states that "facilitate the operation of reciprocity" (Keohane & Martin, 1995:42).

What leaves neorealists firmly in the realist camp is their doubt that there is any escape from the anarchistic world. Both types of realist scholars are, for example, skeptical about the ability of international organizations to promote cooperation (Cox, 1997). Instead, one scholar argues, "the most powerful states in the system create and shape [international] institutions so that [the states] can maintain their share of world power, or even increase it." Therefore, he concludes gloomily, whatever cooperation that does occur "takes place in a world that is competitive at its core—one where states have powerful incentives to take advantage of other states" (Mearsheimer, 1995:7, 12, 13).

THE ROLES OF POWER AND JUSTICE: REALISM AND IDEALISM

Realists and idealists also disagree in their descriptions of and, especially, their prescriptions about the roles of power and justice as standards of international conduct. Realists could be styled the "might makes right" school of thought. Idealists would contend that "right makes right."

Realism: An Emphasis on Power

Realists believe that struggles between states to secure their frequently conflicting national interests are the main action on the world stage. Since realists also believe that power determines which country prevails, they hold that politics is aimed at increasing power, keeping power, or demonstrating power. This is hardly a new thought. Over 2,000 years ago, Kautilya, minister to the first Maurya emperor of India, wrote, "The possession of power in a greater degree makes a king superior to another; in a lesser degree, inferior; and in an equal degree, equal. Hence a king shall always endeavor to augment his own power."

Given the view that the essence of politics is the struggle for power, realists maintain that countries and their leaders, if prudent, are virtually compelled to base their foreign policy on the existence of what realists see as a Darwinian, country-eat-country world in which power is the key to the national survival of the fittest. In the words of one scholar, "In an environment as dangerous as anarchy," those who ignore realist principles "would ultimately not survive" (Sterling-Folker, 1997:18). From this point of view, the national interest can be defined for the most part as whatever enhances or preserves the state's security, its influence, and its military and economic power. In the world that exists and probably has always existed, realists would argue, might makes right—or at least it makes success.

Morgenthau (1986:39), for one, reasoned that it is unconscionable for a state to follow policy based only on morality because "while the individual has a moral right to sacrifice himself" in defense of a moral principle, "the state has no right to let its moral disapprobation... get in the way of successful political action, itself inspired by the moral principle of national survival." This does not mean that realists are amoral (Murray, 1996). Indeed, they argue that the highest moral duty of the state is to do good for its citizens. More moderately, many other realists argue that surviving and prospering in a dangerous world requires that morality be weighed prudently against national interest. One scholar has summed up this realist rule of action with the maxim, "Do 'good' if the price is low" (Gray, 1994:8).

Idealism: An Emphasis on Justice

Idealists do not believe that acquiring, preserving, and applying power must be the essence of international relations. Idealists argue that, instead of being based on power, foreign policy should be formulated according to cooperative and ethical standards. Jimmy Carter is an idealist. As president, Carter (1979:2) declared himself in favor of pursuing human rights as "part of a broad effort to use our great power and our tremendous influence in the service of creating a better world in which human beings can live in peace, in freedom, and with their basic needs met. Human rights is the soul of our foreign policy." Bill Clinton also regularly expressed his idealist philosophy while he was in office. He asked Americans to support sending U.S. troops to Bosnia because "it is the right thing to do." He called up images of "skeletal prisoners caged behind barbed-wire fences, women and girls raped as a tool of war, [and] defenseless men and boys shot down in mass graves.... We cannot save all these people," Clinton declared, "but we can save many of them..., [so] we must do what we can."[8]

The views of Carter, Clinton, and other idealists do not mean that they are out of touch with reality. Carter admitted that, as president, "seldom do circumstances permit me... to take actions that are wholly satisfactory," but he tried. Clinton, too, had to moderate his fundamental idealist predilections with the realpolitik demanded of presidents.

Idealists also dismiss the realists' warning that pursuing ethical policy often works against the national interest. The wisest course, idealists contend, is for Americans and others to redefine their interests to take into account the inextricable ties between the future of their country and the global pattern of human development.

PROSPECTS FOR COMPETITION AND COOPERATION: REALISM AND IDEALISM

The previous two sections have examined how realists describe the nature of politics and the respective roles of power and justice. This section takes up the prescriptive issue introduced in the last section: Should countries follow the dictates of realpolitik or strive to establish a new world order based on greater international cooperation?

Realism and the Competitive Future

There are many implications to the view of most realists that the drive for power and conflict are at the heart of politics and that there is "little hope for progress in international relations" (Brooks, 1997:473). Based on this view, realists advocate a relatively pragmatic approach to world politics, sometimes called *realpolitik*. One principle of realpolitik is to secure your own country's interests first and worry about the welfare of other countries second, if at all, on the assumption that other countries will not help you unless it is in their own interest. This makes realists very wary of what is sometimes termed *idealpolitik*. Self-sacrificing policies are not just foolish but dangerous, according to Morgenthau (1986:38), because countries that shun realpolitik will "fall victim to the power of others."

A second tenet of realpolitik holds that countries should practice *balance-of-power* politics, which is explained further in chapter 3. This tenet counsels diplomats to strive to achieve an equilibrium of power in the world in order to prevent any other country or coalition of countries from dominating the system. This can be done through a variety of methods, including building up your own strength, allying yourself with others, or dividing your opponents.

A third realist policy prescription is that the best way to maintain the peace is to be powerful: "Peace through strength," as President Ronald Reagan was fond of saying. Realists believe that it is necessary for a country to be armed because the world is dangerous. Idealists would reply that the world is dangerous because so many countries are so heavily armed.

It is important to say that this does not cast realists as warmongers. Instead, a fourth realist tenet is that you should neither waste power on peripheral goals nor pursue goals that you do not have the power to achieve. This frequently makes realists reluctant warriors. It is worth noting, for instance, that Morgenthau was an early critic of U.S. involvement in the war in Vietnam. He thought it was a waste of U.S. resources in a tangential area: the wrong war, with the wrong enemy, in the wrong place. Prudence, then, is a watchword for realists.

Idealism and the Cooperative Future

Idealists believe that humanity can and must successfully seek a new system of world order. They have never been comfortable with a world system based on sovereignty, but they now argue that it is imperative to find new organizational paths to cooperation. Idealists are convinced that the spread of nuclear weapons, the increase in economic interdependence among countries, the decline of world resources, the daunting gap between rich and poor, and the mounting damage to our ecosphere mean that humans must learn to cooperate more fully because they are in grave danger of suffering a catastrophe of unparalleled proportions.

Idealists are divided, however, in terms of how far cooperation can and should go. Classic idealists believe that just as humans learned to form cooperative societies without giving up their individuality, so too can states learn to cooperate without surrendering their independence. These idealists believe that the growth of international economic interdependence or the spread of global culture will create a much greater spirit of cooperation among the world countries.

Neoidealists are more dubious about a world in which countries retain full sovereignty. These analysts believe that countries will have to surrender some of their sovereignty to international organizations in order to promote greater cooperation and, if necessary, to enforce good behavior. "The fundamental right of existence," Pope John Paul II told the UN General Assembly, "does not necessarily call for sovereignty as a state." Instead, the pontiff said, "there can be historical circumstances in which aggregations different from single state sovereignty can... prove advisable."[9] This point of view holds that humans have found advancement by being nonsovereign members of domestic societies governed through central authority. Similarly, states may well benefit from giving up some or all of their sovereignty to form hierarchically structured regional and global organizations.

The world has not become what idealists believe it could be, but they are encouraged by some trends in recent years. One of these is the growth of interdependence. Idealists also support their case by pointing to the willingness of countries to surrender some of their sovereignty to improve themselves. The European Union (EU), for instance, now exercises considerable economic and even political authority over its member-countries. They were not forced into the EU; they joined it freely. This and other diminutions of sovereignty will be discussed at length later in the text.

Idealists also condemn the practice of realpolitik. They charge that power politics leads to an unending cycle of conflict and misery, in which safety is temporary at best. They look at the last century with its more than 111 million deaths during two world wars and innumerable other conflicts and deride realists for suggesting that humanity should continue to rely on a self-help system that has so often and so cataclysmically failed to provide safety. Idealists further assert that the pursuit of power in the nuclear age may one day lead to ultimate destruction.

This does not mean that idealists are unwilling to use military force, economic sanctions, and other forms of coercion. They are not so naive as to think that the potential for conflict can be eliminated, at least in the foreseeable future. Therefore most idealists are willing to use coercion when necessary to halt aggression or to end oppression. The use of coercion to restore right is especially acceptable to idealists if it is accomplished through cooperative efforts such as UN peacekeeping forces or sanctions.

ASSESSING REALITY: REALISM AND IDEALISM

Before we leave our discussion of realism and idealism, it is worth pausing to ask which theory better explains how the world has operated and how it operates now. On balance, it is safe to say that throughout history competition rather than cooperation has dominated international relations. Not being at war is not necessarily the same as being at peace in a cooperative way, and suspicion, tension, and rivalry, rather than cooperation, have been the most common traits of what we euphemistically call international peace.

It is also the case that realpolitik is still usually the order of the day, especially where important national interests are involved. Most political leaders tend toward realism in their policies, and even those who lean toward idealism often take the realpolitik road (Elman, 1996). The idealist in President Bill Clinton prompted him as a presidential candidate to object to China's human rights policies and to charge that the unwillingness of President George Bush to punish China demonstrated that Bush had an "unconscionable" propensity to "coddle tyrants."[10] Once he became president, though, Clinton changed to a realpolitik policy that dealt with China as a major power (Rourke & Clark, 1998). Indeed, in March 2000 Clinton persuaded Congress to end the yearly review of China's human relations and to grant China "permanent normal trade relations" (PNTR). The reason, Clinton told Congress, was that "integrating China more fully into the Pacific and global economies... will strengthen China's stake in peace and stability. Within China, it will help to develop the rule of law; strengthen the role of market forces; and increase the contacts China's citizens have with each other and the outside world."[11]

The short answer to the "what is" question almost certainly is that both realism and idealism influence policy. Realpolitik self-interest has been the dominant impulse of countries. Still, it is also true that countries can be cooperative and even altruistic at times. Moreover, it may well be that the idealist approach is gaining ground as states recognize that competition and conflict are increasingly dangerous and destructive and that peaceful cooperation is in everyone's self-interest. It would be naive to argue that the world is anywhere near the point of concluding that self-interest and global interests are usually synonymous. But it is not fatuous to say that an increasing number of people have come to the conclusion that working toward the long-term goal of a safe and prosperous world is preferable to seeking short-term national advantage. Thus, while the question "what is" should engage our attention, the far more important questions are "what should be" and "what will be." What should be is for you to decide after reading this book and consulting other sources of information. What will be is for all of us to see and experience.

HOW TO STUDY WORLD POLITICS

"Well, OK," you may say, "international politics is important and it affects me. And, yes, there are important choices to make. So I'll agree that I should know more about it and get active in the world drama. But where do I start?" Ah, I am glad you asked!

The first thing you should do, if you have not already, is to read the preface. This will tell you how I have structured this text and will help you understand what follows. The next chapter will give you more help in establishing a base to understanding world politics by laying out a brief history of and the current trends in the world system.

POLITICAL SCIENTISTS AND WORLD POLITICS

Before getting to the chapter on global history and trends, it is important that you understand something about what political scientists are attempting to do and how they go about doing it. This knowledge is important to help understand the efforts and goals of the many studies that are cited in this text and others that you may read. Evaluating the research of scholars may also help you construct and conduct your own studies of international relations or any other subject.

Why Political Scientists Study World Politics

There is a long history of international relations as an intellectual focus, and concepts such as anarchy and sovereignty were at its core long before realism, idealism, and other schools of thought were articulated and labeled (Schmidt, 1997). Like all political scientists, scholars study world politics in order to formulate theories—generalizations—about politics. Therefore, what concerns political scientists is understanding patterns that occur over time or that occur in many places at the same time. There are many ways to acquire this understanding, but, whatever the approach, theory is at the heart of political science (Hermann, 1998; Lepgold, 1998).

Within this emphasis on theory, international relations scholars have three subsidiary goals in mind: description, prediction, and prescription. *Description* is the oldest and most fundamental of these three goals. This task sounds a whole lot easier than it is. Not only are events complex and information often difficult to obtain, but political science description should focus on patterns. When a political scientist studies a single event (a case study) or, better yet, a series of events across time or over space, the object is not to just describe the event(s). Instead, the goal is to relate them to a pattern of other events. One illustrative area of political science research has been to try to prove or disprove the hypothesis, "Democracies do not fight each other" (Gartzke, 1998; Gleditsch & Hegre, 1997; Thompson & Tucker, 1997). By studying history, many political scientists have concluded that, indeed, democracies tend not to go to war with one another. This research is discussed fully in chapter 8.

Prediction is even more difficult than description because of the complexity of human nature. Nevertheless, political scientists can use careful research as a basis for "analytical forecasting [by which to] give a reasoned argument for what they expect to happen" (George, 1994:172). If, for instance, we believe the descriptive studies that conclude that democracies are peaceful toward one another, then it is possible to predict that a democratic Russia will be less likely to be antagonistic toward the United States and other democracies than was the nondemocratic Soviet Union.

Prescription is a third goal. Some political scientists go beyond their objective studies and come to normative (what is right or wrong) conclusions and prescribe policy. Those who believe that democracies have not been (description) and will not be

Did You Know That:

The first political scientist to become U.S. president was Woodrow Wilson, who received his Ph.D. (1886) from Johns Hopkins University and taught political science at several colleges. The second was Bill Clinton, who graduated with a specialization in international relations from Georgetown University (1968). Of the two major party candidates in 2000, Al Gore has a B.A. in government from Harvard University (1969), while George Bush inexplicably majored in history instead of political science at Yale University.

Political scientists sometimes practice world politics, as well as study it. Before heading into politics, and finally to Washington, President Bill Clinton and Vice President Al Gore both majored in political science, and Secretary of State Madeleine Albright was a professor of the subject. Yasser Arafat, alas, is not a political scientist. He studied civil engineering at Cairo University.

(prediction) aggressive toward one another, may wish to advocate (prescription) policies that promote the adoption or preservation of democracy. Such advocates might, for example, urge extending massive economic aid to Russia in order to avoid the economic turmoil that is so often associated with a slide toward authoritarian government.

Political scientists, it can be added, do more than talk to students and write about their theories. Some political scientists enter directly into the policy-making realm. Among them is former Georgetown University professor of political science and U.S. secretary of state Madeleine K. Albright and undergraduate political science majors Bill Clinton and Al Gore. Other political scientists try to influence policy indirectly through such methods as serving in so-called think tanks dedicated to policy advocacy, writing op-ed pieces in newspapers, and testifying before legislatures.

How Political Scientists Conduct Research

The most fundamental thing that political scientists need to gather is evidence. They gather evidence by three basic research methodologies: logic, traditional observation, and quantitative analysis. All research should apply logic, but valuable contributions can be made by relatively pure logical analysis (Bueno de Mesquita & Morrow, 1999). Aristotle and the other great political philosophers who are mentioned in this book relied primarily on logical analysis to support their political observations. This technique is still important. Some of the best work on nuclear deterrence has been done by analysts who employ *deductive logic* (from the general to the specific) to suggest specifically how nuclear deterrence works.

A second methodology, traditional observation, uses a variety of techniques to study political phenomena. One method is historical analysis, using sources such as archives, interviews, and participant observation. Traditional observation is an old and still valuable methodology. There are many modern studies of why wars occur, but we can all still learn much by reading *The Peloponnesian War*, written by the Greek historian Thucydides in about 410 B.C. Realists, for instance, are persuaded by his analysis that a struggle for power caused the Peloponnesian War (intermittently between 460 and 404 B.C.) between Athens and Sparta. "What made war inevitable," Thucydides wrote, "was the growth of Athenian power and the fear which this caused in Sparta" (Genest, 1994:71). What the historian did is called a case study, and many modern studies use this method to look at one or more events or other political phenomena in order to add to what we can say about international relations theory.

Quantitative analysis is a third methodology. Political scientists who use this method are interested in measurable phenomena and use mathematical techniques. The studies on war and democracy cited in chapter 8 are able to use quantitative methods because countries and wars are relatively measurable.

WHAT TO STUDY: LEVELS OF ANALYSIS

Another major division among analytical approaches used by political scientists has to do with the level of focus. The essential question here is "what do we study?" One approach by political scientists has been to divide the study into **levels of analysis.** These refer to the level of the factors that affect international politics. Scholars have suggested anywhere from two to six possible levels to analyze world politics. Most commonly, analysts use three levels, and that number will be used here. The three levels are:

1. **System-level analysis**—a worldview that takes a "top-down" approach to analyzing global politics. This level theorizes that the world's social-economic-political structure and pattern of interaction (the international system) strongly influence the policies of states and other international actors. Therefore, understanding the structure and pattern of the international system will lead to understanding how international politics operates.
2. **State-level analysis**—a view in which the concern is with the characteristics of an individual country and the impact of those traits on the country's behavior. This level theorizes that states (countries) are the key international actors. Therefore, understanding how states as complex organizations decide policy will lead to understanding how international politics operates.
3. **Individual-level analysis**—a view in which the focus is on people. This level argues that in the end people make policy. Therefore, understanding how people (individually, in groups, or as a species) decide policy will lead to understanding how international politics operates.

Focus on one level of analysis does not mean exclusion of the others. Indeed, it would be best to think of the levels as occurring along a scale from the general (system-level analysis) to the specific (individual-level analysis). It is possible to focus on one level and still use elements of the others. In the following four chapters, we will examine extensively the implications of each of these levels. After chapter 2 and its discussion of the history of and current trends in the international system, chapter 3 takes up system-level analysis, including the evolution of the world system and theories about how systems operate. Then chapter 4 discusses state-level analysis, followed by chapter 5 on individual-level analysis.

CHAPTER SUMMARY

1. This book's primary message is captured by Shakespeare's line, "All the world's a stage, and all the men and women merely players." This means that we are all part of the world drama and are affected by it. It also means that we should try to play a role in determining the course of the dramatic events that affect our lives.

2. Economics is one way that we are affected. The word *intermestic* was coined to symbolize the merging of *inter*national and *do*mestic concerns, especially in the area of economics. Countries and their citizens have become increasingly interdependent.

3. Economically, trade both creates and causes the loss of jobs. International investment practices may affect your standard of living in such diverse ways as determining how much college tuition is, what income you have, what interest rate you pay for auto loans and mortgages, and what income you can look forward to in retirement. The global economy also supplies vital resources, such as oil. Exchange rates between different currencies affect the prices we pay for imported goods, the general rate of inflation, and our country's international trade balance.

4. Our country's role in the world also affects decisions about the allocation of budget funds. Some countries spend a great deal on military functions. Other countries spend relatively little on the military and devote almost all of their budget resources to domestic spending.

5. World politics also plays an important role in determining the condition of your living space. Politics has not, for the most part, created environmental degradation, but political cooperation will almost certainly be needed to halt and reverse the despoiling of the biosphere.

6. Your life may also be affected by world politics. You may be called on to serve in the military. Whether or not you are, war can kill you.

7. There are many things any of us can do, individually or in cooperation with others, to play a part in shaping the future of our world. Think, vote, protest, support, write letters, join organizations, make speeches, run for office—do something!

8. There are demands for and predictions of a new world order. The future path of the world can be thought about as analogous to Robert Frost's poem about two roads diverging in a wood. As the poet wrote, so too will the road that the world chooses make all the difference. Therefore it is important to think about the direction in which you want the world to go.

9. One road is the traditionalist approach, which focuses on the continuing sovereign role of the state as the primary actor in the international system. The traditionalist approach is associated with many terms; "realism" may be the best known. Realism focuses on the self-interested promotion of the state and nation. Realists believe that power politics is the driving force behind international relations. Therefore, realists believe that safety and wisdom lie in promoting national interest through the preservation and, if necessary, the application of the state's power.

10. The second, alternative road is advocated by those who stress the need for significant change, including both a restructuring of power within states and international cooperation and global interests. Of the terms associated with this approach, "idealism" is used herein. Idealists believe that realpolitik is dangerous and outmoded and that idealpolitik should be given greater emphasis because everyone's "real" interest lies in a more orderly, humane, and egalitarian world.

11. Political scientists have numerous orientations, including realist, idealist (and their variations including neorealist and neoidealist), feminist, and political economist.

12. Political scientists study international relations to describe and predict political phenomena, and to prescribe courses of action. Scholars use a variety of methodologies, including logic, traditional observation, and quantitative techniques, to analyze phenomena and test hypotheses. Scholars also have several orientations, which include focusing on power, human social relations, and economics.

13. There are three levels of analysis from which world politics can be studied. They are system-level analysis, state-level analysis, and individual-level analysis. They are not mutually exclusive. Each of these levels is discussed in detail in the next several chapters.

CHAPTER 2

THE EVOLUTION OF WORLD POLITICS

I am amazed, methinks, and lose my way among the thorns and dangers of the world.

Shakespeare, *King John*

Whereof what's past is prologue, what to come, In yours and my discharge.

Shakespeare, *The Tempest*

All true histories contain instruction; though, in some, the treasure may be hard to find.

Anne Brontë, *Agnes Grey*

We have need of history in its entirety, not to fall back into it, but to see if we can escape from it.

José Ortega y Gasset, *The Revolt of the Masses*

CHAPTER OBJECTIVES

After completing this chapter, you should be able to:

- Recognize major trends in the evolving world system from the birth of states to the present.
- Understand the origin of the current world system and the importance of the Treaty of Westphalia (1648).
- Identify the changes that occurred during the eighteenth and nineteenth centuries and continue to have an important impact on the international system.
- Discuss the pace of world political evolution at the beginning of the twentieth century and describe the weakening of the multipolar system.
- Discuss the transition from a bipolar system to the most likely form of a modified multipolar system.
- Analyze the potential shift in the international system away from a strictly Western orientation.
- Identify both international and domestic challenges to the authority of the state.
- Discuss the implications of following either the traditional national security or alternative international security approach in the quest for peace.
- Understand the implications of economic interdependence and the counterpressures to pursue more traditional national economic policies.
- Discuss the implications of the growing economic disparity between the North and South.
- Analyze the future of human rights and environmental issues in the face of national resistance to international solutions.

This chapter has two purposes. The first is to establish a historical foundation on which to build our analysis of international relations. To this end the following pages give a brief historical narrative that emphasizes the themes and events you will encounter repeatedly in this book.

The second goal of this chapter is to sketch the evolution of the current, rapidly evolving world political system (Robertson, 1997). The concept of an **international system** represents the notion that the world is more than just a sum of its parts, such as countries, and that world politics is more than just the sum of the individual interactions among those parts. The idea of an international system is also based on the belief that there are general patterns of actions among the system's actors. These patterns can be explained in part by the distribution of power and several other factors that we will explore in chapter 3.

It is advisable to be patient as you read through the following overview of the evolution of the international system. You will find that this chapter will often introduce a topic briefly and then hurry on to another point. "Wait a minute," you may think, "slow down and explain this better." Hang in there! Later chapters will fill in the details.

It would also be wise to keep your mind open to change. The current international system evolved relatively slowly for several centuries, then shifted rapidly during the twentieth century. Warp-speed technological innovation is the most important source of change. It has brought benefits such as nearly instantaneous global communications, rapid travel, less disease and longer lives, and enhanced material well-being. Breakneck technological change has also created or intensified many new problems, such as global warming, the expanding population, and nuclear weapons. Whether these changes are good or bad, there can be little doubt that, as one scholar has written, there is "turbulence in world politics" as "Spaceship Earth daily encounters squalls, downdrafts, and windshears as it careens into changing and uncharted realms of experience" in the twenty-first century (Rosenau, 1990:4, 7).

THE EVOLVING WORLD SYSTEM: EARLY DEVELOPMENT

The evolution of the current world political system began in about the fifteenth century. It was then that modern states (countries) began to coalesce. The emergence of states as the focus of political authority involved two contradictory trends—one of integration, the other of disintegration—that transfigured the system that had existed for the preceding millennium.

The *integration process* began in part due to the weakening of small feudal units (such as baronies, dukedoms, and principalities) and city-states (such as Venice), which could no longer maintain their political viability and autonomy. They declined because of a series of changes in technology and economics that diminished their strength. As these small units faltered, kings gained enough power to consolidate their authority and to end the virtual independence of the feudal states and city-states.

The *disintegration process* involved the growing unwillingness of people to accept distant, overarching authority. Some of this had to do with the secularization of politics, especially the resistance in Europe to the political authority of the pope and the Roman Catholic Church. Disintegration also included revolts against, and the eventual collapse of, huge multinational empires. This was a long process that began in Europe with the decline and fall of the Holy Roman Empire in the sixteenth and seventeenth centuries and arguably also included the collapse of the Soviet Union in 1991. More than any other event, the Treaty of Westphalia (1648) has come to symbolize this eclipse of overarching authority and the founding of modern states. This treaty ended the Thirty Years'

War and established the independence of the Netherlands, several German states, and a number of other Protestant political entities from the secular authority of the Holy Roman Empire and its Roman Catholic dynasty (the Hapsburgs) and, by extension, from the religious authority of the pope in Rome.

The story of the origins of the modern state is told in greater detail in chapter 8, but it is appropriate to make a few essential points here about the growth of states and their place in the international system. First, in the post-Westphalia system, states became the primary **actors** in the international system. This leading role remains today. A great deal, although not all, of the action on the world stage is about states and groups of states interacting with one another.

Second, the operation of the post-Westphalia system is partly the result of the fact that states came to possess **sovereignty.** This means that they do not recognize any higher legitimate authority. The pivotal role of the sovereign state has had a defining influence on the international system because the system has no central authority to maintain order and dispense justice. As such, international relations occur within an **anarchical political system.** This does not mean that the international system is a scene of unchecked chaos. To the contrary, the system operates with a great deal of regularity. It exists, however, mostly because countries find it in their interest to act according to expectations. But when a state decides that it is in its interests to break the largely informal rules of the system, as Iraq did in 1990 when it invaded Kuwait, there is little to stop it except countervailing power. The point is that in the international system, anarchy does not mean chaos; it means the lack of a central authority.

THE EVOLVING WORLD SYSTEM: THE EIGHTEENTH AND NINETEENTH CENTURIES

The emergence of the sovereign state as the primary actor was just the beginning of the evolution of the modern international system. The pace of change began to quicken in the eighteenth century. Many of the events that occurred between 1700 and 1900 and many of the attitudes that developed during this time helped shape the structure and operation of the international system as it exists currently. Three themes stand out: the coming of popular sovereignty, the Westernization of the international system, and the culmination of the multipolar system.

Popular Sovereignty The establishment of the concept of **popular sovereignty** marked a major change in the notion of who owned the state and how it should be governed. Prior to the late 1700s and early 1800s, the prevailing principle of governance was the theory of the divine right of kings, which held that the monarch was the sovereign and that the people in the sovereign's realm were subjects. The political identification of individuals tended to have a local orientation. It was the monarch, not the people, who owned the state and in whom legitimate political authority rested (Guibernau, 1996). The American (1776) and French (1789) Revolutions challenged this philosophy. *Democracies* were established on the principle that sovereign political power rests with the people rather than with the monarch. The notion of popular sovereignty also changed and expanded the concept of *nationalism* to include mass identification with and participation in the affairs of the state (country). If the people owned the state, then they had both a greater emotional attachment to it and a greater responsibility to support it. One symbol of this change was that Napoleonic France (1799–1815) was the first country to have a true patriotic draft that raised an army of a million strong.

From its beginnings in America and, particularly, in France, democratic nationalism spread throughout Europe and steadily undermined monarchical government and its concept of divine right. The collapse of the dynasties in China, Germany, *(continued on page 30)*

World Countries

The international system includes many types of actors. Of these, states (or countries) are the most important. National boundaries are the most important source of political division in the world, and for most people nationalism is the strongest source of political identification.

Scale: 1 to 125,000,000

Note: All world maps are Robinson projection.

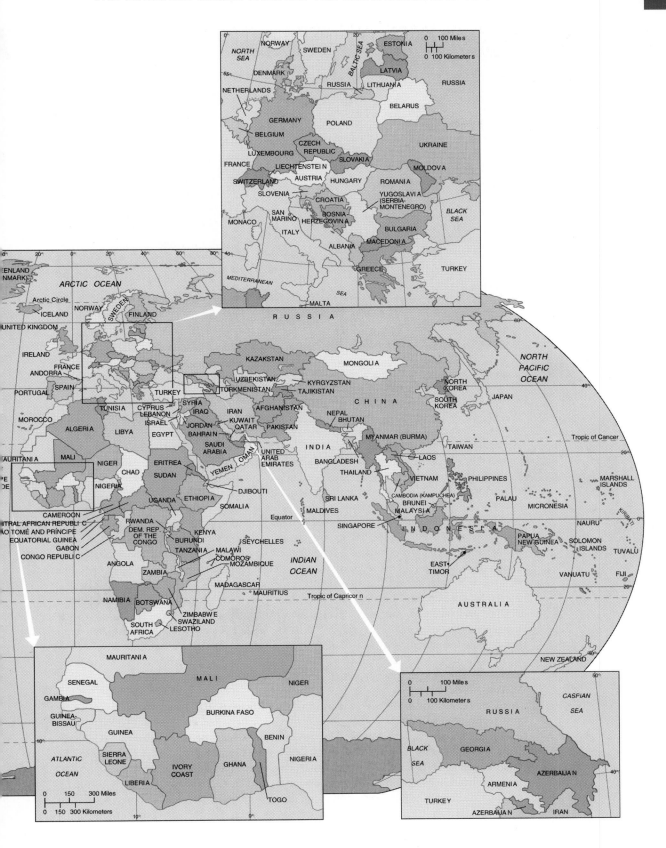

The French Revolution of 1789 was a key event in the growth of democratic nationalism, which embodies the idea that the state is a possession of the people rather than the king. Therefore, all political authority resides with the people. Here Eugène Delacroix's painting *Liberty Leading the People* symbolizes the overthrow of the French monarchy by the French nation.

Austria-Hungary, Russia, the Ottoman Empire, and elsewhere early in the twentieth century marked the real end of strong monarchical government. The multiethnic, in some cases colonial, empires held by several of these monarchies also disintegrated, and the British, French, and other empires would not last much longer.

Westernization of the International System The domination and shaping of the international system by the **West** was a second important characteristic of the eighteenth and nineteenth centuries. Somewhat earlier, the growth of European power had enabled Great Britain, France, and other European countries to thrust outward and take control of North and South America and some other regions. The Arab, Aztec, Chinese, Incan, Mogul (Indian), Persian, and other non-European empires or dynasties began to decline and fall. The process accelerated in the nineteenth century. The result of the transformation of the international "scene... by the expansion of the Europeans over the rest of the globe," as two scholars have observed, is that "a cardinal rule" of the system was that the European states came "to conceive [of] themselves as forming an exclusive club enjoying rights superior to those of other political communities" (Bull & Watson, 1982:425).

One reason for the **Westernization of the international system** was the scientific and technological advances that sprang from the Renaissance (about 1400–1650) in Europe. This sparked the **industrial revolution,** which began in the mid-1700s in Great Britain and then spread to the rest of Europe, Canada, and the United States. The rapid industrialization of the 1800s also occurred elsewhere, such as Japan. Mostly, though, industrialization was a Western phenomenon, and in the few non-Western countries where it did occur, industrialization came later and usually much less completely.

Industrialization and associated advances in weaponry and other technology had a profound impact on world politics. The European powers gained in strength compared

(continued on page 31)

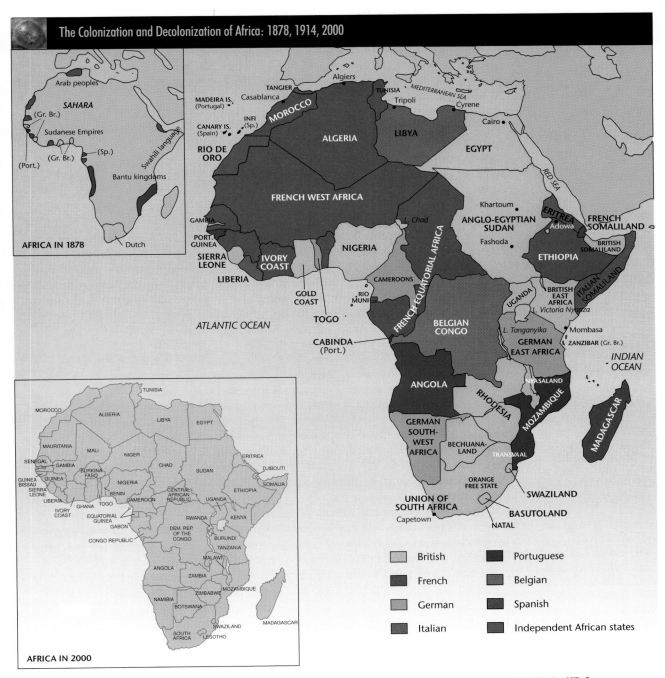

The Colonization and Decolonization of Africa: 1878, 1914, 2000

AFRICA IN 1878

AFRICA IN 2000

Legend:
- British
- French
- German
- Italian
- Portuguese
- Belgian
- Spanish
- Independent African states

Source: Marvin Perry, Myra Chase, James R. Jacob, Margaret C. Jacob, and Theodore H. Von Laue, *Western Civilization: Ideas, Politics, and Society,* Fourth Edition. Copyright 1992 by Houghton Mifflin Company. Used with permission.

The industrialization of the West was one factor that caused the colonization of Asia and Africa in the late 1800s and early 1900s. This map and its insets show that Africa was largely controlled by its indigenous peoples in 1878 (inset) but had, by 1914 (larger map), become almost totally subjugated and divided into colonies by the European powers. Then, after World War II, the momentum shifted. Independence movements led to decolonization. By 2000 there are no colonies left in Africa. Thus the West's domination of the world has weakened.

with nonindustrialized Asia and Africa. Since the industrialized countries needed to find resources and markets to fuel and fund their economies, industrialization promoted colonialism. Many industrialized countries also coveted colonies as a matter of prestige. The result was an era of Euro-American **imperialism** that subjected many people to colonial domination. The fate of Africa is graphically displayed in the map on page 31. Many Asian cultures were similarly subjected to **Eurowhite** domination. China, it should be noted, was never technically colonized, but after the 1840s it was divided into spheres of influence among the Western powers and lost substantial territories to Great Britain (Hong Kong), Japan (Taiwan/Formosa), and Russia (about 1 million square miles).

Americans soon joined in the scramble for colonial possessions. The United States acquired such Pacific territories as Hawaii and Samoa in the 1890s. Victory in the Spanish-American War (1898) added Guam, Puerto Rico, and the Philippines. Additionally, during the next several decades, U.S. domination over many of the Caribbean and Central American countries became so strong that their true independence was in doubt.

As noted earlier, these colonial empires were, for the most part, not long-lived. Still, they had a major and deleterious impact on the subjugated areas that continues to affect world politics. The imperialist subjugation of Asians, Africans, and others by Europeans and Americans set the stage for what became the **North-South Axis.** Indeed, in the overlapping currents of history, the anticolonial movement had begun. An earlier imperial era, which had brought European control to the Western Hemisphere, began to crumble rapidly. In 1804 Haiti won its independence from France, and by 1824 all of Spain's colonies in Central and South America as well as Portugal's colony of Brazil had thrown off colonial rule. The North-South Axis had begun to form.

Growth of the Multipolar System A third characteristic of the 1700s and 1800s is that the multipolar system reached its zenith. The **multipolar system,** which governed political relations among the major European powers from the Treaty of Westphalia in 1648 through the mid-twentieth century, peaked in the 1700s and 1800s because of the global dominance of the European powers. The international system was multipolar in the sense that political affairs were dominated by numerous major powers. For example, in the century between the final defeat of Napoleon (1815) and the outbreak of World War I (1914), the major powers were Great Britain, France, Prussia/Germany, Austria-Hungary, Russia, and to a lesser extent Italy and the Ottoman Empire/Turkey.

The multipolar system that existed between 1648 and 1945 was characterized by shifting alliances designed to preserve the **balance of power** by preventing any single power or combination of powers from dominating the European continent and, by extension, the world. Prime Minister Winston Churchill once clearly enunciated balance-of-power politics as a governing principle of British foreign policy when he explained that "for four hundred years the foreign policy of England has been to oppose the strongest, most aggressive, most dominating power on the Continent" (Walt, 1996:109).

The balance-of-power process succeeded for three centuries in preventing any single power or coalition from controlling Europe and perhaps the world. It did not, however, persist or keep Great Britain and the other dominant European countries from falling from the ranks of major powers.

THE EVOLVING WORLD SYSTEM: THE TWENTIETH CENTURY

The twentieth century was a time of momentous and rapid global change (Chan & Weiner, 1998; Keylor, 1996). The *rapid pace of change* in our time is an important theme for you to keep in mind as you read the balance of this chapter and, indeed, of this book. It is hard for almost any of us to grasp how rapidly things are changing compared

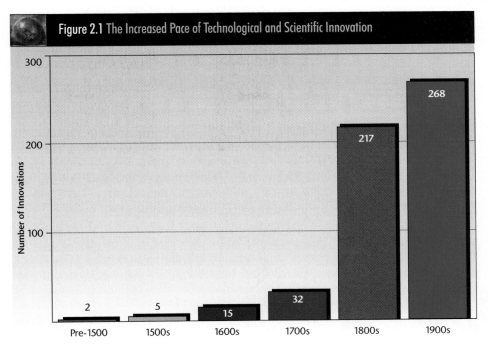

Figure 2.1 The Increased Pace of Technological and Scientific Innovation

Data source: World Almanac (2000).

The escalating pace of technological and scientific change has had a major impact on human beings in general and on world politics in particular. This figure depicts important innovations whose dates of discovery or invention are known. As you can see, only about 10 percent of these occurred before 1800. Another 40 percent occurred in the 1800s, and about 50 percent during the 1900s.

to the earlier pace of social, political, and technological evolution. When the twentieth century began there were no airplanes; monarchs ruled Russia, Germany, Italy, and most other countries; there were no important, global organizations; uranium was a little-known metallic element; and there were about 1.5 billion people in the world. A hundred years later humans can rocket into space and deliver their weapons by intercontinental ballistic missile; elected officials govern most countries; the United Nations, World Bank, World Trade Organization, and other international organizations play important roles in the world; nuclear energy lights our cities and fuels our industries while simultaneously threatening the environment and our very lives through nuclear weapons; and the world population has quadrupled to 6 billion people. All this has happened in just one century, a time period that represents only about 3 percent of the approximately 3,500 years of recorded human history.

Technology has been the prime mover of this rapid change. The twentieth century saw the creation of radio, television, and Internet communications, nuclear power, computers, power chain saws, air and space travel, intercontinental ballistic missiles, effective birth control, antibiotics, crack cocaine, and a host of other innovations that can benefit or bedevil us—keep us together or tear us apart. The world's economy has expanded vastly. Some of the changes have been positive. Many of us have material possessions that a person living a century ago would not have been able even to imagine. But economic expansion has also brought ills, including pollution, deforestation, ozone buildup, and the extinction of untold animal and plant species.

It seems that the world is evolving much faster than ever before. That is evident in part in Figure 2.1, which shows the increased pace of technological and scientific innovation. Technology is both creating and solving problems. Whether the positive or negative results predominate depends in part on our ability to address the issues in a

Did You Know That:

The world is changing at an amazing pace. The world's oldest people may be Mohammed El-Wasimy of Kum Asfin, Egypt, and Elizabeth "Ma Pampo" Israel of Portsmouth, Dominica. Each is thought to have been born in 1875 when Ulysses S. Grant was president of the United States. The two centenarians-plus were 28 years old when Orville and Wilbur Wright first flew and 94 when Neil Armstrong stepped on the moon. They are older than more than 75 percent of the countries in the world.

politically responsible way. But with the accelerated pace of change, there is not time for a leisurely, evolutionary search for solutions.

THE TWENTIETH CENTURY: THE YEARS TO WORLD WAR II

The pace of world political evolution began to speed up even more by the beginning of the 1900s. Democracy was rapidly eroding the legitimacy of dynastic monarchs. In 1900 there were still czars and kaisers; they would be gone in less than two decades. *Nationalism* increasingly undermined the foundations of multiethnic empires. World War I was a pivotal point. Two major empires, the Austro-Hungarian and Ottoman, were among the losers. The result was the (re)establishment of countries such as Czechoslovakia, Poland, and Yugoslavia. Other countries like Jordan, Lebanon, Syria, and Palestine/Israel came under the mandate (control) of the League of Nations and finally became independent after World War II.

The end of the balance of power that had governed European relations during the 1800s was marked by the tragedies of two world wars. The reasons for the end of the multipolar system are still subject to dispute. We can say, however, that the European system changed from being one that was fluid and permitted shifting alliances and pragmatic cooperation to a system dominated by two increasingly rigid and hostile alliances. In World War I (1914–1918) the Central Powers included Germany, Austria-Hungary, and Turkey. The Allied Powers consisted of France, Russia, and Great Britain, which were joined by Italy just after the outbreak of the war. After its defeat in the war, Germany was at first treated severely, but the multipolar system soon led to a **realpolitik** attempt to reestablish balance by allowing Germany in the 1930s to rebuild its strength. With Germany defeated, the British worried that France might once again dominate Europe and threaten them as it had under Napoleon. Therefore, the British tried to offset French power by acquiescing to German rearmament and diplomatic demands. It was, for the British, a near-fatal mistake.

The overthrow of the czarist government in Russia in March 1917 was applauded widely in the West. But when the Bolsheviks, as the early communists were called, came to power in November of that year, the specter of communism alarmed many Europeans and Americans. This early cartoon (1920) depicts the frightening image of Soviet communism common in the West at the time.

Events in Russia also prompted the British and, especially, the French to tolerate German revitalization. The seizure of power by Lenin's Bolsheviks in 1918 evoked horror in the West. Communist ideology combined with Russian military might seemed to threaten the Western powers. Some saw a rearmed Germany serving as a bulwark against the "Red menace."

The grotesqueness of World War I was another reason why Great Britain and France did not seriously try to restrain resurgent Germany. The two victors had each lost almost an entire generation of young men. When Adolf Hitler came to power (1933) and rearmed his country, they vacillated timorously over taking action. The **Munich Conference** (1938) became synonymous with this lack of will when Great Britain and France gave way to Hitler's demands for the annexation of part of Czechoslovakia. British prime minister Neville Chamberlain and other leaders held the false hope that an **appeasement policy** toward Germany would maintain peace.

While all this was occurring in Europe, the rest of the world community expanded and changed during the first 40 years of the twentieth century. Some states gained independence; other existing states, especially Japan and the United States, gradually began to play a more significant role and to undercut European domination of the international system. China began the century saddled with a decaying imperial government and foreign domination, but it overthrew its emperor in 1911 and started a long struggle to rid itself of foreign domination and to reestablish its role as a major power. Also during the first four decades of the century, the League of Nations was established, and many other non-European countries joined world diplomacy through membership in the League. Although international relations still focused on Europe during the first four decades of the 1900s, a shift was under way. The voices of Africa, Asia, and Latin America began to be heard on the world stage.

MAP
Sovereign States: Dates of Independence, p. 136

THE TWENTIETH CENTURY: THE COLD WAR BEGINS AND ENDS

World War II was a tragedy of unequaled proportions. It also marked major changes in the nature and operation of the world political system. This section will focus on the shifts in the polar structure of the system through the end of the cold war. There are a number of other changes that began or accelerated during this period that continue to affect us all as we enter the twenty-first century. These will be taken up in the following section that discusses the issues and choices that lie before us.

On the political front, a series of shifts in the system occurred in the decades after 1945 that involved the actors and, indeed, the polar structure of the system itself. World War II finally destroyed the long-decaying, mostly European-based multipolar structure. It was replaced by a bipolar system dominated by the Soviet Union and the United States. To those who experienced its anguished intensity, East-West hostility seemed to augur an unending future of bipolar confrontation and peril. As is often true, the view that the present will also be the future proved shortsighted. The bipolar era was brief. Significant cracks in the structure were evident by the 1960s; by 1992 the bipolar system was history.

The Rise and Decline of the Bipolar System

World War II devastated most of the existing major actors. In their place, the United States emerged as a military and economic **superpower** and the leader of one power pole. The Soviet Union, though incredibly damaged, emerged as leader of the other pole. The USSR never matched the United States economically, but the Soviets possessed a huge conventional armed force, a seemingly threatening ideology, and, by 1949, atomic weapons. **The East-West Axis** was established.

The exact causes of the confrontation, termed the **cold war,** are complex and controversial. It is safe to say, however, that varying economic and political interests and the power vacuum created by the collapse of the old balance-of-power structure created a bipolar system in which a great deal of world politics was centered on the confrontation between the two superpowers.

The American reaction to the perceived world Soviet/communist threat was the **containment doctrine.** This principle transformed U.S. foreign policy from a prewar norm of isolationism to a postwar globalism, opposing the Soviet Union (and later Communist China) diplomatically and militarily around the world. The United States sponsored a number of regional alliances, most notably the North Atlantic Treaty Organization (NATO, established in 1949). The Soviets responded in 1955 with the Warsaw Treaty Organization (or Warsaw Pact). Both sides also vied for power in the developing countries, and both Soviet and American arms and money flowed to various governments and rebel groups in the ongoing communist-anticommunist contest.

Despite intense rivalry marked by mutual fear and hatred, the reality that both superpowers possessed nuclear weapons usually led them to avoid direct confrontations. There were a few, however, including the scariest moment of the bipolar era, the Cuban missile crisis of 1962. The Soviets had begun building nuclear missile sites in Cuba, and President John F. Kennedy risked nuclear war to force them out.

The containment doctrine also led to the U.S. involvement in Vietnam. Vietnamese forces led by nationalist/communist Ho Chi Minh defeated France's colonial army in 1954 and achieved independence. But the country was divided between Ho's forces in the north and a pro-Western government in the south. The struggle for a unified Vietnam soon resumed, and the United States intervened militarily in 1964. The war, though popular at first, quickly became a domestic trauma for Americans as casualties mounted on both sides. Perhaps the most poignant symbol of opposition to the war was the death in May 1970 of four students at Kent State University during clashes between antiwar demonstrators and Ohio National Guardsmen. War-weariness finally led to a

Few events symbolize the end of the cold war more than the destruction of the Berlin Wall in 1989. It not only divided Berlin and (symbolically) Germany, but represented the divide between the American-led West and the Soviet-led East. The man pictured here was both destroying the wall and collecting a souvenir. As the writing on the wall wisely notes, "Walls are not everlasting."

complete U.S. disengagement. Within a short time Ho's forces triumphed and Vietnam was unified in 1975.

Vietnam caused a number of important changes in American attitudes. One was increased resistance to the cold war urge to fight communism everywhere. Second, Americans saw more clearly that the bipolar system was crumbling, especially as relations between the Soviet Union and China deteriorated.

Beginning approximately with the administrations of Soviet leader Leonid I. Brezhnev (1964–1982) and American president Richard M. Nixon (1969–1974), East-West relations began to improve, albeit fitfully. Nixon accurately assessed the changing balance of power, especially the rise of China, and he moved to better relations through a policy of **détente** with Moscow and Beijing. They came to similar realpolitik conclusions about the changing power configuration of the international system and sought improved relations with Washington.

The End of the Bipolar System

During the 1970s and early 1980s, East-West relations continued to warm, although there were cool periods. Then relations began to change more rapidly. Mikhail S. Gorbachev became the Soviet leader in 1985 and moved to ease the Soviet Union's oppressive political system and to restructure the country's cumbersome bureaucratic and economic systems. While Gorbachev's goals were limited, he opened a Pandora's box for the communist Soviet Union and unleashed forces that were beyond his control.

Gorbachev also sought better relations with the West in order to allow him to reduce the military's burdensome share of the USSR's economy, to receive more favorable trade terms, and to accrue other economic benefits. With this in mind, Gorbachev, among other things, announced that the USSR was willing to let Eastern Europeans follow their own domestic policies. Eastern Europeans moved quickly to escape Moscow's orbit. This was symbolized most dramatically in East Germany, where the communist government fell rapidly apart. East Germany dissolved itself in October 1990, and its territory was absorbed by West Germany into a newly reunified Germany. Other communist governments in the region also fell, and the Warsaw Pact dissolved in early 1991.

It was hard to believe then, but the Soviet Union was next. The USSR soon collapsed, as its constituent republics declared their independence. On December 25, 1991, Gorbachev resigned his presidency of a country that no longer existed. That evening, the red hammer-and-sickle Soviet flag was lowered for the last time from the Kremlin's spires and replaced by the red, white, and blue Russian flag. Few novelists could have created a story of such sweep and drama. The Soviet Union was no more.

THE TWENTY-FIRST CENTURY BEGINS: CHANGES AND CHOICES

"What is past is prologue," Shakespeare comments in *The Tempest*. That is as true for the real world of today and tomorrow as it was for the Bard's literary world of yesterday. One hopes that no future historian will be able to write a history of the coming century under the title *The Tempest*. Titles such as *As You Like It* or *All's Well That Ends Well* are more appealing possibilities for histories yet to be.

Whatever the future will bring, we are in a position similar to that of Banquo in *Macbeth*. He sought to know the future, and we can sympathize with him when he pleads with the Witches of Endore, "If you can look into the seeds of time, And say which grain will grow and which will not, Speak then to me." In Banquo's case, the witches gave him a veiled prophecy that he neither understood nor was able to escape. We are luckier; we have an ability to shape the harvest if we mind another bit of advice that Shakespeare gives, this time in *Much Ado about Nothing*. Our ability to achieve a favorable future, he advises, is determined "by the fair weather that you make yourself: it is needful that you frame the season for your own harvest."

The sections that follow are meant to help you determine your harvest during the coming decades by examining the factors and trends that will benefit or beset the world as it passes into the next century and the next millennium. To facilitate the discussion here, these topics are divided into four areas of changes and choices: political structure and orientation, security, international economics, and the quality of life.

POLITICAL STRUCTURE AND ORIENTATION: CHANGES AND CHOICES

There are a number of important changes occurring in the political orientation and organization of the international system. A new polar structure is emerging, the Western orientation of the system is weakening, and the authority of the state is being challenged from without and from within.

The Emerging Polar Structure

For all the significance of the collapse of the Soviet Union and the bipolar structure, an even more important change is the now-evolving international system. The crucial question is, What will it be like?

One possible answer is that the system will revert to a *traditional multipolar system*, one that is structured and operates much like the system that existed until World War II. The countries that are most likely to play a polar role include the United States, China, Germany, Japan, and Russia. A few other countries, most notably India, with its huge population and nuclear weapons, may join that group. As chapter 3 will explain, a future multipolar system, like past multipolar configurations, would be characterized by patterns of alliances and enmity that are more fluid and complicated than the relationships in the bipolar system. "It is no longer the simple world it once was," one adviser to President Bill Clinton commented. "It is a complex world and we've got to

The international system has become less Westernized in the last several decades as more and more African, Asian, and other countries have gained independence and strength. Fifty years ago, non-Western Kenya was a British colony. Now its ambassador to the United Nations sits as an equal with Great Britain, the United States, and, indeed all other countries.

deal with it the way it is."[1] Who is allied with whom and in opposition to whom will depend more on individual issues and on shifting circumstances than on fixed alliance systems. Old enemies are finding new accommodation. The United States has extended aid to Russia. Old friends have experienced new or intensified tensions. Trade relations among countries of the West are strained, and one scholar predicts that the twenty-first century could experience "capitalist cold war."[2]

Another possible answer is that the system will evolve into a *modified multipolar system*. Many scholars believe that a multipolar system is forming, but they also think that the system will not look or operate like a traditional multipolar system. Instead, these analysts believe that a system is forming in which states and alliances are joined by regional and global international organizations, such as the European Union and the United Nations, as major power centers. This image of the future also holds that the power of even the major states will be considerably restrained by international organizations, international law, and interdependence. It might be that a global or regional organization could become a pole. In any case, this change of cast is modifying the political script, and the dynamics of the modified multipolar system that is emerging will differ from those of a traditional multipolar system.

The Weakening Western Orientation of the International System

The dominant Western orientation of the international system is weakening as a result of the expansion of the number and power of non-Western states. The colonial empires established by the imperial Western powers collapsed after World War II, and in the ensuing years over 100 new countries have gained independence (more than tripling the previous number). The vast majority of these new countries are located in Africa, Asia, and other non-Western regions. Wherever they are, non-Western countries have become a stronger voice in international affairs, and a few, especially China, have achieved enough power to command center stage. These countries have also joined together in such movements and organizations as the Group of 77 in order to promote their causes. Moreover, they have also gained considerable sway in other international organizations. For example, non-Western countries now command a majority in the United Nations General Assembly (UNGA).

While these countries have many differences, they share several commonalities. Most are not well-off economically, earning them the commonly used sobriquet of less developed countries (LDCs). Most of these countries have an ethnic or racial makeup that is not Eurowhite, and they share a history of being colonies of or being dominated by Eurowhites. Furthermore, many of these countries have value systems that differ from the Western values that form the basis of current international law, concepts of human rights, and other standards in the international system (Neuman, 1998).

It should not be surprising, then, that many of these new or newly empowered countries support extensive changes in the international system. The result of all this is that the perspectives and demands of these countries are considerably changing the focus and tone of world political and economic debate.

Challenges to the Authority of the State

While the dynamics of the emerging international system are being determined in part by the changing polar configuration of states and by the rise in importance of non-

Western states, the system is also being affected by the fact that states are no longer virtually the only important actors in the world drama. Instead, as Benjamin Barber (1995) contends in a book entitled *Jihad vs. McWorld,* national states and the state-based structure of the world are being eroded by antithetical forces, some of which are splintering states into fragments (Jihad) and others of which are merging states into an integrated world (McWorld). As Barber (p. 4) puts it, if the first set of forces prevail, there is a "grim prospect of a retribalization of large swaths of humankind by war and bloodshed: a threatened balkanization of nation-states in which culture is pitted against culture, people against people, tribe against tribe, a Jihad in the name of a hundred narrowly conceived [identifications and loyalties]." The other trend, if it triumphs, melds "nations into one homogeneous global theme park, one McWorld tied together by communications, information, entertainment, and commerce." For now, Barber believes, "Caught between Babel and Disneyland, the planet is falling precipitously apart and coming reluctantly together at the very same moment."

The Forces of McWorld   Many analysts believe that there are political, economic, and social pressures, the forces of **McWorld,** which are breaking down the importance and authority of states and moving the world toward a much higher degree of political, economic, and social integration. *Political integration,* for example, is evident in the increasing number and importance of international organizations, such as the United Nations and the World Trade Organization (WTO). When there are trade disputes, countries are no longer free to impose unilateral decisions. Instead, they are under heavy pressure to submit disputes to the WTO for resolution.

Economic interdependence, the intertwining of national economies in the global economy, means that countries are increasingly less self-sufficient. As we noted in the last chapter, national governments have a decreasing ability to manage their own economies. Instead, global trade, international monetary exchange, and other financial flows in the global marketplace play a strong part in determining the jobs we have, whether our investments rise or fall, our country's inflation rate, and many other economic matters. This loss of economic controls diminishes the general authority of a state. There is a lively debate over what this means for the future of states (Hout, 1997; Strange, 1997; Hirst & Thompson, 1996). But some scholars believe, as one puts it, "Globalization will markedly constrain the autonomy and effectiveness of states and, at a minimum, raise serious questions about the meaning of internal and external sovereignty" (Korbin, 1996:26).

Social integration is also well under way in the view of many scholars. They believe that the world is being integrated—even homogenized—by the habits of cooperation and cross-cultural understanding that result from rapid travel and communication and from increased economic interchange of goods and services. People of different countries buy and sell each other's products at an ever-increasing rate; Cable News Network (CNN) is watched worldwide; the World Wide Web gives us almost instant global access to a wealth of information; e-mail has revolutionized communications; English is becoming something of a lingua franca for diplomacy, business, and other forms of international interaction. At a less august level, it is possible to travel around the world dining only on Big Macs, fries, and shakes at the 14,700 McDonald's outlets in 118 countries beyond the United States, which dispense about $20 billion in fast food (accounting for more than half of McDonald's $38.5 billion total sales). Thus, amid some worrisome culinary trends, there are indications that we, the world's people, are moving toward living in a more culturally homogenized global village. This outward trend works to weaken inward-looking nationalism, the primary basis of identification with and loyalty to one's country.

The Forces of Jihad   States are also being tested by and are sometimes collapsing because of a number of pressures, including erosive ethnic rivalries, which Barber refers to as **Jihad** (an Arabic word that means struggling to spread or defend the faith). The

Did You Know That:

Television is promoting transnational culture and a common global frame of reference. CNN, for example, is now available in virtually every country through some 400 million television sets that are watched, at least occasionally, by more than one billion people.

Soviet Union dissolved into 15 independent countries in 1991, and some of them are ethnically unstable. Similarly, Yugoslavia broke apart, and one of its new republics, Bosnia, itself collapsed in ethnic warfare. In 1998 what was left of Serb-dominated Yugoslavia further convulsed when ethnic Albanians, who are a majority in Kosovo Province, rose up against Serb control. Elsewhere, what was Czechoslovakia is now two countries; the people of East Timor declared independence from Indonesia; Somalia exists as a unified state in name only; Turkey's army wages war against separatist Kurds; the Hutu massacre of Tutsis exposed the myth of a single Rwandan people; the list could go on. Moreover, fragmentation and refugees are not faraway phenomena. In the Western Hemisphere, for example, there is a persistent movement in Quebec to achieve autonomy, perhaps even independence, from Canada.

SECURITY: CHANGES AND CHOICES

Military security in today's world is provided primarily by individual countries. Each state is responsible for its own protection and tries to maintain a military capability to defend its national interests. Other countries normally come to the aid of a country that has been attacked only if they find it in their national interest to become allies of that country or to otherwise support the beset country. Kuwait provides a good example. The United States came to Kuwait's aid mostly because of oil. If Kuwait produced tropical fruit, it is unlikely that a half million U.S. troops would have rushed to defend the world's banana supply.

Whatever the advantages of national security based on self-reliance may be, there are also disadvantages. One is the cost. During the decade 1989–1998, total world military expenditures amounted to $9.2 trillion, about one-third of which was U.S. military spending. A second drawback to the traditional way of providing security is that it is hard to say that it works very well when, during the twentieth century alone, over 111 million people were killed in wars. That is almost 6 times as many people as were killed in the nineteenth century and approximately 16 times the number of people slain during the century before that. Even more ominously, the advent of nuclear weapons, heralded by the atomic flash over Hiroshima on August 6, 1945, means that the next war could bring down the final curtain on humankind.

Did You Know That:

Total world military expenditures in 1998 were $884 billion. That was about equal to that year's combined GDPs of the following 23 countries: Albania, Bulgaria, Cambodia, Chile, El Salvador, Ethiopia, Finland, Hungary, Ireland, Malta, New Zealand, Oman, Peru, Rwanda, Somalia, Sri Lanka, Tanzania, Togo, Uganda, Uruguay, Zambia, and Zimbabwe.

In the face of these realities, the world is beginning to work toward new ways of providing security, as chapter 13 will detail. *Arms control* is one trend. The high cost of conventional war and the probable cataclysmic result of a war using weapons of mass destruction (nuclear, biological, chemical) have forced the political system toward trying to avert Armageddon. During the last decade alone, new or revised treaties have been concluded to deal with strategic nuclear weapons, chemical weapons, land mines, nuclear weapons proliferation, and several other weapons issues.

International security forces are another relatively new thrust in the quest for security. United Nations peacekeeping forces provide the most prominent example of this alternative approach to security. Fifty years ago there were none and there never had been a UN peacekeeping mission. In 1988 there were 5; in 2000 there were 15 under way. Using such forces is in its infancy, but they may eventually offer an alternative to nationally based security. There are even calls for a permanent UN army that would be available for immediate use by the UN.

INTERNATIONAL ECONOMICS: CHANGES AND CHOICES

The years since World War II have included a number of trends in international economics that will continue to affect the international system as it moves into the next century. Economic interdependence and economic disparity between the wealthy North and the relatively less developed South are two matters of particular note.

Economic Interdependence

One important economic change in the international system that has gained momentum since World War II is the growth of economic **interdependence.** The trade in goods and services during 2000 exceeded $7.5 billion; Americans alone own more than $2.5 trillion in assets (companies, property, stock, bonds) located in other countries and foreigners own more than $1.8 trillion in U.S. assets; the flow of currencies among countries now exceeds $1.5 trillion every day.

This increasingly free flow of trade, investment capital, and national currencies across national borders has created such a high level of economic interdependence among countries that it is arguably misleading to talk of national economies in a singular sense. The impact of interdependence on virtually every citizen in every country was discussed briefly in the preceding chapter and will be examined in depth in chapter 14. Suffice to say here, then, that whether you realize it or not, global finance affects everything from the price of the clothes that you wear, through the jobs that are available (or not) to you, to the interest you will pay on mortgages, car loans, and other debts.

Even citizens of the United States, the world's most powerful economy with an $8.5 trillion GDP, have their prosperity heavily entwined with the global economy. The figure of $8.5 trillion (or 8.5 thousand billion) is impressive, but so are figures that relate to foreign economic interchange. For 1999, U.S. exports and imports of goods combined came to $1.7 trillion, and the combined export and import of services totaled $475 billion; what Americans earned on their assets overseas and paid to foreign owners of assets in the United States combined for $528 billion; and the net increase in the amount of U.S. assets abroad and foreign-owned assets in the United States came to $796 billion. Other data could be added, but that is not needed to see the key point. The figures related to foreign economic interchange are a significant percentage of the GDP. Moreover, most other countries have economies that are much more enmeshed with the global economy than the immense, still relatively insular U.S. economy.

To deal with this interdependence, the world during the last half-century has created and strengthened a host of global and regional economic organizations. The three most important global economic organizations are the World Bank, the International Monetary Fund (IMF), and the World Trade Organization (WTO), originally called the General Agreement on Tariffs and Trade. There are also numerous economic agencies associated with the UN. Such regional initiatives as the Association of Southeast Asian Nations (ASEAN), the European Union (EU), Mercosur in South America, and the North American Free Trade Agreement (NAFTA) both respond to and further interdependence.

Before leaving our discussion of economic interdependence, it should be noted that the road to integration is neither smooth nor is its future certain. There are numerous difficulties. Trade and monetary tensions exist among countries. Many people are opposed to surrendering any of their country's sovereignty to the UN, the WTO, or any

Multinational corporations dominate the world economy. Globally omnipresent PepsiCo is only the 203rd largest MNC in terms of revenues, but that income came to $20.4 billion in 1999. The company employs 118,000 people, has assets in excess of $17 billion (Fortune 500 Rank: 76), and derives about 30 percent of its revenue from its international operations.

MAP
International Trade
Organizations, p. 219

The poor have little control over their lives. These three girls are sitting dejectedly in the rubble of Saidpur, Pakistan, where the average annual per capita income had been about $50. The children's village had just been leveled for being an "eyesore along a VIP route travelled by Pakistani officials and foreign visitors." "For the poor there is no democracy," lamented Nisar Ahmad, whose house and shop were razed. "For us [there is] only trouble and oppression."

other international organization. Other people, concerned about workers' rights, product safety, and the environment, worry that free trade has allowed multinational corporations to escape effective regulation (Cutler, Haufler, & Porter, 1999). As one analyst puts it, the move to create an unfettered global economy "pulls capital into corners of the globe where there is less regulation, which in turn makes it harder for advanced nations to police their capital markets and social standards" (Kuttner, 1998:6). Indeed, these and other worries have sparked a growing countermovement against further interdependence. When the trade ministers of the countries in the WTO met in Seattle in late 1999, they were faced with 30,000 protesters from labor, environmental, human rights, and other groups. There are, in short, significant choices to be made in how to order financial relations among countries.

Economic Disparity between North and South

There is a wide disparity in economic circumstance between the relatively affluent life of a small percentage of the world population who live in a few countries and the majority of humanity who live in most countries. The terms North and South are used to designate the two economic spheres. The North symbolizes the wealthy and industrialized **economically developed countries (EDCs)**, which lie mainly in the Northern Hemisphere. By contrast, the South represents the **less developed countries (LDCs)**, the majority of which are near or in the Southern Hemisphere. The acronyms EDC, LDC, and associated designations are discussed in Explanatory Notes on page 557.

The economic and political ramifications of the North-South divide are discussed extensively in chapters 14, 15, and 16, but a few basic points are appropriate here. One is that the economic circumstances of countries are not truly dichotomized. Instead they range from general opulence (the United States) to unbelievable poverty (Bangladesh). There are some countries of the South that have achieved substantial

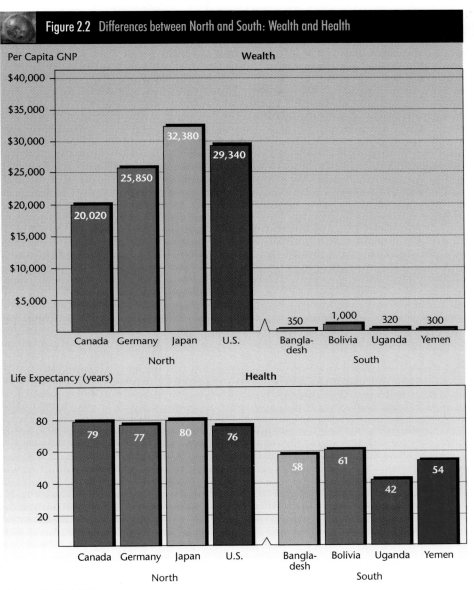

Figure 2.2 Differences between North and South: Wealth and Health

Data source: World Bank (2000).

The difference between the lives of the people in the North and those in the South is measured by per capita GNP wealth and life expectancy. By these, and many other standards, the people of the South are severely disadvantaged compared to those who live in the North.

industrialization and whose standards of living have risen rapidly. These countries are called **newly industrializing countries (NICs).** Moreover, there are some wealthy people in LDCs and numerous poor people in EDCs.

Yet, it is also the case that such details cannot disguise the fact that there is a vast economic gap between North and South. The per capita **gross national product (GNP)** in 1998 of the North was $25,510. At $1,250, the per capita wealth of those in the South was a mere 4.9 percent of that of their contemporaries in the North. This immense gulf in wealth has devastating consequences for the poor. Their children, for instance, suffer an unconscionable mortality rate that is almost 7 times greater than the infant mortality rate in the wealthiest countries. As Figure 2.2 shows, and as the box The 6 Billionth Baby relates, by economic and health measures, the countries of the

(continued on page 45)

MAP
Gross National Product Per
Capita, p. 395

THE 6 BILLIONTH BABY

October 12, 1999, was a Tuesday, and for the most part, it was not an unusual day. The twelfth of October was Columbus Day in many of the Spanish-speaking countries in the Americas and had once also been in the United States until the holiday had been shifted by law to the nearest Monday to stretch out the weekend. Elsewhere the people of Equitorial Guinea and Spain were celebrating their respective national days. Individually, the day marked the birthdays of some 16,438,356 people, give or take a few, around the world.

For all the prevailing "just another day" sense of October 12, though, it was a day of importance to humans and the Earth they inhabit. Somewhere in the world on that day, a first cry heralded the arrival of the baby who brought the global population to 6 billion. Carol Bellamy, executive director of UNICEF, dubbed the infant, the "6 Billionth Baby."[1]

When the world population reached 5 billion just 12 years, 3 months, and 1 day earlier on July 11, 1987, the UN decided to designate a child born on that date as the 5 billionth baby. The chosen symbol was Matej Gaspar, an infant born in Zagreb, in what was then Yugoslavia and what is now the capital of Croatia. One hopes that Matej is now a teenager and has escaped the killing that engulfed and still plagues some parts of crumbling Yugoslavia.

In the intervening 12 years, the UN thought better of bestowing what is not necessarily an accolade of being the next billionth baby on another child. Thus there was no symbolic baby named, and, in truth, there is no way to tell which of the approximately 358,988 babies born on October 12, 1999, was, indeed, the 6 billionth baby.

Thus it is impossible to know for sure if the child was a boy or a girl, whether he or she was born to wealth or poverty, or even if the baby lived or died quickly. Statistically, however, we can conclude that the chances are that the child's health, educational, economic, and other prospects are not very good. How could they be when only about 15 percent of the world's population lives in the relatively prosperous North and 85 percent lives in the less economically developed South? In fact, so many of the people in the South are so poor—often living on less than a two or three dollars a day—that there is a 30 percent chance the 6 billionth baby was born into extreme poverty.

If in the birth lottery the baby was born in the South, then he or she, compared to a child in the

The world population reached 6 billion on October 12, 1999, according to UN calculations. The child, who might be called the "6 billionth baby," marked a 400 percent increase in the world population during the twentieth century alone. Perhaps the baby, one of about 358,988 born that day, came to an economically secure family. But with 85 percent of the world population living in less developed countries, the odds are great that the child, like the Cambodian baby in the picture, was born to a family that has to struggle against poverty and disease.

North, is half as likely to have been delivered by a health professional, is twice as likely to have had a dangerously low birth weight, and is four times more likely to die before age 5. The baby is also 16 times more likely to have had his or her mother die from pregnancy or delivery complications, is 30 percent less likely to learn how to read and write, and, even if he or she does survive infancy, is still likely to live 11 years less than if he or she had been born in the North.

Whoever the 6 billionth baby is, then, we should all wish him or her luck. He or she will probably need it given the vast gap between the economic, health, educational, and other conditions in the North and South.

North and those of the South live in virtually different worlds. The North is predominantly a place of reasonable economic security, literacy, and adequate health care. By contrast, the lives of the people of the South are often marked by poverty, illiteracy, rampant disease, and early death.

One ramification of the weakening Western orientation of the international system discussed earlier is that this economic inequity is causing increased tension along the so-called North-South Axis. The LDCs are no longer willing to accept a world system in which wealth is so unevenly distributed.

They blame much of their poverty on past colonialist suppression and on what they believe are current efforts by the EDCs to keep the LDCs economically and politically weak—as sources of cheap raw materials and labor. They also rebel against the North's control of the IMF and other international financial organizations. When the economies of several Asian nations collapsed in late 1997, some people in that region suspected the EDCs had conspired to thwart their booming development. The demands of the North-dominated IMF that Asian recipients of assistance adopt the North's model of economic development led one major newspaper in Thailand to editorialize in 1998 that, "Just as the fall of the Berlin wall represents a political and ideological victory for the U.S. over socialism, the collapse of the economies in Asia marks another, more subtle triumph of U.S. financial imperialism over this region."[3]

Whether or not one accepts this conspiracy theory is not the issue here. The point is that choices must be made in the face of the changes that are occurring. One option for the wealthy countries is to ignore the vast difference in economic circumstances between themselves and the LDCs. The other option is to do more, much more, to help. Both options carry substantial costs.

THE QUALITY OF LIFE: CHANGES AND CHOICES

The last few decades have spawned several changes involving the quality of human life that will continue to affect world politics in the new century and the choices we must face. Preserving human rights and the environment are two matters of particular note.

Human Rights

It borders on tautology to observe that violations of human rights have existed as far back into history as we can see. What is different is that the world is beginning to take notice of human rights violations across borders and is beginning to react negatively to them.

The change involves the *norms of behavior* that help regulate and characterize any political system. Behavior in virtually all political systems is governed by a mix of coercion and voluntary compliance. Norms, or values, are what determine voluntary compliance. For example, the values about the conduct of war are changing, and attacks on civilians are losing whatever legitimacy they may once have had. The international tribunals trying war crimes and crimes against humanity in Bosnia and in Rwanda and the treaty now before the world to establish a permanent International Criminal Court all exemplify this. Unpunished mistreatment of some or all of one's citizens under the guise of sovereignty has also lost considerable legitimacy. The international community used sanctions to force the white government in South Africa to allow all the people in the country to vote and hold office. And more recently the former brutal dictator of Chile, Augusto Pinochet, escaped being tried in a Spanish court for his actions only after it was ruled amid controversy that he was too ill to stand trial.

There are numerous other areas in which the demand for the protection of human rights is louder and stronger. The rights of women are just one of the subjects that have recently become a focus of international concern and action. The largest and most widely noted in a series of international conferences on the status of women met in

1995 in Beijing. Gertrude Mongella, a Tanzanian serving as secretary-general of the UN **fourth World Conference on Women,** brought the global conclave into session with the ringing declaration that women are "no longer guests on this planet. This planet belongs to us too. A revolution has begun."[4] It is a revolution that will almost certainly have a profound impact on the conduct of international as well as domestic policy in the twenty-first century.

As with many of the other issues that challenge us, it would be naive to pretend that the end of human rights abuses is imminent or that progress has not been excruciatingly slow. Yet it would also be wrong not to recognize that there is movement. Leaders at least discuss human rights concerns; that was virtually unheard of not many years ago. Sometimes, if still not usually, countries take action based on another country's human rights record. Human rights conferences are no longer unnoticed, peripheral affairs. A significant number of human rights treaties have been signed by a majority of the world's countries. In sum, what was once mostly the domain of do-gooders has increasingly become the province of presidents and prime ministers.

The Environment

The mounting degradation of the biosphere has its origins in the industrial revolution and, therefore, like the abuse of human rights, is not new to the world stage. Like human rights, what has changed is the attention that is now being paid to the subject and the international efforts to protect the environment that have begun.

MAP
World Ecological Regions,
pp. 518–519

The greatest challenge is to achieve **sustainable development,** that is, to (a) continue to develop economically while (b) simultaneously protecting the environment. As with human rights, you will see in a later chapter that while progress on the environment has been slow, progress is being made. Among other advances, the subject has shifted from the political periphery to presidential palaces. What leaders have come to realize is that their national interests are endangered by environmental degradation, as well as by military and economic threats. This view was expressed by President Bill Clinton when he told President Jiang Zemin of China that:

> I think the greatest threat to our security [that] you present is... that all of your people will want to get rich in exactly the same way we got rich. Unless we try to triple automobile mileage and to reduce greenhouse gas emission, if you all get rich in that way we won't be breathing very well... [because] you will do irrevocable damage to the global environment.... I think that other countries will support your development more if they don't feel threatened by the environment.[5]

The need to balance economic development and environmental protection is recognized, even by those countries that are struggling to alleviate widespread poverty and its associated ills. "Family planning and environmental protection are of vital importance to sustainable economic growth," President Jiang acknowledged to reporters.[6]

Yet for China and all other countries, achieving sustainable development will not be easy. Among other challenges, China and the other LDCs will need extensive assistance to develop in an environmentally responsible way. UN officials have placed that cost as high as $125 billion a year, and many observers believe that the North should bear a great deal of the cost for three reasons. One is that the North is much wealthier than the South. The second reason is that the North has historically emitted 70 percent of the carbon dioxide (CO_2) and a majority of most other pollutants, despite having less than one-quarter of the world population. "You can't have an environmentally healthy planet in a world that is socially unjust," Brazil's president Fernando Collor de Mello noted at one point.[7]

Third, even if you do not agree with the social justice view, it is arguable that the North should assist the South out of sheer self-interest. To better understand the North's stake in LDC development and its impact on the environment, consider Figure 2.3. On

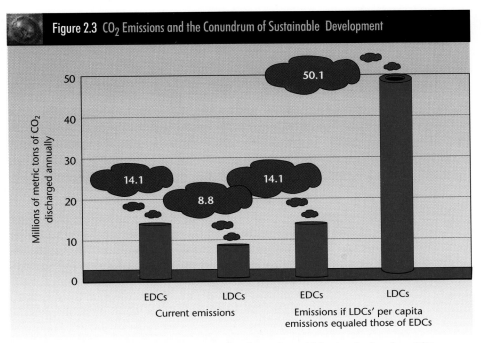

Figure 2.3 CO_2 Emissions and the Conundrum of Sustainable Development

EDCs = economically developed countries   LDCs = less developed countries

Data source: UNDP (1999).

The small percentage of the world's population who live in EDCs currently produce 63 percent of the carbon dioxide (CO_2) emissions. If the LDCs were to reach the same level of development as the EDCs, their CO_2 emissions would increase 569 percent and total world emissions would increase 280 percent. That would be an environmental disaster. The conundrum of sustainable development is how to help the LDCs develop in an environmentally acceptable way.

the left you can see that with about four times as many people, the LDCs only produce a little more than half as much CO_2 as the EDCs. On the right you can see that if the LDCs produced on a per capita basis the same amount of CO_2 as the EDCs, then the annual discharges of the LDCs would soar to 50.1 billion tons, an environmental disaster.

CHAPTER SUMMARY

1. This chapter has two primary goals. One is to establish a reference framework from which the historical examples used to illustrate the theoretical points made in this book can be understood in context. The second goal is to sketch the evolution of the current world political system.

2. The current world system began to develop in about the fifteenth century, when modern states started to form due to a process marked by both integration and disintegration of earlier political authority. The Treaty of Westphalia (1648), more than any other event, demarcated the change between the old and the new systems. With the sovereign state at its center, the newly evolving system is anarchical.

3. Several changes occurred during the 1700s and 1800s that had an important impact on the international system. The emergence of the concept of popular sovereignty involved a shift in the idea of who legitimately controls the state. The divine right of kings gave way to the notion that political power does, or ought to, come from the people. During these two centuries, the system also became Westernized and the multipolar configuration reached its apogee.

4. The twentieth century witnessed the most rapid evolution of the system. The multipolar system tottered, then fell. The bipolar system declined as other countries and transnational actors became more important, as the expense of continuing confrontation strained American and Soviet budget resources, and as the relative power of the two superpowers declined. The bipolar system ended in 1991 when the Soviet Union collapsed.

5. During this century, nationalism also undermined the foundations of multiethnic empires. European contiguous empires, such as the Austro-Hungarian Empire, disintegrated. The colonial empires dominated by Great Britain, France, and other Eurowhite countries also dissolved.

6. There are numerous new trends, uncertainties, and choices to make as we enter the twenty-first century. One significant question is what will follow the bipolar system. The most likely possibility is some form of modified multipolar system. But even though there are likely to be four or more major powers, as in a multipolar system, the system is unlikely to parallel earlier multipolar systems because of the other significant changes that have occurred in the international system. One such change is that international organizations have become much more numerous and more central to the operation of the international system.

7. Another shift in the international system is its weakening Western orientation. The number and strength of non-Western countries have grown substantially, and the strength of these states will almost certainly continue to grow in the next century. These countries often have values that differ from those of the Western countries.

8. Challenges to the authority of the state represent a third shift in the international system, which has strong implications for the next century. There are both disintegrative internal challenges to the state and integrative external challenges.

9. The pursuit of peace is also at something of a crossroad. The destructiveness of modern weaponry has made the quest for peace even more imperative. The issue is whether to follow traditional national security approaches or alternative international security approaches.

10. The international economy is also changing in ways that have important implications for the twenty-first century. Economic interdependence has progressed rapidly. The transnational flow of trade, investment capital, and currencies has economically entwined all countries. There are, however, counterpressures, and an important issue in the near future is whether to continue down the newer path to economic integration or to halt that process and follow more traditional national economic policies.

11. The effort to resolve the wide, and in many ways growing, gulf between the economic circumstances of the countries of the economically developed North and the less economically developed South is also a mounting issue in the new century.

12. A final set of issues that must be addressed in the new century involve the quality of life: human rights and the environment. Both issues have become the subject of much greater international awareness and interaction. Yet ending the abuses of human rights and protecting the environment will be difficult in the face of national resistance to international solutions.

CHAPTER 3

SYSTEM-LEVEL ANALYSIS

Mad world! Mad kings! Mad composition!

Shakespeare, *King John*

If you live among wolves you have to act like a wolf.

Soviet leader Nikita Khrushchev, 1971

CHAPTER OBJECTIVES

After completing this chapter, you should be able to:

- Describe what international systems are and how they help the political scientist understand the world.
- Analyze systemic factors and understand their application to international politics.
- Characterize national and supranational actors in the international system.
- List the types and characteristics of transnational actors, including intergovernmental and nongovernmental organizations.
- Understand the international system's scope and level of interaction.
- Distinguish among the kinds and operations of the different system poles and discuss the effects of varying relative power concentrations.
- Explain how power assets, norms of behavior, and geographic characteristics affect the distribution and exercise of power in the system. Address how changes in the number or power of major actors can alter the international system.
- Discuss how changes in power are related to system stability.
- Understand how a system's economic patterns affect the operation of the system.
- Understand the norms that help determine patterns of behavior and system stability and why those norms may be changing.
- Explore some possible directions of the future international system.
- Understand the strengths and shortcomings of a system-level analysis.

The discussion in chapter 1 of how to study international politics introduced levels of analysis as an analytical concept. The issue is where to focus our study of world politics. Is it most fruitful to study the nature of the world (system-level analysis), to study how countries make foreign policy (state-level analysis), or to study people as individuals or as a species (individual-level analysis)? The best answer is to understand all three levels. The preceding chapter began our survey of system-level analysis through a brief survey of the evolution of the current world system. This chapter will continue examining system-level analysis by discussing it as a theory. Then chapter 4 will take up state-level analysis, followed by chapter 5 on individual-level analysis.

UNDERSTANDING POLITICAL SYSTEMS: THE WORLD AND YOUR SCHOOL

System-level analysis adopts essentially a "top down" approach to studying world politics. It begins with the view that countries and other international actors operate in a global social-economic-political-geographic environment and that the specific characteristics of the system help determine the pattern of interaction among the actors. Systems analysts believe that any system operates in somewhat predictable ways—that there are behavioral tendencies that the actor countries usually follow.

Most people do not think much about systems, but they are an ever-present part of our lives. Although each of us has free will, each of us is also part of many overlapping systems that influence our behavior and make it reasonably predictable. These systems range from very local ones, such as your family and school, to much larger systems, such as your country and the world. Whatever their size, though, how each of these systems operates is based on four factors: structural characteristics, power relationships, economic realities, and norms. Before analyzing the international system according to these four factors, it might be helpful to see how they determine the operation of a nearer, more familiar system: your college.

Structural characteristics are one key to understanding a system. One of these characteristics is how authority is organized. In your college, authority is hierarchical. There is a central governing body that sets down authoritative rules about graduation requirements, when semesters begin and end, the parameters for determining grades, and many other factors. Instructors have considerable, but not complete, freedom inside the classroom. They may not, for one, solicit bribes in return for A+ grades. Students are also restrained. They may not, for instance, seek good grades by threatening their professors. In an anarchic structure without authoritative rules and enforcement, the wealthiest or the biggest students might be the ones who received A+ grades.

Power relationships also help shape the conduct of any system, including your college. Most classes are unipolar systems. They have one major power center (the instructor), who plays a dominant role in the day-to-day conduct of the course. Even if less powerful actors (individual students) do not like how the instructor is conducting the course, it is unlikely that any one of them will stand up in class and demand loudly that the instructor do a better job. The reason is that the instructor has the power to reward and punish. If the students united and staged a walkout or went en masse to protest to the dean, they might have enough strength to become a pole (a power center). This would create a bipolar situation, in which the dynamics would be altered.

Economic patterns are a third factor in most systems. Many students go to college and even read this book because getting a degree is strongly related to getting a job that pays well. Studying is hard and sometimes boring. Watching television, skiing, or lolling at the beach are more fun; but they will not get you a decent job. So for much of the year you try to get good grades rather than a good tan. Things might be very different if professional success were not usually related to going to college.

Norms of behavior are a fourth systemic factor that govern your class. Just think about the way people dress in your class. Last semester this author noticed one day that not only was every student in class in clothes but that most had chosen to wear jeans of exactly the same faded blue denim; all had on either sneakers or hiking boots; and about 75 percent were wearing sweatshirts. Many students had topped off their uniform with ball caps. There was not a tux or ball gown to be seen. The reason for this conformity of dress was not any formal rule mandated by the university. Rather it was the result of the norms that students share about what they wear to class.

If you think about it, you could, as a person with free will, angrily confront professors who do not teach well; you could drop out of school and become a bag person; you could come to class in formal wear or your "birthday suit." But it is reasonably predictable that neither you nor any of your classmates will do any of these things. The reason is that the system at your college influences your behavior.

Just as the nature of your local socioeconomic, political system restrains the behavior of students, instructors, and other actors in that system, so too does the nature of the international system influence states and other system-level actors.

A final thought is that no system, whether it is the one in which your college operates or the one that helps structure global interactions, operates with perfect predictability. Exceptions do not disprove general rules, however, and the existence of occasional aberrant behavior does not disprove the case that a system operates with a degree of regularity based on its structural characteristics, its power relationships, its economic patterns, and its norms. Let us turn to examining each of these factors and how they affect the international system.

STRUCTURAL CHARACTERISTICS

All systems have identifiable structural characteristics. These include how authority is organized, who the actors are, and what the scope and level of interaction among the actors is.

THE ORGANIZATION OF AUTHORITY

The authority structure of a system for making and enforcing rules, for allocating assets, and for conducting other authoritative tasks can range from very hierarchical to anarchical. Most systems, like your university and your country, are hierarchical. They have a **vertical authority structure** in which subordinate units answer to higher levels of authority. Vertical systems have central authorities that are responsible for making, enforcing, and adjudicating rules that restrain subordinate actors. Other systems have a **horizontal authority structure** in which authority is fragmented. The international system is one such system with a mostly horizontal authority structure. It is based on the sovereignty of states. Sovereignty means that countries are not legally answerable to any higher authority for their international or domestic conduct (Jackson, 1999). As such, the international system is anarchic; it has no overarching authority to make rules, settle disputes, and provide protection.

To see how horizontal and vertical structures operate differently, ask yourself why all countries are armed and why few students bring guns to class. The reason is that states in the international system (unlike students in your college) depend on themselves for protection. If a state is threatened, there is no international 911 number that it can call for help. Given this self-help system, each state feels compelled to be armed.

While the authority structure in the international system remains decidedly horizontal, change is under way. Many analysts believe that sovereignty is declining and that even the most powerful states are subject to an increasing number of authoritative rules made by intergovernmental organizations (IGOs) and by international law. In February 2000, for example, the World Trade Organization (WTO) ruled in favor of a complaint brought by the European Union (EU) against the United States. The EU charged that the U.S. practice of giving tax breaks to U.S. companies for goods they sold in Europe and elsewhere abroad amounted to a government subsidy of exports, which is not allowed under world trade rules. Offsetting the sting of such losses, the United States has at other times prevailed in the WTO. One of these victories came in February 1998, when the WTO found in favor of a U.S. complaint that the European Union was illegally barring certain U.S. computer technology in an effort to protect Europe's software companies. Countries still resist and often even reject IGO governance when it touches on sensitive political issues, but that does not negate the slowly growing authority of IGOs in the international system.

Countries are also no longer totally free to make internal policy on even purely domestic matters. For example, the UN condemned the military overthrow of democracy in Haiti and authorized the U.S.–led intervention in 1994 that toppled the military junta. International tribunals sitting in Tanzania and the Netherlands are trying individuals for atrocities committed within Rwanda and the Balkans (including Bosnia and now Kosovo) respectively. Sovereignty certainly continues as a cornerstone of the authority structure of the international system. There is, however, a growing view among many that sovereignty is and ought to be limited. This sense was captured by Pope John Paul II, who told the UN General Assembly that while every country has "the right to shape its life according to its own traditions," this sovereign authority excluded "of course, every abuse of basic human rights and in particular the oppression of minorities."[1]

THE ACTORS

Another characteristic of any system is its actors. What organizations operate in the system, and what impact do they have on the course of international relations? We can answer these questions by dividing actors into three general categories: national actors, international actors, and transnational actors.

National Actors: States

States are the principal actors on the world stage. Therefore, the current configuration is termed a **state-centric system.** The leading role that states play in the international system is determined by several factors, including state sovereignty, the state's status as the primary focus of people's political loyalty, and the state's command of the preponderance of economic and military power.

Inasmuch as the nature and operation of states will be dealt with extensively in chapters 4 and 8, we will not detail them here. What is important for this discussion, though, is that states dominate the action and act with independence. Yet for all this talk of the pivotal role of sovereign states in a largely anarchical international system with a vertical authority structure, it is also true that states are not the only system-level actors. Moreover, there are significant centralizing forces in the system that are slowly moving it, at least somewhat, toward a vertical authority structure.

MAP
World Countries, pp. 28–29

It is also worthwhile at this point to take a moment to understand how this book and many other works in political science use three important terms: state, nation, and government. They are not synonymous.

States are tangible political entities also referred to as countries. A state is a territorially based political organization that possesses sovereignty. States can generally be identified by such objective criteria as having a defined territory and a government.

The United Nations is an important example of the many international organizations that have come on to the world scene since 1945. Their roles, importance, and authority in the international system have increased greatly.

Nations are cultural entities. A nation is a group of people who identify with one another politically because of common characteristics, such as shared history, language, culture, religion, or race. Americans are a nation; the United States is a state. Carefully note the word "identify" in the definition of nations. It means that they are not based on objective criteria. Rather, nations are intangible and are based on a people's mutual perceptions of cultural kinship. The line between an ethnic group and a nation is often hazy, but the basic difference is that a nation has active or latent aspirations for independence or autonomy, whereas an ethnic group does not. Not all nations are defined by ethnic identity, but many are. These are called ethnonational groups. Canada, for example, is a state that contains both an English-speaking and a French-speaking nation.

Government can be used in two ways. It can refer to a type of government, such as the democratic system in Canada or the authoritarian system in China. Government can also designate the specific regime, such as the government of Prime Minister Jean Chrétien in Canada or that of Premier Zhu Rongji in China (whose surname is Zhu, not Rongji; see the section on Explanatory Notes on page 557).

International Governmental Actors

A second group of system-level actors are made up of an array of international organizations. These actors are also called **intergovernmental organizations (IGOs)**. Almost all IGOs have a central administrative structure. The UN is headquartered in New York City and has an administrative staff headed by a secretary-general.

A significant thing to remember about IGOs is that more and more in the past century, states have come to share the stage with this relatively new type of actor. One indication of the enhanced role of IGOs is the steep rise in their number. In 1900 there were 30 IGOs. That number has increased approximately tenfold, with nearly 300 IGOs now in existence. Chapter 9 will deal extensively with IGOs, but here we can preview IGOs by classifying them and considering their membership, roles, and authority.

IGO Membership The key defining characteristic of IGOs that distinguishes them from other types of international organizations is that IGOs have individual countries as members. Some IGOs, such as the United Nations, the International Monetary Fund (IMF), and the World Bank have member-countries from all parts of the world and, in fact, are approaching universal membership. The membership of the UN, for instance, consists of 188 countries. Other IGOs have a more limited geographic scope to their membership. Regional organizations are a rapidly growing phenomenon and include, among others, the Organization of African Unity (OAU), the Organization of American States (OAS), and the Association of Southeast Asian Nations (ASEAN). An IGO's membership may also be based on a common interest among members. The Organization of Petroleum Exporting Countries (OPEC) includes such oil-producing and exporting countries as Indonesia, Nigeria, and Venezuela, in addition to its members from the Middle East.

IGO Roles There are IGOs involved in a wide array of activities. Some IGOs have multiple functions. The UN, for one, is a general-purpose IGO that works to protect or

Table 3.1 Sample Intergovernmental Organizations, 2000

Organization	Members	Headquarters	Chief Officer
International Atomic Energy Agency	130	Austria	Egyptian
International Civil Aviation Organization	185	Canada	Brazilian
International Criminal Police Organization (INTERPOL)	178	France	British
International Fund for Agricultural Development	161	Italy	Kuwaiti
International Maritime Organization	158	United Kingdom	Canadian
International Monetary Fund	182	United States	German
United Nations	188	United States	Ghanian
World Bank	181	United States	American
World Health Organization	191	Switzerland	Norwegian
World Meteorological Organization	188	Switzerland	Nigerian
World Trade Organization	135	Switzerland	New Zealander

Intergovernmental organizations perform a wide variety of functional, or nonpolitical, tasks in the world today, whether they concern themselves with catching criminals, regulating civil aviation, or promoting health.

improve the environment, human rights, and economic conditions, as well as to promote peace and to address other more traditional political matters. Other IGOs are more specialized. The World Health Organization (WHO) is an example. For the IGOs listed in Table 3.1, take note of the wide range of their activities, the diversity of the locations of their headquarters, and the various nationalities of the administrators who head them.

Alliances are a special type of IGO. Most alliances are merely military treaties, but a few, such as the North Atlantic Treaty Organization (NATO), also have organizational structure and evolve roles beyond their original military purpose. This evolution may occur because the commonalties that led initially to the formation of an alliance lead to further bonding among the members through greater trade and other exchanges and through the desire of the members to increase their influence in the global system through mutual diplomatic support (Bennet, 1997; Mansfield & Bronson, 1997). Indeed, it is possible for alliances to survive even after the reason for their formation has been eliminated. A prime example is NATO, which is altering both its functions and its geographic scope (Glennon, 1999; Gordon, 1996). Some people question the need for and the future of the alliance. This issue is discussed in the box, The New NATO Marches East (page 56).

IGO Authority A key issue for IGOs is the basis of their authority. Are they merely shells for national diplomacy and policy or do IGOs make policy independently? Traditionally, IGOs have had little independent authority. Instead they have been and remain primarily vehicles for the diplomacy of their member-states. Countries try to build a coalition IGO in order to garner enough votes to have it pursue a particular policy. This is called parliamentary diplomacy and is discussed in chapter 10. Iraq and the United States, for example, vie within the UN to loosen or retain the UN economic sanctions on Iraq that were imposed after the Persian Gulf War (1990–1991).

Many observers believe, however, that the authority of IGOs is growing and that they are beginning to constitute a centralizing force in the international system by becoming important actors that exercise authority in their own right. It can even be said that some IGOs demonstrate early signs of becoming **supranational organizations.** Such organizations are those whose authority, at least in theory, supersedes the sovereignty of their individual members. We noted earlier, for instance, that the WTO has the ability to review the laws and policies of the United States and other member-countries to ensure that they meet the standards agreed to in the General Agreement on Tariffs and Trade (GATT), which the WTO administers.

The 15-member EU has evolved further than any other IGO toward supranational authority. In addition to achieving a high degree of economic integration, including a new common currency called the euro, the EU has created a quasi-government with limited decision-making authority. Some Europeans favor the development of the EU into a true federal European government. Germany's chancellor once boldly declared, "We favor the political unification of Europe."[2] Not all Europeans agree, and the future is uncertain. Despite such reservations, it is remarkable how far the once divided, often warring countries of Europe have moved toward a supranational "United States of Europe" (Preston, 1998).

Transnational Actors

A third category of actors in the international system is **transnational actors,** organizations that operate internationally, but whose membership, unlike IGOs, is private. To provide an introduction to transnational actors, we can briefly examine the two most numerous and most organized types: nongovernmental organizations and multinational corporations.

Nongovernmental Organizations This type of organization, like an IGO, operates across borders but is different from IGOs in that it has individuals as members. Amnesty International and Greenpeace are examples. Both the number and importance of **nongovernmental organizations (NGOs)** on the world stage is increasing. In 1900 there were 69 NGOs. Since then the number of NGOs has expanded 70-fold to approximately 5,000. Furthermore, the influence and range of activities of these transnational actors are growing as their numbers increase and as technological advances allow them to operate more effectively across political boundaries. The most important aspect of NGOs, according to one analyst, is that their "role in global negotiations and global governance has been emerging stealthily and slowly over the last quarter century" (Phan, 1996:2). This role most commonly occurs when numerous NGOs that have an interest in one aspect or another of global society link together with supportive national organizations, sympathetic government agencies, and IGOs to form what one study refers to as **transnational advocacy networks (TANs).** The IGOs that constitute a TAN have "shared values" and exchange "information and services" related to their mutual concern with human rights, the environment, or some other subject (Keck & Sikkink, 1998:2; Hawkins, 1999).

The place of NGOs on the world stage has become so established that they have achieved a degree of formal recognition by the UN and other international actors (Raustiala, 1997; Weiss, 1996). For example, major UN conferences on world problems now have two centers. One is the IGO meeting itself, to which countries send delegates. The other is a parallel NGO meeting attended by representatives of private groups. This practice began with the UN–sponsored Earth Summit held in Brazil in 1992, and it is now a part of virtually all major UN–sponsored conferences. For example, when in 1995 the UN's Fourth World Conference on Women met in China, the official IGO conference met in Beijing and was attended by some 3,000 delegates from 180 countries

(continued on page 56)

THE NEW NATO MARCHES EAST

The North Atlantic Treaty Organization was formed in 1949 to save Western Europe from what many believed to be a threat from the Soviet Union. Then, after NATO had stood guard for 45 years, the USSR collapsed and, thus, the original purpose of NATO disappeared. One might think that NATO would have soon disbanded amid praise for a job well done.

Such has not been the case, however. Instead, NATO is undergoing a metamorphosis in which it is expanding both its role and its membership. When this transformation is complete, NATO may well emerge as a Pan-European, multipurpose security organization that little resembles its earlier, cold war character.

The first way that NATO has sought new life is by expanding its mission to include peacekeeping (Yost, 1999). The goal, according to NATO deputy secretary-general Sergio Silvio Balanzino (1996:87), is "to move beyond [NATO's] core principle of collective defense" in order to make the alliance "available for collective security tasks such as crisis management and peacekeeping." Bosnia provided the first test of the alliance's new mission. After several years of internal disagreement and ineffective action, NATO finally moved more resolutely in 1995. Military action by NATO air power against the Bosnian Serbs helped bring them to the peace table. The multinational Implementation Force (IFOR) that moved into Bosnia, and remains there, in accordance with the November 1995 Dayton Peace Accord is essentially a NATO operation.

Soon, NATO forces once again found themselves at war and then trying to restore the peace in the Balkans. In this case, Kosovo was the focus of NATO action. It is important to know that the reason NATO intervened was not because of a military threat to the alliance. Rather, according to Lord Robertson of Port Ellen, NATO's secretary-general, there was "a shocking picture of a planned campaign of violence against Kosovar Albanian civilians." Recalling that "it was Edmund Burke who said that for evil to triumph it

is only necessary for good men to do nothing," Lord Robertson proclaimed, "NATO's 19 nations acted."[1] Between March and June, 1999, NATO warplanes and cruise missiles conducted over 10,000 strikes that pummeled targets in Serbia, Montenegro, and Kosovo (all provinces of Yugoslavia) in an effort to force the Serbs to end their attempt to ethnically cleanse Kosovo of its majority Albanian ethnic population. Once that succeeded, approximately 45,000 troops (mostly from NATO, with small contingents from other countries) formed the Kosovo Force, or KFOR, entered Kosovo, and remain there to maintain order.

The second aspect of NATO's evolution involves expanding its membership. The designation "North Atlantic" is being strained by the admission of states in Eastern Europe. The first step came in 1997 when the annual NATO summit meeting extended a membership invitation to the Czech Republic, Hungary, and Poland. They became members in 1999 despite Russia's vehement objections. Also that year, in the words of a NATO fact sheet leaders of the member-countries meeting in Washington, D.C., "reaffirmed... their enduring commitment to NATO's Open Door policy, pledging that this round of NATO enlargement will not be the last." According to the fact sheet, nine countries (Albania, Bulgaria, Estonia, Macedonia, Latvia, Lithuania, Romania, Slovakia, and Slovenia) have declared their wish to join NATO, and the alliance intends to "help these states build the strongest possible candidacy for future membership."[2]

The first round expansion of NATO touched off a heated debate in academic circles, but it did not stir much controversy beyond that realm in the NATO member-countries (Walt, 1998; Perlmutter & Carpenter, 1998). In the United States, for example, the president argued strongly for NATO's expansion; one poll found only 19 percent of Americans opposed; and the U.S. Senate ratified by a vote of 80 to 19 the amendment to the NATO treaty clause that specifies the member-countries. The strategic implications of

(Clark, Friedman, & Hochstetler, 1998). As large as that gathering was, however, it was dwarfed by the approximately 30,000 delegates representing the Asian Foundation on Women, Law, and Development, the Women's Environment and Development Organization, and some 2,000 other NGOs who attended the simultaneous NGO conference in Huairou, a village 30 miles from Beijing. To a degree, this meeting constituted a gathering of the TAN concerned with the rights and status of women.

Ecstasy and Agony: For the ethnic-Albanian Kosovar boy on the left, the arrival of this British soldier and other NATO troops in Kosovo was a cause for joy. For the despondent ethnic-Serb Kosovar woman on the right, the arrival of the Italian soldier behind her and other NATO troops was a tragedy. The Serbs lost control of Kosovo Province, which is central to their history, and many Serb Kosovars left their homes and fled to what remains of Yugoslavia.

expanding NATO were largely ignored (Goldgeier, 1999; Boyer & Rourke, 1988). One of the few senators who opposed the treaty lamented that he had felt "like a voice in the wilderness."[3]

What remains unclear is what the expansion of NATO's role and membership will mean in the future. The change in role may well mean that American, Canadian, and European forces will engage in more peacekeeping missions, like the one in Bosnia. In this sense, NATO is no longer exclusively, or even primarily, an alliance designed to ward off an outside threat. Instead, at least for now, it is a regional peacekeeping organization dedicated to keeping stability within its region by intervening in civil wars and other internal disturbances.

The expansion of NATO's membership also means that the United States and other members are now required to come to the defense of Poland and other states far from the North Atlantic. Nine other countries are seeking admission to NATO, and the inclusion of some of those will bring the NATO (and, therefore, the U.S.) defensive commitment to the very border of Russia. How Americans will react if the need arises to defend Poland from an invasion by the Russians or some other aggressor remains to be seen.

If you had been a member of the U.S. Senate in 1998, would you have voted for the expansion of NATO? Would you vote to allow Estonia, Bulgaria, and other interested countries to join in the future?

The women brought their views to bear on the official meeting and also broadcast their collective and individual messages to the world through the 2,500 reporters who covered the conference (Riddell-Dixon, 1996). Because they were not bound by the diplomatic niceties that restrained the official representatives in Beijing, the NGO delegates spoke their minds on a number of sensitive issues. Tibetan women protested against China's occupation of their homeland; 1992 Nobel Peace Prize winner Rigoberta

International nongovernmental organizations (NGOs) are important global actors. In 1995, for example, representatives of over 2,000 NGOs concerned with the status and rights of women gathered in conjunction with a UN conference on Women held in China. The delegates who attended, represented by those in this photograph, came from all parts of the world but were united by their common political identification as women.

Menchú promoted the rights of indigenous people; a group called Women in Black marched against domestic violence; sexual-choice advocates published a lesbian manifesto in Chinese; activists showed a specially taped message by Burmese political dissident and 1991 Nobel Peace Prize winner Aung San Suu Kyi, in which she castigated male-dominated governments for tolerating Asia's sex trade and subjecting "so many of our young girls... to a life of sexual slavery where they are subject to constant humiliation and ill treatment."[3]

The NGO conference also continued to build the TAN by expanding the network of contacts, organizations, and knowledge that women can use to promote their efforts. "I don't think the world will ever be the same again," predicted American delegate Brownie Ledbetter. "Here we have women networking from all over the world, across incredible barriers. And with faxes and the Internet, it will grow even more."[4]

Multinational Corporations A second important type of transnational actor consists of **multinational corporations (MNCs),** also sometimes referred to as transnational corporations (TNCs). By whatever name, the expansion of international trade, investment, and other financial interactions has brought with it the rise of huge MNCs. These businesses have production and other operations that extend beyond mere sales in more than one country. The role of MNCs is discussed in detail in chapter 14, but suffice it to say here that the economic power of these corporate giants gives them a substantial role in international affairs. Some idea of the economic power of the MNCs can be gained from comparing their gross corporate product (GCP, sales, and other revenues) to the **gross domestic product** (GDP: a measure of all goods and services produced within a country) of various countries (Figure 3.1). The biggest 1999 MNC, General Motors, had a GCP of $161.3 billion that was about equal to the GDP of

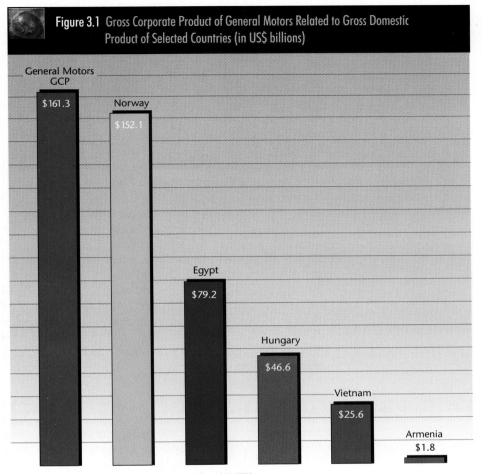

Figure 3.1 Gross Corporate Product of General Motors Related to Gross Domestic Product of Selected Countries (in US$ billions)

Data source: *Fortune* (magazine) Web site: http://www.fortune.com/fortune/global500/.

Multinational corporations (MNCs) are one category of NGO. Some idea of the enormous economic power of MNCs can be illustrated by comparing General Motors' 1999 gross corporate product to the gross domestic product of selected countries.

Norway ($152.1), more than twice Egypt's GDP ($79.2 billion), more than 3 times the GDP of Hungary ($46.6 billion), more than 6 times greater than Vietnam's GDP ($25.6 billion), and about 90 times Armenia's GDP ($1.8 billion).

SCOPE AND LEVEL OF INTERACTION

A third structural characteristic of any political system is the range (scope) of areas in which the actors interact and the frequency and intensity (level) of those interactions. One key to understanding the evolution of the international system is to see that the scope and level of international interaction are very much higher now than they were during the 1800s or even in the first half of the 1900s.

Economic interdependence provides the most obvious example of the escalating scope and level of interaction. It is nonsense today to imagine that any country can go it alone in splendid isolation. Even for a powerful country like the United States, a "fortress America" policy is impossible. Without foreign oil, to pick one obvious illustration, U.S. transportation and industry would literally soon come to a halt. Without extensive trade, the U.S. economy would stagger because exports are a key factor in economic growth. American exports during the period 1990–1998 grew at an annual average of 8.1 percent, more than two and one-half times faster than the 2.9 percent growth rate of the U.S. GDP for the same period. This is not atypical. What this means is that exports are an increasingly important factor in the health of the U.S. economy.

Data about expanding trade does not, however, capture fully the degree to which the widening scope and intensifying level of global interaction is increasing transnational contacts among people. Modern telecommunications and travel, for example, are making once relatively rare personal international interactions commonplace. Foreign travel is just one telling indication of this change. Between 1990 and 1997 the number of foreign visitors to the United States jumped 21 percent from 39.4 million to 47.8 million. During the same period, the number of Americans traveling overseas increased 18 percent from 44.6 million to 52.7 million. People used to talk about the "mysterious Orient" or "darkest Africa." Now Americans by the millions visit these places, and people from abroad are regular visitors to the United States.

It is important to note that the range and intensity of interaction has important political implications. Some theorists argue that large-scale, extended war is becoming difficult or impossible between economically interdependent countries. According to this theory, for example, the world should be safe from the scourge of general war in Europe that earlier led to two world wars. A related theory holds that the chance of war has decreased because of increased cultural contact among countries through modern travel and communications. Insofar as either of these theories is true, interdependence will bring greater peace. But it may be that the converse is also true: If conflict does erupt in an interdependent world, it will be harder to stand apart from the fray, as the Persian Gulf War demonstrated in 1991.

 POWER RELATIONSHIPS

Having examined the structural characteristics of the international system, we can turn our attention to another key set of factors: power relationships. We will in chapter 10 examine the nature of power. What is important to understand here, though, is that the distribution of power within a system affects the way that the system operates. To see this, we can look at three topics: the number of poles, the concentration of power, and the causes and effects of changes in power.

NUMBER OF SYSTEM POLES

Many analysts believe that a pivotal determinant of how any given system operates is the number of major power poles that it has. Traditionally, a system **pole** has consisted of either (1) a single country or empire or (2) a group of countries that form an alliance or a bloc. It is possible that in the future a global IGO, such as the UN, or a regional IGO, such as the EU, might acquire enough power and independence from its member-states to constitute a pole. While we will concentrate on global polar relations, it is worth noting that regions also have more localized polar structures. In the words of one recent study, "the international system is composed of multiple, overlapping systems. The global system encompasses all the states in the world, while regional systems comprise only local members" (Lemke & Warner, 1996:237). China, Japan, and the United States, for instance, constitute what has been termed a "triad of another kind" in the Asia-Pacific region (Zhang & Montaperto, 1999). It also may be that a country such as India can be a regional pole without being a global power.

There are several ways that the number of poles affects the conduct of the international system. To see this, we can examine two factors that may vary according to the number of poles in a system. One is the rules of the game of power politics. The second is the propensity of a system for instability and war.

The Rules of the Game

Some political scientists believe that the pattern of interaction varies according to the number of poles that a system has. It is possible, for example, to identify patterns or rules of the game for unipolar, bipolar, tripolar, and multipolar systems. It is especially interesting to compare bipolar and multipolar systems in order to contrast the rules of the system that has just passed with the rules of the system that is now evolving. Figure 3.2 displays four types of system structures and ways in which the patterns of interaction differ across them.

Unipolar Systems An international **unipolar system** would occur if a country achieved complete global hegemony. This has never really happened, although in ancient times the Roman, Mongolian, and Chinese empires incorporated or controlled all or most of the established societies in the world. There have been times, however, when one country came close to dominating international relations. Great Britain stood as a hegemonic power for a good part of the eighteenth and nineteenth centuries. The United States, in the view of many, currently holds a similar position. "The United States of America predominates on the economic level, on the monetary level, on the military level, on the technological level, and in the cultural area in the broadest sense," France's foreign minister, Hubert Védrine, commented recently. "It is not comparable, in terms and power of influence, to anything we know in modern history."[5] Most analysts classify the current system as a multipolar (four or more major power centers) system. Yet the reality that one of those, the United States, is so much more powerful than any of the others leads some observers to believe that something approaching a unipolar system, with the United States as the sole hegemonic power, has existed from the 1990s through the present. Reflecting the current system's somewhat dual-personality structure, one scholar has characterized it as "uni-multipolar" (Huntington, 1999:36).

A unipolar system could occur through the establishment of a world government. In the latter case, subordinate actors, such as the current states, might have a level of autonomy, but they would not be sovereign. If you live in a country with a federal system, such as Canada (provinces), Germany (lander) or the United States (states), think about how the unipolar rules parallel the operation of your country's national government in its relation to its provinces, lander, states, or other political components that are substantially, but not totally, subordinate to the central government.

The exact rules would depend on how centralized a unipolar system was and the degree of autonomy of subordinate units. In rough approximation, though, and depending on how dominant the hegemonic power or other power center was, the rules might be: (1) The central power plays a dominant role in establishing and enforcing rules for matters that affect the system. The central power especially dominates or even monopolizes military and economic instruments. (2) The central power plays a key role in settling disputes between subordinate units. (3) The central power resists attempts by subordinate units to achieve greater autonomy or, and especially, to create a rival pole. Indeed, the central power may gradually attempt to lessen or eliminate the autonomy of subordinate units. (4) The subordinate units, especially if their status is involuntary, seek to lessen or even escape the authority of the hegemonic power. The view that the United States has or could attain hegemonic power has prompted France's foreign minister, Hubert Védrine, to comment that one of his country's primary foreign policy objectives is ensuring that "the world of tomorrow [is] composed of several poles, not just a single one."[6]

Bipolar Systems This type of system is characterized by two roughly equal actors or coalitions of actors. There may be important nonaligned actors, but they are neutral and

Did You Know That:

The Punic Wars (264–146 B.C.) between Rome and Carthage typified the intense hostility in bipolar systems. The Roman war cry was *Carthago delenda est!* (Carthage must be destroyed!) And so it was. When Rome finally vanquished Carthage, the victors razed the city to the ground, sold its citizens into slavery, and decreed that no one could ever again live where Carthage had once stood.

(continued on page 63)

Figure 3.2 Models and Rules of the Game of Various International System Structures

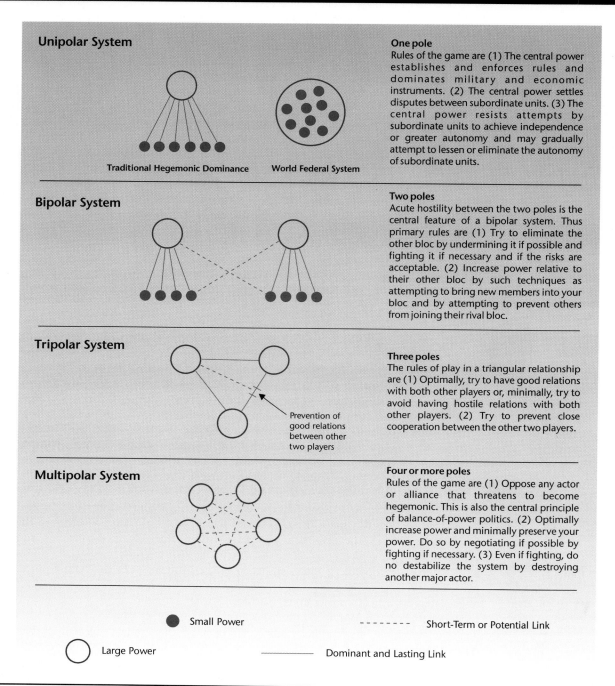

Unipolar System

Traditional Hegemonic Dominance   World Federal System

One pole

Rules of the game are (1) The central power establishes and enforces rules and dominates military and economic instruments. (2) The central power settles disputes between subordinate units. (3) The central power resists attempts by subordinate units to achieve independence or greater autonomy and may gradually attempt to lessen or eliminate the autonomy of subordinate units.

Bipolar System

Two poles

Acute hostility between the two poles is the central feature of a bipolar system. Thus primary rules are (1) Try to eliminate the other bloc by undermining it if possible and fighting it if necessary and if the risks are acceptable. (2) Increase power relative to their other bloc by such techniques as attempting to bring new members into your bloc and by attempting to prevent others from joining their rival bloc.

Tripolar System

Prevention of good relations between other two players

Three poles

The rules of play in a triangular relationship are (1) Optimally, try to have good relations with both other players or, minimally, try to avoid having hostile relations with both other players. (2) Try to prevent close cooperation between the other two players.

Multipolar System

Four or more poles

Rules of the game are (1) Oppose any actor or alliance that threatens to become hegemonic. This is also the central principle of balance-of-power politics. (2) Optimally increase power and minimally preserve your power. Do so by negotiating if possible by fighting if necessary. (3) Even if fighting, do no destabilize the system by destroying another major actor.

● Small Power   - - - - - - - - Short-Term or Potential Link

○ Large Power   ————————— Dominant and Lasting Link

The relationships that exist among the actors in a particular type of international system structure vary because of the number of powerful actors, the relative power of each, and the permitted interactions within that system. This figure displays potential international system structures and the basic rules that govern relationships within each system. After looking at these models, which one, if any, do you think best describes the contemporary international system?

Bipolar systems are often characterized by intense conflict between the two major powers, which has been equated to the death struggle of two scorpions trapped together in a bottle.

do not threaten the two dominant poles. Acute hostility between the two poles is the central feature of a **bipolar system.** Thus primary rules are: (1) Eliminate the other bloc by techniques including war, if it is necessary and the risks are acceptable. (2) Increase power relative to the other bloc by such techniques as bringing new members into your bloc and preventing others from joining the rival bloc.

One way to see how bipolar systems operate is to compare two that existed almost two and one-half millennia apart: The first is the bipolar system centered on the Athenian Empire and on Sparta and its allies. The second is the struggle between the two blocs led by the United States and the Soviet Union, which dominated the last half of the twentieth century.

Predictably, relations between the two blocs were bitter in both systems. The Greek historian Thucydides wrote in his *History of the Peloponnesian War* (400 B.C.), which chronicled the struggle between the two Greek city-states from 432 B.C. to 404 B.C., that "what made war inevitable was the growth of Athenian power and fear which this caused Sparta." The fear and counterfear was also evident in the United States and USSR, which, atomic scientist J. Robert Oppenheimer wrote, were like "two scorpions in a bottle, each capable of killing the other" (Jones, 1988:523).

Also, in the way that bipolar systems operate, both eras saw an either-you're-for-us-or-against-us intolerance of neutralism. In a segment of his epic work called the "Melian Debate," Thucydides reports the Athenians are pressing a small city-state, Melos, to subordinate itself to Athens. The Melians ask, "So, you would not agree to our being neutral... allies of neither" Athens or Sparta? "No," the Athenian ambassador replies, because "our subjects would regard that as a sign of weakness in us." When Melos refused to submit, Athens attacked and, when the Melians surrendered, "slew all the men of military age... and sold the women and children as slaves." This ancient hostility toward neutralism was expressed in more modern times by, for one, U.S. secretary of state John Foster Dulles (1953–1959), who condemned neutrality as an "immoral and shortsighted concept" (Paterson, Clifford, & Hagen, 2000:279).

Tripolar Systems Among the various permutations of a triangular relationship, one analysis postulated that the ideal position for any country is to be the "pivot player" in the triangle. This occurs when the country has good relations with both other countries, which, in turn, are hostile toward one another. In this position, the other two need you, and you can gain concessions for your continued friendship. The least favorable position is to be the "odd country out" in a triangle, where the other two players are friendly, and both are hostile toward you. Based on these calculations, the rules of play in a triangular relationship are: (1) Optimally, try to have good relations with both other players or, minimally, try to avoid having hostile relations with both. (2) Try to prevent close cooperation between the other two players.

There has not been an exact historical example of a **tripolar system**, but many observers believe that from the late 1960s through the beginning of the 1990s, a "strategic-triangle" system existed. The players were the United States, the Soviet Union, and China, which the two superpowers perceived as an emerging superpower. To a degree, the interaction of these three adhered to the rules of a tripolar system. Rule 1, for example, may explain why two strongly anticommunist U.S. presidents, Richard M. Nixon and Ronald Reagan, moved to better relations with Communist China. The reasoning was that China's growing strength created a strategic triangle that left the U.S. presidents little choice. Both presidents also improved relations with the USSR. Nixon followed a détente policy; Reagan moved from overt hostility toward cordiality with Soviet leaders during his presidency. The point is that whatever the personal antipathies of Nixon and Reagan toward communism, system realities pressured them to maintain good relations with at least one of the two communist giants (to avoid being odd

BALANCE OF POWER

Any discussion of how international systems operate must address the concept of balance of power. There are variations in the way that scholars use the term and there is broad disagreement between realists and idealists about the degree to which balance-of-power politics does and should affect world politics (Vasquez, 1997; Waltz, 1997; Christensen & Snyder, 1997; Elman & Elman, 1997; Scheweller, 1997; Walt, 1997). In essence, realists believe that the practice of balance-of-power politics is necessary and proper; idealists disagree on both counts.

Whatever one's views, though, it is important to look at basic balance-of-power politics and its impact on world politics. Fundamentally, those who believe in the efficacy of balance-of-power theory assume that:

1. There is a possibility, and perhaps a natural tendency, for some states to seek regional or even global hegemony.
2. Other states will seek to prevent hegemony by strengthening themselves or entering antihegemonic alliances with other threatened states.

3. A balance of power, therefore, is desirable because it (a) preserves the independence of countries and (b) creates an equilibrium that promotes order and peace.

Balance-of-power theory is applicable to any of the polar configurations, but it is most often associated with multipolar systems. Advocates of balance-of-power politics also believe that leaders will be well advised to continue to practice its principles in the evolving multipolar system. These realists reject the idealist contention that power politics is outmoded because of such factors as the growth of international organizations and independence and that power politics is a failed and increasingly dangerous way of trying to achieve stability and peace. Henry Kissinger, for one, counsels that "in the next century American leadership will have to articulate for their public a concept of the national interest and explain how that interest is served—in Europe and in Asia—by the maintenance of the balance of power."[1]

country out) and preferably to have good relations with both China and the USSR (to try to position the United States as the pivot player).

Multipolar Systems As the number of poles in a system increases, the dynamics of the system become concomitantly more complex. A **multipolar system** containing four or more major powers is a relatively fluid and competitive system in which the countries involved form shifting alliances. Since the amassing of too much power by any one actor or alliance threatens all the other actors, there is a tendency to form counterbalancing alliances and to try to win allies away from the predominant coalition. This type of system is also sometimes characterized as a **balance-of-power** system, a concept discussed in the above box of the same name.

The multipolar rules of the game are: (1) Oppose any actor or alliance that threatens to become hegemonic. This is also the central principle of balance-of-power politics. (2) Increase power or, at least, preserve your power. Do so by negotiating if possible but by fighting if necessary. (3) Even if fighting, do not destabilize the system by destroying another major actor. Therefore, permit defeated major actors to maintain/regain their status. This third rule is based on the recognition that today's opponent may be tomorrow's partner in a coalition to block the hegemonic ambitions of today's ally. Among other things, the flexibility of a multipolar system also means that major actors can rise or fall without significantly changing the basic multipolarity of the system. In the European multipolar system that extended roughly from 1648 to 1945, there were occasional shifts in which countries were poles. Spain and Sweden were early major powers. They eventually declined to secondary status but were replaced by other rising powers, such as Prussia (later Germany). Other countries, such as Great Britain and France, remained powers throughout the period. In this case, the number of major

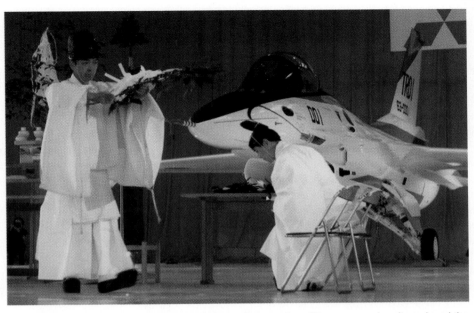

Japan took a major step toward once again becoming a major military power when it produced the FSX, the first warplane to be manufactured in Japan since 1945. A prototype of the FSX is shown here being blessed by Shinto priests in a purification ceremony. The symbol above the tail of the fighter is the logo of the Mitsubishi Corporation, the company that built the famous Japanese "Zero" fighter during World War II.

powers remained above four, and, therefore, the system continued to operate as a multipolar system.

One way to see how these rules of the game are affecting policy in the evolving international system is to consider this question: Why, after opposing the Soviet Union for over 40 years during the bipolar era and finally seeing it fall, has the United States been willing, even eager, to aid Russia? For system-level analysts, the answer is that the West has extended billions of dollars in aid to Russia and taken other steps to prop it up because the hostility dictated by bipolar system rule 1, "try to eliminate the other bloc," has been supplanted by multipolar system rule 3, "do not destabilize the system by destroying another major actor."

The fluidity that rule 3 promotes does not just mean keeping an open mind about one's adversaries. It also means not assuming that one's allies cannot become opponents. This is very unlike the rigid alliances of a bipolar system. American officials are usually loath to say it, but one reason for U.S. reluctance to confront China over the many issues that divide Washington and Beijing is the prospect that a more assertive, even remilitarized, Japan might become a Pacific region antagonist. It is revealing that President Bush defended his forgiving posture toward Beijing less than a year after the Tiananmen Square massacre in 1989 on the grounds that, "I want to retain contacts [with China] because, as you look around the world.... Take a look at Japan. Take a look at a lot of countries in the Pacific. China is a key player."[7] For more on the future of Japan as a major power, see the box, Japan: A Rising Sun?

The Propensity of a System for Instability and War

A second possible impact of the number of poles is the propensity of a system for instability and war. There is a lively academic debate about whether or not the number of poles in a system has an impact on the likelihood of war. Some scholars have found that

(continued on page 66)

JAPAN: A RISING SUN?

In a world in which only the United States has both the economic and military strength to warrant the title superpower, Japan is one of the few countries with the potential to achieve that rank in the foreseeable future. The question is whether it can and wants to assert itself and acquire the military tools to do so.

The first concern is Japan's economy. The country seemed to be an unending economic success story during the 1980s and into the 1990s. For example, Japan's annual real GDP growth rate during the 1980s averaged 3.8 percent, compared to 2.9 percent for all developed countries. Japanese investors snapped up foreign companies and real estate, the country was lauded for its production and management expertise, and many pundits proclaimed that the center of the economic world was shifting from Washington, D.C., to Tokyo.

Then fortunes reversed, and Japan fell into, and continues in, a prolonged economic slump. From 1996 through 1999, Japan's real GDP increased by an annual average of just 1.5 percent, compared to 2.5 percent for all industrialized countries. Part of the problem has been that a series of ineffectual governments have been unable to revitalize Japan. Prime Minister Ryutaro Hashimoto (1996–1998) was dubbed "Herbert Hoover" Hashimoto after the U.S. president whom many blame for failing to avert the Great Depression. His successor, Keizo Obuchi (1998–2000), did little to alleviate Japan's economic woes. One news report characterized him as "remarkably dull, even by the stodgy standards of senior Japanese politicians," and another commentator described Obuchi as having "the pizzazz of a cold pizza."[1] Obuchi was followed by Yoshiro Mori. He hardly seemed a scintillating choice. A news report termed him "a man with no discernible ideology"; and an academic expert at Keio University observed that, "if you prefer the status quo, Mori is the choice."[2]

Can Japan now be written off as hopelessly mired? It would not be wise to do so. Whatever its current economic woes, Japan's $4.1 trillion GDP (second only to the U.S. GDP) makes it an economic powerhouse. It also possesses many other economic assets, including an educated and able population and technological sophistication. Thus it is probable, although not certain, that the economic sun will eventually rise again on Japan.

What is a great deal cloudier is whether Japan will acquire the military forces and the political will to use those forces in a way that realists would argue is necessary to achieve the uncontested status of major power.

There are several factors at work against the possibility of Japan rebuilding and using its military. Internally, the horrific suffering, including atomic bomb attacks, that the Japanese endured in World War II has left them profoundly pacifistic. One indication is that Japan unofficially limits spending on the Self-Defense Force (SDF) to no more than 1 percent of the GDP. Furthermore, the SDF has neither long-range offensive systems such as bombers or aircraft carriers, nor nuclear weapons. There is also a clause (Article 9) in Japan's constitution that bars the "use of force as a means of settling international disputes." Japanese pacifism is also evident in a survey that found only 10 percent of Japanese willing to fight for their country if a war occurred, with 41 percent saying no, and 49 percent unsure (Ladd & Bowman, 1996:32, 109). The Japanese are also very reluctant to see the SDF deployed. According to a 1997 poll, only 20 percent of the population favored (and 69 percent opposed) amending Article 9. Moreover, when asked what their preferred role of the SDF was, more than twice as many Japanese picked "disaster rescue" (46 percent) as "national defense" (20 percent).[3]

For all this aversion to militarism, changes in the international system and in Japanese attitudes are creating a new assertiveness that could lead to an increase in the size and capacity of the SDF. While "Japan's reemergence as an independent military power would be unsettling," notes one commentator, "it may not be preventable" (Menon, 1997:34).

To begin with, one should not underestimate the existing size and strength of the SDF. Even with the 1 percent of GDP restriction, Japan has the world's

unipolar systems are relatively peaceful; that a system with two poles (bipolar) has a medium chance of war; that a three-pole (tripolar) system has a relatively low propensity toward war; and that systems with four or more poles (multipolar) have the highest probability of war. Systems with five poles were found to be the most unstable (Rasler & Thompson, 1992; Ostrom & Aldrich, 1978).

second-largest military budget. From that base, one factor that is working to push Japan toward enhancing its military involves changes in the international system. With the cold war over, the Japanese worry that isolationist pressures in the United States are weakening its commitment to defend Japan and, more generally, to promote the stability of Asia. There is a "nagging feeling," one Asian diplomat has commented, "that after the cold war America isn't going to have the will or the wallet to make the sacrifices that a superpower has to make."[4] Similarly, polls have found that between 1992 and 1997, the percentage of Japanese who believe that the United States would honor its alliance and defend Japan against an aggressor fell from 68 percent to 53 percent.[5]

A second factor affecting Japan's international policy is growing nationalism. The passage of time since World War II and an increased sense of national pride are changing Japanese attitudes. Some observers worry about the rise of "revisionists" in Japan who contend that Japan was trying in the 1930s and early 1940s to liberate Asia from Western colonialism and that, therefore, Japan should shed its guilt for the war. This faction is still small, but, one Japanese observer warns, "The revisionists are rapidly increasing their influence on public opinion,... particularly in education circles and in the media" (Kunihiro, 1997:36). There are also recurrent examples of troubling disdain for non-Japanese. In a recent example, Shintaro Ishihara, the governor of Tokyo, used the derogatory word *sangokujin* in a public speech to refer to people of Korean and Chinese descent living in Japan. Ishihara warned listeners that "atrocious crimes have been committed again and again by sangokujin [which literally means "people from third countries"] and other foreigners," and predicted that in the event of a natural disaster, "We can expect them to riot."[6]

Another indication of changing Japanese attitudes is that in 1999, the parliament officially designated the rising sun emblem (red dot on a white background) as Japan's official flag and "Kimigayo" (His Majesty's Reign) as the national anthem. At one level, the designation of a flag simply recognized what had been the unofficial symbol of Japan since ancient times, the official symbol from 1870 to the end of World War II, and in legal limbo since then. Yet the step to reaffirm the flag and to institute an anthem also reflects growing nationalism. The Education Ministry has directed schools to display the flag and sing the anthem during ceremonies, practices hitherto unusual. Some teachers objected. Said one, "I teach my students that the flag and anthem were tools of Japan's wartime aggression and used to brainwash the Japanese people."[7] Despite such protests, almost 90 percent of Japan's schools now comply with Tokyo's directive.

The combination of external and internal pressures has weakened Japan's official pacifism. Reacting to foreign criticism about its unwillingness to play a military role in the Persian Gulf War, Japan's parliament voted to allow noncombat units of the SDF to participate in UN peacekeeping missions. Soon some 1,000 Japanese soldiers were on their way to take part in the UN operations in Cambodia.

Many observers applauded Japan's willingness to act. Others worried. The step "sets a precedent," fretted scholar Motofumi Asai. "People will get used to the idea, and then [Japan] will take the next step toward engaging the military with the world," Asai predicted. "I don't think that's to the advantage of the United States or other countries. Eventually they will find out," he concluded ominously.[8]

How far Japan will go in building and using its military forces cannot yet be predicted, but there is no question that it continues to consider its options. For many years "it was a taboo to discuss" enhancing Japan's forces and their role, former prime minister Yasuhiro Nakasone has commented. "But now it is not a taboo, and people are thinking about it seriously."[9] Even the possibility of acquiring nuclear weapons is beginning to be occasionally discussed. As political scientist Seizaburo Sato notes, "Russia is still there [powerful and near Japan]. If the U.S. did withdraw [from the Western Pacific], if China continues to mobilize its military forces, if North Korea goes nuclear, then Japan would go nuclear. You would have to prepare yourselves against Japanese forces. And we are pretty efficient."[10]

Does this mean that the world is becoming more dangerous as it moves toward some variation of multipolarity? Not necessarily. In the first place, political scientists disagree about the relative volatility of the various polar configurations. A second reason not to be unduly alarmed about a multipolar world is that the global polar structure is just one of many factors that affect the level of violence in the world. Third, there are scholars who question the impact of poles at all. A variation of this argument is that poles may have been important in the past but that their impact on the action of the major powers has declined and will continue to do so as the world becomes more interdependent and as other actors, such as IGOs, play a greater role.

CONCENTRATION OF POWER

A pole is a major power center, but not all major powers are equal. This inequality affects how the system operates because system stability varies in part according to the degree to which power is concentrated or diffused among the various poles. This finding leads to questions about the stability of the system when two or more poles (countries or alliances) are in a condition of relative *power equality* or *power inequality* (Schweller, 1998; Gochman & Hoffman, 1996; Schampel, 1996).

Some scholars argue that war is more likely when antagonistic poles have relatively equal power, creating "a situation in which [every power] can perceive the potential for successful use of force" (Geller, 1993:173). By this logic, war is less likely when power is concentrated in one camp, because the weaker poles will be deferential. Other scholars disagree. They believe that conflict is more likely between countries of unequal power. The reasoning is that when two antagonists are equal in power, they are deterred from war by the fear of being defeated or by the mauling they will take even if they are victorious. Why, you might ask, would an obviously weaker country fight rather than compromise or give way? One reason is that an aggressor may attack and leave the country no choice. Emotions are another reason. "Live free or die," as the New Hampshire license plate proclaims. What occurs, research shows, is that decision makers are willing to accept much greater risks to prevent losses than to gain an advantage.

Still other scholars conclude that conflict is least likely when power is equal or very unequal and most likely when there are moderate power differences between antagonists (Powell, 1996). Less dramatic differences may lead countries either to miscalculate their power relative to that of their opponent or to gamble.

POWER CHANGES: CAUSES AND EFFECTS

The power equation in the international system is seldom stable for very long. The power of countries rises and falls relative to one another. Major powers sometimes decline to the point that they are no longer a pole, and they may even cease to exist, as did the USSR. Other countries may come into existence and later rise to the rank of major power, as did the United States. New poles could even be an alliance or an international organization, as suggested in the map on the adjacent page, NATO and the EU March East.

There are a number of highly debated general theories about power-based changes in the international system. Some scholars propound "cycle theories" (Pollins, 1996). Some of these theories hold that cycles occur over a period of a few decades; others suggest as much as a century. The cycles are demarcated by great-power or "systemic" wars that reflect strains created by power shifts within the system. They might be equated to earthquakes in the geological system. The systemic wars, in turn, further alter the system by destroying the major power status of declining powers and elevating rising powers to pole status. Then the process of power decay and formation begins anew. Another study uses the idea of "chaos theory" to argue that while there is an evolution to power in the system, "this evolution is *chaotic* [in that] the patterns of global power are not strict chronological cycles, but variable patterns influenced by... small random... effects" that can change the timing and impact of the cycle (Richards, 1993:71).

(continued on page 70)

NATO and the EU March East

1990

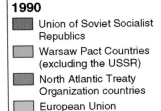

- Union of Soviet Socialist Republics
- Warsaw Pact Countries (excluding the USSR)
- North Atlantic Treaty Organization countries
- European Union

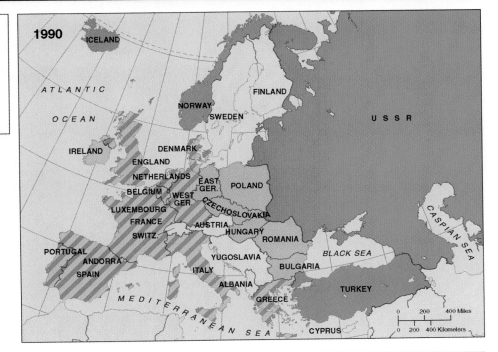

2000

- North Atlantic Treaty Organization countries
- European Union
- European Union applicant countries
- North Atlantic Treaty Organization applicant countries
- North Atlantic Treaty Organization and European Union applicant countries

Power shifts do not necessarily involve just countries. The expansion of both NATO and the European Union and the shrinkage of the USSR/Russia indicate the significant power changes since 1990.

AUTH © 1999 *The Philadelphia Inquirer.*

VICTORY PARADE

Many analysts believe that a hegemonic power helps provide global stability, and they worry that the current superpower, the United States, does not have the political will to fulfill that role. The U.S. willingness to commit ground troops and sustain casualties is especially questionable, and that concern was reconfirmed in many minds by the events in Kosovo. As reflected in this cartoon, the U.S. military, backed by American public opinion, supported the air war against Yugoslavia but opposed sending in American soldiers.

Whatever their view, analysts agree that the international system does change and that the shifts are important. Therefore, how power changes is a key concern. Since the current polar structure of the international system is clearly in flux, it is especially timely to consider the causes and effects of power transitions (Tammen, et al., 2000).

The Causes of Changes in Power

Power changes in three ways. First, change may occur in the sources of power or in their relative importance. Second, power shifts may occur when conditions change within the major actors. Third, the dynamics of balance-of-power politics prompts countries to try prevent dominance by others and to build their own power.

The Sources of Power Power is based on many factors. Developments in any one of them can affect the international system. Occasionally, the change may be sudden. For example, nuclear weapons that can rapidly strike anywhere in the world dramatically changed the system from what it had been in the 1930s.

More often, sources of power and their importance evolve slowly. For all the revolutionary impact of nuclear weapons, a more important evolutionary change may be the gradual decline of the usefulness of military might. Some analysts believe that military power is becoming less important because of the astronomical economic costs of wars and their potential cataclysmic effect. The decrease in the importance of military force as a policy instrument has, according to this line of thought, increased the importance of economics as a source of power. Most observers would agree, for instance, that Japan is a major power even though its military forces remain very limited. Russia still possesses a fearsome nuclear arsenal, yet its economy and society are in such disarray that its status as a major power has plummeted.

Advancing interdependence may also mean that even other forms of coercive power, such as economic sanctions, are gradually becoming less relevant. The reasoning for this is that a country that applies the sanctions may do as much harm to itself as to the country it is trying to punish. Certainly military might and economic capacity remain the cornerstones of state power, but such factors as technological sophistication and leadership capacity may be growing in importance.

Conditions within Major Actors While the system influences the actions of states, conditions within countries and the resulting policy decisions made by them can also change the system. The fate of the Soviet Union provides a dramatic example of the impact of domestic factors on foreign policy and, in turn, on the international system. The disintegration of the Soviet Union stemmed in part from such domestic factors as its inefficient economic and political system, separatist demands by the national groups within it, and a crushing military budget.

Conditions within a state may also affect its willingness to act "abnormally," that is, not play an expected role in global affairs. Sometimes countries are abnormally aggressive, as were Japan and Germany leading up to World War II. This can upset or even transform the system, as occurred when World War II shattered most of the major powers and led to the bipolar era.

At other times, major powers can act with abnormal passivity, which can also "undermine the global balance of power" (Cederman, 1994:528). Some people believe, for example, that the United States does not have the political will to fulfill its super-power role in the post–cold war world. One bit of evidence is a 1999 survey that found that 77 percent of Americans thought that the United States should "pay less attention to problems overseas and concentrate on problems here at home."[8] President Clinton sent American forces into Haiti in 1994 and into Bosnia in 1995, but most Americans favored neither deployment. A majority of Americans did favor using air-strikes and missile-strikes during the crisis with Yugoslavia in 1999, over the fate of Kosovo. But when asked if they would support sending ground forces to fight in that region in the southern Balkans, a strong majority of Americans opposed sending troops.[9]

Such responses have persuaded some foreign observers that Americans no longer have the will to lead. André Fountain, the editorial chief of the French newspaper, *Le Monde*, contends that having won the cold war, the United States, "deprived of its enemies," has fallen "back on its internal problems" and "no longer has the money or the public backing to play a prominent role abroad."[10] American officials share this worry. A few months before she became U.S. secretary of state, Madeleine K. Albright told a college commencement audience, "Today the greatest danger to America is not some foreign enemy; it is the possibility… that we will crawl into a shell… and forget the fundamental lesson of the century, which is that problems abroad, if left unattended, will all too often come home to America."[11]

Some scholars also worry that the United States is not willing to play its expected role as a hegemon (superpower) in the international system (Wohlforth, 1999). Richard Haass (1997) depicts the United States as "The Reluctant Sheriff" and writes that "what the United States does and does not do can help determine history."[12] What many realists like Haass contend is that according to the balance-of-power theory, the United States should exercise its formidable power to preserve stability and to shape the world system to the U.S. design. "There can be no peace in the Balkans unless Washington is fully engaged," a French diplomat commented.[13] Expressing the same view from the Middle East, a former Israeli diplomat opined that in the search for peace, "Nothing can happen without the Americans. Everything can happen with them."[14] And in Asia, a diplomat explained, "We cannot antagonize the Chinese by saying it publicly, but everybody will be more comfortable with American ships in place [in the Pacific]."[15]

Did You Know That:

The hegemonic position of the United States is evident statistically. With 4.6 percent of the world's population, the United States accounts for 21.5 percent of the world's combined GDPs, 18.7 percent of world trade, and 34 percent of world military expenditures.

This desired U.S. role also extends to socioeconomic issues. When in 1995 President Clinton decided not to attend the UN–sponsored conference on human welfare held in Copenhagen, Mahbub ul Haq of the UN Development Programme complained that "this summit without Clinton will be like staging *Hamlet* without the Prince of Denmark."[16]

Such concerns need to be viewed with some caution, however. One recent study of post–cold war changes concludes, "Put simply, the relative decline of American power has not led to a prolonged, across-the-board decrease in efforts to maintain the stability of the international system" (Bobrow & Boyer, 1998:286). Thus there seems to be no immediate danger of general system instability.

Balance-of-Power Politics As the box Balance of Power notes, countries resist the domination of others and may seek to establish themselves as a power pole. This dynamic of resisting the power of others and seeking power for yourself can be pursued unilaterally or in alliance with others. In either case, however, the dynamic, if successful, shifts the power equation. It may be that diplomats from around the world recognize that U.S. power is important to system stability, but it is also true that the governments of these diplomats will struggle to undermine U.S. hegemony. German chancellor Gerhard Schröder warns, "That there is a danger of unilateralism, not just by anybody but by the United States, is undeniable."[17]

The Effects of Changes in Power

There are many ways that changes in power affect the system. System-level analysts examine both the specific effects of alterations in the sources and distribution of power and the degree to which power transitions create dangerous instability in the system.

Specific Effects of Changes in Power Any significant change in the sources of power or the distribution of power among the major actors is likely to alter the operation of a system. The development of nuclear weapons provides an example of the impact that a change in the *sources of power* has on the system. Nuclear weapons altered, perhaps permanently, which states could claim to be a hegemonic power, or in more modern terms, a superpower. Another impact of nuclear weapons and the development of missiles to deliver them, systems analysts would say, was to compel the United States to abandon its isolationist stance and become an active internationalist actor. Americans realized that whatever their preferences might be, they could no longer be secure behind their flanking oceans.

Nuclear weapons technology may have also shifted the rules of the game by which a system operates. Three earlier bipolar systems—those that pitted Athens against Sparta, Macedonia against Persia, and Rome against Carthage in ancient times—were marked by warfare between the two "superpowers" and the eventual defeat of one by the other. Yet the recent, cold war bipolar system did not result in the military death struggle that has characterized earlier bipolar systems. The nuclear devastation that each superpower could wreak on the other worked to keep the two powers from attacking each other directly because the outcome was predictable: mutual annihilation.

Changes in the *distribution of power* also affect the system. This occurs when the system shifts from one polar configuration to another. The recent move from a bipolar to a multipolar configuration is an example. Another way that the changing distribution of power is affecting the system is in the weakening of the system's Western orientation. Until well into the twentieth century, most power in the international system was held by European and European-heritage countries. This resulted in a system based mainly on European organizational, legal, and normative traditions. The way that democracy is defined in terms of a legal procedure, rather than by equitable outcome, and the elevation of individual rights over community welfare are, for instance, both much more strongly rooted in Western tradition than they are in other cultures.

Power Transitions and System Stability "Great powers are like divas. They enter and exit the stage with great tumult," one analyst observes (Zakaria, 1996:37). What this means, and many studies have concluded, is that the world is most prone to violence during times of system transitions (Kugler & Lemke, 1996). That is, wars between major powers are most likely when the power of one or more of them is declining and the power of the other(s) is rising. In such situations it is harder for antagonists to judge their relative power. Furthermore, the declining power may try to maintain its dominant position by attacking the rising power before it becomes too powerful. Simultaneously, the rising power, dissatisfied with its secondary status, may try to improve it by confronting the dominant but declining country. One recent study has concluded that war is most likely when the power of a rising, dissatisfied country nears or becomes equal to that of a dominant state. Then, "power parity provides the opportunity to act for those who are committed to changing the status quo" (Lemke & Warner, 1996:256).

The origins of World Wars I and II provide, in the estimate of some social scientists, a historical example of the effect of power transitions. Early in the twentieth century, power was shifting rapidly. As the twentieth century began, Germany was newly united, and its power was increasing. So was American power, although the country remained largely isolationist. Japanese power was also beginning to grow. Other great powers were beginning to fade. Imperial China, the Austro-Hungarian Empire, and the Ottoman Empire were in states of terminal decay. Russia was also tottering, although the communists would eventually reestablish the power that the czarist government was losing. Germany and Austria-Hungary provide apt illustrations of the calculations of a rising and a declining power. By the beginning of the twentieth century, Germany was ready to challenge the previously dominant states, primarily Great Britain, for ascendancy. By contrast, Austria-Hungary was trying desperately to preserve a shadow of its former glory as the Holy Roman Empire. The result of these two opposite motives was that Germany and Austria-Hungary joined in an alliance that turned aggressive in 1914 and helped ignite World War I. Alas, the "war to end all wars" wasn't the end of war at all; it was just the first round in a power transition. World War II was the second round. It broke out after a breathing space, and it finally spelled an end not only to the power of most of the remaining major European actors but to the multipolar system itself.

A final thought on transitional systems is that they tend toward instability when hegemonic powers are no longer able or willing to control events in countries that were once part of their bloc or in their sphere of influence. Some scholars believe, for example, that the collapse of Soviet/Russian power allowed the simmering ethnic tensions in the formerly communist-dominated Balkans to erupt into the violence that occurred during the 1990s.

By the same logic, according to one study, "increased hegemonic control is associated with fewer wars [and] crises" (Volgy & Imwalle, 1995:819). This may help explain why a settlement was achieved in the Balkans once the United States exerted itself there. The reality, commented former British foreign secretary David Owen, is that "when the most powerful country in the world decides to lead the negotiations and adopt a realistic posture, it's just a different ballgame."[18]

ECONOMIC PATTERNS

How the international system works is based in part on its economic patterns. We can gain a sense of the impact of these patterns by touching on just three of them: interdependence, natural resource location and use, and the maldistribution of development.

Economic interdependence is one pattern that we have noted repeatedly (Jones, 1999). There is some controversy over whether or under what conditions interdependence promotes peace or creates tensions. One study concludes, for instance, that established powerful states (status quo powers) are most likely to join together to deter aggression "when there are extensive ties among the status quo powers *and* few or no such links between them and the perceived threatening powers." By contrast, "When economic interdependence is not strong between status quo powers or if the status quo powers have significant links with threatening powers, [status quo] leaders' capacities to balance are limited," which leads to "weak responses" and "a greater likelihood of aggression by the [threatening] power" (Papayoanou, 1997:135).

Whatever the specific impacts of economic interdependence may be, there is no disagreement that it profoundly affects the international system. This is evident, among other ways, in the refusal of President Clinton to use economic sanctions to pressure China to improve its checkered human rights record. Commenting on the president's stand, the *New York Times* has written with only some hyperbole that Clinton was recognizing "the underlying shift evident in all the industrial democracies today: economic concerns have taken center stage in foreign affairs decision-making. This is the age of the Finance Minister.... The game of nations is now geo-Monopoly, and it is first and foremost about profits, not principles."[19]

The pattern of *natural resource production and consumption* also influences the operation of the system. The strong reaction of the industrialized (and petroleum import–dependent) countries to Iraq's aggression in 1990 was based on the distribution of

The gas pump is one place the world economy affects you. Price hikes for crude oil by the Organization of Petroleum Exporting Countries (OPEC) in 1999 and 2000 drove up gasoline prices to nearly $2 a gallon in the United States and $4 to $6 in Europe. Such prices not only affect your personal driving costs, they also add to manufacturing, shipping, and other commercial costs, which in turn increase the price you pay for many products. The sign on the window of a trucker protesting fuel prices makes that point vividly.

resources. Turmoil in the Persian Gulf region threatened vital oil supplies. While the Bush administration could have decided not to intervene, a system-level analyst would point out that it had little choice. American presidents as far back as Harry S. Truman had pledged U.S. protection of the West's primary petroleum source. Even the usually conciliatory Jimmy Carter had declared during his January 1980 State of the Union message that any attempt "to gain control of the Persian Gulf will be regarded as an assault on the vital interests of the United States of America." Given the distribution of system resources, then, Iraq's invasion of Kuwait and threat to Saudi Arabia and other oil producers brought what a system-level analyst would say was a predictable reaction from the powerful petroleum-importing states. Led by the United States, they moved militarily to end the threat to their supplies because, as U.S. secretary of state James A. Baker III explained to reporters, "The economic lifeline of the industrial world runs from the gulf, and we cannot permit a dictator… to sit astride that economic lifeline."[20]

The *maldistribution of development* is a third economic pattern that has consequences for the international system. States, which are the main actors in the system, are divided into relative haves and have-nots. At the most general level, this economic division pits the less developed countries (LDCs) of the South and their demands for equity against the economically developed countries (EDCs) of the North along the North-South Axis. More specifically, as we shall see, there is a connection between the poor economic conditions in LDCs and such problems as rapid political oppression and instability, population growth, and environmental degradation. These problems harm the people of the South and, by their spillover effect, are detrimental for the people of the North as well. An economic pattern in which a small minority of people and countries enjoy high standards of living while the vast majority of people and countries are relatively impoverished both creates a drag on the world economy and is morally questionable. The disparity also creates resentments rooted in desperation, fertile ground that could one day yield systemic violence—a reminder of Abraham Lincoln's maxim that "a house divided against itself cannot stand."

Did You Know That:

Bill Gates, the Microsoft magnate, is the world's richest person. His estimated worth in 2000 was $49.1 billion, an amount greater than the 1998 GDP of Bangladesh ($44 billion), the world's eighth most populous country with 126 million inhabitants.

NORMS OF BEHAVIOR

The widely accepted standards of behavior that help regulate behavior are the fourth major element of any system. These standards, or values, constitute the **norms** of a system. A caveat is that to be valid, norms must be generally recognized and followed, but they need not be either accepted or practiced universally.

Systems develop norms for two reasons. First, various psychological and social factors prompt humans to adopt values to define what is ethical and moral. Second, humans tend to favor regularized patterns of behavior because of the pragmatic need to interact and to avoid the anxiety and disruption caused by the random or unwanted behavior of others. Over the centuries, for instance, pragmatism led to norms (now supplemented by treaties) about how countries treat each others' diplomats even in times of war. When conflict broke out in the Persian Gulf in 1991, U.S. and other enemy diplomats in Baghdad were not rounded up and executed. Iraqi diplomats in Washington, D.C., and elsewhere were similarly safe from official reprisal.

Changes that occur in the norms of the international system are an important aspect of how the system evolves. What is evident in the current system is that norms are becoming more universal while they are simultaneously being challenged.

The uniformity of norms is the result of the McWorld effect, the homogenization of global culture because of economic interdependence, global communications, and other factors. It would be a vast overstatement to say that capitalist (free-market) economies, democracy, and the precepts of individual human rights reign triumphant throughout the world. But these and other beliefs about the "right way" to do things have certainly become the dominant theme.

Yet it is also true that the exact nature of these precepts is being modified as a result of the de-Westernization of the international system. Norms that have heretofore influenced the system were established by the dominant countries of the West. Now the countries of Asia, Africa, and elsewhere have become more assertive, and they sometimes disagree with and challenge some of the established values (Lensu & Fritz, 1999). For example, some cultures in Asia and elsewhere stress the good of society, whereas American and some other political cultures emphasize the rights of the individual. Reflecting this, the rights of the accused are less extensive and punishments are often harsher in Asia and other countries that take the more communitarian view. Punishment in Singapore, for one, can be quite draconian by American standards and range from $100 fines for failing to flush a public toilet, through being beaten on the buttocks with a bamboo cane for vandalism, to death sentences for 20 different offenses. Americans can be quite critical of these punishments as violations of human rights, especially when they are imposed on Westerners. One instance of this view of Southeast Asian justice is evident in the film *Return to Paradise*, with Anne Heche, which takes a critical view of Malaysian justice. Yet the view is different from that part of the world. "We believe that the legal system must give maximum protection to the majority of our people," says Shanmugan Jayakumar, Singapore's foreign minister. "We make no apology for clearly tilting our law and policy in favor of the majority."[21]

Another important change in the nature and role of norms is that the international cast of actors is more willing than it used to be to take action to enforce changing norms. The strengthening norms of democracy and human rights, for one, prompted global economic sanctions and other pressures that eventually forced South Africa's white government to end apartheid and eventually to turn political power over to the black majority (Klotz, 1997). Changing norms about how we use the biosphere also persuaded Japan to pledge to end drift-net fishing because of its destruction of all forms of marine life caught up in the giant nets. After a UN debate on the issue, a Japanese official explained that his country gave way because, "Since no other country sided with us, we have to consider Japan's position in international society and yield."[22]

The willingness to countenance war, especially unilateral action by an individual country, is also weakening. Wars still occur, but they are being perceived as less legitimate and are more widely condemned in principle. The U.S. invasion of Panama in 1989 was, for example, condemned by both the UN and the Organization of American States (OAS). During the later crisis over government repression in Haiti, the United States was careful to garner UN and OAS support for economic sanctions and for military intervention. The intervention in Bosnia was not the act of a single country, but an international effort sanctioned by the UN and conducted by NATO.

SYSTEM-LEVEL ANALYSIS: PREDICTING TOMORROW

We have, in the preceding pages, examined the international system and how it is shaped by its characteristics: global authority structure, power relationships, economic patterns, and norms of behavior. We have also seen that all these factors are in flux. The question is, then, whether system-level analysis can give us some clues about the world we will experience tomorrow. What do these changes portend for the system during the twenty-first century?

The changes that we have been discussing seem to be simultaneously pulling the international system in different directions. One direction is along the traditional, state-centric road that the system has traveled for centuries. Nationalism, as we shall see,

Globalization has arguably increased the power of multinational corporations and to a degree has homogenized world culture. Some people are uneasy that they are losing political control and that their culture is being diluted. This has sparked increasing protests in recent years. Obvious symbols of global business and acculturation, such as McDonald's outlets, often bear the brunt of this dissatisfaction. In this photo, Ronald McDonald has been symbolically toppled by an avalanche of apples dumped by French farmers in Cavaillon, France, who were angered over their loss of sales to imported food.

MAP
Global Distribution of Minority
Groups, p. 146

remains the most potent political idea in the world today, and the number of sovereign states has tripled since 1945.

Then there is the alternative road. For all the strength of states as the principal actors in the international system, many scholars conclude that the dominance of states as the focus of political authority is in decline. The issue is what will fill this power vacuum. For the moment, one scholar sees "a ramshackle assembly of conflicting sources of authority" and argues that, "The diffusion of authority away from national governments has left a yawning hole of nonauthority" (Strange, 1997:199, 14). If this is true, where does the alternative road take us?

The answer is uncertain because the state-centric system is in some disarray due to pressures from two directions (Hoffmann, 1998; Kaufman, 1997). Some pressures are pushing the system toward greater international cooperation and even supranational governance. This movement toward more global structures is the "McWorld" tendency that we explored in chapter 2. It is based on the buildup of economic and ecological forces that demand cooperation and integration and, thus, are pressing us all into one commercially homogenous global network tied together by technology, ecology, communications, and commerce.

Other pressures, the Jihad tendency, are promoting subnational or transnational political organizations that are vying for the loyalty of individuals and, therefore, undermining the state. Most obviously, there is a strengthening of subnational movements such as **ethnonational groups** that demand autonomy or even independence from the states in which they reside. This is evident in the breakups of Czechoslovakia, the Soviet Union, and Yugoslavia, the separatist movement in Quebec, and ethnic conflict in Burundi, Chechnya, and elsewhere. There is also, as we shall see in chapter 7, an increase in the appeal of such transnational identifications as religion and even gender, as the primary political identification of some individuals.

Where will all this lead? There is broad disagreement (Modelski & Thompson, 1998; Neumann & Weaver, 1997). Some analysts believe that states will remain strong, integral units and that the system will remain state-centric. Another school of thought believes that the world's complex interdependence will result in a much higher level of global authority. Barber (1995:20) agrees that "in the long run, the forces of McWorld... may be unstoppable." A third school of thought argues that disintegration, not integration, will prevail (Enriquez, 1999). At the pessimistic extreme, an article entitled "The Coming Anarchy" predicts that the current system "is going to be replaced by a jagged-glass pattern of city-states, [poor] shanty-states, [and] nebulous and anarchic regionalisms," a virtual nonsystem in which "war and crime become indistinguishable" as "armed bands of stateless marauders clash with the private forces of the elites" (Kaplan, 1994:72). Yet another pessimistic view envisions a future in which there is a "clash of civilizations," as religious, ethnic, and cultural conflict replace state rivalries (Huntington, 1996).

The estimation of most scholars incorporates both views. According to this synthesis, states will still be important, but so will be supranational and subnational structures. Scholars have not settled on a name for what they foresee. Chapter 2 used the term "modified multipolar." The term "modified" reflects the belief of many scholars that the state will have to compete for political legitimacy and power with rising subnational, transnational, and international actors (Rosenau, 1997). This view has led some scholars to envision a "postinternational" era in which the **politics of identity** will make traditional national political identification just one of many ways that people define their primary sense of political identity (Hobbs, 2000).

One study uses "polyarchy" to describe such a system, one made up of "many communities, spheres of influence, hegemonic imperiums, interdependencies, trans-state loyalties" but with "no clearly dominant axis of alignment and antagonism and [with] no central steering group or agency" (Brown, 1988:242). Like Barber, Brown (pp. 260, 263) thinks that the future could hold either a system of "anarchy, where raw power is the principal social arbiter" or a hierarchical system dominated by "international and transnational webs of political accountability, many of them global in scope." Unlike Barber, Brown is unsure about which will prevail. Brown (p. 243) can only tell us that the future "has not been predetermined" and that "which of the variants does emerge will depend on the choices and commitments made by politically influential groups in the years ahead." On that we can all agree.

 # CHAPTER SUMMARY

1. System-level analysis is an approach to the study of world politics that argues that factors external to countries and the world political environment combine to determine the pattern of interaction among countries and other transnational actors. Countries are often compelled to take certain courses of action by the realities of the world in which they exist.

2. Many factors determine the nature of any given system. Systemic factors include its structural characteristics, power relationships, economic patterns, and norms of behavior.

3. One structural characteristic is how authority is organized. The international system is based on state sovereignty and, therefore, is anarchical. There are, however, relatively new centralizing forces that are changing the system.

4. Another structural characteristic is determined by who the major actors in the system are. Currently these are sovereign states, but intergovernmental actors and transnational actors are becoming more numerous and important.

5. A third structural characteristic is a system's scope and level of interaction. The current system is becoming increasingly interdependent, with a rising number of interactions across an expanding range of issues. Economic interdependence is especially significant.

6. Among power relationships, an important factor is the number of poles in a system. Bipolar systems, for instance, may operate differently and be more or less stable than multipolar systems.

7. The pattern of concentration of power is another system characteristic. Whether poles are relatively equal or unequal in power, the shifts in relative strength influence behavior in the system.

8. Power changes in the system when there are shifts in the sources of power or when conditions within major actors affect their tangible or intangible power assets.

9. A system's economic patterns also affect the operation of the system. For instance, the inequitable distribution of wealth among the countries of the world has created tension along what is known as the North-South Axis.

10. Changes in power cause specific changes, for example, the possible impact of nuclear weapons on wars between great powers. Changes in power are also related to system instability.

11. Norms are the values that help determine patterns of behavior and create some degree of predictability in the system. The norms of the system are changing. Many newer countries are, for instance, challenging some of the current norms of the system, most of which are rooted in Western culture.

12. It is clear that there are significant changes occurring in all the determining elements (structural characteristics, power relationships, economic patterns, and norms of behavior) of the international system. What is not clear is exactly what the new system will look like and how it will operate. Scholars use terms such as uni-multipolar, modified multipolar, postinternational, and polyarchal to describe the system that is currently evolving.

13. The view of this book is that system-level analysis is a valid approach to the study of world politics. It must, however, be used in conjunction with other approaches in order to understand world politics fully.

CHAPTER 4

STATE-LEVEL ANALYSIS

An old man, broken with the storms of state, Is come to lay his weary bones among ye; Give him a little earth for charity.

Shakespeare, *Henry VIII*

Oh, that lovely title, ex-president.

Dwight D. Eisenhower, just before leaving office

CHAPTER OBJECTIVES

After completing this chapter, you should be able to:

- Understand the major emphases of state-level analysis.
- Understand various factors affecting foreign policy, including the type of government, domestic factors, gender, and the type of situation and issue.
- Explain how a state's internal dynamics influence foreign policy.
- Understand the importance of political culture on foreign policy.
- Evaluate the role and influence of various subnational actors, including political leaders, bureaucratic organizations, legislatures, political parties, interest groups, and the people.

State-level analysis, a second approach to understanding world politics, emphasizes the national states and their internal processes as the primary determinants of the course of world affairs. As such, this approach focuses on mid-range factors that are less general than the macroanalysis of the international system but less individualistic than the microanalytical focus of human-level analysis.

UNDERSTANDING STATE-LEVEL ANALYSIS

State-level analysts, like system-level analysts, believe that states have long been and continue to be the most powerful actors on the world stage. The two approaches differ, however, on how much freedom of action states have.

Unlike system-level analysts, who believe that the international system pressures states to behave in certain ways, state-level analysts contend that states are relatively free to decide what policies to follow. A state-level analyst would say, "Yes, all countries must deal with the realities of the world system," but, "No, not even the least powerful state is a puppet on the string of the international system." In sum, state-level analysts concentrate on what countries do and how they decide which policy to follow.

Studying *what countries do* is based on the view, as one study puts it, that "much of what goes on in world politics revolves around interactions between governments—two or more states trying to gauge the rationales behind the other's actions and anticipate its next move" (Hermann & Hagan, 1998:133). These interactions are called events, and these events and subsequent events (reactions and counter-reactions) are studied through **event data analysis.** This approach is useful for analyzing matters such as reciprocity between countries. For example, if country A upgrades its military (event), how will country B respond (event)? Will an arms race occur?

Decision-making analysis, or investigating how countries make policy choices, is the second concern of state-level analysts. Once again to contrast system- and state-level analyses, a system-level analyst would contend that, for example, the U.S. military response to Iraq's invasion of Kuwait was almost inevitable, given the realities of where oil was produced and consumed in the system. A state-level analyst would differ strongly and insist that the U.S. response depended on the presidential-congressional relations, the strength of public opinion, and other factors internal to the United States. Therefore, state-level analysts would conclude that to understand the foreign policy of any country, it is necessary to understand that country's domestic factors and its foreign policy–making processes (Milner, 1997; Maoz, 1996). These factors, state-level analysts say, combine to determine how states act and, by extension, how the international system works as a sum of these actions.

MAKING FOREIGN POLICY: TYPES OF GOVERNMENT, SITUATIONS, AND POLICY

If you were to ask people how foreign policy is made, many would reply that presidents or prime ministers decide, and it is done. In reality, decision making is usually a complex process. Sometimes the national leader may be pivotal, but more often the leader does not play a decisive role. One way to begin to see the limits of even powerful leaders is to examine the authority of President Franklin Delano Roosevelt and the power of Lilliputians.

Roosevelt was an epic leader who led his country to victory over both the Great Depression and Hitler. Historians have rated him as one of the three best American presidents. To us, FDR seems to have been very much in charge. Roosevelt was, however, less assured. He often felt fettered by the restraints put on him by the bureaucracy, Congress, public opinion, and other factors.

FDR grumbled often about the bureaucracy, especially the N-A-A-A-V-Y, as he sometimes pronounced it derisively. "To change anything in the N-A-A-A-V-Y," Roosevelt once lamented, "is like punching a feather bed. You punch it with your right and you punch it with your left until you are finally exhausted, and then you find the damn bed just as you left it before you started punching" (DiClerico, 1979:107). Sometimes the Navy would not even tell him what it was up to. "When I woke up this morning," FDR fumed on another occasion, "the first thing I saw was a headline… that our Navy was going to spend two billion dollars on a shipbuilding program. Here I am, the Commander-in-Chief of the Navy, having to read about that for the first time in the press" (Sherill, 1979:217).

Congress also restrained Roosevelt. Isolationist legislators hampered his attempts to aid the Allies against the Axis powers before Pearl Harbor. Toward the end of the war, Congress threatened to block his dream of a United Nations. Diplomat Charles Bohlen (1973:210) has recalled FDR bitterly denouncing senators as "a bunch of obstructionists" and declaring that "the only way to do anything in the American government [is] to bypass the Senate."

Public opinion was also isolationist and further restrained Roosevelt in his desire to help the Allied powers. As late as October 1941, FDR warned the British ambassador that if "he asked for a declaration of war, he wouldn't get it, and opinion would swing against him." (Paterson, Clifford, & Hagan, 2000:182).

Roosevelt did not see himself, then, as the dominant figure that we remember him to be. He knew that to lead the country he had to get it to follow him and that getting it to do so could be difficult and take time. Speaking of his desire to move Americans away from isolationism and toward ever greater support of Great Britain, Roosevelt told one confidante, "The government… cannot change [directions] overnight… Governments, such as ours, cannot swing so far or so quickly" (Paterson, Clifford, & Hagan, 2000:112). Indeed, he might have compared himself to Gulliver in Jonathan Swift's classic tale. The shipwrecked Gulliver was washed ashore in Lilliput. Although the Lilliputians were only a few inches high, Gulliver awoke to find himself bound by countless tiny ropes. He could have broken any one of them, but he could not free himself from all of them.

The point is that, like Gulliver, the freedom of all foreign policy decision makers, whether in democratic or dictatorial states, is limited by an intricate web of governmental and societal restraints. To understand this web, we will explore three general aspects of foreign policy making. This section focuses on how differences in the type of government, the type of policy, or the type of situation influence the policy process. Then the next two sections will deal with the impact of political culture on foreign policy and the roles of the various political actors in making foreign policy.

TYPES OF GOVERNMENT

One variable that affects the foreign policy process is a country's type of domestic political system. Classifying political systems, such as democratic and authoritarian governments, is an important preliminary step to studying how they vary in policy and process because there is strong evidence that differences in the process (how policy is decided) will result in differences in policy substance (which policy is adopted).

Democratic and Authoritarian Governments

The line between **democratic governments** and **authoritarian governments** is not precise. One standard that differentiates the two types, however, is *how many and what*

China considers these people dangerous. One thing that marks a country as authoritarian is severe restrictions on political participation. The people in this photograph are in a Beijing park practicing Falun Gong, a spiritual movement practiced through martial arts and exercise. Chinese leaders, who fear the movement as a potential rival, have banned it and arrested many of its members.

MAP
Political Systems, p. 202

types of people can participate in making political decisions. In countries such as Canada, political participation is extensive, with few adults formally excluded from the political process. In other countries, such as China, participation is limited to an elite based on an individual's political party, economic standing, or some other factor (Nathan, 1998).

How many forms of participation are available is a second criterion for judging forms of government. Political dissent in the United States is public, frequent, often strident, and touches on issues ranging from the president's foreign and domestic policies through his personal life. The seemingly unending spotlight on the relationships between President Clinton and Gennifer Flowers, Paula Jones, Monica Lewinsky, and other women certainly demonstrated this. China, by contrast, tolerates very little open disagreement with policy. This was illustrated dramatically in 1999 when the government cracked down on the banned Falun Gong spiritual movement and arrested 111 members on charges such as disrupting state security and stealing state secrets. The government in Beijing had become alarmed at the growth of the movement, which blends traditional exercises with Buddhism and Taoism, with a bit of mysticism added in. Government leaders labeled the Falun Gong "an evil sect," and President Jiang Zemin was quoted in a government-sponsored book, *Falun Gong and Cults*, as warning, "We must not underestimate it, and even more so, should not be gullible. If this problem is not swiftly solved, it will become a major social disaster."[1] In July 1999 the government banned the group, and the November arrests came after several weeks during which small groups of members sat in Tiananmen Square and meditated in silent protest of having their movement declared illegal.

Before leaving this tale of the Falun Gong and the intolerance of the Chinese government, it must be said that despite the demands by dissidents for greater democracy, it is not certain that most Chinese yearn for democracy, at least Western-style democracy. One factor is the great fear of chaos in China. The Chinese adage, *Yi fang, jiu luan*, which warns, "When control eases, chaos occurs," is based, according to one U.S.

official, on the sense that "all the time in Chinese history, when you don't have strong rule, you get chaos and warlords" (Rourke, 1994:156). Furthermore, the people of China are aware that the people of democratic Russia are worse off economically than were the people of the authoritarian Soviet Union. As one observer commented, "Yes, there are lots of problems, but that doesn't mean [that] the [Communist] party is about to fall. The people reckon their life is getting better [economically], so why change?" Underlining that quiescence, one survey found that by more than two to one, respondents felt that economic development, not democracy, was the country's greatest need.[2]

Democracy and Foreign Policy Choices

As we noted, differences between democracy and autocracy are important to international relations because they can have a foreign policy impact. One reason relates to how many and what types of people can participate effectively in making political decisions. There are a number of ways to explore this impact. One way, which you will see later in this chapter, is to examine differences between average citizens and leaders. There frequently is a gap.

The **leader-public opinion gap** was evident in one recent survey that contrasted the opinions of American leaders from government, business, and other areas with the opinions of the general public. For instance, one series of questions asked whether U.S. troops should be used to counter invasions of Israel, Poland, Saudi Arabia, South Korea, and Taiwan. A majority of the leaders favored using troops in each scenario; a majority of the public opposed intervention. Most Americans favored assassination of terrorist leaders; most leaders did not. Most leaders would give more U.S. funds to the International Monetary Fund to help it react to international financial crises; most of the public would not. Most of the public would impose economic sanctions on China for its human rights abuses; most of the leaders opposed the idea (Rielly, 1999).

Gender provides another relevant standard of democracy. Despite some progress by women, males continue to dominate political decision making globally. Some scholars argue that the underrepresentation of women in the political process has substantive impacts on policy. There is, for example, the view that aggression is associated with maleness. The feminist perspective, in the words of one advocate, "strips the [state] security core naked so that we can see its masculine-serving guises." These, the analyst comments, are "all gussied up with holsters bristling nuclear weapons, spittoons ready to catch the waste (maybe)," and other affectations that strike her as a macho effort to "continually restage the oft-caricatured OK Corral scene in Tombstone, Arizona, where believers now gather to hear soulful renditions of a shoot-out in a lawless place" (Sylvester, 1993:823). If this is the case, then the greater the role of women in policy making, the less likely a country is to be bellicose.

There is at least some empirical evidence to support this view. In the United States, for example, polls going back as far as World War II and extending to the present have found women less ready than males to resort to war or to continue war (Rourke, Carter, & Boyer, 1996:376). During the early days of the Persian Gulf War in 1991, for example, 69 percent of the men thought that the benefits of war would be worth the cost in lives; only 49 percent of women agreed.[3] The gender difference was again evident in 1999 as the United States debated whether to launch air strikes against and even send ground troops to attack Yugoslavia over its ethnic cleansing policy in Kosovo. Neither option was supported by either American men or women, but 46 percent of men favored air strikes, while only 39 percent of women did; and 46 percent of men favored using ground forces, while only 36 percent of women did.[4]

This **gender opinion gap** was not confined to Americans. A survey that studied the opinions of men and women in another 11 countries about the Persian Gulf War found that, with one exception, a greater percentage of men than women favored using force.

What is missing from this photograph of world leaders? Women! There are real, if not legal, restrictions on political participation by women in even the most democratic governments. This is a photograph of five of the leaders of the G-8, the seven major economic powers and Russia. All are men. The missing three would not have changed the picture; they are also men.

This pattern is shown in Figure 4.1. Take note of several things in this figure. One is the gender opinion gap. The men in all but one of the countries, Turkey, were more likely to favor war than were the women. The pro-war average across the 11 societies was 55 percent for men and 47 percent for women. Second, notice the variations between countries. Women, on average, cannot be described confidently as antiwar, because a majority of women in three countries favored using military force. The pattern between countries also shows the possible impact of other factors. National interest may account for the results in Israel and Russia. In Israel, which was threatened, then attacked, by Iraq, an overwhelming majority of both men and women favored force. It may be that the Soviet Union's longtime support of Iraq persuaded the majority in the USSR to oppose force. Cultural beliefs may have also played a role. The pacifistic leanings of the Japanese are probably the reason that a vast majority of both Japanese men and women opposed using the military. The fact that, like Iraqis, most Turks and many Nigerians are Muslims may help explain why a majority in both these countries were unwilling to support the use of force. Perhaps the reason the Mexicans were so bellicose is that they, like the Kuwaitis, were overshadowed by a large neighbor to the north and had empathy for Kuwait.

Such evidence has led one scholar to conclude that women were more averse to supporting military action because "in international conflict situations, females may tend to perceive more negative risk, more potential harm, and they also may view such losses as more certain than do males" (Brandes, 1993:5).

TYPES OF SITUATIONS

Whatever the form of government, the policy-making process is not always the same (Amadife, 1999; Astorino-Courtois, 1998). Situation is one variable that determines the

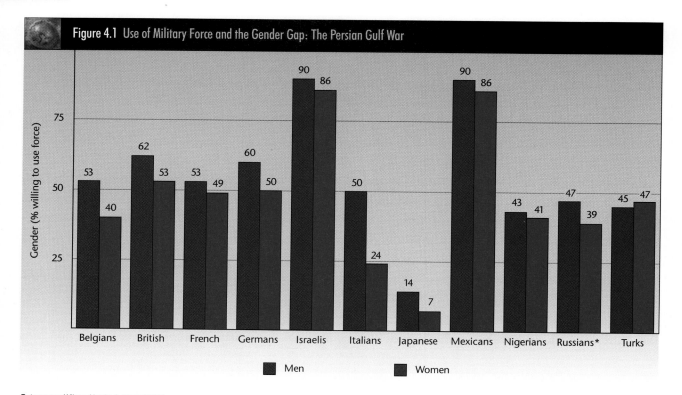

Figure 4.1 Use of Military Force and the Gender Gap: The Persian Gulf War

Data source: Wilcox, Hewitt, & Allsop (1996).
The question was: Should UN soldiers fight if the [economic] embargo [on Iraq] fails?
*The Soviet Union still existed, but the survey was taken in Moscow. Respondents were almost certainly Russians.

Women are less likely than men to favor the use of military force. This was true for each of the 11 nationalities shown here except the Turks, when asked about going to war against Iraq in 1991. It was also true for Americans. Also note the considerable variations among countries in the willingness to endorse war.

exact nature of the foreign policy process. **Crisis situations** are one factor that affects how policy is made. A crisis is a circumstance in which decision makers are 1) surprised by an event, 2) feel threatened (especially militarily), and 3) believe that they have only a short time in which to make a decision (Brecher & Wilkenfeld, 1997). The more intense each of the three factors is, the more acute the sense of crisis. One trait of the policy process during a crisis is that decisions tend to be made by relatively small groups of high-level political leaders. Public opinion is apt to rally in support of whatever action the political leaders take (James & Rioux, 1998). During noncrisis policy making, other subnational actors (such as the legislature, interest groups, and the public) are more likely to be active and influential.

Also, leaders usually strive during a crisis to make rational decisions, but their ability to gather and analyze information is hampered by the exigency of time. This and the anxiety or anger engendered by a crisis often increase the emotional content of decisions. With limited information, little time to think, and with elevated emotions, decision makers rely heavily on preexisting images. "During fast-moving events those at the center of decision are overwhelmed by floods of reports compounded of conjecture, knowledge, hope, and worry," Henry A. Kissinger (1979:627) has recalled from his years as U.S. national security adviser and secretary of state. "These must then be sieved through [the decision makers'] preconceptions. Only rarely does a coherent picture emerge."

What this means is that decision makers will respond to a situation according to the images they already have. If leaders perceive another country as aggressive and if that country mobilizes its forces during a crisis, then decision makers will probably see that act as preparation for attack rather than as preparation for defense. The onset of World War I, for example, can be traced in part to the series of mobilizations and countermobilizations by Austria-Hungary, Germany, Great Britain, France, and Russia. Most of these calls to arms were arguably defensive, but they resulted in a spiral of hostility based on misperceptions. Each country steadily increased its readiness in the belief that it must mobilize to defend itself, while, simultaneously, other countries were viewing the increased readiness as preparations to strike.

Another situational variable that scholars have explored distinguishes between whether the situation fits the existing pattern of relations or portends a radical change. **Status quo situations** are those that fall within existing world patterns. Since there is an inertia in all large organizations, governments are likely to analyze problems in terms of the conventional wisdom and to choose policies that follow established precedent or make only minor changes. This is called incremental policy. It tends to evoke little dissent and to rest with the executive. **Non–status quo situations,** by contrast, occur when a country faces circumstances that diverge markedly from previous, familiar patterns. Such situations require significant changes in policy direction and tend to evoke much stronger debate and to involve a wider array of subnational actors, such as legislatures.

American foreign policy went through a period of sharp division right after World War II as the United States found itself one of two superpowers in a new bipolar world. The divisive issue was whether Americans should abandon isolationism and take on the role of world power. They did play that role, and with a cold war consensus established, U.S. policy entered a status quo era in which many policy choices were analyzed in terms of the cold war. Containment became the predetermined answer to almost any strategic situation. Now U.S. policy makers once again face a time of many non–status quo situations. As could be expected, there is no consensus about what the U.S. role in the world should be. This is one reason why the foreign policies of the first post–cold war president, Bill Clinton, drew so much criticism. His nine immediate predecessors had all enjoyed a central defining issue, the cold war, to anchor their foreign policies. Clinton had no such focus available to him, making it understandable, then, that he once lamented, "Gosh, I miss the cold war" (Patterson, Clifford, & Hagan, 2000:498).

TYPES OF POLICY

How foreign policy is decided also varies according to the nature of the **issue area** involved. This type of analysis rests on the idea that issues that address different subject areas will be decided by different decision makers and by different processes. One theory about policy making holds that presidents and other leaders have greater power to decide foreign policy than they do to determine domestic policy. The latter area is one in which legislatures, interest groups, and even public opinion play a greater role. Agreement on whether this theory is true or not has so far eluded scholars.

One explanation for this lack of consensus may be that many policies are neither purely domestic nor purely foreign. Instead they have elements of both policy types and constitute a third type called **intermestic** policy. Foreign trade is a classic example of an intermestic issue because it affects both international relations and the domestic economy in terms of jobs, prices, and other factors. The influence of political leaders is less on such intermestic issues because they, like domestic issues, directly impact and activate interest groups, legislators, and other subnational actors more than do foreign policy issues. It follows that presidential leadership is strongest on pure foreign/defense policy issues, weaker on mixed (intermestic) issues, and weakest on pure domestic issues.

MAKING FOREIGN POLICY: POLITICAL CULTURE

To repeat an important point, the state is not a unitary structure. Even authoritarian states are complex political organisms. Therefore, as one scholar notes, "All foreign policy decisions occur in a particular domestic context. This environment includes the... political culture... of a society" (Gerner, 1995:21).

Political culture refers to a society's general, long-held, and fundamental practices and attitudes. It has two main sources. One is the *national historical experience*: the sum of events and practices that have shaped a country and its citizens. The fact that the United States has been invaded only once (in 1812) while China has been invaded many times makes American and Chinese attitudes about the world very different. The second source of political culture is the *national belief system*: the ideas and ideologies that people hold. Whether it is capitalism in the United States, Shiism in Iran, Sinocentrism in China, Zionism in Israel, or Russia's sense of its greatness, these intellectual orientations are important determinants of how a country defines itself and decides its policy (Cooper, 1999; Hudson, 1997; Lapid & Kratochwil, 1996).

Before proceeding, several comments should be made. First, political culture does not usually create specific policy. Instead, political culture is apt to pressure leaders or allow them to move or not move in a general direction (Breuning, 1995). In this sense, political culture is important in establishing a country's broad sense of its national interest. Second, political culture changes. Shifts are usually evolutionary, though, because much of a country's political culture is rooted far back in its history and is resistant to change.

Third, a society's political culture is not monolithic. American political culture, for example, includes both liberal humanitarian and isolationist impulses. These have created inconsistency in American feelings about whether or not to intervene in such places as Bosnia. Moreover, the leadership of a country may come from a limited segment of the society that does not share the values of the general public. Some people question, for instance, how accurately American political culture is reflected in the U.S. government.

Even those who study political culture are apt to concede that "demonstrating in a convincing fashion the independent influence of culture on political behavior is difficult" (Gaenslen, 1997:272). To begin to overcome this challenge and to ascertain its impact on policy, we can divide political culture into attitudes about (1) protecting and enhancing the national core, that is, the country's territory and population; (2) creating and maintaining a favorable world order; and (3) projecting values, that is, judging others by and converting them to those values. These three categories can be used to examine the role of any country's political culture in its foreign policy. But for the sake of illustration, the impact will be clearer if we concentrate on just one country: China. China's history is truly ancient, even if some of its belief system dates back only to the communist victory in 1949. The Chinese have a tremendous consciousness of and pride in their nearly 3,000-year-old culture and history. It is a "culture that thinks in terms of dynasties," one observer has noted.[5] This sense of history creates, according to one scholar, a "compressed conceptualization" of time that, compared to the Western conceptualization of time, "renders the past closer to someone standing in the Chinese present than in the Western present" (Katzenstein, 1997:55). Thus, the values and practices of the Chinese are heavily influenced by their sense of their ancient and remarkable civilization.

NATIONAL CORE

An official publication of China proclaims that its first foreign policy principle is "Maintaining Independence, Self-Reliance and National Sovereignty" (China, 1993:3). This

One aspect of political culture that affects China's foreign policy is Sinocentrism, the tendency of the Chinese to see themselves and their country as the center of the political and cultural world. This self-image is represented by these Chinese characters. They are Zhong Guó, the Chinese name for their country, which translates as middle (Zhong, on the left) place (Guó, on the right).

encapsulation of China's attitudes toward its national core reflects a number of interrelated traits of Chinese political culture, including Sinocentrism, insistent sovereignty, and a sense of being beset.

Sinocentrism

The notion of Sinocentrism is an expression of the tendency of the Chinese to see themselves as the political and cultural center of the world. The Chinese word for their country is "Zhong Guó." It means "middle place" and symbolizes the Chinese image of themselves. (For a discussion of the spelling and pronunciation of Chinese and the format of non-Western names, see the section on Explanatory Notes on page 557.)

China has been relatively weak and in turmoil for most of the last century, and Chinese assertions of their centrality have been and remain muted. President Jiang Zemin has reassuringly pledged, "China will never seek hegemony" (May, 1998:52). Some analysts worry, however, that such assurances are merely tactical, and that the middle kingdom complex can be seen in statements such as those of General Mi Shenyu, who counsels, "For a relatively long time it will be absolutely necessary that we quietly nurse our sense of vengeance. We must conceal our abilities and bide our time" (Bernstein & Munro, 1997:22). Some analysts also believe China's intentions are evident in its mounting defense expenditures. Most experts agree that Beijing grossly underreports what it spends on its military, but even by the government figures, China's increase of 12.7 percent for the year 2000 was large, especially given that it marked the 11th straight year of double-digit increases in defense spending.

Sinocentrism also leads the Chinese to consider their principles immutable and not subject to negotiation or compromise. "Traditionally, other nations and people were expected to conform with China's norms and values," one study comments. That "basic attitude that the rest of the world should conform has changed little" (Wilhelm, 1994:25).

Some observers suspect that Sinocentrism will also prompt a rejuvenated China to seek to once again dominate its traditional sphere of influence in neighboring areas, especially Southeast Asia. In the view of one scholar, "From Beijing's post-cold war perspective, Asia is the center of Chinese power and influence, the calculus of ever-expanding circles radiating outward in all directions" (Kim, 1997:248). To promote greater influence, the analysis continues, "China's military power in quantitative and qualitative terms is growing," while the size and budgets of most other countries' military forces have been declining. Beijing has alarmed other capitals in the region by claiming sovereignty over the Paracel Islands and the Spratly Islands in the South China Sea and by slowly building structures and communications capabilities and occasionally sending military units for brief visits in what the defense minister of the Philippines has called a "creeping invasion."[6] Indeed, China claims control over almost all of this sea, with its potential to produce oil and other riches, an area extending southward nearly 1,500 miles from the Chinese mainland. These claims, one scholar writes, are part of a "remarkable and potentially dangerous" new Chinese concept of *haiyang guotu guan*, or "sea as territory" (Kim, 1997:248). What creates the peril is that the Paracels are also claimed by Vietnam and Taiwan. The Spratly Islands are also claimed by Brunei, Malaysia, the Philippines, Taiwan, and Vietnam.

China has moved gradually to reassert its authority over its former territories and over areas that once fell within China's sphere of influence. Its claims include the Paracel Islands and the Spratly Islands. Both island groups are also claimed by neighboring countries. Such claims have convinced many observers that China seeks regional dominance.

Of limited immediate concern, but of great possible portent, China also has laid claim to a small group of islands to the northeast of Taiwan. These are called the Senkaku Islands by Japan, which currently controls them, and the Diaoyu Islands by China (Downs & Saunders, 1999). So far, Tokyo and Beijing have not clashed openly, but one scholar believes that "there's potential here for more than just diplomatic wrangling." Furthermore, the analyst says, "the disputed areas are part of a larger danger of tensions between China and Japan" as two major powers with conflicting interests.[7]

Insistent Sovereignty

Chinese political culture is also marked, in the words of former U.S. secretary of state Henry Kissinger, by a "prickly insistence on sovereignty."[8] The stress that China puts on its sovereign control over what it defines as its territory stems from the fact that during the 1800s and early 1900s China was coerced into surrendering considerable territory to European countries and to Japan. Those countries and the United States also established de facto control over extensive areas in China. China never lost its theoretical independence, but in practice it was divided and dominated by outside powers. The Chinese refer to the period of outside domination as a "period of humiliation." One Chinese official recollected that in Shanghai during this period there was a sign on a park gate reading "No Permission [Entry] for Chinese and Dogs." "Even when I was in the primary and middle school fifty years ago," the official continued, "I exactly knew that this was a gross insult for [the] Chinese people" (Yu, 1994:1). From this perspective, a great deal of China's history in this century can be interpreted as part of the struggle of the Chinese people to regain their pride and to rid their country of the last vestiges of outside influence.

One very important aspect of this struggle has been China's effort to regain the territories it lost during its period of weakness. Tibet, which had earlier escaped all but technical Chinese suzerainty and which claims to have become fully independent in 1911, was invaded by and incorporated into China in 1950. Great Britain's Hong Kong reverted by treaty to China in 1997 and Portugal's Macau followed suit in 1999. Other major territorial claims remain unfulfilled. Taiwan is the most important. The issue of what Taiwan is to be or not to be is detailed in the box on page 92 (Yu, 1996).

It is important to note that China is not fanatical about lost territory. During its period of weakness, China was forced to cede to Russia approximately 1.5 million square kilometers along its northern and western frontiers. After years of negotiations and even armed clashes, the last disputes were settled in 1997, with China relinquishing its claim to most of the territory it had once controlled. The agreement between China and Russia and three other former Soviet Republics (Kazakhstan, Kyrgyzstan, and Tajikistan) also reduced troops along the 4,500 mile-long border.

The Chinese sense of sovereignty also has ramifications beyond territory. They reject, for example, the right of the United States or anyone else to comment on human rights in China. Exemplifying this, President Jiang has depicted the international calls for human rights reform by China as part of a neoimperial plan by "certain big powers for encroaching on the sovereignty of others under the pretext of promoting human rights and democracy."

Sense of Being Beset

A sense of being beset by foreign peril is a third core orientation of Chinese political culture. This trait springs from a combination of Zhong Guó's sense of being the middle place and a history marked by foreign invasions. These include the conquest by Mongols under Ghenghis Khan (1167–1227) and the establishment of the Yuan dynasty (1260–1368) by his grandson, Kublai Khan. The Ming dynasty (1368–1644) reestablished Han Chinese control, but it was toppled by the Manchus, who invaded from the north and ruled China until the fall of the last emperor in 1911.

All of this and more has created a mind-set in China that it is beset by potentially hostile outsiders. The country's most famous symbol, the Great Wall of China, epitomizes this sense of being besieged. The wall stretches 1,500 miles, is on average 25 feet high, and is the only human-made structure visible from outer space. It was begun under the Chin dynasty in the third century B.C. and was periodically extended and reinforced over the next 1,800 years to wall out the "barbarians" to the north. Indeed, until modern times, the Chinese used the word barbarian for all non-Chinese, especially non-Asians, along with a geographic designation (such as north barbarians) to indicate which foreigners were meant.

More recently, the Chinese feeling of peril was given substance when much of China fell under de facto colonial domination by Japan and several European powers during the period of humiliation beginning in the mid-1800s, as noted earlier. Then, from 1949, China's sense of being beset was further reinforced by the communist ideological view that the imperialistic capitalists would inevitably attempt to destroy the communist movement before it could bring about capitalism's downfall.

From Beijing's perspective, the end of the cold war has not lessened the international threat to China. This wary view was evident in a booklet, "Can the Chinese Army Win the Next War?" with an introduction signed by President Jiang. The tract argued that "because of serious... differences in ideology, social systems and foreign policies... it would be impossible to improve fundamentally Sino-U.S. relations" and warned that "the United States still considers China a hypothetical target in its regional defense strategy."[9] China also worries about the prospects of a more forceful, even rearmed, Japan asserting itself alone or in concert with its ally the United States (Shambaugh, 2000).

With increasing frequency, Beijing charges that the United States is "extremely nervous about China becoming [more] powerful day by day" and, therefore, is trying to "contain" China by "attempting to instigate hostile relations between China and neighboring countries." It is also common for the Chinese to argue that the established powers are urging the nonproliferation of nuclear weapons and environmental protection as pretexts to limit China's growth. Scholar Wang Jisi, for example, explains that "the Chinese have a hard time understanding why they cannot do things that other powers did before, such as test nuclear weapons, sell arms, recover lost territories, [and] pollute the environment."[10]

Washington denies such charges, but whatever U.S. intentions are, China's suspicion is understandable. "China sees America snuggling up to India..., recognizing Vietnam, selling F-16s to Taiwan, walking hand in hand with Japan into the 21st century, wanting a united Korea under Seoul allied with the U.S," comments James Lilley, former U.S. ambassador to Beijing. What that looks like to the Chinese, says Lilley, is "a ring around China."[11]

FAVORABLE WORLD ORDER

China is a curious mixture of a former great power that once dominated its region and a currently developing and still officially communist country (Karmel, 2000; Johnston & Ross, 1999; Murray, 1998). These factors dispose China toward favoring changes in the status quo. One shift that China is seeking is an *enhanced world role* for itself. During the last two decades, China's diplomatic activity has expanded considerably. Its most important concerns have been regional, but as China's power grows, its focus will extend beyond its region to include a greater array of global concerns. The regular increases in China's military spending noted above have emphasized power-projection forces designed to apply military power at a distance. For example, as Lieutenant General Liu Shunyao put it in late 1999, China's air force is striving to "realize as soon as possible a change from territorial defense to a combination of defense and offense."[12]

China's view of the proper world order leaves some leaders in Southeast Asia and other observers to suspect that Beijing may try to reassert Zhong Guó's historical geopolitical domination over the Southeast Asian **sphere of influence.** As Lee Kuan Yew, a former prime minister of Singapore, has observed, "Many medium and small countries in Asia are uneasy that China may want to resume the imperial status it had in earlier centuries and have misgivings about being treated as vassal states having to send tribute to China, as they used to in past centuries" (Bernstein & Munro, 1997:20).

(continued on page 94)

TAIWAN: TO BE OR NOT TO BE

"To be or not to be, that is the question," Prince Hamlet muses in one of Shakespeare's oft-quoted lines. It is that President Chen Shui-bian and the other citizens of Taiwan might ask of themselves.

Taiwan (also called Formosa) is located 100 miles to the east of south-central China, has a total land area of 13,969 square miles (about the size of Maryland and Delaware combined), and a current population of 21.7 million. The island was part of China until it was seized by Japan in 1895. China regained the island after World War II, but Taiwan again became politically separated when the Nationalist government led by Chiang Kai-shek fled to Taiwan in 1949 after being ousted by the communist forces of Mao Zedong. Both Mao's government and Chiang's government agreed that there was only one China and that Taiwan was an integral part of China. The two disagreed about which government legitimately represented China. For years, the United States and most other countries recognized Taiwan (Nationalist China, the Republic of China) as the legitimate government of all China, and Taiwan held the China seat in the United Nations.

Over time, though, most countries shifted their diplomatic recognition to Beijing. The UN seated Beijing's representative and, in effect, expelled Taiwan's in 1972; Washington shifted its recognition to the mainland in 1978. Still, Taiwan has continued to exist independently, even though, in essence, it had become a vague diplomatic entity.

For about two decades after the shifts in the 1970s, the issue of Taiwan's status remained relatively moot. More recently, though, two factors have heightened tensions as Taiwan flirts with seeking recognition as a sovereign, separate state and China threatens war, if necessary, to stop any such move. One factor is the growing confidence of Taiwan. It has prospered. Taiwan's $261 billion GDP makes it the world's nineteenth largest economy; its combined merchandise exports and imports of $236 billion make it the world's eighth largest trader. Taiwan also has a formidable military, spending some $7.5 billion a year on its more than 400,000 troops and impressive array of armaments. "The realities are that Taiwan is large, does exist, and is a force to be reckoned with in economic terms," an Asian diplomat has commented. "Now they feel they should be given

She is banned in China. Beijing was so incensed at the pro-independence leanings of Taiwan's president, Chen Shui-bian, that it banned advertising featuring Taiwanese pop star Chang Hue-mei because she sang at President Chen's inauguration. This ad in Shanghai, which shows Ms. Chang promoting a local electric company, was soon removed by Chinese police.

some international space. It is an emotional, psychological thing. They feel inferior. They feel they are being treated as pariahs."[1]

The passage of time has also changed attitudes in Taiwan. The country has two ethnic groups: the traditional Taiwanese, who make up 85 percent of the population, and the closely related mainland Chinese, many of whom arrived in 1949 and who, thereafter, dominated politics. Among the Chinese, the old guard from the mainland has given way to Chinese born on Taiwan. Their attachment to the mainland is less pronounced than that of their elders. Also, the ethnic Taiwanese have become more prominent politically. In 1988, Lee Teng-hui became the first president of Taiwan of ethnic Taiwanese heritage. Lee, however, was the leader of the Nationalist Party, which was established by those who had fled China in 1949. In yet another step away from China, the Nationalists lost the power they had held for over a half century. In the presidential election held in March

2000, the Nationalist candidate finished a distant third in a three-way race. The victor was Chen Shui-bian. Like his predecessor, Chen is Taiwanese. Also, signaling Taiwan's continued political drift away from the mainland, Chen, who was born in 1951, is the first president of the postseparation generation: those who have lived neither in China itself nor in Taiwan during a period when it was united with the mainland.

Over the past decade or so, there have been numerous signs that Taiwan is cautiously seeking legal independence. President Lee's statements often seemed to favor that end. He sought to promote Taiwan's membership in the United Nations and took a number of other actions to try to enhance Taiwan's image of independence. Lee particularly outraged Beijing in 1999 when he asserted Taiwan's de facto independence by declaring that he favored "state-to-state" relations with China and that "under such special nation-to-nation relations, there is no longer any need to declare Taiwanese independence."[2] Lee was regularly condemned by Beijing, but he seemed relatively palatable compared to the prospect in 2000 that Chen, the candidate of the pro-independence Democratic Progressive Party, would be elected.

Any move toward independence is anathema to Beijing. China has repeatedly vowed to use force to reincorporate Taiwan if the island declares its independence. This stand and candidate Lee's leanings toward independence sparked a crisis in the months preceding Taiwan's March 1996 presidential election. In an attempt to intimidate Taiwan, China conducted large military maneuvers in the Taiwan Strait that included firing missiles into "test areas" near Taiwan's main ports. A foreign ministry official told the press, "There is no flexibility on this issue," and that if Taiwan opted for independence, "I am afraid there is going to be war, because this is how our policy dictates we must respond."[3] In the end, China's fear campaign failed. The United States sent two aircraft carrier–led flotillas to the area. Washington warned Beijing not to be rash and simultaneously cautioned Taipei not to be provocative. The election proceeded peacefully.

Tension soared again as the 2000 election approached. In February, the mainland government released a report entitled "The One-China Principle and the Taiwan Issue" that, for the first time, implied ominously that China would not wait forever for reunification. If Taiwan refuses "indefinitely" to agree to "reunification through negotiation," the report warned, "then the Chinese government will be forced to adopt all drastic measures possible, including the use of force, to safeguard China's sovereignty and territorial integrity."[4] Further raising the heat, the military, in an editorial in the *Liberation Army Daily*, pledged to "spare no effort in a blood-soaked battle" to protect China's territorial integrity if Taiwan formally declared independence.[5]

Such threats brought a series of counterwarnings from Washington officials. Undersecretary of State William B. Slocombe, for example, cautioned China that it faced "incalculable consequences" if it took military action. What ensued was a complex, three-sided, Beijing-Taipei-Washington negotiation involving China's trade relations with the United States; China's desire to have the United States support its admission into the World Trade Organization; China's objection to the proposed U.S. sale to Taiwan of certain weapons systems (especially Arleigh Burke class warships); the United States assuring China and warning Taiwan that it did not support an independence move; the willingness of candidate, then newly elected president, Chen to back away from his earlier pro-independence statements and at least rhetorically adhere to the principle of One-China and peaceful negotiations on reunification; and Taiwan undercutting the efforts of Republicans in the U.S. Congress to give it greater military support than the Clinton administration was willing to offer. Unlike what occurred in 1996, there were no overt demonstrations and counterdemonstrations of Chinese and American military muscle. This diplomacy will be covered in detail in chapter 10 on that subject.

Thus, the waters in the Taiwan Strait calmed in the weeks after the election of President Chen, but the issue is far from resolved and remains potentially dangerous. Taiwan remains an "other," neither a state nor a dependent territory. China's determination to regain all its lost territories remains unfulfilled. The reversion to China's control of Hong Kong in 1997 and of Macau in 1999 leaves Taiwan as the last remaining unreclaimed territory. Now, as Foreign Ministry spokesman Chen Jian has said, "the settlement of the motherland" is "on the top of the agenda."[6]

Another aspect of China's worldview is increased *international economic interchange*. China is intent on modernizing itself economically and has come to realize that it needs Western technology and investment to do so. As a result, China has moderated some of its disputes with the capitalist-industrial countries and has established "special economic zones" to promote greater trade and foreign investment, and even now has decidedly capitalist stock exchanges in Shanghai and Shenzhen, as well as in the recently acquired territory of Hong Kong. China is also a member of the IMF, the World Bank, and other international economic institutions that it once condemned as tools of capitalist imperialism. This is a fairly recent orientation, and it conflicts somewhat with China's traditional self-reliance. China also campaigned to become a charter member of the World Trade Organization (WTO), and after long being blocked by the United States and other countries, the way for Beijing's membership was cleared by agreements with the United States and the European Union in mid-2000.

PROJECTING VALUES

The political culture of a nation determines the degree to which it applies its own values to judge others. For example, Americans have a missionary zeal to reshape the world in the American image in the belief that the more other countries resemble the United States the better off they will be (Latham, 1997). This can lead to cultural imperialism. It also means that, more than most other countries, the United States champions human rights (albeit its own interpretation of rights) and, to some degree, applies those standards in making foreign aid and other foreign policy decisions. In the words of one study, national security interests play "the most prominent role" in determining U.S. aid policy, but "human rights do [also] play a role in the decision of who receives U.S. bilateral foreign assistance and how much aid they are allotted" (Apodaca & Stohl, 1999:195).

Chinese political culture attitudes about projecting values are very different from those of Americans. Despite China's immense pride in its culture, there is no history of trying to impose it on others. Even when communist ideology (with its element of exporting the revolution) was a much stronger part of China's foreign policy, Beijing was much less active than was Moscow in trying to convert others. This is a long historical orientation that existed even when China dominated much of the world that it knew. The orientation is based in part on Confucianism's tenet of leading by example rather than by forceful conversion. It also has to do with the Sinocentric attitude that the "barbarians" are not well suited to aspire to the heights of Chinese culture and are best left to themselves as much as possible. Among other current ramifications, this nonmissionary attitude makes it very hard for the Chinese to understand why Americans and some others try to insist that China adopt what it sees as foreign values and standards of behavior on human rights and other issues. Instead of taking these pressures at face value, the Chinese see them as interference or, worse, as part of a campaign to subvert them.

MAKING FOREIGN POLICY: ACTORS IN THE PROCESS

No state (national actor) is a unitary structure, a so-called black box. Instead, the state is more of a "shell" that encapsulates a foreign policy process in which a variety of **subnational actors** take part. These subnational actors include political executives, bureaucracies, legislatures, political opposition, interest groups, and the people. It is the pattern of cooperation and conflict among these subnational actors that constitutes the internal foreign policy–making process.

POLITICAL EXECUTIVES

The beginning of this chapter showed President Franklin Roosevelt's frustrations with the limitations on his authority. Yet it can also be said that **political executives** (officials whose tenure is variable and dependent on the political contest for power in their country) are normally the strongest subnational actors in the foreign policy process. These leaders are located in the executive branch and are called president, prime minister, premier, chancellor, or perhaps king or emir.

Whatever their specific title, political executives have important legal, or *formal*, powers. Most chief executives are, for example, designated as the commanders in chief of their countries' armed forces. This gives them important and often unilateral authority to use the military. Political executives also frequently possess important *informal* powers. Their personal prestige is often immense, and skillful leaders can use their public standing to win political support for their policies.

The foreign policy–making predominance of political executives even in democratic countries has many causes. First, kings traditionally directed foreign and military affairs, and they kept that authority long after they began to lose control of domestic affairs to parliaments. Second, there is a widespread (albeit controversial) feeling, one analysis contends, that "the [successful] conduct of foreign policy... requires a concentration of executive power" (Spanier & Uslaner, 1993:1). Third, foreign policy often sparks only limited activity by other subnational actors, who tend to concentrate instead on domestic issues that affect them directly. The growing intermestic nature of issues is, however, encouraging wider subnational-actor participation in foreign policy making. Fourth, most political leaders have important advantages over other subnational actors. One edge that presidents have is the ability to act, while legislatures can only debate and vote. Another advantage is that heads of government can command much greater information-gathering and analysis resources than any other actor.

Yet it is also true that presidents and premiers are not absolute monarchs. The spread of democracy and the increasingly intermestic nature of policy in an independent world mean that political leaders must often be in a **two-level game** in which "each national leader plays both the international and domestic games simultaneously" (Trumbore, 1998:546; Boyer, 1996). The strategy of a two-level game is based on the reality that to be successful, diplomats have to negotiate at the *international level* with the representatives of other countries and at the *domestic level* with legislators, bureaucrats, interest groups, and the public in the diplomat's own country. The object is to produce a "win-win" agreement that satisfies both the international counterparts and the powerful domestic actors so that both are willing to support the accord. Reflecting this reality, one former U.S. official has recalled that "during my tenure as Special Trade Representative, I spent as much time negotiating with domestic constituents (both industry and labor) and members of the U.S. Congress as I did negotiating with our foreign trading partners" (Lindsay, 1994:292).

TOM
TROUW
Amsterdam
NETHERLANDS

© 2000 CARTOONISTS & WRITERS SYNDICATE http://CartoonWeb.com

When President Clinton began to consider building a missile defense system, he not only received strong criticism from within the United States; he also aroused opposition from the Russians and even from the U.S. allies in Europe, as this Dutch cartoon depicts. Leaders engage in a "two-level game." In this case, one level is negotiating with the other countries that consider the plan destabilizing to nuclear deterrence. The second level involves dealing with Congress and other powerful domestic actors over the wisdom and details of the plan.

BUREAUCRACIES

Every state, whatever its strength or type of government, is heavily influenced by its **bureaucracy.** Although the dividing line between decision makers and bureaucrats is often hazy, we can say that bureaucrats are career governmental personnel, as distinguished from those who are political appointees or elected officials.

Although political leaders legally command the bureaucracy, they frequently complain that it is difficult to control the vast understructure of their governments. "One of the hardest things" about being president, Ronald Reagan grumbled, "is to know that down there, underneath, is a permanent structure that's resisting everything you're doing." Similarly, Mikhail Gorbachev lashed out against a bureaucracy dominated by "conservative sentiments, inertia, [and] a tendency to brush aside everything that does not fit into conventional patterns." And China's Zhao Ziyang agreed that the "unwieldiness of government organs, confusion of their responsibilities, and buck-passing" are "a serious problem in the political life of our party and state" (Rourke, 1990:131). Each of these leaders cast a long shadow on the world stage in his day; each also felt beset by his supposedly subordinate bureaucracy. Our discussion of the foreign policy role of bureaucracies will focus on two points: bureaucratic perspective and bureaucratic methods.

Bureaucratic Perspective

Bureaucrats often favor one policy option over another based on their general sense of their unit's mission and how they should conduct themselves. How any given policy will affect the organization is also an important factor in creating bureaucratic perspective. Often what a given bureaucracy will or will not favor makes intuitive sense. The military of any country will almost certainly oppose arms reductions or defense-spending cuts because such policies reduce the military bureaucracy's resources and influence. But the stereotypic view that the military is always gung ho to go to war is not accurate. Whether the area was Kosovo, Bosnia, Haiti, or elsewhere, the U.S. military has been a main center of opposition to intervention within the government, and especially to the use of ground forces. A common view, expressed by former chairman of the Joint Chiefs of Staff General Colin Powell, is that "politicians start wars. Soldiers fight and die in them."[13]

Bureaucratic Methods

An organization's perceptions will cause it, consciously or not, to try to shape policy according to its views. Bureaucracies influence policy decisions by filtering information, tailoring recommendations to fit the bureaucracy's preference, and implementing policy in ways that alter policy direction.

Filtering information is one method that bureaucracies use to influence policy. Decision makers depend on supporting organizations for information, but what facts they are told depends on what subordinates believe and what they choose, consciously or not, to pass on. Occasionally, for example, a bureaucracy suppresses information that would embarrass the agency or undermine its policy preference. One of the notable disasters in U.S. foreign policy was the Bay of Pigs operation of 1961. A landing of U.S.–trained, anti-Castro Cuban exiles at La Bahía de Cochinos in Cuba was quickly defeated, with most of the invaders killed or captured, by Cuban forces. Recently declassified information indicates at least one cause for the debacle: The Soviets had learned the exact date of the invasion and, presumably, had passed it on to Castro. Even more troubling, the CIA knew the Soviets knew, yet did not warn either the White House or the Cuban exiles of the security breach. Since, according to the CIA agent in charge of the operation, the exiles had not been told of the invasion date and so "the leak could not have been Cuban," it was almost certainly American.[14] Therefore, it is reasonable to suspect that the CIA kept silent and almost certainly doomed the operation rather than disclose that the agency may have been penetrated by Soviet agents.

Subordinates also filter information because they may be afraid that unwelcome news will endanger their careers. In the 1960s, amid the anticommunist consensus of the cold war, one U.S. official recalls, "candid reporting of the strengths of the Viet Cong and the weaknesses of the [U.S.–backed South Vietnamese] Diem government was inhibited" by the fear that any diplomat or intelligence analyst who suggested that the communists might win would be dismissed as weak-minded or, worse, as "soft on communism" (Thompson, 1989:593).

Recommendations are another source of bureaucratic influence on foreign policy. Bureaucracies are the source of considerable expertise, which they use to push the agency's preferred position. One scholar, after analyzing bureaucratic recommendations in several countries, concluded that leaders often faced an "option funnel." This means that advisers narrow the range of options available to leaders by presenting to them only those options that the adviser's bureaucratic organization favors. The options and capabilities developed according to the bureaucracy's "cultural penchant," the analyst continued, "often decided what national leaders would do even before they considered a situation" (Legro, 1996:133).

Implementation is another powerful bureaucratic tool. There are a variety of ways that bureaucrats can influence policy by the way that they carry it out. To a substantial degree, bureaucrats have discretion to carry out policy within broad parameters set down by decision makers. When they have options, it is normal for an official to choose the one that fits with his or her policy outlook. That implementation may inadvertently vary from what policy makers might have wished. At times, however, a bureaucrat can consciously attempt to delay, change, or ignore a decision or try to seize the initiative and act on their own. A fascinating example of both options occurred in Kosovo in 1999. Russia was attempting to play a role in the creation of the largely NATO (North Atlantic Treaty Organization) peacekeeping force that was moving to take up positions in Kosovo after Yugoslavia had given way in the face of the concerted bombing campaign. Fearing they would be shut out by the NATO allies, the Russians landed a force at the airport in Pristina, the capital of Kosovo, and took up positions. The NATO commander, General Wesley Clark, an American, responded by ordering Lieutenant General Mike Jackson, the British commander in the area, to move his tanks to the airport and to block the runways to prevent Russia from flying in supplies or reinforcements. Clark's goal was to force the unwanted Russians out. General Jackson refused, telling Clark, "No, I'm not going to do that. It's not worth starting World War III."[15]

These events demonstrate several aspects of implementation. One was the initiative of General Clark. Washington and the other NATO capitals were negotiating with Moscow about the Russian role when Clark, on his own initiative, decided to try to force the Russians to leave Kosovo and made a move that could conceivably have led to combat between Russian and NATO troops. Second, and adding another bureaucratic twist to the tale, Clark's initiative was trumped when his subordinate, General Jackson, refused to implement the order. One wonders whether Jackson should have been court-martialed, hailed for averting World War III, or both. In any case, whatever the political leaders might have wished, it was the generals in the field who made policy.

LEGISLATURES

In all countries, the foreign policy role of legislatures is less than that of executive-branch decision makers and bureaucrats. This does not mean that all legislatures are powerless. They are not, but their exact influence varies greatly among countries. Legislatures in nondemocratic systems generally rubber-stamp the decisions of the political

Legislatures and even individual legislators can play a strong foreign policy role in some countries. The United States is far behind in paying its assessment to the United Nations. A good part of the reason is the opposition of Senate Foreign Relations Committee chairman Jesse Helms to full payment. He is pictured here being courted by UN secretary-general Kofi Annan on the left and, on the right, Richard Holbrooke, the U.S. ambassador to the UN.

leadership. China's National People's Congress, for example, does not play a significant role in foreign policy making.

Even in democratic countries, however, legislatures are inhibited by many factors. One of these is tradition. The leadership has historically run foreign policy in virtually all countries, especially in time of war or other crises. Second, there is the axiom that "politics should stop at the water's edge." The belief is that a unified national voice is important to a successful foreign policy. This is particularly true during a crisis, when there is the aforementioned tendency to support the political leaders and to view dissent as bordering on treason. This rally effect applies to more than specific issues; it extends to a more general support of presidential foreign policy, at least for a short time. Third, the tradition of executive dominance has led to executives normally being given extensive constitutional power over foreign policy. In Great Britain, for example, a declaration of war does not require the consent of Parliament. Fourth, legislators tend to focus on domestic affairs because, accurately or not, voters perceive domestic issues as more important and make voting decisions based in part on the legislator's domestic record rather than on his or her foreign policy stands. Indeed, paying too much attention to international affairs leaves legislators open to the electoral charge that they are not sufficiently minding their constituents' interests.

None of this means that legislatures do not sometimes play an important role in foreign affairs and have a range of potent powers, such as the ability to appropriate or withhold funds (Bacchus, 1997). Legislative activity is especially likely and important when a high-profile issue captures public attention and public opinion opposes the president's policy. Congress was one of the factors that pushed the Nixon administration to get out of Vietnam and the Clinton administration to withdraw from Somalia. In the earlier case, as is typical, members of the president's own political party were worried that continuing the war would spell disaster to Republican electoral fortunes. "We have got to have the people of the United States convinced that the war is over by this fall, or we [Republicans] are out of business," the Republican Senate leader, Howard Baker, told President Nixon in 1971. "I agree with your political assessment," Nixon replied. "I am keenly aware of the problem."[16]

Even more commonly, intermestic issues are involved that directly affect constituents and interest groups in the legislators' electoral districts and spark legislative activity. As one member of the U.S. Congress put it, "Increasingly all foreign policy issues are becoming domestic issues. As a reflection of the public input, Congress is demanding to play a greater role."[17]

POLITICAL OPPOSITION

In every political system, those who are in power face rivals who would replace them, either to change policy or to gain power. In democratic systems, this opposition is legitimate and is organized into political parties (Breuning, 1996; Noél & Thérien, 1996). Rival politicians may also exist in the leader's own party. Opposition is less overt and/or less peaceful in nondemocratic systems, but it exists nonetheless and in many varied forms. One distinction divides opposition between those who merely want to change policy and those who want to gain control of the government. A second division is between those who are located inside and outside of the government. Just one example of how political opposition can influence foreign policy is contained in the box entitled Frustration-Aggression Analysis and the Rise of Vladimir Putin, in chapter 5.

INTEREST GROUPS

Interest groups are private (nongovernmental) associations of people who have similar policy views and who pressure the government to adopt those views as policy. Traditionally, **interest groups** were generally considered to be less active and influential on foreign policy than on domestic policy issues because foreign policy often had only a limited effect on the groups' domestic-oriented concerns. The increasingly intermestic nature of policy is changing that, and interest groups are becoming a more important part of the foreign policy–making process. We can see this by looking at several types of interest groups.

Cultural groups are one type. Many countries have ethnic, racial, religious, or other cultural groups that have emotional or political ties to another country. For instance, as a country made up mostly of immigrants, the United States is populated by many who maintain a level of identification with their African, Cuban, Irish, Mexican, Polish, and other heritages and who are active on behalf of policies that favor their ancestral homes.

The Cuban American community well illustrates the impact of cultural groups. The group is represented by a number of organizations, especially the Miami-based Cuban American National Foundation, which one report has called not only "the most potent voice on U.S. policy toward Cuba," but "dollar for dollar, arguably the most effective" lobbying force in Washington[18] (Haney & Wanderbush, 1999). The community, and its sentiment against the communist government of Fidel Castro, is a key factor in the continuing U.S. refusal to recognize the Cuban government or allow most forms of economic interchange with Cuba. Part of the group's political power stems from the fact that most of the approximately 1.3 million Cuban Americans live in Florida, which is a key state in U.S. presidential elections. As a Clinton administration official explained, "There are no votes riding on how we deal with Indonesia,... [but] Castro is still political dynamite."[19]

The Cuban American community is also able to influence Congress. Most members have few or no Cuban American constituents, but those who do are passionate in the defense of the group's dominant point of view. "You know that if you kick the Cuba issue, you're going to have a bad day," said a former congressman. "Other than to about

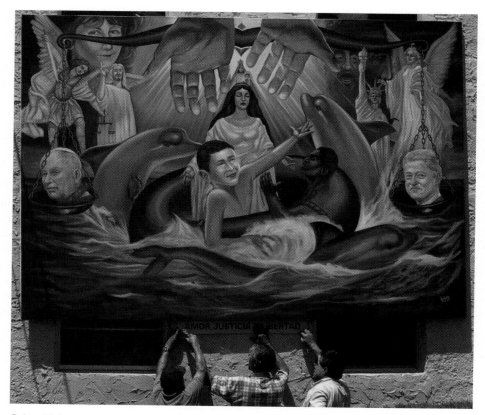

Cultural interest groups can play a strong role in foreign policy. The controversy that erupted over whether Elián González should be treated as a political refugee or returned to his father in Cuba showed the strength of the Cuban American community. This mural in Miami depicts Elián being saved after the boat in which he was fleeing Cuba sank. The woman immediately behind him is his mother, who drowned along with most of the others in the boat. The scale is weighing Pope John Paul II (left) and President Clinton (right). The sign reads "Love, Justice and Liberty."

10 members, it doesn't matter that much. [But] when there are a few people who will die for the issue, and nobody else gets anywhere close to that, they can have their way."

The controversy over the fate of Elián González illustrates the political power of cultural interest groups, in this case the Cuban Americans. On November 22, 1999, Elián's mother took him and joined 11 other people trying to get to the United States from Cuba in a small boat. The boat capsized, drowning most of its occupants, including Señora González. One of the survivors, Elián, was found floating in an inner tube near Fort Lauderdale, Florida, by two fishermen on November 25. The boy was temporarily placed with his great uncle, Lazaro González and other relatives living in the "Calle Ocho" section of Miami; Elián's father, Juan, demanded that the boy be returned to Cuba; and the fate of the child became a front-page political struggle. Both the Cuban government and, eventually, the U.S. government came down on the side of returning the boy to Cuba. On January 14, 2000, U.S. Immigration and Naturalization Commissioner Doris N. Meissner decided that Elián "belongs with his father" and should be returned promptly to Cuba. Even President Clinton declared that father and son "should be reunited.... That is the law."[20] Much of the Cuban American community and its supporters disagreed, however, and demanded that the boy be declared a political refugee and be permitted (or forced, depending on one's view) to remain in Miami with his great uncle.

The details of the struggle that went on for months before Elián was removed by a U.S. marshal's SWAT team from the home of his Miami relatives, reunited with his

Did You Know That:

The score: 25–0. The 25 business leaders and 0 human rights leaders invited to the White House state dinner for President Jiang Zemin of China in 1997 demonstrate the relative influence of business groups and human rights groups on U.S. policy toward China. Among the business guests were representatives of American International Group, Apple Computers, Asea Brown-Boveri, AT&T, Atlantic Richfield, Bell Atlantic, Boeing, Dreamwork Films, Eastman Kodak, General Electric, General Motors, IBM, International Corporation, Oracle, PepsiCo, Proctor & Gamble, U.S. China Business Council, United Technologies, Viacom, Westinghouse, and Xerox.

father, and returned to Cuba are not as important as seeing the intensity with which a cultural group took up an issue related to the country of its heritage and how the group was able to use its political and legal power.

Economic groups are another prominent form of interest activity. They make contradictory demands for both protection from foreign competition and for pressure on other governments to open up their markets (Chrystal, 1998). As international trade increases, both sales overseas and competition from other countries are vital matters to many companies. They lobby their home governments for favorable domestic legislation and for support when a company is having a dispute with the government of a host country in which it is operating. Strong pressure from a generally united business community, for example, was the key element in ending the annual review by Congress of U.S. trade relations with China and securing U.S. support of China's entry into the WTO. This tale is told in the box, The Power of the Purse.

Labor unions also affect trade issues and some other types of foreign policy. For example, labor unions are at the forefront of the forces in the United States that oppose rapid expansion of free trade and the empowerment of international economic organizations, which, according to AFL-CIO president John Sweeney, represent the "capstone of the corporate-dominated world marketplace."[21] Union members were among those who demonstrated against the WTO meeting in Seattle, Washington, in late 1999 and against the IMF and World Bank in Washington, D.C., in April 2000.

Another economic group, farmers and other agricultural producers, are active in many countries in vigorous opposition to policies that would open their countries to increased competition from foreign agricultural sources. The North American Free Trade Agreement (NAFTA) has farmers worried. Mexican milk producers feel engulfed by a flood of milk from American cows. "If something isn't done about this soon," said Maria Teresa Berisain, a dairy farmer, "in three to four years no [Mexican] milk producers will be left."[22] To the north, brussels sprout farmer Steve Bontadelli worries at his farm in central California, "It's simple math. In Mexico, they pay workers $6 a day. That's what we're paying per hour. We just can't keep up."[23] And yet further to the north, the National Farmer's Union of Canada claims that "NAFTA and [other free trade] agreements... have led to lower and more volatile [agricultural] prices. It is unacceptable that these agreements also limit Canada's ability to deal with those low and volatile prices through the design and implementation of effective safety net programs."[24]

Issue-oriented groups make up another category of interest group. Groups of this type are not based on any narrow socioeconomic category such as ethnicity or economics. Instead they draw their membership from people who have a common policy goal. The concerns of issue-oriented groups run the gamut from the very general to the specific. Some groups concentrate on one or a few specific issues. The United Nations Association of the United States brings together Americans who support the UN. At the general end of the spectrum, the Council on Foreign Relations draws together some 1,500 influential (elite) Americans who hold an internationalist point of view, and the council's journal, *Foreign Affairs*, serves as a forum for circulating the view of the elite. As Deputy Secretary of State Strobe Talbott said of the journal, "Virtually everyone I know in the foreign policy/national security area of government is attentive to it."[25]

Transnational interest groups also deserve mention. Some of these are nongovernmental organizations (NGOs) of like-minded individuals from many countries who pool their resources to press their own and other governments to adopt policies desired by the group. Transnational corporations also conduct extensive lobbying efforts in countries where they have interests. Many foreign countries also try to influence spe-

(continued on page 102)

THE POWER OF THE PURSE: INTEREST GROUPS AND U.S. RELATIONS WITH CHINA

The often used phrase "power of the purse" may have first been uttered on January 4, 1788, by Oliver Elsworth in Hartford, Connecticut. Elsworth, who had represented his state at the Constitutional Convention in Philadelphia, was addressing Connecticut's convention to debate whether to ratify the proposed federal constitution. He argued, in part, that to ensure the financial resources to provide for national defense, "Government must ... be able to command the whole power of the purse."

The Constitution was indeed ratified and went into effect, giving Washington the power of the purse. More than two centuries later, some observers worry that it is also true that "the power of the purse is able to command the whole of Government." The degree to which this fear has an element of truth was evident in the intense battle in early 2000 over whether to grant China permanent normal trading relations (PNTR) and clear the way for it to join the World Trade Organization (WTO).

To start with the climax of the drama, a front-page story in the *New York Times* on May 25, 2000, told readers, "In a stunning victory for the Clinton administration and corporate America, the House today swept aside economic restrictions on China that were part of anti-Communist policy for two decades. By a surprisingly wide margin, 237 to 197, lawmakers voted to give Beijing permanent normal trading privileges after months of fierce lobbying that pitted business against organized labor."[1] Later that year, the Senate went along with few dissenting votes, and President Clinton signed the act into law.

The beginning of at least part of the story dates back to 1989 and what has become known as the Tiananmen Square Massacre, representing the attack on antigovernment demonstrators by People's Liberation Army troops in Beijing's main square and many other sites in China. In the aftermath, Congress enacted legislation requiring that the president report every year on China's human rights record, giving Congress an annual opportunity to revoke China's Most Favored Nation (MFN) trade status with the United States. It is worth noting that the MFN designation was misleading, because it really meant normal trade relations at tariff rates no higher than those of most other countries, which presumably were also MFNs.

Each year during the 1990s the president reported, somewhat disingenuously, that China's human rights record had improved. Each year Congress was the scene of numerous speeches castigating China. Each year Congress then voted to continue the status quo.

It became apparent that this annual ritual would no longer suffice when, in late 1999, Washington and Beijing reached an agreement after long negotiations on trade relations that included U.S. support for China's admission into the WTO. Although President Clinton could support China's entry into the WTO without congressional approval, it was necessary to grant China the same permanent trade privileges extended to other U.S. trading partners to avoid violating WTO rules.

That set the stage for one of the most intensely fought legislative conflicts of Clinton's eight years in office. With the Senate expected to vote for PNTR, the battlefield was the House of Representatives. Many of the arguments pro and con had little or nothing to do with economics.

Among others, opponents of PNTR included human rights advocates dismayed by China's abuses, environmentalists worried about China's poor record in that area, and continuing cold war warriors opposed to China's communist government.

Proponents used other arguments. "We're all horrified by what happened at Tiananmen Square," said Julie Moore, president of the Chamber of Commerce for Decatur and Macon County, Illinois. "But we have a better chance of helping the Chinese people if we are there," presumably to keep an eye on the gov-

cific policy in other countries or, more generally, to project a positive image. Taiwan, for one, is active in this way as part of its effort to improve its international standing. To coordinate its activities in the United States, Taiwan operates from the Taipei Economic and Cultural Representative office in Washington, D.C., which employs about 200 people and has 13 regional offices. The Taiwanese spent $1.2 million in 1999 on traditional forms of lobbying politicians and much more on cultural liaison activities such as sponsoring Americans on visits to Taiwan, making a donation of $100,000 to the Friends of

ernment and set a good example.[2] Even more important was the national security argument. As National Security Adviser Sandy Burger put it during one speech, "Rejection [of PNTR] will set off a downward spiral that could disrupt stability in Asia, diminish the chance of dialogue across the Taiwan Strait and deflate hopes for a more constructive relationship between the U.S. and China.[3] That theme was hammered home not only by President Clinton, but by every living former president and by such luminaries as former secretary of state Henry Kissinger and former chairman of the Joint Chiefs of Staff Colin Powell.

Within the skein of controversy, the final decision came down to one of economic strength, of business versus labor. This line-up was evident in that, despite President Clinton's advocacy of PNTR, House Democrats voted 138 to 73 against the measure, while supposedly opposition Republicans voted in favor of PNTR by 164 to 57.

Manufacturing, service industries (such as banking and insurance), and agricultural leaders lined up solidly for the bill, which they believed would bring them better investment opportunities and sales. Some 200 top executives signed a letter in support of PNTR. The industry-backed Business Roundtable and the U.S. Chamber of Commerce spent an estimated $10 million on a television, radio, and print advertising campaign that focused on the districts of uncommitted House members. Individual legislators were visited by hordes of economic leaders from their home districts. "It seems like there have been hundreds of them," one congressman sighed.[4]

Labor mounted a countercampaign. "This is a betrayal of workers' interests," said George Becker, president of the United Steelworkers of America. "This is about moving factories from the U.S. so that they can export back here.[5] Union lobbyists worked the halls of Congress and labor supporters and others descended on Washington to demonstrate. In the end, they did not prevail. "A few thousand people

One of the most difficult campaigns of Bill Clinton's presidency was his successful effort in 2000 to win congressional approval of permanent normal trading relations status for China. Among those who lobbied Congress to defeat the bill was Shengde Li-an, a leader of the Tiananmen Square protesters in 1989, now living in the United States. He is pictured here holding his baby son, Harrison, who is demonstrating support for his dad's views by wearing a sticker demanding "NO Blank Check for China."

bused to Washington today by A.F.L.-C.I.O. labor bosses can't change the fact that the sky is blue, the earth is round and trade is the key to [American prosperity]," countered Representative David Dreier, a California Republican.[6] And so it was that the support of PNTR status for China—and, by inference, U.S. support for its entry into the WTO—was passed by the House. John J. Sweeney, president of the A.F.L.-C.I.O. gave the epitaph for the efforts of the unions and other opponents to the measure. "We mounted a forceful and nearly successful challenge to an array of money and forces unlike any before seen in a lobbying campaign," he said.[7] They had come close, but that only counts in horseshoes.

Animals to help curtail the poaching of elephants and rhinoceroses, and sponsoring a Houston production of *King Lear* set in the Chou dynasty (1027–256 B.C.).

THE PEOPLE

The vast majority of citizens in any country do not have a direct say in policy making. Yet they play a role. This role is obviously more important in democratic systems than

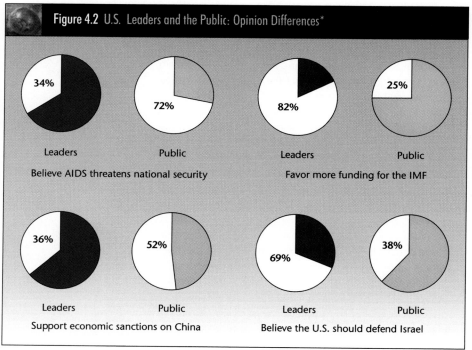

Figure 4.2 U.S. Leaders and the Public: Opinion Differences*

Leaders — 34% — Public — 72%
Believe AIDS threatens national security

Leaders — 82% — Public — 25%
Favor more funding for the IMF

Leaders — 36% — Public — 52%
Support economic sanctions on China

Leaders — 69% — Public — 38%
Believe the U.S. should defend Israel

Data sources: "American Public Opinion and U.S. Foreign Policy, 1999," Chicago Council on Foreign Relations Web site, http://www.ccfr.org/publications/opinion/opinion.html.
*Questions: Do AIDS and other diseases pose a vital threat to the United States? Should the United States give more funds to the IMF to meet world financial crises? Should the United States impose economic sanctions on China for human rights abuses? Should the United States send troops if Arab forces invade Israel?

Even in a democracy, the policy preferences of the citizenry and its leaders often differ. This figure shows that, compared with U.S. leaders, the American public is more apt to see AIDS as a national security threat, less inclined to fund the IMF, more favorable to sanctions against China in response to its human rights abuses, and less willing to commit U.S. troops to the defense of Israel. Whose opinion should usually prevail? Whose opinion usually does?

in authoritarian systems, but there is no system in which the public is totally ignored by leaders. To discuss the people's role, we will look at four factors: variations in interest in foreign affairs, dimensions of public opinion, the quality of public opinion, and the influence of public opinion on foreign policy (Powlick & Katz, 1998).

Variations in Interest in Foreign Affairs

International events and issues do not consistently command the attention of most citizens. Insofar as people are concerned with politics, they are normally focused on domestic pocketbook issues such as unemployment and taxes or social issues such as abortion. This domestic focus means, among other things, that foreign affairs issues do not normally determine how the average citizen votes. The U.S. presidential election of 2000 was no exception. One poll asked Americans how important each of five issues (education, health care, Social Security and Medicare, the economy and jobs, and America's role overseas) would be in their deciding whom to support for president. More than 75 percent of the respondents said each of the four domestic issues would be very important; only 43 percent said the U.S. global role would be very important.[26]

Sometimes, however, the broad public focus is on foreign policy. There is also a segment of the public, the "attentive public," that regularly pays attention to world events (Krosnick & Telhami, 1995). It is accurate to say, then, that public opinion runs the gamut from being interested in to being oblivious to foreign policy, depending on the situation and the issues. Crises will engage a significant segment of the population's attention. So will intermestic policies. Pure foreign policy issues that are not crises will engender much less attention.

Dimensions of Public Opinion

It is also important to note that the generic term public opinion disguises many variations in opinion. Ideology is one source of division. Public opinion ranges across ideology or values scales, such as isolationism-internationalism, militancy-cooperativeness, and multilateralism-unilateralism. Studies show that the specific opinions of individuals are strongly influenced by their general ideological orientation and other basic values. Opinion also often varies by economic circumstance, gender, age, and other demographic characteristics. A third variation is between a society's **elites** (social-economic-political leaders) and the **mass** (the public). Among other differences between the two groups, the public tends to be less internationalist than is the elite (Murray, 1997). This difference is made clear in Figure 4.2.

The Quality of Public Opinion

Another important aspect of public opinion to consider is its quality (Holsti, 1997). Some analysts dismiss the public as uninterested in and ignorant about foreign policy. They contend that, if too closely heeded by policy makers, the uninformed whims of public opinion create dangerous instability in foreign policy. Others disagree and hold that public opinion is both reasonable and stable.

The resolution of this disagreement depends in part on the questions that are asked. The view that the public is apathetic and uninformed is best supported by studies that show that people do not pay close attention to the news and by surveys that ask the public for specific information about world politics and find that it is largely absent. Figure 1.1 on page 3, for instance, shows that when people in eight countries were asked if they knew four specific facts, an average of only 45 percent of the respondents were able to supply the correct answer to any one of the questions. The data also shows, though, that what people know varies significantly from country to country. Germans scored highest, with a 68 percent correct response rate, and two other nations (the French and the Italians) also scored better than 50 percent. The British, Canadians, Spaniards, Americans, and Mexicans were, in descending order, all under 50 percent.

Research that takes a broader perspective is more charitable about the quality of public opinion. Studies that examine long-term trends in public opinion and studies that compare shifts in opinion to events in order to see if opinion moves in a reasonable way find that public opinion is neither erratic nor unreasonable. For example, a review of studies of American opinion on the use of military force found that "the public evaluates the use of America's armed forces pragmatically and in a way consistent with fundamental international principles regarding sovereignty and self-determination.... The public is 'pretty prudent'" (Oneal, Lian, & Joyner, 1996:274).

The Influence of Public Opinion on Foreign Policy

Whatever the divisions or quality of public opinion may be, the key matter is its impact on foreign policy. To a degree, the interest of the public and impact of its opinion rise and fall according to the situation and the policy issue, and the type (democratic, authoritarian) of government, as discussed earlier.

There are direct and indirect channels, as noted in chapter 1, of public influence on policy. Occasionally, the public gets to decide an issue directly through the use of referendums. Use of **direct democracy** is still limited, but it is growing. During the last decade, for example, voters in Austria, Finland, and Sweden voted to join the EU; Norwegian and Swiss voters rejected membership; and Danish voters rejected replacing the

Using direct-democracy techniques, people can make decisions for themselves and world politics. This agitated individual is a pro-independence supporter in Dili, capital of East Timor, who has been clashing with anti-independence advocates off camera. The people of East Timor voted in 1999 to declare independence from Indonesia. Opponents, probably supported by the Indonesian military, waged a bloody (and unsuccessful) campaign attempting to disrupt democracy.

kroner with the euro. Australians decided to continue to recognize the British monarch as their head of state; the people of East Timor voted for independence from Indonesia; a majority of Hungarians cast ballots in favor of joining NATO; residents of Quebec voted against seeking autonomy or independence from Canada; a majority of voters in Nevis cast ballots in favor of their island seceding from the federation of St. Kitts and Nevis, but failed to get the required two-thirds vote for independence; the Swiss voted against a proposed ban on exporting arms; and there have been a variety of other referendums in which citizens, rather than legislatures, decided policy.

Indirect influence is more common and occurs in several ways. Most foreign policy makers, especially those in democratic countries, are politicians. First, voters sometimes get to choose among candidates who have different foreign policy goals and priorities. The decision by Israeli voters in 1996 to replace Shimon Peres with Benjamin Netanyahu as prime minister had a great deal to do with the candidates' divergent views about how to deal with security and with the Arab world; as did, with a reverse of the pendulum's swing, the defeat of Netanyahu by Ehud Barak in 1999. Second, whatever the exact level of public interest may be, politicians are prone to believe that the public is watching and that if they ignore it or have it turn against them, they will suffer during the next election. Secretary of State James A. Baker III recalls in his memoirs that during the Persian Gulf crisis in 1990 he told President Bush that it "has all the ingredients that brought down three of the last five presidents: a hostage crisis, body bags, and a full-fledged recession caused by $40 [a barrel] oil."[27] Third, policy makers believe that the chances of foreign policy success overseas are enhanced by public opinion support at home. Fourth, in democracies, most policy makers believe that public opinion is a legitimate factor that should be considered when determining which policy is to be adopted. For all these reasons, public opinion does count, particularly when the people are strongly for or against a policy (Foyle, 1997; Powlick, 1995).

CHAPTER SUMMARY

1. States are traditionally the most important political actors. States are political organizations that enjoy at least some degree of sovereignty.

2. Foreign policy is not formulated by a single decision-making process. Instead, the exact nature of that process changes according to a number of variables, including the type of political system, the type of situation, the type of issue, and the internal factors involved.

3. Many scholars believe that the fact that democracies include a greater diversity of subnational actors in the foreign policy arena has an impact on policy. It is also the case that as current democracies become more democratic by, for example, ensuring more and more authoritative participation of women, this will also affect policy.

4. States are complex organizations, and their internal, or domestic, dynamics influence their international actions.

5. One set of internal factors centers on political culture, which is the fundamental, long-term beliefs. China is used to illustrate the impact of political culture attitudes toward the national core, about what is perceived as a favorable world order, and about the degree to which a nation should project its values.

6. Another set of internal factors centers on the policy-making impact of various subnational actors. These include political leaders, bureaucratic organizations, legislatures, political parties and opposition, interest groups, and the public. Each of these influences foreign policy, but their influence varies according to the type of government, the situation, and the policy at issue. Overall, political leaders and bureaucratic organizations are consistently (though not always) the strongest subnational actors.

CHAPTER 5

INDIVIDUAL-LEVEL ANALYSIS

There is history in all men's lives.

Shakespeare, *Henry IV, Part II*

Be not afraid of greatness. Some are born great, some achieve greatness, and some have greatness thrust upon 'em.

Shakespeare, *Twelfth Night*

My mind-set is Munich; most of my generation's is Vietnam.
U.S. secretary of state Madeleine Albright

Toughness doesn't have to come in a pinstripe suit.

U.S. senator Dianne Feinstein

CHAPTER OBJECTIVES

After completing this chapter, you should be able to:

- Define what is meant by individual-level analysis in world politics and outline the nature-of-humankind approach.
- Identify the roles of psychological and biological factors in the nature-of-humankind approach.
- Discuss the humans-in-organizations approach and consider role factors in this context.
- Explain how group-behavior factors function in the humans-in-organizations approach.
- Describe the psychological focus of the idiosyncratic-behavior approach.
- Consider how political and personal history can shape political leaders' decision making.
- Outline major sources and characteristics of decision makers' perceptions and assess the impact of those perceptions.
- Understand the impact of operational reality.

This chapter analyzes humans as actors on the world stage. The focus on humans lies at the micro end of the scale that ranges from macroscopic, system-level analysis detailed in chapter 3, through mid-range, state-level analysis discussed in chapter 4, to this chapter's microscopic, individual-level analysis.

The fundamental task of this chapter is to identify the characteristics of the complex process of human **decision making**. This includes gathering information, analyzing that information, establishing goals, pondering options, and making policy choices.

The human role in the world drama can be addressed from three different perspectives. One is to consider *human nature*, to examine fundamental human characteristics that affect decisions. *Organizational behavior* is the second perspective. This looks at how humans interact within organized settings, such as a decision-making group. Third, the human behavior perspective explores how the *idiosyncratic behavior* of specific humans affects foreign policy.

INDIVIDUAL-LEVEL ANALYSIS: HUMAN NATURE

The central question is this: How do fundamental human characteristics influence policy? To answer that, a first step is to understand that humans have limited and flawed decision-making abilities because people are unable intellectually and physically to learn and process all the information required to make fully rational decisions. Moreover, we humans have emotions that warp our judgment. Sometimes, for instance, presidents simply get angry. President Jimmy Carter was frustrated over his inability to free the hostages whom Iran seized in 1979. His anger was compounded by protesting Iranian students who had traveled from their U.S. colleges to Washington. Carter fumed at having "to sit here and bite my lip… and look impotent" while "those bastards [are] humiliating our country in front of the White House." If I "wasn't president," Carter growled to an aide, I would go "out on the streets myself" and "take a swing" at any demonstrator "I could get my hands on" (Vandenbroucke, 1991:364). Of course Carter was president and could not punch out an Iranian demonstrator. Instead, he sent an ill-fated hostage rescue mission. Pent-up anger was certainly part of that decision. The point is that there is no such thing as a truly rational decision, be it your decision about which college to attend or President Carter's plan to rescue the hostages in Tehran. To study the limits on rationality, we can examine cognitive, psychological, and biological factors in decision making.

COGNITIVE FACTORS

Decision making is one of the most complex things that political scientists study (Vertzberger, 1998). At its most abstract, decision-making analysis is involved with *cybernetics*, which is the study of control and communications systems. Since no human even approaches being a perfect cybernetic system, another important term to note is **cognitive decision making.** This means that humans necessarily make decisions within the limits of what they consciously know and are willing to consider (Geva & Mintz, 1997). Since there are many external and internal barriers or boundaries to what a decision maker knows or even can know, cognitive decision making is also called "bounded rationality." External boundaries include such factors as missing or erroneous information and the inability of any decision maker to know for sure what decision makers in another country are thinking or how they will react to various policy options. Internal boundaries that account for cognitive limits include every decision maker's intellectual and physical limits. No decision maker has the vast intellectual or physical capacity to analyze completely the mass and complexity of information that is available.

Emotions are another all-too-human internal restraint on rational decision making. People regularly ignore information that they find emotionally unacceptable.

To see the difficulty of making a purely rational decision, recall your decision about which college to attend. Surely you did not just flip a coin, but did you consider all colleges worldwide, analyzing each according to cost, location, social atmosphere, class size, faculty qualifications, living arrangements, and program requirements? Did you consult a wide range of experts? Did you ignore such emotional factors as how far away from home the school was and how that interacted with your desire to be near, or perhaps far away from, your family, friends, or romantic partner? The answer, of course, is that you did not do all these things fully. Instead, you probably conducted a relatively limited rational review of information and options, then factored in irrational emotional considerations. You also relied on fate, because part of your happiness and success at college depend on things (such as with whom you would share your dorm room) that were unknowable when you applied. Thus you made one of the more important decisions of your life within a significant degree of bounded rationality.

Foreign policy decisions are also made within the limits of bounded rationality. Therefore, a key issue involves how policy makers cope with various cognitive limits on rational decision making. Four of the many mental strategies for coping with cognitive limits are seeking cognitive consistency, wishful thinking, limiting the scope of the decision, and using heuristic devices.

Numerous psychological factors can affect a leader's decision. Here a crowd of Iranians has gathered outside the U.S. embassy in Tehran, where Americans were being held hostage in 1980. The Iranians are holding a sign caricaturing President Jimmy Carter and taunting his inability to free the captives. Carter's frustration, anger, and wishful thinking all contributed to his ordering the ill-fated mission to try to rescue the hostages.

Seeking Cognitive Consistency Decision makers tend to seek cognitive consistency by attempting to suppress ideas and information that run counter to accepted interpretations of events and actors or counter to the policy path that a policy maker is determined to follow. Avoiding uncomfortable information is one way to do this. Later in this chapter we will look at the 1980 attempt by the Carter administration to rescue U.S. hostages from Iran. It was a disaster. What is revealing is that there was information beforehand that the attempt would probably fail. The mission commander put the probability of success at "zero." The CIA estimated that at least 60 percent of the hostages would be killed, and one observer reported that a dress rehearsal for the rescue attempt was "the sorriest display of professionalism I've ever seen" (Smith, 1984:118). Carter and most of his aides ignored the forboding signs because they were frustrated by deadlocked negotiations and concerned over the president's political vulnerability. Because they could not simultaneously favor a rescue attempt and believe that it would fail, they achieved cognitive consistency by discounting negative information.

Wishful Thinking A second mental strategy to cope with cognitive limits is wishful thinking. Once humans make a decision they acquire an emotional stake in its wisdom, and they are apt to believe increasingly that their choice will succeed. This is the reason why it is so hard to reverse a decision once it is made. President Carter's chief of staff, Hamilton Jordan, later wrote that he realized that it would be "Carter's ass if it [the mission] fails. But I couldn't even contemplate failure.... I couldn't get my mind off the helicopters lifting off from the embassy grounds with the hostages. I wanted desperately for this Godforsaken crisis to be over and done with" (Vandenbroucke, 1991:419).

Limiting the Scope of Decisions A third way that decision makers cope with cognitively complex problems is by limiting the scope of decisions. Deciding small things is easier than deciding big ones. Incrementalism is one way to limit what must be decided. Because they cannot know everything, decision makers will most often make what seems to be the safest choice by following established policy or only making small (incremental) changes. "Satisficing" is a related strategy. This means adopting the first option that is presented that minimally meets your goals rather than continuing to search for an optimum solution.

Using Heuristic Devices The use of heuristic devices is a fourth strategy to deal with cognitive limits. A heuristic device is a mental tool or frame of reference that helps an individual sort and evaluate information. In this sense, people use heuristic devices as shortcuts that allow them to skip long and detailed gathering and analyses of information and come to decisions quickly.

There is a wide variety of heuristic devices that humans use to reach decisions quickly. We will discuss three: national belief systems, stereotypes, and analogies.

National belief systems are based in political culture. Part of U.S. policy during the cold war stemmed from the fact that most Americans shared a national belief system that saw the authoritarian, communist, and officially atheistic Soviet Union as antithetical to everything they valued. This cold war consensus made decisions easy: oppose any advance by the communists. For example, Americans went to war in Vietnam with relatively little dissent. As then Secretary of Defense Robert McNamara later explained, there was a widespread belief that "the loss of Vietnam would trigger the loss of Southeast Asia, and conceivably even the loss of India, and would strengthen the Chinese and the Soviet position across the world, weakening the security of Western Europe and weakening the security of North America.... I'm not arguing [we viewed it] correctly—don't misunderstand me," McNamara conceded, "but that is the way we viewed it."[1] Given this orientation, it is not surprising that when President Lyndon Johnson asked Congress to pass the Tonkin Gulf Resolution (1964) authorizing military action in the region, legislators passed the measure unanimously in the House and by 88 to 2 in the Senate. Public opinion supported the intervention; there were no major protests on the country's campuses or streets. All that came later.

Stereotypes are a second heuristic device that sometimes stem from political culture. For example, Western attitudes toward the Middle East are shaped in part by stereotypes. It is relatively easy to identify with the distinctly Western-looking, often English-speaking Israelis. After Israeli prime minister Benjamin Netanyahu spoke to a joint session of the U.S. Congress, one legislator gushed, "This man, he speaks English with no accent. He seems like one of us."[2] It is harder to relate to Arabs, who less often speak unaccented English, and who, in many minds, evoke images of camels, veiled women, Bedouin raiding parties, and other distinctly non-Western traits.

Analogies are a third heuristic shortcut. We make comparisons between new situations or people and situations or people that we have experienced or otherwise have learned about (Peterson, 1997). How decision makers use analogies will be discussed in depth later, but, in essence, what happens is this: An issue, such as Saddam Hussein threatening Kuwait in 1991, is associated with a known historical event, such as Adolf Hitler threatening Czechoslovakia in 1938. Given the analogy, the course of action is clear: stand up to Iraq, just as we should have stood up against Nazi Germany. The trick, of course, is selecting the right analogy.

PSYCHOLOGICAL FACTORS

Theories that focus on the common psychological traits of humankind also help explain political behavior. **Frustration-aggression theory** is one such approach. It contends that

(continued on page 112)

FRUSTRATION-AGGRESSION ANALYSIS AND THE RISE OF VLADIMIR PUTIN

Like Germans decades ago, Russians today cannot understand how they fell so far, so fast from the rank of superpower to international hardship case. "We've become a Third World country—nobody looks at us with respect any more," one Russian worker frets.[1] As occurred in Germany, hyperinflation ruined Russia. Averaging 554 percent a year during 1991–1997 price increases have left 22 percent of Russians below the poverty line. Conditions have improved, but only from terrible to merely bad. During 1999, for example, prices still rose almost twice as fast as wages. To make matters even worse, three-quarters of all Russian workers report delays of weeks and even months in receiving their meager wages.

Russians are also plagued by violent crime, vast corruption, and other socially destabilizing forces. Partly out of despair, suicide has soared, as has the death rate (often from alcohol abuse) of Russians under 60 years of age. Concomitantly, the birthrate has dropped to one of the world's lowest, and there are many other signs of a sick society. It is not surprising, then, that a 1999 survey found that 71 percent of Russians thought, "The last year or two have been the hardest of my life" (ADL, 1999:16).

As may happen in times of frustration, it is easy for many Russians to imagine, just as Germans did in the 1930s, that malevolent forces are responsible for their trouble. One poll taken in early 2000 found that the percentage of Russians who believe that the United States was trying to reduce Russia to a second-rate power had increased to 81 percent from 59 percent in 1995.[2]

As Germans once did, Russians are also prone to look internally for people and groups to blame for their misery. Unsettlingly, anti-Semitism has become more pronounced. A survey that presented respondents with 11 negative statements about Jews (sample: "Jews have many irritating traits.") found that 44 percent of Russians agreed with 6 or more of the statements, and another 37 percent agreed with between 2 and 5 of the statements (ADL, 1999: 36).

Russia's leadership has failed for the most part to ease the travails that have engendered despair and negativism among its people. President Boris Yeltsin loomed larger than life during the collapse of the Soviet Union and the rebirth of an independent Russia. By the late 1990s, however, he had been reduced to a virtual shell by the ravages of heart disease, apparent alcoholism, and other ailments. This left Russians anxious to have strong leadership. When one survey asked whether "order or democracy" was "more important," Russians chose order over democracy by a ratio of almost 9 to 1.[3]

All these factors leave some analysts worried that Russia's woes are fertile ground for a more oppressive domestic policy and a more aggressive foreign policy. The meteoric rise during 1999 and 2000 of Vladimir Putin from relative obscurity to the presidency of Russia gives such analysts pause. When in August 1999, President Yeltsin named Putin as yet another in a merry-go-round of prime ministers, few observers thought the 47-year-old head of the Russian Security Council had much of a future. That proved wrong.

When he took office, the new prime minister was asked what his mood was like. Putin's curt reply: "Combative."[4] Demonstrating that, he moved decisively against Chechnya, a Muslim area in the Caucasus region that had won autonomy in 1996 after a bloody conflict. Fighting had flared anew, and Prime Minister Putin declared, "Only one thing can be effective in such circumstances—to go on the offensive. You must hit first, and hit so hard that your opponent will not rise to his feet."[5] The ensuing Russian military campaign in Chechnya, which included indiscriminate assaults on civilian areas, was so brutal that many world leaders condemned it. Putin was undeterred, however, and his popularity in Russian opinion polls soared to as much as 80 percent.

Then, in a stunning event, Putin became acting president when Yeltsin resigned on December 31, 1999. The change brought to Russia's presidency an individual who spent most of his professional career in the KGB (the Soviet secret police), who headed its successor (Russia's FSB), and whose hobby is judo. Once again Putin moved decisively, this time to win the presidential election in March 2000. He made

frustrated societies sometimes become collectively aggressive. It is possible to argue, for example, that mass frustration promoted the rise of Adolf Hitler and German aggression in World War II. Germany's capitulation at the end of World War I left many Germans bewildered. They had defeated Russia earlier, and their army was still in France when the war ended. Germans were embittered further by the harsh economic and political

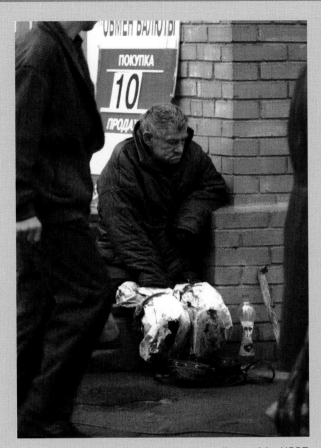

The economic plight of Russians since the collapse of the USSR is symbolized by this recent photograph of a homeless, disabled man in Moscow begging for coins from passers-by. Frustration-agression theory argues that when a nation is suffering, it may become aggressive. There is concern that the inflation and other economic ills that have devastated the lives of many Russians could lead to pent-up anger that could explode, with Russians venting their frustrations on others.

special efforts to visit Russian soldiers in Chechnya and to allow photo opportunities showing himself seated in Russian fighters and in other military poses. The acting president pledged to take strong control internally, to reassert Russia's world position, and to rebuild the country's economy. "Our country Russia was a great, powerful, strong state," Putin told Russians on national television. "It is clear this is not possible [to restore] if we do not have strong armed forces, powerful armed forces," he continued. "We will not achieve this if we do not solve a range of problems in the economic and social spheres."[6] In sum, Putin told another audience, "Russia needs a strong state power."[7]

Such aggressive stands were well received by Russians. "I could never imagine," commented Professor Andrei Zorin of the Russian State University, that "there is such a strong desire [among Russians] for a powerful leader." There is an "incredible consensus," Zorin continued. "Everybody wants to have a fist before his nose. Then maybe people are going to behave accordingly when someone shows this fist."[8]

The combination of Putin's image of strength and the search of Russians for economic and political resurrection led to a resounding win for Putin in the March election. Whereas Yeltsin had been forced into a run-off election in 1996, Putin won a majority (53 percent) of the vote, far outdistancing his only serious opponent, Communist Party head Gennadii Zyuganov (29 percent), and nine other candidates.

It is too early in Putin's term to predict whether he will try to capitalize on the frustrations Russians feel and undermine the country's democracy, rebuild Russia's military, and reassert Russia's strength internationally. What is certain, however, is that Russians are very frustrated. Similar feelings once led to aggression against supposed enemies, foreign and domestic, in Germany. It is not inconceivable to imagine Russia following a similar path. Thus far, most of Putin's statements have been soothing. Yet there also have been some ominous signs. Most alarmingly, within days of the inauguration, masked and armed FSB forces raided the offices of Russia's largest private news and multimedia company looking for evidence of unspecified criminality. The mayor of Moscow called the raid "a powerful and vulgar attack" and warned, "Russia faces a real danger of seeing its freedom of the press stifled."[9] Putin assured Russians that he supports a free press, but the raid and earlier actions tended to belie that claim. For example, a Russian correspondent who criticized the campaign in Chechnya was detained. Putin explained to Western reporters that the journalist's criticism was "much more dangerous than firing a machine gun" and that, "We interpret freedom of expression in different ways [from the West]."[10]

terms imposed by victors, the resulting 1,700 percent inflation and economic devastation of Germany during the 1920s, and the treatment of the country as a political pariah. Germany's increasingly doddering President Paul von Hindenburg, an august field marshal during World War I, and other democratically elected leaders were unable to restore Germany's pride, position, or economy. Entering this turmoil, Hitler capitalized on the Germans' pent-up anger by telling them that their defeat in the war and their subsequent plight were caused by Jewish and Bolshevik conspirators. Rearm and reclaim your proud heritage! Hitler told the Germans. There are only two choices, he proclaimed in *Mein Kampf*: "Germany will be either a world power or it will not be at all." The frustrated German people rallied behind the call to conquest, and World War II ensued.

Similarities between today's Russia and interwar Germany are worrisome. During the 1990s, Russian (Soviet) power collapsed suddenly, just as Germany's did. The Soviet economy staggered under hyperinflation, just as Germany's had. Russia's society is in turmoil, just as Germany's was. And Russia found itself adrift under the leadership of a once heroic, but increasingly weak and aging president, just as Germany did. Entering this turmoil, Vladimir Putin assumed the presidency of Russia. His rise and the situation in Russia are related in the box, Frustration-Aggression Analysis and the Rise of Vladimir Putin.

BIOLOGICAL FACTORS

Various biological theories provide yet another way to explain human behavior (Somit & Peterson, 1997). One of the most important issues in human behavior is the so-called "nature versus nurture" controversy. The question is the degree to which human actions are based on animal instinct and other innate emotional and physical drives (nature) or based on socialization and intellect (nurture). With specific regard to politics, **biopolitics** examines the relationship between the physical nature and political behavior of humans. Biopolitics can be illustrated by examining two approaches: ethology and gender.

Ethology

The comparison of animal and human behavior is called **ethology.** Konrad Lorenz (*On Aggression*, 1969), Desmond Morris (*The Naked Ape*, 1967), Robert Ardrey (*The Territorial Imperative*, 1961), and some other ethologists argue that like animals, humans behave in a way that is based partly on innate characteristics. Ardrey (pp. 12–14), for example, has written that "territoriality—the drive to gain, maintain, and defend the exclusive right to a piece of property—is an animal instinct" and that "if man is a part of the natural world, then he possesses as do all other species a genetic… territorial drive as one ancient animal foundation for that human conduct known as war."

Did You Know That:

Animals have wars. Primatologist Jane Goodall discovered this in 1974 when chimpanzees from one tribe in Tanzania waged war on neighboring chimps. The aggressors moved stealthily through the forest, set up ambushes, and eventually annihilated the beset tribe. Since the well-fed attackers did not take over the territory, and also killed the females, the aggression could not be explained by the usual territorial need based on food and mating. The fighting was no more explicable than some human wars.

It is clear that territorial disputes are a common cause of war. To begin with, one study points out, "Most interstate wars are fought or begin between neighbors" (Vasquez, 1995:277). Furthermore, another study concludes that since 1945, "war is a highly probable event in cases where contiguous states… disagree about the location of their shared boundary" (Kocs, 1995:173).

There are some territorial clashes that might seem rational to an outsider, but other disputes defy rational explanation. One recent war that was hard to comprehend by anyone but those involved was the fighting in 1998 and again in 2000 between two desperately poor countries, Ethiopia and Eritrea, over tiny bits of territory along their border. The land was described in one press report as "a dusty terrain of termite mounds, goatherds, and bushes just tall enough for a camel to graze upon comfortably."[3] It was, said one observer, "like two bald men fighting over a comb."[4] Even the leaders of the two countries could not explain why war was waged. "It's very difficult to easily find an answer," Eritrea's president, Isaias Afwerki, admitted. "I was surprised, shocked, and puzzled," added a perplexed Meles Zenawi, the prime minister of Ethiopia.[5]

Waiting in the wings to escalate is the dispute over a group of five islets and three barren rocks 200 miles off China's central coast. Japan calls the islets Senkakus; China

It may be that primordial territorial instincts cause humans to sometimes fight wars over virtually use-less territory. Here we can see a dead Ethiopian soldier lying on barren land that is typical of the area over which Ethiopia and Eritrea were at war in 2000. Was the decision to wage this war that killed thousands on both sides based on rational goals or animal instincts?

calls them Diaoyu. Japan has controlled the islands since the 1895 Sino-Japanese war, but China asserts that they "have been Chinese territory since ancient times." It is tempting to treat such contretemps with amusement, and, to paraphrase a game, ask "Where in the World Is Senkakus?" Unfortunately, it is no joke. One person has already drowned as con-testing groups of Japanese and Chinese patriotic zealots have planted their country's respective flags on the tiny dots of land. Also, the rhetoric between Tokyo and Beijing has heated up, with, for instance, China declaring that the "Chinese people are outraged and want to issue a strong protest" against Japanese flag-waving on the islets.[6] It is possible, of course, to offer various rationales for every territorial war that has occurred. Still, one has to wonder whether many such confrontations are not prompted by some primordial impulse about territory that growls "Mine!" from deep within the human psyche.

Gender

A second biopolitical factor that interests many analysts is the possibility that some dif-ferences in political behavior are related to gender. An adviser to President Lyndon Johnson has recalled that once when reporters asked him why the United States was waging war in Vietnam, the president "unzipped his fly, drew out his substantial organ, and declared, 'That is why.'"[7] Such earthy sexual explanations by male leaders are far from rare in private, and they lead some scholars to wonder whether they represent gender-based aggressiveness to policy making or are merely gauche.

The connection, according to some analysts, is that power seeking is a particularly male sexual impulse. One study of primates has commented on the "remarkable par-allels in male primate behavior" and on the "observed pattern of power seeking or status striving that appears to hold across species among males." The reason, the study continues, is that "males tend to act to increase power as a means of increasing their reproductive success." Moreover, the connection with politics is that "statesmen, who think and act in terms of interests defined as power, should be no exception" to this pri-

Female Heads of State or Government, 1950s, 1970s, 1990s

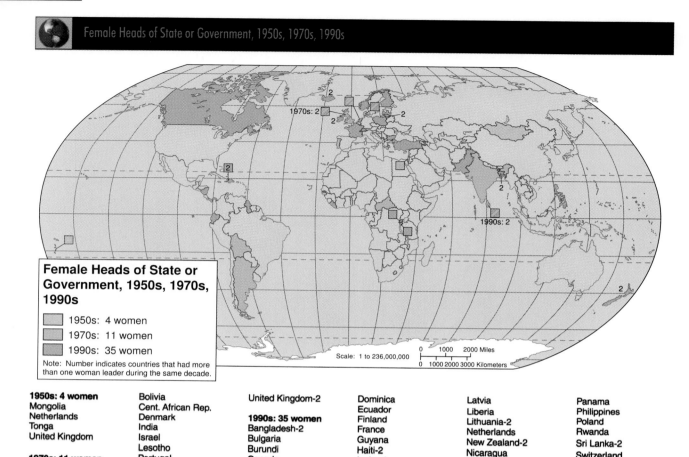

Female Heads of State or Government, 1950s, 1970s, 1990s

	1950s: 4 women
	1970s: 11 women
	1990s: 35 women

Note: Number indicates countries that had more than one woman leader during the same decade.

1950s: 4 women
Mongolia
Netherlands
Tonga
United Kingdom

1970s: 11 women
Argentina

Bolivia
Cent. African Rep.
Denmark
India
Israel
Lesotho
Portugal
Sri Lanka

United Kingdom-2

1990s: 35 women
Bangladesh-2
Bulgaria
Burundi
Canada
Denmark

Dominica
Ecuador
Finland
France
Guyana
Haiti-2
Iceland
Ireland-2

Latvia
Liberia
Lithuania-2
Netherlands
New Zealand-2
Nicaragua
Norway
Pakistan

Panama
Philippines
Poland
Rwanda
Sri Lanka-2
Switzerland
Turkey
United Kingdom

Some analysts believe that gender influences policy attitudes. One limit on the ability to be certain about this issue is the fact that relatively few women have led their countries. Still, that number is growing. This map demonstrates across time the increase in number of women leaders as heads of state and heads of government (such as presidents, prime ministers, and queens). During the 1950s, only 4 women led their countries; during the 1970s, the number increased to 11; during the 1990s, that number more than tripled to 35. Though the 1960s and 1980s are not included, each of those two decades also advanced over the preceding decade. Women have come a long way politically toward numerical parity with men; they have even further to go.

mordial drive (Schubert, 1993:29, 21). From this perspective, Napoleon's claim that "power is my mistress," or Henry Kissinger's confession that "power is a great aphrodisiac," can be construed as deep-seated revelations rather than mere rhetorical flourishes.[8]

Political scientists are just beginning to examine the questions of whether or not gender makes a difference in the political attitudes and actions of policy makers. A related, more general question is whether any gender differences that do exist are inherent (biological, genetic) or the product of differences in male and female socialization (Ember & Ember, 1996). The ultimate question is whether an equal representation (or perhaps dominance) of women in foreign and defense policy making would make an appreciable difference in global affairs. Many scholars answer yes and say that the change would be for the good. Francis Fukuyama (1998:33), for one, contends that political violence is a product, in part, of male-dominated politics because, "statistically speaking it is primarily men who enjoy the experience of aggression and the camaraderie it brings and who revel in the reutilization of war." By contrast, Fukuyama believes, a world dominated by women "would be less prone to conflict

"SO SAY THE MAMAS": A FEMINIST WORLD

The assignment for my undergraduate honors course in international relations one semester was to do a project that involved almost anything but the standard 15-page, go-to-the-library, don't-forget-the-bibliography research paper. The results were fascinating. Among others, the submitted projects included a short story entitled "So Say the Mamas" by one of the women students.

The year was 2050 as "So Say the Mamas" opened. A number of women from around the world decided that the violence and inequality of the male-dominated world would never change and that it would be easier to forge a new civilization than try to fix the existing one. So they gathered a racially and ethnically representative group of women from around the world, acquired a spaceship, and left Earth, bound for the uninhabited, but habitable, planet of Xylos.

The women landed on Xylos and set about establishing a new society. Among the other provisions that they had brought from Earth, the women possessed a large quantity of frozen sperm that they could use for artificial insemination. By analyzing the sperm before implantation, the women could ensure that only female babies were born, thereby preserving forever an all-female population on Xylos.

At first, with relatively few women, the society on Xylos was governed by the "founding mothers" who had initiated the interplanetary move. This group was universally called the Mamas, and the rules that they established were promulgated with the declaration, "So Say the Mamas."

In time the women of Xylos multiplied and moved beyond their initial political structure and, by dint of sheer numbers, beyond their original, close-knit society. The author of "So Say the Mamas" went on to consider the nature of Xylos a millennium after its founding. Had the women established a world in which racial and ethnic differences had disappeared or were irrelevant? Or had racial and ethnic divisions built up? Was there equality on Xylos? Or had women established hierarchies based on race or some other characteristic? Was there a global government of Xylos? Or had the women divided themselves into sovereign states? Was there cooperation and peace on Xylos? Or had competition and warfare overtaken the planet? In short, was Xylos a brave new world, or had it become just like male-dominated Earth, which the Mamas had fled a thousand years earlier?

What the woman who wrote the story concluded is not as important here as what you think. The year is 3050. How does humanity fare on Xylos?

and more conciliatory and cooperative than the one we inhabit now." Other scholars classify such views as part of the "myth of women's pacifism," and contend that a future world dominated by women "would not be as rosy as Fukuyama suggests" (Caprioli, 2000:271; Ehrenreich & Pollitt, 1999). Certainly there is good evidence, as noted in chapter 4, that women in the mass public are less likely to countenance war than men. The attitudes of women in positions of authority may be much different, though. So far only about two dozen of them have been elected to lead countries, although that number is slowly growing, as is evident in the map on p. 116. Yet, even when past queens who had real power—such as Elizabeth I of England and Catherine the Great of Russia—are included, the relative scarcity of female international leaders makes comparisons with their male counterparts difficult. There can be no doubt, though, that able, sometimes aggressive, leadership has been evident in such modern heads of government as Israel's Golda Meir, India's Indira Gandhi, and Great Britain's Margaret Thatcher.

The so-called **nature versus nurture debate** will undoubtedly continue far into the future and presents some fascinating questions. One of these is the basis of the box, "So Say the Mamas": A Feminist World. Whatever the exact role of biological factors may be, though, it is important to bear in mind that no one argues that biology is the sole cause of behavior or even that most human behavior is instinctual rather than learned. Furthermore, learning can modify behavior even if it is partly genetic. This is demonstrated by the basically peaceful conduct of interpersonal relations in most societies.

INDIVIDUAL-LEVEL ANALYSIS: ORGANIZATIONAL BEHAVIOR

A second approach within individual-level of analysis examines how people act in organizations. Just as our overall cultural setting influences how we behave, so do the more specific pressures of our positions and the dynamics of group interaction affect how we behave. Thus the **organizational behavior** of humans significantly influences the decision-making process of governments, as well as the operation of clubs, businesses, and other types of groups. Two concepts, "role behavior" and "group decision-making behavior," are useful to discuss how humans act in organizational settings.

ROLE BEHAVIOR

We all play a variety of roles. They are based on the attitudes and behaviors that we adopt given the position that we hold. Your attitudes and how you act—whether you are in class, on the job, or in a family situation—depends on your role, on whether you are the professor or a student, a manager or a worker, or a parent or child.

Presidents and other policy makers also play roles. The script for a **role** is derived from two sets of expectations about how an actor should think and behave. *Self-expectations* are one important source of role. Behavior in a given position is based partly on what an individual expects of himself or herself. *Expectations of others* are the second important source of role behavior. We behave in certain ways because of what others expect of us in a particular role. Such expectations are transmitted by cues that leaders receive from advisers, critics, and public opinion about how they, in the role of leader, should act. One common role expectation is that leaders be decisive and do things. A leader who approaches a problem by saying "I don't know what to do" or "we can't do anything" will be accused of weakness. Therefore, leaders tend to take action even when it might be better to wait or not to act at all. Reflecting this, former secretary of state Dean Rusk (1990:137) recalled, "We tended then—and now—to exaggerate the necessity to take action. Given time, many problems work themselves out or disappear."

The Iranian hostage crisis (1979–1981) provides an informative case study of the impact of roles. The positions of the principal U.S. decision makers influenced their respective views about whether or not to attempt an armed rescue of the hostages. National security adviser Zbigniew Brzezinski told President Carter that "your greater responsibility [than protecting the hostages] is to protect the honor and dignity of our country" (Glad, 1989:47). Carter agreed that it is the role of a president to take action. "I am the president of a great country. I would like to continue to be patient, but it is difficult to do so," he said (Vandenbroucke, 1991:366). The secretary of defense, the CIA director, and the chairman of the Joint Chiefs of Staff (JCS) were also, as might be expected, proponents of using force to free the hostages. The president's press secretary and his chief of staff also supported the fateful rescue attempt, but for a different reason. They defined their roles as boosting the president's political popularity, and for them the rescue of the hostages would have been a political bonus—one that might have even gotten Carter reelected. The only opposition to action came from the secretary and deputy secretary of state, who cast themselves in the roles of diplomats instead of warriors. It was role-playing, then, that helped determine the course of action that each of the players advocated.

A last point about role is that it is not immutable for any given position. Instead, there is "a more complex, less rigid relationship between role and issue position" than is implied in the old maxim "Where you stand depends on where you sit" (Ripley, 1995:91). For example, an analysis of decision making in the Dutch government found that while "some ministers consistently took positions that can be explained by their bureaucratic interest [which helps define role]," the views of other ministers "could be better understood in terms of [such factors as] moral commitment.... It is therefore not possible to portray Cabinet decision making as simply a clash between diverging bureaucratic interests" (Metselaar & Verbeek, 1996:25).

GROUP DECISION-MAKING BEHAVIOR

People behave differently in organizations than they would act if they were alone. There are complex and extensive theories about decision making in a group setting, but for our purposes here, the most important aspect of organizational decision making is the tendency toward **groupthink** (Hart & Stern, 1997).

Causes of Groupthink

The primary cause of groupthink is pressure within decision-making groups to *achieve consensus*. Consensus may be a true meeting of minds, but it also may be the product of leaders and groups ignoring or suppressing dissidents, discordant information, and policy options, or of subordinates being afraid to offer discordant opinions or information.

Ignoring or suppressing dissidents, discordant information, and policy options Groupthink creates an atmosphere in which *discordant information or advice is rejected or ignored*. Furthermore, dissenters risk rejection by the group and its leaders. This pattern was evident in the Carter administration during the hostage crisis with Iran. Carter and his aides waited to make their decision to attempt a rescue mission until that option's chief opponent, Secretary of State Cyrus Vance, was out of town. When he learned that he had been left out, Vance insisted on another meeting to press his case. He persuaded no one; he only engendered derision. White House chief of staff Hamilton Jordan has remembered Vance's "eyes begging for support. I fidgeted, feeling sorry for Cy." National security adviser Zbigniew Brzezinski's evaluation of Vance was even more patronizing: "A good man who has been traumatized [and made weak] by his Vietnam experience." And the president wrote Vance off as "extremely despondent lately" and "deeply troubled and heavily burdened." It turned out that Vance had been right; the raid was a disaster. That did not make any difference, however. Within a month he was forced out of office, and Carter announced that he was appointing a new, "more statesmanlike figure" as secretary of state (Glad, 1989:50–56).

Reluctance of subordinates to offer discordant opinions While the Vance case shows that overt suppression of dissent occurs, it is not the norm. Usually subordinates are careful not to contradict what they know or think to be the preferences of the group and, especially, their superiors. Experienced officials understand that dissenting, especially once the leader has taken a position, is risky. Therefore, they avoid it.

The U.S.–backed Bay of Pigs operation in 1961 to topple Fidel Castro ended quickly in utter disaster. A number of advisers thought the plan highly dubious, but as presidential confidant Theodore Sorensen later lamented, "Doubts were entertained, but never pressed." Admiral Arleigh Burke recalled that the JCS was skeptical of the operation but that President Kennedy told the military that since it was a CIA operation, "you're not involved in this." This attitude, according to the admiral, had "a very strong effect on the whole damn thing. We *did* keep our hands off... didn't pound the table" (Vandenbroucke, 1991:110). In the end, the ill-fated operation went forward, Assistant Secretary of State Thomas Mann has recalled, because when "President Kennedy asked each of those present [at a crucial meeting] to vote for or against" the invasion, "everyone present expressed support." Mann admits, "I did the same. I did this because I did not wish to leave the impression that I would not support whatever the president decided to do" (Gleijeses, 1995:32).

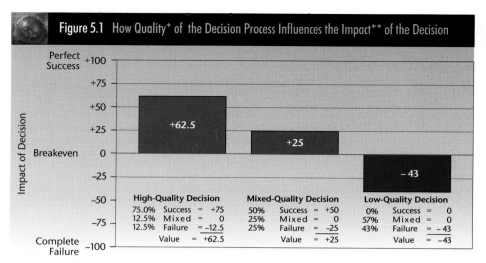

Figure 5.1 How Quality* of the Decision Process Influences the Impact** of the Decision

Data sources: Herek, Janis, & Huth (1987:217). Also see Purkitt (1990) and Welch (1989).

* High Quality = 0 or 1 symptom of defective decision making.

Medium Quality = 2 or 3 symptoms of defective decision making.

Low Quality = 4 or more symptoms of defective decision making.

** Success = Experts agreed that outcome was favorable for U.S. interests = +1.

Mixed = Experts disagreed on whether or not outcome was favorable to U.S. interests = 0.

Failure = Experts agreed that outcome was unfavorable for U.S. Interests = –1.

The quality of the decision-making process affects the quality of the decisions, as this figure shows. For this figure, successes were assigned an abstract value of +1, mixed results received a null value of 0 (zero), and failure received a value of –1.

Effects of Groupthink

The urge for consensus that characterizes groupthink limits the policy choices available. It also decreases the chances that the policy chosen will prove successful.

Limited policy choices Anthony Lake, who served as national security adviser to President Clinton, recognized that "there is a danger that when people work well together [that] you can take the edge off options." This can lead, Lake says, to "groupthink... [with] not enough options reaching the president."[9] One way that groupthink may limit policy choices is through **incremental decision making,** which adheres to established policy or makes only marginal changes. One of Lake's predecessors, Zbigniew Brzezinski, has compared foreign policy to "an aircraft carrier. You simply don't send it into a 180-degree turn; at most you move it a few degrees to port or starboard" (Paterson, Clifford, & Hagan, 2000:414).

Lowest common denominator policy Another way that groupthink's drive for consensus limits policy choices is that decision makers often adopt the policy that is least objectionable rather than the optimal policy. During the Cuban missile crisis, President Kennedy and his advisers did not decide to blockade Cuba because they thought it was the best thing to do. In fact, few of the decision makers really liked the idea of a blockade. Instead, it was a compromise between those who wanted to use military force to destroy the missiles and those who preferred to use diplomacy to persuade Moscow to withdraw the missiles.

Poor policy A review of the decisional inadequacies brought on by groupthink leads to the question, *Do poor decisions result in policy failures?* The answer is yes.

Decision making that falls victim to groupthink invariably does not achieve optimal foreign policy. This was confirmed by three scholars who studied nineteen crisis decisions and rated them for evidence of 7 different symptoms of defective decision making (Herek, Janis, & Huth, 1987). Eight decisions had either 0 or 1 symptom and were rated "high quality." Four decisions with 2 or 3 symptoms were rated "medium quality," and seven decisions with 4 or more symptoms were rated "poor quality." The researchers then asked experts to evaluate the impact of each decision as positive or negative in its effects on U.S. national interest. As Figure 5.1 indicates, there is a distinct relationship between the quality of the decision process and the effectiveness of the policy adopted.

INDIVIDUAL-LEVEL ANALYSIS: IDIOSYNCRATIC BEHAVIOR

A third approach to individual-level analysis focuses on humans as individuals. This approach emphasizes the idiosyncratic characteristics of political leaders. Note that idiosyncratic means individual, not odd. **Idiosyncratic analysis** assumes that individuals make foreign policy decisions and that different individuals are likely to make different decisions. In its simplest form, this approach includes examining biographies and memoirs as political histories. More recently, analysts have written sophisticated "psychobiographies" that explore the motivations of decision makers. Scholars are also using increasingly sophisticated methodologies such as content analysis, which involves analyzing the content of a decision maker's statements and writings to understand the basic ways he or she views the world.

Whatever the specific methodology of such studies, the point is not *what* a leader decided. Rather, the fundamental question is *why* the leader chose certain paths. What are the internal factors that motivated the decision maker? The list of possible psychological factors is long, but for our discussion we will consider five basic characteristics of individual decision makers: personality, physical and mental health, egos and ambitions, political history and personal experiences, and perceptions.

PERSONALITY

The study of personality stems from the belief that, in the end, decisions are made by individuals and that the personalities of those decision makers affect what they do. One scholar writes that after years of studying why wars occur, he is convinced that "the personalities of the leaders... have often been decisive.... In all cases [studied], a fatal flaw or character weakness in a leader's personality was of critical importance. It may, in fact, have spelled the difference between the outbreak of war and the maintenance of peace" (Stoessinger, 1998:210).

When studying personality types and their impact on policy, scholars examine a leader's basic orientations toward self and toward others, behavioral patterns, and attitudes about such politically relevant concepts as authority. There are numerous categorization schemes. The most well-known of these places political personality along an active-passive scale and a positive-negative scale (Barber, 1985). Active leaders are policy innovators; passive leaders are reactors. Positive personalities have egos strong enough to enjoy (or at least accept) the contentious political environment; negative personalities are apt to feel burdened, even abused, by political criticism. Many scholars favor active-positive presidents, but all four types have drawbacks. Activists, for example, may feel compelled to try to solve every problem even though not doing something might be preferable. That was arguably true in some cases for President Clinton, whom most political psychology studies categorize as an extremely activist

Did You Know That:

Former Bosnian Serb president Radovan Karadzic, who has been indicted by the international war crimes tribunal in The Hague, Netherlands, has an extremely active-negative personality. Among other evidence of Karadzic's personality is a poem he wrote in 1971 entitled "Let's Go Down to the Town and Kill Some Scum."

personality, and who himself admitted to being "almost compulsively overactive" (Renshon, 1995:59).

Whatever the best combination may be, there is wide agreement that the worst is active-negative. The more active a leader, the more criticism he or she encounters. Rather than taking criticism in stride, though, the leader assumes that opponents are enemies and may withdraw into an inner circle of subordinates who are supportive and who give an unreal view of events and domestic and international opinion. Adolf Hitler and Josef Stalin and, to a lesser degree, Lyndon Johnson and Richard Nixon were all active-negative personalities who showed symptoms of delusion, struck out at their enemies, and generally developed bunker mentalities.

PHYSICAL AND MENTAL HEALTH

A leader's physical and mental health can be important factors in decision making (Park, 1994). In a book entitled *The Dying President* (1998), noted historian Robert Farrell details the diplomacy of Franklin Delano Roosevelt during the pivotal period toward the end of World War II. Farrell concludes that the president was so ill from hypertension that he was "in no condition to govern the republic." This period included such critical junctures as Roosevelt's meeting with British prime minister Winston Churchill and Soviet leader Josef Stalin at Yalta in February 1945. Some analysts believe that the ailing president, who by that time was unable to concentrate for long periods or work more than four hours a day, was too debilitated to resist Stalin's demands for U.S. acquiescence to Soviet domination of Poland and the rest of Eastern Europe. Less than two months after returning, FDR's blood pressure soared even higher to 300/190, and on April 12, the president suffered a massive brain hemorrhage and died.

A few leaders may even have acute mental problems. Stalin probably suffered from clinical paranoia, and a psychiatrist who has studied Hitler concludes that he was "very disturbed," although not legally insane.[10] To make matters worse, alcohol or (in Hitler's case) drugs may also occasionally affect a decision maker's judgment. As World War II turned against the Germans, Hitler's drug intake for a panoply of real and imagined illnesses reached epic proportions. Barbiturates, laxatives, cardiac stimulants, opiates, desoxycorticosterone (for muscle weakness), hormones from female placentas and from the testes and prostates of young bulls, caffeine, Pervitin (an amphetamine), and Eukodal (a morphine equivalent) all coursed through his blood. After mid-1944 Hitler also received multiple daily cocaine treatments for sinusitis. One analysis notes, "The precise effects of this pharmaceutical cocktail on Hitler's mental state [are] difficult to gauge. Suffice it to say, in the jargon of the street, Hitler was simultaneously taking coke and speed."[11] The drug combinations Hitler used would almost certainly generate a high-low cycle, producing euphoria and delusions of grandeur followed by paranoia and irrational anger. This bizarre pattern closely resembles Hitler's wildly inconsistent moods and decisions late in the war. It is probably too much to argue that a more lucid Hitler would have won the war or achieved a stalemate, but the conflict would almost certainly have gone on longer (L'Etang, 1970).

Alcohol abuse can also lead to problems. For example, there are persistent stories that President Richard Nixon, who Secretary of State Henry Kissinger once called "my drunken friend," alarmed advisers with his drinking and was once incapacitated during an international crisis with the Soviet Union (Schulzinger, 1989:178). Alcohol also impaired President Boris Yeltsin's ability to govern. His bouts with alcohol led to a number of incidents of bizarre public behavior, such as loudly singing a song that was different from what the band was playing at a public ceremony. Fortunately, especially for a man who had command over nuclear weapons, there were no major incidents. Still, the alcohol plus Yeltsin's heart condition (which required quadruple bypass heart surgery in 1996), so weakened the president that Russia was virtually leaderless during

The health of leaders can affect their ability to govern and to make policy decisions. President Boris Yeltsin of Russia (1991–1999) clearly had a problem with alcohol, symbolized in this image of the new president Vladimir Putin asking an aide to remove the vodka source from the presidential suite in the Kremlin. Not the least of the concerns about Yeltsin's frequent inebriation was the fact that he controlled Russia's strategic nuclear weapons.

his second term. One poll found that 92 percent of Russians had an unfavorable opinion of him, and he resigned before his term was complete (ADL, 1999:28).

EGO AND AMBITION

The egos and personal ambitions of political leaders can also influence policy. *Ego*, especially the male variety, sometimes works to make leaders want to appear tough. This trait may well have figured in the onset of the Persian Gulf War. There is something revealing in the name of Iraq's president, Saddam Hussein. His original name was Hussein al-Takrit, but once in power, he dropped al-Takrit and added Saddam, an Arabic word that means "one who confronts." The ego of Saddam Hussein's nemesis, George Bush, also may have influenced policy. Bush came to office with a reputation for being wishy-washy, and the "wimp factor" became a regular subject of journalistic comment. *Newsweek* magazine, for example, ran a picture of Bush and a banner, "The Wimp Factor" on the cover of a 1989 issue. It is possible that an ego-wounded Bush responded by being too tough. He soon invaded Panama, and the following year, during the Persian Gulf crisis, some analysts argued that Bush's fierce determination not to negotiate with Iraq left Baghdad little choice but to fight or capitulate. Certainly, it would be outrageous to claim that Bush decided on war only to assuage his ego, but to ignore the possible role of this factor would be naive. In fact, even after defeating Panama and Iraq, Bush remained testy about the wimp image. Addressing a California audience in June 1991, Bush expostulated with prickly pride, "You're talking to the wimp… to the guy that had a cover of a national magazine, that I'll never forgive, put that label on me" (Rourke, 1993:31).

Ambition is another driving force that sometimes affects decision makers (Renshon, 2000). The ambition to remain in power is, according to two scholars, "the very essence of the office-holding *homo politicus*" and can influence foreign policy (Bueno de Mesquita & Siverson, 1993:30). The policy of President John F. Kennedy toward the USSR and other communist nations was driven, in part, by Republican charges that he and other Democrats were "soft on communism." The president was determined not to let such accusations hurt his reelection chances. Soviet leader Nikita S. Khrushchev recalled that at his first meeting with Kennedy (in Vienna, Austria, in 1991), Kennedy had pleaded, "Don't ask for too much. Don't put me in a bind. If I make too many concessions, I'll be turned out of office." "Quite a guy," was Khruschev's sarcastic evaluation of Kennedy. "He comes to a meeting but can't perform. What the hell do we need a guy like that for? Why waste time talking to him?" (Fursenko & Naftali, 1997:134).

The following year during the Cuban missile crisis, electoral politics once again influenced Kennedy's actions. The crisis occurred just before the November congressional elections, and there is considerable evidence that the White House was aware of the implications of the crisis for the upcoming legislative elections and for the prospects of Kennedy's being reelected in 1964. "It was election time," the president's brother, Robert F. Kennedy (1969:25), begins his memoir of the crisis. The president certainly did not risk nuclear war with the Soviet Union solely because of his sense of ego and his concern about his and the Democratic Party's political future. But it would be naive to imagine that those factors were absent from the decisions that brought the world closer to nuclear destruction than at any time before or since. "If you hadn't acted, you would have been impeached," the president's brother Robert observed just after the crisis. "That's what I think," brother John agreed (Kennedy, 1969:67).

POLITICAL HISTORY AND PERSONAL EXPERIENCES

The past is a fourth factor that shapes a political leader's approach to world problems. Philosopher George Santayana wrote in *The Life of Reason* (1905) that "Those who cannot remember the past are condemned to repeat it." Contemporary policy makers frequently echo that sentiment. "History is a strange teacher," Secretary of State Madeleine Albright mused. "It never repeats itself exactly, but you ignore its general lessons at your peril."[12] The trick of letting history be one's teacher is learning the right lesson. The ability of decision makers to wisely apply the lessons of history is not, however, always evident, as we will see by examining lessons drawn from political history and personal experience.

Political History

Historical analogies that are based on how individuals or even societies interpret historical events and apply their supposed lessons are a regular part of policy making. The **Munich analogy** is one such history lesson that figures frequently in policy debates and rationale. When Germany threatened Czechoslovakia in 1938, France and Great Britain were unwilling to confront Hitler to risk war on behalf of what Prime Minister Neville Chamberlain told the British was "a faraway country about which we know little." The British and French therefore agreed at the Munich Conference to appease the Germans by letting them annex the Sudetenland region of Czechoslovakia. The traumatic events of World War II followed, and that experience "taught" that compromise with aggressive dictators would only encourage them.

During the intervening years leaders have repeatedly cited the lesson of the 1930s as justification for confronting international opponents and, if necessary, going to war. "If history teaches us anything, it is that... appeasement does not work," President Bush declared to the American people when Saddam Hussein's forces attacked Kuwait. "As

The personal experiences of leaders can affect their perceptions and decisions. Secretary of State Madeleine Albright, who is seen receiving a bouquet from Afghan refugees at a temporary camp in Pakistan, was especially sensitive to the plight of these young women because of their shared experience of being female in a world dominated politically by males.

was the case in the 1930s," Bush instructed, "we see in Saddam Hussein an aggressive dictator threatening his neighbors. Half a century ago the world had a chance to stop a ruthless aggressor and missed it. I pledge to you: We will not make that mistake again" (Rourke, 1993:30). War followed.

Lessons of history often fade as those who remember them become fewer and as more recent history teaches new lessons. One such new lesson for Americans is the **Vietnam analogy.** This is almost the antithesis of the Munich syndrome. Now when there is the possibility of an intervention, especially in a civil war, the cry "no more Vietnams" is heard (Simons, 1998). The image of Vietnam was, for instance, raised frequently by those who opposed U.S. intervention in Bosnia. "Most of us hark back to Vietnam and have faint enthusiasm for punching somebody to see what happens," one senior U.S. military officer commented on the possibility of sending U.S. troops to the Balkans.[13]

Two subsidiary comments about the use of historical analogies are important. First, as a heuristic device, historical analogies are too often used to avoid thinking rather than to inform decisions. Saddam Hussein is certainly an aggressive dictator, just as Hitler was. The Persian Gulf in 1990 was not, however, Europe in 1938. Nor, it can be added, did the difficult terrain and the irregular forces in the Balkans in the 1990s mean that it was like Vietnam in the 1960s. The point is that a historical analogy should be the beginning, not the end, of a political discussion, and it is the responsibility of the individual using the analogy to demonstrate its applicability.

Second, policy makers sometimes make a decision, then select a likely historical analogy to justify their position. A study of the congressional debate on the Persian Gulf War resolutions in 1991 found that almost all foreign policy conservatives and Republicans (who were predisposed toward military action) used the Munich example to argue for war. By contrast, almost all foreign policy liberals and Democrats (who were predisposed to continue economic sanctions) used the Vietnam example to argue against quick military action. The data led to the conclusion that the Munich and

Vietnam analogies were "used by members of Congress as post-hoc justifications for policy choices and [did] not help determine them" (Taylor & Rourke, 1995:467).

Personal Experiences

Decision makers are also affected by their personal experiences. Madeleine Albright's experiences as a woman clearly made her more sensitive as U.S. secretary of state to the plight of women around the world. Under her leadership, the United States has brought increased pressure on the conservative Muslim Taliban government of Afghanistan to ease its repression of women. Albright traveled to Pakistan in 1997 to meet with refugee Afghani women. Clearly identifying with the women from the other side of the world, she condemned the government in Kabul for its "despicable treatment of women and children and lack of respect for human dignity," and told a group of Afghani women assembled in a mud-brick building, "I especially wanted to come to meet with you and to hear your stories." Even though she acknowledged her relatively privileged life, the secretary of state went on to say that "I find that women have the same stories.... I know we are all the same, and we have the same feeling. We all suffer when we hurt and we all suffer for each other.... We really are all sisters."[14]

PERCEPTIONS

A decision maker's images of reality constitute a fifth idiosyncratic element that influences their approach to foreign policy. These images are called **perceptions.** Images and reality may be the same; they may be dramatically different. Some factors in world politics, such as the existence of Kashmir in Asia, are in the realm of objective reality. Other factors are subjective. India perceives Kashmir as an integral and proper part of the country. Pakistan perceives Kashmir to be a territory whose largely Muslim population has been illegally annexed by India—a territory that should be part of Pakistan. Since India's and Pakistan's perceptions are mutually exclusive, it follows that perceptions sometimes distort reality.

Perceptions have a multitude of sources. Many, such as belief systems and historical analogies, are related to the cognitive limits discussed earlier in this chapter or to the idiosyncratic characteristics of decision makers that we have been analyzing in this section. The information that decision makers receive from their bureaucracies or elsewhere, as discussed in chapter 4, is another important source of perceptions. Whatever their source, though, perceptions have a number of characteristics and impacts that are important to world politics (Blanton, 1996).

Characteristics of Perceptions

There are numerous common perceptual characteristics that influence policy making, and we can highlight a few of the distortions they cause. One common perceptual characteristic is that *we tend to assume that other people and leaders see the world in the same way that we do.* George Bush dealt with Saddam Hussein, and with Arabs in general, on the assumption that they operated from the same mental framework that he had. When, for example, the U.S.–led coalition amassed a huge military force and gave Iraq an ultimatum to get out of Kuwait or suffer the consequences, Bush assumed that the Iraqis could count, would realize they would be flattened, and would give way. Just three weeks before that perception was proven false by the onset of war, a reporter asked President Bush if he thought that Iraq would quit Kuwait. "Some leaders tell me [that Iraq] cannot get out," he replied. "I do not have much of a feel" for the Arab point of view, Bush conceded, but, he went on, Saddam Hussein "must understand what he is up against in terms of power.... Oh God," Bush concluded hesitantly, "my gut says he will get out of there" (Rourke, 1993:37).

Second, *we tend to see other countries as more hostile than our own.* This tendency is particularly strong when there is a lack of knowledge about others. When Ronald Reagan took office in 1981 he was prone to demonizing the USSR, once even calling it an evil empire. Similarly, soon after Soviet president Mikhail Gorbachev came to power in 1985 he characterized President Reagan as a prisoner of the military-industrial complex who "couldn't make peace if he wanted to."[15] Neither Reagan's nor Gorbachev's image was especially accurate, and history records that by 1987 the two had signed the Intermediate-Range Nuclear Forces (INF) treaty and were well on their way to concluding a strategic nuclear weapons treaty. By the end of Reagan's tenure the two had met so often and so cordially that they were dubbed the Ron and Gorby Show.

Third, *we tend to see the behavior of others as more centralized, disciplined, and coordinated than ours.* During the cold war, both the Americans and the Soviets imagined that the other side had a carefully planned, well-executed master strategy to expand its power and influence and to frustrate and defeat its opponents. By contrast, each side saw itself as on the defensive and as responding on a piecemeal basis to the aggressive thrusts of the other side. Former secretary of state Henry Kissinger (1979:1202) has described the two superpowers as behaving like "two heavily armed blind men feeling their way around a room, each believing himself in mortal peril from the other whom he assumes to have perfect vision." Each, according to Kissinger, "tends to ascribe to the other side a consistency, foresight, and coherence that its own experience belies. Of course, over time even two armed blind men in a room can do enormous damage to each other, not to speak of the room."

Fourth, *we tend to assume that the other side sees our good intentions and thus is not suspicious or afraid of us.* Not only is each side convinced that it wears the white hats and that the other side wears the black hats, but it is hard to believe that the other side can doubt our sincerity. During the cold war, Americans supported an immense military buildup because, they were told, it was the only way to fend off the communist Soviet Union. "Peace through strength," is how President Ronald Reagan put it. Perhaps, but there are indications that the Soviets felt the same way: imperiled and defensively armed. "We have to conduct our policies from a position of strength," Nikita Khrushchev told a Soviet audience. "There can't be any other policy. Our opponents don't understand any other language.... If I took any other view," Khrushchev concluded, "I'd be a jellyfish" (Fursenko & Naftali, 1997:134).

The Impact of Perceptions

The most obvious impact of perceptions is that they form a "lens" or "prism" through which we perceive reality. When our perceptions are inaccurate they distort our images both of ourselves and of others. Try borrowing a pair of glasses from a friend. Look at the world around you. It becomes distorted, with the degree of distortion depending on how thick the lenses are. Similarly, the degree of perceptual distortion relates to the strength of the beholder's beliefs. Such misperception can cause us to misjudge the actions of others and to fail to understand how our own actions are perceived by others. If this were the only extent of the impact of perceptions, their role would be limited, but it is not. Perceptions affect how we act on the world stage.

The link between perception and policy is the concept of **operational reality.** Policy makers tend to act, or operate, based on perceptions, whether they are accurate or not. We noted earlier in this chapter that American perceptions of communist hostility dominated U.S. policy making during the cold war and led, among other things, to the U.S. government supporting numerous right-wing dictatorships whose internal practices contravened core values of American political culture about democracy, human rights, and other matters. As one critic put it, if the U.S. government "hated tyranny enough to invade or attempt to overthrow" numerous "presumably tyrannical"

In the 1960s the cold war perception was that a communist victory in Vietnam might have a domino effect, leading all of Southeast Asia, and perhaps beyond, to fall to communism. This brought the United States to war in the region. The communists won, but the perception proved false. Instead, Vietnam and the rest of the region have become increasingly capitalist and, to a degree, Westernized. That is symbolized by the amused reaction of these Vietnamese women to a statue of Colonel Sanders outside a KFC restaurant in Ho Chi Minh City (formerly Saigon, the capital of South Vietnam).

left-wing regimes (such as Nicaragua in the 1980s), "one might wonder why [the United States] never moved against Chile, South Africa, Indonesia, Zaire, Paraguay, Turkey, and a host of other terribly repressive [rightist] regimes" (Parenti, 1992:187). Another critic charges that U.S. policy was too ready to commit vast resources to defend strategically remote places against communism. A prime example is Vietnam, where the United States spent billions of dollars and tens-of-thousands of lives in a war over what President Lyndon Johnson once called "a raggedy-ass fourth rate country."

The answer to the seeming contradictions between U.S. policy and both American values and U.S. strategic interests is based in the way, one study has found, that perceptions can shape perceived interests. One way is that an image of an enemy, such as the Soviet Union and world communism, can create a felt need for allies, even if they are brutally authoritarian or of peripheral strategic value. "The enemy image thus produces interests in other countries that would not follow from the intrinsic qualities of the other country and may disappear as soon as the enemy image erodes" (Herrmann, et al., 1997:423). The validity of this conclusion is certainly upheld by U.S. post–cold war policy. Now, the U.S. government cares little about the form of Vietnam's political system (still communist), and it is hard to imagine even a foreign invasion (say, by China) causing the United States to send in a half-million troops, as it did in the 1960s.

There is a related perceptual phenomenon called an **operational code.** This idea describes how an individual acts when faced with specific types of situations, given a "leader's philosophical propensities for diagnosing" how politics works and the "leader's instrumental propensities for choosing" rewards, threats, force, and other methods of diplomacy as the best way to be successful (Walker, Schafer, & Young, 1998:176). Because of their different operational codes, decision makers differ, for example, in their responses to situations. President Nixon, for instance, believed that foreign relations "are a lot like poker—stud poker with a hole card. The hole card is all-important because without it your opponent… has perfect knowledge of whether he can beat you. If he knows he will win he will raise you. If he cannot, he will fold and get out of the game." Nixon thought, therefore, that a diplomatic strategy of keeping an opponent uncertain was necessary because "the United States is an open society. We have all but one of our cards face up on the table. Our only covered card is the will, nerve, and unpredictability of the President—his ability to make the enemy think twice about raising the ante" (Rogers, 1987:31).

That poker image helps explain why Nixon raised the ante in Vietnam by, for example, unleashing in 1972 such a tremendous "Christmas bombing" offensive against North Vietnam's cities that one U.S. official described it as "calculated barbarism" (Paterson, Clifford, & Hagan, 2000:392). Nixon believed that these actions would help persuade the North Vietnamese and their Soviet backers to cash in their chips and agree to more serious negotiations. Actually, the terms Nixon got after the bombing were not much different from those offered before. Be that as it may, the point is that the president's crisis-operational code caused his violent reaction, which he later claimed was a major turning point to end the war.

CHAPTER SUMMARY

1. Individual-level analysis studies international politics by examining the role of humans as actors on the world stage.

2. Individual-level analysis can be approached from three different perspectives. One is to examine fundamental human nature. The second is to study how people act in organizations. The third is to examine the motivations and actions of specific persons.

3. The human nature approach examines basic human characteristics. Cognitive, psychological, and biological factors influence decision making. Cognitive factors include cognitive decision making, cognitive consistency, wishful thinking, limiting the scope of decision, and using heuristic devices. Frustration agression is the primary psychological factor considered, while biological factors include ethology and gender.

4. The organizational-behavior approach studies role factors; that is, how people act in certain personal or professional positions. The approach is also concerned with how groups behave and how the interactions affect decisions.

5. Groupthink is one possible outcome of organizational behavior, in most cases leading to bad decisions. Ignoring or suppressing dissidents, discordant information, and policy options are all causes of groupthink. Another is the reluctance of subordinates to offer discordant opinions. Among the effects of groupthink are limited policy choices, lowest common denominator policy, and poor policy.

6. The idiosyncratic-behavior approach explores the factors that determine the perceptions, decisions, and actions of specific leaders. A leader's personality, physical and mental health, ego and ambitions, understanding of history, personal experiences, and perceptions are all factors.

7. Perceptions are especially important to understanding how leaders react to the world. These spring from such sources as a group's or an individual's belief system, an individual's values, and the information available to the individual.

8. Perceptions can be explained by exploring operational reality. How a group or an individual perceives a situation, another individual, or another country is often a distortion of reality. Distorted perceptions are important because leaders act on what they perceive to be true rather than on what is objectively true.

CHAPTER 6

NATIONALISM: THE TRADITIONAL ORIENTATION

I do love My country's good with a respect more tender, More holy and profound, than mine own life.

Shakespeare, *Coriolanus*

If he govern the country, you are bound to him indeed; but how honourable he is in that, I know not.

Shakespeare, *Pericles, Prince of Tyre*

Our country! In her intercourse with foreign nations may she always be in the right; but our country, right or wrong.

Stephen Decatur, 1816

You're not supposed to be so blind with patriotism that you can't face reality. Wrong is wrong, no matter who does it or who says it.

Malcolm X, *Malcolm X Speaks*, 1965

CHAPTER OBJECTIVES

After completing this chapter, you should be able to:

- Define nationalism.
- Identify the elements that make up a state.
- Describe how a nation differs from a state.
- Identify and explain the ideal concept of nation-state and its relationship to nationalism.
- Discuss why nationalism may be said to be both a cohesive and a divisive force.
- Understand nationalism as the product of historical development.
- Identify arguments predicting the end of nationalism and the demise of the territorial state, and note post–World War II trends that have contradicted these predications.
- List and discuss positive and negative aspects of nationalism.
- Identify the ideal and actual relationships between nation and state.
- Define multistate nationalities and explain when they occur.
- Understand the origins of microstates and the problems that their existence presents to the state-centric system.
- Explain the place of nationalism and the nation-state in today's world where transnational and other structures and identifications are also increasing in scope and intensity.

Aliens fascinate us. Not the aliens that immigration officials worry about, but the ones that come from other planets. Whether it is the comical others in *3rd Rock from the Sun* or the aggressive aliens in the sci-fi thriller *Independence Day*, our entertainment media are filled with "others." These others can do more than amuse or scare us; they can tell us something. For instance, take E.T.—the extraterrestrial being. Now, there was one strange-looking character. He—she?—had a squat body, no legs to speak of, a large shriveled head, saucer eyes, and a telescopic neck. And the color! Yes, E.T. was definitely weird. Not only that; there was presumably a whole planet full of E.T.'s—all looking alike, waddling along, with their necks going up and down.

Or did they all look alike? They might have to us, but probably not to one another. Perhaps on their planet there were different countries, ethnic groups, and races of E.T.'s. Maybe they had different-length necks, were varied shades of greenish-brown, and squeaked and hummed with different tonal qualities. It could even be that darker-green E.T.'s with longer necks from the country of Urghor felt superior to lighter-green, short-necked E.T.'s from faraway and little-known Sytica across the red Barovian Sea. If E.T. was a Sytican, would the Urghorans have responded to the plaintive call, "E.T., phone home"?

We can also wonder whether E.T. could tell Earthlings apart. Was he aware that some of his human protectors were boys and some were girls and that a cross section of racial and ethnic Americans chased him with equal-opportunity abandon? Maybe we all looked pretty much the same to E.T. If he had been on a biological specimen–gathering expedition and had collected a Canadian, a Nigerian, and a Laotian, he might have thrown two of the three away as duplicates.

The point of this whimsy is to get us thinking about our world, how different from and how similar to one another we humans are, and how we categorize ourselves. What we will see is that we do not have an image of ourselves as humans. Rather, we divide

Nationalism tends to make us view people from other cultures and countries as different from ourselves. These figures are part of the 1001 statues created by Indonesian sculptor Dadang Christianto as part of his "1001 Earth Humans" exhibit near Jakarta. One has to wonder whether a being from another world, such as E.T., would have seen all humans as basically the same, just as Christianto depicts them here.

up ethnically into Chinese, Irish, Poles, and a host of other "we-groups." Despite our manifest human similarities, we usually identify and organize ourselves politically around some "we-group" subdivision of humanity. If you think about it, you see yourself politically as a citizen of the United States, or some other country. You might even be willing to fight and die for your country. Would you do the same for your hometown? Or Earth?

Nationalism is the country-level focus that makes most people feel patriotic about their country, but not their hometown or their planet. This identification is our traditional political orientation. It has helped configure world politics for several centuries and will continue to shape people's minds and affairs in the foreseeable future. Few would argue with the observation that "nationalism has been… the nineteenth and twentieth centuries' most powerful political idea" (Taras & Ganguly, 1998:xi). Despite its strength, however, nationalism today is not as unchallenged as it once was. Some even doubt whether it will or should continue and predict or advocate various transnational alternative orientations.

This juxtaposition of the traditional nationalist orientation and the alternative transnational orientation represents one of this book's main themes: that the world is at or is approaching a critical juncture where two roads diverge in the political wood. The two paths to the political future—traditional and alternative—were mapped out briefly in chapter 1.

This chapter and those that follow will explore the two roads, usually by comparing them in successive chapters. This chapter, for example, takes up nationalism, the traditional way we identify ourselves politically. Then, in chapter 7, we will turn to alternative, transnationalist orientations.

UNDERSTANDING NATIONS, NATION-STATES, AND NATIONALISM

Three concepts will help explain the divisions that characterize traditional global politics. Those three concepts are: nation, nation-state, and nationalism (Mortimer & Fine, 1999; Barrington, 1997).

NATIONS

A **nation** is a people who mutually identify culturally and politically to such a degree that they want to be separate and to control themselves politically. As such, a nation is intangible. A nation, of course, includes tangible people, but the essence of a nation is its less tangible elements, such as similarities among the people, their sense of connection, and a desire of the people to govern themselves. A state is an institution; a nation is "a soul, a spiritual quality," a French scholar once wrote (Renan, 1995:7).

Demographic and Cultural Similarities The similarities that a people share are one element that help make them a nation. These similarities may be demographic characteristics (such as language, race, and religion), or they may be common culture or historical experiences. When such commonalities are strongly present, the formation of the nation precedes that of the state. In Europe, nations generally came together first and only later coalesced into states. Germans, for instance, existed long before they came together as Germany in the 1860s and 1870s. Germany was again divided in 1945, but Germans, east and west, felt that there should be *ein Deutschland*, one Germany. Eventually the East German Communist regime collapsed because its legitimacy among the East German people evaporated. Beginning on October 3, 1990, there was once again *ein Deutschland*.

In other regions and circumstances, the formation of the state comes first. In such cases, a critical task of the state is to promote internal loyalty and to create a process whereby its diverse citizens gradually acquire their nationalism through common historical experiences and the regular social/economic/political interactions and cooperation that occur among people living within the same state (Barkey & von Hagen, 1997). This is very difficult. For example, many states in Africa are the result of boundaries that were drawn earlier by colonial powers and that took in people of different tribal and ethnic backgrounds. These former colonial states often do not contain a single, cohesive nation, and the diverse cultural groups find little to bind them to one another once independence has been achieved. Rwanda and Burundi are neighboring states in which Hutu and Tutsi people were thrown together by colonial boundaries that, with independence, became national boundaries, as depicted in the map of Africa on page 31. The difficulty is that the primary political identifications of these people have not become Rwandan or Burundian. They have remained Hutu or Tutsi, and that has led to repeated, sometimes horrific, violence.

It should be added that nation-building and state-building are not necessarily locked in a strict sequential interaction, where one fully precedes the other (Cederman, 1997). Sometimes they evolve together. This approximates what occurred in the United States, where the idea of being American and the unity of the state began in the 1700s and grew, despite a civil war, immigration inflows, racial and ethnic diversity, and other potentially divisive factors. The point is that being within a state sometimes allows a demographically diverse people to come together as a nation through a process of *e pluribus unum* (out of many, one), as the U.S. motto says. It could be said that the American nation is the outcome of Valley Forge, Martin Luther King, the interstate highway system, McDonald's, CBS, the Super Bowl, Gloria Estefan, and a host of other people, events, and processes that make up the American experience.

MAP
World Countries, pp. 28–29

Feeling of Community A second thing that helps define a nation is its feeling of community. Perception is the key here. For all the similarities a group might have, it is not a nation unless it feels like one. Those within a group must perceive that they share similarities and are bound together by them. Unfortunately, groups also often define themselves by how they differ from other groups of "strangers" (Guibernau, 1996:49). Whether a group's sense of connection comes from feeling akin to one another or different from others, it is highly subjective.

Desire to Be Politically Separate The third element that defines a nation is its desire to be politically separate. What distinguishes a nation from an ethnic group is that a nation, unlike an ethnic group, has a desire to be self-governing or at least autonomous. In the United States there are many groups, such as Italian Americans, who share a common culture and have a sense of identification. They are not, however, nations because they are not separatists. In nationally divided states (like Cyprus, with its majority-Greek and minority-Turkish communities), the minority nationalities refuse to concede the legitimacy of their being governed by the majority nationality.

Sometimes the line between ethnic groups and nations is not clear. In many countries there are so-called *ethnonationalist* groups that either teeter on the edge of having true nationalist (separatist) sentiment or that have some members who are nationalists and others who are not. Canada is one such country where the line between ethnic group and nation is uncertain. There is an ongoing dissatisfaction among many French Canadians in the province of Quebec about their status in the Canadian state. Some Québécois favor separation, others do not.

NATION-STATES

A second element of our traditional way of defining and organizing ourselves politically is the **nation-state.** This combines the idea of a nation with that of a state.

The possibility of peace in the Middle East exists on the knife edge of Israeli-Palestinian relations. During the past few decades there have been some times of great hope, such as after the Camp David accords (1978) and Oslo accords (1993). There have also been times when peace seemed impossible, as symbolized by this photograph of a Palestinian policeman and an Israeli soldier angrily confronting each other in the West Bank city of Hebron during the violence that occurred in 2000.

Did You Know That:

Flags as national symbols are relatively modern inventions. Earlier, most countries' flags were really those of the royal dynasties. The French tricolor, for example, dates only to the time of the French Revolution, when it replaced the white flag with fleur-de-lis of the royal house of Bourbon.

A nation-state (more commonly called a state or country), is a tangible entity. It has territory, people, organization, and other reasonably objective characteristics. Canada and China are states.

The nation-state is the ideal joining of nation and state, the notion of a unified people in a unified country. There are two ways in which this can occur. One is where a state is created by a nation that wishes to govern itself independently. A second scenario for the creation of a nation-state is when once-diverse people within a state learn to identify with one another and with the country in which they reside.

The nation-state is represented by many symbols, such as flags, national anthems, or animals (eagles, bears, dragons). It is the object of patriotic loyalty, and most people view it as the highest form of political authority.

In practice the nation-state concept diverges from the ideal in two ways. First, many states, such as Canada, contain more than one nation. Second, many nations overlap one or more international borders and may not even have a state of their own. The presence of Palestinians in Egypt, Israel, Jordan, and elsewhere is a current illustration. This lack of "fit" between nations and states is often a source of international conflict, as discussed later. Indeed the gap between the theory of nation-states and the reality of ethnically and nationally divided states is so great that some scholars prefer the term *national state* to emphasize the idea of a state driven by nationalism.

NATIONALISM

The third aspect of our traditional political orientation is **nationalism** itself. It is hard to overstate the importance of nationalism to the structure and conduct of world politics (Beiner, 1999). Nationalism grows from the sense of community and turns it into "a principle of political loyalty and social identity" (Gellner, 1995:2). Nationalism does this by merging the three concepts of state, nation, and nation-state in a way that is personally related to citizens. The transformation occurs when individuals (1) "become sentimentally attached to the homeland," (2) "gain a sense of identity and self-esteem through their national identification," and (3) are "motivated to help their country" (Druckman, 1994:44). This merging of the three concepts means that nationalism is an ideology that holds that the nation, embodied in its agent, the sovereign nation-state, should be the paramount object of the political loyalty of individuals.

THE EVOLUTION OF NATIONALISM

The evolution of nationalism and the development of the state-centric international system are intertwined. Neither states nor nationalism nor the state-centric system have always existed. This is important because if something has not always been, it does not necessarily always have to be. It is also important to note that nationalism has evolved and continues to do so. Understanding the historical dynamics of nationalism will assist you to evaluate its current status and its value and will help you to form preferences about the future of nationalism.

THE RISE OF NATIONALISM

Nationalism is such a pervasive mindset in the world today, that it may be difficult to believe that it has not always existed. It has not. Indeed, most scholars contend that nationalism is a relatively modern phenomenon. It is certainly the case, one scholar notes, that "there have always... been distinctive cultures." It is also the case that in some very old societies the "upper classes have had some sense of shared ethnic solidarity." What is modern, the scholar continues, is the "nationalist idea," the belief that people who share a culture should "be ruled only by someone co-cultural with themselves" (Hall, 1995:10).

Early Nationalism It is impossible to precisely establish when nationalism began to evolve, but one early step occurred in Europe toward the end of the Dark Ages. Charlemagne became king of the Franks in 768, and during his long reign he gained control over most of western and central Europe. The extent of his empire was recognized officially in 800 when Pope Leo III proclaimed him emperor of Romans, a symbolic title denoting the universal empire that had been Rome's. Whatever unity Charlemagne brought to the West did not long exist after his death in 814. What followed was a fragmentation of the empire into different cultures. The use of Latin as a language spoken by all elites across Europe declined. Localized languages took Latin's place and divided the elites. This was but the first step in a process that eventually created a sense of divergent national identities among the upper classes.

The growth of nationalism became gradually intertwined with the development of states and with their synthesis, the national state. We will review the history of states in chapter 8, but we can say here that some of the earliest evidence of broad-based nationalism occurred in England at the time of King Henry VIII (1491–1547). His break with the centralizing authority of the Roman Catholic Church and his establishment of a national Anglican Church headed by the king were pivotal events. The conversion of English commoners to Anglicanism helped spread nationalism to the masses, as did the nationalist sentiments in popular literature. In an age when most people could not read, plays were an important vehicle of culture, and one scholar has characterized the works of William Shakespeare (1564–1616) as "propagandist plays about English history" (Hobsbawm, 1990:75). "This blessed plot, this earth, this realm, this England," Shakespeare has his *King Richard II* exalt. In another play, *Henry VI*, Shakespeare notes the end of the authority of the pope in Rome over the King in London by having Queen Margaret proclaim "God and King Henry govern England." This sounds commonplace today, but omitting mention of the authority of the papacy was radical stuff 450 years ago. (Alulis & Sullivan, 1996).

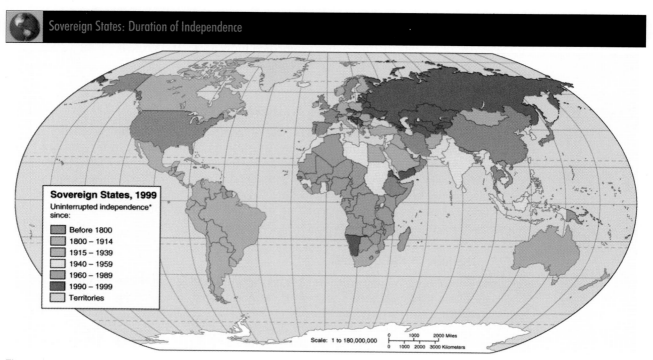

Sovereign States: Duration of Independence

Sovereign States, 1999
Uninterrupted independence*
since:

- Before 1800
- 1800 – 1914
- 1915 – 1939
- 1940 – 1959
- 1960 – 1989
- 1990 – 1999
- Territories

Scale: 1 to 180,000,000

Figure 6.1 on the opposite page gives you a sense of the recent rapid growth in the number of countries. This map gives you an opportunity to see the geographic dimensions of that growth. Notice that Asia and Africa have seen the most change. Most of the countries that now exist on those continents were colonies of a European country in 1940.

Modern Nationalism The evolution of nationalism took an important turn in the 1700s and began to change into its modern form based on the close association of the people and the state. Until that time, the link between the states and their inhabitants was very different. Most people were emotionally unconnected to the state in which they lived. As one study points out, "The Medieval Frenchman was a *subject* of the… monarch, not a *citizen* of France" (Guibernau, 1996:52). This changed once the people took control of the state and, therefore, identified with it. **Popular sovereignty** had been evolving slowly in Switzerland, England, and a few other places. But it accelerated when the American and French Revolutions dramatically shifted the basis of theoretical political authority in states away from the divine right of kings and toward the idea, as the American Declaration of Independence proclaimed, that governments derive their "just powers from the consent of the governed." While impact of the American Revolution took time to spread from the isolated United States, the French Revolution's doctrine of "liberty, equality, fraternity" was more immediate. The pens of such French philosophers as Rousseau, Voltaire, and Montesquieu spread the idea of popular sovereignty far beyond France's borders. Soon France's powerful legions added the sword to the tools that spread the philosophy of the national state throughout Europe.

From these beginnings, the idea of popular sovereignty and the belief in the right to national self-determination began to spread around the globe. Some countries were formed when a nation coalesced into a national state. This was true for Germany and Italy in the 1860s and 1870s. In other cases, national states were established on the ashes of empire. The Spanish empire fell apart in the 1800s, and the Austro-Hungarian and Ottoman empires collapsed after World War I. By the mid-twentieth century, nearly all of Europe and the Western Hemisphere had been divided into nation-states, and the colonies of Africa and Asia were beginning to demand independence. The doomed British and French empires soon vanished also. Only the Russian-Soviet empire survived—but not for long. Nationalism reigned virtually supreme around the world.

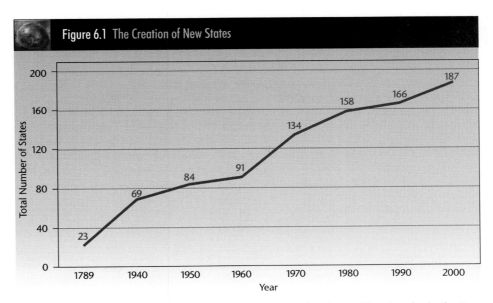

Figure 6.1 The Creation of New States

Data sources: CIA (2000); author's calculations. The numbers should be taken as approximate because of the controversies about how to count countries that merge, divide, or lose and regain independence.

This figure and the map on the opposite page portray the rapid growth in the number of countries in the international system. From the beginning of the sovereign state about 500 years ago, it took until 1940 for 69 states to evolve. In the intervening 60 years, that number has nearly tripled.

These developments were widely welcomed. An image of "populist-romantic nationalism" appealed to liberals on two grounds (Gellner, 1995:6). First, the idea of a nation contains an implied equality for all members. Liberal philosophers such as Thomas Paine in *The Rights of Man* (1791) depicted the nation and democracy as inherently linked in the popularly governed nation-state. Liberals also welcomed nationalism as a destroyer of empires. One well-known expression of this view was the call in 1918 of President Woodrow Wilson for the recognition of the right of people within empires to choose independence, if they wished, through a process of self-determination.

THE PREDICTED DEMISE OF NATIONALISM

World War II marked a sharp change in liberal philosophy about nationalism. Fascism and other forms of virulently aggressive nationalism helped bring about the horrors of the war and cast a pall on the concept of nationalism. Some observers believed that the war demonstrated that the state system was not only anachronistic but dangerous. The development of nuclear weapons, in particular, led some analysts to conclude that the sovereign state could no longer carry out the primary task of protecting the nation and therefore was doomed. The emphasis on free trade and growing economic interdependence also seemed to augur an end to the nationalist age. Indeed, the newly established (1945) United Nations symbolized the desire to progress away from conflictive nationalism and toward cooperative universalism.

The thrust of this thinking led numerous scholars to predict the imminent demise of the national state or, at least, its gradual withering away. As it turned out, such retirement announcements and obituaries proved reminiscent of the day in 1897 when an astonished Mark Twain read in the paper that

Some analysts predicted after World War II that nationalism was dying. The obituary notice proved premature, and nationalism continues to determine most people's political identification. Now, however, there are signs that nationalism and the related concept of sovereignty are weakening.

he had died. Reasonably sure that he was still alive, Twain hastened to assure the world: "The reports of my death are greatly exaggerated." Rather than retire or die, nationalism gained strength as a world force.

PERSISTENT NATIONALISM

The continued strength of nationalism is summarized in Figure 6.1, which shows that between 1940 and 2000 the number of states increased 271 percent. This growth is also evident in the color map, Sovereign States: Duration of Independence. For most of this time, the primary force behind the surge of nationalism was the anti-imperialist independence movements in Africa, Asia, and elsewhere. More recently, nationalism has reasserted itself in Europe. Germany reemerged when West Germany and East Germany reunited. More commonly, existing states disintegrated. Yugoslavia dissolved into 5 countries and Czechoslovakia became 2 states. Soon another state became 15 countries when the last great multiethnic empire, the vast realm of Russia, then the USSR, sank under its own ponderous weight like a woolly mammoth in the La Brea tar pits. Except for East Timor, Eritrea, Namibia, and Palau, all of the states that have achieved independence since 1989 are in Eastern Europe or are former Soviet republics (FSRs). There are also nationalist stirrings—in some cases demands—among the Scots, Irish, and Welsh in Great Britain, the Basques and Catalans in Spain, and among other ethnonational groups elsewhere in Europe (Caplan & Feffer, 1996).

It may seem contradictory, but the continuing strength of nationalism does not mean that those who earlier predicted its demise were wrong. It may only mean that they were premature. For all the continuing strength of nationalism, there are numerous signs that nationalism is waning and that states are weakening. In the last section of this chapter we will turn to the future course of nationalism. To help evaluate the current role of nationalism and to decide whether it is a good standard for the future, we should consider the positive and negative roles that nationalism plays in world politics.

NATIONALISM: BUILDER AND DESTROYER

When Pope John Paul II addressed the UN General Assembly in 1995, he spoke of the "difference between an unhealthy form of nationalism which teaches contempt for other nations or cultures, and... proper love of one's country."[1] What the pope could see about nationalism is that, like the Roman god Janus, it has two faces. Nationalism has been a positive force for political democratization and integration. It has also brought despair and destruction to the world. It is, in essence, both a uniting and a dividing force in international politics (McKim & McMahan, 1997).

THE BENEFICENT FACE OF NATIONALISM

Most scholars agree that in its philosophical and historical genesis, nationalism was a positive force. It has a number of possible beneficial effects.

Nationalism promotes democracy. The idea that the state is the property of its citizens is a key element of nationalism. This idea received a strong boost from the American and French Revolutions. If the state is the agent of the people, then the people should decide what policies the state should pursue. This is democracy, and, in the words of one scholar, "Nationalism is the major form in which democratic consciousness expresses itself in the modern world" (O'Leary, 1997:222). In short, nationalism promotes the idea that political power legitimately resides with the people and that governors exercise that power only as the agents of the people. Therefore, two Spanish scholars conclude, "Democracy is unimaginable without the notion of a sovereign people" (Cardús & Estruch, 1995:352).

Nationalism encourages self-determination. In modern times, the notion that nationalities ought to be able to preserve their cultures and govern themselves according to their own customs has become widely accepted. The English utilitarian philosopher John Stuart Mill's essay *On Liberty* (1859) argued that "where the sentiment of nationality exists... there is a prima facie case for unity of all the members of the nationality under... a government to themselves apart." Self-determination was also, as noted earlier, a key element of Woodrow Wilson's Fourteen Points (1918). Most recently, the ideal of self-determination led to the belief that people in colonies and those in multinational states such as Yugoslavia and the Soviet Union should be able to choose whether or not to become independent.

Nationalism discourages imperialism. A related impact of nationalism is that it strengthens resistance to outside occupation. One example is the recent history of the Chechens in the box, The Chechens: Death or Freedom.

Nationalism allows for economic development. Many scholars see nationalism as both a facilitator and a product of modernization. Nationalism created larger political units in which commerce could expand. The prohibition of interstate tariffs and the control of interstate commerce by the national government in the 1787 American Constitution are examples of that development. With the advent of industrialization and urbanization, the local loyalties of the masses waned and were replaced by a loyalty to the national state.

Subordinate nations have usually been shortchanged economically. This has been true in colonial empires, like those once controlled by the British and French, and in theoretically integrated multiethnic empires, such as the Soviet Union. This economic exploitation of colonized peoples is one cause of the poverty that persists in much of the world today. Similarly, many of the FSRs are, by political experience and economic circumstance, also less developed countries (LDCs). Most of the non-Russian peoples were conquered by and incorporated into Russia. Their languages, customs, and religions were often suppressed. Like other people in LDCs, their socioeconomic standards are lower than those in the country that once controlled them. The six predominantly Muslim FSRs (Azerbaijan, Kazakhstan, Kyrgyzstan, Tajikistan, Turkmenistan, and Uzbekistan) have an average per capita GDP that is only about 32 percent of Russia's. By another telling standard, the infant mortality rate in the six Muslim republics is 65 percent higher than it is in Russia. It is certain that these new countries face years of economic hardship, but, from their perspective, at least their efforts will be devoted to their own betterment.

Nationalism allows diversity and experimentation. It has been argued that regional or world political organization might lead to an amalgamation of cultures or, worse, the suppression of the cultural uniqueness of the weak by the strong. By contrast, diversity of culture and government promotes experimentation. Democracy, for instance, was an experiment in America in 1776 that might not have occurred in a one-world system dominated by monarchs. Diversity also allows different cultures to maintain their own values. Political culture varies, for example, along a continuum on which the good of the individual is on one end and the good of the society is on the other end. No society is at either extreme of the continuum, but Americans and people in some other nations tend toward the individualism end and its belief that the rights of the individual are more important than the welfare of the society. Chinese and people in yet other countries tend more toward the communitarian end of the continuum and hold that the rights of the individual must be balanced against those of the society and sometimes even be subordinated to the common good.

THE TROUBLED FACE OF NATIONALISM

The benevolent view of nationalism that dominated the earlier part of this century is no longer commonly held. President Woodrow Wilson may have promoted national self-

(continued on page 140)

The earlier, multinational state of Yugoslavia collapsed because it did not command the internal loyalty of most of its people. Instead, Yugoslavia atomized amid deadly conflict into the states and restive provinces shown here.

THE CHECHENS: DEATH OR FREEDOM

That nationalism is an antidote for imperialism is amply demonstrated by the Chechens. The approximately one million Chechens are a largely Islamic people living in the northern Caucasus region just west of the Caspian Sea. Chechnya (or the Chechen Republic) encompasses about 6,000 square miles (a bit larger than Connecticut). Imperial Russia began a campaign in 1783 to conquer the Chechens that went on for so long and was so fierce that the Russian poet Mikhail Lermontov wrote in 1832 of the badly outnumbered Chechens, "Their god is freedom, their law is war." Even after Russia finally established control in the mid-1800s, rebellions were a regular event. It seemed, as one military governor warned, that the Russians and their czar "would find no peace as long as a single Chechen remains alive."[1]

The same might have been said about the peace of Soviet commisars. During World War II, Moscow deported the entire Chechen population to the east and away from the invading Germans. Stalin suspected the Chechens might assist the Germans under the old theory that my enemy's enemy is my friend. Even though one-third of all Chechens died during their time in the gulag (an acronym for "Main Directorate of Corrective Labor Camps"), they remained defiant. As Aleksandr Solzhenitsyn wrote in *The Gulag Archipelago* (1973), "There was one nation that would not give in... [to] submission—and not just individual[s]..., but the whole nation to a man. These were the Chechens.... And here is an extraordinary thing—everyone was afraid of them. No one could stop them from living as they did. The [Soviet] regime which had ruled the land for thirty years could not force them to respect its laws."[2]

The Chechens were allowed to return to their native land in the mid-1950s but remained restive. Once the USSR dissolved, the Chechen quest for self-rule redoubled, and in a ferocious clash that cost between 60,000 to 100,000 lives, they achieved a level of autonomy in 1996. After a brief interlude, fighting resumed in 1999, and in early 2000 they were again overrun by Russian arms. The struggle continues, however, as it has for over two centuries. Current

One benefit of nationalism is that it encourages people to resist outside domination. That reality is portrayed here by two dead Russian soldiers sprawled amid rubble in Grozny, the Chechen capital. A grimly determined Chechen rebel and a burning Russian armored vehicle are in the background. The Russians have been trying to break the Chechens' national spirit for almost 200 years; the effort has failed.

Russians leaders, like czars and commissars before them, must think ruefully of their attempts to subdue the Chechens, a people whose national anthem goes in part:

> We were born at night, when the she-wolf whelped.
> In the morning, as lions howl, we were given our names.
> In eagles nests, our Mothers nursed us,
> To tame a stallion, our Fathers taught us....
> Granite rocks will sooner fuse like lead,
> Than we lose our Nobility in life and struggle....
> Never will we appear submissive before anyone,
> Death or Freedom—we can choose only one way....
> We were born at night, when the she-wolf whelped.
> God, Nation, and the Native land.

determination as a basic political principle, but recent American presidents have warned of the ills of unrestrained nationalism. "Militant nationalism is on the rise," President Clinton cautioned, "transforming the healthy pride of nations, tribes, religious, and ethnic groups into cancerous prejudice, eating away at states and leaving their people addicted to the political painkillers of violence and demagoguery."[2] Clinton's

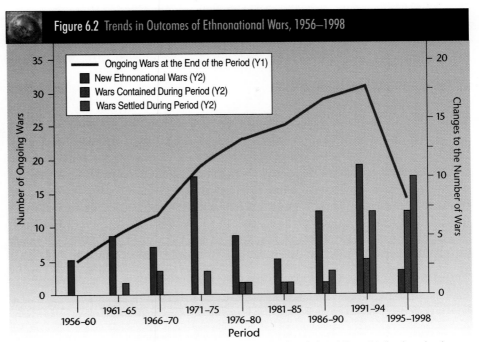

Figure 6.2 Trends in Outcomes of Ethnonational Wars, 1956–1998

Source: Ted Robert Gurr, "Global Conflict Trends, 1946–1999," Reprinted by permission of the Center for Systemic Peace at http://members.aol.com/CSPmgm/conflict.html.

Ethnopolitical conflict within countries escalated sharply through most of the 1990s and was much more common than conflict between countries. There was a marked decline in ethnopolitical conflict toward the end of the decade, as can be seen in this figure. Whether that drop is a short-term anomaly or represents a new period of much reduced domestic conflict remains to be seen.

warning was based on fact. The number of ongoing ethnonational conflicts rose steadily from 5 in 1960 to 18 in 1975, to 31 in 1994. Then the number of conflicts declined sharply to 14 in 1998. Some analysts suggest that ethnonational conflict has peaked and will continue to decline (Gurr, 2000a). Perhaps; but it is probably too early to tell whether this sharp drop is an anomaly or a positive sign. Unfortunately, whatever the number of conflicts, the intensity and magnitude of ethnonational conflicts remain high, as evident in Figure 6.2 (Gurr, 2000; Saideman, 1997). The ills that nationalism brings can be subdivided into how we relate to others and the lack of fit between states and nations.

How We Relate to Others

By definition, nationalism is feeling a kinship with the other "like" people who make up the nation. Differentiating ourselves from others is not intrinsically bad, but it is only a small step from the salutary effects of positively valuing our "we-group" to the negative effects of devaluing the "they-group." Four aspects of negative nationalism are xenophobia, internal oppression, external aggression, and lack of concern for others.

Xenophobia   One too-frequent product of nationalism is **xenophobia,** the suspicion, dislike, or fear of other nationalities. Negative nationalism also often spawns feelings of national superiority and superpatriotism, and these lead to internal oppression and external aggression. It is this reality that moved Voltaire to lament in 1764 that "it is sad that being a good patriot often means being the enemy of the rest of mankind."[3]

Feelings of hatred between groups are especially apt to be intense if there is a history of conflict or oppression. Past injuries inflicted "by another ethnic group [are] remembered mythically as though the past were the present," according to one scholar.[4]

Nationalism can cause ethnic hatred and other types of xenophobia. Many people might think of Fiji as a South Pacific paradise. That image was damaged, however, when ethnic hatred spurred indigenous Fijians to overthrow the government of an ethnic Indian Fijian prime minister and to attack Indo-Fijians and their property. The violence is apparent in this photograph of a guard protecting what is left of an Indo-Fijian-owned store in the capital city of Suva after it was ransacked in May 2000 by indigenous Fijians.

For Serbs, this heroic lore centers on the battle of Kosovo in 1389, in which the Ottoman Turks defeated Serbia's Prince Lazar, thus beginning five centuries of Muslim domination. The battle, according to one commentary, is "venerated among the Serbs in the same way Texans remember the Alamo." Adds Serb historian Dejan Medakovic, "Our morals, ethics, mythology were created at that moment, when we were overrun by the Turks. The Kosovo cycle, the Kosovo myth is something that has permeated the Serbian people."[5]

It is a tragic irony that the symbolic battle of Kosovo is now entwined with the future of Kosovo Province in what is left of Yugoslavia. As a result of the ethnic ebb and flow over the centuries in the region, 90 percent of Kosovo is made up of ethnic Albanians, who are mostly Muslims, rather than the predominately Christian Orthodox Serbs.

Internal Oppression Negative nationalism can frequently lead to internal oppression because, as one scholar puts it, "Nationalism is a scavenger [that] feeds upon the pre-existing sense of nationhood" in an effort "to destroy heterogeneity by squeezing" diverse ethnic groups "into the Nation," by trying to suppress the culture of minority groups, or by driving them out of the country (Keane, 1994:175). The ethnic cleansing frenzy in Bosnia-Herzegovina between 1992 and 1995, the genocidal attacks on the Tutsis by the Hutus in Rwanda in 1994, and the attacks on ethnic Albanian Kosovars by Serbian Kosovars and Serbian Yugoslav troops in 1998 and 1999 are the most recent horrific outbreaks of xenophobic violence, but there are many other lesser instances.

For example, trouble erupted in Fiji, which has an image of near paradise, when in May 2000 a group claiming it was acting in the name of ethnic Fijians (49 percent of the population) overthrew the government headed by the country's first prime minister from the ethnic Indian (46 percent of the population) minority. The Indo-Fijians are descendants of sugar plantation workers brought into the Pacific island republic when it and India were both British colonial possessions. Shops and other property owned by those of Indian heritage were looted and burned in some areas, and, in the words of one

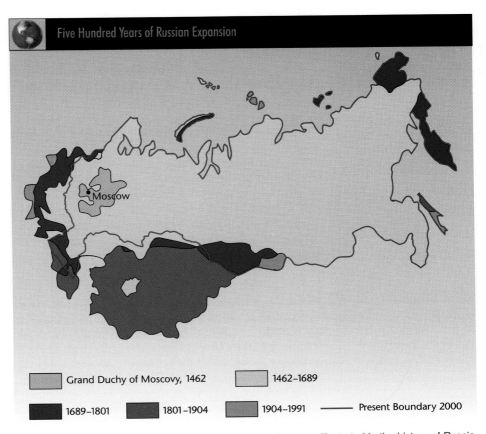

Five Hundred Years of Russian Expansion

Moscow

Grand Duchy of Moscovy, 1462   1462–1689

1689–1801   1801–1904   1904–1991 —— Present Boundary 2000

Nationalism has positive and negative effects, and both these are illustrated in the history of Russia. Among the negative effects, nationalism often prompts expansionism. The Grand Duchy of Moscovy was about half the size of Maine when it was founded in about 1480. It expanded under Russian czars and then Soviet commissars to become what was the world's largest country.

Indo-Fijian leader, "The future is very clear now. This [coup] proves Indians will have to make their way out of this country."[6]

At its extreme, nationalism engenders the sense of superiority and hatred that festered in Nazi Germany. The Germans thought that their "Aryan nation" was at the top of a ladder that descended downward to where, at the bottom, Slavic peoples were considered marginal humans and were to be kept as virtual and expendable slaves in segregated and degrading conditions. Jews and Gypsies were "nonpeople" and "racial vermin" to be exterminated, along with the insane and homosexuals. "The highest purpose of a *folkish state*," Hitler preached in *Mein Kampf*, is "preservation of those original racial elements which bestow culture and create the beauty of a higher humanity. We, as Aryans, can conceive of the state only as a living organism of [German] nationality." Whatever the toll in human life and suffering, and whether it is Indian businesses being ransacked in Suva, the capital of Fiji, in 2000, or Jewish businesses being destroyed in Berlin in 1938, the intolerance is driven by the same force: xenophobia.

External Aggression This sense of superiority and devaluing of other people, which is so often part of fervent nationalism, can also become an excuse for the conquest and domination of neighbors. Underneath its ideological trappings, the Soviet Union was a classic multiethnic empire built on territories seized by centuries of czarist Russian expansion and furthered by Soviet arms. From its beginning 500 years ago as the

Did You Know That:

Russians have traditionally seen themselves as the successor to the earlier great Western empires centered in Rome and Constantinople. In fact the Russian royal title of *czar* (tsar) is a derivative of Caesar.

15,000-square-mile Duchy of Moscovy (half the size of Maine), Russia, and then the USSR, ultimately grew to be the world's largest country. This expansion is shown in the map on page 143.

Many of those territories have been lost, but there are strong suspicions that a rejuvenated Russia will try to reclaim them. Such concerns have been heightened by a number of actions or statements, including the 1996 passage by Russia's parliament, the Duma, of a resolution expressing the view that the dissolution of the Soviet Union had been illegal and, by inference, that all the now-independent FSRs should once again come under Moscow's control.

For now Russia's economic and other travails mean that it is not in a position to even consider trying to reassert the earlier domination of its neighbors that it had in the days of czars and comrades. Indeed, old-fashioned imperialism may have become too costly economically and diplomatically to pursue in the future. Yet there is gnawing concern that the German theoretician Karl Marx was prescient when he warned long ago that "the policy of Russia is changeless. Its methods, its tactics, its maneuvers may change, but the polar star of its policy—world domination—is a fixed star."[7]

Lack of Concern for Others The mildest, albeit still troubling, trait of negative nationalism is a lack of concern for others. Because we identify with ourselves as the we-group, we tend to consider the they-group as aliens. Our sense of responsibility—of even human caring—for the "theys" is limited. People in most countries accept the principle that they have a responsibility to assist the least fortunate citizens of their national we-group. All of the economically developed countries (EDCs) have extensive social welfare budgets, and the people in those countries engage in countless acts of charity, from donating blood to distributing toys for tots. The key is that we not only want to help others in our we-group, we feel that we have a duty to do so.

Internationally, most of us feel much less responsible. Horrendous conditions and events can occur in other countries that evoke little notice relative to the outraged reaction that would be forthcoming if they happened in our own country. For example, average income for the poorest 20 percent of the world population is just a little more than a dollar a day and accounts for a miniscule one percent of the world GDP. The grueling lives of these people stand in stark contrast to what life is like for the wealthiest 20 percent, who have 86 percent of the globe's wealth. The wealthy countries conduct massive public efforts to assist their own poor. International efforts pale in comparison. Chapter 15 will discuss foreign aid in detail, but the bottom line is that in 1998 the EDCs through bilateral aid and through international organizations donated $57.9 billion in aid to LDCs. That is a laudable figure, but it is less stellar when you consider that the amount equaled only about one-quarter of one percent (0.0028) of their collective GDPs. The $11.5 billion U.S. effort was especially dismal compared to its wealth and, at about one-eighth of one percent (0.0013) of its GDP, placed last among EDCs. Indeed, compared to a per capita U.S. foreign aid expenditure of $42, Americans spent $309 per person on alcoholic beverages, over 7 times as much as they spend on the world's poor.

Even when sudden violence or other types of calamities occur that bring suffering and death to the innocent, our reactions differ greatly when the victims are "others." More than one observer commented sardonically that at the same time in late 1999 and early 2000 when Americans were gripped with the drama of the fate of the Cuban refugee child, Elián González, tens of thousands of Ethiopian children were suffering, and often dying, from starvation and its related diseases in drought-stricken Ethiopia. Yet this catastrophe drew little press coverage and even less public notice in the United States. "I'm afraid," Ethiopia's foreign minister, Sayoum Mesfim, noted accurately, that "Africa gets a response from [the wealthy countries] only when people see the skeletons on their [television] screens and in their newspapers."[8]

Nationalism leads us to focus on ourselves and be much less concerned with others. Americans were captivated for months in late 1999 and early 2000 with the fate of one refugee child, Elián González, and whether he would be granted political asylum in the United States or returned to his father in Cuba. Most Americans paid no attention to the tens of thousands of Ethiopian children who, at the same time, were starving to death or succumbing to diseases related to inadequate nutrition.

The Lack of Fit between Nations and States

The spaces occupied by nations and states often do not coincide (MacIver, 1999). In fact, most states are not ethnically unified, and many nations exist in more than one state. This lack of "fit" between nations and states is a significant source of international (and domestic) tension and conflict. There are four basic disruptive patterns: (1) one state, multiple nations; (2) one nation, multiple states; (3) one nation, no state; (4) multiple nations, multiple states.

One State, Multiple Nations The number of **multinational states** far exceeds that of nationally unified states. Indeed, only about 10 percent of all countries truly fit the nation-state concept. The rest of the countries fall short of the ideal by at least some degree, with, at the extreme, 30 percent having no national majority. The map on the next page showing the degree of demographic unity of each country indicates racial and ethnic, as well as national, diversity. Most of these minority groups do not have separatist tendencies, but many do or could acquire them.

Canada is one of the many countries where national divisions exist. About 27 percent of Canada's 31 million people are ethnically French (French Canadians) who identify French as their "mother tongue" and first language (Francophones). The majority of this group reside in the province of Quebec, a political subdivision rather like (but politically more autonomous than) an American state. Quebec is very French. Of the province's 7.1 million people, 83 percent are Francophones, Catholic, and culturally French.

Many French Canadians have felt that their distinctive culture has been eroded in the predominantly English-culture Canada. There has also been a feeling of economic and other forms of discrimination. The resulting nationalist sentiment in the province gave rise to the separatist Parti Québécois and to a series of efforts in the 1980s and

Global Distribution of Minority Groups

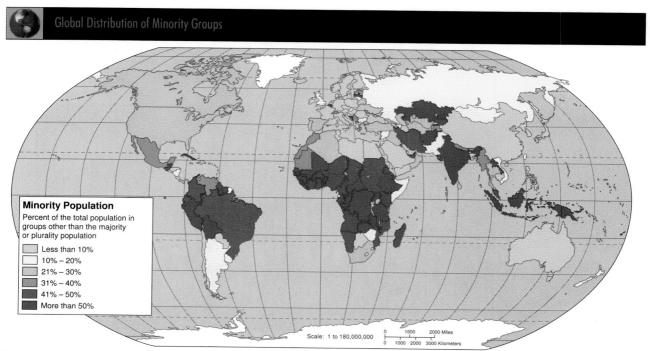

Minority Population

Percent of the total population in groups other than the majority or plurality population

- Less than 10%
- 10% – 20%
- 21% – 30%
- 31% – 40%
- 41% – 50%
- More than 50%

Scale: 1 to 180,000,000

0   1000   2000 Miles
0   1000   2000   3000 Kilometers

The concept of a nation-state envisions political states, each of which contains just one nation. Moreover, virtually all of the people of that nation would live within the state. In reality, few countries fit this ideal. As this map shows, most countries are ethnically and nationally diverse. Because they do not have aspirations for independence or autonomy, not all minority populations are nations, but many are.

1990s to obtain autonomy, even independence, for the province. The most recent of these was a referendum on separation held in 1995. The voters in Quebec rejected independence, but this time with only a razor-thin majority of 50.6 percent voting *non* to sovereignty and 49.4 percent voting *oui*.

It is too early to tell when, or even if, another referendum will occur (Seymour, 2000). Nationalist feelings continue in Quebec, but they have eased based on better economic and cultural conditions for the Francophones and, perhaps, the (at least temporary) reluctance to continue an unsuccessful struggle. One poll has found that the percentage of those in Quebec favoring independence or autonomy fell from 50 percent in 1995 to 38 percent in 1999.[9] "The sense of anger that allowed Quebecers to contemplate a break with Canada just isn't there any more," comments one observer. "The movement is a little bit stalled," concedes the editor of the pro-independence newspaper. "Even a lot of [separatist] organizers are asking themselves publicly whether it is possible to win. That's quite a change."[10]

Many multinational states have not been as fortunate as Canada, which has largely avoided bloodshed over its national division. Other states have suffered extraordinary violence. The death and destruction spawned by clashing ethnonationalist groups was given voice by Prime Minister Agathe Uwilingiyamana when the killing began in Rwanda in 1994. "There is shooting. People are being terrorized. People are inside their homes lying on the floor. We are suffering," she said in a broadcast from the capital, Kigali, appealing for help.[11] Those were her last public words; soon after, she was dragged from her refuge in a UN compound and murdered by marauding Hutus.

One Nation, Multiple States A second departure from the nation-state ideal occurs when nations overlap the borders of two or more states. When **multistate nationalities** exist, nationalist sentiments create strong pressures to join the politically separate nation within one state. This impulse has frequently played a role in recent international politics when a nation was divided into two states, as indicated by the examples of North and South Vietnam, North and South Korea, East and West Germany, and the two Yemens. Ireland and Northern Ireland provide another possible example, although the Scottish heritage of many of the Protestants in the North makes the existence of a single Irish nationality in two states controversial. In any case, a single nation that dominates two states has an urge to unite the states and, thus, itself. Today only Korea (and arguably Ireland) remains as an example of such a division, and the two Koreas have begun a dialogue that may eventually erase first their hostility and then their border. But there is often conflict over union, a tension that led to fighting in four of the examples (Vietnam, Korea, Ireland, and Yemen).

Another recipe for trouble is where most members of a nation live in their own state while other members of the nation live as a minority population in one or more adjoining states. This creates conflict when those minority populations wish to join the motherland or when the motherland claims the area in which they live. This demand is called **irredentism.** Even if a nation-state is not (yet) seeking to incorporate all the members of the nation, surrounding states with minority segments of that nationality may react with worried hostility.

The long-standing instability in the southern Balkans is based in large part on such overlapping ethnonational and state boundaries. One reason for concern about the fate of Kosovo Province, given its majority Albanian population and the Serb-dominated government of Yugoslavia, is that if fighting were to resume, neighboring Albania might be drawn into the conflict on the side of the Kosovan Albanians. The urge for a greater Albanian state that includes all the region's Albanians could also destabilize neighboring Macedonia, which is about 22 percent Albanian. "We must also fight for our freedom in Macedonia, just as Albanians are fighting for their freedom in Kosovo," proclaimed one ethnic Albanian in Macedonia.[12]

To complicate matters further, the Macedonians themselves might be the source of irredentist conflict with Greece. The Macedonians in Yugoslavia declared their independence in 1991 and, reasonably, named their country Macedonia. This, however, angered and worried Greece, just to the south. The most northern part of Greece is its Macedonian region, and Athens is worried that independent Macedonia might have irredentist designs on the Macedonians in Greece. The Greeks and the Macedonians also squabble over which culture can properly claim to trace part of its lineage to ancient Macedon and its hero Alexander the Great (356–323 B.C.).

One Nation, No State A third pattern where the state and nation are not congruent occurs when a national group is a minority in one or more states, does not have a nation-state of its own, and wants one. The Palestinians are a familiar example of a *stateless nation*; their status is detailed in the box, Palestinians: A Nation without a State.

Yet another stateless nation is that of the Kurds, an ancient, non-Arab people of the Mesopotamian region, who are mostly Sunni Muslims. The most famous of all Kurds was Saladin, the great defender of Islam who captured Jerusalem from the Christians (1187) and who then defended it successfully against England's King Richard I (the Lion-Heart) and the other invading Christians during the Third Crusade (1189–1192). Estimates of the Kurdish population range between 14 million and 28 million. About half the Kurds are in Turkey; Iran and Iraq each have another 20 to 25 percent; and smaller numbers reside in Syria and Armenia. Sporadic and continuing attempts to establish an independent Kurdistan have caused conflicts with the countries in which the Kurds live. These disputes also sometimes involve outside countries, such as when the United States launched cruise missile attacks on Iraq in September 1996 after Baghdad's forces attacked one of the Kurdish groups in northern Iraq. Also, concern

(continued on page 150)

PALESTINIANS: A NATION WITHOUT A STATE

Two nations, Israeli and Palestinian, both have long existed in the same area. Most of that territory is now controlled by Israelis; the Palestinians mean to get enough of it back to create a Palestinian state.

The dispute goes back to Abraham and his two sons: Isaac, who founded the Jewish nation, and Ishmael, the symbolic father of all Arabs. Such biblical stories are important because the Jews base their claim to Israel partly on Jehovah's promise to Moses that he would deliver the Hebrews out of Egypt to "a land flowing with milk and honey" (Exodus 3:8). The catch is that God directed the Hebrews "unto the place of the Canaanites"—occupied territory. Jewish fortunes changed, though, and after a millennium the last vestige of their control in the region was ended by the Romans in A.D. 70. During the diaspora that followed, most Jews were scattered throughout the world (Farsoun, 1997).

The Palestinians have existed in the region for centuries and may date back to the pre-Hebrew tribes in the area. In any case, Palestinian Arabs were the area's primary inhabitants for many centuries and comprised 90 percent of the population in 1920. Most Palestinians are Muslims, but many are Christians.

In Europe, however, Zionism gathered strength in the nineteenth century. **Zionism** is the nationalist, not strictly religious, belief that Jews are a nation that should have an independent homeland (Shlaim, 1999; Wheatcroft, 1996). After the British captured Palestine from Turkey during World War I, they allowed limited Jewish immigration into the territory. The trickle became a flood when those fleeing Nazi atrocities swelled the Jewish population in Palestine from 56,000 in 1920 to 650,000 by 1948 (compared to nearly 1 million Arabs). In rapid succession, fighting for control erupted, Britain turned the issue over to the UN, and Arab leaders rejected a UN plan to partition Palestine into a Jewish state and an Arab state. Israel won the ensuing war in 1948 and acquired some of the areas designated for the Arab state. At least 500,000 Palestinians fled to refugee camps in Egyptian-controlled Gaza and elsewhere; another 400,000 came under the control of Jordan in an area called the West Bank (of the Jordan River).

Since then, Israel has fought and won three more wars with its Arab neighbors. In the 1967 war Israel captured considerable territory, including the Sinai Peninsula and Gaza from Egypt, the Golan Heights from Syria, and the West Bank (including East Jerusalem) from Jordan. Victory, however, did not bring Israel peace or security. The most important reason is the unresolved fate of the West Bank, which is central to the quest of Palestinians for their own autonomous, even independent, homeland.

Israel has retained control of the West Bank for two

Sometimes, it is not clear when a state comes into existence or whether it exists at all. The Palestinians have territory they govern. As he does here reviewing Palestinian troops, their leader Yasser Arafat projects the image of a head of state. Moreover, a number of countries have diplomatic relations with the Palestinian National Authority. Yet most experts would say that Palestine is not a state, at least not quite.

reasons. One is security. The West Bank thrusts far into Israel's central region, and Israel has refused to withdraw before peace is fully achieved. Part of the full-scale peace, the Israelis say, is the cessation of terrorist acts against them. Israel is also reluctant to quit the West Bank because the territory is emotionally central to many, especially very conservative Jews, who call the West Bank by its biblical names of Judea and Samaria. Israel would find it especially difficult to surrender control of East Jerusalem, which is a holy city for Jews, as it also is for Muslims and Christians.

The fate of Israel, the Palestinians, and the occupied territories has created an explosive mix. In addition to the wars, there have been numerous terrorist attacks against Israel and against Jews and others around the world, Israeli incursions into Lebanon, and repeated clashes between Israelis and West Bank Palestinians.

There have also been positive developments. Pressures from outside countries and war weariness among both Israelis and Arabs created the incentive to try to settle their differences. Peace agreements were reached between Israel and Egypt in 1979, after meetings with President Carter at the presidential retreat at Camp David, and between Jordan and Israel in 1994. Additionally, Israelis and

Palestinians have searched to find common ground. Progress has been made. Most Arabs no longer advocate the dissolution of Israel. An increasing number of Israelis are willing to admit that the Palestinians cannot be kept a stateless people in perpetuity.

Yet as the last decade or so illustrates, the peace process has been maddeningly slow and uncertain. The 1990s began positively with a Middle East peace conference in Madrid in 1991 and the election in 1992 of Israeli prime minister Yitzhak Rabin. He advocated compromise with the Arabs and authorized secret talks held in Norway with the Palestine Liberation Organization (PLO). In the resulting Oslo agreement, (1) Israel recognized the PLO as "the representative of the Palestinian people"; (2) the PLO renounced violence and recognized Israel's right to exist; and (3) the two sides agreed to a plan to create Palestinian self-rule in the West Bank and Gaza by century's end. Rabin and PLO chairman Yasser Arafat signed the pact before a beaming President Clinton, who waxed eloquently. "The children of Abraham... have embarked together on a bold journey."[1] Soon thereafter, Israel turned over some of its authority in Gaza and parts of the West Bank to the Palestinians, and Arafat became the first head of the Palestinian National Authority (Robinson, 1997).

Peace soon retreated, however, under extremist attack. Rabin was assassinated in 1995 by a fanatical Israeli, who denounced his victim for "setting up a Palestinian state [in the West Bank] with an army of terrorists... [that Israelis soon] will have to fight."[2] Arab extremists also struck out to murder the peace. Hezbollah and other groups launched terrorist attacks that increased Israeli doubts about whether Arabs could be trusted (Arian, 1996).

A year later, these worries helped conservative Benjamin Netanyahu come to power in Israel. He argued that the Oslo pact had "brought neither peace to Israel nor real security" and dismissed the idea of an independent Palestine. He pledged to expand existing Jewish settlements in the West Bank and declared undivided Jerusalem to be "the eternal capital of the Jewish people."[3]

Relations between the Palestinians and Israelis once again plummeted. The Palestinians accused Netanyahu of reneging on the Oslo Accords. Israel countered that the Arafat government had not, as promised, prevented terrorist attacks on Israelis or punished the perpetrators.

In the 1999 elections, the Israelis' longing for peace won out over their simultaneous suspicion and fear of the Palestinians and other Arab neighbors, and Netanyahu was defeated by Ehud Barak. A protégé of the slain Yitzhak Rabin, Barak told his followers, "If Yitzhak is looking down on us from where he may, he knows that we together will fulfill his legacy. We need to strengthen our country's security by moving forward to peace agreements."[4]

Whatever Barak's intentions, his path was uncertain. Hopes rose when talks with Syria began over the Golan Heights, but fell when the negotiations stalled. Israel withdrew in May 2000 from the security zone it had occupied for 18 years in southern Lebanon, but whether that will increase stability by eliminating a sore point or increase conflict by bringing militant Arabs to Israel's northern border is unclear. Renewed talks with the Palestinians led President Clinton to invite Arafat and Barak to Camp David for intensive negotiations. The hope was to recreate the success of the first Arab-Israeli meeting there. Camp David II failed, however, primarily over the seemingly intractable issue of Jerusalem. Arafat insisted on claiming East Jerusalem; Barak was equally adamant that Israel would not give it up.

Whatever their personal views may be, both Barak and Arafat face strong pressures from within their own camps that make compromise and progress difficult (Barzilai, 1999). Some Israelis see the Palestinians as evil. Orthodox Rabbi Ovadia Yosef, spiritual adviser to the Shas political party thundered, "You are bringing snakes beside us.... Will you make peace with snakes?"[5] Moreover, Barak heads a government made up of a seven-party coalition. That weak position led him, for example, to agree that any transfer of the Golan Heights back to Syria could only come after a referendum. One of the parties left his coalition when Barak went to Camp David, and he was rebuked by an opposition leader for abandoning the idea of "Zionist Jewish" Israel.[6]

Similarly, Arafat has been attacked by Arab hard-liners (Shikaki, 1998). For example, one critic has written that Arafat is too willing to "surrender with a fig leaf of dignity" to achieve "an unjust peace" so that he could fly "flags of fantasy," that is, imagine himself the leader of a Palestinian state.[7] It is also the case that the Israeli withdrawal from Lebanon increased the pressure on Arafat. As he explained, "My public sees Hezbollah as heroes who succeeded in getting the Israeli arm out of Lebanon, and believes that this is the route we should take as well."[8]

Negotiations between Israel and the Palestinians continued after Camp David II, perhaps because the alternative was too terrible to contemplate. As one senior U.S. official put it, "The entire Middle East is standing at the edge of a cliff."[9] The Palestinians deferred in September 2000 their threat to declare independence, but they will not be put off forever. A unilateral declaration could bring war once again to the region. So could the kind of intense violence that erupted in October 2000 in the West Bank and Gaza and spread to the Lebanese border. That dangerous place is not new in the ancient history of the Middle East. One can but hope that the leaders on both sides will step away from the precipice and, instead, look to antiquity to remember the words of the book of Isaiah (52:7), "How beautiful upon the mountains are the feet of him that bringeth good tidings, that publisheth peace."

that Turkey is sometimes brutal in its campaign to quell its restive Kurds is one factor standing in the way of Turkey's wish to join the European Union.

Overall, then, the lack of fit between nations and states has been and is a major source of conflict. Given the rampant nationalism that still exists, it is likely to continue as a problem. Africa is such a patchwork quilt of nations and states that the Organization of African Unity has refused to give aid to secessionist movements. As President Julius K. Nyerere of Tanzania put it, "African boundaries are so absurd that they need to be recognized as sacrosanct" (Jensen, 1982:58). That may be good policy for existing states, but it will surely be challenged by nations that desire self-determination.

Multiple Nations, Multiple States When one examines the global demographic and political map closely, it becomes clear that the most common pattern is a complex one in which several states and nations overlap. This labyrinth of people and places is well illustrated by the ethnonational composition of many of the former Soviet republics.

India is so divided by various religious, ethnic, language, and social groups that it is a wonder that the country exists at all. To focus on just one ethnonational group, the Hindu Tamils, who are split between India and Sri Lanka, are a stateless nation. The Tamils in Sri Lanka have fought a long, bloody guerrilla war against the Buddhist Sinhalese majority there. After losing ground, the Tamils staged a strong offensive in early 2000, cutting off a large government force in Jaffna, the most likely Tamil capital. This fighting raised the possibility of outside intervention by India, which is worried about the possible slaughter of Tamils if the tide of war changes, and about Tamil separatism spreading to India's Tamils if the Sri Lankan Tamils gain independence or autonomy.

The FSRs make up another hodgepodge of nations and states. Only about half the people in the Soviet Union were Slavic Russians. Twenty percent were related Slavic peoples, and another 20 percent were Turkic and other traditionally Muslim peoples ethnically related to the peoples in nearby countries such as Turkey, Iran, and Afghanistan. Caucasus-region Indo-Europeans, Balts, and Finno-Karelian people each constituted about 3 percent of the population, and the Romanian-related Moldovans were about 1 percent. In all, the USSR contained 58 ethnic/national groups of 100,000 or more people.

In the aftermath of the breakup of the USSR, this overlap of ethnonational groups and states became a volatile mixture. The most widely reported conflict began in 1991 when, once again, the approximately one million Muslim Chechen people in Russia revolted, as discussed in the box, The Chechens: Death or Freedom page 140. That gruesome struggle continues. In addition to this struggle, Armenians (Christian Orthodox) and Azerbaijanis (Muslim) fought bitterly over the territory of Nagorno-Karabakh, a predominantly Armenian enclave that was placed entirely within Azerbaijan by Moscow in 1923. The Armenians won, but at great cost to both sides. Georgians (Christian Orthodox) fought with the Abkhazians after that Muslim group declared their independence from Georgia. The Moldovans are eager for close ties, perhaps unification, with their ethnic kin in Romania.

The dissolution of the USSR left many Russians in other FSRs. A large number have returned to Russia, but many

Many countries face problems when they contain more than one nation. Sri Lanka has endured a civil war between its dominant (mostly Buddhist) Sinhalese majority and its (mostly Muslim) Tamil minority. The conflict has lasted almost two decades and has claimed more than 50,000 lives. The hostility between the two ethnonational groups is evident in this photo taken in the capital city, Colombo, of a Sri Lankan soldier in front of a sign saluting Sri Lanka's largely Sinhalese army for its (so far unsuccessful) efforts to destroy the opposing Tamil force, called the Tamil Tigers.

remain in other FSRs. Therefore, another problem could arise through Moscow's intervention on behalf of Russians who are being maltreated or who Moscow, for its own purposes, claims are suffering. Such a pretext took Germany into Czechoslovakia's German-populated Sudetenland in 1938, and it could be used by Russia as an excuse to move against, dominate, and perhaps reincorporate one or more FSRs. This has not yet occurred, but there have been threats. President Yeltsin once cautioned that "it is our duty" to pay "close attention to the problems of [Russians] living in neighboring states."[13]

NATIONALISM AND THE FUTURE

Now that we have seen the benign and malevolent faces of nationalism past and present, we can turn to the future of nationalism. We should ask ourselves (a) whether we favor the spread or curtailment of nationalism and (b) whether it will persist or wane as the primary focus of political identity for most people.

SELF-DETERMINATION AS A GOAL

One way to examine your feelings about nationalism is to extend the concept to every group that wishes to be sovereign (Moore, 1997). If being a proud member of a nation is good for you, and if the nationalistic urge of your people to govern itself in its own nation-state is laudable, then should not that privilege—or perhaps right—be extended to everyone? Americans, for one, asserted in 1776 that their nation had a right to have its own state, and they have fiercely defended it ever since.

Although it is impossible to determine exactly where the ultimate limits of national identification are, one study estimates that "there are over 5,000 ethnic minorities in the world" (Carment, 1994:551). Each of these groups has the potential to develop a national consciousness and to seek independence. Before dismissing such an idea as absurd, recall that political scientists widely recognize the existence of Barber's (1995) Jihad tendency: the urge to break away from current political arrangements and, often, to form into smaller units. World politics in the last decade or so has been marked by strong nationalist movements (Musgrave, 1997). Many of these have waged bloody campaigns of separation, and the incidence of protest, rebellion, and communal conflict, and the magnitude and intensity of these conflicts, has risen markedly during the past half-century (Gurr, 2000; Gurr & Haxton, 1996).

There are numerous good reasons to support **self-determination**. In addition to the benefits of nationalism noted earlier, self-determination would end many of the abuses that stem from ethnic oppression. If all ethnic groups were allowed to found their own sovereign units or join those of their ethnic brethren, then the tragedies of Bosnia, Chechnya, East Timor, Kosovo, Rwanda, and many other strife-torn peoples and countries would not have occurred.

Did You Know That:

There is an active native Hawaiian independence movement. Haunai-Kay Trask, who heads Kalahui Hawaii, the largest Hawaiian nationalist group, contends that her group's aim is "decolonization in the last area of the world to decolonize—the Pacific Basin."[1] The state of Hawaii held a referendum in 1996 among native Hawaiians to determine their preferences for the future. The result was a resounding 73 percent "yes" for independence.

There are also, however, numerous problems associated with the unlimited extension of self-determination. *Untangling groups* is one problem. Various nations are intermingled in many places. Bosnia is such a place; Bosnian Muslims, Croats, and Serbs often lived in the same cities, on the same streets, in the same apartment buildings. How does one disentangle these groups and assign them territory when each wants to declare its independence or to join with its ethnic kin in an existing country?

The *dissolution of existing states* is a second problem that the principle of self-determination raises for many states, ranging from Canada about Quebec, through Great Britain about Scotland, to Spain about the Basque region and Catalonia (Keating, 1996).

Table 6.1 Characteristics of a Microstate, a U.S. State, and a U.S. City

	Kiribati	Rhode Island	Dayton
Population	79,500	990,225	178,540
Territory (sq. mi.)	226	1,545	55
Per Capita Wealth*	920	24,765	23,238

*Per capita GDP for Kiribati; per capita personal income for Rhode Island and Dayton, Ohio.

Data source: World Almanac (2000).

Some analysts worry about instability associated with the limited ability of microstates to sustain themselves economically or to defend themselves. The sovereign state of Kiribati is smaller in most ways than the geographically smallest U.S. state, Rhode Island, and Dayton, Ohio, the U.S. city with only the one-hundredth largest population.

Americans also need to ponder this problem. They have long advocated the theory of a right of self-determination. The Declaration of Independence asserts just this when it declares that "When in the course of human events, it becomes necessary for one people to dissolve the political bands which have connected them with another" and to assume "separate and equal" status, then it is the "right of the people to alter or to abolish [the old government] and to institute [a] new government." President Woodrow Wilson made much the same claim when he told Congress in 1918 that "self-determinism is not a mere phrase. It is an imperative principle of action."[14] One has to wonder, however, how Wilson would have applied this principle to national minorities in the United States. Do, for instance, Wilsonian principles mean that all Americans should support those native Hawaiians who claim correctly that they were subjugated by Americans a century ago and who want to reestablish an independent Hawaii?

Microstates present a third problem related to self-determination. The rapidly growing number of independent countries, many of which have a marginal ability to survive on their own, raises the issue of the wisdom of allowing the formation of what have been called microstates. These are countries with tiny populations, territories, and/ or economies. Such countries have long existed, with Andorra, Monaco, and San Marino serving as examples. But in recent years, as colonialism has become discredited, more of these **microstates** have become established.

Many **microstates** lack the economic or political ability to stand as truly sovereign states. One set of measures can be seen in Table 6.1's comparison of a tiny Western Pacific island country, the smallest U.S. state, and the one-hundredth most populous U.S. city. There are 40 microstates, countries with populations of less than 1 million. These microstates comprise more than one-fifth of all the world's countries. In fact, as Figure 6.3 depicts, if you added up all their populations, they would amount to just 12.4 million people, smaller than Ecuador's population; about 45 percent that of Tokyo, the world's most populous city; and only 38 percent of California's population.

The perplexity about microstates is that one can simultaneously support the theory of self-determination and worry about the political liability that microstates cause. This quandary is exacerbated by the fact that larger predatory powers, not the microstates, are the real source of danger. In a perfect world, the military and economic strength of a state would not matter. But the world is not perfect, and therefore it is reasonable to evaluate microstates within the reality of the international system that exists. Most microstates have scant ability to defend themselves against internal or external attack. That was amply demonstrated in 2000 when a handful of indigenous Fijians lead by a failed insurance salesman managed to seize the country's prime minister and a number of ministers, to force the resignation of the president, and to force an agreement barring Fijians of ethnic Indian descent from political power. After a prolonged crisis, the rebel leader was arrested, but some of his

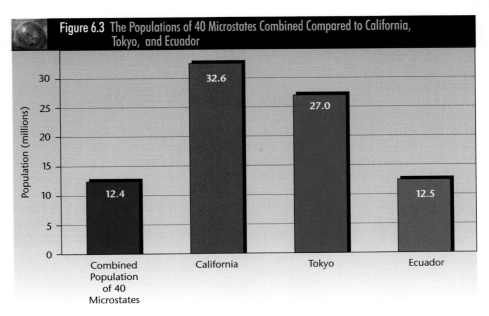

Figure 6.3 The Populations of 40 Microstates Combined Compared to California, Tokyo, and Ecuador

Data sources: *World Almanac (2000)*, author's calculations.

oppressive actions stood. This was evident in the fact that he was charged with treason for overthrowing the ethnic Fijian president, but no charges were filed for ousting the Indo-Fijian prime minister.

Many microstates also lack a sustainable economic base. The sovereign state of Nauru, a tiny (8 square miles) island country of some 10,000 people, which lies 300 miles to the northeast of Papua New Guinea, bases virtually its entire economy on the export of phosphates, used for fertilizer. This product is derived from guano, the droppings of seabirds, which covered most of the island and has provided Nauruans with considerable income. Unfortunately, 80 percent of the island has been strip-mined to its rock base, leaving it, in one description, "a pitted, ghostly moonscape." Worse, what is left of the guano will soon be gone, and Nauru will have no economy at all. Nauruans may have to accept Australia's offer to resettle them on an island off its east coast. "It would be very sad to leave our native land; but what else can we do?" grieves 84-year-old James Aingimea. "The land of our ancestors has been destroyed."[15]

Thus the exigencies of the real world suggest that some standard has to be applied to independence movements. There is a large array of ethnonational groups with aspirations that arguably are just as legitimate as were American goals in 1776 or East Timorese desires were in 1999. Which independence movements should be favored? Which should not? There are critics of self-determination who charge that "liberalism's embrace of national self-determination [has] raised more questions than it [has] answered" (Hoffmann, 1995:163). Or, as another scholar puts it, "Self-determination movements... have largely exhausted their legitimacy.... It is time to withdraw moral approval from most of the movements and see them for what they mainly are—destructive" (Etzioni, 1993:21).

By contrast, some commentators advocate broad support of self-determination, which one analyst calls "the most powerful idea in the contemporary world" (Lind, 1994:88). Between these two ends of the spectrum of opinion, many seek a set of standards by which to judge whether or not a claim to the right of secession is legitimate. One such standard is whether a minority people is being discriminated against by a majority population (Hannum, 1998). Perhaps it would be wiser for the international community to guarantee human and political rights for minority cultural groups than to support self-determination to the point of *reductio ad absurdum*. Whatever the standard though, it is certain that applying the principle of self-determination is difficult in a complex world (Talbott, 2000).

NATIONALISM: WILL THE CURTAIN FALL?

A critical question in the future of nationalism, and indeed the course of world politics, is whether nationalism will significantly weaken or even die out. The answer is unclear. The existence of divergent identities based on language and other cultural differences extends as far back into time as we can see. From a biblical perspective, there may have been a single people at the time of Adam and Eve and their immediate descendants. But later in the first book of the Bible, God reacts with dismay by the attempt of humans to build the Tower of Babel up to the heavens in an effort to elevate themselves to the deity's level. To defeat that pretentious plan, God creates different languages to complicate communication. "Behold," God commands, "the people is one, and they have all one language.... [L]et us go down, and there confound their language, that they may not understand one another's speech" (Genesis 11:6-7).

Whether this tale is taken literally or symbolically, the point is that diverse cultural identities are ancient and, some analysts would say, important, perhaps inherent, traits of humans that stem from their urge to have the psychological security of belonging to a we-group. One scholar contends, for example, that being a member of a nation both "enables an individual to find a place... in the world [in] which he or she lives" and, also, to find "redemption from personal oblivion" through a sense of being part of "an uninterrupted chain of being" (Tamir, 1995:432). Yet it must also be said that group identification and nationalism are not synonymous. The sense of sovereignty attached to cultural identification is relatively modern. "Nationalism and nations have not been permanent features of human history," as one scholar puts it (O'Leary, 1997:221). Therefore, nationalism, having not always existed, will not necessarily always be the world's principal form of political orientation.

What does the future hold? Some scholars believe that nationalism will continue to flourish as the main source of political identification; other scholars expect nationalism to eventually cease to be an important political phenomenon. The most common view among political scientists is a middle position that holds that nationalism will persist for the foreseeable future as a key sense of the political identification of most people, but that nationalism will not enjoy the unrivaled center stage presence it has had for several hundred years (Ishiyama & Breuning, 1998; Eley & Suny, 1996).

Also unclear is what would follow if state-centric nationalism were to die out. Some scholars believe that it will be replaced by culture, religion, or some other demographic characteristic as the primary sense of political self. Yet another group of scholars argues that a sense of global nationalism could emerge based on the similarities among all humans and their common experiences, needs, and goals. This envisages "a nation coextensive with humanity" that would then come together in a "United States of the World" (Greenfeld, 1992:7).

What can we conclude from this scholarly disagreement? Will nationalism persist "until the last syllable of recorded time," to borrow words from Shakespeare's *Macbeth*? The answer is that the script for tomorrow's drama on the world stage is still being written by the world's political playwrights. If we think the world drama important, each of us should lend a hand to establishing the plot, casting the actors, and writing the dialogue.

CHAPTER SUMMARY

1. Nationalism is one of the most important factors in international politics. It defines where we put our primary political loyalty, and that is in the nation-state. Today the world is divided and defined by nationalism and nation-states.

2. Nations, nation-states, and nationalism are all key concepts that must be carefully defined and clearly differentiated and understood.

3. The political focus on nationalism has evolved over the last five centuries.

4. After World War II, some predicted an end to nationalism, but they were wrong. Today nationalism is stronger, and the independence of Afro-Asian countries, the former Soviet republics, and other states has made it even more inclusive.

5. Nationalism has both positive and negative aspects.

6. On the plus side, nationalism has promoted democracy, self-government, economic growth, and social/political/economic diversity and experimentation.

7. On the negative side, nationalism has led to isolationism, feelings of superiority, suspicion of others, and messianism. Nationalism can also cause instability when there is a lack of fit between states and nations. Domestic instability and foreign intervention are often the result of such national instability. Nationalism has also led to a multiplicity of microstates.

8. There are many enthnonational groups that are seeking or may seek independence. Among other considerations, this could lead to the further multiplicity of microstates.

9. In a world of transnational global forces and problems, many condemn nationalism as outmoded and perilous. Some even predict its decline and demise. Such predictions are, however, highly speculative, and nationalism will remain a key element and powerful force in the foreseeable future.

CHAPTER 7

TRANSNATIONALISM: THE ALTERNATIVE ORIENTATION

A speedier course than lingering languishment
Must we pursue, and I have found the path.

Shakespeare, *Titus Andronicus*

Not all those that wander are lost.

J. R. R. Tolkien, *The Fellowship of the Ring*

An invasion of armies can be resisted, but not an idea whose time has come.
Victor Hugo, *Histoire d'un Crime*, 1852

CHAPTER OBJECTIVES

After completing this chapter, you should be able to:

- Understand the concept of transnationalism.
- Examine and discuss transnational ideas and ideologies.
- Understand the underpinnings of transnationalism.
- Understand the origins of globalism and how it relates to idealism, postmodernism, and postinternationalism.
- Identify evidence for the increasing level of transnational interaction.
- Discuss the growth of transnational movements and organizations.
- Understand the transnational feminist philosophy.
- Identify transnational feminist activity and trace its progress.
- Discuss the transnational elements of religion.
- Examine both the positive and negative roles of religion in world politics.
- Analyze, as a case study, the role of Islam in world politics.
- Examine the cohesive and divisive effects of transnational culture.
- Discuss the future role of global political and cultural organization.

Breathtaking change has been the most common theme in books about international politics written during the last decade. "The onset of the post-Cold War era in 1990 entailed far more sweeping and revolutionary changes than were even apparent at the time," one study begins (Klare & Chandrani, 1998:vii). "These are exciting times to study global politics.... We have entered into a period of turbulent transitions," another study declares on the first page of its preface (Mansbach & Rhodes, 2000:xi).

Such sentiments are not new. We humans have often chafed at the world in which we live and have yearned to change it. "Had I been present at the creation, I would have given some useful hints for the better ordering of the universe," a dismayed King Alfonso the Wise (1221–1284) of Castile and León (in what is now Spain) once mused.

One of the suggestions heard often over the course of human history is that people take a broader, more inclusive view of humanity. This call for change reflects frustration with the traditional way that we humans organize ourselves politically along ethnonational lines. Whether that political organization is the modern nation-state or some earlier form, such as the city-state, there have been critics who urge that we look beyond such territorially bounded structures. These critics urge us to adopt transnational affiliations as an alternative to traditional identification with and loyalty to the nation-state.

THE ORIGINS AND IMPACT OF TRANSNATIONALISM

The concept of **transnationalism** includes a range of loyalties, activities, and other phenomena that connect humans *across nations and national boundaries*. Transnationalism is, therefore, inherently counternationalist in that it undermines nationalism (and its tangible manifestation, the national state) by promoting cross-national political activity. These interactions, in turn, raise the possibility of people adopting a sense of primary political identification that does not focus on the nation-state.

This chapter will explore the bases and evidence of transnationalism in the world. We shall see that the origins of transnationalist thought are ancient. It is also the case, though, that transnationalism is today, more than in the past, a real process rather than just a philosophical perspective. As this chapter will make clear, transnationalism is multifaceted; it is potentially unifying and divisive; it is both praised and vilified.

Some streams of transnational thought are referred to as globalism, cosmopolitanism, or other such encompassing words. The globalist school of thought is closely associated with the idealist approach to politics, discussed in chapter 1, and is the primary focus of this chapter. There are, however, other transnational movements, such as transnational religion and the transnational women's movement, that are both transforming and undermining the state. For all their diversity, what these transnational beliefs and activities have in common is that they offer alternative political orientations to traditional nationalism. Thus, this chapter surveys part of the political road less traveled by.

Transnationalism springs from two sources. Global interaction is one. The degree to which economic interdependence, mass communications, rapid travel, and other modern factors are intertwining the lives of people around the world is a constant theme of this book. Human thought is the second source of transnationalism. The philosopher René Descartes argued in *Discourse on Method* (1637) that intellect is the essence of being human. "I think, therefore I am," he wrote. People can think abstractly, can conceive of what they have not experienced, and can group ideas together to try to explain existence and to chart courses of action.

The idea of a universal community of humankind is an ancient one that extends back to the Roman emperor Marcus Aurelius (A.D. 121–180) and other followers of the philosophy of Stoicism. Nationalism, the view of political loyalty tied to the territorial state, is a relatively modern political focus.

TRANSNATIONAL THOUGHT

Our ability to think beyond our personal experiences is important in understanding current transnationalism because until recently it has persisted on the periphery of world politics. Therefore we need to spend time examining transnational ideas and ideologies. Whether or not it is literally true, as Ecclesiastes (I:9) tells us, that "There is no new thing under the sun," it is often profitable to understand that many very modern ideas have very ancient origins.

Early Transnational Thought

Transnational thought in Western culture can be traced to the Stoics of ancient Greece and Rome. Stoicism flourished from about 300 B.C. to A.D. 200, a period marked by the eclipse of the small Greek city-states and the rise of the large Macedonian, then Roman, empires. This expansion of political boundaries was accompanied by a new school of thought founded in about 300 B.C. by the Cypriot philosopher Zeno.

The word stoicism has come to mean accepting one's burdens without complaint, but the philosophy of classical Stoicism embodies much more. Stoicism appealed to people to see themselves as individuals who are part of humanity, not as members of one or another smaller political community. Thus, Stoic outlook was cosmopolitan, a word derived from combining the Greek *cosmos* (world) and *polis* (city). This view is central to our discussion of transnationalism. It is not too much of a stretch to say that Stoics had a sense of themselves as global citizens. Reflecting this, the Roman emperor Marcus Aurelius wrote of himself in *Meditations*, "my... country, so far as I am [the emperor] is Rome, but so far as I am a man, it is the world."

In time, Stoicism declined, but its influence did not vanish. To the contrary, the writings of the Stoic philosophers influenced later thinkers, as we shall see. Also, some elements of Stoicism were incorporated into early Christian thought in the West. These

Christians often passively resisted the Romans and other persecutors; they practiced a communitarian lifestyle; they held a universal view of humankind.

It is important to note that other ancient, non-Western great philosophical traditions contain teachings that are similar to the cosmopolitan thrust of Stoicism. Philosophies such as Confucianism and religions such as Buddhism and Hinduism all contain transnational elements that parallel those in Stoicism. For example, Siddhartha Gautama (ca. 563–483 B.C.), who became known as the Buddha, urged that we adopt a universal perspective. "Whatsoever, after due examination and analysis, you find to be conducive to the good, the benefit, the welfare of all beings," he taught, "that doctrine believe and cling to, and take it as your guide."

Later Transnational Thought

The idea of transcending local political structure and power remained alive over the centuries. "We have it in our power to begin the world over again," the revolutionary Thomas Paine proclaimed in *Common Sense* (1776). We remember Paine as an American patriot, but that is an ill-fitting description. He was, in fact, what one analyst has called "the kind of man who would today be forced to inscribe 'Revolutionary' in the box asking for his profession."[1] Paine was committed to a philosophy, not to any country. He described himself as a "citizen of the world" and was dubious about countries because they "limited citizenship to the soil, like vegetation." It is true that Paine's writing helped galvanize Americans during their struggle for independence from the British, but of that effort, Paine wrote in 1779 that he would have "acted the same part in any other country [if] the same circumstances [had] arisen there which have happened here."[2] Paine supported the American Revolution not to establish yet another narrow nationality but because he believed, as he wrote in *The Rights of Man* (1779), that it represented a "new method of thinking" and was "in great measure the cause of mankind." Paine also supported the French Revolution, which he saw as continuing the work of its American counterpart and leading a "march on the horizon of the world" that "neither the Rhine, the [English] Channel, or the ocean... can arrest." That transnational march, Paine predicted, would lead to free trade and to establishing an international congress to resolve differences among states (Fitzsimons, 1995:579). Thus today's World Trade Organization and United Nations would not have surprised him.

During the same revolutionary period in which Paine was writing, the philosopher Immanuel Kant took the idea of international cooperation for peace even further. Kant wrote in *Idea for a Universal History from a Cosmopolitan Point of View* (1784) that countries should abandon their "lawless state of savagery and enter a federation of people in which every state could expect to derive its security and rights... from a united power and the law-governed decisions of a united will."

Early communist theory also contained a strong element of transnational thought that stressed the commonality of humankind and foresaw a global community. To understand this aspect of communism, it is important to put aside its application in authoritarian states such as the Soviet Union and China and, instead, to examine the thinking of nineteenth-century German communist philosophers such as Friedrich Engels and Karl Marx. They believed that the economic classes inherent in capitalism were the source of human divisions and that states were capitalist tools that the wealthy class, the bourgeoisie, used to keep control of the working class, the proletariat. The "history of all hitherto existing society is the history of class struggles," *The Communist Manifesto* (1848) explained; "workingmen have no country." What Engels foresaw was that once communism was triumphant, "as soon as class rule... [is] removed, nothing more remains to be repressed, and a special repressive force, a state, is no longer necessary." This means, Engels reasoned, that the state becomes "superfluous, and then dies out of itself."

Contemporary Transnational Thought

After existing on the periphery of political thought during the halcyon days of nationalism, transnational thought came increasingly to the fore in the twentieth century. The main thrust of this perspective was covered in the extensive discussion of idealism in chapter 1. As noted there, idealists contend that a transition from a conflictive, state-centric system to a cooperative, interdependent system is both under way and is desirable.

Another perspective that is related to transnationalism is called **postmodernism.** At its core, postmodernism contends that reality is subjective rather than objective. This view holds that reality is created by the ways that we think and by our discourse (writing, talking) about our world. Postmodernists believe that we have become trapped by stale ways of conceiving of how we organize and conduct ourselves.

As such, postmodernism is especially important for transnationalism because it seeks to examine the ways we organize ourselves politically. Postmodernists believe that organizing ourselves politically around a geographically defined country is only an image in our mind reinforced by the way that we discuss politics. Postmodernists believe, for instance, that political identity is structured by such national identities as American or Mexican, and they want to change the discourse on political identity so that it could also include, for instance, being a woman or a human as a focus of political identity.

A closely related concept is **postinternationalism** (Hobbes, 2000). This idea holds that in a turbulent world, people have begun to change their political identity and, in many cases, are giving much greater weight to subnational political identities, such as their ethnic group, or to transnational political identities, such as their gender. From this perspective, we are entering an era where "international" is becoming an outmoded concept that misses the multiple levels, from local to global, with which people identify and around which they organize themselves politically.

Whether it be Stoic transnationalism, idealism, postmodernism, or postinternationalism, such seemingly radical ideas have often alarmed those who trod the traditional path. Paine's revolutionary fervor was welcomed by Americans in rebellion, but once the United States was established, Paine seemed dangerous to many. Former president John Adams wrote in 1807 that he doubted that "any man in the world has had more influence on its inhabitants or affairs for the last thirty years than Tom Paine." That worried Adams, though, and he condemned Paine's efforts to revolutionize the world as being "a career of mischief" conducted by "a mongrel between pig and puppy, begotten by a wild boar and a bitch wolf" (Fitzsimons, 1995:581).

Despite the fulminations of Adams and other traditionalists about the alternative path propounded by philosophers such as Zeno and Paine, the idea has persisted. "Nationalism is an infantile disease. It is the measles of the mind," Albert Einstein wrote in 1921. Such ideas remained on the periphery, however, until the years following World War II. Since then, theory has begun to assume at least limited reality. In fact, it may be that the ideas of Paine and similar thinkers, no matter how much they were dismissed in their own eras as odd, even dangerous, have better stood the test of time than the views of their detractors. As Paine foresaw, one scholar notes, "the world today [is] moving gradually toward greater integration and homogenization through the lowering of trade barriers, the growing significance of communication networks, international financial and legal agreements, and transnational bodies such as the European Union and the United Nations" (Fitzsimons, 1995:582). It would surely have pained John Adams to see this.

TRANSNATIONAL INTERACTION

Whatever we may wish, transnationalism is occurring. Its existence is more than a matter of intellect; it stems from myriad interactions across national borders. Such contacts have certainly always existed, but they have grown at an explosive rate during the past fifty years or so. What is even more significant is that the scope and level of these international interactions will continue to expand exponentially in the foreseeable future. The change is being driven by or made possible by a range of factors—economics, communications, transportation, and organizations. You will see, among other things, that each of these factors both promotes and is dependent on the others.

TRANSNATIONAL ECONOMICS

Economic interchange among people is bringing the world together in many ways. The intensifying reality of economic interdependence was addressed in chapter 1 and, thus, need not be taken up here beyond iterating two basic points. The first is that the international economy affects each of us through our jobs, what we pay for the goods and services we consume, the interest rates we pay on loans, for school, and a broad array of other economic aspects of our lives. Second, as economically intertwined as we are today, there is every prospect that the connections will grow even more complex and comprehensive.

What is important to see here is that economic interchange has a transnational impact that extends beyond dollars and cents. Many analysts believe that economic interchange is bringing people together transnationally through a familiarity with each other and each other's products. Some of these contacts are interpersonal; more have to do with the role of international economics in narrowing cultural differences and creating a sense of identification with trading partners. This is illustrated by Japan. In 1999, 51 percent of Japan's trade was with the Western industrialized countries. By contrast, Asian countries accounted for only 37 percent of Japan's trade. The impact of this trade flow on Japan's sense of identity is evident in one recent study. It found that when Japanese were asked whether they felt Japan was more closely associated with Asian or Western countries, 40 percent replied "Western countries," compared to 34 percent who replied "Asian countries," with the rest divided or unsure. When those who answered "Western countries" were asked why they identified that way, 89 percent said it was because of "economic interaction" (Namkung, 1998:46). The degree to which we are absorbing each other's products is evident in Figure 7.1, which shows the increased amount of the wealth that Americans produce that is spent on imported goods and services.

> **Did You Know That:**
> The basic unit of the metric system, the meter, was named and defined by the French in 1793 as one ten-millionth of the distance between the Equator and the North Pole. To increase accuracy using atomic clocks, the meter was redefined by the International Bureau of Weights and Measures in 1983 as the distance that light will travel through a vacuum in one-299,792,458th of a second. For those who are without an atomic clock, a meter is equal to 39.37 inches.

MAP
Dependence on Trade, p. 5

Some integrative changes also occur because of technical matters, such as the need to standardize products so that, in a sense, one size fits all countries. Despite determined resistance, for instance, Americans are gradually being edged toward adopting the metric measure system used by most of the rest of the world. Americans now commonly buy 2-liter bottles of soda rather than half-gallons; it is hard to fix a car these days without a metric socket wrench set; and since the passage of the North American Free Trade Agreement (NAFTA), the instructions to many U.S.–made products are now in Spanish (for Mexico) and French (for Quebec and elsewhere in Canada) as well as English. These changes stem from the rigors of economic competition. As one U.S. senator wrote to President Clinton, urging him to promote adopting the metric system, "In order for this nation's business to be truly competitive with the rest of the world, we must play by the same rules."[3]

TRANSNATIONAL COMMUNICATIONS

It is almost impossible to overstate the impact that modern communications have had on international relations (Tehranian, 1999; Vlahos, 1998; Deibert, 1997). In only a century and a half, communications have made spectacular advances, beginning with

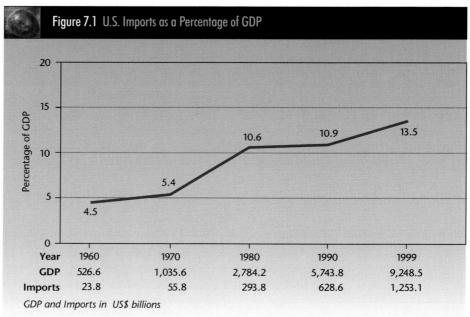

Figure 7.1 U.S. Imports as a Percentage of GDP

Year	1960	1970	1980	1990	1999
GDP	526.6	1,035.6	2,784.2	5,743.8	9,248.5
Imports	23.8	55.8	293.8	628.6	1,253.1

GDP and Imports in US$ billions

Data sources: Bureau of the Census (1999); IMF (2000).

This figure shows that an increasing percentage of the wealth produced in the United States (GDP) is spent on imports, which means that more and more of what Americans own and consume comes from abroad. The mounting expenditures on imports are a part of the impact of the transnational economic interdependence on the globalization process.

the telegraph, followed by photography, radio, the ability to film events, telephones, photocopying, television, satellite communications, faxes, and now computer-based Internet contacts and information through e-mail and the World Wide Web.

One of the impacts of global communications is to undermine authoritarian governments. As such, the rapid mass communications that are taken for granted in the industrialized democracies are still greeted with suspicion by authoritarian governments. In China, those with Internet access must register with the police, and China's State Bureau of Security warns that "All organizations and individuals are forbidden from releasing, discussing, or transferring state secret information on bulletin boards, chat rooms, or in Internet news groups."[4] Penalties include imprisonment and heavy fines for the use of the Internet to "split the country" (air dissent). Whatever Beijing's hopes are to control "leaks" in and out of the country, they are probably roughly akin to Peter trying to hold back the sea by putting his finger in the dike.

In a process that has been labeled "democratic internationalism," transnational communications have also provided citizens from different countries with the ability to interact, exchange views, organize political activity, and undertake political action (Gilbert, 1999). In one example, activists mobilized transnationally to oppose the proposed Multilateral Agreement on Investment (MAI) designed to ease the flow of investment capital among the 29 countries in the Organization for Economic Cooperation and Development (OECD). Opponents claimed that the MAI would, among other negative aspects, allow corporate investors to move money too freely in and out of countries to the disadvantage of workers in those countries. Among other places, the Internet presence established by the anti-MAI movement can be found at the "Stop MAI" Web site of the group Public Citizens: Global Trade Watch at: http://www.citizen.org/pctrade/MAI/maihome.html. The opposition helped stall the MAI in the late 1990s, but the anti-MAI forces are wary that there will be an attempt to revive it.

Did You Know That:

Communications technology is spreading with increasing speed. From the technology's inception to its use by 50 million people, it took radio 28 years, television 13 years, and the Internet a mere 4 years.

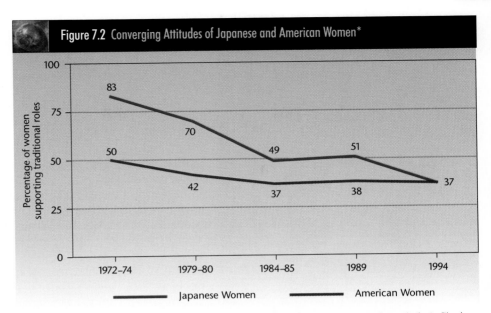

Figure 7.2 Converging Attitudes of Japanese and American Women*

*This figure incorporates data from surveys that asked similar, but not always the same, questions about accepting or rejecting traditional roles for women and men. Questions were not always asked in the same year in both countries.

Data source: Ladd and Bowman (1996).

Transnational communications help create similar values across national boundaries. Changes in attitudes about the roles played by women began earlier in the United States, Canada, and Europe than elsewhere. Feminist attitudes have, however, spread globally to even very traditional societies, such as Japan's, as this figure shows.

Transnational communications also have enabled women to learn more about their relative societal status in other countries and to forge transnational action networks, all of which has arguably helped change women's attitudes, as evident in Figure 7.2. In another realm, images from Somalia, Bosnia, and elsewhere of starving, slain, brutalized fellow humans have helped create pressures to intervene. It is also the case that more and more people around the globe are getting their news from the same sources. The most obvious omnisource is CNN, which now reaches virtually every country in the world.

Modern communications are also bringing the gruesome realities of war into people's living rooms and the earlier sanitized, even sometimes heroic, image is largely a thing of the past. While televised pictures of starving Somalis helped propel U.S. troops into Somalia in 1993, later-televised images of a slain, nearly naked U.S. soldier being dragged by a rope through the dusty streets of Mogadishu created a public uproar that soon forced President Clinton to withdraw the troops.

TRANSNATIONAL TRANSPORTATION

Just as transnational communication rapidly transmits our images and thoughts across national borders, transnational transportation carries our products and people with a speed that would have been incomprehensible not very long ago. This point about the advent of rapid, mass transnational transportation makes it worth thinking about the lives of Mohammed El-Wasimy of Egypt and Elizabeth "Ma Pampo" Israel of Dominica. They are both thought to have been born in 1875 and are reputed to be the world's oldest people.

One thing that modern transportation has done during the life of the two modern Methuselahs is to make the world more familiar and interdependent by creating the ability to move huge amounts of what we produce across borders and oceans. Just before

A sense of how quickly the world is changing can be gained by thinking of the life of the world's oldest man, Mohammed El-Wasimy, who was reputedly born in 1875. He is seen here with his young wife, Fatma, age 75, at their home in Egypt. El-Wasimy was already 28 years old when the first airplane flew, 43 when the communists took over Russia, 94 when a human walked on the moon, and 116 when communism fell in the USSR. He is older than most countries and virtually all international organizations. More and more people will live as long as El-Wasimy. If you do, what will your world be like when you reach his current age early in the twenty-second century?

they were born, the most famous merchant vessel of its time, the *Flying Cloud*, (1851–1874) was 229 feet long. In the youth of these very senior citizens, the world's largest ship was the then-immense *Great Eastern*, which was 693 feet long. Now if the two gazed seaward, they might spot the modern tanker *Seawise Giant*, which at 1,504 feet long (almost one-third of a mile) is so large that crew members often use bicycles to travel from one point to another on the ship. This ship is part of the world merchant fleet that is made up of almost 28,000 freighters and tankers, which have a total capacity to carry, at any one moment, over 733 million tons of goods.

Air transportation also brings our national products to one another, but it is even more important as a way of carrying people between countries. When El-Wasimy and Ma Pampo were 20 years old, Lord Kelvin, president of the Royal Society, Great Britain's leading scientific advisory organization, dismissed as "impossible" the idea of "heavier-than-air flying machines."[5] Just eight years later, in 1903, Orville and Wilbur Wright proved Lord Kelvin wrong. Now international air travel has become almost routine, and each year rapidly carries hundreds of millions of travelers between countries. Caracas, Venezuela, is closer in travel time to New York than is Los Angeles, and London is not much farther. In 1997 about 22 million Americans flew overseas, and about 24 million people flew in the opposite direction. It strains the imagination, but given the speed of the supersonic transport (SST) and the time-zone differences, it is possible to fly across the Atlantic from London to New York, and when you land the local time in New York will be earlier than the time in London when you took off.

TRANSNATIONAL ORGANIZATIONS

The growth in the number and activities of private transnational organizations, called nongovernmental organizations (NGOs), was introduced in chapter 3. What is important here about NGOs is that many of them reflect a disenchantment with existing political organizations based in or dominated by states. "Stifled by the unwillingness of nations and international organizations to share decision making, and frustrated by the failure of political institutions to bring about reform," one study explains, "political activists began to form their own cross-border coalitions in the 1970s and 1980s" (Lopez, Smith, & Pagnucco, 1995:36). These coalitions born of frustration led to an upsurge in the founding of NGOs to act as the organizational arm of transnational social movements, such as those that promote women's rights, nuclear disarmament, or environmental protection.

The global women's movement provides an illustration of the process. First, as with many causes, the advances that women have made internationally have not generally come at the initiative of national governments. Instead, the place of women's issues on the international political agenda is largely the result of women's groups pressing governments and international organizations to address their concerns.

Second, NGOs facilitate the building of networks of contacts and interaction across borders. The networks of NGOs and national organizations that share an interest in a specific aspect of global society are called transnational advocacy networks (TANs). This networking function was one of the valuable benefits for the approximately 30,000, mostly female delegates from some 2,000 NGOs who met in Huairou, China. The meeting paralleled the **fourth UN World Conference on Women (WCW)**, which met in Beijing in 1995. "The real action here," said Sri Lankan delegate Hema Goona-tilake, "is hearing and learning, forming networks."[6]

Third, NGOs bring pressure on governments to support the NGOs' various trans-national programs. Reviewing the impact of the successive World Conferences on Women, the New York-based Women's Environment and Development Organization (WEDO) reported recently that 70 percent of the world's national governments have now drawn up plans to advance women's rights, and 66 countries have established national offices of women's affairs. "What's happened... could not have happened without Beijing," one scholar notes. "The energy, the activity of Beijing has not gone away."[7]

Modern transnational trade, communications, transportation, and organizations would not be relevant here if they merely brought people into contact and had no political impact. The fact is, though, that these transnational phenomena are important politically. They facilitate links among people that transcend state boundaries and help establish identifications that supplement or sometimes even take the place of nation-alism. Some of these connections are global; others are narrower. But they are all trans-national and are creating a different political mind-set. To explore these transnational links further, we can look in more depth at the transnational women's movement and also explore transnational religion and transnational culture.

TRANSNATIONAL WOMEN'S MOVEMENT

It strains the obvious to point out that women globally have been and remain second-class citizens economically, politically, and socially. Historical data is scant, but there are stark current statistics. No country has achieved socioeconomic or political gender equality. There are relative differences between countries, with the gap between men

This is a rare photograph indeed. Normally, pictures of world leaders are made up entirely, or nearly so, of men. This photograph of world leaders gathered at Harvard University is composed exclusive-ly of women, all but two of whom have been prime ministers of their countries. From left to right those standing (and their country) are: Tansu Ciller (Turkey), Hanna Suchocka (Poland), Kazimiera Prun-skiene (Lithuania), Benazir Bhutto (Pakistan), Mary Eugenia Charles (Dominica), and Kim Campbell (Canada); seated are Violetta de Chamorro (Nicaragua), Vigdis Finnbogadottir (president, Iceland), and Laura Liswood (executive director, Council of Women World Leaders). That there are enough women leaders to form a council represents change and progress.

The Gender Gap: Inequalities in Education and Employment

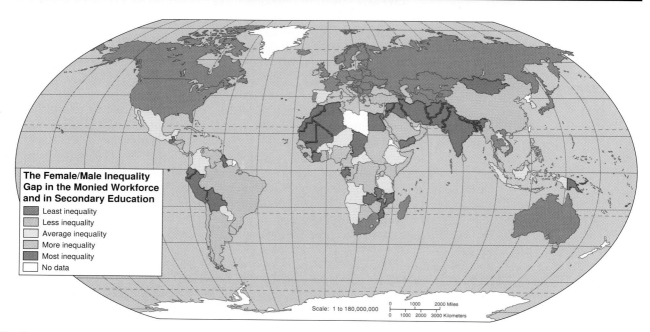

The Female/Male Inequality Gap in the Monied Workforce and in Secondary Education

- Least inequality
- Less inequality
- Average inequality
- More inequality
- Most inequality
- No data

Scale: 1 to 180,000,000

The day may come when one end of a scale of male/female equality is labeled "equal." That time has not arrived yet, and this map classifies countries on a scale of relative inequality, ranging from least inequality to most inequality. All societies are held back by legally or socially restricting the educational and work opportunities of females, who make up half the population. While every country does this, the less developed countries, those that need "people power" the most, tend to be the most restrictive.

and women generally greater in less developed countries (LDCs) than in economically developed countries (EDCs). Still, the country-to-country differences are not all explained by economics. Socioeconomic gender differences are represented in the accompanying color map.

We will say much more about the status of women later, but for now consider the following barrage of facts: Women constitute 70 percent of the world's poor and two-thirds of the world's illiterates. They occupy only 14 percent of the managerial and administrative jobs, constitute less than 40 percent of the world's professional and technical workers, and garner a mere 35 percent of the earned income (money wages) in the world. One reason that women are poor is that 66 percent of the work that they do is unpaid. Only 34 percent of the work done by men is unpaid. The UN estimates that if women were paid for their household and other uncompensated work, they would earn an additional $16 trillion a year.

Life for women is, on average, not only hard and poorly compensated; it is dangerous. "The most painful devaluation of women," the UN reports starkly, "is the physical and psychological violence that stalks them from cradle to grave" (UNDP, 1995:7). Among other signs of violence against women are the fact that about 80 percent of the world's refugees are women and their children. Statistics also show, the UNDP report (p. 44) continues, that annually "an estimated one million children, mostly girls in Asia, are forced into prostitution. And an estimated 100 million girls suffer genital mutilation."

Such economic, social, and political abuses of women are not new. What has changed is women's ability to see their common status in global terms through transnational communication and transportation. What is also new is the focused determination of women and the males who support the cause of gender equality to work together through transnational NGOs to address these issues. As the UNDP report (p. 1) points out, "Moving toward gender equality is not a technocratic goal—it is a political process."

The global women's movement is the driving force in this political process. We can examine this effort by looking first at the feminist philosophy and goals, then turning to the efforts of the women's movement.

THE TRANSNATIONAL WOMEN'S MOVEMENT: PHILOSOPHY AND GOALS

The first thing to note about the women's movement is that whether it is termed feminism or some other name, its adherents share some common views, but also vary considerably in their attitudes and emphases. Indeed, even the term feminism is an issue; for a variety of reasons, some women find what they see as the feminist ideology to be fully relevant to their experiences. Others are put off by the unfortunate stereotype of feminism as necessarily radical. "I think [women do] not feel as passionately militant thirty years later," one woman comments.[8] Also, the genesis of the feminist movement is rooted mostly in the United States and other industrialized, Western countries. As such, many of its primary concerns and values (such as individualism) understandably spring from the dominant Eurowhite cultures of those countries. For example, at the meeting in 2000 of the so-called **Beijing + 5 Conference** at the UN in New York City, to review progress since the 1995 Beijing conference, one group of women from LDCs complained that the agenda was too Western dominated and did "not reflect the reality of [some LDC] women's concerns nor the very real challenges they have to meet on a daily basis in trying to work for the implementation of the Beijing recommendations."[9] The same cultural issue was also evident when the classic feminist book *Our Bodies, Ourselves* was issued for the first time in Spanish. That edition, published in 2000, is entitled *Nuestros Cuerpos, Nuestras Vidas (Our Bodies, Our Lives)*. The title change, according to the book's latina author, reflects the different cultural views of its readers. As she explains it, "In Latin cultures relationships come first. The individualistic focus of North American feminism is not in keeping with the views of many women of color that their whole society is what's most important."[10]

It is also the case, however, that these criticisms are rejected by some feminists. "The oft-heard argument that feminism (read the struggle for women's equality) is a struggle pursued primarily by elite women is simply another example of the traditional demeaning of women," one study argues (Fraser, 1999:854). "History is replete with examples of male leaders who are not branded with this same charge, even though much of history is about elite men."

It is not the place of this text to attempt to settle this dispute among women. Instead we will adopt the strategy of a feminist author and use the term feminism "in its original meaning: the theory of, and the struggle for, equality for women" (Fraser, 1999:855). From this perspective, it is possible to highlight a number of common points in feminist thought about world politics.

First, those in the women's movement feel left out of the process and even the conceptualization of world politics. Feminist scholars maintain that the definition of what is relevant to the study of international relations, as presented in textbooks and most other scholarship written by men, is a product of the male point of view and ignores or underrepresents the role of women, their concerns, and their perspectives (Scott, 1996). The problem, women's equality advocates say, is that the scholarly definition of international relations has "excluded from that conception, quite comprehensively,... the [lives] of most women," who "experience societies and their interactions differently" than do men (Grant & Newland, 1991:1).

Concepts such as peace and security are prime examples of how, according to feminists, men and women perceive issues differently. One feminist scholar suggests that "from the masculine perspective, peace for the most part has meant the absence of war

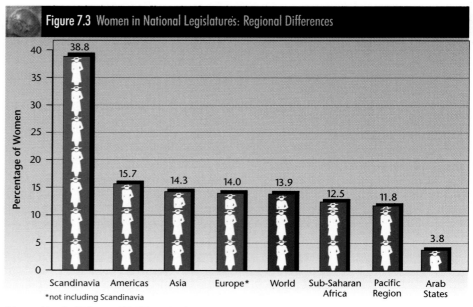

Figure 7.3 Women in National Legislatures: Regional Differences

Data source: International Parliamentary Union Web site at http://www.ipu.org/.

By one measure, women have come a long way, increasing their global share of national legislative seats from 3 percent in 1955 to 13.9 percent in 2000. But there is a long way, 36.1 percent, to go to reach 50 percent and equality. Clearly this goal is closer in some regions than in others.

and the prevention of armed conflict" (Reardon 1990:137). She terms this "negative peace." By contrast, Reardon (p. 138) continues, women think more in terms of "positive peace," which includes "conditions of social justice, economic equity and ecological balance." Women, more than men, are also apt to see international security as wider than just a military concept; as also including security from sexism, poverty, domestic violence, and other factors that assail women (Razavi, 1999). Women favor this more inclusive view of security because, according to another study, "the need for human security through development is critical to women whose lives often epitomize the insecurity and disparities that plague the world order" (Bunch & Carillo, 1998:230).

A second central point about the philosophy of the women's movement is that it is normative and includes an agenda for change. One obvious goal is to increase the participation of women in the political process and the positions they hold at all levels. In mid-2000, only 8 women were serving as the presidents or prime ministers of their countries, just 8 percent of all cabinet ministers were women, and women made up a scant 14 percent of the members of the world's national legislatures. Moreover, these overall figures do not reveal that women have an even smaller political presence in some regions, as Figure 7.3 indicates.

International organizations are no less gender skewed. No woman has ever headed the UN, the International Monetary Fund (IMF), the World Trade Organization (WTO), or the World Bank, and women occupy only about 15 percent of the senior management positions in the leading IGOs. Like male political leaders, some females have been successful in office; others have not. Yet, as the longtime (1980–1996) president of Iceland, Vigdis Finnbogadottir, has remarked, the stereotype remains that "women are not competitive enough or women do not understand economics." "If you do something wrong," she warned other women at a conference, "you will be attacked with the strongest weapon—mockery."[11]

The derogatory whisper campaign that women make weak leaders has been repeatedly disproved by the records of female leaders such as Prime Minister (1966–

1977, 1980–1984) Indira Gandhi of India, Prime Minister (1969–1974) Golda Meir of Israel, and Prime Minister (1979–1990) Margaret Thatcher of Great Britain, each of whom led her country to victory in war (with, respectively, Pakistan in 1971, several Arab states in 1973, and Argentina in 1982). Madeleine Albright, the first woman to serve as U.S. secretary of state, was also not afraid to use military power when necessary. In fact, one Pentagon official fretted that "Madeleine... feel[s] we should get involved [militarily] in many more things than this building thinks."[12] A similar evaluation was held by chairman of the Joint Chiefs of Staff Colin Powell, who remembers that when he expressed reluctance to send U.S. troops to Bosnia, Albright asked him heatedly, "What's the point of having this superb military... if we can't use it?" General Powell recalls thinking he "would have an aneurysm."[13]

Oddly, Saddam Hussein and the Iraqis shared the Pentagon's worry about Albright's willingness to use force. This was evident when one Baghdad newspaper published a scathing poem, the first stanza of which read:

> Albright, Albright,   Why do you throw over the peace leaves
> Alright, alright.   And maintain the papers of flight?
> You are the worst   Why do you hate the day and love the night?
>   in the night.   Don't put out the light.[14]

Advocates of women's political activism see their goal as more than simply a drive for power. They also see power for women as a way to change policy based on the view of at least some feminists that, overall, women have somewhat different values than men on a variety of issues. While the governance of Margaret Thatcher and other women demonstrate that women leaders can and have used military force, it is also the case, as discussed in chapter 4, that women have been generally less inclined to advocate force than men have been. There also are other differences. A recent poll found, for instance, that American women consistently place more emphasis than do men on international social and economic programs. One illustrative question asked men and women to prioritize whether countries should get U.S. foreign aid based on whether the recipient was important to U.S. security, was important as a U.S. trading partner, or was poor.[15] The rankings (and percentages) were:

Men	*Women*
1. Security (37%)	1. Poverty (35%)
2. Trade (34%)	2. Security (34%)
3. Poverty (25%)	3. Trade (26%)

The transnational women's movement additionally addresses the normative issue of how to improve the lot of women—and everyone else—in the international system. As such, the concern extends beyond sexism's deleterious effect on women to include the impact of discrimination on the entire society. Feminists point out correctly that keeping women illiterate retards the entire economic and social development of a society. It is not a coincidence, for example, that the percentage of women in the paid workforce is lowest in those countries where the gap between male and female literacy is the highest. Educating these illiterate women would increase the number of ways that they could contribute to their countries' economic and social growth. Beyond this, there is a correlation between the educational level of women and their percentage of the wage-earning workforce, on the one hand, and restrained population growth, on the other. In other words, one good path to population control is creating a society of fully educated men and women who are employed equally in wage-earning occupations.

THE TRANSNATIONAL WOMEN'S MOVEMENT: PROGRAMS AND PROGRESS

Programs to promote gender equity are making progress, but they also have a long way to go. As the concluding report of the Beijing + 5 Conference put it, "Even though significant positive developments [during the last five years] can be identified, barriers remain, and there is still the need to further implement the goals and commitments made in Beijing."[16] While reviewing the progress and the distance yet to go, it is important to remember that just 30 years or so ago, gender equality was not even a prominent political issue in the various countries, much less on the world stage. Inasmuch as chapter 17 of this book will spend considerable time discussing the progress of women in the area of human rights, we will focus in this section on political advances that women are making.

Women have been and are politically active in a large number of national and transnational organizations that focus all or in part on women's issues. These organizations and their members have interacted transnationally at many levels ranging from the Internet through global conferences. Individually, women with Internet access can now, for instance, find out more about their common concerns through such sites as the home page of WomenWatch: The UN Internet Gateway on the Advancement and Empowerment of Women at http://www.un.org/womenwatch/. Collectively, women are now frequently gathering in such global forums as the UN Conference on Population and Development (UNCPD), held in Cairo in 1994, the fourth WCW, and the Beijing + 5 Conference. Beyond the substantive proceedings of such conferences, they facilitate transnational contacts among women. Parma Khastgir, a Supreme Court justice in India and a delegate to the 1995 WCW, stressed this contribution in her observation that "what appealed to me most [about the WCW] was that people overcame their ethnic barriers and were able to discuss universal problems. They showed solidarity."[17]

It is difficult to measure the precise impact on women's views of themselves and politics that transnational communications through individual interactions, world and regional conferences, and the mass media are having (Shaheed, 1999). There is, however, evidence that cultural differences among women relating to their roles are narrowing. Figure 7.2 on page 163 shows, for example, that the views of Japanese women, who have been very traditional, are beginning to parallel the attitudes of American women.

Another standard by which to judge the impact of the transnational feminist movement is the advancement of women in politics. "Never before have so many women held so much power," writes one scholar. "The growing participation and representation of women in politics is one of the most remarkable developments of the late twentieth century" (Jaquette, 1997:23). Both these statements are certainly factual, but it is also the case that progress is slow and that women are a distinct political minority. As former Norwegian prime minister (1981, 1986–1989, 1990–1996) Gro Harlem Brundtland commented dryly, "I was the first woman in 1,000 years [to head Norway's government]. Things are evolving gradually."[18]

To add a bit of historical perspective: women only began to be able to vote in national elections a little more than a century ago. In 1893 New Zealand was the first country to recognize the right of women to vote. Other countries followed suit slowly. Switzerland in 1971 was the last EDC to allow female suffrage. Now, almost all countries do, although there are still some exceptions. One is Kuwait, where in 1999 the legislature rejected a bill to give women the right to vote.

Voting was a significant political step for women, but access to political office has come more slowly. Women won seats in Finland's parliament in 1907, making them perhaps the first elected female national legislators anywhere. The first woman other than a monarch to become a head of state was President of the Presidium Yanjamaa Nemendeyen Sbaataryn of Mongolia in 1953, and the first woman prime minister, Sirimavo Ratwatte Dias Bandaranaike of Ceylon (now Sri Lanka), did not take office until 1960. From these beginnings, the ranks of female political leaders have grown, but their still limited numbers reflect the continuing formidable barriers to full political participation by women (Reynolds, 1999).

The path to political power in international organizations has also been an uphill climb (Meyer & Prgel, 1999). The UN Charter pledges equal opportunity for men and women. The reality a half century after the Charter was adopted is that women hold just 15 percent of all top UN administrative posts. "We are a collection of all the world's chauvinisms," one UN staff member has commented bluntly.[19] Still, progress is being made. The secretary-general has appointed a number of women to high UN posts. Most notably, Kofi Annan in 1998 named Canadian diplomat Louise Fréchette as deputy secretary-general, the UN's second highest post. Other recent additions to the ranks of women in top UN posts include Carol Bellamy (former U.S. Peace Corps director, now director of the UN Children's Fund, or UNICEF); Gro Harlem Brundtland (former prime minister of Norway, now director general of the World Health Organization); and Mary B. Robinson (former president of Ireland, now UN High Commissioner for Human Rights). Thus, things are changing. Nafis Sadik has recalled that in the 1970s, when she first came to work at the UN Population Fund (UNFPA), "Western men saw me as an Asian woman; very decorative, but I couldn't possibly have any ideas."[20] As it turned out, she is not an adornment; Director Sadik now heads the UNFPA.

The accomplishments of these women have been, of course, personal. Many of the other advances of women have been made through national efforts. It is also the case, however, that the progress of women almost everywhere has been facilitated by and, in turn, has contributed to, the transnational feminist movement. Women have begun to think of themselves politically not as only American, or Canadian, or Zimbabwean women, but as women with a transnational identity and ties. This is both transforming national politics and weakening the hold of nationalism.

TRANSNATIONAL RELIGION

Most of the world's great religions have a strong transnational element. At its most expansive, religion can assert universalistic claims. More modestly, religion creates an urge to unite all the members of the religion or, failing that, to support coreligionists in other countries. Religions are not political ideologies in the strictest sense. Nevertheless, many religions have all the characteristics of an ideology and have an impact on the secular world as well as on spiritual life. This is particularly true when the adherents of a spiritual concept actively apply their beliefs to secular political goals, such as Pan-Islamic pride and solidarity.

RELIGION AND WORLD POLITICS

"You're constantly blindsided if you consider religion neutral or outside world politics," cautions international relations scholar the Reverend J. Bryan Hehir of Harvard. It is "better to understand the place that religion holds in the wider international framework," the Roman Catholic theologian observes wisely.[21]

Religion has played many roles in world politics. Certainly, it has often been and continues to be the source of peace, humanitarian concern, and pacifism. It is also true, though, that religion has been at the center of many bloody wars. The establishment and expansion of Islam beginning late in the sixth century and the reaction of Christian Europe set off a series of clashes, including the eight Crusades (1095–1291), between the equally combative Islamic and Christian worlds. The Protestant Reformation (1517) divided Christianity, and the resulting rivalry between Protestants and Catholics was one cause of the Thirty Years' War (1618–1648) and other conflicts. Religion also played a role in the imperial era. Catholic and Protestant missionaries were early

European explorers and colonizers. Whatever the missionary movement's good intent and works were, it also often promoted and legitimized the political, economic, and cultural subjugation of local people by outsiders.

Religion-based political conflict continues. It is an element of the conflict between Israelis, who are mostly Jewish, and Arabs, who are mostly Muslim. When Great Britain gave up its colonial control of the Indian subcontinent in 1947, that area was divided between the Hindus and the Muslims. Countless members of each faith were killed in the ensuing conflict and in the subsequent wars between India and the newly created state of Pakistan. That tension continues, with a particular focus on India's predominantly Muslim border territory of Kashmir.

Did You Know That:

Mohandas K. Gandhi, a Hindu and the leader of India's independence movement, was assassinated in 1948 by Nathuram Vinayak Godse, a Hindu fundamentalist who opposed Gandhi's insistence that India be a secular state that did not discriminate against Muslims.

Religion also causes or exacerbates conflict within countries. What was Yugoslavia disintegrated in part along religious lines. The people living in Bosnia-Herzegovina were of the same Slavic stock and spoke the same Serbo-Croatian language, but being Catholic Croats, Muslim Bosnians, and Eastern Orthodox Serbs divided them into fratricidal factions. More recently, religion plays a role in the cultural divide between Serbs and Muslim Albanians in Kosovo Province. Yet another example is the long struggle between the Roman Catholics and Protestants of Northern Ireland that killed over 3,000 people between 1969 and the establishment in 1998 of a still tenuous peace.

Organized religion also plays a range of intermediate roles as a transnational actor, projecting its values through a range of intergovernmental organizations (IGOs). Among Christians, the World Evangelical Alliance, founded in 1846, is an early example of a Protestant NGO. The Roman Catholic Church is by far the largest and most influential of current religion-based NGOs. The Vatican itself is a state, and the pope is a secular as well as a spiritual leader. The political influence of Roman Catholicism, however, extends far beyond the Vatican. Under the first Polish-born pope, John Paul II, the Church was active both internationally and within Poland in trying to topple the communist government there and dissuading the Soviet Union from intervening. Many years ago, when a subordinate cautioned Joseph Stalin about risking the displeasure of the Church, the Soviet leader reportedly dismissed the Church's influence with the sarcastic question, "How many [army] divisions does the pope have?" The Soviet and Polish communists found out that the pope may have no military divisions, but his legions of devout followers are many.

More recently, the Church sparked international controversy when it opposed pro-abortion rights language at UN conferences on women held in Egypt in 1994, in China in 1995, and in New York City in 2000. A Church representative claimed that the language was "a United Nations plan to destroy the family" by seeking to legitimize "abortion on demand, sexual promiscuity, and distorted notions of the family."[22] Not unexpectedly, many women at the conferences disagreed. Sally Ethelson of Population Action International, for one, accused the pontiff and his cardinals of insensitivity and argued that "women should not die or suffer irreparable physical harm as a result of unsafe abortions because of [the opposition of] a group of 114 celibate men."[23] Nevertheless, backed by some Catholic countries and in alliance with delegations from some Muslim countries, the Church was able to prevent language that specifically advocated abortions, homosexual unions, or other practices to which the Church objected.

The Vatican is also active on a wide variety of other issues. From the beginning of his time as pope through June 2000, John Paul II had made 91 apostolic visits to countries outside the Vatican. The Church has also been active on such issues as seeking an end to economic sanctions against Iraq and Cuba as injurious to civilians, pressing for nuclear arms restraint, and calling on the world's wealthy countries to do more to aid the developing countries.

THE STRENGTH OF RELIGIOUS FUNDAMENTALISM

One aspect of religion that appears to have gained strength in many areas of the world is **fundamentalism.** This phenomenon is also called religious traditionalism and religious nationalism. At least in the way that it is used here, a religious fundamentalist is someone who holds conservative religious values and wishes to incorporate those values into otherwise secular political activities, such as making laws that would apply not only to the faithful who agree with them, but to everyone. There is also a transnational element to some fundamentalists, who believe that loyalty to the religion should supersede patriotism and that all adherents of their religion should be united politically. That may mean bringing people together across borders; it may also mean driving out people of another or no faith or suppressing their freedoms within borders.

There is considerable debate over whether the rise of fundamentalism is a series of isolated events or related to a larger global trend. Taking the latter view are scholars who believe that at least part of the increase in the political stridency of religion is based on two factors: first, the mounting failure of states to meet the interests of their people, and, second, a resistance to the cultural blending that has come with modern trade, communications, and transportation. This leads people to seek a new source of primary political identification. Frequently, that is with their religion and with their coreligionists across national borders.

As part of this process, political conservatism, religious fundamentalism, and avid nationalism often become intertwined. For example, Israel's politics are strongly influenced by the role of orthodox Jewish groups. As a result of the 1999 election, Israel's Shas Party, which is mostly supported by orthodox Israelis, became the third largest party in Israel's parliament, the Knesset. The religious parties have pressed the government to limit travel on Saturday, the Jewish Sabbath, and to implement other regulations based on orthodox Jewish observances. Indeed, whether Israel's law should be based on religious or secular principles is one of the core issues in that country. In mid-2000, for example, Israelis were heatedly debating the justice of McDonald's Israeli franchise being fined $20,000 for employing Jewish workers on the Sabbath. The fine was levied when a Shas Party member became minister of labor in return for the party supporting the coalition government of Prime Minister Ehud Barak.

The volleys back and forth say a great deal about the depth of feeling in Israel about the religious-versus-secular debate. The local owner of the franchise protested in an Israeli newspaper ad that, "Religious coercion in Israel must be stopped," and called on the government of Prime Minister Barak to "stop capitulating to [the ultra-orthodox] Shas [Party] or else Israel will become Iran." In reply, a Shas spokesperson accused the owner of "turning his hamburgers into a political beef." Then, turning serious, the Shas representative told reporters that for such acts as employing Jews on the Sabbath and violating Jewish dietary law by mixing meat and dairy on cheeseburgers, "McDonald's to me is a symbol of the war against the things that are most sacred for the Jewish people."[24]

More specifically related to international affairs, the religious right in Israel also claims that the West Bank and the Golan Heights are part of the ancient land given in perpetuity to the Jewish nation by God. Among other things, the conservative parties pushed legislation through the Knesset in 2000 that will require a national referendum to approve the return of any portion of the Golan Heights to Syria. Whether the policy ramifications are domestic or international, however, "The issue," according to a Hebrew University scholar, "is whether Israel will shape a way of life according to Western, democratic concepts, or one infected by Middle Eastern fundamentalism and theocratic impulse." Others dismiss such concerns. "We're not going to make a second Iran in the Middle East," a rabbi who also heads a religion-oriented political party assures listeners.[25]

Waving a sword presented to celebrate his election was undoubtedly a photo opportunity gesture for India's prime minister Atal Behari Vajpayee. Yet this militant image symbolizes the worry of some observers that Vajpayee and his nationalist Hindu Bharatiya Janata Party will create a more aggressive foreign policy for India. The explosion of India's first nuclear weapons four months after this picture was taken accentuated these fears.

India has also seen the rise of religious traditionalism. A Hindu nationalist party, the Bharatiya Janata Party (BJP), came briefly to power in 1996, then lost power when its coalition government collapsed, only to regain and hold onto power as head of an unsteady coalition government through elections in 1998 and 1999. Unlike some of the religions being discussed here, the vast majority of Hindus live in one country, India. Indeed, tiny Nepal is the only other country with a Hindu majority. As such, the Hindu traditionalism of the BJP has a strong nationalist content and is part of the fragmentation, Jihad tendency that is struggling against the McWorld impulse. This will be discussed later in this chapter. There we will see, among other things, that the resurgence of religious traditionalism in India played a role in its decision in 1998 to test nuclear weapons.

While a number of the world's major religions illustrate the intersection of religion and global politics, more can be gained from a closer examination of one religion. To that end, we can turn our attention to Islam because of its growing sociopolitical impact and because its history and tenets are too often unknown or misrepresented in the Western world.

ISLAM AND THE WORLD

Islam is a monotheistic religion founded by Muhammad (ca. 570–632). The word *Islam* means "submission" to God (Allah), and *Muslim* means "one who submits." Muslims believe that Muhammad was a prophet who received Allah's teachings in a vision. These divine instructions constitute the Koran (or Qur'an), meaning "recitation."

It is the political application of Islam by Muslims that interests us here (Esposito, 1997). A central Islamic concept is the *ummah*, which encapsulates the idea that Muslims are or should be a united spiritual, cultural, and political community. Muhammad was the first leader of the ummah. Muslims distinguish between Muslim-held lands, which they call *dar al-Islam* (the domain of Islam), and non-Muslim lands, which are termed *dar al-harb* (the domain of unbelief). One of the tenets of Islam is the jihad, "struggle" in the name of Allah. Those who struggle to defend or promote Islam are sometimes called *mujahedin*. It is important to stress that jihad does not necessarily mean either expansionist or armed struggle. It can also mean peacefully spreading Islam or defending the faith (Johnson, 1997).

The political ramifications of Islam are important because there are over one billion Muslims spread widely over the world, as demonstrated by the accompanying map of the Organization of the Islamic Conference. They are a majority among the Arabs of the Middle East and also in non-Arab countries like Algeria, Bangladesh, Iran, Pakistan, Sudan, Turkey, several of the former Soviet republics (FSRs: Azerbaijan, Kazakhstan, Kyrgyzstan, Tajikistan, Turkmenistan, and Uzbekistan), and Indonesia (whose 207 million people make it the most populous Muslim country). There are other countries, such as Nigeria and the Philippines, in which Muslims constitute an important political force. Indeed, only about one of every four Muslims is an Arab. To explore political Islam, we can examine five factors: the political heritage of Muslims, Islam and nationalism, Islam and the non-Islamic world, Islamic sectarianism, and Islamic traditionalism and secularism.

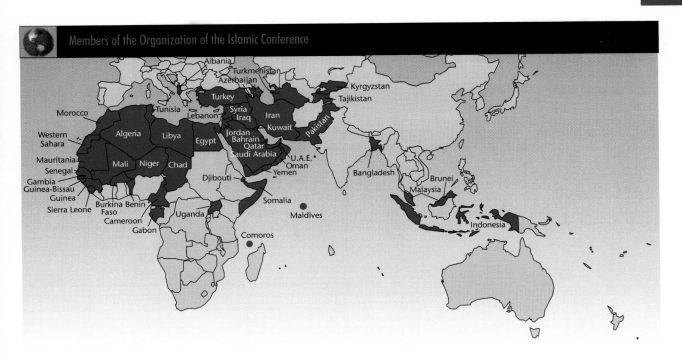

Members of the Organization of the Islamic Conference

*United Arab Emirates

This map of the Islamic Conference illustrates that Islam is not confined to the Arab states in the Middle East. In fact, most Muslims are not Arabs. The largest predominantly Muslim state is Indonesia, where 87 percent of the country's 206 million people are Muslims. The people of Pakistan and Iran, the second and third most populous predominantly Muslim countries, are also not Arabs.

The Political Heritage of Muslims

The attitudes of Muslims toward the non-Muslim world are shaped by three historical elements (Lewis, 1996). The first is a *triumphant past*. During Islam's early period, Muslim zeal sparked rapid religious and political expansion by peaceful conversion and violent conquest. This drive was led at first by Arabs, then by Ottoman Turks and other Muslim dynasties. At their farthest, the boundaries of Muslim domination encompassed the Middle East, North Africa, southwestern Asia to the Ganges River, Spain, and central Europe to just south of Vienna.

Conflict with Christian powers, especially those of Europe, is a second element of Muslim political heritage. At the urging of Catholic popes, the Christian kings of England, France, and the Holy Roman Empire led the Crusades against the Muslims. Muslims also clashed for hundreds of years with Christianity's Orthodox emperors of Byzantium and later with the Orthodox czars of Russia. Later still, most Muslim lands fell under the colonial rule of Christian European powers. Even today, in the view of many Muslims, Christian powers still dominate the world and beset them. Many Muslims are dismayed, for example, by the fact that all of the UN Security Council's permanent members except China are countries with a Christian heritage. Moreover, two council members, Great Britain and France, are the same countries that led the Crusades and later colonized a good portion of the Muslim world.

The third element of Muslim political heritage is the decline of their power and the eventual *domination of Muslims by others*. After about the year 1500, Muslim secular strength declined slowly over the centuries. A variety of European powers had by the late 1800s come to dominate many of the Muslim areas from Mauritania in Africa to Indonesia in Asia. The last vestige of Muslim power was eclipsed when the Ottoman Empire was defeated in World War I. In the aftermath, the British and the French became the colonial overlords of the Middle East. As a result, most Muslim countries, whatever their location, share an experience of recent colonial domination by mostly European, Christian-heritage powers (Lustick, 1997).

During the last half century, direct political domination ended with the collapse of colonialism. New countries came into being; others moved from autonomy to full independence. As with most new countries, the Muslim states fiercely guard their sovereignty. Most Muslims also chafe under the foreign control that has frequently persisted through economic dominance and other neocolonialist techniques exercised by the Western powers. In recent years, this indirect domination has been eased by the growth of oil power, and there has been a concurrent growth of Islamic fundamentalism, pride, and militancy that has interacted with and supplemented the nationalism of Islamic countries.

Islam and Nationalism

There are elements of the reawakening of Muslim assertiveness that support the unification in the ummah. After centuries of outside political, economic, and cultural domination, the people in the region that stretches from Morocco to Afghanistan have begun to reclaim their heritage in what might be called a "Muslim pride" movement.

The resurgence of Islam also includes international support for the strengthening of Muslims. Islamic solidarity efforts have ranged from coordination in protecting Islamic holy places, through support of the Palestine Liberation Organization, to some Muslim leaders' support of Pakistan's possession of nuclear weapons (referred to by some as "Islamic bombs"). Among Arab Muslims, the common tie of Islam has helped promote Pan-Arab sentiment. This Pan-Arab feeling has led to the establishment of some regional cooperation (the Arab League, for example) and even attempts to merge countries.

Despite all of these elements of Pan-Muslim and Pan-Arab sentiment, it is unlikely that Muslims will reestablish the ummah in the foreseeable future. Ethnonationalism is one factor that will prevent this. Many Muslim countries have sharp differences and vie with one another for regional influence (Tibi, 1997; Lefebvre, 1996). Some Muslims, notably the Kurds who live in Turkey, Iraq, Iran, and elsewhere, want to form their own countries. Further solidifying nationalism, there are major ethnic differences within Islam. Culturally, Indonesians are no more like Syrians than are Canadians.

Indeed, Indonesians are ethnically not even like one another, and their political views are more strongly tied to ethnicity and other factors than to religion. According to a study of Indonesia's 1999 elections, there was a "lack of strongly positive relationship between religion, especially Muslim variants, and partisan choice." By contrast, the identification of voters as Javanese, Sudanese, Batak, Balinese, Malay, or one of the other linguistically and culturally distinct groups in Indonesia "played a larger independent role" in the elections than expected (Liddle & Mujani, 2000:37, 25).

Islam and the Non-Islamic World

Muslim political history influences current Muslim attitudes toward the domain of unbelief in several ways. One is the frequent evidence of anti-Western feeling. In the eyes of many Muslims, the United States is the most recent dominant Euro-Christian power. Americans have therefore inherited Muslim resentment based on what one Arab leader describes as "Western behavior over centuries that has been unfair to Muslims."[26] Muslims also see the struggle with Israel, especially the issue of Jerusalem, as part of a long, ongoing history. They tend to view Israel as partially a creation of the Western powers in the latest round of the ancient contest for control of Jerusalem and the surrounding region.

The Muslims' often unhappy history of interaction with the West also explains why so many of them were ambivalent about Iraq's aggression. Many Muslims were appalled when Iraq invaded Kuwait, yet they also admired Saddam Hussein because, as a rug merchant in Damascus proclaimed colorfully, "He is breaking the head of the U.S. He is sticking his finger up its nose. He has made America crazy."[27] These attitudes have persisted during the recurrent U.S.–led confrontations with Iraq over its alleged attempts to hide weapons of mass destruction from UN inspectors. Arabs often note, for example, that the United States has never protested against Israel's nuclear weapons capability, and they suspect that racism is the reason. "There is a deep feeling that when it comes to the Arabs, it's always very harsh treatment, and when it comes to the Israelis, it's easy," notes an Egyptian analyst.[28]

Islamic Sectarianism

Religion is not always a source of Islamic unity. Instead, religious conflict has been sparked by sectarian splits. The most important of these separates the majority Sunnis and the minority Shiites (Francke & Fuller, 1999). The issues between the two sects involve doctrinal matters beyond our scope of inquiry here. What is important here is that the sometimes quiescent Sunni-Shiite rivalry was reignited in 1979 when the Ayatollah Ruhollah Khomeini led fundamentalist Shiites to power in Iran. One of Khomeini's proclaimed goals was to reestablish Islamic unity under Shiite leadership by displacing Sunni control of Saudi Arabia (which controls Mecca, the holiest of Muslim places) and other countries. The most serious clash was Iran's war with Iraq (1980–1988). There were territorial and other nationalistic causes behind the war, but Khomeini's determination to overthrow Iraq's Sunni-dominated regime was also a cause of the war and of the millions of casualties that occurred.

The death of Khomeini in 1989 eased, but did not end, Sunni-Shiite strife. Among other places, Muslim sectarianism has spelled continuing tragedy for Afghanistan. Various rebel factions fought together in a 14-year effort to evict the Soviet invaders and to oust Afghanistan's communist government. Then, with victory in 1992, rebel unity dissolved, and the various factions have continued to fight a civil war that has taken countless lives and utterly destroyed the country's cities and infrastructure. Ethnic divisions were one source of the trouble, but these intermingle with and are supplemented by the contest for power between Sunni and Shiite factions. The Sunni Taliban government of Afghanistan has also had numerous border clashes with Shiite Iran.

Islamic Traditionalism and Secularism

A second point of division within Islam separates Muslim traditionalists and secularists. Traditionalist (fundamentalist) Muslims want to resurrect many of the cultural traditions, such as banning alcohol and having women cover their faces, which were weakened under the influence of Western culture. Fundamentalists also want to establish legal systems based on the *shari'ah* (the law of the Koran) rather than on Western legal precepts. The traditionalists also look forward to the reestablishment of the ummah. "The notion that a majority should rule and the notion of the political party are all Western notions," explains one ranking Muslim theologian. What "Islam calls for," he continues, is "obedience to the ruler, the unification of the nation and advice by religious scholars."[29]

While traditional religion has gained political strength in a number of countries, it has declined in a few others. This picture shows Iran's president, Mohammed Khatami, soon after the moderate candidate was elected by a landslide in May 2000. Behind him, and seeming to scowl disapprovingly, is an image of the fervent religious leader, Ayatollah Ruhollah Khomenei, who came to power in 1979 and ruled until his death in 1989. For another 11 years Iran remained largely controlled by religious conservatives, but the 2000 election raised hopes that Iran's policy would moderate.

Secularists, by comparison, believe that within Islam there can be many Muslim states and that religious and secular law should be kept separate. A top Arab jurist argues, for example, that "politicized Islamic groups proclaim Islam to be a nation when in fact Islam is a religion."[30] Whatever may be theologically correct, the fact is that traditionalist Muslim movements during the 1990s gained strength in Algeria, Iran, Turkey, and several other Muslim countries.

Does any or all of this mean that there is a "green peril," a term that relates to the traditional association of the color green with Muslims? Not necessarily. Just as it would be wrong to ignore the role of religion in politics, it would be misleading to make dire predictions (Faksh, 1997). One limit is that there is an ebb and flow of the strength of traditionalism and secularism. Moreover, as one study has recently found, "Democracy itself and Islam are not mutually exclusive," although there are often cultural differences about how democracy is understood and implemented (Midlarsky, 1999:504). For example, the balance has begun to shift away from traditionalism in Iran, which for more than 20 years was dominated by conservative Shiite clerics. The parliamentary elections in Iran in February 2000 resulted in serious losses for religious conservatives and gains for the more secular opposition, which won 59 percent of the seats in the parliament. Subsequently, in the May presidential election, the moderate candidate, Mohammad Khatami, won 70 percent of the votes cast, trouncing his conservative opponent.

Another reason to be wary about alarmist views of religious traditionalism is that mixing any religion, including Islam, with politics is not inherently explosive. Religion most often promotes peace. Certainly, as with any movement, there are extremists who have lost their sense of proportion. But there are also many devoutly religious people who think and act with moderation. It should also be remembered that, where it exists, fanaticism is often a by-product of deprivation, frustration, and other ills. To a substantial degree, Muslims are merely reacting against what they believe are the wrongs of the recent past and are attempting to uplift the circumstances of Muslims everywhere. Perhaps the best lesson to draw is that religion is a significant factor in international relations. Like any set of coherent ideas, religion helps define who is on which side and thus often plays a powerful role in shaping the perceptions of political leaders and the actions of the countries they command.

TRANSNATIONAL CULTURE

Having examined the transnational aspects of the specific identifications of gender and religion, we can now turn our attention to the transnationalization of culture (Iriye, 1997). The idea of culture is difficult to deal with for several reasons. First, the often-seen phrase "distinct culture" is somewhat misleading. Cultures evolve, intermingle, and sometimes even merge. Second, because culture is an amalgam of many components (such as language, religion, and a common history), it is impossible to discuss culture without overlapping discussions of its component parts. You will see in the following discussion, for example, that the Pan-Arab culture impulse is closely related to the Muslim faith that most Arabs share and that the various Eastern Orthodox denominations are very much part of Pan-Slavism, which we address later. Moreover, you will see that transnational acculturation is moving the world in two divergent directions. One is associated with Barber's (1995) concept of McWorld. It is too early to speak of a world uniculture, but we have in the last half century moved quickly and substantially in that direction. The other culture direction relates to Barber's concept of Jihad. There is substantial resistance to McWorld. Furthermore, some observers believe that the world is moving to reorder itself away from national conflict and toward a world of cultural clash.

THE CULTURE OF McWORLD

Discussions of the evolution of an amalgamated global culture inevitably include a great deal about McDonald's, basketball, rock music, e-mail, and other such aspects of pop culture as well as commentary about more overtly political transnational phenomena such as the global reach of CNN. It would be an error to suppose that such a discussion of the impact of burgers and the Chicago Bulls on global culture is an attempt to trivialize the subject. Indeed, the potential impact of common culture on cooperation set off a series of columns in the *New York Times* entitled "Big Mac I" and "Big Mac II." The columnist formulated a quasi-tongue-in-cheek "Golden Arches Theory of Conflict Prevention" based on the observation that no two countries with McDonald's had ever fought a war. Not all analysts, it should be noted, agreed with the theory. Scholar Francis Fukuyama, for one, commented that "I would not be surprised if in the next 10 years several of these McDonald's countries go to war with each other."[31]

More substantively, there is a long line of political theory that argues that the world will come together through myriad microinteractions rather than through such macroforces of political integration as the United Nations. This school of thought believes that political communities are built by social communities and that those social communities come together through a process of interaction, familiarization, and amalgamation of diverse existing communities. Scholars who examine this bottom-up process look for evidence in such factors as the flow of communications and commerce between countries and the spread across borders of styles of dress, similarities in what people eat, and what people do for recreation. It is not inconsequential, from this perspective, that the New York Mets and Chicago Cubs opened the 2000 season of America's "national pastime," baseball, at the Tokyo Dome, rather than at Shea Stadium or Wrigley Field.

The Spread of Common Culture

There is significant evidence of cultural amalgamation in the world. The leaders of China once wore "Mao suits"; now they wear Western-style business suits. When dressing informally, people in Shanghai, Lagos, and Mexico City are more apt to wear jeans, T-shirts, and sneakers than their country's traditional dress. A young person in Kyoto is more likely to be listening to The Smashing Pumpkins than to traditional Japanese music. Big Macs, "fries," and milk shakes are consumed around the world.

Before looking further at the evidence, one caution is in order. You will see that a great deal of what is becoming world culture is Western, especially American, in its origins. That does not imply that Western culture is superior; its impact is a function of the economic and political strength of Western Europe and the United States. Nor does the preponderance of Western culture in the integration process mean that the flow is one way. The West is being influenced by material things and philosophical values from other parts of the world. The United States, for example, is influenced by many "imports," ranging from pasta, through increasingly popular soccer, to Zen Buddhist meditation.

Language One of the most important aspects of converging culture is English, which is becoming the common language of business, diplomacy, communications, and even culture. President Jiang Zemin of China and many other national leaders can converse in English. Indeed, a number of them, including Jacques Chirac of France and Alberto Fujimori of Peru, learned or improved their English while enrolled at U.S. universities. UN secretary-general Kofi Annan received his B.A. and M.S. degrees from U.S. universities.[32]

Modern communications are one driving force in the spread of English. Whether you watch CNN in Cairo or Chicago, it is broadcast in English. There are certainly sites on the World Wide Web in many languages, but most of the software, the search engines, and information in the vast majority of Web sites are all in English. One estimate is that 90 percent of all Internet traffic is in English. As the Webmaster at one

The global popularity of American movies is one of the many ways that the world is being homogenized culturally. Walking along a street in Beijing, this Chinese man is perhaps thinking of going to see the movie *Notting Hill*, starring Julia Roberts and Hugh Grant.

site in Russia comments, "It is far easier for a Russian... to download the works of Dostoyevsky translated in English to read than it is for him to get [it] in his own language."

Business is also a significant factor in the global growth of English. The United States is the world's largest exporter and importer of goods and services, and it is far more common for foreign businesspeople to learn the language of Americans than it is for Americans to learn Chinese, German, Japanese, and other languages. A report issued by the Japanese government in early 2000 declared that "achieving world-class excellence demands that all Japanese acqure a working knowledge of English."[33]

In a related way, the current ascendancy of capitalism on the world stage is bringing vastly increased numbers of foreign students to the United States to study business, with students taking bachelor of business and MBA degrees constituting 21 percent of all foreign students enrolled in U.S. universities and colleges. Moreover, the fact that U.S. higher education attracts many foreign students helps spread English and the American culture. Some 481,000 foreign students are now studying in the United States, with Japan's 47,000 students being the most numerous.

Consumer products The interchange of popular consumer goods is another major factor in narrowing cultural gaps. American movies are popular throughout much of the world. Hollywood is pervasive, earning 50 percent of its revenue abroad—a 20 percent jump in twenty years. American movies dominate many foreign markets, earning 50 percent of all film revenues in Japan, 70 percent in Europe, and 83 percent in Latin America. By contrast, foreign films account for just 3 percent of the U.S. market. It is not surprising, then, that at one point in early 2000, some top grossing films overseas were France: *Taxi 2*, Turkey: *Erin Brockovich*, and Hong Kong: *Shanghai Noon* (something of an irony, given its stars, Jackie Chan and Lucy Liu). Joining the tidal wave of visual common culture, American television programing is also increasingly omnipresent. For example, only about 30 percent of all television programs in Latin America originate in that region, while 62 percent come from the United States, and 8 percent are made elsewhere.

Older American movies are available, among other places, through the more than 1,000 stores that Blockbuster Video has in 27 countries outside the United States. And if non-Americans want to look authentic at an American movie, they can get a pair of jeans distributed through Levi Strauss's 34 regional headquarters, which employ about half the company's workers and earn Levi Strauss about one-third of its annual sales. Even if the product is not Western, the style often is. Kuwaiti radio now airs a call-in show called *Love Line*. Host Talal al-Yagout tells listeners in a soothing voice that "we get to talk about love, broken hearts, getting married."[34] This is not a translation from Arabic; the host and his callers converse in English. Chinese culture has also succumbed to many things American, as related in the box, And Never the Twain Shall Meet: Until Now.

To return to and reemphasize the main point here, there is a distinct and important intermingling and amalgamation of cultures under way. For good or ill, Western, particularly American, culture is at the forefront of the beginning of a common world culture. The observation of the director-general of UNESCO, that

(continued on page 181)

AND NEVER THE TWAIN SHALL MEET: UNTIL NOW

"Oh, East is East, and West is West, and never the twain shall meet." Perhaps these words seemed true when Rudyard Kipling penned them in *The Ballad of East and West* (1889), but they hardly apply anymore.

As in many countries, Western pop culture is making significant inroads in China. Children there successfully pester their parents into buying 180,000 Mi Loushu (Mickey Mouse) comic books each month, and the mayor of Shanghai traveled to Los Angeles to try to convince Disney officials to build a Disneyland in his city. Kentucky Fried Chicken is also winning many converts to its American specialty with 250 outlets in more than 50 cities. McDonald's, with 200 outlets in 17 cities, is the second largest fast-food company in China, and it and KFC dominate the market (Watson, 2000). Together they serve up, for instance, an estimated 70 percent of the french fries sold annually in China. An order of fries costs an average $1.20, equal to about a half-day's pay for the average Chinese worker. "It's a bit expensive to eat here," one diner commented about McDonald's, "but I guess for a high-fashion restaurant like this, the prices are O.K."[1] After indulging in a *jishi hanbao* (cheeseburger), hungry Chinese might go to Dairy Queen to get a *sheng dai* (sundae) for dessert. Following such a gastronomic tour de force, the calories can be worked off by dancing at Beijing's Hard Rock Cafe to rockers such as Cui Jian and his top single "Rock on the New Long March." Finally, exhausted by the night's adventures, revelers might choose to get some rest at Beijing's Hilton, Holiday Inn, Radisson, or Sheraton hotel.

While at the hotel relaxing, patrons can turn on the television and watch CNN in English or change channels to catch a National Basketball Association (NBA) game. Finding one will be easy, because state television often carries two NBA games each weeknight and more on the weekends. Fans shout *pee-ow liang*! (pretty) for 3-point jump shots, but their favorite is the awesome *kou qui* (slam dunk).

It may be a while, however, before fans see a Chinese player in an NBA uniform. In March 2000, Beijing refused to let star player Yao Ming, a 7-foot, 6-inch center for the Shanghai Sharks, travel to the

Those who made this unlicensed sweatshirt may not have known how to spell the team of Air Jordan and company, but they did know that the Chicago Bulls are the favorite professional team of Chinese basketball fans.

United States to play in the Nike Hoop Summit in Indianapolis. The official reason was that Yao needed rest for the approaching Olympics; the probable real reason was fear that he would be lured away from his current $8,000 salary by a multimillion dollar NBA contract with the Dallas Mavericks, which drafted him in 1999. Still, despite such matters, the NBA has teamed up with sneaker producers Nike and Reebok to ride the popularity of present and past NBA stars in China. Michael "Air" Jordan and others promote the sport to sell a bonanza of merchandise to what they hope will be more than one billion fans. "We are really bullish—if you'll excuse the term—on basketball in China," says an NBA executive stationed in Hong Kong.[2] Of course in China, like most countries, not all the merchandise is licensed, but, as the boy's sweatshirt in the accompanying photo shows, it is often possible to tell the difference between the authorized and knock-off goods.

"America's main role in the new world order is not as a military superpower, but as a multicultural superpower," is probably an overstatement, but it captures some of what is occurring (Iyer, 1996:263).

What is most important is not the specific source of common culture. Rather it is the important potential consequences of cultural amalgamation. There are, as noted, analysts who welcome it as a positive force that will bring people and, eventually, political units together. There are other people who see transnational culture as a danger to desirable diversity.

The Resistance to a Common Culture

Those who resist a common culture in the world worry about what Barber (1995) refers to as the "yawn" of cultural homogeneity—McWorld—that may accompany globalization. Consider, for example, the plight of France as it struggles to preserve its cherished and concededly glorious culture in the face of the engulfing tide of foreign culture, especially of Anglo-Saxon origin. The French worry, for instance, that the 570 McDonald's outlets in France represent what an editorial in the newspaper *Le Figaro* called gastronomic "new terrorism." "America, imperial power, doesn't just intend to stuff our heads with its diplomatic obsessions," the editorial complained, "It also means to cram our bellies in its own way."[35] This sense has led to numerous attacks in France on the McDonald's outlets. One such "culture commando" is José Bové, a French sheep farmer, who in 1999 bulldozed a McDonald's outlet in the region in the south of France famous for its sheep's milk–based Roquefort cheese. "McDonald's is one culture—in Singapore in Texas and in France—and we don't want that," Bové explained. "Each people have the right to eat what it wants."[36] Unimpressed, a French court in September 2000 sentenced Bové to six months in prison.

The French language is also under siege, and French president Chirac has condemned the rising English-language domination of the Internet and other forms of international communication as a "major risk for humanity" through "linguistic uniformity and thus cultural uniformity."[37] There are even those guardians of all that is French who view the invasion of alien words as more than a simple linguistic sacrilege. "The use of a foreign language is not innocent," France's minister of culture has warned. In reality, he has declared, it is part of the "considerable efforts" to infiltrate French culture by the "Anglo-Saxons" as one prong of attack in their "hegemonic drive."[38]

All is not lost yet, though, for French traditionalists have fought back (Carruthers, 1998; Grantham, 1998). France has amended its constitution to declare: "The language of the republic is French."[39] The national Assembly has enacted laws requiring that English words not be used in teaching, business, and government, and to assist in modernizing French, numerous agencies work to find French substitutes. The Ministry of Finance, for example, has decreed *non* to "e-mail" and *oui* to *message electronique. Jeunes pousses* (green shoots, as in young plants) is mandated instead of "start up," an adjective for a new company. And stock option is *option sur titres* (option on titles).

In the skies above France, a great furor broke out in early 2000 when Air France ordered its pilots to follow international rules (which require using English in all pilot-to-air controller communications during international flights) at Charles de Gaulle airport. "These people are jerks," thundered one member of France's parliament, condemning those who "tirelessly ape the Anglo-Saxon world.... After all," he added, "French is the language of civilization."[40] It was too much for the pilots to contemplate speaking in English to the tower at an airport in Paris named after the French general and president who not only was dedicated to restoring France's glory but who once observed, "You may be sure that the Americans will commit all the stupidities they can think of, plus some that are beyond imagination."[41] Many of the pilots and controllers refused to comply, and after two weeks Air France retreated. The company vowed to try again to institute the global standard, but one controller's union official warned, "They were made to go backward, and it's not easy to turn that around."[42]

Lest one think that the emphasis on the value of the state to protect cultural diversity is all a matter of silliness about invasions of Anglo-Saxon hamburgers and the like, consider the fact that 19 countries met in Ottawa, Canada, in 1998 to discuss how to distinguish culture from commerce so that countries could protect their cultures from exported American movies, CDs, and similar items. The worry that these delegates and others have, according to one scholar, is that "if national identities are indeed being eroded, what is likely to take their place is not rich cultural pluralism..., but a world market as the distributor of cultural resources" that will tend toward "a lowest-common-denominator mass culture exemplified by Disney, McDonald's, and Australian soap operas." That, he concludes, "will be bad news" (Miller, 1995:187).

Thus, fear of cultural erosion is not limited to France. It exists broadly. It was evident in the Russian who characterized the English-dominated Internet as "the ultimate act of intellectual colonialism."[43] The worry also surfaced after three Israeli teenagers died in a stampede at a rock music festival in their country. President Ezer Weizman charged that the tragedy had occurred because "the Israeli people are infected with Americanization. We must be wary of McDonald's; we must be wary of Michael Jackson. We must be wary of Madonna."[44]

Cultural fear and protectionism can also be found in Asia. The Vietnamese government warns against the "poisonous" foreign corruption of Vietnamese culture and has particularly targeted imported magazines and videotaped movies that emphasize sex and violence. "It is the right time to make pure again our cultural life," says Tran Binh, an official with the Ministry of Culture.[45] Similarly in India, the campaign platform of the BJP attacked the inroads of foreign culture. Kentucky Fried Chicken outlets became the centerpiece of what Indian newspapers dubbed "The Chicken War" when government health inspectors shut down the KFC in New Delhi after two flies were found on the premises. The *New Delhi Times* editorialized sarcastically that the restaurants should have been given an award "because only two flies were found."[46] Flies, of course, were not the issue. Rather it was the sense that tandoori chicken, a classic Indian dish, and the rest of Indian culture is being eaten away by fried chicken and the rest of American culture. As the BJP campaign slogan went, "Send us microchips, not potato chips."

THE CULTURE OF JIHAD

There is another, nearly antithetical negative image of transnational culture that envisions a world divided and in conflict along cultural lines. The best-known thesis of this view is Samuel P. Huntington's (1996, 1993) image of a coming **"clash of civilizations."** Huntington's (1993:22) thesis is that "the fundamental source of conflict" in the future will "be cultural" and that "the battle lines of the future" will pit "different civilizations" against one another. He projects (p. 25) that world politics will be driven by the "interactions among seven or eight major civilizations," including "Western, Confucian, Japanese, Islamic, Hindu, Slavic-Orthodox, Latin American, and possibly African."

Like many analysts, Huntington (p. 26) believes that various modern forces work to "weaken the nation-state as a source of identity" and that new cultural identifications will emerge "to fill this gap" and to group countries into cultural blocs. His prediction for such alignments is dark. "Over the centuries," according to Huntington (pp. 25–27), "differences among civilizations have generated the most prolonged and the most violent conflicts," because "cultural characteristics and differences are less mutable and hence less easily compromised and resolved than political and economic ones."

What should we make of this image of a future world torn asunder by the clash of civilizations? One unsettling sign that Huntington's theory is not totally unthinkable is the coming together of Hinduism and nationalism in India. That development is related in the box, *Hindutva* and the Bomb, on the next page.

Along with the example of India, there is plenty of circumstantial evidence to support Huntington's thesis. The strengthening of religious fundamentalism, which we

(continued on page 184)

HINDUTVA AND THE BOMB

At 3:45 P.M. on May 11, 1998, the ground near Pokharan in northwest India shook ominously, causing seismographs around the world to jump with justifiable alarm. India had exploded its first nuclear weapon in a test series. Seventeen days later, neighbor and rival Pakistan answered with its own tests. "I cannot believe that we are about to start the twenty-first century by having the Indian subcontinent repeat the worst mistakes of the twentieth century," a distressed President Clinton said.[1]

The meaning of these events for global security and arms control will be discussed in chapters 12 and 13. What is important here is to see how India's nuclear tests relate to the rise of nationalist religious traditionalism in India and the vision of *Hindutva*, a concept that mixes Hindu theology and nationalism.

Eighty percent of India's one billion people adhere to Hinduism, a religion at least 3,500 years old. Another 14 percent, mostly in the northwest, are Muslims. Religious tensions are not new in India, but the rise of a Hindu fundamentalist movement, politically represented by the Bharatiya Janata Party (BJP), is both a symptom and a cause of increased religious tensions.

The BJP came to power in 1998 amid frustration over general government ineffectiveness and continued nationalist sentiment. Statistically, the BJP won only 26 percent of the popular vote and one-third of the seats in the 543-member Lok Sabha, the dominant chamber in India's parliament. That was enough, however, to establish a coalition government and install its leader, Atal Behari Vajpayee, as prime minister.

Muslims and many Hindus fear that a government controlled by the BJP might try to suppress religious and cultural diversity in India. Vajpayee has regularly tried to dispel such concerns, and BJP policy has been restrained by the fact that it heads an unstable coalition government (re-elected in 1999 with similar percentage of the votes and legislative seats). Still, many Hindu nationalists are virulently strident (Bouton, 1998).

The rise of the BJP has caused concern in India and abroad. The party's platform advocates the re-creation of an idealized *Akband Bharat* (Old India), a concept that envisions the unification of the Indian subcontinent (Bangladesh, Bhutan, India, Nepal, and Pakistan) under Indian leadership and the Hindu religion. According to one nationalist leader, Srikanth Joshi, "Muslims are converted Hindus, but they have forgotten their Hinduness. So we will awake them to their Hinduness."[2] Prime Minister Vajpayee is a moderate, at least by BJP standards, but even he has warned that "appeasement" of Muslims and other minorities would "injure the Hindu psyche" and has spoken repeatedly of Hindutva.[3] The BJP has pledged to deal with Pakistan more sternly about the disputed region of Kashmir, which separates them. Vajpayee and other BJP leaders also hinted that they would make India a declared nuclear power, and they kept their word.

While security issues pushed India to nuclear testing, it is also true that the decision to become a nuclear power grew from the traditionalist, nationalist thinking among India's leadership. Vajpayee evoked India's "past glory and future vision to become strong."[4] He also contended, "The greatest meaning of the tests is that they have given India shakti," a Hindi word for power commonly used to refer to the strength of Hindu gods.[5] It is also worth noting that the code name for the nuclear devices was Shakti. Other Indian leaders also took that nationalist line. The defense minister dismissed threatened international sanctions by telling Indians, "We have become a very soft people, and we must realize that nations are not built through soft options. One has to be willing to live a hard life."[6] And the BJP's Bombay boss Balasaheb Thackeray declared "We have to prove that we are not eunuchs."[7]

It must be said that there was dissent in India, but the many Indians celebrating in the streets and shouting "Bharat mata ki jai" (victory to mother India) drowned out the voices of the few who dared to speak. Hindutva and the glory—or perhaps destruction—of Bharat came a little closer.

discussed earlier, lends credence to his belief. So does the persistence of racism and other forms of intolerance. There are, for example, many observers who believe that widespread racism, which in its broadest sense can be called "culturalism," will exacerbate clashes in the future. The inaction during the early 1990s of Western powers, while Christians were slaughtering Muslims; the barring of Muslim Turkey from the mostly Christian EU; and the vigorous opposition of the largely Christian West to Muslims (or Hindus) getting nuclear weapons, while ignoring the Israeli nuclear

Some analysts believe that racism influences the decisions of the powerful, mostly Eurowhite developed countries about where they will intervene to stop violence. This picture could be a prop room for Shakespeare's play, *Hamlet,* in which the young prince holds the skull of the court jester, and laments, "Alas! poor Yorick. I knew him,… a fellow… of most excellent fancy." Sadly, this photograph represents reality. It is an image of death from Rwanda, where Hutu militias massacred a half-million people. The Eurowhite world stood by and did nothing.

stockpile, cause some Muslims to suspect that culturalism is the cause of inaction. Such views are not confined to Muslims. Just before his death, Richard Nixon wrote, "It is an awkward but unavoidable truth that had the citizens of Sarajevo [the capital of Bosnia] been predominantly Christian or Jewish, the civilized world would not have permitted [the atrocities that occurred]."[47]

Similarly, latent racism may account for the limited responses, in some cases near nonresponses, to crises in Africa and other non-Eurowhite regions and countries. UN secretary-general Boutros-Ghali (1992–1997) once charged that "Eurocentrism" prompted the major powers to leave Africans to the "cruelties of fate." When Boutros-Ghali's comments brought angry protests, especially in the British press, he retorted that their critical attitude might be "because I'm a wog" (a British pejorative for nonwhite colonial subjects).[48] The secretary-general was referring to Somalia, but the virtual nonresponse of the West to the unimaginable slaughter in Rwanda in 1994, the ongoing bloody fratricide in Liberia, the mounting ethnic killing in Burundi and along the Rwanda-Zaire border in 1996, and the mass maimings and other ghastly events in Sierra Leone in recent years also have evoked suspicion of Eurowhite racism. Typically, Ghanaian diplomat Victor Gbeho observes, "If I were paranoid, I would say the delays [in getting a response by the big powers] we always face here are due to the fact that we are dealing with Africa."[49]

On a different front, evidence of potential cultural clash may be apparent in what some observers see as a rebirth of "Slavophilism," or the support of Slavic-Orthodox culture to which Huntington refers. This impulse helped set off World War I when Slavic Russia sided with Slavic Serbia against Austria-Hungary. More recently, Russia was more sympathetic during the fighting in Bosnia and, later, in Kosovo to the Serbs than were most other countries. Explaining Russia's view at one point, its foreign minister argued that atrocities were being committed by all sides, and that a bias was being created by the Western media focusing only on abuses by the Serbs. The opposite was occurring in Russia, the foreign minister noted, where "there is a mirror situation" in which the Russian media stressed "the hardships suffered by the Serbs." The result, he said, is that "when I deliver mild criticism of Serbs here [in Russia], I am seen as a betrayer of our Slavic brotherhood."[50]

Whether such evidence presages a future that fits with Huntington's prediction is highly speculative. Numerous analysts disagree with Huntington (Walt, 1997). Some point out that while racism, ethnic and religious intolerance, and other forms of culturalism are unsettling, they have persisted throughout human history and, thus, do not augur increased cultural clashes. Other analysts believe that the forces that are bringing the world together will overcome those that are driving it apart. Another scholar contends that "the real clash of civilizations will not be between the West and one or more of the Rest," but will occur within Western civilization as it struggles with itself over the postmodernist tendency toward "marginalizing Western civilization" as the work of "dead white European males" and other "boring clichés of the deconstructionists" (Kurth, 1994:14–15).

One bit of good advice comes from Kishore Mahbubani, a diplomat from Singapore. "Huntington was right," Mahbubani (1994:10) has written, insofar as he realized that "power is shifting among civilizations." What worries the Singaporean is that in response to the reemergence of non-Western cultures, a "siege mentality is developing" in the West. What is best, he argues (p. 14) is for those in the West to dispense with the "hubris" that assumes Western values are the best and to adopt some of the values of other civilizations, just as they have adopted some of the positive values of Western culture.

TRANSNATIONALISM TOMORROW

It is impossible to predict how far transnationalism will progress. It is not inconceivable that a century from now humans will share a common culture and perhaps even a common government. That is, however, far from certain. There are those who doubt that the trend of today toward transculturalism will continue into the future. Some analysts believe, for example, that English will cease to be the common language of the Internet as more and more non-English-speaking people gain access. "Be careful of turning astute observations about the current state of the Web into implications for the future," one observer cautions wisely.[51]

E Pluribus Unum?

Moreover, nationalism, as we saw in the last chapter, is proving to be a very resilient barrier to globalization and to such transnational movements as Islam. Whether it is based on political nationalism or on simple cultural familiarity, there is also strong resistance to cultural homogenization. However rational it might be to use the metric system, the bulk of Americans still seem to agree with the publisher of the anti-metric newsletter *Footprint*, who rejects "the folly of adopting faddish European units of measure."[52]

It is also very evident, however, that nationalism organized in the nation-state is under assault. One direction of attack is from the various jihad movements, secular and religious. Nation-states are splintering as people increasingly identify with smaller national units, ethnic groups, religions, and other demographic units. From the opposite direction, the forces of globalization press nations to assimilate with one another economically, socially, and politically. "We have to learn to push our politics in two directions at once: upward beyond the nation-state and downward below the nation-state," writes one scholar who advocates diminished nationalism. "For purposes of dealing with global issues [such as the environment], we need to inspire a large sense of global citizenship, because these are global problems with only global solutions." He adds, though, that people are seeking smaller units of political reference because they realize that "the planet is no substitute for a neighborhood," and that it is only in associations smaller than states, much less the globe, that "people can have a direct hand in exercising responsibility for their communities."[53]

CHAPTER SUMMARY

1. This chapter explores the bases and evidence of transnationalism in the world. Transnationalism includes a range of loyalties, activities, and other phenomena that connect humans across nations and national boundaries.

2. Some streams of transnational thought are referred to as globalism, cosmopolitanism, or some other such encompassing word. Other transnational movements, such as religion and gender, have a more limited focus.

3. The development of transnationalism springs from two sources: human thought and global interaction.

4. The lineage of the globalist strain of transnational thought extends in Western culture back to the Stoics of ancient Greece and Rome and to Buddhism in Eastern culture. Transnationalist thought is evident today in idealism, postmodernism, and postinternationalism.

5. Transnational interaction is increasing, as evident in changes in economics, communications, transportation, and organizations. International economic interdependence, mass communications, the ease of travel across borders, and the growth of transnational organizations are all helping to break down national barriers.

6. An important modern trend in international relations is the growth of transnational movements and organizations that are concerned with global issues. This includes the transnational women's movement and its associated organizations.

7. Though women's attitudes and emphases may vary, the transnational women's movement shares a similar philosophy and goals. These center on the idea that women around the world should cooperate to promote gender equality and to transform the way we think about and conduct politics at every level, including the international level.

8. Feminists, both women and the men who support gender equity, are pursuing numerous projects and making progress. The fourth World Conference on Women and its follow-up Beijing +5 Conference are just examples of activity in this area.

9. Most religions have a strong transnational element. Some religions assert universalistic claims; other religions create an urge to unite all the members of that religion across countries.

10. Religion has played many roles in world politics. The roles have been both positive and negative. The current rise in religious fundamentalism in many areas of the world is worrisome.

11. To understand the role of religion in world politics, a case study of Islam discusses the global impact of a transnational religion.

12. Transnational culture is both bringing the world together and dividing it. The movement of goods, ideas, and people across national boundaries is helping to create what is perhaps the beginning of a common global culture. Some people see this as a positive development; others oppose it.

13. Some observers believe that we are not moving toward a common culture but, instead, toward a future in which people will identify with and politically organize themselves around one or another of several antagonistic cultures or so-called civilizations.

CHAPTER 8

NATIONAL STATES: THE TRADITIONAL STRUCTURE

For the whole state, I would put mine armour on,
Which I can scarcely bear.

Shakespeare, *Coriolanus*

Something is rotten in the state of Denmark.

Shakespeare, *Hamlet*

Who saves his country, saves himself, saves all things, and all things saved do bless him! Who lets his country die, lets all things die, dies himself ignobly, and all things dying curse him!

Senator Benjamin H. Hill Jr., 1893

Man exists for his own sake and not to add a laborer to the state.

Ralph Waldo Emerson, *Journals*

CHAPTER OBJECTIVES

After completing this chapter, you should be able to:

- Understand how states as political organizations are defined.
- Examine the origins of states.
- Understand various theories of governance.
- Analyze forms of authoritarian governance.
- Analyze standards of democracy.
- Discuss the importance of balancing individualism and communitarianism in democracies.
- Examine the drive to institute democracy globally and the related implications for global and national security.
- Understand various types of interests in determining international activity.
- Discuss the future of states as principal actors in the world system.
- Understand the democratic peace thesis.

This chapter and the next one examine two divergent roads that we can take toward politically organizing the world stage. This chapter will take up the traditional organization: the state. Then, chapter 9 will examine the alternative type of organization: international governmental organizations.

THE NATURE AND ORIGINS OF THE STATE

In considering states, it is important to understand how their existence as sovereign actors affects world politics and also what their political future is. Discussing these matters, however, requires that we first establish a foundation of knowledge about what states are and how they came into being and have evolved.

THE STATE DEFINED

States are territorially defined political units that exercise ultimate internal authority and that recognize no legitimate external authority over them. States are also the most important units in defining the political identity of most people. When an Olympian steps atop the ceremonial stands to receive his or her gold medal, the flag of the victor's country is raised and its national anthem is played. States are also the most powerful of all political actors. Some huge companies approach or even exceed the wealth of some poorer countries, but no individual, company, group, or international organization approaches the coercive power wielded by most states. Whether large or small, rich or poor, populous or not, states share all or most of six characteristics: sovereignty, territory, population, diplomatic recognition, internal organization, and domestic support.

Sovereignty

The most important political characteristic of a state is **sovereignty.** This term means that the sovereign actor (the state) does not recognize as legitimate any higher authority. Sovereignty also includes the idea of legal equality among states. As we shall discuss further, sovereign states developed late in the Middle Ages (ca. 500–1350) from a consolidation and simultaneous expansion of political power. First, the rulers of Europe expanded their political authority by breaking away from the secular domination of the Holy Roman Empire and the theological authority of the pope. Second, the kings also consolidated political power by subjugating feudal estates and other competing local political organizations within their realms. The resulting states exercised supreme authority over their territory and citizens; they owed neither allegiance nor obedience to any higher authority.

It is important to note that sovereignty, a legal and theoretical term, differs from independence, a political and applied term (James, 1999). Independence means freedom from outside control, and in an ideal, law-abiding world, sovereignty and independence would be synonymous. In the real world, however, where power is important, independence is not absolute. Sometimes a small country is so dominated by a powerful neighbor that its independence is dubious at best. Especially in terms of their foreign and defense policies Bhutan (dominated by India), the Marshall Islands (dominated by the United States), Monaco (dominated by France), and other such countries can be described as having only circumscribed sovereignty (Clapham, 1999).

While independence has always been relative, the weakening of the doctrine of state sovereignty is more of a recent phenomenon. It is one of the most important changes under way in the international system (Hashmi, 1997). The world community is beginning to reject sovereignty as a defense for a government's mistreatment of its citizens. South Africa long oppressed its non-European-heritage citizens, especially its blacks. What changed was world norms. The United Nations condemned South Africa

The principle that sovereignty means that countries can do whatever they wish within their borders is beginning to fray. Protests broke out in many places in Europe, and the European Union imposed diplomatic sanctions on Austria in early 2000, when it appeared that Austria would include the neo-fascist Freedom Party led by Jörg Haider in the coalition government. This photograph shows an anti-Haider demonstration in front of Austria's parliament building in Vienna attended by at least 20,000 protesters. The placard shows, from left, Nazi Germany's führer (1933–1945) Adolf Hitler, fascist Italy's leader (1922–1943) Benito Mussolini, Yugoslavia's president (1989–2000) Slobodan Milosevic (who has been indicted for war crimes by the international tribunal in The Hague), and Haider. The German translates, "Faces change… not the message." The outrage across Europe and the diplomatic pressure kept Haider out of the government.

and suspended its membership. Countries imposed escalating economic and other sanctions to force reforms on the white government. Finally, in 1992 South African whites agreed to share political power with the country's black citizens, and in 1994 the country's first black president, Nelson Mandela, took office.

The events in Haiti in 1994 highlight another diminution of sovereignty. The UN condemned the coup that had overthrown Haiti's elected president and imposed sanctions. When those failed the Security Council authorized UN members "to form a multinational force… [and] to use all necessary means" to topple the military junta. Soon thereafter, a U.S.–led force sent the generals packing into exile.

On another issue, the international community in the late 1990s brought strong pressure on the Yugoslav government to cease its brutal attacks on rebellious towns in Kosovo, even though that province is clearly part of Yugoslavia. When diplomacy and sanctions failed, NATO warplanes went into action. The Serbs were driven from Kosovo, and the province was occupied by KFOR, the multinational Kosovo Force.

Even more recently, Europe demonstrated sharp unwillingness to tolerate Austria's movement toward what many saw as a neofascist government. Following national elections in February 2000, Wolfgang Schüssel, the leader of the conservative People's Party, formed a government coalition with the ultra right-wing Freedom Party, led by Jörg Haider. Europe broke into an uproar. Haider is often accused of being sympathetic to Nazism. He has, among other things, defended Nazi Germany's murderous Waffen SS as simply part of the Wehrmacht [the World War II German army] and hence deserving of "all the honor and respect of the army in public life" and referred to Hitler's concentration camps as "the punishment camps of National Socialism."[1] The partnership with Chancellor Schüssel gave the Freedom Party important power and put Haider in line to be deputy chancellor.

In response, the European Union (EU), of which Austria is a member, moved to downgrade the relations among Austria and its other members to the "technical level." The EU members suspended high-level contacts with Austria, and in some cases recalled ambassadors and left lower-level diplomats in charge of embassies in Vienna. "This is about Europe and its values," said an adviser to the German chancellor; "We cannot have business as usual with an Austrian government that would allow the far right to be legitimized."[2] The action was also an important step whereby, for the first time, the EU overrode the doctrine of sovereignty by interfering in the internal political processes of one of its members. "We are moving swiftly to the reduction of sovereignty in the political field," noted one French foreign policy analyst.[3]

Haider accused the EU of engaging in a "medieval exorcism" and predicted that a wave of "ideological change" would soon sweep Europe, but stepped down as leader of the Freedom Party and, thus, out of the government.[4] After six months of watchfulness, the EU members were assuaged that the Freedom Party would not be part of the Austrian coalition government, and normal relations were reestablished in September 2000.

What should we make of these restraints on internal sovereignty in South Africa, Haiti, Yugoslavia, and Austria? It would be naive to imagine they mean that in the foreseeable future the world community will regularly ignore sovereignty to take a stand against racism or authoritarianism whenever and wherever they occur. It would be equally wrong, however, not to recognize that the actions against racial oppression, military coups, ethnic cleansing, and neofascism were important steps away from the doctrine of unlimited state sovereignty.

Sovereignty also implies legal *equality* among states. That theory is applied in the UN General Assembly and many other international assemblies, where each member-state has one vote. Are all states really equal, though? Compare San Marino and China (Table 8.1). San Marino lies entirely within Italy and is the world's oldest republic, dating back to the fourth century A.D. After years of self-imposed nonparticipation, the San Marinese decided to seek membership in the UN. "The fact of sitting around the table with the most important states in the world is a reaffirmation of sovereignty," explained Giovanni Zangoli, the country's foreign minister.[5] The General Assembly seated San Marino in 1992 as a sovereign equal. Nevertheless, it is obvious that whatever sovereignty may mean legally, in many ways the two countries are not equal.

Table 8.1 San Marino and China: Sovereign Equals

	San Marino	China	Ratio
Territory (sq. mi.)	24	3,705,400	1:154,392
Population	25,061	1,246,872,000	1:49,753
GDP ($ millions)	500	4,500,000	1:9,000
Military Personnel	0	2,300,000	1:∞
Vote in UN General Assembly	1	1	1:1

China includes data for now-incorporated Hong Kong. San Marino has a police force with an annual budget of about $37 million.

∞ = infinity

Data sources: World Almanac (2000); CIA (2000).

The legal concept of sovereign equality is very different from more tangible measures of equality, as is evident in this comparison of two countries: San Marino and China.

Territory

A second characteristic of a state is territory. It would seem obvious that a state must have physical boundaries, and most states do. On closer examination, though, the question of territory becomes more complex. There are numerous international disputes over borders; territorial boundaries can expand, contract, or shift dramatically; and it is even possible to have a state without territory. Many states recognize what they call Palestine as sovereign, yet the Palestinians are scattered across other countries such as Jordan. An accord that the Israelis and Palestinians signed in 1994 gave the Palestinians a measure of autonomy in Gaza (a region between Israel and Egypt) and in parts of the West Bank, and these areas have increased through subsequent negotiations. Therefore, depending on one's viewpoint, the Palestinians have some territory, no territory, or have been expelled from the territory now occupied by Israel. It is also possible to maintain, as the United States and most other countries currently do, that the Palestinians still have no state of their own.

Population

People are an obvious requirement of any state. The populations of states range from the 860 inhabitants of the Holy See (popularly referred to as the Vatican) to China's 1.3 billion people, but all states count this characteristic as a minimum requirement.

What is becoming less clear in the shifting loyalties of the evolving international system is exactly where the population of a country begins and ends. Citizenship has become a bit more fluid than it was not long ago. For example, a citizen of one European Union (EU) country who resides in another EU country can now vote in local elections and even hold local office in the country in which he or she resides. Similarly, a reform accord reached in 1996 by the political parties of Mexico allows Mexicans who have emigrated to the United States to vote in Mexican presidential elections.

Diplomatic Recognition

A classic rhetorical question is: If a tree fell in the forest and no one heard it, did it make a sound? The same question governs the issue of statehood and the recognition by others. If a political entity declares its independence and no other country grants it diplomatic recognition, is it really a state? The answer seems to be no.

How many countries must grant recognition before statehood is achieved is a more difficult question. When Israel declared its independence in 1948, the United States and the Soviet Union quickly recognized the country. Its Arab neighbors did not extend recognition and instead attacked what they considered to be the Zionist invaders. Was Israel a state at that point? It certainly seems so, because which countries, as well as how many of them, extend recognition is important.

Yet a lack of recognition, even by a majority of other countries, does not necessarily mean a state does not exist. Diplomatic recognition by most countries of the communist government of Mao Zedong in China came slowly after it took power in 1949. U.S. recognition was withheld until 1979. Did that mean that the rechristened People's Republic of China did not exist for a time? Clearly the answer is no because, as one scholar comments, "power capabilities are equally or more important than outside recognition" in establishing the existence of a state (Thompson, 1995:220).

The issue of recognition remains a matter of serious international concern. Taiwan is for all practical purposes an independent country, and it is recognized by more than two dozen countries. Yet, Taiwan itself does not claim independence, and thus is a *de facto* (in fact), but not *de jure* (in law) state.

Another contemporary issue involves the Palestinians. Many states recognize a Palestinian state and did so even before the Palestinians acquired any autonomous territory in Gaza and the West Bank beginning in the mid-1990s. Currently, according to the Palestine National Authority (PNA), almost 100 countries (including China and India) recognize an "independent State of Palestine," some 79 (including the United States) accept Palestinian passports, and 22 countries maintain representative missions in Gaza or the West Bank. Since the PNA has not declared an independent Palestine, it would be hard to construe these diplomatic ties as recognizing Palestinian sovereign statehood. Yet if the PNA and its president, Yasser Arafat, do declare independence, as he has said will soon happen, then the degree to which these countries recognize that independence and establish full diplomatic relations will have important legal and political ramifications for the nascent state of Palestine.

Did You Know That:

Countries other than the United States, where the Internet started, have a national "domain" designation of the state's cyberspace territory. A modern indication of evolving statehood for Palestine is that the Internet's international coordinating authority, the Internet Corporation for Assigned Names and Numbers, has granted a domain designation ".ps" to the Palestinian National Authority. Soon one may be able to visit the Web site of the Palestinian president at yasserarafat.gov.ps.

Certainly, the standard of diplomatic recognition remains hazy. Nevertheless, it is an important factor in the international system for several reasons. One is related to psychological status. History has many examples of new countries and governments, even those with revolutionary ideology, that have assiduously sought outside recognition and, to a degree, moderated their policies in order to get it. Second, external recognition has important practical advantages. Generally, states are the only entities that can legally sell government bonds and buy heavy weapons from another state. Israel's chances of survival in 1948 were enhanced when recognition allowed the Israelis to raise money and purchase armaments in Europe, the United States, and elsewhere. Also, it would be difficult for any aspirant to statehood to survive for long without recognition. Economic problems resulting from the inability to establish trade relations is just one example of the difficulties that would arise. The case of Taiwan shows that survival while in diplomatic limbo is not impossible, but it is such an oddity that it does not disprove the general rule.

Internal Organization

States must normally have some level of political and economic structure. Most states have a government, but statehood continues during periods of severe turmoil, even anarchy. Afghanistan, Liberia, Sierra Leone, Somalia, and some other existing states dissolved into chaos for an extended time during the last decade, and had no functioning national government. Yet none of these "failed states" ceased to exist legally. Each, for instance, continued to sit as a sovereign equal, with an equal vote in the UN General Assembly.

An associated issue arises when what once was and what still claims to be the government of a generally recognized or formerly recognized state exists outside the territory that the exiled government claims as its own. There is a long history of recognizing governments-in-exile. The most common instances have occurred when a sitting government is forced by invaders to flee. A current and controversial example of what claims to be a government-in-exile involves Tibet, as explained in the box, The Dalai Lama in Dharamsala.

Domestic Support

The final characteristic of a state is domestic support. At its most active, this implies that a state's population is loyal to it and grants it the authority to make rules and to govern (legitimacy). At its most passive, the population grudgingly accepts the authority of the government. For all the coercive power that a state usually possesses, it is difficult for any state to survive without at least the passive acquiescence of its people. The dissolution of Czechoslovakia, the Soviet Union, and Yugoslavia (and, in turn, Bosnia) are illustrations of multinational states collapsing in the face of the separatist impulses of disaffected nationalities.

(continued on page 196)

THE DALAI LAMA IN DHARAMSALA

The Chinese describe him as a "traitor," a "splittist," and "a wolf in monk's clothing."[1] Others exalt him as a living god, a symbol of enlightened peace, and representative of an oppressed people. Indeed, the Dalai Lama and the fate of his native Tibet have become a cause célèbre among Americans and many others through such sympathetic movies as *Seven Years in Tibet*, with Brad Pitt, and director Martin Scorsese's *Kundun*. Other film notables, such as Richard Gere, who is Buddhist, have taken up the cause, and the Students for a Free Tibet have chapters on many U.S. college campuses. Indeed the Dalai Lama's image is generally so benign that one news magazine has dubbed him the "Teflon Lama."[2] The Dalai Lama himself chuckles disarmingly, "In reality, I am just an ordinary human being."[3]

Whatever the character or theological nature of the Dalai Lama, his roles include those of spiritual leader of Tibetan Buddhism and head of what many consider to be Tibet's government-in-exile located in Dharamsala, India. The tale of Tibet presents an interesting case study for what constitutes a state.

Tibet is large (471,000 square miles, almost twice the size of Texas) and sits 15,000 feet high in the Himalayas between India and China. Population data varies greatly by source, but perhaps 3 million Tibetans and an equal number of Chinese live in Tibet. Another 2 million or so Tibetans live in adjacent areas in China or are refugees in northern India. China claims them as Chinese, but the Mongolian-stock Tibetans are distinct from the Han, the dominant Chinese ethnic group. Also, the Tibetan language is related more to Burmese than it is to the major Chinese dialects (Mandarin, Cantonese, Fukienese).

Tibetans are Buddhists, but their form of Buddhism has its roots in India, not China. Tibetan Buddhism and Tibetan ethnonational identity are closely connected. Perhaps one-sixth of the adult male population of Tibet were monks (lamas) in 1950. For over a thousand years, Tibet was a theocracy, ruled spiritually and politically by the Dalai Lama and other lamas. The current, fourteenth Dalai Lama was just five years old when he was enthroned in 1940.

Tibet was an independent kingdom from the 800s to the 1300s. It then came under the sway of Ghengis Khan and the Mongols. The dynasty founded by his grandson, Kublai Khan, also ruled China. The Mongols were expelled from China after about a century, but they continued to rule their homeland and Tibet. As Mongol power ebbed, Tibet exercised increased autonomy, and in 1577 the Mongol emperor Altan Khan gave political authority in Tibet to the ranking lama and designated him *Dalai Lama* (lama of all within the seas). Soon, however, Tibet's autonomy was eclipsed. Chinese influence grew, and a massive invasion by China in 1751 established the Chinese emperor's suzerainty over Tibet.

Thus Tibet was independent for about 600 years, then for another 600 years was in a political twilight zone, neither fully sovereign nor completely subordinate to the Mongols, or, later, to the Chinese. A new era of independence began in 1911, when imperial China collapsed, and lasted until 1950, when Chinese forces again seized control. At first, the Dalai Lama remained in Lhasa, Tibet's capital, and exercised some local authority. Then in 1959 the Tibetans revolted against China. They were bloodily crushed, and the Dalai Lama and his supporters fled south to India and established a government-in-exile at Dharamsala. China revoked Tibet's autonomy and demolished or seized almost all of its important monasteries in an effort to wipe out Tibetan religion and culture. The Dalai Lama claims (and China denies) that 6,000 monasteries have been closed or destroyed and 1.2 million Tibetans have been killed by the Chinese since 1950.

The issue of Tibet's statehood is complicated (Goldstein, 1997). Beijing traces its authority back through centuries of Chinese emperors, who, depending on their own fortunes, exercised greater or lesser control over Tibet. The Tibetans concede that they were subjects of the imperial dynasties but maintain that Tibet was autonomous. Moreover, Tibetans argue that they were under the suzerainty of the emperor, not China. They note that the connection between monarchs and national countries is a relatively modern phenomenon. In an earlier era, emperors ruled subjects in various lands, but that rule was personal. In this case, while the Chinese emperor ruled Tibet, that did not make Tibet part of China. Tibetan claims also rest on their cultural distinctiveness, including the nearly inseparable spiritual and temporal intertwining of the Dalai Lama and Tibet.

China also contends that its control is valid because Tibet was ruled by an oppressive theocracy that kept the country backward and in poverty. "When the Dalai Lama ruled Tibet there were few schools in the region, and 95 percent of the people were illiterate," Beijing has argued. By comparison, China's justification went on, "Tibet now has thousands of schools... drastically reducing the illiteracy rate."[4] Perhaps, but Tibetans do not seem to feel liberated by the Chinese. "As soon as we can, we'll regroup, demonstrate, and drive the Chinese out," says a female stallholder in a Lhasa market.[5]

One strategy that China has adopted to deal with the

issue of Tibet has been to try to undermine Tibetan identity by destroying or closing the monasteries and repressing political activity. "Everyone is so nervous here," says a Lhasa shopkeeper. "No one knows what the Chinese are going to do next. They have destroyed the underground movement. All the monks and nuns are terrified."[6] Beijing is also trying to mute Tibetan identity by diluting the population with emigrant Han Chinese and their culture. The Dalai Lama condemns the "mass influx of Chinese" along with "the destruction of [Tibetan] cultural artifacts and traditions" as "cultural genocide."[7]

Additionally China is trying to create a future rival to the Dalai Lama by kidnapping a six-year-old boy who had been identified by a group of lamas in 1995 as the eleventh Panchen Lama,

The Dalai Lama

Tibet's second most important lama. China then announced that other, more cooperative lamas had found another boy to be the true Panchen Lama. The whereabouts of the first boy, perhaps the world's youngest political prisoner, remain unknown.

Despite these efforts to undercut the Dalai Lama, he remains a threat to China's control of Tibet. To support Tibet's cause, the Dalai Lama has traveled extensively, and his self-effacing demeanor and advocacy of nonviolence have won Tibet considerable sympathy. Not only has he gained a star-studded galaxy of supporters in the West, but in 1989 the Dalai Lama received the Nobel Peace Prize.

The Dalai Lama has also worked to win official international support for Tibet, but neither he nor any of his earlier incarnations have enjoyed much success. For instance, in 1909, with the Chinese imperial court in its death throes, the thirteenth Dalai Lama appealed to Great Britain for support. This was rejected by London, according to a British document, on the grounds that Tibet was a "worthless piece of territory" (Heberer, 1995:303). The British were not alone in this view. During the 1911–1950 period of Tibetan independence, no

country extended diplomatic recognition to Lhasa.

The unwillingness to recognize Tibet has not changed. For example, speaking in Beijing in 1998 at a joint press conference with President Jiang Zemin of China, President Clinton stated, "I agree that Tibet is a part of China.... And I can understand why acknowledgment of that would be a precondition of dialogue with the Dalai Lama."[8]

This does not mean that the status quo is immutable. While it is improbable that China will surrender its claim to Tibet, it is not unthinkable that China might allow Tibet some autonomy and even permit the return of the Dalai Lama to Lhasa. At his press conference with President Clinton, President Jiang commented that "as long as the Dalai Lama can publicly make a... commitment that Tibet is an inalienable part of China..., then the door to dialogue and negotiation is open."[9] This brought a positive response from the Dalai Lama. "I have made it very clear that I'm not seeking independence for Tibet," he told reporters. "I am seeking genuine autonomy; and this indirectly recognizes Chinese sovereignty."[10]

The Dalai Lama's offer of what he calls "the middle way" of domestic autonomy, but not sovereignty, for Tibet, has, however, been condemned both by China as "a disguised form of independence," and by those (mostly younger) Tibetans who reject nonviolence.[11] Says one 32-year-old Tibetan, "If we wait for nonviolence to work, maybe I will spend my whole life here [in Dharamsala]. We need a stronger way."[12] Even the Dalai Lama concedes that he has lost some influence among Tibetans. "For many years, I'd been able to persuade the Tibetan people to eschew violence in our freedom struggle," he said recently. "Today, it's clear that a sense of urgency is building up. In that sense my efforts have failed," he concluded pessimistically.[13]

It is important to note for our discussion of the future of states that domestic support is based on pragmatic considerations as well as on emotional attachment to the national state. Those who study the origins of the sovereign state point out that states developed in part "as the result of a social coalition based on the affinity of interests and perspective" between emerging kings and important elements of the population (Spruyt, 1994:79). The point is that states are political organizations created to perform tasks, to "establish Justice, insure domestic Tranquillity, provide for the common defense, promote the general Welfare, and secure the Blessings of Liberty," as the Preamble to the U.S. Constitution puts it. Because states are meant to provide such benefits, states derive part of their domestic support from their ability to deliver the proverbial goods. When states are unable to meet important needs (and some analysts say states now cannot do so), the domestic support of the state weakens. This observation about the founding and evolution of the sovereign state leads to a further discussion of origins of the modern state.

THE ORIGINS OF THE STATE

In the last chapter we noted the decline of the Greek city-states as the center of political organization in the West and the eventual domination of the universalistic Roman Empire. After more than five centuries as the hub of the known Western world, Rome fell in 476. Thereafter, secular political power in the West was wielded for almost a millennium by two levels of authority—one universal, the other local. On the universalistic *macrolevel*, international organizational authority existed in the form of the Roman Catholic Church. Christianity as interpreted by the Catholic Church and its pope served as the integrating force in several ways. The Church kept Latin alive, which provided a common language among intellectuals. Christian doctrine underlay the developing concepts of rights, justice, and other political norms. Even kings were theoretically (and often substantially) subordinate to the pope. It was, for example, Pope Leo III who crowned Charlemagne "Emperor of the Romans" in 800. Charlemagne's empire did not last, but the idea of a new Christian-Roman universal state was established, and was strengthened further when in 936 Otto I was crowned head of what became known as the **Holy Roman Empire.**

Centuries later, the overarching authority of the Catholic Church was supplemented and, in some cases, supplanted, by great multiethnic empires. These political conglomerations came to exercise control over many different peoples. The Austro-Hungarian, British, Chinese, Dutch, French, German, Ottoman, Russian, Spanish, and other empires controlled people in their immediate continental areas and on other continents. Most of the people within these empires did not feel a strong political identification with or an emotional attachment to them. Many of these empires lasted into this century; but the collapse of the Soviet Union, which had inherited the Russian empire, marked the end of the last of the great multiethnic empires that had provided an earlier degree of macrolevel integration.

The local, *microlevel* of authority centered on political units that were smaller than the states that would one day evolve. The **feudal system** was characterized by principalities, dukedoms, baronies, and other such fiefdoms, which were ruled by minor royalty who provided local defense. This warrior elite was largely autonomous, even though individual nobles were theoretically vassals of a king or an emperor.

It is important to understand here, as one scholar explains it, that systems of governance "had vastly different characteristics" than they do today. "They were nonterritorial, and sovereignty was, at best, disputed" (Spruyt, 1994:35). Certainly rulers, from emperors to barons, controlled specific pieces of territory. The land that a feudal lord controlled, though, was mostly a function of his individual power and his relationship to other feudal lords and, thus, was not fixed. The Church and the Holy Roman Empire by definition sought to include all Christians, not a defined territory. Furthermore, the

MAP
Sovereign States: Dates of Independence, p. 136

very nature of the feudal system, in which vassals were theoretically subservient to kings and kings were theoretically subservient to emperors and popes, meant that sovereignty did not exist legally and often did not exist in fact.

By the thirteenth century the fabric of universalism and feudalism had begun to fray. In the words of one scholar, "At the end of the Middle Ages, the international system went through a dramatic transformation in which the crosscutting jurisdictions of feudal lords, emperors, kings, and popes started to give way to territorially defined authorities" (Spruyt, 1994:1). The existing nonterritorially defined, hierarchical system was replaced by a system based on territorially defined sovereign states.

The Decline of the Feudal System

The forces of change in the Middle Ages that eroded the feudal system were many. Of these, two factors stand out—military technology and economic expansion.

States became the dominant form of political organization for several pragmatic reasons. One of these was that once gunpowder began to be used militarily in the 1300s, territorially larger states proved more defensible than were feudal realms and their castles.

Military Technology Advances in military capabilities, especially the introduction of gunpowder, diminished the ability of the relatively small feudal manors to provide security. The first mention of guns in Europe is contained in a manuscript written in Florence in 1327. Thereafter, an armored knight, the epitome of the feudal warrior elite, could be shot off his horse by a quickly trained commoner armed with a primitive firearm; the castle, the centerpiece of feudal defense, could be demolished easily by cannons. These and other factors meant that static defenses of small territories needed to be replaced by defense based on the ability to maneuver, which could be provided only by a territorially larger unit, the state.

Economic Expansion The growth of Europe's economy undermined the feudal system and promoted the state system. *Improved trade* was one factor. The decline of the Viking maritime menace to the north of Europe and the easing of Muslim barriers to trade with Asia increased trade with lands to the east of Europe and brought in new wealth. This in turn led to the building of larger ships, which created even greater possibilities for trade. The journeys of Marco Polo to China and other lands far from his native Venice between 1271 and 1295 were an early manifestation of this new commercial activity. Soon thereafter, the search for trade was a major focus of Europeans and led, among other things, to the journey of Christopher Columbus to the Caribbean in 1492.

The beginning of early *mass production* was a second factor driving economic expansion. Individual craftsmen began to give way to primitive factories. The full-scale **industrial revolution** did not take place for several hundred more years, but by the 1200s the early stages of this new mode of production already required larger markets and larger sources of supply for raw materials than the limited territory of the feudal realm provided.

The rise of trade and manufacturing and, consequently, the accumulation of new wealth resulted in important changes in political power. Increased trade and manufacturing added to the size, wealth, and, therefore, power of the commercial class, the burghers. In the same way, the need for trading centers and manufacturing centers led to the increase in the size and importance of towns. Neither burghers nor towns fit with the feudal system, which was based on the authority of the local lord over mostly agricultural peasants. The economic needs of the burghers and towns led them to support the creation of larger political units more suited for uninterrupted commerce. In this desire the burghers found ready allies in kings. The kings wanted to increase their control over their often-fractious feudal lords but needed money to finance the men and arms to overcome local resistance. The burghers wanted to destroy local restraints and had the money to loan the kings. The resulting alliance helped create the modern state. In fact, the burghers became so powerful in their own right that, much later, they were part of the elite that resisted the king and launched democracy in the United States and elsewhere.

Did You Know That:

The most successful of the new economic elite of the Middle Ages was the Italian family founded by Giovanni di Bicci de' Medici (1360–1429). The immense wealth gained by this family of bankers and merchants led to political power. They dominated the city-state of Florence from the 1400s until 1737 as dukes and duchesses; two de' Medicis became queens of France (Catherine in 1547, Marie in 1610); and three de' Medicis became popes (Leo X in 1513, Clement VII in 1523, and Leo X in 1605).

In sum, changes in military technology rendered the feudal manor obsolete as a defensive unit and changes in manufacturing and commerce rendered the feudal manor obsolete as an economic unit. Larger political units were needed to provide protection and to operate efficiently. Furthermore, improved communications and transportation made people more aware of and cooperative with their ethnic kin in other areas. The feudal system was doomed.

The Decline of Universalistic Authority

At the same time that the micropolitical feudal system was decaying, the macropolitical claims of universalistic authority by the pope and the Holy Roman emperor were also being increasingly challenged. In part, political-religious authority began to decline as the authority of kings grew through the just-discussed process of subduing feudal manors and incorporating them into their kingdoms. As kings became more powerful, they began to reject the real, or even titular, political authority of the pope.

The decline of papal authority and the increase in royal power were reinforced by a period of cultural and intellectual rebirth and reform called the **Renaissance** (about 1350–1650). Educated people looked to the classical Hellenic and Roman cultures as models and developed a concept of personal freedom that ran counter to the authority of the Church.

One significant outcome of this secular movement was the **Protestant Reformation.** Influenced in part by Renaissance thinking, Martin Luther rejected the Catholic Church as the necessary intermediary between people and God. In 1517 Luther protested Catholic doctrine and proclaimed his belief that anyone could have an individual relationship with God. Within a few decades, nearly a quarter of the people of Western Europe became Protestants.

The first great secular break with the Catholic Church occurred in England, where King Henry VIII (1509–1547) rejected papal authority and established the Anglican Church. The Reformation also touched off political-religious struggles elsewhere in Europe. The ostensible issue was religious freedom, but there were also important political causes and consequences. When the century-long struggle between the imperial and Catholic Holy Roman Empire and the nationalist and Protestant ethnic groups ended with the **Treaty of Westphalia** (1648), centralized political power in Europe was over. The Holy Roman Empire had splintered into two rival Catholic monarchies (Austria and Spain); a number of Protestant entities (such as Holland and many German states) gained independence or autonomy; and other countries, such as Catholic France and Protestant England, were more secure in their independence. Thus, many scholars regard 1648 as marking the births of the modern national state and of the world political system based on sovereign states as the primary political actors (Philpott, 1999).

The Victory of the Sovereign State

The breakdown of the feudal-universalistic systems did not, however, lead immediately to the uncontested growth and political dominance of states. Instead, the people of the

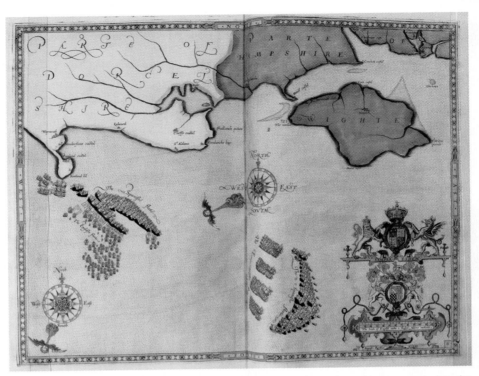

One of the events that secured the future of the evolving sovereign state system occurred when the Spanish Armada dispatched in 1588 by Phillip II, king of Spain and ruler of the Holy Roman Empire, failed in its attempt to conquer Protestant England in the name of the Roman Catholic empire. This antique map from a museum in Madrid shows the 125-ship Armada and the smaller opposing English fleet commanded by Sir Francis Drake in the English Channel just before the pivotal Battle of Gravelines, which Drake won. Thereafter, much of what was left of the Armada was swept away by powerful storms off the coasts of Scotland and Ireland.

Middle Ages experimented with several types of political organizations to see how well they met the security and economic needs of the time.

The Early State and its Competitors The revival of city-states, such as Florence and Venice, was one alternative scheme of political organization. Another was the formation of loosely confederated city-leagues based on common economic interests. The most famous of these mercantile alliances was the Hanseatic League (*hanse*, German for "merchant guild"). Founded in 1358 to protect commerce against piracy, and eventually including 70 north-central European cities such as Hamburg and Lübeck, the city-league became a major economic force.

Neither the city-league nor city-state form of organization persisted; the state did. The Hanseatic League ended in 1667, when its council met for the last time. The fortunes of Florence and other city-states ebbed more slowly, but they eventually faded also. What is important is that states bested city-states and city-leagues to become the successor of the feudal-universalistic system of political organization. This occurred for identifiable, pragmatic reasons. A review of the complex factors involved in this victory of the state is beyond our telling here, but the essential point, as one scholar puts it, is that in time "sovereign states displaced city-leagues and city-states... because their institutional logic gave them an advantage in mobilizing their societies' resources" (Spruyt, 1994:185). States were best equipped to conduct commerce and to provide defense.

We can see two key points from the foregoing. First, sovereign, territorial states as we know them have not always been the basis of international political organization

Monarchs once claimed that they ruled by divine right and "owned" the state. Through the French Revolution (1789) and the execution of Louis XVI, who is receiving the last rites in this engraving, the French people claimed France for themselves.

(Opello & Rosow, 1999). Second, states did not succeed earlier systems and prevail over competing systems or organizations because states were inevitable or because they had some special moral or philosophical claim as the ultimate expression of human political organization. Rather, states won out because they worked better at a particular time in history. Remembering this point about the pragmatic origins of the state will be crucial to judging the contemporary argument about the future of the state when we take that matter up later in the chapter.

Evolution of States toward Democracy To round out this survey of the founding and evolution of the state, we can note that during the several centuries that followed the Peace of Westphalia, the genesis of national states continued as economic and social interaction grew, and monarchs such as Louis XIV of France (1643–1715), Frederick II of Prussia (1740–1786), and Peter the Great of Russia (1682–1725) consolidated their core domains and even expanded them into empires. In the development of the modern national state, however, one key element was yet to come. Missing was the concept that the state is an embodiment of the nation (the people). Kings claimed to rule their realms by "divine right"; thus France's Louis XIV could proclaim, "*L'état, c'est moi*" (I am the state). Perhaps it was so then, but in 1793 another French king, Louis XVI, lost his head over this presumption, and the people claimed the state for themselves.

The coming of democracy, exemplified by the American (1776) and French (1789) Revolutions promoted the creation of the national state. The fixed territory of modern states and their sense of sovereign singularity had already begun to create a spirit of nationalism in England and elsewhere. Still, the attachment of most individuals to the state was limited by the theory that the state was the property of the monarch and the people were the crown's subjects. Democracy changed the theory of who owns the state from monarch to citizen, and that solidified nationalism. Now the state was the possession of the people, who, therefore, were obliged to support it emotionally and materially.

Once this occurred, all the basic parameters for the modern state that exists today were in place. Certainly, new states continued to evolve into being as older systems slowly disintegrated. Important states like Germany and Italy did not exist a century and a half ago; other states like Vietnam did not exist 50 years ago; still other states like Ukraine did not exist a decade ago. The idea that people own and are tied to their countries also continued to evolve. A century ago, monarchs ruled nearly everywhere. Now they rule almost nowhere, and even authoritarian governments claim power in the name of the people.

THE STATE AS THE CORE POLITICAL ORGANIZATION

Having explored the evolution of states, our next task is to look at the state as our primary political organization. Chapter 4 pointed out that the anarchical nature of the international system stems from the fact that the sovereign state is the key actor in the system. Then chapter 5 looked inside the state to illuminate the foreign policy-making process. What we can add here are examinations of differing theories of governance and of national and other interests.

THEORIES OF GOVERNANCE

It is possible to divide theories of governance into two broad categories. One includes types of **authoritarian government**, which allow little or no participation in decision making by individuals and groups outside the upper reaches of the government. The second category includes **democratic government**, which allows much broader and more meaningful participation. As with many things we discuss, the line between authoritarian and democratic is not precise. Instead, using broad and meaningful participation as the standard, there is a scale that runs from one-person rule to full, direct democracy (or even, according to some, to anarchism). The map on p. 202 provides one way to order types of government, with the countries in shades of green being generally democratic and the countries in other colors being generally authoritarian.

Authoritarian Theories of Governance

The world has witnessed the coming, dominance, and the passing of a number of nondemocratic political theories about how societies should be organized and governed. The idea of *theocratic rule* by spiritual leaders is ancient. Now, however, it has almost disappeared, although there are some elements of **theocracy** left in the popular, if not the legal, status of Japan's emperor, Thailand's king, and (most strongly) Tibet's exiled Dalai Lama. Iran's government also contains an element of theocracy, and the increased strength of religious fundamentalism in many places means that it is not unthinkable that a rejuvenation of theocracy might occur. Similarly, strong **monarchism** resting on the theory of the divine right of kings is as old as human organization. But it has also declined almost to the point of extinction, with only a few strong monarchs (such as Saudi Arabia's king) scattered among a larger number of constitutional monarchies that severely restrict the monarch's power.

    Communism as it originated in the works of Friedrich Engels and Karl Marx is essentially an economic theory. As applied, however, by Vladimir Lenin and Joseph Stalin in the USSR, by Mao Zedong in China, and by other Communist leaders in those countries and elsewhere, communism also falls squarely within the spectrum of authoritarian governance. Even Marx expected that a "dictatorship of the proletariat" over the bourgeoisie would follow communist revolutions and prevail during a transitional socialist period between capitalism and communism. Lenin institutionalized this view. His concept of dictatorship meant, in the words of one study, "the dictatorship of the Communist Party over the proletariat, since [Lenin] had little faith that the working class had the political understanding or spontaneous organizational ability to secure the existence and expansion of a communist state" (Ebenstein, Ebenstein, & Fogelman, 1994:125). Stalin further concentrated political authority in his person and in a small group of associates. Even the Communist Party lost its control, and, another study explains, "After 1930, not a single protest was raised; not a single dissenting voice or vote expressed" any difference with what Stalin decided (Macridis & Hulliung, 1996:117). Indeed the encompassing social, economic, and political control that Stalin claimed was termed "totalitarian."

    Fascism is another authoritarian political philosophy that in some of its manifestations embraces totalitarianism. The term fascism is often used loosely to describe almost anyone far to the right. That approach is wrong, for the term should be used with some precision. Modern fascism can be traced to Italy and the ideas of Benito Mussolini and to a variant, National Socialism and Adolf Hitler and his Nazi followers in Germany. There were some differences between Italian Fascism and German Nazism, but they were similar enough so that, one study commented, "It is not too difficult to state the basic elements of the fascist outlook" (Ebenstein, Ebenstein, & Fogelman, 1994:87). These include (1) a rejection of rationality and a reliance on emotion to govern; (2) a belief (especially for Nazis) in the superiority of some groups and the inferiority of others;

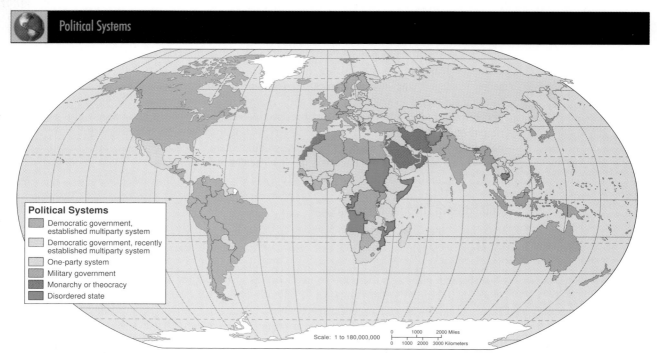

The democratization of the world's countries, which began symbolically with the American (1776) and French (1789) Revolutions, progressed slowly for 150 years, then accelerated after World War II. Now, as this map and Figure 8.1 on the next page indicate, the majority of countries are full-fledged– or quasi-democracies.

(3) advocacy of the legitimacy of subjugating countries of "inferior" people; (4) a rejection of the rights of individuals in favor of a "corporatist" view that people are "workers" in the state; (5) gearing all economic activity to the support of the corporatist state; (6) an anthropomorphic view of the state as a living thing (the organic state theory); (7) belief that the individual's highest expression is in the people (*volk* in German); and (8) belief that the highest expression of the volk (and, by extension, the individual) is in the leader (*führer* in German, *duce* in Italian), who rules as a totalitarian dictator.

This approach, which we will generically call fascism, spread beyond Italy and Germany to include such other countries as Spain under Francisco Franco (1939–1975) and Argentina under Juan Perón (1946–1955). What makes fascism of more contemporary interest is that it is again astir in a variety of countries. The term fascist is so tainted by history that few concede to being fascist. But under the old rubric that if something waddles and quacks like a duck, it probably is a duck, there are a number of movements that goose-step and espouse political and social quackery that is suspiciously fascist. There are a number of such movements in Western Europe and elsewhere that have achieved unsettling success in recent years.

Xenophobia directed at foreigners, Jews, and Gypsies (more properly Roma) have marked the recent upswing in the fortunes of several right-wing parties in Europe. The success of Jörg Haider and the Freedom Party in Austria came in part through virulent anti-immigrant rhetoric. During the elections in late 1999, Freedom Party posters warned against *überfremdung*, a term coined in Nazi Germany, which translates as "foreign infiltration." Among Haider's views: "The Africans who come here are drug dealers and they seduce our youth. We've got the Poles who concentrate on car theft. We've got the people from the former Yugoslavia who are burglary experts. We've got the Turks who are superbly organized in the heroin trade. And we've got the Russians who are experts in blackmail and mugging."[6]

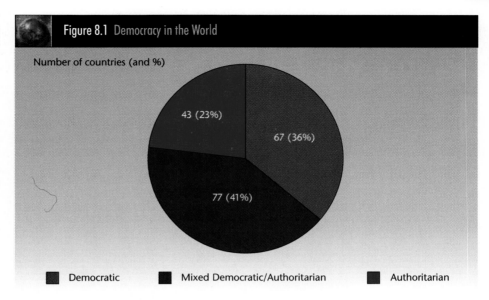

Figure 8.1 Democracy in the World

Number of countries (and %)

43 (23%)

67 (36%)

77 (41%)

■ Democratic   ■ Mixed Democratic/Authoritarian   ■ Authoritarian

Data source: Freedom House Website at http//:www.freedomhouse.org/survey99.

Note: Status as democratic, mixed democratic/ authoritarian, and authoritarian is based on evaluations of 187 countries by the organization Freedom House using two scales of 1 (most free) to 7 each to designate the degree of civil liberties and political rights in those countries. Countries with a combined score of 4 or less are counted here as democratic; countries scoring 5 through 10 are categorized as mixed; countries scoring 11 or more are labeled authoritarian.

Despite progress, democracy is not as fully rooted or as widespread as we might wish. Only about 4 in 10 countries are fully democratic. About 1 in 4 countries is still strongly authoritarian; and the rest are mixed systems with some democratic and some authoritarian aspects.

In France, Jean-Marie Le Pen, who heads the Front National (FN), received 15 percent of the vote in the presidential elections in 1995, and he was also elected to the European Parliament. He has dismissed the extermination of 6 million Jews and others in the Holocaust as a mere "detail" of history.[7] The FN proclaims that it sees itself as "the stronghold and bastion of national identity against cosmopolitan projects aimed at mixing peoples and cultures."[8] In one last example, anti-immigration also helped the nationalist Swiss People's Party (SPP) to garner the second-largest percentage of votes in the 1999 election. One of the country's main problems according to SPP leader Christoph Blocher: "90 percent of the immigrants who are here are abusing the system."[9]

Thus, as we begin the twenty-first century, it is possible to give only a mixed report on the prospects for the end of authoritarian government. It is true that fascists have fallen far short of electoral victory. No ultranationalist leader has recently won the title of president, prime minister, or chancellor. Yet, it is also the case that the political philosophies that focus on xenophobia and authoritarianism are far from moribund in Europe and elsewhere. As one analysis notes gloomily, "ideologies often go through a process of ebb and flow. Right-wing extremism and authoritarianism have deep roots" (Macridis & Hulliung, 1996:183). Democracy has become more prevalent, but it is also far from triumphant.

Democratic Theories of Governance

The existence of democratic government (which is derived from the Greek word *demos*, meaning "the citizenry") dates from the ancient Greek city-states circa 500 B.C. For more than 2,000 years, however, democracy existed only sporadically and usually in isolated locations. The gradual rise of English democracy, then the American and French Revolutions in the late eighteenth century, marked the change of democracy from a mere curiosity to an important national and transnational political idea. Still, the spread of democracy continued slowly. Then, during the late 1980s and early 1990s, dictatorship fell on hard times, and many observers tentatively heralded the coming of a

The growth of democratic governance has not been fast or steady, but there has been an important expansion in the number of countries and people who enjoy democracy. The spread of democracy is symbolized by this photograph of native Arctic region people on the Yamal peninsula some 1,400 miles north of Moscow, voting in Russia's presidential election.

democratic age. This view was captured by Francis Fukuyama's (1989:3) essay, "The End of History?" In it he suggests that we may have come to "the end of mankind's ideological evolution and the universalization of Western liberal democracy as the final form of government." Other observers are less optimistic about democracy's strength or the future spread of democracy (Attali, 1997).

Whoever is correct in the long run, data shows that for now the spread of democracy has not stalled. One periodic study has found that both the number and percentage of democratic countries increased between 1989 and 1999. At the same time, the number and percentage of authoritarian countries declined, with most of those that changed transitioning to the mixed category. The current status of global democracy is evident in the map on p. 202 and Figure 8.1 on p. 203.

STATE GOVERNANCE AND WORLD POLITICS

How states are governed has a number of ramifications for world politics. We will explore two: the drive to institute democracy globally and the related implications of democratization for global and national security.

The Drive for Universal Democracy: Issues

When President Woodrow Wilson asked on April 2, 1917, for a declaration of war against Germany, he told Congress that America should fight because, among other reasons, "The world must be made safe for democracy." Clarion calls to defend and expand democracy continue. Yet, without denying the benefits of democracy, several issues exist with regard to the efforts to export it. Three such difficulties relate to the standards of democracy, the possibility of democracy, and the impact of democracy on domestic security.

Standards of Democracy One difficulty with promoting democracy is that it is not always clear what is democratic and what is not. Americans, Canadians, Western Europeans, and some others tend to emphasize **procedural democracy.** If citizens periodically choose among competing candidates and follow other such procedures, then there is democracy. Many other cultures in the world stress **substantive democracy.** They see democracy as a substantive product associated with equality.

Critics of American-style democracy comment, for example, that a country has failed democratically if, despite meeting procedural requisites, it produces a perpetual socioeconomic underclass, based on race, ethnicity, gender, or some other factor, such as exists in the United States. Such a system, they contend, although going through the motions of democracy, in the end, denies the most important element of democracy: the substantive human right to equality. Critics further argue that any system with such vastly different economic circumstances is inherently undemocratic because the theory of government "of, by, and for the people" is undercut by the ability of wealthy individuals, groups, and corporations to spend large sums to hire professional lobbyists, to wage public relations campaigns, to donate money to electoral campaigns, to pay attorneys to sue opponents in court, and otherwise to use economic muscle unavailable to most citizens. This, the critics say, makes the contest unfair and undemocratic, no matter what the theory may be.

Defining democracy is also complicated by a second set of standards. **Individualism** argues that the rights and liberties of the individual are paramount. By contrast, **communitarianism** contends that the welfare of the collective (the community, the society) must be valued over any individual's benefit. Leaders of economically disadvantaged countries often argue that their struggle to feed, clothe, and otherwise attend to the needs of their people does not allow the "luxury" of Western-style democracy, with its incessant political bickering and its attention to the individual.

The Possibility of Democracy Yet another conundrum when promoting democracy as a norm in the international system involves whether democracy is always possible. In most of the West, where democracy has existed the longest and seems the most stable, it evolved slowly and often fitfully. More recently, other parts of the world have experienced increased degrees of democratization, but the likelihood that any single country will adopt democratic values and practices is at least partly linked with internal factors, such as attitudes about democracy and a country's educational and economic level.

With regards to attitudes, it would be a mistake to assume that everyone, everywhere is yearning to be free. For instance, a 1999 survey that asked Russians to indicate which of 10 things (ranging from good health to life without war) was most important to them found that "freedom" was most important to only 6 percent of respondents, placing it a poor eighth. When asked which of the ten was least important, freedom ranked third at 20 percent.[10]

As for economic and education level, it may be that attempting to promote full-fledged democracy in countries with poor economic and educational conditions is tantamount to trying to impose an alien political system on a socioeconomic system that is not ready for it. Doing so may even prove counterproductive. As one analyst has put it, "The democracy we are encouraging in many poor parts of the world is an integral part of a transformation toward new forms of **authoritarianism**" (Kaplan, 1999:178).

There are other scholars who take exception to this view and argue that democracy enhances development. The recipient of the 1998 Nobel Prize in economics, for one, contends that democracy promotes economic growth by pressing leaders to invest their countries' capital in education, consumer production, and other areas that will build economic strength and stimulate production instead of in military spending and other less productive economic paths (Sen, 1999).

Democracy and Domestic Security Some observers also contend that the move from authoritarian to democratic government can produce very negative side effects. It is possible to argue, for example, that the turmoil that has engulfed what was once a much larger Yugoslavia is a result of the end of the authoritarian control of the communist government, especially under strongman Josip Broz Tito during his long (1945–1980) rule. Once Tito died, the ethnonational rivalries among Serbs, Croats, Slovenians, Bosnian Muslims, Macedonians, Kosovar Albanian Muslims, and Montenegrins began to simmer and, in the ensuing years, heated up to the point of boiling over into conflict. Only the Montenegrins have not yet revolted against the Serbs, and that is a crisis waiting to happen. Similar patterns can be seen in several African countries, in the former Soviet Union, and elsewhere in cases where independence or the coming of democracy has unleashed bloody ethnic clashes.

To this contention, supporters of global democratization respond that any bloodshed that it brings pales when compared to the brutality inflicted by authoritarian regimes. One study of "democide," the killing of unarmed residents by governments, demonstrates that the degree to which a government is totalitarian "largely accounts for the magnitude and intensity of genocide and mass murder" committed by that government. Therefore, the study reasons, "the best assurances against democide are democratic openness, political competition, leaders responsible to their people and limited government. In other words, power kills, and absolute power kills absolutely" (Rummel, 1995:25).

Democracy and International Security

The impact of democracy on global security centers on the question of whether, if all states became democracies, the chance of war would decrease to near zero. It is not a new question. The German philosopher Immanuel Kant argued in *Perpetual Peace* (1795) that the spread of democracy would change the world by eliminating war. This is called **democratic peace theory**. Kant reasoned that a democratic peace would occur because "if the consent of the citizens is required in order to decide that war should be declared…, nothing is more natural than that they would be very cautious in commencing such a poor game, decreeing for themselves all the calamities of war." Modern scholarship has taken up this question of whether democratic regimes are more peaceful, especially with one another (Chan, 1997; Elman, 1997; Brown, Lynn-Jones, & Miller, 1996). Using empirical methods, contemporary scholars have established that "democracies are unlikely to engage in any kind of militarized disputes *with each other* or to let any such disputes escalate into war. They rarely even skirmish." (Russett, 2000:232; Oneal & Russett, 1999). This view is accepted by many scholars "as 'the closest thing to an empirical law' in world politics" that exists (Henderson, 1999:482; Thompson & Tucker, 1997).

Scholars are less unified about why democracies do not fight with one another. *Institutional explanations* focus on the way that democracies operate (Schultz, 1999). One such explanation is that democracies are "quite likely to avoid wars against one another for reasons ultimately based on the desire of their elected leaders to keep themselves in power" (Ray, 1997:60; Bueno de Mesquita, et al., 1998).

Normative explanations hold that democracies both become allies of one another and are less likely to fight one another because they share similar values and, therefore, share benign images of each other (Gaubatz, 1996). It may also be that democratic societies and leaders, being used to settling domestic differences peacefully, are more likely to settle international disputes in the same way. Yet another normative explanation about domestic democracy and external war is based on the view that violence is pervasive. As such, countries that are repressive internally are more apt to be violent externally.

Interest explanations attribute the democratic peace phenomenon to the fact that democracies and their citizens tend to be "satisfied." They are neither interested in upsetting the established order nor willing to accept the risks of doing so. Since there is some relationship between a country's level of economic development and the likelihood of that country being a democracy, it arguably follows that those who are relatively satisfied economically (and who have more to lose) are less bellicose than poorer, less democratic countries (Lemke & Reed, 1996; Rousseau, et al., 1996).

It should be noted that not all scholars agree with the theory of democratic peace (Caprioli, 1998). For example, some analysts are skeptical that the absence of war between democracies is anything more than a historical anomaly that may not persist in the future (Gartzke, 1998).

Before concluding this discussion of democracy and peace, it is important to stress that the findings are about relations among democracies. In other contexts, democracy may not necessarily be a force for peace. Some analysts maintain (and others dispute), for instance, that as countries transition to democracy, they may be more unstable and aggressive than either when they were clearly autocratic or than they will be when they become established democracies (Ward & Gleditsch, 1998; Gleditsch & Hegre, 1997). There is also some evidence that the behavior of democracies can become more aggressive under certain internal conditions, such as economic hardship. Other studies find that public pressure sometimes pushes democratic leaders toward war rather than away from it. To return to the main point, though, there is broad, albeit not complete, agreement among scholars that democracies have more peaceful relations with each other than do democracies with authoritarian states or authoritarian states with one another. From this perspective, even if a world in which all countries were democratic did not produce perpetual peace, as Kant thought, it might produce preponderant peace and, thus, should be promoted (Huntley, 1998).

NATIONAL AND OTHER INTERESTS

Whatever the system of governance of any state, a key factor that governs its affairs and interactions on the global stage are its interests. The concept of national interest is used almost universally to argue for or against any given policy. Most political leaders and citizens still argue that it is paramount. Certainly, most Russians thought it laudable when President Boris Yeltsin proclaimed that "the main goal of our foreign policy is consistent promotion of Russia's national interests."[11] Indeed, it is hard to imagine a national leader announcing that he or she had taken an important action that was counter to the national interest but in the world's interest. Even if such an aberration occurred, it is improbable that the leader would remain in office much longer.

National Interest as a Standard of Conduct

The use of national interest as a cornerstone of foreign policy is a key element of the road more traveled by in world politics. Realists contend that it is a wise basis for foreign policy. Henry Kissinger (1994a:37), for one, regrets what he sees as the current U.S. "distrust of America's power, a preference for multilateral solutions and a reluctance to think in terms of national interest. All these impulses," Kissinger believes, "inhibit a realistic response to a world of multiple power centers and diverse conflicts."[12]

Realpolitik nationalists further contend that we live in a Darwinian political world, where people who do not promote their own interests will become prey for those who do. Nationalists further worry about alternative schemes of global governance. One such critic of globalism notes that in intellectual circles "anyone who is skeptical about international commitments today is apt to be dismissed as an isolationist crank." Nevertheless, he continues, globalization should be approached with great caution because "it holds out the prospect of an even more chaotic set of authorities, presiding over an even more chaotic world, at a greater remove from the issues that concern us here in the United States" (Rabkin, 1994:41, 47).

There are other analysts who reject the use of national interest as a guide for foreign policy. The first criticism is that there is no such thing as an objective national interest. Instead, these critics say, what is in the national interest is totally subjective and "approximates idiosyncrasy" (Kimura & Welch, 1998). Analysts can accurately point out that national interest has been used to describe every sort of good and evil. As used by decision makers, it is a projection of the perceptions of a particular regime or even a single political leader in a given international or domestic environment. Consider again the 1994 U.S. invasion of Haiti. President Clinton told the American people that what happens in Haiti "affects our national security interests" and it was therefore imperative that "we must act now" to "protect our interests."[13] A majority of the American people disagreed with Clinton. A survey just before Clinton's speech found that only 13 percent of respondents believed that "U.S. interests are threatened" and that only 34 percent favored U.S. participation in a multinational invasion."[14]

A second criticism of using national interest as a basis of policy is that it incorrectly assumes that there is a common interest. The contention here is that every society is a collection of diverse subgroups, each of which has its own set of interests based on its political identity (Chafetz, Spirtas, & Frankel, 1999). Furthermore, the concept of national interest inherently includes the assumption that if a collective interest can be determined, then that interest supersedes the interests of subgroups and individuals. Writing from the feminist perspective, for example, one scholar has noted that "the presumption of a similarity of interests between the sexes is an assumption" that cannot be taken for granted because "a growing body of scholarly work argues that... the political attitudes of men and women differ significantly" (Brandes, 1994:21).

A third difficulty with the idea of national interest is the charge that operating according to one's self-defined, inherently selfish national interest inevitably leads to conflict and inequity on the world stage. The logic is simple. If you and I both pursue our national interests and those objectives are incompatible, then one likely possibility is that we will clash. Another possibility is that the interest of whichever of us is the more powerful will prevail. That is, power, not justice, will win out. Certainly, we might negotiate and compromise, as countries often do. But in an anarchical international system that emphasizes self-interest and self-help, the chances of a peaceful and equitable resolution are less than in a hierarchical domestic system that restrains the contending actors and offers institutions (such as courts) that can decide disputes if negotiation fails.

A fourth common charge is that the way that national interest is applied frequently involves double standards. This violates a political golden-rule principle, at least for idealists, who believe that a country should do unto other countries

Critics of the concept of national interest claim that it makes people indifferent to the world around them. There is a strong U.S. strain of isolationism that persuades some Americans that their country has few global interests or responsibilities. That persistent feeling is epitomized by this 1924 poster reacting to U.S. losses during World War I, in which, presumably, the United States had unwisely tried to be its brother's keeper. Showing some ignorance of the book of Genesis (4:11), the poster misses the point that God did not curse Cain for being his brother's keeper, but for killing him and then lying to God. The Creator had asked Cain where his brother Abel was, and had been told by Cain, "I do not know; am I my brother's keeper?" One has to wonder whether God or nature considers allowing one's brothers (and sisters) to die by refusing to help to be any better than killing them.

what it would have done unto itself. One current controversy has to do with the U.S. insistence that the treaty to establish the International Criminal Court (ICC), which is now open for countries to sign and ratify, be amended to shield U.S. military from the court's jurisdiction unless Washington agrees otherwise on a case-by-case basis. As a U.S. diplomat explained to the Senate Foreign Relations Committee, the worry is that, "multinational peacekeeping forces… can be exposed to the [ICC's] jurisdiction… [and] U.S. armed forces operating overseas could be conceivably prosecuted by the international court."[15] To many Americans, the U.S. position seems reasonable. Many others wonder why Americans cannot remember the old maxim that what is good for the goose ought also to be good for the gander.

A fifth objection to national interest and the way that it is applied contends that it is too often shortsighted. Concerned with their immediate, domestic needs, for example, most economically developed countries (EDCs) give precious little of their wealth to less developed countries (LDCs) in the form of foreign aid. This is shortsighted, some analysts contend, because in the long run the EDCs will become even more prosperous if the LDCs also become wealthy and can buy more goods and services from the EDCs. Furthermore, the argument goes, helping the LDCs now may avoid furthering the seething instability and violence born of poverty. "As images of life lived anywhere on our globe become available to all, so will the contrast between the rich and the poor" become a "force impelling the deprived to demand a better life from the powers that be," President Nelson Mandela of South Africa warned a joint session of the U.S. Congress.[16] He might also have added another old maxim: Avoid being "penny wise and pound foolish."

Alternatives to National Interest

One alternative to national interest is to adopt a standard of *global interest*. Proponents of this standard contend that the world would be better served if people defined themselves politically as citizens of the world along with, or perhaps in place of, their sense of national political identification. Writes one such advocate, "The apparent vast disjunction between what humankind must do to survive on the planet in a reasonably decent condition… and the way world society has typically worked throughout history… points to the need… for substantial evolution of world society in the direction of world community" (Brown, 1992:167).

A significant point in this internationalist argument is that its advocates claim that they do not reject national interest as such. Instead, they reject national interest in the shortsighted, narrowly self-interested way that the globalists think it is usually construed. In the long run, globalists argue, a more enlightened view of interests sees that the nation will be more secure and more prosperous if it helps other states also achieve peace and prosperity. This approach suggests that national interests and human interests are closely related, perhaps even synonymous. For example, one scholar calls for "international communitarianism" to become the new agenda of world politics. "The primary moral tenet of communitarianism," he urges, "is that states should pursue their interest responsibly, that is, with attention to the consequences for other states" (Haas, 1994:7). What this means is that leaders should consider the consequences of a proposed action on the global village as well as on their own state.

Individual interests are another alternative to national interest. Virtually all individuals are rightly concerned with their own welfare. To consider your own interests could be construed as the ultimate narrow-mindedness, but it also may be liberating. It may be that your interests, even your political identification, may shift from issue to issue.

It is appropriate to ask, then, whether your individual interests, your nation's interests, and your world's interests are the same, mutually exclusive, or a mixed bag of congruencies and divergences. Only you, of course, can determine where your interests lie.

STATES AND THE FUTURE

Sovereign, territorially defined states have not always existed, as we have noted. Therefore, they will not necessarily persist in the future. The questions are: Will they? Should they? The future of the state is one of the most hotly debated topics among scholars of international relations. As one such analyst explains, "Central to this future is the uncertain degree to which the sovereign state can adapt its behavior and role to a series of deterritorializing forces associated with markets, transnational social forces, cyberspace, demographic end environmental pressures, and urbanism" (Falk, 1999:35).

THE STATE: THE INDICTMENT

In rough division, there are two main lines of reasoning by those scholars who foresee or advocate the decline, perhaps the demise, of states as principal actors on the world stage. One contention is that states are obsolete; a second argument is that states are destructive (Lugo, 1996).

States Are Obsolete

The argument that states are obsolete begins with the premise that they were created in the middle of the last millennium as utilitarian political organizations to meet security, economic, and other specific needs and replaced the feudal and other forms of political organization that no longer worked effectively. "The nation-state is a rough and ready mechanism for furnishing a set of real services," one scholar writes. The problem, he continues, is that "the relation between what a state is supposed to do and what it actually does is increasingly slack" (Dunn, 1995:9). There is an interesting line of reasoning that suggests that states are too large to do the small things people want and need and too little to do the big things.

States Are Too Large   Some scholars believe that one reason that the claim of states to be sole legitimate international representative of their citizens is weakening is the feeling of many people that their interests are ignored or subverted by states and other mega-organizations (such as big corporations) of the modern world. Political minorities are especially likely to feel powerless. This sense of loss of individual and group power and people's concern about their diversity being homogenized into a bland monoculture intensify when talk about world or regional government and a uniculture in the global village begins. This may lead to the Jihad tendency and propel people to join or identify with movements or organizations that are more accessible and that share their values.

States Are Too Small   It may also (or alternatively) be that states are too limited to deal with the greatest problems facing humankind (Cusimano, 1998). As one study puts it, "the separate nation-states have become ever more impotent in dealing on their own... with material and political realities that are increasingly threatening the safety and well-being of their citizens" (Brown, 1998:3).

Providing physical safety is one key role of the state. Yet the ability of states to protect their citizens is limited at best (Betts, 1998; Keller & Rothchild, 1996). If we date the sovereign-state system to its symbolic beginning in 1648 with the Treaty of Westphalia, it is possible to argue that the record that states have of protecting their people is horrendous and getting worse. Since the mid-1600s, as shown in Figure 12.1 on page 322, there have been almost 600 wars that have killed around 144 million people. Moreover, the victim totals have risen rapidly through the centuries as humankind "improved" its killing capabilities. Therefore, the question is, in an era of nuclear, chemical, and bio-logical weapons of mass destruction, against which there is little or no defense, does the

Modern transportation has made health a growing global concern because diseases can rapidly spread around the world. Beginning in 1999, birds, horses, and a few humans in the U.S. northeast began dying from West Nile virus, a mosquito-borne infection. The mosquitoes in this container were captured for testing in New Jersey.

state protect people or simply define them as targets for other states in an anarchical international system?

Providing economic prosperity is a second key role of the state. The same genre of questions applies to the economic functions of a state. The tidal wave of trade and capital that moves across national borders means that states are increasingly less able to provide for the prosperity of their residents. Jobs are won or lost depending on a variety of factors, such as where transnational corporations decided to set up manufacturing, over which national governments have little or no control.

Providing for the general welfare is a third key role of the state. Health is one such concern, and states as independent entities are finding themselves increasingly unable to contain the spread of disease in an era when people and products that may carry the threat of disease with them move quickly and in massive numbers around the globe. During 1999, 62 people in the New York City area were infected with the West Nile virus, a mosquito-borne disease that can cause encephalitis. Seven died. The disease also kills birds, which are thought to provide a host for the virus. By 2000, the disease, which had never before been detected in the Western Hemisphere, had spread. Scientists found birds infected with the West Nile virus as far away as Boston, creating concern that migrating birds may spread the disease beyond the northeastern United States.

AIDS is another transnational health danger. Thought to have originated in Africa, it threatens people everywhere and is so severe in parts of sub-Saharan Africa that it could destabilize that region. The Clinton administration declared in April 2000 that AIDS was a threat to national security. "The heart of the security agenda is protecting lives," explained Vice President Al Gore speaking at the United Nations, "and we now know that the number of people who will die of AIDS in the first decade of the twenty-first century will rival the number that died in all the wars in all the decades of the twentieth century."[17]

Whether it is West Nile virus, AIDS, or another microbial enemy, the reality, according to a U.S. physician, is that, "Today, in 30 hours, you can literally travel to the other side of the world. And likewise, while you are there, you can pick up a germ or a micro-organism that may not exist on this side of the globe and within 30 hours you can have that back in the United States."[18] National borders provide increasingly scant protection to these globally transportable diseases, which, if they are to be contained, must be attacked through an international effort.

States Are Destructive

The essence of the sovereign state is to pursue its interests. Those interests clash. There is little in the system other than power to determine which states' interests will prevail. Therefore, the argument continues, states too often use economic coercion or military force to settle disputes. Critics of the state system contend that whatever the wins and losses for states, the most likely losers are average citizens, who bear the brunt of war and economic sanctions to a far greater degree than do leaders.

To make matters worse, states are often perpetrators of violence on those they are supposed to protect (Burgess, 1998). "Political regimes—governments—have probably murdered nearly 170 million of their own citizens and foreigners in this century—about four times the number killed in all international and domestic wars and revolutions," one scholar charges (Rummel, 1995:3).

THE STATE: THE DEFENSE

While those who predict or advocate the diminishment or demise of the state as a primary political organization are able to make a strong case, it is hardly an open-and-shut case leading to a verdict against the state.

First, as we noted in chapter 6, nationalism has proven resilient, and its political vehicle, the state, still has many resources at its disposal. This leads some analysts to doubt the substantial weakening, much less the disappearance, of states as sovereign actors. As two such scholars write, "Reports of its demise notwithstanding, sovereignty appears to us to be prospering, not declining.... It still serves as an indispensable component of international politics" (Fowler & Bunck, 1995:163). "Although the evidence is not decisive," another scholar writes, "I am skeptical that state sovereignty has eroded" (Thompson, 1995:231).

Second, it may be possible that states can adjust to the new realities by learning to cooperate and live in peace with other countries. Analysts who hold this view point to the increasing creation of and membership in numerous IGOs, like the WTO, as evidence that states are willing to give up some of their sovereignty in return for the benefits provided by free trade and other transnational interactions.

Third, states are arguably being strengthened as increasingly complex domestic and international systems create new demands for services. From this perspective, globalization and the strength of states "may be mutually reinforcing rather than antagonistic" (Weiss, 1998:204). "Empirical evidence demonstrates that the roles of the state are changing rather than diminishing," according to two scholars. "The state remains crucially involved in a wide range of problems," they continue, and "in each of these areas, specific initiatives may make state policies more efficient... as the roles of the nation-state continue to evolve" (Turner & Corbacho, 2000:118–119).

Fourth, sovereignty has always been a relative, not an absolute principle and a dynamic, rather than static concept (Sorensen, 1999). States and their leaders have long violated the principle when it suited their interests in what one scholar terms "organized hypocrisy" (Krasner, 1999). This leads some analysts to conclude that states will survive by adapting the parameters of sovereignty to international norms.

Fifth, it is possible to defend sovereign states as better than the other forms of political organization. States do provide some level of defense, and some states have been relatively effective at shielding their citizens from the ravages of war. Sometimes, as with the United States, that is a matter of power. But in other cases, it is related to geography, diplomatic skill, or a simple resolution not to take sides under almost any circumstances. Sweden and Switzerland, for example, managed to avoid becoming involved in any war, including either world war, during the twentieth century.

Sixth, it is yet to be proven that international governmental organizations (IGOs) provide an effective alternative to the state. Peacekeeping by the United Nations and other IGOs has had successes, but also notable failures. The WTO and other economic IGOs are under attack for benefiting rich countries, corporations, and individuals at the expense of less developed countries, small businesses, and workers. It may well be, as we will discuss in the next chapter, that IGOs can prove to be more effective and just instruments of governance as they evolve. That remains an open question, though.

THE STATE: THE VERDICT

For now, the jury is still out on whether states will and should continue to dominate the political system and be the principle focus of political identity. States continue to exercise great political strength and most of them retain the loyalty of most of their citizens. Yet it is also true that the state exists in a rapidly changing political environment that is creating great pressures, whether they be those of Jihad or McWorld. The state will not survive based on its record or on residual loyalties. Instead, as one scholar notes, "history sides with no one.... [The] lesson to be drawn [from the rise and evolution of states] is that all institutions are susceptible to challenges." Therefore, the sustainability of states depends in substantial part on whether or not they provide "efficient responses to such challenges" (Spruyt, 1994:185).

Where does this leave the future of sovereign states at the dawn of the twenty-first century? The answer that most political scientists would probably give is that "although the system of sovereign states is likely to continue [in the foreseeable future] as the dominant structure in world politics, the content of world politics is changing" (Keohane & Nye, 1999:118). Those changes are well captured in the view of one scholar that "a new epoch is evolving. It is an epoch of multiple contradictions:... States are changing, but they are not disappearing. State sovereignty has eroded, but it is still vigorously asserted. Governments are weaker, but they can still throw their weight around.... Borders still keep out intruders, but they are also more porous. Landscapes are giving way to ethnoscapes, mediascapes, ideoscapes, technoscapes, and financescapes, but territoriality is still a central preoccupation for many people" (Rosenau, 1998:18).

CHAPTER SUMMARY

1. States are the most important political actors. States as political organizations are defined by having sovereignty, territory, population, diplomatic recognition, internal organization, and domestic support.

2. The sovereign territorial state is a relatively modern form of political organization. States emerged in the West in the aftermath of the decline of the local authority of the feudal system and the universalistic authority of the Roman Catholic Church and the Holy Roman Empire.

3. There are various authoritarian and democratic theories of governance that shape the state as a core political organization.

4. Monarchism, theocracy, and communism applied politically, and fascism are four forms of authoritarian governance. The percentage of countries ruled by authoritarian regimes has declined, but dictatorial governments are still common.

5. Democracy is a complex concept. Different procedural and substantive standards serve as a basis to determine whether or not a political system is democratic.

6. There are also disputes over when it is possible or advisable to press all countries to quickly adopt democratic forms of government.

7. Democratic theorists and societies also disagree over the proper balance between individualism and communitarianism in a democracy.

8. Democratic peace theory argues that democracies are unlikely to enter into conflict with one another. Why democracies do not fight one another remains disputed among scholars, with explanations given from institutional, normative, and interest perspectives.

9. There are many types of interests—national, state, governmental, global, and individual—and it is important to distinguish among them. National interest has been and is the traditional approach to determining international activity, but there are some people who contend that national interest is synonymous with destructive self-promotion and should be diminished or even abandoned.

10. The future of the state is a hotly debated topic among scholars of international relations.

11. Some analysts predict the demise of states as principal actors, claiming that states are obsolete and destructive.

12. Other analysts of nationalism contend that the state is durable and has many resources at its disposal. These analysts doubt that the states will weaken substantially or disappear as sovereign actors.

13. One key question that will help determine the fate of states is whether they can cooperate to address global problems, such as environmental degradation.

14. A second key question that will help determine the fate of states is whether they can remain at peace in an era of nuclear arms and other weapons of mass destruction.

CHAPTER 9

INTERNATIONAL ORGANIZATION: THE ALTERNATIVE STRUCTURE

Friendly counsel cuts off many foes.

Shakespeare, *Henry VI, Part 1*

[The United Nations is] group therapy for the world.
Antonio Montiero, Portuguese ambassador to the UN

No nation needs to face or fight alone the threats which this organization was established to diffuse.

UN secretary-general Kofi Annan

CHAPTER OBJECTIVES

After completing this chapter, you should be able to:

• Examine the nature and development of international organization as an alternative form of organizing and conducting international relations.
• Characterize the roots of international organization as a primarily modern phenomenon.
• Trace the growth of intergovernmental organizations and nongovernmental organizations during the twentieth century.
• Summarize the traditional goals and activities of international organizations.
• Examine and discuss the current and expanding roles of IGOs.
• Discuss the concept of world and regional government.
• Explain the prospect of effective supranational organizations for international governance, making reference to the evolution of the European Union.
• Describe IGO structure by evaluating the experience of the United Nations.
• Identify the promotion of international peace and security as the primary IGO activity, as exemplified by the United Nations.
• Outline major social, economic, environmental, and other roles of intergovernmental organizations.
• Speculate regarding the shape of international organization in the future.

Γhe sovereign state has been the primary actor in world politics and the essential building block of the state-based international system. Indeed, it is hard to conceive of any other form of organizing and conducting international relations. Yet there are alternatives.

International organization is one of these alternatives (Diehl, 1996). As we have seen, there are many drawbacks to basing global relations on self-interested states operating in an anarchical international system. Many observers believe that global, regional, and specialized international organizations can and should begin to authoritatively regulate the behavior of often-conflicting states. Advocates of strengthened international organization believe that it is time to address world problems by working toward global solutions through global organizations. Those who take this view would join in the counsel given by Shakespeare in *Henry VI, Part III*: "Now join your hands, and with your hands your hearts." Such advice may be right. It is just possible that ongoing organizations will serve as prototypes or building blocks for a future, higher form of political loyalty and activity.

It is all too easy to dismiss the notion of international organizations as idealistic dreaming. But there was also a time when we believed that the world was the center of the universe. We now know that is not true; perhaps we can also learn that the national state need not be the center of the political cosmos. Surrendering some of your country's sovereignty to an international organization may seem unsettling. But it is neither inherently wrong, nor unheard of in today's world. In fact, the growth in the number, functions, and authority of international organizations is one of the most important trends in international relations. To explore this change in governance, this chapter will take up international organizations. The European Union, as a regional organization, and the United Nations, as a global organization, will be given particular attention to illustrate what is and what might be. Shakespeare tells us in *Hamlet* that "we know what we are, but not what we can be." Perhaps he was correct in saying that we cannot know for sure what we can be, but we surely can imagine what we *might* be if we keep our minds open to new ideas.

THE NATURE AND DEVELOPMENT OF INTERNATIONAL ORGANIZATION

The concept of international organization is not a new one, although the practice of having a continuous international organization is a relatively recent advance in the conduct of international relations. Now there are a growing number of permanent international organizations. The size and scope of these international organizations vary greatly, ranging from multipurpose, nearly universal organizations like the United Nations to single-purpose organizations with very few member-countries.

TYPES OF INTERNATIONAL ORGANIZATIONS

The term *international organization* tends to bring the United Nations to mind. There are many more, however. They can be divided geographically into global or regional organizations and grouped by functions into general or specialized international organizations, as shown in Table 9.1. Whatever their specifics, though, all the organizations that we will discuss in this chapter share the fact that their memberships consist of national governments. Therefore, they are termed international **intergovernmental organizations (IGOs)** to distinguish them from the transnational (or international) **nongovernmental organizations (NGOs)** discussed in several other chapters.

Table 9.1 Types and Examples of IGOs

	Purpose	
Geography	General	Specialized
Global	United Nations	World Trade Organization
Regional	European Union	Arab Monetary Fund

International organizations (IGOs) can be classified according to whether they are general purpose, dealing with many issues, or specialized, dealing with a specific concern. Another way of dividing IGOs is into global and regional organizations.

THE ROOTS OF INTERNATIONAL ORGANIZATION

International organization is primarily a modern phenomenon. One thing that you can note about IGOs is that nearly all of them were created in the last 50 years or so. It is also true, though, that the origins of international organizations extend far back in history. Three main root systems have nourished the current growth of international organizations.

Belief in a Community of Humankind

The first branch of the root system is the universal concern for improving the condition of humanity. The idea that humans share a common bond is not new. Philosophers such as William Penn and Immanuel Kant argued that the way to accomplish this end was through general international organizations (Pagden, 1998; Bohman & Lutz-Bachmann, 1997). The first example of an IGO based on this goal was the **Hague system,** named for the 1899 and 1907 peace conferences held at that city in the Netherlands (Best, 1999). The 1907 conference was more comprehensive, with 44 European, North American, and Latin American states participating. Organizationally, the Hague system included a rudimentary general assembly and a judicial system. The conferences also adopted a series of standards to limit the conduct of war. World War I destroyed the plans for a third Hague conference in 1915, but the move toward universal organization was under way.

The next step on the path was the creation of the **League of Nations** after World War I. The League was intended mainly as a peacekeeping organization, although it did have some elements aimed at social and economic cooperation. Despite the hopes with which it was founded, the League could not survive some of its own organizational inadequacies, the unstable post–World War I peace, the Great Depression, and the rise of militant fascism. After only two decades of frustrated existence, the League died in the rubble of World War II.

The **United Nations (UN)** is the latest, and most advanced, developmental stage of universal concern with the human condition. Like the League of Nations, the UN was established mainly to maintain peace. Nevertheless, it has increasingly become involved in a broad range of issues that encompasses almost all the world's concerns. In addition, the UN and its predecessor, the League, represent the coming together of all the root systems of international organizations. They are more properly seen as the emergent saplings of extensive cooperation and integration.

Big-Power Peacekeeping

The second branch of the root system is the idea that the big powers have a special responsibility to cooperate and preserve peace. Hugo Grotius, the "father of international law," suggested as early as 1625 in his classic *On the Law of War and Peace* that the major Christian powers cooperate to mediate or arbitrate the disputes of others or even, if required, to compel warring parties to accept an equitable peace.

This idea took on substance with the Congress of Vienna (1814–1815), which led to the Concert of Europe. This informal coalition of the major European powers and the following balance-of-(big-) power diplomacy managed generally to keep the peace for the century between the fall of Napoleon in 1815 and the outbreak of World War I in 1914.

The philosophy of big-power responsibility (and authority) carried over to the Council of the League of Nations. It had authority (Covenant Article 4) to deal "with any matter within the sphere of activity of the League or affecting the peace of the world." Significantly, five of the nine seats on the council were permanently assigned to the principal victors of World War I. The council was thus a continuation of the Concert of Europe concept.

When the United Nations succeeded the League of Nations, the special status and responsibilities of the big powers in the League's council were transferred to the UN Security Council (UNSC). Like its predecessor, the UNSC is the main peacekeeping organ and includes permanent membership for five major powers (China, France, Great Britain, Russia, and the United States). We will further explore the Security Council, but for now we should notice that a conceptual descendant of the Concert of Europe is alive and well in the UNSC.

Functional Cooperation

The third branch of our root system is composed of the specialized agencies that deal with specific economic and social problems. The six-member Central Commission for the Navigation of the Rhine, established in 1815, is the oldest surviving IGO, and the International Telegraphic (now Telecommunications) Union (1865) is the oldest surviving IGO with global membership. As detailed below, the growth of specialized IGOs and NGOs has been phenomenal. This aspect of international activity is also reflected in the UN through the 20 specialized agencies associated with the world body.

THE EXPANSION OF IGOs

An important phenomenon of the twentieth century is the rapid growth in the number, activities, and importance of intergovernmental and nongovernmental organizations.

Quantitative Expansion

The twentieth century saw rapid growth in the number of all types of IGOs. By one calculation, the number of well-established IGOs increased sevenfold from 37 in 1909 to 251 in 1999, according to the Union of International Associations.

Figure 9.1 gives another view of this rapid expansion that focuses on the major IGOs. It is worthwhile to think about the fact that the average major IGO represented in Figure 9.1 had been in existence in 1999 for only 33 years. That made them, on average, younger than the average American, whose age in 1999 was 34.

Expansion of Roles

Even more important than the growing number of IGOs is the expanding roles that they play. There are several aspects to this. First, more and more common governmental functions are being dealt with by IGOs. If you reviewed the major departments and ministries of your national government and the subjects they address, it is almost certain that you would be able to find one or more IGOs that deal with the same subjects on the international level. Second, some of these expanding roles are dealt with by creating new IGOs. For example, the development of satellites and the ability to com-

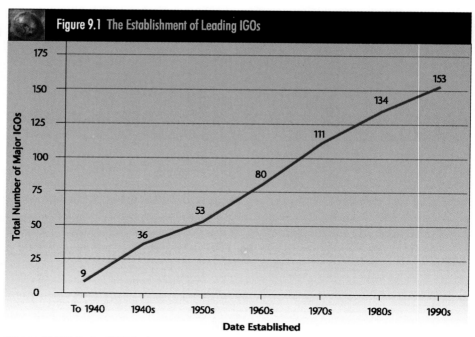

Figure 9.1 The Establishment of Leading IGOs

Data source: CIA (2000). Based on 153 IGOs listed and author's calculations.

The growth of IGOs is primarily a modern trend. Of the 153 most important IGOs on one list, 76 percent have been established during the last 50 years.

municate through them and the need to coordinate this capability led to the establishment of the International Mobile Satellite Organization (IMMARSAT) in 1979.

Third, the increasing need for IGO activity is leading existing IGOs to take on new functions beyond their initial roles. Few IGOs better illustrate this than the European Union (EU). It is the product of the expanded functions of the European Community, which, in turn, was the result of the 1967 merger of the European Economic Community, the European Coal and Steel Community, and the European Atomic Energy Community. Furthermore, the scope of EU activities is expanding beyond its original economic focus to a wider range of political and social concerns. The EU is also developing an increasingly important organizational structure, and some Europeans hope that it will evolve into a United States of Europe.

Reasons for Expansion

The twentieth century's rapid growth of international organizations, both in number and in scope of activity, is the result of a number of forces. Those forces were summarized by two scholars who examined why states act through international organizations. Their conclusion was that "by taking advantage... of IO's, states are able to achieve goals that they cannot accomplish [alone]" (Abbot & Snidal, 1998:29). In other words, the growth of international organizations has occurred because countries have found that they need them and that they work. We can note six specific causes for this expansion:

Increased international contact is one cause. The revolutions in communications and transportation technologies have brought the states of the world into much closer contact. These interchanges need organizational structures in order to become routine and regulated. The International Telegraphic Union, founded over a century ago, has been joined in more modern times by the IMMARSAT and many others.

International Trade Organizations

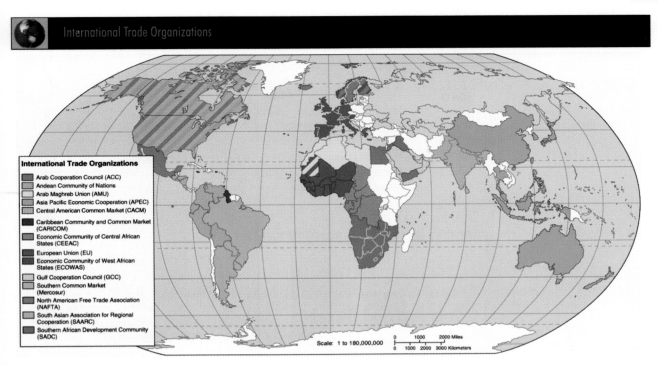

International Trade Organizations

- Arab Cooperation Council (ACC)
- Andean Community of Nations
- Arab Maghreb Union (AMU)
- Asia Pacific Economic Cooperation (APEC)
- Central American Common Market (CACM)
- Caribbean Community and Common Market (CARICOM)
- Economic Community of Central African States (CEEAC)
- European Union (EU)
- Economic Community of West African States (ECOWAS)
- Gulf Cooperation Council (GCC)
- Southern Common Market (Mercosur)
- North American Free Trade Association (NAFTA)
- South Asian Association for Regional Cooperation (SAARC)
- Southern African Development Community (SADC)

Scale: 1 to 180,000,000

Pragmatic necessity is one reason for the rapid growth of many types of IGOs. One response to the fast expansion of global trade has been the establishment of a large number of regional trade organizations. None of these existed fifty years ago; now virtually every country is in at least one of them. The term "national economy" is rapidly becoming outmoded.

Second, the world's *increased interdependence*, particularly in the economic sphere, has fostered a variety of IGOs designed to deal with this phenomenon (Diehl, 1997). The International Monetary Fund (IMF) and the World Bank are just two examples. Regional trade and monetary organizations, cartels, and, to a degree, multinational corporations are other examples.

A third cause of the growth of international organizations is the *expansion of transnational problems* that affect many states and require solutions that are beyond the resources of any single state. One such issue (and its associated IGO) is nuclear proliferation (International Atomic Energy Agency).

A fourth incentive for the expansion of IGOs is the *failure of the current state-centered system* to provide security. The agony of two world wars, for instance, convinced many that peace was not safe in the hands of nation-states. The United Nations is the latest attempt to organize for the preservation of peace. The continuing problems in health, food, human rights, and other areas have also spurred the organization of IGOs.

A fifth factor is the *effort of small states to gain strength through joint action*. The concentration of military and economic power in a handful of countries has led less powerful actors to join coalitions in an attempt to influence events. Vulnerability has, thus, motivated countries to come together in such organizations as the 113-member Nonaligned Movement (NAM) and the Group of 77, a now-132-member organization of less developed countries (LDCs) interested in promoting economic cooperation and development. In some ways the end of the cold war has increased this vulnerability. As a Western diplomat attending a NAM meeting commented, "A lot of these tiny nations are praying the movement and organizations like it can survive and advocate on their behalf.... No one pays attention to them any more."[1]

Sixth and last, the existence and successes of international organizations provide *role models* that have generated still other IGOs and NGOs. People and countries have learned that they can sometimes work together internationally, and this has encouraged them to try new ventures in international organization and cooperation.

GOALS OF INTERNATIONAL ORGANIZATION

Given the expanding number and importance of international organizations, we should ask ourselves what it is that we want international organizations to accomplish ultimately. The various ideas about the proper and possible goals of IGOs can be grouped into two broad categories. One category includes relatively limited and traditional goals. The second category is much more far-reaching and includes international organizations moving toward assuming the roles of regional governments or even of a global government.

EXISTING AND POSSIBLE ROLES OF IGOs

The roles of IGOs have been defined mostly in limited, traditional ways. There are, however, a range of more far-reaching activities that some people believe IGOs can and should take up. It is possible to arrange these roles along a scale that measures how close each is to the traditional road or to the alternative road of international politics. Starting at the traditional end of the scale and moving toward the alternative end, the four roles are: interactive arena, creator and center of cooperation, independent international actor, and supranational organization.

Before moving to these four roles, it should be noted that they are evaluated quite differently by realists and idealists. *Realists* portray IGO policy making and activity as simply an extension of the power diplomacy of self-interested states. As one realist scholar puts it, IGOs "are basically a reflection of the distribution of power in the world. They are based on the self-interested calculations of the great powers,… have no independent effect on state behavior,… [and] therefore… are not an important cause of peace" (Mearsheimer, 1995:7).

Idealists have a very different view. They reject realist analysis of IGOs as "incomplete and logically unsound" because, in part, it does not offer "a plausible account of the investments that states have made in such international institutions as the EU, NATO, GATT, and the regional trading organizations." Furthermore, idealists contend that IGOs are "essential if states are to have any hope of sustained cooperation" and that "international institutions… will be components of any lasting peace" (Keohane & Martin, 1995:47, 50).

Interactive Arena

The most common use of IGOs is to provide an interactive arena in which member-states pursue their individual national interests. This approach is rarely stated openly, but it is obvious in the struggles within the UN and other IGOs, where countries and blocs of countries wage political struggles with a vengeance. For example, research on the UN General Assembly since the end of the cold war indicates that its principle dimension of conflict is between the dominant West, led by the United States, and a "counterhegemonic" bloc of countries (Voeten, 2000:185).

The use of IGOs to gain national advantage is somewhat contradictory to the purpose of these supposedly cooperative organizations and has disadvantages. One negative factor is that it sometimes transforms IGOs into another scene of struggle rather than utilizing them to enhance cooperation. Furthermore, countries are apt to reduce or withdraw their support from an international organization that does not serve their narrow national interests.

The use of IGOs as an interactive arena does, however, have advantages. One is based on the theory of international integration called *intergovernmentalism*, which argues that integration can advance even when IGOs are the arena for self-interested national interaction. The reasoning is that even when realpolitik is the starting point, the process that occurs in an IGO fosters the habit of cooperation and compromise.

A second advantage is that sometimes, as in the case of reversing Iraq's aggression, using the IGO makes it politically easier to take action. Third, debate and diplomatic maneuver may even provide a forum for diplomatic struggle. This role of providing an alternative to the battlefield may promote the resolution of disputes without violence. As Winston Churchill put it once, "To jaw-jaw is better than to war-war."[2]

Creator and Center of Cooperation

A second role that IGOs perform is to promote and facilitate cooperation among states and other international actors. Secretary-General Kofi Annan has observed correctly that the UN's "member-states face a wide range of new and unprecedented threats and challenges. Many of them transcend borders. They are beyond the power of any single nation to address on its own."[3] Therefore, countries have found it increasingly necessary to cooperate to address physical security, the environment, the economy, and a range of other concerns. The Council of the Baltic Sea States, the International Civil Aviation Organization, the International Organization for Standardization, and a host of other IGOs were all established to address specific needs and, through their operations, to promote further cooperation.

What sometimes occurs is that narrow cooperation expands into more complex forms of interdependence. International regimes are one such development (Hasenclever & Mayer, 1997). A regime is not a single organization. Instead, a **regime** is a collective noun that designates a complex of norms, rules, processes, and organizations that, in sum, have evolved to help to govern the behavior of states and other international actors in an area of international concern such as the use and protection of international bodies of water (Cortell & Davis, 1996). Some regimes may encompass cooperative relations within a region. Other regimes are global, and we will use one of these, the regime for oceans and seas, as an example.

The regime that is currently evolving to govern the uses of the world's oceans and other bodies of international water is represented in Figure 9.2. Note the regime's complex array of organizations, rules, and norms that promote international cooperation in a broad area of maritime regulation. Navigation, pollution, seabed mining, and fisheries are all areas of expanded international discussion, rule-making, and cooperation. The Law of the Sea Treaty proclaims that the oceans and seabed are a "common heritage of mankind," to be shared according to "a just and equitable economic order." To that end, the treaty contains provisions for increased international regulation of mining and other uses of the oceans' floors. It established (as of 1994) the International Seabed Authority, headquartered in Jamaica, to supervise the procedures and rules of the treaty.

In addition to the Law of the Sea Treaty, the regime of the oceans and seas extends to include many other organizations and rules. The International Maritime Organization has sponsored agreements regarding safeguards against oil spills in the seas. As a result, the average amount of yearly spills into the oceans and seas fell from 302,000 tons (1970–1974) to 38,000 tons (1995–1999). The International Whaling Commission, the Convention on the Preservation and Protection of Fur Seals, the Commission for the Conservation of Antarctic Marine Living Resources, and other efforts have begun the process of protecting marine life and conserving resources. The Montreal Guidelines on Land-Based Pollution suggest ways to avoid fertilizer and other land-based pollutants from running off into rivers and bays and then into the oceans. Countries have expanded their conservation zones to regulate fishing. The South Pacific Forum has limited the use of drift nets that indiscriminately catch and kill marine life.

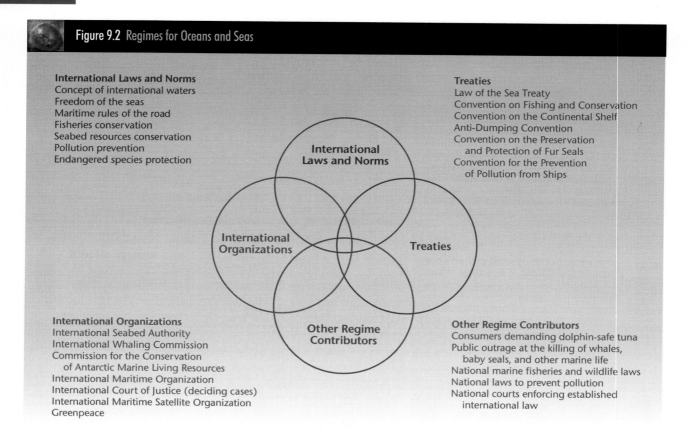

Figure 9.2 Regimes for Oceans and Seas

International Laws and Norms
Concept of international waters
Freedom of the seas
Maritime rules of the road
Fisheries conservation
Seabed resources conservation
Pollution prevention
Endangered species protection

Treaties
Law of the Sea Treaty
Convention on Fishing and Conservation
Convention on the Continental Shelf
Anti-Dumping Convention
Convention on the Preservation
   and Protection of Fur Seals
Convention for the Prevention
   of Pollution from Ships

International Organizations
International Seabed Authority
International Whaling Commission
Commission for the Conservation
   of Antarctic Marine Living Resources
International Maritime Organization
International Court of Justice (deciding cases)
International Maritime Satellite Organization
Greenpeace

Other Regime Contributors
Consumers demanding dolphin-safe tuna
Public outrage at the killing of whales,
   baby seals, and other marine life
National marine fisheries and wildlife laws
National laws to prevent pollution
National courts enforcing established
   international law

Entries are only a sample of all possibilities.

The concept of an international regime represents the nexus of a range of laws and actors that regulate a particular area of concern. This figure shows some of the elements of the expanding regime for oceans and seas.

NGOs such as Greenpeace have pressed to protect the world seas. Dolphins are killed less frequently because many consumers only buy cans of tuna that display the "dolphin safe" logo. The list of multilateral lawmaking treaties, IGOs, NGOs, national efforts, and other programs that regulate the use of the seas could go on. The point is that while each activity and organization is separate, they are, in combination, an ever-expanding network that constitutes a developing regime of the seas. Gradually, what swims in the sea, what lies under it, the availability of international waters as a dumping ground, the conduct of ships on the seas, and myriad other matters that were once the focus of international struggles over sovereign utilization are falling within the regime for oceans and seas.

Independent International Actor

The third of the existing and possible IGO roles is that of an independent international actor. This role is located toward the alternative end of the traditional-alternative scale of IGO activities. Technically, what any IGO does is controlled by the wishes and votes of its members. In reality, many IGOs develop strong, relatively permanent administrative staffs. These individuals often identify with the organization and try to increase its authority and role. Global expectations—such as "the UN should do something"—add to the sense that an IGO may be a force unto itself. Soon, to use an old phrase, the whole (of the IGO) becomes more than the sum of its (member-country) parts. We will

Activists with Greenpeace, an international environmentalist organization, are trying to prevent the Japanese whaler *Nishin Maru* from hoisting a minke whale carcass aboard in January 2000. Greenpeace is a part of a complex group of international and national actors, treaties, international norms, and other elements that make up the regime for oceans and seas, as illustrated in Figure 9.2.

explore this role more fully when we discuss the United Nations later in the chapter. But insofar as IGOs do play an independent role, proponents of this approach argue that it should be one mainly of mediation and conciliation rather than coercion. The object is to teach and allow, not to force, states to work together.

To a degree, organizational independence is intended and established in the charters of various IGOs. The International Court of Justice (ICJ) was created to act independently. The UN Charter directs that the secretary-general and his or her staff "shall not seek or receive instructions from any government or from any other authority external to the organization." And the European Parliament is a unique example of an IGO assembly whose representatives are popularly elected rather than appointed and directed by national governments.

Supranational Organization

It may also be possible for IGOs to play a fourth role: **supranational organization.** This means that the international organization has authority over its members, which, therefore, are subordinate units. Theoretically, some IGOs possess a degree of supranationalism and can obligate members to take certain actions. In reality, supranationalism is extremely limited. Few states concede any significant part of their sovereignty to any IGO. But there are some signs that this is giving way to limited acceptance of international authority. As we will see in chapter 11 on international law, for instance, countries normally abide by some aspects of international law, even at times when it conflicts with their domestic law or their immediate interests.

The extreme limits on supranationalism now does not mean, however, that the authority of IGOs cannot expand. There are many people who believe that the world is moving and should continue to move toward a more established form of international government. Such supranational government could be regional or global in scope. There are two schools of thought, functionalism and neofunctionalism, about how the world can move toward increasing supranationalism.

Functionalism The term **functionalism** represents the idea that the way to global cooperation is through a "bottom-up," evolutionary approach that begins with limited, pragmatic cooperation on narrow, nonpolitical issues. One such issue was how to deliver the mail internationally. To solve that problem, countries cooperated to found the Universal Postal Union in 1874. Each such instance of cooperation serves as a building block to achieve broader cooperation on more and more politically sensitive issues. Plato's description of "necessity" as "the mother of invention" in *The Republic* (ca. 380 B.C.) might well serve as a motto for modern functionalists.

Functionalists support their view about how global cooperation has been and is being achieved by pointing to hundreds, even thousands, of IGOs, multilateral treaties, NGOs, and other vehicles that have been put in place to deal with specific international concerns. Functionalists further hold that by cooperating in specific, usually nonpolitical areas, countries and people can learn to trust one another. This, in turn, will lead to ever broader and ever higher levels of cooperation on the path to comprehensive cooperation or even global government.

Neofunctionalism The "top-down" approach to solving world problems is called **neofunctionalism.** Its advocates are skeptical about the functionalist belief that nonpolitical cooperation can, by itself, lead eventually to full political cooperation and to the elimination of international conflict and self-interested state action. Neofunctionalists also worry that even if the evolutionary approach favored by functionalists might someday work, it will not move quickly enough to head off many of the world's looming problems. Therefore, neofunctionalists argue for immediately establishing IGOs and treaties that can address political issues with an eye to fostering even greater cooperation. They argue that this speeds up the timetable of addressing the most important questions.

Most people who wish to follow this alternative approach to political organization believe that IGOs ought to have real authority to solve problems when states cannot or will not do so. To accomplish this, the current national states would have to give up at least some of their sovereignty to one or more global or regional supranational organizations that would have lawmaking, enforcing, and adjudicating authority.

Gradually through history our focus on primary loyalty has shifted from smaller units such as tribes and villages to larger units, especially countries. Some people believe that this trend should continue and that a world government should be established. The image of children starting out their day by saying "I pledge allegiance to the flag of the United States of the World" may seem strange, but a global government may evolve.

World Government as an Alternative The most far-reaching alternative to the current state-based international system is the possibility of a powerful **world government** that governs a global political system (Zolo, 1997). Such a global government might be a highly *centralized* structure, one in which countries are nonsovereign subunits that serve only administrative purposes. A less dramatic alternative is *federalism*, in which the central authority and the member units share power. Models of federalism include the relations between the United States and its 50 states and Canada and its 10 provinces. *Confederalism* would provide an even less centralized structure, one in which the members are highly interdependent and join together in a weak directorate organization while retaining all or most of their sovereign authority. The European Union provides a current example of what is or, at least, approaches a **confederation.**

There is a strong opposition to the one-world idea. Critics argue that, first, there are *practical barriers* to world government. The assumption here is that nationalism has too strong a hold and that neither political leaders nor masses would be willing to surrender independence to a universal body (Taylor, 1999). Are we ready to "pledge allegiance to the United States of the World"? Second, critics of the world government movement pose political objections. They worry about the concentration of power that would be necessary to enforce international law and to address the world's monumental economic and social problems. A third doubt is whether any such government, even given unprecedented power, could succeed in solving world problems any better than states can. Fourth, some skeptics further argue that centralization would inevitably diminish desirable cultural diversity and political experimentation in the world. A fifth criticism of the world government movement is that it diverts attention from more reasonable avenues of international cooperation, such as the United Nations and other existing IGOs.

Regional Government as an Alternative The idea of **regional government** meets some of the objections to global government. Regions would still have to bring heterogeneous peoples together and overcome nationalism, but the regional diversity is less severe than is global heterogeneity. Moreover, regional governments would allow for greater cultural diversity and political experimentation than would a global government. Some proponents of regional governments also suggest that they might serve as a stepping-stone toward world government.

Whatever one's views about whether international governance should occur at the regional or global level—or at all, for that matter—the reality is that there is movement toward supranational organization. To further explore the current and expanding roles of IGOs, we can break them down into two groups, regional IGOs and global IGOs, with a focus on the most prominent regional IGO, the European Union, and the most important global IGO, the United Nations.

REGIONAL IGOS: FOCUS ON THE EUROPEAN UNION

The growth of regional IGOs has been striking (Mansfield & Milner, 1999; Mace & Therien, 1996). Prior to World War II there were no prominent regional IGOs. Now there are many. Most of these are relatively specialized, with regional economic IGOs, such as the Arab Cooperation Council, the most numerous. Other regional IGOs are general purpose and deal with a range of issues. These include, for example, the Organization of African Unity (OAU) and the Organization of American States (OAS).

Another noteworthy development regarding regional IGOs is that some of them are transitioning from specialized to general purpose organizations. The Association of Southeast Asian Nations (ASEAN) was founded in 1967 to promote regional economic cooperation. More recently, though, ASEAN has begun to take on a greater political tinge, and, in particular, may serve as a political and defensive counterweight to China in the region (Ahmad & Ghoshal, 1999). A more obvious change in role is evident for the Economic Community of West African States (ECOWAS). It was established in 1975 to facilitate economic interchange, but in the 1990s ECOWAS took on a very different function when it intervened in the civil war raging in Liberia. Approximately 8,000 troops from five African countries moved to end the fighting, and they eventually were able to help provide stability. Troops from ECOWAS were also deployed in Sierra Leone in the late 1990s when that country fell into chaos. They had some temporary success there but were withdrawn in favor of a UN force in March 2000, when Sierra Leone again slipped into brutal chaos.

Beyond any of these examples of regional IGOs, the best example of what is possible is the regionalism in Europe. There, the European Union, with its 15 member-countries, has moved toward full economic integration. It has also traveled in the direction of considerable political cooperation (McCormick, 1999).

THE ORIGINS AND EVOLUTION OF THE EUROPEAN UNION

The **European Union (EU)** has evolved through several stages. One way to keep track of the changes in the structure and purpose of the EU described in the following paragraphs is to note the changes in the names of the successive organizations. "What's in a name?" you might ask, echoing Shakespeare's heroine in *Romeo and Juliet*. As she discovered, the names Capulet and Montague proved important. So too, the name changes leading up to the current EU are important in the tale they tell.

Economic Integration

The organizational genesis of the EU dates back to 1952 when Belgium, France, (West) Germany, Italy, Luxembourg, and the Netherlands joined together to create a common market for coal, iron, and steel products called the European Coal and Steel Community (ECSC). It proved so successful that in 1957 the six countries signed the Treaties of Rome that created the **European Economic Community (EEC)** to facilitate trade in many additional areas and the European Atomic Energy Community

(EURATOM) to coordinate matters in that realm. Both new communities came into being on January 1, 1958.

Interchange among the 6 countries expanded rapidly, and they soon felt that they should coordinate their activities even further. Therefore, the 6 created the European Communities (EC), which went into operation in 1967. Each of the 3 preexisting organizations became subordinate parts of the EC. Success brought new members. Denmark, Ireland, and Great Britain were admitted in 1973. Greece became the 10th member in 1981; Spain and Portugal joined in 1986. Then in 1995 Austria, Finland, and Sweden became members of the (by then) EU, bringing its membership to 15. Most of the other countries of Europe have expressed interest in joining the EU, and as of early 2000 negotiations were underway between the EU and 12 applicants (Bulgaria, Cyprus, the Czech Republic, Estonia, Hungary, Latvia, Lithuania, Malta, Poland, Romania, Slovakia, and Slovenia).

The eventual, if not quite stated, goal of the EU is to encompass all the region's countries. Jacques Santer, president of the European Commission (1995–1999), insisted that no country that met the EU economic and political standards should be kept out. "There will be no such things as 'in countries' and 'out countries'; rather there will be 'ins' and 'pre-ins'," he said.[4] He might have added that within a decade or two, all the countries of Europe may well be "ins."

For about 30 years, the integrative process in Europe focused on economics. Members of the EC grew ever more interdependent as economic barriers were eliminated. In 1968 the members of the EC abolished the last tariffs on manufactured goods among themselves and established a common EC external tariff. The EC also began to bargain as a whole with other countries in trade negotiations. On another economic front, members agreed in 1970 to fund the EC with a virtually independent revenue source by giving it a share of each country's value-added tax (VAT, similar to a sales tax) and all customs duties collected on imports from non–EC countries. The last major step in the pre–EU evolution toward economic integration was the Single European Act (SEA) of 1987. The SEA amended the basic EC agreement and committed the EC to becoming a fully integrated economic unit.

Political Integration

There comes a point in economic integration when pressure builds to take steps toward political integration. One reason this occurs is that it is impossible to reach full economic integration among sovereign states whose domestic and foreign political policies are sometimes in conflict. Moreover, as the people unite economically, it is easier to think of becoming one politically.

Europe entered a new, more political phase of integrative evolution in 1993 when the far-reaching Treaty on European Union (known as the **Maastricht Treaty**) went into effect. The treaty had important economic provisions that called for monetary integration, the coordination of social policies (such as labor conditions and benefits), and other steps to increase economic integration further. Of even greater importance were the political changes that began under the treaty. The concept of European citizenship has been expanded. Citizens of EU countries can now travel on either an EU or a national passport, and citizens of any EU country can vote in local and European Parliament elections in another EU country in which they live. There are a growing number of joint European enterprises. The European Space Agency, for one, develops commercial rocket and satellite ventures. The European Investment Bank lends about $30 billion a year to promote economic growth within the EU. Also, the EU is the prime supporter of the European Bank for Reconstruction and Development, which finances development projects in Eastern Europe (about $2 billion in 1999).

Figure 9.3 Membership and Organizational Structure of the European Union

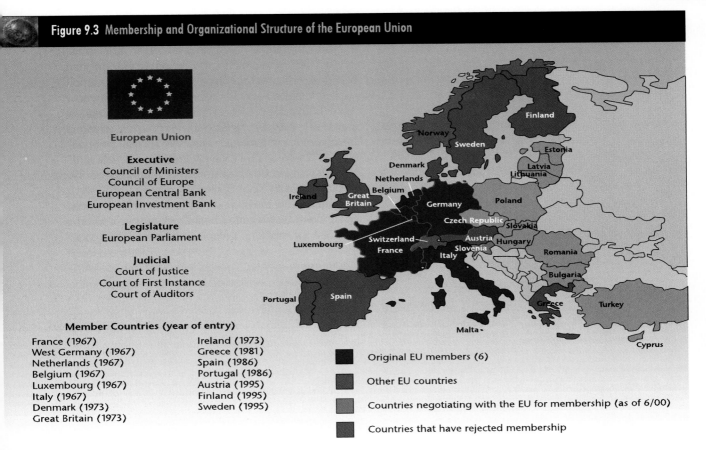

European Union

Executive
Council of Ministers
Council of Europe
European Central Bank
European Investment Bank

Legislature
European Parliament

Judicial
Court of Justice
Court of First Instance
Court of Auditors

Member Countries (year of entry)

France (1967)	Ireland (1973)
West Germany (1967)	Greece (1981)
Netherlands (1967)	Spain (1986)
Belgium (1967)	Portugal (1986)
Luxembourg (1967)	Austria (1995)
Italy (1967)	Finland (1995)
Denmark (1973)	Sweden (1995)
Great Britain (1973)	

■ Original EU members (6)

■ Other EU countries

■ Countries negotiating with the EU for membership (as of 6/00)

■ Countries that have rejected membership

The world's most advanced regional organization is the European Union. It has expanded from the 8 original countries that created the European Community in 1967 to 15 countries today. Thirteen others await admission. The EU's focus is primarily economic, but it is also involved in a variety of political, social, and environmental issues and reflects a greater level of integration than can be found in any other region.

In addition, the EU acts increasingly as a political unit (Piening, 1997; Rhodes, 1997). The Maastricht Treaty called for the eventual creation of a common foreign and defense policy and common policy relating to such issues as crime, terrorism, and immigration. Gradually, such ideas have begun to become reality. The EU and the United States exchange ambassadors. To a degree, the recognition by EU member-states of Bosnia, Croatia, Macedonia, and other countries that seceded from Yugoslavia was undertaken with EU coordination. The EU was also active, albeit unsuccessfully, in trying to mediate the disputes in the Balkans.

The most recent agreement to further economic and political integration is the Treaty for Europe, known as the **Treaty of Amsterdam.** The treaty was completed in 1997, ratified by the parliaments of 14 member-states and by Ireland's voters in a referendum, and went into effect on May 1, 1999. The treaty, in the words of EU president Santer, "sets out the rules of the game governments have to observe and... establishes rights for all the citizens [of the EU]."[5] Among other things, the treaty requires member-states to align their employment policies according to EU guidelines, furthers the sense of EU citizenship in a number of ways, and establishes a new external policy planning unit that could be construed as an early first stage of a EU foreign ministry. The Treaty of Amsterdam also limits the ability of any single member or a few members to block EU policy, increases the power of the president of the EU and the European Parliament, brings patents and intellectual property rights further into the EU's realm, and encourages the development of the Western European Union (WEU, a long-standing but little-used defense arrangement), which could lead to an EU defense ministry and military force.

THE GOVERNMENT OF EUROPE: A PROTOTYPE

The EU's organizational structure is extremely complex, but a brief look at it is important to illustrate the extent to which a regional government has been created (Hix, 1999; Peterson & Bomberg, 1999). As with all governments, the structure and the authority of the various EU units play an important part in determining how policy is made and which policies are adopted (Meunier, 2000). Figure 9.3 gives a brief overview of this structure. The EU's government can be divided for analysis into the political leadership, the bureaucracy, the legislature, and the judiciary (Richardson, 1997).

Political Leadership

Political decision making occurs within the Council of the European Union, usually called the **Council of Ministers.** The council meets twice a year as a gathering of the prime ministers and other heads of government and decides on the most important policy directions for the EU. The council meets more often with lesser ministers (often finance ministers) in attendance to supplement the prime ministerial meetings. Most sessions are held in Brussels, Belgium, which is the principal site of the EU administrative element. Originally, each country had one vote on the council, but the SEA and the Treaty of Amsterdam began and expanded decision making by a weighted-vote plan (termed "qualified majority voting"). Under this plan the larger EU countries have more votes on some matters. There are a total of 87 votes, with each country's allocation ranging from 10 votes for France, Germany, Great Britain, and Italy to 2 votes for Luxembourg. Unanimity is often required, but 62 of the 87 votes are sometimes sufficient to make policy.

Bureaucracy

Bureaucracy in the EU is organized within the **European Commission.** The 20-member commission administers policy adopted by the council. Individual commissioners are selected from the member-states on the basis of two each from France, Germany, Great Britain, Italy, and Spain and one commissioner from each of the other members. The commissioners are not, however, supposed to represent the viewpoint of their country. They serve five-year terms and act as a cabinet for the EU, with each commissioner overseeing an area of administrative activity. One of the commissioners is selected by the Council of Europe to be the commission president. This official serves as the EU's administrative head and is the overall director of the EU bureaucracy headquartered in Brussels (Cini, 1997; Nugent, 1997).

The post of **President of the Commission** has evolved into one of the most significant in the EU, arguably something like a president of the European Union. A great deal of that evolution can also be attributed to Jacques Delors, a French national who served as president from 1985 through 1994 and who became known as "Mr. Europe" because of his strong advocacy of European integration. Delors and his staff created a core structure, informally referred to as "Eurocracy," which has a European point of view, rather than a national orientation.

The growing importance of the post of president of Europe and of the Eurocracy was evident in the sharp battle that occurred within the European Council over a successor to Delors. This struggle is taken up later in the chapter in the box Much Ado about Something, which examines the frequent struggles over who will head various IGOs. The essence of the EU controversy was the insistence of the British and some

The 626-member European Parliament (EP) located in Strasbourg, France, is the first truly international legislature. In other IGO models, countries send diplomatic representatives to the UN General Assembly and other such plenary bodies, and those individuals take instructions from their government. By contrast, the members of the EP are elected by voters across Europe, and they tend to group themselves and vote by ideological leanings and policy preferences, rather than by national origin.

others that the EU's bureaucracy and its president needed to be more restrained. Germany and other countries disagreed. In the end the Council of Europe compromised on Luxembourg's prime minister, Jacques Santer, whom Prime Minister John Major of Great Britain described as a "decentralizer."[6] True to this description, Santer took a lower profile than did Delors and Santer's successor, Romano Prodi of Italy, has followed suit. Nevertheless, the size and power of the EU bureaucracy mean that anyone serving as its president will be a person of significant influence.

Yet another indication of the importance of the commission, as well as the political integration of Europe, is the emergence of an ever larger, more active, and more powerful EU infrastructure. The EU's administrative staff has almost quintupled from a little over 5,000 in 1970 to about 29,000 today. The number of EU regulations, decisions, and directives from one or the other EU body has risen from an annual 345 in 1970 to over 600. The EU's 2000 budget is about $83 billion, raised from tariff revenues, from contributions based on each member's gross domestic product, and from part of each member's VAT.

Legislative Branch

The **European Parliament (EP)** serves as the EU's legislative branch and meets in Strasbourg, France. It has 626 members, apportioned among the EU countries on a modified population basis and elected to five-year terms. The most populous country (Germany) has 99 seats; the least populous country (Luxembourg) has 6 seats. Unlike most international congresses, such as the UN General Assembly, the EP's members are elected by voters in their respective countries. Furthermore, instead of organizing themselves within the EP by country, the representatives have tended to group themselves by political persuasion. The 1999 elections, for example, resulted in the moderately conservative coalition, called the European People's Party (EPP) winning 224 seats and the moderately liberal coalition, the Socialist Party of Europe (SPE) winning 180 seats. It was the first time in the EU's history that the EPP had gained more seats than the SPE. The remaining seats were scattered among seven identifiable groupings of legislators and a few dozen unaffiliated members.

The EP has had mostly advisory authority, but it is struggling to carve out a more authoritative role. That goal was advanced under the Treaty of Amsterdam, which extends the EP's "co-decision" authority with the Council of Ministers to a greater number of matters. The EP can also veto some regulations issued by the commission and it confirms the President of the Commission. A key power, albeit one that is so far little used, is the EP's ability to accept or reject the EU budget proposed by the commission.

Judicial Branch

The Court of Justice is the main element of the judicial branch of the EU (Alter, 1998; Garrett, Kelemen, & Schulz, 1998; Mattli & Slaughter, 1998). The 15-member court hears cases brought to it by member-states or other EU institutions and sometimes acts as a court of appeals for decisions of lower EU courts. The treaties of the EU are often styled its "constitution." Like the EU's other institutions, the courts have gained authority over time. In one illustrative case, the Court of Justice ruled that certain VAT exemptions in Great Britain violated EU treaties and would have to be eliminated. The ruling prompted some members of the British Parliament to grumble that it was the first time since Charles I's reign (1625–1649) that the House of Commons had been compelled to raise taxes. Another bit of evidence of the mounting influence of the court is that its workload became so heavy that the EU created a new, lower court, the Court of First Instance, which hears cases related to the EU brought by corporations and individuals. The judicial branch also includes the Court of Auditors, which monitors budget spending. There is also a **European Ombudsman,** an office that acts as a mediator between government agencies and citizens who bring complaints. The office of the Ombudsman can demand information from and make recommendations to agencies and can also recommend corrective legislation to the Council of Ministers and the European Parliament.

THE FUTURE OF THE EU

There is in Europe both a sense that the EU should continue to press economic and political integration forward and a hesitancy to move toward becoming the United States of Europe (Wallace, 1999). This duality was evident in a June 2000 speech by France's president Jacques Chirac to Germany's parliament. "Those countries that want to proceed further with integration, on a voluntary basis and in specific areas, must be allowed to do so without being held back," he declared. But, he added, his image was of a "united Europe of states rather than a United States of Europe."[7] How much further and how fast the EU proceeds down the road of integration and expansion rests on a number of factors (Gabel, 1998; Cafruny & Lankowski, 1997; Landau & Whitman, 1997).

Popular Support for EU Integration The level of public support for EU integration is one factor that will determine the EU's future. A poll, the *Eurobarometer*, that tracks opinion in Europe finds somewhat mixed signals about how Europeans feel about the EU.[8] For example, popular support for their country's membership in the EU can be viewed in two ways. From one perspective, only a thin majority (51 percent) of Europeans voice support. But only 13 percent voice opposition, with others uncertain. Over time, average support increased from about 50 percent in the early 1980s to approximately 70 percent during 1989–1991, then dropped back to about 50 percent in the late 1990s.

There are numerous indications, however, that Europeans support EU integration, want it to proceed further, and want it to proceed faster. For instance, people are relatively comfortable with EU governance of at least some areas once exclusively the realm of national governments. Asked about a list of 25 policy areas (such as foreign policy and education) over which the EU has some authority, the average support of Europeans for EU decision making in these areas was 53 percent, compared to only 17 preferring exclusive national decision making (and the rest undecided). Support of EU decision making ranged widely by issue, with 69 percent support for EU decision making in foreign policy compared to only 34 percent for education policy.

Europeans also give a slight nod to faster integration. A *Eurobarometer* measure asked people to place on a 1 (not moving) to 7 (racing) scale how fast integration was moving and how fast they wished it to move. The study found that, on average, respondents perceived integration to be moving at 4.0 and wished it to move at a 4.8 rate. Yet somewhat oddly, given the desire to speed up integration, there has been a slight downward trend in the sense that there are benefits to EU membership. From 1983 through 1991, a majority of poll respondents usually said their country had benefited from EU membership. From 1992 through 1999, the level was consistently below 50 percent, dipping to a low of 40 percent in 1997 and standing at 46 percent in 1999.

The EU Economy The economic prosperity of EU members and their citizens is a second factor in course of EU integration. Whether Europeans feel that the EU is beneficial is based in part on their perceptions of its impact on their prosperity. The drop-off in perceived benefits of the EU that occurred after 1991 came at the same time as the combined EU economy slowed from an annual growth rate of 2.9 percent in 1990, to 1.4 in 1991, 1.0 in 1992, and a negative (–)1.8 in 1993. Then the economy started to slowly improve, and after a slight lag, so did the percentage of people seeing the EU as beneficial.

While the EU economy is better, it has not been as robust in the recent past as the U.S. economy. Between 1995 and 1999, the U.S. GDP increased an average annual of 4.1 percent, compared to 2.1 percent for the EU. Unemployment is particularly troublesome for the EU, and stood at 9 percent in mid-2000, compared to 4 percent in the United States. When asked which of a series of issues should be an EU priority, 90 percent of Europeans selected "fighting unemployment" as a priority.

While the potential for the European economy is immense, there are numerous possible obstacles to overcome. One is economic disparity. The original six members were relatively close in their economic circumstances. The addition of new countries has changed that and will continue to do so. As it stands, the average annual per capita GDPs of EU countries range from Luxembourg's $33,700 to Greece's $13,000. Adding East European countries, such as Bulgaria ($4,100), which applied to join the EU, will further complicate the integration of the EU's diverse economies.

Just as expanding EU membership has potential pluses and minuses, so does the ongoing implementation of the euro as the official currency and the planned abolishment of the German mark, French franc, Italian lira, and the other national currencies of the EU members (McKay, 1999; Overturf, 1997). Having a common currency is necessary to achieve full economic integration and to move further toward political integration. Still, the creation of the euro has created major issues as the EU struggles to resolve longstanding national differences over fiscal policy. Four EU countries are not in the "euro zone," that is, they will not generally use the euro. Moreover, the currency was not received with confidence in the world financial markets. When the euro was put into circulation on January 1, 1999, it was pegged at 1 euro = $1.17. From that point, the euro's exchange rate by late 2000 had fallen to about $0.87, a 26 percent drop, creating inflationary pressures in the euro zone. The falling value of the euro also had the effect of driving up the price of gasoline and other imported products (which are valued

The European Union's new currency, the euro, is already used in many government and business transactions in the EU, and will enter general use in 2002. Replacing French francs, German marks, Italian lira, and many other familiar national currencies with the euro will be perhaps the greatest test so far of the EU. This picture shows the euro symbol in the center, surrounded by a star for each of the EU's 15 member-countries.

on the international market in U.S. dollars) even faster than in the United States. The price of gasoline per gallon reached $4 to $5 in various EU countries (depending on taxes), setting off massive protests, especially by truckers who blocked roads, ports, and other transportation hubs. This caused the European Central Bank (the EU's equivalent of the U.S. Federal Reserve Board) to raise interest rates to stem inflation, but that threatened to dampen Europe's economy.

Satisfaction with EU Institutions The degree to which the EU's rule-making and administrative institutions function effectively is a third factor that will affect the future of EU integration. Overall, only 38 percent of citizens in the EU say they tend to trust the European Commission, European Parliament, and other EU institutions. This, however, may reflect global attitudes toward government. For instance, only 30 percent of Americans say they trust their government to do the right thing all or most of the time.[9]

Some European voters oppose expansion of EU functions because of their sense that so-called Eurotaxes are too high and that the EU bureaucracy, the "Eurocracy," is too powerful, unresponsive, and even corrupt. This feeling was substantiated in March 1999 when all 20 members of the European Commission, including its president, Jacques Santer, resigned amid allegations of mismanagement and cronyism and were replaced by a new set of commissioners headed by Italy's Romano Prodi. Some of the tales of Eurocratic excess that circulate are related in the box, When Is a Banana a Banana?

Political Identity How Europeans identify politically is a fourth factor that will impact EU integration (Zielonka, 1998). An increase in the transfer of authority from national governments to the EU will require citizens to shift their loyalties to an equal degree from their national states to the EU. Some analysts conclude that Europeans are doing so. "There has been a qualitative jump in the sense of European identity," according to a German expert on international affairs. "What you are seeing are the first signs of shared beliefs, rights and responsibilities among young Europeans no longer ready to sit passively as America protects them or as the Union grows."[10]

Recent polls give some credence to this view. While almost no one considers themselves, politically, a North American or an African, 52 percent of people in the EU countries indicated they see themselves, at least partly, as European. But the sense of Euronationalism is also limited in several ways. Only 10 percent of EU citizens see themselves as European only or European more than national. Forty-five percent identify with their nationality only, and national identity is stronger than European identity for 42 percent. Three percent were unsure. Furthermore, most Europeans also express strong national pride, with a strong majority in all EU contries saying they are proud or fairly proud of their countries. It is also the case that while Europeans are far more likely now than earlier to see Europe as a cultural whole, that is still a minority feeling at 38 percent.

Nationalism-based resistance is especially evident in the newer EU members, but it is an important emotion in even the original six EU members. "Our nations are the source of our identities and of our roots," President Chirac recently proclaimed. "The diversity of our political traditions, cultures and languages is one of the strengths of the union. In the future, our nations will stay the first reference point for our people."[11]

WHEN IS A BANANA A BANANA?

Tales of attempts by EU bureaucrats to regulate everything have become part of the political lore of Europe. One field of contest has been the great EU food wars. Skirmishes have been fought over what food can be called.

Greece, for example, persuaded the EU to bar Denmark from exporting what it called feta cheese. Denmark swallowed that, but Danes nearly left the EU when the pride and joy of their apple crop, the Queen Bridgette, was declared too small to move in trade among EU members. Intense negotiations repolished Danish–EU relations, and Denmark remains a core EU member.

Many Europeans also reacted with bemusement at the EU's banana contretemps. The details are slippery, but it all stemmed from a bunch of regulations promulgated by the EU bureaucracy that, among other things, specified that imported bananas had to be at least 5.5 inches long and 1.1 inches wide, and could not be abnormally bent. Great Britain, where archeologists in 1999 uncovered the remains of a banana skin dating back to the mid-1400s, was especially offended. "Brussels bureaucrats proved yesterday what a barmy bunch they are—by outlawing curved bananas. The crazy laws were drawn by thumb-twiddling EU chiefs who spent thousands on a yearlong study," protested the British newspaper, the *Sun*. An EU spokesperson replied that while, indeed, bananas of an abnormal shape could not be imported, that "in no sense" meant that EU regulation banned "curved bananas because a curve is a normal shape for a banana."[1]

Once the Europeans agreed on what a banana was, they also agreed to impose lower tariffs on bananas from their former colonies than on bananas from other places. That drove Americans bananas because many of those other places were Caribbean and Central American countries with close ties to the United States. Washington then butted heads with the EU by threatening to retaliate by barring cashmere and other EU products. This got the goat of Scottish cashmere producers. In the end, the two economic superpowers were able to escape the horns of this dilemma by agreeing that the EU would gradually end its preferences for its bunch of favored countries and equally admit the bananas from the U.S.–favored bunch of countries.

The reputation of the Eurocracy was further darkened by the chocolate imbroglio. Having decided that bananas could indeed be bent, at least somewhat, and in the right places, EU policymakers turned to the sticky issue of what constitutes chocolate. The battle line was drawn between the eight EU countries that require chocolate to consist entirely of cocoa butter and the other seven EU members that allow up to 5 percent vegetable oil in chocolate. Representing the purists, the head of the Belgian chocolate company, Godiva, proclaimed that only "100 percent chocolate should be called... chocolate." Answering back for the nondoctrinaire chocolatiers, a representative of Great Britain's largest chocolate maker, Cadbury, urged, "Let's celebrate Europe's regional diversity and recognize that there are different ways of making chocolate." The purists won the first round when the European Parliament voted 306 to 112 in favor of their position. But the war was not over, for the European Council of Ministers had to make the final gooey decision. "Whatever we do will be attacked from one side or the other," an EU spokesperson has complained. Compromise was the sweet solution. An early 2000 ruling declared that chocolate with vegetable oil could be shipped throughout the EU. Moreover it could be labeled chocolate, but only in the seven nonpurist countries. In the purist eight, it would have to be labeled "family milk chocolate." Not that it has anything to do with families or milk. Ah well, as Forrest Gump mused, "Life is like a box of chocolates."

Perceptions of Germany Wariness of Germany is a fifth factor that impinges on EU integration. Germany accounts for 21 percent of the EU's population, 25 percent of the GDP, and 22 percent of total EU merchandise exports. One survey of British, French, German, and Italian citizens asked which country, if any, "will become the dominant power" in the EU. A majority of the British, French, and Italians, and even a plurality of the Germans, replied "Germany." When asked if they liked the idea of Germany dominating, 91 percent of the British, 73 percent of the French, and 71 percent of the Italians said "no."[12]

Furthering the disquiet in some, Germany has been a leading proponent of ever greater economic and political integration. In May 2000 German foreign minister

Joschka Fischer commented in a speech that the current EU structure was too cumbersome to achieve a fully integrated Europe and should be replaced by "nothing less than a European Parliament and a European government which really do exercise legislative and executive power within [a]... federation."[13] In short, Fischer proposed creating a more powerful European government and a federal United States of Europe. Reaction was swift and sharp. "There is a tendency in Germany to imagine a federal structure for Europe which fits in with its own model," warned France's interior minister, Jean-Pierre Chevènement. "Deep down, [Germany] is still dreaming of the Holy Roman Empire. It hasn't cured itself of its past derailment into Nazism."[14] Fischer later protested he was speaking as an individual, not as German foreign minister, and Chevènement apologized for his undiplomatic reference to Germany's Nazi past. Still, the incident reflected a concern that is not far below the surface in Europe.

Expanded Membership Popular willingness to accept new members into the EU is a sixth pivotal issue in the future of the EU and is also related to nationalism. Support for integration does not necessarily mean support for expansion, and the latter is being limited by the recent upsurge in antiforeigner sentiment in Europe. As a result, public support for the enlargement of the EU is mixed. Asked about a list of 13 countries that have applied to join the EU, respondents gave majority support to only two, Norway and Switzerland. It should be noted, however, that "don't know" responses were high, and none of the 13 countries registered majority opposition.

In sum, the evolution of the EU has been one of the remarkable events of the past half century. It does not take much imagination to foresee a day when the once antagonistic states of Europe are a United States of Europe. That is just one possibility, however, and what is certain is that the progress of the EU toward further economic and political integration, whether or not it leads to true federation, will be difficult.

GLOBAL IGOs: FOCUS ON THE UNITED NATIONS

The growing level and importance of IGO activity and organization at the regional level is paralleled by IGOs at the global level. Of these, the United Nations is by far the best known and most influential (Ryan, 2000). Therefore, we will focus in this section on the UN, both as a generalized study of the operation of IGOs and as a specific study of the most prominent member of their ranks.

IGO ORGANIZATION AND RELATED ISSUES

Many people assume that the study of organizational structure is dry and meaningless, but the contrary is true. Constitutions, rules of procedure, finance, organization charts, and other administrative details are often crucial in determining political outcomes. It is, for example, impossible to understand how the UN works without knowing that five of its members possess a veto in the Security Council and the other 183 do not. An outline of the UN's structure is depicted in Figure 9.4.

Organizational structure is also important because it must reflect realities and goals and have the flexibility to change if it becomes outmoded. "Clearly we cannot meet the challenges of the new millennium with an instrument designed for the very different circumstances of the middle of the twentieth century," the UN's secretary-general, Kofi Annan, points out.[15] To examine structure and rules, the following discussion of IGOs will take up matters relating to general membership, the structure of representative bodies, voting formulas, the authority of executive leadership, and the bureaucracy. Then we will turn to the matter of IGO finance.

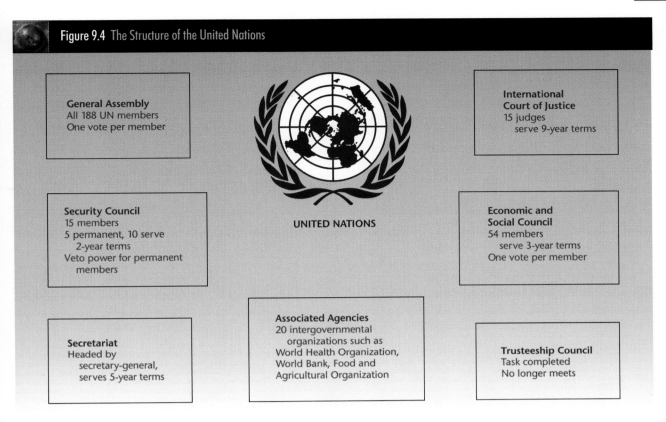

Figure 9.4 The Structure of the United Nations

General Assembly
All 188 UN members
One vote per member

International Court of Justice
15 judges
serve 9-year terms

Security Council
15 members
5 permanent, 10 serve
2-year terms
Veto power for permanent
members

UNITED NATIONS

Economic and Social Council
54 members
serve 3-year terms
One vote per member

Secretariat
Headed by
secretary-general,
serves 5-year terms

Associated Agencies
20 intergovernmental
organizations such as
World Health Organization,
World Bank, Food and
Agricultural Organization

Trusteeship Council
Task completed
No longer meets

The United Nations is a complex organization. It has 6 major organs and 20 associated agencies.

General Membership

Theoretically, membership in most IGOs is open to any state that is both within the geographic and/or functional scope of that organization and subscribes to the principles and practices of that organization. In practice, a third standard, politics, often becomes a heavy consideration in membership questions. Today the UN has grown to nearly universal membership, as Figure 9.5 shows, but that was not always the case. One point of occasional controversy is the standards for *admitting new members*. One instance occurred in mid-1998 when the General Assembly voted by an overwhelming margin of 124 to 4 (with others abstaining or not voting) to give the Palestinians what amounts to an informal associate membership. Only the Marshall Islands, Micronesia, and the United States joined Israel on the losing side. The Palestinians do not have the right to vote, but they do have the ability to take part in debates in the UN and perform other functions undertaken by states. Nassar al-Kidwa, the head of the Palestinian delegation, told the General Assembly, "A small victory was achieved for Palestine today, and we thank you for that.... However,... it is our hope that our reliance on this resolution passed today will not last for a long time, as we hope that the United Nations will accept Palestine as a member state in the near future."[16]

The issue of *successor states* has also been quite political. With little fanfare, the UN agreed to recognize Russia, rather than one of the other former Soviet republics, as the successor state to the Soviet Union. This meant, among other things, that Russia inherited the USSR's permanent seat and veto on the Security Council. Taking the opposite approach, the UN in 1992 refused to recognize the Serbian-dominated gov-

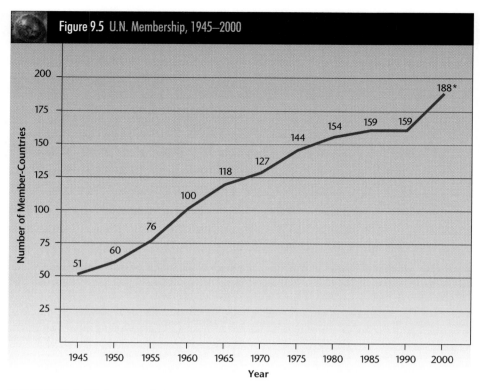

Figure 9.5 U.N. Membership, 1945–2000

Data source: UN Web site at: http://www.un.org. and author.

*The Security Council in February 2000 voted to recommend that the application of Tuvalu to join the UN be approved. The expected final approval of the General Assembly will bring UN membership to 189.

Membership in the United Nations has risen rapidly. The 269 percent rise in UN membership is an indication of the increased number of states in existence and also of the UN's nearly universal membership.

ernment in Belgrade as the successor to Yugoslavia once that country broke apart. Instead, the General Assembly required Yugoslavia to (re)apply for admission. Yugoslavia has not and remains in a nonparticipating status at the UN.

Withdrawal, suspension, and expulsion is another membership issue. At times members have withdrawn from IGOs. Indonesia withdrew from the UN in 1965 for one year amid turmoil in that country. Members have withdrawn from UN agencies. The United States and Great Britain quit UNESCO in 1984 amid charges of waste. Reforms were implemented, and the British rejoined in 1997. The Clinton administration indicated that it wished to rejoin, but did not because it did not think it could get Congress to appropriate the dues for UNESCO.

Countries can also be suspended or expelled from IGOs. Nationalist China (Taiwan) was, in effect, ejected from the UN when the "China seat" was transferred to the mainland. In a move close to expulsion, the General Assembly refused between 1974 and 1991 to accept the credentials of South Africa's delegate because that country's apartheid policies violated the UN Charter.

Representative Bodies

There are important issues that relate to how to structure the representative bodies of international organizations. Most IGOs have a **plenary representative body** that includes all members. The theoretical basis for plenary bodies is the mutual responsibility of all members for the organization and its policies. The **UN General Assembly (UNGA)** is the UN's plenary organ, but in other IGOs it may be termed a council, a conference, a commission, or even a parliament. These plenary bodies normally have the authority to involve themselves in virtually all aspects of their organizations. Thus, in theory, they are the most powerful elements of their organizations. In practice, however, the plenary organization may be secondary to the administrative structure or some other part of the organization.

A second type of representative organization body is a **limited membership council.** The theory here is that some members have a greater stake, responsibility, or capacity in a particular area of concern. The **UN Security Council (UNSC)** has 15 members. Ten are chosen by the UNGA for limited terms, but five are permanent members (Barber, 1996). These five (China, France, Russia, the United Kingdom, and the United States) were the five leading victorious powers at the end of World War II and were thought to have a special peacekeeping role to play. During the UN's more than 50 years, these five countries have served continuously as permanent members on the Security Council. Of the other 183 members, more than half have never served on the Council (Russett, 1997).

The special status enjoyed by the five permanent members of the UNSC has become a simmering issue in the UN. The most common argument against the arrangement is that the existing membership has never been fully realistic and is becoming less so as time goes by. Many global and regional powers that do not have permanent seats are beginning to press for change (Drifte, 1999). Japan's prime minister declared his country "ready to take up the challenge" of a permanent seat.[17] Similarly, Germany's foreign minister avowed that "Germany is... prepared to assume responsibility as a permanent member of the Security Council."[18] India's delegate to the UN has said that when a new formula is reached to determine which powerful countries should have permanent seats, "We believe that India will be among them."[19]

Less powerful countries are also urging reform. The president of Sri Lanka, for one, has called on the UNSC to "become more representative and more responsible to the general membership of the United Nations." Similarly, the president of Zambia has declared that the Council "can no longer be maintained like the sanctuary of the Holy of Holies with only the original members acting as high priests, deciding on issues for the rest of the world who cannot be admitted."[20]

Dissatisfaction with the Security Council has spawned many plans to revise it. Whatever the plan, however, change will be hard to achieve. One difficulty is that any Charter revision must be recommended by a two-thirds vote of the UNSC (where each of the five permanent members has a veto), adopted by a two-thirds vote of the UNGA, and ratified by two-thirds of the members according to their respective constitutional processes. The permanent UNSC members are opposed to surrendering their special status. It will also be difficult to arrive at a new formula that satisfies the sensitivities of other countries and regions. For example, the thought of India having a permanent seat alarms Pakistan, whose UN representative has characterized those seeking permanent status as motivated by "an undisguised grab for power and privilege."[21] Therefore, the prospects for reform remain dim. As an Italian diplomat has noted, "The only matter that we would seem to have agreed on is that we are in profound disagreement on how to enlarge the Council."[22]

Voting Formulas

One of the difficult issues that any international organization faces is its formula for allocating votes (Bohman, 1999). Three major alternatives as they exist today are majority voting, weighted voting, and unanimity voting. The implications of various voting formulas are evident in Figure 9.6.

Majority voting is the most common formula used in IGOs. This system has two main components: (1) each member casts one equal vote, and (2) the issue is carried by either a simple majority (50 percent plus one vote) or, in some cases, an extraordinary

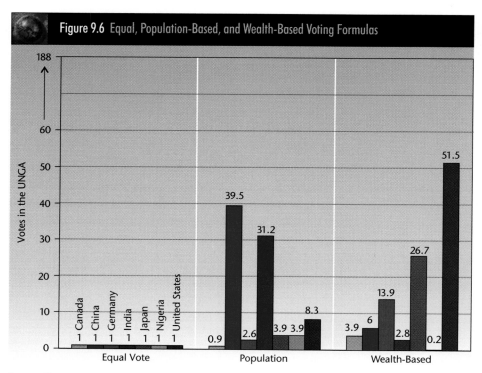

Figure 9.6 Equal, Population-Based, and Wealth-Based Voting Formulas

Data source: World Bank (1999) and author's calculations.

To see the impact of various voting formulas, imagine that the current 188 votes in the UNGA were allocated on the basis of equality, population, and wealth. Voting power would vary widely. For example, the United States would have one vote under equal voting, 8.3 votes under population-based voting, and 51.5 votes under wealth-based voting. Nigeria would gain votes under population; lose votes under wealth. Canada would lose under population; gain under wealth. Are any of these formulas fair? What would be a fair formula?

majority (commonly two-thirds). The theory of majoritarianism springs from the concept of sovereign equality and the democratic notion that the will of the majority should prevail. The UNGA and most other UN bodies operate on this principle.

The problem with the idea of equality among states is that it does not reflect some standards of reality. Should Costa Rica, with no army, cast an equal vote with the powerful United States? Should San Marino, with a population of thousands, cast the same vote as China, with its more than one billion people? It might be noted, for example, that in the UNGA, some 125 states, whose combined populations are less than 15 percent of the world's population, account for two-thirds of members and, thus, the available votes. By contrast, the 10 countries with populations over 100 million (Bangladesh, Brazil, China, India, Indonesia, Japan, Nigeria, Pakistan, Russia, and the United States), which combine for 68 percent of the world's population, have less than 6 percent of the available votes in the General Assembly.

Another impact of the one-country-one-vote formula in the UNGA has been a marked change in the voting power of regions and blocs. When the UN began operation, for example, Europe and four other predominantly Eurowhite countries (Australia, Canada, New Zealand, and the United States) held 37 percent of the UNGA vote. These countries now command only 24 percent of the vote. By contrast, Africa's vote, which stood at 8 percent in 1945, is now 28 percent of the UNGA total. The percentage of votes wielded by the Asian-Pacific countries has increased from 16 percent to 28 percent.

Weighted voting, or a system that allocates unequal voting power on the basis of a formula, is a second voting scheme. Two possible criteria are population and wealth. As noted earlier, the European Parliament provides an example of an international representative body based in part on population. A number of international monetary organizations base voting on financial contributions. Voting in the World Bank and the International Monetary Fund is based on member contributions. The United States alone commands about 17 percent of the votes in the IMF, and it and France, Germany, Great Britain, and Japan together can cast almost 40 percent of the votes in that IGO. This "wealth-weighted" voting is especially offensive to LDC states, which contend that it perpetuates the system of imperial domination by the industrialized countries.

Unanimity voting constitutes a third scheme. This system requires the assent by all, although sometimes abstaining from a vote does not block agreement. The Organization for Economic Cooperation and Development (OECD) and some other IGOs operate on that principle. Unanimity preserves the concept of sovereignty but can easily lead to stalemate.

The voting formula in the UNSC by which some countries can **veto** proposals while others cannot is an unusual variation on the unanimity scheme. In the UN Security Council, any of the 5 permanent members (the P5) can, by casting a negative vote, veto a resolution favored by the other 14 members (O'Neill, 1997). During the cold war between 1946 and 1990, the veto was cast 264 times. Since then, vetoes have been much less frequent, but the power remains important. First, a veto is still sometimes cast. China in 1999 forced an end to the UN peacekeeping mission in Macedonia by vetoing a continuing resolution. Second, the veto remains important as a threat. Many votes are never taken because they face a certain veto by one or more of the P5. There was, for example, no formal U.S. veto in 1996 of the reelection of Secretary-General Boutros-Ghali. Nevertheless, despite all 14 other council members supporting him, the U.S. veto power ended his tenure. Indeed, the continuing importance of the veto in practice and its value as a symbol of big-power status have made it a target of the many countries that are proposing reforms for the Security Council. From the perspective of some LDCs, for example, the UNSC is a vehicle for domination by the big powers. President Fidel Castro of Cuba, for one, has condemned "the obsolete veto privilege" as an "ill use of the Security Council by the powerful" aimed at "exalting a new colonialism" through the UN.[23]

Voting formulas are important politically because they have a major impact on who will be powerful, who will not, and what policies will be adopted (Holloway & Tomlinson, 1995). Furthermore, how to apportion representation in the parliamentary bodies of such IGOs as the UN will become increasingly important and contentious as the IGOs become more powerful, especially if and when they begin to have true supranational power to compel states to act in certain ways. As noted, one way to think further about the ramifications of various voting schemes is to examine Figure 9.6 on page 238. It shows the number of votes each of six countries would have in the current 188-vote UNGA using equality, population, or wealth as the determinant.

Political Leadership

It is difficult for any organization to function without a single administrative leader, and virtually all IGOs have a chief executive officer (CEO). The UN's administrative structure is called the **Secretariat**, and the secretary-general is the CEO. In this section we will take up the selection and role of the UN secretary-general and other CEOs of IGOs. Then, in the next section, we will address the bureaucratic understructure of IGO secretariats (Barnett & Finnemore, 1999).

Selection The UN secretary-general is nominated by the UNSC, then elected by the General Assembly for a five-year term. This simple fact does not, however, adequately emphasize the political considerations that govern the appointment of administrators.

(continued on page 240)

MUCH ADO ABOUT SOMETHING

The argument that IGOs are marginal to world politics is belied by the frequent conflict over who will head them. Clearly, there must be much ado about something.

The post of UN secretary-general has quite often been the focus of sharp clashes. Because the secretary-general is nominated by the UNSC and only one nomination is forwarded to the UNGA for election, the five permanent members with their veto power can, in effect, select the secretary-general. To pick up the saga of struggle with the fifth secretary-general, Javier Pérez de Cuéllar (1982–1992), won office only after a protracted stalemate in which various UNSC permanent members vetoed each others' preferred candidates. The selection of his successor, Boutros Boutros-Ghali (1992–1997) was also controversial.

No African had yet been secretary-general, and the countries of that continent insisted that it was their turn. The United States and some other countries were dubious about the potential priorities of an African secretary-general but did not want to alienate Africa. "We weren't going to be the 900-pound gorilla" on this issue, commented one U.S. official.[1] In this atmosphere, Boutros-Ghali, an Egyptian and the only non–sub-Saharan African candidate, was an ideal compromise. He was the most Westernized of all the African candidates, spoke several languages, and had been a professor of international law in Egypt and a Fulbright scholar at Columbia University. Any possible alarm that Boutros-Ghali was an Arab was eased by the fact that he is a Coptic Christian, not a Muslim, and his wife, Leah, is Jewish.

In office, Boutros-Ghali proved to be an assertive, sometimes acerbic secretary-general who often rankled some members, especially the United States. President Clinton branded the secretary-general as ineffective and claimed that if he remained, it would be impossible to persuade Congress to appropriate funds for the UN. For these and other reasons, Washington, in effect, vetoed a second term for Boutros-Ghali.

Since most recent secretaries-general have served two terms, the African countries felt that it was still their "turn," and the names of potential African candidates began to circulate. The process in the Security Council involved a search for consensus that Italy's representative likened to selecting a pope. The only difference, said the ambassador, was that in the UN "if you stare at the ceiling, there are no frescoes by Michelangelo to inspire you."[2] In a series of straw votes, two names emerged: Kofi Annan, a career UN diplomat from Ghana, and Amara Essy, the foreign minister of the Ivory Coast. Annan was favored by the United States. He had a reputation as a capable and moderate diplomat and administrator, and his personal history (a B.A. degree in economics from Macalaster College in St. Paul, Minnesota, M.A. in management from MIT) helped assuage Washington's concern that a secretary-general from black Africa might prove too radical. Annan is married to Nane Lagergren, a Swedish lawyer, who is a niece of Raoul Wallenberg, the heroic Swedish diplomat noted for trying to save Jewish lives during World War II.

France was the primary supporter of Essy, based on the fact that he spoke fluent French (but only halting English), had earned his law degree from Poitiers University in France, and came from a former French colony. The French threatened initially to veto Annan, and the Americans and British indicated they would veto Essy. In the end, with Annan clearly ahead in the straw votes, and given that he speaks at least some French, France gave way.

The maneuvering to pick several secretaries-general underlines the importance of that office, and this standard can also be applied to the heads of other IGOs. For example, the creation of the World Trade Organization in 1995 set off a spirited contest for the top spot, with Europe, Asia, and the United States each backing one or more candidates from their respective regions. What looked to be building toward a momentous clash between the EU and the United States over who would lead the WTO suddenly went in favor of the EU candidate, Italy's Renato Ruggiero, when the U.S.–backed candidate, Carlos Salinas de Gortari, who had just retired as president of Mexico, was discredited by the precipitous devaluation of the Mexican peso in December 1994 and by rumors of corruption. When Ruggiero resigned in 1999, the next round of struggle featured a determined effort by the LDCs to break the EDCs' monopoly on the top jobs in the leading financial IGOs. The

One sign of the importance of IGOs is that who will head them has often been, and seems increasingly to be, the subject of intense struggle among member-countries. This is taken up in the box, Much Ado about Something.

Role: Activism versus Restraint An issue that swirls around IGO executives is their proper role. The role orientations of the UN secretary-general and other IGO leaders

result was a compromise: an EDC national, Mike Moore of New Zealand, was selected with the understanding that in 2002 he would step down in favor of Thailand's Supachai Panitchtpakdi, who would serve until 2005.

The selections for the top job at the World Bank have also been influenced by domestic politics. By tradition, the president of the World Bank is an American, and the last two presidents, Lewis T. Preston and James D. Wolfensohn, were both selected because they would please members of Congress who wanted the bank to fund more businesslike projects and who threatened to cut U.S. funding of the bank unless it reoriented its lending policies.

The selection of a new managing director of the IMF to replace Michel Camdessus of France also became a complex imbroglio. Germany wanted one of its nationals to fill the position and nominated Chio Koch-Weser, Germany's deputy finance minister. Washington argued he was too junior, but what the White House really wanted was to have a European of a less financially powerful country in the post. Other European countries backed the German candidate, but some did so unenthusiastically because they shared Washington's concern with empowering Germany. Understandably, the Germans were offended, with one official complaining that the United States "sees its global role not only in the military area but also in setting the rules of globalization through the IMF." Washington could oppose, but it could not propose because it did not want to offend the Europeans by nominating an American. Nevertheless that happened when the African and Arab countries backed the number two official at the IMF, Stanley Fisher, who, ironically, is a Jewish American and is seen as a friend to the less developed countries. Japan nominated one of its own finance ministry officials, Eisuke Sakakibara. Tokyo apparently did not expect him to win, but wanted to position Japan for the job when it next opens up. Finally, the standoff ended when Germany shifted its support to another German, Horst Köhler, president of the European Bank for Reconstruction and Development (EBRD). Washington was not enthusiastic about Köhler either, but did not want to deny the Germans again and reasoned that, as head of the ERBD, Köhler is more European and less German than is Koch-Weser. Thus it was when the IMF met behind closed doors in Washington, amid noisy street protests, that Herr Köhler was quietly selected as the IMF's new managing director.

Issues of diversity have also become a factor in the selection of IGO heads. Women have headed few IGOs, and the last time the top position at UNICEF, which has traditionally been held by an American, was open, Washington favored an American male. Sensing an opportunity, the Europeans nominated several women to fill the vacancy. "We think it's time for a change," France's delegate declared.[4] Only when the Clinton White House retreated and submitted a new name, that of Peace Corps director Carol Bellamy, was the post kept in American hands. Even more recently, Japan led a fight to capture for the first time the top spot of an IGO for an Asian, when in 1999 it used its economic muscle in UNESCO to secure the director-generalship of UNESCO for Koichiro Matsuura, a career diplomat in Japan's foreign ministry. Japan was not trying "to antagonize one civilization over another," explained a Japanese official, "but it is simply not sound to have such a gross number of directors-general coming from European-based civilizations."[5] That will be corrected in 2002 in the WTO, as noted above.

The regional level has also been the scene for spirited contests over leadership positions. For one, the decision in 1994 of Jacques Delors to retire as president of the European Commission sparked such a struggle. Most EU members supported Belgian prime minister Jean-Luc Dehaene, but he was opposed by Great Britain for being too strong an advocate of increased EU integration. British opposition sparked an angry reaction. For one, France's president, François Mitterrand, charged that "the British conception [of the EU] does not correspond to that of the founding countries."[6] The upshot of the imbroglio was a month of maneuvering that led to the selection of Prime Minister Jacques Santer of Luxembourg as a compromise between the forces of integration and restraint in Europe.

To return to the point with which we started this review of the contest over recent appointments to head leading IGOs, the jostling among the major powers to appoint one of their own or someone of their liking to the top jobs indicates how important these IGOs are. All that sound and fury must signify something.

can range between activism and restraint. For the most part, the documents that established IGOs anticipated a restrained role. In the UN Charter, for example, the Secretariat is the last major organ discussed. That placement indicates the limited, largely administrative role that the document's drafters intended for the secretary-general.

Whatever was intended, the first two secretaries-general, Trygve Lie of Norway (1946–1953) and Dag Hammarskjöld of Sweden (1953–1961), were activists who steadily expanded the role of their office. Hammarskjöld believed that he had a "responsibility" to act to uphold the peace even if the UNGA and UNSC would not or could not and, he said, "irrespective of the views and wishes of the various member governments" (Archer, 1983:148). The height of Hammarskjöld's power came during the crisis that followed the independence of the Belgian Congo in 1960. The secretary-general used UN military forces to avert outside intervention, to suppress the attempt by Katanga Province to secede, and to restore peace. It is somehow sadly fitting that he died when his plane crashed during a mission to the area in 1961. It is widely thought that Hammarskjöld's plane was shot down by mercenaries fighting for Katanga.

Hammarskjöld's independence was not appreciated by all the big powers. The Soviets were so upset at the activist and what they saw as a pro-Western stance of Hammarskjöld that in 1961 they proposed a "Troika" plan to divide the office into three parts. At one point, the visiting Soviet leader, Nikita S. Khrushchev, became so worked up over such issues that he literally took off his shoe and pounded the General Assembly podium with it. Moscow was not able to change the structure of the UN Secretariat or oust Hammarskjöld, but the USSR's stance did lead to a tacit pruning of the powers of his immediate successor.

Over time, however, secretaries-general have once again tended toward activism. The sixth secretary-general, Egypt's Boutros Boutros-Ghali (1992–1996), believed that "if one word above all is to characterize the role of the secretary-general, it is independence. The holder of this office must never be seen as acting out of fear or in an attempt to curry favor with one state or groups of states."[24] Just as Hammarskjöld's activism had led him into disfavor, so to did Boutros-Ghali's views. In this case it was the United States and Great Britain that were dismayed. They were particularly piqued by his criticism of the Eurowhite-dominated Security Council for what he saw as a racially tinged tendency to pay more attention to some matters (such as the Balkans crisis in Europe) than others (such as the crises in Somalia and Rwanda in Africa). Whatever the validity of such charges, the result was that the United States tacitly vetoed a second term for Boutros-Ghali.

In the aftermath of the ouster of Boutros-Ghali, the Security Council nominated and the General Assembly elected Kofi Annan of Ghana as the UN's seventh secretary-general. He brought a number of qualifications to the post. Annan is the first secretary-general to have spent almost his entire career as a UN diplomat rather than as a diplomat for his country. He joined UN service at age 24, and served in a variety of positions, including under secretary-general for peacekeeping. Annan has an exceptionally quiet demeanor, and many observers speculated when he was first selected as secretary-general that he would not act independently.

Those predictions were inaccurate. Since taking office in 1997, Annan has demonstrated a willingness to exercise leadership and even differ with the United States. He has done so more diplomatically, however, than the sometimes sharp-tongued Boutros-Ghali, earning Annan generally smooth relations with Washington and other major capitals. Certainly he is soft-spoken; but that does not mean soft. Annan strongly supports the idea that the UN and its secretary-general should act with independence when necessary. During a commencement speech at the Massachusetts Institute of Technology (MIT), Annan told graduates that his years at MIT had given him "not only the analytical tools but also the intellectual confidence... to be comfortable in seeking the help of colleagues, but not fearing, in the end, to do things my way."[25]

Early in this tenure, Annan had the opportunity to demonstrate his willingness to live up to his words about doing it "my way" if necessary. A crisis boiled up in early 1998 over Iraq's refusal to allow UN weapons inspectors free access to some sites. Both Baghdad and Washington seemed to be spoiling for a fight. Annan worked with the Security Council members to derive a UN position, but the United States let it be

Since coming to office in 1997, Secretary-General Kofi Annan of Ghana has shown himself to be a skilled and assertive leader. The UN secretary-general and the heads of many other international organizations are more than mere administrators; many of them are important diplomatic figures in their own right.

known that they would oppose Annan's intervention unless the UNSC position was acceptable to Washington. The Clinton administration's position was too obdurate, in the view of some, and Annan forced the issue by indicating that he would go to Iraq with or without U.S. approval. Sounding much like Dag Hammarskjöld might have in a similar situation, Annan avowed, "I had a constitutional duty to avert this kind of tragedy [renewed war with Iraq] if I could." When asked whether the maneuvering that forced the U.S. hand had been unintended, the secretary-general laughed softly and replied, "To some extent, no, it wasn't."[26] One senses that when his time as secretary-general is over, Annan will leave softly humming the famous Frank Sinatra refrain, "I did it my way."

Similar tensions over the role of top officials exist in other IGOs, as discussed in the box, Much Ado about Something. Such clashes are in substantial part a struggle between the traditional approach versus the alternative approach to world politics. Traditionally, national states have sought to control IGOs and their leaders. As IGOs and their leaders have grown stronger, however, they have more often struck out independently down the alternative path. As Secretary-General Annan has commented, he and his predecessors have all carried out their traditional duties as chief administrative officer, but they have also assumed another, alternative role: "an instrument of the larger interest, beyond national rivalries and regional concerns."[27] Presidents and prime ministers are finding, comments one U.S. diplomat, that "you can't put the secretary-general back in the closet when it's inconvenient."[28]

Bureaucracy

The secretary-general appoints the other principal officials of the Secretariat, but he must be sensitive to the desires of the dominant powers in making these appointments and must also pay attention to the geographic and, increasingly, gender composition of the Secretariat staff. Controversies have occasionally arisen over the distributions, but in recent years the focus of criticism has been the size and efficiency of the staffs of the UN headquarters in New York and its regional offices (Geneva, Nairobi, and Vienna). In this way, the UN is like many other IGOs and, indeed, national governments, whose allegedly bloated, inefficient, and unresponsive bureaucracies have made them a lightning rod for discontent with government.

Certainly, as with almost any bureaucracy, it is possible to find horror stories about the size and activities of IGO staffs. It is also the case, however, that the charges that the UN and its associated agencies are a bureaucratic swamp need to be put in perspective.

For instance, the UN has substantially trimmed its staff. The Secretariat staff, which peaked at about 12,000 in 1985, declined 28 percent to 8,700 in 2000. Some perspective on such data can also be gained by comparing the UN bureaucracy to local governments and to companies. The city of Minneapolis (population: 352,000), for instance, employs more people (9,000) than does the UN (population: 6,100,000,000). Even if one were to count all 52,100 employees of the UN and its 29 affiliated agencies (like the World Health Organization), they would only be roughly equal in number to the municipal employees of Los Angeles or the combined workers at Disney World and Disneyland. Indeed, MacDonald's has more than five times as many employees devoted to serving the world hamburgers, french fries, and shakes than the UN has people devoted to serving the world's needs for peace, health, dignity, and prosperity.

IGO FINANCING AND RELATED ISSUES

All IGOs face the problem of obtaining sufficient funds to conduct their operations. National governments must also address this issue, but they have the power to impose and legally collect taxes. By contrast, IGOs have very little authority to compel member-countries to support them.

The United Nations Budget The United Nations is beset by severe and controversial financial problems. There are several elements to the extended UN budget. The first is the *core budget* for headquarters operations and the regular programs of the major UN organs. Second, there is the *peacekeeping budget* to meet the expenses of operations being conducted by the Security Council. These two budgets were, respectively, $1.2 billion and $940 million in FY1999. Supporting the UN budgets respectively cost each American $1.11 and $1.07, for a total of $2.18—or would have if the United States fully paid its share of UN costs. The third budget element is called the *voluntary contributions budget*, which funds a number of UN agencies such as the United Nations Children's Fund (UNICEF) and the United Nations Environment Program (UNEP). The combined FY1999 expenditures of these agencies are about $3.6 billion.

The UN is almost entirely dependent on the *assessment* it levies on member-countries to pay its core and peacekeeping budgets. This assessment is fixed by the UNGA based on a complicated formula that reflects the ability to pay. According to the UN Charter, which is a valid treaty binding on all signatories, members are required to meet these assessments and may have their voting privilege in the General Assembly suspended if they are seriously in arrears. There are eight countries that each have assessments of 2 percent of the budget or higher. They and their percentages of the budget assessment are: the United States (25.0 percent), Japan (19.0 percent), Germany (9.8 percent), France (6.5 percent), Italy (5.4 percent), Great Britain (5.1 percent), Canada (2.8 percent), and Spain (2.6 percent). At the other end of the financial scale, there are a large number of countries that pay very little, with 142 countries assessed below .01 percent, including 37 UN members paying the minimum assessment of 0.001 percent ($10,391 for FY1999). The "target" voluntary budget payments are the same as the core budget. Because of their special responsibility (and their special privilege, the veto), permanent UNSC members pay a somewhat higher assessment for peacekeeping, with the U.S. share at 31 percent.

The assessment scheme is criticized by some on the grounds that while the eight countries with assessments of 2 percent or higher collectively paid 76.2 percent of the UN budget in FY1999, they cast just 4.3 percent of the votes in the UNGA. By contrast, the 142 countries with a 0.01 percent assessment or less account for less than 4.1 percent of the UN budget, but they command 75.5 percent of the votes in the General Assembly. One result of the gap between contributions and voting power has been disenchantment with the organization by a number of large-contributor countries who sometimes find themselves in the minority on votes in the UNGA.

Such numbers are something of a fiction, however, because some countries do not pay their assessment. In early 2000 member-states were in arrears by $1.76 billion. As a result, the UN's financial situation constantly teeters on the edge of crisis at the very time it is being asked to do more and more to provide protection and help meet other humanitarian and social needs. "It is," said a frustrated Boutros-Ghali just before he stepped down, "as though the town fire department were being dispatched to put out fires raging in several places at once while a collection was being taken to raise money for the fire-fighting equipment."[29] The analogy between the UN's budget and fire fighting is hardly hyperbole. During FY1999, for example, the UN's peacekeeping budget was about 25 percent smaller than the budget for the New York City fire department.

The United States and the UN Budget The key to the UN's financial difficulties is the United States, which is the largest debtor. In early 2000, it owed $1.2 billion to the UN, accounting for more than two-thirds the UN deficit. Various U.S. administrations have made some effort to pay their country's bills, but they have made little headway.

The U.S. Congress has been the main stumbling block. Members of Congress oppose some or all funding for a variety of reasons including charges that the UN is wasteful, that it undermines U.S. sovereignty, that it drains funds from U.S. domestic needs, and that it supports programs (especially abortion) that some representatives oppose.

Finally, in 1999, with the United States facing a loss of its vote in the UN for non-payment of its obligations, Congress authorized making up $819 million of the arrearage in three installments. The first, "no-strings" payment of $100 million was sent to the UN in December 1999. The other installments are, however, contingent on the UN meeting congressional demands. To get the second installment ($475 million) in 2000, the UN must agree to write off an additional $107 million debt for peacekeeping arrears and to drop the U.S contribution to 22 (from 25) percent of the regular budget assessment rate and to 25 (from 31) percent of the peacekeeping budget. The third payment ($244 million) in 2001 is contingent on the UN taking a number of steps, such as further reducing the size of its staff. The UN has resisted taking these steps.

The unwillingness of the U.S. Congress to meet the U.S. assessment and its insistence on placing conditions upon paying the arrears, particularly combined with the criticism of the UN heard in the United States, has opened the floodgates to a torrent of criticism from even staunch U.S. allies. "We are growing tired of UN bashing," Prime Minister Jean Chrétien of Canada reproved, "and it is especially irritating when it comes from those who are not paying their bills." Critics also charge that the U.S. conditions on the UN are roughly equivalent to private U.S. citizens telling the Internal Revenue Service that what they owe is based on a rate calculated by the individuals themselves rather than on the tax laws enacted by Congress. And, in a line that British diplomats had been waiting for over 200 years to deliver, the British foreign secretary said that for Americans to continue to vote in the UN without paying their assessment was tantamount to "representation without taxation."[30]

IGO ACTIVITIES AND RELATED ISSUES

The most important aspects of any international organization are what it does, how well this corresponds to the functions we wish it to perform, and how well it is performing its roles. The following pages will begin to explore these aspects by examining the scope of IGO activity, with an emphasis on the UN. Much of this discussion will only begin to touch on these activities, which receive more attention in other chapters.

Promoting International Peace and Security

The opening words of the UN Charter dedicate the organization to saving "succeeding generations from the scourge of war, which… has brought untold sorrow to mankind." The UN attempts to fulfill this goal by creating norms against violence, by providing debate as an alternative to fighting, by intervening diplomatically to avert the outbreak of warfare or to help restore peace once violence occurs, by instituting diplomatic and economic sanctions, by dispatching UN military forces to repel aggression or to act as a buffer between warring countries, and by promoting arms control and disarmament.

Creating Norms against Violence   One way that the United Nations helps promote international peace and security is by creating norms (beliefs about what is proper) against aggression and other forms of violence. To accomplish this, the UN works in such areas as promoting the concept of nuclear nonproliferation through the International Atomic Energy Agency, limiting chemical and biological weapons, and promoting rules for the restrained conduct of war when it occurs.

Countries that sign the Charter pledge to accept the principle "that armed force shall not be used, save in the common interest" and further agree to "refrain in their international relations from the threat or the use of force except in self-defense." Reaffirming the Charter's ideas, the UN (and other IGOs) have condemned Iraq's invasion of Kuwait, Serbian aggression against its neighbors, and other such actions. These denunciations and the slowly developing norm against aggression have not halted violence, but they have created an increasing onus on countries that strike the first blow. When, for example, the United States decided in 1989 to depose the regime of Panama's strongman, General Manuel Noriega, it acted unilaterally. Noriega was toppled, but Washington's action was condemned by both the UN and the OAS. Five years later, Washington again decided to overthrow the regime of a small country to its south. But before U.S. troops landed in Haiti, Washington took care to win UN support for its action.

Providing a Debate Alternative   A second peace-enhancing role for the United Nations and some other IGOs is serving as a passive forum in which members publicly air their points of view and privately negotiate their differences. The UN thus acts like a safety valve, or perhaps a sound stage where the world drama can be played out without the dire consequences that could occur if another "shooting locale" were chosen. This grand-debate approach to peace involves denouncing your opponents, defending your actions, trying to influence world opinion, and winning symbolic victories. The British ambassador to the UN has characterized it as "a great clearing house for foreign policy," a place where "We talk to people… whom we don't talk to elsewhere because we have fraught relations with them."[31]

Diplomatic Intervention   International organizations also regularly play a direct role in assisting and encouraging countries to settle their disputes peacefully. Ideally this occurs before hostilities, but it can take place even after fighting has started. The United Nations and other IGOs perform the following functions: (1) *Inquiry*: Fact-finding by neutral investigators; (2) *Good Offices*: Encouraging parties to negotiate; acting as a neutral setting for negotiations; (3) *Mediation*: Making suggestions about possible solutions;

acting as an intermediary between two parties; (4) *Arbitration*: Using a special panel to find a solution that all parties agree in advance to accept; and (5) *Adjudication*: Submitting disputes to an international court such as the ICJ. These activities do not often capture the headlines, but they are a vital part of maintaining or restoring the peace.

It is possible, even probable, that renewed fighting between Iraq and the United States and some other countries was averted in early 1998 because of Secretary-General Annan's personal mediation and his ability to fashion a solution acceptable to all. According to the UN ambassador at the time, "Annan's personal diplomacy coupled with a formula that only he, through his stature, could sell to the Iraqis" was the difference between war and peace.[32]

Sanctions The increased interdependence of the world has heightened the impact of diplomatic and economic sanctions. In recent years, these have been applied by the UN, the OAS, and other IGOs on such countries as Haiti, Iraq, Libya, South Africa, and Yugoslavia. As we will see in chapter 15, sanctions are controversial and often do not work. But there have been successes. Sanctions against South Africa helped ease apartheid there; they helped force Iraq to grudgingly give up some of its hidden remaining arms and arms production facilities and to allow UN military inspectors to search for other violations; and they were a factor in finally persuading Libya to surrender for trial two men accused of masterminding the plot that in 1988 blew up Pan-American Flight 103 over Lockerbie, Scotland, killing 270 people. The trial began in May 2000.

Peacekeeping The United Nations additionally has a limited ability to intervene militarily in a dispute. Other IGOs, such as the OAS, have also occasionally undertaken collective military action. In the UN, this process is often called peacekeeping. It is normally conducted under the auspices of the UNSC, although the UNGA has sometimes authorized action.

Peacekeeping as a form of international security will be extensively covered in chapter 13, but a few preliminary facts are appropriate here. Through mid-2000, the United Nations had mounted 53 peacekeeping operations that had utilized about 800,000 military and police personnel from 118 countries. These operations ranged from very lightly armed observer missions, through police forces, to full-fledged military forces. Never before have international forces been so active as they are now. The number of UN peacekeeping operations has risen markedly in the post–cold war era, as shown in Figure 9.7. In mid-2000, there were 15 UN peacekeeping forces of varying sizes in the field at locations throughout the world. These forces totaled about 40,000 troops and police. As the UN took on more missions, peacekeeping costs rose sharply from $235 million in FY1987 to about $3.5 billion for FY1996. From there they fell off for the next two years, but an upsurge of turmoil in Sierra Leone, the Congo, and other trouble spots led the UN to project a $1.9 billion peacekeeping budget for FY2000.

This Indian soldier is part of the UN force dispatched to Sierra Leone in 2000. There is a significant debate over the structure and mission of UN forces. To date, most UN forces have been small, lightly armed, and limited to peacekeeping activities. Secretary-General Kofi Annan and many others believe that UN forces should more closely mirror the powerful image presented by this soldier and be large enough and well enough armed to engage in peacemaking if necessary.

United Nations peacekeeping seldom involves a stern international enforcer smiting aggressors with powerful blows. Few countries are willing to give any IGO much power and independence. Rather, UN peacekeeping is usually a "coming between," a positioning of a neutral force that creates space and is intended to help

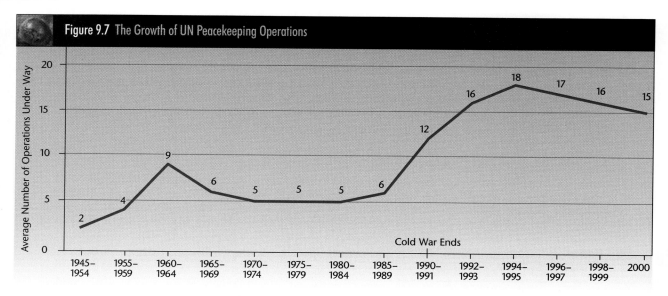

Figure 9.7 The Growth of UN Peacekeeping Operations

Data source: UN, Department of Peacekeeping Web site, http://www.un.org/depts/dpko/

The end of the cold war and its standoff between the United States and the Soviet Union in the Security Council has allowed the UN to mount a significantly increased number of peacekeeping operations in the 1990s.

MAP
United Nations Peace-
keeping Missions, p. 381

defuse an explosive situation. This in no way lessens the valuable role that the UN has played. In the early 1960s, UN troops kept the Congo from exploding into a cold war battlefield, and UN forces were an important factor in allowing the disengagement of Egyptian and Israeli troops in 1973. After many years of violence, the people of Cyprus live in peace under the watch of UN forces there.

United Nations peacekeepers alone could not stop the killing in Bosnia, but many fewer died than would have been the case without a UN presence. Fortunately, UN peacekeeping forces have suffered relatively few casualties, but almost 1,700 have died in world service. For these sacrifices and contributions to world order, the UN peacekeeping forces were awarded the 1988 Nobel Peace Prize.

Arms Control and Disarmament Promoting arms control and disarmament is another international security function of IGOs. The International Atomic Energy Agency, an affiliate of the UN, helps promote and monitor the nonproliferation of nuclear weapons. The UN also sponsors numerous conferences on weapons and conflict and has also played an important role in the genesis of the Chemical Weapons Convention and other arms control agreements.

Social, Economic, Environmental, and Other Roles

In addition to maintaining and restoring the peace, IGOs engage in a wide variety of other activities. During its early years, the United Nations' emphasis was on security. This concern has not abated, but it has been joined by social, economic, environmental, and other nonmilitary security concerns. This shift has been a result of the ebb and eventual end of the cold war, the growing number of LDCs since the 1960s, realization that the environment is in danger, and changing global values that have brought an increased focus on human and political rights. "Peacekeeping operations claim the headlines," Secretary-General Annan has observed astutely, "but by far the lion's share of our budget and personnel are devoted to the lower-profile work of... helping countries to create jobs and raise standards of living; delivering relief aid to victims of famine, war and natural disasters; protecting refugees; promoting literacy; and fighting disease. To most people around the world, this is the face of the United Nations."[33]

It would be impossible to list here, much less fully describe, the broad range of endeavors in which the UN and other IGOs are involved. Suffice it to say that they cover most of the issues that humans address at all levels of government. Many of these activities will be highlighted in subsequent chapters, so this discussion is limited to a few of the programs and successes of the United Nations and other IGOs.

IGOs and Economic Development The United Nations Development Programme (UNDP), the World Bank, and a significant number of other global and regional IGOs work to improve the economic well-being of those who are deprived because of their location in an LDC, gender, or some other cause. The UNDP alone supports more than 5,000 projects globally with a budget of $1.3 billion. The UN Development Fund for Women (UNIFEM) focuses on the betterment of women in LDCs.

IGOs and Human Rights Beginning with the Universal Declaration of Human Rights in 1948, the UN has actively promoted dozens of agreements on political, civil, economic, social, and cultural rights. The UN Commission on Human Rights has used its power of investigation and its ability to issue reports to expose abuses of human rights and to create pressure on the abusers. Currently, for example, the UN is at the heart of the global effort to free the estimated 250 million children who are forced to work instead of being sent to school, to end the sexual predation of children that is big business in some parts of the world, and to eliminate other abuses that mock the meaning of childhood.

Did You Know That:

The UN and its associated agencies, such as UNICEF, have about 81 cents per human to spend on economic and social development. The world defense ministries have about $135 per human for military expenditures.

IGOs and the Environment Beginning with the UN Conference on Environment and Development (dubbed the Earth Summit) in 1992, the UN has sponsored several global meetings on the environment. These have resulted in the initiation of programs that will slow down, stop, or begin to reverse the degradation of the environment. IGOs are increasingly also requiring that environmental impact statements accompany requests for economic development aid, and in some cases refusing to finance projects that have unacceptable negative impacts on the biosphere.

IGOs and International Law and Norms An important and increasing role of the UN and other IGOs is defining and expanding international law and international norms of cooperation. International courts associated with IGOs help establish legal precedent. Also, the signatories to the UN Charter and other IGO constitutions incur obligations to obey the principles of these documents. International organizations additionally sponsor multinational treaties, which may establish the assumption of law. Over 300 such treaties have been negotiated through the UN's auspices. As one scholar sees the norm-building function of IGOs, "The procedures and rules of international institutions create information structures. They determine what principles are acceptable as a basis for reducing conflicts and whether governmental actions are legitimate or illegitimate. Consequently, they help shape actors' expectations" (Keohane, 1998:91).

IGOs and the Quality of Human Existence More than 30 million refugees from war, famine, and other dangers have been fed, given shelter, and otherwise assisted through the UN High Commissioner for Refugees. A wide variety of IGOs also devote their energies to such concerns as health, nutrition, and literacy. For example, UNICEF, WHO, and other agencies have undertaken a $150 million program to develop a multi-immunization vaccine. This vaccine program is designed to double the estimated 2 million extra children who now annually survive because of such international medical

This elderly ethnic Albanian refugee from Kosovo is carrying a box of soap and other hygiene products supplied by the UN High Commissioner for Refugees. The UNHCR has given food, shelter, and other assistance to over 30 million refugees. As a guide to its efforts, the organization cites on its Web home page the words of the Athenian playwright Euripides written in 431 B.C., "There is no greater sorrow on Earth than the loss of one's native land."

assistance. The Food and Agriculture Organization (FAO) has launched a program to identify, preserve, and strengthen through new genetic techniques domestic animals that might prove especially beneficial to LDCs. Western breeds of pigs, for example, usually produce only about 10 piglets a litter; the Taihu pig of China manages 15 to 20. The FAO hopes to use the latter and other appropriate animals to increase protein availability in the LDCs.

IGOs and Independence   Yet another role of IGOs has been to encourage national self-determination. The UN Trusteeship Council once monitored numerous colonial dependencies, but the wave of independence in recent decades steadily lessened its number of charges. Then, in October 1994, the United States and Palau notified the council that, as Kuniwo Nakamura, Palau's president, put it, "We have made our own decision that we are ready to embark on the journey of independence with confidence."[34] Inasmuch as Palau was the last trust territory, the announcement meant that the Trusteeship Council's mission was fulfilled and, while it continues to exist technically, it no longer meets.

EVALUATING IGOs AND THEIR FUTURE

The United Nations has existed for more than fifty years. Most other IGOs are even younger. Have they succeeded? The answer depends on your standard of evaluation.

Ultimate goals are one standard. Article 1 of the UN Charter sets out lofty goals such as maintaining peace and security and solving economic, social, cultural, and humanitarian problems. Clearly, the world is still beset by violent conflicts and by ongoing economic and social misery. Thus, from the perspective of meeting ultimate goals, it is easy to be skeptical about what the UN and other IGOs have accomplished.

One has to ask, however, whether the meeting of ultimate goals is a reasonable standard. There is, according to one diplomat, a sense that "failure was built into [the UN] by an extraordinary orgy of exaggerated expectations."[35]

Progress is a second standard by which to evaluate the UN and other IGOs. The question is, Is the world better off for their presence? That is the standard Kofi Annan appeals for when he implores people to "Judge us rightly... by the relief and refuge that we provide to the poor, to the hungry, the sick and threatened: the peoples of the world whom the United Nations exists to serve."[36] Between its 40th and 50th anniversaries, the United Nations surpassed all previous marks in terms of numbers of simultaneous peacekeeping missions, peacekeeping troops deployed, and other international security efforts. Such UN–sponsored conferences as those on environment (Rio de Janeiro, 1992), human rights (Vienna, 1993), population (Cairo, 1994), women's issues (Beijing, 1995), social needs (Stockholm, 1995), food (Rome, 1996), and living conditions (Istanbul, 1996) have all focused attention on global problems and have made some contribution to advancing our knowledge of and enhancing our attempts to deal seriously with a wide range of economic, social, and environmental global challenges. Moreover, the people of the world tend to recognize these contributions. A recent survey of people in 60 countries around the world found that 60 percent of the respondents evaluated the UN as "very" or "somewhat" satisfactory. More than 80 percent of respondents in Africa, the world's most troubled region, gave the UN positive marks.[37] Thus, by the standard of progress, UN and other IGOs have made a contribution.

What is possible is a third standard by which to evaluate the UN and other IGOs. Insofar as the UN does not meet our expectations, we need to ask whether it is a flaw of the organization or the product of the unwillingness of member-states to live up to the standards that countries accept when they ratify the Charter. Simply paying their assessments is one thing more countries could do. Congress refuses to do that because it says the UN does not work very well. Many Americans have the same opinion of Congress, but they may not withhold their taxes. The UN will also work better if countries try to make it effective. It is a truism, as Kofi Annan put it, that there is a "troubling asymmetry between what the member-states want of the [UN] and what they actually allow it to be."[38]

Whether alternatives exist is a fourth standard by which to evaluate the UN and other IGOs. One must also ask, If not the UN and other international organizations, then what? Can the warring, uncaring world continue unchanged in the face of nuclear weapons, persistent poverty, an exploding population, periodic mass starvation, continued widespread human rights violations, resource depletion, and environmental degradation? Somehow the world has survived these plagues, but one of the realities that this book hopes to make clear is that we are hurtling toward our destiny at an ever-increasing, now exponential speed. In a rapidly changing system, doing things the old way may be inadequate and may even take us down a road that, although familiar, will lead the world to cataclysm. At the very least, as Secretary of State Madeleine Albright noted, "The United Nations gives the good guys—the peacemakers, the freedom fighters, the people who believe in human rights, those committed to human development—an organized vehicle for achieving gains."[39] This returns us to the question, If not the UN, then what? In reply, there may be considerable truth in the view of the British ambassador to the UN that "it's the UN, with all its warts, or it's the law of the jungle."[40] It is through this jungle that the road more familiar has passed, and following it into the future may bring what Shakespeare was perhaps imagining when he wrote in *Hamlet* of a tale that would "harrow up thy soul, [and] freeze thy young blood."

To repeat an important point, the UN and other IGOs are, in the end, only what we make them. They do possess some independence, but it is limited. Mostly their successes and failures reflect the willingness or disinclination of member-countries to cooperate and use them to further joint efforts. Kofi Annan urged support of the UN by quoting what Winston Churchill said to Franklin Roosevelt in 1941, "Give us the tools and we will do the job."[41] In the same vein, Dag Hammarskjöld aptly predicted, "Everything will be all right—you know when? When people, just people, stop thinking of the United Nations as a weird Picasso abstraction and see it as a drawing they made themselves."[42]

Whether that occurs is uncertain. What is clear is that critics of IGOs are too often narrowly negative. They disparage the organizations without noting their contributions or suggesting improvements. IGOs hold one hope for the future, and those who would denigrate them should make other, positive suggestions rather than implicitly advocate a maintenance of the status quo. There is a last bit of Shakespeare's wisdom, found in *Julius Caesar*, that is worth pondering. The playwright counsels us that:

> There is a tide in the affairs of men
> Which, taken at the flood, leads on to fortune;
> Omitted, all the voyage of their life
> Is bound in shallows and in miseries.

CHAPTER SUMMARY

1. One sign of the changing international system is this century's rapid rise in the number of intergovernmental organizations (IGOs).
2. There are many classifications of international organizations, including global, regional, and specialized IGOs.
3. Current international organization is the product of three lines of development: the idea that humans should live in peace and mutual support, the idea that the big powers have a special responsibility for maintaining order, and the growth of specialized international organizations to deal with narrow nonpolitical issues.
4. The rapid growth of all types of international organizations stems from increased international contact among states and people, increased economic interdepen-

dence, the growing importance of transnational issues and political movements, the inadequacy of the state-centered system for dealing with world problems, small states attempting to gain strength by joining together, and successful IGOs providing role models for new organizations.

5. There are significant differences among views on the best role for international organizations. Four existing and possible roles of IGOs are: providing an interactive arena, acting as a center for cooperation among states, evolving into an independent national actor, and becoming a supranational organization.

6. Some observers argue that international organizations are best suited to promoting cooperation among states rather than trying to replace the state-centered system. Still others contend that international organizations should concentrate on performing limited functional activities with the hope of building a habit of cooperation and trust that can later be built upon. Finally, many view international organizations as vehicles that should be manipulated to gain national political goals. The UN serves as an example of how current IGOs are organized and operate.

7. Some observers favor moving toward a system of supranational organization, in which some form of world government, or perhaps regional governments, would replace or substantially modify the present state-centered system.

8. The EU provides an example of the development, structure, and roles of a regional IGO. The EU has evolved considerably along the path of economic integration. The movement toward political integration is more recent and is proving more difficult than economic integration.

9. The United Nations provides an example of the development, structure, and roles of a global IGO.

10. There are several important issues related to the structure of international organizations. One group of questions relates to membership and criteria for membership.

11. Voting schemes to be used in such bodies are another important issue. Current international organizations use a variety of voting schemes that include majority voting, weighted voting, and unanimity voting.

12. Another group of questions concerns the administration of international organizations, including the role of the political leaders and the size and efficiency of IGO bureaucracies. The source of IGO revenue and the size of IGO budgets are a related concern.

13. There are also a number of significant issues that relate to the general role of international organizations. Peacekeeping is one important role. Others include creating norms against violence, providing a debate alternative, intervening diplomatically, imposing sanctions, and promoting arms control and disarmament.

14. Other roles for the UN and other international organizations include promoting international law, promoting arms control, bettering the human condition, promoting self-government, and furthering international cooperation.

15. However one defines the best purpose of international organization, it is important to be careful of standards of evaluation. The most fruitful standard is judging an organization by what is possible, rather than setting inevitably frustrating ideal goals.

CHAPTER 10

NATIONAL POWER AND DIPLOMACY: THE TRADITIONAL APPROACH

Then, everything includes itself in power,
Power into will, will into appetite.

Shakespeare, *Troilus and Cressida*

Bid me discourse, I will enchant thine ear.

Shakespeare, *Venus and Adonis*

We thought, because we had power, we had wisdom.

Stephen Vincent Benét, *Litany for Dictatorships*, 1935

All politicians make their decisions on the basis of national or political interest
and explain them in terms of altruism.

Former Israeli diplomat Abba Eban, 1996

CHAPTER OBJECTIVES

After completing this chapter, you should be able to:

- Characterize diplomacy as an activity conducted by a state to further its interests.
- Understand power as the foundation of diplomacy.
- Analyze the characteristics of power.
- Understand the major elements of a country's power.
- Explain the functions of diplomacy.
- Describe the various settings of diplomacy.
- Summarize the evolution of diplomacy from ancient Greece to nineteenth-century Europe.
- Describe and characterize diplomatic practice in the modern era.
- Explain the increase in high-level, leader-to-leader diplomacy.
- Consider the growing importance of public diplomacy in world politics.
- Explain the art of diplomacy and the importance of choosing among various options in its practice.
- Consider the various rules of diplomacy.
- Identify various diplomatic alternatives.

O nce upon a time," began a fable told by the great British diplomat and prime minister Winston Churchill, "all the animals in the zoo decided that they would disarm." To accomplish that laudable goal, the animals convened a diplomatic conference, where, Churchill's tale went:

> The Rhinoceros said when he opened the proceeding that the use of teeth was barbarous and horrible and ought to be strictly prohibited by general consent. Horns, which were mainly defensive weapons, would, of course, have to be allowed. The Buffalo, the Stag, the Porcupine, and even the little Hedgehog all said they would vote with the Rhino, but the Lion and the Tiger took a different view. They defended teeth and even claws, which they described as honourable weapons of immemorial antiquity. The Panther, the Leopard, the Puma, and the whole tribe of small cats all supported the Lion and the Tiger. Then the Bear spoke. He proposed that both teeth and horns should be banned and never used again for fighting by animals. It would be quite enough if animals were allowed to give each other a good hug when they quarreled. No one could object to that. It was so fraternal, and that would be a great step toward peace. However, all the other animals were very offended by the Bear, and the Turkey fell into a perfect panic. The discussion got so hot and angry, and all those animals began thinking so much about horns and teeth and hugging when they argued about the peaceful intentions that had brought them together, that they began to look at one another in a very nasty way. Luckily the keepers were able to calm them down and persuade them to go back quietly to their cages, and they began to feel quite friendly with one another again.[1]

Sir Winston's allegory is instructive, as well as colorfully entertaining. It touches on many aspects of diplomacy discussed in this chapter. We will begin by looking at *power*, which remains an essential element of diplomacy in a system based on self-interested sovereignty. In our world, like the zoo, the actors that possess the power to give rewards or inflict punishment are able to influence other actors. Power has many forms. Physical strength is one, and the rhino and the lion were both powerful in this way. Skill is another aspect of power. The turkey had little tangible strength, but perhaps it possessed guile and other intangible diplomatic skills to persuade the other animals to adopt its views. Economic power is also important in diplomacy. The zookeepers controlled the food supply, and may have used food as a positive incentive (more food) or negative sanction (less or no food) to persuade the animals to return to their cages.

Having established the power foundations of diplomacy, we will turn to the general *nature of diplomacy*. This involves the overall system, the setting in which modern diplomacy occurs. The zoo was the system in which the animals negotiated. Like the current international system, the zoo system was based on self-interest, with each group of animals selecting goals that were advantageous to itself with little thought about how they affected others. The zoo system also apparently allowed some potential for fighting and thus based success in part on the Darwinian law of the jungle. Yet it is the case that the animals were also partly constrained by the zookeepers with, perhaps, some protection afforded by cages.

The third part of this chapter will examine *modern diplomacy* by looking at how it has evolved and at some of its characteristics. Multilateral diplomacy, for example, has become a much more prominent part of diplomacy than it once was. In Churchill's story, the animals conducted multisided negotiations instead of bilateral diplomacy between, say, just the rhino and the tiger. Those two animals might have made a bilateral agreement that both horns and fangs were acceptable; once hedgehogs, turkeys, and others became involved, the diplomatic dynamic changed greatly. In such a circumstance, diplomatic coalition building is one aspect of support gathering. It may well have been that, before the conference, the rhino had met with the buffalo, stag, porcupine, and hedgehog to convince them that they should support the rhino's position that horns were defensive weapons, while teeth and claws were offensive weapons.

Finally, the fourth part of the chapter will turn to options in the conduct of diplomacy. Direct negotiation is one method, and the animals were engaged in that. Signaling is another method. This occurred when the animals "began to look at each other in a very nasty way." Public diplomacy to win the support of public opinion is another diplomatic method, and it is possible to see in Churchill's story how a clever diplomatic proposal can create an advantage. One can imagine the bear's proposal emblazoned in the *Zoo News* headline the next day: "Bear Proposes Eliminating All Weapons. Suggests Hugging as Alternative to Fighting." World opinion might have rallied to the bear; this would have put pressure on the other negotiators to accede to a seemingly benign proposal to usher in a new world order based on peace, love, and hugging.

Before proceeding, we should take a moment to put this chapter in context. It is the first of two chapters that look at the traditional and the alternative bases for establishing what policies will prevail in the world. The traditional approach involves countries' practicing national diplomacy by applying power in the pursuit of their self-interest. This approach does not mean that might makes right, but it surely means that might usually makes success. The alternative approach, discussed in chapter 11, is to apply the standards of international law and justice to the conduct of international relations so that right, rather than who is mightiest, will more often determine who prevails.

NATIONAL POWER: THE FOUNDATION OF NATIONAL DIPLOMACY

"Until human nature changes, power and force will remain at the heart of international relations," a top U.S. foreign policy adviser commented.[2] Not everyone would agree with such a gloomy realpolitik assessment, but it underlines the crucial role that power plays in diplomacy. When the goals and interests of states conflict, states often struggle to determine whose interests will prevail. The resolution rests frequently on who has the most power. During 1998 and early 1999, the United States and most European countries diplomatically pressed Yugoslavia to end its attacks on ethnic Albanians in Kosovo. When diplomacy failed, military might prevailed. It is impossible to tell what the course of events would have been if Yugoslavia was a superpower or the United States was not. But neither was the case, and the United States and its allies bombed Yugoslavia, occupied Kosovo, and imposed their will.

THE NATURE OF POWER

Social scientists struggle to define and measure power and to describe exactly how it works. Harvard University dean and former top U.S. Defense Department official Joseph Nye (2000:55) writes that power "is like the weather. Everyone talks about it, but few understand it." Alluding to an even greater mystery, Nye confides that power is "like love... easier to experience than to define or measure." He also warns that if we always try to intimidate others, "we may be as mistaken about our power as was the fox who thought he was hurting Brer Rabbit when he threw him into the briar patch." Weather, love, briar patches? Yes, power is perplexing! If its intricacies can throw a Harvard dean and assistant secretary of defense into such a morass of mixed metaphors and similes, then how can we understand power? The first step is to define the way this text uses the word, so that we can proceed from a common point.

Power as an Asset

The term **power** can be understood to equal national capabilities. Power is a political resource, which encompasses the sum of the various attributes of a state that enable it to achieve its goals even when they clash with the goals of other international actors. Power is multifaceted. It includes tangible elements, such as numbers of weapons; it also includes intangible elements, such as public morale.

One way to comprehend power is to think about *power as money*, as a sort of political currency. Equating power and money is helpful because both are assets that can be used to acquire things. Money buys things; power causes things to happen. Like money, power is sometimes used in a charitable way. But also like money, power is more often used for self-interest. It is also true that acquiring money and power both often require sacrifices. Furthermore, those who use their financial or power assets imprudently may lose more than they gain. As with any analogy, however, you should be wary of overusing the comparison. There are differences between money and power. One is that political power is less liquid than money; it is harder to convert into things that you want. A second difference is that power, unlike money, has no standard measurement that allows all parties to agree on the amount involved.

As with money, one of the confusions about power is whether it is an asset (an end, goal) that you try to acquire and maintain or a tool (a means, instrument) that you use. It is both. Countries seek both to acquire power and to use it in international politics. While this chapter concentrates on power as an asset, it is important to realize that countries sometimes treat power as a goal.

One important issue about any asset is, "How much is enough?" If you think about money as a physical object, it is pretty useless. It is inedible, you cannot build anything useful out of money, and it will not even burn very well if you need to keep warm. Yet some people are obsessed with having money for its own sake. For them, acquiring money is an end in itself. Literature is full of such stories, ranging from Moliére's *The Miser* to Dickens's classic *A Christmas Carol* and its tragic tale of Ebenezer Scrooge. The misers give up love, friendships, and other pleasures to get and keep money only to discover, in the end, that their money becomes a burden. Similarly, some people believe that countries can become fixated on acquiring power, especially military power, beyond what is prudently needed to meet possible exigencies. This, critics say, is unwise because power is expensive, it creates a temptation to use it, and it spawns insecurity in others.

Measuring Power

At a general level, it is possible to measure or at least estimate power. There can be no doubt, for example, that China is more powerful than Mongolia. Beyond such broad judgments, however, scholars and policy makers have not been successful at anything approaching precise measurements of power. One problem is creating a formula that properly weights military might, economic capacity, leadership capability, and other factors in the power equation. This was well illustrated by a study that reviewed four attempts by various scholars to devise formulas to measure national power (Taber, 1989). There were numerous disagreements based on the imprecise ability to measure power. Two studies rated the Soviet Union the most powerful. One each rated the United States and China most powerful. One ranked China only seventh. Brazil ranked number three in one study, and India ranked number four in another study; yet two studies did not place either country in the top ten. The list need not go on to make the point that different formulas for measuring power yielded very different results.

A second problem with measuring power precisely is a result of the fact that many aspects of power are difficult to quantify. Gathering data on some aspects of power (such as number of weapons, GDP, or population) is easy. Quantifying other aspects of power, such as leadership, borders on the impossible.

Does this mean that we should abandon trying to estimate national power? No, it does not. To repeat a point, there are clearly differences in national power. Ignoring them would be foolish, but it would also be a mistake to ignore the complexity and fluidity of power and to underestimate or overestimate the power of others based on one or more simple calculations.

Characteristics of Power

Power is not a simple and stable phenomenon. Indeed, it is very much a political chameleon, constantly changing even while it remains the same. The last task of this section is to explore the impact of the various characteristics of power.

Power Is Dynamic Even simple measurements show that power is constantly in flux. Economies prosper or lag, arms are modernized or become outmoded, resources are discovered or are depleted, and populations rally behind or lose faith in their governments. The USSR was a superpower; it collapsed; its successor state, Russia, is far from a superpower status.

Adding to the dynamism of power, some scholars believe that its very nature is changing. They contend that military and other assets that contribute to **coercive power** (also called "hard power," the ability to make another country do or not do something) are declining in importance as military force and economic sanctions become more costly and less effective. Simultaneously, according to this view, **persuasive power** (also called "soft power," assets such as moral authority or technological excellence that enhance a country's image of leadership) are increasing in importance (Nye, 2000; Hall, 1999).

Some scholars even believe that war has become so destructive that it is a fading phenomenon, especially among economically developed countries (EDCs). That thought is given some credence by the fact that the 1990s were not a time of interstate warfare, with the major exception of Iraq's invasion of Kuwait and a few relatively minor border clashes. Perhaps coercive diplomacy will sometime become a relic of humankind's barbaric past, but that day, if it comes at all, is probably far in the future for two reasons. First, as one study notes, the incidence of violence during the 1990s was so high and so often brought outside intervention that conflict was a "growth industry" (Bloomfield & Moulton, 1997:34). Second, there are still times when force or the threat of force is needed to resolve an international crisis. After an agreement that averted war in 1998 over Iraq's refusal to allow continued UN arms inspections, Iraqi foreign minister Tarik Aziz and UN secretary-general Kofi Annan held a joint press conference. Aziz contended that it was "diplomacy that reached this agreement, not the saber-rattling." To which Annan chimed in, "You can do a lot with diplomacy, but of course you can do a lot more with diplomacy backed up by firmness and force."[3]

Power Is Both Objective and Subjective We have seen on several occasions that international politics is influenced both by what is true and by what others perceive to be true. **Objective power** consists of assets that you objectively possess and that you have both the capacity and the will to use. As such, it is a major factor in determining whose interests prevail, as Iraq found out in 1991 in its war with the U.S.–led coalition of forces.

Subjective power is also important. It is common to hear politicians argue that their country cannot back down in a crisis or get out of an ill-conceived military action because the country's reputation will be damaged. Research shows that concern to be overdrawn (Mercer, 1996). Still, a country's power is to a degree based on others' perceptions of its current or potential power or its reputation for being willing (or not

Power is relative. The relative power of India compared to potential opponents, such as China, has increased now that India has tested nuclear weapons and has also built missiles, such as the Agni seen here on display during a military parade in New Delhi. The Agni can carry a nuclear warhead to a target 1,500 miles away.

willing) to use the power it has. Sometimes the perception that a country is not currently powerful can tempt another country. When asked for his evaluation of the U.S. military in 1917, a German admiral replied, "Zero, zero, zero." Based on this perception of U.S. power, Germany resumed the submarine warfare against U.S. merchant shipping, a move that soon led to war with the United States. At other times, the perception of current power that really does not exist can deter another country. During the 1950s and early 1960s, U.S. nuclear deterrence rested in significant part on the advertised ability of the Strategic Air Command to get its bombers that were on "ready alert" off the ground quickly in case of a nuclear attack. Subsequent information has shown that much of this claimed ability did not really exist. But since almost everyone believed it did, deterrence was served. Perceptions of potential power can also be important. Decision makers in the United States and other countries have long given China a degree of deference, in part because of its potential to become a true superpower.

Power Is Relative Power does not exist in a vacuum. Since power is about the ability to persuade or make another actor do or not do something, calculating power is of limited use except to measure it against the power of the other side. When assessing capabilities, then, **relative power,** or the comparative power of national actors, must be considered. We cannot, for example, say that China is powerful unless we specify in *comparison to whom.* Whatever Beijing's power resources may be, China's relative power compared to another major power, such as Japan, is less than is China's relative power compared to a smaller neighbor, such as Vietnam.

A related issue is whether power is a *zero-sum game.* If a gain in power of one actor inevitably means a loss of power for other actors, the game is zero-sum. If an actor can gain power without the power of other actors being diminished, then the game is non–zero-sum. Realists tend to see power as zero-sum; idealists usually portray it as non–zero-sum. Without delving too far into this controversy, we can say that the relative nature of power implies that sometimes, especially between antagonists, power approaches zero-sum. When China's Asian rival India tested nuclear weapons in 1998, it decreased

China's relative power compared to India and arguably reduced China's influence in the countries to its southwest. Yet India's advance in power was non–zero-sum relative to another of its regional rivals, Pakistan, because that country tested its own nuclear weapons almost simultaneously with India. When the nuclear dust settled, India and Pakistan were in the same relative power position vis-à-vis one another as they had been before the blasts.

Power Is Situational A country's power varies according to the situation, or context, in which it is being applied. A country's **situational power** is often less than the total inventory of its capabilities. Military power provides a good example. If we agree that, even if provoked, India is unlikely to use nuclear weapons against Sri Lanka no matter what occurs there in the civil war between the majority Buddhist Sinhalese and the minority Hindu Tamils, then India's becoming a nuclear weapons state has not affected the Sri Lanka/India power relationship.

Power Is Multidimensional Power is multifaceted. Therefore, to analyze power well it is important to consider *all* the dimensions of power *and* to place them in their proper relative and situational contexts. Only then can we begin to answer the question of who is powerful and who is not. To help with that process, our next step is to identify the various determinants of national power.

THE ELEMENTS OF POWER

There are many ways to categorize the multitudinous elements of power. One common way that we have mentioned is to distinguish between objective (easily measurable, tangible) elements of power and subjective (hard-to-measure, intangible) facets of power. Another approach is to group both the tangible and the intangible power assets into various functional categories. Two such categories, the national core and the national infrastructure, are central to the power of all countries because they serve as a foundation for the more utilitarian categories of national power, specifically military power and economic power. We will, in the following sections, analyze these two central categories of national power; military and economic power will be discussed in chapters 12 and 15 respectively.

THE NATIONAL CORE

The national state forms the basis of this element of power. The essence of a state can be roughly divided into three elements: national geography, people, and government.

National Geography

Shakespeare's King Henry VI proclaimed:

> Let us be backed with God and with the seas
> Which He hath given for fence impregnable,…
> In them and in ourselves our safety lies.

It is not clear what, if anything, God has done for England over the centuries, but King Henry's soliloquy reminds us that the English Channel has helped save England from European conquest for nine centuries. The country's most important physical characteristic is being separated from the continent by a narrow expanse of water. Without it the British might have been conquered by Napoleon in the early 1800s or by Hitler's army in 1940. Geographic factors include location, topography, size, and climate.

The *location* of a country, particularly in relation to other countries, is significant. The Chinese army's significance as a power factor is different for the country's relations with the United States and with Russia. The huge Chinese army can do little to threaten the United States, far across the Pacific Ocean. By contrast, Russia and China share a border, and Chinese soldiers could march into Siberia. Location can be an advantage or a disadvantage. Spain was able to avoid involvement in either world war partly because of its relative isolation from the rest of Europe. Poland, sandwiched between Germany and Russia, and Korea, stuck between China and Japan, each has a distinctly unfortunate location. The Israelis would almost certainly be better off if their promised land were somewhere—almost anywhere—else. And the Kuwaitis probably would not mind moving either, providing they could take their oil fields with them.

A country's *topography*—its mountains, rivers, and plains—is also important. The Alps form a barrier that has helped protect Switzerland from its larger European neighbors and spared the Swiss the ravages of both world wars. Topography can also work against a country. The broad European plain that extends from Germany's Rhine River to the Ural Mountains in central Russia has been an easy invasion avenue along which the armies of Napoleon, Kaiser Wilhelm II, and Hitler have marched.

A country's *size* is important. Bigger is often better. The immense expanse of Russia, for example, has repeatedly saved it from invasion. Although sometimes overwhelmed at first, the Russian armies have been able to retreat into the interior and buy time in exchange for geography while regrouping. By contrast, Israel's small size gives it no room to retreat.

A country's *climate* can also play a power role (Eichengreen, 1998). The tropical climate of Vietnam, with its heavy monsoon rains and its dense vegetation, made it difficult for the Americans to use effectively much of the superior weaponry they possessed. At the other extreme, the bone-chilling Russian winter has allied itself with Russia's geographic size to form a formidable defensive barrier. Many of Napoleon's soldiers literally froze to death during the French army's retreat from Moscow, and 133 years later Germany's army, the Wehrmacht, was decimated by cold and ice during the sieges of Leningrad and Stalingrad. In fact the Russian winter has proved so formidable that Czar Nicholas I commented, "Russia has two generals we can trust, General January and General February."

People

A second element of the national core is a country's human characteristics. As President Clinton put it, "The currency of national strength in this new [technological, interdependent] era will be denominated not only in ships and tanks and planes, but in diplomas and patents and paychecks" (Paterson, Clifford, & Hagan, 2000:504). Tangible demographic subcategories include number of people, age distribution, and such quantitative factors as health and education. There are also intangible population factors such as morale.

Population As is true for geographic size, the size of a country's population can be a positive or a negative factor. Because a large population supplies military personnel and industrial workers, sheer numbers of people are a positive power factor. It is unlikely, for instance, that Tonga (pop. 109,000) will ever achieve great-power status. A large population may be disadvantageous, however, if it is not in balance with resources. India, with 1 billion people, has the world's second-largest population, yet because of the country's poverty ($440 per capita GDP), it must spend much of its energy and resources merely feeding its people.

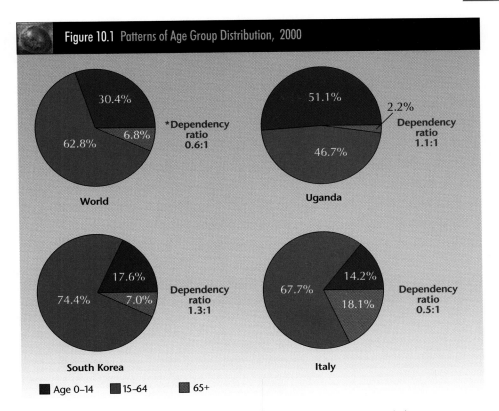

Figure 10.1 Patterns of Age Group Distribution, 2000

World
- 30.4%
- 62.8%
- 6.8%
- *Dependency ratio 0.6:1

Uganda
- 51.1%
- 46.7%
- 2.2%
- Dependency ratio 1.1:1

South Korea
- 17.6%
- 74.4%
- 7.0%
- Dependency ratio 1.3:1

Italy
- 14.2%
- 67.7%
- 18.1%
- Dependency ratio 0.5:1

■ Age 0–14   ■ 15–64   ■ 65+

Data sources: World Bank (2000a); U.S. Census Bureau, International Data Base at: http://www.census.gov/ipc/www/idbnew.html.

*Dependency ratio is a World Bank calculation of the ratio of the dependent population (age 14 and under plus age 65 and older) to the working-age population (15–64). Generally, the lower the ratio, the more economically disadvantaged a country is.

The age group distribution of a country's population can be a source of strength or weakness. Relatively large percentages of children and old people, who consume more economic resources than they produce, leave countries like Uganda (for children) and Italy (for senior citizens) disadvantaged compared to South Korea with its higher percentage of working-age people.

Age Distribution It is an advantage for a country to have a large number and percentage of its population in the productive years (15–64 by international reporting standards). Some countries with booming populations have a heavy percentage of children who must be supported. In other countries with limited life expectancy, many people die before they complete their productive years. Finally, some countries are "aging," with a geriatric population segment that consumes more resources than it produces.

Worldwide, 30.4 percent of the Earth's population in 2000 was less than 15 years old; 6.8 percent was 65 or over; 62.8 percent was in the working-age years (15–64). Figure 10.1 shows the age distributions of several countries, which you should compare. The figure also shows the dependency ratio of young and old people combined compared to the working-age population. Many analysts would contend that South Korea is relatively advantaged by its large working-age population, while Uganda, with numerous children, and Italy, with a high percentage of senior citizens, are relatively disadvantaged.

Countries like Italy that have such low birthrates that they are in a zero or even a negative population growth pattern are also disadvantaged in that they may experience economic difficulty because of future labor shortages. A growing geriatric population also means that the cost of providing pensions and other services to retired citizens will strain a country's capacity. By 2015, for instance, an estimated 24.7 percent of Japan's

MAP
Population Growth Rate,
pp. 524–525

Table 10.1 Health and Education in Canada and Senegal

	Canada	Senegal
Health and Education Spending	$2,251	$25
Life Expectancy	79	52
Children Dying before Age 5	0.7%	12.1%
Population per Physician	410	6,250
Adult Literacy	99%	35%
Secondary School Enrollment	95%	20%

Public spending for health and education is per capita; life expectancy is years; secondary school enrollment is the percentage of youths in that age group.

Data source: World Bank (2000a).

Canada's power is enhanced by its educated and healthy population, especially relative to Senegal's disadvantaged population.

population will be age 65 and older. Most European countries, such as Italy (23 percent), will also have high percentages of retirees. Even at 13 percent, the U.S. social security and health care systems will face a formidable challenge. That was evident in the presidential election in 2000, when one of the key issues between George W. Bush and Al Gore was how to finance these systems and at what level to set benefits. Indeed, for much of Europe, Japan, and some other countries, a combination of low birthrates and increasing longevity presents a serious threat to their future economic prosperity.

Health and Education An educated, healthy population is important to national power. Although there are health and education variations among all countries, less developed countries (LDCs) are especially disadvantaged compared to economically developed countries (EDCs), as illustrated by the contrasts between Canada and Senegal in Table 10.1. It will be hard, for example, for LDCs to create educational programs that will close the gap in research and development (R&D) scientists and technicians, who number 41 per every 10,000 people in the EDCs and only 4 per 10,000 people in the LDCs. To make matters worse for LDCs, many of them suffer a substantial "brain drain," an "outflow of highly educated individuals," to EDCs, where professional opportunities are better (Carrington & Detragiache, 1999:1).

The quality of a country's education system is also important. For example, almost all Americans are literate, yet, there is growing concern that the U.S. educational system is not adequately preparing students to meet the requirements of the modern world. It may be that the basic 3 Rs—reading, 'riting, and 'rithmetic—that once served to train a workforce will no longer suffice in the twenty-first century. Instead, the requirements will be more like the 3 Cs—computers, calculus, and communications.

There is even concern that not enough students are learning the old 3 Rs, much less the new 3 Cs. In the 1950s, the United States, with a high school graduation rate of 77 percent, ranked first among a list of 29 countries. That percentage had slipped to 72 in 1998. That absolute drop and the increased graduation rates in other countries put the United States at twenty-eighth on the list, ahead of only Mexico and well behind leading countries (90+ percent) such as Finland, Poland, and South Korea.[4]

As for those American students who do stay in school, there are indications that they learn less than their contemporaries in other countries. A recent study showed that for general mathematics, American high school seniors finished behind those in 13 other countries, equal to seniors in 4 countries, and ahead of seniors only in Cyprus and

Did You Know That:

A survey taken in 2000 asked seniors at 55 top U.S. universities to answer 34 multiple-choice questions drawn from high school history exams. The average score was 53 percent. Only 23 percent could pick out James Madison as the "father of the Constitution," and only 34 percent could select George Washington as the victorious general at the Battle of Yorktown. But 99 percent knew that Bevis and Butt-Head were "television cartoon characters," and an equally impressive 98 percent correctly identified Snoop Doggy Dog as a "rap singer."

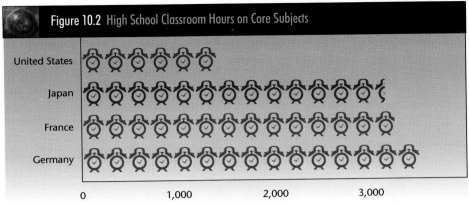

Figure 10.2 High School Classroom Hours on Core Subjects

Data source: "Prisoners of Time," The Report of the National Education Commission on Time and Learning, at http://www.ed.gov/pubs/Prisoners OfTime/.
The graph above indicates the number of hours students spend on core academics in their four years of high school.

An educated populace is a key element of a country's infrastructure. American students, compared to students in many other countries, score lower on mathematics and some other academic achievement tests. One possible cause is that U.S. students spend fewer hours on these core subjects than do students in many other countries.

South Africa. General physics yielded about the same results, with American students far behind most of their contemporaries and, again, only ahead of those in Cyprus and South Africa. Perhaps even more worrisome were the results from some of the best and brightest students, those taking advanced mathematics and physics tests. Among these students, who presumably receive the best their educational systems have to offer, American high school seniors finished last in both areas. Given the wealth of the United States, President Clinton was belaboring the obvious when he declared "There is something wrong with the system.... You cannot blame the [students]."[5]

Expenditure on education is just one factor in determining national achievement. There are some countries, such as Japan, that spend considerably less of their GDP on education than does the United States and yet have students that score better than U.S. students. Another provocative fact is that the tests showed that U.S. fourth graders finished above average in math and science, U.S. eighth graders finished about average, and U.S. high school seniors finished below average. One clue to why this occurs may be in Figure 10.2, which shows that American students during their four years of high school spend an average of less than 1,500 hours in classes dealing with core subjects. This contrasts with the 3,000 to 3,500 hours spent on core subjects during average four-year curriculums in Japan, France, and Germany.

Yet another way to break down general educational statistics is to see how well a country trains various segments of its population. Most countries limit their power potential by underutilizing major elements of their population. For example, sexism limits the possible contribution of women in virtually all countries. In Bangladesh, 42 percent more male than female teenagers are enrolled in secondary school. Racial, ethnic, and other bases of discrimination add to this failure to maximize a population's potential. The fact that (of American adults over age 24) just 15 percent of blacks and 11 percent of Hispanics, compared to 25 percent of whites, have completed college means that the potential of a significant number of these disadvantaged people has been lost to the country.

Health problems can also sap a country's power. The health data shown in Table 10.1 can be supplemented by such information as the specific health problems that some countries face. AIDS is a world scourge, but it is particularly devastating in Africa. About 50 percent of the world's 40 million HIV-infected people live in Africa. Over 25 percent of the population of Botswana is HIV positive, as is at least 10 percent of the adult population in 15 other sub-Saharan African countries. The toll on the region is

The quality of a country's population is an important element of national power. The Russian population, especially its males, is suffering from a variety of problems, including excessive alcohol consumption, which has sharply shortened the life span of Russian men. Given the amount the average Russian man drinks, the 12-liter case of vodka that each of these two Muscovites are taking home is only about six weeks' worth of alcohol.

immense. The disease is killing more than 2 million people a year there, and there are some 11 million AIDS orphans, some of whom are themselves infected and will meet an early death.

Alcohol and other attacks on health are devastating Russia and some other countries. Chain smoking, a deficient diet, and the ravages of alcohol are decimating Russia's male population. Two-thirds of all adult Russian males smoke (2.5 times the U.S. rate), and there are estimates that the average Russian adult male drinks almost two quarts of vodka a week. "Sobriety is no longer the moral norm in Russia," says one health official there.[6]

The attitude of Russian men, President Boris Yeltsin once explained, is "What kind of Russian man are you if you cannot drink?"[7] One answer is a healthy man, because a huge number of the estimated 60 percent of Russian men who do drink to excess die from alcohol-related diseases and accidents. Others kill themselves in despair, with Russian males having the world's highest reported annual suicide rate (73 per 100,000 males). This compares to a rate of 14 for Russian women and 28 for American men. As a result, the longevity of Russian males has actually declined substantially, and now only 59 percent of them (compared to 79 percent of Russian women) live to age 65. Indeed a smaller percentage of Russian males reach retirement age than do males in profoundly poor Bangladesh. The threat to Russia's national strength is so palpable that one Russian government study calls it "the clearest possible threat to national security."[8]

Morale A final factor that affects the population element of national power is the morale of a country's citizens. World War II demonstrated the power of strong civilian morale. Early in the war, Great Britain and the Soviet Union reeled under tremendous assaults by the Nazi forces. Yet the Allies hung on. Winston Churchill proclaimed in Parliament on October 9, 1940, during the darkest days of the war, that for the British people "Death and sorrow will be the companions of our journey; hardship our garment; constancy and valor our only shield. We must be united, we must be undaunted, we must be inflexible." The British answered Sir Winston's call. They remained undaunted; they held; they prevailed.

Conversely, the collapse of national morale can bring about civil unrest and even the fall of governments. The end of the USSR in 1991 provides an example. Polls in 1990 showed that 90 percent of Soviets believed that the country's economic situation was bad or critical, and 57 percent had no confidence in the future. This pessimism, which persisted throughout the 1990s, served to intensify the normally gloomy Russian outlook, which novelist Fyodor Dostoyevsky (1821–1881) described as "almost a Russian disease," and spawned dark humor. According to one such joke, a Russian meets another and asks, "How are things?" The comrade replies, "Well, it appears I've hit rock bottom," to which the first Russian says, "Ah, you always were an optimist" (Javeline, 1999).

Government

The quality of a country's government is a third power element associated with the national core. The issue is not what form of government, such as a democracy or an authoritarian system, a country has. Instead the issue is *administrative competence*: whether a state has a well-organized and effective administrative structure to utilize its power potential fully. The collapse of the Soviet Union stemmed in part from its massive and inefficient bureaucratic structure, and Russia continues to struggle under poor governance. President Vladimir Putin candidly told the Duma in July 2000 that "government lies have become the norm," and that earlier pledges to build a strong state had proven "hollow." Putin went on to warn the legislators that Russia was at risk of becoming a "derelict nation.... We have created islands, separate islets of government, but we have not built any bridges to them." Among the other impacts of this ineptitude, he added, was continued economic disarray, creating a "growing gap between the advanced nations and Russia [that] is pushing us into the group of Third World countries."[9]

Leadership skill also adds to a government's strength. Leadership is one of the most intangible elements of national power. Yet it can be critical, especially in times of crisis. For example, Prime Minister Winston Churchill's sturdy image and his inspiring rhetoric well served the British people during World War II. By contrast, the presidency of Boris Yeltsin, which had begun with such heroics as he faced down tanks in the streets of Moscow, dissolved into incompetence as the ailing, often inebriated Yeltsin became an increasingly sad caricature of his former self.

THE NATIONAL INFRASTRUCTURE

Another group of elements that form the foundation of state power is related to a country's infrastructure. The infrastructure of a state might roughly be equated with the skeleton of a human body. For a building, the infrastructure would be the foundation and the framing or girders. To examine the infrastructure of the state as an element of national power, the following sections will discuss technological sophistication, transportation systems, and information and communications capabilities. Each of these factors strongly affects any country's capacity in the other elements of power.

Technology

"Everything that can be invented has been invented," intoned Charles H. Duell, commissioner of the U.S. Office of Patents in 1899.[10] Commissioner Duell was obviously both in error and in the wrong job. Most of the technology that undergirds a great deal of contemporary national power has been invented since his shortsighted assessment. Air conditioning modifies the impact of weather, computers revolutionize education, robotics speed industry, synthetic fertilizers expand agriculture, new drilling techniques allow for undersea oil exploration, microwaves speed information, and lasers bring the military to the edge of the Luke Skywalker era. Thus, technology is an overarching factor and will be discussed as part of all the tangible elements.

One source of U.S. strength is the considerable money that its government, corporations, and universities spend on R&D. During 1997, the United States spent $169 billion. That was more than the combined spending of $161 billion of the next four highest countries (Japan, Germany, France, and Great Britain). Another good measure of technological sophistication and capability is computing capacity. Needless to say, the business, education, science, and other key elements of national power depend on computers, and, as Figure 10.3 shows, there is a vast disparity in national capabilities.

Transportation Systems

The ability to move people, raw materials, finished products, and sometimes the military throughout its territory is another part of a country's power equation. The collapse of public support for the Soviet Union and its subsequent demise was partly a result of the lack of enough affordable food. Just before the USSR ceased to exist, its official news agency, Tass, reported that 29 million tons of grain, 1 million tons of meat, and 25 percent of vegetables were lost between farm and table. Tass also reported that 1,700 trains were stalled because of lack of fuel or repair parts. The same sort of discouraging figures also applied to the country's trucks. Thus, one major hurdle that the FSRs face to restore their

Information and communications capabilities are a key element of a country's power. Contrary to the incongruous image of this Samburu warrior talking on a cell phone, his native Kenya and other less developed countries are hampered by a lack of sophisticated and extensive information and communications technology.

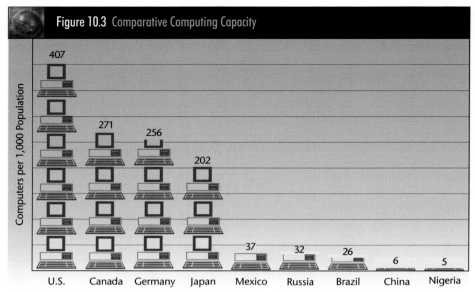

Figure 10.3 Comparative Computing Capacity

Data source: World Bank (2000).

Computer capacity is a key element of a country's technological infrastructure. As this figure shows, there is a huge gap in global computing power.

economic vitality is repairing and expanding their relatively limited transportation systems. As one standard, for every 1,000 square miles of its territory, Russia has but 84 miles of paved roads and 14 miles of railroad track. The United States has 1,049 miles of paved roads and 45 miles of railroad track for the same amount of territory. Inadequate transportation systems are also a problem for LDCs. Nigeria, for one, has just 213 miles of paved roadway and only 6 miles of railroad track for each 1,000 square miles.

Information and Communications Systems

A country's information and communications capabilities are becoming increasingly important (Rothkopf, 1998). The advent of satellites and computers has accelerated the revolution begun with radio and television. Photocopying machines, then fax machines, and now the Internet have dramatically changed communications. Enhanced communications technology increases the ability of a society to communicate within itself and remain cohesive. It also increases efficiency and effectiveness in industry, finance, and the military.

Here again, the gap between LDCs and EDCs is wide. There are, for example, 2.6 times more televisions, 5.5 times more radios, and 14 times more cell phones per capita in Canada than in China. Another way to see the extent of the LDCs' limitations in communications technology is to contrast the people and telephones in the United States with those of China, India, Bangladesh, Indonesia, Pakistan, and Nigeria. These six countries have a combined population that is more than 10 times larger than the U.S. population and amounts to nearly half the world's population. Yet the United States (183 million phones) has 50 percent more telephones than these six countries combined (122 million phones).

THE NATURE OF DIPLOMACY

Now that we have explored the core and infrastructure elements of the power foundation on which much of national diplomacy rests, we can turn to the conduct of national diplomacy. At its core, diplomacy is a basic human activity. As one study notes, "The desire to resolve problems amicably pervades all arenas of social organization. It is the function of negotiation to provide a channel for peaceful dispute resolution" (Starkey, Boyer, & Wilkenfeld, 1999:1). To see how this occurs and to provide a level of continuity in our discussion of diplomacy, this chapter will make frequent, although not exclusive, use of illustrations from four diplomatic events.

The U.S.–North Korea nuclear crisis of 1993 and 1994 is one of the events. This occurred when the United States moved to force North Korea (the Democratic People's Republic of Korea, DPRK) to give up its alleged nuclear weapons program. Alarm that North Korea was developing a nuclear bomb rang out in 1993 when North Korea announced its withdrawal from the Nuclear Non-Proliferation Treaty (NPT) and the press reported that the CIA believed that the DPRK probably had one or two nuclear weapons. The image of a nuclear-armed North Korea created grave concerns because of the possibility of a nuclear nightmare occurring on the ever-tense Korean peninsula and because, in the estimate of former U.S. defense secretary Harold Brown, "A few nuclear weapons in North Korea could have a significant effect on the possibility of nuclear programs in Japan, South Korea, and Taiwan."[11]

What followed was a series of diplomatic moves and countermoves during a 19-month-long confrontation that focused on persuading North Korea (1) to allow the resumption of inspections by the UN–associated International Atomic Energy Agency (IAEA) and (2) to dismantle those nuclear reactors that the DPRK had or was building that were capable of producing nuclear weapons-grade uranium or plutonium. The confrontation escalated to the point that between April and June 1994 there were dire threats, military moves, and an open discussion of the possibility of war in the capitals of Pyongyang, North Korea, Seoul, South Korea, and Washington, D.C.

Then diplomacy lowered the flame of crisis. All the parties eased their stands to facilitate agreement. North Korea agreed to suspend work on the nuclear reactors it had under construction, to dismantle its current nuclear energy program over 10 years, and to allow the IAEA inspections to resume. The United States and its allies pledged that they—principally Japan and South Korea—would spend approximately $4 billion to build in North Korea two nuclear reactors that were not capable of producing plutonium for bomb building. The West also agreed to help meet North Korea's energy needs by annually supplying it with about 138 million gallons of petroleum until new reactors are on line. The issue resurfaced in 1998 when U.S. intelligence agencies discovered what they charged was a massive effort by North Korea to build an underground nuclear facility, so this tale of diplomacy may not yet be over.

The crises between China and Taiwan in 1996 and in 2000 are the second and third events that will be used to illustrate various aspects of diplomacy. These two events, which featured diplomatic interplay between China and the United States during the periods just before Taiwan's two most recent presidential elections, were detailed in the chapter 4 box, To Be or Not To Be, on pages 92–93.

The U.S.–Iraq inspection crisis of 1997–1998 is the fourth diplomatic event used extensively in the discussion of diplomacy that follows. Iraq had agreed in the aftermath of the Persian Gulf War of 1991 to allow UN inspectors to ensure that the Iraqis had destroyed all their nuclear, biological, and chemical weapons capabilities. Over the years there was frequent friction between Iraq and the UN inspection team, and this escalated to crisis level when, in late 1997, Iraq refused to allow the inspectors access to large facilities that Baghdad claimed were presidential palaces.

Like the crisis on the Korean peninsula four years before, the confrontation with Iraq teetered on the edge of war. Finally, however, the diplomatic maneuvering again avoided war. The crisis subsided after a trip by UN secretary-general Kofi Annan to Baghdad, where he negotiated an agreement acceptable to both sides. Among other things, Saddam Hussein agreed to let the UN inspectors enter the supposed presidential palaces and Annan held out the hope that the long-standing economic sanctions on Iraq would be eased, perhaps even ended. As with the North Korean nuclear issue and many other sagas of diplomacy, the agreement in early 1998 was not the end of the story. Later in the year, perhaps trying to take advantage of President Clinton's embroilment in the Monica Lewinsky affair, Iraq again defied UN inspectors. Once again the world sought a solution somewhere between acquiescence and war.

THE FUNCTIONS OF DIPLOMACY

National diplomats serve as communication links between their country and the rest of the world. As one scholar puts it, "Diplomats not only seek to represent their states to the world, but also seek to represent the world back to their respective states, with the objective of keeping the whole ensemble together" (Sharp, 1999:53).

Traditionally, diplomacy has focused on the national interest. Writing in the 1400s, Venetian ambassador Ermolao Barbaro asserted that "the first duty of an ambassador is... to do, say, advise, and think whatever may best serve the preservation and aggrandizement of his own state" (Craig & George, 1995). More sardonically, Sir Henry Wotton, the English ambassador to Venice, wrote in *Reliquae Wottonianae* (1651) that "an ambassador is an honest man sent to lie abroad for the commonwealth [state]." Whether it is conducted with honor or deceit, diplomacy is carried on by officials with a variety of titles such as president, prime minister, ambassador, or special envoy, and it is worthwhile to explore the roles that these officials and other diplomats play in promoting the national interest (Berton, Kimura, & Zartman, 1999).

Observer and reporter is one role. A primary diplomatic role has always been to gather information and impressions and to analyze and report these back to the home office. This mostly includes routine activity, such as reading newspapers and reporting observations. Many embassies also contain a considerable contingent of intelligence officers who are technically attached to the diplomatic service but who are in reality a part of their country's intelligence service. Whatever the method, it is important for policy makers to know both the facts and the mood of foreign capitals, and the embassy is a primary source.

The value of this function is especially evident when it is absent. The internal politics and international intentions of North Korea, for example, are largely shrouded from outside view. Many countries, including the United States, do not have embassies in Pyongyang, and those diplomats who are there are generally restricted in their travel and contacts in North Korea. One U.S. official noted that "compared with North Korea, the Soviet Union was a duck-soup intelligence target."[12] This lack of good information was particularly worrisome during the events of 1993 and 1994 that involved North Korea's nuclear program. "The fact of the matter is that we don't really understand what they are doing," a U.S. official commented at one point.[13]

Even in less critical times, the day-to-day contacts that an ambassador has may be important, and the knowledge that a diplomat gains from being present in a country and interacting regularly with its leaders and people may be better than the secondhand knowledge of more distant experts and centers of analysis. The continuing importance of ambassadors and other diplomatic personnel regularly stationed in another country is also a function of the expansion of diplomatic focus. On-scene diplomatic reporting remains important to keep track of such intangibles as the mood of a country and to ascertain and analyze a country's economics and culture as well as its politics.

For all of this continued value, it is also the case that the importance of the ambassador as an observer and reporter has declined. High-level policy makers are more likely to visit countries themselves, and they also bring back and share valuable insights and information. Countries are also far less isolated from one another than they once were, and there are many new ways, using advanced technology, to gather information about other countries. The result is that diplomatic reports compete with many other sources of information. This frustrates diplomats. As one U.S. official put it, "There is a diminished value in classical diplomatic reporting. If you had a choice

Did You Know That:

Perhaps reflecting a convention that diplomats and other political leaders need all the help they can get, Pope John Paul II canonized Thomas More (1478–1535) and named him patron saint of politicians. More entered the kings's diplomatic corps, was knighted, and became chancellor of England in 1529. The comfort that political leaders gain from having a patron saint may be offset, however, by the fact that the career of Sir, now Saint, Thomas ended when he was beheaded by King Henry VIII.

between reading the [diplomatic] cables in your box and tuning in to CNN three times a day, you'd tune in to CNN."[14]

Negotiator is a second important role of a diplomat. Negotiation is a combination of art and technical skill that attempts to find a common ground among two or more divergent positions (Hopmann, 1996). For all of the public attention given to meetings between national leaders, the vast bulk of negotiating is done by ambassadors and other such personnel. The early negotiations between U.S. and North Korean diplomats resembled two boxers feeling each other out in the early rounds. "The whole idea is to test the proposition that the North Koreans are willing to deal," observed the chief American negotiator, Assistant Secretary of State Robert L. Gallucci. "And I always put it in terms of 'test the proposition' because I don't have… high confidence that we actually can resolve this through negotiations."[15]

Substantive and symbolic representative is a third role of a diplomat. Substantive representation includes explaining and defending the policies of the diplomat's country. Misperception is dangerous in world politics, and the role that diplomats play in explaining their countries' actions and statements to friends and foes alike is vital to accurate communications. Diplomats, to a degree, also personify, and thus symbolically represent, their countries. For example, ambassadors who have historical ties to the country to which they are accredited are apt to be received enthusiastically, enhancing the image of their country. Reverse characteristics can alienate people. The appointment in 1997 of Felix Rohatyn, who speaks fluent French and was awarded the Legion of Honor by France, as U.S. ambassador to Paris was warmly greeted by the French. Whatever the other fine qualifications of Ambassador Daniel Kurtzer, many Egyptians were dismayed when in 1998 president Clinton named him the first Jewish U.S. ambassador to an Arab country. "A Rabbi in the Robes of a Diplomat," grumbled the headline of one Egyptian news magazine.[16] Other Egyptians sprang to Ambassador Kurtzer's defense and the imbroglio eventually died down. A few diplomats, however, have managed to offend nearly everyone in their host country. Few Italians were able to appreciate the American humor of President Bush's ambassador to Italy, who joked before going to Rome that the modern Italian navy had to have glass-bottom boats "so they can see the old Italian navy."[17] Certainly, with today's rapid, multichannel communications and transportation, there are many images of any one country that are projected. But day in and day out, the ambassador represents *the* official image of his or her country and society.

Diplomats can sometimes *intervene* to tell a weaker country what to do. When, in 1972, South Vietnam resisted the U.S.–negotiated settlement, President Nixon cabled President Thieu that "all military and economic aid will be cut off… if an agreement is not reached" and that "I have… irrevocably decided to proceed… to sign [the agreement]. I will do so, if necessary, alone [and] explain that your government obstructs peace." As the United States' chief diplomat, Nixon was being distinctly undiplomatic. "Brutality is nothing," he told Kissinger. "You have never seen it if this son-of-a-bitch doesn't go along, believe me" (Kissinger, 1979:1420, 1469). Thieu went along.

Finally, diplomacy is also sometimes conducted for its *propaganda value*. Even where there is little hope for settlement, it may benefit a country's image to appear reasonable or to make opponents seem stubborn. As Soviet leader Nikita Khrushchev told a diplomat, "Never forget the appeal that the idea of disarmament has to the outside world. All you have to say is 'I'm in favor of it,' and it pays big dividends" (Shevchenko, 1985:246).

THE DIPLOMATIC SETTING

The nature of diplomacy and how it is carried out are also affected by its setting. The setting can be roughly divided into three parts: the international system, the diplomatic environment, and the domestic connection.

The International System

One aspect of the setting is the system. As we have noted many times, the nature of the anarchical international system creates a setting in which self-interested actors pursue their diplomatic goals by, if necessary, using power to ensure that their goals prevail over the goals of others. That emphasis on national interest is why this chapter discusses national diplomacy and national power.

Moreover, there are no authoritative outside actors to resolve disputes in the system among the main actors, the states. What is important to see about the system is that there was no supranational force to unravel the complex situations, such as the one in which China, Taiwan, and the United States found themselves during the crises that arose over China's attempt to influence Taiwan's 1996 and 2000 presidential elections. Taipei and Washington could only look to themselves to forestall any military attempt by Beijing to reincorporate Taiwan. China was similarly limited to self-reliance. In the current system, the only recourse for China if Taiwan were to declare its independence would be to try to reincorporate Taiwan militarily. Thus, when tension occurred, the actors had little choice but to rely on their own power to protect their divergent national interests.

The Diplomatic Environment

A second part of the diplomatic setting is determined by the relationships among the various actors who are involved in a particular matter. This part of the setting can be subdivided into four diplomatic environments: hostile, adversarial, coalition, and mediation diplomacy.

Hostile Diplomacy Where one or more countries are engaged in armed clashes or when there is a substantial possibility that fighting could result, diplomacy is conducted in a hostile environment. The maneuvering surrounding the U.S.–Iraq inspection crisis of 1997–1998 fell distinctly within the range of **hostile diplomacy.** The United States increased its firepower in the region to include 300 warplanes in Saudi Arabia, Kuwait, and Bahrain and on the aircraft carriers USS *Nimitz* and USS *George Washington* in the Persian Gulf. The U.S. fleet in the Gulf was joined by a British aircraft carrier HMS *Invincible* and included nine ships able to fire Tomahawk cruise missiles deep into Iraq. To underline the possibilities, U.S. secretary of defense William Cohen told reporters that "If one has to resort to military options… they will be substantial. They are something that Saddam Hussein should understand, and something a great deal more than any pinprick that might have been delivered in the past."[18]

Adversarial Diplomacy An environment of **adversarial diplomacy** occurs at a less confrontational level when two or more countries' interests clash but when there is little or no chance of armed conflict. A great deal of diplomacy involving economic issues occurs in adversarial circumstances as countries press other countries to accede to their wishes. During the 1990s, for example, there was a somewhat adversarial—but not hostile—relationship between Japan and the United States over Washington's efforts to get Tokyo to lower its trade barriers and stimulate its lagging economy so that the Japanese could buy more American exports. The thought of either Tokyo or Washington threatening to use force, much less actually doing so, is inconceivable in the foreseeable future. Yet relations between the two capitals have often been tense; overt and, more often, implied threats of economic sanctions and other forms of coercive diplomatic action have sometimes volleyed back and forth across the Pacific. At one point, for example, Washington threatened to impose a 100 percent tariff on imported Japanese luxury cars if Japan did not agree to further open its markets. To ensure that Japan got the point, then Vice President Al Gore used the imagery that once governed the cold war's eyeball-to-eyeball confrontations with the Soviet Union to warn, "We're not going to blink."[19]

Image: When Palestinian leader Yasser Arafat and Israeli leader Ehud Barak joined President Bill Clinton at the presidential retreat at Camp David, Maryland, in July 2000, Clinton, and indeed much of the rest of the world, was gladdened to see the two former enemies engaged in friendly horseplay as Barak jokingly pushed Arafat to take the honor of entering Clinton's quarters first.

Reality: Once the negotiations began, the earlier joviality of Arafat and Barak disappeared. The Camp David negotiations ended in failure, with each side bitterly accusing the other of trying to push it too far. From there relations worsened, and during the violence that erupted in October 2000, Israel rocketed Arafat's headquarters on the West Bank.

Coalition Diplomacy When a number of countries have similar interests, often in opposition to the interest of one or more other countries, then **coalition diplomacy** becomes a significant aspect of international activity. National leaders spend a good deal of time and effort to build coalitions that will support the foreign policy initiatives of their country or of other international actors that they support. When, for instance, Iraq invaded Kuwait in August 1990, President George Bush spent much time and effort in rounding up international support for military action against Iraq. During the first four days of the crisis Bush made 23 phone calls to a dozen foreign leaders, and personally flew to Colorado to consult with British prime minister Margaret Thatcher, who was coincidentally speaking at a conference there.

Bush and his advisers also rallied support against Iraq under the auspices of the United Nations. The UN Security Council passed a series of resolutions approving economic sanctions and the deployment of military forces in the Gulf region. The Security Council later approved the action taken in January and February by the American-led coalition forces to push Iraq out of Kuwait. These efforts did more than just build multinational support for the U.S. goal of ousting Iraq from Kuwait. The use of multilateral organizations also lent an air of legitimacy to a war that, if the United States had waged it unilaterally, would have created much more furor than was the case as a UN–sponsored operation.

Mediation Diplomacy Unlike hostile, adversarial, or coalition diplomacy, the use of **mediation diplomacy** occurs when a country that is not involved directly as one of the parties tries to help two or more sides in conflict resolve their differences. In July 2000, President Clinton decided on a bold and risky strategy to advance peace in the Middle East by inviting Israel's prime minister Ehud Barak and Palestinian National Authority (PNA) head Yasser Arafat to meet with him at the presidential retreat at Camp David in Maryland. The meeting inevitably evoked images of a similar event in 1979, during which President Jimmy Carter successfully served as mediator, and Prime Minister Menachem Begin of Israel and President Anwar Sadat of Egypt negotiated a historic peace treaty between their two countries. The situation in 2000 was fluid. In the weeks before the meeting Israel had withdrawn from Lebanon, and Syria's long-serving president, Hafez al-Assad, had died and been succeeded by his son, Bashar. Moreover, Prime Minister Barak's coalition government had become increasingly shaky, partly because of his willingness to compromise with the Palestinians. Adding to the drama, PNA head Arafat, under pressure from within his own ranks, declared that the Palestinians would soon declare the territory they controlled to be a state, with or without Israeli concurrence. The chances for success were slim. Knowing that it was his last chance as president to make a difference, Clinton decided to go ahead anyway. "If the parties do not seize this moment to make more progress, there will be more hostility and more bitterness—perhaps even more violence," he explained. As for the dim prospects, Clinton reasoned, "While there clearly is no guarantee of success, not to try would guarantee failure."[20]

The Domestic Connection

Domestic politics provide the third part of the diplomatic setting. The concept of **two-level game theory,** discussed in chapter 4, holds that to be successful a country's diplomats must find a solution that is acceptable to both the other country at the international level and, at the domestic level, to the political actors (legislators, public opinion, interest groups) in the diplomat's own country. From this perspective, the diplomatic setting exists at the domestic as well as at the international level, and is influenced by the interplay of the two levels when leaders try to pursue policies that satisfy the actors at both levels (Trumbore, 1998; Peterson, 1996).

During the Taiwan crises, the leaders of China and the United States not only had to find a point of agreement between themselves, they also had to fend off domestic forces that were pushing to escalate the crisis. Prior to the 1996 crisis, President Jiang Zemin told the U.S. ambassador, "Any leader who let this pass [Taiwan's independence] would be overthrown."[21] Similar tensions surfaced within the Chinese government in 2000 over how to respond to the seemingly pro-independence stance of Taiwanese presidential candidate Chen Shui-bian, who subsequently won the election. "We are painting ourselves into a corner," one official in Beijing told a reporter. "We are being tough when we should be soft and passive when we should be taking the initiative."[22] The issue, one political scientist explained, was Beijing's worry that Taiwan would evolve gradually into a recognized state without Beijing being able to stop it. "It has become imperative," the scholar continued, "not only to not be the leader who lost Taiwan, but not to be the leader who allowed this slow drift [toward independence] to continue."[23]

President Clinton also had to deal with strong domestic forces. In 1996 House Republicans urged Clinton to commit the United States "to the defense of Taiwan."[24] Keeping the pressure up in 2000, Republican Senate leader Trent Lott condemned the "threats emanating from Beijing" and suggested that the Clinton "administration should worry more about protecting and promoting Taiwan's democracy than offending the communist dictators in Beijing."[25] To ensure that Clinton did not ignore their views, congressional Republicans threatened to block the pending extension of permanent normal trading relations to China, a move that would have derailed China's entry into the World Trade Organization (see the box, The Power of the Purse, on p. 102). GOP legislators also introduced the Taiwan Security Enhancement Act, which would have substantially increased the U.S. commitment to Taiwan and, thus, outraged China. "There is a lot of pent-up frustration about the administration's policy approach to China," a GOP aide noted. "Either that gets vented in terms of the World Trade Organization and permanent normal trade relations or on the [Taiwan] Security Enhancement Act."[26]

THE EVOLUTION OF DIPLOMACY

Diplomacy is an ancient art. Because of the economic and political world dominance of Europe and European-heritage countries for the past several centuries, a great deal of modern diplomatic practice can be traced through its evolution in Western practice. Still, diplomacy predates the West.

EARLY DIPLOMACY

The genesis of diplomacy can be traced to the Eastern Mediterranean and the region around the Tigris and Euphrates valleys, the so-called cradle of civilization, north of the Persian Gulf. Diplomatic records in the region date back almost four millennia, and records from what appear to be embassies can be found from as far back as the time of the great Babylonian emperor, Hammurabi (1792–1750 B.C.). These beginnings found continuance and advancement in ancient Greece and Rome, which originated many of the concepts and practices used in modern diplomacy. Diplomatic missions are described in Homer's *Iliad* (about 850 B.C.), and the Greeks, followed by the Romans, wrote treaties, established the rudiments of international law, initiated or revived other aspects of diplomatic practice, and used ambassadors to negotiate disputes. The Byzantine Empire, which flourished after Rome's collapse, added further to the evolution of diplomacy by specifically training negotiators and by establishing the first department of foreign affairs.

The diplomacy of the Italian city-states beginning in the fifteenth century contributed to the evolution of diplomacy through the establishment of the first permanent diplomatic missions since Hammurabi's time, more than 3,000 years earlier. Italians also introduced summit meetings as a diplomatic practice and became particularly known for diplomatic artifice. Indeed, the unflattering adjective, Machiavellian, is an eponym after Niccolò Machiavelli of Florence, who counseled in *The Prince* (1532) that it was best to be as powerful as a lion and as sly as a fox, and who summed up his estimation of human nature with the observation that one "must start with assuming that all men are bad and ever ready to display their vicious nature whenever they may find occasion for it."

Did You Know That:

The oldest surviving diplomatic document is a cuneiform tablet written about 2,500 B.C. It is a message sent by Ibubu, chief minister to the king of Ebla (in modern Lebanon), to King Zizi of Hamazi (in modern Iran), some 1,200 miles away. In it Ibubu pledges goodwill, relates that he is sending Zizi a quantity of rare wood, and says that he wants him to "give me good mercenaries. Please send them" (Cohen, 1996:2).

The French system is the direct predecessor of modern diplomacy. Cardinal Richelieu, who served as chief minister (1624–1642) to King Louis XIII, was the first to see diplomacy as an ongoing process rather than as an expedience, and he consolidated all foreign affairs functions under one ministry. Later, during the reign (1643–1715) of Louis XIV, the minister of foreign affairs became a member of the king's cabinet, and permanent embassies were established in all the major capitals, with lesser-ranked missions in minor capitals. It was also at the end of this era that the first diplomatic manual, *On the Manner of Negotiating with Sovereigns* (1716), was written by François de Callierres.

In general, the old diplomacy that developed mostly in Europe had several traits. One was elite domination. "L'état c'est moi" (I am the state), Louis XIV supposedly proclaimed with some justification, and true to that assertion, foreign policy was almost exclusively dominated by the monarch and ministers and diplomatic corps recruited from the nobility and gentry. Democracy had begun in a few places, but the say of the people in foreign affairs was still minimal. As conducted by the elite, diplomacy was further marked by secrecy. Even treaties were often secret. Although there were a few multilateral conferences, such as the Congress of Vienna (1815), **bilateral diplomacy** (direct negotiations between two countries) was the normal form of negotiation.

MODERN DIPLOMACY

Although diplomatic practice has evolved slowly, the World War I (1914–1918) era serves as a benchmark in the transition to modern diplomacy. It was the beginning of the end of European world dominance. It also marked the fall of the German, Austrian, Ottoman, and Russian emperors. Nationalistic self-determination stirred strongly in Europe and other parts of the world. New powers—the United States, Japan, and China—began to assert themselves and they joined or replaced the declining European countries as world powers. The "old diplomacy" did not vanish, but it changed substantially. The "new diplomacy" includes seven characteristics: expanded geographic scope, multilateral diplomacy, parliamentary diplomacy, democratized diplomacy, open diplomacy, leader-to-leader diplomacy, and public diplomacy. These new practices have been greeted as "reforms," but many also have drawbacks.

Expansion of Geographic Scope

The diplomacy of the twentieth century has been marked by expansion of its geographic scope. The two Hague Conferences (1899, 1907) on peace, particularly the second, with its 44 participants, included countries outside the European sphere. President Wilson's call for national self-determination foreshadowed a world of almost 200 countries. Today, the United Nations, with its nearly universal membership, symbolizes the truly global scope of diplomacy.

Multilateral Diplomacy

Although conferences involving a number of nations occurred during the nineteenth century, that practice has expanded greatly in the modern era (Best, 1999). Woodrow Wilson's call for a League of Nations symbolizes the rise of **multilateral diplomacy.** There are now a number of permanent world and regional international organizations. Ad hoc conferences and treaties are also more apt to be multilateral. Before 1900, for example, the United States attended an average of one multilateral conference per year. Now, the United States is a member of scores of international organizations and American diplomats participate daily in multilateral negotiations.

Multilateral diplomacy has increased for several reasons. Technological progress is one. Advances in travel and communications technology allow faster and more frequent contacts among countries. Second, multilateral diplomacy has increased because more countries and leaders recognize that many global concerns, such as the environment, cannot be solved by any one country or through traditional bilateral diplomacy alone. Instead, global cooperation and solutions are required. Third, diplomacy through multilateral organizations is attractive to smaller countries as a method of influencing world politics beyond their individual power.

A fourth factor promoting multilateral diplomacy is the rise of expectations that important international actions, especially the use of military force, will be taken within the framework of a multilateral organization. An important point to make about multilateral diplomacy is that participation in a global setting does not mean that countries usually pursue policies for the global good. Instead, as we saw in the preceding chapter, countries most often try to achieve their self-interests by manipulating multilateral organizations and conferences.

Parliamentary Diplomacy

Another modern practice is **parliamentary diplomacy.** This includes debate and voting in international organizations and sometimes supplants negotiation and compromise.

The maneuvering involved in parliamentary diplomacy was strongly evident in the UN with regard to North Korea during 1993 and 1994. The United States had to proceed cautiously with threats of UN–endorsed sanctions against North Korea because both China and Russia were averse to sanctions and each possessed a veto. "What will the Chinese do?" Assistant Secretary Gallucci rhetorically asked reporters at a briefing. "Will you be able to pass a sanctions resolution? If there is anybody in this room who knows things they know, if they are willing to give me odds, and I do not care in which direction, I'll take them. I do not know what the Chinese are going to do."[27]

Despite the reluctance of China and Russia to act, parliamentary diplomacy did eventually play a role in putting pressure on North Korea. In May 1994, the five permanent members of the Security Council issued a joint statement calling on North Korea to provide evidence that it was not reprocessing spent nuclear reactor fuel rods into plutonium for weapons. Among other benefits, this statement signaled to Pyongyang that the five permanent members (P5) of the Security Council were united in opposition to a North Korean nuclear-weapons capability and that even Chinese and Russian patience was not inexhaustible.

Democratized Diplomacy

The elite and executive-dominant character of diplomacy has changed in several ways. One result of **democratized diplomacy** is that diplomats are now drawn from a wider segment of society and, thus, are more representative of their nations. It also means, though, that diplomats have lost the common frame of reference once provided by their similar cosmopolitan, elite backgrounds. Diplomats now have their attitudes rooted in their national cultures and are more apt to suffer from the antagonisms and misperceptions that nationalistic stereotyping causes.

A second democratic change is the rise of the roles of legislatures, interest groups, and public opinion. Executive leaders still dominate the foreign policy–making process, but it is no longer their exclusive domain. Now, as discussed in the earlier section on the domestic setting, national executives often must conduct two-level diplomacy by negotiating with domestic actors as well as other countries to find a mutually agreeable solution to outstanding issues.

The democratization of diplomacy means, among other things, that diplomats conduct public diplomacy aimed at influencing not just leaders, but also the legislatures, interest groups, and public opinion in other countries. UN secretary-general Kofi Annan has reportedly said, "If I can't get the support of governments, then I'll get the support of the people. People move governments."[28]

Open Diplomacy

Of Woodrow Wilson's Fourteen Points, his call for "open covenants, openly arrived at" is the best remembered. As such, Wilson would have approved of the fact that, much more than before, diplomacy and even international agreements are widely reported and documented. One advantage of **open diplomacy** is that it fits with the idea of democracy. Secret diplomacy more often than not is used by leaders to "mislead the populations of their own countries" rather than to keep information from international opponents (Gibbs, 1995:213).

There are, however, advantages to secret diplomacy. Most scholars and practitioners agree that public negotiations are difficult. Early disclosure of your bargaining strategy will compromise your ability to win concessions. Public negotiations are also more likely to lead diplomats to posture for public consumption. Concessions may be difficult to make amid popular criticism. In sum, it is difficult to negotiate (or to play chess) with someone kibitzing over your shoulder. Indeed, domestic opposition to dealing with an adversary may be so intense that it may be impossible to negotiate at all.

COME ABROAD TO SEE THE WORLD

To the outsider, the thought of being a president or prime minister engaged in world diplomacy seems pretty attractive. Your personal plane flies you to interesting places where you meet important people. You stay in the best hotels or official residences and are the host or the guest at lavish banquet after lavish banquet. Not a bad deal, most people would say.

Amazingly, though, leaders often complain bitterly about the rigors of travel and ceremony. Tight schedules and jet lag are often so exhausting that, to cite one example, Ronald Reagan once fell asleep while listening to a speech by the pope.

Then there is the culinary challenge. Dining can be a delicious part of diplomacy, but there are many hazards to what has been waggishly labeled "meal-politik" and "gravy-boat diplomacy." One peril is having to eat odd things to avoid injuring local sensitivities. President Bush dined on boar's penis soup while visiting China in 1989. One American at the dinner recalls hoping that there had been a translation error, but finding out it was "what everyone thought it was."[1] Only slightly more palatable were the moose lips that appeared on Bill Clinton's presidential plate during a 22-course dinner hosted by President Boris Yeltsin in Russia. "This was not a chocolate dessert," joked one American official.[2] Even if the food is not exotic, the hectic pace can lead to gastric distress. One victim was Jimmy Carter, who was felled in Mexico City by what he undiplomatically called Montezuma's revenge. And while in Tokyo, George Bush was so indisposed that he threw up on the Japanese prime minister and fainted. It is no wonder, then, that presidents may often think of Shakespeare's *Comedy of Errors* and the lament of Dromio, "For with long travel I am stiff and weary."

Yet despite the perils of globe-trotting, presidents and prime ministers do so at a near frenetic pace. Before becoming president, Bill Clinton criticized the incumbent, George H. W. Bush for being abroad too much. "It is time," Clinton asserted while campaigning in New Hampshire, "for us to have a president who cares more about Littleton [NH] than Liechtenstein or more about Manchester [NH] than Micronesia."[3] As president, however, Clinton soon began to act, according to one congressional critic, "like the Energizer Bunny, he has continued to keep on going, and going and going."[4] Indeed, Clinton's "goings" eventually made him the most-traveled U.S. president. The old marks were surpassed in October 1997, when Clinton departed from Andrews Airforce Base in Maryland for a trip to South America, bringing his total to 26 trips, 66 countries. Clinton's wanderlust was hardly sated though. During 1998, 1999, and the first 10 months of 2000, he made another 15 trips, visiting 33 countries. In addition to those, foreign travel has become so common that quick trips for meetings, such as Clinton's travel to the Middle East for an emergency summit meeting in October 2000, are not even counted on the White House's Web site of overseas presidential travel. A finishing record of at least 40 state visits, not to mention numerous less formal business trips, to about a third of the world's countries will be hard for a future president to top.

Both the undemocratic downside of secret diplomacy and its facilitating upside can be seen in the negotiations that led to the Oslo Accords, which were discussed in the box Palestinians: A Nation without a State in chapter 6. It is probable that the peace agreements between Israel and the Palestine Liberation Organization (PLO) in 1993 could not have occurred without secret diplomacy. For Israel, direct contact with the PLO would have raised a riot of protest. The PLO leadership would also have faced opposition from the die-hard elements of the Palestinian movement. To get around such domestic barriers, Norway's foreign minister initiated and acted as mediator during secret negotiations between Israel and the PLO. A total of 14 meetings took place in a large farmhouse near Oslo and elsewhere in Norway between Israelis and Palestinians of ever-increasing rank. "We [created] a very informal atmosphere—to build personal confidence. They were actually living in the same house, living very closely together," one of the Norwegian diplomats has recalled.[29] "We [also] closed off large areas to allow for walks in the woods." Lights burned late into the night; the occupants were seen wandering in the woods. Neighbors were told that the seemingly eccentric people

Despite the fact that President Clinton averaged about 40 days a year, or 11 percent of his time, abroad during his second term, it is almost certainly just political rhetoric to charge that paying attention to Moscow, Russia, and Athens, Greece, means that the president is paying too little attention to Moscow, Idaho, and Athens, Georgia. A bit more substantive, however, are concerns about the cost of presidential travel abroad.

President Clinton's 10-day trip to China in 1998 provides a case in point. Accompanying the president were his wife and daughter, 5 cabinet secretaries, 6 members of Congress, 86 senior aides, 150 civilian staff (doctors, lawyers, secretaries, valets, hairdressers, and so on), 150 military staff (drivers, baggage handlers, snipers, and so on), 150 security personnel, several bomb-sniffing dogs, and many tons of equipment, including 10 armored limousines and the "blue goose," Clinton's bulletproof lectern. The cost of the expedition was almost $19 million dollars according to the U.S. General Accounting Office.[5] This figure represents what is called "incremental costs," that is, costs in addition to the salaries of the federal employees who accompanied the president and the costs of planning the trip. The reported costs also did not include the expense of protecting the president, a figure that is classified for national security reasons.

The bulk of costs accrue to the Defense Department (DOD), which some critics charge is an unwise way to spend the country's defense dollars. To get the presidential entourage and its vast array of equipment to China and back, the Air Force flew 36 airlift missions using Boeing 747, C-141, and C-5 (the largest transport, with a capacity of 145 tons of cargo) aircraft. The cost to DOD of the China trip was $14 million. Indeed operating Air Force One alone costs over $34,000 an hour.

China was neither the least nor the most expensive presidential trip per day. That record was probably set by the $42.8 million, 1,300 person, 10-day trip to Africa in March 1998. But if China can be used as an average, the cost of $1.8 million per day for a presidential trip overseas means that the incremental costs of President Clinton's foreign travel during his eight years in office came to more than $500 million.

Why do presidents and other leaders travel so much? Certainly there is a value to leader-to-leader diplomacy, whether it be a dramatic breakthrough or the ability to meet other leaders and, as one scholar puts it, to "see how they talk, how they laugh... if they laugh."[6] It is also the case that presidents can escape the voracious press at home and the difficulty of working with a cantankerous Congress and bureaucratic barons. President Clinton once explained that foreign policy was more "fun" because he could make policy "with less interference and static in Congress," whereas in domestic policy even the president was but "one of a zillion decision makers."[7] Thus, like Petruchio in Shakespeare's *Taming of the Shrew*, presidents outward bound on Air Force One may muse to themselves:

> Crowns in my purse I have and goods at home,
> And so am come abroad to see the world.

were professors writing a book. Free from outside kibitzing, the two sides went over page after page of detailed proposals and counterproposals. Given the historic enmity of the two sides, the end result was almost unimaginable. Israel's prime minister Yitzhak Rabin and the PLO's chairman Yasser Arafat, the two leaders of "the children of Abraham," as President Clinton called them, met on the White House lawn, signed a cooperation agreement, and thus, as Clinton waxed eloquently, "embarked together on a bold journey."[30] As noted earlier, the road that journey has traversed has proven rocky indeed, but at least the first steps were taken.

Leader-to-Leader Diplomacy

Modern transportation and communications have spawned an upsurge of high-level diplomacy (Dunn, 1996). National leaders regularly hold bilateral or multilateral summit conferences, and foreign ministers and other ranking diplomats jet between countries, conducting shuttle diplomacy. One hundred thirty years of American history

One advantage of summit diplomacy is that it sometimes allows leaders to establish a personal rapport that can help ease negotiations. President Jiang Zemin of China and President Bill Clinton had many meetings during the eight years (1993–2001) Clinton was in office, and this picture of the two leaders during a press conference in Washington, D.C., captures their relaxed familiarity with one another.

Did You Know That:

For reaching out to North Korea and for helping to create democracy in South Korea President Kim Dae Jung of South Korea won the Nobel Peace Prize for 2000.

passed before a president (Woodrow Wilson) traveled overseas while in office. Richard Nixon departed on his first state visit to Europe only 33 days after his inauguration, and each president has surpassed his predecessor's record of foreign travel, as the box, Come Abroad to See the World, discusses. The once-rare instances of leader-to-leader diplomacy meetings between heads of state have become so common that in some cases they have become routine. For example, the leaders of the Group of Eight (G–8, the largest industrialized countries plus Russia) meet annually; the leaders of the European Union's countries meet at least twice a year.

The advent of globe-trotting, leader-to-leader diplomacy, or **summit meetings,** and the increased frequency of telecommunications diplomacy are mixed blessings. There are several *advantages*. The first is that meetings between leaders can demonstrate an important symbolic shift in relations. For fifty years after the outbreak of the Korean War, relations between Pyongyang and Seoul were unrelentingly hostile. Symbolically, that changed in June 2000, when President Kim Dae Jung of South Korea and President Kim Jong Il of North Korea met in Pyongyang. Some agreements were reached, but their importance paled compared to the symbolic televised image of the two shaking hands, smiling, bantering, and drinking champagne. "Maybe nothing dramatic will happen right away," a clerk in Seoul noted wisely, "but most people would agree that a surprising amount of progress and understanding has been achieved already."[31]

Second, leaders can sometimes make dramatic breakthroughs. The 1978 Camp David Accords, which began the process of normalizing Egyptian-Israeli relations after decades of hostility and three wars, were produced after President Carter, Egyptian president Sadat, and Israeli prime minister Begin isolated themselves at the presidential retreat in Maryland. A third advantage is that rapid diplomacy can help dispel false information and stereotypes. President Bush lauded the telephone as a helpful tool. "If [another leader] knows the heartbeat a little bit from talking [with me]," the president explained, "there's less apt to be misunderstanding."[32]

A fourth advantage of personal contact among leaders is that mutual confidence or even friendships may develop. It would be an overstatement to say that President Clinton and President Jiang Zemin of China became friends, but they did establish a level of ease with one another. As one U.S. aide put it, "I think there has developed over these... meetings a bond. I think when Jiang talks about 'my friend Bill Clinton' and having met with him five times, he's doing more than going through the motions."[33]

Clear vision and good feelings are laudable, but there are also several potential *disadvantages* to leader-to-leader diplomacy. One problem is that summits may lead to ill-conceived agreements. According to Kissinger (1979:142), "Some of the debacles of our diplomatic history have been perpetrated by presidents who fancied themselves negotiators." An irony of modern diplomacy is that the interdependent and technical natures of global issues are making them increasingly complex at the very time when leader-to-leader diplomacy is becoming more frequent. There is, one Bush administration official worried, a tendency to oversimplify problems: "We assume five or six people can do anything, and it makes it a lot easier. But," the official warned, "if we push the experts aside, we suffer in the end."[34]

A second problem with leader-to-leader diplomacy is that it may lead to misunderstandings. There are numerous instances where leaders have made and reached what each thought was a mutual understanding, only to find to their equally mutual surprise and anger that they had misunderstood one another. Furthermore, as tricky as personal contacts may be, the telephone may present even greater difficulties. Henry Kissinger, for example, argues that "the telephone is generally made for misunderstanding. It is difficult to make a good record. You can't see the other side's expressions or body language."[35]

Third, while mistakes made by lower-ranking officials can be disavowed by their superiors, a leader's commitments, even if not well thought out, cannot be easily retracted. "When Presidents become negotiators no escape routes are left," Kissinger (1979:12) warns. "Concessions are irrevocable without dishonor."

Fourth, specific misunderstanding and general chemistry can work to damage working relations between leaders instead of improving them. Kissinger (1979:142), who should know, has observed that most world leaders are characterized by a "healthy dose of ego," and when two such egos collide, "negotiations can rapidly deteriorate from intractability to confrontation."

Public Diplomacy

The communications revolution has placed leaders and other diplomats in public view more than ever before, and their actions have an impact on world opinion that is often distinct from their negotiating positions. Among other things, this means that diplomacy is often conducted under the glare of television lights and almost everything that officials say in public is heard or read by others. Additionally, a country's overall image and the image of its leaders have become more important because of the democratization of the foreign policy process discussed above.

These changes have meant that international relations are also increasingly conducted through **public diplomacy.** The concept of public diplomacy can be defined as a process of creating an overall international image that enhances a country's ability to achieve diplomatic success. This is akin to propaganda. Public diplomacy includes traditional propaganda, but goes beyond that: it also includes what is actually said and done by political figures, practices of national self-promotion that are much the same as advertising, and other forms of public relations that are utilized by business. In practice, as we shall see, propaganda and public diplomacy overlap substantially. One scholar's concept of public diplomacy envisions a "theater of power" that is a "metaphor for the repertoire of visual and symbolic tools used by statesmen and diplomats." As players in the theater of power, leaders "must be sensitive to the impression they make on

Leaders increasingly engage in public diplomacy by reaching out to the people of other countries instead of just to their leaders. Not long ago it would have been nearly unthinkable for a Kremlin leader to address the American public. Now it seems almost natural for President Vladimir Putin of Russia to appear as an interview guest on the Larry King show, as happened in September 2000.

observers.... They surely [are] subject to the same sort of 'dramatic,' if not aesthetic, criticism of other kinds of public performances" (Cohen, 1987:i–ii).

Governments also recognize this change. President Clinton's visit to China in 1998 was a tour de force of public diplomacy. He spoke to crowds on several stops, engaged in a question-and-answer session with students at Beijing University, and, most importantly, held a joint press conference with President Jiang that was broadcast live on China's state television. The White House had pressed hard to have Clinton permitted significant opportunities to speak to the Chinese public, and the unprecedented decision by China's government to let a foreign leader have direct access to a national audience left U.S. officials elated. The Chinese government "recognized that the price of engagement with us was giving us access to their people. Jiang knew he needed to do that to make this a successful summit," one U.S. official commented. The press conference began somewhat stiffly, but then became more spontaneous and important as the two leaders publicly exchanged views on such sensitive topics as Taiwan, Tibet, U.S.–China economic relations, and human rights in China. It was the first time that the Chinese had seen their government's policies openly criticized on national television, not to mention their president debating those policies. With China still a politically controlled society, it was hard to judge the immediate impact of the exchange on China. But, observed a U.S. diplomat, "The real answer is going to come…, of course, from the people of China. And we've seen repeated quotes in the press from people indicating that it [the press conference] will have profound reverberations from here."[36]

There is also an element of public diplomacy that goes beyond presenting one's best face and that involves distortions through propaganda and even outright lying. *Propaganda* is an attempt to influence another country through emotional techniques rather than logical discussion or presentation of empirical evidence. It is a process of appealing to emotions rather than minds by creating fear, doubt, sympathy, anger, or a variety of other feelings. Although the use of propaganda is as old as history, advances in communication, democratization, and the understanding of psychology have made propaganda increasingly important. In essence, if you cannot persuade another country's leaders through force or diplomacy, you can try to affect policy by persuading its people through propaganda.

By any standard, propaganda is big business. The United States, for one, operates or sponsors the Voice of America, Radio Free Europe/Radio Liberty, and Radio Martí. The U.S. Information Agency also produces Worldnet, a television service available globally, provides Web sites, and has other modern communications capabilities. Still, the end of the cold war has dealt harshly with most such efforts. Radio Free Europe/Radio Liberty, for example, has just 200 employees, down from 1,700 in the 1980s.

This does not mean that propaganda is dying. It is not. Instead, it is becoming more subtle. For instance, countries now often hire private public relations firms to present their image. One of the reasons that Taiwan has been more effective than China in pressing its case in the United States is that Taipei pays the Washington firm of Cassidy & Associates some $1.5 million a year to promote Taiwan's image and interests. The Taiwanese government also spends much more time reaching out to Americans in many ways, from donating to U.S. charities to sponsoring trips of up-and-coming people to Taiwan. As for China, a former White House adviser on Asia has commented, "It's hard to think of anybody who does this kind of thing worse. The Chinese come in and tell you what they want and you're supposed to say, 'good.' They... do not recognize that the key to lobbying is education over time."[37] That image of ineptness is beginning to change, however, amid swirling charges that China donated money to the Democratic National Committee to influence the 1996 U.S. presidential and congressional campaigns and the slick performances of President Jiang Zemin during his visit in 1997 to the United States and President Clinton's return visit to China in 1998.

THE CONDUCT OF DIPLOMACY

Diplomacy is a complex game of maneuver in which the goal is to get other players to do what you want them to do. The players can number from two, in bilateral diplomacy, to many, in multilateral diplomacy. The rules of diplomacy are, at best, loose. The norms of the system set down some guidelines to diplomacy, but they are ever-evolving and even the ones that exist are not always followed. The unilateral, aggressive use of force, for instance, is now widely considered a violation of the rules. Yet players still sometimes employ it, and the penalties for rules violations are uncertain.

Another factor that adds to the complexity of the often multisided, loosely constrained diplomatic game is that it is multidimensional. There is not just one mode of play. Instead, like all the most fascinating games, diplomacy is intricate and involves considerable strategy that can be employed in several ways. Thus, while diplomacy is often portrayed by an image of somber negotiations over highly polished wooden tables in ornate rooms, it is much more than that. Modern diplomacy is a far-ranging communications process.

Diplomacy as a communications process has three elements: negotiation, signaling, and public diplomacy. *Negotiation* occurs when two or more parties are talking with one another, either directly or through an intermediary. *Signaling* entails saying or doing something with the intent of sending a message to another government. When leaders make bellicose or conciliatory speeches, when military forces are deployed or even used, when trade privileges are granted or sanctions invoked, or when diplomatic recognition is extended or relations are broken, these actions are, or at least should be, signals of attitude and intent to another country. *Public diplomacy* moves away from its traditional mode of government-to-government communication. Instead, as we noted earlier, public diplomacy involves the more modern practice of trying to influence a wider audience, including public opinion in another country or throughout the world.

THE RULES OF EFFECTIVE DIPLOMACY

Delineating the three modes of diplomatic communications is easy. Utilizing them effectively is hard. There is no set formula that will ensure victory. There are, however, several considerations that affect the chances of diplomatic success. We can examine some of these considerations by looking, in this section, at the rules of effective diplomacy, then, in the next section, by turning to the various options available for playing the great game of diplomacy. Some basic rules of effective diplomacy are:

Be realistic. It is important to have goals that match your ability to achieve them. "The test of a statesman," Kissinger (1970:47) has pointed out, "is his ability to recognize the real relationship of forces." Being realistic also means remembering that the other side, like yours, has domestic opponents. During discussions with North Korea in 1994, U.S. negotiator Robert Gallucci avoided pressing for nonvital, albeit desirable, concessions that, he said, "we recognized [as] serious [domestic] issues for [North Korea, but which] needed not be undertaken immediately."[38] Critics charged that the Clinton administration was being too soft, but to apply the test of pragmatism, final judgment of the pact's wisdom might best be based, as one U.S. official noted, on the "question of whether this is better than war."[39]

Be careful about what you say. The experienced diplomat plans out and weighs words carefully. When the Korean nuclear crisis first flared up, President Clinton stated spontaneously, "North Korea cannot be allowed to develop a nuclear bomb; we have to be very firm about it."[40] The danger of ad-libbing became apparent the next month when the CIA reported that North Korea might already have one or two nuclear weapons. Faced with this fait accompli, Clinton either had to retreat from his words or risk war with North Korea. He chose retreat. "Our policy right along," announced an obviously backpedaling senior official, "has been oriented to try to keep North Korea from getting a significant nuclear-weapons capability."[41] Later, when a reporter asked Clinton about his early penchant for off-the-cuff statements, the president replied, "I've completely stopped that. I think that is a mistake."[42]

Seek common ground. Disputes begin negotiations; finding common ground ends them successfully. Almost any negotiation will involve some concessions, so it is important to maintain a degree of flexibility. An important start on the road to common ground is to be wary of dogmatic statements. A Japanese diplomat criticized President Clinton's initial hard line that North Korea could not be allowed to have a nuclear bomb as "drawing a line in the sand." "You should be softer," the diplomat counseled; "Clinton... should have told Kim, 'You say you don't have the Bomb. O.K., we believe you.' Then, quietly, he should have begun to deal."[43]

Flexibility also involves compromise on minor points. Concessions, even unilateral ones, are likely to engender positive responses that can help build a spirit of cooperation (Bennett, 1996). Even if one country has the upper hand, it may be unwise to press the advantage too far. One study of how peace is made and maintained, concludes, "Wars are seldom a struggle between total virtue and vice.... But when so conceived, they become crusades that remove the possibility of finding common ground after the battles are over" (Kegley & Raymond, 1999:249).

Understand the other side. There are several aspects to understanding the other side. One is to appreciate an opponent's perspective even if you do not agree with it. Just four months after Ronald Reagan was inaugurated and began an arms buildup, the Soviet leader, Leonid Brezhnev, wrote to his American counterpart to protest the military expansion "aimed against our country." "Try, Mr. President," Brezhnev asked Reagan, "to see what is going on through our eyes" (Kriesberg, 1992:12). It was good advice. As a corollary, it is also wise to make sure that thine enemy knows thee. Errors that result from misperceptions based on cultural differences and the lack of or wrong information are a major cause of conflict.

Be patient. It is also important to bide your time. Being overly anxious can lead to concessions that are unwise and may convey weakness to an opponent. As a corollary, it is poor practice to set deadlines, for yourself or others, unless you are in a very strong position or you do not really want an agreement. Throughout the negotiations with North Korea, which were frustrating and included many setbacks, the Clinton administration was patient and used gradual offers of rewards and threats of punishments. Critics called for stronger action. The steady course eventually carried the day.

Leave avenues of retreat open. It is axiomatic that even a rat will fight if trapped in a corner. The same is often true for countries. Call it honor, saving face, or prestige; it is important to leave yourself and your opponent an "out." Ultimatums, especially public ones, often lead to war. During the crisis with Iraq in 1998, Secretary-General Kofi Annan sought face-saving compromises that would allow Iraq to back away from its refusal to let inspectors into so-called presidential palaces. "Talk to some of your Arab friends," he suggested to a journalist. "Ask them to talk about dignity. It's like Chinese losing face—it's that important. It's not a joke. The sense of humiliation or losing your dignity or losing face—they would die or go to war over that."[44]

OPTIONS FOR CONDUCTING DIPLOMACY

While the above rules are solid guidelines to effective diplomacy, the practice is still more art than science. Therefore, effective diplomacy must tailor its approach to the situation and the opponent. To do this, diplomats must make choices about the channel, level, visibility, type of inducement, degree of precision, method of communication, and extent of linkage that they will use (Feron, 1997).

Direct or Indirect Negotiations

One issue that diplomats face is whether to negotiate directly with each other or indirectly through an intermediary. *Direct negotiations* have the advantage of avoiding the misinterpretations that an intermediary third party might cause. As in the old game of "Gossip," messages can get garbled. Direct negotiations are also quicker. An additional plus is that they can act as a symbol.

Indirect negotiations may also be advisable. Direct contact symbolizes a level of legitimacy that a country may not wish to convey. Israel, for instance, long refused to openly and directly negotiate with the PLO. Indirect diplomacy can also avoid the embarrassment of a public rebuff by the other side. During the opening moves in 1970, exploring diplomatic relations, the United States and China sent oral messages through the "good offices" (friendly intermediaries) of Pakistan and Romania, and written messages were exchanged on photocopy paper with no letterheads or signatures.

High-Level or Low-Level Diplomacy

The higher the level of contact or the higher the level of the official making a statement, the more seriously will a message be taken. It implies a greater commitment, and there will be a greater reaction. Therefore, a diplomat must decide whether to communicate on a high or a low level.

A high level of diplomacy has its advantages. Verbal and written statements by heads of government are noted seriously in other capitals. At one point in 1998 during the confrontation with Iraq, President Clinton personally and publicly commented on a UN Security Council resolution stating that Iraq faced "severest consequences" if it continued to block arms control inspections. "The government of Iraq should be under no illusion," Clinton said. "The meaning of severest consequences is clear. It provides [the United States and other countries] authority to act" if Iraq does not reverse its policy. Just in case Baghdad had any doubts, a State Department spokesman defined severest to mean, "There is no more severe consequence, which makes quite clear that what we're talking about here is military force."[45]

There are other times when *low-level communications* are wiser. Low-level communications avoid overreaction and maintain flexibility. Dire threats can be issued as "trial balloons" by cabinet officers or generals and then, if later thought unwise, disavowed by higher political officers. During the Taiwan crisis of 2000, the principal leaders tended to avoid military threats, leaving that role to lesser officials. For example, an editorial in the Chinese military's newspaper, *Liberation Army Daily*, was far enough removed from official policy makers to warn provocatively that China would "spare no effort in a blood-soaked battle" if Taiwan declared independence.[46] From a position safely distant from the pinnacle of U.S. authority in the Oval Office, Under Secretary of Defense for Policy Walter Slocombe growled back that China would face "incalculable consequences" if it attacked Taiwan.[47]

Sometimes it is even prudent to use a representative who is not in the government at all. During the 2000 crisis it was diplomatically difficult for China and Taiwan officials to meet face-to-face, so, apparently, Jeremy Stone, president of the American Federation of Scientists and a close friend of Taiwan's new president, was used as an intermediary. Stone, who also has a diplomatic background in arms control, visited President-elect Chen in Taiwan. He then flew to Beijing as an "unofficial representative of Taipei," according to one Chinese official. "What we're trying to do is find ways to communicate," explained a Taiwanese source.[48]

During the diplomacy surrounding Taiwan's presidential election in 2000, China was alarmed by the seemingly pro-independence stance of Taiwanese presidential candidate Chen Shui-bian. By threatening war if Taiwan declared itself an independent state, China hoped to frighten the Taiwanese into defeating Chen. Some Taiwanese, including the man holding this sign, were intimidated and probably voted against Chen. Many other citizens of Taiwan were not worried. Chen won the election.

Using Coercion or Rewards to Gain Agreement

Yet another diplomatic choice is whether to brandish coercive sticks or proffer tempting carrots. To induce an opponent to react as you wish, is it better to offer rewards or to threaten punishment?

Coercive diplomacy can be effective when you have the power, will, and credibility to back it up. Verbal threats and military maneuvering were central to the diplomatic interplay among the United States, North Korea, and the other countries embroiled in the 1993–1994 confrontation. Perhaps because it was the weaker side, North Korea was particularly bombastic. Its main newspaper, *Rodong Sinmum*, declared that if "war breaks out," the "reactionaries" would be "digging their own grave."[49] Given the long and bloody Korean War (1950–1953) and North Korea's considerable military might, such rhetoric was believable. There was a consensus, one Pentagon source put it, that "it's going to be a bloody, bloody mess if [war] happens. A real tragedy."[50] The United States and its allies also practiced coercive diplomacy. They threatened economic sanctions and at least refused to rule out military action. After Pyongyang refused to allow inspections, a stern U.S. official announced, "This time the North went too far. There are no more carrots."[51]

There are also a number of drawbacks to coercive diplomacy. If it does not work, then those who have threatened force face an unhappy choice. On the one hand, not carrying out threats creates an image of weakness that may well embolden the opponent in the crisis at hand. Opponents in other ongoing and future confrontations may also be encouraged. On the other hand, putting one's military might and money where one's mouth is costs lives and dollars and is not necessarily successful either. Even if coercion does work, it may entail a long-term commitment that was not originally planned or desired. The war with Iraq ended in February 1991, but U.S. forces have remained enmeshed in the region, have been on the verge of renewed war with Iraq on several occasions, and have spent many billions of dollars patrolling the region.

There are many times when *offers of rewards* may be a more powerful inducement than coercion. Threats may lead to war, with high costs and uncertain results. It may also be possible to "buy" what you cannot "win." One song in the movie *Mary Poppins* includes the wisdom that "a spoonful of sugar helps the medicine go down," and an increase in aid, a trade concession, a state visit, or some other tangible or symbolic reward may induce agreement. The incentive approach was evident during the negotiations with Iraq in 1998. In February 1998 the UN Security Council agreed to allow Iraq to increase to $5.2 billion the amount of oil it could sell every six months to pay for food and medical care. Secretary-General Annan also appealed to Iraq and its president, Saddam Hussein, through positive statements. Annan publicly praised the Iraqi leadership for its "courage, wisdom, flexibility." It was "homage to Saddam," according to one UN diplomat, and it brought down a torrent of criticism on the secretary-general from those who favored a hard-line approach.[52] Still, in the end, the carrots that Annan offered played a role in resolving the immediate crisis peacefully.

Often, the best diplomacy mixes carrots and sticks (O'Reilly, 1997). In contrast to the mixture of carrots and sticks that resolved the crisis with Iraq in 1998, U.S. diplomacy during the 1990–1991 Persian Gulf crisis offered virtually no positive incentives to Iraq. President Bush declared that "Iraq will not be permitted to annex Kuwait. That's not a threat, not a boast. That's just the way it's going to be." Some commentators criticized what they saw as a one-sided approach. In an article entitled "For Saddam, Where's the Carrot?" Roger Fisher, coauthor of the book on bargaining, *Getting to Yes*, argued that coercion was "barely half" of what was needed to resolve the crisis. He maintained that the United States should be "building a golden bridge for Saddam's retreat" and contended that Bush had erred by increasing the level of threat without providing simultaneous positive signs of what would happen if Iraq withdrew.[53]

Being Precise or Being Intentionally Vague

Most diplomatic experts stress the importance of being precise when communicating. There are times, however, when purposeful vagueness may be in order.

Precision is a hallmark of diplomacy. Being precise in both written and verbal communications helps avoid misunderstandings. It can also indicate true commitment, especially if it comes from the national leader. At times, however, *vagueness* may be a better strategy. Being vague may paper over irreconcilable differences. "The Saudis have a nice way of doing things" when they do not wish to agree, says one U.S. official. "They say, 'we'll consider it.' It is not their style to say no."[54] Lack of precision also can allow a country to retreat if necessary or permit it to avoid being too provocative. During the Taiwan elections in 1996 and 2000, the United States accomplished both goals by refusing to say exactly what it would do if China attacked Taiwan. When in 1996 a reporter asked Secretary of State Warren Christopher what would occur, he pushed aside the possibility of a Sino-American war as mere "operational details."[55]

Communicating by Word or Deed

Diplomacy utilizes both words and actions to communicate. Each method has its advantages. *Oral and written communications*, either direct or through public diplomacy, are appropriate for negotiations and also can be a good signaling strategy. They can establish positions at a minimum cost and are more apt to maintain flexibility than active signaling. Sometimes communications can even be indirect. After many years of hostile relations since the seizure of the U.S. embassy in 1979, Iran and the United States have been cautiously probing better relations. Observers considered it very significant when the President of Iran, Ayatollah Mohammad Khatami, agreed to an interview on CNN and made a number of conciliatory remarks about the United States. "When the President of Iran, a country with whom we've had a very bad relationship for a long time, gets on CNN and addresses the American people... and says he regrets the hostage-taking [and seizure of the U.S. embassy in 1979] and talks about America as a great civilization..., it is an indication to us that he's interested in breaking down this distrust and finding a way to engage with us," a U.S official observed.[56]

Signaling by action is often more dramatic than verbal signaling and it has its uses. Some signals can be fairly low level. The Clinton administration in 2000 signaled its displeasure with China's threats by, among other things, threatening to sell advanced warships to Taipei. Beijing objected that the move would inflate "the arrogance of the separatist forces in Taiwan."[57] A U.S. spokesperson signaled to China how it could avoid the sale by commenting, "The greater the threat posed by China, the greater Taiwan's defensive needs will be."[58] China moderated its tune; the ships were not sent.

Other actions can be stronger, but they are perilous because it is harder to retreat from dramatic deeds than from words or even subtle acts. When, in 1961, the East Germans and Soviets threatened to blockade Berlin, President John F. Kennedy took the risky step of going there and, before a throng of West Berliners, proclaimed himself a symbolic fellow citizen. "*Ich bin ein Berliner*," Kennedy's words rang out. Both sides understood the import of the president's putting his personal honor on the line, and the crisis eased. Germans on both sides of the Wall also got a good chuckle, because the president's speech writers had made a minor grammatical error. "*Ich bin Berliner*" (I am a Berliner) is what he had wanted to say. By adding the "*ein*," however, Kennedy had inadvertently changed the meaning of Berliner from citizen to jelly doughnut, locally called a berliner. Thus what the leader of the free world actually declared was "I am a jelly doughnut."[59]

Various military actions, ranging from alerting forces, through deploying them, to limited demonstrations of force, can also be effective (albeit perilous) signals. Such maneuvers were especially evident during the Taiwan imbroglio in 1996. Just before the election in Taiwan, Beijing announced that it was going to "conduct joint ground, naval, and air exercises in and over a sea area near Taiwan."[60] This demonstration of military might included, among other things, China's firing six powerful missiles into the seas near Taiwan's two major ports, Kaohsiung and Keelung. Chinese television showed the launch of the M-9 and M-11 missiles, which can carry nuclear or conventional warheads. As breathlessly described by the Chinese narrator, "Milky-white missiles were seen deployed, nested in a mountain range. Officers and men were in full battle array. In the middle of the night, the command post issued the orders of operation. Amid the uproar of the launch came the reports: 'The first missile hits the target, the second missile hits the target.'"[61]

For its part, the United States responded to the implied Chinese threat by utilizing its aircraft carriers. President Clinton ordered a major naval flotilla, centered around the carriers USS *Nimitz* and USS *Independence*, into the waters off Taiwan. The commanding admiral of the U.S. Seventh Fleet explained that "we do not want to see an escalation. China has said [it is] not going to attack Taiwan, and that's exactly what we want to see happen."[62]

Linking Issues or Treating Them Separately

A persistent dispute is whether a country should deal with other countries on an issue-by-issue basis or link issues together as a basis for a general orientation toward the other country. Advocates of *linking issues* argue that it is inappropriate to have normal relations on some matters with regimes that are hostile and repressive. Those who favor *treating issues separately* claim that doing so allows progress on some issues and keeps channels of communications and influence open.

During the crisis in 2000, China's stand on Taiwan became enmeshed with the fate of China's permanent normal trade relations with the United States and with China's admission to the WTO. A Chinese foreign ministry official objected that his country "firmly opposes any attempt to link these issues," and claimed that China's stand on Taiwan and "the issue of normal trade relations [are] two entirely separate issues."[63] That protest was in vain, however, and the issues remained tied together.

On a more general basis, linkage remains an ongoing and inconsistent issue in U.S. foreign policy. President Clinton argued that China's poor human rights record and authoritarian form of government should not be linked to China's trade status. One reason to delink the issues, according to Clinton, was that regular interaction would be a "force for change in China, exposing China to our ideas and ideals." The president also argued that "our engagement with China serves American interests.... [by promoting] stability in Asia, preventing the spread of weapons of mass destruction, combating international crime and drug trafficking, [and] protecting the environment."[64] Not mentioned, but a factor, were the billions of dollars in U.S. exports and investments that go to China.

Cuba has been another matter, though, and delinking issues has not extended to that country. There are a number of U.S. measures, including the Helms-Burton Act (1996), that institute economic sanctions on Cuba and foreign companies doing business with Cuba in an attempt to weaken the government of President Fidel Castro. Why delinking would promote change in China and not in Cuba remains unexplained.

Maximizing or Minimizing a Dispute

Diplomats face a choice over whether to put a confrontation in a broad or narrow context. The advantage of maximizing a dispute by invoking national survival, world peace, or some other major principle is that it increases credibility. During the 1996 Taiwan Strait crisis, China maximized the stakes by having the country's second-ranking official, Premier Li Peng, publicly depict the matter as a "core principle" involving China's "territorial integrity and the cause of reunification."[65]

Yet the advantages of *minimizing a dispute* were also evident in both the Taiwan crises. To ease the crisis in 2000, Chinese officials in March seemed to disavow a policy paper issued in February that escalated tension by declaring for the first time that "all drastic measures" would be used if Taipei refused "indefinitely" to rejoin the mainland. Responding to the furor, China's deputy prime minister reassuringly said on television that the document merely "reiterates the government's consistent stance" and that, "some foreign media have regarded China as making a major change to its policy on the Taiwan issue. This is incorrect."[66]

The United States also sought to minimize the dispute. "We will continue to insist that the Taiwanese... not seek independence," Secretary of Defense William S. Cohen told reporters during the confrontation in 2000.[67] Washington was also careful to downplay any U.S. military threat to China. "Our decision to deploy naval forces to the region was one with the intent to defuse tension, not to raise tension," a senior White House official publicly assured China and the world in 1996.[68]

A final note is that despite the recitation of diplomatic rules and analysis of the advantages and disadvantages of various diplomatic options in the preceding two sections, there is no substitute for skill and wisdom. Understanding how the game ought to be played does not always produce a win on the playing field of sports or a success at the negotiating table of diplomacy. Certainly you are advantaged if you know the fundamentals, but beyond that, individual capacity and field savvy provide the margin of victory.

CHAPTER SUMMARY

1. National diplomacy is the process of trying to advance a country's national interest by applying power assets to attempt to persuade other countries to give way.

2. Power is the foundation of diplomacy in a conflictual world. National power is the sum of a country's assets that enhance its ability to get its way even when opposed by others with different interests and goals.

3. Measuring power is especially difficult. The efforts to do so have not been very successful, but they do help us see many of the complexities of analyzing the characteristics of power. These characteristics include the facts that power is dynamic, both objective and subjective, relative, situational, and multidimensional.

4. The major elements of a country's power can be roughly categorized as those that constitute (1) its national core, (2) its national infrastructure, (3) its national economy, and (4) its military. The core and infrastructure are discussed here and form the basis for economic and military power, which are analyzed in later chapters.

5. The national core consists of a country's geography, its people, and its government.

6. The national infrastructure consists of a country's technological sophistication, its transportation system, and its information and communications capabilities.

7. The functions of diplomacy include advancing the national interest through such methods as observing and reporting, negotiating, symbolically representing, intervening, and propagandizing.

8. Diplomacy does not occur in a vacuum. Instead it is set in the international system, in a specific diplomatic environment (hostile, adversarial, coalition, and mediation diplomacy), and in a domestic context.

9. Diplomacy is an ancient art, and some of the historical functions of diplomacy are still important. Diplomacy, however, has also changed dramatically during the past century. Seven characteristics describe the new approach to diplomacy: expanded geographic scope, multilateral diplomacy, parliamentary maneuvering, democratized diplomacy, open diplomacy, leader-to-leader communications through summit meetings, and public diplomacy.

10. These changes reflect the changes in the international system and in domestic political processes. Some of the changes have been beneficial, but others have had negative consequences. At the least, diplomacy has become more complex with the proliferation of actors and options. It has also become more vital, given the possible consequences should it fail.

11. Diplomacy is a communication process that has three main elements. The first is negotiating through direct or indirect discussions between two or more countries. The second is signaling. The third is public diplomacy.

12. Good diplomacy is an art, but it is not totally freestyle, and there are general rules that increase the chances for diplomatic success. Among the cautions are to be realistic, to be careful about what you say, to seek common ground, to try to understand the other side, to be patient, and to leave open avenues of retreat.

13. There are also a wide variety of approaches or options in diplomacy. Whether contacts should be direct or indirect, what level of contact they should involve, what rewards or coercion should be offered, how precise or vague messages should be, whether to communicate by message or deed, whether issues should be linked or dealt with separately, and the wisdom of maximizing or minimizing a dispute are all questions that require careful consideration.

CHAPTER 11

INTERNATIONAL LAW AND MORALITY: THE ALTERNATIVE APPROACH

Which is the wiser here, Justice or Iniquity?

Shakespeare, *Measure for Measure*

The law hath not been dead, though it hath slept.

Shakespeare, *Hamlet*

I establish law and justice in the land.

Hammurabi, king of Babylon, circa 2100 B.C.

Power not ruled by law is a menace.

Arthur J. Goldberg, U.S. Supreme Court justice

CHAPTER OBJECTIVES

After completing this chapter, you should be able to:

- Discuss the dynamic nature of law by addressing the concept of a primitive but evolving legal system.
- Evaluate the effectiveness of international law.
- Distinguish between the different sources of international law.
- Discuss the role of morality in the international system and in international law.
- Understand the four essential elements of the international legal system.
- Identify and examine the roots and characteristics of international law.
- Discuss adherence to international law.
- Describe the process of adjudication in international law.
- Enumerate problems in applying international law to different cultures.
- Identify the international legal issues that have developed during the twentieth century and explain how changes in the world system have affected these issues.
- Illustrate how and why international law has been applied increasingly to individuals rather than only to states.
- Examine issues of morality in the modern international legal system and the role of morality in a future system.

The focus of this chapter is the notion that world politics can be conducted with a greater emphasis on following international law and attempting to ensure justice. This is an alternative approach to national diplomacy and its power-based pursuit of self-interest discussed in the last chapter. It would be naive to think that the actors in any system would not be motivated in significant part by what is good for themselves. Most individuals and groups in domestic political systems emphasize their own welfare, just as states do in the international system. There are differences, however, in how domestic and international systems work. What is of interest here is the way domestic systems, compared to the international system, restrain the pursuit of self-interest.

Legal systems are one thing that helps limit the role of pure power in a domestic system. The Fourteenth Amendment to the U.S. Constitution, for example, establishes "the equal protection of the laws" as a fundamental principle. Certainly, powerful individuals and groups have distinct advantages in every domestic system. Rules are broken and the guilty, especially if they can afford a high-priced attorney, sometimes escape punishment. Still, in the United States, laws cannot overtly discriminate and an attorney is provided to indigent defendants in criminal cases. Thus, the law evens the playing field, at least sometimes.

Morality is a second thing that restrains the role of power in domestic systems. We are discussing what is "right" here, not just what is legal. Whether the word is moral, ethical, fair, or just, there is a greater sense in domestic systems than there is in the international system that appropriate codes of conduct exist, that the ends do not always justify the means, and that those who violate the norms should suffer penalties. Surely, there is no domestic system in which everyone acts morally toward everyone else. Yet the sense of morality and justice that citizens in stable domestic systems have does have an impact on their behavior.

Most importantly, what all this means is that politics does not have to work just one way. There are alternatives. *Idealists* envision and prescribe a system of international law that covers more and more aspects of international interchange and that contains strong mechanisms to resolve disputes and enforce the law. *Realists* do not believe that this goal is attainable and suspect that national states will follow the dictates of national interest, ignore the law, and act in a self-serving way, especially on national security and other vital matters. Idealists reply that they are not so foolish as to imagine a perfect world, only a better one.

FUNDAMENTALS OF INTERNATIONAL LAW AND MORALITY

What actors may and may not legitimately do is based in both international and domestic law systems on a combination of expectations, rules, and practices that help govern behavior. We explore the fundamental nature of these legal systems and moral codes by looking first at the primitive nature, growth, and current status of international law; then by turning to issues of morality (Ku & Diehl, 1998).

THE PRIMITIVE NATURE OF INTERNATIONAL LAW

No legal system, domestic or international, emerges full blown. Each one grows, advancing from a primitive level to ever more sophisticated levels. As such, any legal system can be placed on an evolutionary scale ranging from primitive on one end to modern on the other. Note that modern does not mean finished; people in the future may shake their heads in disbelief over how rudimentary current legal systems are. This is speculative, but what is certain is that the concept of a *primitive but evolving legal system* is important to understanding international law.

The current international legal system falls toward the primitive end of the evolutionary scale of legal systems. First, as a primitive law system, the international system does not have a formal rule-making, or legislative, process. Instead, codes of behavior are derived from custom or from explicit agreements among two or more societal members or groups. Second, there is little or no established authority to judge or punish violations of law. Primitive societies, domestic or international, have no police or courts. Moreover, a primitive society is often made up of self-defined units (such as kinship groups), is territorially based, primarily governs itself, and resorts to violent "self-help" in relations with other groups.

Viewing international law as a primitive legal system has two benefits. One is that we can see that international law does exist, even if it is not as developed as we might wish. The second benefit is that it encourages us with the thought that international society and its law may evolve to a higher order.

THE GROWTH OF INTERNATIONAL LAW

The beginning of international law coincides with the origins of the state. As sovereign, territorial states arose, they needed to define and protect their status and to order their relations. Gradually, along with the state-based political system, elements of ancient Jewish, Greek, and Roman practice combined with newer Christian concepts and also with custom and practice to form most of the rudiments of the prevailing international system of law (Van Dervort, 1997).

A number of important theorists built on this foundation. The most famous of these was the Dutch thinker Hugo Grotius (1583–1645), whose study *De Jure Belli et Pacis* (On the Law of War and Peace) earned him the title "father of international law." Grotius and others discussed and debated the sources of international law, its role in regulating the relations of states, and its application to specific circumstances such as the justification and conduct of war and the treatment of subjugated peoples. From this base, international law expanded and changed slowly over the intervening centuries, as the interactions between the states grew and the expectations of the international community became more sophisticated.

It has been during the last century or so, however, that the most rapid expansion by far of concern with international law and its practical importance has occurred. Increasing international interaction and interdependence have significantly expanded the need for rules to govern a host of functional areas such as trade, finance, travel, and communications (Armstrong, 1999). Similarly, our awareness of our ability to destroy ourselves and our environment and of the suffering of victims of human rights abuses has led to lawmaking treaties on such subjects as genocide, nuclear testing, use of the oceans, and human rights. Even the most political of all activities, war and other aspects of national security, have increasingly become the subject of international law. Aggressive war, for example, is outside the pale of the law. The UN's response of authorizing sanctions and then force against Iraq after it invaded Kuwait reflected, in part, a genuine global rejection of aggression (Linklater, 1999).

THE PRACTICE OF INTERNATIONAL LAW

One of the charges that realists make against international law is that it exists only in theory, not in practice. As evidence, critics cite ongoing, largely unpunished examples of "lawlessness" such as war and human rights abuses. The flaw in this argument is that it does not prove its point. In the first place, international law *is* effective in many areas. As one scholar notes, "the reality as demonstrated through their behavior is that states do accept international law as law, and, even more significant, in the vast majority of instances they... obey it" (Joyner, 2000:243). Furthermore, the fact that law does not cover *all* problem areas and that it is not *always* followed does not disprove its existence. There is, after all, a substantial crime rate in the United States, but does that mean there is no law?

International law is *most effective* in governing the rapidly expanding range of transnational **functional relations**. Functional interactions are those that involve "low politics," a term that designates such things as trade, diplomatic rules, and communications.

International law is *least effective* when applied to "high-politics" issues such as national security relations between sovereign states. When vital interests are involved, governments still regularly bend international law to justify their actions rather than alter their actions to conform to the law.

This does not mean, however, that the law never influences political decisions. To the contrary, there is a growing sensitivity to international legal standards, especially insofar as they reflect prevailing international norms. Both international law and world values, for instance, are strongly opposed to states unilaterally resorting to war except in self-defense. Violations such as Iraq's invasion of Kuwait still occur, but they are met with mounting global condemnation and even counterforce. Now even countries as powerful as the United States regularly seek UN authorization to act in cases such as Haiti in 1994, when not long ago they would have acted on their own initiative.

THE FUNDAMENTALS OF INTERNATIONAL MORALITY

As with international law, it would be equally erroneous to overestimate the impact of morality on the conduct of states or to dismiss the part that morality plays. As one scholar notes, "Contrary to what the skeptics assert, norms do indeed matter. But norms do not necessarily matter in the ways or often to the extent that their proponents have argued" (Legro, 1997:31).

Concepts of moral behavior may stem from religious beliefs, from secular ideologies or philosophies, from the standard of equity (what is fair), or from the practice of a society. We will see in our discussion of roots of international law that what a society considers moral behavior sometimes becomes law. At other times, legal standards are gradually adopted by a society as moral standards. Insofar as moral behavior remains an imperative of conscience rather than law, we can consider morality in a broad sense. There are distinctions that can be made between moral, ethical, and humanitarian standards and behavior, but for our purposes here, the three terms—morals, ethics, and humanitarianism—are used interchangeably.

It would be madness—given recurring war, gnawing human deprivation, persistent human rights violations, and debilitating environmental abuse—to imagine that morality is a predominant global force. Yet moral considerations do play a role in world politics (Frost, 1996). Even more important, there is a growing body of ethical norms that help determine the nature of the international system. Progress is slow and inconsistent, but it exists. The UN–authorized force did not drop nuclear weapons on Iraq in 1991, even though it arguably could have saved time, money, and the lives of Americans and their allies by doing so. Many countries give foreign aid to less developed countries. National leaders, not just philosophers and clergy, regularly discuss and sometimes even make decisions based on human rights. Consumers have rallied to the environmentalist cause to protect dolphins by purchasing only cans of tuna on which dolphin-safe logos are featured.

The reality is that world politics operates neither in a legal vacuum nor in a moral void. To understand the current course of world interactions and events we will turn in the following pages to an examination of the international legal system and then to a discussion of the application of law and morality in the international system.

THE INTERNATIONAL LEGAL SYSTEM

International law, like any legal system, is based on four critical considerations: the philosophical roots of law, how laws are made, when and why the law is obeyed (adherence), and how legal disputes are decided (adjudication).

THE PHILOSOPHICAL ROOTS OF LAW

Before considering the mechanics of the legal system, it is important to inquire into the roots of law. Ideas about what is right and what should be the law do not spring from thin air. Rather, they are derived from sources both external and internal to the society that they regulate.

External Sources Some laws come from sources external to a society. The idea here is that some higher, metaphysical standard of conduct should govern the affairs of humankind. An important ramification of this position is that there is or ought to be one single system of law that governs all people.

Those who believe in the external sources can be subdivided into two schools. The **ideological/theological school of law** is one. This school of thought holds that law is derived from an overarching ideology or theology. For instance, a substantial part of international legal theory extends back to early Western proponents of international law who relied on Christian doctrine for their standards. The writings of Saint Augustine and Saint Thomas Aquinas on the law of war are examples. There are also elements of long-standing Islamic, Buddhist, and other religions' law and scholarship that serve as a foundation for just international conduct.

The **naturalist school of law** relies on a second source of external principles. This view holds that humans, by nature, have certain rights and obligations. The English philosopher, John Locke, argued in *Two Treatises of Government* (1690) that there is "a law of nature" that "teaches all mankind, who will but consult it, that all [people] being equal and independent [in the state of nature], no one ought to harm another in his life, health, liberty, or possessions." Since countries are collectives of individuals, and the world community is a collective of states and individuals, natural law's rights and obligations also apply to the global stage and form the basis for international law.

Critics of the theory of external sources of law contend that standards based on ideology or theology can lead to oppression. The problems with natural law, critics charge, are both that it is vague and that it contains such an emphasis on individualism that it almost precludes any sense of communitarian welfare. If a person's property is protected by natural law, then, for instance, it is hard to justify taking any individual's property through taxes levied by the government without the individual's explicit agreement.

Internal Sources Some legal scholars reject the idea of divine or naturalist roots and, instead, focus on the customs and practices of society. This is the **positivist school of law,**

International law is not abstract. Just like the outlaws of old American western movies, many of the Serbs who committed war crimes in Bosnia in the early 1990s have found their faces on reward posters. The three wanted men on this poster in Sarajevo, Bosnia, have been indicted for war crimes by the international tribunal in The Hague, the Netherlands. They are Yugoslavia's former president, Slobodan Milosevic, who is a Serb (top); Radovan Karadzic, the Bosnian Serbs' political leader (lower left); and General Ratko Mladic, the commander of the Bosnian Serb army (lower right). The reward is "5 million American dollars." Anyone with information is instructed to contact the U.S. Department of State.

CORRUPTION AND INTERNATIONAL LAW

The growing global movement against corruption is one way to see the sources and evolution of positivist international law. The growth of economic interdependence has made corruption increasingly intolerable to those doing business across international borders. International financial agencies such as the World Bank are also critical of corruption because it hinders development (Elliot, 1997).

At the heart of the movement against corruption is a relatively new international nongovernmental organization (NGO) called Transparency International (TI). It was founded in 1993, has its headquarters in Berlin, Germany, has national chapters in 78 countries, and is financed mainly by governmental agencies (like the U.S. Agency for International Development, USAID), and by corporations (such as General Electric). The Advisory Council of TI includes such luminaries as former president of Costa Rica and Nobel Peace Prize laureate Oscar Arias Sánchez and former U.S. president Jimmy Carter. According to its Web page (http://www.transparency.de/index.html), TI "is a non-governmental organization dedicated to increasing accountability and curbing both international and national... corruption."

Perhaps TI's most effective public relations tool is the annual Corruption Perception Index that it began publishing in 1994. According to TI chairman, Peter Eigen, a former World Bank official, the index measures "how business people around the globe perceive levels of corruption."[1] The results of the 1999 index, which scored 99 countries from 0 (most corrupt) to 10 (least corrupt), found Cameroon (1.5) to be the world's most corrupt country. Being labeled one of the world's most corrupt places brings responses ranging from outrage to a kind of grim humor. After the 1997 survey, which ranked Nigeria and Pakistan the most corrupt and second most corrupt countries, one Pakistani quipped, "Actually we were number one, but we bribed the Nigerians to take first place."[2] Denmark finished best in 1999 with a perfect 10. The United States (7.5) came in eighteenth.

TI has been able to move the issue of corruption onto the international political and legal agenda. For example, the Organization for Economic Cooperation and Development (OECD), which includes the world's economically developed countries (EDCs) and a number of other countries, adopted in 1997 the Convention on Combating Bribery of Foreign Public Officials in International Business Transactions. The 21 countries that have ratified the treaty so far agree to a number of steps, such as passing national laws to, among other things, end the ability to take tax deductions for bribes paid in international business transactions. There is also now a periodic International Anti-Corruption Conference. The 1999 meeting, which was held in Durban, South Africa, drew over 1,600 delegates from 135 countries and the 2001 meeting is scheduled to convene in Prague, Czech Republic.

It is too early to predict exactly the degree to which corrupt practices will become the subject of international law, but the activities of TI are arguably part of the genesis of turning what not long ago was an exclusive concern of national law into a matter of international law.

which advocates that law reflects society and the way people want that society to operate. Therefore, according to positivist principles, law is and ought to be the product of the codification or formalization of a society's standards.

Critics condemn the positivist approach as amoral and sometimes immoral, in that it may legitimize immoral, albeit common, beliefs and behavior of a society as a whole or of its dominant class. These critics would say, for instance, that slavery was once widespread and widely accepted, but it was never moral or lawful, by the standards of either divine principle or natural law.

HOW INTERNATIONAL LAW IS MADE

Countries usually make domestic law through a constitution (constitutional law) or by a legislative body (statutory law). In practice, law is also established through judicial decisions (interpretation), which set guidelines (precedent) for later decisions by the courts. Less influential sources of law are custom (common law), and what is fair (equity).

Compared to its domestic equivalent, modern international lawmaking is much more decentralized. There are, according to the Statute of the International Court of Justice, four sources of law: international treaties, international custom, the general principles of law, and judicial decisions and scholarly legal writing. Some students of international law would tentatively add a fifth source: resolutions and other pronouncements of the UN General Assembly. These five rely primarily on the positivist approach but, like domestic law, include elements of both external and internal sources of law.

International Treaties Treaties are the primary source of international law. A primary advantage of treaties is that they **codify,** or write down, the law. Agreements between states are binding according to the doctrine of **pacta sunt servanda** (treaties are to be served/carried out). All treaties are binding on those countries that are party to them (have signed and ratified or otherwise given their legal consent). Moreover, it is possible to argue that some treaties are also applicable to nonsignatories. Multilateral treaties, those signed by more than two states, are an increasingly important source of

international law. When a large number of states agree to a principle, that norm begins to take on system-wide legitimacy. The 1948 Convention on the Prevention and Punishment of the Crime of Genocide, for example, has been ratified by most states. Some would argue, therefore, that genocide has been "recognized" and "codified" as a violation of international law and that this standard of conduct is binding on all states regardless of whether or not they have formally agreed to the treaty. Now people are being tried, convicted, and sentenced for genocide, as we shall discuss presently.

International Custom The second most important source of international law is custom. The old, and now supplanted, rule that territorial waters extend three miles from the shore grew from the distance a cannon could fire. If you were outside the range of land-based artillery, then you were in international waters. Maritime rules of the road and diplomatic practice are two other important areas of law that grew out of custom. Sometimes, long-standing custom is eventually codified in treaties. An example is the Vienna Convention on Diplomatic Relations of 1961, which codified many existing rules of diplomatic standing and practice.

General Principles of Law The ancient Roman concept of *jus gentium* (the law of peoples) is the foundation of the general principles of law. By this standard, the International Court of Justice (ICJ) applies "the general principles of law recognized by civilized nations." Although such language is vague, it has its benefits. It encompasses "external" sources of law, such as the idea that freedom of religion and freedom from attack are among the inherent rights of people. More than any other standard, it was these general principles that Iraq's aggression in 1990 violated. Even if he was being hyperbolic, U.S. secretary of state James Baker's worry that "if might is to make right, then the world will be plunged into a new dark age" catches something of the international reaction.[1] The principle of *equity*, what is fair when no legal standard exists, also has some application under general principles.

Judicial Decisions and Scholarly Writing In many domestic systems, legal interpretations by courts set precedent according to the doctrine of *stare decisis* (let the decision stand). This doctrine is specifically rejected in Article 59 of the Statute of the International Court of Justice, but as one scholar points out, "The fact is that all courts... rely upon and cite each other [as precedent] abundantly in their decisions" (Levi, 1991:50). Thus, the rulings of the ICJ, other international tribunals, and even domestic courts

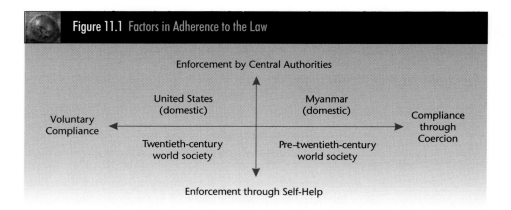

Figure 11.1 Factors in Adherence to the Law

Two crucial factors in international law are how the law is enforced and what encourages compliance. These factors differ over time and for different societies.

when they apply international law, help shape the body of law that exists. Judicial review is another possible role of international judicial bodies, and one that is exercised by many domestic courts. This is a court's authority to rule on whether the actions of the executive and legislative branches violate the constitution or other charter under which the court operates. The European Court of Justice has exercised that authority, and some scholars believe that the ICJ is moving cautiously toward a similar stand.

International Representative Assemblies The preceding four sources of international law are generally recognized. The idea that laws can come from the UN General Assembly or any other international representative assembly is much more controversial. Clearly, to date, international law is nonlegislative. The General Assembly cannot legislate international law the way that a national legislature does. Yet, UN members are bound by treaty to abide by some of the decisions of the General Assembly and the Security Council, which makes these bodies quasi-legislative. Some scholars contend that those resolutions that are approved by overwhelming majorities of the General Assembly's nearly universal membership constitute international law. The reasoning here is that such votes reflect international custom and/or the general principles of law and, therefore, they subtly enter the stream of international law. We may, then, be seeing the beginnings of legislated international law, but, at best, it is in its genesis. Certainly, UN resolutions and mandates are often not followed, but some would argue that this means that the law is being violated rather than that the law does not exist.

ADHERENCE TO THE LAW

Adherence to the law is a third essential element of any legal system. What makes the law effective in any legal system is a mixture of compliance and enforcement. As Figure 11.1 represents, people obey the law because of a mixture of voluntary and coerced compliance, and they enforce the law through a mixture of enforcement by central authorities and enforcement through self-help (Hurd, 1999).

Compliance Obedience in any legal system—whether it is international or domestic, primitive or sophisticated—is based on a mix of voluntary compliance and coercion. *Voluntary compliance* occurs when the subjects obey the law because they accept its legitimacy. This means that people abide by rules because they accept the authority of the institution that made the rules (say, a legislature or a court) and/or agree that the rules are necessary to the reasonable conduct of society. *Coercion* is the process of gaining compliance through threats of violence, imprisonment, economic sanction, or other punishment.

Any society's legal system can be placed somewhere along the compliance scale between complete reliance on voluntary compliance and complete reliance on coercion. Voluntary compliance is usually more important, but the mixture of it and coercion varies widely among societies. Americans tend to obey the law voluntarily; in Myanmar (Burma) obedience to the laws of the country's military junta is primarily a function of force.

The overall degree of compliance to the law is lower in the international system than in most domestic systems, but insofar as adherence to international law has grown, it has been based more on voluntary compliance than on coercion. Legitimacy, based primarily on pragmatism, is the key to international voluntary compliance. Countries recognize the need for a system that is made predictable by adherence to laws. As we saw earlier, functional international law governing day-to-day relations between states has expanded rapidly because of their need to regulate complex international interactions such as trade, finance, communications, and diplomacy. Legitimacy based on norms is less well established, but it has also grown. Aggression, violation of human rights, and other unacceptable practices still occur, but they increasingly meet with widespread international and domestic condemnation. Unilateral military action is, for example, becoming ever more difficult for a country to launch without meeting severe criticism. The unilateral U.S. invasion of Panama in 1989, for example, was condemned by the United Nations and the Organization of American States as a violation of international law and the UN Charter. American leaders have also found that the public increasingly is adverse to unilateral military action. Recent U.S. presidents have found repeatedly that the public and Congress have been more averse to unilateral action than to intervention within the context of a multilateral force sanctioned by an international organization. As one study puts it, "the domestic salience of the United Nations and collective security may help to explain… [the current] U.S. reliance on the United Nations framework for action," in contrast to its earlier, often unilateral approach to military intervention (Cortell & Davis, 1996:472).

Enforcement In all legal systems, enforcement relies on a combination of *enforcement by central authorities* and *enforcement through self-help*. In more sophisticated legal systems, most enforcement relies on a central authority such as the police. Still, even the most sophisticated legal system recognizes the legitimacy of such self-help doctrines as self-defense. Primitive societies rely primarily on self-help and mediation to enforce laws and norms. As a primitive society evolves, it begins to develop enforcement authorities. Domestic systems have done this, and the international system is now just beginning to take this evolutionary path.

In the primitive international legal system, enforcement by central authorities has been slow to develop. Domestic societies rely on central authorities to provide law enforcement organizations (usually the police) and sanctions (fines, prison) to compel compliance with the law. Neither law enforcement organizations nor sanctions are well developed at the international level, but both have begun to evolve. International law continues to rely mainly on self-help to enforce adherence, as reflected in the UN Charter's recognition of national self-defense. There have been, however, instances of enforcement and the number is growing. War criminals were punished after World War II, and indictments have been handed down for war crimes in Bosnia. Economic and diplomatic sanctions are becoming more frequent and are sometimes successful. Armed enforcement by central authorities is even less common and sophisticated. The UN–authorized military action against Iraq (1991) and the NATO intervention in Kosovo in 1999 were more akin to an Old West sheriff authorizing posses to chase the outlaws than true police actions, but they did represent a step toward enforcement of international law by central authorities.

The International Court of Justice (ICJ)

J Countries with judges on the ICJ in 2000: Algeria, Brazil, China, France, Germany, Hungary, Japan, Jordan, Madagascar, the Netherlands, Russia, Sierra Leone, the United Kingdom, the United States, and Venezuela.

Countries involved in cases brought to, decided by, or pending before the ICJ, 1993–2000: Australia, Bahrain, Belgium, Bosnia-Herzegovina, Botswana, Burundi, Cameroon, Canada, Chad, Congo (Kinshasa), Croatia, Denmark, France, Germany, Guinea, Guinea-Bissau, Honduras, Hungary, Indonesia, Iran, Italy, Libya, Malaysia, Namibia, Nauru, New Zealand, Nicaragua, Nigeria, Norway, Portugal, Qatar, Rwanda, Senegal, Slovakia, Spain, Uganda, the United Kingdom, the United States, and Yugoslavia.

Countries both with ICJ judges in 2000 and involved in ICJ cases: France, Germany, Hungary, the United Kingdom, and the United States.

The International Court of Justice (ICJ), which sits in The Hague, the Netherlands, draws both its judges and its caseload from around the world. This map shows the home countries of the ICJ's 15 judges and the 39 countries involved in one or more cases before the ICJ during 1993–2000.

ADJUDICATION OF THE LAW

How a political system resolves disputes between its actors is a key element in its standing along the primitive-to-modern evolutionary scale. As primitive legal systems become more sophisticated, the method of settling disputes evolves from (1) primary reliance on *bargaining* between adversaries, through (2) *mediation/conciliation* by neutral parties, to (3) **adjudication** (and the closely related process of arbitration) by neutral parties. The international system of law is in the early stages of this developmental process and is just now developing the institutions and attitudes necessary for adjudication (Roht-Arriaza, 1999).

International Courts There are a number of international courts in the world today. The genesis of these tribunals extends back less than a century to the Permanent Court of

International courts are beginning to have greater importance. When Germany refused to allow Tanja Kreil to serve in an army combat position, she sued for sex discrimination in the European Court of Justice. The court found in Kreil's favor in January 2000, and Germany's military forces may soon have many more members that look like this Bundeswehr soldier. When the photo was taken she was barred from carrying arms; now she can.

International Arbitration established by the Hague Conference at the turn of the century. In 1922 the Permanent Court of International Justice (PCIJ) was created as part of the League of Nations, and in 1946 the current **International Court of Justice (ICJ)**, which is associated with the UN, evolved from the PCIJ. The ICJ, or so-called World Court, sits in The Hague, the Netherlands, and consists of 15 judges, who are elected to nine-year terms through a complex voting system in the UN. By tradition, each of the five permanent members of the UN Security Council has one judge on the ICJ, and the others are elected to provide regional representation, as is evident in the map on page 298.

In addition to the ICJ, there are a few regional courts of varying authority and levels of activity, including the European Court of Justice (ECJ), the European Court of Human Rights, the Inter-American Court of Human Rights, the Central American Court of Justice, and the Community Tribunal of the Economic Community of West African States. None of these has the authority of domestic courts, but like the ICJ, the regional courts are gaining more credibility. In 2000, for example, Tanja Kreil, a 23-year-old German woman, brought a case to ECJ seeking to overturn a German law that bars women from holding combat positions in the military. Germany argued that it was within its sovereign discretion to determine the composition of its armed forces, and Great Britain and Italy filed briefs supporting Germany's position.

In the end, it was Fräulein Kreil who prevailed. The court ruled that the German "national authorities could not... adopt the general position that the composition of all armed units in the Bundeswehr had to remain exclusively male."[2] The court also found historic discrimination against women in hiring and promotion stemming "from deep-rooted prejudices and from stereotypes" and declared that Germany must "restore the balance."[3] "It was... a very good discovery, the existence of this European court," said

Kreil, after the decision. "I used to think of myself as German. Now I feel a little European, too."[4]

Also, as with domestic courts, the mere existence of international courts sometimes has an impact by making people or governments change their behavior rather than face an adverse ruling. In one such instance, Great Britain established the age of consent at 16 for heterosexuals and 18 for homosexuals. Euan Sutherland, a 17-year-old British homosexual, sued in the ECJ, arguing that the differentiation of two years was discriminatory. Rather than contest a case the British would probably have lost, Prime Minister Tony Blair persuaded the House of Commons to lower the age of consent for homosexuals to 16. Great Britain's upper house of Parliament, the House of Lords, blocked the measure. One opponent, the Earl of Longford, reasoned that "A girl is not ruined for life by being seduced. A young fellow is." This logic escaped many. "Lord Longford is 92," wrote a columnist in *The Observer* of London, "but he acts like a man twice his age."[5] The issue remains unresolved, but in 2000 the House of Commons voted once again to equalize the age of consent, and British analysts consider it probable that this time the House of Lords will also approve the legislation.

Did You Know That:

When a lesbian couple recently sued the British government of Prime Minister Tony Blair in the European Court of Justice on the grounds of gender discrimination in the workplace, the plaintiffs' lawyer was Cherie Booth, Prime Minister Blair's wife. The court dismissed the complaint, ruling that the issue was not gender discrimination, which is against European Union law, but sexual-orientation discrimination, which is not barred.

Jurisdiction Although the creation of international tribunals during this century indicates progress, the concept of sovereignty remains a potent barrier to adjudication. The authority of the ICJ extends in theory to all international legal disputes. There are two ways that cases come before the ICJ. One is when states submit contentious issues between them. The second is when one of the organs or agencies of the UN asks the ICJ for an advisory opinion.

From 1946 through the present, the court has annually taken up only about two new contentious cases submitted by states or advisory cases involving issues submitted by organs of the United Nations. This is obviously relatively few cases, given the ICJ's broad jurisdiction and the number of issues facing the world and its countries. More than any other factor, the gap between the court's jurisdiction and its actual role is a matter of the willingness of states to submit to decisions of the ICJ. First, states must agree to be subject to the ICJ. Although all UN member-countries are technically parties to the ICJ statute, they must also sign the so-called *optional clause* agreeing to be subject to the compulsory jurisdiction of the ICJ. Many countries have not done so. For example, the court recently had to dismiss a case brought by Portugal against Indonesia because Jakarta is not a signatory of the optional clause.

Second, irrespective of their agreement to accept ICJ jurisdiction, countries can reject it or the court's decisions in specific cases. When, in 1984, Nicaragua filed a case with the ICJ charging that U.S. support of the Contra rebels and its mining of Nicaraguan harbors violated international law, the United States argued that the charges were political and, therefore, that the court had no jurisdiction. When the ICJ rejected the U.S. objections and decided to hear the case, the United States terminated its agreement to submit to the compulsory jurisdiction of the ICJ.

Third, even if countries are signatories of the optional clause, they can attach "reservations" to their agreement. While the United States was a party to the optional clause, for example, it reserved the right to reject ICJ jurisdiction in any "domestic matter... as determined by the United States." This is an extremely broad disclaimer and, in effect, means that the United States can reject ICJ jurisdiction on virtually any issue.

Fourth, in addition to jurisdiction, it is important to note that the ICJ has little power to enforce its decisions. While domestic courts rely heavily on the willingness of those within its jurisdiction to comply voluntarily, the courts are also usually backed up

One benefit of the International Court of Justice is that it allows countries to seek a judicial solution to disputes. Nicaragua and Honduras disagree over the maritime border between the two countries in the shrimp-rich Gulf of Fonseca. Each has seized the other's shrimp boats in the disputed waters, and the possibility of war between the two neighbors is represented here by the armed Honduran patrol near a buoy that Honduras claims (and Nicaragua denies) marks the boundary. Fortunately, the two countries decided that suing was preferable to shooting, and they have taken their case to the ICJ for resolution.

by powerful executive branches that can enforce decisions when necessary. By contrast, with the UN Secretariat as its executive branch, the ICJ does not have a source of strong support to back up its decisions.

Use and Effectiveness of International Courts Given the real limits on the jurisdiction of the ICJ and other international courts, it is tempting to write them off as having little more than symbolic value. Such a judgment would be in error. The ICJ, for instance, does play a valuable role. Its rulings help define and advance international law. Furthermore, the court can contribute by giving countries a way, short of war, to settle a dispute once diplomacy has failed. The current ICJ case between Nicaragua and Honduras over their maritime border provides a good example. In its complaint to the ICJ, Nicaragua argued that the "maritime Caribbean border with Honduras has not been determined." Honduras responded that "there in fact exists a delimitation line [established by] an [arbitration] award of... 1906 made by the King of Spain." Nicaragua's petition also pointed out that the dispute "has brought repeated confrontations and mutual capture of vessels of both nations in and around the general border area" and that "diplomatic negotiations have failed."[6] Throughout history, many land and maritime border disputes have resulted in failed diplomacy, in each side seizing the other's people and property, and in war. Without an ICJ to appeal to, that might have been the outcome of the boundary dispute between Nicaragua and Honduras. With an ICJ there is an alternative option that may well lead to a peaceful settlement.

Even when countries reject ICJ jurisdiction, the court's decisions may have some effect. In the Nicaragua versus United States case, discussed earlier, the court heard the case anyway and ruled in Nicaragua's favor. This decision gave a black eye to the United States in the court of world opinion and strengthened the U.S. domestic opponents of the Reagan administration's policy. The United States stopped mining Nicaragua's harbors.

The ICJ's advisory opinions also help resolve issues between IGOs and may even help establish general international law. In separate actions, the UN General Assembly and the World Health Organization each asked the ICJ to rule on the legality of using nuclear weapons (Matheson, 1997). The court ruled in 1996 that "the threat or use of nuclear weapons would generally be contrary to the rules of international law applicable in armed conflict," but went on to say that it was unable to "conclude definitively whether the threat or use of nuclear weapons would be lawful or unlawful in an extreme circumstance of self-defense, in which the very survival of a state would be at stake."[7] While the ICJ's ruling was not as all-encompassing as some antinuclear advocates hoped, the decision does put any leader considering the use of nuclear weapons except in extremis on notice that he or she could wind up the defendant in some future war crimes trial.

Finally, there is evidence that the willingness of countries to utilize the ICJ, the ECJ, and other international courts and to accept their decisions is slowly growing. The map of the ICJ's justices and cases on page 298 shows that countries around the world serve on the court and are party to its cases. Now more than 50 countries, including Canada and the United Kingdom, adhere to the optional clause giving the ICJ compulsory jurisdiction over their international legal disputes. It is true that the international judicial system is still primitive, but each of the more than 150 opinions issued by the PCIJ and the ICJ in the twentieth century is one more than the zero instances of international adjudication in previous centuries.

 # APPLYING INTERNATIONAL LAW AND MORALITY

Law and morality are easy to support in the abstract, but it is much more difficult to agree on how to apply them. To examine this, we will look at issues of cultural perspective, issues of applying international law and standards of morality equally to states and individuals, and issues of prudence.

LAW AND MORALITY: ISSUES OF CULTURAL PERSPECTIVE

As primitive political systems evolve and expand to incorporate diverse peoples, one problem that such legal systems encounter is the "fit" between differing culturally based concepts of law and morality. The evolving international system of law faces the same difficulty. Most of international law and many of the international standards of morality that currently exist and influence world politics are based on the concepts and practices of the West. This is a result of U.S. and European dominance, though, and does not mean that Western concepts are superior to those held in other parts of the world. Now, in a changing international system, Africans, Asians, Latin Americans, and other non-Westerners are questioning and sometimes rejecting law based on Western culture.

Western and Non-Western Perspectives

There are numerous points on which Western and non-Western precepts of law and morality differ. The *Western view* of law is based on principles designed to protect the long-dominant power of this bloc of states. Order is a primary point, as is sovereignty. Closely related is the theory of property, which holds that individuals (and states) have a "right" to accumulate and maintain property (wealth). This is a major philosophical underpinning of capitalism. Western law also relies heavily on the process and substance of law rather than on equity. Thus, there is an emphasis on courts and what the law is rather than on what is fair.

The *non-Western view* of international law is influenced by the different cultural heritage of non-Western states, by the recent independence of those states, and by the

Cultural differences make it difficult to resolve standards of legality and morality. Here you can see the father of a murdered boy using an assault rifle to execute his son's killer in Afghanistan. A court convicted the man and sentenced him to death, then immediately turned him over to the boy's family for execution. All this is shocking by Western standards. By Afghani cultural standards, the method of execution and how quickly it was carried out were justified. Was this a human rights violation?

history of exploitation their people have often suffered at the hands of the West. The newer, mostly non-Western, and mostly less developed countries (LDCs) claim that since they had little or no role in determining the rules that govern the international system, they are not bound by preexisting agreements, principles, or practices that work to their disadvantage. These countries support sovereignty and reject aspects of international law that they claim are imperialistic abridgments of that principle. They insist on noninterference and support, for example, the "Calvo Clause," named after Argentine diplomat and legal scholar Carlos Calvo, and enunciated in his book, *International Law of Europe and America in Theory and Practice* (1868). Even though it is well over a hundred years old, the clause can be found regularly in such documents as the 1996 amendments of Mexico's Foreign Investment Law. One part of the new language specifies, "In all cases relating to foreign investment... it is necessary for the investor to make a covenant, known as a 'Calvo Clause' [thereby agreeing]... to be (i) treated as a Mexican national (i.e., to accept the application of Mexican laws..., as well as to accept the jurisdiction of the Mexican courts), and (ii) renounce the right to invoke diplomatic intervention by such person's national government."[8]

The LDCs also reject weighted voting schemes, such as those in the UN Security Council, the World Bank, and the International Monetary Fund, that favor the rich and powerful. The LDCs often emphasize equity over the substance and process of law. For them, the important standard is fairness, especially in terms of economic maldistribution.

Moreover, Western and non-Western law and morality differ considerably on the *rights of the individual* versus the *rights of the community*. Imagine a scale that ranges, on one end, from a value system in which the rights of an individual are always more important than those of the community to, at the other end, a value system in which the good of the community always takes precedence over the good of the individual. Western states would generally fall toward the individualistic end of the scale; non-Western states would generally fall farther toward the communitarian end of the scale.

There is, for example, a long list of rights afforded in the United States to individuals accused and even convicted of crimes. Non-Western cultures tend to think this practice gives the society too little protection; they therefore favor a more communitarian approach to ordering their society. That perspective was expressed succinctly by Singapore's foreign minister, Shanmugam Jayakumar, who defended what Americans might see as draconian laws by explaining, "We believe that the legal system must give maximum protection to the majority of our people. We make no apology for clearly tilting our laws and policy in favor of the majority."[9]

What constitutes a human rights abuse and what is merely a matter of clashing cultural values has been a particular sore point between the United States and China. American criticism of China on a wide range of rights issues is reflected in the U.S. State Department's review of global human rights issued in 2000. It reported that in China, "Citizens lack both the freedom peacefully to express opposition to the Party-led political system and the right to change their national leaders or form of government." In sum, the report charged, China has "continued to commit widespread and well-documented human rights abuses, in violation of internationally accepted norms."[10]

China rejects such criticisms. In reality, one spokesperson contends, such human rights criticisms "arise largely from the fact that East and West have different conceptions of human rights. For Asians," the official continued, "human rights do not mean the privileges of the few but of the many."[11] Using its more communitarian standards, China also accuses the United States of its own range of human rights violations. "Human rights protection provided by the U.S. Constitution is very limited," a Chinese government report asserts. It notes, for instance, that in the United States there is no right to "food, clothing, shelter, education, work, rest, and reasonable payment." The report also criticizes widespread racism as "the darkest abyss in American society" and points out that democracy is limited because "running for office requires large sums of money."[12]

The Chinese communitarian view of human rights also tends to value order and social control, as reflected in the Chinese adage, *yi fang, jiu luan*, which means "as soon as control eases, there is chaos." Applying that adage to the 1989 massacre in Tiananmen Square, a Chinese diplomat argued recently that "the Chinese government was forced to take radical measures to maintain order and society's stability so that our economic development would not be interrupted."[13] Even to the degree that the Chinese government is willing to accommodate Western demands for reform, there is concern about adopting Western values, especially too quickly. This was evident in an exchange of aphorisms during one meeting between U.S. secretary of state Madeleine Albright and China's premier Zhu Rongji. Albright urged China to leap forward toward reform, telling Zhu, "You cannot cross an abyss by taking only two steps." The premier responded with the advice, "You don't get fat if you eat only one spoonful at a time."[14]

APPLYING INTERNATIONAL LAW AND MORALITY IN A MULTICULTURAL WORLD

Given the differences in perspective between cultures, the question arises as to whether it is reasonable to try to apply the standads of law and morality at all. Those who deny that any common principles exist contend that no single standard does (or, they suspect, can) exist, at least not without global cultural homogenization, and imposing that would be **cultural imperialism.** Chinese scholar Li Zhongcheng (1994:1) has, for instance, criticized the UN's Universal Declaration of Human Rights (1948) as a document that has only "affirmed the traditional dominant status of the basic Western liberalist concepts" and given "priority to [individual] civil and political rights" while ignoring collective "social and economic rights."

Others reject such claims as poor attempts to justify the unjustifiable. President Chandrika Kumaratunga of Sri Lanka, for one, has expressed the opinion that "of course, every country has its own national ethos, but... when people talk about a conflict of values, I think it is an excuse that can be used to cover a multitude of sins" (Franck, 1997:627). Seconding this view, Secretary-General Kofi Annan told an audience in Iran, there is "talk of human rights being a Western concept,... [but] don't we all suffer from the lack of the rule of law and from arbitrariness? What is foreign about that? What is Western about that? And when we talk of the right [of people]... to live their lives to the fullest and to be able to live their dreams, it is universal."[15]

APPLYING INTERNATIONAL LAW AND MORALITY TO STATES

Traditionally, the application of international law and of standards of moral behavior in the international system has focused primarily on states. The actions of individuals have not been subject to judgment. Now that is changing rapidly, as we shall see presently. This section will deal with states and, with regard to them, the first thing to address is whether states and individuals can be held to the same standards of law and morality. Then we can look at the specific issues of law and morality as they relate to states.

Should States Be Held to the Same Standards as Individuals?

It is common for states to act legitimately in ways that would be reprehensible for individuals. If you are in your country's air force and shoot down five enemy pilots, you are an "ace"; if you, as an individual, shoot five people, you are a mass murderer. Of course, we recognize differences between justifiable and inexcusable actions, but where do you draw the line? Some have argued that the state cannot be held to individual moral standards. Realist philosopher and statesman Niccolò Machiavelli wrote in *The Prince* (1517) that a ruler "cannot observe all those things which are considered good in men, being often obliged, in order to maintain the state, to act against faith and charity, against humanity, and against religion."

Proponents of state morality disagree and argue that neither national interest nor sovereignty legitimizes immoral actions. A philosopher and statesman who took this view was Thomas Jefferson. While secretary of state (1789–1793), Jefferson argued that since a society is but a collection of individuals, "the moral duties which exist between individual and individual" also form "the duties of that society toward any other; so that between society and society the same moral duties exist as between the individuals composing them" (Graebner, 1964:55).

This debate about joint or separate standards of morality for states and individuals can also be applied to international law. Should states, individually or collectively, be legally able to do what it would be inadmissible for an individual to do? One provocative example of this issue that involves both the morality and legality of international action is provided by policy toward Iraq: The West has continued economic sanctions on Iraq until it abides by arms inspections and other terms imposed by the victorious UN coalition powers in 1991. Studies have shown that the lack of food, medicine, and other basics have contributed to the deaths of several hundred thousand more Iraqi children than would have otherwise died. The intransigence of the government of Iraq and its internal food and medicine allocation policies bear some of the responsibility. But does that settle the question? It is hard to conceive of a circumstance where we as individuals could legally or morally take action against a person that would injure that person's children. Is it moral, should it be legal, that we—as the collective of states in the UN—assail the Iraqi children to punish Iraq's regime?

The immediacy of this question with regard to Iraq was eased in part in late 1996 when the UN and Iraq had reached an agreement that allows Iraq to sell enough oil each year to buy, under UN supervision, food, medicine, and other humanitarian supplies. This has somewhat improved life in Iraq, but it does not bring back the Iraqis who have died or suffered permanent physical losses; nor does it address the ongoing question of whether sanctions, which almost always inflict the most damage on those with the least political voice, are morally justified.

States and Issues of Law and Morality

Traditionally, international law has concerned itself with the actions and status of states. Some of the most prominent issues are sovereignty, war, the biosphere, and human rights.

Issues of Sovereignty Sovereignty continues to be a cornerstone of the state system, but sovereignty is no longer a legal absolute. Instead, it is being chipped away by a growing number of law-creating treaties that limit action. Sovereignty is also being slowly restricted by the international community's growing intolerance of human rights abuses and other ills inflicted by governments on their people. As Secretary-General Annan puts it, sovereignty "was never meant as a license for governments to trample on human rights and human dignity. Sovereignty implies responsibility, not just power."[16] Views such as this led, for instance, to international action that ended apartheid in South Africa (1993) and forced the military junta in Haiti to flee (1994), and to the NATO bombardment of Yugoslavia until it ceased its ethnic cleansing policy in Kosovo (1999).

Issues of War Most of the early writing in international law was concerned with the law of war, and this issue continues to be a primary focus of legal development. In addition to issues of traditional state-versus-state warfare, international law now attempts also to regulate revolutionary and internal warfare and terrorism.

To illustrate these diverse concerns, we can focus on the long debate on when and how war can morally and legally be fought. "Just war" theory has two parts: the cause of war and the conduct of war. Western tradition has believed in *jus ad bellum* (just cause of war) in cases where the war is (1) a last resort, (2) declared by legitimate authority, (3) waged in self-defense or to establish/restore justice, and (4) fought to bring about peace. The same line of thought maintains that *jus in bello* (just conduct of war) includes the standards of proportionality and discrimination. Proportionality means that the amount of force used must be proportionate to the threat. Discrimination means that force must not make noncombatants intentional targets (Barry, 1998).

As laudable as limitations on legitimate warfare may seem, they present problems. One difficulty is that the standards of when to go to war and how to fight it are rooted in Western-Christian tradition. The parameters of jus in bello and jus ad bellum extend back to Aristotle's *Politics* (ca. 340 B.C.) and are especially associated with the writings of Christian theological philosophers Saint Augustine (Aurelius Augustinus, A.D. 354–430) and Saint Thomas Aquinas (1226–1274). As a doctrine based on Western culture and religion, not all the restrictions on war are the same as those derived from some of the other great cultural-religious traditions, including Buddhism and Islam.

Another difficulty with the standards of just war, even if you try to abide by them, is that they are vague. What, for example, is proportionally in line with jus in bello? Almost everyone would agree, for instance, that France, Great Britain, and the United States would not have been justified in using their nuclear weapons against Yugoslavia in 1999 to force it to withdraw from Kosovo. But what if Iraq had used chemical weapons against the forces of those three countries during the Persian Gulf War in 1991? Would they have been justified if they had retaliated with nuclear weapons? Some people even argue that using nuclear weapons under any conditions would violate the rule of discrimination and would thus be immoral.

The jus in bello standard of discrimination also involves matters of degree rather than clear lines. Many observers have assailed Russia for some of its tactics in Chechnya during the especially vicious war being waged by both sides. At one juncture, for

This dead ethnic Albanian lying in the rubble was one of 64 people killed in April 1999 by a NATO air strike that inadvertently shattered a refugee convoy. Troubling issues about just war standards arose over NATO's willingness to rain bombs on targets in Kosovo and elsewhere in Yugoslavia, sometimes killing the innocent (including those NATO was trying to help) compared to NATO's unwillingness to risk the lives of its troops.

instance, Russian aircraft dropped leaflets into the nearly razed Chechen capital, Grozny, telling inhabitants to flee or face death. "Those staying in the city will be regarded as terrorists and gangsters and will be destroyed by artillery and air force," the fliers warned.[17]

The U.S.–led actions in Kosovo in 1999 also raised troublesome issues of discrimination for some observers. One retired U.S. Marine colonel has decried the "willingness-to-kill-but-not-to-die" that prompted the United States and its NATO allies to launch a major bombing campaign against the Serbs instead of sending in ground troops. This policy, he charges, led to unnecessary civilian casualties. Yugoslavia claims that thousands of noncombatants were killed, but the colonel contends, "Whether one believes these statistics is a moot point." The crux of the matter, he writes, is that "the allies' resolve was greater than the resources [troops] they were willing to commit to the action." Therefore, the colonel concludes, "Immorality resided in the mismatch" (DeCamp, 2000:43). Did Russia violate the laws of war in Chechnya? Did the United States and its NATO partners do so in Kosovo?

As these examples illustrate, the law and morality of war remain highly controversial. Still, progress has been made to set down rules. The Hague Conferences near the turn of the century and the Geneva Convention of 1949 set down some rules about jus in bello regarding impermissible weapons, the treatment of prisoners, and other matters. Other treaties have banned the possession and use of biological and chemical weapons, and the ICJ has ruled that in most circumstances the use of nuclear weapons would be illegal. Jus ad bellum is addressed by the UN Charter, by which members agree that the only legitimate reasons to resort to interstate violence are (1) in self-defense and (2) as part of a UN or regional military effort. Violating this standard has brought condemnation and sometimes action, as Iraq found out when it was expelled from Kuwait by a force authorized by the global community through the UN. Also in the realm of jus ad bellum, individuals are now sometimes held accountable for war crimes. That happened after World War II and, as related later, it is occurring once again for the horrendous violations of international law that were committed in Bosnia and Rwanda.

Issues of the Biosphere Another important and growing area of international law addresses the obligation of states and individuals to use the biosphere responsibly on the theory that it belongs to no one individually and to everyone collectively. This area of law is aptly illustrated by the law of the sea.

The status of the world's oceans is a long-standing subject of international law. The international maritime rules of the road for ships have long had general acceptance. The extension of a state's territorial limits to 3 miles into the ocean was another widely acknowledged standard based, as noted, on international custom.

In recent years, the resource value of the seas has grown because of more sophisticated harvesting and extraction technology, and this has created uncertainty and change. Undersea oil exploration, in particular, is the source of serious dispute among a number of countries. As early as 1945, the United States claimed control of the resources on or under its continental shelf. In 1960 the Soviet Union proclaimed the extension of its territorial waters out to 12 miles, a policy that has been imitated by

Table 11.1 Eight Important Multilateral Human Rights Treaties

Multilateral Treaty	Year	Countries* (2000)
Convention on the Prevention and the Punishment of the Crime of Genocide	1949	130
Convention Relating to the Status of Refugees	1951	136
International Convention on the Elimination of All Forms of Racial Discrimination	1965	156
International Covenant on Civil and Political Rights	1976	144
International Covenant on Economic, Social, and Cultural Rights	1976	142
Convention on the Elimination of All Forms of Discrimination Against Women	1979	165
Convention Against Torture and Other Cruel, Inhuman, or Degrading Treatment or Punishment	1984	119
Convention on the Rights of the Child	1989	191

*Indicates number of countries that have ratified or otherwise agreed to abide by the treaty.
Data source: United Nations Treaty Collection at: http://untreaty.un.org/English/treaty.asp.

Most countries have signed a variety of multilateral treaties, thereby agreeing to abide by the treaties' various human rights standards. Even though not all countries have signed every treaty, and while there have also been numerous violations, many analysts argue that such treaties take on the characteristic of international law once they have been ratified by the preponderance of the world's states. As such, the standards set in these treaties may be used in a number of ways, including through international courts and tribunals, to judge the cases of states and individuals.

others, including the United States as of 1988. Several Latin American countries claimed a 200-mile territorial zone, and the United States not only established a 200-mile "conservation zone" in 1977 to control fishing but in 1983 extended that control to all economic resources within the 200-mile limit.

In an ambitious attempt to settle and regulate many of these issues, the Law of the Sea Convention (1982) defines coastal zones, establishes the International Seabed Authority to regulate nonterritorial seabed mining, provides for the sharing of revenue from such efforts, and establishes the International Tribunal for the Law of the Sea to settle disputes. As of 2000, 133 countries had ratified the convention. Canada and the United States have signed the treaty, but their national legislatures have not ratified it amid concerns that they could lose control of, or revenues from, offshore activities through decisions of the International Seabed Authority. The absence of a few countries—even a few powerful ones—should not take away from the growing body of law that protects the oceans and seas.

Issues of Human Rights International law is developing affirmatively in the area of defining human rights. International attention to the law of human rights has grown because of many factors, including the horror of the images of abuses that television reveals, the expanding efforts of individuals and organizations that promote human rights, and the growing awareness that human rights violations are a major source of international instability.

The UN Charter supports basic rights in a number of its provisions. This language was expanded in 1948 when the UN General Assembly passed the Universal Declaration of Human Rights. No country voted against the declaration, although a few did abstain. Since then, the growth of global human rights has also been enhanced by a number of important global multilateral treaties. The most important of these treaties are listed in Table 11.1. In addition to global treaties, there have been a number of

Some people doubt whether all the world's diverse cultures can agree on one system of international law. It will be difficult, but in some areas there is growing agreement on at least fundamental principles. One such area is human rights. Most of the world's countries have agreed to the Universal Declaration of Human Rights.

regional multilateral treaties, such as the Helsinki Accords (1977), which address European human rights and the African Charter on Human and Peoples' Rights (1990).

Much, however, remains to be done. Canada and several other countries have signed all the human rights treaties found in Table 11.1; many other countries have not. There are also many countries, including the United States, whose legislatures have not ratified some of the treaties because of fears that they might be used as platforms for interfering in domestic affairs or for pressing demands for certain international policy changes, such as a redistribution of world economic resources. For instance, it took the U.S. Senate almost 40 years to ratify the Convention on the Prevention and Punishment of the Crime of Genocide (signed December 1948, ratified November 1988), and the Senate still has not consented to the Convention on the Elimination of All Forms of Discrimination against Women (signed 1979).

The gap between existing legal standards and their application is the area of greatest concern. Gross violations of the principles set down in the multilateral treaties continue to occur. And the record of international reaction to violation of the standards and enforcement of them through sanctions and other means is very sporadic and often weak. "We have not traveled as far or as fast as we had hoped," UN deputy secretary-general Margaret J. Anstee has commented on the convention to protect women.[18] To varying degrees, this could be said about all human rights treaties. Yet their existence provides a constant reminder that most of the world considers certain actions to be reprehensible. The treaties also serve, in the view of many, as a standard of international law and conduct for which states and individuals can be held accountable. Thus, the growth of human rights law has just begun. The acceptance of the concept of human rights has gained a good deal more rhetorical support than practical application, and enforcement continues to be largely in the hands of individual states with a mixed record of adherence. For all these shortcomings, though, human rights obligations are now widely discussed, and world opinion is increasingly critical of violations.

APPLYING INTERNATIONAL LAW AND MORALITY TO INDIVIDUALS

International law has begun recently to deal with the actions of individuals. A series of precedents in the twentieth century have marked this change. It is possible to divide these developments into four topics: Post–World War II Tribunals, the National Enforcement of International Law, Current International Tribunals, and the International Criminal Court (Beigbeder, 1999).

Post–World War II Tribunals

The first modern instances of individuals being charged with crimes under international law came in the aftermath of the horrors of World War II. In the Nuremberg and Tokyo war crimes trials, German and Japanese military and civilian leaders were tried for waging aggressive war, for war crimes, and for crimes against humanity. Nineteen Germans were convicted at Nuremberg; 12 were sentenced to death. Similar fates awaited convicted Japanese war criminals. Seven were hanged. Many Germans and Japanese also went to prison. Some important precedents were established. One was that those who ordered criminal acts or under whose command the acts occurred were just as liable to punishment as those who actually carried out the crimes. Another important precedent was that obeying orders was not a defense for having committed atrocities (Osiel, 1999).

There were efforts in the UN as early as 1948 to establish a permanent international tribunal to deal with genocide and other criminal affronts to humankind. Little came of the effort, however, and there were no subsequent war crimes tribunals for almost the next half-century.

National Enforcement of International Law

The lack of international tribunals did not mean that crimes went completely unpunished. Although trials have been unusual, a number of states have used their national courts to try those accused of crimes under international law.

One reason that countries began capturing and trying individuals for crimes that had occurred in another country was the inability of the international system to bring such criminals to justice. Germans who eluded prosecution immediately after the war were a special target for prosecution. Perhaps the most famous incident was Israel's abduction from Argentina of a top Nazi, Adolf Eichmann. He was charged, tried, convicted, and hanged in 1962 by Israel for crimes that not only had not occurred in Israel, but for crimes committed before Israel even existed. More recently, Germany tried and convicted two Serbs for committing war crimes in Bosnia. Both men were arrested in Germany after having unwisely fled there, and the German courts rejected the claim of the accused that Germany had no jurisdiction over what they might have done in another country.

Taking yet a further step, a Spanish court in 1999 sought the extradition of former Chilean dictator (1973–1989) General Augusto Pinochet from Great Britain, where he was receiving treatment for cancer. The Spanish judge charged that Pinochet not only had ordered the murders of Spanish citizens in Chile, but also had committed crimes against humanity through the murder and torture of British, American, and Chilean citizens. It is important to see the implications of the charges for the traditional sovereign immunity of current or former heads of state. Another aspect of the case with great importance for international law was the effort to bring to trial in Spain a former Chilean president for crimes committed in Chile against, among others, Chileans.

During more than a year of legal maneuvering, British legal officials agreed to extradite Pinochet. His British lawyers then argued that their client was too ill with cancer to stand trial. Perhaps in recognition of the immense implications of an extradition order, the British government accepted this maneuver and ordered the general out of the country and back to Chile. When Pinochet arrived back in Santiago, the sup-

A potentially momentous legal precedent was set when a Spanish judge sought to extradite Chile's former dictator Augusto Pinochet from Great Britain, where he was staying. The Spanish court wanted to try Pinochet charging that he had blood on his hands for crimes against Chileans and others in Chile. This picture of a "bloody" hand raised by a protester before a poster bearing Pinochet's image was taken outside the London courtroom where his extradition hearing was being held. Pinochet was eventually able to avoid extradition and return to Chile by claiming he was ill. But once in Santiago he was indicted by Chile and awaits trial there.

posedly near-death man arose suddenly from his wheelchair, greeted friends heartily for ten minutes, and climbed unaided into a waiting helicopter. "Pinochet is in perfect shape, as anyone can see. All humanity should feel cheated by this sham," charged a woman representing families of Chileans who disappeared during Pinochet's rule.[19] Many other Chileans felt the same, and the government revoked Pinochet's immunity and moved to try him for his alleged crimes (Weller, 1999). The general appealed to Chile's Supreme Court; in August 2000 it rejected his appeal. Pinochet now awaits trial, but there is concern that Chile's military might intervene to protect him.

The portent of the Pinochet case became rapidly evident in a much less-publicized case in Africa. In early 2000, Hissene Habre, the former dictator of Chad, who was living in exile in Senegal, was indicted by a Senegalese judge for human rights crimes that Habre had committed in Chad. It was the first time a former African head of state has been charged in one African country for atrocities alleged in another, making Habre what the press labeled as "Africa's Pinochet."[20]

Current International Tribunals

After languishing for nearly 50 years, the idea of international tribunals to deal with criminal violations of international law was resurrected by the atrocities that occurred in Bosnia and in Rwanda during the 1990s. In both places, people on all sides were abused, injured, and killed, although in Bosnia it was the Muslims who were the principal victims and the Serbs who inflicted the most death and degradation between 1990 and 1995. In Rwanda, the Hutus did most of the killing in 1994, and the Tutsis did most of the suffering and dying.

The evil that befell Bosnia and Rwanda strains credulity. Bosnian Serb forces carried out a ghastly campaign that created a humanitarian Bermuda Triangle where the decency of aggressors and the dignity of victims vanished. Children were gunned down by snipers or fell victim to the shelling of their homes, schools, and playgrounds. Women were beset by a systematic campaign of rape and other degradations. Men were slaughtered wantonly. One Muslim woman remembered the nightmare she and others endured after they were captured: "I was raped. I was beaten. One night [the Serbs] built an enormous bonfire outside and pushed men into it. I was forced to watch... and was told, 'Look how they're all singing and dancing,' as the men hopped around, burning alive."[21]

Human decency also deserted Rwanda. Smoldering ethnic tensions erupted into a firestorm of carnage that turned the country into a charnel house in 1994 when the majority ethnic group, the Hutus, set out to destroy the minority Tutsi population. "The Tutsis must be driven out," one Hutu leader proclaimed, "and we are going to find a shortcut... by throwing them into the Nyabarongo River.... Wipe them all out!" (Rieff, 1996:27). The call for genocide was meant literally. Marauding Hutus killed some 500,000 Tutsis, often dumping them into the crocodile-infested Nyabarongo. One eyewitness wrote that the scenes he encountered "had the sense of life stopped in a freeze-frame. There was the mission school house, the lesson half-written on the blackboard, the notebooks still on the desks. And there were the rotting bodies, lying where they had fallen, while lurking at the edge of the compound were packs of dogs, well-fed dogs" (Rieff, 1996:31).

The atrocities in Bosnia and Rwanda shocked the conscience of the world and made it obvious, as a former UN official put it, that "a person stands a better chance of being tried and judged for killing one human being than for killing 100,000."[22] This jarring reality led to the establishment in 1994 of a tribunal for Bosnia and another for Rwanda to prosecute those who committed atrocities. The tribunal for the Balkans sits in The Hague, the Netherlands. The Rwanda tribunal is located in Arusha, Tanzania.

The Hague tribunal has indicted about 60 individuals, and more than 30 have been arrested. A growing number of these accused war criminals have been convicted and sentenced to prison for genocide, murder, rape, and torture. Serbian officer Goran Jelisic, for one, was convicted for war crimes he committed as senior commander at the Luka concentration camp. He received a 40-year sentence from presiding judge Claude Jorda of France, who called Jelisic's behavior "repugnant, bestial and sadistic."[23] Not all those convicted have been Serbs. In March 2000, for example, a former Croatian general, Tihomir Blaskic, received a prison term of 45 years for ordering a series of attacks on Muslim villagers in Bosnia between 1992 and 1994 while trying to secure the area for Croatia. Adding to its jurisdiction, The Hague tribunal has announced it has expanded its investigation to include war crimes in Kosovo.

The Rwanda tribunal has made headway more slowly than its counterpart in The Hague, but an important step occurred in 1998 when the tribunal obtained its first conviction. Former Rwandan prime minister Jean Kambanda pleaded guilty to genocide and was sentenced to life in prison. Through mid-2000, the tribunal had convicted 8 people and was holding another 43 suspected genocide leaders. Hutu civilian and military leaders have made up most, but not all, of the convicted and accused. For instance, a Belgian-born Italian citizen, Georges Henry Joseph Ruggiu, who was a radio journalist in Rwanda, was sentenced in June 2000 to 12 years in prison for inciting genocide. Among the many other chilling calls to mayhem he broadcast in 1994: "You [Tutsi] cockroaches must know you are made of flesh.... We will kill you."[24]

Other such tribunals may be created. Cambodia and the United Nations reached an agreement in 2000 to create a joint tribunal to bring to justice some of the former Khmer Rouge officials responsible for the death of upwards of 1.5 million Cambodians in the late 1970s. Also, in August 2000 the Security Council agreed to establish a war crime tribunal for Sierra Leone. In that afflicted country, rebels killed and mutilated many thousands of noncombatants in an attempt to terrorize the population. The rebels' favorite gruesome tactic was to hack off part of one or more of their victims' limbs so that the maimed individuals would serve as living reminders not to oppose the Revolutionary United Front. The RUF leader, Foday Sankoh, is in custody and will almost certainly be one of the first to face the bar of international justice.

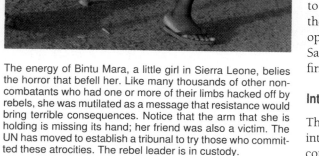

The energy of Bintu Mara, a little girl in Sierra Leone, belies the horror that befell her. Like many thousands of other non-combatants who had one or more of their limbs hacked off by rebels, she was mutilated as a message that resistance would bring terrible consequences. Notice that the arm that she is holding is missing its hand; her friend was also a victim. The UN has moved to establish a tribunal to try those who committed these atrocities. The rebel leader is in custody.

International Criminal Court

The temporary international tribunals and the enforcement of international law by national courts have signaled those who commit genocide and other atrocities that they are at peril. But the world community has also begun to recognize, as President Clinton told a University of Connecticut audience in 1995, that "the signal will come across even more loudly and clearly if nations all around the world… establish a permanent international court to prosecute… serious violations of humanitarian law."[25]

To that end, a UN–sponsored conference soon convened to create a permanent International Criminal Court (ICC). The final work was undertaken in June 1998 when most of the world's countries met in Rome. A bloc of about 50 countries, with Canada as its informal leader, favored establishing a court with broad and independent jurisdiction. Secretary-General Kofi Annan supported this position, calling on the delegates in Rome to "not flinch from creating a court strong and independent enough to carry out its tasks. It must be an instrument of justice, not expediency."[26]

Other countries wanted a much weaker ICC. For example, U.S. opposition to a strong ICC rested on two concerns. One was the fear that U.S. leaders and military personnel might become targets of politically motivated prosecutions. "The reality is that the United States is a global military power and presence…. We have to be careful that it does not open up opportunities for endless frivolous complaints to be lodged against the United States as a global military power," explained the chief U.S. delegate to the talks.[27] Senate ratification will also be a hurdle, with Foreign Relations Committee chairman Jesse Helms having announced himself "unalterably opposed to the creation of a permanent UN criminal court" and proclaiming that the treaty would be "dead on arrival" in the Senate.[28]

The U.S. stand drew strong criticism. Canada's foreign minister accused the United States of wanting "a Potemkin village," and an Italian diplomat expressed disbelief "that a major democracy… would want to have an image of insisting that its soldiers be given license never to be investigated."[29]

In the end, some of the reservations of the United States and some other countries were met, but the conference opted to create a relatively strong court by a vote of 120 for to 7 against (including China, India, and the United States), and 21 abstentions. Secretary-General Annan told the delegates in Rome, "Two millennia ago one of this city's most famous sons, Marcus Tullius Cicero, declared that 'in the midst of arms, law stands mute.' As a result of what we are doing here today, there is real hope that that bleak statement will be less true in the future than it has been in the past."[30]

The treaty gives the ICC jurisdiction over genocide and a range of other "widespread and systematic" crimes committed as part of "state, organization, or group policy," during international and internal wars. National courts will remain the first point of justice, and the ICC will be able to try cases only when they fail to do so. The UNSC can delay a prosecution for up to a year, but the vote to delay will not be subject to veto.

There the matter rests for now. As of July 2000, 98 countries had signed the ICC treaty, and 14 had ratified it. Momentum to reach the required 60 ratifications for the treaty to go into effect is building. In June 2000, France became the first permanent member of the Security Council to ratify the treaty, and in July Canada gave its final agreement. The issue in the United States remained on the sidelines, but that is unlikely to persist. "It is no longer something that's going away; in fact it's probably something that's coming quicker than most people would anticipate," Canada's foreign minister, Lloyd Axworthy, commented sagely. "Our strategy is to keep the U.S. engaged," he continued, and "to work and massage and accommodate" Washington's fears. "But," Axworthy concluded, "the U.S. side [has] to adjust… and recognize that they are not going to get an exemption from this court. That's pretty clear."[31]

Would you shoot this man? If it were the 1930s and you could foresee the horrors of World War II and the Holocaust, and you were standing just out of this picture with a gun in your hand, would you assassinate Adolf Hitler? Would the end justify the means? This and other issues are raised if one attempts to apply moral standards to the formation and conduct of foreign policy.

LAW AND MORALITY: ISSUES OF PRUDENT JUDGMENT AND APPLICATION

In a perfect world, everyone would act morally, obey the law, and insist that others conduct themselves in the same way. Moreover, what is legal and what is not, and what is moral and what is not, would be clear. Finally, our choices would be between good and evil, rather than between greater and lesser evils. In our imperfect world, standards and choices are often much murkier, which leads to several questions regarding the prudence of applying our standards of law and morality.

Can Ends Justify Means? One conundrum is whether an act that, by itself, is evil can be justified if it is done for a good cause. There are those who believe that ends never justify means. The philosopher Immanuel Kant took a position of **moral absolutism** in his *Groundwork on the Metaphysics of Morals* (1785) and argued that ends never justify means. He therefore urged us to "do what is right though the world should perish."

In practice, the primitive international political system can make applying strong moral principles strictly, adhering to international law, and other such altruistic acts unwise and even dangerous. Clearly, most of us do not adhere to such an absolute position. Nor do we practice **amorality.** Instead, most people adhere to **moral relativism.** They believe that actions must be placed in context. For example, most Americans explicitly or implicitly accept capital punishment and the atomic bombings of Hiroshima and Nagasaki as somehow justified as retaliation or even as an unfortunate necessity to a better end. The problem, again, is where to draw the line. How about assassination? Think about the smiling Adolf Hitler in the photograph here. What if you had a time machine? Given what you know of World War II and of the genocide of 6 million Jews, would you be justified in traveling back to 1932 and assassinating Hitler?

Should We Judge Others by Our Own Standards? The issue about whether to judge others morally rests on two controversies. The first, which we have already addressed, is whether it is supportable to apply standards of international law and morality given the divergent values of a multicultural world. Some claim that doing so is cultural imperialism; others believe that at least some universal standards exist.

The second objection to any country or even the UN imposing sanctions or taking any other action based on another country's supposed morality or lack thereof is that it violates the sovereignty of the target country. Many Americans have few qualms about criticizing the human rights record of other countries, but they become outraged when others find American standards lacking. Capital punishment is legal and on the rise in most U.S. states, but many other countries find the practice abhorrent. Therefore they refuse to extradite accused criminals to the United States if there is a possibility of capital punishment. The opposition to capital punishment is intensified by the belief that there are demographic injustices in who gets executed. The UN Commission on Human Rights (UNCHR) passed a resolution in 1998 calling for a moratorium on exe-

Did You Know That:

Human rights groups criticize China as the country that executes the most prisoners. At least 1,769 Chinese were executed in 1998 for crimes ranging from murder to drunk driving. This compares to 68 U.S. executions that year and zero in most countries.

cutions because, in part, of a UNCHR report that found that in the United States "race, ethnic origin and economic status appear to be key determinants of who will and will not receive a sentence of death."[32] Americans have regularly rejected such refusals to extradite and questioning of fairness as gross outside interference.

What If Moral and Legal Standards Clash? Another dilemma occurs when two choices, both of which we can define as desirable, clash. Or, what does one do when the choice you face is not between good and bad, but, from your point of view, between bad and worse?

Consider Algeria. In 1990, after more than two decades of one-party rule, Algeria held free elections and the opposition party gained control of the national legislature. Democracy clearly was working. Good! Well, perhaps. The coalition of groups that won formed the Front for Islamic Salvation (FIS), an Islamic fundamentalist movement. It campaigned on the platform of instituting the *shari'ah*, the law of the Koran. Among other things, such a change would have severely restricted the freedom of women. One Algerian woman objected that the fundamentalists are "not democrats interested in dialogue," but "little fascists" and a bunch of "bearded, sexually frustrated men" who wanted to take away the freedom that Algerian women had gained under the more secular, but less democratic, government that had preceded the fundamentalists.[33] What happened was that the military staged a coup, and the brief experiment with democracy ended. Some women's rights were preserved, but democracy was short-circuited (Bova, 1997). What should policy be in such circumstances?

Is It Prudent to Apply Moral and Legal Standards? Another objection to trying to apply moral principles is based on self-interest. Realists maintain that national interest sometimes precludes the application of otherwise laudable moral principles. They further contend that trying to uphold abstract standards of morality casts a leader as a perpetual Don Quixote, a pseudo knight-errant whose wish "To dream the impossible dream; To fight the unbeatable foe;.... [and] To right the unrightable wrong" while appealing romantically, is delusional and perhaps dangerous. One danger is that you waste your reputation, your wealth, and the lives of your soldiers trying to do the impossible. A second peril springs from the reality that since not all states act morally, those who do are at a disadvantage: "Nice guys finish last."

Those who disagree with this line of reasoning contend that it fails the test of courageously standing up for what is right. They might even recall the remonstration of President John Kennedy, who, evoking Dante Alighieri's *The Divine Comedy* (1321), commented, "Dante once said that the hottest places in hell are reserved for those who in a period of moral crisis maintain their neutrality."[34]

More pragmatically, advocates of applying principles of law and morality contend that greater justice is necessary for world survival. This argument deals, for example, with resource distribution. It contends that it is immoral to maintain a large part of the world both impoverished and without self-development possibilities. The inevitable result, according to this view, will be a world crisis that will destroy order as countries fight for every declining resource.

One way out of the dilemma about when and how great a degree of law, morality, and other principles to apply to foreign policy may be to begin with the observation that it is not necessary to choose between moral absolutism and amorality. Instead, there is a middle ground of moral relativism that relies on **moral prudence** as a guiding principle. There is a secular prayer that asks for the courage to change the wrongs one can, the patience to accept the wrongs that one cannot change, and the wisdom to know the difference. From this perspective, a decision maker must ask, first, whether any tangible good is likely to result from a course of action and, second, whether the good will outweigh negative collateral consequences. By the first standard, taking high-flown principled stands when it is impossible or unlikely that you will affect the situation is quixotic. By the second standard, applying morality when the overall consequences will be vastly more negative also fails the test of prudence. But not taking action when change is possible and when the good will outweigh the bad fails the test of just behavior.

THE FUTURE OF INTERNATIONAL LAW AND MORALITY

The often anarchic and inequitable world makes it easy to dismiss talk of conducting international relations according to standards of international law and morality as idealistic prattling. This view, however, was probably never valid and certainly is not true now. An irreversible trend in world affairs is the rapid acceleration of states and people interacting in almost all areas of endeavor. As these interactions have grown, so has the need for regularized behavior and for rules to prescribe that behavior. For very pragmatic reasons then, many people have come to believe, as one analyst notes, that "most issues of transnational concern are best addressed through legal frameworks that render the behavior of global actors more predictable and induce compliance from potential or actual violators" (Ratner, 1998:78). The growth of these rules in functional international interactions has been on the leading edge of the development of international law. Advances in political and military areas have been slower, but here too there has been progress. Thus, as with the United Nations, the pessimist may decry the glass as only half full, whereas, in reality, it is encouraging that there is more and more water in the previously almost empty glass.

All the signs point to increasing respect for international law and a greater emphasis on adhering to at least rudimentary standards of morality. Violations of international standards are now more likely to draw criticism from the world community. It is probable, therefore, that international law will continue to develop and to expand its areas of application. So too will moral discourse have increasing impact on the actions of the international actors. There will certainly be areas where growth is painfully slow, and there will also be those who violate the principles of law and morality and who sometimes get away with their unlawful and immoral acts. But, just as surely, there will be progress.

CHAPTER SUMMARY

1. International law can be best understood as a primitive system of law in comparison with much more developed domestic law. There are only the most rudimentary procedures and institutions for making, adjudicating, and enforcing international law. This does not mean, however, that international law is impotent, only that it is in an earlier stage of development than domestic law.

2. As a developing phenomenon, international law is dynamic and has been growing since the earliest periods of civilization. This growth has accelerated in the twentieth century because the increasing level of international interaction and interdependence requires many new rules to govern and regularize contacts in trade, finance, travel, communication, and other areas. The possible consequences of war have also spurred the development of international law.

3. Thus far, international law is most effective when it governs functional international relations. International law works least well in areas of "high politics," where the vital interests of the sovereign states are at stake. Even in those areas, though, international law is gradually becoming more effective.

4. Morality is another factor in establishing the rules of the international system. It acts as a guide to action and as the basis for some international law.

5. The international legal system has four essential elements: its philosophical roots, lawmaking, adherence, and adjudication.

6. The roots of law for any legal system may come from external sources, such as natural law, or from within the society, such as custom.

7. Regarding lawmaking, international law springs from a number of sources, including international treaties, international custom, general principles of law, and international representative assemblies. Some scholars argue that resolutions and other pronouncements of the UN General Assembly should be included as a significant influence.

8. Regarding adherence, international law, again like primitive law, relies mainly on voluntary compliance and self-help. Here again, though, there are early and still uncertain examples of enforcement by third parties, a feature that characterizes more advanced systems.

9. The fourth essential element of a legal system, adjudication, is also in the primitive stage in international law. Although there are a number of international courts in the world today, jurisdiction and the use and effectiveness of these courts are limited. The existence of the International Court of Justice and other such international judicial bodies represent an increasing sophistication of international law in this area as well.

10. In a still culturally diverse world, standards of international law and morality have encountered problems of fit with different cultures. Most current international law and many concepts of morality, such as the stress on individualism, are based on Western ideas and practices, and many states from the South object to certain aspects of international law as it exists.

11. The changes in the world system in this century have created a number of important issues related to international law. Among these are status of sovereignty, the legality of war and the conduct of war, rules for governing the biosphere, and observing and protecting human rights.

12. International law has been interpreted as applying to states. Now it is also concerned with individuals. Primarily, it applies to the treatment of individuals by states, but it also has some application to the actions of individuals. Thus people, as well as countries, are coming to have obligations, as well as rights, under international law.

13. It is not always possible to insist on strict adherence to international law and to high moral standards, yet they cannot be ignored. One middle way is to apply principles prudently.

NATIONAL SECURITY: THE TRADITIONAL ROAD

[W]hen the blast of war blows in our ears,
Then imitate the tiger:
Stiffen the sinews, conjure up the blood,
Disguise fair nature with hard-favour'd rage;
Then lend the eye a terrible aspect.

Shakespeare, *King Henry V*

We make war that we may live in peace.

Aristotle, *Nichomacean Ethics*, circa 325 B.C.

An eye for an eye only winds up making the whole world blind.

Mohandas K. (Mahatma) Gandhi

CHAPTER OBJECTIVES

After completing this chapter, you should be able to:

- Identify reasons for studying war and summarize the human record of war, including the incidence, death toll, frequency, and severity.
- Discuss the causes of war from three levels of analysis: system, state, and individual.
- Understand force as a political instrument and its limitations.
- Explain the escalating use of a country's military power, from intimidation to attack.
- Analyze the effectiveness of the threat and use of force in the international system.
- Consider how the nature of war has changed as a result of nationalism and technology.
- Describe the destinations, sources, motives, and impact of international arms transfers.
- Characterize covert intervention and terrorism and distinguish between them.
- Define and describe the goals and conduct of war.
- Discuss limited nuclear-biological-chemical war as part of a battlefield strategy.
- Examine the major issues surrounding strategic nuclear war.
- Summarize strategic nuclear weapons and strategy as ongoing factors in international politics.

War is an enigma. We bewail its existence and consequences while we regularly battle with exhilaration. Those who have fought and seen war often speak of its tragedy. "I am tired and sick of war," General William Tecumseh Sherman told military cadets in 1879. "Its glory is all moonshine. It is only those who have neither fired a shot nor heard the shrieks and groans of the wounded who cry aloud for more blood, more vengeance, more desolation. War is hell!" General of the Army Dwight David Eisenhower agreed with his historical comrade in arms: "I hate war as only a soldier who has lived it can, as only one who has seen its brutality, its futility, its stupidity." From their experience, the generals would have surely agreed with the lament of English poet Wilfred Owen in 1914:

> War broke: and now the Winter of the world
> With perishing great darkness closes in.

War may be hell, but we are too often attracted to it like moths to the flame. "I have loved war too much," King Louis XIV of France confessed in 1710. "It is well that war is so terrible—we should grow too fond of it," General Robert E. Lee wrote similarly in 1862. More than a century later, President George Bush paced the White House grounds, carrying a handheld television to follow live reports from the Persian Gulf War. When miniature images flickered on the screen of U.S warplanes attacking Iraqi targets, "Bush jabbed his index finger at each target on the screen as though silently declaring 'Gotcha!'" as "smart bombs" obliterated buildings and bodies.[1] Perhaps, then, there is something to Henry Ward Beecher's observation in *Proverbs from Plymouth Pulpit* (1887): "It is not merely cruelty that leads men to war, it is excitement."

WAR AND WORLD POLITICS

Whether one considers war a tale of tragedy or a saga of heroism, there is resonance to scholar Max Weber's (1864–1920) classic observation: "The decisive means for politics is violence. Anyone who fails to see this is… a political infant" (Porter, 1994:303). Realists would agree that war is an inherent part of politics. Idealists would rejoin that humans can learn to live without war. Whoever is right, the fact for now is that countries continue to rely on themselves for protection and sometimes use threats and violence to further their interests. Thus, it is important to grasp the role of force to understand the conduct of international politics.

WAR: THE HUMAN RECORD

War is as ancient as humanity (Cioffi-Revilla, 1996). There are varying estimates of the number of wars that have occurred throughout history, but there can be little doubt that the number is high. One reasonable number, as shown in Figure 12.1, is that there were almost 1,000 wars during the millennium that just ended. Looking even farther back, it is possible to see that the world has been totally free of significant interstate, colonial, or civil war in only about 1 out of every 12 years in all of recorded human history.

The data also shows that war is not a tragic anachronism waged by our less civilized ancestors. To the contrary, political violence continues. Two ways to gauge this are frequency and severity. *Frequency* provides bad news. Over the last ten centuries, as Figure 12.1 on page 322 shows, wars have become more frequent, with some 30 percent occurring in just the last two centuries. It is true that the frequency of war in the 1900s declined somewhat from the horrific rate in the 1800s, but it is also the case that the number of civil wars increased. This means that the overall incidence of interstate and intrastate warfare remains relatively steady (Pickering & Thompson, 1998).

Severity is the truly terrible news. Again, as Figure 12.1 shows, over 147 million people have died during wars since the year 1000. Of the dead, an astounding 75 percent perished in the twentieth century and 89 percent since 1800. Not only do we kill more soldiers, we also now kill larger numbers of civilians. During World War I, 8.4 million soldiers and 1.4 million civilians died. World War II killed 16.9 million troops and 34.3 million civilians. Thus the ratio of soldiers to civilians killed went from six soldiers to every civilian (6:1) during WW I to two civilians for every soldier (1:2) in WW II. The worst news may lie ahead. President John F. Kennedy observed in 1961 that "mankind must put an end to war, or war will put an end to mankind." A nuclear war would escalate the casualty count from millions per year to millions per minute, and Kennedy's cataclysmic characterization could literally come to pass.

THE CAUSES OF WAR: THREE LEVELS OF ANALYSIS

Why war? This question has challenged investigators over the centuries (Geller & Singer, 1998). Philosophers, world leaders, and social scientists have many theories. It may be that further research can identify a single root cause of war, but it is more likely that there is no single reason why people fight. Given this, one way to discuss the multiple causes of war is to classify them according to the three levels of analysis: system-level analysis, state-level analysis, and individual-level analysis detailed in chapters 3, 4, and 5.

System-Level Causes of War

Wars may be caused by balance-of-power politics and a number of other factors that are related to the general nature of the world's political system (Cashman, 1999; Rosecrance & Lo, 1996). The *distribution of power* in the world is one possible system-level cause of conflict. Recall from chapter 3 that some analysts believe that the propensity for warfare to occur within the international system is related to factors such as the system's number of poles (big powers), their relative power, and whether the poles and their power are stable or in flux (Maoz, 1996; Walt, 1996a). When, for example, a system is experiencing significant power transitions (that is, when some powers are rising and others are declining or even vanishing), power vacuums often occur. These can cause conflict, as opposing powers move to fill the void. Postwar alliances that concentrate power by bringing victorious, major countries together have also been found to be "war prone" (Gibler & Vasquez, 1998:805).

The *anarchical nature of the system* is also cited as a cause of conflict. Some systems analysts argue that wars occur because there is no central authority to try to prevent conflict and to protect countries. Unlike domestic societies, the international society has no effective system of law creation, enforcement, or adjudication. This causes insecurity, and, therefore, countries acquire arms in part because other countries do, creating a tension-filled cycle of escalating arms ⟶ tensions ⟶ arms ⟶ tensions until a flash point is reached.

System-level economic factors can also cause conflict. The distribution of oil is one factor, as the defense of oil sources by the U.S.–led coalition in the 1991 Persian Gulf War shows. The global gap between wealthy and poor countries is another system-level factor, and some analysts are concerned that the highly uneven distribution of wealth between countries and regions could spark conflict along the North-South axis as the resentment of the relatively poor countries rises.

System-level biosphere factors are yet another possible cause of conflict. Water provides one example. This basic resource is becoming so precious in many areas that, as you will see in chapter 18, there are growing concerns that countries might soon go to war with one another over disputes about water supplies. According to one scholar,

WAR IS HELL!

War is hell! Burned in a misdirected American napalm attack on the pagoda in which she had sought refuge, 9-year-old Phan Thi Kim Phuc (right) flees in terror near the town of Trang Bang, South Vietnam. Over half of the girl's body was charred by third-degree burns from the jellied-gasoline inferno; her two little brothers were instantly incinerated and a third brother also suffered excruciating burns. War is hell!

Nick Ut, the photographer who took this Pulitzer Prize–winning picture, rushed the girl to a hospital and may have saved her life. But it has not been an easy life. Kim Phuc spent over a year in the hospital recovering from her immediate wounds, and she still has massive scars over most of her upper body. Most of her oil and sweat glands were also burned away, and she continues to be assailed by migraine headaches, diabetes, breathing difficulty, and chronic pain associated with her trauma.

Some 24 years after the searing napalm attack, Ms. Kim Phuc came to lay a wreath at the Vietnam Veterans Memorial in Washington, D.C. She sought reconciliation, not recrimination, and hugged American veterans. "I have suffered a lot [of] physical and emotional pain. Sometimes I could not breathe. But God saved my life and gave me faith and hope," she told the audience to several standing ovations. "Even if I could talk face to face with the pilot who dropped the bomb," she went on, "I would tell him, 'We cannot change history, but we should try to do good things for the present and for the future to promote peace.'" Said one tearful American Vietnam veteran, "It's important to us that she's here, part of the healing process. We were just kids doing our job. For her to forgive us personally means something." Kim Phuc said that she also had accepted the invitation by a Vietnam Veterans group to speak at the memorial in order to tell the world that "behind that picture of me [at age 9], thousands and thousands of people suffered more than me. They died. They lost part of their bodies. Their whole lives were destroyed, and nobody took [their] picture."[1] War is hell!

"When the empire of man over nature can no longer be easily extended, then the only way for one people to increase its standard of living is by redistributing the sources or fruits of industry from others to themselves. The surest way to do this is by extending man's empire over man" (Orme, 1998:165).

State-Level Causes of War

War may also result from the very nature of states and from their internal political dynamics (Auerswald, 1999; Dassel, 1998). Some scholars believe that states inherently tend toward *militarism*. One such analyst writes that "it is impossible to understand the nature of modern politics without considering its military roots" (Porter, 1994:xix). The argument is that as warfare required more soldiers and more increasingly expensive

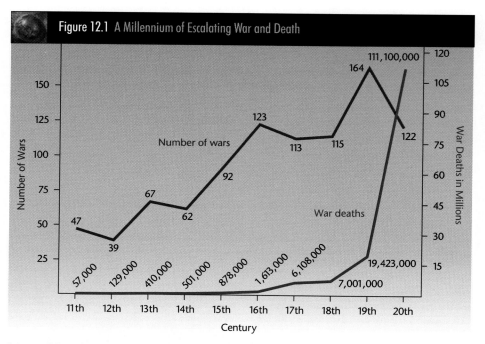

Figure 12.1 A Millennium of Escalating War and Death

Data sources: Eckhardt (1991); author. Eckhardt defines a war as a conflict that (1) involves a government on at least one side and (2) accounts for at least 1,000 deaths per year of the conflict.

This figure shows the long-term trend in the rise of both the frequency and severity of war. Beginning in the year 1000, the number of wars in each century has usually increased. The soaring death toll of the twentieth century's wars, which accounted for 75 percent of the millennium's total, is a truly alarming figure.

weapons, it created a need for political units with larger populations and economies. This gave rise to the state.

There are also several theories of state-related causes of war that have to do with the internal processes and conditions of countries (Morgan & Anderson, 1999; Fordham, 1998). First, there are times when external aggression is linked to domestic unrest. This linkage is called *diversionary war* or the *externalization of internal conflict*. Social scientists know that sometimes governments engage in war to rally the populace and divert attention from domestic problems. Evidence indicates, for instance, that revolutionary regimes will attempt to consolidate their power by fomenting tension with other countries (Snyder, 1999). It is also the case that countries are more likely to go to war while they are experiencing times of economic distress (Gelpi, 1997; Wang, 1996). Just as occurred in the movie *Wag the Dog*, starring Dustin Hoffman, analysts believe that when leaders fear they may lose power, they are tempted "to engage in international crises" (Smith, 1996:147).

Second, there are analysts who believe that some *types of countries*, because of their political structure (democratic, authoritarian) or their economic resources and wealth, are more aggressive than others. Chapter 8 discussed, for example, the democratic peace theory, the conclusion of most analysts that democratic countries are not prone to fighting with one another. Third, there are scholars who believe that a nation's *political culture* is correlated to warlike behavior. No nation has a genetic political character. Nations, however, that have had repeated experiences with violence may develop a political culture that views the world as a hostile environment (Ember & Ember, 1996). It is not necessary for the list to go on to make the point that how states are organized and how they make policy can sometimes lead to conflict and war among them.

Individual-Level Causes of War

It may be that the causes of war are linked to the character of individual leaders or to the nature of the human species. "In the final analysis," one scholar writes, "any contemplation of war must return to... the nature of humanity, which yet stands as the root cause of war and the wellspring of History's inestimable tragedy" (Porter, 1994:304).

Those who have this perspective believe that although it is clear that human behavior is predominantly learned, there are also behavioral links to the primal origins of humans. Territoriality, which we examined in chapter 5, is one such possible instinct, and the fact that territorial disputes are so frequently the cause of war may point to some instinctual territoriality in humans (Huth, 1996; Vasquez, 1996). Another possibility, some social psychologists argue, is that human aggression, individually or collectively, can stem from stress, anxiety, or frustration. The reaction of the German society to its defeat and humiliation after World War I is an example. A sociopsychological need for power is yet another possibility. At least some leaders have a power drive that may cause aggressive behavior. While discounting some of the more strident characterizations of Saddam Hussein as a madman, most personality analyses of Iraq's leader characterize him as driven to seek power and to dominate.

FORCE AS A POLITICAL INSTRUMENT

It may be that future social scientists will be able to write of war in the past tense, but for the present we must recognize conflict as a fact of international politics. For this reason, having discussed the human record and causes of war, we should also consider levels of violence, the diplomatic and military effectiveness of force, the changing nature of warfare, and the classification of wars. Before delving into those topics, however, it is appropriate first to consider the nature of military power that provides the sword for policy makers to wield.

NATIONAL MILITARY POWER

For good or ill, military power adds to a country's ability to prevail in international disputes. Military power is based on an array of tangible factors, such as spending and weapons levels, and intangible factors, such as leadership, morale, and reputation. Military power is not free, though. To the contrary, acquiring it and using it can be costly in many direct and indirect ways.

Levels of Spending

One of the largest categories in any nation's budget is the amount spent on national security. In times of peril, the amount may account for more than half of all government spending. During the tense years of the cold war, global military spending soared, peaking at just under $1 trillion a year in the late 1980s. Since the end of the cold war, defense spending has dropped significantly. The 1998 global figure was about $750 billion, a decrease of more than 25 percent in current dollars and even more in real dollars (value controlled for inflation). Projections for defense spending are, of course, tricky, but the UN estimated that in the year 2000 world defense spending, in constant dollars, would be 36 percent lower than it was in 1987. This decline is shown in Figure 12.2, and data through 1998 tends to confirm the projection.

As might be expected, the decline in military spending has included a substantial drop in the number of troops. From a peak of 28.7 million soldiers in 1988, the total number of troops in the world dropped almost 22 percent to 22.3 million in 1997. The biggest personnel declines have been in the economically developed countries (EDCs). Their forces declined 37 percent from 12 million to 7.6 million.

Did You Know That:
The 1998 U.S. defense budget was about equal to the combined official budgets of the next six biggest countries, which were (in descending order) Russia, Japan, France, Germany, Great Britain, and China.

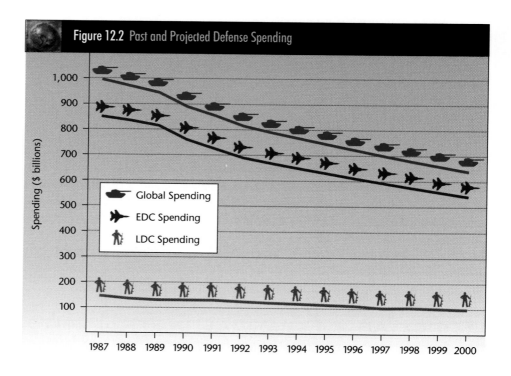

Figure 12.2 Past and Projected Defense Spending

Expenditures are calculated in billions of 1991 dollars. Dollar amounts for all years are not shown. Data for 1998 through 2000 are UN projections.

Data sources: UNDP (1997), ACDA

There are two ways to look at global defense spending. One way is that it has dropped off significantly since 1987. The other way is that the world's countries still spend huge amounts on weapons and soldiers.

Overall figures, however, disguise some less positive data and trends. The military spending (in real dollars) and number of troops of the world's economically less developed countries (LDCs) have declined only marginally, as is evident in Figure 12.2. The LDCs spent over $232 billion (current dollars) on their militaries in 1997. The amount was equivalent to 2.7 percent of their collective GDPs and some 50 percent of the LDCs' combined spending on health and education. This means that without the need for military forces, these developing countries could substantially increase spending to create a healthier, more educated population. The 45 economically poorest countries, the so-called least developed countries (LLDCs), have the most troublesome recent pattern. These countries have reduced military spending somewhat, but their armed forces actually increased 47 percent to 1.6 million. Because these soldiers are often ill-supported and dissatisfied, they are prone to taking action against the governments and civilians in the countries that the soldiers are supposed to safeguard.

A final troubling point is that the military budgets of some regions and countries have increased amid the general global decline in military spending. Military expenditures in South and East Asia increased about 25 percent in the 1990s, and there is an escalating arms race in the region, with China, India, and Pakistan the main contenders. China's defense spending has increased substantially in the past few years (for example, up 13 percent in 2000) and India has moved to match it. "We shall not shrink from making any sacrifice to guard and protect every inch of our beloved motherland," India's finance minister declared in 2000 when he announced a military spending hike of 28 percent, the largest increase in India's history.[2]

Weaponry: Quantity versus Quality

Very often when you see a comparison of two countries' or alliances' military might, you see a map with an overlay of small figures representing troops, tanks, planes, and other weapons. Such graphics emphasize quantity, and it always seems as if the other side's figures far outnumber your own.

Quantity is an important military consideration, but the relative value of these figures must be modified by the cost and quality of the weapons and troops. The West, especially the United States, has tended to favor acquiring fewer but superior high-technology weapons. Moving in the same direction, France, Great Britain, and other countries have announced during the past few years that they will significantly thin their already-reduced post–cold war military forces and emphasize technological sophistication and mobility, both expensive goals. "The truth is that we do not have an... intervention force that is up to our diplomatic ambitions," said one French legislator.[3] By contrast, China and other countries, because of their technology lag and preferences, have favored masses of weapons. There is a general agreement that most important Western military weapons systems are technologically superior to any other country's weapons. The war in the Persian Gulf was, for example, a showcase for high-technology warfare. In that war, U.S. main battle tanks maneuvered at nearly highway speeds, coalition pilots used laser guidance systems to maneuver "smart bombs" to their targets, and cruise missiles used a satellite-based Global Positioning System (GPS) to find their own way to their targets.

The seemingly triumphant technology lesson of the Persian Gulf War must, however, be considered carefully. In the first place, high technology is very expensive. A single U.S. B-2 bomber costs $2.1 billion. That is more than the yearly defense budgets of two-thirds of the world's countries.

Second, it is difficult to calculate with any precision the relative worth of masses of weapons versus fewer, more sophisticated, weapons. The newest U.S. fighter, the F-22, is a technological marvel that can defeat any other fighter flying. One has to wonder, though, whether one $127 million F-22 could defeat, say, four Iraqi-flown, Russian-built MiG-29 fighters (available for $30 million). Such calculations about quantity versus quality are even murkier given the fact that the military sometimes inflates the success rates of their high-tech weapons. During the Persian Gulf War, for instance, the Pentagon claimed that the Patriot antimissile missile had a 96 percent success record against Scud missiles fired by the Iraqis. Later analyses concluded, to the contrary, that the Patriots may not have brought down any Scuds at all. In fact, according to the U.S. General Accounting Office (GAO), there has been a "pattern of overstatement" about how effective weapons are by the U.S. military and the arms industry. A 1997 GAO report concluded that "the gap between what has been claimed [for weapons success] and what actually occurred was sometimes substantial."[4]

Third, high-technology weapons are also less durable and are more difficult to fix under battle conditions than are low-tech weapons. The $2.1 billion B-2 bomber cannot be left outside in the rain. The GAO reports that the warplane "must be sheltered or exposed to [only] the most benign environments—low humidity, no precipitation, moderate temperatures" because even mildly adverse weather makes the plane's skin, which is made of thermoplastic-composite material, deteriorate and lose the qualities that supposedly make the B-2 invisible to radar. Even the Air Force has had to admit that "it would be difficult to operate the B-2 from a deployed location," meaning near where the war is.[5]

It should also be remembered that the effectiveness of soldiers and military hardware is very situational. Therefore, a country's military systems need to be appropriate to the challenges they will face. American technology easily overwhelmed the Iraqis in the relatively open terrain near the Persian Gulf but was not able to prevail

The low morale of Russia's military forces sank further when one of Russia's most modern nuclear submarines, the *Kursk*, went to the bottom with all hands in August 2000. The decrepit shape of even Russia's newest weapons was exposed when the ship was destroyed by an internal explosion, probably from an unstable torpedo. To make matters worse, the Russian navy was unable to get divers or rescue apparatus to the *Kursk*. Once Russia belatedly appealed for help, Norwegian divers took less than a day to reach the stricken vessel. Sadly, everyone on board was dead. One can only imagine the foreboding that these events created for navy personnel, such as this young Russian sailor, who is lighting memorial candles for the crew of the *Kursk* in a St. Petersburg cathedral.

during the war in densely forested Vietnam against an even less sophisticated opponent than Iraq.

Military Morale and Leadership

Morale is a key element of military power. An army that does not fight well cannot win. Historian Stephen Ambrose, who served as a consultant for the film *Saving Private Ryan*, reflects that "in the end success or failure on D-Day [came] down to a relatively small number of junior officers, noncoms, and privates." According to Ambrose, "If the men coming in over the beaches [had] flopped down behind the seawall and refused to advance, if the noncoms and junior officers [had] failed to lead their men up and over the seawall… in the face of enemy fire—why, then, the Germans would [have won] the battle and thus the war."[6]

Morale, of course, is not inherent. Russian soldiers fought with amazing valor during World War II despite conditions that, in many cases, were far worse than those that American troops faced. Yet in more recent times, the morale of Russia's soldiers has been sapped by being left poorly paid, housed, equipped, and trained. "My heart aches for our hungry soldiers, for our officers who do not receive their pay on time, for their families roaming about for years with nowhere to live," Russia's president told a radio audience.[7] Such heartaches have left the once-vaunted Soviet/Russian army a dispirited shell. What should have been an overpowering Russian force could not batter the outnumbered, outgunned Chechen rebels into submission in 1996. And even after a second attempt waged with horrendous brutality in 2000, the Chechens fight on. One reason is the poor morale of Russia's troops. As one Chechen rebel said of his opponents, "They have very strong weapons— but not very strong spirits."[8]

Military leadership, in the form of both inspirational and tactical skills, plays a significant role (Taylor & Rosenbach, 1996). It is difficult, for instance, to understand the long resistance of the U.S. Southern Confederacy to the overwhelming numerical superiority of the Union unless the brilliant generalship of Robert E. Lee is considered. By contrast, French generals in this century made a series of classic errors. Marshal Ferdinand Foch, who commanded Allied forces on the Western Front during World War I, was of the opinion that "airplanes are interesting toys, but of no military value."[9] Continuing this old mindset into the 1930s, French generals relied on the fortified, but static, Maginot Line and were routed in 1940 by the Germans, who did not think their Stuka dive bombers were toys and who created a highly mobile and mechanized army with air support. In 1954, still relying on a static defense, the French garrison at Dien Bien Phu in Indochina was surrounded and decimated by Vietnamese forces under the command of the able General Giap.

Military and Political Reputation

Another power consideration is a country's reputation. Whatever real power a country may possess, its ability to influence others will depend partly on how those others perceive its capacity and will. National leaders commonly believe that weakness tempts their opponents, while a reputation for strength deters them. "Real leadership requires a willingness to use military force," argues one former White House aide.[10]

Some analysts believe, as one French general put it, that Americans want "zero-dead wars," as demonstrated by U.S. withdrawals in the face of casualties in Lebanon in 1983 and Somalia in 1993.[11] This reputation, the analysts say, is undermining U.S. power because opponents often do not take American threats seriously. "The nature of American society makes it impossible for the United States to bear tens of thousands of casualties," Saddam Hussein calculated when he invaded Kuwait.[12] Similarly, Bosnian Serbs for years asked, in the words of one, "Are Americans prepared to send their own sons into a war in Bosnia?... and face graves and body bags for [American] soldiers?"[13] And Haiti's military junta long persisted because they thought that, as one officer reasoned, even if a U.S. intervention came, "It'd be just like Somalia. [The Americans] will run away when the first U.S. soldier is returned in a body bag."[14]

Military Power: The Dangers of Overemphasis

Given the importance of military power as a tool of national defense and diplomacy, it is not uncommon for people to assume that the phrase "too much military power" must be an oxymoron. Exactly how much is enough is a complex question, but it is certain that there are clear dangers associated with overemphasizing military power. Three such perils deserve special mention. They are insecurity, temptation, and expense.

Military power creates insecurity. One result of power acquisition is the "spiral of insecurity." This means that our attempts to amass power to achieve security or gain other such ends are frequently perceived by others as a danger to them. They then seek to acquire offsetting power, which we see as threatening, causing us to acquire even more power... then them... then us, ad infinitum, in an escalating spiral. As we will see in chapter 13's review of disarmament, the arms race is a complex phenomenon, but the interaction of one country's power and other countries' insecurity is an important factor in world politics.

Military power creates temptation. A second peril of amassing excess military power is the temptation to use it in a situation that is peripheral to the national interest. The United States went to war in Vietnam despite the fact that President Lyndon Johnson derided it as a "raggedy-ass fourth-rate country." One reason Americans intervened in Vietnam was because of a so-called arrogance of power. Had U.S. military power been more modest, the United States might have emphasized diplomacy or maybe even acquiesced to the reunification of North and South Vietnam. One can never be sure, but it is certain that it is hard to shoot someone if you do not own a gun.

Military power is expensive. A third problem with acquiring power for its own sake is that it is extremely expensive. Beyond short-term budget decisions about spending (domestic or defense programs) and how to pay the bills (taxes or deficits), there is a more general, longer-range concern. One scholar who studied the decline of great powers between 1500 and the 1980s concluded that "imperial overstretch" was the cause of their degeneration (Kennedy, 1988). Kennedy's thesis is that superpowers of the past poured so many resources into military power that, ironically, they weakened the country's strength by siphoning off resources that should have been devoted to maintaining and improving the country's infrastructure. Kennedy's study did not include the Soviet Union, but it is arguable that the collapse of the USSR followed the pattern of overspending on the military, thereby enervating the country's economic core. Declinists warn that the United States is also guilty of imperial overstretch and could go the way of other great powers that rose, dominated, then fell from the pinnacle of power.

The **imperial overstretch thesis** has many critics (Knutsen, 1999). At the strategic level, some critics argue that far more danger is posed by a "lax Americana" than by any

The drawing of Uncle Sam reaching beyond his grasp illustrates the view that U.S. power is declining because of "imperial overstretch," whereby the country spends too much on military power in an effort to become and remain a superpower. Other observers argue that any decline that has occurred is the result of overspending on what they see as economically unproductive programs such as care for the elderly. This might be called "social overstretch."

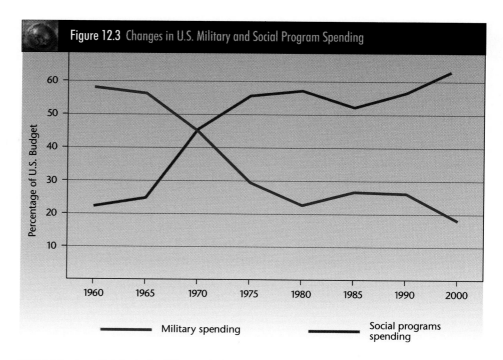

Figure 12.3 Changes in U.S. Military and Social Program Spending

Military spending

Social programs spending

Social spending does not include education. Military spending includes Department of Defense, Department of Energy nuclear weapons programs, and veterans' programs.

Data source: U.S. Bureau of the Census (1999).

Many analysts agree that a country's power declines if it does not invest in its infrastructure, but they disagree about what diverts funds from that investment. Imperial overstretch theory argues that defense spending is the drain; Social overstretch theory contends that appropriations for welfare, old-age care, and other such programs are sapping the economy. This figure shows the relative changes in U.S. military and social spending, but it does not answer whether either or both are too high, too low, or about right.

effort to create a "pax Americana." The reasoning is that if the United States does not exercise certain leadership as hegemon, then the international system is in danger of falling into disorder.[15] Similarly, some scholars warn that a rush to peace is only slightly less foolish than a rush to war. One study that reviewed the sharp cuts in U.S. military spending after World War II, the Korean War, and the Vietnam War, concluded, "In each case the savings proved only temporary, as declining defense budgets eroded military readiness and necessitated a rush to rearm in the face of new dangers abroad" (Thies, 1998:176).

Critics of Kennedy's thesis also say that it is wrong about the economic cause of decline. These critics agree with Kennedy that *overconsumption* (spending that depletes assets faster than the economy can replace them) at the expense of reinvestment (spending that creates infrastructure assets) causes decline. Whereas Kennedy argues that excessive military spending causes overconsumption, his critics say that the villain is too much social spending. This might be termed the **social overstretch thesis.** "Whether in the form of bread and circuses in the ancient world or medical care for the lower classes and social security for the aged in the modern world," the argument goes, it is social spending on the least productive elements of a society that financially drains a society (Gilpin, 1981:164). It is a harsh judgment, but its advocates believe that the economic reality is that such altruistic programs may leave our spirits enriched but our coffers depleted. Consider, for example, Figure 12.3. It shows that U.S. military spending has declined while spending on social programs has increased steadily as a percentage of the U.S. budget. It is also the case, however, that U.S. military spending accounts for about one-third of all military spending in the world. Which, if either, category would you cut to increase spending on education, transportation, communications, and other infrastructure programs? Indeed, as chapter 10 related, the aging population of most of the current EDCs is a major concern and could threaten the economic capacity of many countries in the not-too-distant future. Social Security, Medicare, and related issues were key points of controversy in the 2000 presidential campaign between Al Gore and George Bush, and the cost of sustaining the elderly promises to be a central concern for at least the next several decades.

LEVELS OF VIOLENCE: FROM INTIMIDATION TO ATTACK

A country's military power may be used in several escalating ways: (1) as a diplomatic backdrop that creates perceived power through military potential; (2) as a source of supply to another government or an insurgency group; (3) by explicitly threatening its use against an opponent; (4) through limited demonstrations of violence; and (5) by direct use of military forces to defeat an opponent. It also should be noted that the options provided by the five levels of violence form a *multiple menu*. That is, they are often exercised concurrently.

Military power does not have to be used or even overtly threatened to be effective. Its very existence establishes a *diplomatic backdrop* that influences other countries (Freedman, 1998). "Diplomacy without force is like baseball without a bat," one U.S. diplomat has commented.[16] One obvious role of military strength is to persuade potential opponents not to risk confrontation. Military power also influences friends and neutrals. One reason why the United States has been, and remains, a leader of the West is because massive U.S. conventional and nuclear military power creates a psychological assumption by both holder and beholder that the country with dominant military power will play a strong role.

Another way to use military power without actually having to fight is to serve as a *source of supply* to another government or an insurgency group. This approach is utilized in two related ways. One way is to supply an ally with arms during times of peace in order to strengthen a mutual position. The United States, for example, is a major supplier of arms to Israel. Arms are also regularly supplied overtly or covertly to a government or insurgent group that is embroiled in a war.

A step up the escalation ladder is *overtly threatening* an opponent. This may be done verbally, or it may involve shifts in the readiness or deployment of a country's armed forces. As the crisis with Iraq over UN arms inspections peaked in early 1998, President Clinton warned, "Either Saddam acts [to allow inspections] or we will have to."[17] To give substance to the president's threat the Pentagon leaked the outlines of the planned Operation Desert Thunder, which included a salvo of about 300 sea-based and 100 air-launched cruise missiles, and a round-the-clock campaign of 1,200 combat sorties against Iraq over four days, to be carried out by Air Force and Navy carrier-based warplanes.

Limited demonstration of your capability and commitment is a third military option. This involves wielding restrained force to intimidate or harass rather than defeat an opponent. One way to do this is by covert action such as hit-and-run, guerrilla-style attacks or terrorism. A second method is using very limited forces in an overt way. American threats were sufficient in 1998, but actual force in a limited demonstration was used in September 1996 when the United States attacked Iraqi military installations with about 30 cruise missiles in an effort to persuade Baghdad to end its military operations against Kurdish areas in the northern part of Iraq.

Direct action is the most violent option and involves using full-scale force to attempt to defeat an opponent. Within this context, the level of violence can range from highly constrained conventional conflict to unrestricted nuclear war.

(continued on page 332)

International Conflicts in the Post–World War II World

War is a continuing reality in the international system. The conflicts since World War II have been less cataclysmic than that global conflagration, but the ongoing use of force means that the world cannot be sure World War III does not lie in the future. The possibility of conflict also means that the military instrument is used in many ways, ranging from an intimidating diplomatic backdrop to a full-scale assault on an opponent.

	Conflict[1]	Start Date	Major Belligerent Countries[2] (in alphabetical order)	
1	Palestine	1948	Egypt Iraq Israel	Jordan Lebanon Syria

2	Korean	1950	China
			North Korea
			South Korea
			United Nations:
			  United States and 11 other
			  countries	

3	Soviet-Hungarian	1956	Hungary	Soviet Union
4	Sinai	1956	Egypt France	Israel United Kingdom
5	Sino-Indian	1962	China	India
6	Kashmir	1965	India	Pakistan
7	Vietnam	1965	Australia North Vietnam South Korea	South Vietnam United States
8	Six-Day	1967	Egypt Israel	Jordan Syria
9	Soviet-Czech	1968	Czechoslovakia	Soviet Union
10	Football	1969	El Salvador	Honduras
11	Indo-Pakistani	1971	India	Pakistan
12	Yom Kippur	1973	Egypt Israel	Syria
13	Cyprus	1974	Cyprus	Turkey
14	Ogaden	1977	Ethiopia	Somalia
15	Cambodian-Vietnamese	1978	Cambodia China	Vietnam
16	Ugandan-Tanzanian	1978	Tanzania	Uganda
17	Afghanistan	1979	Afghanistan	Soviet Union
18	Persian Gulf	1980	Iran	Iraq
19	Angola	1981	Angola Cuba	South Africa
20	Falklands	1982	Argentina	United Kingdom
21	Saharan	1983	Chad	Libya
22	Lebanon	1987	France Israel Lebanon	Syria United States
23	Panama	1989	Panama	United States

24	Persian Gulf	1990	Iraq
			United Nations:
			  United States and 7 other
			  countries	

25	Yugoslavia	1990	Bosnia-Herzegovina	Croatia Serbia
26	Peruvian-Ecuadorian	1995	Ecuador	Peru
27	Albania	1995	Albania	Yugoslavia (Serbia-Montenegro)
28	Rwanda	1995	Burundi	Rwanda
29	East Timor	1995	Indonesia	New Guinea insurgency
30	Cameroon	1996	Cameroon	Nigeria
31	Northern Iraq	1996	Iraq	Kurdish insurgency
32	Eritrea	1997	Eritrea	Yemen
33	Iraq	1998	Great Britain Iraq	United States
34	Kosovo	1999	Albania NATO	Yugoslavia
35	Ethiopia	2000	Ethiopia	Eritrea

[1] "Conflict" implies at least 1,000 battle deaths.
[2] "Belligerent" implies country supplied at least 5% of the combat troops in the conflict.

International Conflicts in the Post-World War II World

✦ Area of conflict

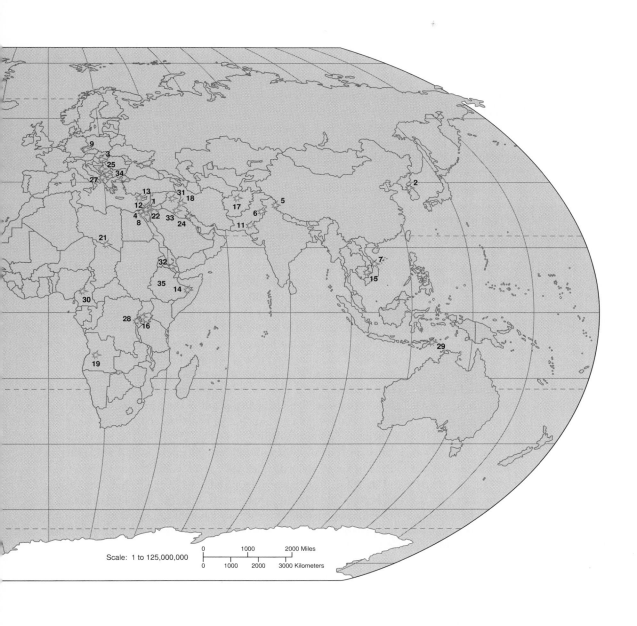

Scale: 1 to 125,000,000

EFFECTIVENESS OF FORCE

Another aspect of the threat and use of force is the question of whether or not it works in a utilitarian way. It does, and one of the reasons that weapons and war persist in the international system is that they are sometimes successful. This continuing use of force is evident in the map of international conflicts between the end of WW II and 2000 on pages 330–331. The threat of violence may successfully deter an enemy from attacking you or an ally. The actual use of force also sometimes accomplishes intended goals. Given these realities, we should ask ourselves how to determine if force will be effective by utilitarian standards. Answering this question necessitates looking at measurements and conditions for success.

Measurement

There are two ways of measuring the effectiveness of war. One is by trying to apply *cost/benefit analysis*. War is very expensive. There is no accurate count of the deaths in the Persian Gulf War, but 100,000 is a reasonable estimate. The UN–coalition countries spent $60 billion to oust Iraq from Kuwait. Estimates of the costs to both sides (including the physical destruction and lost oil revenues) are as high as $620 billion. Were the results worth the loss of life, human anguish, and economic destruction? Although such trade-offs are made in reality, it is impossible to arrive at any objective standards that can equate the worth of a human life or political freedom with dollars spent or territory lost.

The second way to judge the effectiveness of force is in terms of *goal attainment*. The issue is whether the accumulation and use of military power achieve the desired results. Wars are often caused by specific issues and fought with specific goals. Furthermore, the choice for war is not irrational because leaders usually calculate, accurately or not, their probability of success (Nevin, 1996). This calculation is called the *expected utility* of war. In the words of one study, "Initiators [of war] act as predators and are likely to attack [only] target states they know they can defeat" (Gartner & Siverson, 1996:4). An interesting related finding that helps to explain the different pattern of war exhibited by democratic countries compared to authoritarian countries is that "democratic leaders select wars to participate in that have a lower risk of defeat than is true for their authoritarian counterparts." The reason democratic leaders are more war averse, two scholars say, is because they fear that defeat will result in their losing office, thereby threatening "the very essence of the office-holding *homo politicus*" (Bueno de Mesquita & Siverson, 1995:852; Bennett & Stam, 1996).

Of course, as Miguel de Cervantes noted in *Don Quixote* (ca. 1615), "There is nothing so subject to inconsistency of fortune as war." Leaders often miscalculate and, as Saddam Hussein did in 1990, start a war they ultimately lose. The vagaries of war also mean that the government of a country that goes to war and fails to win stands a good chance of being overthrown electorally or through revolution by its citizens. That is, for example, what happened to the military government of Argentina after it attacked Great Britain's Falkland Islands in 1982.

Even given the costs and the risks, the utilitarian rationality of threatening or using force is supported by the fact that it sometimes does work. Haiti's military junta surrendered power in 1994 because of the threat of massive U.S. military power, not because the generals had a sudden burst of democratic conscience. The expected utility of force is especially apt to be positive when a major power starts the war. One study found that from 1495 to 1991, great powers that initiated wars won 60 percent of them (Wang & Ray, 1994). What is more, the initiators' success rate is going up. During the first three centuries (1495–1799), the initiators won 59 percent of the wars they fought. But during the last two centuries (1800–1991), the success rate increased, with the initiators winning 75 percent of the wars.

Conditions for Success

The next question, then, is, When does force succeed and when does it fail to accomplish its goals? There is no precise answer, but it is possible to synthesize the findings of a variety of studies and the views of military practitioners (see the Explanatory Notes section on p. 557) to arrive at some rudimentary rules for the successful use of military force, especially in cases of intervention when a country has not been directly attacked. In cases of intervention, success is most likely when:

1. A country takes action in areas where it has a clearly defined, preferably long-standing, and previously demonstrated commitment.
2. Government leaders are strongly committed to military action and have said so publicly.
3. Military force is used to counter other military force rather than to try to control political events.
4. Military force is used early and decisively (with sufficient force), rather than through extended threatening and slow escalation.
5. Goals are clearly established and adhered to, even if success seems to open other possibilities.
6. Use of military action and the announced goals both enjoy widespread domestic support.

These correlations between military action, political circumstances, and success are only preliminary and do not guarantee success. They do, however, indicate some of the factors that contribute to successful use of the military instrument.

THE CHANGING NATURE OF WAR

The scope and strategy of war have changed greatly over the centuries (Lawrence, 1998). Two factors are responsible: technology and nationalism.

It goes without saying that the *technological ability to kill* has escalated rapidly. Successive "advances" in the ability to deliver weapons at increasing distances and in the ability to kill ever more people with a single weapon have resulted in mounting casualties, both absolutely and as a percentage of soldiers and civilians of the countries at war.

Nationalism has also changed the nature of war. Before the nineteenth century, wars were generally fought between noble houses with limited armies. The French Revolution changed that. War began to be fought between nations, with increases in intensity and in numbers involved. France's Grand Army was the first to rely on a mass draft and the first to number more than a million men (Avant, 2000).

As a result of technology and nationalism, the *scope* of war has expanded. Entire nations have become increasingly involved in wars. Before 1800, no more than 3 of 1,000 people of a country participated in a war. By World War I, the European powers called 1 of 7 people to arms. Technology increased the need to mobilize the population for industrial production and also increased the capacity for, and the rationality of, striking at civilians. Nationalism made war a movement of the masses, increasing their stake and also giving justification for attacking the enemy nation. Thus, the lines between military and civilian targets have blurred.

Finally, the *strategy* of war has changed. Two concepts, the power to defeat and the power to hurt, are key here. The **power to defeat** is the ability to seize territory or overcome enemy military forces and is the classic goal of war. The **power to hurt,** or coercive violence, is the ability to inflict pain outside the immediate military sphere. It means hurting some so that the resistance of others will crumble. The power to hurt has become increasingly important to all aspects of warfare because the war effort depends on a country's economic effort and, often, the morale of its citizens. Perhaps the first military leader to understand the importance of the power to hurt in modern warfare was General William Tecumseh Sherman during the U.S. Civil War. "My aim was to whip the rebels, to humble their pride, to follow them to their inmost recesses, and [to] make them fear and dread us," the general wrote in his memoirs.[18]

Traditionally wars were fought with little reference to hurting. Even when hurting was used, it depended on the ability to attack civilians by first defeating the enemy's military forces. During the American Revolution, for example, the British could have utilized their power to hurt—to kill civilians in the major cities they controlled—and they might have won the war. Instead they concentrated on defeating the American army (which they could not catch, then grew too strong to overpower), and they lost.

In the modern era, the power to defeat has declined in importance relative to the power to hurt. Guerrilla and nuclear warfare both rely extensively on terror to accomplish their ends. Even conventional warfare sometimes uses terror tactics to sap an opponent's morale. The use of strategic bombing to blast German cities during World War II is an example.

CLASSIFYING WARS

The changing nature of war, the increased power of weapons, and the shifts in tactics have all made classifying wars more difficult. Studies of war and other uses of political violence divide.these acts into a variety of categories. Whatever the criteria for these categories, though, the exact boundaries between various types of wars or other political phenomena are imprecise. Therefore, you should be concerned mostly with the issues involved in planning for and fighting wars. With recognition of their limits, this chapter will rely on a mix of geographical scope and weaponry to divide international conflict into three categories: local conflict, regional conflict, and strategic nuclear conflict.

 LOCAL CONFLICT

Of our three categories of international conflict, the one that has the most limited geographical scope and that involves the least powerful weapons is local conflict involving, at most, a very few countries. It is possible to use a variety of the instruments of violence at this level. Three ways for an outside country to apply its military power in local conflict are through (1) arms transfers, (2) covert operations and terrorism, and (3) direct and overt military intervention.

ARMS TRANSFERS

The international supply of arms is big business, involving tens of billions of dollars annually. There are several motivations to export arms that we will explore. Whatever the cause, however, the global flow of arms can be properly considered as a form of intervention because, whether intended or not, it has an impact on events within countries and between countries (other than the supplier). This is particularly true where the exports are to LDCs.

Arms Transfers: Destinations and Sources

The export and import of arms has long been important economically and politically, but it reached new heights during the cold war as the two hostile superpowers struggled for influence. World arms exports during the 1980s alone amounted to $490 billion. The arms that flowed in the world during the cold war came largely from the superpowers, with the United States and Soviet Union accounting for about two-thirds of all arms transfers. The LDCs were the destination of about two-thirds of the flow of weaponry.

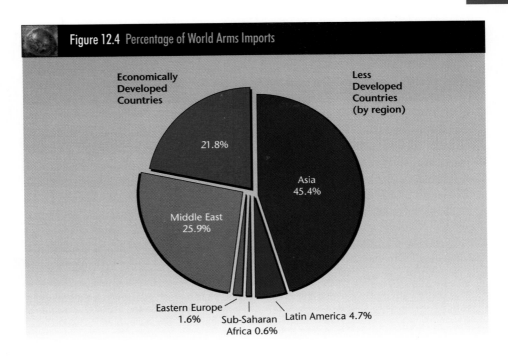

Figure 12.4 Percentage of World Arms Imports

Economically Developed Countries

21.8%

Middle East 25.9%

Eastern Europe 1.6%

Sub-Saharan Africa 0.6%

Latin America 4.7%

Less Developed Countries (by region)

Asia 45.4%

Data source: Stockholm International Peace Research Institute (SIPRI) Web site at: http://projects.sipri.se/armstrade/atfproj.html.

World arms imports in 1999 came to about $45 billion. LDCs buy most of the weapons; a similar pie chart of exports would show that EDCs sell most of the arms.

More recently, the end of the cold war, the drop in military aid, and the easing of tensions in the Middle East have combined to decrease the arms trade. Overall, annual world arms transfers (sales and military aid) dropped 39 percent (to $45 billion) from 1989 to 1999. Still, the movement of arms that continues is substantial. Figure 12.4 shows the percentage of arms imports of various global regions. The most worrisome region is Asia, with the arms imports of East Asia increasing nearly 40 percent during the decade.

As for arms exports, the EDCs are the dominant exporters, with 97 percent of the market. The United States is by far the world's leading arms merchant, with 58.3 percent of the market. Other countries with more than 1 percent are Great Britain (12.1 percent), France (10.8 percent), Russia (4.2 percent), China (1.8 percent), Sweden (1.6 percent), Germany (1.4 percent), and Italy (1.3 percent).

Arms Transfers: Motives

There are several motives that prompt countries to sell and give weapons to other countries or to insurgent groups. One is to *support allies* with arms during peacetime. A second reason countries supply weapons is to *intervene in a conflict*. Rebel groups in Afghanistan that are fighting the fundamentalist Taliban regime, for example, receive support from Pakistan and other bordering countries with more moderate Muslim governments, which fear that they might be destabilized by Taliban influence.

A third motive for supplying arms is to wield *diplomatic influence* over the recipient by befriending it or by creating a dependency relationship. Sometimes the strategy works, but often it does not. One study of U.S. policy between 1950 and 1992 found that influence was most likely to be gained through the arms trade under four conditions: (1) when the approach was positive (selling arms rather than withholding them); (2) when the arms were used to change the recipient's foreign policy (rather than to promote democracy or human rights); (3) when the recipient's government was civilian;

Arms proliferation occurs in part through massive international sales of conventional weapons. Now that the cold war is over and the United States, Russia, and some other countries are buying fewer weapons for their own use, they are especially eager to support their defense industries and workers by selling arms abroad.

and (4) when the United States exercised greater hegemonic power earlier in the 42-year period (Sislin, 1994).

A fourth motive for selling weapons is to *preserve the defense production infrastructure*. Declining military budgets lead to the closing of defense plants and the movement of scientists, engineers, and skilled plant workers into other fields. Arguably, this loss of capacity weakens a country because it will be difficult to replace if necessary in the future, especially if it is needed quickly. One way to have both a low defense budget and continued weapons production capability is to keep the weapons industry and its workers busy making arms for other countries and groups.

National economic benefit is a fifth, and now perhaps the predominant, motive behind arms exports. As one Russian official noted candidly, "The arms trade is a highly profitable business."[19] This is especially true to the world's leading arms merchant, the United States. There have been some years since the end of the cold war in which the U.S. defense industry has sold more warplanes to other countries than to the U.S. government. Such weapons production keeps workers on the job, taxes from their incomes flowing to the government, and profits from sales rolling in to corporations and their investors. When the United Arab Emirates announced in 1998 that it would buy 80 U.S. F-16 fighters for $7 billion, the deal was hailed personally by Vice President Al Gore and meant that the plane's manufacturer, Lockheed Martin, could reverse its plan to lay off 2,000 of the 11,000 workers at its Fort Worth plant and, instead, add 2,000 workers.

Other countries are also eager to sell their military wares, and for some, foreign sales are a critical part of their exports. Arms are North Korea's leading export, and it has been developing such missiles as the Taepodong, with a 2,000-to-3,000 mile range, more to market them than for Pyongyang's own use. "Our military exports are aimed at obtaining foreign money we need at present," the offical Korean Central News agency admitted recently in a moment of candor.[20]

Arms Transfers: Dangers

It is worth belaboring the obvious to point out that selling or giving arms to other countries is not like other trade and aid transfers. There can be little doubt that countries

Even if imported weapons do not cause civil wars, they certainly fuel them. One troubling aspect of these internal conflicts is the phenomenon of "boy soldiers," such as this 11-year-old boy in Sierra Leone who, with an imported assault rifle, is on guard at an army checkpoint in May 2000. The weapons trade that armed this boy raises difficult moral issues for countries that export weapons.

have legitimate defense needs and that sometimes arms transfers help stabilize situations. It is also true, however, that the massive flow of arms entails dangers to both the importing and to the exporting countries.

Cost One danger of the weapons trade is cost. As noted earlier, countries, especially poorer ones, face classic "guns or butter" budget decisions about whether to spend on defense or domestic programs. At least some of the more than $25 billion a year in weapons that LDCs import could be devoted to domestic infrastructure or social programs.

Increased Violence A second danger, according to many scholars, is that the arms flow increases the level and perhaps frequency and intensity of violence between countries and within countries. A study found that the U.S. and Soviet transfer of arms to rival client states during the cold war was "profoundly destabilizing" (Sanjian, 1999:641). Another recent study concludes that the consequences of the continuing flow of weapons, especially to the LDCs, is "likely to be severe.... Third World countries now possess the capacity to conduct wars of greater intensity, duration, and reach." The study notes that "while no one can predict that the growing availability of modern weapons will lead to an increased frequency of armed conflict, there is a high correlation between the growing diffusion of war-making material and the increased tempo of global violence" (Klare & Lumpe, 2000:173; Parker, 1999, Hashim, 1998).

Moral Corruption A third peril of the weapons trade, according to some critics, is that supplying weapons for others to kill with is immoral. Whether or not you agree with that, it is hard not to give some credence to the rueful observation of Samuel Cummings, president of Interarms, a major private arms dealer, that "the arms business is based on human folly, and folly has yet to be measured nor its depths plumbed."[21] One

(continued on page 338)

THE KILLING FIELDS

Whatsoever a man soweth, that shall he also reap.
Galatians 6:7

They wait with menacing silence and near invisibility in the fields of Cambodia, on the paths of Angola, in the hills of Bosnia, and elsewhere around the globe. Land mines are patient. They kill and maim today; they will wait until tomorrow or for many years to claim a victim. Land mines are nondiscriminatory; they care not whether it is a military boot or a child's bare foot that causes them to sprout their deadly yield of shrapnel.

The civil war in Angola is now over; land mines there still randomly kill an average of 120 people a month. According to UNICEF, 75 percent of mine victims in El Salvador are children. Mines have taken a limb or an eye from one out of every 236 Cambodians; 80,000 have been killed. Sam Soa was trying to find his cow in a field near his village when he stepped on a mine. "It knocks you down," he remembers. "I didn't realize what had happened, and I tried to run away."[1] Sam Soa could not run away, though; the bottom of his left leg was gone.

Land mines also attack those who come to help. Ken Rutherford, an American worker with the International Rescue Committee, was traveling a dusty rural road in Somalia when a blast tore off his right foot. "I was trying to put it back on," he recalls. "It kept falling off."[2] On another continent, the first American soldier killed in Bosnia was Sergeant Donald Dugan. The assailant was a mine. Globally, perhaps 1,000 people a month share the fate of Sam Soa, Ken Rutherford, and Donald Dugan, and at least 300 of them die.

It is impossible to know exactly how many land mines lie in wait around the world, but a U.S. State Department report, "Hidden Killers 1998: The Global Landmine Crisis," puts the figure at 60 to 70 million

in 60 countries.[3] Egypt, with 23 million mines dug into its soil, many dating back to World War II, has the most land mines on its territory. Bosnia-Herzegovina, with 176 mines per square mile, has the densest concentration of mines and also the highest ratio of mines to population (two mines per Bosnian).

One reason that mines litter the earth is that they cost as little as $2 to make. They are, one U.S. senator observed, the "Saturday night specials of warfare."[4] Unfortunately, mines are difficult and expensive to remove. Kuwait spent $800 million on mine removal after the Persian Gulf War, and the UN estimates that with current technology, it would take $33 billion and 1,100 years to purge the world of its land mines.

The ghastly toll of mines spurred the formation of the International Campaign to Ban Land Mines (ICBL), an NGO alliance of more than 1,000 citizen-groups from 60 countries. The effort of the ICBL and supportive countries such as Canada eventually led to a conference that met in Olso, Norway, then in Ottawa, Canada, in 1997 to negotiate and sign a treaty banning the production, use, or sale of land mines. Most countries responded favorably, but China and Russia did not. The United States also opposed an immediate ban on land mines, arguing that they were still necessary along the border between North and South Korea and could once again be needed there and elsewhere in times of war. Retired general H. Norman Schwarzkopf, who commanded the UN coalition forces in the Persian Gulf War, and retired general David Jones, former chairman of the U.S. Joint Chiefs of Staff (JCS), wrote an open letter to President Clinton telling him that, "given the wide range of weaponry available to military forces today, antipersonnel land mines are not essential."[5] The existing JCS opposed a ban, however, and Clinton was not willing to ignore them. "I can't afford a breach

---

of several especially troubling ramifications of the arms trade is the merciless maiming and death caused by land mines, as discussed in the box The Killing Fields.

Another shameful phenomenon is boy soldiers. Children, usually small boys, are often persuaded or forced to fight for one rebel group or another. These groups would find it difficult or impossible to wage war without an outside supply of weapons. Experts estimate that up to 300,000 children in 50 countries are involved in fighting as soldiers or support workers. For example, during the grueling civil war (1989–1997) that decimated Liberia, Charles Taylor, the leader of one of the Liberian factions (and now the country's president), created a special fighting force of child fighters called the

with the Joint Chiefs," Clinton told the head of the Vietnam Veterans of America.[6]

The opposition of the United States and a few other countries was not enough to stem the momentum. With the U.S. delegate looking somberly on, an overwhelming majority of delegates from the more than 120 countries at the conference agreed to submit a treaty to the countries of the world for signature and ratification. Those countries that adhere to the treaty commit themselves never to use, produce, stockpile, or transfer antipersonnel land mines; and they agree to destroy current inventories and remove all mines they have planted. Countries have the right to withdraw from the treaty with six months' warning. China, Russia, the United States and a few other countries declined to sign the treaty, but that did not dampen the enthusiasm in Ottawa. Canada was the first country to sign, and after affixing his signature, Lloyd Axworthy, Canada's foreign minister, turned to hug American Jody Williams, who won the Nobel Peace Prize for her work with the ICBL. Kofi Annan also honored Williams and the NGO. The work of the ICBL, said the secretary-general, made "the international community a living, thriving reality, and not just the hope of a distant future." "Together we are a superpower," Williams said to the national and NGO representatives alike. "It's a new definition of superpower. It's not one of us, it's everyone."[7]

The Anti-Personnel Mine Treaty became effective on March 1, 1999, six months after the 40th country had ratified it. By mid-2000, 137 countries had signed, and 100 had ratified it. China, Russia, and the United States remain among the holdouts, but the growing norm against land mines will probably pressure them to come along eventually. Clinton unilaterally declared that by 2003 the United States will stop using land mines, except in Korea, and will sign the treaty in 2006. The president pledged to spend $100 million a year on land mine clearance; Canada

The refusal of the United States to sign the treaty to ban land mines has drawn many protests, including this one by the Land Mine Survivors Network in front of the White House. To make their point about the danger of land mines to innocent victims long after a war is over, the protesters piled up their prosthetic devices on the sidewalk and asked, "Why not sign?"

pledged $15 million a year; and other countries joined in the effort to speed up the removal of the stealthy killers that made the admonition, "Watch your step," deadly serious advice.

Small Boy Unit. Samuel Bull joined the unit when he was eight years old. He later recalled being given Valium tablets, known locally as "bubbles," before battles. The boy also admits to killing many people, including one woman whom he machine-gunned with his AK-47 assault rifle because she refused to hand over food. "I liked the sound of the gun," remembered Sam, who had entered a UN rehabilitation program. But observers were worried that Sam and the others who have been turned into killers before puberty are scarred for life. At the UN compound, Sam discovered that someone had taken a pair of his socks. "The next time someone comes into my sock drawer, I'll take my knife and kill him," Sam snarled. "I knew he meant it," said a UN social worker.[22]

Another troubling moral issue is based on the fact that supplying arms to an oppressive government sometimes helps it to stay in power. Although studies show that human rights factors do play a role in determining whether or not the United States will supply another country with weapons, it is also true that "a nondemocracy still has roughly a [50 percent] chance of receiving U.S. arms" (Blanton, 1998:15).

Intervention Pressure A fourth danger in the arms trade is that the country supplying the weapons begins to be identified with the recipient country or rebel group. If things begin to go badly for the recipient, and even more and more powerful weapons do not reverse the tide, then the supplier may be tempted to send advisers, engage in limited combat support, and, finally, commit to a full-scale military intervention with its own troops. This is how the United States waded ever deeper into the quagmire in Vietnam and how the Soviet Union fell into the abyss in Afghanistan.

Facing One's Own Weapons A fifth danger is that an arms-exporting country may eventually find itself facing its own weapons. This occurred during the Persian Gulf War. In the decade before its invasion of Kuwait, Iraq bought fighter aircraft from Egypt and France; antitank weapons from Egypt, France, and Italy; tanks from Egypt and Kuwait; armored personnel carriers from France and Great Britain; artillery from Egypt, France, and Saudi Arabia; and bombs from Saudi Arabia. None of the combat systems came directly from the United States, but some (such as the Saudi-supplied howitzers and bombs) were U.S. weapons that had been resold to Iraq. The upshot of these sales was that Kuwait had supplied Iraq with some of the tanks in its invasion force; and when American, British, Egyptian, and French troops moved to liberate Kuwait, they faced weapons that their own countries had supplied to Iraq.

Exported weapons, especially those sent to insurgent groups, also regularly wind up on the vast black market. Only about 30 percent of the $2 billion in the U.S. arms sent to the Afghan rebels during the 1980s ever arrived at their destination. Some of the diverted weapons (such as sophisticated, shoulder-fired Stinger surface-to-air missiles) were so dangerous that, in a bizarre twist, the CIA tried to buy them back on the subterranean arms market. Unfortunately for global safety, the missiles were in such demand that even though the CIA offered to pay more than twice what a Stinger originally cost, the agency was considerably outbid by eager rebels, terrorists, and other arms shoppers willing to pay six to seven times the official price for one of the missiles.

Hypocrisy A sixth problem with the arms trade is that, however laudable you think your goals are, it is hard to persuade others not to do what you are doing. Massive U.S. arms sales, says one analyst typically, "give a green light to other weapons sellers in the world."[23] Moreover the U.S. contention that it sells arms only to responsible recipients strikes others as patently self-serving. One effort by Washington to prevent the sale of weapons to Iran by the Czech Republic left one of that country's officials fuming that the Americans "are preaching that we drink water while they drink wine. I consider it hypocritical."[24]

COVERT OPERATIONS AND TERRORISM

A second form of intervention involves supporting dissident forces in another country or directly intervening through special operations, such as guerrilla forces, intelligence operatives, or other clandestine agents. When such covert activities extend beyond attacking a certain range of clearly military targets—and the line is thin—the operations move into the realm of terrorism.

What concerns us most here is **state terrorism**. This is terrorism carried out directly by, or specifically encouraged and funded by, an established government. Exactly what

It is easy to write off terrorists as lunatics, but they are not. Osama bin Laden, who is the alleged mastermind behind several terrorists attacks, including those in 1998 on the U.S. embassies in Kenya and Tanzania, holds fervent religious views, but he is almost certainly not psychotic. Instead, he claims that he is fighting the corrupting influence of U.S. power and culture with the only methods available to him and his cause.

the line is between terrorism and military action, and who is guilty or not of terrorism are not, however, matters of universal agreement. From the U.S. perspective, the State Department's annual terrorist report for 1999 lists Cuba, Iran, Iraq, Libya, North Korea, Sudan, and Syria as countries guilty of state terrorism.

Others condemn the U.S. approach to defining terrorism as self-serving and hypocritical. Osama bin Laden, who allegedly masterminded the attacks on the U.S. embassies in Kenya and Tanzania in August 1998, charges that "American history does not distinguish between civilians and military, and not even women and children. [Americans] are the ones who used the [atomic] bombs against [the Japanese]."[25]

From this perspective, one has to wonder about the U.S. retaliation for the attack on its embassies. The response included a Tomahawk cruise missile attack that destroyed an alleged chemical weapons factory in Khartoum, Sudan. American officials claimed that the factory supplied explosives to bin Laden. Sudan denied the U.S. charge and claimed that the plant was a pharmaceutical company. President Omar Hassan el-Bashir of Sudan called the attack, which killed many Sudanese, an act of terrorism. He charged that "the American president has violated international law. He meant to destroy a civilian establishment and to kill innocent people.... He is a war criminal of the first degree."[26] Among those who were not sure which government was right was former U.S. president Jimmy Carter, who called for an international investigation to determine what, in fact, the factory produced. During the ensuing controversy, no credible evidence to support the U.S. contention was ever found or made public.

Questions have also been raised about American complicity in the alleged state terrorism practiced by some U.S. client states, especially during the anticommunist fervor of the cold war. A secret document that was declassified in 1999 records the anguished views expressed in 1968 by Peter Vaky, the second-ranking U.S. diplomat in Guatemala. American support was flowing through the embassy to the Guatemalan military's campaign against Marxist guerrillas and their civilian supporters. Vaky wrote that the military was "guilty of atrocities. Interrogations are brutal, torture is used, and bodies are mutilated." The guilt-ridden diplomat went on, "We have not been honest with ourselves [about our complicity]. We have condoned counter-terror, we may even in effect have encouraged and blessed it." That occurred because, "We have been so obsessed with the fear of insurgency that we have rationalized away our qualms and uneasiness.... Murder, torture, and mutilation are all right if our side is doing it and the victims are Communists."[27]

The Record of Covert Operations and Terrorism

The use of covert military intervention by countries has increased in recent decades for several reasons. First, there has been an increase in civil strife within countries. Second, attempts to topple governments or to create separatist states are now usually waged using guerrilla tactics, rather than conventional tactics, as occurred during the U.S. Civil War. More than any single reason, this change in tactics has occurred because the preponderance of high-tech weapons available to government forces makes it nearly suicidal for opposition forces to fight conventionally. Third, covert intervention avoids the avalanche of international and, often, domestic criticism that overt interventions set off. Fourth, clandestine operations allow the initiating country to disengage more easily, if it wishes, than would be possible if it overtly committed regular military forces.

Terrorism: The Recent Record There are different estimates of the number of covert military operations, but it is safe to say that the number of paramilitary operations has been extensive since World War II. The United States and, while it existed, the Soviet Union stand first in the ranks of countries that have participated in such activities, but many countries have sent military special operations forces or intelligence operatives into other countries.

International terrorism has also become a regular occurrence. The number of attacks rose from 165 in 1968 to peak at 666 in 1987. Since then terrorist attacks have been somewhat less frequent (Enders & Sandler, 1999). Such incidents averaged 543 annually during the 1980s and 382 in the 1990s, with 397 terrorist acts in 1999. During the period 1994 through 1999, international terrorist attacks injured 19,207 people, of whom over 2,000 died.

Geographically, international terrorism has been widespread, with all regions other than North America suffering frequent terrorist attacks. International terrorists have perpetrated some attacks in the United States, such as the spectacular bombing of the World Trade Center in New York City that killed six people in 1993. A much greater danger, however, has been domestic terrorists, such as the militia zealots who bombed the Oklahoma City federal building in 1995, killing 168 people.

The ultimate goal of the terrorists who planted the bomb that destroyed this bus and its occupants in Jerusalem, Israel, was not to kill these people. Instead it was to create publicity for the terrorists' cause and to breed fear among surviving Israelis.

Terrorism: The Future Record The explosion that tore apart the Federal Building in Oklahoma City and buried its victims under tons of rubble, the mangled remains of Israeli civilians in a bomb-shattered bus, the hollow stares of hostages held as pawns in the macabre game that terrorists play—these are the images of terrorism that have too often gripped us. For all the ghastly history of terrorism, what the future may record is more disturbing. Now there is a new, more terrible possibility—nuclear, biological, and chemical terrorism (Gurr & Cole, 2000; Tucker, 2000).

The concern over the possibility of terrorists acquiring a nuclear weapon has grown in recent years as authorities in the Czech Republic, Germany, and elsewhere have seized several small (up to 12 ounces) shipments of plutonium and several larger quantities (up to 6 pounds) of uranium-235 (Cameron, 1999). Even such small amounts, if made into a bomb, would cause severe blast damage over roughly a 40-block area and spread radiation far beyond. Moreover, it is also possible to conduct nuclear terrorism through such methods as water-supply contamination.

The sources of the fissionable material were not certain, but Russia was widely suspected. With that country, as well as the United States, dismantling many of its nuclear weapons, there are tons of plutonium and uranium that have to be stored. Adding to that is Russia's desperate economic condition. One potential deal that German intelligence agents prevented would have exchanged 4 kilograms of plutonium for $250 million (or $28.4 million a pound), and such figures are especially tempting to impoverished Russian military and scientific officials.

The possibility of chemical or biological attack is also increasing. A chemical attack is the most likely because the chemicals are not difficult to obtain and to combine into lethal mixtures. In 1995 a Japanese cult, Aum Shinrikyo (Supreme Truth), used nerve gas in an attack on a Tokyo subway station that killed 12 people and injured 5,000. Police later discovered that the group had been working to create a biological agent. Two of the involved cult members were sentenced to death by Japanese courts in mid-2000, and others face trial and possible capital punishment.

Biological weapons are also a threat. A report by the U.S. Office of Technology Assessment (OTA) worries about the possibility of terrorists spreading plague, botulism, or anthrax. With regard to anthrax, the process of turning *bacillus anthracis*, a disease of sheep, into a pneumonic form that kills more than 90 percent of the humans it infects is not extremely difficult. The OTA anticipates that on a calm night, a light plane flying over Washington, D.C., and releasing just 220 pounds of anthrax spores using a common crop sprayer could deliver a fatal dose to 3 million people.[28]

What defenses can countries erect against such terrorist attacks? The answer, CIA director John M. Deutch told Congress, is that "the ability of our country, or, I might say, any other country in the developed world to protect its infrastructure from a terrorist attack based on nuclear, chemical, and biological weapons is very, very small indeed."[29] To test the U.S. ability to respond, the government conducted a mock biological attack. A genetically engineered virus designed to be invulnerable to existing cures was supposedly spread in the exercise along the U.S.–Mexico frontier. "You could make such a virus today," said a leading expert on genetic engineering. "Any trained molecular virologist with a really good lab can do it."[30] The results of the exercise remain secret, but they reportedly confirm CIA director Deutch's earlier testimony that the country was unprepared.

The Causes and Effects of Covert Operations and Terrorism

It is important to understand why terrorism occurs and what impact it has. While the causes and effectiveness of terrorism are controversial, there is wide agreement among serious analysts that it is misleading to treat terrorism as the irrational acts of crazed fanatics. To the contrary, terrorism occurs because many of those who use it consider it a necessary, legitimate, and effective tool to rid themselves of what they consider oppression. It is necessary, its proponents say, because it may be the only way for an oppressed group to prevail against a heavily armed government.

The effectiveness of terrorism has been further enhanced by modern conditions. Modernity has created an ever-greater number of targets for terrorists. Urbanization brings people together so that they are more easily attacked. Modern transportation also provides ready opportunity, as does modern dependence on electric generation and transmission facilities, water supplies, and other utilities that can be disrupted. Modern communications have also made terrorism more efficacious because the goal of the terrorist is not to kill or injure, as such. Instead, the aim of terrorism is to gain attention for a cause and to create widespread anxiety that will, in turn, create pressure on governments to negotiate with terrorists and accede to their every demand. Without the media to transmit the news of their acts, terrorists would affect only their immediate victims, which would not accomplish the terrorists' goals.

In the end, terrorism, like most forms of violence, exists because terror tactics sometimes do accomplish their goals. However much one may condemn the acts themselves, it is also accurate to say that over the years Palestinian terrorists almost certainly played a role in increasing the willingness of Israel to deal with them, in enhancing global awareness of and concern with the Palestinian cause, and in bringing pressure on Israel by the international community to reach an agreement with them (Guelke, 1998; Reich, 1998).

DIRECT MILITARY INTERVENTION

The most overt form of coercive intervention is for a country to dispatch its own forces to another country. The junctures where military aid becomes military intervention and where limited military intervention becomes full-scale war are debatable. What is implied here, though, is the direct but limited use of military personnel on one side or the other of another country's internal conflict.

Beyond the cost in lives and wealth to the intervening country, there is the danger that direct military intervention will fail or that it will escalate into a full-scale war that, in turn, may itself fail. The U.S. experience in Vietnam is an example of an intervention that both escalated and failed, as is the long, and ultimately unsuccessful, Soviet involvement in Afghanistan throughout most of the 1980s.

The legitimacy of intervention is also controversial. Panama provides a good case in point. General Manuel Noriega was abhorrent by almost any political or ethical standard. The U.S. intervention in 1989 ended his rule, and Panama is well rid of him. Does this legitimize the U.S. intervention? Certainly President Bush thought so, and others agreed. Yet intervening in the internal affairs of another country is troubling. It may well be, as Senator Edward M. Kennedy observed, that "the United States [or anyone else] does not have the right under international law… to roam the hemisphere to bring dictators to justice or… to impose democracy by the barrel of a gun on Panama or any other nation."[31]

 ## REGIONAL CONFLICT

War sometimes involves entire regions. Geographically, even the two conflicts labeled "world wars" in this century were, in a sense, regional conflicts. The vast majority of the fighting in World War I took place in Europe and its surrounding waters. The scope of combat in World War II was broader, but the conflict can also be seen as two great regional wars. One, in Europe and North Africa, primarily pitted the Germans and the Italians against the Americans, British, Canadians, French, and Russians. The second, in Asia, was mostly a struggle between the Americans, Australians, British, and Chinese on one side and the Japanese on the other. Other regions remained largely unscathed.

Regional conflicts often include the use of more and more powerful weapons. Such wars used to be called "conventional wars" or "traditional wars" to distinguish them, in part, from "nuclear wars." That distinction makes less sense to some observers now because a few countries possess an array of tactical (battlefield) nuclear weapons. The availability of chemical and biological weapons and the ongoing development of electronic and other weapons that, not long ago, were the stuff of science fiction also render inadequate the use of the adjectives *conventional* or *traditional* to describe regional wars.

GOALS AND CONDUCT

The classic statement on the proper goal of war was made by German strategist Carl von Clausewitz in *On War* (1833). He argued that "war is not merely a political act, but also a political instrument, a continuation of political relations, a carrying out of the same by other means." Note that Clausewitz's point implies several principles that civilian and military decision makers should keep in mind.

First, *war is a part of diplomacy, not a substitute for it*. Therefore, channels of communication to the opponent should be kept open in an attempt to limit the conflict and to reestablish peace. Second, *wars should be governed by political, not military, considerations*. Often commanders chafe under restrictions, as General Douglas MacArthur did during the Korean War (1950–1953) over his lack of authority to attack China. When generals become insubordinate, as MacArthur did, they ought to be removed from command, as he was.

Third, Clausewitz held that *war should be fought with clear political goals*. When goals are not established or are later ignored, disaster looms. The stated U.S. goal at the beginning of the Korean War in 1950 was to drive North Korea's forces out of South Korea. That was soon accomplished, but instead of declaring victory, an emboldened President Truman ordered U.S. forces to move northward to "liberate" North Korea from communism. That brought China into the war. As a result, a war that arguably had already been won dragged on for two more years and cost tens of thousands more lives. For all the later criticism of George Bush for not driving on to Baghdad and unseating Saddam Hussein, the U.S. president should get credit for not repeating Truman's mistake. The stated UN goal in 1991 was to liberate Kuwait. When that was accomplished, Bush halted hostilities. In so doing, he ended the killing and stayed within the legal confines of the UN resolution that authorized the action.

The fact that most wars are fought within limits does not mean that those boundaries are never violated. **Escalation** occurs when the rules are changed and the level of combat increases. Increasing the scope and intensity of a war, however, has always been dangerous, and it is particularly so in an era of nuclear, biological, and chemical (NBC) weapons. Not long after their entry into the war in Vietnam in the mid-1970s, Americans began to realize that continuing the war within the limits it was being fought offered little chance of victory and carried a heavy cost in lives and economics. Escalating the war by invading North Vietnam might have brought China into the war and increased the cost monumentally. Also, many Americans were sickened by the human cost to both sides; if the war had been continued or escalated, there would have surely been an increase of deep divisions within the United States. Ultimately, the United States could have achieved a military victory by "nuking" North Vietnam and killing everyone there. Americans finally accepted, though, that victory was not the only thing. American troops began to withdraw from Vietnam in 1969; all U.S. troops were gone by 1973; Vietnam was reunited under Hanoi's control in 1975.

AVOIDING UNCHECKED ESCALATION

The dangers of escalation and the prudence of keeping limited wars limited make it important to understand how to avoid unchecked escalation. As with most things political, there is no set formula. There are, however, a few useful standards.

Keep lines of communication open. The basic principle is that escalation (or de-escalation) should be a deliberate strategy used to signal a political message to the enemy. Accordingly, it is also important to send signals through diplomatic or public channels so that the opponent will not mistake the escalation as an angry spasm of violence or misconstrue the de-escalation as a weakening of resolve.

Limit goals. Unlimited goals by one side may evoke unlimited resistance by the other, so limiting goals is another way to avoid unchecked escalation. It is usually appropriate, for instance, that a goal should fall short of eliminating the opponent as a sovereign state! Even where unconditional victory is the aim, obliteration of the enemy population is not an appropriate goal.

Restrict geographical scope. It is often wise to limit conflict to as narrow a geographical area as possible. American forces refrained from invading China during the Korean War. Similarly, the Soviets passed up the temptation to blockade Berlin in 1962 in response to the U.S. blockade of Cuba.

Observe target restrictions. Regional wars can be controlled by limiting targets. Despite their close proximity, the Arabs and Israelis have never tried to bomb each other's capitals. Iraq's launch of Scud missiles against Tel Aviv and other Israeli cities in 1991 was, by contrast, a serious escalation.

Limit weapons. Yet another way to keep war limited is to adhere to the principle that the level of force used should be no greater than the minimum necessary to accomplish war aims. The stricture on weapons has become even more important in an era when there is such a great potential for the use of limited, on-the-battlefield NBC weapons. In addition to moral issues, even the limited use of NBC weapons might well set off a serious escalation that could lead to strategic nuclear war or massive biological and chemical attacks.

REGIONAL CONFLICT AND NBC WEAPONS

The principle of avoiding the use of NBC weapons in order to prevent escalation leads to a discussion of these armaments. Most of those who read this text will have some knowledge of the availability and use of atomic/nuclear weapons, which date back to 1945. Much more will be said presently about these weapons. For here, though, we can note that the United States, Russia, and other countries have a range of relatively low-yield (blast equivalents as low as 0.3 tons of TNT) warheads and bombs designed for tactical (battlefield) use. In mid-2000, Russia had about 4,000 and the United States had about 1,700 tactical nuclear weapons in their respective arsenals. Fewer people are familiar with biological and chemical weapons. They have long existed.

Biological Weapons Many historians trace the use of biological warfare to 1763 when, during an Indian uprising, the British commander in North America, Sir Jeffrey Amherst, wrote to subordinates at Fort Pitt, "Could it not be contrived to send the smallpox among those disaffected tribes of Indians?"[32] As it turns out, Sir Jeffrey's prompting was unnecessary. Soldiers at the fort had already given disease-infected blankets to members of the Shawnee and Delaware tribes.

Although the 1972 Biological Weapons Convention bans their production, possession, and use, germ-based *biological weapons* continue to be a threat. For example, Russia's deputy foreign minister admitted in 1992 that "the Soviet Union was violating [the BW] convention and was running a program in the sphere of offensive biological research and development" from 1946 until 1992 and had amassed 20 tons of smallpox.[33] The UN–led inspections of Iraq since the Persian Gulf War indicate that the country also had a germ warfare program that had, at minimum, produced 132,000 gallons of anthrax and botulism toxins. According to one expert, "it's far more likely than not" that, in addition to Russia, such countries as Iran, Iraq, and North Korea also have biological weapons.[34]

Chemical Weapons Of the three components of NBC warfare, chemical weapons are the most prevalent because they are relatively easy and inexpensive to produce. Indeed, they have earned the sobriquet of "the poor man's atomic bomb." As CIA director John M. Deutch told Congress, "Chemicals used to make nerve agents are also used to make plastics and [to] process foodstuff. Any modern pharmaceutical facility can produce biological warfare agents as easily as vaccines or antibiotics."[35]

Most ominously of all, chemical weapons have been used recently. Both Iran and Iraq used them during their grueling war (1980–1988), and Iraq used them to attack rebellious Kurds in Iraq's northern provinces. The UN inspections in Iraq after the Persian Gulf War also discovered huge stores of chemical weapons, including over 105,000 gallons of mustard gas; 21,936 gallons of tabun, sarin, and other nerve gases; and over 453,000 gallons of other chemicals associated with weapons. Some of this supply was contained in munitions, such as 12,786 artillery shells filled with mustard gas and 18 warheads or bombs filled with nerve agents. There is no evidence that any chemical weapons were used during the war, but traces of mustard gas and sarin were detected on the battlefield. These may have released inadvertently when the allied attacks destroyed Iraqi weapons depots, and some analysts suspect that exposure to these chemicals may be the cause of Gulf War Syndrome, which has afflicted many veterans of the war.

STRATEGIC NUCLEAR WAR

The Bible's Book of Revelation speaks of an apocalyptic end to the world: A "hail of fire mixed with blood fell upon the earth; and... the earth was burnt up.... The sea became blood... and from the shaft rose smoke like the smoke of a great furnace and the sun and the air were darkened." Revelation laments, "Woe, woe, woe to those who dwell on earth," for many will die a fiery death, and the survivors "will seek death and will not find it; they will long to die, and death will fly from them." Whatever your religious beliefs, such a prophecy is sobering. We now have the capability to sound "the blast of the trumpets" that will kill the living and make those that remain wish to die.

The world joined in a collective sigh of relief when the Soviet Union collapsed and the cold war between the two great nuclear powers ended. Almost overnight, worry about the threat of nuclear war virtually disappeared from the media and general political discussion. Unfortunately, the perception of significantly greater safety is illusory. It is certainly true that the number of strategic nuclear weapons has declined since the end of the cold war. Nevertheless, there remains a huge number of extremely powerful nuclear weapons.

The United States and Russia remain the nuclear Goliaths. In mid-2000, the U.S. deployed strategic (intercontinental-range) arsenal included 7,206 nuclear warheads and bombs and 1,055 missiles and bombers to carry them to destinations anywhere in the world. Russia's deployed strategic inventory was 5,906 weapons and 1,173 delivery vehicles. Each country also has thousands of nuclear devices in storage. China, France, Great Britain, India, and Pakistan all openly have nuclear weapons, and Israel and (perhaps) North Korea have undeclared nuclear weapons, adding another 1,300 or so nuclear devices to the volatile mix of over 31,000 deployed or reserve tactical and strategic nuclear devices. The largest of the warheads has an explosive power up to 50 times that of the bombs dropped on Japan in 1945. Additionally, several countries have or are suspected of having nuclear weapons development programs, and another 30 countries have the technology base needed to build nuclear weapons. Moreover, countries continue to "improve" their weapons. For example, China, Russia, and the United States have all developed nuclear-explosion activated neutron bombs, which kill people and many other life forms, but which have a limited blast effect. Thus, nuclear weapons proliferation is a global concern.

Given this reality, it would be unwise to discount the continuing impact of nuclear weapons on world politics. One role that nuclear weapons play is to be a part of the "backdrop" of power and influence. There can be little doubt that the massive nuclear capability of the United States is part of what makes it a superpower. Similarly, the continuing importance of Russia, despite its tremendous travails, rests in part on its still immense nuclear arsenal. Deterrence is a second role played by nuclear

The United States and Russia still have by far the largest arsenal of nuclear weapons and strategic range missiles. But China's inventory is growing, as symbolized in this photo of a People's Liberation Army soldier contemplating a display of Chinese missiles in Beijing. The end of the cold war may have eased the threat of nuclear war, but it did not eliminate it.

weapons. Whether or not nuclear weapons will always deter conventional or nuclear attack is uncertain, but they have at least sometimes been and remain a restraining factor that deters an opponent from attacking in the first place or that limits an opponent's weapons or tactics. It is not unreasonable to conjecture, for instance, that the nuclear option that the United States, France, and Great Britain all had in the Persian Gulf War may have helped deter Saddam Hussein from using his chemical weapons. Actual use is a third role for nuclear weapons. The atomic attacks on Hiroshima and Nagasaki demonstrate that humans have the ability and the will to use weapons of mass destruction. Therefore, it is naive to imagine that nuclear war cannot happen. To the contrary, there are several ways that a nuclear war could break out.

HOW A NUCLEAR WAR MIGHT START

For all its potential horror, nuclear war is within the realm of possibility. Strategic analysts envision many possible scenarios, including (1) an accident, (2) an irrational leader, (3) an unprovoked attack, (4) a last-gasp defense, (5) an inadvertent error in judgment, and (6) an escalation.

Before we examine these scenarios, two preliminary points should be made here. One is that these scenarios are not equally likely. Inadvertent war and escalation, for instance, are much more likely than an accident. Second, the six are not necessarily mutually exclusive. They may combine into *multipath scenarios*. For example, a crisis on the China-Russia border with the possibility of escalation to war could lead to a partial release of nuclear weapons safety controls, thereby increasing the chances of accidental war.

Accident. An accident caused by a technical malfunction or a human technical error is one way a nuclear war could start. In 1995, for example, Russian radar detected what appeared to be an incoming missile fired, presumably, by an American submarine. A nuclear alert was flashed to Russian missile silos and submarines; an aide with President Yeltsin opened the briefcase carrying Russian nuclear release codes; the president stared at a screen showing a bright dot representing the suspected launch site in the Norwegian Sea and pondered a row of buttons that would begin one or another of the Soviet nuclear counterattack options. Twelve minutes passed and the last moment to respond approached before it was determined that the radar blip was an outgoing Norwegian scientific rocket, not an incoming U.S. D-5 missile. The Norwegians had notified the Soviet embassy in Oslo, but the information had not been relayed to Moscow. "For a while," said a Russian defense official, "the world was on the brink of nuclear war."[36] This was neither the first, nor was it likely to be the last, such close call. Overall, the chance of an accidental nuclear detonation is slight, but an accident at a time of high international tension might cause a spasm reaction that could take the world across the nuclear firebreak.

Irrational leader. A leader who was fanatical, deranged, drunk, or otherwise out of control is another possible cause of nuclear war. What if Adolf Hitler had had the bomb? Were Russia's weapons safe under the control of the country's hard-drinking president, Boris Yeltsin? According to reports, worried Russian generals told the Duma in secret that they were unsure of what could be expected of their often drunken president during a crisis.[37] It is also possible that a berserk military officer might try to use nuclear weapons, although there are numerous safety devices such as the "dual key" system and electronic "permissive action links" designed to limit such a possibility. Moreover, the danger of an unbalanced leader controlling nuclear weapons increases with proliferation. The odds of such a scenario based on irrationality leading to nuclear war are slim, but in a time of crisis, with tensions high and safety systems partially or fully relaxed, the probability would rise sharply.

MAP
The Spread of Nuclear Weapons, p. 368

Unprovoked attack. A "bolt out of the blue" nuclear attack could also happen. This might occur if one country felt that it could deliver a first strike that would disable all or most of its opponent's strategic forces. Such an attack could come if a country believed that, combined with defensive measures, the strike would result in a victory with "acceptable losses." An unprovoked nuclear attack could also come as a result of a nuclear country attacking a nonnuclear country. Perhaps the most likely preemptive scenario is a preemptive nuclear attack on a country that is just about to develop or has just developed nuclear weapons. Currently, the small, easily targeted nuclear arsenals of countries like India and Pakistan are especially apt to invite such an attack because there is the possibility of eliminating them. Moreover, such scenarios are not mere speculation. Secret documents declassified in 1998 indicate that the United States seriously considered in 1964 a preemptive nuclear strike on China's nuclear arms development facility at Lop Nor. That did not occur, but five years later the Soviets also came close to launching their own strike on Lop Nor.

Last gasp. Nuclear war could come as a final attempt to fend off conventional defeat. One scenario with real possibilities is to imagine a beleaguered Israel, its vaunted conventional forces finally overwhelmed by numerically superior Arab invaders, launching a last-gasp strike against Egyptian, Jordanian, and Syrian armies pounding the last Israeli defensive positions in Jerusalem near the Wailing Wall on Temple Mount, the holiest place of the Jewish people.

Inadvertent nuclear war. Of the various triggers of a nuclear war, misperception is one of the two most likely causes. The limits of rationality in decision making mean that those who command nuclear weapons can make mistakes. False intelligence that a nuclear attack is imminent, for example, might cause a leader to strike first. There is a nuclear strategy called "damage denial" that looks to reduce a country's damage by, among other things, destroying an opponent's offensive capability before it is launched. Such decisions involve three different launch strategies: Launch on warning (LOW, use your missiles when you receive a warning that an enemy attack is about to commence), launch under attack (LUA, launch once an enemy launches its missiles, but before the strike), and launch on impact (LOI, launch a counterstrike only after a missile strike has impacted your territory or forces).

The time for American and Russian leaders to make decisions in a nuclear crisis is short enough, about 30 minutes given the flight time of a nuclear missile between the two countries. Leaders of countries close to one another, like Pakistan and India, would have much, much less time to respond. This will decrease the time to confirm reports that a nuclear attack has been launched or is about to be launched. It will also vastly increase the pressure to (perhaps mistakenly) launch what the leaders sees as a counter-strike (but which may be a first strike) under the rubric "use them or lose them." This means that if I do not launch my missiles before the missiles of the enemy land, I will not have any missiles to launch at all. The options are laid out further in the accompanying box, It's Your Call, Mr./Madam President.

Escalation. A deadly spiral is a final, not unlikely, single path to nuclear war. History has demonstrated that leaders are willing to risk nuclear war even when there is no immediate and critical threat to national security. During the Cuban missile crisis, when the Soviets were placing missiles with nuclear warheads in Cuba, both Soviet leader Nikita Khrushchev and U.S. president John Kennedy risked nuclear war. When the Soviet defense minister asked why the missiles and warheads were being sent to Cuba, Khrushchev replied, "Why not throw a hedgehog at Uncle Sam's pants?" in an attempt to offset the U.S. strategic nuclear advantage.[38] Once the Soviet plan was discovered, the Americans also evidenced a willingness to risk nuclear war. Kennedy's national security adviser, McGeorge Bundy, asked in a top-level meeting, "What is the strategic impact [of the Soviet missiles]? How gravely does this change the strategic balance?" Secretary of Defense Robert McNamara replied, "My own personal view is 'not at all.'"

IT'S YOUR CALL, MR./MADAM PRESIDENT

Imagine that you are the U.S. (or British, Chinese, French, Indian, Pakistani, or Russian) president (or prime minister). You are absolutely convinced that an enemy is about to launch a major nuclear strike. What do you do? You can wait and pray; you can surrender; you can contact the other country's leader on the telephone. If you call, though, isn't the other leader likely to just deny your accusation? Moreover, if you call, do you tip them off and eliminate your chance of a pre-emptive, damage-denial strike? Perhaps you should strike first to destroy as many enemy missiles as possible, thereby hoping to limit the damage to your country. You will have greater confidence that you are not inadvertently starting a nuclear war if you wait until the enemy actually launches their missiles but then those missiles will certainly devastate your country and your counterstrike will only have the effect of "taking them with you." Or you can be sure that you are not mistakenly starting a nuclear war by waiting until the strike actually hits your territory and forces, but your ability to counterstrike may be diminished or obliterated. But,

then again, what do you gain by retaliating at that point, anyway?

Or imagine that you are the president and military warning systems flash that an attack is under way. You know that such warnings have sometimes proven false, but the time is short. Do you ask for confirming intelligence so you can be pretty sure? Do you wait until the enemy missiles have landed so you can be absolutely sure? Do you launch now and, if the warnings are false, start a nuclear war where none existed?

Mr./Madam President, your aide who carries the nuclear release codes and accompanies you everywhere has just handed them to you. Your advisers are in turmoil and shouting conflicting advice. Your generals stand before you ready to carry out your orders. Your time is limited: 30 minutes at most if you are in Washington or Moscow; perhaps no more than 5 or 10 minutes if you are in New Delhi or Islamabad. What do you order the general to do? It's your call, Mr./Madam President.

"What difference does it make?" Kennedy put in. "They've got enough to blow us up now anyway.... This is a political struggle as much as a military struggle."[39] Thus for political reasons, the United States confronted the Soviet Union and readied for an invasion of Cuba. We know now that Soviet nuclear warheads were already in Cuba. Once even low-yield tactical weapons are used on a battlefield, the breakdown in communications and the psychological pressure on decision makers could easily lead to wider strikes. Thus a U.S. step against Cuba might well have been the first of an escalatory ladder from conventional fighting between Soviet and invading U.S. troops, to the use of tactical nuclear weapons by the Soviets, to a general nuclear exchange between the United States and the Soviet Union.

Multiple path. A mixture of events and real or imagined provocations leading to nuclear war is more likely than any single path. It is possible to imagine many such combinations of accident, irrationality, and other factors, but to consider just one, watch perhaps the best of all nuclear war films, *Dr. Strangelove, or: How I Learned to Stop Worrying and Love the Bomb.* In the 1964 film, a demented U.S. general orders the bombers he commands to attack the USSR because, he suspects, the communists are working to pollute the "precious bodily fluids" of the American people. It turns out that the U.S. attack will set off a Soviet "Doomsday Device," destroying all life on Earth. A drunken Soviet leader is among the hurdles to overcome in order to avoid nuclear war. The outcome can remain a mystery to those who have not seen the film, but it and other films, such as *Crimson Tide* (1995), are worth viewing, and then asking yourself: Could it happen? What would I do if I had to make the ultimate decision? In *Crimson Tide*, would you have sided with Lieutenant Commander Hunter (Denzel Washington) and not launched the submarine's missiles or with Captain Ramsey (Gene Hackman) and fired your weapons?

THE IMPACT OF NUCLEAR WAR

If nuclear war is possible, then we should know what the impact of nuclear weapons would be. The trouble is that we do not know—precisely. Certainly, it would be terrible for those in immediate blast areas. More broadly, some scholars predict that a massive exchange of nuclear weapons would have dire global consequences, ranging from biological devastation to a modern ice age (nuclear winter) caused by dust clouds screening the sun's rays. Other analysts are dubious about such end-of-the-world scenarios. Specifically commenting on nuclear winter, for instance, one eminent scientist has characterized "all the hype about a lot of freezing following a nuclear exchange" as "hyperbole."[40]

There is no doubt about the immediate effect of a nuclear attack. Let us assume a 1-megaton warhead. Its detonation a mile above your city creates a huge fireball with temperatures in the range of 20 million degrees Fahrenheit. Within 2.5 miles everything and everyone is set on fire. All is quickly snuffed out, however, by an atomizing blast. Death and destruction are total. In a second 2-mile ring, flesh is charred, blast winds reach 160 mph, and collapsing buildings and flying glass and metal crush and shred nearly everyone. Yet another 2 miles out, most homes are on fire, half the population is dead, and the remainder are probably lethally exposed to radiation. Still another 4 miles out, a third of the population is wounded, normal services are destroyed, and civil chaos threatens as panic sets in and people fight for medicine, food, and water. Those who survive will face uncertain futures of psychological trauma and devastated lifestyles. It strains the imagination to call them the lucky ones.[41]

STRATEGIC NUCLEAR WEAPONS AND STRATEGY

The reality that nuclear weapons exist and could be used make it important that we briefly examine strategic nuclear weapons and strategy. There are issues of what a country's nuclear arsenal and doctrines should be that seldom enter the public debate, but that are crucial to an effective and stable arsenal. Furthermore, the post–cold war changes have brought on new challenges in strategic planning. As one expert has noted, within the declared nuclear weapons countries, it "is clear that there is a great debate... over who is the enemy and what is the target."[42] Within the debate, the two main issues are (1) how to minimize the chance of nuclear war and (2) how to maximize the chance of survival if a nuclear exchange does occur. It is not possible here to review all the factors that impinge on these issues, but we can illustrate the various concerns by examining deterrence and then several specific issues about weapons systems and strategy.

Deterrence

The concept of deterrence has been and remains at the center of the strategy of all the nuclear powers. **Deterrence** is persuading an enemy that attacking you will not be worth any potential gain. Deterrence is based on two factors: capability and credibility.

Capability. Effective deterrence requires that you be able to respond to an attack or impending attack on your forces. This capability is what India claimed it was seeking when it openly tested nuclear weapons in 1998. "Our problem is China," said an Indian official. "We are not seeking [nuclear] parity with China.... What we are seeking is a minimum deterrent."[43] Just having weapons, however, is not enough. Since there is no way to defend against a missile attack once it is launched, deterrence requires that you have enough weapons that are relatively invulnerable to enemy destruction so that you can be assured that some will survive for a counterattack. Submarine-launched ballistic missiles (SLBMs) are the least vulnerable; fixed-site, land-based intercontinental ballistic missiles (ICBMs) are the most vulnerable. Air-launched (bombs, short-range missiles) and mobile ICBMS (such as the Russian SS-25) are in the midrange of vulnerability.

(continued on page 352)

THE FLYING GARBAGE CAN

The official U.S. designation is "exoatmospheric kill vehicle" (EKV). Among other unflattering names, its critics have dubbed it "the flying garbage can" based on its shape and, one suspects, their estimation of its value. The object is a 55-inch long, 120-pound canister full of sensors, explosives, and rocket thrusters. It is meant to be launched by missile, then to separate and hurtle through space at 14,000 mph to intercept and destroy enemy warheads streaking toward the United States. The commonly used name for the overall program is the national missile defense system (NMDS).

The simmering debate over whether to try again to build a BMD system gained full force in 1998 after a report by the Commission to Assess the Ballistic Missile Threat to the United States chaired by former secretary of defense (1975–1977) Donald Rumsfeld. The so-called Rumsfeld Report concluded that: (1) "Concerted efforts by a number of overtly or potentially hostile nations to acquire ballistic missiles with biological or nuclear payloads pose a growing threat to the United States"; (2) "The threat to the U.S. posed by these emerging capabilities is broader, more mature and evolving more rapidly than [previously estimated]"; and (3) "The warning times the U.S. can expect of new, threatening ballistic missile deployments are being reduced."[1]

The Clinton administration was pushed toward going ahead with the development and deployment of the NMDS by the concerns expressed in the Rumsfeld report, by the threat that the Republicans would make the supposed vulnerability of the United States an issue in the 2000 presidential campaign, by a strong push for the system from the military, and by other factors.

The argument for building a limited BMD system rests on the three basic points made by the Rumsfeld report. Those who oppose the system claim that it will cost too much, will not work, and should not be built even if it could work because it will harm national security.

Cost. The Congressional Budget Office estimates

The most important consideration regarding building a national missile defense system (NMDS) is whether it will create greater safety or will destabilize deterrence. This photograph of the vapor trail of an outgoing missile carrying a test antimissile weapon over Victorville, California, forms something of a question mark in the sky. That ? underlines the uncertainty about the wisdom of building an NMDS.

that building the proposed NMDS, including 250 missiles and an early warning system (radar and infrared detection and tracking capabilities), will cost $60 billion. The cost is perhaps the least salient criticism, given the fact that U.S. liquor stores took in almost that amount in 1999.

Reliability. A more cogent criticism centers on whether the system can work. Through mid-2000 the progress was not promising. The first test in October 1999 was successful, but critics point out that the inter-

Credibility. It is also necessary for other states to believe that you will actually use your weapons. Perception is a key factor. The operational reality will be determined by what the other side believes rather than by what you intend. We will see, for example, that some analysts believe that relying on a second-strike capability may not always be credible.

This two-part equation for deterrence sounds simple enough on the surface, but the question is how to achieve it. The debate can be roughly divided into two schools of

ceptor had been preprogrammed with the path of the supposed attacking warhead. Two later tests in 2000 failed completely. More important than these early problems, however, is the contention that it will be easy for potential enemies to develop counter-measures to render the EKVs ineffective. One approach would be to deploy ionized balloons along with the real warheads to confuse the EKVs' sensors. "What advocates of the system want you to believe is that adversaries will be smart enough to build intercontinental ballistic missiles and nuclear warheads but not smart enough to figure out ways of foiling the EKV," contends MIT's Professor Ted Postol. "That doesn't sound plausible."[2] Advocates of the NMDS say they can overcome its current technical flaws and future enemy countermeasures; critics doubt it.

President Clinton cited cost and reliability when, in September 2000, he told his military advisers that he would not support an immediate effort to deploy the NMDS. According to one adviser, "[Clinton] said he did not want to pay the big front-end costs if he was not sure this thing would work."[3] The White House treated the announcement as a major decision but, in truth, it was not. Testing will continue, and what Clinton really did was to leave the ultimate decision on deployment to his successor.

Impact on National Security. The most important debate about the proposed NMDS is whether it will improve or harm national security. The Rumsfeld report did not advocate building a missile defense system. Nevertheless, the report, in the view of others, does lead inexorably to the conclusion that such a system is necessary. In this "new strategic environment," two analysts argue, the United States should hasten "to develop and to deploy ballistic-missile defenses. Such defenses would inure us to the threat of an attack on American soil and enable us to protect our forces and our allies overseas" (Kagan & Schmitt, 1998:23).

Critics charge that deploying the NMDS would harm national security because, in the opinion of experts, it would mean a U.S. unilateral breaking of the Anti-Ballistic Missile (ABM) Treaty of 1972, which forbids the deployment of such systems. That would put all other arms reduction treaties in jeopardy and set off an arms race.

Russia's foreign minister, Igor Ivanov, has taken this view, pointing out that "the prevailing system of arms control agreements is a complex and quite fragile structure." Therefore, he has argued, "Once one of its key elements has been weakened, the entire system is destabilized. The collapse of the ABM treaty would, therefore, undermine the entirety of disarmament agreements concluded over the last 30 years."[4] On behalf of China, Sha Zukang, the director general for arms control, has commented that the NMDS would destroy the "balance of terror" that has arguably deterred nuclear war for decades. "We will not sit on our hands," Sha told U.S. diplomats. Instead, he said, "To defeat your defenses we'll have to spend a lot of money, and we don't want to do this. But otherwise, the United States will feel it can attack anyone at any time, and that isn't tolerable. We hope you'll give this up. If not, we'll be ready."[5]

It is easy to write off these views of past and potential U.S. enemies. But most of the rest of the world and the U.S. intelligence community also agree that an NMDS could reignite a nuclear arms race. In January 2000, a resolution in the UN General Assembly supporting the ABM Treaty passed by a lopsided vote. That was followed in August 2000 by a worrisome, highly classified intelligence report, "Foreign Responses to U.S. National Missile Defense Deployment," authored by the CIA and other U.S. intelligence agencies. The National Intelligence Estimate reportedly warned that deploying the NMDS could lead China to expand its nuclear arsenal ten-fold and prompt Russia to place multiple warheads on ballistic missiles that now carry only one.[6] It may be, then, given the odd logic of deterrence, that no defense is the best defense.

nuclear strategy. They are characterized by the bizarrely colorful acronyms of **MAD** (Mutual Assured Destruction) and **NUT** (Nuclear Utilization Theory).

Those who favor the mutual assured destruction strategy (the MADs) believe that deterrence is best achieved if each nuclear power's capabilities include (1) a sufficient number of weapons that are (2) capable of surviving a nuclear attack by an opponent and then (3) delivering a second-strike retaliatory attack that will destroy that opponent. MADs believe, in other words, in *deterrence through punishment*. If each nuclear power has these three capabilities, then a mutual checkmate is achieved. The result, MAD theory holds, is that no power will start a nuclear war because doing so will lead to its own destruction (even if it destroys its enemy).

Those who favor nuclear utilization theory (the NUTs) contend that the MAD strategy is a mad gamble because it relies on rationality and clear-sightedness when, in reality, there are other scenarios (discussed earlier in the section "How a Nuclear War Might Start") that could lead to nuclear war. Therefore, NUTs prefer to base deterrence partly on *deterrence through damage denial* (or limitation), in contrast to the punishment strategy of MADs. This means that NUTs want to be able to destroy enemy weapons before the weapons explode on one's own territory and forces. One way to do this is to destroy the weapons before they are launched.

Nuclear Weapons and Strategy Issues

The rapid reconfiguration of the political world and nuclear weapons inventories has muted the MAD-NUT debate, but there are still echoes in current weapons and strategy issues. To illustrate these issues, we can examine two weapons systems: first-strike weapons and missile-defense systems. Note that the launch doctrines discussed in the box It's Your Call, Mr./Madam President, are also part of the MAD-NUT debate, with the MADs favoring LOI and the NUTs favoring LOW (with LUA as a fallback).

First Use One long-standing debate is when, if ever, to be the first to use nuclear weapons, especially to escalate from nonnuclear to nuclear warfare. The NATO alliance long held that it might launch a nuclear strike to destroy oncoming, overwhelming Soviet ground forces. More recently, President Bush reportedly warned Saddam Hussein that if Iraq used biological or chemical weapons in the impending Persian Gulf War, Iraq faced U.S. nuclear retaliation. Similarly, a U.S. nuclear strategy presidential decision directive issued in 1997 anticipates the possible use of nuclear weapons in the face of biological or chemical attack. MAD advocates are very leery of first-use, warning that using nuclear weapons against a nuclear power could lead to uncontrolled escalation. Using nuclear weapons against a nonnuclear power could undermine the norm against nuclear warfare and make it easier in the future for other nuclear powers to use their weapons against still other nonnuclear powers (Tannenwald, 1999). NUT advocates argue that, just like nuclear weapons, biological and chemical weapons are weapons of mass destruction and, therefore, deterring their use with nuclear weapons is valid.

First-Strike Weapons Another controversy centers on first-strike weapons. These are warheads and delivery systems designed to destroy an enemy's "hardened" targets such as missile silos and command centers, thereby making it impossible for an opponent to attack or counterattack. Weapons with first-strike potential include some very powerful ICBMs and SLBMs. One such weapon is the D-5 missile, which is carried on *Ohio*-class U.S. nuclear ballistic missile submarines (SSBNs). Each such SSBN carries 24 D-5 missiles, each of which contains 8 warheads, with an explosive power of 475 kilotons apiece. This means that each such submarine can fire nuclear warheads with a combined explosive power equal to some 6,080 of the 15-kiloton-yield atomic bombs dropped on Japan in 1945. There is no need to have such powerful warheads to erase cities and other "soft" targets. Instead, such huge warheads are most valuable for "hard-target kill" (such as missile silos, and command centers) capability that is most advantageous during a first strike.

NUTs favor first-strike weapons as part of a damage-denial strategy. They believe that one path to safety is to be able to destroy enemy missiles, bombers, and leadership capabilities before an attack occurs. MADs disagree. They claim that first-strike weapons dangerously undermine mutual assured destruction by threatening to destroy an opponent's retaliatory system, thereby creating instability. MADs oppose such weapons on two grounds: they create a temptation to strike first and they also create instability by making the ability of other nuclear powers to launch a counterattack less than assured.

Missile Defense Systems Another long-standing controversy in the area of nuclear planning is whether or not to build a ballistic missile defense (BMD) system. There were some thoughts of mounting such an effort in the 1960s, but high costs and technical unfeasibility led the United States and the Soviet Union to sign the Anti-Ballistic Missile (ABM) Treaty in 1972, largely banning the testing and development of such a system. Ronald Reagan renewed the controversy when he proposed building the Strategic Defense Initiative (SDI), also labeled "Star Wars" by its critics. Reagan's vision of a comprehensive shield from missile attack was abandoned as too expensive and technically infeasible.

After a lull, the Clinton administration reopened the BMD by debate proposing a limited national ballistic missile defense system to counter attacks by such states as North Korea if they were to develop nuclear weapons and the means to deliver them. This latest round in the debate is related in the box, The Flying Garbage Can, on pages 352–353.

As the box indicates, NUTs favor building a BMD system because it fits in with the damage-denial strategy by, perhaps, allowing you to destroy all or some of your opponent's weapons in flight. NUTs also argue that if your opponent believes that its weapons may not get through, the opponent is less likely to launch them and risk retaliation. MADs adamantly oppose BMD capability as dangerously destabilizing. They argue that a defensive system detracts from assured retaliatory destruction, since second-strike missiles would be destroyed in flight. MADs also worry that a BMD system might tempt its possessor into a first strike, since the BMD system would be most effective against a reduced retaliatory strike rather than a full-scale first strike by an opponent. This double-edged element of a BMD, its critics say, means that it would inevitably push other nuclear powers to develop a massive number of new nuclear delivery devices capable of overwhelming any defensive system.

CHAPTER SUMMARY

1. War is organized killing of other human beings. Virtually everyone is against that. Yet war continues to be a part of the human condition, and its incidence has not significantly abated. Modern warfare affects more civilians than it traditionally did; the number of civilians killed during war now far exceeds that of soldiers.

2. The study of force involves several major questions. When and why does war occur? When it does happen, how effective is it, what conditions govern success or failure, and what options exist in structuring the use of force?

3. Although much valuable research has been done about the causes of war, about the best we can do is to say that war is a complex phenomenon that seems to have many causes. Some of these stem from the nature of our species, some from the existence of nation-states, and some from the nature and dynamics of the world political system.

4. Miltary power is both tangible and intangible. Tangible elements of power, such as tanks, are relatively easy to visualize and measure. Intangible elements of military power, such as morale and reputation, are much more difficult to operationalize.

5. Acquiring military power also has drawbacks. It creates the temptation to use it, it makes others insecure, and it is costly. Some people argue, and others disagree, that spending too many resources on military power is a major factor in the decline of

once-mighty countries. Another argument debates whether quantity or quality provides the best defense.

6. Force can be used, threatened, or merely exist as an unspoken possibility. When it is used, its success requires much planning and skill. Studies have determined the ideal conditions for successful use of military force. If force *is* to be used, it should be employed as a means, or tool, rather than, as sometimes happens, as an end in itself.

7. Force does not have to be used to have an impact. The possession of military power creates a backdrop to diplomacy, and the overt threat of force increases the psychological pressure even more. The tools of force can be applied through arms sales and other methods of intervention. When it is used, force can range from a very limited demonstration to a full-scale nuclear attack.

8. The nature of war is changing. Technology has enhanced killing power; nationalism has made war a patriotic cause. As a result, the scope of war has expanded, which has also changed the strategy of war. The power to defeat is a traditional strategy of war, while the power to hurt has increased in significance and incidence.

9. Wars can be classified into three categories: local conflict, regional conflict, and strategic nuclear conflict. To look at the conduct of war, we examined intervention, traditional warfare, limited nuclear-biological-chemical (NBC) war, and strategic nuclear war.

10. For each of the types of conflicts examined in this chapter, we looked at a variety of factors such as weapons and strategy. The MAD versus NUT debate, for instance, involves how to structure nuclear weapons systems and doctrines. We also saw that the ability to conduct war is continuing to change as new technology develops new weapons.

CHAPTER 13

INTERNATIONAL SECURITY: THE ALTERNATIVE ROAD

Weapons! arms! What's the matter here?

Shakespeare, *King Lear*

He's mad that trusts in the tameness of a wolf.

Shakespeare, *King Lear*

As the bomb fell over Hiroshima and exploded, we saw an entire city disappear. I wrote in my log the words: "My God, what have we done?"

Capt. Robert Lewis, U.S. Army Air Corps, copilot of the *Enola Gay*

A world without nuclear weapons would be less stable and more dangerous for all of us.

British prime minister Margaret Thatcher

CHAPTER OBJECTIVES

After completing this chapter, you should be able to:

- Think about the issue of security by considering what insecurity means.
- Discuss limited self-defense as an approach to security.
- Characterize arms control as an approach to achieving security by limiting the numbers and types of weapons that countries have.
- List major events and themes in the history of arms control.
- Explain the limitation and reduction of arms as important aspects of arms control.
- Discuss limits on arms transfers, focusing on the issues of proliferation and nonproliferation of weapons, including biological, chemical, and conventional weapons.
- Summarize and evaluate political, technical, and domestic barriers to arms control.
- Describe the role that international security plays in world politics.
- Consider the abolition of war as an approach to security, focusing on disarmament and pacifism.

Security is the enduring yet elusive quest. "I would give all my fame for a pot of ale, and safety," a frightened boy cries out before a battle in Shakespeare's *King Henry V.* Alas, Melpomene, the muse of tragedy, did not favor the boy's plea. The English and French armies met on the battlefield at Agincourt. Peace—and perhaps the boy—perished. Today most of us similarly seek security. Yet our quest is tempered by the reality that while humans have sought safety throughout history, they have usually failed to achieve that goal for long.

THINKING ABOUT SECURITY

Perhaps one reason that security from armed attack has been elusive is that we humans have sought it in the wrong way. The traditional path has emphasized national self-defense by amassing arms to deter aggression. Alternative paths have been given little attention and fewer resources. From 1948 through 2000, for example, the world states spent 1,500 times as much on their national military budgets (about $36 trillion) as on UN peacekeeping operations (about $24 billion). It just may be, then, that the first secretary-general of the United Nations, Trygve Lie, was onto something when he suggested that "wars occur because people prepare for conflict, rather than for peace."[1]

The aim of this chapter is to think anew about security from armed aggression in light of humankind's failed effort to find it. Because the traditional path has not brought us to a consistently secure place, it is only prudent to consider alternative, less-traveled-by, paths to security. These possible approaches include limiting or even abandoning our weapons altogether, creating international security forces, and even adopting the standards of pacifism.

A TALE OF INSECURITY

One way to think about how to increase security is to ponder the origins of insecurity. To do that, let us go back in time to the hypothetical origins of insecurity. Our vehicle is a parable. Insecurity may not have started exactly like this, but it might have.

A Drama and Dialogue of Insecurity

It was a sunny, yet somehow foreboding, autumn day many millennia ago. Og, a caveman of the South Tribe, was searching for food. It had been a poor season for hunting and gathering, and Og fretted about the coming winter and his family. The urge to provide security from hunger for his family carried Og northward out of the South Tribe's usual territory and into the next valley.

It was the valley of Ug of the North Tribe. The same motivations that drove Og also urged Ug on, but he had been luckier. He had just killed a large antelope. Ug, then, was feeling prosperous as he used his large knife to clean his kill. At that moment, Og, with hunting spear in hand, happened out of the forest and came upon Ug. Both the hunters were startled, and they exchanged cautious greetings. Ug was troubled by the lean and hungry look of the spear-carrying stranger, and he unconsciously grasped his knife more tightly. The tensing of his ample muscles alarmed Og, who instinctively dropped his spear point to a defensive position. Fear was the common denominator. Neither Og nor Ug wanted a confrontation, but they were trapped. Their disengagement negotiation went something like this (translated):

Ug: You are eyeing my antelope and pointing your spear at me.

Og: And your knife glints menacingly in the sunlight. But this is crazy. I mean you no harm; your antelope is yours. Still, my family is needy and it would be good if you shared your kill.

Ug: Of course I am sympathetic, and I want to be friends. But this is an antelope from the North Tribe's valley. If there is any meat left over, I'll even give you a little. But first, why don't you put down your spear so we can talk more easily?

Og: A fine idea, Ug, and I'll be glad to put down my spear, but why don't you lay down that fearful knife first? Then we can be friends.

Ug: Spears can fly through the air farther.... *You should be first.*

Og: Knives can strike more accurately.... *You should be first.*

And so the confrontation continued, with Og and Ug equally unsure of the other's intentions, with each sincerely proclaiming his peaceful purpose, but with each unable to convince the other to lay his weapon aside first.

Critiquing the Drama

Think about the web of insecurity that entangled Og and Ug. Each was insecure about providing for himself and his family in the harsh winter that was approaching. Security extends further than just being safe from armed attacks. Ug was a "have" and Og was a "have-not." Ug had a legitimate claim to his antelope; Og had a legitimate need to find sustenance. Territoriality and tribal differences added to the building tension. Ug was in "his" valley; Og could not understand why unequal resource distribution meant that some should prosper while others were deprived. The gutting knife and the spear also played a role. But did the weapons cause tension or, perhaps, did Ug's knife protect him from a raid by Og?

We should also ask what could have provided the security to get Og and Ug out of their confrontation. If Og's valley had been full of game, he would not have been driven to the next valley. Or if the region's food had been shared by all, Og would not have needed Ug's antelope. Knowing this, Ug might have been less defensive. Assuming, for a moment, that Og was dangerous—as hunger sometimes drives people to be—then Ug might have been more secure if somehow he could have signaled the equivalent of today's 911 distress call and summoned the region's peacekeeping force, dispatched by the area's intertribal council. The council might even have been able to aid Og with some food and skins to ease his distress and to quell the anger he felt when he compared his ill fortune with the prosperity of Ug.

The analysis of our parable could go on and be made more complex. Og and Ug might have spoken different languages, worshipped different deities, or had differently colored faces. That, however, would not change the fundamental questions regarding security. Why were Og and Ug insecure? More important, once insecurity existed, what could have been done to restore harmony?

SEEKING SECURITY: APPROACHES AND STANDARDS OF EVALUATION

Now bring your minds from the past to the present, from primordial cave dwellers to yourself. Think about contemporary international security. The easiest matter is determining what our goal should be. How to do that is, of course, a much more challenging question.

Approaches to Security

There are, in essence, four possible approaches to securing peace. The basic parameters of each is shown in Table 13.1. As with many, even most, matters in this book, which approach is best is part of the realist-idealist debate.

Unlimited self-defense, the first of the four approaches, is the traditional approach of each country being responsible for its own defense and amassing weapons it wishes for

Table 13.1 Four Approaches to Security

Security Approach	Sources of Insecurity	World Political System	Armaments Strategy	Primary Peacekeeping Mechanism	Strategy
Unlimited Self-Defense	Many; probably inherent in humans	State-based; national interests and rivalries; fear	Have many and all types to guard against threats	Armed states, deterrence, alliances, balance of power	Peace through strength
Limited Self-Defense	Many; perhaps inherent, but weapons intensify	State-based; limited cooperation based on mutual interests	Limit amount and types to reduce capabilities, damage, tension	Armed states; defensive capabilities, lack of offensive capabilities	Peace through limited offensive ability
International Security	Anarchical world system; lack of law or common security mechanisms	International political integration; regional or world government	Transfer weapons and authority to international force	International peacekeeping/peacemaking force	Peace through law and universal collective defense
Abolition of War	Weapons; personal and national greed and insecurity	Various options from pacifistic states to libertarian global village model	Eliminate weapons	Lack of ability; lack of fear; individual and collective pacifism	Peace through being peaceful

Concept source: Rapoport (1992).

The path to peace has long been debated. The four approaches outlined here provide some basic alternatives that help structure this chapter on security.

that defense. The thinking behind this approach rests on the classic realist assumption that humans have an inherent element of greed and aggressiveness that promotes individual and collective violence. This makes the international system, from the realists' perspective, a place of danger where each state must fend for itself or face the perils of domination or destruction by other states.

Beyond the traditional approach to security, there are three alternative approaches: *limited self-defense* (arms limitations), *international security* (regional and world security forces), and *abolition of war* (complete disarmament and pacifism). Each of these will be examined in the pages that follow. Realists do not oppose arms control or even international peacekeeping under the right circumstances. Realists, for instance, recognize that the huge arsenals of weapons that countries possess are dangerous and, therefore, there can be merit in carefully negotiated, truly verifiable arms accords. But because the three alternative approaches all involve some level of trust and depend on the triumph of the spirit of human cooperation over human avarice and power-seeking, they are all more attractive to idealists than to realists.

Standards of Evaluation

Now that we have identified the approaches to seeking security, the question is which one of them offers the greatest chance of safety. There is no clear answer, so it is important to consider how to evaluate the various possibilities.

To evaluate the approaches to security, begin by considering the college community that you are living in while taking the course for which this book is being used. The next time you are in class, look around you. Is anyone carrying a gun? Are you? Probably not. Think about why you are not doing so. The answer is that you feel relatively secure.

The word "relatively" is important here. There are, of course, dangerous people in your community who might steal your property, attack you, and perhaps even kill you.

Security is partly a state of mind. Like this man who is being held hostage by an armed robber in Argentina, an individual in domestic societies can suddenly fall victim to a violent crime. Yet most people do not carry guns because they feel safe in their domestic system with its law enforcement system and norms against violence. By contrast, the anarchical international system relies mostly on self-protection, which is why most countries are heavily armed.

There were 16,910 killings, 93,100 reported rapes, and 1,531,040 other violent crimes in the United States during 1998. Criminals committed another 10,944,600 burglaries, car thefts, and other property crimes. Thus, with one crime for every 22 Americans, it is clear that you are not absolutely secure. Yet most of us feel secure enough to forgo carrying firearms.

The important thing to consider is why you feel secure enough not to carry a gun despite the fact that you could be murdered, raped, beaten up, or have your property stolen. There are many reasons. *Domestic norms* against violence and stealing are one reason. Most people around you are peaceful and honest and are unlikely, even if angry or covetous, to attack you or steal your property. Established *domestic collective security forces* are a second part of feeling secure. The police are on patrol to deter criminals, and if anyone does attack you or steal your property, you can call 911; criminal courts and prisons deal with convicted felons. *Domestic disarmament* is a third contributor to your sense of security. Most domestic societies have disarmed substantially, shun the routine of carrying weapons, and have turned the legitimate use of domestic force beyond immediate self-defense over to their police. *Domestic conflict-resolution mechanisms* are a fourth contributor to security. There are ways to settle disputes without violence. Lawsuits get filed, and judges make decisions. Indeed, some crimes against persons and property are avoided because most domestic political systems provide some level of social services to meet human needs.

To return to our stress on relative security, it is important to see that for all the protections and dispute-resolution procedures provided by your domestic system, and for all the sense of security that you usually feel, you are not fully secure. Nor are countries and their citizens secure in the global system. For that matter, it is unlikely that anything near absolute global security can be achieved through any of the methods offered in this chapter or anywhere else. Therefore, the most reasonable standard by which to evaluate approaches to security is to compare them and to ask which makes you more secure.

LIMITED SELF-DEFENSE THROUGH ARMS CONTROL

The first alternative approach to achieving security involves limiting the numbers and types of weapons that countries possess. This approach, commonly called **arms control,** aims at lessening military (especially offensive) capabilities and lessening the damage even if war begins. Additionally, arms control advocates believe that the decline in the number and power of weapons systems will ease political tensions, thereby making further arms agreements possible (Gallagher, 1998).

METHODS OF ACHIEVING ARMS CONTROL

There are a number of methods to control arms in order to limit or even reduce their number and to prevent their spread. These methods include numerical restrictions, research, development, and deployment restrictions; categorical restrictions; and transfer restrictions. Several of the arms control agreements that will be used to illustrate the restrictions are detailed in the following section on the history of arms control, but to familiarize yourself with them quickly, it would be wise to peruse the agreements listed in Table 13.2.

Numerical Restrictions

Placing numerical limits on existing weapons, or weapons that might be developed, is the most common approach to arms control. This approach specifies the number or capacity of weapons and/or troops that each side may possess. In some cases the numerical limits may be at or higher than current levels. For example, both the first and second Strategic Arms Limitations Talks (**SALT I** and **SALT II**) Treaties listed in Table 13.2 relied heavily on numerical limits to cap future expansion rather than to reduce existing levels.

Numerical limits may also be lower than existing arsenals. The two Strategic Arms Reduction Talks (START I and START II) Treaties significantly reduced the number of American and Russian nuclear weapons.

Development, Testing, and Deployment Restrictions

A second method of limiting arms involves a sort of military birth control that ensures that weapons systems never begin their gestation period of development and testing or, if they do, they are never delivered to operational sites used by the military. The advantage of this approach is that it stops a specific area of arms building before it starts. The Antiballistic Missile (ABM) Treaty of 1972 put stringent limits on U.S. and Soviet efforts to build a ballistic missile defense (BMD) system, which many analysts believe could destabilize nuclear deterrence by undermining its cornerstone, mutual assured destruction (MAD). The restrictions on long-range BMD systems are now subject to international controversy and debate within the United States over the prospect of a U.S. national missile defense system, as discussed in the box, The Flying Garbage Can, in chapter 12.

Some restrictions aim to stop **weapons proliferation.** One common element of the Biological Weapons Treaty (BWT), the Chemical Weapons Convention (CWC) Treaty, and the Nuclear Nonproliferation Treaty (NPT) is that all the countries that have ratified them and that do not have the weapons covered in them agree not to develop such weapons. A related initiative is the Comprehensive Test Ban Treaty (CTBT), which is designed to end all forms of nuclear tests. The testing of nuclear weapons by India and Pakistan in 1998 demonstrates that neither the NPT nor the CTBT is fully effective; yet,

(continued on page 364)

Table 13.2 Selected Arms Control Treaties

Treaty	Provisions	Date Signed	Number of Signatories
Geneva Protocol	Bans using of gas or bacteriological weapons	1925	125
Antarctic Treaty	Internationalizes and demilitarizes the continent	1959	42
Limited Test Ban	Bans nuclear tests in the atmosphere, outer space, or under water	1963	123
Outer Space Treaty	Internationalizes and demilitarizes space, the moon, and other celestial bodies	1967	94
Non-Proliferation Treaty (NPT)	Prohibits selling, giving, or receiving nuclear weapons, materials, or technology for weapons	1968	187
Seabed Arms Control	Bans placing nuclear weapons in or under the seabed	1971	92
Biological Weapons	Bans the production and possession of biological weapons	1972	131
Strategic Arms Limitation Talks Treaty (SALT I)	Limits the number and types of U.S. and USSR strategic weapons (expired 1977)	1972	2
ABM Treaty	U.S.–USSR pact limits antiballistic missile testing and deployment	1972	2
Threshold Test Ban	Limits U.S. and USSR underground tests to 150 kt	1974	2
Environmental Modification	Bans environmental modification as a form of warfare	1977	48
SALT II	Limits the number and types of USSR and U.S. strategic weapons	1979	2
Intermediate-Range Nuclear Forces (INF)	Eliminates all U.S. and Soviet missiles with ranges between 500 km and 5,500 km	1987	2
Missile Technology Control Regime (MTCR)	Limits transfer of missiles or missile technology	1987	25
Conventional Forces in Europe Treaty (CFE)	Reduces conventional forces in Europe. Nonbinding protocol in 1992 covers troops	1990/ 1992	20 30
Strategic Arms Reduction Talks Treaty (START I)	Reduces strategic nuclear forces between the United States and the USSR/Russia	1991	2
START II	Reduces U.S. and Russian strategic nuclear forces	1993	2
Chemical Weapons Convention (CWC)	Bans the possession of chemical weapons after 2005	1993	165
Comprehensive Test Ban Treaty (CTBT)	Bans all nuclear weapons tests	1996	155

Notes: SALT II was never ratified; the MTCR is a negotiated understanding, rather than a treaty as such; the NPT was renewed and made permanent in 1996; the CTBT is open for ratification.
Data sources: Numerous news and Web sources, including the United Nations Treaty Collection at: http://untreaty.un.org/.

Progress toward controlling arms has been slow and often unsteady, but each agreement listed here represents a step down the path of restraining the world's weapons.

as we will discuss further below, it would be an error to dismiss the importance of these and other sometimes-violated, but also often-honored, treaties (Speirs, 2000).

Even if weapons are developed, it is possible to control them by geographic barriers on their operational placement. The deployment of military weapons in Antarctica, the seabed, space, and elsewhere is, for example, banned.

Categorical Restrictions

A third approach to arms control involves limiting or eliminating certain types of weapons. The Intermediate-Range Nuclear Forces (INF) Treaty eliminated an entire class of weapons—intermediate-range nuclear missiles. The START II Treaty will erase multiple-independent-reentry-vehicle (MIRV) warhead ICBMs from the nuclear arsenals. The new Anti-Personnel Mine (APM) Treaty will make it safer to walk the Earth. A number of other treaties are also aimed at eliminating types of weapons. In addition to trying to halt proliferation, the BWT and CWC require the countries that have ratified them to forswear having or using these weapons.

Transfer Restrictions

A fourth method of arms control is to prohibit or limit the flow of weapons and weapons technology across international borders. Under the NPT, for example, countries that have nuclear weapons or nuclear weapons technology pledge not to supply weapons or the technology to build them to nonnuclear states.

Limiting the transfer of missile technology and missiles capable of attacking distant points is another arms control area that focuses on transfer restrictions. The primary effort to stem missile proliferation centers on an informal 1987 multilateral agreement, styled the **Missile Technology Control Regime (MTCR).**

India, Japan, and a few other countries have developed missiles capable of launching satellites that, as a side effect, have intercontinental capability. Just one step down, there are a number of countries with nuclear weapons or a desire to have them that have also developed or purchased long-range missiles. These countries include, among others, Iran, Iraq, Israel, North Korea, and Pakistan. The MTCR has not stopped the spread of missiles but has certainly slowed it down. The countries with the most sophisticated missile technology all adhere to the MTCR, and they have brought considerable pressure to bear on China and other missile-capable countries that do not. There have been repeated charges that China has violated the MTCR by selling missiles to Pakistan and elsewhere. China rejects such charges and refuses to formally join the MTCR, but when President Clinton was in China in 1998, President Jiang Zemin did agree to abide by the MTCR principles. Still it is not clear that China has desisted. A senior U.S. official recently commented that China's record in "the missile area remains a particular concern," and cited Pakistan as a prime example of China's violation of the MTCR's rules.[2]

This review of the strategies and methods of arms control leads naturally to the question of whether they have been successful. And if they have not been successful, why not? To address these questions, we will, in the next two sections, look at the history of arms control, then at the continuing debate over arms control.

THE HISTORY OF ARMS CONTROL

Attempts to control arms and other military systems extend almost to the beginning of written history. In 431 B.C. Sparta and Athens negotiated over the length of the latter's defensive walls, and the Greeks also prohibited incendiary weapons. More recently, the Rush-Bagot Treaty (1817) between the United States and Canada continues to secure the world's longest undefended border. In Europe, it was not until the Hague Conferences (1899, 1907) that the first multilateral arms negotiations took place. Those meetings did nothing about general arms levels, but some restrictions were placed on poison gas and the use of other weapons (Croft, 1997).

The horror of World War I increased world interest in arms control. The Washington Naval Conference (1921–1922) established a battleship tonnage ratio among the world's leading naval powers and, for a time, headed off a naval arms buildup. There were a number of other bilateral and multilateral arms negotiations and agreements in the 1920s and 1930s, but they all had little impact on the increasing avalanche of aggression that culminated in World War II.

Arms control efforts were spurred by the unparalleled destruction by both conventional arms during World War II and by the atomic flashes that leveled Hiroshima and Nagasaki in 1945. In January 1946, for example, the UN created a commission, now called the International Atomic Energy Agency (IAEA), to try to limit the use of nuclear technology to peaceful purposes.

Progress during the ensuing 40 years was slow, but it occurred, as Table 13.2 on page 363 shows. The first major step occurred in 1963, when most countries agreed to cease testing nuclear weapons in the atmosphere. Between 1945 and 1963, 449 nuclear devices were detonated in the open air, an average of 24.9 per year. After the treaty was signed, these tests by nonsignatories declined to about three a year, then ended in the 1980s. Thus, the alarming threat of radioactive fallout that had increasingly contaminated the atmosphere was largely eliminated.

Negotiations to limit the number, deployment, or other aspects of nuclear weapons also began to take place. The most important of these were the SALT I and SALT II treaties (1972, 1979). The ABM Treaty (1972) was also important, and it is still significant today, given the U.S. effort to build a missile defense system.

Arms control momentum picked up even more speed beginning in the mid-1980s. There were many reasons for this acceleration. First, the mounting number of weapons and their increasing power made even supporters of nuclear armament wonder if the levels had not well exceeded any conceivable need. Second, the high cost of weaponry was straining many economies. Third, the cold war thawed considerably, taking the impetus out of the U.S.–Soviet arms race. Fourth, the mounting number of countries building or capable of building weapons of mass destruction led to a concern about the proliferation of nuclear and chemical weapons and the proliferation of missiles that could deliver them.

The U.S.–Soviet INF Treaty (1987) was one product of these changes. Because the treaty eliminated an entire class of nuclear delivery vehicles (missiles with ranges between 500 and 5,500 kilometers), it was the first pact to actually reduce the globe's nuclear arsenal. Other agreements, such as the SALT I and II treaties, had only limited the growth of the number of nuclear weapons.

Nuclear Arms Control in the 1990s and Beyond

The most significant arms control during the 1990s involved efforts to control nuclear arms (Larsen & Rattray, 1996). To review the changes, and the controversy associated with them, we can examine the START I and START II Treaties, the renewal of the NPT, and the efforts to conclude a CTBT.

The START I Treaty After a decade of negotiations, Presidents George Bush and Mikhail Gorbachev signed the **START I Treaty** in 1991. The treaty mandated significant cuts in U.S. and Soviet strategic nuclear forces, including a limit of 1,600 delivery vehicles and 6,000 strategic explosive nuclear devices each. Thus, the START I Treaty began the process of reducing strategic range (over 5,500 kilometers) delivery systems and warheads. Both the United States and Russia have used dynamite to destroy hundreds of ICBM silos, have cut up ICBMs, dismantled bombs and warheads, and have with-

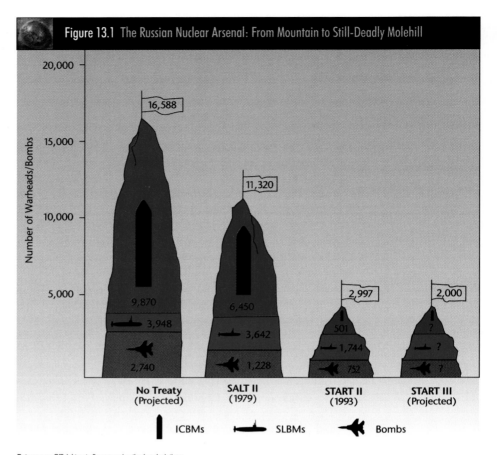

Figure 13.1 The Russian Nuclear Arsenal: From Mountain to Still-Deadly Molehill

Data source: Official treaty figures and author's calculations.

You can see the impact of arms control efforts by comparing the data from the projection of what Russia's nuclear forces might have become without any arms control treaties, through the SALT II and START II Treaties, to the projected totals of the START III Treaty. The projections here for the START III Treaty use the low end of the range (2,500–2,000) of weapons, which Russia and the United States agreed should be the goal when the talks commence.

drawn nuclear weapons from numerous sites. The silos at several former U.S. ICBM sites are now completely empty, and some of the bases have even been sold. Perhaps they will revert to farming, bringing to fruition the words from the Book of Isaiah (2:4), "They shall beat their swords into plowshares, and their spears into pruning hooks."

The START II Treaty Presidents Boris Yeltsin and George Bush took a further step toward reducing the mountain of nuclear weapons when they signed the **START II Treaty** in 1993. The impact of this change of direction is evident in Figure 13.1, which shows four alternatives: no limits, limits at or above existing arms (SALT II), reductions of existing arms (START II), and projected further reduction under START III. Under the START II Treaty, Russia and the United States agree that by 2003 they will (1) reduce their nuclear warheads and bombs to 3,500 (for the United States) and 2,997 (for Russia); (2) eliminate all MIRV ICBMs and retain only about 500 single-warhead ICBMs; (3) limit SLBM warheads (U.S.: 1,728; Russia: 1,744); and (4) reduce air-launched nuclear weapons (bombs, cruise missiles) to 1,272 for the United States and 752 for Russia.

The U.S. Senate ratified the treaty in 1997, but anger in Russia over the expansion of the North Atlantic Treaty Organization (NATO), the air war against Yugoslavia, and other issues delayed ratification by Russia's parliament until May 2000. Even then, the ratification was conditional on a series of complex legal protocols that, in effect, delays final agreement until the United States abandons the possibility of building the national missile defense system discussed in the chapter 12 box, The Flying Garbage Can. Indeed, Russia has threatened to withdraw from the START I Treaty as well if the U.S. missile defense system goes forward.

The START III Treaty Although Russia had not yet ratified the START II Treaty, Presidents Clinton and Yeltsin agreed in 1997 on the broad principles for a third round of START aimed at further cutting the number of nuclear devices mounted on strategic-range delivery systems by one-third of the START II Treaty limits. The preliminary goal is to reduce the number of such weapons to between 2,000 to 2,500.

Formal negotiations were not possible, however, until Russia ratified the START II Treaty. Once that occurred, even if only conditionally, a U.S. State Department official declared that, "now we can move in an accelerated way to negotiations on START III." And in Moscow, President Vladimir Putin commented that "ratification of the START II Treaty opens a way to the start of official talks on further reduction of strategic arsenals of Russia and the U.S.A. in the framework of a START III Treaty."[3]

The Nuclear Nonproliferation Treaty Renewal Nuclear weapons proliferation ranks high among the nuclear arms control challenges facing the international community. There is an occasional argument that universal nuclear armament would create a stable nuclear checkmate system based on mutual assured destruction, but most observers consider the mere existence, and even more so the proliferation, of nuclear weapons to be dangerous. "I think it's a bloody miracle that one of these eggs has not gotten loose," former CIA director William E. Colby has observed. "The subject of control over nuclear weapons is so awful a problem that there aren't any real solutions to them, and you can't relax about it at all."[4]

The stark fact is that nuclear weapons are proliferating, as indicated in the map on the next page. Less than 50 years ago there were no countries with nuclear arms. Now there are seven countries that openly possess nuclear weapons, one country (Israel) whose nuclear arsenal is an open secret, and one country (North Korea) that may well have nuclear weapons. Several other countries such as Iran and Iraq have or recently had active programs to develop nuclear weapons.

The cornerstone of the effort to control the spread of nuclear weapons is the NPT. The treaty was originally signed in 1968; it was renewed and made permanent in 1995, and it has now been signed by more than 85 percent of the world's countries. The signatories agree not to transfer nuclear weapons or in any way to "assist, encourage, or induce any nonnuclear state to manufacture or otherwise acquire nuclear weapons." Nonnuclear signatories of the NPT also agree not to build or accept nuclear weapons and to allow the IAEA to establish safeguards to ensure that nuclear facilities are used exclusively for peaceful purposes. These efforts have been successful insofar as there are many countries with the potential to build weapons that refrain from doing so.

For all its contributions, the NPT is not an unreserved success. The U.S.–led effort to renew it and make it permanent met with numerous criticisms. Several Muslim countries threatened to block the treaty unless Israel agreed to it and gave up its nuclear weapons. Many nonnuclear countries resisted renewal unless the existing nuclear-weapons countries set a timetable for dismantling their arsenals. Malaysia's delegate to the NPT conference charged, for instance, that without such a pledge, renewing the treaty would be "justifying nuclear states for eternity" to maintain their monopoly.[5]

Gradually, however, the objections were overcome. One important factor was a pledge by the nuclear-weapons states to conclude the Comprehensive Test Ban Treaty. Another factor was determined by U.S. diplomacy. "It would have been political suicide to oppose" the NPT, observed a Mexican diplomat. "We used to play in the stadium of

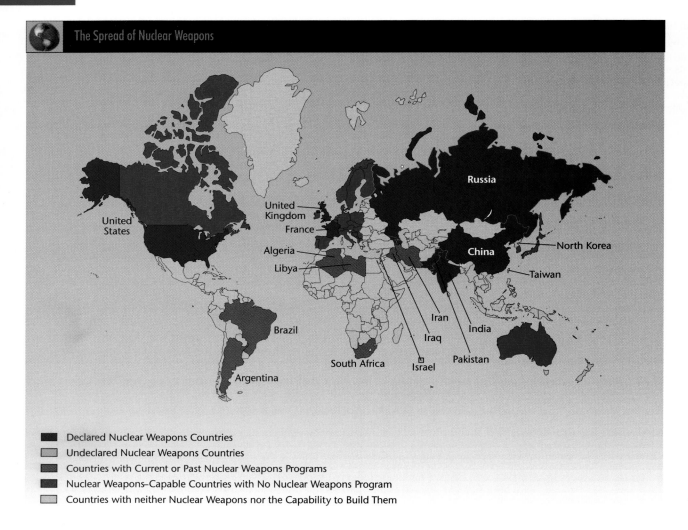

The Spread of Nuclear Weapons

- ■ Declared Nuclear Weapons Countries
- ▢ Undeclared Nuclear Weapons Countries
- ■ Countries with Current or Past Nuclear Weapons Programs
- ■ Nuclear Weapons–Capable Countries with No Nuclear Weapons Program
- ▢ Countries with neither Nuclear Weapons nor the Capability to Build Them

Data sources: Author's evaluation based on press reports and on SIPRI information, on the Web (http://www.sipri.se), and on MILNET-Nuclear Weapons on the Web (http://www.onestep.com/milnet/nukeweap/).

Efforts such as the Nuclear Nonproliferation Treaty have slowed, but not stopped, the proliferation of nuclear weapons. There are now nine declared and undeclared nuclear weapons countries. Numerous other countries have the ability, and in some cases the desire, to acquire nuclear weapons.

the cold war. Now we are playing in Yankee Stadium."[6] In 1995 the delegates of 170 countries approved the NPT, which now will exist in perpetuity.

Nevertheless, proliferation has continued, as witnessed in 1998 by the nuclear tests of India and Pakistan. This fact makes it easy to deride the NPT as a failure, but that judgment is probably too facile. For every country like India and Pakistan that can develop nuclear weapons and has, there are many other technologically advanced countries that have remained nonnuclear. These countries adhere to the NPT, which is both an expression of their animus toward proliferation and a treaty that supports their determination to remain without nuclear weapons.

Another outcome of the NPT renewal resulted from the allegation that the nuclear-weapons powers were attempting to maintain a nuclear monopoly. This and similar charges during the CTBT and other arms negotiations finally led in 2000 to a global conference held at the UN during which the five long-standing nuclear-weapons powers (China, France, Great Britain, Russia, and the United States) agreed to "an unequivocal undertaking by the nuclear-weapon states to accomplish the total elimination of their nuclear arsenals leading to nuclear disarmament."[7] This pledge would only be implemented as part of global nuclear disarmament, but it was the first time the United States and the others clearly stated that their ultimate goal is to eliminate all nuclear weapons.

The Comprehensive Test Ban Treaty Effort   Another important effort toward arms control involves the testing of nuclear warheads. The permanent UN Conference on Disarmament in Geneva attempted to agree on a complete test ban, in part as a response to the pledges made during the NPT negotiations. The negotiations were derailed, however, by the opposition of several countries, most notably India. New Delhi's main concerns were the treaty's lack of a timetable committing current nuclear-weapons states to disarm and that it might be left vulnerable to nuclear threat or attack by China and Pakistan (Walker, 1998; Arnett, 1997).

This setback did not, however, constitute a death certificate for the CTBT. Led by Australia, 116 countries moved to have the UN General Assembly endorse the CTBT, after which they could sign it with or without India's agreement. Even though the treaty would not be fully effective without India's eventual signature, the 116 countries reasoned that all states that did sign it would be obligated not to test their weapons. Moreover, the treaty has a clause stating that three years after it becomes effective, countries that have signed it may consider sanctions against those that have not.

The General Assembly endorsed the CTBT in 1996 by a vote of 158 to 3 (India, Libya, and Nepal opposed; 24 other countries abstained or were absent). President Clinton called the CTBT "the longest-sought, hardest-fought prize in arms control history" and predicted that it would "immediately create an international norm against nuclear testing even before the treaty formally enters into force."[8]

By mid-2000, 155 countries had signed the CTBT and 51, including Russia, had ratified it. Still, the future of the CTBT is unclear. A mushroom cloud cast a shadow over the prospects for the treaty when in 1998 India and Pakistan both conducted nuclear weapons tests, as discussed in the box, Chained to the Nuclear Rock, on page 370. Further darkening the umbra, the Republican-controlled U.S. Senate rejected the treaty in 1999. President Clinton had signed the CTBT in 1996 and continued to support it, and a majority of senators voted to ratify it. But enough legislators viewed the treaty as antithetical to U.S. national security so that it failed to obtain the two-thirds vote required for ratification. Since all 44 countries designated by the treaty as having or capable of building nuclear weapons are required to ratify it for it to go into effect, the U.S. action dealt CTBT's prospects a heavy blow. A resolute President Clinton denounced the Senate's rejection as a "reckless" and "partisan" act and vowed to continue to pursue a ban on testing. "I assure you the fight is far from over," he said. "When all is said and done, the United States will ratify the treaty."[9] Perhaps, but not in his administration, and Clinton left office on January 20, 2001, with the CTBT in limbo.

In the decades following the advent of nuclear weapons in 1945, arms control efforts focused mostly on restraining these awesome weapons and, to a lesser degree, the other weapons of mass destruction (biological and chemical weapons). In the 1990s, the world also began to pay more attention to conventional weapons inventories and to the transfer of conventional weapons.

Conventional Weapons Inventories   The virtual omnipresence of conventional weapons and their multitudinous forms makes it more difficult to limit conventional weapons than nuclear weapons (Pierre, 1997). Still, progress has been made.

One major step is the Conventional Forces in Europe (CFE) Treaty. After 17 years of wrangling between the countries of NATO and the Soviet-led Warsaw Treaty Organization (WTO), the two sides concluded the CFE Treaty in 1990. The treaty, which has

Did You Know That:
The most powerful nuclear weapon ever tested was a 50-megaton device detonated by the USSR in 1961. Equivalent to 50 million tons of TNT, the yield was about 350 times larger than the bomb dropped on Hiroshima in 1945.

(continued on page 372)

CHAINED TO THE NUCLEAR ROCK

There are many mythological tales warning of the dangers of hubris, the arrogance of seeking godlike power. In one such Greek myth, the Titan Prometheus stole fire from the gods and gave it to humankind. An angry Zeus chained Prometheus to a rock and each day sent an eagle to tear open his abdomen. To punish humans for receiving the fire, Zeus created the deceitful Pandora. He gave her a box containing all the travails that could plague humankind and sent her to live in the household of the brother of Prometheus. There Pandora succumbed to the human trait of seeking the unknown despite its risks. She opened the box; evil escaped to bedevil the world.

There are echoes of this fable in the development of atomic energy and weapons. It is a tragic tale about the folly and hubris that led humans to develop the atomic fire that has given them the god-like power to destroy the Earth and all of its creatures and that has left the world unable to escape the nuclear rock that could be the site of humanity's final agony. In the modern replay of the hubris and agony of Prometheus and the folly of Pandora, the box was opened with the first atomic blast at Alamogordo, New Mexico, on July 16, 1945. Humankind now possessed the atomic fire; humankind has arguably been chained to the rock of potential nuclear destruction ever since.

After that first detonation, the number of tests, like the ominous cloud that symbolizes them, kept mushrooming, peaking in 1962 at 171 blasts. Then the flood tide of testing began to ebb in response to the negotiation of a number of treaties restricting testing (see Table 13.2), a declining need to test, and unilateral restraints.

By the early 1990s, the number of nuclear weapons tests had declined to the point where they were unusual. Moreover, when tests did occur, they were greeted with rancor. France detonated four underground nuclear blasts in 1995 on uninhabited atolls in the South Pacific and set off an explosion of criticism. "Lamentable and detestable," charged Argentina's president.[1] "An act of stupidity," thundered the prime minister of Australia. "Crazy," was the word chosen by Japan's finance minister.[2] A resolution in the UN condemning the French tests garnered the support of 95 countries, with only 2 opposed (others abstained). Even the people of France said *non*. A poll by *Le Monde* found that 60 percent of the French people opposed the test.

The following year China, contending that it, too, needed tests to modernize its weapons, exploded two bombs at its test facility under Lop Nor. They were the world's 2,044th and 2,045th nuclear weapons tests. Once again, the world was dismayed.

The total rose to 2,050 after India conducted five underground tests in May 1998. The largest explosion had a yield equivalent to 25 kilotons, nearly twice the size of the Hiroshima atomic bomb. The blast left a crater that was seven stories deep and several hundred yards wide, bearing mute testimony to the continuance of nuclear proliferation and testing.

India argued that the tests were needed for national security. A particular concern is China, which India's defense minister termed his country's "potential number one enemy."[3] This reasoning was rejected by many observers. "There has been no major change in the disposition of Chinese or Pakistani force in at least two years," said a Western military attaché in New Delhi. "India's making the bomb has nothing to do with military needs."[4] An alternative explanation is that Prime Minister Atal Behari Vajpayee was trying to shore up his shaky governing coalition by whipping up nationalist fervor. Yet other theories were more visceral. One line of thought attributed India's tests to the religious-traditionalist/ultranationalist orientation of Vajpayee and his Bharatiya Janata Party (BJP). This is reviewed in the box, *Hindutva* and the Bomb, in chapter 7. And some critics implied that the urge to nuclear power was a derivative of aggressive male impulses, as discussed in chapter 5. "Made with Viagra," is how one editorial cartoon in India labeled the bomb.[5]

Prime Minister Vajpayee rejected the outside criticism as hypocritical. "Some of the countries which have... criticized our action have themselves not only conducted far more nuclear tests than we have done, but they have also built huge stockpiles of nuclear weapons and delivery systems," Vajpayee argued accurately.[6]

Whatever the reasons for India's decision to acquire nuclear weapons, it is debatable whether India's security improved. One U.S. expert commented that the region running from China to Pakistan, Iran, Iraq, Israel, and Egypt "is a nuclear powder keg, and India just lit the fuse. All those countries are connected. They all have, want to have, or have thought about having nuclear weapons programs."[7] That observation was rapidly confirmed when, on May 28, 1998 Pakistan began its own series of tests, the largest of which measured about 12 kilotons. "Today we have evened the score with India," Prime Minister Nawaz Sharif declared.[8] When the dust settled, the total read 2,056 tests.

What comes next is extremely important. One scenario includes more tests, more countries with nuclear arms and, perhaps, nuclear war. Many experts believe that we will witness a nuclear arms race in Asia, with both India and Pakistan testing to improve their weapons and China joining in to maintain its existing superiority. "The logic of nuclear weapons does not respect minimalists," warns retired Indian general V. R. Raghavan.[9]

The tests may also encourage further proliferation. Secretary of Defense William S. Cohen was almost certainly correct when he told a U.S. Senate committee that "there will be other countries that see this [testing] as an open invitation to try to acquire [nuclear weapons] technology. We have a real proliferation problem that's taking place globally. This is only going to contribute to that."[10] If India and Pakistan have the bomb, will Iran and other countries soon follow? The urge will be strong. Libya's leader, Muammar Qaddafi, once thought, "We should be like the Chinese—poor and riding donkeys, but respected and possessing an atom bomb." He is now almost certainly recalling those words (Manning, 1998:75).

The darkest part of the scenario is nuclear war. Analysts point out correctly that the ability of the United States and the Soviet Union to avoid nuclear war despite intense antagonism does not mean India and Pakistan can do the same. One reason is that the two superpowers did not share a common border; India and Pakistan do. Second, the two superpowers never fought one another; India and Pakistan have had three wars (1948, 1965, 1971). Third, U.S. and Soviet/Russian territory are so far apart that a sneak nuclear attack would be difficult, and there is time to check and dismiss or verify warnings of an incoming attack. By contrast, the decision/response time between neighboring India and Pakistan will be almost nil, thereby vastly increasing the chance of inadvertent war. Fourth, the superpowers took decades to develop a sophisticated command and control system; there is no evidence that either India or Pa-

kistan has one. When one reporter asked a ranking military officer how prepared India was to be a nuclear power, he replied, "On the record we are working on it,... and I've no doubt we will rise to the occasion." Then he added disconcertingly, "Off the record, we are totally unprepared."[11] These factors have persuaded one expert that if both India and Pakistan were to deploy their nuclear weapons, "I think it would almost certainly lead to a nuclear exchange in combat."[12] With India and Pakistan each having enough nuclear material to make 50 or more nuclear weapons, and with that number growing, the outcome of such an exchange would be cataclysmic.

It did not take long for the rivalry of nuclear India and nuclear Pakistan to flare anew. Attacks by Pakistani-backed Muslim rebels in Kashmir in 1999 brought a strong military reaction from India. The two countries teetered on the brink of war. American intelligence officials reportedly told the White House that the chance of war between India and Pakistan was in the "50–50 range," and that if war did break out, "there is a serious threat" that it could escalate to a nuclear exchange.[13] Reflecting that view, President Clinton described the region as "perhaps the most dangerous place in the world today because of tensions over Kashmir and the possession of nuclear weapons."[14] War was averted, but the issue of Kashmir remains an open sore that, unless settled, will almost certainly once again bring India and Pakistan to or into the abyss in the most dangerous region in the world.

A less gloomy scenario is that having assuaged whatever drove them to acquire nuclear weapons, India and Pakistan will not unleash a nuclear holocaust on one another, will join the effort to make the NPT fully effective, and will ratify the CTBT. In September 1998 the prime ministers of India and Pakistan both announced they might soon sign the CTBT, but two years later that had not occurred. Prime minister Vajpayee told President Clinton during his trip to the region in March 2000 that India would not conduct further tests. That remains to be seen. In Greek mythology, the agony of Prometheus ends when Hercules frees him from his chains. Perhaps the world will one day escape its nuclear rock, but no modern-day Hercules is likely to come to the rescue. Perhaps the best path is to follow the wisdom of Gandhi: "You must be the change you wish to see in the world."

been reaffirmed by the various former Soviet Republics (FSRs), cuts conventional military forces in Europe from the Atlantic to the Urals (the ATTU region). This geographic focus excludes forces in the United States and Canada and also does not affect FSR forces in Asia (east of the Ural Mountains).

The arms reductions under the CFE Treaty have been impressive. By mid-1997, forces in the ATTU region had been reduced by approximately 53,000 units of the covered weapons systems (artillery tubes, tanks, other armored vehicles, combat helicopters, and fixed-wing combat aircraft).

A supplementary step was taken in 1992 when 29 countries at the Helsinki, Finland, meeting of the Organization for Security and Cooperation in Europe (OSCE) signed a nonbinding, but still important, agreement that established the goal of reducing their troop strengths in the ATTU region. For the larger countries, the troop limits in the ATTU region now are: France (325,000), Germany (345,000), Great Britain (260,000), Russia (1,450,000), Ukraine (450,000), and the United States (250,000). The agreement, said chief U.S. negotiator Lynn Hansen, is "unprecedented in the history of Europe, [or] as far as I know, anywhere."[10]

An additional step in conventional weapons arms control came in 1997 when most of the world's nations signed the Anti-Personnel Mine (APM) Treaty during ceremonies in Ottawa, Canada. The details of that pact and the negotiations leading up to it can be found in the chapter 12 box, The Killing Fields.

Conventional Weapons Transfers

Another thrust of conventional arms control in the 1990s and beyond has been and will be the effort to limit the transfer of conventional weapons. To that end, 31 countries in 1995 agreed to the Wassenaar Arrangement on Export Controls for Conventional Arms and Dual-Use Goods and Technologies. Named after the Dutch town where it was organized, the "arrangement" is an agreement directing its signatories to limit the export of some types of weapons technology and to create an organization to monitor the spread of conventional weapons and **dual-use** (peaceful and nonpeaceful potential) **technology.**

An even more recent attempt to control conventional weapons is the effort to stem the international flow of "light arms," such as assault rifles and machine guns. This effort is sometimes referred to as "micro-arms control." Although such weapons are often used in domestic conflicts that relate to international relations, the issue is being handled in Vienna under the aegis of the UN Commission on Crime Prevention and Criminal Justice. This meeting and subsequent activities resulted in the UN General Assembly resolving in 1999 to convene in mid–2001 the United Nations Conference on the Illicit Trade in Small Arms and Light Weapons in All Its Aspects.

Biological and Chemical Arms Control in the 1990s and Beyond

Despite control agreements dating back to the Geneva protocol of 1925 that forbade the use of gas or bacteriological warfare, such weapons still threaten security. Several of the major powers have (or are suspected of having) such weapons. Additionally, there are reportedly between 15 and 24 LDCs with chemical weapons programs and 6 to 16 such countries with biological weapons programs. Moreover, chemical weapons have been used in some recent conflicts, as chapter 12 related. There is no firm evidence that biological warfare has ever been waged, but the world was put on notice about the possibilities when UN inspectors found evidence that Iraq had earlier been engaged in a biological warfare development program aimed at producing anthrax, botulism, and a gangrene-inducing toxin.

Biological Weapons Arms Control Most countries have signed the Biological Weapons Convention of 1972. Events have demonstrated, however, that the development of biological weapons continues. The Iraqi biological warfare program was discussed in the last chapter. There is also concern that Syria, Iran, and Libya have biological weapons development programs and that Egypt, Iraq, and Russia may still have remnants of previous such programs.

Chemical Weapons Arms Control The growing threat and recent use of chemical weapons sparked a series of UN–sponsored international conferences that culminated in 1993 with the signing of the **Chemical Weapons Convention (CWC).** The signatories pledged to eliminate all chemical weapons by the year 2005 and to submit to rigorous inspection. The signatories also agreed "never under any circumstance" to develop, produce, stockpile, or use chemical weapons. The transfer of chemical weapons to another country is also prohibited, as is any activity that assists or encourages another country to acquire such weapons (Price, 1997). Some 160 countries soon signed the treaty, and when in 1996 Hungary became the 65th country to also ratify the treaty, it went into full effect. Almost as importantly, the U.S. Senate ratified the CWC in mid-1997 and Russia's Duma followed suit later that year.

As with all arms control treaties, the CWC represents a step toward, not the end of, dealing with a menace. One issue is that Libya, Syria, North Korea, and several other countries with demonstrated or suspected chemical weapons programs did not sign the treaty. Not all these refusals were necessarily sinister. Some nonnuclear states view chemical weapons as a way to balance the nuclear weapons of other countries. Some Arab nations, for instance, are reluctant to give up chemical weapons unless Israel gives up its nuclear weapons.

A second problem with implementing a chemical weapons treaty is that many common chemicals also have weapons applications. Furthermore, some chemicals are deadly in such minute quantities that verification is extremely difficult. Perfluoroisobutene, for one, is a gas that causes pulmonary edema (the lungs fill with fluid). The chemical is clear and odorless and therefore hard to detect, has a toxic effect when dispersed in minute levels, and can be formed from the same chemical (polytetrafluoroethene) used to make nonstick frying pans.

THE BARRIERS TO ARMS CONTROL

Limiting or reducing arms is an idea that most people favor. Yet arms control has proceeded slowly and sometimes not at all. The devil is in the details, as the old maxim goes, and it is important to review the continuing debate over arms control to understand its history and current status. None of the factors that we are about to discuss is the main culprit impeding arms control. Nor is any one of them insurmountable. Indeed, important advances are being made on a number of fronts. But together, these factors form a tenacious resistance to arms control.

Security Barriers

Perhaps the most formidable barrier to arms control is thrown up by security concerns. Those who hold to the realist school of thought have strong doubts about whether countries can maintain adequate security if they disarm totally or substantially. Realists are cautious about the current political scene and about the claimed contributions of arms control.

The Possibility of Future Conflict Some analysts argue, "Serious military threats to U.S. security have diminished dramatically since the end of the cold war."[11] Others see the world situation very differently, and argue for keeping defenses up. Testifying before the U.S. Senate Armed Services Committee in 1999, CIA director George J. Tenet

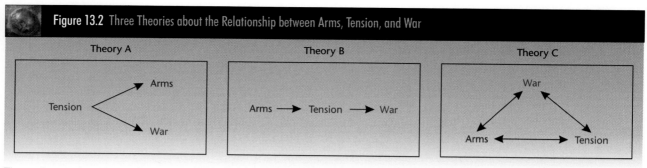

Figure 13.2 Three Theories about the Relationship between Arms, Tension, and War

Theory A approximates the realist view, and Theory B fits the idealist view of the causal relationship between arms, tension, and use. Theory C suggests that there is a complex causal interrelationship between arms, tension, and war in which each of the three factors affects the other two.

remarked to the panel, "In this last annual threat assessment of the twentieth century, I must tell you that U.S. citizens and interests are threatened in many arenas and across a wide spectrum of issues." Tenet went on to portray threats from terrorism; the "challenge" of Russia and China; threats from "regional troublemakers" Iraq, North Korea, and Iran; national security worries about the India-Pakistan confrontation; unrest in the Balkans; potential hot spots in the Aegean Sea region, Haiti, and Africa; and the "continued and growing risk of attack by **weapons of mass destruction**" (which include some exceptionally devastating conventional arms, such as fuel-air explosives, as well as nuclear, biological, and chemical weapons). "The world seen from my window is far from placid," Tenet concluded; "It is becoming a vastly more challenging place for those of us whose job it is to warn our nation's leaders and to protect American lives."[12]

Doubts about the Value of Arms Control Those who have doubts about arms control are skeptical about its supposed benefits. They tend to disbelieve the often heard arguments that arms races occur and that reducing arms will increase security. The skeptics therefore reject the idea that arms control agreements necessarily represent progress (Kydd, 2000).

Does acquiring arms set off arms races? Arms control skeptics doubt it. Instead, a classic tenet of realpolitik is that humans arm themselves and fight because the world is dangerous, as represented by Theory A in Figure 13.2. Given this view, realists believe that political settlements should be achieved before arms reductions are negotiated. Idealists, by contrast, agree with Homer's observation in the *Odyssey* (ca. 700 B.C.) that "the blade itself incites to violence." This is represented by Theory B in Figure 13.2.

While the logic of arms races seems obvious, and, indeed occurs in some specific cases, it is also true that empirical research has not confirmed the arms race model as an overall phenomenon (Koubi, 1999; Li, 1996). Similarly, it is not clear whether decreases in arms cause or are caused by periods of improved international relations. Instead, a host of domestic and international factors influence a country's level of armaments. What this means is that the most probable answer to the chicken-and-egg debate about which should come first, political agreements or arms control, lies in a combination of these theories. That is, arms, tension, and wars all promote one another, as represented in Theory C of Figure 13.2.

Does arms control increase security? The number of nuclear weapons has dropped 55 percent since the 1980s. Does this make the world safer? Many arms control advocates take it as a given that fewer nuclear weapons make the world more secure. Arms control skeptics take the opposite view. They argue that without political agreements, arms reductions only serve to make one more vulnerable.

It is even possible that arms, especially nuclear arms, have increased security. Early in the atomic age, Winston Churchill observed that "it may be that we shall by a process of sublime irony" come to a point "where safety will be the sturdy child of terror and survival the twin brother of annihilation" (Nogee & Spanier, 1988:5). His point was that nuclear weapons may have made both nuclear war and large-scale conventional war between nuclear powers too dangerous to fight. There are also scholars whose work supports this view. One study suggests that, "peace... may depend on the maintenance of credible deterrent policies.... Consequently, the great powers... should not... undermine the potency of their nuclear deterrent" (Huth, Gelpi, & Bennett, 1993:619). Similarly, another study concludes that without proportionate decreases by all nuclear powers, "U.S. and Russian force reductions below 1,000 warheads are [only] ambiguously stable" (Cimbala, 1995:165). If such views are correct, then eliminating or perhaps even substantially reducing nuclear weapons levels could make war more possible and decrease security (Feaver & Niou, 1996).

Are the doubts valid? While these suspicions about the supposed value of arms control merit consideration, you should be chary of too easily accepting them. One caution is that such conclusions are disputed by other studies. It is also important to be wary of the implication that idealists who advocate arms control are confined to academia and other places outside the "real" realm of the military and policy-making professions. That is not true. For example, General George Lee Butler, a former commander of the U.S. Strategic Command, with overall responsibility for U.S. nuclear forces, and 56 other retired generals and admirals from the various nuclear weapons countries issued a manifesto in 1996, which declared that nuclear weapons are now "of sharply reduced utility"; it called for "substantially reducing their numbers," and proclaimed that "the ultimate objective of phased reduction should be the complete elimination of nuclear weapons from all nations" (Schultz & Isenberg, 1997:87).

Technical Barriers

How to compare weapons systems is one technical problem. Numbers alone mean little in arms negotiations because similar weapons have varying quality, capability, capacity, and vulnerability characteristics. When reducing ICBMs, for example, how does one equate a fixed-site U.S. Minuteman ICBM versus a road-mobile Russian SS-25 ICBM? If you were a U.S. negotiator, would you eliminate one of your Minuteman for each SS-25 the Russians scrapped?

Verification difficulties pose another technical barrier to arms control. Countries suspect that others will cheat. One common complaint about the CTBT that led to its rejection by the U.S. Senate was, "While the treaty will constrain the United States from modernizing and developing weapons, it will be possible for other nations to cheat with little or no risk of being caught because the CTBT cannot be verified" (Bailey, 1999:2).

Possible cheating can be divided into two levels: *break-out cheating* and *creep-out cheating*. A violation significant enough by itself to endanger your security would constitute a break-out. This possibility worries skeptics of arms control. Some are also hesitant about arms control because of what they believe would be the reluctance of democracies to respond to creep-out cheating. In this scenario, no single violation would be serious enough by itself to create a crisis or warrant termination of the treaty. Yet the impact of successive and progressive violations might seriously upset the balance of forces.

There have been great advances in verification procedures and technologies. The most important recent procedural advance is increased **on-site inspection (OSI)**. Countries are increasingly willing to allow others to inspect their facilities. Yet as the problems UN inspectors have had in Iraq illustrate, even OSI is not foolproof, especially if the other side is not cooperative. **National technical means (NTM)** of verification using satellites, seismic measuring devices, and other equipment have also advanced rapidly. These have been substantially offset, however, by other technologies that make

NTM verification more difficult. Nuclear warheads, for example, have been miniaturized to the point where ten or more can fit on one missile and could literally be hidden in the back of a pickup truck or even in a good-sized closet. Therefore, in the last analysis, virtually no amount of OSI and NTM can ensure *absolute verification*.

Because absolute verification is impossible, the real issue is which course is more dangerous: (1) coming to an agreement when there is at least some chance that the other side might be able to cheat or (2) failing to agree and living in a world of unrestrained and increasing nuclear weapons growth? Sometimes, the answer may be number 2. Taking this view while testifying in 1996 before the U.S. Senate about the pending Chemical Weapons Convention, former secretary of state James A. Baker III counseled, "The Bush administration never expected the treaty to be completely verifiable and had always expected there would be rogue states that would not participate." Nevertheless, Baker urged the Senate to ratify the treaty on the grounds that "the more countries we can get behind responsible behavior around the world..., the better it is for us."[13]

Domestic Barriers

As we saw in chapter 4, all countries, and especially democracies, are complex decision making organizations. Even if they favor arms control, leaders have numerous other powerful domestic political actors that they must work with or, perhaps, overcome in the policy-making process. Some of the opposition that leaders face when they try to restrain or reduce arms comes from the ideological differences and policy doubts expressed above. In addition to these security and technical issues, other domestic opposition to arms control often stems from national pride and from the interrelationship among military spending, the economy, and politics.

National Pride The Book of Proverbs tells us that "pride goeth before destruction," and this statement is equally applicable to modern arms acquisitions. Whether we are

Although Pakistan and India are desperately poor countries, they both spent huge sums of money to develop nuclear weapons and the missiles to deliver them. Whatever rational reasons might be given, it is also true that emotional national pride played a role in the decisions of Islamabad and New Delhi to build nuclear weapons. As this protest sign in India indicates, not everyone agreed that building the bomb was wise.

Building weapons is big business. The corporations, unions, and other economic interests associated with the arms industry join with the military to put great pressure on governments to maintain or even increase military spending. The missile pictured here in front of the U.S. Capitol is part of a display designed to convince members of Congress to appropriate funds to build an antimissile missile system.

dealing with conventional or nuclear arms, national pride is a primary drive behind their acquisition. For many countries, arms represent a tangible symbol of strength and sovereign equality. EXPLOSION OF SELF-ESTEEM read one newspaper headline in India after that country's nuclear tests in 1998.[14] LONG LIVE NUCLEAR PAKISTAN read a Pakistani newspaper headline soon thereafter. "Five nuclear blasts have instantly transformed an extremely demoralized nation into a self-respecting proud nation... having full faith in their destiny," the accompanying article explained.[15]

Military Spending, the Economy, and Politics "Every gun that is made, every warship launched, every rocket fired signifies, in the final sense, a threat to those who hunger and are not fed, those who are cold and are not clothed," President Dwight D. Eisenhower once told Americans.[16] The trouble with this charge is that for all its stirring emotion, it may not be true.

Critics and supporters of defense spending have long argued over whether it harms or contributes to the economic health of the world and its individual countries. Critics charge that because military expenditures are in capital-intensive industries (require large sums of money but employ relatively few people to produce relatively few products), they create fewer jobs per dollar spent than more labor-intensive enterprises, such as education or construction (Henderson, 1998).

Such arguments about the negative impact of arms spending have an element of truth. Still, they should be accepted only with caution. The relationship between defense spending and the overall economy is extremely complex, and scholars differ widely on specific impacts. First, lower defense expenditures do not necessarily mean higher budget funds for nondefense programs. Nor is it always true that increased defense spending leads to cuts in domestic programs. It is more accurate to say that defense spending may affect domestic spending but that the impact is inconsistent, both over time and among programs.

Moreover, whatever the objective truth may be, it is perceptions and politics that often dominate the arms control debate within countries. Economically, arms are big business, and economic *interest groups* pressure their governments to build and to sell weapons and associated technology (Keller & Nolan, 1997). American industry, its workers, and the cities and towns in which they reside, for example, have been prime supporters of military spending and foreign sales. Additionally, there are often *bureaucratic* elements in alliance with the defense industry and its workers. Finally, both interest groups and bureaucratic actors receive support from *legislators* who represent the districts and states that benefit from military spending. This alliance between interest groups, bureaucracies, and legislators forms a military-industrial-congressional complex that has been termed the **iron triangle.**

A good example is the story of the V-22 Osprey, which is a virtual sequel to the movie *Pentagon Wars* starring Kelsey Grammer as the U.S. Army general in charge of developing the ill-designed Bradley fighting vehicle. The new movie might be titled *Clinton versus the Iron Triangle*. In the real story on which the movie would be based, the Clinton administration tried hard to kill the $37 billion program to build V-22s. In addition to the high expense, the cross between a helicopter and conventional airplane does not seem to work. The General Accounting Office has found that the V-22's major components "remain inadequate or untested," and the Pentagon's civilian analysts have criticized the testing of the plane by its manufacturer as "extremely artificial." Two test planes crashed. So did one of the initial Ospreys delivered to the Marines in an accident in Arizona that killed 19 soldiers in April 2000. None of this has spelled a death knell for the V-22. The Marines, who desperately want to add it to their arsenal, shrug off the plane's record and proclaim, "We're confident in the program." They are supported by the prime contractor, Boeing, by numerous subcontractors, and by labor unions whose members work in the plants that will build the V-22 and its parts. Moreover, Boeing astutely gave subcontracts for parts to companies in 40 states, which helped numerous legislators see the benefit of the Osprey. "Those who come out... and question the program, they don't know what they're talking about," charges Representative Curt Weldon.[17] The district of the Pennsylvania Republican coincidentally includes Boeing's helicopter division. In the end the iron triangle won out. Just as the colonel who opposed the Bradley was forced to retire, so too the Clinton administration passed into history. Just as the Bradley fighting vehicle survived, so too the V-22 continues to roll off the production lines.

INTERNATIONAL SECURITY FORCES

The idea of forming international security forces to supplement or replace national military forces is a second approach to seeking security on the road less traveled by. This approach would enhance, not compete with, the first approach, arms control. Organizing for international security would emphasize international organizations and de-emphasize national defense forces. Thus, the creation of international security forces and the first approach, arms control, are mutually supportive.

INTERNATIONAL SECURITY FORCES: THEORY AND PRACTICE

The idea of seeking security through an international organization is not new. Immanuel Kant foresaw the possibility over two centuries ago in *Idea for a Universal History from a Cosmopolitan Point of View* (1784). "Through war, through the taxing and never-ending accumulation of armament... after devastations, revolutions, and even complete exhaustion," Kant predicted, human nature would bring people "to that which reason could have told them in the beginning": that humankind must "step from the lawless condition of savages into a league of nations" to secure the peace. These ideas have evolved into attempts to secure the peace through such international structures as the Concert of Europe, the League of Nations, and the United Nations. An increased UN peacekeeping role has been especially evident, and other international governmental organizations (IGOs) also have occasionally been involved in international security missions (Roberts, 1996). The far-reaching language in the UN Charter related to peacekeeping can be found in the box, The UN Charter and International Security.

An important point is that while our discussion here will focus on the UN as a global organization, much of what is said is also applicable to regional IGOs and their security forces. NATO is providing international security forces in Bosnia-Herzegovina. Also in Europe, the **Organization for Security and Cooperation in Europe (OSCE)** shows signs of evolving into a regional security structure. Established in 1973, the OSCE now has 55 members, including almost all the countries of Europe, Kazakhstan and several other states in Central Asia, and Canada and the United States (Flynn & Farrell, 1999). Operationally, it has begun limited field activities to, in the words of the OSCE, "work 'on the ground' to facilitate political processes, prevent or settle conflicts, and inform the OSCE community."[18] These efforts primarily involve sending monitors and other personnel to try to resolve differences, and as of mid-2000, OSCE missions

THE UN CHARTER AND INTERNATIONAL SECURITY

The fundamental idea of international security is contained in the UN Charter. Article 1 commits all members "to maintain international peace and security, and to that end, to take effective collective measures" to preserve or restore the peace. Article 24 gives to the Security Council the "primary responsibility for the maintenance of international peace and security," and by Article 25 members "agree to accept and carry out the decisions" of the council. Article 42 gives the Security Council the authority to "take such action by air, sea, or land forces as may be necessary to maintain or restore international peace and security." Key language in Article 43 requires members to "undertake to make available to the Security Council, on its call... armed forces... necessary for the purposes" of peace maintenance. The forces are subject to "special agreements" between the UN and member-countries, but the article (as written in 1945) states that the "agreements shall be negotiated as soon as possible." If you think about the implications of this language, clauses to which virtually all countries are bound legally, it is very powerful.

were operating in Albania, Bosnia, Latvia, Macedonia, Moldova, Tajikistan, and more than a dozen other countries or hotspots. The largest OSCE peacekeeping effort involved the dispatch of 6,000 troops from eight countries to Albania in April 1997 when that country's political system collapsed into anarchy amid factional fighting. Beyond Europe, troops from the Economic Community of West African States (ECOWAS) helped return Liberia to some semblance of normalcy after a particularly horrendous civil war, and were also able in 1998 to restore a measure of unfortunately temporary peace in Sierra Leone (Love, 1996). And in the Western Hemisphere, the Organization of American States (OAS) has advanced peace on a number of fronts, including helping to settle the long and seemingly intractable border dispute between Ecuador and Peru. The potential cause of war was eliminated in October 1998 when the presidents of the two countries met in Brazil to sign the *Acta de Brasilia* demarcating their border and establishing Argentina, Brazil, Chile, Spain, and the United States as the guarantors of the pact.

To organize our discussion of global and regional international security forces, we can examine the theory and practice of their use according to three essential concepts: collective security, peacekeeping, and peacemaking.

Collective Security

One theory behind use of international security forces through the UN and other IGOs is the concept of **collective security**. This idea was first embodied in the Covenant of the League of Nations and is also reflected in the Charter of the United Nations. Collective security is based on three basic tenets. First, all countries forswear the use of force except in self-defense. Second, all agree that the peace is indivisible. An attack on one is an attack on all. Third, all pledge to unite to halt aggression and restore the peace by supplying to the UN or other IGOs whatever material or personnel resources are necessary to deter or defeat aggressors and restore the peace.

This three-part theory is something like the idea that governs domestic law enforcement. First, self-defense is the only time an individual can use force legally. Second, acts of violence are considered transgressions against the collective. If one person assaults another in, say, Ohio, the case is not the victim versus the aggressor but the society (Ohio) versus the aggressor. Third, domestic societies provide a collective security force, the police, and jointly support this force through taxes.

Collective security, then, is not only an appealing idea but one that works—domestically, that is. It has not, however, been a general success on the international scene. In part, applying collective security is limited by problems such as how, in some cases, to tell the aggressor from the victim. But these uncertainties also exist domestically and are resolved. The more important reason that collective security fails is the unwillingness of countries to subordinate their sovereign interests to collective action. Thus far, governments have generally maintained their right to view conflict in terms of their national interests and to support or oppose UN action based on their nationalistic points of view. Collective security, therefore, exists mostly as a goal, not as a general practice. Only the UN–authorized interventions in Korea (1950–1953) and in the Persian Gulf (1990–1991) came close to fulfilling the idea of collective security.

Peacekeeping

What the United Nations has been able to do more often is implement a process commonly called **peacekeeping.** Apart from using military force, peacekeeping is quite different from collective security. The latter identifies an aggressor and employs military force to defeat the attacker. Peacekeeping takes another approach and deploys an international military force under the aegis of an international organization such as the UN to prevent fighting, usually by acting as a buffer between combatants. The international force is neutral between the combatants and must have been invited to be present by at least one of the combatants.

Some of the data regarding the use of UN peacekeeping forces and observer groups to help restore and maintain the peace were given in chapter 9 but bear repeating briefly here. During its first 55 years (1945 through mid-2000), the United Nations sent over 800,000 soldiers, police officers, and unarmed observers from 118 countries to conduct 53 peacekeeping or truce observation missions. Over 1,650 of these individuals have died in UN service. The frequency of such UN missions has risen sharply, as can been seen in Figure 9.7 on p. 248. In 2000 there were 14 different armed UN forces of varying size, totaling 40,000 troops and police, in the field in Africa, Asia, the Caribbean, Europe, and the Middle East. The cost of these operations peaked at about $3.5 billion for 1996, dropped to under $1 billion, and stood at somewhat more than $2 billion in 2000.

Several characteristics of UN peacekeeping actions can be noted. First, most have taken place in LDC locations, as evident in the map on page 381. Second, UN forces have generally utilized military contingents from smaller or nonaligned powers. Canada and Fiji have contributed personnel to virtually all peacekeeping efforts, and the Scandinavian countries and Ireland have also been especially frequent participants. The end of the cold war has made it possible for the troops of larger powers to take a greater part in international security missions, and in 2000, American, British, French, German, and Russian troops and police personnel were in the field as UN peacekeepers.

Peacemaking

Did You Know That:

The 10 countries with the most troops/police serving with the UN in late 2000 were: India (4,507), Nigeria (3,439), Jordan (3,400), Bangladesh (2,362), Ghana (1,906), Australia (1,710), Pakistan (1,209), Kenya (1,197), Poland (1,077), and Nepal (1,037).

For all the contributions that UN peacekeeping efforts have made, they have sometimes been unable to halt fighting quickly (or even at all) or to keep the peace permanently. The numerous reasons for the limited effectiveness of UN forces can be boiled down to two fundamental and related problems: The first problem is that countries frequently do not support UN forces politically or financially. It is often difficult to get the self-interested UN Security Council members, especially the five, veto-wielding permanent members, to agree to authorize a UN mission. Even when the mission is authorized, it is often given a very narrow scope of authority to act and few troops. When the UN initially sent forces to the Balkans, the secretary-general asked for 35,000 peacekeepers. He got only 7,000, and their lack of heavy weapons and lack of authority to take strong action led, at one point, to UN troops being taken hostage and chained to potential targets to deter threatened action by NATO forces.

United Nations Peacekeeping Missions

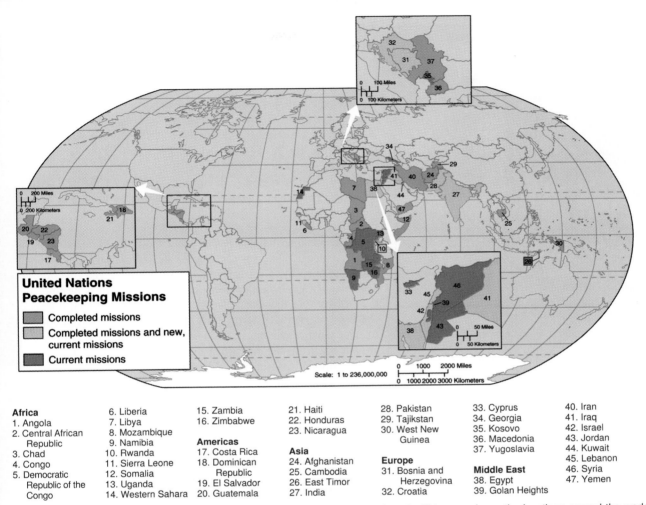

United Nations Peacekeeping Missions

- Completed missions
- Completed missions and new, current missions
- Current missions

Scale: 1 to 236,000,000

Africa
1. Angola
2. Central African Republic
3. Chad
4. Congo
5. Democratic Republic of the Congo
6. Liberia
7. Libya
8. Mozambique
9. Namibia
10. Rwanda
11. Sierra Leone
12. Somalia
13. Uganda
14. Western Sahara

15. Zambia
16. Zimbabwe

Americas
17. Costa Rica
18. Dominican Republic
19. El Salvador
20. Guatemala
21. Haiti
22. Honduras
23. Nicaragua

Asia
24. Afghanistan
25. Cambodia
26. East Timor
27. India
28. Pakistan
29. Tajikstan
30. West New Guinea

Europe
31. Bosnia and Herzegovina
32. Croatia

33. Cyprus
34. Georgia
35. Kosovo
36. Macedonia
37. Yugoslavia

Middle East
38. Egypt
39. Golan Heights
40. Iran
41. Iraq
42. Israel
43. Jordan
44. Kuwait
45. Lebanon
46. Syria
47. Yemen

The United Nations has played a valuable peacekeeping and collective security role. This map shows the locations around the world where UN forces have been or are active. The 1988 Nobel Peace Prize was awarded to the soldiers who have served, some of whom have been wounded or lost their lives, in the interest of international peace.

Peacemaking: Support Surges The mounting frustrations with the reactive, passive peacekeeping approach of UN forces led to an upsurge of support for the idea of proactive **peacemaking**. This new role would involve heavily armed UN forces with the authority to restore and maintain the peace. Such UN units would not only intervene where fighting had already broken out. They could also be deployed to imperiled countries before trouble starts, thereby putting an aggressor in the uncomfortable position of attacking UN forces as well as national defense forces. The UN Security Council called on the secretary-general to examine such a possibility by suggesting ways, including a permanent UN force, to strengthen the UN's capacity for "preventative diplomacy, for peacemaking and for peacekeeping."[19]

Secretary-General Boutros Boutros-Ghali soon responded in a report entitled "Agenda for Peace" that, among other things, asked for the establishment of a $1 billion contingency fund that would allow the UN to dispatch forces to troubled areas quickly. To create such a force, Boutros-Ghali requested member-states to commit a total of

UNCLE SAM OWES YOU

PETERSON
THE SUN
Vancouver
CANADA

I.O.UN
$1.7 BILLION
IN BACK DUES.
Sam

© 2000 CARTOONISTS & WRITERS SYNDICATE http://CartoonWeb.com

Even though the annual U.S. assessment ($300 million–$800 million in recent years) for UN peacekeeping operations only averages about one-quarter of the cost of a single B-2 bomber ($2.1 billion), Washington refuses to pay what it owes. This has left the UN short of the funds necessary to operate effectively.

Did You Know That:

The U.S. assessment for UN peacekeeping operations in 1999 cost each American about $1.37—less than the price of a Big Mac—or would have if Congress had appropriated all the funds.

100,000 troops that could be deployed by the UN as a rapid-response force to intervene early during crises in the hopes of containing them.

Initially, the international response was positive. Numerous countries, including the United States, indicated a willingness to have their units train with units from other countries so that they could rapidly join in a UN force. Within two years, 15 countries had pledged 54,000 troops for a rapid-response force. The goal was not to create a standing UN army. Instead, the units of participating countries would have specialized training that would enable them to assemble quickly and operate effectively as a UN force. As such, according to one analyst, the ready force would be a half step toward a standing UN force "in the hopes [that] countries get half-pregnant with the idea of committing forces to the UN."[20] Whatever the strategy, however, the gestation is proving to be long and difficult.

Peacemaking: Support Wanes Soon, however, the momentum lost steam. One damper was the variety of barriers, especially nationalism and sovereignty, to an expanded UN role. As one analysist explained, "Robust peace enforcement is beyond the capacity of the United Nations. The Security Council does not have the stomach for it, contributing countries don't want to put their troops under other commanders and then have to answer questions at home when their troops get killed."[21]

Additionally, as discussed in chapter 9, the UN has continued to be hobbled by the unwillingness of many countries to pay their assessment. In early 2000 member-states were in arrears on their peacekeeping obligations by $1.5 billion. The United States was the largest debtor, with a shortfall of over half the total. Moreover, all indications are that the deficit will get worse. Increased needs for UN intervention in Sierra Leone and elsewhere during 2000 increased the costs for that year to about $2.2 billion. Yet there was no hope that Congress would appropriate the funds to meet the U.S. share of those costs. The problem for Clinton administration officials was, one analyst noted, "If they go to congressional leaders and say they are revising the number [need for the U.S. assessment for peacekeeping] upward to $1 billion, they will be laughed out of the room."[22]

Peacemaking: Humanitarian Intervention or Neocolonialism? Doubts about a more aggressive UN military role are not just based on nationalism and other such factors. There is also a concern that creating a more powerful, proactive UN will undermine the sovereignty of the smaller LDCs and that the UN will become a neocolonial tool of the big powers. The chaos and death that often engulf some countries create powerful emotional and political incentives to intervene in these so-called failed states. One observer urges, for instance, that the UN "must begin to systematically exercise its mandated political authority *within* nations, when nations have disintegrated into warring factions." That goal requires the UN "to abandon some of its most cherished notions regarding the inviolate nature of national sovereignty," the analyst continued (Chopra, 1995:31).

Other commentators worry that once the barrier of sovereignty is breached, the powerful countries will have license through the UN to impose their will on weaker countries. That suspicion is not only voiced by some people in LDCs. It also receives support from a recent review of UN peacekeeping activity. The analysis of the record from 1945 to 1990 led the scholar to conclude that the "interests that have been served by UN peacekeeping are those of the Western states whose interests are served by the status quo and a few non-Western states that lay claim to some prestige in international affairs through their UN activities." This use of the UN, the scholar continues, may "amount to Western interventionist foreign policy bordering on imperialism. The recent expansion of UN peacekeeping activities may indeed signal an era in which sovereignty is eroded, but only for non-Western states" (Neack, 1995:194).

International Security and the Future

What does the future hold for international security? While there are certainly many impediments on the path to international security, it would be foolish to dismiss the idea as impossible. First, it is in almost everyone's interest to prevent or contain crises, and there is a growing recognition that cooperation through the use of an international security force may often be a more effective way to maintain or restore peace than is continued reliance on unlimited national self-defense in a world capable of producing and using nuclear, biological, and chemical weapons. As such, the existence of peace-keeping has been largely a functional response to an international problem, and the increased number of missions, whether by the UN or one of the regional organizations, is evidence that the international security efforts are necessary and almost certainly have become a permanent part of world politics.

Second, it is important to see that many of the shortcomings of previous international security missions have not been due to an inherent failure of the UN (Wesley, 1997). Certainly the UN has problems, as any large political and bureaucratized organization does (Jett, 2000). The central problem, at least in Kofi Annan's view, is that the UN has "been asked to do too much with too little."[23]

Efforts to create the nucleus of a UN ready force continue but remain controversial (Rosenblatt & Thompson, 1998; Ratner, 1996). Events in the first year of the new millenium somewhat revived interest in strengthening UN forces and giving them more proactive authority. As has occurred too often, UN forces, this time in Sierra Leone in 2000, were outnumbered and outgunned by hostile forces and suffered other problems inherent in trying to deploy an army made up of various national contingents with little ability to work as a unified force. The worst moment came when several dozen Kenyan and Zambian soldiers serving with the UN force were taken hostage by rebels. In the aftermath of this humiliation, there have been renewed calls to invigorate the UN's capabilities. For one, Richard C. Holbrooke, the U.S. ambassador to the UN, advised, "Peacekeeping needs three things: More financial resources, more and better-trained military and civilian personnel in the field and a coherent command structure overseas with better central direction out of [UN headquarters in] New York."[24] Whether that view has survived the intervening U.S. presidential election remains to be seen.

Another approach for the immediate future may be to distinguish types of international security efforts, including peacekeeping and peacemaking missions, and to handle them differently (Mockaitis, 1999; Diehl, Druckman, & Wall, 1998). The UN's under secretary-general for peacekeeping has contended that "peace enforcement and serious peace restoration campaigns will... be the responsibility of a coalition of interested countries using their own forces but with a green light from the Council."[25] This model is much like the NATO–led interventions in Bosnia in 1995 and in Kosovo in 1999 and the International Force in East Timor (INTERFET). This Australian-led multinational force moved to restore stability in East Timor beginning in September 1999 before handing over responsibility for the territory to the UN. According to this model, peacemaking would be up to heavily armed regional forces and peacekeeping to lightly

It is easy to disparage UN peacekeeping forces for sometimes being weak and ineffective. These children in East Timor, walking safely with a Portuguese soldier attached to the UN command there, would probably disagree about the value of UN forces. Moreover, the shortcomings of UN peacekeeping forces have mostly been caused by the inadequate support they have received.

armed UN contingents. As one U.S. diplomat explains it, "There has to be a peace to keep before the blue helmets are put on the ground."[26]

Whatever the model, talk of an international security force may sound outlandish, but this is one of those junctures when it is important to remember the events during the lives of Egypt's Mohammed El-Wasimy and Dominica's Elizabeth Israel. When they were reputedly born in 1875, the Hague Conferences, the League of Nations, and the United Nations were all in the future. When they reached 65, retirement age for many, talk of international peacekeeping forces in Bosnia, Cyprus, Haiti, and other far-flung places would have been greeted with incredulous shakes of the head. Yet all these things exist today. The world needed them. Some say the world also needs an international security force.

ABOLITION OF WAR

The last of the four approaches to security that we will examine in this chapter looks toward the abolition of war. For our purposes, we will divide the discussion into two parts: complete disarmament and pacifism.

COMPLETE DISARMAMENT

The most sweeping approach to arms control is simply to disarm. The principal argument in favor of disarmament is, as noted, the idea that without weapons people will not fight. This rests in part on sheer inability. **General and complete disarmament (GCD)** might be accomplished either through unilateral disarmament or through multilateral negotiated disarmament.

In the case of *unilateral disarmament*, a country would dismantle its arms. Its safety, in theory, would be secured by its nonthreatening posture, which would prevent aggression, and its example would lead other countries to disarm also. Unilateral disarmament draws heavily on the idea of pacifism, or a moral and resolute refusal to fight. The unilateral approach also relies on the belief that it is arms that cause tension rather than vice versa.

Negotiated disarmament between two or more countries is a more limited approach. Advocates of this path share the unilateralists' conviction about the danger of war. They are less likely to be true pacifists, however, and they believe one-sided disarmament would expose the peace pioneer to unacceptable risk.

The GCD approach has few strong advocates among today's political leaders. Even those who do subscribe to the ideal also search for intermediate arms limitation steps. Still, the quest goes on. The UN Disarmament Committee has called for GCD, and the ideal is often a valuable standard by which to judge progress as "real."

PACIFISM

The second war-avoidance approach, pacifism, relies on individuals. As such, it very much fits in with the idea that people count and that you can affect world politics if you try. Unlike other approaches to security, **pacifism** is a bottom-up approach that focuses on what people do rather than a top-down approach that stresses government action.

Pacifism begins with the belief that it is wrong to kill. Leo Tolstoy, the Russian novelist and pacifist, told the Swedish Peace Conference in 1909 that "The truth is so simple, so clear, so evident... that it is only necessary to speak it out completely for its full significance to be irresistible." That truth, Tolstoy went on, "lies in what was said thousands of years ago in four words: *Thou Shalt Not Kill.*"

Pacifism, simply refusing to fight physically, is one way to halt violence. Mohandas K. Gandhi, who freed what is now India, Bangladesh, and Pakistan from British colonial rule through passive resistance, would smile benignly, if somewhat incredulously, at the argument that pacifists are hopelessly idealistic.

Beyond this starting point, pacifists have varying approaches. There are *universal pacifists*, who oppose all violence; *private pacifists*, who oppose personal violence but who would support as a last resort the use of police or military force to counter criminals or aggressors; and *antiwar pacifists*, who oppose political violence but would use violence as a last resort for personal self-defense.

The obvious argument against pacifism is that it is likely to get one killed or conquered. Those who support pacifism make several countercontentions. One is that there is a history of pacifism's being effective. As one scholar points out, "Nonviolence is as old as the history of religious leaders and movements." The analyst goes on to explain that "traditions embodied by Buddha and Christ have inspired successful modern political movements and leaders [such as]... the Indian struggle for independence under the leadership of [Mohandas K.] Gandhi [in India] and the struggle of the American Blacks for greater equality under the leadership of Martin Luther King Jr." (Beer, 1990:16).

Gandhi was the great Indian spiritual leader (Burrowes, 1996). He began his career as a London-trained attorney earning what was then an immense sum of £5,000 annually practicing in Bombay. Soon, however, he went to South Africa, where, earning £50 a year, he defended Indian expatriates against white legal oppression. Gandhi returned to India in 1915 to work for its independence. He gave up Western ways for a life of abstinence and spirituality. Gandhi believed that the force of the soul focused on, to use the Hindi, *satyagraha* (truth seeking) and *ahimsa* (nonviolence) could accomplish what a resort to arms could not. He developed techniques such as unarmed marches, sit-downs by masses of people, work stoppages, boycotts, and what might today be called "pray-ins," whereby truth seekers (*satyagrahi*) could confront the British nonviolently. "The sword of the *satyagrahi* is love," he counseled the Indian people (Lackey, 1989:14). Gandhi became known as Mahatma (great soul) and was the single most powerful force behind Great Britain's granting of independence to India in 1947. The Mahatma then turned his soul toward ending the hatred and violence between Hindus and Muslims in independent India. For this, a Hindu fanatic, who objected to Gandhi's tolerance, assassinated him in 1948. Earlier, after the United States had dropped atomic bombs on Japan, Gandhi was moved to write that "mankind has to get out of violence only through nonviolence. Hatred can be overcome only by love. Counter-hatred only increases the surface as well as the depth of hatred." One has to suspect that had he been able to, Gandhi would have repeated this to the man who shot him.

Pacifists, especially antiwar pacifists, would also make a moral case against the massive, collective violence that is war. They would say that no gain is worth the loss. This view, pacifists would argue, has become infinitely more compelling in the nuclear age. Consider the description of Nagasaki filed by the first reporter who flew over the city after a U.S. bomber dropped an atomic bomb, killing at least 60,000 people. "Burned, blasted, and scarred," the reporter wrote, "Nagasaki looked like a city of death." It was a scene, he continued, of "destruction of a sort never before imagined by a man and therefore is almost indescribable. The area where the bomb hit is absolutely flat and only the markings of the building foundations provide a clue as to what may have been in the area before the energy of the universe was turned loose" (Lackey, 1989:112). Pacifists contend that even by the standards of just war conduct (*jus in bello*) adopted by nonpacifists, any nuclear attack would be unconscionable.

A final point about pacifism is that it is not an irrelevant exercise in idealist philosophy. There are some countries, such as Japan, where at least limited pacifism represents a reasonably strong political force. Moreover, in a changing world, public opinion, economic measures, and other nonviolent instruments may create what is sometimes called a "civilian-based defense." Indeed, there are efforts, such as the Program on Nonviolent Sanctions in Conflict and Defense at Harvard University's Center for International Affairs, which are working to show that those who favor nonviolence should not be considered "token pacifists" who are "tolerated as necessary to fill out the full spectrum of alternatives, with nonviolent means given serious considerations only for use in noncritical situations" (Bond, 1992:2). Instead, advocates of this approach believe that the successes of Gandhi, King, and others demonstrate that proactive techniques, including nonviolent protest and persuasion, noncooperation, and nonviolent intervention (such as sit-ins), can be successful (Bock & Young, 1999).

It is true that pacifists are unlikely to be able to reverse world conflict by themselves. They are a tiny minority everywhere. Instead, pacifism may be part of a series of so-called "peace creation" actions. It is an idea worth contemplating.

CHAPTER SUMMARY

1. The goal of the chapter is to discuss alternative paths to security. Security is not necessarily synonymous with either massive armaments or with disarmament. There are four approaches to security: unlimited self-defense, limited self-defense, international security, and abolition of war. The first was the subject of the last chapter. This chapter investigates the other three.

2. There are four possible approaches to ensuring security. They involve restrictions on the number of arms; their development, testing, and deployment; restrictions on certain types of weapons; and the transfer of weapons. Additionally, the stan-

dards of evaluation are determined by domestic norms, domestic collective security forces, domestic disarmament, and the established domestic conflict-resolution mechanism. Despite all of the protections and dispute-resolution procedures provided by a domestic system, security is a relative term, thus making full security impossible.

3. There are some people who believe that, because of the nature of humans and the nature of the international system, unlimited self-defense is the prudent policy. Advocates of this approach are suspicious of arms control.

4. Limited self-defense is one means of alternative security. People who favor limited self-defense would accomplish their goals through various methods of arms control.

5. From the standpoint of pure rationality, arms control, or the lack of it, is one of the hardest aspects of international politics to understand. Virtually everyone is against arms; virtually everyone is for arms control; yet there are virtually no restraints on the explosive arms escalation in which we are all trapped. It is a story that dates back far into our history, but unless progress is made, we may not have a limitless future to look forward to.

6. There are many powerful arguments against continuation of the arms race. Arms are very costly, in direct dollars and in indirect impact on the economy. Arms are also very dangerous and add to the tensions that sometimes erupt in violence.

7. During the 1990s, efforts increased to regulate arms. Several START treaties, renewal of the Nuclear Nonproliferation Treaty (NPT), the Comprehensive Test Ban Treaty (CTBT), conventional weapons inventories, conventional weapons transfer regulation, and biological and chemical arms control efforts are among the efforts made. There are heavy domestic pressures from the military-industrial complex and sometimes from the public against arms control.

8. There are a number of ways to implement approaches to arms control, including arms reductions, limits on the expansion of arms inventories, and prohibitions against conventional arms transfers and nuclear proliferation.

9. Some people favor trying to achieve security through various international security schemes. Collective security, peacekeeping, and peacemaking are among the most significant attempts of an international security effort. The most likely focus of this approach would be the United Nations with a greatly strengthened security mandate and with security forces sufficient to engage in peacemaking, rather than just peacekeeping.

10. Abolition of war is a fourth approach to security. One way to avoid war is through general and complete disarmament. This makes violence difficult and may also ease tensions that lead to violence. Individual and collective pacifism is another way to avoid violence. Pacifists believe that the way to start the world toward peace is to practice nonviolence individually and in ever-larger groups.

CHAPTER 14

THE INTERNATIONAL ECONOMY: A GLOBAL ROAD MAP

O, behold, the riches of the ship is come onshore.

Shakespeare, *Othello*

They are sick that surfeit with too much, as they that starve with nothing.
Shakespeare, *The Merchant of Venice*

You don't make the poor richer by making the rich poorer.

Winston Churchill

If we make the average of mankind comfortable and secure, their prosperity will rise through the ranks.

Franklin D. Roosevelt

CHAPTER OBJECTIVES

After completing this chapter, you should be able to:

• Explain why politics and economics are intertwined aspects of international relations.
• Understand international political economy (IPE).
• Discuss the economic nationalist doctrine.
• Discuss the economic internationalist approaches to IPE.
• Discuss the economic structuralist approaches to IPE.
• Analyze the economic elements that form the base of the North-South axis.
• Consider the three explanations offered for the existence of the economic gap between the North and South.
• Understand the history of IPE while focusing on the effect of changes during the last 50 years.
• Discuss how the expansion of IPE continues to be dominated by the North.
• Note the growth of trade, rapid expansion of international financial ties, and economic importance of monetary relations.
• Analyze the effect of increasing economic interdependence on both countries and individuals.

Given the degree to which this text has already discussed the interplay of politics and economics, you have probably concluded correctly that, to a significant extent, economics is politics and vice versa. This chapter and the two that follow it will continue to explicate how economics and politics intertwine. The subject of this chapter is the general nature of **international political economy (IPE)**, including IPE theories, and the situation of the economically developed countries (EDCs) of the North and the less developed countries (LDCs) of the South. Chapter 15 will examine the traditional political path of national economic competition. Finally, chapter 16 will discuss the alternative path of international economic cooperation.

It is important before delving into the subject to familiarize yourself with the distinctions between gross national product (GNP) and gross domestic product (GDP), between either of those adjusted for purchasing power parity (GNP/PPP, GDP/PPP), and between **current dollars** and **real dollars.** It is also important that you understand how to read graphs (including 100-as-baseline graphs) and that you gain a sense of the origin and reliability of economic statistics. To do so, go to Explanatory Notes on page 557, and review "Economics: Technical Terms and Sources."

THEORIES OF INTERNATIONAL POLITICAL ECONOMY

Before getting into the details of current global economic conditions, it is appropriate to examine the broad theories about the connection between economics and politics (Burch & Denemark, 1997; Pettman, 1996). As chapter 1 discussed, many political scientists believe that economic forces and conditions are the key determinants of the course of world politics. One scholar observes, "Clearly, a state perceives its international economic interests on the basis of a set of ideas or beliefs about how the world economy works and what opportunities exist within it" (Woods, 1995:161). We also noted in chapter 1 that there are a variety of approaches to IPE and that they can be roughly divided into mercantilism, liberalism, and structuralism.

All of the three approaches are descriptive, in that they all purport to describe how and why conditions occur. The three approaches are also prescriptive, in that they make arguments about how policy should be conducted. These descriptions and prescriptions are summarized in Table 14.1 on page 390. You should further note that economic nationalism is a realpolitik school of IPE, while economic internationalism and, especially, economic structuralism are idealist schools.

ECONOMIC NATIONALISM

The core of **economic nationalism** is the belief that the state should use its economic strength to further national interests. By extension, economic nationalists also advocate using a state's power to build its economic strength. This approach is also called *economic statecraft* and, classically, *mercantilism.* Economic nationalists are realists who believe that conflict characterizes international economic relations and that the international economy is a zero-sum game in which one side can gain only if another loses. From the economic nationalist perspective, political goals should govern economic policy because the aim is to maximize state power in order to secure state interests.

Alexander Hamilton was an early mercantilist. "The love of wealth," he wrote in *Federalist* No. 6, is "as domineering and enterprising a passion as that of power or glory." Therefore, he asked rhetorically, "Have there not been as many wars founded upon commercial motives... [as there have been] occasioned by the cupidity of territory or dominion?" The answer was yes, he thought. Based on this view, that economic rivalry was the cause of conflict, Hamilton also believed that economic strength was necessary to national survival and greatness, and to advance American interests he

Table14.1 Approaches to International Political Economy

	Economic Nationalism	Economic Internationalism	Economic Structuralism
Associated terms	Mercantilism, economic statecraft	Liberalism, free trade, free economic interchange, capitalism, laissez-faire	Marxism, dependencia, neo-Marxism, neo-imperialism, neo-colonialism
Primary economic actors	States; alliances	Individuals, multinational corporations, IGOs	Economic classes (domestic and state)
Current economic relations	National-based conflictual; all countries compete with all other countries; zero-sum game	National conflict but cooperation increasing; non–zero-sum game	Structural conflict based on classes of countries; wealthy states exploit poor ones; zero-sum game
Goal for future	Preserve/expand state power, secure national interests	Increase global prosperity	Eliminate internal and international classes
Prescription for future	Follow economic policies that build national power; use political power to build national economy	Eliminate/minimize role of politics in economics; use politics	Radically reform system to end divisions in wealth and power between wealthy and poor countries
Desired relationship of politics and economics	Politics controls economic policy	Politics used only to promote domestic free markets and international free economic interchange	Politics should be eliminated by destruction of class system
View of states	Favorable; augment state power	Mixed; eliminate states as primary economic policy makers	Negative; radically reform states; perhaps eliminate states
Estimation of possibility of cooperation	Impossible; humans and states inherently seek advantage and dominance	Possible through reforms within a modified state-based system	Only possible through radical reform; revolution may be necessary

Conceptual sources: Balaam & Veseth (1996); Gilpin (1996); author.

Analysts take very different approaches in describing how the international political economy works and in prescribing how it should work.

advocated harnessing the economy to build national strength. "It is evident" argued Hamilton as U.S. secretary of the treasury, "that the interference and aid of [the U.S.] government are indispensable" to protect American industry and to build U.S. economic strength (Balaam & Veseth, 1996:23).

To accomplish their ends, economic nationalists rely on a number of political-economic strategies. These include:

Imperialism and neoimperialism are one set of economic nationalist practices. Imperialism is the direct control of another land and its people for national economic gain. It was this motive that propelled Europeans outward to conquer the great colonial empires that dominated so much of the world until recent decades. Direct colonial control has largely died out, but many observers charge that neoimperialism (indirect control) continues to be a prime characteristic of the relationship that exists, or that EDCs try to achieve, between themselves and LDCs.

Economic incentives and disincentives provide a second set of economic nationalist practices. Countries that offer economic carrots, such as foreign aid and favorable trade policies, or that use economic sticks, such as sanctions, to promote the state's national

The slogan on the back of a construction worker's shirt during a September 2000 campaign stop by presidential candidate Al Gore in Philadelphia gives voice to the sentiment that buying American products supports American workers and, for this man, his union. Actually, economic reality is more complex. Among other things, it is hard to tell where many products are made. For instance, Ford produces many cars in Mexico; many Hondas are made in Ohio.

interests are practicing economic nationalism. For example, a State Department official justified what he depicted as putting "pressure on the Cuban government through the embargo and [other economic measures]" on the grounds that "economic sanctions can be and are a valuable tool for... protecting our national interests."[1]

Protectionism and domestic economic support are a third set of tools that economic nationalists believe should be used to promote national power. "I use not porter [ale] or cheese in my family, but such as is made in America," George Washington once avowed.[2] From this perspective, economic nationalists are suspicious of economic interdependence on the grounds that it undermines state sovereignty and weakens the national economic strength. Economic nationalists would prefer that their respective countries use trade barriers, economic subsidies, and other policies to protect national industries, especially those with military value.

Although the rationale is often muted, it is important to realize that national leaders most often make economic decisions based on what is good for their country in the short run. It is also worth noting that while economic nationalists in the United States and many other countries are apt to describe themselves as believers in capitalism (free enterprise, a free-market economy), that self-image is inaccurate because economic nationalism requires government manipulation of the economy. Such interference violates the principles of the theory of capitalism, which hold that business should proceed largely or completely unimpeded by government.

ECONOMIC INTERNATIONALISM

A second major theoretical and policy approach to IPE is **economic internationalism.** This approach is also associated with such terms as capitalism, laissez-faire, economic liberalism, and free trade. Economic internationalists are idealists. They believe that international economic relations should and can be conducted cooperatively because, in their view, the international economy is a non–zero-sum game in which prosperity is available to all.

Economic internationalists contend that the best way to create prosperity is by freeing economic interchange from political restrictions. Therefore, economic internationalists (in contrast to economic nationalists) oppose tariff barriers, domestic sub-

Did You Know That:

The phrase "laissez-faire" originated with an eighteenth-century group of French capitalist philosophers called *les Économistes*. Reflecting their objection to government interference in the economy, their motto was *laissez-faire, laissez-passer* (let be, let pass). The views of *les Économistes* influenced the noted English capitalist philosopher Adam Smith in his writing of *The Wealth of Nations* (1776).

sidies, sanctions, and any other economic tool that distorts the free flow of trade and investment capital.

The origins of economic liberalism lie in the roots of capitalism. In one of the early expositions of capitalist theory, *The Wealth of Nations* (1776), Adam Smith wrote that "it is not from the benevolence of the butcher, the brewer, or the baker, that we expect our dinner, but from their regard to their own interest." Smith believed that this self-interest constituted an "invisible hand" of competition that created the most efficient economies. Therefore, he opposed any political interference with the operation of the invisible hand, warning, "The statesman, who should attempt to direct private people in what manner they ought to employ their [finances] would assume an authority which... would nowhere be so dangerous as in the hands of a man who had folly and presumption enough to fancy himself fit to exercise it."

The pure capitalism advocated by Smith has few adherents today. Instead, most modern economic liberals favor using the state to modify the worst abuses of capitalism by ensuring that monopolies do not form and by taking other steps to ensure that the competition and unequal distribution of wealth inherent in capitalism is not overly brutal. Writing in the 1930s, the British economist John Maynard Keynes found classic capitalism "in many ways objectionable" but believed that "capitalism, wisely managed, can probably be made more efficient for attaining economic ends than any alternative system." What Keynes suggested was "to work out a social organization which shall be as efficient as possible without offending our notions of a satisfactory way of life" (Balaam & Veseth, 1996:49).

At the international level, Keynesian economics has influenced economic internationalists and the changes they advocate to traditional economic nationalist policies. They are moderate reforms, though, which would alter, but not radically change, either capitalism or the state-based international system. For example, the efforts in the 1940s to set up organizations such as the International Monetary Fund (IMF) and to promote trade through the General Agreement on Tariffs and Trade (GATT) reflect the Keynesian idea of using intergovernmental organizations (IGOs) and agreements to promote and, when necessary, to regulate international economic interchange. Modern liberals also favor such government interference as foreign aid and, sometimes, concessionary trade agreements or loan terms to assist LDCs to develop.

Still, modern liberals are capitalists, albeit modified ones, who are willing to use IGOs to promote the capitalism that they believe is the best engine of economic prosperity. The IMF, for example, presses countries to adopt capitalism in exchange for loans to help stabilize their currencies. Russia and the other former communist countries are among those who have experienced such pressure. In the words of the IMF's managing director, "the stronger the program [of capitalist reform], the stronger the financing will be."[3]

In sum, modern economic liberals generally believe in eliminating political interference in the international economy. They also favor, however, using IGO and national government programs for two ends: (1) to ensure that countries adopt capitalism and free trade and (2) to ease the worst inequities in the system so that future competition can be fairer and current LDCs can have a chance to achieve prosperity. Thus economic liberals do not want to overturn the current political and economic international system. This support of a modified status quo is quite different from the more far-reaching changes advocated by economic structuralists.

ECONOMIC STRUCTURALISM

The third major approach to IPE is called **economic structuralism.** Like the other two approaches, economic structuralism has both descriptive and prescriptive elements.

Economic structuralists believe that economic structure determines politics. That is, the conduct of world politics is based on the way that the world is organized economically. Structuralists contend that the world is divided between have and have-not countries and that the "haves" (the EDCs) work to keep the "have nots" (LDCs) weak and poor in order to exploit them. To change this, economic structuralists favor a radical restructuring of the economic system designed to end the uneven distribution of wealth and power.

Economic structuralists can be divided into two major camps: Marxist theorists and dependencia theorists. Marxists see the state and capitalism as inherent sources of economic evil; dependencia analysts do not necessarily share this view. Instead, they advocate radical reforms to end economic oppression. Both types of economic structuralists believe that significant changes have to be made in the way international politics works in order to promote LDC development, but they disagree about how radical the change must be. Marxists believe that the entire capitalist-based system must be overturned and replaced with domestic and international socialist systems before economic equity can be achieved. Less radical economic structuralists stress reform of the current market system.

Marxist Theory

Marxism is perhaps the best-known strand of structuralist thought. Communist ideology, associated with Karl Marx, maintains that history proceeds by means of a historical dialectic, or clash of opposing ideas (thesis versus antithesis), with a resulting new order (synthesis). **Marxism** also holds that the economic (material) order determines political and social relationships. Thus, history, the current situation, and the future are determined by the economic struggle, termed dialectical materialism. The first Soviet Communist Party chief, V. I. Lenin, applied dialectical materialism to international politics. He argued in *Imperialism: The Highest Stage of Capitalism* (1916) that capitalist, bourgeois leaders had duped their proletariat workers into supporting the exploitation of other proletariat peoples through imperialism. Thus, the material dialectic was transformed, in part, from a domestic class struggle to an international class struggle between bourgeois and proletariat countries and peoples. Since Marx saw the state as a creation and tool of the monied class, Marxism includes a level of hostility toward the state and holds that it will no longer exist once communism is fully realized.

Dependencia Theory

A second variation of structuralist thought is the **dependencia theory,** which is also referred to as neo-Marxist theory and economic radical theory. Dependencia theorists argue that the exploitation of the LDCs by the EDCs is exercised through indirect control and is driven by the EDCs' need for cheap primary resources, external markets, profitable investment opportunities, and low-wage labor. The South produces low-cost, low-profit **primary products** such as agricultural products and raw materials. These help supply the EDCs' production of high-priced, high-profit manufactured goods, some of which are sold to the LDCs. It is, therefore, in the interest of capitalist exploiters to keep LDCs dependent. For this reason, economic structuralists say, **neocolonialism** (neoimperialism), which operates without colonies but is nevertheless imperialistic, has created a hierarchical structure in which the rich states in the center of the world economic system dominate the LDCs on the periphery of the system. The dependency of LDCs is maintained in a number of ways, such as structuring the rules and practices of international economics to benefit the North. The economic structuralists further contend that neoimperial powers corrupt and co-opt the local elite in LDCs by allowing them personal wealth in return for the governing of their countries in a way that benefits the North.

GOMAA
AL AHRAM WEEKLY
Cairo
EGYPT

This Egyptian editorial drawing captures the view of economic structuralists, who believe that the world's wealthier countries want the world's less developed countries to remain poor in order to dominate and exploit them.

An economic radical would argue, for example, that the U.S. role in the Persian Gulf region dating back to World War II epitomizes neoimperialism. The devil's bargain, in the view of structuralists, is this: The United States protects or tries to protect the power of obscenely rich, profoundly undemocratic kings of oil-rich states. These would include, among others, the king of Saudi Arabia and the emir of Kuwait. For economic radicals, the U.S.–led intervention to restore the emir of Kuwait to power in 1991 and the continued presence of the U.S. military in the Persian Gulf region are just the latest examples of U.S. protection of the rich and undemocratic. The other half of the bargain is what the United States gets in return: cheap oil. Dependencia theorists say that the oil potentates pay back the United States for its protection of their marble palaces, Rolls Royces, and Swiss bank accounts by ensuring that the price of petroleum stays low. This ensures the continued prosperity of the economy of the United States and the other EDCs. There can be little doubt that throughout the 1990s petroleum was a relative bargain, selling in 1999 at only 74 percent of its 1990 price measured in current dollars. There was an upsurge in the price of crude oil in 2000 to about $36 a barrel, but in real dollars prices were still little more than what they had been a decade before. It is possible to argue that the bargain basement price of petroleum has been based on supply and demand. Structuralists would differ, though, and argue that those market forces have been manipulated through a greedy conspiracy between capitalist oil consumers and despotic oil producers.

TWO ECONOMIC WORLDS: NORTH AND SOUTH

Whether or not you subscribe to economic nationalist, internationalist, or structuralist theory, it cannot be denied that the world is generally divided into two economic spheres: a wealthy North made up of EDCs and a less wealthy South composed of LDCs. The two geographical designations result from the fact that most EDCs lie to the north in North America and Europe and most LDCs are farther to the south in Africa, Asia, and Central and South America. There are exceptions, however, and what is important is that the North and the South are distinguished from each other by economic and political factors more than by their geographical position.

TWO ECONOMIC WORLDS: ANALYZING THE DATA

The economic factor is the most objective distinction between North and South. The North is much wealthier than the South, as can be ascertained by examining countries (and the 1998 per capita GNP of each). That year the 22 wealthiest countries had an average per capita GNP of $25,510; the South's average per capita GNP was $1,250. The structure of the economy is another factor that generally differentiates EDCs from LDCs. The countries of the North tend to have more diverse economic bases that rely for their income on the production of a wide variety of manufactured products and the provision of diverse and sophisticated services. The countries of the South usually depend on fewer products for their income; these are often agricultural produce or raw materials, such as minerals. In 1998, for example, agriculture accounted for 12 percent of the GDPs of the South and only 2 percent of the GDPs of the North.

It is important to note that these two classifications and the overall numbers contain some difficulties. One is that, as with most attempts to categorize the world's political and economic divisions, the classifications are imprecise and subject to change. On the sole basis of per capita GDP, for example, the World Bank divides countries into four economic groups: low-income ($760 or less), lower-middle-income ($761–$3,030), upper-middle-income ($3,031–$9,360), and high-income (more than $9,361). These groupings are illustrated in the accompanying map.

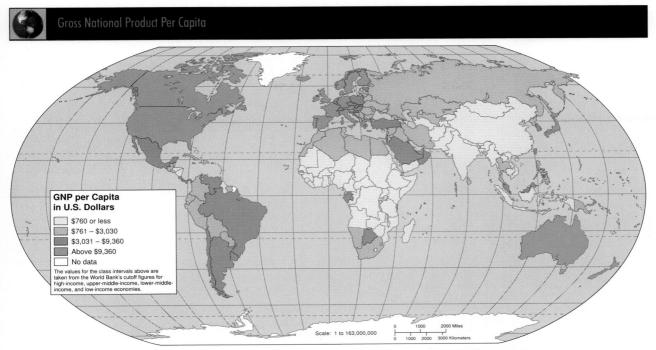

Gross National Product Per Capita

GNP per Capita in U.S. Dollars

☐ $760 or less
☐ $761 – $3,030
☐ $3,031 – $9,360
☐ Above $9,360
☐ No data

The values for the class intervals above are taken from the World Bank's cutoff figures for high-income, upper-middle-income, lower-middle-income, and low-income economies.

Scale: 1 to 163,000,000

0   1000   2000 Miles
0   1000   2000   3000 Kilometers

There is a great disparity in the world between a handful of countries that have a relatively small percentage of the world population but possess a huge proportion of global wealth (measured here in per capita GNP) and everyone else. The dollars that the legend uses to divide countries into economic categories do not truly convey the impact of the differences in economic circumstance. Especially if you are living in one of the poorest countries, you are much more likely to be illiterate, ill-housed, malnourished, and ill, and to die earlier than your contemporaries in the wealthy countries.

These two classifications (North-South, and the four World Bank income groups) generally coincide, but not completely. One difference is that four countries (Israel, Kuwait, Singapore, and the United Arab Emirates), which are usually classified as part of the South, fall into the high-income group. It is also important to note that some LDCs have moved a significant distance toward achieving a modern economic base. The **newly industrializing countries (NICs)** are still usually placed in the South by analysts, but countries such as South Korea ($8,600) and Argentina ($8,030) could be classified as developed market economies. The NICs are also sometimes referred to as NIEs (newly industrializing economies) to accommodate the inclusion of Taiwan ($13,928).

A second issue of classifying countries economically relates to how to treat Russia, the other former Soviet republics (FSRs), and the former communist region of Eastern Europe. The World Bank designates these countries as transition economies (from communism to capitalism). They are also referred to as **countries in transition (CITs).** Some of these transition economies have a reasonable industrial base, although all of them have experienced significant economic difficulties during the transition. Of them, only one, Slovenia (GNP: $9760) falls in the high income group. Others, such as Hungary ($4,510), fall into the upper-middle-income group, but most CITs, including Russia ($2,260), are in the lower-middle-income group, and five of the Asian FSRs are all in the low-income category. Of this group of FSRs, Tajikistan ($370) is the poorest. Given the economic data, all these countries except Slovenia are treated here as LDCs.

A third concern centers on the difficulty of measuring and reporting economic data. All the statistics are only an approximation. If, for instance, you have ever had an odd job babysitting or raking leaves, have been paid for it, and have not reported your income to the government, then the GDP for your country is slightly lower than it should be. All countries, especially LDCs, have significant unrecorded economic

Classifying countries economically is complex. We are used to thinking of Russia as an industrialized country, yet by some objective economic criteria, it is a less developed country. The dire economic condition of many Russians is symbolized by an elderly woman counting coins she has received by begging near St. Basil's Cathedral in Moscow.

activity. For this reason, major differences in economic circumstances, economic trends, and other macroeconomic indicators are more important than specific dollar figures.

Fourth, the cost of many items varies tremendously from country to country, undermining part of the relevance of some data, such as GNP. This issue is explored in the box, GNP-PPP: The Big Mac Standard.

For all of these difficulties, the classification of the world into a North and a South is still useful. One reason is that the classification anomalies do not disguise the fact that, as a rule, the countries of the South are poorer and less industrialized than those of the North. The data can be dry to read, but the reality behind the data is that, on average, the conditions of life for the citizens in the countries of the industrialized North are dramatically better than the living standards of the relatively deprived people who reside in the LDCs of the South.

Economic vulnerability is a second factor that unites most of the South and distinguishes it from the North. Even many upper-middle-income countries of the South have a shaky economic base that relies on one or a few products. For example, those LDCs that rely on petroleum production and export are at substantial risk when the price of oil is exceptionally low, as it was throughout most of the 1990s.

Common political experiences of the LDCs are a third reason that the North-South distinction continues to be applicable. Most LDCs share a history of being directly or indirectly dominated by the EDCs of Europe and North America or, in the case of the former communist countries, by Russia.

TWO ECONOMIC WORLDS: HUMAN CONDITIONS

Sensationalism is not the aim of this book. Still, it is hard to recount conditions of impoverishment in neutral, academic terms. Approximately 85 percent of the world's people live in the South, yet they produce only 22 percent of the global GNP. Far outpacing the fortunes of those who reside in LDCs, the 15 percent of the people who are fortunate enough to reside in the North produce 78 percent of the world's measurable GNP. Another telling calculation is that on a per capita basis, the richest 15 percent of the world's citizens produce $49 for every $1 produced by the 60 percent of the world's population who live in the poorest countries (the low-income or **least developed countries, LLDCs**). Perhaps worse, this 60:1 ratio has doubled from a 30:1 ratio in 1960. As stark as these statistics are, their true meaning is in their social impacts. Compared with those who live in an EDC, a person who lives in an LLDC is:

- 3 times more likely to be illiterate if adult.
- 14 times more likely to die before age 5.
- 27 times more likely not to have access to basic sanitation services.
- 28 times more likely to have to work full-time as a child.
- 15 times more likely to die during childbirth.
- 14 years earlier in the grave.

The scope of the deprivation that many in the South suffer also boggles the mind when the total number of humans affected is calculated. About 25 percent of all the

GNP-PPP: THE BIG MAC STANDARD

The existence of about 180 national currencies and their fluctuation in values against one another make it difficult to evaluate any country's financial status by using standard measures, such as gross national product (GNP). Using the U.S. dollar as a base to calculate exchange rates, some countries' 1998 per capita GNPs were: United States ($29,340), Germany ($25,850), Kenya ($330), and Russia ($2,300). Many economists argue that these figures do not present an accurate picture because they do not reflect the prices for commonly consumed local products such as housing, public transportation, movies, and fast food. One way the Union Bank of Switzerland (one the world's largest banks) keeps track of these relative factors is by using the ubiquitous Big Mac as a standard to measure relative prices. According to data on 30 countries compiled by the *Economist* (a leading financial journal), the average 1998 Big Mac cost $2.43 in the base-price United States, and ranged from $1.19 in Malaysia to $3.97 in Switzerland.[1] The currency of a country is overvalued by the Big Mac standard if the Big Mac costs more than it does in the United States and undervalued if the deluxe hamburger costs less. The Swiss franc, for example, would be judged overvalued by 64 percent and the Malaysian ringgit undervalued by 51 percent.

To adjust GDP to reflect the actual cost of living in various countries, the World Bank and other financial institutions use GNP-PPP (Purchasing Power Parity), which uses a "market basket" of items "not traded on international markets" (that is, like Big Macs, locally produced and consumed) as one way to compare standards of living. By this standard (and again using the United States as the base), the above countries' (per capita GNP-PPPs) in 1998 were: United States ($29,340), Germany ($20,810), Kenya ($1,130), and Russia ($3,950). Note that, compared to the U.S. data, Germany had a higher GNP and lower GNP-PPP, whereas the GNP-PPPs of Kenya and Russia were higher than their GNPs. One of the most dramatic differences is Japan, which had a per capita GNP of $32,380, some 10 percent larger than the U.S. Japan's very high prices, however, put its GNP-PPP at $23,180, about 21 percent lower than the U.S. GNP-PPP.

It is important to see that neither the standard GNP nor the newer GNP-PPP is a fully accurate measure. GNP does not take prices of locally produced and consumed items into account. But GNP-PPP misses the fact that many items we all consume come through international trade, and the price of a barrel of imported petroleum, an imported Toyota, or an imported Mac—in this case the computer—is pretty much the same, whether you are paying for it in U.S. dollars, German marks, Kenyan shillings, or Russian rubles.

people in the LDCs live on less than $1 a day. Literacy and education are beyond the dreams of many. There are 842 million illiterate adults and 80 million children in the South who are not in school. The North's per capita spending on education is $1,377; the South has but $51 to spend. The perils to health are everywhere. Some 1.2 billion people in LDCs do not have access to safe drinking water. The South can afford to spend a mere $13 a year on health care per person; $1,531 is spent on health care in the North. Even those medical facilities that do exist in the South are overwhelmed. Each physician in the South is responsible for 5,833 people, compared to only 350 people for a physician in the North; 766 million people in the South have no access to any kind of health care. These conditions lead to disease and death on a wide scale. Some 158 million children in the South are malnourished; more than 12 million toddlers die each year. Half the people in LLDCs (compared to 11 percent of the people in EDCs) do not live to age 60.

Beyond the overall North-South statistics, it is also instructive to compare lives in two countries: Japan of the North and Nigeria of the South. The two countries have approximately equal populations, yet the statistical comparison of the two reflects a life of advantage for the Japanese and of disadvantage for the Nigerians, as shown in Figure 14.1 on the next page.

Did You Know That:

Worldwatch Institute estimates that 1.2 billion people around the world are underfed and undernourished. It also reports that during 1999, some 400,000 Americans underwent liposuction procedures to siphon excess fat from their bodies. "It shows how out of balance things are," Worldwatch president Lester R. Brown comments.

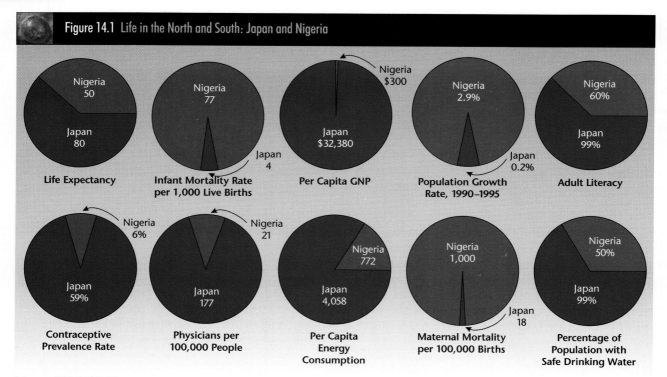

Figure 14.1 Life in the North and South: Japan and Nigeria

Data sources: UNDP (1999); World Bank (2000).

Infant mortality measures deaths before age 5 per 1,000 live births; maternal mortality measures deaths during childbirth; per capita energy consumption is measured by kilograms of oil consumption or equivalents; contraceptive prevalence rate is the percentage of couples using any form of contraceptive practice. Each pie chart reflects each country's relative share of the sum of both numbers/percentages.

By most measures, life is vastly better in EDCs like Japan than in LDCs like Nigeria. These pie charts show the relative deprivation of Nigerians compared to Japanese, but no statistical representation can capture the stark realities. Just one example is that Nigerian children are 19 times more likely to die before age 5 than are Japanese children.

Nor is the future bright for many in the South in spite of some improving indicators of social conditions. Overall, though, the economic gap between North and South is widening. In 1990 the per capita GNPs of the South ($840) and the North ($19,590) left a gap of $18,750. That gap—gulf is a better word—had spread to $24,260 in 1998 between the North ($25,510) and the South ($1,250).

The worst news is that conditions are declining in some countries. One-third of the LLDCs have had their per capita GNPs decline over the last 25 years. Sub-Saharan Africa is a particularly depressed region. The combined per capita GNP of the region's countries declined by an annual average of −0.3 percent between 1965 and 1998. Even though the United States and sub-Saharan Africa have approximately equal populations, the U.S. total GDP is 23 times larger than that of sub-Saharan Africa. A horrific 46 percent of its population lives on less than $1 a day. The region has the world's highest birthrate, and the rapidly rising population is outpacing agricultural production. Only 47 percent of the region's population has access to basic sanitation; there is but one physician for every 18,514 people; adult illiteracy is 42 percent; life expectancy is only 50 years. It is unnecessary to recite more grim statistics in order to document that—relatively speaking and, in some cases, absolutely—the rich are getting richer and the poor are getting poorer.

TWO ECONOMIC WORLDS: APPROACHES TO NORTH-SOUTH RELATIONS

Documenting the plight of the South is easier than agreeing on the causes or the remedies. An initial question is, Why did the gap between North and South develop? One factor was circumstance. The industrial revolution came first to Europe and, by

While tractors and other mechanical farm equipment in the North produce so much food that farm surpluses and obesity are problems, the South has difficulty feeding itself. This Vietnamese rice farmer and his horse are struggling to harvest the crop, but there is only so much they can do. The farmer would have preferred to use a 64-horsepower, John Deere 5310 farm tractor. But given the tractor's $24,000 price tag, it would take the average Vietnamese 73 years to earn enough money to buy one.

extension, to North America. Industrialization brought the North both wealth and technology that, in part, could be turned into sophisticated weapons that overpowered the more rudimentarily armed people of the South. The need for primary products to fuel the North's factories and the search for markets in which to sell those products led to increased direct colonization and indirect domination. Nationalism intensified this process as countries also sought colonies to symbolize their major-power status. As a result of all these factors, Asians, Africans, Latin Americans, and others were exploited to benefit the industrialized, imperialist countries. This pattern existed for a century and in some cases much longer. Politically, most of the LDCs achieved independence in the decades following World War II. Economically, though, the South remains disadvantaged in its relationship with the North. In many ways that we will explore later, the international economic system remains stacked against the LDCs. What can and should be done? More specifically, what can and should the countries of the North do to assist the countries of the South?

The Economic Nationalist Approach

Economic nationalists operate from a realpolitik orientation and believe that each country should look out for itself first and foremost. Therefore, economic nationalists argue that an EDC should be governed by its own national interest when formulating trade, investment, and aid policies toward the South. Furthermore, economic nationalists suspect that the South's calls for greater equity are, in essence, attempts to change the rules so that the LDCs can acquire political power for themselves.

Economic nationalists view the political economy as a zero-sum game in which gains made by some players inevitably mean losses for other players. It is a perspective that leads economic nationalists to worry that extensive aid to LDCs may be counterproductive for both the donor and the recipient. This reasoning often uses a *lifeboat analogy*. This image depicts the world as a lifeboat that can support only so many passengers. The people of the EDCs are in the boat. The billions of poor are in the sea, in peril of drowning and clamoring to get aboard. The dilemma is that the lifeboat is incapable of supporting everyone because there are not enough resources. Therefore, if everyone gets in, the lifeboat will sink and all will perish. The answer, then, is to sail off with a sad but resolute sigh, saving the few at the expense of the many in the interest of common sense. An extension of this logic, economic nationalists suggest, is that providing food and medicine to the already overpopulated LDCs only encourages more childbearing, decreases infant mortality, and increases longevity, and thereby worsens the situation by creating more people to flounder and drown in the impoverished sea.

The Economic Internationalist Approach

Economic internationalist theorists believe that development can be achieved within the existing international economic structure. This belief is related to the idealist approach to general world politics. Economic internationalists believe that the major impediments to the South's development are its weakness in acquiring capital, its shortage of skilled labor, and some of its domestic economic policies, such as centralized planning and protectionism. These difficulties can be overcome through free trade and foreign investment supplemented by loans and foreign aid and through reduced government interference in the economy. Such policies, economic internationalists believe, will allow unimpeded international economic exchange among states, which will eventually create prosperity for all. Thus, for economic internationalists, the global economy is a non–zero-sum game. They look to integrate LDCs into the world economic system by eliminating imperfections in the current system while maintaining the system's basic structure and stability.

As for the lifeboat analogy, economic internationalists contend that we are not in (or out of) a lifeboat at all. Instead, they say, we are all inescapably sailing on the same vessel, perhaps the SS *World*, to a common destiny. From this perspective, we can all reach the home port of prosperity, or we can all suffer the fate of the *Titanic*, which struck an iceberg and sank in the North Atlantic in 1912. The 1,513 passengers who drowned came from both luxurious first-class and steerage accommodations, but they found in death the equality inherent in all humans. Commenting in this vein about Brazil, one reformer noted that the country, with its gulf between rich and poor, "is like a huge ocean liner that has been slowly sinking. The elite are in the top cabins, so they haven't been noticing as the rest of us have been going under water. But now the water is beginning to tickle their feet and they see that they're on the same sinking ship."[4]

The Economic Structuralist Approach

Structuralist scholars believe that the political-economic organization of the world patterns of production and trade must be radically altered for the LDCs to develop. In terms of the lifeboat analogy, economic structuralists believe that not only should the poor be allowed into the boat but that they should also at least share command with, and perhaps supplant, the wealthy captains who have been sailing the vessel in their own interests and at the expense of others. Marxists would not shun a peaceful change of command if that were possible, but they are not averse to a mutiny if necessary.

It is obvious that the three different IPE approaches to the general conduct of global economic affairs and to North-South relations present markedly different descriptions of, and even more dramatically different prescriptions for, the conduct of political-economic relations. To help decide which of the three contains the greatest element of truth, it is appropriate to turn to an examination of the history of international political economy.

THE GROWTH AND EXTENT OF INTERNATIONAL POLITICAL ECONOMY

Economic interchange between politically separate people predates written history. Trading records extend back to almost 3000 B.C., and archaeologists have uncovered evidence of trade in the New Stone Age, or Neolithic period (9000–8000 B.C.). Since then, economics has become an ever more important aspect of international relations. This is evident in expanding trade and the resulting increased interrelationship between international economic activity and domestic economic circumstances. We can see this by examining trade, investment, and monetary exchanges and by looking at both the general expansion of each of these factors and the uneven pattern of each.

TRADE

Before beginning our discussion of the historical growth and the current extent of trade, it is necessary to note the two elements that compose trade: goods and services. **Merchandise trade** is what people most frequently associate with imports and exports. These goods are tangible items and are subdivided into two main categories: *primary goods* (raw materials) and *manufactured goods*. **Services trade** is less well known but also important. Services include things that you do for others. When American architects receive pay for designing foreign buildings, when U.S. insurance companies earn premiums for insuring foreign assets or people, when American movies and other intellectual properties earn royalties abroad, when U.S. trucks carry goods in Mexico or Canada, the revenue they generate is payment for the export of services. These services are a major source of income for countries, amounting to more than $1.5 billion, or 20 percent of the entire flow of goods and services across international borders.

Did You Know That:

The early economic and military empire of Assyria extended between the Black, Caspian, and Mediterranean Seas. At the empire's height under Ashurbanipal (669–633 B.C.), it welded vassal states into a single monetary system that facilitated trade. The recent excavation of the Philistine vassal-city of Ekron in modern Israel revealed 105 olive-oil pressing sites capable of producing 290,000 gallons annually for the empire.

The trade in services can also have a significant impact on a country's balance of trade. The United States in 1999 had a merchandise-trade deficit of $347 billion. This was somewhat offset by a $76 billion services-trade surplus, which reduced the overall U.S. trade deficit by 21 percent. It is also worth pointing out that exported services do not have to be performed overseas. American colleges and universities, for example, are one of the the country's largest exporters of services. More than 491,000 foreign students spent over $8 billion for tuition, room, and board at U.S. institutions of higher learning and at least another $3 billion on other aspects of college life ranging from textbooks to pepperoni pizzas.

A General Pattern of Expanding Trade

Trade is booming, and the international flow of goods and services is a vital concern to all world states (Moon, 1996). World trade in 1913 totaled only $20 billion. In 2000 world trade stood at over $7.5 trillion. Even considering inflation, this represents a tremendous jump in world commerce. Figure 14.2 depicts the rise in the dollar volume of trade. Trade growth has been especially rapid during the post–World War II era of significant tariff reductions. During the 1913 to 1948 period of world wars, depression, and trade protectionism, trade increased at an average annual rate of only 0.8 percent. The postwar period has seen average annual increases at a rate of approximately 9 percent. The rapid growth of trade has been caused by a number of factors, including productive technology, resource requirements, materialism, transportation, and free trade philosophy.

Productive Technology The industrial revolution, which began in eighteenth-century Europe, is one factor behind increased trade. As productivity increased, so did the supply

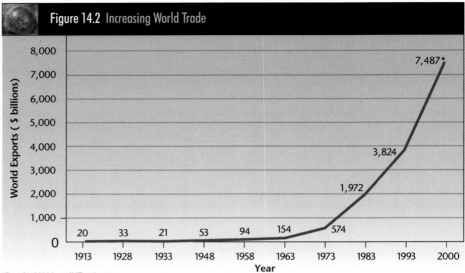

Figure 14.2 Increasing World Trade

*Data for 2000 is an IMF estimate.

Data source: IMF, *World Economic Outlook,* on the Web at: http://www.imf.org/.

Trade, measured here in current dollar exports, has grown meteorically during recent decades. This growth is one sign of the vastly increased importance of international economic relations to the individual countries and their citizens.

of goods. From 1705 to 1780, prior to industrialization, world industrial production increased only slowly at an annual rate of only 1.5 percent, and trade increased at only about 1 percent a year. In the years that followed industrialization, productivity rapidly increased and so did the volume of trade.

The age of machine production of goods, such as textiles, meant that more manufactured products were available and that they were available at lower prices. These manufactured goods, then, formed the "supply" side of trade development. For a time, industrial production grew faster than trade as a society with more money (due to manufacturing earnings) consumed what was produced. Then, beginning in about 1840, the need to import raw materials and the availability of surplus manufactured goods for export boosted annual trade growth beyond annual industrial production growth. Figure 14.3 shows this relationship.

This pattern of increases in both industrial output and trade has generally continued to the present, as you can see in Figure 14.4 on page 404. The figure demonstrates that trade growth helps drive economic expansion by comparing the growth of two inflation-adjusted measures: the volume of trade (exports) and real GDP. Again, the importance of these numbers is that trade consumed more and more of what countries and their workers produced. Without trade, then, or with a marked decline in trade, national economies would slow, perhaps stall, or might even decline.

MAP
International Trade
Organizations, p. 219

Resource Requirements Industrialization and other technological advances also affected the "demand" side of international trade. During the nineteenth century and through World War II, importation of raw materials by the industrialized European countries was a primary force in trade as manufacturing needs both increased demand for raw materials and outstripped domestic resource availability. During the late 1800s, for example, raw materials accounted for 97 percent of all French and 89 percent of all German imports.

In the post-1945 world economy, primary resources have declined both as a percentage of total world trade and as a percentage of the imports of the EDCs. With respect to merchandise trade, primary resources decreased globally from one-half of all

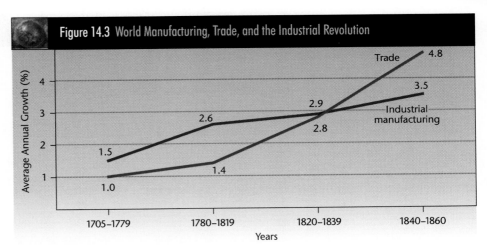

Figure 14.3 World Manufacturing, Trade, and the Industrial Revolution

Data source: Rostow (1978).

Manufacturing and trade both grew rapidly once the industrial revolution began in the 1700s, but trade came to expand even faster than manufacturing. This meant that more and more goods were sold abroad and that the prosperity of countries, their businesses, and their workers became increasingly dependent on foreign markets.

imports in 1960 to only about one-fifth in the late 1990s. In 1999, for instance, 85 percent of all U.S. imported goods were manufactured products, while only 15 percent were agricultural and mineral products. If petroleum imports were excluded, this figure would fall to 6 percent. This shift is due to the increased value of manufactured goods, however, rather than to a decline in the demand for primary resources, which over the long term has remained strong, if often unstable in price.

Materialism The rise in the world's standard of living, especially in the industrialized countries, has also contributed to "demand" pressure on international trade. More workers entered the wage-producing sector, and their "real" (after inflation) wages went up. The real wages of English craftspersons held relatively steady between 1300 and 1800, for instance, but beginning in 1800, after the industrial revolution, more than doubled by the 1950s.

Here again, the trend has continued into the current era. The workers of the wealthier countries have especially enjoyed increased real wages. The average real wage in the industrialized countries, for example, rose 1.8 percent annually between 1980 and 1998. This strengthens demand because individuals have more wealth with which to purchase domestic and imported goods.

Transportation Technology has also increased our ability to transport goods. The development of railroads and improvements in maritime shipping were particular spurs to trade. They both increased the volume of trade that was possible and decreased per-unit transportation costs. Less than two centuries ago, all exported products were carried abroad in sailing ships or in wagons. Now foreign commerce is carried around the world by about 28,000 oceangoing merchant vessels and a vast number of trains and trucks; in just the United States, it is delivered by over one million large trucks and by more than 19,000 locomotives pulling almost 1.3 million freight cars.

Free Trade Philosophy The 1930s and early 1940s were a period of global trauma, marked first by great economic depression and then by World War II. One cause for these miseries, it was said, was the high tariffs that had restricted trade and divided nations. To avoid a recurrence, the United States took the lead in reducing barriers to

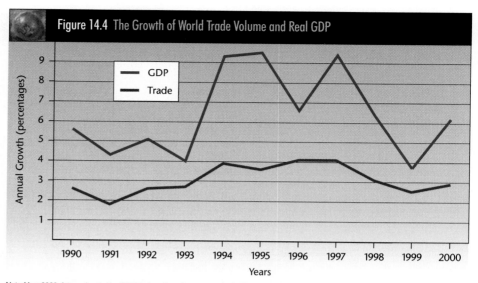

Figure 14.4 The Growth of World Trade Volume and Real GDP

Note: Year 2000 data estimated by IMF. Trade volume is a measure of inflation, exchange rates, and unit prices.

Data source: IMF, *World Economic Outlook,* on the Web at: http://www.imf.org/.

As it long has, the growth of trade continued to outpace the growth of national economies measured in GDP during the 1990s and in 2000. This means that more and more of what countries produce is sold abroad. Therefore, national economic health is ever more dependent on trade.

international trade. The General Agreement on Tariffs and Trade (GATT) came into being in 1947 when countries accounting for 80 percent of world commerce agreed to work to reduce international trade barriers. As a result of this and a series of related efforts, world tariff barriers dropped dramatically. American import duties, for example, dropped from an average of 60 percent of the product's wholesale price in 1934, to 25 percent in 1945, to a current level of less than 4 percent. The tariffs of other EDCs have similarly dropped. Tariffs, as we will soon see, are not the only trade barrier, but their sharp reductions have greatly reduced the cost of imported goods and have strongly stimulated trade.

Uneven Patterns of Trade: North and South

MAP
Exports of Primary Products,
p. 433

The historical growth of trade, it is important to note, has not occurred evenly throughout the world. Instead, three facts about the patterns of international commerce stand out. First, as depicted in Figure 14.5, trade is overwhelmingly dominated by the EDCs in the North. These countries amass 67 percent of the merchandise exports and 76 percent of the exports in goods and services combined. The percentage of world trade shared by the LDCs is relatively small, especially in per capita figures.

A second, and related, pattern of world trade is that only a small percentage of global commerce occurs among LDCs. The merchandise trade among LDCs in 1999 accounted for a scant 14 percent of the world total. Moreover, the handful of EDCs bought 54 percent of all LDC exports. This pattern of trade leaves the LDCs heavily dependent on the EDCs for export earnings and, thus, in a vulnerable position.

A third important trade pattern involves types of exports. EDCs predominantly export manufactured and processed products. LDCs export mostly primary products, such as food, fibers, fuels, and minerals. The United States and Chile provide a good comparison. Of all U.S. goods exported, manufactured products account for 82 percent and primary products for 18 percent. Chile's exports are just about the opposite, with manufactured goods at 17 percent and primary products at 83 percent. To make matters worse, just one primary product, copper, accounts for about 40 percent of Chile's exports. This dependence on primary products for export earnings leaves the

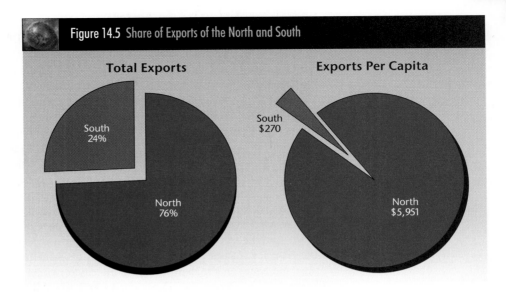

Figure 14.5 Share of Exports of the North and South

Total Exports

South 24%

North 76%

Exports Per Capita

South $270

North $5,951

Data source: World Bank (2000).

The pattern of world trade is very uneven. The North exports more than three times as much in goods and services as does the South in overall dollars and 22 times as much on a per capita basis.

LDCs in a disadvantaged position because the prices of primary products increase more slowly than those of manufactured goods and also because the price for primary products is highly volatile. In this case, Chile's economy in the late 1990s was rocked by the plummeting price of copper, which was $1.33 a pound in 1995 and sank to $0.66 a pound in early 1999 before beginning to recover slowly.

INTERNATIONAL INVESTMENT

Trade has not been the only form of international economic activity that has grown rapidly. There also has been a parallel expansion of international financial ties. This flow of investments can be examined by reviewing types of foreign investments and multinational corporations.

Foreign Direct and Portfolio Investment

One aspect of increased financial ties is the growth of investment in other countries. When Americans invest in British or Nigerian companies, or when Canadians invest in U.S. corporations, a web of financial interdependency is begun. Such international investment has long existed but has accelerated greatly since World War II. In 1950 U.S. direct investment abroad was $11.8 billion. By 1998 that figure had skyrocketed to $2.1 trillion. Investors in other industrialized countries and a few investors from LDCs have added to the international flow of investment capital. Currently, total world **foreign direct investment (FDI),** buying a major stake in foreign companies or real estate, is well over $10 trillion, including $2.2 trillion in direct investments in the United States. **Foreign portfolio investment (FPI)** in stocks and bonds that does not involve the control of companies and real estate is measured in the trillions. For the United States alone, foreign investors hold just over $3.4 trillion in U.S. assets, and Americans own over $1.9 trillion in foreign portfolio investment.

Like most areas of international economics, the movement of investment in the world is not evenly distributed. Since few investors are from the South, the flow of profits from investment mostly benefits the North. Certainly, the flow of investment capital has benefits for recipient countries, but even here the distribution is mixed. About two-thirds of all FDI, and an even greater percentage of FPI, is made in EDCs. Not only does a minor proportion of FDI and FPI go to the LDCs, but the flow is highly uneven. If we consider just the LLDCs, for example, about 81 percent of the FDI and 66 percent of the FPI in those 49 countries goes to China, leaving relatively little funding for the other LLDCs.

The flow of investment capital into and out of countries is an important factor in their economic well-being. FDI and, to a degree, FPI helps support and expand local businesses. For example, foreigners hold about $2.3 trillion in U.S. debt instruments (mostly public and corporate bonds), and these loans to Americans help finance both U.S. businesses and private consumption. Foreign capital also helps support government spending through the purchase of bonds that governments sell to cover their budget deficits. Looking again at the United States, foreigners in 1999 held 35 percent ($1.3 trillion) of the U.S. national debt. Without these purchases, U.S. interest rates would have risen as the Treasury Department would have had to hike its rates to attract alternative purchasers of treasury bonds and other instruments. This would have meant that the cost of consumer loans and mortgages to individual Americans and business loans to American companies would have increased, with a concomitant negative effect on the overall U.S. economy and individual standards of living.

International Investment and Multinational Corporations

To understand the flow of international investment, it is especially important to analyze the growth and practices of **multinational corporations (MNCs)**. These firms, also called transnational corporations (TNCs), are at the forefront of the international movement of investment capital and private loans among countries.

An MNC is a private enterprise that includes subsidiaries operating in more than one state. This means more than merely international trading. Rather, it implies ownership of manufacturing plants and/or resource extraction and processing operations in a variety of countries. Additionally, MNCs conduct businesses abroad that supply services, such as banking, insurance, and transportation. Many observers therefore contend that MNCs are transnational organizations with operations that transcend national boundaries (Pauly & Reich, 1997).

The roots of modern MNCs extend back to Europe's great trading companies, beginning with the Dutch East India Trading Company in 1689. The level of multinational enterprise grew slowly, then expanded more quickly along with the increased European industrialization in the nineteenth century. By the end of that century, burgeoning American industry began to be a force, and it was not long after Henry Ford began building Model T's that his corporation had its first subsidiary in Europe. Indeed, as early as 1902 one British author wrote a book, *The American Invaders*, warning against the takeover of the European economy by such American predators as Singer Sewing Machine, Otis Elevator, and General Electric.

Then, after World War II, the development of MNCs truly accelerated. Since 1945 direct private investment in international ventures has increased, on average, about 10 percent annually, and it is currently expanding at over $200 billion a year. In the process, modern MNCs became economic goliaths that account for a growing percentage of trade and other forms of international commerce.

There are now tens-of-thousands of MNCs operating in more than one country. Not only are MNCs numerous; they also pack enormous economic muscle. Just the top 50 world corporations in 1997 had combined assets of $8.8 trillion, a combined gross corporate product (GCP) of $2.7 trillion, and over 7.1 million workers. Moreover, the size of some individual MNCs is immense. Using a company's revenue (GCP) as a standard, the biggest manufacturing MNC in 1999 was General Motors with a GCP of $176.6 billion. About 30 percent of GM's GCP came from foreign sales, and over a quarter of GM's $273

Did You Know That:

There are 57 multinational corporations that employ 100,000 or more people. General Motors is the MNC with the largest number of employees. There are 53 countries whose populations are smaller than GM's 709,000 employees.

billion in assets were located outside the United States. And if GM's GCP counted as its GDP, the company would have been the world's nineteenth largest economy. Its workforce of 388,000 is larger than the populations of about two dozen small countries.

It is also worth noting that the MNCs are overwhelmingly based in the North. Therefore they contribute to the wealth and economic power of the EDCs at, some analysts would say, the expense of the South. All of the top 50 MNCs are headquartered in an EDC, with the majority based in the United States. Of the top 500 MNCs, more than half are American or Japanese. The remaining EDCs combine for another 40 percent of the top 500. Thus, about 95 percent of the top 500 are based in the North, with only a few of the biggest corporations in LDCs.

MONETARY RELATIONS

The increased flow of trade and capital means that **monetary relations,** including exchange rates, interest rates, and other monetary considerations, have become an increasingly significant factor in both international and domestic economic health. This has always been true, but as trade and other economic relations have expanded, the importance of monetary interchange has increased proportionately. To begin to explore the complex area of monetary relations here and in later chapters, we can look at the evolution of the monetary system, how exchange rates work, and the calculation and impact of the balance of payments.

The Evolution of the Monetary System

The dramatic growth of world trade, international investment, and other aspects of international economic interchange have already been detailed in this chapter. The point to stress is that there has been a true explosion in the volume of such interchange. Even the world's largest economy, the United States, is now thoroughly enmeshed in the complex web of international monetary relations. What you should draw from this discussion of the pluses and minuses of fluctuating national currencies is that world monetary relations are a crucial aspect of international relations. This has always been true, but as trade and other economic relations have expanded, the importance of monetary interchange has increased proportionately (Eichengreen, 1996).

Toward the end of World War II, the United States and its allies met at Bretton Woods, New Hampshire, to establish a system of international monetary regulation. We will explore the Bretton Woods System and other efforts to regulate the international monetary system in chapter 16. For now, the important point is that the Bretton Woods System eventually failed and was abandoned in the early 1970s. The value of a country's currency (compared to other countries' currencies) is now basically left to supply and demand modified by various international cooperation agreements and by the intervention of government through such international monetary organizations as the IMF. This free market approach to currency regulation has often not worked well either, and the world continues to seek a way to stabilize currency exchange in an era of monetary interdependence marked by a globalization of money and of banking.

The international flow of currency is so immense that there is no truly accurate count. But at least $1.5 billion a day are converted from one currency to another, and the rise and fall of exchange rates has a significant impact on the economies of all countries and their citizens.

The Globalization of Money Increased trade, investment, and other factors have set off a torrent of money moving in international channels. The amount of currency exchange has reached such a point that it is impossible to calculate very accurately, but it is not unreasonable to estimate that the currency flow is at least $1.5 trillion a day, or $548 trillion a year. About two-thirds of this moves through the banking centers in just four countries: Germany, Japan, the United Kingdom, and the United States. With just these four leading banking centers exchanging at least $1 trillion a day, this represents a phenomenal increase from the 1989 levels of $550 billion a day, or $201 trillion a year in currency exchanges. Central banks use their monetary reserves (foreign currencies and gold) to try to control exchange rates by buying or selling currency. The rapid rise in the rate of currency exchange means, however, that in 2000, with the combined total currency and gold reserves of the world's countries and of the IMF and other financial IGOs at $1.9 trillion (equal to about two days of currency exchanges), the ability to control currency fluctuations is limited. This endangers monetary exchange stability and, by extension, economic prosperity.

The Globalization of Financial Services To accommodate the globalization of money, there has been a parallel globalization of banking and other financial services. In a relatively short period of time, banks have grown from hometown to national to multinational enterprises. Another indicator of increased international financial ties is the level of international lending by private banks. Multinational banks make up 64 of the 500 largest MNCs (the Global 500), and they amassed a combined GCP of $1.3 trillion in 1999. The largest of these banks, Germany-based Deutsche Bank, is the 31st largest MNC and had 1999 revenues of $58 billion. The largest U.S.–based international bank in 1999 was BankAmerica, with $51 billion in revenues. These and other banks hold over $10 trillion in foreign deposits and have about the same amount in outstanding international loans. Beyond the banks, there are numerous other huge MNCs in the areas of insurance, stocks and bonds, and other financial services. Finally it is worth noting that many MNCs are merging into immense, multipurpose financial service conglomerates. The merger in 1998 of Citicorp and Travelers Group into Citigroup is one example. Citicorp included Citibank, the second largest U.S. bank, which operates in nearly 100 countries, and Global Consumer Business, the world's largest issuer of credit cards (about 60 million). The Travelers Group included the insurance company and such subsidiaries such as Primerica Financial Services, and the now-merged major brokerage houses, Salomon Brothers and Smith Barney. The trend, then, is toward multipurpose financial MNCs that have a major impact on the global economy based on to whom they loan their money, for what purposes they loan it, and what interest rates they charge.

North-South Patterns of Money and Banking As with most other sources of economic power, the control of money and banking is largely dominated by the North and little influenced by the South. The 13 percent of the countries that are EDCs hold 42 percent of all foreign reserves. With the exception of a few offshore banking havens controlled by the North, the banks of the LDCs hold only 5 percent of all foreign deposits and have made only about 3 percent of all foreign loans. Of the 64 banks that are among the Global 500, all but 5 are based in EDCs, with 75 percent based in just five countries: France, Germany, Japan, the United Kingdom, and the United States.

Exchange Rates

Of all the facets of international economic relations, one of the least understood is the importance of the ebb and flow of the world's currencies. **Exchange rates** are, very simply, the values of two currencies in relation to each other—for example, how many U.S. dollars per Japanese yen and vice versa. Exchange rates are important because they affect several aspects of the balance of payments and the health of domestic economies. Fundamentally, a decline in the exchange rate of your country's currency in relation to

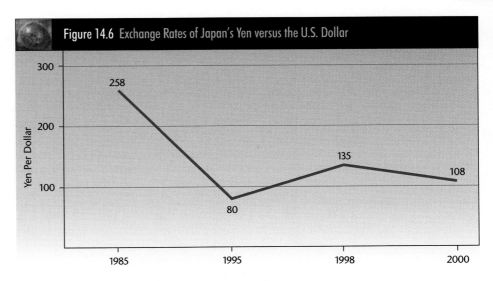

Figure 14.6 Exchange Rates of Japan's Yen versus the U.S. Dollar

The changes in the yen/dollar exchange rate illustrate currency fluctuations.

another country's currency means that things you buy in or from that country will be more expensive and things that the other country buys in or from you will be less expensive. If your country's currency increases in value, things you buy in or from that country will be less expensive and things that the other country buys in or from you will be more expensive. For a fuller explanation of this, see the entry "How Exchange Rates Work" in the Explanatory Notes on page 557.

One example of the dramatic change in the value of a currency involves the exchange rate of the U.S. dollar versus Japan's yen (¥) since 1985, as shown in Figure 14.6. In January of that year, one dollar was worth 258 yen ($1 = ¥258). Then the dollar's value declined 70 percent to a low of $1 = ¥80 in 1995, rose to $1 = ¥135 in late 1998, then declined again to $1 = ¥108 in mid-2000. The normal way of discussing this change would be to say that the U.S. dollar in 1995 was 68 percent weaker versus the yen than it was in 1985 and in 2000 was 35 percent stronger than it was in 1995. Does weak equal bad and strong equal good, though? That depends.

If you are an American, a relatively strong dollar versus the yen is good news if you are going to buy a Japanese automobile. It will cost less. But if you are a U.S. worker producing cars, you may get laid off because relatively inexpensive foreign cars cut into the domestic market. If you are a traveler and the dollar is strong, going to Japan will be less costly because your dollar will be worth more there. If you are in the American tourist industry, however, you will be harmed by the strong dollar since fewer Japanese will visit the United States because their yen will be worth less there. The list need not go on to make the point that currency fluctuations are a two-edged sword that have both financial benefits and drawbacks no matter which way it swings.

On a more general level, if your national currency is strengthening, inflation will probably go down in your country because the foreign products you buy will be less expensive. Also, your standard of living may go up because you can buy more imported goods to improve your material well-being.

If, on the other hand, you are a U.S. manufacturer trying to sell something to the Japanese, the dollar's rise is bad news because your product's price will rise in those countries and you will probably export less. If you work for one of those companies, your standard of living could plummet if you are laid off. A declining currency, then, benefits businesses that export and may also translate into more jobs as factories expand to meet new orders.

Balance of Payments

Along with exchange rates, another complicated aspect of the international political economy that is central to understanding a country's overall health in the global economy is that country's balance of payments. Many of the matters that we have already discussed, including exports and imports, the ebb and flow of investment capital and investment returns, and international borrowing and other financial flows, combine to determine a country's **balance of payments,** a figure that represents the entire flow of money into and out of a country—that is, credits minus debits.

It is important to understand the components of the overall balance of payments to determine whether a country has a net inflow or a net outflow of financing. The United States has since 1989, when it had a balance-of-payments surplus of $15.3 billion, steadily amassed larger and larger balance-of-payments deficits, reaching $220 billion in 1998. The primary cause has been the mounting U.S. merchandise trade deficit, which grew from $101 billion in 1990 to 347 billion in 1999, the largest in U.S. history. Payments on the national debt are a second factor in the growing U.S. balance-of-payments deficit. With an accumulated federal debt over $5 trillion, the annual interest payment for FY1999 came to $363 billion. Of that, about one-third ($121 billion) went to foreign bondholders.

Credits (Money Entering the Country)	Debits (Money Leaving the Country)
1. Export of goods	1. Import of goods
2. Export of services	2. Import of services
3. Foreign visitors (military, tourists)	3. Citizens' travel abroad
4. Foreign aid received	4. Foreign aid given
5. Inflows of capital (loans, investments)	5. Outflows of capital
6. Profits and interest earned from foreign investments	6. Profits and interest paid to foreigners
7. Government receipts from abroad	7. Government overseas expenditures

The dollar amounts of the deficit seem huge, but so is the U.S. economy. A relative comparative standard shows that the U.S. deficit was a not-too-worrisome 1.8 percent of the U.S. GDP in 1990. From there it inched upwards to 2.2 percent of the U.S. GDP in 1996. Then it fell back to 2.0 percent in 1998, aided by the robust U.S. economy and the end of federal budget deficits. The recent record-breaking U.S. prosperity will almost certainly suffer future reverses, and that worries analysts (Krugman, 1998). They ask, "How much longer can the United States continue to spend more than it earns and support the resumption of global growth?" The answer is that "At some point... the United States' [current account deficit]... will become too great a burden on the U.S. economy," touching off severe financial repercussions.[5]

It is also worth noting that a positive balance-of-payments does not automatically mean prosperity. Beset by lagging domestic demand, poor banking practices, and other problems, Japan's economy was stagnant through most of the mid- and late 1990s, despite an average balance-of-payments surplus (1994–1998) of $105 billion, equal to 1.8 percent of GDP. Still, a chronic deficit or one that is a high percentage of GDP eventually depletes a country's financial strength (Lincoln, 1998).

THE IMPACT OF EXPANDED ECONOMIC INTERCHANGE

The expansion of world trade and investment has profoundly affected countries and their citizens. Economic interdependence has inexorably intertwined national and international economic health.

Increased Economic Interdependence

One result of increased international trade, financial, and monetary interchange is that the subjects of national economic health and international economics have become increasingly enmeshed (El-Agraa, 1997; Macesich, 1997). Domestic economics, employment, inflation, and overall growth is heavily dependent on foreign markets, imports of resources, currency exchange rates, capital flows, and other international economic factors. The rise in trade is both a cause and a result of this increased international economic **interdependence.**

The impact of already-extensive and continuously growing economic interdependence has been repeatedly discussed in chapter 1, earlier in this chapter, and elsewhere in this book. It will suffice, therefore, to recount briefly the main ways that the global economy affects almost all of us at one point or another.

Trade is the most obvious, but far from the only, way that national prosperity and the international economy are connected. We need many foreign goods, such as oil. Others, such as toys and clothes, are often cheaper if imported. Exports create jobs; imports sometimes threaten jobs.

Foreign investment in U.S. government debt instruments helps keep interest rates down by increasing demand for those instruments. Without that demand, interest rates would rise, harming business expansion and the standard of living of many individuals. For example, on a $100,000, 30-year mortgage, an increase of just 1 percent in the interest rate increases the yearly payment by $897 and would put a home out of the reach of some potential buyers.

Exchange rates are also a significant determinant of domestic economic circumstances in an interdependent world. We have already noted the impact of exchange rates on prices, on trade, and therefore, on employment. There are numerous other examples. A strong currency, for instance, makes it more expensive for foreign tourists to visit. The strengthening of the U.S. dollar versus the Japanese yen between 1995 and 2000 means that if you are in the U.S. tourist business you will be hurt, because it is likely that fewer Japanese will visit and spend their money. Japanese visitors spent more than $13 billion in the United States in 1996; they will spend much less in 2000.

Foreign direct investment also influences the domestic economy. The global flow of investment capital affects you in more ways than you probably imagine. Many familiar U.S. companies are owned by foreign investors, and the product and marketing decisions they make have a wide impact. For example, the Burger King chain is owned by British investors, Gerber's foods are produced by a Swiss-owned company, and Chrysler Motors is controlled by German investors. Some resent foreign control, but the infusion of foreign capital sometimes keeps foundering U.S. companies in business and U.S. workers on the job. In other cases, foreign investors make investments that create new jobs for Americans. There are tens-of-thousands of Americans who make Nissan automobiles in Tennessee, Hondas in Ohio, Toyotas in Kentucky, Mitsubishis in Illinois, and other foreign brand name products in U.S. plants. These American workers all owe their jobs to foreign investment.

Foreign portfolio investments are another part of the skein of international economic interdependence. Americans own nearly $2 trillion in foreign stocks and bonds, and those assets and earnings from other foreign investments enriched Americans by $258 billion in 1998.

Domestic portfolio investments and the money they earn or lose for Americans are also related strongly to the international economy. About 43 percent of all adult Americans own stock through the purchase of individual equities or mutual funds or through individual retirement plans. Companies that make up the Standard & Poor's 500, one of the key indices of the U.S. stock market, do 40 percent of their business overseas.

When the world economy is good, the profits they earn result in part in dividends and capital gains for Americans, either directly or through such vehicles as retirement funds.

The list of ways that the domestic and international economies intertwine could go on interminably! That is not necessary, though, to stress the point that the idea of **autarky,** the notion of any country's being truly economically independent, has long since ceased to be a realistic concept. The strength and weakness of the international economy have a significant impact on national economies. By the same token, the strength and weakness of the individual major EDCs and, collectively, of the smaller EDCs and the LDCs, affect the prosperity of the international economy and, by extension, one another. Most important, when all is said and done, how prosperously or poorly each of us lives is determined in significant part by the state of the global economy.

CHAPTER SUMMARY

1. Economics and politics are closely intertwined aspects of international relations. Each is a part of and affects the other. This interrelationship has become even more important in recent history. Economics has become more important internationally because of dramatically increased trade levels, ever-tightening economic interdependence between countries, and the growing impact of international economics on domestic economics.

2. The study of international political economy (IPE) examines the interaction between politics and economics.

3. There are many technical aspects to explaining and understanding the international political economy, and those not familiar with economic terms and methods should review the listing called Economics: Technical Terms and Sources found in the section toward the end of the book entitled Explanatory Notes on pages 557–559.

4. The approaches to IPE can be roughly divided into three groups: economic nationalism (mercantilism), economic internationalism (liberalism), and economic structuralism.

5. The core of the economic nationalist doctrine is the realist idea that the state should harness and use national economic strength to further national interest. Therefore, the state should shape the country's economy and its foreign economic policy to enhance state power.

6. Economic internationalists are idealists who believe that international economic relations should and can be harmonious because prosperity is available to all and is most likely to be achieved and preserved through cooperation. The main thrust of economic internationalism is to separate politics from economics, to create prosperity by freeing economic interchange from political restrictions.

7. Economic structuralists hold that world politics is based on the division of the world into have and have-not countries, with the EDCs keeping the LDCs weak and poor in order to exploit them. There are two types of economic structuralists. Marxists believe that the entire capitalist-based system must be replaced with domestic and international socialist systems before economic equity can be achieved. Less radical economic structuralists stress reform of the current market system by ending the system of dependencia.

8. Whether or not you subscribe to economic structuralist theory, it is clear that the world is generally divided into two economic spheres: a wealthy North and a much less wealthy South. There are some overlaps between the two spheres, but in general the vast majority of the people and countries of the South are much less wealthy and industrially developed than the countries of the North and their

people. The South also has a history of direct and indirect colonial control by countries of the North.

9. Economic nationalists, economic internationalists, and economic structuralists all offer different explanations of why the relative deprivation of the South exists. The three schools of thought also have varying prescriptions about what, if anything, to do to remedy the North-South gap in economic development.

10. The history of international economics is ancient, but a change that has occurred since the second half of the twentieth century is that the level of economic interchange (trade, investments and other capital flows, and monetary exchange) has increased at an exponential rate.

11. Within the overall expansion of the international economy, there is, however, a pattern in which most of the trade, investment, and other aspects of international political economy are dominated by the North and work to its advantage.

12. Trade in goods and services is booming, having grown 2,600 percent from $20 billion in 1913 to nearly $7.5 trillion in 2000.

13. There has also been a rapid expansion of international financial ties. This flow of investment can be examined by reviewing types of foreign investments and multinational corporations.

14. The increased flow of trade and capital means that monetary relations, including exchange rates, interest rates, and other monetary considerations, are a significant economic factor. It is not unreasonable to estimate that the daily currency flow is $1.5 trillion, or some $548 trillion a year.

15. The expansion of world trade and investment has profoundly affected countries and their citizens. Economic interdependence has inexorably intertwined national and international economic health.

CHAPTER 15

NATIONAL ECONOMIC COMPETITION: THE TRADITIONAL ROAD

I greatly fear my money is not safe.

Shakespeare, *The Comedy of Errors*

Having nothing, nothing can he lose.

Shakespeare, *Henry VI, Part III*

No one can... love his neighbor on an empty stomach.

Woodrow Wilson, speech, May 23, 1919

As the images of life lived anywhere on our globe become available to all, so will the contrast between the rich and the poor become a force impelling the deprived to demand a better life from the powers that be.

Nelson Mandela, to a joint session of the U.S. Congress, October 7, 1994

CHAPTER OBJECTIVES

After completing this chapter, you should be able to:

- Explain why politics and economics are intertwined aspects of international relations.
- Describe how economics has taken on a more important role in international relations.
- Understand the source of economic power.
- Analyze the use of economic statecraft.
- Describe the economies of the North and their current political issues.
- Describe the economies of the South and their current political issues.
- Discuss the sources of hard currency.
- Consider the effects of debt crisis on the global financial community and the role of loans.
- Discuss LDCs' need for investment capital and the difficulty in acquiring it.
- Understand the role of foreign aid in the global political community.
- Analyze the demand for a New International Economic Order.
- Describe the various impediments to free trade.
- Discuss the arguments for and against free international economic interchange.

Economic nationalism—the state-centric approach to the international political economy—is the traditional road that countries have long followed. While it is true that there has been considerable movement toward liberalizing international economic relations in recent decades, economic nationalism remains the dominant practice in global economic affairs for two reasons: First, states remain the principal actors on the world stage. Second, these states most often use economic tools and formulate economic policy to benefit themselves, not the global community. This chapter will explore the economic nationalist approach, including discussions of national economic power assets and the ways that countries utilize their economic power (Milner, 1998).

NATIONAL ECONOMIC POWER: ASSETS AND UTILIZATION

The use of political power to achieve national economic goals and the reciprocal use of economic power to gain national political goals is at the core of economic nationalism. This orientation, which is also called "economic statecraft" or "mercantilism," remains in one form or another the basic approach of states to international political economy in the current state-based, quasi-anarchical system. The reason states take this self-serving approach is understandable. Each state is largely responsible for its own economic well-being. Certainly there is foreign aid and other forms of financial assistance are available from states and from international governmental organizations (IGOs) such as the United Nations, the International Monetary Fund (IMF), and the World Bank. Such assistance, however, is neither guaranteed nor munificent. Thus, as is true for military security, economic security is based mostly on self-help.

NATIONAL ECONOMIC POWER

It is axiomatic that to pursue economic statecraft effectively, a country needs to possess considerable economic power. Chapter 10 has already reviewed the national infrastructure (technological sophistication, transportation systems, information and communications capabilities) that provides part of the basis for building a powerful economy. To these factors this chapter will add as determinants of national power the following: financial position, natural resources, industrial output, and agricultural output.

Financial Position

The center of any country's economic power is its basic financial position. To think about that, consider Table 15.1 and the six criteria of financial strength detailed there for the United States and Russia. Neither country has an enviable record on all points. Still, the United States is in vastly better financial shape than is Russia. The U.S. economy is huge, has experienced moderate growth and low inflation, and the American dollar is backed by substantial international reserves. In 1998, the United States had both a negative balance of payments and a budget deficit, but they were relatively small as a percentage of the GNP. Moreover, the U.S. budget deficit continued to decline, and there is now a substantial federal budget surplus, while Russia struggles with ongoing deficit spending.

Russia is in financial shambles—especially compared to the United States. The 1998 figures show that Russia's GNP was relatively small and had declined steadily since the Soviet Union dissolved. Russia had scant international reserves and a gaping budget deficit. With the Russian government virtually broke and with industry staggering, many workers remained unpaid. Soaring inflation wiped out much of the purchasing power of people's savings and the fixed pensions of retired Russians. The salaries of those

MAP
GNP Per Capita, p. 395

Table 15.1 Measures of National Financial Power

Country	1998 GNP ($ billions)	Annual GNP Growth 1990–1998	Annual Inflation 1990–1998	International Reserves, 1998 ($ billions)	Balance of Payments as % of GNP, 1998	Government Budget Balance as % of GNP, 1998
Russia	$338	–7.0%	235.6%	$12	+3.6	–4.7
United States	$7,921	+2.9%	2.2%	$146	–2.0	–0.3

Note: GNP growth rate is per capita and calculated in real, not current, monetary terms; budget balance is for the central government.
Date Sources: World Bank (2000a), IMF (1999).

Every country's power rests in part on its financial strength. Notice the U.S. and Russian comparative data for each column. In each, except balance of payments, the U.S. financial situation is considerably stronger than is Russia's position.

who did get paid often did not keep up with inflation. Rampant corruption has made a bad situation much worse. The result is that about one-third of all Russians are living in poverty.

A weak financial position makes it difficult for an economy to provide the solid infrastructure required for prosperity or to provide adequately for national defense. Financial weakness also saps a country's diplomatic influence. During the 1990s, Russia objected to the expansion of NATO, the intervention in Kosovo, and a number of other initiatives taken by the United States and its allies. There was only so far Moscow could go in opposition, though, as long as it needed infusions of cash from the West-dominated IMF to keep the Russian economy from total collapse.

Additionally, financial weakness exposes a country to attacks on its economy. Economic sanctions against Yugoslavia in the early 1990s for its support of the atrocities in Bosnia drove up the inflation rate mercilessly. In late 1992 a U.S. dollar was equal to 1,000 Yugoslav dinars. A year later the currency collapsed and inflation hit an annual rate of 600,000 percent. A dollar was equal to 180 trillion dinars, and Yugoslavia set a record by printing the first 500 billion (dinar) bank note. With it, Yugoslavs could buy a gallon of milk. More recently, Iraq and Afghanistan have suffered hyperinflation because of economic sanctions. The Iraqi currency, also called the dinar, traded against the U.S. dollar in early 1990 at one dinar = $3.10. By 1999 it took 5,580 dinars to equal $3.10. Similarly, the financial pressure on Afghanistan, because of the Taliban regime's repressive policies and its harboring of terrorists, has driven that country's currency, the afghani, to the point of not being worth the paper it is printed on. The largest bank note, the 10,000 afghani, is worth about 40 cents, requiring people to carry huge stacks of currency to transact business. Indeed, when in 2000 the country's main currency bazaar was robbed at night of $200,000 worth of afghanis, money traders calculated that even if all the bills had been 10,000 afghani notes, the thieves would have had to truck away 12 tons of currency.

Did You Know That:

On August 31, 2000, at 3:03 P.M. EDT, the U.S. national debt was $5,664,426,601,630.23. Each American's share of the debt was $20,430.55. You can find one of the national debt clocks on the Web at: http://www.brillig.com/debt_clock/.

Natural Resources

The possession of or lack of energy, mineral, and other natural resources has become an increasingly important power factor as industrialization and technology have advanced. Natural resources affect power in four related ways: (1) The greater a country's *self-sufficiency* in vital natural resources, the greater its power. (2) Conversely, the greater a country's *dependency* on foreign sources for vital natural resources, the less its power. (3) The greater a country's *surplus* (over domestic needs) of vital resources needed by other countries, the greater its power.

Financial strength, including currency stability, is one aspect of national economic power. Under the pressure of international sanctions since the Persian Gulf War (1990–1991), the value of Iraq's currency, the dinar, has plummeted to about one-sixteen-thousandth of its 1990 value against the U.S. dollar. The changing value is represented by the large American $100 bill behind this Iraqi money trader and the 100-note bundles of 250 dinar notes, Iraq's largest domination. Each bundle is worth $14, and it would take more than 7 bundles to exchange for the $100.

Each of these three related points plays a key role in determining international relationships. Self-sufficiency and dependency are inexorably linked. The key here is not just production; it is production compared to consumption. The United States, for example, produces about 10 percent of the world's zinc but accounts for 22 percent of the world's total consumption. This level of use, combined with a dearth of some other minerals, creates a marked U.S. dependency on a variety of minerals designated by the government as "federal strategic and critical minerals." Of the 11 such minerals, the United States depends on imports of more than 70 percent of 9 of them (bauxite, chromium, cobalt, industrial diamonds, manganese, platinum, tin, tungsten, and zinc), and is self-sufficient (under 10 percent imported) in just 2 of the minerals (silver and titanium). By contrast, there are some countries, such as Russia and Canada, that are relatively more resource sufficient. Still other countries are almost totally dependent on foreign sources for their natural resource requirements. Japan, for one, imports virtually all of its primary energy supplies (oil, natural gas, and others) and 90 percent or more of most critical minerals.

A second factor involves avoiding energy or other resource dependency. It can be difficult to do so in a modern economy. Energy is used both to fuel economic production and to provide for citizen comfort and mobility. These uses make significant conservation efforts economically and politically difficult. Some countries have chosen to rely on nuclear power to decrease their energy dependency. France generates 76 percent of its commercial energy by nuclear power. Concerns about the safety of nuclear power keep other countries' efforts more limited, with the United States, for example, generating only 19 percent of its commercial energy by nuclear power. One downside of this lower reliance on nuclear energy is a heavy reliance on petroleum. About 39 percent of U.S. energy consumption is generated from petroleum. To meet energy needs beyond what domestic production can supply, Americans annually import some 131 billion gallons of petroleum. This accounts for 53 percent of all U.S. petroleum use and over 30 percent of

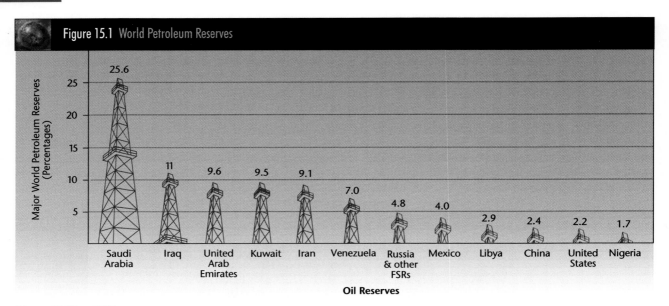

Figure 15.1 World Petroleum Reserves

Data source: World Almanac (2000).

The concentration of over two-thirds of the world's oil reserves in the Middle East gives that region not only significant wealth but also enhances the political importance of the region and adds to the power of its countries.

all energy consumption, which leaves the United States vulnerable to an interruption of its energy supplies or to price hikes, such as those that occurred in 1999 and 2000.

Possessing a surplus of a vital resource is a third power factor. The global imbalance of oil production, as is evident in Figure 15.1, has dramatically underlined this point. Oil resources have been the chief source of export revenue for many countries in the Middle East and, despite the depressed oil market during most of the 1990s, so-called black gold has allowed some of that region's countries to amass huge financial reserves. In 1999, for example, Saudi Arabia earned $39 billion from petroleum products. Oil has also increased the global political focus on and the diplomatic power of the petroleum-producing countries, especially those in the Middle East, which account for about two-thirds of world petroleum reserves.

Industrial Output

Even if a country is bountifully supplied with natural resources, its power is limited unless it can convert those assets into industrial goods. Both China and India have extensive reserves of iron and coal, and China is finding new oil possibilities, but because of their limited industrial capacity, these countries have not been effectively able to transform potential into power.

Japan, by contrast, efficiently converts imported resources into manufactured products and has become an industrial power despite its lack of natural assets. Japan has 0.0002 percent of the world's reserves of iron, the main ingredient of steel. Yet Japan is the world's leading steel producer, accounting for 12 percent of the world total.

On a global basis, industrial production is highly concentrated. The European Union, Japan, and North America (the United States and Canada) alone produce over 47 percent of the world's total steel output. Vehicle production is another indication of industrial concentration, as indicated in Figure 15.2. It shows that the three biggest vehicle manufacturers (Germany, Japan, and the United States) made 51 percent of the global total. Another 11 countries combined for 39 percent with a mere 10 percent manufactured by 14 other countries. About 85 percent of the world countries (including all those in Africa) produce no or only a negligible number of vehicles.

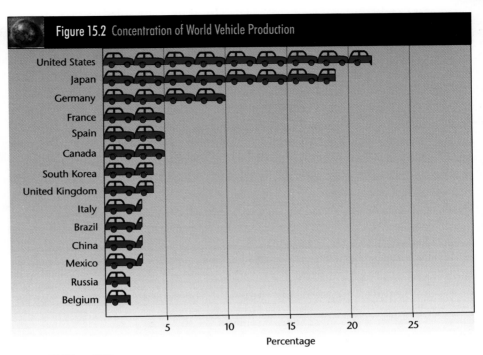

Figure 15.2 Concentration of World Vehicle Production

Percentage

Data source: World Almanac (2000).

Global industry is highly concentrated. The 14 countries that produced 2 percent or more of the 55.4 million vehicles manufactured in 1998 accounted for 90 percent of the world's production. The biggest three producers combined for just over half of all the cars and trucks produced.

Agricultural Output

It is not common to equate food production with power. Yet a country's agricultural capacity is an important factor. The contribution of agriculture to power depends on whether a country can adequately supply its domestic needs, whether it has a surplus of a commodity that others need, and the percentage of its total economic energy that a country must devote to feeding its own people.

Self-sufficiency varies widely in the world. The United States is basically able not only to supply its own needs but to earn money from agricultural exports. With less than 5 percent of the world's population, it produces 16 percent each of the world's cereal grains and meat. Other countries are less fortunate. Some have to use their economic resources to import food. Yet others have insufficient funds to buy enough food and face widespread hunger. Many parts of Africa are in particularly desperate shape.

Another significant agricultural factor is the percentage of economic effort that a country must expend to feed its people. Countries are relatively disadvantaged if they have larger percentages of their workforce in agriculture (and thus not available for the manufacturing and service sectors); they have to spend a great deal of their economic effort (measured as a percentage of GDP) to feed their people; they use a small number of tractors and other mechanical farming machines per agricultural worker; and they cannot afford to use significant amounts of fertilizer to boost per acre productivity. Table 15.2 on page 420 uses these four standards to contrast the agricultural efficiency of an EDC (Canada) to that of an LDC (Nigeria). On each measure Nigeria is disadvantaged agriculturally.

POLITICAL USES OF THE ECONOMIC INSTRUMENT

States possess a variety of economic tools. It is possible to divide the economic instruments available to countries into economic incentives and economic sanctions.

Table15.2 Agricultural Effort of Canada and Nigeria

Agricultural Effort	Canada	Nigeria
Agriculture as % of GDP	3	32
% of workforce in agriculture	3	43
Tractors per 1,000 agricultural workers	1,642	2
Pounds of fertilizer used per acre	348	30

Data Sources: World Bank (2000a); CIA (2000); U.S. State Department Country Reports at: http://www.state.gov/www/issues/economic/trade_reports/99_toc.html.

Many LDCs have to spend an inordinate amount of their economic effort to feed themselves. Nigerians devote 32 percent of their economic activity and 43 percent of their workers to this task. Canadians expend a mere 3 percent each of their economic effort and their workforce to feed themselves. Among the most important reasons that Canadian agriculture is so much more efficient than Nigeria's is that Canada can afford to enhance its yield by equipping its workers with more agricultural machinery and by using more fertilizers.

Economic Incentives

States regularly offer economic incentives to induce other states to act in a desired way. Incentives include providing foreign aid, giving direct loans or credits, guaranteeing loans by commercial sources, reducing tariffs and other trade barriers, selling or licensing the sale of sensitive technology, and a variety of other techniques. Not all incentives are successful in changing another country's behavior, but they certainly do work some of the time. For example, the United States in 1998 offered the Russians (and they tacitly accepted) more opportunities to get involved with the lucrative satellite launching business if Moscow agreed to stop supplying Iran with missile technology. "We are prepared to go forward and enhance cooperation in this area [satellite launches], but we cannot do it in the absence of progress on the Iran ballistic missile front," a senior U.S. official told reporters. Understanding the message, a top Russian official commented, "The increase of the quota [of launches] is an important and necessary issue for us."[1]

Other incentives have been less successful. The details remain hazy, but it is clear that the United States supplied money and perhaps even arms to Iraq during the late 1980s. The U.S. rationale, according to the presidential directive that authorized the aid, was that it would serve as a "means of developing access to and influence with" Iraq and that "normal relations between the U.S. and Iraq would serve our longer-term interests and promote stability in both the [Persian] gulf and the Middle East."[2] Iraq's invasion of Kuwait in 1990 and the ensuing Persian Gulf War signaled the clear failure of the U.S. strategy.

Economic Sanctions

Countries and alliances can use their economic power in a negative way by applying sanctions. Research indicates that countries are especially likely to do so "if there are expectations of frequent conflict with the target" (Drenzer, 1998:728). Methods include raising trade barriers, cutting off aid, trying to undermine another country's currency, and even instituting blockades.

The History of Sanctions The Book of Exodus records what may have been the first attack on a country's economic (and social) infrastructure in order to overthrow imperial domination. To persuade the pharaoh to release the Israelites from their Egyptian captivity, Moses (with God's help) turned the Nile "to blood.... And all the fishes died; and the Nile became foul so that the Egyptians could not drink water." When that failed, Moses dispatched successive plagues of frogs, gnats, and flies to bedevil the Egyptians. The pharaoh still refused to release the Israelites. Next a plague was visited on Egypt's livestock, and all the Egyptians were infected with boils. A wise pharaoh would have relented, but this one did not. So, at Moses' command, "thunder and hail and fire... rained upon the land of Egypt" and struck down every man, beast, and plant. Adding to the Egyptians' misery, Moses then dispatched a swarm of locusts that "covered the face of the land" and "ate all the plants in the land and all the fruits on the trees... not a green thing remained." When even the locusts plus three solid days of darkness failed to convince the pharaoh to let the Israelites go, God decided to slay the firstborn of every Egyptian family. Finally, a shattered pharaoh begged Moses to lead his people out of Egypt quickly lest all Egyptians perish.

The point of this story is that the use of economic instruments to promote policy is ancient. In more modern times, sanctions are becoming more frequent policy tools. There were only 8 incidents of economic sanctions (0.3 per year) from 1914 through 1939. This increased to 44 incidents of sanctions (1.5 per year) during the 1940–1969 period; and rose again to 71 incidents (3.6 per year) during the two decades of the 1970s and 1980s (Rothgeb, 1993). The increased use of sanctions has occurred, in part, because people are more aware of events in the world around them and more intent on influencing how other governments act both domestically and internationally. Sanctions are also more frequent because economic interdependence makes target countries more vulnerable to sanctions. The increased use of sanctions additionally reflects the search for ways to pressure other countries without going to war (Doxey, 1996).

Before leaving the history of sanctions, it should be noted that they are used by international organizations as well as by individual countries. The 1990s have seen sanctions imposed by the UN on Libya for supporting terrorism; on Yugoslavia (Serbia-Montenegro) for aggression in the Balkans; on Iraq for aggression against Kuwait and for failing to live up to the cease-fire agreement of 1991; on Haiti for toppling its democratic government and substituting a military regime; and, for the first time, on a rebel group, UNITA, in Angola (Cortright & Lopez, 2000; Brown, 1999).

The Effectiveness of Sanctions Economic sanctions are a blunt instrument that attempts to economically bludgeon a target country into changing some specific behavior. As such, the effectiveness of sanctions is mixed. Sometimes they can be effective. Sanctions cost South Africa tens of billions of dollars and helped push the country's white leadership to end the apartheid system. The harsh sanctions on Yugoslavia arguably helped cause the downfall of President Slobodan Milosevic in October 2000.

It is also the case, though, that, more often than not, sanctions fail to accomplish their goal, with some analysts placing their success rate as low as 5 percent (Elliott, 1998; Pape, 1997). Sanctions imposed by international organizations may be even less effective than those levied by states (Kaempfer & Lowenberg, 1999). Given this paltry success rate, a reasonable question is, When do they accomplish their goals? Sanctions are most likely to be effective in certain circumstances (Drezner, 2000; Shambaugh, 2000; Brawley, 1996). These include instances where (1) "the goal is relatively modest," thereby minimizing the need for multilateral cooperation; (2) "the target is politically unstable, much smaller than the country imposing sanctions, and economically weak"; (3) "the sender and target are friendly toward one another and conduct substantial trade"; (4) "the sanctions are imposed quickly and decisively to maximize impact"; and (5) "the sender avoids high costs to itself," such as the loss of substantial export revenue (Elliott, 1993:34).

Still, sanctions remain a regular tool, especially for the United States. "Therein is the great paradox," says one expert on sanctions. "While unilateral embargoes are less and less of an effective force in an integrated world economy, American enthusiasm for

Economic sanctions often hurt people who have little or no say in national policy. The sanctions imposed on Iraq beginning in 1990 have caused increased malnutrition, death, and disease among Iraqi children because of a lack of food and medicine. This Iraqi mother is weeping after taking her 15-month-old-child to a doctor. The little girl, like many children in Iraq, is malnourished and half the weight she would be if she were an average American kid. She is suffering from bronchitis and chronic diarrhea. Her prognosis was not encouraging.

them has not diminished."[3] There are a number of possible explanations for this paradox. One is that tangible success is not the only standard by which to measure sanctions. They also have a symbolic value that has nothing to do with whether they actually cause another country to change its behavior. Simply put, just as you might choose not to deal with an immoral person, so too, countries can express their moral indignation by reducing or severing their interactions with an abhorrent regime (Baldwin, 2000).

The Drawbacks of Sanctions Especially given the high failure rate of sanctions, countries that apply them must be wary of the negative impact of sanctions on unintended victims. One such difficulty is that sanctions may harm economic interests other than those of the intended target. The UN sanctions imposed on Iraqi oil exports have cost Jordan and Turkey many millions of dollars by way of lost revenues that they would have earned for the use of pipelines that run from Iraq through them and on to ports from which the oil is shipped.

Another drawback is that threatening or implementing sanctions can damage those who impose them. For instance, calls for U.S. sanctions on China in response to its alleged human rights abuses and other objectionable practices have been rejected in part because, explains a top presidential adviser, "the main victim [of sanctions] is U.S. business, and China doesn't suffer."[4] In one case, amid a flurry of threatened U.S. sanctions, Beijing used Boeing Aircraft as an example of what could occur, by choosing unexpectedly to place a $1.5 billion aircraft order with Airbus Industrie, the European consortium, rather than with Boeing. "There's no doubt we are being punished," said a dejected Boeing official. In fact, he continued, Boeing had been warned by a top Chinese official that if "your government constantly chooses to kick us and harass us, many, many business opportunities that should go to the U.S. [could go] elsewhere."[5]

A third criticism of sanctions is that they are often the tool used by EDCs to continue their dominance of LDCs. Of the 71 incidents of sanctions applied during the 1970s and 1980s, 49 of the cases (69 percent) involved EDCs placing sanctions on LDCs (Rothgeb, 1993). A fourth charge against sanctions is that they can dismay countries that do not support them. Continuing U.S. sanctions against Cuba are viewed as particularly offensive by many U.S. allies and other countries.

A fifth criticism of sanctions is that they often harm the very people whom you want to assist. President Fidel Castro of Cuba has called sanctions "noiseless atomic bombs" that "cause the death of men, women, and children."[6] Iraq provides a good example of Castro's point. There, persistent UN sanctions and a defiant government in Baghdad have had a brutal impact. Scant supplies of food and medicine for the civilian population are among the hardships. The effects are especially devastating for children. Various studies by the UN, Harvard University's School of Public Health, and others have all found that the sanctions have caused (beyond normal expectations) over one million Iraqi children to be malnourished and upwards of 500,000 to have died. The sanctions have been relaxed in recent years to allow Iraq to sell some oil and, under supervision, to use the proceeds to buy food and medicine. Still, serious human damage

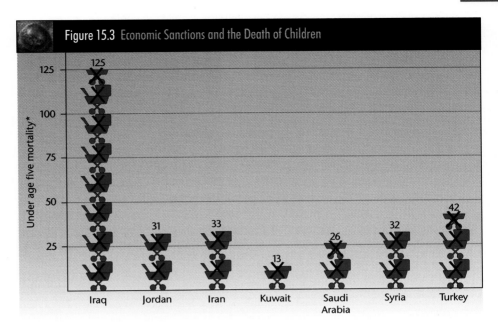

Figure 15.3 Economic Sanctions and the Death of Children

*The number of children who die before age five per 1,000 children born.

Data source: World Bank (2000a).

One objection to economic sanctions is that they often have the most deleterious impact on those who have the least responsibility for the actions of their government. There is little doubt that the economic sanctions that were imposed on Iraq beginning in 1990 has caused many young children to die. The average death rate of small children for Iraq's 6 neighbors dropped markedly from 83 in 1990 to 30 in 1998, while Iraq's rate rose from 95 to 125.

continues. This deleterious effect is evident in Figure 15.3, which compares the child mortality rate in Iraq to its neighbors.

Now, having reviewed national economic assets and the use of the economic instrument, we can turn to specific national economic concerns and policies. This discussion will be divided into two parts: the national economic issues and policies of the North and the national economic issues and policies of the South.

THE NORTH AND INTERNATIONAL POLITICAL ECONOMY

By many standards, the economic position of the North is enviable. Its 1998 per capita GDP was $25,442 compared to $1,236 each for the people of the South. Between 1980 and 1998, the combined GDPs of the EDCs jumped from $7.7 trillion to $22.5 trillion. That was monumental compared with a rise in the combined GDPs of the LDCs from $3.2 trillion to $6.2 trillion. Yet all is not well in the North.

THE NATIONAL ECONOMIES OF THE NORTH

The fundamental cause of concern among EDCs is that the North's economic growth rate has slowed considerably from its earlier high levels. The average annual real GDP growth rate of the EDCs during the 1970s and 1980s was 3.1 percent; during the 1990s that declined to 2.4 percent. Per capita GDP, which had risen 2.4 percent annually in the 1980s, went up by only 1.8 percent a year in the 1990s. The number of new jobs being created in the North increased an annual average of 1.3 percent in the 1980s; during the 1990s average job growth was but 0.7 percent.

There are many reasons for the deceleration of the North's economy. One is the beginning of competition from a few newly industrializing countries (NICs) of the South in the manufacturing, industrial, and service sectors. Also, the post–cold war drop in defense spending has caused some dislocation.

Yet another adjustment for the EDCs involves their entering a period that some analysts call the **postindustrial economy.** What this means is that through the use of robotics and other techniques, fewer and fewer workers are needed to produce more and more manufactured goods. Companies need to reduce their workforces to stay competitive internationally. Downsizing is a relatively new, and unwelcome, word in the economic vocabulary of the North. Many of the displaced workers are either unemployed or find jobs in the usually lower-paying service sector. Indeed, the shift away from manufacturing has added a whole new class of economies, service economies, to such traditional designations as primary product (agriculture, minerals) economies and industrialized economies.

Service economies are those countries that derive at least a plurality of their earnings from performing services (such as banking, education, insurance, and transportation). For most countries, domestic services (everything from flipping burgers, through almost all government activity, to acting in movies) are already the biggest part of their internal economic activity. Such services make up 71 percent of the U.S. GDP, compared to just 24 percent for industry, and 5 percent for primary products. Services are also becoming a more important part of exports and, therefore, the international economy. The services that Americans exported in 1980 were just 17 percent of all U.S. exports; in 1998 that percentage was up to 26 percent. Thus other countries increasingly import what Americans know and do, rather than just what they harvest, mine, and make.

At the beginning of the first decade of the twenty-first century, the overall economic numbers for the North are good, but much of the rosy picture stems from the longest and one of the most robust periods of American economic expansion in history. Other parts of the North are having a more difficult time. Japan's economy is stagnant, with GDP growth for 1998–2000 at (–)0.3 percent. The growth rate for the European Union (EU) was 2.4 percent, compared to 3.4 percent for the United States. Unemployment in the EU (9.6 percent in 1999) was more than twice the rate in the United States (4.3 percent). As for Japan, its unemployment rate doubled during the 1990s to 5 percent, and for the first time in decades exceeded the U.S. rate.

In sum, the economy of the North is not in immediate trouble, but it is not as healthy as it could be or has been. Moreover, it is uncertain how long the unbroken period of U.S. strong growth can continue. An optimistic analysis entitled "A Second American Century" concludes, "If anything, American business should widen its lead over the rest of the world. France had the seventeenth century, Britain the nineteenth, and America the twentieth. It will also have the twenty-first" (Zuckerman, 1998:31). Other analyses are more cautious. In the words of one, "The current sense that the United States is on the top of the world is based on a huge exaggeration of the implications of a few good years here and a few bad years elsewhere.... Future historians will not record that the twenty-first century belonged to the United States" (Krugman, 1998:45).

Whatever the future may hold, the record of the 1990s accentuated the concern of each EDC with its own economy, and has sometimes strained economic relations within the North. It is to these concerns and policies that we now turn our attention.

NATIONAL ECONOMIC ISSUES AND POLICIES OF THE NORTH

Because they make up such an overwhelming percentage of the world's economic enterprise, the economic issues and policies of the North are a key determinant of the course of the global economy. For an extended period after World War II, the EDCs enjoyed good growth and were generally united politically with the United States and under its leadership. Now, with both economic and political factors changing, tensions among the EDCs are increasing.

Changes in the Economic and Political Climate in the North

The 1990s were a time of significant shifts in the international economic relations and policies of the countries of the North. There were several causes of these shifts. One, as noted, was the unsteady economic fortunes of the North. During the decades of booming prosperity following World War II, the rapidly expanding international economy minimized any pressures for economic rivalry among the developed countries. Now, in a less robust economic climate, there is increased protectionist sentiment.

A second factor is the end of the cold war. The resulting changes in the international system have lessened the need for strategic cooperation among the industrialized Western allies. With no common enemy to bind them together, the long-standing trade disputes among the **trilateral countries** (Japan, the United States/Canada, Western Europe) that had once been suppressed in the name of allied unity have become more acrimonious.

A third and related factor that has further complicated matters is that central direction has declined in the North. The United States once provided that direction. But with an upsurge in economic rivalries among the EDCs and with the American people less willing to support U.S. internationalism, Washington has lost some of its ability to lead. The seven most economically powerful Western countries (Canada, France, Germany, Great Britain, Italy, Japan, and the United States) have met annually since 1975 as an informal economic directorate called the **Group of Seven (G-7).** Then in 1998 the G-7 officially became the **Group of Eight (G-8),** at least sometimes, when the G-7 leaders added Russia as a member. In some sense, however, the G-7 continues to exist because the original seven agreed they would meet as the G-7 without Russia on financial issues and with the Russian president as the G-8 on political issues. To avoid confusion, the groups will be referred to as the G-8 in all their activities.

The meetings of the G-8 leaders have been effective in several ways. The conferences have promoted communication among the eight, have reinforced and advanced the theme of EDC cooperation to promote globalization, and have established in broad terms a determination to address numerous global problems. The 2000 meeting in Okinawa, Japan, for instance, stressed efforts to fight AIDS globally and to help LDCs address their low level of computerization. What the G-8 has done less well is achieving concrete results. For this reason, meetings of the G-8, which were once major news stories, have more recently been far from front-page news. To return to the headlines, two scholars observe, "the group needs to show that its initiatives are not spinning into oblivion, leaving behind only lengthy communiqués."[7]

Whatever the efforts of the G-8, the reality is that the EDCs continue to act with a sort of dual personality in the realm of international economic affairs. There is one set of forces within most EDCs that has pressed with significant success for the continued expansion of **free economic interchange** among nations. The EU has continued to integrate; Canada, Mexico, and the United States joined together in the North American Free Trade Agreement (NAFTA); and the world extended and enhanced the General Agreement on Tariffs and Trade (GATT) and created the World Trade Organization (WTO) to administer it. All these efforts in the 1990s toward economic cooperation will be discussed in the next chapter.

Simultaneously, however, **protectionism** remains a powerful countervailing force, and there has been increased pressure within countries to follow economic nationalist policies. This pressure has been occasioned by the sagging economies of the North, by increased economic competition not only from other EDCs but also from NICs, and by a gnawing sense of economic insecurity among many people of the North. When the

American public was presented with a list of policy options and asked which they thought were important, 80 percent said that "protecting the jobs of American workers should be a very important U.S. foreign policy goal" (Rielly, 1999). Only 45 percent of American leaders gave job protection a high priority. It follows, then, that public attitudes have pushed national leaders to follow policies of economic nationalism (Cohen, 2000).

The result of these countervailing internationalist and nationalist economic pressures within the EDCs gives something of a schizophrenic pattern to the foreign economic policies of the North's countries. They profess support of the further internationalization of the world economy while at the same time trying to promote and protect their own national economies.

Economic Disputes among the EDCs

Trade relations among the EDCs have become more difficult in the past decade. One source of tension is that some countries have chronic trade surpluses, while others regularly run trade deficits. Japan and the United States are the two countries at the opposite ends of the scale. During the 1990s, Japan accumulated a global goods and services trade surplus of just over $1.1 trillion, while the U.S. trade balance was the reverse—a $1.1 trillion deficit. Although trade is but one aspect of a country's overall international balance of payments, it is an important one. This is reflected in Japan having a balance-of-payments surplus that averaged $108 billion annually during 1993–1999, and the United States averaging an annual balance-of-payments deficit of $165 billion for the same period.

A particular point of friction during the 1990s was U.S.–Japan trade relations. The greatest source of Japan's trade and balance-of-payment surpluses and of the U.S. deficits has been the bilateral merchandise trade between the two countries. In 2000, for instance, the estimated $40 billion U.S. trade deficit with Japan accounted for about 20 percent of the overall U.S. deficit.

The already substantial U.S. trade deficit with Japan worsened even more when Asia's NICs and LDCs experienced a financial downturn in 1997. This further weakened Japan's moribund economy, for which exports to the rest of Asia are very important. As a result, the Japanese reduced imports from the United States. Moreover, U.S. exports to the troubled Asian countries also declined. This led U.S. leaders to press Japan to spend billions of yen on domestic programs in an attempt to stimulate Japan's economy and to take other steps that would promote consumer spending by the Japanese on, in part, imported U.S. products. The Japanese government, in turn, resented what it saw as U.S. meddling, and tension continued just below the surface.

THE SOUTH AND INTERNATIONAL POLITICAL ECONOMY

The economic goals of the North and South are both very much alike and very different. They are alike in that both the EDCs' and the LDCs' goals have to do with prosperity. They are different in that the North's goal is to preserve and enhance prosperity; the South's goal is to achieve it.

To further understand the economic position, goals, and policies of the LDCs, the following sections will examine economic development by looking first at the LDCs' sources of development capital and then by turning to the perspective of the LDCs on development issues. Before taking up these matters, though, it is important to look at the status of LDC development.

There is significant economic disparity within all countries, but the gap between the wealthy few and the many poor people tends to be greater in less developed countries. Despite the fact that Vietnam (an LDC) is supposedly an egalitarian communist country, the wealthiest 20 percent of Vietnamese have 45 percent of the national income, while the poorest 20 percent have just 8 percent. The per capita GNP of Vietnam is $350, yet some Vietnamese, such as the businessman talking on his cell phone, can afford cars like this gold 1930 Citroen worth about $30,000.

DEVELOPMENT IN THE SOUTH: STATUS

MAP
Human Development Index, p. 496

There can be little doubt that on many statistical bases there has been improvement in the socioeconomic development of the South. Over the last few decades, the infant mortality rate has been cut by one-third; the percentage of people with access to safe water has grown 70 percent; the adult literacy rate is up 35 percent; and the people live an average of 43 percent longer. Between 1980 and 1998, the real GDP of the South grew an annual average of 3.3 percent. Annual real per capita GDP growth was a slower 2.5 percent, but it did advance (Dickson, 1997; Hoogvelt, 1997).

The progress in the South, however, has also had its drawbacks. What these averages for the South disguise is a highly variegated pattern of development.

Development: A Mixed Pattern

There is a diverse pattern of development in the South. The disparity in development has occurred both between and within countries.

Disparity between countries is one characteristic of uneven economic growth in the South. Although it is possible to show, for example, that for LDCs the aggregate manufacturing output, GDP, and some other factors have expanded considerably during the last 25 years, these averages are misleading. This is because much of the progress was confined to a relatively few newly industrializing countries (NICs). During 1998, these NICs (Argentina, Brazil, China, Malaysia, Mexico, Singapore, South Korea, Taiwan, and Thailand) accounted for about half of all the goods exported by all LDCs as well as half of the South's combined GDPs. Excluding China, the NICs also had an average per capita GDP that is much greater than that of the average LDC.

For most LDCs, by comparison, development has been much slower. While LDCs generally have a positive growth rate in per capita GDP, many—31 LDCs during

Did You Know That:
Between 1989 and 2000, the number of billionaires in the world increased from 157 to 555. The net wealth of this exclusive club was about $1.1 trillion. That equaled about three times the combined GNPs of the countries of sub-Saharan Africa.

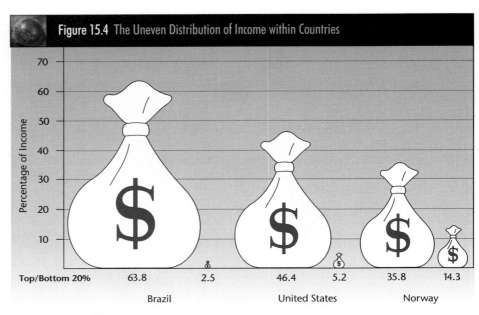

Figure 15.4 The Uneven Distribution of Income within Countries

Top/Bottom 20%	63.8	2.5	46.4	5.2	35.8	14.3
	Brazil		United States		Norway	

Data source: World Bank (2000a).

The figure shows one comparative indication of the uneven distribution of wealth within countries. The money bags represent the incomes of the wealthiest 20 percent of a country's income-earners and the poorest 20 percent in Brazil (which has one of the greatest disparities), the United States (the largest economy), and Norway (which has one of the narrowest gaps). All countries have disparities, but they tend to be much wider in the LDCs.

1999—have had a negative growth rate. Among the worst was Indonesia at (–)18 percent. Indeed, if the strong economic growth rate that a few LDCs, such as China, have had were factored out of the LDC data, the growth rate for the rest hovers near zero. The point is that a few LDCs (the NICs) are making progress economically; most LDCs are either nearly static or actually experiencing long-term economic decline.

Disparity within countries is a second characteristic of LDC economic development. Economic class, sometimes based on race or ethnicity, is one division. Within the South there are cities with sparkling skyscrapers and luxuriant suburbs populated by well-to-do local entrepreneurs who drive Mercedes-Benzes and splash in marble pools. For each such scene, however, there are many more of open sewers, contaminated drinking water, distended bellies, and other symptoms of rural and urban human blight. In short, the scant economic benefits that have accrued in the South are not evenly distributed.

Figure 15.4 shows the percentage of income earned by the wealthiest and poorest 20 percent of income earners in an LDC (Brazil), an EDC (Norway), and the world's largest economy (the United States). Notice how unevenly Brazil's income is distributed, especially relative to Norway. The wealthiest Norwegians make only 2.5 times as much as the country's poorest citizens. In Brazil the top 20 percent of income earners make more than 25 times what the poorest 20 percent of Brazilians receive. When Pope John Paul II visited Brazil, he spoke of "the contrasts between the two Brazils: one is highly developed, strong, and launched on the path of progress and riches; the other is seen in untold zones of poverty, suffering, illiteracy, and marginalization."[8]

If all countries could have been crammed into Figure 15.4, you would have seen that while they all have income distribution disparities, the gaps tend to be larger in the South than in the North. It might be noted, however, that the U.S. disparity is greater than that of any other major industrialized economy and approaches the difference one would expect to find in an LDC rather than in an EDC.

MAP
The Gender Gap,
p. 166

Gender is another basis of economic disparity within countries. Women make up 59 percent of those people living in absolute poverty in the LDCs. One reason is that women comprise only 39 percent of the wage earners in LDCs. Adding to the disparity, data shows that women perform many more hours of unpaid household labor than do men. If this labor is included, women do 62 percent of the total work and (if salaries were equal, which they are not) receive only 32 percent of the wages.

Modernization: A Mixed Blessing

In addition to its more traditional woes, the South also suffers many negative side effects from the process of modernization. Medical advances have led to decreased infant mortality and increased longevity, but one result has been an *explosive population growth*. The population of sub-Saharan Africa, for instance, rose 299 percent from 210 million in 1960 to 628 million in 1998, and the region is expected to add another 206 million people by 2015.

Economic change has also brought *rapid urbanization* as the hope of finding jobs and better health, sanitation, and other social services has set off a mass migration from rural areas to cities in the South. Between 1965 and 1998 the percentage of the South's population living in urban areas grew from 22 to 41 percent, and it is projected to reach 53 percent in the year 2020. There are now a total of approximately 175 cities in LDCs with populations over 1 million. Tokyo is the world's largest metropolitan area (the core city and its suburbs) with 27 million people. Mexico City and São Paulo, Brazil, are the most populous LDC cities, with about 15.3 million inhabitants each. Twelve of the sixteen cities with populations above 10 million are in LDCs.

This rapid urbanization process has created a host of problems. One is the weakening of social order. Older tribal, village, and extended-family loyalties are being destroyed, with few new offsetting values and other social support systems to take their place. Second, the hope of employment is often unfulfilled, and unemployment and poverty in many cities is staggering. Third, struggling LDC governments are often unable to meet the sanitary, housing, and other needs of the flood of people moving to or being born in the cities. Twenty-eight percent of the South's urban population is living in what the World Bank terms "absolute poverty," with nutritional, sanitary, and housing conditions below the minimum standard for health. At least a third of all urban dwellings in sub-Saharan Africa have no running water, toilets, or electricity. By one count, only 8 of India's 3,000 large towns and cities have sewage treatment facilities capable of handling all the effluents of the population.

Development has also brought industrial and *environmental dangers*. The impact of development on the environment will be detailed in chapter 18, but some brief note of the dangers is appropriate here. One problem is deforestation. This is especially critical in the South, where increased demand for wood, expanding farm and ranch acreage, and general urban growth are rapidly depleting the forests. Loss of these forests increases soil erosion, decreases oxygenation of the air, lessens rainfall, and has numerous other deleterious effects. It is also the case that LDC industrial development is adding to air, water, and soil pollution. This is a problem of industrialization in general, but pollution growth is especially acute in developing countries, which often cannot afford the expensive processes to cleanse emissions and dispose of waste.

DEVELOPMENT IN THE SOUTH: CAPITAL NEEDS

Whatever the problems and drawbacks of industrialization, the LDCs are justifiably determined to increase their development. Because of their poor economic base, most LDCs find it difficult to raise capital internally. Incomes are so low in India, for example, that less than 1 percent of the country's people pay income taxes. Many things

The ability of many less developed countries to develop economically is being hindered by their heavy foreign debt. These countries use such a high percentage of what they take in from exports and other external sources of capital to pay the principal and interest on their debt that they have insufficient funds remaining to invest in the development of their economies. The debt crisis has eased somewhat in the past few years, but the debt burden remains a major problem for many LDCs.

can be accomplished with domestic resources and drive, but the LDCs also need massive amounts of **development capital** in order to expand and diversify their economies. "Uganda needs just two things," says its president, Yoweri Museveni. "We need infrastructure and we need foreign investment. That is what we need. The rest we shall do ourselves."[9]

Obtaining these resources is difficult. The LDCs are constrained by limited financial reserves, especially **hard currency.** American dollars are the standard currency of international exchange. British pounds, German marks, French francs, Japanese yen, and a handful of other currencies are also widely convertible. Guatemalan quetzals, Iraqi dinars, Malaysian ringgits, and Nigerian nairas are another story. They and most LDC currencies are not readily accepted in international economic transactions. Since most of the world's hard-currency reserves are concentrated in the EDCs, the LDCs struggle to purchase needed imports.

A primary issue for LDCs, then, is the acquisition of hard-currency development capital. Four main sources of convertible currencies are available: loans, investment, trade, and aid. Unfortunately, there are limitations and drawbacks to each. Unless significant changes are made to increase the flow of development capital to the LDCs and to distribute it more broadly among all LDCs, the majority of them are destined for the foreseeable future to remain relatively poor.

Loans

One source of hard currency is loans extended by private or government sources. Based on a number of economic factors, the LDCs in the 1970s moved to finance their development needs by borrowing heavily from EDC banks, other private lenders, national governments, and international organizations. The upshot was that by 1982 LDC international debt had skyrocketed to $849 billion. While the rate of increase has eased, the total debt owed by the LDCs has continued to grow and stood at $2.5 trillion in 1998. Banks and other private institutional and individual bondholders are the largest creditors, followed by IGOs (such as the IMF and World Bank) and governments.

A Debt Crisis Breaks Out Most countries borrow money. During the 1800s when the United States was developing, it and its major enterprises (such as railroads) borrowed heavily from abroad to help finance expansion. More recently, the United States borrowed over a trillion dollars from foreigners to help pay for the budget deficit that persisted for thirty years. Thus, the recent borrowing by LDCs is neither remarkable nor necessarily irresponsible.

Both borrowers and lenders must manage money carefully, however, and in the 1980s, as evident in Figure 15.5, an unwise spiral of lending and borrowing occurred. The reasons are complex, but suffice it to say that LDCs were in dire need of funds and the lenders in the EDCs had surplus capital, which they urged the LDCs to borrow. Then a global economic downturn undercut the LDCs' ability to repay their loans. At its 1987 peak, debt was nearly twice the total of the LDCs' export earnings, and the LDCs had to pay 26 percent of all their export earnings just to meet the annual principal and interest payments.

Argentina, Brazil, Mexico, Nigeria, and several other LDCs verged on the edge of bankruptcy and faced a seemingly lose-lose choice. They could either halt payments and thereby ruin their credit. Or they could continue to try to meet their **debt service** (principal

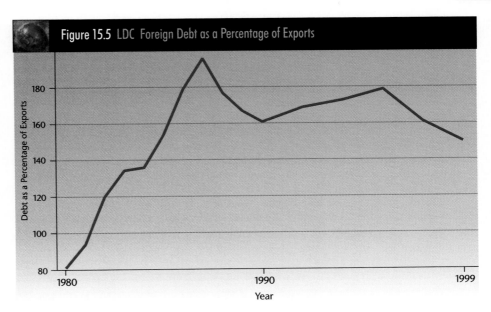

Figure 15.5 LDC Foreign Debt as a Percentage of Exports

Data source: World Bank (2000a).

Export earnings are a key source of capital that LDCs use to pay debt. This ability was severely strained during the 1980s as the LDCs' debt as a percentage of export earnings soared. Financial cooperation between the LDCs and EDCs along with an improved global economy have eased the crunch since its peak in 1987. Still, the 1999 level of debt at 132 percent of export earnings remains too high.

and interest payments) even though that meant an annual outflow of $100 billion that the LDCs desperately needed to provide domestic services and to develop their economies.

The North was also threatened. Banks and other creditors faced potential losses of hundreds of billions of dollars that might have driven some huge banks into insolvency. That would have cost the governments of the EDCs billions, as they intervened to fend off bank failures or to repay depositors under government insurance plans.

The Debt Crisis Eases The mutual danger of the debt crisis to both the North and South led them to search for solutions. The details are complex, but a plan proposed in 1989 by U.S. secretary of the treasury Nicholas Brady began to ease the debt crisis. Under the Brady Plan during the 1990s, banks forgave over $100 billion of what the LDCs owed, lowered interest rates, and made new loans. In return, the governments of the EDCs, the IMF, and the World Bank guaranteed the loans and have increased their own lending to the LDCs. The Brady Plan has also required that the LDCs meet fiscal reform requirements negotiated with the IMF and other lenders.

The Current Debt Situation The immediate LDC debt crisis has abated, but the debt situation remains troublesome. One concern is that the LDCs still have a towering debt. Earnings from exports are one source of revenue to service debt, and the 1999 debt as a percentage of export earnings was a burdensome 132 percent. Among other things, this meant that the LDCs paid out $292 billion (18.4 percent of their annual export earnings) that year to meet their principal and interest obligations. While the debt service is much below its 30 percent peak in 1985, it still represents a loss of much-needed capital for the LDCs.

Private Investment

A second source of capital for LDCs is private investment through **foreign direct investment (FDI)** and **foreign portfolio investment (FPI)**. The flows of FDI and FPI are growing in importance as capital sources for the LDCs. Figure 15.6 shows that the

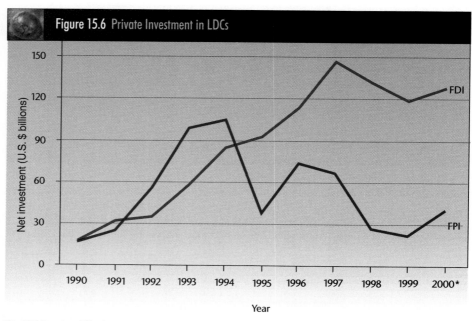

Figure 15.6 Private Investment in LDCs

*The 2000 figure is an IMF estimate.
Data source: IMF (2000 and 1999a).

Foreign direct investment and foreign portfolio investment are important sources of development capital for LDCs. Notice that, compared to FDI, the flow of FPI is relatively unstable and thus, less desirable as a source of external financing. The sharp decline in net FPI beginning in1995 and continuing through the rest of the 1990s was a reaction first to Mexico's currency crisis in the late 1994, then to the onset in 1997 of the Asian and Russian financial crises. These latter two crises also depressed the net flow of FDI to the LDCs. The first year of the new millennium, however, brought a welcome, if still uncertain, upswing in net investment flows.

combined net FDI and FPI in the LDCs skyrocketed during the 1990s. By another measure, there is an upward trend in the proportion of global FDI that they receive. While it is still a minority, with most funds being invested in EDCs, the LDCs' proportion of FDI increased from 16 percent in 1990 to 27 percent in 1998.

There are several factors that temper the developmental impact of the rising flow of investment capital. First, most investment capital goes to only a handful of LDCs. During 1998, for example, China and Brazil alone received almost 44 percent of the FDI flow to the LDCs, and those two and another six countries (Argentina, South Korea, Malaysia, Mexico, Singapore, and Thailand) took in 68 percent of the available FDI capital. By contrast, Africa received only 2.5 percent of the capital. Second, as evident in Figure 15.6, FPI is volatile. Third, the net increase of FPI each year during the 1990s disguises the fact that for individual countries, the net flow can turn sharply negative. The serious consequences that such a negative shift can cause were illustrated when worried investors withdrew a net $9.5 billion from Mexico in the mid-1990s and caused a "peso crisis."

Trade

MAP
Dependence on Trade,
p. 5

Export earnings are a third possible source of development capital. In light of the vast size of the world market, and because earnings from trade can be utilized by LDCs according to their own wishes, trade is theoretically the optimal source of hard currency for LDCs. Yet, in reality, the LDCs are severely disadvantaged by the pattern and terms of international trade.

There are several sources of LDC trade weakness. First, they command only 24 percent of the world goods and services export market. Second, as noted earlier, just a

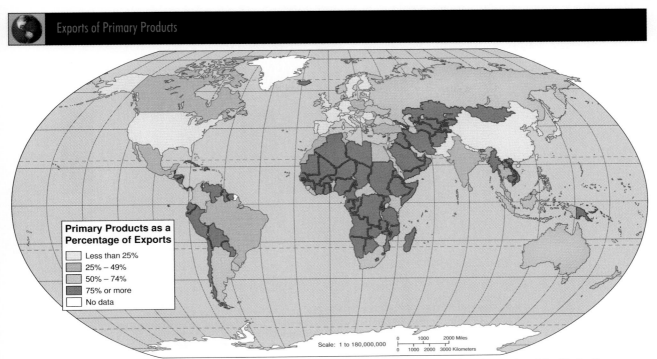

Exports of Primary Products

Primary Products as a Percentage of Exports
- Less than 25%
- 25% – 49%
- 50% – 74%
- 75% or more
- No data

Scale: 1 to 180,000,000

| 0 | 1000 | 2000 Miles |
| 0 | 1000 | 2000 | 3000 Kilometers |

The less developed countries of the South are disadvantaged compared to the economically developed countries of the North. One reason is that the LDCs are much more reliant on primary products for export earnings. This dependency is a disadvantage because the demand for and price of primary products is unstable. Also, over the long term the value of primary products rises more slowly than manufactured products. Therefore most LDCs have increasing difficulty earning the foreign capital needed for economic development. This map shows the distribution of countries according to the percentage of their exports accounted for by primary products.

few NICs account for a lion's share of all the goods exported by the South. Third, most LDCs suffer a chronic trade deficit. Only a handful of the 62 poorest LDCs (the least developed countries, LLDCs) had a positive trade balance in 1998. Many of the other LLDCs had staggering trade deficits that debilitated their national economies. For example, Mozambique's imports were 200 percent of its exports.

Fourth, LDC trade weakness stems from the heavy dependence of these countries on the export of primary products, including fibers, foodstuffs, fuels, and other minerals and raw materials. The more a country depends on primary products for export earnings, the less wealthy it tends to be. For the average LDC, primary products are the most important component of its exports. A general rule of thumb is that the more dependent it is on the export of primary products other than petroleum, the poorer a country is likely to be. This compares unfavorably to the diversified composition of EDC goods and services exports, of which only 5 percent are primary products. Moreover, many LDCs are export-dependent on one or just a few primary products. Dependency on a few products, especially primary products, for export earnings leaves LDCs disadvantaged because of several factors.

Product instability is one factor. Countries that rely on fish and other marine foodstuffs for export are endangered by the declining fish stocks in the world's oceans. When a freeze damages Colombia's coffee crop, a drought devastates the groundnut crops that Ghana relies on, or floods wipe out the Bangladesh jute crop, then trade suffers greatly.

Market and price weaknesses are also common for primary products. A downturn in world demand can decimate markets. During the past decades, world trade in products such as cotton, sisal, jute, wool, and other natural fibers has been harmed by the development of synthetics. Sugar sales have been undercut by artificial substitutes and by dietary changes. Minerals such as tin and lead have also experienced market declines. Despite its recent rise, even the oil market was depressed during most of the 1990s.

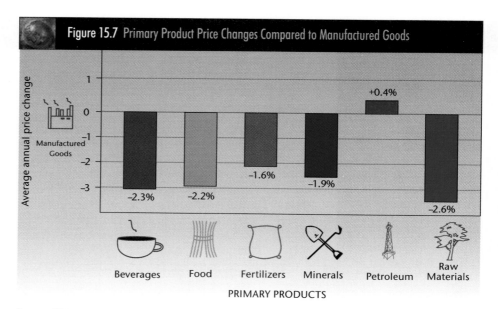

Figure 15.7 Primary Product Price Changes Compared to Manufactured Goods

Data source: World Bank (2000a); percentage calculations by author.

*Reading the chart: In this chart the horizontal line "0" represents the price of manufactured goods held constant during the 1990s to allow a price comparison with primary products. If in one year, manufactured goods went up 2 percent and food went down 1 percent, the manufactured goods price would be "zeroed" (−2) and the −1 percent food price would be decreased by another 2 percent to −3 percent.

When the percentage of annual price changes of primary products and, of manufactured goods are compared, it is evident that the value of almost all primary products has declined relative to the value of manufactured goods. This means that since the majority of LDCs rely on primary products for export earnings, the LDCs have an increasingly difficult time earning enough foreign capital through trade to modernize their economies.

Price weakness for primary products is the response to the classic economic relationship of too much supply and too little demand. According to the World Bank, the real dollar price of 28 of the 36 commodities it tracks declined between 1990 and 1999. Figure 15.7 shows the average annual change between 1960 and 1999 in the prices brought on the world market by several categories of primary products compared to manufactured goods. As you can see, the prices of all the primary products except petroleum declined, and oil increased only a miniscule 0.9 percent. These price differentials are debilitating to the economies and development programs of the LDCs that export primary products. Chile provides one example. The price of Chile's main export, copper, plummeted by 43 percent in the 1990s. Therefore Chile in 1999 would have had to sell almost twice as much copper as it did in 1990 to purchase machinery to build a manufacturing plant in order to industrialize and diversify its economy.

The use of trade, then, to acquire capital and to improve economic conditions has not been highly effective for most LDCs. Their pattern of merchandise trade deficits, export dependence on primary products, and market and price weaknesses all disadvantage LDCs in their trade relations with the EDCs.

Foreign Aid

A fourth possible external source of capital for LDCs is foreign aid (Hook, 1996). In some ways the flow of official development assistance (ODA) to LDCs has been impressive, amounting to over half a trillion dollars since World War II. Official ODA for 1998 was $52.9 billion. Currently, almost all foreign aid that is given comes from the 21 EDCs that are members of the Development Assistance Committee (DAC) of the Organization for Economic Cooperation and Development (OECD). Most assistance is

Table 15.3 Recipient Foreign Aid Data, 1998

Recipient	Received ($ billions)	% of GNP	Per Capita ($)
Bangladesh	1.3	2.8	9.93
Cambodia	0.3	11.9	30.64
Ghana	0.7	9.3	38.94
Guatemala	0.2	1.2	21.18
All LLDCs	20.3	4.7	10.65

Note: LLDCs are the least developed countries—those with per capita GNPs under $761. The data here omits India and China, whose huge populations skew LLDC data.
Date source: World Bank (2000a).

It is impressive to talk about foreign aid in the tens of billions of dollars; it is less impressive when aid is measured on a recipient per capita basis. For example, Bangladesh, one of the world's poorest countries, received per capita aid of only $9.93, not quite enough in the United States for a large cheese pizza.

extended through **bilateral aid** (country to country), with a smaller amount being channeled through **multilateral aid** (via the United Nations, the World Bank, and other IGOs).

Limitations on the Impact of Aid

Without disparaging the value or intent of past or current efforts, aid is neither a story of undisguised generosity nor one of unblemished success (Katada & McKeown, 1998; Schraeder, Hook, & Taylor, 1998). Factors that reduce the impact of aid include political considerations, the military content of aid, recipient per capita aid, donor aid relative to wealth, and aid application.

Political considerations are one factor that limits the effectiveness of aid. The bilateral aid that makes up the bulk of all foreign aid is often given more on the basis of political-military interest than to meet economic needs or to promote human rights. A very high percentage of all U.S. bilateral foreign aid during 1998 went to just two countries: Israel (23 percent) and Egypt (17 percent). By contrast, the countries in sub-Saharan Africa received only 10 percent of U.S. bilateral aid. Most other countries also give aid selectively. Great Britain and France have a special interest in their former colonies. Japan focuses on Asia and elsewhere where it has special economic interests. In fairness it should be pointed out that promoting democracy, human rights, and other such standards also influence foreign aid policy.

Even multilateral aid has political overtones because most of the international aid-giving organizations, such as the World Bank, are dominated by the countries of the North. Turkmenistan and Iran, for example, are attempting to develop rail, gas pipeline, and other links to help Turkmenistan to export its products, but attempts to secure loans from the World Bank to help fund the projects have been blocked by the United States, based on its opposition to the regime in Iran.

Military content is another factor that limits the impact of the aid figures that are sometimes reported. Egypt certainly needs aid, but of the total U.S. aid to that country in 1998, about half was military aid. Indeed, over 25 percent of all American bilateral assistance that year was military aid (Blanton, 2000).

Measuring recipient per capita aid, rather than gross aid, is also useful to gain a truer picture of the impact of economic foreign aid. In 1998 the LLDCs (excluding China and India) received about $16 per person. Some representative aid recipients are shown in Table 15.3.

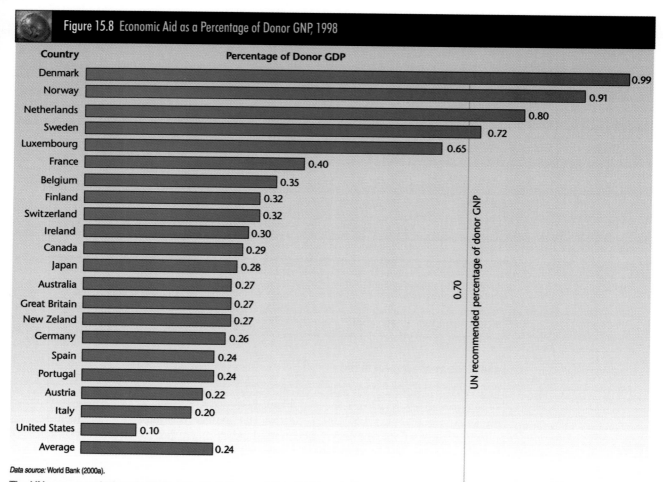

Figure 15.8 Economic Aid as a Percentage of Donor GNP, 1998

Data source: World Bank (2000a).

The UN recommends that the EDCs allocate 0.7 percent of their respective GNPs to economic aid. Only four EDCs meet that mark. The U.S. percentage of its wealth devoted to foreign economic aid is by far the lowest.

Donor aid relative to wealth is another analytical approach that lessens the seeming significance of aid figures. This compares aid given to the donor's wealth. Overall, aid as a percentage of EDCs' total GNP has been steadily declining for a quarter century. In 1965 aid equaled 0.46 percent of the OECD's total GNP. That percentage declined to 0.24 in 1998. Americans are particularly apt to think that their country is a sort of Santa Claus, beneficently sending massive amounts of foreign aid down the chimneys of deserving LDCs in an act of self-sacrifice that unmercifully burdens American taxpayers (perhaps portrayed as elves in the stage version). The image is a delusion. It is true that the $8.8 billion in U.S. bilateral and multilateral economic aid for 1998 ranked second among the DAC countries after Japan ($9.4 billion). But, from the perspective of U.S. wealth, American aid was truly paltry. It equaled a tiny one-tenth of 1 percent (0.1 percent) of the U.S. GDP. As Figure 15.8 shows, this placed the United States dead last among the EDCs in terms of generosity measured against wealth. Indeed, the U.S. percentage was only half that of the next stingiest EDC. The United Nations recommends that each EDC use 0.7 percent of its GNP for economic assistance. As the figure shows, only 4 of the 21 countries meet or exceed that standard. If they had given the recommended 0.7 percent, economic aid in 1998 would have risen to $216 billion, with a U.S. share at $62 billion.

The way aid is applied is a final factor that limits its impact (Koehn & Ojo, 1999). Too often in the past aid has been used to fund highly symbolic but economically unwise projects such as airports and sports arenas. Inefficiency and corruption have also sometimes drained off aid. There is criticism, too, on the grounds that aid is used to maintain the local elite, does not reach the truly poor, and, therefore, continues the dependencia relationship between North and South. In fact, some critics argue that aid can actually retard growth, contending, for example, that giving poor people food reduces their incentive to farm. These charges are not universally accurate, but aid donors and recipients have moved to address problems that do exist. Among other changes, donors are now working to ensure that the aid is used wisely. "For too long development cooperation has focused on the economy and not the polity," the head of United Nations Development Programme (UNDP) has conceded. "Without a functioning political system and effective governance, the best-lain economic plans are not going to succeed."[10] To address this issue, aid is now being aimed at what is called "capacity building." This means creating a political and business structure to use aid more effectively to build a recipient's economic infrastructure.

DEVELOPMENT IN THE SOUTH: LDC PERSPECTIVES AND POLICIES

While the gap in wealth between the North and South has long existed, relations between the two economic spheres have not been static. The LDCs are now asserting with mounting intensity the proposition that they have a right to share in the world's economic wealth. They have acted on a number of fronts to enhance their own economic situations and to pressure the EDCs to redistribute part of their wealth. We will examine these views and efforts in terms of the LDCs' expectations, organizational movement, demands, and actions.

Rising Expectations

One of the most important developments in the last half of the twentieth century was the independence movement among LDCs. Dozens of colonies in Africa and Asia demanded and won political sovereignty. Even after independence, though, many LDCs remained in an economically subservient and disadvantaged position in relation to their former colonial masters or to other dominant EDCs. Most people in LDCs are not willing to accept such manipulation. The resistance to a dependencia relationship with the North is the result of a number of factors.

Nationalism is one factor. LDC leaders recognize that true sovereignty cannot exist without economic independence. *Relative deprivation* is a second factor. The rapid increase of communications technology has brought the image of the North's relative richness to the South. Whether or not their lot has improved in objective terms, the impoverished people of the South are more aware of their relative deprivation and therefore are more discontent.

Increased moral/cooperative rhetoric is a third factor that has promoted LDC assertiveness. From the time of the League of Nations, and accelerating during and after World War II, there has been increased lip service paid to the idea of fostering international cooperation and responsibility and promoting peace, economic well-being, and human rights. This rhetoric is symbolized by chapters IX and X of the United Nations Charter, which dedicate that organization to cooperative principles and establish the Economic and Social Council. Whatever sincerity the North has in upholding these ideas, the South takes them seriously and is demanding that the industrialized states practice what they have so nobly preached.

Transnational ideology is a fourth factor that has contributed to the South's assertiveness. Marxism may be largely moribund, but LDC leaders are well aware of, and often sympathetic to, the international economic structuralist perspective that condemns what it sees as continuing capitalist/imperialist exploitation of the South. *Eco-*

nomic turmoil is a fifth factor motivating the South. A variety of related and destabilizing economic events, including the periodic worldwide economic downturns and gyrating energy costs, occurred during the past several decades. Conditions in the South often went from bad to worse, and the affected countries responded with a series of declarations of economic rights and responsibilities, detailed in the following sections.

Development of the LDC Movement

The developing identity of the South first took the form of *political nonalignment*. In 1955, 29 African and Asian countries convened the Bandung Conference in Indonesia to discuss how to hasten the independence of colonial territories and how to be nonaligned in the cold war. Most of the colonies are now independent, and the cold war is over. But the Bandung Conference remains an important mark of the ongoing sense of identity among the LDCs.

The South's concerns soon also turned to economic development. Political demands for an end to colonialism provided a role model for similar economic assertiveness. A coalition of disadvantaged countries, the **Group of 77,** emerged and called for creation of the first United Nations Conference on Trade and Development (UNCTAD), which met in Geneva in 1964. This conference and the Group of 77 (which has grown to 133 members) evolved into an ongoing UNCTAD organization. UNCTAD, which has 190 members, has served as a vehicle for the LDCs to discuss their needs and to press demands on the North.

UNCTAD and the Group of 77 have also promoted many other discussions of the South's economic position. The first formal meeting between North and South occurred in a 1981 meeting at Cancún, Mexico, and others have been held in sites around the world. The details are not important to make the point that the results have generally been the same. For instance, the UNCTAD meeting in 2000, which convened in Bangkok and was billed as a meeting that would help build bridges between the EDCs and LDCs. Instead, it ended in acrimony when the EDCs refused to make concrete commitments to open their markets more fully to the exports of the LDCs. It would to too strong to say that the EDCs are unwilling to help their poorer brethren, but the largesse of the EDCs is certainly very limited.

LDC Demands

The development of LDC consciousness and assertiveness has led to a series of demands on the industrialized North. These calls for reform are collectively known as the **New International Economic Order (NIEO).** More than any other single document, the Declaration on the Establishment of a New International Economic Order outlines and symbolizes the South's view, and its calls for reform, of the "old" international economic order. This declaration, adopted as a resolution by the UN General Assembly in 1974, begins by protesting the North's domination of the existing economic structure and the maldistribution of wealth. To remedy this situation, the NIEO declaration called for a number of reforms:

1. *Trade reforms.* The NIEO envisions improved and stabilized markets for primary products. This would include removal of trade barriers and the regulation of prices and supplies.
2. *Monetary reforms.* Reforms in monetary relations include stabilization of inflation and exchange rates and increased funding from the IMF and other international monetary agencies. The NIEO also includes demands for greater LDC participation in the decision making of the IMF and other such international agencies.
3. *Industrialization.* The 1974 resolution also calls on the North to assist the South in gaining technology and in increasing industrial production.

As this editorial cartoon from France suggests, the people of the economically less developed countries of the South are demanding that they receive a greater share of the world's wealth, which is largely possessed by a minority of people who live in the economically developed countries of the North.

4. *Economic sovereignty.* The South asserts its right to control its own resources and to regulate the activities of MNCs.

5. *Economic aid.* Finally, the LDCs have called on the EDCs to increase economic aid to at least be equivalent to 0.7 percent of their respective GDPs. Only four EDCs now meet that standard, as detailed in Figure 15.8 on p. 426. There are also calls for more nonpolitical multilateral aid to be given through the World Bank and other such IGOs.

These changes have regularly been reiterated by UNCTAD and other LDC organizations, but none of the reforms have been truly implemented. Indeed the onward march of globalization has in many ways sharpened the demands for what UN secretary-general Annan has termed a "Global New Deal" for the LDCs, one in which "large parts of the world are [no longer] excluded from the benefits of globalization."[11]

LDC Action

The LDCs have not waited passively for the EDCs to respond to their demands. They have instead taken action on a number of fronts. Not all these moves have succeeded, but they indicate the South's growing assertiveness.

Early LDC Development Policy One early LDC approach was *nationalization of MNCs* operating within their borders. The oil-producing countries, for example, made Western producers surrender all or majority control of their fields and processing facilities. Many LDCs reasoned that if they controlled an industry it would operate in their interest rather than in the interest of foreign companies, investors, and governments. Perhaps, but these drastic measures caused considerable backlash and dried up the inflow of new investment money. As a result, the practice of nationalization has largely been abandoned.

Establishing cartels was a second tactic that LDCs tried initially. A **cartel** is an international trading agreement among producers who hope to control the supply and price of a primary product. The first cartel was established in 1933 to regulate tea, but the decade of the 1960s, when 18 came into existence, was the apex of cartel formation. They ranged in importance from the Organization of Petroleum Exporting Countries (OPEC) to the Asian and Pacific Coconut Community.

Cartels, however, have proven generally unsuccessful, as illustrated by the limited impact of even OPEC. During the 1970s OPEC seemed almost invincible. With its 12 members in control of most of the oil needed by the seemingly insatiable EDCs, OPEC manipulated supplies and prices, which sent the cost of a barrel of oil from $1.35 (or 3.2 cents per gallon) skyrocketing 2,500 percent to $34 per barrel in 1981. Money poured into the OPEC treasuries as black gold flowed out. During the 1970s more than $1 trillion was accumulated, and the OPEC countries' balance-of-payments surplus peaked at an annual $109 billion in 1980.

The dominance of OPEC was, however, only temporary. The high price of oil sparked massive quests to find new sources of oil. With new discoveries in the North Sea, the Gulf of Mexico, and elsewhere, the supply of oil increased. Also a greater percentage of oil came from non–OPEC countries. On the demand side, the high price of oil encouraged conservation and alternative energy measures and drove down oil consumption. The result of increased supply and decreased demand weakened prices, which sharply dropped prices in both real and current dollars. By 1998, oil prices had sunk to a miniscule $14.50 a barrel (34.5 cents a gallon). Prices in 1999 and 2000 shot upward, as OPEC reduced production, but even at $32 a barrel the price has to be kept in perspective. In the first place, in real dollars, oil at that price was only marginally more expensive than it had been in 1989, and much less expensive than during some earlier periods. Moreover, compared to many other commodities, oil was cheap. At $32 a barrel, crude oil in 2000 cost $.0078 an ounce. Using that price per ounce, a gallon of milk would have cost $1, not $2.49 (the price at a local store in Connecticut in August 2000), a two-liter bottle of Coke would have cost 53 cents, not $1.39; and a six pack of beer would have cost 56 cents, not $5.19.

The upshot is that although OPEC continues to supply about 39 percent of the world's petroleum, and while OPEC members possess approximately 80 percent of the world's proven oil reserves, the cartel has not been successful in sustaining dramatically increased oil prices. The inability of OPEC to keep prices up has been caused by political pressure by the United States and other EDCs, by the continuing oversupply of oil compared to demand, and by numerous political strains among the OPEC members. The Persian Gulf War, which involved Iraq, Kuwait, and Saudi Arabia among other OPEC members, is the most obvious example (Lynn, 1999; Morse, 1999).

Protectionism was a third, and now also rapidly declining, thrust of early LDC activity. The temptation and domestic political pressure for developing countries to use tariff and nontariff barriers to protect infant industries are strong and may, in the earliest stages, even have some merit. It is also understandable, given the common fear, as one Indian economist explains, "that the foreigners will exploit, dominate, and control us."[12] Protectionist policies, however, have numerous drawbacks. Most important, there is evidence that for LDCs protectionism does not work and that economic growth is positively associated with eliminating trade impediments. Moreover, whether protectionism works or not, EDCs are less willing to tolerate it and have used a variety of approaches to entice or coerce the LDCs to open their markets.

More Recent LDC Development Policy With nationalization, cartels, and protectionism not helping, and even proving counterproductive, and under pressure from the United States, the IMF, and other bastions of free-market advocacy, many LDCs have turned toward trying to compete with the EDCs on their own terms. Even most of the few remaining communist countries, such as China and Vietnam, have succumbed to capitalism. Moreover, there have been some remarkable success stories, as our earlier discussion of NICs indicates. Singapore's per capita GNP is the ninth highest in the world, and South Korea's is just short of World Bank's "high income" category.

Yet for the LDCs, including the countries in transition (CITs, the former communist countries) that are struggling to develop their economies, the capitalist path to development has several negative by-products. One is control. To a degree, some LDCs have achieved development by suppressing democracy in favor of the political stability that outside investors favor. Second, some LDCs have also followed anti–labor union practices and other policies in order to keep wages low so that export prices can be kept down. A third drawback is that some LDCs have attracted foreign investment by having lax environmental, safety, and other regulations. Some LDCs are among the world's most polluted countries. Japan, for instance, produces 4.6 times more manufactured goods than does China; yet China's industrial emissions of carbon dioxide are 2.8 times higher than are Japan's.

Fourth, CITs and even those, such as China, that remain officially communist, have found that capitalism and international economic liberalism have negative social consequences. China once stressed socioeconomic equality. Now some Chinese drive imported Mercedes, while others live in the shantytowns that have sprung up around Chinese cities. The wealthiest 20 percent of Chinese now take in 47 percent of the country's income; the poorest 20 percent make only 6 percent of the national income. That is about the same income disparity as the quintessential capitalist country, the United States. There also are indications that women are losing some of their standing in the Chinese economy as it changes its emphasis to maximize profits. In the words of one Chinese businesswoman, "These days if you're a woman, you're as good as a commodity. You're either worth six pounds of gold or two tons of aluminum."[13]

THE FUTURE OF NATIONAL ECONOMIC POLICY

There can be no doubt that the economic story of the last half century has been marked by two important and related trends. The first has been the almost complete triumph of **capitalism** over competing economic models, especially Marxism and socialism. One measure of this change is the Index of Economic Freedom, which has been calculated since 1995 by the Heritage Foundation, a conservative think tank. The index measures 50 variables that, according to the study, are "factors of economic freedom... the higher the score on a factor, the greater the level of government interference in the economy and the less economic freedom in the economy" (O'Driscoll, Holmes, & Kirkpatrick, 2000:1). By 1995 the movement toward capitalism was well underway, but even since then, there has been a noticeable shift in the economic orientation of countries. As evident in Figure 15.9, the percentage of countries in the economically "free" category (1–1.99) remained steady, but there was a marked increased in the "mostly free" category (2–2.99) and a decrease in the "repressed" category (3–3.99), with the unfree category (4–5) unchanged. According to the survey, Singapore (1.45) was the freest economy, North Korea (5) the least free.

The second important trend has been a steady movement toward ever greater economic interdependence based on an increasingly free exchange of trade, investment, and other financial activity. An array of statistics presented in this and the preceding chapter show conclusively that the movement of goods, services, investment capital, and currencies across borders has expanded exponentially. Furthermore, as we shall take up in the next chapter, the international system has created the EU, IMF, NAFTA,

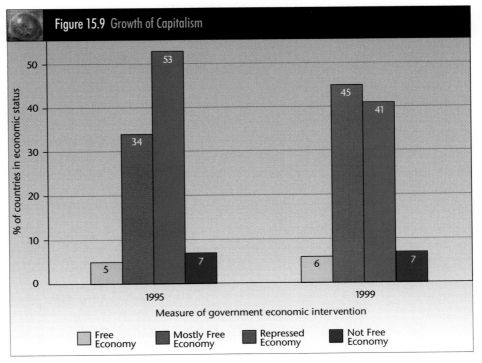

Figure 15.9 Growth of Capitalism

% of countries in economic status

Measure of government economic intervention

□ Free Economy   ■ Mostly Free Economy   ■ Repressed Economy   ■ Not Free Economy

Data source: O'Driscoll, Holmes, & Kirkpatrick, 2000.

A significant change in the past few decades had been a surge in the capitalist approach to national economic management and a decline in the prevalence of other models, particularly Marxism and socialism. The shift is evident in this figure based on data from the Heritage Foundation. Notice especially the shift in percentages from the Repressed Economy category to the Mostly Free Economy category.

MAP
International Trade
Organizations, p. 219

World Bank, WTO, and numerous global and regional organizations and arrangements to facilitate and promote free international economic interchange.

For all this evidence, it would be erroneous to conclude that the world is on a path to inevitable economic integration and the eclipse of economic nationalism. Indeed, there are powerful arguments against and forces opposed to globalization. "We have sunlight, but we have shadows, too," the head of the WTO commented.[14] Those shadows are cast, according to one analyst, by the fact that "today many people think that globalization is going to destroy their life as they know it. We have gotten used to the idea that globalization will inevitably succeed, but I am not so sure anymore."[15]

The trend toward free economic interchange and the opposing powerful forces of economic nationalism mean that one of this century's critical debates will be whether to continue, halt, or even reverse economic integration. We will explore that debate by looking at the arguments for and against free economic interchange. First, however, it is appropriate to review the barriers that countries can and do erect to affect the flow of goods, services, and capital.

BARRIERS TO FREE ECONOMIC INTERCHANGE

Some years ago, Paul Simon recorded a song that told us, "There must be 50 ways to leave your lover." Insofar as countries have increasingly vowed to reduce trade barriers and to be bound together economically—for richer, for poorer; for better, for worse—there are at least 50 ways to get out of, or perhaps cheat on, that relationship.

Barriers to Merchandise Trade

There are numerous ways that countries can restrict trade. **Tariffs** are the most familiar trade barrier. While these are generally low, tariff hikes are still occasionally either threatened or used. Most often this occurs over economic issues. Not long ago, for example, the United States threatened to impose 100 percent tariffs on some Chinese goods if Beijing did not end the piracy of U.S. intellectual property (copyrights and patents) by Chinese manufacturers. China pledged to crack down on those producing bootleg copies of music and video compact discs and other violators. The practices continue, however, and the tariff club remains in the U.S. closet. *Import prohibitions* based on political sanctions, such as the ban against importing Iraqi oil, is another method. At the extreme, trade *embargoes*, such as the one that the United States has imposed on Cuban goods, may totally bar trade.

Nontariff barriers (NTBs) are a less well-known but more common and important way of restricting trade. These NTBs are sometimes reasonable regulations based on health, safety, or other considerations. More often they are simply protectionist. *Quotas* that limit the number of units that can be shipped are one form of NTB. Some quotas are imposed by importing countries; others are self-imposed by exporting countries in preference to facing imposed restrictions. One reason Japanese auto manufacturers built plants in the United States was the threat of U.S. quotas on the importation of Japanese vehicles.

Pricing limits are another way to restrain trade. During the 1996 election campaign, President Clinton pleased Florida tomato farmers by successfully pressuring the Mexican government to agree not to export tomatoes to the United States for less than 20.86 cents per pound. The U.S. growers complained that they were unable to compete with Mexican imports. The pressure on Mexico violated the spirit of NAFTA, but, one U.S. official commented, "This was Mexico's moment to pay [Clinton] back for the bailout" of the Mexican economy after the peso collapse. Besides, the official said, "the math was pretty simple. Florida has 25 electoral votes, and Mexico doesn't."[16]

Technical restrictions, such as health and safety regulations, are sometimes really meant to bar imports or increase their cost considerably. Even though NAFTA allows the trucks of its member-countries to carry goods across borders, many Mexican trucks are barred from the United States because they do not meet the stricter U.S. safety regulations. *Subsidization* allows a domestic producer to undersell foreign competition at home. Many governments, for instance, heavily subsidize their agriculture industries. Efforts to reduce agricultural subsidies have met with fierce domestic resistance in France, Japan, and elsewhere.

Dumping is yet another variant of an NTB. The tactic is prohibited by GATT rules, but there are frequent charges that it happens. Dumping occurs when a company sells its goods abroad at a price lower than what it sells them for at home. Mexico, for example, recently placed an added duty of 1,105 percent on Chinese shoes after finding that China was dumping them on the Mexican market.

Barriers to the Trade in Services and to Investment

Just as there are a wide array of merchandise trade barriers, so too are there multitudinous ways to restrict the trade in services and the flow in investment. Of the few that we can sample here, *licensing requirements* are one way to make it difficult for foreign professionals and companies to provide services in another country. Many countries license architects, engineers, insurance agents, stock and bond traders, and other professionals. *Majority ownership requirements* are a way to bar the foreign ownership of businesses within a country. India, for example, requires that all companies located in India have at least 51 percent Indian ownership.

FREE ECONOMIC INTERCHANGE: THE DEBATE

There is a crucial debate being held across the world in government councils, academic circles, the media, and elsewhere about the advantages and disadvantages of economic globalization. Supporting globalization, President Clinton told the World Economic Forum, which brings together many of the globe's business and political leaders, "Those who wish to roll back the forces of globalization because they fear its disruptive consequences… are plainly wrong. Fifty years of experience shows that greater economic integration and political cooperation are positive forces."[17] Others are opposed to or very cautious about globalization. "Our global village has caught fire, from where we do not know," President Hosni Mubarak of Egypt told the same conclave. "In the emerging world," Mubarak continued, "there is a bitter sentiment of injustice, a sense that there must be something wrong with a system that wipes out years of hard-won development because of changes in market sentiment."[18]

The main points of that debate are reviewed in the following two sections that outline the case for and against free economic interchange. Think about these points as you read them and decide whether the view of President Clinton or that of President Mubarak is closer to your own.

The Case for Free Economic Interchange

Advocates of free economic interchange argue from a series of economic and political propositions. Some of these involve trade or some other single aspect of international economic exchange. Other arguments are more general.

Benefits of Specialization One economic theory supporting free trade holds that each country should efficiently do what it does best. Free trade theory dates back at least to Edward Misselden's *Free Trade or the Means to Make Trade Flourish*, published in England in 1632. Free trade theory is also associated with the ideas presented in Adam

The role of multinational corporations in our lives is ubiquitous. Problems with Firestone tires, which caused many accidents and, reportedly, 100 deaths and 400 injuries, necessitated a massive recall of 6.6 million tires in 2000. Critics charge that the tires were poorly made to maximize profits. Firestone is a name that for over 100 years has been associated with the U.S. tire industry, but in fact the company is a subsidiary of Bridgestone, a Japanese MNC. Here, Masatoshi Ono, the president of Firestone, is framed by one of his company's failed tires as he waits to testify before the U.S. Senate in September 2000.

Smith's *Wealth of Nations* (1776) and David Ricardo's *Principles of Political Economy and Taxation* (1817). Starting from the premise that economies are most efficient when governments do not intervene, these theorists argued that everyone would benefit if countries produced and sold freely what they did most efficiently. This specialization would benefit everyone based on human and natural resource availability and an "economy of scale" that reduces per unit costs and, thus, provides goods to everyone at the lowest possible price.

The Cost of Protectionism The reverse side of specialization is the cost of protectionism to the country erecting barriers. Tariffs and NTBs result in higher prices. This occurs because the tariff cost is passed on to consumers or because consumers are forced to buy more expensive domestically produced goods. A study that examined 21 protected U.S. industries with annual sales of more than $1 billion in the United States found that the protectionism added an average of 35 percent to the prices of the products of those industries. The protection saved an estimated 191,000 jobs but cost American consumers $170,000 per job saved. Even when the cost of unemployment, other payments to displaced workers, lost taxes from unemployed workers, and lost tariff revenues were deducted from the $170,000, the net loss per job saved was still $54,000.[19]

Moreover, the economists found that the benefits from protection did not principally aid the workers. The average hourly pay in the 21 protected industries was only $7.76. One of the economists used the sugar industry, which is one of the most heavily protected in the United States, to illustrate this point. "If protection were a boon to low-skill workers," he asked rhetorically, "how is it that we have extremely bad working conditions and low pay in sugar plantations in Florida and Louisiana?" Answering his own question, the economist argued that "basically, if protection helps anybody, it's the owners. It doesn't trickle down."[20]

Promotion of Competition A third economic free trade argument focuses on competition (Crystal, 1998). Without foreign competition, domestic manufacturers have a captive market. However, a variety of ill effects, from price fixing to lack of innovation, may occur, especially if one corporation dominates its field or if there is monopolistic collusion among supposed competitors. American automakers seemingly refused to offer U.S. consumers well-built, inexpensive, fuel-efficient small cars until pressure from foreign competition forced them to reshape their product and modernize their production techniques.

Competition has also spurred American manufacturers to modernize and streamline their operations to boost productivity, reduce costs, and improve competitiveness. There can be little doubt that the beating that U.S. manufacturers took at the hands of their foreign competitors, especially during the 1970s and 1980s, forced Chrysler, Ford, and General Motors to be more efficient and to offer better products.

Providing Development Capital Fourth, those who favor free economic interchange contend that the flow of investment capital is an important source of development capital for LDCs. The IMF calculates that during the 1990s, more than $1.3 trillion in net foreign direct and portfolio investment flowed into the LDCs to bolster their economic development. It is also the case that MNC–directed investments provide EDCs with a wide variety of economic benefits. Jobs are one example. Foreign-owned MNCs employ 4.9 million people in the United States, or about 4 percent of the U.S. workforce. They pay those workers over $200 billion a year and contribute tens of billions of dollars in U.S. federal, state, and local taxes. At least some of these jobs would not have existed without foreign investment.

World Cooperation A fifth, and this time political, argument claims that free economic interchange promotes world cooperation. *Functionalism* argues that cooperating in certain specific functions, such as trade, can lead to cooperation in more political areas. If countries can trade together in peace, the interactions will bring greater contact and understanding. Cooperation will then become the rule rather than the exception, and this, it is thought, will lead to political cooperation and interaction. The move toward the political integration of Europe, which began with economic cooperation, is the most frequently cited example.

By a similar logic, supporters of free economic interchange also contend that the flow of investment capital around the world through MNCs promotes transnational cooperation and additionally serves the function of bringing people together through regular contact, cooperation, familiarity, and friendship.

Conflict Inhibition A sixth, and again political, argument for free economic interchange is that it restrains conflict by promoting interdependence, which makes fighting more difficult and more unlikely (Mott, 1997). In the words of one study, "Higher levels of economically important trade... are associated with lower incidences of militarized interstate disputes and war" (Oneal & Russett, 1997:288). The trade-peace link is based on several factors. One is that if countries become highly dependent on each other for vital resources and products, then the countries' interdependence would dissuade or even prevent them from fighting. If oil and iron are necessary to fight, and if Country A supplies Country B's oil, and B supplies A's iron, then they are too enmeshed to go to war. Moreover, trade brings harmonious economic relations, which extend into equally harmonious political relations.

Much the same case is made for international investment as a restraint on conflict. Arguably, the more we own of each other, the more self-damaging it is to engage in economic or other sorts of aggression. Americans have long grumbled about the trade deficit with Japan, and there have been occasional calls to retaliate strongly against alleged unfair Japanese economic practices. Any chance of the United States acting on such impulses, however, is inhibited by the nearly $200 billion in foreign direct and portfolio investment that the Americans and Japanese have each invested in the other's country. Whatever the cause and whatever the outcome, both sides would suffer cataclysmic economic damage. As the somewhat grim joke goes, if the Japanese were ever again to bomb Pearl Harbor, they would be blowing up their own property.

In reality, a very high level of specialization and integration would be required to make this idea work perfectly. Moreover, the relationship between political behavior and trade relations is complex. Indeed, dependency can cause conflict in some cases. One study has even found that while "low to moderate degrees of interdependence reduce the likelihood of... disputes" between two countries, "extensive economic linkages increase the probability of militarized disputes" (Barbieri, 1996:29). This may be because dependence also creates vulnerability. The United States repeatedly threatened military action to protect oil supplies from the Persian Gulf, and in 1991 it went to war there to protect its interests.

Promoting Democracy

A seventh, and once more political, argument advanced by some advocates of economic liberalization is that the openness required for free economic exchange promotes democracy. During the past few years, such NICs as South Korea, Taiwan, and Mexico have had their first truly democratic elections either ever or in many decades. The collapse of the repressive regime of President Suharto in Indonesia in 1998 and the country's first democratic elections in 1999 were, in the view of some observers, a result of the country's exposure to the liberalizing dictates of free trade and capital movements. Suharto had ruled as a despot for 30 years; in 2000 he was ordered to stand trial for looting his country's economy. In short, a South Korean political scientist explains, "Corrupt, authoritarian governments cannot adjust to the demands of the new globalized world, where you have to have a more transparent, competitive, and rational economic structure."[21]

The Case against Free Economic Interchange

There are also several political and economic arguments for economic nationalism. Some of these involve trade or some other single aspect of international economic exchange; other arguments are more general (Greider, 1997).

Protecting the Domestic Economy The need for economic barriers to protect threatened domestic industries and workers from foreign competition is a favorite theme of domestic interest groups and politicians (Milner & Rosendorff, 1997). "I'm not a free trader," a U.S. secretary of commerce once confessed. "The goal," he said, "is to nurture American workers and industry. It is not to adhere to some kind of strict ideology."[22] An associated argument seeks protection for new or still small, so-called infant industries. This is an especially common contention in LDCs trying to industrialize, but it is also heard worldwide. Many economists give the idea of such protection some credibility but argue that supposedly temporary protection too often becomes permanent.

Opponents of the free flow of investment capital also argue that the positive impact of creation or preservation of jobs by the inflow of investment is offset by the loss of jobs when MNCs move operations to another country or when MNCs create new jobs in another country rather than in their own home country. American MNCs, for example, employ about 500,000 more workers in other countries than foreign MNCs employ American workers in the United States. Furthermore, these opponents say, forcing well-paid workers in the United States and elsewhere to compete with poorly paid workers in LDCs depresses the wages and living conditions in EDCs. As a general statement the statistics show that this is not the case, but some types of workers, such as those in manufacturing that directly competes with foreign sources, are especially hard hit. The U.S. apparel industry, for one, has been devastated. The U.S. government estimates that from 1983 to 2005, the number of textile and garment workers will decline from 1.9 million to 1.3 million. For the regions in the U.S. south, where these plants are concentrated, the consequences are especially serious.

Lost jobs and wages must also be measured in terms of the ripple effect that multiplies each dollar several times. A worker without a job cannot buy from the local merchant, who in turn cannot buy from the building contractor, who in turn cannot buy from the department store, and so on, rippling out through the economy. Displaced workers also collect unemployment benefits and may even wind up on public assistance programs. These costs are substantial, and although some economists find that they are less than the cost of protecting jobs, the economic costs of unemployment diminish the gains derived from free trade. Finally, there is the psychological damage from being laid off and from other forms of economic dislocation that cannot be measured in dollars and cents.

Diversification Another economic nationalist argument holds that economic diversification should be encouraged. Specialization, it is said, will make a country too dependent on a few resources or products. If demand for those products falls, then economic catastrophe will result. In reality, no modern, complex economy will become that specialized, but the argument does have a simplistic appeal.

Compensating for Existing Distortions Yet another economic nationalist argument is that real-world trade distortions exist that are unaccounted for by pure economic theory. When the oil-producing countries set prices, authoritarian governments control exports and imports (state trading), protectionist countries erect NTBs, and governments subsidize producers of export items or items that compete with imports, then, the argument goes, nice-guy free-traders will finish last.

Free trade advocates reply that the answer to such distortions is to correct them rather than to retaliate. There has been, for example, progress made through negotiations between the United States and Japan to remedy the informal barriers in Japan that Americans have long complained about. Still, many existing distortions (such as consumer attitudes) are difficult to remedy by governmental action. It is also fatuous to imagine that countries will not control trade at least to some degree for economic, strategic, or domestic political reasons. Therefore, many argue that it is prudent to continue to compensate for existing distortions and that it is imprudent to take too far a lead in free trade and suffer negative consequences while others hold back.

Social, Economic, and Environmental Protection The chairman of Dow Chemical Company once confessed, "I have long dreamed of buying an island owned by no nation and establishing the world headquarters of the Dow company on... such an island, beholden to no nation or society" (Gruenberg, 1996:339). Critics of MNCs claim that such statements confirm their suspicions that these global enterprises use their ability to move operations around the globe to undercut protections relating to child labor, minimum wages, employment benefits, the ability of workers to organize, and many other socioeconomic standards (Rodrik, 1998). In the estimate of one analyst, "National governments have lost much of their power to direct their own economies because of the power of capital to pick up and leave." The result of the "quantum leap in the ability of transnational corporations to relocate their facilities around the world," he continues, is to make "all workers, communities and countries competitors for these corporations' favor." This competition, he worries, has set off "a 'race to the bottom' in which wages and social and environment conditions tend to fall to the level of the most desperate" (Brecher, 1993:685).

Critics of globalization also charge that, among other evils, the race to the bottom will mean gutting desirable social programs. Europe has built an extensive social welfare support system through government programs and mandates on industries (such as health insurance for workers, paid vacations, and other benefits). Such programs and benefits are costly, however, and European economies are struggling to meet them while also keeping the price of their products low enough to be competitive in the world markets or even at home compared to imported goods and services.

National Sovereignty One of the fastest-growing sources of sentiment against free economic interchange is the realization of many people that the process is eroding their country's

BOLIGAN
EL UNIVERSAL
Mexico City
MEXICO

CARTOONISTS & WRITERS SYNDICATE http://CartoonWeb.com

GLOBALIZATION

Many Americans are alarmed by the impacts of globalization on the U.S. ability to control its economy, environment, and, in general, to exercise sovereignty. As represented by this editorial cartoon from the Mexico City newspaper *El Universal*, the plunge into globalization for smaller countries is even more worrisome.

national sovereignty. Many people are shocked to find that sometimes their country's laws and regulations must give way when they clash with rules of the WTO or some other international organization or agreement.

A closely related phenomenon involves the fear that foreign investors will gain control of your country's economy and will be able to influence your political processes and your culture (Bartlett & Seleny, 1998). In the 1960s U.S. investment capital seemed ready to engulf other countries' economies; Jean-Jacques Servan-Schreiber's best-seller, *The American Challenge* (1968), called on Europeans to resist foreign domination. Then, in the second half of the 1980s, when the value of the dollar plunged, the tide of foreign investment reversed, and the United States was seemingly flooded with foreign investors. During the period 1987–1990, foreigners invested $124 billion more in U.S. assets than Americans invested in foreign assets. Foreign investors acquired quintessential American brand names. The British controlled Capitol Records; Canadians ran Roy Rogers; the Germans directed Alka-Seltzer. Cries rang out that the British, among others, were coming. One member of Congress fretted that "for the first time since the Revolution, Americans are being subjected to decisions and dictates from abroad."[23] Japanese investment was a particular source of anxiety. Japanese FDI soared by over 400 percent between 1985 and 1990 and included the purchase of Columbia Pictures, Rockefeller Center, 7–11 Stores, and many other seemingly all-American businesses.

Then, in the ceaseless ebb and flow of international finance, the tide turned again. Beginning in 1991, changes in the global economy resulted in a flood tide of American direct investment (FDI) abroad once again outpacing FDI coming into the United States. During the years 1991–1996, the net total outflow was $128 billion. A sort of slack tide occurred in 1996 with the net inflows and outflows even at $109 billion each, followed by a new ebb tide, with more FDI being invested in the United States than being invested abroad by Americans.

The ebb and flow of FDI and the fears occasioned by foreign ownership have to be put in some perspective. For a country as large as the United States, the economy is so huge that foreign investment is still a minor aspect of the overall economic enterprise. Total foreign investment is just .02 percent (two one-hundredths) of the estimated $24 quadrillion worth of privately held tangible U.S. assets. Also, foreign investment is spread broadly among many countries. In 1998, the British were the largest direct investors in the United States with $151 billion in assets, and the Japanese were second with $132 billion in FDI. All totaled, though, there were 27 countries with $1 billion or more FDI in the United States. With such diversity, control by any outside country is impossible. It must also be remembered that Americans control more of other people's assets than others hold in U.S. assets. The $796 billion in FDI controlled by Americans in 1996 was 26 percent more than the $630 billion in U.S. direct investment assets owned by foreigners.

National Security A related political economic nationalist argument involves national defense. The contention is somewhat the reverse of the "conflict inhibition," pro–free trade argument made earlier. Protectionists stress that the country must not become so dependent on foreign sources that it will be unable to defend itself. In recent years, the U.S. government has acted to protect industries ranging from specialty steels to basic textiles, partly in response to warnings that the country was losing its ability to produce weapons systems and uniforms.

Also under the rubric of national security, there is the issue of what can be called strategic trade. The question is how far a country should go in restricting trade and other economic interchanges with countries that are or may become hostile. Currently, the primary focus of the strategic trade debate is on **dual-use technology** that has peaceful uses but also has military applications. Trying to maintain the U.S. lead in the $27 billion commercial satellite industry, the Clinton administration authorized sales to

China for what Beijing and Washington claimed were civilian use. Critics charged that the technology could be and probably was being diverted in part to China's military. The issue well illustrates the tug of selling billions of dollars of aircraft and other equipment abroad versus the pull of supplying a less than friendly country with the capacity to increase the sophistication of its military equipment. "The U.S. faces excruciating trade-offs," observed one former ranking U.S. trade official. "On the one hand, we have overwhelming commercial goals. On the other, we have to be careful about transferring technology, first because there could be unintended military consequences, and secondly because we could be transferring our competitiveness."[24]

Policy Tool A seventh economic nationalist argument maintains that trade is a powerful political tool that can be used to further a country's interests. The extension or withdrawal of trade and other economic benefits also has an important—albeit hard-to-measure—symbolic value. Clearly, economic tools can be used to promote a country's political goals and free economic interchange necessarily limits the availability of economic tools to pursue policy.

To return to the point with which we began this section, the clash between the forces that favor the advancement of free economic interchange and those that oppose it will be one of the most pivotal struggles in the years ahead. Secretary-General Kofi Annan is correct in his observation that while the world has moved toward ever greater globalism, "we have underestimated its fragility. The problem is this: The spread of markets far outpaces the ability of societies and their political systems to adjust to them let alone guide the course they take. History teaches us that such imbalances between the economic, social and political realms can never be sustained for very long."[25]

Economic nationalism, the traditional path in world politics, remains the prevailing approach to the global economy. But there has also been great change. The countries of the world have adopted a vast array of policies, have concluded numerous economic agreements, and have created many international organizations to promote and facilitate free economic interchange. These policies, agreements, and organizations all represent an alternative approach to the international political economy, and it is to this newer path that we will turn our attention in the next chapter.

 ## CHAPTER SUMMARY

1. Economics and politics are closely intertwined aspects of international relations. Each is a part of and affects the other. This interrelationship has become even more important in recent history. Economics has become more important internationally because of dramatically increased trade levels, ever-tightening economic interdependence between countries, and the growing impact of international economics on domestic economics.

2. The stronger role played by international economics means that political relations between countries have increasingly been influenced by economic relations. Conversely, politics also significantly affects economic relations. Domestic political pressures are important determinants of tariff policies and other trade regulations. Trade can also be used as a diplomatic tool.

3. Economic strength is a key element of every country's overall power. Economic power is based on financial position, natural resources, industrial output, agricultural output, and international competitiveness.

4. Countries use their economic power through a mixture of positive incentives and negative sanctions. While each approach is sometimes successful, both incentives and, particularly, sanctions are difficult to apply successfully and have numerous drawbacks.

5. The economies of the North are prosperous compared to those of the South. With the end of the cold war and with a variety of changing economic circumstances, however, the situation has changed greatly. The EDCs are experiencing a number of economic difficulties, including the pressure of entering into a period of postindustrial economy, and economic tensions among them have increased.

6. The economies of the South are relatively weak compared to those of the North. Also, in the South there is great disparity in wealth among and within countries. A few NICs have expanding and modernizing economies. There is also, in most LDCs, a small wealthy class of people and a much larger class of impoverished people.

7. The LDCs need hard currency capital to buy the goods and services that will allow them to develop their economies. There are four basic sources of hard currency: loans, foreign investment, trade, and foreign aid. There are, however, problems with each of these sources.

8. Loans are unsatisfactory because of high repayment costs. The debt crisis has eased, but LDC debt is growing once again and could threaten the global financial community.

9. Investment capital has grown in amount and importance in recent years. Still, investment capital flows mostly into just a few LDCs.

10. The catch-22 of trade is that the primary products that LDCs mainly produce do not earn them enough capital to found industries to produce manufactured goods that would earn more money.

11. Foreign aid is minor compared with world needs and is often given on the basis of political expediency rather than economic necessity.

12. In recent years, the countries of the South have begun to make greater demands for economic equity to press the North to join in establishing a New International Economic Order.

13. There are a variety of barriers to the unimpeded international movement of trade and capital. These include such barriers as tariffs, nontariff barriers, and licensing requirements.

14. There are significant arguments on both sides of the question of whether or not to continue to expand free international economic interchange. Advocates of doing so contend that it results in greater efficiency and lower costs and that international commerce promotes world cooperation and inhibits conflict. Opponents argue that economic barriers are needed to protect domestic industry, that overreliance on other countries is dangerous for national security reasons, and that trade can be a valuable policy tool.

CHAPTER 16

INTERNATIONAL ECONOMIC COOPERATION: THE ALTERNATIVE ROAD

The gods sent not
Corn for the rich men only.

Shakespeare, *Coriolanus*

Happy are they that can hear their detractions, and can put them to mending.
Shakespeare, *Much Ado About Nothing*

If a house be divided against itself, that house cannot stand.

Mark 3:25

The Lord so constituted everybody that no matter what color you are you require
the same amount of nourishment.

Will Rogers, *The Autobiography of Will Rogers*

CHAPTER OBJECTIVES

After completing this chapter, you should be able to:

- Explain why economic cooperation and integration will prove to be pivotal determinants of future international relations.
- Describe the specialized cooperative efforts currently at work on the world stage.
- List and describe the most significant development agencies involved in granting loans and aid to less developed countries.
- Discuss the reasons leading to growing international monetary cooperation, giving special attention to the International Monetary Fund.
- Evaluate how the European Union exemplifies efforts at international or regional economic integration.
- Trace the evolution of the North American Free Trade Agreement and assess its effects on the region and the world.
- Describe efforts at regionalism that have emerged at least partly in response to the economic integration occurring in Europe and North America.

This chapter is the last one of three that examine international political economy. The first of the trio laid out the global economic road map. The second took up economic nationalism, which is characterized by self-interested economic competition among and between the states of the North and of the South. Economic nationalism persists and, in some aspects, is on the rise. It may even eventually provide prosperity to all states and peoples. Yet there is a gnawing doubt about the harvest that we reap from this economic strategy. There are numerous scholars, political leaders, and others who maintain that economic nationalism underlies many of the current economic difficulties and tensions discussed in chapters 14 and 15. These critics favor economic internationalism. As we have noted, however, that approach faces its own challenges and detractors.

These sharp disagreements between economic nationalists and internationalists are one aspect of the overarching reality that the world is at the juncture of two political roads that diverge. One path is national self-interest, the other is international cooperation. Whatever may come, it is clear that the degree to which countries can or cannot cooperate economically, or even integrate their economies, is going to be a pivotal determinant of future international relations. This is true whether the issue is relations among the economic titans of the developed North, the struggle of the poorer countries of the South to improve their lot, or the willingness of the North to help the South develop. Having reviewed the traditional road of economic nationalism in the last chapter, this chapter will assess economic internationalism and the cooperative international economic policies and organizations that this school of thought favors.

THE ORIGINS OF ECONOMIC COOPERATION

While economic nationalism has long been the prevailing reality, it is also true that economic cooperation and regulation have become increasingly commonplace, albeit still limited, elements of national and international economics. The liberal idea of creating a global economy based on free economic interchange and interdependence dates back over two centuries to Adam Smith, who wrote *The Wealth of Nations* (1776), and the French capitalist philosophers called *les Économistes*. Their views also found adherents on the other side of the Atlantic, such as Benjamin Franklin, who wrote in "Thoughts on Commercial Subjects" (1780) that "no nation was ever ruined by trade." This view was slow to take hold, though, and did not begin to shape international economic relations to any great extent until the 1930s and 1940s. A combination of the strife that had marked the twentieth century to that point and the Great Depression that was gripping the world in the 1930s led an increasing number of leaders to agree with the view of the longest-serving U.S. secretary of state (1933–1944), Cordell Hull, that "international commerce is not only calculated to aid materially in the restoration of prosperity everywhere, but it is the greatest civilizer and peacemaker in the experience of the human race" (Paterson, Clifford, & Hagan, 2000:121).

While the tensions that led to World War II kept international economic reform on the political back burner for a decade, the war added to the impetus to change the structure and course of world politics. With the United States leading the anti-Axis alliance and then the anticommunist West, the capitalist EDCs moved during the years 1943–1948 to create the foundation for a new international economic order. The EDCs reached several accords, such as the General Agreement on Tariffs and Trade (GATT), to reduce national economic barriers. The EDCs also created a number of global and regional intergovernmental organizations (IGOs) to handle a range of economic interactions across national boundaries. The most prominent of these IGOs are the World

Bank, the International Monetary Fund (IMF), and the United Nations, with its numerous economic agencies and responsibilities.

Thus began the current era of enhanced global and regional economic cooperation. Trade and the flow of international capital grew rapidly. These successes and the need to further regulate the increased economic interchanges led to yet more agreements and IGOs dedicated to still further reductions of national economic barriers. The European Union (EU), the World Trade Organization (WTO), and the North American Free Trade Agreement (NAFTA) are just three of the more recent IGOs or treaties that facilitate and further the free flow of goods, services, and capital. We will examine them by first taking up global efforts, then by turning to regional ones.

🌐 GLOBAL ECONOMIC COOPERATION

The effort to create global economic cooperation led to two types of IGOs. One type addresses a wide range of economic and, sometimes, other issues. The UN is the best example. The second type is specialized and focuses on just one aspect of international economics. The WTO, which concentrates on the trade of goods and services, is one such specialized economic IGO.

GENERAL ECONOMIC COOPERATION: THE UN

The UN serves as a global umbrella organization for numerous agencies and programs that deal with economic issues through the UN General Assembly (UNGA), the United Nations Economic and Social Council (UNESCO), and other UN divisions and associated agencies. The economic focus of the UN can be roughly divided into two categories: global economic regulation and the economic development of the South.

The UN and Global Economic Regulation

The UN is involved in a number of areas related to global economic cooperation. The regulation of transnational (or multinational) corporations (TNCs/MNCs) is one such area. The need to regulate business first became apparent at the national level. As a result, the sometimes predatory practices of capitalist corporations have been partially restrained by domestic laws enacted over the past century or so. In the United States, for instance, the Progressive Era of the late 1800s and early 1900s led to efforts to rein in the so-called robber barons of big business through the passage of such legislation as the Sherman Antitrust Act (1890) and the establishment of such agencies as the Federal Trade Commission (1914).

Now, some people worry that internationalization has allowed business to escape regulation. These critics, therefore, favor creating global regulations and oversight ("watchdog") agencies similar to those in most EDCs. "Are we really going to let the world become a global market without any laws except those of the jungle?" President François Mitterrand of France once asked a UN–sponsored economic conference. "Should we leave the world's destiny in the hands of those speculators who in a few hours can bring to nothing the work of millions of men and women?"[1] In response to such concerns, the UN's Center for Transnational Corporations was established as part of the effort to create global standards and regulations to limit the inherently self-serving practices of capitalist corporations.

Creating global labor standards is a related area of economic regulation. At the national level, for example, it was during the American Progressive Era that workers began to organize widely into unions. The American Federation of Labor, for one, was established in 1886. The U.S. government also began to regulate labor through such statutes as the Federal Child Labor Law (1916) and to create agencies such as the

This young girl in the slums of Khulna, Bangladesh, making matchboxes to sell, evokes images of *My Fair Lady*. In the 1964 movie, a young street vendor in London, Eliza Doolittle (played by Audrey Hepburn), is rescued from her desperate poverty and transformed into a refined belle of the ball by phonetics expert Professor Henry Higgins (Rex Harrison). Alas, it is extremely unlikely that there will be a story-book ending for this Bengali girl or for the millions of children who, like her, labor daily to eke out a meager existence instead of going to school.

Department of Labor (1913) to promote the welfare of workers. Similarly, the UN is trying to make progress on labor conditions at the international level through such affiliated specialized agencies as the United Nations Children's Fund (UNICEF) and the International Labor Organization (ILO).

Child labor is one of the principal current concerns of the ILO. Most EDCs protect children by setting strict standards on when and under what conditions they may be employed and by banning the manufacture, transportation, or sale of goods produced by child labor. Unfortunately, many LDCs either do not have such laws or they are ineffective. Therefore goods produced by child workers, often under horrible conditions, are sold through international trade and circulate with impunity even in those importing countries where child labor is illegal. The shirt on your back, the sneakers on your feet, the toys you give children for holidays and birthdays may have been produced by children elsewhere who get no toys, who have no shoes, and whose clothes are in tatters.

The ILO estimates that 13 percent (73 million) of the world's children between the ages of 10 and 13 go to work, not to school. Furthermore, "this is only part of the picture," reports an ILO official, because "no reliable figures" exist on the "significant" numbers of child workers under 10 or the even larger number of 14- and 15-year-olds who must work. "If all of these could be counted and if proper account were taken of the domestic work performed full-time by girls," says the official, "the total number of child workers around the world today might well be in the hundreds of millions."[2]

There were several early efforts, including the Minimum Age Convention (1973), to ease the worst abuses of child labor. It is only in the past few years, however, that the world community has turned more seriously to addressing the issue. For example, an ILO–sponsored international conference meeting in 1999 led to an agreement known as the Worst Forms of Child Labour Convention. The convention bars countries from inflicting on children any form of compulsory labor similar to slavery (including being forced to become a child soldier), using children for illicit activities (prostitution, pornography, drug trafficking), and having children do work that is inherently dangerous. As of late 2000, the treaty had been ratified by 35 countries and was well on its way to becoming part of international law.

The UN and the Economic Development of the South

The second focus of UN economic activity has been on the economic development of the LDCs. One role that the UN plays is providing a forum where world leaders from North and South occasionally come together. During the Millennium Summit sponsored by the UN in September 2000, one lunch table included Nigeria's president, Olusegun Obasanjo, U.S. president Bill Clinton, UN secretary-general Kofi Annan, China's president Jiang Zemin, British prime minister Tony Blair, and several other leaders. "The wishes of the developing world are simple," President Obasanjo told President Clinton and Prime Minister Blair. "We are all living in the same house, whether you are developed or not developed.... [But some of us] are living in superluxurious rooms; others are living in something not better than an unkempt kitchen where pipes are leaking and where there is no toilet. We [in the South] are saying," Obasanjo continued, "Look,... let [those] living in the superluxurious rooms pay a bit of attention to those who are living where the pipes are leaking, or we'll all be badly affected. That's the message."[3]

The UN also has numerous programs to promote development. Many of the UN's programs began during the mid-1960s in response to the decolonization of much of the South and the needs and demands of the new countries. The UN's attempts to foster international cooperation to advance the economic fortunes of the LDCs also reflect the organization's mission, as stated in the preamble to the UN Charter, "to employ international machinery for the promotion of the economic and social advancements of all people." This statement of values was high-flown rhetoric in 1945 and mostly still is. There is, however, a substantial and growing number of people in the North and South who contend that aiding the South to develop is not just a matter of humanitarianism.

MAP
Human Development
Index, p. 496

Factors Urging Development Assistance to the South   Simple humanitarian compassion is one reason to assist the South. There are a number of pragmatic concerns that motivate the UN to try to help the LDCs develop economically. *Decreased international violence* is one way that the North will benefit from increased prosperity in the South, according to aid advocates. This view contends that the poor are becoming increasingly hostile toward the wealthy. In chapter 15 we noted that modern communications have heightened the South's sense of relative deprivation—the awareness of a deprived person (group, country) of the gap between his or her circumstances and the relatively better position of others. Research shows that seeing another's prosperity and knowing that there are alternatives to your own impoverished condition cause frustration and a sense of being cheated that often lead to resentment and sometimes to violence. President Nelson Mandela once warned that Africans and others among the world's poor "wonder why it should be that poverty still prevails [over] the greater part of the globe," and are angry that "many in positions of power and privilege pursue cold-hearted philosophies which terrifyingly proclaim, 'I am not my brother's keeper.'"[4]

Increased economic prosperity for the EDCs is another benefit that many analysts believe will result from the betterment of the LDCs. This view maintains that it is in the North's long-term economic interest to aid the South's development. After World War II, the United States launched the Marshall Plan, which gave billions of dollars to Europe. One motivation was the U.S. realization that it needed an economically revitalized Europe with which to trade and in which to invest. Europe recovered, and its growth helped drive the strong growth of the American economy. In the same way, according to many analysts, helping the South toward prosperity would require an immense investment by the North. In the long run, though, that investment would create a world in which many of the 1.3 billion Chinese could purchase Fords, more of India's 1 billion people could afford to travel in Boeing airplanes, and a majority of the 121 million Nigerians and 161 Brazilians could buy Dell personal computers. It is true that a developed South will compete economically with the North, but economic history demonstrates that increased production and competition bring more, better, and cheaper products that increase the standard of living for all.

The North: The Recalcitrant Rich   Whatever the logic of the pragmatic benefits of increasing LDC prosperity may seem, the North has been slow to respond to the development needs of the South. Traditional narrow self-interest has been strengthened recently by the rising global economic competition among, and economic uncertainty within, the EDCs. One indication of this trend, as we have noted, is that bilateral foreign economic aid–giving by the EDCs has dropped off both in real dollars and as a percentage of their productive wealth.

Efforts to bring the North and South together directly to marshal resources and coordinate programs have also shown very limited results. The initial UN–sponsored

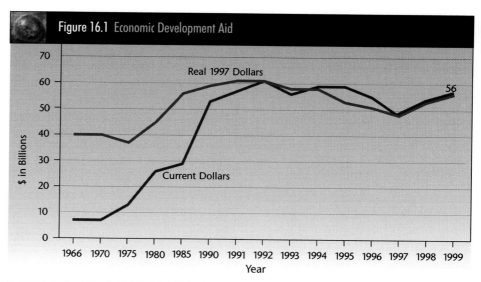

Figure 16.1 Economic Development Aid

For the years 1991 and 1992, the OECD included debt forgiven in its calculations. Therefore the aid flow reported in those years is higher than the actual flow of funds. Real dollars based on 1997.

Data source: OECD, DAC Web site at http://www.oecd.org/dac/htm/HLM2000stats.htm.

Somewhat different perspectives of economic aid are gained by using current and real (controlled for inflation) dollars. The aid flow in real dollars trended upward through the early 1990s, then dropped off for several years, before rising in 1998 and 1999. If a line were added to track the percentage of the EDCs' wealth sent to LDCs, it would show a steady downward trend.

meeting, which was held in 1981 at Cancún, Mexico, yielded little of financial substance. Subsequent global meetings, such as the 1992 conference on the environment in Rio de Janeiro, the 1994 conference on population in Cairo, and the 1995 conference on social development in Copenhagen, also have not moved the North to loosen its purse strings. For example, the last of the UN's planned global conferences of the 1990s, the 1996 World Food Summit in Rome, ended, according to one press report, "on familiar notes: a vague pledge to do better, sharp words from poor nations against rich ones,... and American reservations about the internationally recognized right to be fed." The conference set down a goal to reduce by half by the year 2015 the 840 million people who are malnourished, and it reaffirmed the standard that EDCs should contribute at least 0.7 percent of their GNPs to economic development. Typical of the reactions of the North to such goals and standards, the Clinton administration declared that the United States considered providing adequate nutrition for the world's poor as only "a goal or aspiration" that "does not give rise to any international obligations."[5] Indeed it is possible to argue that the recalcitrance of the rich is unrelenting. As Figure 16.1 demonstrates, economic aid has increased in current dollars, but its progress in real (deflated) dollars has increased only slowly, and suffered a sharp decline in the mid-1990s. Moreover, EDCs are becoming increasingly miserly in the percentage of their wealth that they devote to economic assistance. Just between 1993 and 1998, the percentage of their collective GNPs that the EDCs gave in aid dropped one-third from 0.33 percent to 0.22 percent.

UN Development Programs Given the South's immense development needs and the North's limited response, the UN has become a vital vehicle to provide information, to help obtain available funds, and to coordinate programs for the economic development of the LDCs.

The General Assembly, for example, created the **UN Development Programme (UNDP)** in 1965 to provide both technical assistance (such as planning) and development funds to LDCs. The UNDP's budget of just over $2 billion is obtained through voluntary contributions from the member-countries of the UN and its affiliated agencies. The UNDP especially focuses on grassroots economic development, such as promoting entrepreneurship, supporting the Development Fund for Women, and transferring technology and management skills from EDCs to LDCs.

At the more macro end of the economic spectrum, the **UN Industrial Development Organization (UNIDO)** promotes the growth of industry in LDCs. The suspicion of many in the South that the dependencia-minded North has little true interest in their development was heightened when, in 1967, the LDCs in the UNGA had to overcome considerable opposition by many EDCs in order to create UNIDO. The doubts harbored by the LDCs were inevitably deepened by announcements in the mid-1990s by Australia, Great Britain, and the United States that they were withdrawing from UNIDO. Each of these EDCs argued that its withdrawal was based on UNIDO's inefficiency, but the organization's director-general, Mauricio de Maria y Campos, undoubtedly voiced the view of many in the South when he argued that an "isolationist malaise as regards development assistance is becoming contagious at the multilateral level." This was especially troubling, he said, in light of the fact that "the fruits of globalization have not been equally distributed and poor countries are becoming increasingly marginalized."[6] Most other EDCs remained in UNIDO, and the British eventually decided not to quit the organization. Still, the departure of two important EDCs and the funds they contributed to UNIDO's budget does not bode well for the organization's future.

Another important UN organization, the **United Nations Conference on Trade and Development (UNCTAD)**, was founded in 1964 to address the economic concerns of the LDCs. There is an UNCTAD summit conference every four years, with the tenth and most recent conference held in Bangkok, Thailand, in 2000. The organization has been a primary vehicle for the formation and expression of LDC demands for a New International Economic Order (NIEO), as discussed in chapter 15. For example, at the UNCTAD's gathering in Thailand, the group concentrated on the theme that globalization could not just serve the interests of the EDCs. That view was captured in the report of UNCTAD's secretary-general, Rubens Ricupero. "It is not the amount and pace of international integration that counts, but its quality," he commented. "A world economic system that fails to offer poorer countries, and the poorer parts of the populations within them, adequate and realistic opportunities to raise their living standards will inevitably lose its legitimacy in much of the developing world," Ricupero warned. "And without this legitimacy, no world economic system can long endure."[7]

The report went on to focus on two areas: labor migration and intellectual property rights (especially patents) where the LDCs believe that the EDCs are playing something of a double game. The issue about labor reflects belief of the LDCs that workers, just like goods and services, should face decreasing international barriers. The discontent about patents is based on LDCs' belief that EDCs have adopted excessively long periods of patent protection for new medicines, technology, and other innovations the LDCs need desperately but cannot afford to pay for. The charge is that the EDCs want to profit from patents at the expense of the LDCs and also to use these patents to continue their neocolonial domination of the LDCs. As the UNCTAD secretary-general put it, the LDCs "have been pressured [by the EDCs] to liberalize trade, investment and financial flows. But that liberalizing zeal has been found wanting [in the EDCs] when it comes to labor mobility... [and] promoting unfettered access to knowledge."[8]

While UNCTAD itself includes virtually universal membership and addresses general issues of trade and LDC development, the organization spun off a closely associated bloc called the **Group of 77 (G-77)**, named after the LDCs that issued the Joint Declaration of the Seventy-Seven Countries at the end of the first UNCTAD conference. Since then the G-77 has expanded to include 133 members. In April 2000, the leaders of the G-77 countries gathered in Havana, Cuba, for the organization's first summit meeting since the initial one that founded it in 1964. Much like the UNCTAD meeting in Bangkok, the Havana summit stressed the need to narrow the economic gap between the few EDCs and the many LDCs. In particular, the meeting called for debt relief.

GENERAL ECONOMIC COOPERATION: OTHER IGOs AND PROCESSES

The UN is the best known of the IGOs promoting general economic cooperation, but it is not the only one. The **Organization for Economic Cooperation and Development (OECD)** is another such IGO. It was originally created by several European countries as the Organization for European Economic Cooperation in 1948 to coordinate the foreign aid that the United States extended to Europe under the Marshall Plan. In 1960 the member-countries agreed to ask the United States and Canada to join the organization, to change its name to OECD, and to reorient its mission to coordinating economic policy among the Western EDCs. This led to the subsequent admission of Japan and most other EDCs and, thus, to the OECD's becoming known as a "rich man's club." This has begun to change slightly. In 1994 Mexico became the first new country to be invited to join the OECD in 21 years. Mexico's admission came in light of its link to the United States and Canada under NAFTA. Since then, the Czech Republic, Hungary, Poland, and South Korea have also been admitted to the OECD, and the application of Slovakia for admission is being considered. Thus it is possible to argue that the OECD is once again changing, or at least expanding, its mission to also include the exchange of information and economic policy coordination among some newly industrializing countries (NICs) and **countries in transition (CITs)** that are moving from communism to capitalism.

If the OECD is something of an exclusive club of prosperous member-countries, the **Group of Eight (G-8)** is equivalent to the executive board. The G-8 does not have a formal connection to the OECD, but it does represent the pinnacle of economic power. The G-8 began in 1975 as the G-7, which included the seven most economically powerful Western countries (Canada, France, Germany, Great Britain, Italy, Japan, and the United States). The group's annual meeting in 1997 expanded membership for political matters to include Russia. The group officially became the Group of Eight (G-8) the following year. In some sense, however, the G-7 continues to exist because the original seven agreed they would meet as the G-7 without Russia on financial issues and with the Russian president as the G-8 on political issues. To avoid confusion, the groups will be referred to as the G-8 in all its activities.

Whatever the G-number is, the most important issue is the impact of the process. Many analysts conclude that the annual summits play a positive, if not always clear-cut role. As one scholar writes, the member-countries "do comply modestly with the decisions and consensus generated [at the annual economic summit meetings]. Compliance is particularly high in regard to agreements on international trade and energy." The analyst also points out that the meetings provide "an important occasion for busy leaders to discuss major, often complex international issues, and to develop the personal relations that help them" both to "respond in an effective fashion to sudden crises or shocks" and to "shape the international [economic] order more generally."[9] Also, the group takes up political and social issues. The 2000 meeting of the G-8 in Okinawa, for instance, stressed efforts to fight AIDS globally and to help LDCs address their low level of computerization.

There are other analysts who fault the G-8 for not achieving more concrete results and cite this as a reason why the meetings of the G-8, which were once major news stories, have more recently been far from front-page news. To return to the forefront, two scholars observe, "the group needs to show that its initiatives are not spinning into oblivion, leaving behind only lengthy communiqués."[10]

TRADE COOPERATION: GATT AND THE WTO

While the UN addresses the broad range of global economic issues, there are a number of IGOs that focus on one or another specific area of economic interchange. One of the most prominent of these specialized economic IGOs on the global level is the **General Agreement on Tariffs and Trade (GATT)**. It was founded in 1947 to promote free trade. For most of its existence, the name GATT was the source of considerable confusion because it was both the name of a treaty and the name of the organization headquartered in Geneva, Switzerland. That confusion has now ended. The GATT treaty was amended to create the **World Trade Organization**, which superseded the GATT organization as of January 1, 1995. Therefore, references to the organization (even before 1995) will use WTO; the treaty will be referred to as GATT. Whatever its name, the organization's initial membership of 23 countries has expanded to 136 members. Several other admission negotiations have been concluded that will bring the total membership to at least 140 by 2001, and more than two dozen additional governments are seeking membership. The trade of the full members accounts for more than 85 percent of all world trade. GATT has played an important role in promoting the meteoric expansion of international trade. The organization has sponsored a series of trade negotiations that have greatly reduced tariffs and nontariff barriers (NTBs), such as import quotas.

The Latest Revisions of GATT: The Uruguay Round

The eighth, and most recent round of negotiations to revise GATT in order to further reduce trade barriers was convened in Punta del Este, Uruguay, in 1986. The **Uruguay Round** proved to be the most difficult in GATT history. When, in April 1994, the members of GATT finally gathered in Marrakech, Morocco, to sign an agreement, they broke into thunderous applause. The head of GATT, Peter Sutherland of Ireland, gleefully admitted that he was "tempted" to do "an Irish jig on the table."[11] From Washington, President Clinton hailed the pact as promoting a "vision of economic renewal" for the United States and the rest of the world.[12]

Opposition to the Uruguay Round Revisions Not everyone shared Clinton's rosy view of the agreement. Some businesses that would face increased international competition were unhappy. "I consider this [GATT] to be just a complete sellout of this [the U.S. textile] industry," objected the president of Fruit of the Loom.[13] Other critics focused on the loss of sovereignty that abiding by the treaty necessarily imposes on all signatories. These issues created an odd alliance between the more conservative and liberal wings of American politics. From the right, American commentator (and later Reform Party presidential candidate in 2000) Patrick J. Buchanan condemned the GATT agreement as "a wholesale surrender of American sovereignty and states' rights."[14] From the left, Ralph Nader, Green Party presidential candidate in 2000, charged that, "approval of these [GATT] agreements... makes every government increasingly hostage to an unaccountable system of transnational governance designed to increase corporate profit, often with complete disregard for social and ecological consequences."[15]

These concerns have been confirmed, in the view of some, by such events as the WTO ruling in 1998 that a U.S. law banning shrimp imports from countries whose shrimp nets fail to protect sea turtles violates GATT rules. "This is the clearest slap at environmental protection to come out of the WTO to date," protested the head of one environmental group.[16] It should be noted that not all WTO rulings have dismayed environmentalists. They were buoyed, for example, by a WTO decision in July 2000 to uphold France's ban for health reasons on the importation of asbestos from Canada.

Americans were not the only ones up in arms over the new GATT. Some 200,000 Indian leftists demonstrated in New Delhi, calling on their government to reject GATT lest India's infant industries be bought up or driven out of business by predatory foreign

Did You Know That:
Symbolic of the complexity of modern trade negotiations, the 1994 GATT revision is some 26,000 pages long and weighs 385 pounds.

MNCs. Belgian farmers burned a tractor in front of EU headquarters in Brussels to demonstrate their fear that the livelihood of European farmers is threatened by GATT. South Korean and Japanese rice farmers protested over the elimination of protection for their product.

In the end, the objection from the right and left of the American political spectrum, from India, and from elsewhere all went for naught. The Uruguay Round revisions of GATT were signed and subsequently ratified by most of the world's countries. The new agreement did two important things. The first was to further reduce economic barriers among a vast majority of the world's countries. The second was to establish the World Trade Organization.

Provisions of the New GATT Agreement. The GATT revisions related to reducing economic barriers are complex. They address the nature and trade details of some 10,000 products and myriad businesses and other commercial interchanges. There are, for example, four paragraphs on the importation of "soft-ripened cow's milk cheese" and how to distinguish that kind of cheese from other kinds of cheese.

What is important, though, is that, overall, the countries that signed the Uruguay Round document agreed to reduce their tariffs over a 10-year period by an average of one-third. According to U.S. estimates, these cuts will reduce tariffs globally by $744 billion over 10 years. Agricultural tariffs were included in GATT for the first time, and the agreement also further reduced or barred many NTBs. Japan will have to end its ban on rice imports, for example; the United States will have to end its import quotas on peanuts, dairy products, sugar, textiles, and apparel. The signatories also agreed to institute within five years effective protection of intellectual property, such as patents, copyrights, trade secrets, and trademarks.

The Structure and Role of the WTO

To deal with the complexities of GATT and to deal with the disputes that will inevitably arise, the Uruguay Round also created the WTO. It is headquartered in Geneva, Switzerland, and currently headed by Director-General Mike Moore, a former prime minister and trade minister of New Zealand.

The WTO has the power to enforce the provisions of GATT and to assess trade penalties against countries that violate the accord. While any country can withdraw from the WTO by giving six months' notice, that country would suffer significant economic perils because its products would no longer be subject to the reciprocal low tariffs and other advantages WTO members accord one another. When one country charges another with a trade violation, a three-judge panel under the WTO hears the complaints. If the panel finds a violation, the WTO may impose sanctions on the offending country. Each country will have one vote in the WTO, and sanctions may be imposed by a two-thirds vote. This means, among other things, that domestic laws may be disallowed by the WTO if they are found to be de facto trade barriers.

Despite grumbling by critics about the loss of sovereignty, the WTO judicial process has been busy. From 1995 through January 2000, the WTO handled 203 cases. The United States was the country most frequently involved in the process. It has brought more than 50 complaints to the WTO and has had to answer more than 25 complaints by other countries. Most of these issues are settled "out of court," but of the cases actually decided by the WTO, the United States prevailed more often than it lost. Some, such as the ruling in 2000 that overturned South Korean restrictions on imported U.S. beef cheered interested Americans. Others, such as a WTO ruling dismissing the U.S. complaint that Japan was discriminating against Kodak film, dismayed interested Americans.

The Future of GATT and the WTO

Although the WTO has gotten off to a promising start, its future is not clear. One issue is what will happen if one or more member-countries, especially powerful ones, refuse to abide by the WTO rules and reject the findings of the judicial process. So far, when Washington and the EU have lost a case, they have quietly given way. What remains to be seen, however, is the reaction when a highly sensitive case is brought before the WTO. The United States and the EU barely avoided one such confrontation. Attempts by the United States to punish foreign companies that do business with Cuba, Iran, Libya, and some other countries sparked considerable anger in many countries, and in 1996 the European Union announced it would challenge the legality of these sanctions by bringing the matter before the WTO. When in 1997 the WTO moved to appoint a panel of judges to hear the case, a senior U.S. official said the WTO "has no competence to proceed" and declared, "We will not show up" at the hearing.[17] What could have been a WTO–destroying confrontation was avoided when, in 1998, the EU withdrew its complaint on the tacit understanding that Washington would suspend sanctions while seeking to negotiate a resolution of the dispute with Europe.

A second and related issue for the WTO involves globalization, which the WTO epitomizes, and the strengthening movement against it. When the WTO held its annual summit meeting in Seattle, Washington, in December 1999, President Clinton applauded the progress achieved through GATT and the WTO, but he also cautioned the conclave that, "for 50 years, trade decisions [have been] largely the province of trade ministers, heads of government and business interests. But now, what all those people in the street tell us is that they would also like to be heard, and they're not so sure that this deal is working for them."[18] The people in the streets that Clinton mentioned were the throngs of protesters who had gathered outside the convention center where he was speaking. Their views were captured in two protest placards. One asked, "When Did We Elect the WTO?" The other urged, "Resist Corporate Tyranny. Ban the WTO. The People Have Spoken."[19]

A third issue that the WTO must deal with is the future of reform. The meeting in Seattle launched what may come to be known as the Seattle Round of GATT revisions. Some outstanding economic issues remain outside of the GATT rules because negotiators in the Uruguay Round put them aside when they failed to reach an agreement. Because of its fear of becoming culturally Americanized, Europe, especially France, would not agree to ending limits on the distribution of movies, music, or other cultural products. Fear of losing financial control left many countries, both North and South, opposed to opening completely their insurance, banking, and brokerage service industries. National regulation and protection of the shipping, steel, and telecommunications industries were also largely exempted from GATT provisions. Beyond these specifics, whatever agreements are reached will have to take into account the feelings of those countries, groups, and individuals who believe they are being disadvantaged by globalization in general and GATT and the WTO in particular. Moreover, the WTO will have to balance its traditional focus on free economic interchange with such issues as labor rights, environmental protection, and cultural preservation.

A fourth unresolved issue for GATT involves China's adherence to the treaty and its possible membership in the WTO. China sought membership under the rules that govern LDCs. These rules give them some advantages, such as allowing them to keep tariffs somewhat higher or somewhat longer to protect infant industries from foreign competition. The United States and the European Union had blocked China's entry into the WTO on the grounds that China's total industrial output is so large that it should not be accorded the extra protections. The negotiations with China were long and difficult, but agreements between Beijing and both Washington and Brussels (the seat of the EU's administration) were concluded in 2000. Although a number of issues remain, it is probable that China will become a member of the WTO in 2001 or 2002.

There is a growing debate over whether globalization is a positive or negative trend. The World Trade Organization is one prominent symbol of globalization, and this editorial cartoon negatively portrays those who protested and, in some cases, rioted against globalization during the WTO meeting in Seattle, Washington, in December 1999. To this political cartoonist, the protesters are like Ebenezer Scrooge from Charles Dickens's *Christmas Carol* (1843), who snorted, "Bah, humbug," at the thought of a beneficent Christmas spirit.

This political cartoon takes the opposite view from the one to your left. Here we see global business, vaguely resembling the World Wrestling Federation's 250-pound bad guy Stone Cold Steve Austin, mauling a hapless victim, in this case workers' rights. Just like the WWF matches, the referee stands by passively while flagrant fouls are committed. The turtle that the wrestler is wielding is a reference to a WTO decision that disallowed U.S. trade penalties on countries whose fishing practices harmed sea turtles and other endangered marine species.

MONETARY COOPERATION: THE IMF

As trade and the level of other international financial transactions have increased, the need to cooperate internationally to facilitate and stabilize the flow of dollars, marks, yen, pounds, and other currencies has become vital. To meet this need, a number of organizations have been founded. The **International Monetary Fund (IMF)** is the most important of these.

Early Monetary Regulation

The formation of the IMF stemmed in part from the belief of many analysts that the Great Depression of the 1930s and World War II were partly caused by the near international monetary chaos that characterized the years between 1919 and 1939. Wild inflation struck some countries. Many countries suspended the convertibility of their currencies, and the North broke up into rival American, British, and French monetary blocs. Other countries, such as Germany, abandoned convertibility altogether and adopted protectionist monetary and trade policies. It was a period of open economic warfare—a prelude to the military hostilities that followed.

As part of postwar planning, the Allies met in 1944 at Bretton Woods, New Hampshire, to establish a new monetary order. The **Bretton Woods system** operated on the basis of "fixed convertibility into gold." The system relied on the strength of the U.S. dollar, which was set at a rate of $35 per ounce of gold.

The delegates at Bretton Woods also established the IMF and several other institutions to help promote and regulate the world economy. Thus, like GATT, the IMF was created by the West, with the United States in the lead, as part of the liberalization of international economic interchange. The specific role of the IMF in attempting to provide exchange rate stability will be discussed in the next section.

The Bretton Woods system worked reasonably well as long as the American economy was strong, international confidence in it remained high, and countries accepted and held dollars on a basis of their being "as good as gold." During the 1960s and the early 1970s, however, the Bretton Woods system weakened, then collapsed. The basic cause was the declining U.S. balance-of-payments position and the resulting oversupply of dollars held by foreign banks and businesses. The growth of world competition, U.S. budget deficits being driven by the costs of foreign policy (especially the war in Vietnam), domestic spending, and other factors further lowered confidence in the dollar. Countries were less willing to hold dollars and increasingly redeemed their dollars for gold. U.S. gold reserves fell precipitously, and in 1971 this forced the United States to abandon the gold standard. In place of fixed convertibility, a new system, one of "free-floating" currency relations, was established. The conversion from a fixed standard to floating exchange rates in the international monetary system increased the IMF's importance even more because of the potential for greater and more rapid fluctuations in the relative values of the world's currencies.

In the initial period after the end of the Bretton Woods system, international money managers assumed that exchange rates among the EDCs would fluctuate slowly and within narrow boundaries. This has not been true. Instead, the exchange rates of most currencies have fluctuated greatly. During 1999, for example, the Greek drachma weakened by 12 percent against the U.S. dollar, while the Japanese yen strengthened 14 percent. The currencies of LDCs often are even less stable. For instance, the kip, the currency unit of Laos, tumbled from 4,200 to the dollar to 7,727 to the dollar during 1999, an 84 percent shift.

This occurs because governments have frequently had difficulty managing international monetary exchange rates. To do so, a country's central bank, for example, may choose to create demand by buying its own currency if it wishes to keep its price up. The price goes up because of increased demand for a limited supply of currency. Conversely, a central bank that wishes to lower the value of its currency may create a greater supply by selling its currency. Governments sometimes even cooperate to control any given currency by agreeing to buy or sell it if it fluctuates beyond certain boundaries. Given the more than $1.5 trillion in currency exchanges each day, however, even the wealthiest countries with the largest foreign reserves often find themselves unable to adequately regulate the rise and fall of their currencies.

The Role of the IMF

The IMF began operations in 1947 with 44 member-countries. Since then the IMF has grown steadily, and in 2000 membership stood at 182. Indeed, about the only countries not in the IMF are those few (such as Nauru, which uses the Australian dollar) that do not have their own currency and have adopted the currency of a larger neighbor. The IMF's headquarters are in Washington, D.C. The managing director of the IMF since May 2000 is Horst Köhler, a German and former president of the European Bank for Reconstruction and Development.

The IMF's primary function is to help maintain exchange-rate stability by making short-term loans to countries with international balance-of-payments problems because of trade deficits, heavy loan payments, or other factors. In such times, the IMF extends a country a line of credit that the country can use to draw upon IMF funds in order to help meet debt payments, to buy back its own currency (thus maintaining exchange-rate stability by balancing supply and demand), or take other financial steps.

This display of a few of the world's nearly 200 national currencies makes a colorfully attractive image. As a practical matter, having myriad currencies makes conducting the world's business increasingly difficult. Just as many countries, such as the United States, had to abandon local currencies in order to expand and prosper economically, a unified world currency might be needed to facilitate trade and other international economic transactions. For now, the IMF works to try to keep the exchange rates stable among these currencies.

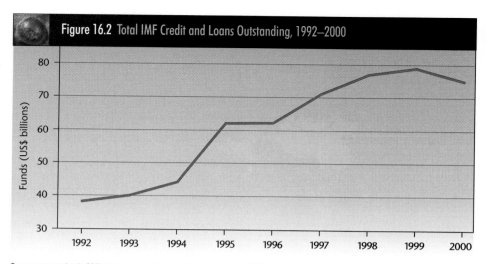

Figure 16.2 Total IMF Credit and Loans Outstanding, 1992–2000

Sources express data in SDRs; conversion to dollars by author using average SDR rate for each year. Data for 2000 is an average through September. *Data source:* IMF (2000) and IMF Web site at: http://www.imf.org/external/index.htm.

The rapid growth of the world economy and the need to keep currencies stable in a free-floating exchange rate environment have led to increasing importance for the IMF. Almost all funds go to developing and transitional economies. As evident, rising levels of IMF intervention are needed.

The IMF receives its usable funds from hard currency reserves ($114 billion in 2000) placed at its disposal by wealthier member-countries and from earnings that it derives from interest on loans made to countries that draw on those reserves. The IMF also holds more than $100 billion in reserves in LDC currencies, but they do not trade readily in the foreign exchange markets and, therefore, are of little practical use.

To help stabilize national currencies, the IMF has **Special Drawing Rights (SDRs)** that serve as reserves on which central banks of needy countries can draw. SDR value is based on an average, or market basket, value of several currencies, and SDRs are acceptable as payment at central banks. In January 2000, one SDR equaled about US$1.35. A country facing an unacceptable decline in its currency can borrow SDRs from the IMF and use them in addition to its own reserves to counter the price change. During 2000, the IMF had, on average, $69 billion in outstanding loans and credit lines to 96 countries. The growth of total outstanding IMF lending from 1992 through 2000 is shown in Figure 16.2.

While SDRs have helped, they have not always been sufficient to halt instability. One problem is that the funds at the IMF's command are paltry compared to the immense daily flow of about $1.5 trillion in currency trading. Also, monetary regulation is difficult because countries often work at odds with one another.

The IMF Focus on LDCs and CITs Over the last two decades, the IMF has especially concentrated on loans to LDCs and to CITs. The IMF typically lends countries money to support their currency or to stabilize their financial situation by refinancing their debt. Representative of this focus, all $77.1 billion of the IMF's outstanding loans in mid-2000 were to LDCs and CITs. Russia, with $14.7 billion in loans and credit, was the IMF's biggest client as of late 2000. Indonesia was second, with its $10.8 billion outstanding credits and loans stemming from the financial crisis that gripped Asia beginning in 1997. We can gain some insight on how the IMF operates and its impact by examining the background relating to the agency's responses to the financial crises in Asia and Russia.

The IMF and the Asian Financial Crisis Asia fell into financial turmoil when the currencies and economies of the Pacific Rim LDCs and NICs—especially Indonesia, Malaysia, South Korea, and Thailand—nosedived in 1997 and 1998. The flow of outside private capital into these countries dropped from a net inflow of $62 billion in 1996 to net outflows of $22 billion in 1997 and $30 billion in 1998. After years of strong growth, the GDP growth of Indonesia, Malaysia, South Korea, and Thailand all fell to near zero in 1997 and all declined in 1998. The four worst were Indonesia, with a 13.2 percent GDP decline in 1998, Thailand (–10.4 percent), Malaysia (–7.5 percent), and South Korea (–6.7 percent). On average, the NICs of Asia declined 2.3 percent. The currencies of the affected countries plunged in value, with, for example, the South Korean won losing nearly half its value versus the U.S. dollar.

This economic implosion led to a massive international effort, with the IMF at the forefront, to help stabilize and restart those economies. From mid-1997 through mid-1998, the Pacific Rim countries were the largest borrowers from the IMF. During that period, some $37 billion in IMF loans went to these countries, as part of an overall international financial assistance package of $82 billion.

The international effort was spurred by the danger that Asia's turmoil would spread throughout the world's interdependent economy. One peril was posed by a contraction of all the Asian NICs' imports. For example, Korea's merchandise imports dropped from $144 billion in 1996 to $90 billion in 1998; Indonesia's imports plummeted from $43 billion to $27 billion over the same period. Such drastic reductions imperiled the economies of even the largest countries.

The United States, for example, exports 27 percent of its merchandise to the Pacific Rim. That region's troubles caused U.S. exports to Indonesia, Malaysia, South Korea, and Thailand to drop 44 percent from $27.8 billion during the first six months of 1997 to $15.9 billion during the first six months of 1998. The impact of this seemingly dry statistic was felt in many American homes. When, for example, United Technologies, headquartered in East Hartford, Connecticut, announced that it was laying off 1,000 workers, the company cited the decrease in aircraft jet engine orders from Asia as a primary cause.

Perhaps even more worrisome from the perspective of the United States and the rest of the world was the fact that the "Asian economic flu" appeared contagious and threatened the health of the rest of the global economy. Chastened by what had happened in Asia, investors pulled money out of Latin America and other LDC regions. These LDCs were also hurt when their imports to Asia declined and when, because several Asian countries had devalued their currencies, some exports of Latin American countries to LDCs were displaced by now-cheaper Pacific Rim exports.

Even more than the United States, Japan's economy is intertwined with the Pacific Rim, and that region's downturn imperiled Japan's already weakening economy. The country's exports to the rest of Asia dropped dramatically, pushing Japan downward from a 2.9 percent real GDP growth rate in 1996, to a near stagnant 0.5 growth rate in 1997, to a recession with a 0.5 percent decline in 1998. This set off loud alarm bells in the other EDCs. "If Japan goes into a tailspin, if the U.S. economy slows down, if there are [currency] devaluations or the governments fail to save the banking systems, then all bets are off," worried one economist.[20]

By 1999, economic conditions had begun to improve. The GDP growth rates of the NICs in Asia were all positive. Imports had also picked up, with, for example, South Korea's rising 33 percent from $90 billion in 1998 to $121 in 1999. The exchange rates of the NICs stabilized and in some cases strengthened against the dollar and other world currencies. Many problems remained, including the political unrest in Indonesia that was caused by the country's economic trauma. Still, at least in part because of the IMF's intervention, Asia appeared to be on the road to economic recovery.

The IMF and the Russian Financial Crisis In addition to its assistance to the LDCs, the second main thrust of the IMF's recent efforts has been to extend assistance to the CITs in their attempts to reorient toward a market economy. In addition to the outstanding loans to Russia of $14.7 billion in 2000, the other former Soviet republics

(FSRs) and the CITs of Eastern Europe had outstanding loans of $7.2 billion. In total, about a third of the IMF's outstanding loans in 1998 were to these countries.

As with the LDCs, the IMF's assistance to the CITs is dependent in part on the recipients' instituting market economy–oriented changes approved by the IMF. Also, just as with the LDCs, these strings attached to the IMF loans and lines of credit are controversial. It is also the case that the IMF and its managing director have responded to political as well as financial considerations in extending assistance to Russia and other CITs. The United States very much wanted to see President Boris Yeltsin reelected in 1996, and there can be little doubt that Washington's thinking helped influence the decision of the IMF to give Yeltsin a strong boost amid the Russian presidential campaign by announcing a further credit line of $10.2 billion for Russia.

These funds, it turned out, were not enough. A new, intense economic crisis broke out in mid-1998 when the inability of the Russian government to pay its bills sparked a precipitous 57 percent drop in the exchange rate of the ruble during July. The IMF responded to Russia's rapidly deteriorating financial instability and to worries that this could lead to political turmoil by approving $11.2 billion to help Moscow try to defend the ruble and to prevent a collapse of Russia's monetary and economic systems. In return, the IMF demanded that Russia continue to institute economic reforms, the most important of which was increasing tax revenues through better enforcement of existing tax laws. The IMF loans to Russia also helped set the stage for the World Bank and other lenders to advance up to another $17 billion to Russia.

As with the ailing economies of Asia, the future of the Russian economy remains unclear. But also like those of Asia, the most recent Russian economic trends are better. The real GDP growth rate went from a recession-level (–)4.6 percent rate in 1998 to a 3.2 percent growth rate in 1999. The IMF also projects Russia's inflation rate for 2000 at a still unhealthy 23 percent, but that is vastly better than the 236 percent average rate for 1990 through 1998. The prospects for Russia's economic future have also improved with the departure from the Kremlin of President Boris Yeltsin, who was as sick as the economy, and the arrival of Vladimir Putin. To prosper again, Russia has even further to go than Asia. There can be little doubt, though, that at least part of the story of getting Russia on the road to recovery has been the intervention of the IMF.

Controversy about the IMF

Although the IMF has played a valuable role and has many supporters, it has not been above criticism (Feldstein, 1998; Hale, 1998). Indeed, in recent years the IMF has been one focus of struggle between the North and the South. It is possible to divide the controversies regarding the IMF into three categories: voting, conditionalilty, and capitalism and social justice.

Voting The first issue centers on the formula that determines voting on the IMF board of directors. Voting is based on the level of each member's contribution to the fund's resources. On this basis, the United States (17.7 percent) and the EU countries (30.6 percent) alone control almost half the votes. This wealth-weighted system has two ramifications. One is that the formula gives the small percentage of the world's people who live in EDCs a solid majority of the votes. Indeed, with just Japan (6.3 percent) added, the major EDCs easily control the decisions of the IMF. Second, the voting formula means that Eurowhites control the IMF. Adding, for example, Canada (3.0 percent) to the combined U.S.–EU total (48.3 percent), creates majority Eurowhite control. This apportionment has led to LDC charges that the fund is controlled by the North and is being used as a tool to dominate the LDCs.

Conditionality The second criticism of the IMF is that it imposes unfair and unwise conditions on countries that use its financial resources. Most loans granted by the IMF to LDCs and CITs are subject to **conditionality.** This refers to requirements that the borrowing country take steps to remedy the situations that, according to the IMF, have caused the recipient's financial problems. Foreign banks and other sources of external funding also base their decisions on the degree to which an applicant country has met the IMF's terms. The IMF's conditions press the LDCs to move toward a capitalist economy by such steps as privatizing state-run enterprises, reducing barriers to trade and to the flow of capital (thus promoting foreign ownership of domestic businesses), reducing domestic programs in order to cut government budget deficits, ending domestic subsidies or laws that artificially suppress prices, and devaluing currencies (which increase exports and make imports more expensive).

On the surface such conditions sound prudent, but in reality they have their drawbacks. First, LDCs charge that the IMF conditions *violate sovereignty* by interfering in the recipients' policy-making processes. "Interference in the internal affairs of a sovereign country... is now admissible in international social and political conduct," one commentator from Nepal complains. "With the emergence of governance as an important domain of international development partnership," he explains, "governments, inter-state institutions like the United Nations and its specialized agencies and multilateral financial establishments [like the IMF] are now increasingly treading on more complex and sensitive areas of domestic governance in the recipient countries."[21]

Second, some critics have contended that conditionality intentionally or unintentionally *maintains the dependencia relationship.* Reacting to the conditions laid down by the IMF in 1997 and 1998 to assist Asia's faltering economies, *Matichon,* a daily newspaper in Thailand, editorialized that the conditions amounted to "economic colonialism" and denounced the "financial and economic wars" that the paper said the EDCs were waging to humble the region.[22] From the same perspective, a South Korean newspaper, *Dong-A Ilbo,* wrote that "It is not desirable that [the EDCs] made use of our desperate situation for their own gains."[23]

Third, critics charge that sometimes the IMF *harms economies* in LDCs and CITs rather than helps them by requiring "cookbook" plans of fiscal austerity and other stringent conditions and by not sufficiently tailoring plans to the circumstances of individual countries. Taking that view, Richard Cooper, a former U.S. undersecretary of state, says the IMF "has the disadvantages of any large organization: inertia, preoccupation with precedent, and [being] encrusted with dated rules of thumb and modes of operation."[24]

Capitalism and Social Justice Another line of criticism aimed at the IMF contends that it pushes countries to adopt fiscal reforms that strengthen the economic elite of the recipient country while ignoring the welfare of workers and others. The view that the IMF has most often taken is clear in the observation of its managing director: "The stronger the program [of capitalist reform], the stronger the financing will be."[25] According to critics, this leads the IMF to demands that force recipient LDC governments to harm the quality of life of their citizens by reducing economic growth and by cutting social services in order to maintain a balanced budget. Often it is the poorest people that are hurt the most, and civil unrest is not uncommon.

A sharp dispute broke out in 2000 between Brazil and the IMF, for example, over just such an issue of conditionality versus social welfare. Brazil has one of the world's greatest gaps between the incomes of its richest citizens and the vast majority of impoverished Brazilians. In February, President Fernando Henrique Cordoso announced plans to spend $22 billion over the following decade in support of the newly established Fund to Combat and Eradicate Poverty. The IMF, which had given Brazil a $42 billion dollar loan in 1998 during the global economic turmoil set off by the Asian financial crisis, objected. "Brazil already spends a significant amount of money on social programs," the IMF's representative to the country chided; "This money has to be used more effectively." The ensuing outrage in Brazil brought support for the beleaguered official from IMF headquarters. "We in the IMF believe that what is important in the strategy of a country is not to get rid of the problems of the poor by doing some charity work from time to time," the IMF's managing director commented.[26] He went on to explain his belief that sacrificing in the short-term would eventually create a sound economy that would, in the long run, give Brazil the best chance of alleviating poverty. This rationale, however, did little to quiet the charges in Brazil that the IMF was insensitive to the plight of the poor and too willing to violate Brazilian sovereignty.

Before concluding our discussion of the IMF, it is important to note that there are several other monetary IGOs that make contributions. On a global scale, the oldest (founded in 1930) and the largest is the Bank for International Settlements (BIS). The BIS has 45 members, including all the major EDCs and a number of economically important LDCs such as China and Saudi Arabia. The BIS serves several functions. One is as a meeting ground where its members' central banks discuss global monetary issues. Second, the BIS provides expertise to assist the central banks of those LDCs and other countries that are struggling with fiscal stability. Third, the BIS has assets ($112 billion in 2000) deposited by the central banks of its members, and it uses these funds for purposes such as maintaining currency exchange stability. Finally, there are a number of regional monetary policies and institutions, such as the European Central Bank and the Arab Monetary Fund, that are affiliated with larger regional organizations.

DEVELOPMENT COOPERATION: THE WORLD BANK GROUP

A third type of multilateral economic cooperation involves granting loans and aid for the economic development of LDCs. The most significant development agency today is the **World Bank Group.** The group has four agencies. Two of them, the International Bank for Reconstruction and Development (IBRD) and the International Development Association (IDA), are collectively referred to as the World Bank. The larger World Bank Group also includes the International Finance Corporation (IFC) and the Multilateral Investment Guarantee Agency (MIGA).

While the World Bank Group operates as a funding agency according to established financial criteria, it, like all the other financial IGOs, is also influenced by the world's political currents. For example, furious opposition arose to China's application for World Bank funds to relocate 58,000 ethnic Chinese into a region near Tibet and traditionally inhabited by ethnic Tibetans. As explained in the chapter 9 box, The Dalai Lama in Dharamsala, no country disputes that Tibet is a legal part of China. Nevertheless, many countries saw the Chinese move as part of its alleged attempt to destroy Tibetan culture by making the Tibetans a minority in their own homeland. In the end, faced with certain rejection, China in July 2000 withdrew its application.

World Bank Group Operations

Of the four World Bank Group agencies, the IBRD, which was founded in 1946, is the oldest and, with 181 members, the largest. All four agencies get their funds from money subscribed by their member-governments, from money the agencies borrow, and from interest paid on the loans they make.

The *International Bank for Reconstruction and Development*, of the four, is the agency whose lending policies most closely resemble those of a commercial bank. The bank applies standards of creditworthiness to recipients and the projects they wish to fund, and charges some interest. In 1999, the IBRD made loans of $22.2 billion to fund 131 projects.

The *International Development Association* was created in 1960 and has a separate pool of funds drawn from member contributions. It has 159 members, and it focuses on making loans, usually at virtually no interest, to the very poorest countries. During 1999, the IDA extended $6.8 billion in loans to fund 145 projects. Given its focus on the LLDCs, about a third of all IDA money went to sub-Saharan Africa, whereas very few loans of the slightly more commercial IRBD went to countries in that region.

The *International Finance Corporation* is a third part of the World Bank Group; it was established in 1957 and has 174 members. The IFC makes loans to LDCs and guarantees private investment aimed at promoting private-sector development, whereas the IBRD and the IDA mostly make loans for public projects. Because of its goal of enhancing capitalism, the IFC, more than any of the other multilateral banks, has been favorably received in the United States. The IFC's loans for 1999 came to $3.5 billion for funding 255 projects in 84 countries. Because of the risky business climates in many countries, many of the IFC's projects are hazardous. But the philosophy at the agency, according to one of its officials, is that "the IFC needs to be ahead of the curve—we need to go where angels fear to tread. As it turns out, angels and devils tread everywhere now."[27]

The Multilateral Investment Guarantee Agency is the fourth and newest of the World Bank Group agencies, having been established in 1988. The agency specializes in promoting the flow of private development capital to LDCs by providing guarantees to investors against part of any losses they might suffer due to noncommercial risks (such as political instability). The agency in 1999 issued $1.3 billion in guarantees on approximately five times that amount of private capital invested in LDCs. Like the IFC, the MIGA, with 149 members, is autonomous from the World Bank, but draws on the bank's administrative, analytical, and other services.

Controversy about the World Bank Group

Like the IMF, the agencies that make up the World Bank Group do a great deal of good, but they have also been the subject of considerable controversy. One point of criticism involves the North's domination of the South. An American runs the World Bank, a New Zealander heads the WTO, and a German directs the IMF. Exemplifying these leaders is the ninth and current (since June 1995) head of the World Bank, James D. Wolfensohn. He holds MBA and J.D. degrees and has been an attorney, a Wall Street investment officer, and a consultant on international investing to more than 30 multinational corporations. As evidence of the North's domination, critics also point out that the World Bank Group, like the IMF, has a board of directors with a voting formula that gives the majority of the votes to the handful of EDCs. The United States has over 15 percent of the votes in both the IBRD and the IDA. The EU and Japan combined account for about another 33 percent of the IBRD and 39 percent of the IDA votes, giving these countries the ability to easily dominate the two organizations.

What all this means, from the perspective of the LDCs, is that the leaders of the World Bank Group and many other financial agencies do not truly understand the development needs of the South. A more dire interpretation of the dominance of the financial IGOs by the North is that they are vehicles for neoimperialist control of the LDCs by the EDCs.

A second complaint about the World Bank is simply that it provides too little funding. Figures such as $34.7 billion in total World Bank commitments to or guarantees of projects in 1999 sound impressive. But they are less so in light of the fact that lending has declined somewhat from the early 1990s when measured in real dollars (adjusted for inflation). Moreover, the repayment of loans means that the net flow of funds to LDCs is lower than it seems. For example, the IRBD's $22.2 billion in loans to LDCs in 1999 was partially offset by the $7.5 billion in principal and interest payments from LDCs. This left the bank's 1999 net disbursements (money given out minus repayments received) at just $14.7 billion or $2.94 per person in the LDCs.

Did You Know That:

Many of the LDC stock exchanges encouraged by the IFC are extremely small. For each dollar's worth of stock traded on the Ivory Coast exchange, $1,547,520 worth of stocks are traded on the New York Stock Exchange.

The terms of the loans are a third sore spot. The World Bank Group is caught between the North's concentration on "businesslike," interest-bearing loans and the South's demands that more loans be unconditionally granted to the poorest countries at low rates or with no interest at all. The World Bank also demands that recipients take sometimes painful measures to correct what the bank judges to be economically damaging policies. Many in the LDCs charge that such policies violate their sovereignty and hurt more than they help. "I think the World Bank is some kind of monster," says Monique Olboudo, a lawyer in Burkina Faso. "It sits on top of Africa like an octopus, sucking us dry. It never looks to see the effects on the lives of the people. It treats us like numbers, economic agents."[28]

A fourth criticism of the World Bank Group has heated up in the post–cold war era as the World Bank Group and other financial IGOs have all allied themselves further with the U.S. desire to promote market economies, foreign direct investment, and other aspects of capitalism. Speaking about the Inter-American Development Bank (IDB), a regional equivalent of the World Bank, one former bank official commented that "the IDB shouldn't be in the business of making life easier for the capital markets. [It should be] in the business of helping development of countries, typically things like water, sanitation, health, and education, not toll roads, telecommunications, or power stations." The crux of the matter is whether the interests of foreign investors, who hope to make a profit, can be balanced with those of the host countries.

Such criticisms and the more general uneasiness about globalization have made the World Bank, like the WTO and IMF, the target of massive street protests. When the World Bank had its annual meeting in April 2000, up to 20,000 demonstrators clogged the streets around its Washington, D.C., headquarters demanding that LDC debt be cancelled and that the World Bank take other steps to alleviate poverty. "It was impossible not to be affected," bank president James Wolfensohn said soon thereafter; "I come to work every day with 10,000 colleagues who think that they are doing what we are being criticized for [not doing]." It would be too strong to say that such protests have an immediate dramatic effect, but they do add to the pressure that affects policy. That is evident in recent shifts in the World Bank and other global financial IGOs, toward a greater willingness to support social programs. At the 2000 meeting, for instance, Wolfensohn announced that the bank would commit "unlimited money" to fight AIDS in the LDCs.[29]

REGIONAL ECONOMIC COOPERATION

For all the far-reaching economic cooperative efforts at the global level, the degree of activity and economic cooperation and integration at the regional level is even more advanced (El-Agraa, 1999). There are a dozen regional development banks. In terms of loan commitments in 1999, the largest regional banks (and their loans) were the just-mentioned, 46-member IDB ($10 billion), the 57-member Asian Development Bank ($6.7 billion), and the 58-member European Bank for Reconstruction and Development ($2.3 billion), which focuses on projects in the European CITs. Many other regional banks are much more limited in their funding. The annual loans of the poorly funded Caribbean Development Bank, for example, amount to less than $100 million, despite its region's pressing needs.

MAP
International Trade
Organizations, p. 219

There are also a large and growing number of regional organizations that promote free trade and other forms of economic interchange. Table 16.1 provides just one index of the interest in regional economic interchange. Note the global diversity of the regional organizations. Some, in truth, are little more than shell organizations that keep their goals barely alive. Yet the very existence of each organization represents the conviction of its members that, compared to standing alone, they can achieve greater economic prosperity by working together through economic cooperation or even economic integration.

Table16.1 Regional Trade Organizations and Agreements

Name	Founded	Membership
European Union and antecedents	1958	15
Latin American Integration Association	1960	11
Central American Common Market	1961	5
Council of Arab Economic Unity	1964	11
Central African Customs and Economic Union	1966	6
Association of Southeast Asian Nations	1967	10
Andean Community of Nations	1969	5
Caribbean Community and Common Market	1973	14
Economic Community of West African States	1975	16
Gulf Cooperation Council	1981	6
Economic Community of Central African States	1983	11
Arab Cooperation Council	1989	4
Arab Maghreb Union	1989	5
Asia Pacific Economic Cooperation	1989	21
Black Sea Economic Cooperation Zone	1992	11
North American Free Trade Agreement	1992	3
South African Development Community	1992	14
Southern Common Market (Mercosur)	1995	5
Free Trade Area of the Americas	1995	34

The geographically diverse, growing number of regional trade organizations testifies to the belief of most countries that they are better able to achieve or preserve prosperity through relatively free trade than through protectionism.

Economic cooperation is a process whereby sovereign states cooperate with one another bilaterally or multilaterally through IGOs (such as the IMF) or processes (such as the G-8 meetings). *Economic integration* means such a close degree of economic intertwining that, by formal agreement or informal circumstance, the countries involved begin to surrender some degree of sovereignty and act as an economic unit. There is no precise point when economic cooperation becomes economic integration. It is more a matter of moving along a continuum ranging from economic isolation, through mercantile policy, then to economic cooperation, and finally to economic integration. The countries joined together in the EU have moved far along this continuum toward integration; the three countries of NAFTA are just beginning this journey. It is also worth noting that the process of economic integration is not the result of a single strand of activity. Rather, integration is a complex phenomenon that results from the interaction and mutual strengthening of transnational trade and finance, of IGOs and NGOs, and of transnational values and international law.

One discussion of transnational economic activity divides economic integration into five different levels (Feld, 1979). These levels (ranging from the least to the most integrated) are (1) a *free trade area*, which eliminates trade barriers for goods between member-countries; (2) a *customs union*, which adds common tariff and nontariff barriers adopted against external countries; (3) a *common market*, which increases integration further by eliminating barriers among members to the free flow of labor, capital, and other aspects of economic interchange; (4) an *economic union*, which proceeds to harmonize the economic policies (such as tax and social welfare policies) of members; and (5) a *monetary union*, which adopts a common currency, a common central bank, and other aspects of financial integration. Feld (p. 272) comments that once monetary union is achieved, "the member states might be very close to political unification." He adds the caveat that this final step "might not really be possible without the unification of political institutions." This comment has proven to be the case for the EU, as we shall explore presently.

To give our discussion of economic integration additional substance, we can now turn our attention to the progress that has been made along the continuum toward integration. This will entail an examination of regional integration in Europe, North America, and the Pacific region.

EUROPE

The **European Union** is by far the most extensive regional effort. This Western European organization of 15 member-countries has moved substantially toward full economic integration. It has also traveled in the direction of considerable political cooperation. The evolution of the EU's economic integration since the early 1950s and its organizational structure and political development were all discussed in chapter 9. Given this background, it is possible to make a few summary points about the current status and future of the EU's progress toward economic and political integration that reflect the earlier discussion.

One such point is that despite the EU's steady progression through the levels of economic integration, the ultimate attainment of economic unification is not assured. Future political integration is even more in doubt. There are a number of roadblocks on the path to further EU integration. Europe is reasonably prosperous, but it faces numerous economic uncertainties that are inhibiting further EU progress. One is the *lagging European economy*, which during the 1990s performed substantially less well than the U.S. economy, as detailed in chapter 15. Unemployment in the EU, which stood at 9.6 percent in 1999 (more than twice the U.S. figure), is one of the more troubling indicators.

Sovereignty is another barrier on the road to further EU integration. Recall from above the comment by Feld that complete economic integration "might not really be possible without the unification of political institutions." This strong probability is the nexus of the difficulty of achieving further integration in Europe. As the discussion of EU politics in chapter 9 indicated, many Europeans, especially in the newer EU countries, retain strong feelings of national identity and are reluctant to adopt a European identity. The EU has also found it hard to act in concert on political matters. "The dream of a unified, decisive Europe, which assumes a major world role is not likely to be realized [soon]," one diplomat has commented.[30]

The *birth pangs of the euro* are the next, and perhaps greatest, test that the EU will face (Ferguson & Kotlikoff, 2000). The question is whether it is possible to successfully implement the European Monetary Union (EMU), including coordinated national fiscal policies, a central bank, and a unified currency (the euro). The EU countries decided in 1995 to work toward complete monetary integration. There would be a number of steps toward establishing the euro as the EU's currency culminating during 2002, with euro coins and bills going into general circulation on January 1 and, after six months, replacing

MAP
Membership and
Organizational Structure of
the European Union, p. 227

ARCADIO
LA NACION
San Jose
COSTA RICA

© 2000 CARTOONISTS & WRITERS SYNDICATE http://CartoonWeb.com

The euro, the unified currency of the European Union, was launched with great fanfare on January 1, 1999. By late 2000, the exchange rate of the euro against the U.S. dollar, Japan's yen, and other major currencies had dropped considerably, and the future of the euro and the EU's monetary unification were in question.

the traditional European currencies such as French francs and German marks. It was a goal that President Jacques Chirac of France called "the greatest collective adventure of Europe."[31]

As of late 2000, the adventure was having its travails. Some EU countries, most notably Great Britain, were not taking part in the experiment. To make matters worse, Denmark held a referendum in September 2000 on whether to adopt the euro as its currency, and the voters defeated monetary unification by a margin of 53 percent to 47 percent. Moreover, there was a lack of confidence in the euro, and, as a result, its exchange rate in September 2000 stood at 1 euro = $0.87, significantly down from its January 1, 1999, opening rate of 1 euro = $1.17. It is also unclear how many Europeans will be willing to abandon the currencies they have grown up with, and which have long symbolized their countries, in favor of the euro. As an EU analysis comments, "The success of the changeover to the single currency will depend on one condition: The euro must win full public acceptance.... [The] switch will indeed be a radical change and will upset people's habits."[32]

The success of the monetary union will also depend on the ability of the EU countries to agree on such issues as whether the euro should be regulated with an eye to restraining inflation by keeping interest rates high, or an eye to promoting economic growth by having relatively low interest rates, even if that risks inflation. This issue, combined with residual nationalism, created a nasty dispute between Germany and France over who would lead the European Central Bank (ECB). Germany, which fears inflation, favored Willem F. Duisenberg, a former president of Germany's central bank. France, which wants a faster growth rate to combat unemployment, backed Jean-Claude Trichet, head of the Bank of France. In the end, the Solomon-like compromise was to have Herr Duisenberg serve the first half of the eight-year term of the European Development Bank (ECB) head, then retire in favor of Monsieur Trichet. That solved the immediate contretemps, but many observers saw such political infighting as ominous for the future of cooperation amid suspicions that one or another country would be trying to force its fiscal philosophy on the others.

THE WESTERN HEMISPHERE

Economic cooperation in the Western Hemisphere does not yet rival the level found in Europe, but the process is under way. The origins of hemispheric distinctiveness and a U.S. consciousness of its connection to the hemisphere date back many years. The United States proclaimed the Monroe Doctrine in 1823. Often that meant gunboat diplomacy: heavy-handed, unilateral U.S. intervention in the region, a practice that continued through the 1989 invasion of Panama. But, slowly, the idea that the United States should help and cooperate with its hemispheric neighbors took hold. The first hemispheric conference met in 1889. A U.S. proposal to establish a customs union was thwarted by the other 17 countries that attended, but they did create the first regional organization, the International Bureau of American Republics. That later became the Pan-American Union, then, by the Rio Treaty of 1948, the Organization of American States (OAS). President Franklin Delano Roosevelt announced the Good Neighbor Policy. John F. Kennedy announced the Alliance for Progress. The first summit of most of the hemisphere's heads of government occurred in Punta del Este, Uruguay, in 1967.

These events and trends have recently led to two important trade efforts. The first was the creation of the North American Free Trade Agreement. The second was a commitment by the hemisphere's countries to create a hemisphere-wide free trade area by the year 2005.

The North American Free Trade Agreement

For good or ill, the United States is the economic hegemon of the Western Hemisphere, and regional integration only truly began when the Americans moved to forge free trade agreements with other countries in the region. That effort began with the formation of the **North American Free Trade Agreement (NAFTA)**, which encompasses much of the northern half of the hemisphere.

The Evolution and Provisions of NAFTA   The first step toward creating NAFTA was the U.S.–Canada Trade Agreement (1988) to eliminate most economic barriers between the two signatories by 1999. Four years later, Mexico was added to the free trade zone when the leaders of the three countries signed the NAFTA documents. After considerable debate, especially in Canada and the United States, each of the countries' legislatures ratified NAFTA, and the treaty went into effect on January 1, 1994.

The agreement, which takes up more than 2,000 pages, established schedules for reducing tariff and nontariff barriers to trade over a 5-to-10-year period in all but a few hundred of some 20,000 product categories. By 2003, almost all U.S. and Canadian tariffs and about 92 percent of all Mexican tariffs on one another's merchandise will have vanished, with all tariffs eliminated by 2009. Also under NAFTA, many previous restrictions on foreign investments and other financial transactions among the NAFTA countries will end, and investments in financial services operations (such as advertising, banking, insurance, and telecommunications) will flow much more freely across borders. This is particularly important for Mexico, which, for example, has not heretofore allowed foreign direct investment in its petroleum industry. Beginning in 2000, American banks, which had been virtually banned from operating in Mexico before NAFTA, were able to hold 15 percent of the Mexican market. Intra–NAFTA transportation has also become much easier. Truck and bus companies now have largely unimpeded access across borders, and starting in 2000, U.S. trucking firms were allowed to become majority owners of Mexican trucking companies. There is a standing commission with representatives from all three countries to deal with disputes that arise under the NAFTA agreement.

The Growth of Intra–NAFTA Trade   The greatest change under NAFTA is that it allows a much freer flow of goods, services, and investment among the three member-countries. Trade among them was extensive even before NAFTA, and has grown even more since then, as can be seen in Figure 16.3. Mexico is the most dependent on intra–NAFTA trade, with 89 percent of its exports going to and 76 percent of its imports coming from Canada and the United States. Canada's level of intra–NAFTA trade is not much less, with 87 percent of exports going to and 71 percent of its imports coming from its NAFTA partners. Another index of the importance of NAFTA is that total U.S.–Canada trade of $356 billion is the world's largest two-way commercial relationship. The United States is least dependent, albeit still heavily so, on NAFTA trade, with 36 percent of U.S. exports going to Canada and Mexico and 29 percent of U.S. imports coming from them.

The Impact of NAFTA   NAFTA is certainly less advanced than the EU, but it is a no less portentous example of regional integration. Indeed, NAFTA is an economic unit that, with 387 million people, a combined 1999 GDP of $9.2 trillion, and 24 percent of

Figure 16.3 Expansion of Intra–NAFTA Trade

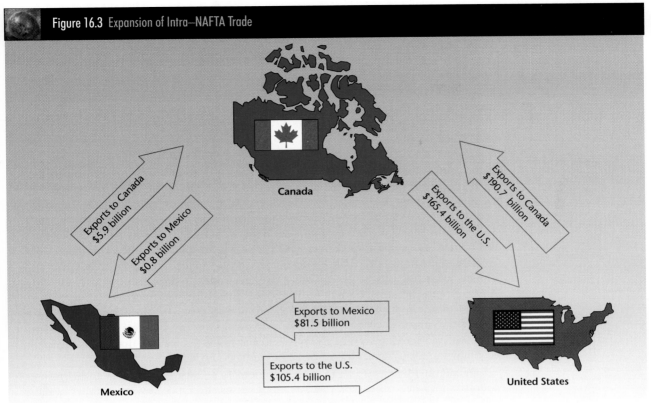

Exports to Canada
$5.9 billion

Exports to Mexico
$0.8 billion

Canada

Exports to Canada
$190.7 billion

Exports to the U.S.
$165.4 billion

Exports to Mexico
$81.5 billion

Exports to the U.S.
$105.4 billion

Mexico

United States

Total Intra–NAFTA Trade for 1999: $549.7 billion

Data source: IMF 2000a.

The North American Free Trade Agreement has accounted for a rapid rise in trade among Canada, Mexico, and the United States since the treaty went into effect in 1994. There are now plans for a Western Hemisphere free trade zone, the Free Trade Area of the Americas.

all world goods exports rivals the EU (371 million people, a GDP of $8.5 trillion, and 37 percent of exports).

Beyond trade expansion, it is difficult to be precise about specific impacts. There was and, to a degree, still is, a vigorous debate going on inside each of the three countries about whether NAFTA will bring boom or bust. The evidence is still coming in, and its analysis has been made especially complex by the collapse of the value of the Mexican peso at the end of 1994, which impeded the ability of Mexicans to import goods from the United States and Canada. By the same token, Mexican goods became much less expensive for Americans and Canadians. Thus, the growth of Mexico's imports from the United States and Canada have lagged behind the solid growth of Mexico's exports to its NAFTA partners.

Another problem is the continuing reservations in each country about NAFTA. Nationalism makes some Americans, Canadians, and Mexicans wary. Canadians and Mexicans are concerned about the possibility of being overwhelmed by American dollars and culture. Sharing the continent with the United States was once likened by then-Canadian prime minister Pierre Trudeau to "sleeping with an elephant. No matter how friendly and even-tempered the beast… one is affected by every twitch and grunt" (Duchacek, 1975:146). Many Mexicans were even more worried than Canadians about the behemoth on their border. This concern is captured in the oft-quoted, if perhaps apocryphal, sigh of an earlier Mexican leader, "Poor Mexico so far from God, so close to the United States." Already, Mexico is being flooded by U.S. products and business ventures. A Mexico City billboard tells those passing by that "It's Time for a Domino's Pizza." Traditional donkey-shaped piñatas have lost favor to Mutant Ninja Turtle and McDonald's "Hamburglar" piñatas. In an odd cultural twist, the American-owned chain, Taco Bell, is opening franchises in Mexico! "The Mexican economy is becoming Americanized,… the culture to a great extent, too," lamented writer Homero Aridjis. "Many Mexicans are becoming aliens in their own country," he continued. "When I ask the question, 'What is going to happen to the tortilla culture?' nobody has an answer."[33]

It is, as noted, too early to tell what the specific impact of NAFTA will be. Some commentators predict that all countries will win. If you believe the naysayers, everyone will lose. What is probably closer to reality is that there will be winners and losers in every country. Consumers in all three countries will almost certainly be helped by having access to more products at lower prices due to specialization and competition. Japanese and other Asian electronics producers such as JVC, Matsushita, and Samsung have rushed to set up plants in Tijuana and other Mexican cities just across the border. These border plants, known as *maquiladoras*, have spurred an employment boom along the border and employ more than 24,000 people in Tijuana alone. The impact of NAFTA on the prosperity of the bulk of Mexico farther to the south is much less certain. The maquiladoras and, in general, freer trade with Mexico have also cost over 60,000 American jobs because of shifts of plants over the border and increased competition from Mexican products (Carr, 1999). Yet, it is also the case that the 1.5 million televisions that Samsung will be producing, employing Mexican workers at about $50 a week, will mean cheaper products for Americans. It will also be true that as the Mexican economy improves, demand for American products and services will increase.

Whatever the effect on the overall economies of each of the three participating countries may be, it is certain that some businesses and types of workers will benefit; others will be harmed. It is also clear that NAFTA reduced the sovereignty of each signatory. So do all trade agreements and, indeed, all international treaties. It is equally sure, though, that Canada and Mexico are not about to become the 51st and 52nd American states. Political integration at some point in the future is not impossible, but it will be many mañanas before that occurs, if it ever does.

The Free Trade Area of the Americas

It is possible that NAFTA may also be another step toward integration of all or most of the Western Hemisphere. Trade cooperation in the hemisphere moved toward a new, higher level in 1994 with the beginning of an effort to create what has been tentatively named the **Free Trade Area of the Americas (FTAA).**

The Origins of FTAA Proposals for a free trade area date back to the 1880s, as noted. The reality of trade zones is more recent. Seven of the regional trade groups listed in Table 16.1 on page 471 are in the Western Hemisphere, and the momentum behind trade cooperation has steadily built up during the past decade. It may be that the creation of a hemispheric trade zone will come through the addition of new members or through the merger of existing regional common markets rather than through the FTAA or some other new trade group.

The most specific precursor of the current efforts to found a hemispheric trade zone occurred in 1990 when President George Bush advocated such a goal. The president said that economic advancement in the hemisphere rested on three pillars: international debt reduction, trade, and investment. Unspoken, but a fourth factor, was the continuing democratization of the hemisphere's countries. Progress was made toward each of these four goals during subsequent years. Debt reduction has proceeded slowly to less perilous, if still unsatisfactory, levels. The debt of Latin America and the Caribbean countries (measured as a percentage of their exports) fell from 384 percent in

1987 to 255 percent in 1999. Trade has grown, with the volume of exports up from an annual average of 4.5 percent during the 1980s to 9.8 percent during the 1990s. Both FDI and FPI have flowed strongly into the region south of the United States, increasing from $24 billion in 1990 to $87 billion in 1998. Democracy has spread. When the Summit of the Americas met, all but one (Cuba) of the hemisphere's countries had democratically elected governments.

The Summit of the Americas The end result of these various efforts was the 1994 meeting of the heads of 34 countries at the Summit of the Americas in Miami, Florida. Only Cuba was excluded. Their agreement was far-reaching. The conference agreed to aim at the creation of a free trade zone in the hemisphere within 10 years. The leaders also agreed to a series of more than 100 specific political, environmental, and economic programs and reforms. "We pushed very, very hard," said one U.S. official, to get a document in which the signatories pledged, among other things, to "strive to make our trade liberalization and environmental policies mutually supportive" and to "secure the observance and promotion of worker rights."[34]

The conference ended in near-euphoria. "The atmosphere was splendid," said José Angel Gurria, Mexico's secretary of foreign affairs. "We now have a flight plan that will keep us busy for years to come."[35] "When our work is done, the free trade area of the Americas will stretch from Alaska to Argentina," said President Clinton. "In less than a decade, if current trends continue, this hemisphere will be the world's largest market."[36]

The Future of FTAA If it proceeds as planned, the FTAA will link the Western Hemisphere in a single market that in 2005 will have an estimated 850 million consumers buying $13 trillion worth of goods and services. The bargaining over the details will be difficult. As excited as they are about access to the U.S. markets, the hemisphere's LDCs are equally as nervous about dropping their protections and being drowned in a tidal wave of American imports, services, and purchases of local businesses and other property. Many Americans are just as sure their jobs will wind up in the hands of an underpaid Bolivian, Honduran, or perhaps Uruguayan worker. President Clinton was fond of recalling an image used often by John Kennedy in which JFK would observe, "As they say on my own Cape Cod, a rising tide lifts all boats. And a partnership, by definition, serves both partners." Another possibility, Prime Minister Owen Arthur of Barbados told President Clinton in Miami, is that "a rising tide can... overturn small boats."[37] Yet for all the difficulty ahead, the momentum in the direction of creating FTAA will probably carry the day. One is tempted to say that the leaders who gathered in Miami did not so much begin the task of creating a regional trade area as to recognize and organize a process that was already under way.

Yet the exact future of the FTAA remains unclear. When in 1998 the second FTAA summit meeting convened in Santiago, Chile, the mood was a good deal more sober than it had been in Miami four years earlier. Expanding trade under U.S. leadership has faltered on several fronts. During his second term, President Clinton had increasing difficulties getting Congress to support the continued expansion of free economic exchange. For example, Congress in 1997 refused to renew the president's "fast-track authority" to rapidly negotiate trade treaties with a reduced chance of Congress rejecting the results. In the aftermath, Clinton seemed to turn his attention on economic affairs away from the region and toward such matters as securing permanent normal trade status for China. The flagging American leadership prompted one observer to compare U.S. efforts to "a guy who starts a brawl in a barroom and then slips out the backdoor."[38] The result was that FTAA negotiations moved to something of a back burner, awaiting the 2000 U.S. presidential and congressional elections for the possibility of renewed U.S. leadership. Given the role of the United States as the hemi-

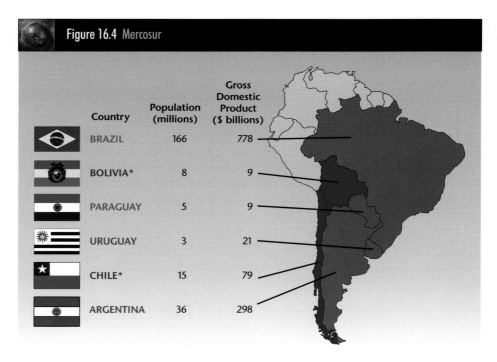

Figure 16.4 Mercosur

Country	Population (millions)	Gross Domestic Product ($ billions)
BRAZIL	166	778
BOLIVIA*	8	9
PARAGUAY	5	9
URUGUAY	3	21
CHILE*	15	79
ARGENTINA	36	298

* associate members

The Southern Common Market (Mercosur, after its Spanish acronym) is an example of one of the several important and growing regional free trade organizations. A key issue for the future of the Western Hemisphere is whether it will unite into a single free trade organization, the Free Trade Area of the Americas (FTAA) or whether the hemisphere will be divided into two rival trade blocs, Mercosur and the North American Free Trade Agreement (NAFTA).

sphere's hegemonic power, it is unlikely that the FTAA idea will progress rapidly or even at all without leadership from Washington (Wrobel, 1998).

Mercosur

Whatever the disposition of the new U.S. president and Congress that took office in January 2001, a number of countries have undertaken or continued efforts to establish or expand their own trade treaties. The **Southern Common Market (Mercosur)** is of particular note. Mercosur was established in 1995 by Argentina, Brazil, Paraguay, and Uruguay. Chile and Bolivia became associate members in 1996 and 1997, respectively. They are negotiating full membership, and Colombia, Ecuador, Peru, and Venezuela have evinced interest in joining Mercosur. Including just its four full members, Mercosur is a market of 210 million people with a combined GDP of $1.1 trillion. Adding in associate members Bolivia and Chile would slightly increase those numbers, as shown in Figure 16.4.

Whether, like NAFTA, Mercosur is a building block toward the FTAA is uncertain. As the president of Argentina explained the relationship between the FTAA's uncertain future and the expansion of Mercosur, "I don't want to rule out the [FTAA],... but charity begins at home."[39] This had led some observers to worry that an expanded Mercosur might even derail the FTAA and compete with NAFTA. Another analyst's more optimistic scenario is that it would be easier to form a hemispheric union after several smaller regional pacts had "ironed out" their problems. The wise advice of this analyst: "I suggest that everybody take a deep breath and calm down. A hemispheric trade agreement is going to take a while."[40]

ASIA, THE PACIFIC, AND ELSEWHERE

The impulse for regional ties has not been confined to Europe and the Americas. Other regions have also begun to form their own groups. There are four Arab and seven sub-Saharan African trade groups. The three Slavic FSRs (Belarus, Russia, and Ukraine) agreed in 1993 to negotiate cooperation agreements with an eye to a future economic union. Adding to that, Belarus and Russia agreed in 1994 to move to unify their monetary systems based on the Russian ruble.

Even more portentous than these efforts is the trend toward regionalism in the Pacific. The **Association of Southeast Asian Nations (ASEAN)** was established in 1967 and now includes Brunei, Cambodia, Indonesia, Laos, Malaysia, Myanmar (Burma), the Philippines, Singapore, Thailand, and Vietnam. The ASEAN countries have a combined population of about 500 million, a GDP of approximately $737 billion, and total exports of about $360 billion. As discussed in chapter 9, ASEAN, like some other trade organizations, is also working to forge greater political cooperation among its members and to try to bargain as a group (as the EU does) with external countries and other trade organizations.

More recently, the **Asia-Pacific Economic Cooperation (APEC),** an oddly named structure, began in 1989 and may be evolving toward becoming a regional trade organization. The 21-member organization includes most of countries of the greater Pacific Ocean region. The members range in the Eastern Pacific from Russia in the north, through Southeast Asia, to Australia in the south. On the other side of the Pacific, members extend from Canada in the north, through Mexico, to Chile in the south. The APEC members account for 42 percent of the world population, 59 percent of the global GDP, and 48 percent of all merchandise trade. APEC has a small secretariat based in Singapore, but it is symbolic of APEC's still-tentative status that it has not added a word such as "organization" or "community" to the end of its name.

The first of what have become annual summit meetings of the APEC leaders took place in Seattle, Washington, in 1993. The United States hoped for an agreement in principle to move toward a free trade zone, an Asia-Pacific Community. That effort was forestalled because, as one Japanese diplomat put it, "there are a variety of concerns, especially among the developing nations, that we proceed with some caution." Delegates from the other countries also doubted U.S. sincerity in light of the bruising battle in Congress over the ratification of NAFTA that was then under way. "If there was this much debate on NAFTA, imagine the debate you would have in America over a free trade area with the whole Pacific," South Korea's foreign minister pointed out cogently.[41]

Progress toward further APEC integration has been slow. There have been agreements in principle, for example, to achieve "free and open trade and investment" in the Asia-Pacific region. Japan and the United States are to remove all their barriers by the year 2010, with the rest of the APEC members achieving a zero-barrier level by 2020. Whether this will occur, given such factors as China's already rising trade surplus with the United States and Japan's faltering economy, remains very unclear. Beyond this, few specific agreements have resulted from these summits, but they are part of a process of dialogue that helps keep lines of communications open.

Beyond Asia, regional trade pacts are even less developed. The various efforts to give life to them in the Middle East have fallen prey to the region's political problems, to the fact that many of the oil production–dependent economies have little to trade with one another, and other problems. Similarly, Africa's regional trade groups have languished in the face of the continent's poverty and frequent political turmoil.

THE FUTURE OF REGIONALISM

The precise role that regional trading blocs will play on the world stage is unclear. Some observers believe that such groupings will help integrate regions, improve and strengthen the economic circumstances of the regions' countries and people, and provide a stepping-stone to world economic integration, just as the EEC was part of the genesis of the EU and just as NAFTA led to the FTAA agreement. Other analysts are worried. Economist Jagdish Bhagwati believes that "the revival of regionalism is unfortunate."[42] While regional blocs (no matter what their level of integration) must still adhere to GATT rules with respect to trade with other blocs and countries, Bhagwati is still afraid that the regions will become increasingly closed trading areas and that competition among the blocs will cause a breakdown of GATT and the construction of higher trade barriers among the blocs.

Such concerns are not far-fetched, given the impetus that is partly responsible for the current rapid regionalization that the world is undergoing. Whatever the negotiation, it is clear that part of the motivation to get together is the urge to defend against the possibility of predatory and protectionist trade practices by other economic blocs. The EU's integration is being driven in part by such fears. From Europe's point of view, competing with the United States alone is unnerving; competing with NAFTA, much less with the newly forming FTAA, is truly alarming. A modern European advocate of unity might echo Benjamin Franklin's warning to the revolutionary American colonies that if we do not all hang together, we will all hang separately, and today's equivalent of Paul Revere might gallop through the European night crying, "NAFTA is coming, NAFTA is coming!" Some Europeans, as one Dutch scholar explained, "want a united Europe out of fear more than out of love."[43]

Similarly, NAFTA and FTAA are in part a response to the EU. "My fear," a U.S. Chamber of Commerce official told Congress, "is that, as European governments seek to balance political interests among [themselves], the legitimate interests of outsiders will be the first to be traded off. 'Fortress Europe' may not be a realistic outcome, but selected protectionism... will be defended as necessary" (Olmer, 1989:133). This concern led the United States to use the threat and reality of regional trade associations to pressure Europe, Japan, and others to open their markets. During the FTAA summit in Miami, Mickey Kantor, the U.S. trade representative, observed that one benefit of the meeting was that "the Europeans will be encouraged, to use a delicate word, to be more open in a number of areas we have been concerned about. And Asians will also be encouraged to go in this direction, or they too will be left behind."[44] Like the regional trends in North America and Europe, the Southeast Asian effort is partly defensive. Explained Prime Minister Goh Chok Tong of Singapore, "Unless ASEAN can match the other regions," it will lose out. By contrast, the free trade agreement would make ASEAN a "strong player in the new world order."[45]

While these defensive reactions and counterreactions are understandable, they also contain a danger. It is that instead of promoting global economic cooperation, the regional organizations that exist or are being created may one day become centers of economic-political-military rivals that are as bitterly locked in contest as individual countries once were. There are already signs that regionalization, rather than globalization, is determining where the investors from various countries put their FDI. The majority of all American FDI in LDCs now goes to Latin America and the Caribbean. Similarly, the majority of Japan's FDI in LDCs is in East Asia and the Pacific; the French put the majority of their FDI investment in the LDCs and CITs of Eastern Europe and Central Asia. There is in George Orwell's novel *1984* an image of the world divided into three hostile blocs—Eastasia, Eurasia, and Oceania. It is a vision with an unsettling geographical resemblance to a possible ASEAN-EU-FTAA tripolar system. Just as it is much too early to predict a merging of the various trade regions into a global free trade economy, so is it premature to assume an Orwellian future. The most likely path lies somewhere between the two extremes, yet either of them is possible (Hanson, 1998).

CHAPTER SUMMARY

1. This chapter discusses the global and regional attempts of countries to cooperate to address the economic issues that face them and to find common interests and solutions.

2. A wide variety of general intergovernmental organizations (IGOs) and efforts are devoted to economic cooperation. The UN maintains a number of efforts aimed at general economic development, with an emphasis on the less developed countries.

3. Many specialized IGOs are also involved in economic cooperation; some examples are the Organization for Economic Cooperation and Development and the Group of Eight.

4. Trade cooperation has grown through the new General Agreement on Tariffs and Trade and its administrative structure, the World Trade Organization, and great strides have been taken toward promoting free trade.

5. Among monetary institutions, the International Monetary Fund is the primary organization dedicated to stabilizing the world's monetary system. The IMF's primary role in recent years has been to assist LDCs and CITs to prosper by reducing their foreign debt.

6. The IMF, however, attaches conditions to its assistance, and this practice has occasioned considerable criticism, especially regarding voting formula, conditionality, capitalism, and social justice.

7. There are a number of international organizations established to provide developmental loans and grants to countries in need. The best known of these is the World Bank Group, which consists of several interrelated subsidiaries. These organizations also primarily extend aid to EDCs, but, like the IMF, the conditions they attach are criticized by some analysts.

8. There are also several regional efforts aimed at economic integration. The European Union and the North American Free Trade Agreement are the most important of these.

9. By far the most developed is the European Union. The EU has been experiencing some sharp difficulties but has also showed great resilience. Whether the EU can integrate its national monetary systems and convert to a single European currency, the euro, is the next great hurdle facing the organization.

10. The new NAFTA regional free trade area will rival the EU in population and combined GDP. The Free Trade Area of the Americas, Mercosur, the Association of Southeast Asian Nations, and the Asia Pacific Economic Cooperation forum are on the horizon as even larger regional organizations.

CHAPTER 17

PRESERVING AND ENHANCING HUMAN RIGHTS AND DIGNITY

The sun with one eye vieweth all the world.

Shakespeare, *Henry VI, Part I*

And your true rights be term'd a poet's rage.

Shakespeare, *Sonnet XVII*

Recognition of the inherent dignity and of the equal and inalienable rights of all members of the human family is the foundation of freedom, justice, and peace in the world.

Preamble to the Universal Declaration of Human Rights, 1948

CHAPTER OBJECTIVES

After completing this chapter, you should be able to:

- Understand the two types of human rights.
- Evaluate the global problems related to population growth and food shortages, and assess international efforts to address them.
- Evaluate the global problems related to health and assess international efforts to address them.
- Discuss the role of education in achieving human rights and the organizations developed to improve levels of education.
- Examine the two types of individual rights.
- Discuss the prevalence of human rights abuses and the ideological justification for those abuses.
- Identify the focus of modern international efforts to ease human rights abuses.
- Analyze the political barriers to human rights efforts and the progress that has been made.

As we near the end of this survey of world politics, it is appropriate to pause momentarily to remember that, amid all the sound and fury, politics ought to be about maintaining or improving the quality of life of people. We have been exploring whether the traditional state-based international system that operates on self-interested competition can best protect and enhance humanity or whether the alternative of global cooperation in an international system with reduced sovereignty will lead to a more felicitous future. This and the next chapter continue that inquiry by addressing the human rights and social dignity of the world's people and the condition of the biosphere that they inhabit. First, this chapter will address preserving and enhancing human rights and dignity by looking at efforts to provide for the human body and spirit. Then chapter 18 will take up environmental concerns and programs.

THE BIOSPHERE AND ITS INHABITANTS: THE ESSENCE OF POLITICS

It is important to stress that while the discussions of the human condition and the environment are divided into two chapters, the two subjects are intrinsically intertwined. The size of the globe's population and the need to feed people and supply their material needs is putting tremendous pressure on the capacity of the biosphere to provide resources and to absorb waste. Indeed, the intersection of people and their environment and the combined impact of the two on the social and economic future are so strong that the World Bank has devised a new way to measure the *comprehensive wealth* of countries. The traditional method relies exclusively on economic production measured by either per capita gross national or domestic product (GNP, GDP). The alternative method introduced by the World Bank in 1995 and dubbed "green accounting" starts with manufactured wealth (products) and adds estimates of "natural capital" and "human capital." Natural capital is divided into two subcategories. One is "land" and includes factors such as the acreage available for farming. The second is "resources," and measures available water, minerals, and other related factors. Human capital measures education, health, and other such criteria. Estimating natural and human capital is even more difficult than arriving at GDP figures, but the results are valuable. Nobel Prize–winning economist Robert M. Solow contends that the new method is more comprehensive because "what we normally measure as capital is a small part of what it takes to sustain human welfare." Therefore, adds another economist, green accounting "is a valuable thing to do even if it can only be done relatively crudely."[1]

Changing the emphasis away from mere production helps us to focus on the economic reality that any economic unit needs to add to its national core and infrastructure in order to remain prosperous. If, for example, the owner of a farm devotes all of the farm's financial and human resources to producing crops, does not take care to avoid depleting the soil and water supplies, and does not devote resources to keeping the workers healthy and to training them in the latest farm methods, then, even though production may soar in the short term, the farm's long-term prospects are not good. Similarly, countries that do not preserve and, when possible, replenish their natural and human capital may face an increasingly bleak future. As one observer put it, such "countries are [inflating] income by selling off the family jewels."[2]

Figure 17.1 helps visualize the different results for six countries derived from calculating only GDP and, alternatively, from calculating comprehensive wealth (production, natural capital, and human capital). Notice, for example, that Australia's percentage of the sum of the six countries' per capita comprehensive wealth is much greater than its share of the combined per capita GDPs. This is primarily because of the estimated value that the World Bank places on Australia's land resources. Japan is also advantaged

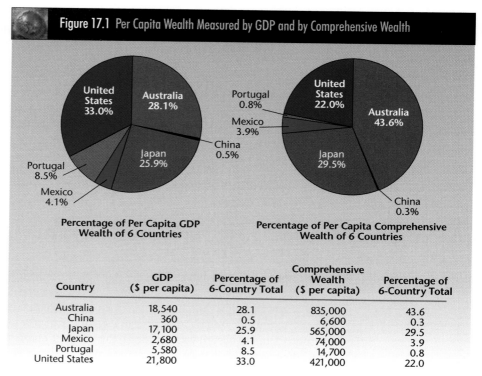

Figure 17.1 Per Capita Wealth Measured by GDP and by Comprehensive Wealth

Percentage of Per Capita GDP
Wealth of 6 Countries

Percentage of Per Capita Comprehensive
Wealth of 6 Countries

Country	GDP ($ per capita)	Percentage of 6-Country Total	Comprehensive Wealth ($ per capita)	Percentage of 6-Country Total
Australia	18,540	28.1	835,000	43.6
China	360	0.5	6,600	0.3
Japan	17,100	25.9	565,000	29.5
Mexico	2,680	4.1	74,000	3.9
Portugal	5,580	8.5	14,700	0.8
United States	21,800	33.0	421,000	22.0

The World Bank data is for 1990 and, for comparability, the GDP data is also for 1990.

Data sources: New York Times, September 19, 1995, for comprehensive wealth; *World Almanac* (1993) for GDP; percentage calculations by author.

The traditional way of calculating a country's per capita wealth is by GDP. The absolute and relative wealth of countries can change significantly when natural and human resources are added to production to calculate wealth.

because of the high value of its human capital. By contrast, the U.S. share of the six countries' per capita comprehensive wealth is much less than the U.S. share of their combined per capita GDPs. The United States produces a great deal, but the World Bank calculates that U.S. per capita resources are low and that U.S. human wealth is below par for such a wealthy country. Of the six countries, Portugal fares worst in percentage of comparative wealth compared to GDP because of its paucity of natural capital.

The complexities of this green-accounting approach to measuring wealth should not obscure its basic message that the richness or impoverishment of the human condition is an amalgam of the human rights people enjoy or are denied and the biosphere's bounty or exhaustion. As noted, we will address human rights in this chapter, then turn to the environment in the next.

THE NATURE OF HUMAN RIGHTS

Before moving to a detailed discussion of human rights, it is important to explain the broad concept of human rights used here. We are used to thinking about human rights in terms of *individual human rights,* that is, freedom from specific abuses or restrictions, especially by governments. The U.S. Bill of Rights, for example, prohibits (except in extreme cases) the government from abridging individual Americans' right to exercise their religion or free speech, from discriminating against citizens based on race and other demographic traits, from being long-imprisoned without a trial, and from a variety of other abuses. Gradually, these constitutional prohibitions have been extended to restrict actions by U.S. state and local governments and even, in some cases, by individuals.

There is a more comprehensive concept of rights. This broader view holds that people and groups not only have the right not to be specifically abused, but that they also have *collective human rights* to a quality of life that, at minimum, does not detract from their human dignity (Felice, 1996). One scholar suggests that the most fruitful way to think about human rights is to begin with the idea that "ultimately they are supposed to serve basic human needs." These basic human needs, which generate corresponding rights, include, among others (Galtung, 1994:3, 72):

- "Survival needs—to avoid violence": The requisite to avoid and the right to be free from individual and collective violence.
- "Well-being needs—to avoid misery": The right to adequate nutrition and water; to movement, sleep, sex, and other biological wants; to protection from diseases and from adverse climatological and environmental impacts.
- "Identity needs—to avoid alienation": The right to self-expression; to realize your potential, to establish and maintain emotional bonds with others; to preserve cultural heritage and association; to contribute through work and other activity; and to receive information about and maintain contact with nature, global humanity, and other aspects of the biosphere.
- "Freedom needs—to avoid repression": The right to receive and express opinions, to assemble with others, to have a say in common policy; and to choose in such wide-ranging matters as jobs, spouses, where to live, and lifestyle.

Few, if any, people would argue that these rights are absolute. As the classic formulation about free speech goes, for example, freedom of speech does not include the right to shout "fire!" in a crowded theater. It is also the case that the legal rights granted and recognized by countries largely include only protections from specific abuses of individuals and groups and do not include the right to certain qualitative standards of life. But it is also arguable that the very nature of being human means that people have the right to exist in at least tolerable conditions as well as the right to be merely free from specific abuses. It is also appropriate to say a bit about the origins of human rights. Recall from chapter 11 that there is an ancient debate about the basis of human rights. Universalists represent one school of thought; relativists represent the other.

Universalists believe that human rights are derived from sources external to society. Depending on the universalist, the source may be one or another theological or ideological doctrine or it may be natural rights. This last concept holds that the fact of being human carries with it certain rights that cannot be violated or can only be violated in extremis. Universalists therefore believe that there is a single, prevailing set of standards of moral behavior on which human rights are based.

Relativists argue from a positivist point of view and claim that rights are the product of a society's contemporary values. Positivists therefore contend that in a world of diverse cultures, no single standard of human rights exists or is likely to exist short of the world becoming completely homogenized culturally. Those who believe in the cultural relativism of rights also tend to view attempts to impose standards of rights by one culture on another as cultural imperialism.

It is not uncommon to hear those in the non-Western world argue that many of the rights asserted in such international documents as the Universal Declaration of Human Rights, which was adopted in 1948 by an overwhelming vote of the UN General Assembly, are based on the values of the politically dominant West. Positivists contend that many of these Western values, such as individualism and democracy, are not held as strongly in other cultures, and that no matter how highminded it is, Western attempts to impose them are imperialist. There are, however, leaders in non-Western cultures who reject these assertions of cultural relativism. Burmese political activist and 1991 Nobel Peace Prize winner Aung San Suu Kyi writes that claims about "the national culture can become a bizarre graft of carefully selected historical incidents and distorted

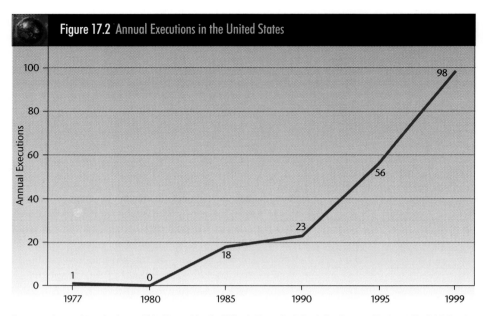

Figure 17.2 Annual Executions in the United States

Data source: Amnesty International report, "United States of America, Failing the Future: Death Penalty Developments, March 1998–March 2000" on the Amnesty International Web site at http://www.amnesty.org/ailib/aipub/2000/AMR/25100300.htm.

The U.S. Supreme Court in 1976 declared that executing prisoners was not "cruel and inhuman punishment," thereby reinstating the death penalty after a four-year moratorium. One prisoner was executed (by firing squad) in 1977. By March 2000 another 624 individuals had been put to death. Many countries and such groups as Amnesty International consider the death penalty to be a violation of human rights. What do you think?

social values intended to justify the policies and actions of those in power." She goes on to argue that, "It is precisely because of the cultural diversity of the world that it is necessary for different nations and peoples to agree on those basic human values which will act as a unifying factor." As for the cultural imperialism argument, Suu Kyi contends that "when democracy and human rights are said to run counter to non-Western culture, such culture is usually defined narrowly and presented as monolithic." To avoid this, she counsels, it is possible to conceive of rights "which place human worth above power and liberation above control" (Suu Kyi, 1995:14, 15, 18). The power and control she wishes to subordinate are not just those of government, but those of one ethnic group, race, religion, sex, or other societal faction over another.

It must be said that differences over what constitutes a human right are not only matters of Western and non-Western philosophies. There are also vigorous disputes between countries of similar cultural heritage. For example, many countries have taken the same position and will not extradite people accused of capital crimes unless assured that the death penalty will not be invoked. In one case, Italy's Constitutional Court cited the alleged barbarity of executions and blocked the extradition of an Italian wanted for first-degree murder in Florida, which has a death penalty. A U.S. Department of Justice official called the Italian court's decision "a bad omen"; Giovanni Leone, a former president of Italy, called the decision "one of historic character that does honor to Italy."[3]

Such views have increased worldwide as the number of executions in the United States has risen, as evident in Figure 17.2. A total of 98 inmates were put to death in U.S. prisons in 1999, and 3,565 other prisoners were under sentence of death. Of these, 77 had been sentenced to death for crimes they had committed as children (under age 18). The U.S. record stands in sharp contrast to the trend worldwide, where the number of countries that prohibit the execution of prisoners increased from 8 in 1948 to 108 in 2000. This difference was one factor that led the UN in late 1997 to name a monitor to report on potential human rights violations by the United States in light of (1) its relatively high rate of executions (fourth in the world in 1999); (2) the execution of individuals for crimes they committed as children; and (3) the high percentage of those executed who are from minority groups (36 percent of all those executed in 1998 were African Americans; adding Latinos, for whom separate data is not compiled, would certainly push the minority rate over 50 percent).

The two matters of whether rights protect only against specific abuses or extend to quality of life criteria and whether rights are culture-based or universal are addressed further in the box, A Global Bill of Rights on the next page. See if you agree with the range of individual and group rights that the UN General Assembly adopted.

HUMAN RIGHTS: QUALITY OF LIFE ISSUES AND PROGRESS

One set of pressing problems for the world community involves preserving and enhancing human dignity by protecting and improving the physical condition of humans (Lauren, 1998). These issues are, in part, economic in nature and are being addressed by the international economic cooperation efforts discussed in chapter 16. There are also, however, specific efforts to deal with such concerns as living conditions and human rights. Note that many of these issues have a strong environmental factor. It is not facile to say that how people are treated has a great deal to do with the way that they treat one another and the ecosphere they share. It is also the case that, in the view of many, food, health, and the other quality of life matters included in this section fall under the rubric of human rights (Speth, 1998). For example, the UN–sponsored World Food Summit that met in 1996 reasserted the principle found in many international human rights documents that there is a "right to adequate food and the fundamental right of everyone to be free from hunger."[4]

FOOD

Some two centuries ago, Thomas Malthus predicted in *Essay on the Principle of Population* (1798) that the world's population would eventually outpace the world's agricultural carrying capacity. For the two centuries since Malthus's essay, human ingenuity has defied his predictions. The question is whether it can continue to do so, given the rapidly increasing global population.

There are two basic food problems. One is the *short-term food supply*. Regional shortages inflict real human suffering. Hunger—indeed, starvation—is most common in Africa, where many countries face a severe shortage of food. In addition to the multitudes that have died from starvation or diseases stemming from malnutrition, agricultural insufficiency has a host of negative economic impacts that range from sapping the vigor of the population to consuming development funds for food relief. The UN's Food and Agricultural Organization (FAO) estimates that around the globe there are 800 million people, one-quarter of them children under age 5, who are undernourished; some 15 million a year die from outright starvation or from diseases brought on by malnutrition.

The *long-term adequacy of the food supply* is also a significant concern. A combination of population control and agricultural development is necessary to ensure that the world's appetite does not outstrip its agriculture. There is, in essence, a race under way between demand and supply. The growing population and the efforts to increase the calorie, protein, and other nutrient intake of chronically underfed people is rapidly increasing demand. On the supply side, food production must rise 75 percent over the next 30 years to meet this escalating demand. Whether that standard can be met is, however, uncertain.   *(continued on page 490)*

A GLOBAL BILL OF RIGHTS

It is easy to assert that people have, or ought to have, rights, especially when we think ours are being violated. It is much harder to agree on what rights all people (regardless of place, status, or demographic trait) should have and which, therefore, we and our governments should respect and protect.

The following list of rights is drawn in close paraphrase from almost all of the clauses of the Universal Declaration of Human Rights. This declaration was adopted in 1948 by the UN General Assembly with no dissenting votes (albeit with abstentions by the Soviet bloc countries, Saudi Arabia, and South Africa). The rights that the UN membership recognized with near unanimity illustrate two of the important controversies about rights. One is the matter of cultural relativism. The Universal Declaration of Human Rights (UNDHR) in its preamble implicitly rejects the positivist concept that rights are culture-based by recognizing the existence of "inalienable rights of all members of the human family." The second controversy is whether rights involve only prohibitions on governments, and perhaps people, against specific abuses (such as abridging free speech), or whether rights extend to quality of life criteria (such as health and economic condition). You will note that beginning with number 20, the rights enumerated by the Universal Declaration include several quality of life standards.

One thing that you can do with this list, in your class or with your friends, is to constitute yourselves as the World Constitutional Convention, debate the various clauses of the UNDHR, and decide whether to ratify or reject each one of them. You might also decide to open them up for amendment. Finally, take note of clause 27 and ponder whether it provides too much of an escape clause that potentially allows governments to violate rights and to assert that doing so is necessitated by "the just requirements of morality, public order, and the general welfare in a democratic society."

How say you to the propositions that:

1. Everyone has the right to life, liberty, and security of person.   Ratify_____ Reject_____

2. No one shall be held in slavery or servitude; slavery and the slave trade shall be prohibited in all their forms.   Ratify_____ Reject_____

3. No one shall be subjected to torture or to cruel, inhuman, or degrading treatment or punishment.   Ratify_____ Reject_____

4. All are equal before the law and are entitled without any discrimination to equal protection of the law.   Ratify_____ Reject_____

5. No one shall be subjected to arbitrary arrest, detention, or exile.   Ratify_____ Reject_____

6. Everyone charged with a penal offense has the right to be presumed innocent until proved guilty according to law in a public trial [and to have] all the guarantees necessary for his [or her] defense.   Ratify_____ Reject_____

7. Everyone has the right to freedom of movement and residence within the borders of each state.   Ratify_____ Reject_____

8. Everyone has the right to leave any country, including his own, and to return to his country.   Ratify_____ Reject_____

9. Everyone has the right to seek and to enjoy in other countries asylum from persecution.   Ratify_____ Reject_____

10. No one shall be arbitrarily deprived of his nationality nor denied the right to change his nationality.   Ratify_____ Reject_____

11. Adults, without any limitation due to race, nationality, or religion, have the right to marry or not to marry and to found a family. They are entitled to equal rights both during marriage and at its dissolution.   Ratify_____ Reject_____

12. Everyone has the right to own property alone. No one shall be arbitrarily deprived of his property.   Ratify_____   Reject_____

13. Everyone has the right to freedom of thought, conscience, and religion; to change religion or belief; and in public or private to manifest that religion or belief in teaching, practice, worship, and observance.   Ratify_____   Reject_____

14. Everyone has the right to freedom of opinion and expression; this includes freedom to hold opinions without interference and to seek, receive, and impart information and ideas through any media and regardless of frontiers.   Ratify_____   Reject_____

15. Everyone has the right to freedom of peaceful assembly and association.   Ratify_____   Reject_____

16. No one may be compelled to belong to an association.   Ratify_____   Reject_____

17. Everyone has the right to take part in the government of his country, directly or through freely chosen representatives.   Ratify_____   Reject_____

18. Everyone has the right to equal access to public service in his country.   Ratify_____   Reject_____

19. The will of the people shall be the basis of the authority of government; this will shall be expressed in periodic and genuine elections which shall be by universal and equal suffrage and shall be held by secret vote or by equivalent free voting procedures.   Ratify_____   Reject_____

20. Everyone has the right to work, to free choice of employment, to just and favorable conditions of work, and to protection against unemployment.   Ratify_____   Reject_____

21. Everyone, without any discrimination, has the right to equal pay for equal work.   Ratify_____   Reject_____

22. Everyone has the right to form and to join trade unions for the protection of his interests.   Ratify_____   Reject_____

23. Everyone has the right to a standard of living adequate for the health and well-being of himself and of his family, including food, clothing, housing and medical care, and necessary social services, and the right to security in the event of unemployment, sickness, disability, widowhood, old age, or other lack of livelihood in circumstances beyond his control.   Ratify_____   Reject_____

24. Motherhood and childhood are entitled to special care and assistance. All children, whether born in or out of wedlock, shall enjoy the same social protection.   Ratify_____   Reject_____

25. Everyone has the right to education. Education shall be free, at least in the elementary and fundamental stages. Elementary education shall be compulsory. Technical and professional education shall be equally accessible to all on the basis of merit.   Ratify_____   Reject_____

26. Parents have a prior right to choose the kind of education that shall be given to their children.   Ratify_____   Reject_____

27. In the exercise of his rights and freedoms, everyone shall be subject only to such limitations as are determined by law solely for the purpose of securing due recognition and respect for the rights and freedoms of others and of meeting the just requirements of morality, public order, and the general welfare in a democratic society.   Ratify_____   Reject_____

OVERABUNDANCE AND SCARCITY

The world is a place of dietary overabundance as well as scarcity. Many in the North die early because they eat too much in general and have fat intakes way beyond what is healthy. Many people in the South die too early or never develop to their full potential because they eat too little and have other nutritional deficiencies. The people with the highest daily per capita caloric intake are the Portuguese (3,658 calories), who just edge out Americans (3,642). Eritreans (1,585) have the lowest calorie consumption. For fat, which is a problem when too much or too little is consumed, the French, whose daily per capita intake is 165 grams, are most in need of watching their diets. The people of Mozambique, who consume just 35 grams of fat daily, are the most deprived. Protein, which is critical for muscle and brain development and maintenance, is also most abundant in France, where people consume 114 grams a day. The people of Burundi suffer the greatest protein deficiency, consuming just 12 grams a day.

One critical determinant will be crop yields. On the positive side, yields have grown over 50 percent since 1970 due to the "green revolution" (the development and widespread introduction of high-yielding rice, wheat, and other grains), the increased use of fertilizers and pesticides, and other agricultural advances. On the negative side, the annual rate at which yields are increasing has been dropping steadily from about 5 percent annually in the 1970s to about 2 percent annually in the 1990s. What is worse, the FAO projects that the increase will drop to 1 percent or less in the first decade of the twenty-first century. This decline is compounded by the loss of land available for farming. Only about 11 percent of the world's land surface was ever well-suited for agriculture to begin with. Some new farmland has been added through irrigation and other methods, but even more has been lost to urbanization, to poor environmental practices that cause erosion, to soil-nutrient exhaustion, to salinization, and to other degradations. The FAO calculates that 38 percent of the world's original cropland (some 2.1 million square miles, almost two-thirds the area of the United States) has been lost to agriculture, and that a combination of increasing population and loss of arable land has cut the world's cultivated land to six-tenths of an acre per mouth to feed.

Causes of the Food Problem

There are several causes of hunger. *Population growth* is one. Production cannot keep up with population in many areas of the world. The result is that LDC per capita food production is barely expanding from its poverty base, and there is the constant threat of calamity. There are 38 countries whose per capita food production declined between 1990 and 1998. Indonesia had the worst record, with a drop of 43 percent in its per capita production.

Maldistribution of food is a second problem. For now at least, the world has the agricultural capacity to feed everyone adequately. Resources and consumption, however, are concentrated in relatively few countries. In the EDCs, daily food consumption averages a waist-expanding 3,377 calories a day, 62 percent more than the average 2,095 calories in the LLDCs.

Nutritional content represents a third, and even greater gap between the ability of the North and South to meet dietary needs. Protein deficiency is particularly common in the LLDCs. Most people in Africa, for instance, consume less than 60 grams of protein per day per capita and in some countries they average as little as 30 grams. The recommended daily intake is about 55 grams for sedentary individuals, which means that in the LLDCs, where manual labor is the norm, protein deficiency is also the norm. The lack of protein is especially detrimental to children because of the role it plays in

The World Food Programme is not well known in the United States and other wealthy countries, but it has been, literally, a life saver in poor countries suffering from food shortages. The WFP's executive director, Catherine Bertini, is trying to shake hands with an obviously shy little boy in Jakarta, Indonesia, where the WFP provides rice for over 5 million of the country's urban poor. The Asian financial crisis of the late 1990s and La Niña–related weather disruptions have beset Indonesia.

developing both healthy bodies and brain tissue. Vitamin A deficiency is also common in LLDCs. About 10 million children a year suffer visual impairment from Vitamin A deficiency and many others fall ill and die because of insufficient quantities of the vitamin, which also promotes the ability of the mucous membranes to resist infection. Some dietary comparisons for specific countries are detailed in the box, Overabundance and Scarcity.

Political strife is a fourth problem. In many countries with severe food shortages, farms have been destroyed, farmers displaced, and food transportation disrupted by internal warfare. Rwanda is one of the recent tragic examples and now produces 19 percent less food than the already-meager supply it managed to do in 1990 before it was overtaken by strife between the Hutus and Tutsis.

The International Response to the Food Problem

A number of international efforts are under way. Some deal with food aid to meet immediate needs, while others are dedicated to increasing future agricultural productivity.

Emergency Food Aid Supplying food aid to areas with food shortages is a short-term necessity to alleviate malnutrition and even starvation (Belgrad & Nachmias, 1997). Grains constitute about 95 percent of food aid. About 7 million tons of grains and more limited amounts of other foodstuffs are donated each year. Some of the aid is given bilaterally, but a good deal of the assistance goes through a number of multilateral food aid efforts. The UN's World Food Programme (WFP) is the largest. It distributes food in crisis situations. About three-quarters of WFP aid goes to countries that have experienced massive crop failures or natural disasters; another 25 percent goes to feed refugees and other displaced persons. In 1998, the WFP received $1.7 billion in grains and other foodstuffs, about half of which came from the United States. While these contributions are laudable, they meet only about two-thirds of the emergency food needs identified by the WFP. There are also a variety of NGOs, such as Food for the Hungry International, that are active in food aid.

Agricultural Development The development of agricultural techniques and capabilities is crucial if there is to be any hope of future self-sufficiency. This is particularly important to the 8 countries that suffer what the FAO labels critical food security (all sources of supply are less than 65 percent of need) and to another 20 countries that have low food security (supply is 65 to 75 percent of need).

On a bilateral basis, many countries' programs include agricultural development aid. There is also a multilateral effort. The oldest agricultural IGO is the FAO. Founded in 1945, it has 174 members and an annual budget of approximately $650 million. The FAO supplies food aid and technical assistance to LDCs. The agency has been criticized for a variety of its policies, including putting too much emphasis on short-term food aid and not enough effort into long-range agricultural growth. This, in addition to the growing recognition of the food problem, has led to the establishment of several other global food efforts.

One of these is the International Fund for Agricultural Development (IFAD), a specialized UN agency. IFAD began operations in 1977 and is particularly dedicated to environmentally sustainable agricultural development projects in the poorest LDCs. The agency raises its funds through the voluntary contributions of its 161 member-countries, and since its establishment has disbursed nearly $6 billion to support almost 500 projects in over 110 countries. These efforts are supplemented by several UN–associated organizations involved in various donor, investment, and research efforts in agriculture. Finally, there are a variety of regional and specialized organizations that address agricultural issues.

World Food Conferences A key event in both the area of short-term aid and, especially, agricultural development effort was the 1974 World Food Conference held in Rome. Among its other actions, the conference sponsored the creation of IFAD and various structures associated with the UN Economic and Social Council to monitor the global food supply and its delivery to needy countries and people.

A second global conference, the 1996 World Food Summit, met at FAO headquarters in Rome and was attended by the heads of more than 80 governments and representatives from more than 100 other governments. Reflecting the declining commitment of the EDCs to foreign aid, though, the leaders of most of the industrialized countries were not present. The United States, for example, was represented by only its secretary of agriculture. The tone of the meeting was set by the first plenary speaker, Pope John Paul II, who called on the world's countries to "eliminate the specter of hunger from the planet" and to "jointly seek solutions so that never again will there be hungry people living side by side with people in opulence.... Such contrasts between poverty and wealth cannot be tolerated."[5]

Without the strong support of the EDCs, though, there was little of immediate substance that the summit could accomplish. It did, however, establish the goal of reducing the number of undernourished people by half before 2015. It also reaffirmed the UN's traditional standard that the EDCs should devote 0.7 percent of their respective GDPs to development aid, including food and agricultural assistance. Third, in a move that rankled Washington and some other capitals, the conference resolved that "food should not be used as an instrument for political and economic pressure."[6] This swipe at economic sanctions came just days after the UN General Assembly voted by 137 to 3 to urge the United States to end its 34-year embargo against Cuba.

HEALTH

The state of medical care, sanitation, and other conditions related to health in some areas of the world is below a level imaginable by most readers of this book. The EDCs spend on average $2,505 per citizen annually on health care, of which about two-thirds is paid for through public funds or private (usually employer-supported) health insurance. By comparison, the countries and the citizens of the South (which have scant public funds and very limited private health insurance) can afford to spend annually an average of just $75 per capita on health care. The amount for LLDCs is a mind-boggling $23. By another measure, there are 17 times as many physicians per person in the EDCs as there are in the LDCs. The health of people within these countries is an international concern for reasons beyond personal well-being. A healthy population is vital to economic growth because healthy people are economically productive and because unhealthy people often consume more of a society's resources than they produce.

The fate of children is one way to think about health care. Children under age 5 die in LDCs at a rate 14 times higher than children in EDCs. The reality that proper medical care, sanitation, and nutrition could reduce the infant mortality rate in the LDCs to that of the EDCs means that each year about 6 million children in LDCs die needlessly from malnutrition. Another 6 million perish from curable or preventable diseases, with acute respiratory and infectious intestinal (diarrheal) diseases being the most common. Overall, some 41 percent of deaths in the LDCs, compared to just 1 percent of deaths in the EDCs, result from such infectious and parasitic diseases. As the director of the UN Children's Fund (UNICEF) has lamented, "No famine, no flood, no earthquake, no war has ever claimed the lives of this many children a year."[7]

As grim as these figures are, they were once much worse. An infant born in an LDC is now 31 percent more likely to live to age 1 than an infant born in 1980. As recently as 1974, only 5 percent of all children in LDCs received any vaccinations; now 80 percent receive protection against diphtheria, whooping cough, and polio. As a result, the health of children in LDCs has improved dramatically. According to UNICEF, 90 percent of the children in LDCs live in countries that are making progress in the area of children's health. This means that about 2.5 million fewer children now die needlessly and almost a million fewer children will be disabled, blinded, crippled, or mentally handicapped than a decade ago.

Much of the credit for these advances goes to the **World Health Organization (WHO).** Headquartered in Geneva, Switzerland, the UN–affiliated WHO was created in 1946. It has 191 members and an annual budget of about $819 million from the UN and from other sources. The crusade against smallpox provides a heartening example of WHO's contributions. Smallpox was a scourge throughout human history. There were over 131,000 cases worldwide in 1976 when WHO began a 10-year campaign to eradicate the disease. By 1987 smallpox was confined to a single case in Somalia; no case has been reported since 1989. Polio is another disease whose death may be imminent. The annual global incidence has been cut from 350,000 reported cases in 125 countries during 1988 to 7,012 cases in 30 countries during 1999. Moreover, WHO hopes to have all children vaccinated by 2005. Among other notable achievements in that quest was the vaccination of 147 million children in India in one day. As one WHO official notes, the approaching eradication of polio "should be a source of pride to all of us, and it shows what can be done when everybody works together for a common cause for the benefit of mankind."[8]

Optimism based on progress is offset by continuing problems and new threats. In LDCs, 18 percent of all children born have low birth weights (less than 5.5 pounds), and the maternal mortality rate in many countries is horrendous. Eleven percent of all pregnant women in the Central African Republic die giving birth. That is 138 times worse than in the United States. Also, diseases once thought to be on the decline can reassert themselves catastrophically. Tuberculosis is one such disease. WHO declared in

1993 that TB had resurged, and there were 33 million people suffering from TB in 1999. Indeed, TB has become the leading cause of death from a single infectious agent and, in WHO's estimate, will kill more than 35 million people between 2000 and 2020.

New problems add to these old worries. The worldwide AIDS epidemic, for one, is a global killer. At least 40 million people worldwide are HIV-positive, and the number of people infected is increasing by 16,000 a day. Of those infected with HIV, over 1.6 million are known to have AIDS, and that figure grew rapidly in the 1990s. So far over 15 million people, including millions of children, have died of AIDS. Some countries are truly devastated. More than 10 percent of the populations of 11 sub-Saharan countries are HIV-positive, with Botswana and Zimbabwe each having over a 25 percent infection rate. Children infected during gestation and birth are among the victims. More than 1 million babies have been born HIV-positive; half die immediately. Other children will fall victim to AIDS in a different way. The UN estimates that by the end of the decade over 10 million children in sub-Saharan Africa alone will lose their mothers to AIDS. As one WHO physician explains the grim logic, "As more women die of AIDS, the number of orphans will rise exponentially."[9]

Yet other horrific emerging diseases lurk in the shadows and threaten to spread, as AIDS has, to a world with few or no natural or manufactured immunological defenses. The mosquito-transmitted West Nile virus began in 1999 to alarm Americans in the Northeast, but its effects are minor compared to such horrors as the Ebola virus. The most recent outbreak of the disease, which was discovered in 1976 and is named for a river in Zaire where it was first detected, was in Uganda in October 2000. The source of the Ebola virus in nature remains unknown, but monkeys, like humans, are susceptible to infection and may serve to transmit the disease. The virus causes a hemorrhagic fever, beginning with fever and chills, then usually progressing to vomiting, diarrhea, and other acute symptoms. Finally, the victim's blood fails to clot, and he or she dies from internal bleeding from the gastrointestinal tract and other internal organs. So far local medical personnel aided by WHO and other international agencies have contained outbreaks of new and recurring horrors such as the bubonic plague, Ebola, monkeypox, and o'nyong-nyong fever. Still, one WHO physician cautions, "There are almost certainly diseases out there waiting to get us. What is happening is that human beings are invading territories where no human beings have been before. We're cutting down forests, we're going to areas to develop agriculture where there wasn't any before. Human beings are coming into contact with animals and insects they never met before."[10]

What makes these diseases even more of a world problem than they once were is the flow of humans and their products around the globe, which means that diseases can be spread very quickly from continent to continent. A person who contracts an exotic disease in one place can board an airplane and, 12 hours later, be stifling a sneeze while sitting next to you in a restaurant. Therefore, the work of WHO has become increasingly pivotal to combating new and persistent diseases worldwide.

Health is an international, as well as national, problem, as the global spread of AIDS grimly demonstrates. Chan Mom, the Cambodian woman in the photograph, is HIV-positive. She is attending one of the thousands of global forums during World AIDS Day, which was held on December 1, 1999. Like many AIDS victims, especially women and children, Chan Mom is a "third-party" victim. She was infected by her husband. The Cambodian forum called the men of the country to use condoms for disease control.

EDUCATION

Education, like health, affects more than just the quality of life. Education is also a key to increased national and international productivity, population control, and other positive social goals. Promotion of education remains primarily a national function, but there are a number of international efforts. For one, the United Nations Educational, Scientific, and Cultural Organization (UNESCO) sponsors several programs. These national and international efforts are slowly paying off. In the 1950s less than 30 percent of all children in LDCs ever attended any school; now almost all children begin the first grade and more than half go on to begin secondary school. Overall, the level of adults with at least rudimentary literacy has increased to about 75 percent in the LDCs. The data is even more encouraging if younger people (age 15–24) are considered. Of this group in LDCs, 80 percent are literate.

The increasing percentages should not disguise the crying needs that still exist. More than 1 billion adults are still illiterate, and their personal and societal productivity is limited. There is also a gender gap in education, especially in LDCs, where males are 19 percent more likely to be literate than females. An optimistic note is that the gap is only 8 percent among people age 15 to 24. The averages also tend to disguise regional areas of profound educational deprivation. In sub-Saharan Africa, adult illiteracy is 41 percent.

The statistics showing an increase of literacy in LDCs also tend to cloud the fact that most children receive just a few years of primary education. Only about 60 percent of the relevant age groups of children in LDCs are in secondary school; that figure drops off to 27 percent in the LLDCs. The postsecondary school level is attained by only 10 percent of LDC students (and 4 percent of the LLDC students), compared with 47 percent of students in EDCs. Expenditures on education also vary widely between EDCs, which annually spend $1,376 per capita, and LDCs, which can manage only $51 in per capita educational funding. In our technological age, the lack of advanced training is a major impediment to development. In the North there are nearly 849 scientists and technicians for each 10,000 people. For each 10,000 inhabitants of the South, there are 88 scientists and technicians; in sub-Saharan Africa there are only 10.

HUMAN RIGHTS ISSUES REGARDING ABUSES OF INDIVIDUALS AND GROUPS

The human condition depends on more than food security, level of education, and degree of health, on the individual level or collectively. There is also a range of rights having to do with the treatment of specific groups or individuals within a society, whether domestic or global, that are subject to abuse. Some legal scholars distinguish between two types of such rights. *Civil rights* (civil liberties) include positive requirements on governments to ensure that all people and groups are treated equally by the government and perhaps by everyone. The Fourteenth Amendment to the U.S. Constitution, which provides to all people in the country "the equal protection of the laws," is a quintessential statement of civil rights. *Civil liberties* are those things that the government (and perhaps anyone) cannot, or should not be able to, prevent an individual or group from doing. Freedom of religion, speech, and assembly are examples.

HUMAN RIGHTS ABUSES: DIVERSE DISCRIMINATION AND OPPRESSION

Intolerance and the abuses that stem from it are ancient and persistent. They also are global and demographically diverse. Whether the focus is race, ethnicity, gender, sexual orientation, religious choice, or some other trait, there are few human characteristics or beliefs that have not been the target of discrimination and abuse somewhere in the world.

The hatred of other humans based on what they are, rather than on what they have done, extends as far back into history as we can see. Genocide is a modern term, but the practice is ancient. The Roman philosopher and statesman Seneca (ca. 8 B.C.–A.D. 65) wrote in *Epistles* that Romans were "mad, not only individually, but nationally" because

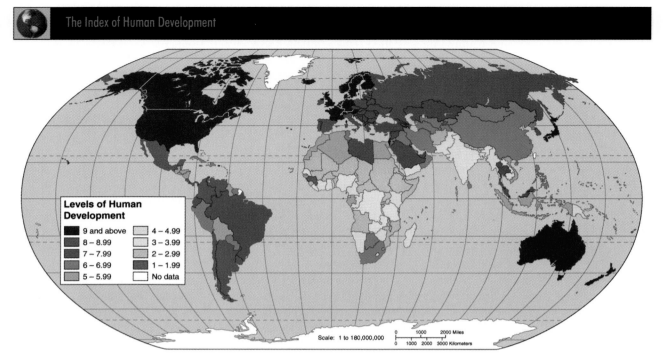

The Index of Human Development

Levels of Human Development

9 and above	4 – 4.99
8 – 8.99	3 – 3.99
7 – 7.99	2 – 2.99
6 – 6.99	1 – 1.99
5 – 5.99	No data

Scale: 1 to 180,000,000

The level of human rights and dignity around the world is measured in part by the Index of Human Development. The index, which was developed by the United Nations Development Programme, includes such gauges as health, literacy, income, and education. As you can see, the level of development that people enjoy or endure, as they case may be, varies greatly.

they punished "manslaughter and isolated murders" but accepted "the much vaunted crime of slaughtering whole peoples."

In the intervening years, attitudes on racial or other forms of demographic superiority have often played a powerful, and always destructive role in history. Many of today's divisions and problems are, for example, a legacy of the racism that combined with political and economic nationalism to rationalize oppression. The ideas of biologist Charles Darwin in *The Origin of Species* (1859) were thoroughly corrupted to allow the exploitation of the "unfit" (nonwhites) by the "fit" (whites). Whites in this context (as used here) means European-heritage whites (Eurowhites) and does not extend to Arabs, Persians, most of the people of India, and other Caucasians. Racism also joined with religion to build a case in the Western mind that subjugation was in the interest of the uncivilized and pagan—that is, nonwhite, non-Christian societies. Symbolic of this racist self-justification is Rudyard Kipling's "White Man's Burden," penned in 1899 to urge Americans to seize the Philippines:

Take up the White Man's burden—
Send forth the best ye breed—
Go bind your sons to exile
To serve your captives' need;
To wait in heavy harness
On fluttered folk and wild—
Your new-caught, sullen peoples,
Half devil and half child.

Take up the White Man's burden—
And reap his old reward:
The blame of those ye better
The hate of those ye guard—
The cry of hosts ye humor
(Ah, slowly!) toward the light:—
"Why brought ye us from bondage,
Our beloved Egyptian night?"

This sort of bastardized **social Darwinism** also reared its head in such brutally repressive ideologies as Italian fascism and the related German credo, National Socialism. The führer proclaimed that war and conquest were "all in the natural order of

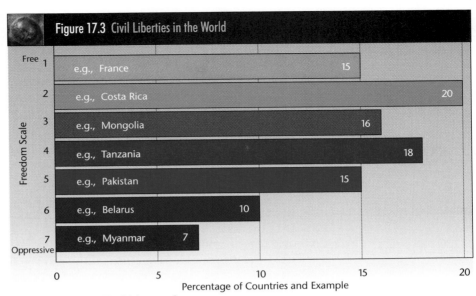

Figure 17.3 Civil Liberties in the World

Note: Percentages do not add to 100 due to rounding.

Data source: Freedom House, *Freedom in the World, 1999-2000*, on the Web at: http://www.freedomhouse.org/survey/2000/method.html.

Oppression of civil liberties remains common. Freedom House evaluates countries for freedom of speech, religion, association, and other aspects of civil liberties and assigns each country a score of 1 (free) to 7 (oppressive) on the freedom scale. Only 35 percent of all countries fall into the most laudable 1 and 2 categories; most countries have a mixed score; and 17 percent fall into the very oppressive 6 and 7 categories.

things—for [they make] for the survival of the fittest." Race was a particular focus of conflict because, Hitler asserted in *Mein Kampf* (1925), "all occurrences in world history are only expressions of the races' instinct of self-preservation." This racist social theory became a key part of the Nazi *weltanschauung* (worldview) and of Hitler's foreign policy.

It must be added that while genocidal attacks are often blamed on leaders who whip their former and otherwise peaceful followers up to murderous frenzy, it is also the case that ordinary common people are often all too willing to join the attacks. For example, Daniel Goldhagen argues in *Hitler's Willing Executioners: Ordinary Germans and the Holocaust* (1996), that the reason "the most committed anti-Semites in history" were able to come to power in Germany and turn a grotesque "private fantasy into the core of the state," was because German culture was "pregnant with murder" and rendered psychopathic by "hallucinatory anti-Semitism." This, Goldhagen concludes, led Germans in general to "believe [that] what they were doing to Jews was the right thing."[11]

The point is to not delude ourselves into thinking that the doctrine of superiority based on ethnic, racial, religious, or other differences died with the Third Reich or that it is always forced on unwilling populations by a few satanic leaders. Instead, hatred remains virulently alive. The many persistent forms of intolerance and oppression have been discussed earlier and will be encapsulated in the next section.

Oppression is also, of course, the tool of dictators, and the degree to which it is all too common is evident in data from one survey that ranked countries' respect for civil liberties on a scale of 1 (free) to 7 (oppressive). Civil liberties include freedoms such as speech, belief, and association that enable individuals to make choices about their lives. Political freedoms involve the right to vote and other factors that contribute to a democratic political process. Figure 17.3 illustrates that civil liberties are still moderately to severely restricted in most of the world's countries.

It is likely that you, like most of the people who read this book, live in the United States, Canada, or some other country that has attained a ranking of 1 on the Freedom

House civil liberties scale and where civil rights, while far from ideal, have progressed over time. Indeed, it is hard for those of us fortunate enough to live in such countries to imagine how widespread and how harsh oppression can be. It is tempting to describe lurid tales of repression, and it would be easy to do so, for there are many. It will suffice, however, to review briefly the many types of oppression and the diversity of victims that have suffered from it by examining some of the human rights issues and violations regarding women, children, ethnic and racial groups, religious groups, indigenous people, and refugees and immigrants.

Women

MAP
The Gender Gap, p. 166

In our discussion of the plight of a diversity of demographic groups, it is appropriate that we begin with the largest of all minority groups, women. Females constitute about half the world's population, but they are a distinct economic-political-social minority because of the wide gap in societal power and resources between women and men. Compared to men, women are much less likely to have a job that pays money, are much less likely to hold a professional position, are much more likely to be illiterate, and are much more likely to be living below the poverty line (Rhein, 1998).

The relative disadvantages of women are, of course, nothing new, but what has changed is that the issues of women's rights and circumstances have moved much higher on the global agenda. For example, it was not until 1994 that the U.S. State Department's annual report on global human rights focused for the first time on the status of women. "Its findings are grim," one news analysis related. "In painstaking detail the report... paints a dreary picture of day-to-day discrimination and abuse."[12] The common theme found in virtually every discussion of women's economic, political, and social status is that females suffer because of their gender. We have noted that women work longer hours than men but earn less; that women are afforded fewer opportunities than men to go to school; and that there is or has recently been a pattern of sexual and other physical assaults, including politically directed rape in Bosnia, forced prostitution in Thailand, bride-burning in India, sexual mutilation in many countries, and wife-beating almost everywhere.

Women in many countries are sold or forced by poverty to go into de facto slavery in their own countries or abroad. These domestic servants are often mistreated. The sale of young women and even girls (and young men and boys) into heterosexual or homosexual slavery is also relatively common in some places. In Pakistan, girls between 8 and 10 years old reportedly brought bids of $397 to $529 at one auction. According to the director of social welfare in Pakistan's Sind province, many men there believe that "since a woman is no better than a dumb, driven chattel, who cares what happens to her? She can be sold, purchased, transferred and bargained off like cows, sheep, goats or some other property."[13] So many women from Russia have been forced, physically or by poverty, into prostitution in other countries that this sad trafficking in women has become known as the "Natasha trade" (Hughes, 2000).

Other assaults on women arguably constitute a form of genocide. UNICEF reports that "In many countries, boys get better care and better food than girls. As a result, an estimated 1 million girls die each year because they are born female."[14] Not only that, but medical advances mean that more female than male fetuses are being terminated by abortion. A UN Population Fund (UNFPA) study of India concluded that the spread of ultrasound technology, by which sex can be determined, has resulted in increased abortions of female fetuses. "It is generally recognized," the report said, "that [the] adverse sex ratio occurs not because fewer girls are born (or conceived) but because fewer are allowed to be born or to survive." This has led some groups in India and elsewhere to campaign against procedures such as ultrasound. "We want to make these sex determination tests illegal," explained a representative of the All-India Democratic Women's

There is a significant movement under way to improve the rights and conditions of women globally. These women and children in Saudi Arabia symbolize two forms of injustice against many women globally. One is oppression. For example, the women of Saudi Arabia are required to wear a *burqa*, the garment that covers them from head to toe. The second injustice is poverty. Despite Saudi Arabia's wealth, many of its people are poor. Moreover, as in all countries, women constitute a significantly higher percentage of the poor than do men.

Association; "we think it is an attack on the existence of women."[15] The groups in India have not been successful, but China, which has the same problem, has banned sex-determination tests.

Sometimes the abuses are sanctioned by law, but more often the rights of women are ignored because male-dominated governments turn a blind eye. In some cases, there are also economic incentives for governments to ignore abuses. Prostitution is a huge business in Southeast Asia, as elsewhere, and the females—often poor girls and women who are forced or duped into sexual slavery—bring in billions of dollars. The UN estimated in 1998, for example, that Thailand's sex tourism and other aspects of the illicit sexual trade earned the country about $25 billion a year. That added roughly 15 percent to Thailand's officially reported GDP. According to the report, "The Sex Sector: The Economic and Social Bases of Prostitution in Southeast Asia," the "revenues [the sex trade] generates are crucial to the livelihoods and earning potential of millions of workers beyond the prostitutes themselves."[16]

Most often, civil law and social strictures reinforce one another. One current place where this is so is Afghanistan. When in late 1996 a fundamentalist Muslim movement, the Taliban, took control of most of the country, the Taliban leaders decreed the *Shari'a* (Islamic law) would be the law of the country. The Taliban interpretation of the Shari'a dictates, among other things, that women should be forced to wear the *burqa* (a head-to-foot garment covering everything but the eyes and hands). "Some women want to show their feet and ankles," worried one Taliban leader. "They are immoral women. They want to give a hint to the opposite sex."[17] Women are also banned from working outside the home and from going to school, which among other deleterious effects has left widows destitute and without any means of support for themselves and their children. The UN pressured the government into lifting the work ban, but it was reimposed in mid-2000.

The Taliban also reintroduced the long-abandoned practice of stoning women, and sometimes couples, who were found to have committed adultery. In this practice, victims

(continued on page 500)

ASYLUM

Fauziya Kassindja arrived at the U.S. border on December 17, 1994, and presented herself to customs officials. The 17-year-old from Togo asked for asylum. She was fleeing her country, she said, to avoid those who wanted "to scrape my woman parts off."[1]

What terrorized Kassindja was female genital mutilation (FGM), or, euphemistically, female circumcision. This traditional rite of puberty is performed widely in central and northern Africa and involves a clitoridectomy (the excision of the clitoris), which deprives a woman of all or most sexual sensation. Sometimes, more drastically, FGM extends to infibulation, the cutting away of all of a female's external genitalia and labial tissue. The UN estimates that as many as 130 million girls and women in the world today have suffered FGM and that each year another 2 million girls are subjected to the knife, shears, or razor blade. The practice is extremely painful. A woman who performs the rite in Togo explains that "young, weak girls are held down by four women. Stronger ones require five women, one to sit on their chests and one for each arm and leg."[2]

Aside from the psychic scars, FGM can be dangerous when carried out, as it usually is, by people who are not medically trained and who operate in unsanitary conditions. Infections and other complications are common; death can result. When a journalist asked the patriarch (senior male) of the Kassindja family in Togo about the danger, he conceded that "there are some girls who die." Still, he insisted, "To me it is not the excision that caused the death." When the reporter asked him what did cause the death, he merely shrugged.[3]

Supporters defend FGM on two grounds. One is tradition. "Since our forefathers' time, this is the law," a village elder said.[4] The second rationale is that it supposedly ensures chaste behavior by girls and women. "Am I supposed to stand around while my daughter chases men?" one African father asked incredulously. "So what if some infidel doctor says it is unhealthy?"

he went on. "Banning it would make women run wild like those in America," added another man to reporters.[5]

It should be noted that some women favor FGM. "During the ceremony they find out if you are a virgin," one Togolese woman explained. "If you are a virgin the man will pay more dowry and your family will be honored by the husband." Other women are merely resigned to their fate and that of their daughters. "I have to do what my husband says," one woman commented. "It is not for women to give an order.... I remember my suffering. But I cannot prevent it for my daughter."[6]

Shielded by her family, Kassindja was able for a time to avoid the rite. But then, at age 15, she was betrothed to 45-year-old man. He demanded that she undergo a clitoridectomy. Rather than face mutilation, Kassindja fled from Togo to Ghana, and through a circuitous route, she eventually tried to use a fake passport to enter the United States, where she had a relative. There she was initially treated as a criminal, and was subjected to treatment that must have made her wonder whether her flight had been from one purgatory to another. "What I hate is when they put 20 or 30 people in a room," Kassindja has recalled. "They strip all of us together. They tell us to turn around, open your legs, squat. They stand looking at you. Sometimes they laugh."[7]

Kassindja's plight gained increasing attention of the national press, however, and in April 1996 she was released after nearly 16 months in prison to await the resolution of her appeal for asylum. The following year, a U.S. court finally granted asylum to Kassindja on the grounds that immigration law allows asylum for those who can show that they have a well-founded fear of persecution because of their race, religion, nationality, political opinions, or membership in a social group. The court found that Kassindja's membership in the Tchamba-Kunsuntu tribe, as a social group, made her subject to persecution. In support, the court quoted

are buried up to their chests, then killed by people who hurl heavy stones at their heads. "Just two people, that's all, and we ended adultery [in Afghanistan] forever," one Taliban member exulted naively after one such execution.[18] Protests from numerous international sources, including the United Nations, were rejected by the Taliban. The Taliban minister of information and culture proclaimed that "there is no possibility of a change in Islamic principles, which have not changed in the last 1,400 years."[19]

Seventeen-year-old Fauziya Kassindja (center) fled Togo to avoid ritual female genital mutilation. When she entered the United States using a fake passport to join a relative who had agreed to shelter her, she asked for asylum. Instead, she was arrested. The relief she felt on being released after 15 months in prison is evident in this picture of Kassindja and some of the women whose support had helped free her, pending an appeal of the decision to deny her application for asylum. She was finally granted asylum, giving hope to other women who wish to escape FGM.

an Immigration and Naturalization Service report that commented, "It remains particularly true that women have little legal recourse and may face threats to their freedom, threats of acts of physical violence, or social ostracization for refusing to undergo this harmful traditional practice."[8]

While Kassindja left the courtroom a free and whole woman, other women have not been and will not be so fortunate. Reportedly, the girls in Kassindja's home village are now being cut at age 4 to 7 instead of 14 or 15. The reason for that change, a male village elder explained, is, "We don't want to let them grow up before we do it because they can run away."[9]

The larger implication of Kassindja's refusal to submit is that it highlights and symbolizes the determination of many people to eradicate the practice of FGM. About a third of the countries where FGM is performed have made it illegal, but these laws have only begun to reduce the incidence of FGM. Some advances have been by individual countries. The ability to seek refuge is clear in Canada, which, like a few other countries, has enacted a law that makes FGM and other acts of gender abuse grounds for asylum. The U.S. court decision in Kassindja's case should have made it easier for other women to claim asylum, but that has not occurred. For example, Adelaide Abankwah, who fled from Ghana to escape FGM, spent two years in a U.S. jail before she was finally granted asylum in 1999.

There is also a determined international effort to end FGM by such global organizations as the International Planned Parenthood Federation and the World Health Organization. Perhaps most prominently, this campaign is represented by Waris Dirie, a women's rights activist, fashion model, and victim of FGM at age 5. One of her contributions has been to publicize her ordeal in an effort to educate others about FGM. Dirie's (1998) story, *Desert Flower,* was published as a book and excerpted in *Reader's Digest.* She also serves as special ambassador for the elimination of female genital mutilation of the United Nations Population Fund. Ambassador Dirie, a native of Somalia, lived through her ordeal, but a sister and several of her cousins did not. Then at age 13, betrothed to a 60-year-old man and facing even more radical FGM, Dirie fled, as Kassindja had, to safety in another country. "Because women and girls are not valued equally as human beings, they are treated as less than such," Dirie charges. "Female genital mutilation is one example of this that has got to be stopped."[10]

The defense of such policies toward females on the grounds of compliance with the Shari'a raises the point of cultural relativism, which is frequently used to justify the differences between how women and men are treated in some Muslim and other societies (Howland, 1999). Cultural relativism is also the crux of debate over another ancient practice—genital mutilation. The story of this African practice and the reaction of U.S. officials to a young woman who fled from Togo to avoid it is told in the box, Asylum.

Children

Children are not commonly considered a minority group. But insofar as they are dominated and sometimes abused by others, children fall well within the range of the groups that suffer because of their lack of economic and political power and because they are often denied rights accorded to the dominant segments of society.

Besides conditions such as lack of adequate nutrition that deny to a vast number of children any opportunity for a fulfilling life, there are a variety of abuses that children endure. Being forced to work is one of them. According to UNICEF's data in 2000, there are 250 million children ages 5 to 14 in LDCs who go to work, not to school, each day. This includes 40 percent of the children in Africa, 20 percent of the children in Asia, and 16 percent of the children in Latin America. Even more disturbing is the fate of the 2 million children who were killed and 6 million who were severely injured during armed conflict in the 1990s.

Yet another repugnant reality is the sexual exploitation of children. Precise information is difficult to gather, but the consensus among those familiar with the problem is that there is a global, multibillion-dollar sex trade, into which about 1 million children are drawn each year. UNICEF has estimated that 200,000 are children being sexually exploited commercially in Thailand, 300,000 in the United States, 400,000 in India, and 650,000 in the Philippines. The estimates of children engaged in commercial sex in Brazil range between 500,000 and 2,000,000. "Brazil may be the worst in the world, but nobody really knows," says UNICEF's representative in Brazil.[20]

There are many reasons ranging from abuse at home to economic desperation why children turn to prostitution; it is also the case that many children are sold by their families to or kidnapped by sex-slavers. An astronomical rate of AIDS and other sexually transmitted diseases are among the dangers these children face.

The treatment of children is certainly the proper concern of national governments, but it is also an international issue. It is estimated that 10 to 12 million men travel each year internationally as "sex tourists" to exploit children. Clothes, shoes, and other products manufactured by children are sold in international trade; you may be wearing one of these products even as you read these words. The wars and civil strife that ruin the lives of boy soldiers and other children are often rooted in world affairs.

Ethnic and Racial Groups

MAP
Global Distribution of Minority Groups, p. 146

Strife and oppression based on ethnicity and race are still unsettlingly common. Until international pressure through economic sanctions and other actions finally compelled South African whites to surrender political power in 1994, racism persisted officially through the apartheid system that permitted 6.5 million whites to dominate the other 29 million black, Asian, and "colored" (mixed-race) people. Also in 1994 the slaughter of Tutsis by Hutus in Rwanda and the recurring violence between these two groups in Burundi and Rwanda provided a terrible example of racial/ethnic hate politics. Throughout the 1990s, various ethnic groups in what was Yugoslavia have beset one another, with the Serbs the main perpetrators, and the Muslim Bosnians and, more recently, the Muslim Kosovars, the main victims. The previous descriptions, especially in chapter 6, of these ethnic and racial tensions mean that here it is only necessary to reiterate that ethnic and racial identification are a key component of the tensions and conflict that make nationalism one of, if not the most, divisive elements of human politics.

Religious Groups

Strife and oppression based all or in part on religion is also common on the world stage, as the conflict in Northern Ireland, the conflict in Sudan between the Muslim government and non-Muslim rebels, the earlier-mentioned slaughter of Bosnian Muslims and Kosovars by Orthodox Bosnian Serbs, and other conflicts attest. There are also, as detailed in chapter 7, numerous efforts by religious fundamentalists in India, Israel, Northern Ireland, several Muslim countries, and elsewhere to align the legal codes and religious laws of their respective countries and to force everyone, regardless of their personal beliefs, to follow those theocratic laws. Even in countries where there is no move to supplant civil with theocratic law, religious intimidation is not uncommon.

Racism, anti-Semitism, and other disturbing forms of hatred are also on the rise in Europe. Russia and Eastern Europe have witnessed the reemergence of overt and not infrequent verbal and physical assaults on Jews. Public opinion surveys in some countries reveal that many negative images of Jews persist. One poll found 59 percent of Russians agreeing with the statement, "Jews have too much power in the world of business" (ADL, 1999:21). Giving voice to that sort of xenophobia, Gennadi Zyuganov, the leader of the still powerful communists in Russia's parliament, has charged that Russia and the rest of Christian civilization was separated from its moral foundations by Jews who "traditionally controlled the financial life of the continent."[21]

Other former communist countries in Europe are also seeing more overt anti-Semitism. A survey in Poland found that one-third of all respondents thought Jewish influence "too great" in the country, and 31 percent admitted to being somewhere between "extremely" and "slightly" anti-Semitic. When the movie *Schindler's List*, depicting the horrors in the Polish ghettos and in the concentration camps, played in Germany, some Germans charged that the movie overdramatized events, and a poll found that 39 percent of the Germans surveyed agreed with the statement, "Jews are exploiting the Holocaust for their own purposes."[22]

Indigenous People

The history of the world is a story of mass migrations and conquests that have often left the indigenous people of a region as a minority in national political systems imposed on their traditional tribal or other political structures. The most familiar of these groups to many readers probably are the numerous native peoples of North and South America commonly lumped together as "Indians," or more contemporarily referred to by such designations as Native Americans and Mezo-Americans. The Eskimos or Inuits of Canada and Alaska (as well as Greenland and eastern Siberia), and native Hawaiians in that U.S. state are also indigenous peoples.

The efforts of various indigenous groups in Central and South America have also become increasingly well known. The unrest in the southern area of Chiapas in Mexico is associated in part with the alienation of the impoverished Mayan and other indigenous people of that region from the Mexican government. This feeling of oppression is supported by UN data that finds that on the UNDP's Human Development Index, the level of development of the Mexican people is 27 percent higher than that of the country's indigenous people. This relative poverty, even in what used to be called **Third World** countries, has led to the term **Fourth World** to designate indigenous people collectively.

One of the particular efforts of indigenous people in recent years has been their effort to protect their traditional home areas politically and environmentally from the incursion of the surrounding cultures. The spread of the people and business of Brazil into the vast interior areas of the Amazon River system has increasingly degraded the health, environment, and other aspects of the life of the indigenous people of that region. The Yanomami people, for one, are being devastated by the diseases carried by miners who have entered their region and, on occasion, by violence aimed at forcing the tribe off its lands. The number of Yanomami has shrunk to just 8,268, with 2,200 of them dying between 1988 and 1995 alone. Similarly, the 1,400 Kaipao people, who live in the Brazilian Mato Grosso region in the 6.4-million-acre Xingu National Park along

These Yanomami boys playing with model airplanes on a landing strip near their home in Brazil's Amazon jungle capture the encroachment of "civilization" on the Yanomami people. They, like many other indigenous people around the world who have tried to maintain their cultural lifestyle, are disappearing as their homelands are invaded by outsiders bringing guns, diseases, and machinery that assail the people and their habitat. In other places, indigenous people who have given up their traditional lifestyle are almost always at the bottom of their country's socioeconomic scale.

with 14 other tribes, are fighting a losing battle to keep outsiders (ranging from miners and loggers to ecotourists) out of their homeland.

Beyond Brazil and the Western Hemisphere, parallel stories are common. Representatives of the Khwe people of Botswana traveled to the annual UN Commission on Human Rights convention in Geneva, Switzerland, to seek help in fending off their threatened expulsion from the Kalahari Desert to make way for tourism facilities. "We came without any promise of getting anything done," said John Hardbattle, leader of the First People of the Kalahari organization. "We felt that if we can't get help at the UN, then we won't get it anywhere else."[23] As Hardbattle recognized, the ability of aboriginal groups to resist the hunger of powerful outside forces for resources and land is limited. They depend in part on gaining world attention and help. That has just begun, as we will see later.

Refugees and Immigrants

Many commentators have accurately noted the rise of ethnic and racial strife, religious fundamentalism, and other xenophobic movements in recent years, but there is much less agreement about the causes. One intriguing explanation is offered by Václav Havel, who suggests that societies "tend to look for pseudo-certainties" and that people everywhere are insecure in this era of immense and rapid political, economic, and social change. One reaction for many people, Havel suggests, is "submerging themselves in a crowd, a community, and defining themselves in contrast to other communities." It is in part for this reason, the Czech president thinks, "that we are now witnessing manifestations of intolerance, xenophobia, racism, and nationalism."[24]

Did You Know That:

The United States admitted a total of just 1.8 million refugees between 1980 and 1997, accounting for less than 12 percent of total immigrants allowed to enter the country. The U.S. immigration rate of 3.4 (immigrants per 1,000 citizens) during 1980–1997 was well below half of what it was (8.0) during the first two decades of the 1900s.

One clear indication of that nativist tendency is evident in the upsurge in negative feeling in many quarters of the world toward immigrants and refugees. The post–cold war spasm of civil wars and other internal violence, added to the economic desperation of many people, has set off a flood of refugees. "Migration is the visible face of social change," as a report by UNFPA puts it.[25] According to the United Nations High Commissioner for Refugees, there were 11.5 million refugees living outside of their native countries at the beginning of 2000. Additionally, there were another 4 million internally displaced persons who, while still living in their own country, had been forced to flee their homes, villages, and cities.

In addition to the people who are overt refugees, there are millions of people who have legally or illegally entered other countries to find work. The tide of refugees and immigrants, legal and illegal, has been met with increasing resistance in the EDCs. The presence of a large number of foreign workers and the influx of Bosnian refugees led Germany to revise its laws and begin to place much greater restrictions on political refugees. That has not stemmed a rising rate of racial/ethnic violence. During June 2000 alone, Germany reported 129 xenophobic offenses, including 28 violent right-wing attacks that left one person dead and 26 injured. That month a German judge told one skinhead who had been convicted of killing an African immigrant that he was imposing a maximum sentence because the murder "was the latest in the long chain of attacks to which we must put an end.… Animals show mercy to opponents lying on the ground, but rightist extremists apparently do not," the judge intoned. "They are pitiless, without mercy."[26]

France in 1994 changed its laws in a way that meant that many foreigners who had earlier entered France legally to work would have to leave. Most of these workers and their families came from former French colonies in Africa. Although most French people would not agree with its stridency, many would find at least some hint of truth in the view of right-wing French political leader Jean-Marie Le Pen, who portrays some parts of France as "literally gangrenous because of the foreign invasion." Beware, Le Pen warned the French of "old origin" (whites, compared to most immigrants, who are Africans), "Tomorrow the immigrants will be moving into your house, eating your food and sleeping with your wife, your daughter, or your son."[27]

Anti-immigrant and anti-refugee opinion has also strengthened in North America. There has been broad political pressure in the United States to reduce legal immigration and illegal workers, and legislation, such as Proposition 187 in California, to deny services, including education for children, to undocumented aliens. Arguably, at least part of the feeling against the arrival or presence of temporary or resident aliens is based on racial and ethnic distinctions. A poll found that, of those Americans with an opinion, half favored making it easier for (generally white) immigrants from Eastern Europe to enter the United States. This contrasts with the percentages that wanted entry to be more difficult for (mostly black) Haitians (73 percent), Africans (59 percent), people from the Middle East (77 percent), Chinese (61 percent), and other Asians (65 percent).[28] Americans also tend to overestimate both the percentage of foreign-born people in the United States and the percentages of specific groups. The percentage of foreign-born people in the United States today is less than half of what it was in 1910. Moreover, when asked what percentage of the U.S. population was made up of which groups, white Americans answered (and the real answer was) Whites 49.9 percent (74 percent), Hispanics 14.7 percent (9.5 percent), Asians 10.8 percent (3.1 percent), and African Americans 23.8 percent (11.8 percent).[29]

Coping with refugees and economically driven illegal immigrants is costing the North many billions of dollars each year. Billions are spend to assist refugees overseas, and many countries are also spending vast sums on their border patrols and on other domestic programs to stem the influx of refugees and undocumented immigrants, to assist those who are admitted or who slip in, and to return some of those who do arrive to their country of origin.

Whatever the impact of programs to lessen the inflow of refugees and immigrants may be, it is certain that they are not only expensive, but that they will be unending as long as people in some countries are subject to endemic violence and poverty. The Kevin Costner movie *Field of Dreams* revolved around the line, "If you build it, they will come." To those who daily face death, disease, and hunger, the EDCs' societies of relative peace and material wealth represent a field of dreams. And people in danger and destitution will come.

One way to avoid perpetually spending vast sums on aid, immigration control, and other programs, some say, is to help the South develop quickly, to at least build a field that meets minimum needs of sustenance and safety. It is arguable that if Mexico's standard of living were to increase substantially, many of its citizens would no longer undergo the dislocation and risk the physical danger that leaving home and slipping into the United States entails. "We have a good argument now, a very concrete one," for helping the LDCs, the prime minister of Denmark told a UN conference, "which is, if you don't help the Third World…, then you will have these poor people in your society."[30]

THE INTERNATIONAL RESPONSE TO INDIVIDUAL AND GROUP HUMAN RIGHTS ISSUES

It would be naive to argue that the world has even begun to come close to resolving its numerous individual and group human rights issues; it would be equally wrong to deny that a start has been made (Moravcsik, 2000). The way to evaluate the worth of the efforts that we are about to discuss is to judge their goals and to see them as the beginnings of a process that only a few decades ago did not exist at all. Whatever country you live in, the protection of human rights has evolved over an extended period and is still far from complete. The global community has now embarked on an effort similar to your country's effort. It will, however, take time and will be controversial.

The United Nations is at the center of global human rights activity (Pace, 1998). The basis for concern is the UN's charter, which touches on human rights in several places (Eide, 1998; Korey, 1998). More specific is the Universal Declaration of Human Rights (1948), which includes numerous clauses discussed in the earlier box, A Global Bill of Rights. These are proclaimed as a "common standard… for all peoples and all nations." Many of the rights contained in the Universal Declaration are also included in two other multilateral treaties: the International Covenant on Civil and Political Rights (1966) and the International Covenant on Economic, Social and Cultural Rights (1966). Most countries have agreed to all three of these pacts. A notable addition to these ranks came in 1998 when China signed the treaty on civil and political rights. In addition, there are 19 other UN–sponsored covenants that address children's rights, genocide, racial discrimination, refugees, slavery, stateless persons, women's rights, and other human rights issues (Kent, 1999). These agreements and human rights in general are monitored by the United Nations Commission on Human Rights (UNCHR).

It would be foolish to imagine that when China or any other country adheres to one or another of these treaties, doing so ends abuses. That has not happened in China, which agreed to become a signatory to the civil and political rights covenant in order to head off the yearly ritual of a U.S.–led move to censure China in the UN. In return for China's agreement and its release of some political prisoners, the United States ended the censure effort. "China still has an enormous way to go," one U.S. official explained, "but in light of these steps, we have decided not to sponsor the resolution [of censure]."[31] It is easy to decry such decisions as cover-ups, but the desire of China to avoid censure and its willingness to formally sign the human rights treaty are also evidence of the impact of changing global norms.

There are also a number of regional conventions and IGOs that supplement the principles and efforts of the UN. The most well-developed of these are in Western Europe and include two human rights covenants. These are adjudicated by the European Court of Human Rights and by the Commission on Human Rights. Additionally, there are a substantial number of NGOs, such as Amnesty International and Human Rights Watch, that are concerned with a broad range of human rights. These groups work independently and in cooperation with the UN and regional organizations to further human rights. They add to the swell of information about and criticisms of abuses. They help promote the adoption of international norms that support human rights (Clark, 1996).

The impact of IGOs and NGOs and general progress in the human rights arena have, as noted, been mixed. Political selectivity and national domestic political concerns are two of the factors that impede the growth of human rights observance and enforcement on the international stage. Both these factors were discussed in chapter 8 and, thus, merit only brief recapitulation. Political selectivity disposes all countries to be shocked when opponents transgress against human rights and to ignore abuses by themselves, by their allies, and by countries that they hope to influence. Nationalism and the standard of sovereignty continue to be used by some countries to reject outside interference of domestic abuses, and by other countries as a reason for ignoring those abuses. An associated issue is the claim that cultural standards are different, and, therefore, what is a human rights violation in one country is culturally acceptable in another.

These and other impediments should not cloud the human rights contributions of the UN, Amnesty International, and other IGOs and NGOs. The frequency and horror of the abuses that they highlight increasingly are penetrating the international consciousness and disconcerting the global conscience. The 1993 UN–sponsored World Conference on Human Rights (WCHR) held in Vienna, Austria, provides an example. As is true for international forums on most issues, the WCHR witnessed political fissures along several lines. Some Asian, Muslim, and other countries resisted broad declarations of human rights based on what they see as Western-oriented values. This charge of cultural imperialism also led them to oppose the appointment of a high commissioner for human rights to head the UNCHR and give it more impact. In the end, though, some advances were made in both defining global human rights and creating and empowering a high commissioner. To clarify human rights, the WCHR declared that "all human rights are universal and indivisible and interdependent and interrelated," while adding that "the significance of national and regional particularities and various historical, cultural, and religious backgrounds must be kept in mind" when defining rights and identifying and condemning abuses (Burk, 1994:201). Those who advocated appointing a high commissioner were able to overcome the roadblocks erected at the WCHR by subsequently bringing the issue before the UN General Assembly, which created the post.

To give a bit more detail on the efforts of the UN, other IGOs, and NGOs in the area of human rights, we can turn to their activities with respect to women, children, ethnic and racial groups, religious groups, indigenous people, and refugees and immigrants.

Women A great deal of the human rights attention and some of the most vigorous international human rights efforts in recent years have focused on women. The most significant progress has been made in the realm of identifying the treatment of women as a global problem, identifying some of the causes and worst abuses, and defining women's rights. This has placed the issue of women solidly on the international agenda. For example, the UN General Assembly's Third Committee, which specializes in social, cultural, and humanitarian issues, spent less than 2 percent of its time discussing women's rights from 1955 to 1965. That percentage had risen almost sevenfold by the mid-1980s, and, indeed, has become the second most extensively discussed issue (after racial discrimination) in the Third Committee.

Crown Prince Abdullah Bin Abdul-Aziz Al-Saud of Saudi Arabia is seen here at the UN in September 2000 signing the Convention on the Elimination of All Forms of Discrimination Against Women. Certainly both the convention and the willingness of the Saudis to sign it are steps forward for women. But implementation of the treaty is the key. For example, the continuing status of Saudi women represented in the photograph on p. 499 is a reminder that deeds, not words and signatures, are the real goal of the convention. Among other things, it might be noted that the phrase "Saudi male leader" is redundant, since women are barred from political participation in that country.

A major symbolic step occurred with the UN declaration of 1975 as International Women's Year and the kickoff of a Decade for Women. Numerous conferences brought women together to document their status. Funding for projects to benefit women was begun through the establishment of such structures as the UN Fund for Women (UNIFEM, after its French initials). The adoption of the Convention on the Elimination of All Forms of Discrimination Against Women in 1979 was a pathbreaking step in defining women's rights on an international level. As of late 2000, 165 countries had agreed to the treaty, but the United States remained among the absent. Progress on women's issues also occurred at the 1993 WCHR. The plan adopted by the conference urged universal adoption of the 1979 treaty and urged the UNCHR to create the post of special rapporteur on violence against women. The commission complied in early 1994, naming a Sri Lankan jurist to the post.

This rise in the level of consciousness also led to a number of other institutional changes at the UN. The organization created the Division for the Advancement of Women, which is responsible for addressing women's issues and promoting their rights. In this role, the division administratively supports both the Commission on the Status of Women (CSW), which is the main UN policy-making body for women, and the Committee on the Elimination of Discrimination Against Women (CEDAW), which monitors the implementation of the 1979 convention on women's rights. The division has also organized four UN world conferences on women.

Of these, the most important was the fourth World Conference on Women (WCW), which convened in Beijing in 1995. During the planning for the conference, its chairwoman urged that "the road to Beijing must be paved with vision and commitment" (Burk, 1994:239). It was, and the story of that conference is told in the box, The Road to Beijing and Beyond.

Finally, there have been advances in other contexts to further the rights of women. One notable stride occurred through the treaty signed by most countries in 1998 to

THE ROAD TO BEIJING AND BEYOND

The most recent well-publicized effort to advance women's rights globally was the fourth World Conference on Women (WCW) that convened in Beijing in September 1995. Building on the third conference, held in Nairobi in 1985, and also on other events such as the 1994 UN Conference on Population and Development (UNCPD) held in Cairo, the WCW had three "priority themes": equality (especially equal pay for equal work), development (with an emphasis on population, nutrition, and health factors), and peace (particularly eradicating societal and family abuse of women).

The 188-page report that emerged from the WCW declared that women have the right to decide freely on all matters related to their sexuality and childbearing. This included a condemnation of forced sterilizations and abortions. The final document denounced rape in wartime as a war crime and called on national governments to intervene to prevent the genital mutilation of girls, bride burning, and all spousal abuse. The conference also called for the economic empowerment of women. To this end, it demanded an end to sexual harassment at work. The document further called for public and private lending organizations to extend credit to low-income women for establishing small businesses and other economic betterment projects and for an end of forbidding women to inherit their husband's property (Scott, 1996).

There were, of course, controversies. The ongoing sensitivities of some Roman Catholic, Muslim, and other countries to the issue of abortion led to language in the final document that was not as strong as some abortion-rights advocates wished. Lesbian rights were debated internationally for the first time, but no language was included in the report.

In many ways, though, the specifics about what the conference said are less important than the fact that it happened and that it voiced the concerns of women and presented their goals to a global audience. The official conference at Beijing was attended by some 3,000 delegates from 180 countries. The U.S. delegation was headed by first lady Hillary Rodham Clinton; UN ambassador and future U.S. secretary of state Madeleine Albright was the deputy head of the delegation. There was also a huge parallel conference for NGOs at nearby Huairou, which drew 30,000 delegates representing some 2,000 NGOs. In short, the meetings in China constituted the largest conclave of women in history. Not only could women meet and strengthen their already formidable network of women's groups, but their collective voice was carried outward by the 2,500 reporters who covered the conferences.

While the Beijing conference's platform of action was not binding on states, it set a standard that has already begun to have an impact. In June 1996, for example, The Hague Tribunal on war crimes in Bosnia declared for the first time in history that rape in war is a war crime by indicting eight Bosnian Serb soldiers for the rape of Bosnian Muslim women. "This is a landmark indictment because it focuses exclusively on sexual assaults, without including any other charges," noted a tribunal spokesperson.[1]

The meetings in China also strengthened the resolve of women to campaign against cultural sexism. Mahnaz Afkhami, an Iranian exile who heads an NGO, the Sisterhood Is Global Institute, and who is a leader of the effort to establish a Muslim women's movement, was able to meet with women from Iran. "The Iranian women were under enormous constraint," she noted, but she also found that while "they may have had to wear the chador (traditional full-cover garment),... they didn't have a conservative line.... That kind of interaction is very important."[2]

create the International Criminal Court. It specifies in Article 7 (Crimes Against Humanity) that such crimes "when committed as part of a widespread or systematic attack directed against any civilian population, with knowledge of the attack" include, among others, acts of "rape, sexual slavery, enforced prostitution, forced pregnancy, enforced sterilization, or any other form of sexual violence of comparable gravity." There are currently war criminals being prosecuted at the existing tribunals in The Hague (for the Balkans) and in Tanzania (for Rwanda) for such depravities, and the world has now served notice that rape and related abuses are war crimes.

There is also evidence that the rising international condemnation of the abuse of women is having some impact on norms and practices within countries. Egypt provides a case study. The country has long been one in which the genital mutilation of women was common. Then its health ministry banned the practice in 1996, setting off a legal struggle. The following year, an Egyptian court overturned the law as a usurpation of power by the government. That ruling was, however, reversed by Egypt's highest court, which held that "circumcision of girls is not an individual right under the Shari'a. There is nothing in the Koran that authorizes it."[32] Egypt has also changed its divorce laws. Beginning in 2000, women gained the ability to file for divorce, an option men alone had possessed.

Children   Serious international efforts to protect the rights of children have only recently begun, but there have already been worthwhile steps. UNICEF is the most important single agency, but it is supported by numerous other IGOs. The efforts of UNICEF are also supported and supplemented by a wide range of NGOs, such as End Child Prostitution in Asian Tourism, which was established in 1991 by child welfare groups in several Asian countries. Their common goal, in the words of UNICEF executive director, is to "ensure that exploitive and hazardous child labor becomes as unacceptable in the next century as slavery has become in this. Children should be students in school, not slaves in factories, fields, or brothels."[33]

The sexual exploitation of children is a global problem that the international community has just begun to address. This little girl in the Brazilian "gold rush" mining town Curionopolis is one of the millions of children around the world who have been physically or economically forced into the sex trade. The Convention on the Rights of the Child, which is now before the world's countries for signature and ratification, is one of the first steps toward ending the sexual exploitation of children.

One noteworthy advance is the Convention on the Rights of the Child (Mower, 1997). Work on it began in 1979, which was designated by the UN as the International Year of the Child. A treaty was adopted unanimously by the UN General Assembly in 1989 and made available for signature and ratification by the world's countries. The convention outlines a wide range of collective and individual rights for all persons under age 18. If all countries and people abided by the convention, the sexual exploitation of children, the use of boy soldiers, the diversion of children from their education to work, and many other abuses would end.

It is a mark of hope that the convention garnered enough ratifications to go into force in less than a year and also quickly became the most widely ratified human rights treaty in history. Indeed, as of mid-2000, of the 191 countries that had signed the treaty or otherwise become a party to it, only one country, the United States, had not ratified it. Among other concerns in the United States was whether the convention would abridge the possibility in some U.S. states that minors convicted of capital crimes can be executed once they reach age 18.

A second important effort on behalf of children was the World Congress Against Commercial Sexual Exploitation of Children, which met in Stockholm, Sweden. The 1996 conference was attended by representatives of 122 national governments, the UN and other IGOs, and 471 NGOs. The authority of such international meetings is severely limited, but they do serve a valuable function by focusing attention on issues. As the congress's general rapporteur, Vitit Muntarbhorn of Thailand, noted, "There can be no more delusions—no one can deny that the problem of children being sold for sex exists, here and now, in almost every country in the world."[34]

Despite the near impossibility of opposing children's rights in theory, the effort to protect them in practice, like most international human rights programs, runs into the problems of nationalism and parochialism. Countries resist being told what to do, and they are better able to see what others should do than what they themselves should do. India's representative to the UNCHR in Geneva, reacted to criticism of the number of children being exploited in her country by lashing out at "finger pointing" by other countries and recounting that when India had tried to garner support for a global ban on sex tourism, the effort had met resistance from Germany, Japan, Korea, and the Netherlands. Displaying ads in German magazines offering "boys of any color, size, or age," the delegate related that other countries had told her, "We are not willing to ban promotion of sex tours."[35]

Ethnic, Racial, and Religious Groups Efforts to define the rights of ethnic, racial, and religious groups have been part of the major human rights documents such as the International Covenant on Economic, Social, and Cultural Rights and the Convention on the Prevention and Punishment of the Crime of Genocide. There have also been some specific agreements, such as the International Convention on the Elimination of all Forms of Racial Discrimination (1969). It is a step forward that 155 countries have been willing to agree to this document, which, among other things, proclaims that its signatories are "convinced that any doctrine of superiority based on racial differentiation is scientifically false, morally condemnable, socially unjust and dangerous, and that there is no justification for racial discrimination, in theory or in practice, anywhere."

These efforts have been supplemented by some levels of enforcement. The earlier international pressure on South Africa to end legal racism was an important step. The international tribunals investigating and trying war crimes committed in the Balkans and in Rwanda are further evidence that persecution based on ethnicity, race, or religion are increasingly considered an affront to the global conscience.

Did You Know That:

The word Eskimo is probably derived from the word *assimew*, which means "she laces a snowshoe" in Montagnais, the Algonquin language of eastern Canada, and from the related Objibwa word for snowshoe, *askime*.

Indigenous People The UN General Assembly proclaimed 1993 to be the International Year of the Indigenous Peoples (Pritchard, 1998). The following year, as part of that year's UNCHR meeting, representatives of the more than 5,000 indigenous peoples agreed to an International Covenant on the Rights of Indigenous Nations and made it available for signature and ratification by the world's countries. The efforts of indigenous people have also been furthered by numerous NGOs, including the International Indian Treaty Council, the World Council of Indigenous Peoples, the Inuit Circumpolar Conference, and the Unrepresented Nations and Peoples' Organization. The causes of indigenous people were also furthered when the Nobel Peace Prize Committee made its 1992 award to Rigoberta Menchú of Guatemala in recognition of her efforts to advance the rights of her Mayan people in her country and to further the welfare of indigenous people globally.

Refugees and Immigrants International efforts on behalf of refugees provide very mixed results. There have been a number of efforts to define the status and the rights of both international and internal refugees. An early effort was the 1951 Convention Relating to the Status of Refugees (1951). This document charged the UN with providing assistance to people who were being persecuted in their countries or who feared persecution if returned to their home countries. The convention also defined the basic rights of refugees and minimum standards for their treatment and has served, among other things, as a foundation for subsequent efforts on behalf of refugees. It is also true, though, that it is one of the least widely ratified of the UN's major human rights treaties. Because of concerns that they might be required to open their borders to refugees or extend rights to those that managed to arrive unbidden, only 134 countries have signed and ratified it, with the United States among the missing countries.

Aid to refugees, while scant compared to their actual need, presents a somewhat brighter picture. The effort on behalf of displaced persons in the early 1950s led to the creation of the UN High Commissioner for Refugees in 1951 with wide responsibility

The world is awash with refugees forced from their homes. These Chechen women peering from the window of a vehicle at a checkpoint in Russia capture some of the sadness of refugees. Indeed, the image of the woman on the right has the air of the somber tones of early Dutch painters, especially Jan Vermeer's *Girl with the Pearl Earring* (c. 1665–1666), which can be found on the Web at: http://members.aol.com/Hilhaud/Vermeer.html.

for refugee rights and needs. Also formed that year was the International Organization for Migration (IOM), a body specifically concerned with the movement of refugees either to new homes or back to their former homes, as appropriate. Additionally, there are a number of IGOs, such as the International Red Cross (and its Muslim counterpart, the International Red Crescent), Oxfam, and others, which are involved in providing food, clothes, shelter, and other necessities.

 CHAPTER SUMMARY

1. This chapter discusses two types of human rights. Individual human rights consist of freedom from specific abuses or restrictions, especially by governments. Collective human rights include the right to a quality of life, including adequate nutrition; reasonable health care; and educational opportunity that, at minimum, does not detract from human dignity.

2. Population growth, the underproduction of food, and the maldistribution of the food that is produced means that there are many people who do not receive adequate nutrition. International organizations, such as the Food and Agriculture Organization, attempt to provide short-term food relief and long-term agricultural assistance to countries facing nutritional shortages.

3. Many people in LDCs face diseases and lack of medical care to degrees that boggle the minds of most people in EDCs. Some of the diseases, such as AIDS, can become a world health threat. The World Health Organization, other IGOs, and many NGOs are attempting to bring better health care to people globally.

4. The ability of individuals to achieve a higher quality of life and the ability of countries to develop economically depend in substantial part on education. More than

1 billion adults are still illiterate, many more have only the most rudimentary education, and the personal and societal productivity of these people is limited. The United Nations Educational, Scientific, and Cultural Organization is one of many international organizations working to improve education in the LDCs.

5. There are two types of individual rights. Civil rights include standards, such as equal standing in the courts, that must exist to ensure that all people and groups are treated equally. Civil liberties are those things, like exercising free speech, which individuals cannot be prevented from doing.

6. Human rights abuses are widespread. They spring from intolerance, authoritarianism, and other causes and are often rationalized by pseudoscientific theories, such as social Darwinism, and by repressive ideologies, such as fascism.

7. The discussion of human rights abuses and the efforts to ease them focuses on women, children, ethnic and racial groups, religious groups, indigenous people, and refugees and immigrants.

8. The area of human rights is one of the most difficult to work in because violations are usually politically based. Therefore, efforts to redress them are often resented and rejected by target countries. The greatest progress has been made in adopting a number of UN declarations, such as the Universal Declaration of Human Rights, and multilateral treaties that define basic human rights. The enforcement of human rights is much less well developed, but the rising level of awareness and of disapproval of violations on a global scale is having a positive impact. There are also many IGOs, such as the UN Human Rights Commission, and NGOs, such as Amnesty International, that work to improve human rights.

CHAPTER 18

PRESERVING AND ENHANCING THE GLOBAL COMMONS

Comfort's in heaven, and we are on the earth.

Shakespeare, *Richard II*

Dear earth, I do salute thee with my hand.

Shakespeare, *Richard II*

Over the long haul of life on this planet, it is the ecologists, and not the bookkeepers of business, who are the ultimate accountants.

Stewart L. Udall, U.S. secretary of the interior

Only in the last moment of human history has the delusion arisen that people can flourish apart from the rest of the living world.

Edward O. Wilson

CHAPTER OBJECTIVES

After completing this chapter, you should be able to:

- Explain the concept of sustainable development and consider whether it is possible or desirable.
- Understand the debate regarding environmental degradation and possible solutions.
- Describe the world's growing population and efforts to control population growth.
- Evaluate the global problems related to population and industrialization, including their causes.
- Discuss current efforts toward international environmental cooperation and speculate about their future role.

This chapter deals with ecological concerns and cooperation, but it is in many ways an extension of the human rights issues in chapter 17. One connection between the two chapters is the normative question, Should we care? Clearly, the view in this text is that we all should care. Self-interest compels us to attend to issues of the world's expanding population, the depletion of natural resources, the increase of chemical discharges into the environment, and the impact of these trends on the global biosphere. You will see that new approaches are needed because solutions attempted by single countries will be insufficient to solve the problems we humans face collectively. The issues discussed in this chapter are transnational problems. Therefore, their solution requires transnational programs achieved through international cooperation (Zurn, 1998; Bellany, 1997).

TOWARD SUSTAINABLE DEVELOPMENT

Before taking up specific issues, it is helpful to understand that they are related. To do this, we can discuss two overarching controversies. One debates the *ecological state of the world*. You will see presently that some analysts are truly alarmed about the future. Other observers believe that worries about the ecosphere are frequently overwrought. The second broad controversy focuses on **sustainable development.** The issue is whether (or perhaps, how) the world can continue simultaneously to sustain development and to protect its environment. Another important term is **carrying capacity,** which is the largest number of humans that the Earth can sustain indefinitely at current rates of per capita consumption of natural resources.

THE ECOLOGICAL STATE OF THE WORLD

There is a book, *The State of the World* (Brown, 2000), published annually.[1] Just as the U.S. president delivers an annual State of the Union address to Congress, the study each year assesses the ecological state of the world. We should follow its lead and regularly take stock of the Earth we all live on.

A good place to start is with the value of Earth's ecological systems. About $33 trillion was the figure one group of scientists came up with. Of course, it is impossible to measure precisely the financial value of the world's ecosystems. Still, there is some food for thought in the estimates of 13 scientists, who assigned a dollar value to 17 different natural functions (such as water supply, soil formation, oxygen generation by plants) based on either the economic value they supply or what it would cost to replicate them artificially.[2] The estimates ranged from $16 trillion to $54 trillion, with $33 trillion as a median figure. Whatever the exact amount, the key point is that in sheer dollars and cents, the globe's ecological systems are extraordinarily valuable. By comparison, the world GDP, that is, all the measurable goods and services produced, was about $18 trillion in 1997.

A second preliminary point about the state of the world's ecological systems is to ask how important they are to us, irrespective of monetary value. The answer is that we cannot get along unless they are in reasonably good working order. Using medical analogies, one scientist refers to the biosphere as "the planet's life-support system," and other scientist calls it humankind's "umbilical cord." Adds the latter scholar, "Common sense and what little we have left of the wisdom of our ancestors tells us that if we ruin the Earth, we will suffer grievously."[3]

There is no controversy over the immense financial value of the biosphere and our dependence on it. Consensus ends, however, when we turn to the question of the current and future ecological state of the world. Here the range of opinions can be roughly divided into two camps: the environmental pessimists and the environmental optimists.

Environmental pessimists aptly describes one group of analysts who assess the state of the world. Lester Brown and the others who contribute to the annual *The State of the World* volume are among this group. Brown (2000:4) writes that the rapidly growing world population combined with the expanding global economy are outgrowing Earth's ecosystems and that "evidence of this can be see in shrinking forests, eroding soils, falling water tables, rising temperatures, dying coral reefs, melting glaciers, and disappearing plant and animal species." Brown draws a grim analogy between the ever expanding economy and human cancer cells. Unless they are checked, such cells continually grow, consuming the resources of the body, until the cancer destroys the human who is its unwilling host. Where will this lead? Brown (p. 16) worries that the world may face "wholesale ecosystem collapse." Avoiding that fate, he writes, requires "a massive undertaking by any historical yardstick." Finally, and echoing this text's theme about becoming actors on the world stage, Brown urges (p. 20) that "saving the planet.... is not a specator sport. It is something everyone can [and should] participate in."

Some pessimistic analysts even foresee "environmental scarcities" as the cause of future warfare among states desperate to sustain their economies and quality of life. According to one study, scarcities of renewable resources are already causing some conflict in the world, and there may be "an upsurge of violence in the coming decades... that is caused or aggravated by environmental change" (Homer-Dixon, 1998:342).

Environmental optimists reject this gloomy view of the world and its future. Indeed, some optimists believe that the pessimists resemble Chicken Little, the protagonist in a children's story who was hit on the head by a shingle that had fallen off the barn roof. Convinced that he had been struck by a piece of the sky, Chicken Little panicked and raced around the barnyard crying, "The sky is falling, the sky is falling," thereby creating unfounded pandemonium. For example, one optimist chastises the ecology movement for promoting "green guilt" by "scaring and shaming people" and falsely contending that there is "little that we in the industrial world... do that... [is not] lethal, wicked, or both."[4]

Optimists say that the sky remains safely in its traditional location and that with reasonable prudence there is no need to fear for the future. They argue that we will be able to meet our needs and continue to grow economically through conservation, population restraints, and, most importantly, technological innovation. They believe that new technology can find and develop oil fields. Synthetics can replace natural resources. Fertilizers, hybrid seeds, and mechanization can increase acreage yields. Desalinization and weather control can meet water demands. Energy can be drawn from nuclear, solar, thermal, wind, and hydroelectric sources. In sum, according to one of the best-known optimists, economist Julian Simon (1994:297), not only do the scientific facts indicate that "the current gloom-and-doom about a 'crisis' of our environment is all wrong," but "almost every economic and social change or trend points in a positive direction." In fact Simon was so sure of his view, that in 1980 he made a $1,000 bet with an equally convinced pessimist, biologist Paul Ehrlich, author of *The Population Bomb*, about the prices of five basic metal ores in 1990. Ehrlich wagered that population demands would drive the prices up; Simon bet they would not. A decade and nearly a billion people later, the prices were all down. Ehrlich sent Simon a check.

It is important to note that most optimists do not dismiss the problems that the world faces. "Progress does not come automatically," Simon wrote (p. 306); "and my message is not complacency. In this I agree with the doomsayers—that our world needs the best efforts of all humanity to improve our lot." That effort will be provided, he continued, expressing his profound optimism, by our "ultimate resource... people—especially skilled, spirited, and hopeful young people... who will exert their wills and imaginations for their own benefit, and so inevitably they will benefit not only themselves but the rest of us as well."

SUSTAINABLE DEVELOPMENT

Industrialization and science have been two-edged swords in their relationship to the environment and the quality of human life. On the positive side, industrialization has vastly expanded global wealth, especially for the economically developed countries (EDCs). Science has created synthetic substances that enhance our lives; medicine has dramatically increased our chances of surviving infancy and has extended adult longevity. Yet, on the negative side, industry consumes natural resources and discharges pollutants into the air, ground, and water. Synthetic substances enter the food chain as carcinogens, refuse to degrade, and have other baleful effects. Decreased infant mortality rates and increased longevity have been major factors behind the world's skyrocketing population growth.

All these phenomena and trends, however, are part of modernization and are unlikely to be reversed. The dilemma is how to protect the biosphere and, at the same time, advance human socioeconomic development. This conundrum overarches specific issues such as population, habitat destruction, and pollution.

Pessimists would certainly see this concern as immediate and critical, but even most optimists would concede that the challenge would be vastly compounded if you were to bring the industrial production and standard-of-living levels of the nearly 5 billion people who live in less developed countries (LDCs) in the South up to the levels enjoyed by the less than 1 billion people who reside in the North.

The Conundrum of Sustainable Development

Here is the problem you should ponder as you read the rest of this chapter: If the minority of the world's population who live in EDCs use most of the resources and create most of the pollution, how can the South develop economically without accelerating the ecological deterioration that already exists? Think about what consumption would be like if China were economically developed and the Chinese per capita consumption of petroleum and minerals and per capita CO_2 emissions were equal to that of Americans. Figure 2.3 on page 47 illustrates this. Given the fact that China's population is about four times that of the United States, a fully developed China with a per capita consumption equal to the United States (compared to current consumption and emissions) would more than triple the two countries' combined petroleum consumption and their combined CO_2 emissions and would more than quadruple their combined mineral consumption. Furthermore, if you were to bring the rest of the LDCs up to the U.S. (as an EDC) level of resource use and emissions discharge, then you would hyperaccelerate the depletion of natural resources and the creation of pollution even more. Clearly, this is not acceptable.

Options for Sustainable Development

What to do? is the question. Apart from doing little or nothing and hoping for the best, there are two options. One is to restrict or even halt economic development. The second option is to make the cooperative political and financial commitment to develop in as environmentally safe a way as is possible.

Severely Restricting Development Preserving the environment by consuming less is the first option. What is necessary, according to one analyst, is to institute "an integrated global program to set permissible levels" for consumption and emission, to mobilize huge financial resources for resource conservation and pollution control, and to create "effective international institutions with legally binding powers... to enforce [the] agreed-upon standards and financial obligations" (Johansen, 1994:381).

(continued on page 520)

World Ecological Regions

The world has many ecological areas. There is one issue that all these diverse areas share: the environmental health of each of them has been degraded and continues to be further threatened by human activity. Without international cooperation, it is improbable that the conundrum of sustainable development can be successfully resolved.

World Ecological Regions

Arctic and Subarctic Zone

- Ice Cap
- Tundra Province: moss-grass and moss-lichen tundra
- Tundra Altitudinal Zone: polar desert (no vegetation)
- Subarctic Province: evergreen forest, needleleaf taiga; mixed coniferous and small-leafed forest
- Subarctic Altitudinal Zone: open woodland; wooded tundra

Humid Temperate Zone

- Moderate Continental Province: mixed coniferous and broadleaf forest
- Moderate Continental Altitudinal Zone: coastal and alpine forest; open woodland
- Warm Continental Province: broadleaf deciduous forest
- Warm Continental Altitudinal Zone: upland broadleaf and alpine needleleaf forest
- Marine Province: lowland, west-coastal humid forest
- Marine Altitudinal Zone: humid coastal and alpine coniferous forest
- Humid Subtropical Province: broadleaf evergreen and broadleaf deciduous forest
- Humid Subtropical Altitudinal Zone: upland, subtropical broadleaf forest
- Prairie Province: tallgrass and mixed prairie
- Prairie Altitudinal Zone: upland mixed prairie and woodland
- Mediterranean Province: sclerophyll woodland, shrub, and steppe grass
- Mediterranean Altitudinal Zone: upland shrub and steppe

Humid Tropical Zone

- Savanna Province: seasonally dry forest; open woodland; tallgrass savanna
- Savanna Altitudinal Zone: open woodland steppe
- Rain Forest Province: constantly humid, broadleaf evergreen forest
- Rain Forest Altitudinal Zone: broadleaf evergreen and subtropical deciduous forest

Arid and Semiarid Zone

- Tropical/Subtropical Steppe Province: dry steppe (short grass), desert shrub, semidesert savanna
- Tropical/Subtropical Steppe Altitudinal Zone: upland steppe (short grass) and desert shrub
- Tropical/Subtropical Desert Province: hot, lowland desert in subtropical and coastal locations; xerophytic vegetation
- Tropical/Subtropical Desert Altitudinal Zone: desert shrub
- Temperate Steppe Province: medium to shortgrass prairie
- Temperate Steppe Altitudinal Zone: alpine meadow and coniferous woodland
- Temperate Desert Province: midlatitude rainshadow desert; desert shrub
- Temperate Desert Altitudinal Zone: extreme continental desert steppe; desert shrub, xerophytic vegetation, shortgrass steppe

NORTH PACIFIC OCEAN

NORTH ATLANTIC OCEAN

Tropic of Cancer

Equator

Tropic of Capricorn

SOUTH PACIFIC OCEAN

SOUTH ATLANTIC OCEAN

Antarctic Circle

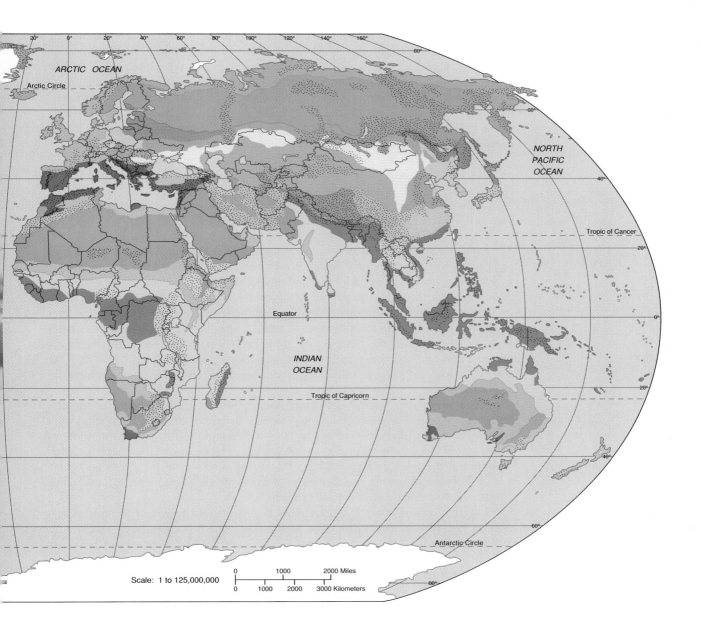

ARCTIC OCEAN

Arctic Circle

NORTH PACIFIC OCEAN

Tropic of Cancer

Equator

INDIAN OCEAN

Tropic of Capricorn

Antarctic Circle

Scale: 1 to 125,000,000

0	1000	2000 Miles
0	1000	2000	3000 Kilometers

Objections to such solutions leap to mind. Are we, for instance, to suppress LDC development? If the Chinese do not acquire more cars, if Indians are kept in the fields instead of in factories, and if Africans continue to swelter in the summer's heat without air conditioners, then accelerated resource use and pollution discharges can be partly avoided. As we saw in chapter 15, however, the LDCs are demanding a New International Economic Order that will allow them to develop industrially and technologically. The EDCs cannot "try to tell the people of Beijing that they can't buy a car or an air-conditioner" because they pollute, said one Chinese energy official; "it is just as hot in Beijing as it is in Washington."[5]

Another possible answer is for the people of the North to use dramatically fewer resources and to take the steps needed to reduce pollution drastically. Polls show that most people favor the theory of conservation and environmental protection. Yet practice indicates that, so far, most people are also unwilling to suffer a major reduction in their conveniences or standards of living. Efforts to get more Americans to use mass transit, for example, have had very little success. Proposals to raise U.S. gasoline taxes (thereby reducing consumption and raising environmental protection revenue) have met with strong political opposition. Laws could be passed mandating compact cars, but Americans would vote anyone out of office who threatened their SUVs and pickup trucks.

Those who advocate stringent programs believe that, eventually, we will be better off if we make the sacrifices necessary to restrain development and preserve the environment. In the end, one advocate asserts, "accepting and living by sufficiency rather than excess" will allow people to return to nonmaterialistic values "that give depth and bounty to human existence" and are "infinitely sustainable."

Paying the Price for Environmentally Responsible Development A second option is to pay the price to create and distribute technologies that will allow for a maximum balance between economic development and environmental protection. Without modern technology and the money to pay for it, China, for example, poses a serious environmental threat. China now stands second behind the United States in terms of national production of carbon dioxide emissions. A primary reason is that China generates most of its commercial power by burning coal, which is very polluting. Moreover, the country's coal consumption is expected to more than double between what it was in 1990 and 2010, and that alone will double China's annual carbon dioxide emissions by the end of the period.

There are options, such as generating more power by burning petroleum or utilizing hydroelectric energy. Each option, however, has trade-offs, which are often win-lose scenarios. For China, consuming more oil would require vastly expensive imports, which could affect the country's socioeconomic development. Increased oil consumption at the level China would need would also accelerate the depletion of the world's finite petroleum reserves. Moreover, the new oil fields that are being found often lie offshore, and drilling endangers the oceans.

A second option, using hydroelectricity to provide relatively nonpolluting energy, requires the construction of dams that flood the surrounding countryside, displace its residents, and spoil the pristine beauty of the river valley downstream. China, for example, is trying to ease its energy crunch and simultaneously develop clean hydroelectric power by building the massive Three Gorges dam and hydroelectric project on the Yangtze River. The engineering project rivals the Great Wall of China in scope. When completed, the project will vastly increase the availability of electric power to rural provinces by generating 18,200 megawatts of electricity without burning highly polluting coal. The dam will also help stem floods that have often caused catastrophic damage downstream. To accomplish these benefits, however, the dam will create a reservoir approximately 400 miles long, thereby flooding 425 square miles of fertile land, inundating 1,500 factories, some 160 towns, 16 archaeological sites, and submerging

Sustainable development—the issue of how to protect the Earth's environment while continuing to develop economically—has become a source of tension between the economically developed countries (EDCs) and the less developed countries (LDCs). The LDCs resent the incessant calls of the EDCs to restrain growth and avoid environmentally damaging practices that the EDCs themselves earlier utilized to achieve prosperity. From the LDCs' point of view, the calls to "do as I say, not as I did" are hypocritical. Some people also suspect the EDCs' calls are neoimperialistically self-serving, inasmuch as they seem to work toward keeping the LDCs poor and subservient to the EDCs.

what many consider one of the most scenic natural areas in the world. The huge reservoir also began in 1997 to force what will become an estimated 1.1 million people from their homes. Thus, the Three Gorges project is an almost perfect illustration of the difficulty of sustainable development. Even though the project will ease some environmental problems (in this case, coal burning) it will also have an adverse impact on people and on the environment.

Even if you can cut such Gordian knots, you will encounter other problems: the short-term costs of environmental protection in terms of taxes to pay for government programs; the high costs of products that are produced in an environmentally acceptable way and that are themselves environmentally safe; and the expense of disposing of waste in an ecologically responsible manner.

Moreover, since the LDCs are determined to develop economically, yet struggle to pay the costs of environmentally sound progress, the North must extend significant aid to the South to help it develop in a relatively safe way. Money is needed to create non-polluting energy resources, to install pollution control devices in factories, and to provide many other technologies. The costs will be huge, approaching, in some estimates, $20 billion a year. Billions more are needed each year to help the LDCs stem their—and the world's—spiraling population.

Is the North willing to pay this price? Polls show that people in many countries are concerned about global warming, ozone layer destruction, deforestation, wildlife destruction, and acid rain. Cross-national polls also regularly find that a majority of respondents say that their governments should do more to protect their country's environment and also to be involved in the global environmental effort. Yet surveys additionally find that a majority of citizens think that their tax burdens are already too heavy and are unwilling to support large expenditures on environmental programs. One illustrative poll asked Americans if they would pay $200 in extra taxes to clean up the environment. A laudable 70 percent said "yes." That was the limit of the majority's financial commitment, though. When the next question raised the cleanup bill to an extra $500, only 44 percent said "yes." This resistance will work against any attempt to amass the funds that need to be spent internationally to help the LDCs simultaneously develop and protect the environment.[6]

The Sustainable Development Debate: What to Believe "Help!" you might exclaim at this point. "Is it necessary to live in unheated tents and abandon our cars to keep the sky from falling?" Fortunately, the answer is "Probably not."

There is a need, though, to consider the problems and possible solutions carefully. The answers are not easy. Indeed, sustainable development is "a Herculean task," as Canadian diplomat Maurice Strong, the secretary-general of the 1992 Earth Summit, put it.[7] Thus, we should now turn our attention to the specific issues surrounding the state of the biosphere and its inhabitants, and the possibility of achieving international cooperation toward sustainable development. We will first consider population. Then we will turn to concerns over such resources as minerals, forests, wildlife, and water. Last, the chapter will take up environmental issues, including pollution of the ground, water, air, and upper atmosphere.

SUSTAINABLE DEVELOPMENT: ISSUES AND COOPERATION

Throughout history, humans have taken their world for granted. They have assumed that it will always be here, that it will yield the necessities of life, and that it will absorb what is discarded. For several millennia this assumption proved justifiable. The Earth was generally able to sustain its population and replenish itself.

Now, the exploding human population and technology have changed this. Not only are there five times as many people as there were just a little more than 150 years ago, but our technological progress has multiplied our per capita resource consumption and our per capita waste and pollutant production. Technological wizardry may bring solutions, as the optimists predict, but such solutions are uncertain; for now the reality is that the world faces a crisis of carrying capacity—the potential of no longer being able to sustain its population in an adequate manner or being able to absorb its waste. To put this as an equation:

| Exploding population | x | Spiraling per capita resource consumption | x | Mounting waste and pollutant production | = | Potential catastrophe |

POPULATION ISSUES AND COOPERATION

Identifying the population problem is simple: There are too many of us, and we are reproducing too quickly. Here are some amazing and, to most people, disturbing, statistics. Stop and think about what they mean for the future.

On Tuesday, October 12, 1999, the population of the world passed the 6 billion mark. That is a stunning number. It took all of human history until 1804 for the population to reach 1 billion. Adding the next billion people took just 123 years. Now we are expanding by 1 billion people about every 13 years. Of all the people who have ever lived, an incredible 25 percent are alive right now. One country, China, with its 1.3 billion inhabitants, has more people than there were humans in the entire world less than 200 years ago. And just since the birth in 1875 of the world's oldest living people (Mohammed El-Wasimy of Egypt and Elizabeth Israel of Dominica) the world population has about quadrupled. At its current growth rate of 77 million per year, the world is annually adding a number of people equal to the combined populations of Canada, Spain, and Sweden. In only the time it took you to take this course, assuming a 15-week semester, the world's population expansion equaled the number of people in Iraq. Indeed, by tomorrow the number of new people in the world will be larger than the current populations of more than a dozen of the world's smaller countries. Almost one in every three people in the world is a child (less than 16 years old). Most of these children will soon become adults and become parents.

Projections of future population trends are not reassuring either. According to the United Nations Population Fund (UNFPA), the world population will reach the 10 billion mark in 2071 and will not stabilize until it reaches about 10.7 billion people in 2200. Thus the population continues to expand rapidly, and the 1999 milestone of 6 billion people means a doubling of the Earth's population in less than 40 years. There are approximately 30 countries with a population growth rate between 3.0 percent and 4.9 percent; they will double their populations in 14 to 22 years. About another 50 countries have population growth rates between 2.0 percent and 2.9 percent; they will double their populations in 23 to 34 years. Such numbers have convinced Pakistani physician Nafis Sadik, the executive director of the UNFPA, that population growth is a "crisis" that "heightens the risk of future economic and ecological catastrophe."[8]

To the extent that anything in the UNFPA data and estimates can be considered good news, it is that the rate of growth has slowed somewhat. As recently as 1994, the population was expanding at 94 million a year, and the UN was estimating that it would reach 11.6 billion by 2150. Even this bit of good news about the decline in the overall growth rate is dampened, however, by the fact that the fastest population increases are occurring in the LDCs, especially those in Africa, which often are the least able to support their people, and whose economic development is further retarded by the burden of the increased population. Moreover, as one demographer commented about the easing of the population growth rate, "The difference is comparable to a tidal wave surging toward one of our coastal cities. Whether the tidal wave is 80 feet or 100 feet high, the impact will be similar."[9] Population increases are shown in Figure 18.1 and the following map.

Causes of the Population Problem

There are several causes of the rapidly expanding population. One is fewer deaths. Infant mortality has decreased; adult longevity has increased. These two factors combine to mean that even in areas where the birthrate declines, the population growth rate sometimes continues to accelerate. Sub-Saharan Africa's birthrate declined from 47 births per 1,000 population in 1980 to 40 in 1998. But during the same period the chances of reaching age 65 increased from 40 to 46 percent, and there has also been a decrease in the child mortality rate (annual deaths per thousand children through age 5) from 188 children to a better, if still tragic, 151 children. Furthermore, the region's overall crude death rate (annual death of people per thousand) dropped from 18 to 15. The net result is that the rapidly declining death rates have more than offset the more slowly declining birthrates and resulted in an annual population growth of 2.7 percent. This means that the region's population jumped from 391 million in 1980 to 628 million in 1998 and is projected to reach 1.2 billion in 2030.

Another reason for the alarming population growth is the huge population base of 6.1 billion. This problem is one of mathematics. Although the global fertility rate (number of expected births per woman) has declined from 4.9 in 1970 to its current rate of 2.7 and continues to ebb, there are so many more women in their childbearing years that the number of babies born continues to go up. During the next decade, some 3 billion women will enter their childbearing years. At the current fertility rate, these

(continued on page 526)

Population Growth Rate

The world's population approximately quadrupled during the twentieth century. We continue to strain the Earth's resources by adding about 1 billion people every 15 years. Although Figure 18.1 and this map use slightly different data parameters, they are complementary. What you can see in this map is a graphic representation that the growth of population is not evenly spread around the globe. The most rapid growth is in less developed countries of the South, which will struggle to house, educate, feed, and otherwise care for their burgeoning populations. At the same time, many of the economically developed countries of the North are near or even below the zero population growth rate. For these countries, an aging population will present a different set of challenges than face the LDCs with their massive number of children.

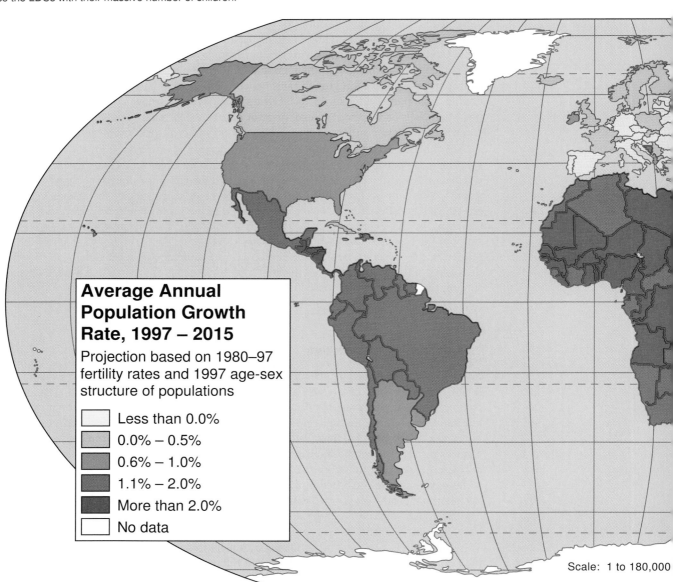

Average Annual Population Growth Rate, 1997 – 2015

Projection based on 1980–97 fertility rates and 1997 age-sex structure of populations

- Less than 0.0%
- 0.0% – 0.5%
- 0.6% – 1.0%
- 1.1% – 2.0%
- More than 2.0%
- No data

Scale: 1 to 180,000

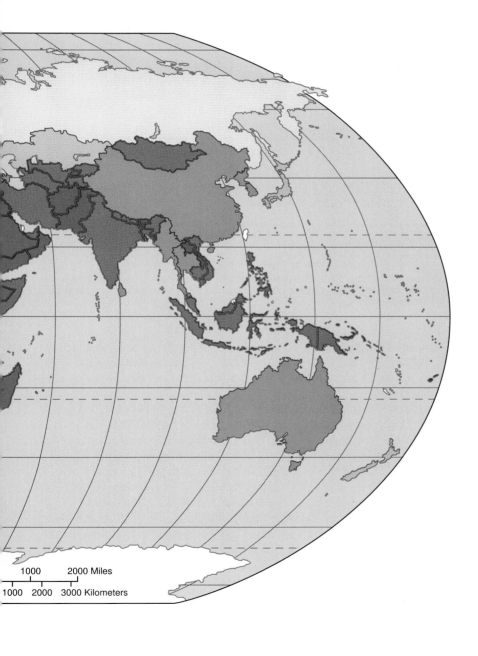

1000 2000 Miles

1000 2000 3000 Kilometers

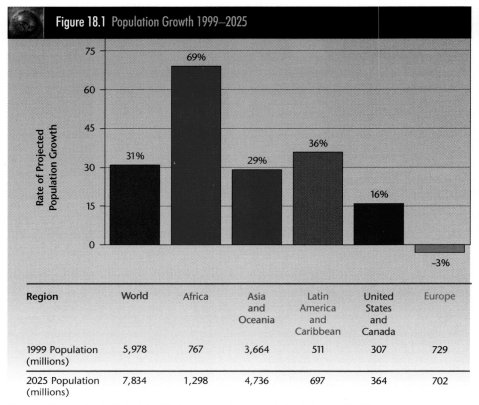

Figure 18.1 Population Growth 1999–2025

Region	World	Africa	Asia and Oceania	Latin America and Caribbean	United States and Canada	Europe
1999 Population (millions)	5,978	767	3,664	511	307	729
2025 Population (millions)	7,834	1,298	4,736	697	364	702

Data source: The State of the World's Population at http://www.unfpa.org. Percentage calculation by the author. Population at mid-year.

World population growth is not even. The burden of additional people will fall most heavily on the regions with a predominance of less developed countries, which have scant resources to support their burgeoning populations.

women will have 8.1 billion children, of which 7.5 billion will live to at least age 5. Thus, happily, most of this tidal wave of children will grow up. Most of them will also one day become parents, which will be a more joyous event for them than for the embattled ecosphere.

There is a clear relationship between poverty and birthrates. Ninety-five percent of global population growth is in the LDCs. In 1998, the fetility rate in EDCs was 1.7. In the LDCs it was 70 percent higher at 2.9. The rate in the poorest countries is even higher. The fertility rate in sub-Saharan Africa is 5.7, more than triple the EDC rate. With a fertility rate of 3.2, India alone accounted for more than 20 percent of the world's population growth between 1980 and 1998, and at current rates will surpass the population of China (fertility rate: 1.9) by 2040 with about 1.5 billion people.

How does one explain the link between population and poverty? One commonly held view is that overpopulation causes poverty. This view reasons that with too many people, especially in already poor countries, there are too few resources, jobs, and other forms of wealth to go around. Perhaps, but that is only part of the problem, because it is also true that poverty causes overpopulation (Catley-Carlson & Outlaw, 1998). The least developed countries (LLDCs) tend to have the most labor-intensive economies, which means that children are economically valuable because they help their parents farm or, when they are somewhat older, provide cheap labor in mining and manufacturing processes. As a result, cultural attitudes in many countries have come to reflect economic utility. Having a large family is also an asset in terms of social standing in many societies with limited economic opportunities.

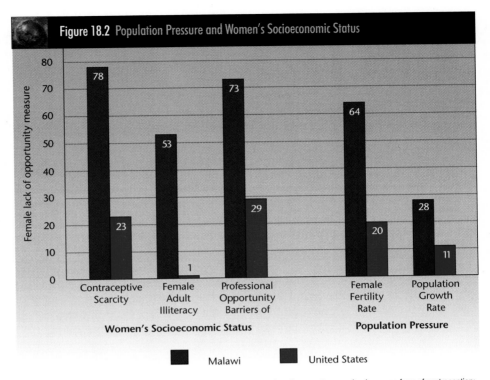

Figure 18.2 Population Pressure and Women's Socioeconomic Status

Notes: Contraceptive Scarcity: percentage of females age 15–49 who are (or whose partners are) using some form of contraception; Female Illiteracy: percentage of age 15 or more; Professional Opportunity Barriers: degree of lack of equality in political, professional, and economic opportunities that make up the gender empowerment measure (GEM) of the UNDP; lower GEM here means a greater degree of equality; Female Fertility Rate: number of children the average woman will have during her childbearing years; all data rounded to the nearest whole number and converted to a 100 base for comparison.

Data sources: World Bank (2000a), UNDP (1999).

There is a strong relationship between the lack of availability to women of contraceptive programs, education, and professional and other economic opportunities (represented by the three categories to the left) and upward population pressures (represented by the two categories to the right.) Notice that compared to the United States, the measures for Malawi related to the lack of opportunities for women in the three left categories are reflected by greater upward population pressures in the two categories on the right. The evidence indicates that the best way to control population growth is to enhance women's opportunities.

Furthermore, women in LDCs have fewer opportunities to limit the number of children they bear. Artificial birth control methods and counseling services are less readily available in these countries. Another fact is that women in LDCs are less educated than are women in EDCs. It is therefore harder to convey birth control information, especially written information, to women in LDCs. Additionally, women in LDCs have fewer opportunities than do women in EDCs to gain paid employment and to develop status roles beyond that of motherhood. The inadequacies in financial, educational, and contraceptive opportunities for women are strongly and inversely correlated to high fertility rates. One way to see relationships is to consider Figure 18.2, which compares Malawi and the United States.

MAP
The Gender Gap, p.166

The International Response to the Population Problem

The world has generally concluded that something must be done to stem population growth. The only option, other than letting disproportionate numbers of poor children die in infancy and allowing impoverished adults to die in their forties and fifties, is to lower the average fertility rate. That has already begun, with the average global rate down from 3.7 in 1980 to 2.7 in 1998. The goal is 2.1, which is considered the stable replacement rate, although as infant mortality and crude death rates continue to drop, it may even be necessary to reach 2.0 or slightly lower to stabilize the population.

While the population problem has been building up momentum for almost two centuries, efforts to deal with the issue through international cooperation are relatively recent. The growth of cooperative efforts is symbolized by the establishment of numerous international governmental and nongovernmental organizations (IGOs, NGOs) concerned with the issue and by a series of world conferences on population.

Unfortunately, not all the news about the effort to constrain population growth is good. Funding to keep programs going is vital, and the downtrend in the foreign aid of many EDCs is imperiling population programs. The U.S. Congress, for example, cut or held up funding to the United Nations, the International Monetary Fund, and U.S. Agency for International Development in an attempt to make the Clinton administration agree to include language that would bar any of the appropriated funds going to any agency that supports abortions overseas or counsels women about their availability. One of the legislators who sponsored the restrictions explained that the move was a message that if population-control organizations want funding they should be "getting out of the abortion business." The impact, according to the UNFPA director, Nafis Sadik, is that even more abortions will be performed because "17 to 18 million unwanted pregnancies are going to take place, a couple of million abortions will take place, and I'm sure that 60,000 to 80,000 women are going to die because of these abortions—and all because the money has been reduced."[10]

International Organizations and the Population Problem The effort to control global population growth is led appropriately by the United Nations. There are a number of associated organizations and programs within the UN's purview. Of these, the UNFPA, a subsidiary organ of the UN General Assembly, is the largest. The agency began operations in 1969 and focuses on promoting family planning services and improving reproductive health in LDCs. During its three decades of operation, the UNFPA has provided a total of over $4.3 billion to support population programs in the vast majority of the world's countries. The organization is funded through voluntary contributions, and in 1999 had a budget of $305 million donated by about 95 countries. This aid currently accounts for about one-fourth of the world's population assistance to LDCs. Beyond that, the agency helps coordinate the programs of other efforts by IGOs, NGOs, and national governments.

Within the UN group of associated agencies, the work of the UNFPA is supported by the United Nations Children's Fund (UNICEF), the World Health Organization (WHO), and other IGOs. These efforts are further supplemented by and often coordinated with NGOs such as the International Planned Parenthood Federation (IPPF). This British-based organization, which was founded in 1952, operates its own international family planning programs and also links the individual planned parenthood organizations of about 150 countries. The IPPF is funded by these national organizations, by private contributions, and by donations from approximately 20 countries. Like a number of other IGOs in the population control and reproductive health area, the IPPF has consultative status with the UN.

World Population Conferences The rapidly rising global population also led the UN to begin the World Population Conference series to focus world attention on the issue, to seek agreement on solutions, and to galvanize international cooperative efforts to address the issue. There have been three conferences, the first two of which met in Bucharest (1974) and in Mexico City (1984).

The most recent of these, the 1994 **United Nations Conference on Population and Development (UNCPD)** met in Cairo, Egypt. It was organized by the UNFPA, and brought together delegates from over 170 countries and a large number of NGOs. The session focused on population control and on reproductive health. Each year, for example, about 413,000 women (99 percent of whom live in LDCs) die from complications of pregnancy and childbirth. Abortion presents a particularly emotional issue for both its supporters and opponents.

Only about 2 percent of all countries ban abortion to protect a woman's life, but beyond that, whether and under what circumstances abortions are legal varies greatly. Abortions to protect a women's physical or mental heath are legally available in 90 percent of the EDCs but in only about 50 percent of LDCs. Among the LDCs, China and India both permit abortions, giving about 75 percent of the world's women access to abortion.

Abortions that are unsafe, either in countries where abortion is illegal or severely restricted or in countries with an inadequate health care system, are a major threat to women's health. The World Health Organization estimates that 70,000 women a year die due to unsafe abortions, accounting for about 13 percent of the maternal mortality rate. There are estimates that in some countries, which both restrict abortions and are exceptionally poor, over half of all maternal mortality is the result of illegal abortions.

Such harsh realities turned the attention of the conference to a third focus, which was, in the words of Nafis Sadik, "gender equality and empowering women to control their lives, especially their reproductive lives."[11] As such, an important, if informal, role of the UNCPD was to bring women together internationally and to promote a shared consciousness of gender as a transnational focus of political identity and activity. "Women have dreams at every level," commented a Pakistani delegate; "when an opportunity [such as the Cairo conference] comes they take it." A Chinese delegate agreed that she had become more aware that "women all over the world have a lot of things in common."[12]

While the related goals of restraining population growth, improving reproductive health, and empowering women were hardly debatable, how to achieve these ends was subject to considerable controversy. The primary dispute centered on the belief of some that the conference was moving toward pressuring husbands and wives to limit their children, supporting birth out of wedlock, advocating abortion, and promoting other practices to which the critics objected. The predominantly Muslim Sudanese government charged that the conference's agenda would result in "the spread of immoral and irreligious ideas."[13] In fact, Iraq, Lebanon, Sudan, Saudi Arabia, and some other countries refused to attend the UNCPD at all.

The Roman Catholic Church was also critical. Pope John Paul II wrote to UNFPA director Nafis Sadik that "parenthood must be free from social and legal coercion" and asserted that the "Cairo draft document ignores the rights of the unborn." The pope additionally emphasized his opposition to methods of "finality," such as sterilization and abortion, calling them a "violation of human rights, especially [those] of women." As an alternate approach, the pontiff contended that the world would be better off if societies promoted development that improved the lot of families, rather than denying the right to be born.

The Vatican's view drew furious criticism. Many at the conference commented that while the pope had a point about development, it had to go hand-in-hand with population control. "If our population policy goes wrong, nothing else will have a chance to go right," contended India's delegate, M. S. Swaminathan.[14] Other critics took an even stronger stand. For one, Prime Minister Gro Harlem Brundtland of Norway, who has since become head of WHO, charged that "morality becomes hypocrisy if it means accepting mothers' suffering or dying in connection with unwanted pregnancies and illegal abortions and unwanted children."[15]

Did You Know That:

A British birth-control advocacy group outraged many in France by offering low-cost vasectomies to Frenchmen. Because of France's law barring "self-mutilation" and cultural attitudes, only 1 percent of men there are sterilized. The Paris metro and French newspapers refused to carry ads for the service, and some press stories treated it as one more Anglo-Saxon attempt to neuter France. Word got out anyway, and the first Frenchman to take advantage of the offer reported, "I feel great."

The result of all this was a series of compromises. The draft document's language on promoting safe abortion added "in circumstances in which abortion is legal." Another change inserted the words that "in no case should abortion be promoted as a method of family planning." These compromises allowed the conference to approve unanimously a "Program of Action" calling for spending $17 billion annually by the year 2000 on international, national, and local programs to foster family planning and on such related areas as the improvement of the education of women. As has been the case with many such calls to action and financial commitment, the funds have not been forthcoming anywhere near the goal. For example, the annual contributions of countries that fund UNFPA have remained virtually unchanged at $270 million since the conference. Nevertheless, the conference, and even the objections of the pope and others, served at the very least to heighten awareness and to set a global debate about how to address the population problem and the closely associated issue of women's reproductive health.

Whether the programs being developed are engendered by IGOs and NGOs or by global conferences such as the UNCPD, there are two basic approaches to reducing the birthrate. One is social, the other is economic.

Social Approaches to Reducing the Birthrate One approach to reducing the birthrate involves social programs such as providing information about birth control and encouragement to practice it. The social approach also involves making birth control devices and pills, sterilization, and, in some cases, abortion programs available. At the national level, many LDCs have made strong efforts, given their limited financial resources. In Thailand, for instance, 72 percent of all couples practice contraception (the contraceptive prevalence rate).

These national efforts are supported by the UNFPA, the IPPF, and other IGOs and NGOs, and their combined efforts have had an impact. During the early 1960s, the contraceptive prevalence rate in the LDCs was only 9 percent. Now about 48 percent of couples in LDCs practice birth control. This contraceptive prevalence rate falls off drastically in the least developed countries (LLDCs), where it is only 24 percent. There are at least 15 countries in which the rate is a mere 10 percent or less.

Economic Approaches to Reducing the Birthrate Population growth can also be slowed through economic approaches. The evidence that poverty causes population increases means that if the poverty gap both between countries and within countries is narrowed, then declining birthrates will be among the benefits. Therefore, efforts must be made to develop the LDCs and to equalize income distribution within countries if population is to be controlled. One economic approach to population control is to improve the status of women, because women who are more fully and equally employed have fewer children.

Those who study population dynamics have found that advancing the economic and educational opportunities available to women needs to be an integral part of population control. This realization was one of the factors that led the UN to designate 1975 as International Women's Year and to kick off the Decade for Women. That year the UN also convened the first World Conference on Women (WCW). These initiatives were followed in 1976 by the establishment of the UN Development Fund for Women (UNIFEM, after its French acronym). The Fund works through 10 regional offices to improve the living standards of women in LDCs by giving them technical and financial support to improve the entry of women into business, scientific and technical careers, and other key areas. UNIFEM also strives to incorporate women into the international and national planning and administration of development programs and to ensure that the issues of particular concern to women such as food, security, human rights, and reproductive health are kept on the global agenda. The UN also established the International Research and Training Institute for the Advancement of Women with the task of carrying out research, training, and information activities related to women and the development process. Headquartered in the Dominican Republic, the institute conducts research on the barriers that impede the progress of women in social, economic, and political development.

RESOURCE ISSUES AND COOPERATION

Recent decades have witnessed increased warnings that we are using our resources too quickly. Most studies by individual analysts, governmental commissions, and private organizations have concluded that the rate at which humans are depleting energy, mineral, forest, land, wildlife, fishery, and water resources is a matter for concern ranging from caution to serious alarm.

Petroleum, Natural Gas, and Minerals

The supply of oil, gas, and mineral resources is one area of concern. At the forefront of these worries are the cost and supply of energy resources. The energy issue has such immense economic and environmental ramifications that it set off a war when Iraq invaded Kuwait in 1990.

World energy needs are skyrocketing. Global commercial energy production increased roughly 39 percent between 1980 and 1997. The burning of fossil fuels (coal, oil, gas) accounts for about 90 percent of output. There has been a growth of geothermal and hydroelectric power generation, but together they still account for 3 percent of world energy production, with nuclear power plants producing the remaining 7 percent of all commercial energy. Of the various sources, nuclear energy production by far increased the most rapidly, growing more than tenfold over the last two decades.

At one time the world had perhaps 2.3 trillion barrels of oil beneath its surface. Roughly half of that has already been consumed. Projections of future use are tricky, as are estimates of future reserves. According to one study, the world consumed 853 billion barrels (or 35.1 trillion gallons) of petroleum between 1961 and 1998. The study forecasts that petroleum production (now about 26 billion barrels a year) will peak at about 31.6 billion barrels in 2007, then rapidly fall off 63 percent to 11.7 billion barrels in 2040, as oil-producing countries scramble to protect their nearly exhausted reserves. At that point, global consumption (1961–2040) is predicted to have been 1.9 trillion barrels.[16] The story for natural gas is nearly the same. New discoveries, enhanced extraction methods, and other factors may have a peripheral impact on the timing, but the bottom line is that by midcentury, petroleum and natural gas production, if this and other forecasts are even nearly correct, will not be able to supply anything but a small fraction of the world's energy needs.

Coal is another and abundant energy source that will last almost 500 years at current consumption rates, but it is a major pollutant if not controlled by expensive technology. The development of hydroelectric power is attractive in some ways, but it is expensive (albeit increasingly less so) to develop. Moreover, as noted, placing of dams on rivers creates environmental and social problems. Nuclear power is yet another alternative, and some countries have become reliant on it. France and Lithuania lead in this category, each generating over 75 percent of its commercial electricity by nuclear power. They are exceptions, however. Only 32 countries generate nuclear power, and on average it amounts to only 27 percent of their total commercial energy production. Additionally, there are high costs and obvious hazards to nuclear power. Some people advocate developing wind, solar, geothermal, and other such sources of power. So far, though, cost, production capacity, and other factors have limited the application of these energy sources and will continue to do so unless there are major technological breakthroughs.

Dealing with the supply and demand for energy also requires understanding of use patterns. The vast majority of all energy is used by the EDCs. Most of the growing demand for energy, by contrast, is a result of increased needs by the countries of the South. During the period 1980–1995, the energy consumption of EDCs increased 21 percent, while the LDCs' energy use increased 43 percent. Among other things, this means that LDC development without proper energy conservation and other environmental safeguards is a serious concern.

The supply of fossil fuel resources has the highest political profile, but there are also many other minerals being rapidly depleted. Based on world reserves and world use, some minerals that are in particularly short supply (and estimates of the year that the Earth's supply will be exhausted) include copper (2056), lead (2041), mercury (2077), tin (2053), and zinc (2042). Moreover, "current use" may well skyrocket as current LDCs develop, and that eventuality would considerably decrease the projected depletion years listed here.

The resource puzzle, as mentioned, is how, all at the same time, to (1) maintain the industrialized countries' economies and standards of living, (2) promote economic development (which will consume increased energy and minerals) in the South, and (3) manage the problems of resource depletion and environmental damage involved in energy and mineral production and use. If, for instance, we were able to develop the South to the same economic level as the North, if the LDCs' energy-use patterns were the same as the North's currently are, and if the same energy resource patterns that exist now persisted, then petroleum reserves would soon be dry. Natural gas and many other minerals would quickly follow oil into the museum of geological history.

Forests and Land

For many who will read this book, the trees that surround them and the very land on which they stand will hardly seem like natural resources and will certainly not seem to be endangered. That is not the case. There are serious concerns about the depletion of the world forests and the degradation of the land.

Forest Depletion The depletion of forests and their resources concerns many analysts. Data compiled by the UN Food and Agriculture Organization (FAO) and other sources indicates that the increase in world population and, to a lesser degree, economic development are destroying the world's forests. Some 1 billion people depend on wood as an energy source, and many forests have disappeared because of such domestic needs as cooking and heating. Forests are also being cleared to make room for farms and grazing lands. Forests and woodland still cover about 25 percent of the Earth's land area. Once, however, they occupied 48 percent of the land area, and tree cover is declining by about one percent every three years. Cash-poor countries are cutting their trees and exporting the wood to earn capital to pay off their international debt and to finance economic development. Forests are also being drowned by hydroelectric projects and being strip-mined for minerals. Acid rain and other environmental attacks increase the toll on trees. Whatever the cause, the result is that some 40,000 square miles of forest are being lost every year. This is a loss roughly equivalent to clear-cutting both Belgium and Ireland. Reforestation replaces only about 10 percent of the loss.

Some areas have already suffered almost total devastation. Madagascar has lost 90 percent of its original vegetation; significant stretches of China, East Africa, Malaysia, and Brazil have been nearly denuded of their forests. The tropical forests, which account for over 80 percent of all forest losses, are of particular concern. Fifty years ago, 12 percent of the Earth's land surface was covered by tropical forest; now just 6 percent is. The Amazon Basin's tropical forest in Brazil and the surrounding countries is an especially critical issue. This ecosystem is by far the largest of its kind in the world, cov-

Did You Know That:

Eating less meat has many environmental benefits. To produce one pound of beef requires 7 lbs. of grain, which take 7,000 gallons of water to grow. For each resulting pound of meat, cattle discharge 12 pounds of feces and other organic pollutants and copious amounts of methane. Of all U.S. grain raised, 70 percent goes to feed livestock.

Each year the world's forests shrink as trees are cut and land is cleared. It is easy to decry this and to advocate a halt to forest destruction, but what does one say to this poor Indonesian farmer standing amid the ruins of the forest he burned to start his farm? "There's no other way of clearing the land," he said. "I've got to grow crops," he might have added, "so that I can earn a living and support my family."

ering 2.7 million square miles, about the size of the 48 contiguous U.S. states. The expanding populations and economic needs of the region's countries have exerted great pressure on the forest. For example, the Amazon Basin has recently been losing 25,000 square miles (an area about the size of West Virginia) of forest every two years, for a rate of more than 15 acres a minute.

Even worse, the FAO projects that harvesting trees for fuel, paper, and wood products will increase 53 percent from 4.3 billion tons in 1990 to 6.6 billion tons in 2010. Clearing land for agriculture will take a further toll on the world's trees. Overall, the FAO estimates that 39 percent of the Earth's remaining relatively pristine "frontier forests" are in severe to moderate danger from agriculture, logging, mining, and other threats. It is easy to blame the LDCs for allowing their forests to be overcut, but many in those countries ask what alternative they have. "Anyone, American, Dutch or whatever, who comes in and tells us not to cut the forest has to give us another way to live," says an official of Suriname (a former Dutch colony). "And so far they haven't done that." Instead, what occurs, charges the country's president, is "eco-colonialism" by international environmental organizations trying to prevent Suriname from using its resources.[17]

Deforestation has numerous negative consequences. One is global warming, which we will discuss in a later section. Another ill effect of forest depletion is that with a shrinking supply of wood and an increased demand for cooking and heating, the cost of wood goes up and may swallow a third of a poor family's income in some African cities. In some rural areas, wood is so scarce that each family must have at least one member working nearly full-time to gather a supply for home use. The devastation of the forests is also driving many forms of life into extinction. A typical 4-square-mile section of the Amazon Basin rain forest contains some 750 species of trees, 125 kinds of mammals, 400 types of birds, 160 different kinds of reptiles and amphibians, and perhaps 300,000 insect species. The loss of biodiversity has an obvious aesthetic impact, and there are also pragmatic implications. Some 25 percent of all modern pharmaceutical products contain ingredients originally found in plants. Extracts from Madagascar's rosy periwinkle, for example, are used in drugs to treat children's leukemia and Hodgkin's disease. A drug called taxol, derived from the Pacific yew, is a promising treatment for breast and ovarian cancer. Many plants also contain natural pesticides that could provide the basis for the development of ecologically safe commercial pesticides to replace the environmental horrors (such as DDT) of the past.

Land Degradation   Not only are the forests in trouble, so too, is the land. Deforestation is one of the many causes of soil erosion and other forms of damage to the land. Tropical forests rest on thin topsoil. This land is especially unsuited for agriculture, and it becomes exhausted quickly once the forest is cut down and crops are planted or grazing takes place. With no trees to hold soil in place, runoff occurs, and silt clogs rivers and bedevils hydroelectric projects. Unchecked runoff can also significantly increase the chances of down-river floods, resulting in loss of life and economic damage.

Honduras is one of the many countries that environmental scientists had identified as endangered by deforestation. As one study relates: "They were right. In October 1998, Hurricane Mitch slammed into the Gulf [of Mexico] coast of Central America and stalled there for four days. Nightmarish mudslides obliterated entire villages," the study continues; "half the population of Honduras was displaced, and the country lost 95 percent of its agricultural production.... And in the chaos and filth of Mitch's wake, there followed tens of thousands of additional cases of malaria, cholera, and dengue fever" (Bright, 2000:23).

Since 1950, according to the United Nations Environmental Program (UNEP), 4.6 million square miles of land have suffered mild to extensive soil degradation. This is an area equal to about the size of India and China. At its worst, *desertification* occurs. More of the world's surface is becoming desertlike because of water scarcity, timber cutting, overgrazing, and overplanting. The desertification of land is increasing at an estimated rate of 30,600 square miles a year, turning an area the size of Austria into barren desert. Moreover, that rate of degradation could worsen based on UNEP's estimate that 8 billion acres are in jeopardy. Some areas are in particular trouble. "All regions of the world suffer from desertification and drought," Arthur Campeau, Canada's ambassador for environment and sustainable development, points out, "but the African nations are the most vulnerable and the least able to combat these problems."[18]

Wildlife

The march of humankind has driven almost all the other creatures of the Earth into retreat and, in some cases, into extinction. Beyond the impact of deforestation, there are many other human by-products, ranging from urbanization to pollution, that destroy wildlife habitat. Whatever its cause, a decrease in the planet's wildlife will be an ineffable loss to humans. The drug Capoten, which is used to control high blood pressure, is derived from the venom of the Brazilian pit viper. And the American Heart Association has identified an anti–blood-clotting drug based on substances found in bat saliva that is effective in preventing heart attacks in humans. Many endangered species have no known immediate pragmatic value. Nevertheless, a world without giant pandas, hooded cranes, Plymouth red-bellied turtles, and Chinese river dolphins will be a less diverse, less appealing place.

Unfortunately, some species do have economic value: The trade in feathers, pelts, ivory, and other wildlife products is endangering indigo macaws, snow leopards, black rhinoceroses, and many other species. In the mid-1980s the legal trade alone of wildlife products included 192,000 wildcat skins, 472.5 tons of ivory, and 10.5 million reptile skins. Poachers added to this grisly business. During the 1980s, legal hunters and poachers seeking ivory, which sold for up to $120 per pound, slaughtered some 650,000 elephants, reducing their number by half. Rhinoceros horns and other products are in demand in Asia because of the belief in *jinbu*, the Chinese word for the notion that inadequacies ranging from poor eyesight to sterility can be remedied by eating parts of various animals. Pollution also threatens wildlife. Birds and fish, for instance, are particularly affected by insecticides that enter their systems directly and through the food they eat.

It should be noted that on the issue of wildlife, like many of the matters discussed in this chapter, there are optimists who believe that the problem is being grossly over-stated. According to Julian Simon "a fair reading of the available data suggests a rate of extinction not even one one-thousandth as great as the one the doomsayers scare us with." Simon was careful to say that he was not suggesting "that we should ignore pos-sible dangers to species." He contended, though, that "we should strive for a clear and unbiased view of species' assets so as to make sound judgments about how much time and money to spend on guarding them."[19]

Human food requirements bring increasing pressure on the ocean's fish, mollusks, and crustaceans. The importance of marine life as food and the demands of a growing world population combined to increase the marine (salt water) catch by 23 percent between 1985 and 1997, to 85 million metric tons. The FAO estimates that the sus-tainable annual yield of the oceans is somewhere between 69 and 96 million tons. Competition is fierce for this resource, and a 1998 report indicates that the world's fishing fleets have the capacity to take 155 percent more fish than can be replaced through natural reproduction.[20] This has already led, according to FAO data, to 69 percent of the commercial species of marine life being fully fished or overfished. Therefore, fishing at current fleet capacity or even continuing the current level of marine harvest will mean that fish, crustaceans, and mollusks are being taken, or soon will be taken, faster than they can replenish themselves. A decline in the marine catch could pose a health threat to countries that rely on fish for vital protein supplies. Espe-cially imperiled would be Asia and Africa, where fish contribute 28 percent and 21 percent respectively of the protein in the diet of the regions' inhabitants.

Water

The final resource that we will examine here is perhaps the most basic of all. Along with oxygen, water is an immediate need for almost all life forms. Seventy-one percent of the Earth's surface may be covered by water, but 96.5 percent is salt water, and 2.4 percent is in the form of ice or snow. This leaves just 1.1 percent readily available for human consumption, a significant part of which is polluted, and drinking it poses serious health risks. Moreover, this scarce water supply is threatened, and the cry "Water, water, everywhere/Nor any drop to drink" of Samuel Taylor Coleridge's Ancient Mariner may foreshadow the shortages of the future. Increased agricultural and industrial use, pol-lution, and other factors are depleting or tainting water supplies. Fresh water use, after tripling between 1940 and 1975, has slowed its growth rate to about 2 to 3 percent a year. Much of this is due to population stabilization and conservation measures in the developed countries. Still, because the population is growing and rainfall is a constant, the world needs to use an additional 7.1 trillion gallons each year just to grow the extra grain needed to feed the expanding population.

Complicating matters even more, many countries, especially LDCs, have low per capita supplies of water, as you can see in the map on p. 536. The world per capita average availability is 8,354 cubic meters. There are currently 25 countries with an annual replenishment rate of less than 1,000 cubic meters of water per person. Given the fact that Americans annually use 1,658 cubic meter of water per capita, the inade-quacy of less than 1,000 cubic meters is readily apparent.

To make matters worse, the water usage in the LDCs will increase as they develop their economies. These increases will either create greater pressure on the water supply

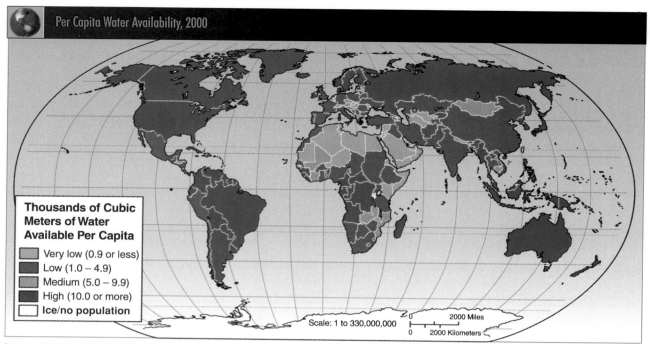

Per Capita Water Availability, 2000

Thousands of Cubic Meters of Water Available Per Capita

- Very low (0.9 or less)
- Low (1.0 – 4.9)
- Medium (5.0 – 9.9)
- High (10.0 or more)
- Ice/no population

Scale: 1 to 330,000,000

0   2000 Miles
0   2000 Kilometers

Data source: World Resources Institute, 1998.

A report by the United Nations Commission on Sustainable Development warns that 1.2 billion people live in countries facing "medium-high to high water stress".

or will limit a country's growth possibilities. Globally, most fresh water is used for either agriculture (70 percent) or industry (22 percent), with only 8 percent for domestic (personal) use. Industrialized countries, however, use greater percentages for industry and more water per capita overall than LDCs. It follows then, that as the LDCs industrialize, their water needs will rise rapidly. China provides an example; water use for industry, which amounted in 1980 to 46 billion cubic meters, increased 107 percent to 95 billion cubic meters in 1998.

Adding to the problem in many countries, a great deal of the water needed for drinking is being contaminated by fertilizer leaching, industrial pollution, human and animal wastes, and other discharges. China, for one, daily discharges 11.7 million pounds of organic pollutants into its rivers, lakes, and coastal waters. This leaves one of every three Chinese without access to safe drinking water, but they fare favorably compared to people in many other countries. For instance, only about one-half of the people in Nigeria, Africa's most populous country, have access to safe drinking water.

Many analysts are worried by the projections that water shortages will increase (Engleman & LeRoy, 1995). The result of the current scarcity of water and the growing pressure on this limited resource could lead to a competition for water and to international tensions. There are, for example, 19 countries that get 20 percent or more of their fresh water from rivers that originate outside their borders. The security of these countries would be threatened if upstream countries diverted that water for their own purposes or threatened to limit it as a political sanction. Such possibilities have led some analysts to suggest that in the not-too-distant future the access to water supplies could bring "thirsty" countries to and over the brink of war.

Before leaving the unhappy catalog of types of environmental abuse and turning to the happier topic of resource conservation, it is worth noting that damage to one aspect

THE DEATH OF A SEA

There are few stories better than that of the sad fate of the Aral Sea to illustrate humankind's abuse of the environment and its devastating consequences. The inland sea is located between Kazakhstan to the north and Uzbekistan to the south. In 1960, when those countries were still part of the Soviet Union, the sea was the fourth largest inland body of water, covering 26,300 square miles, an area about the size of Belgium and the Netherlands combined.

Then, beginning in the 1960s, Soviet agriculture demands and horrendous planning began to drain water from the sea and from the two great rivers that feed it (the Amu Darya from the north and the Syr Darya from the south) faster than the water could be replenished.

The sea started to shrink rapidly. As it did, the level of its salinity rose, and by 1977 the catch from the once-important fishery had declined by over 75 percent. Still the water level continued to fall, as the sea provided irrigation for cotton fields and for other agricultural production. The same Soviet planning that brought the world the Chernobyl nuclear plant disaster in Ukraine, stood by paralyzed as the Aral Sea began to disappear before the world's eyes.

Now, in reality, the geographical name Aral Sea is a fiction, because it has shrunk in size and depth so much that a land bridge separates the so-called

This man and his fishing boat have been left high and dry by the environmental mismanagement that has drained the Aral Sea of 75 percent of its water. The boat, exactly where it lies now, was once tied to a pier in the Aral Sea port of Munak, Uzbekistan. Now the shore is 50 miles away.

Greater Sea to the north from the Lesser Sea to the South. What was a single sea has lost 75 percent of its water and 50 percent of its surface area in the past 40 years. That is roughly equivalent to draining Lake Erie and Lake Ontario. The Uzbek town of Munak was once the Aral Sea's leading port, with its fishermen harvesting the sea's abundant catch. Now there are few fish, but even if there were many, it would not help the people of Munak. The town is now in the middle of a desert; the shoreline of the Lesser Sea is 50 miles away.

of the environment can also adversely affect others. This is readily obvious in the box, The Death of a Sea, which details the impact of poor water conservation. Fishery stock depletion, desertification, and salinization are among other disasters that have befallen the Aral Sea and the countries and people on its shrinking shores.

RESOURCE CONSERVATION: THE GLOBAL RESPONSE

While pessimists and optimists disagree about how serious the problems are and how immediate and drastic remedies need be, it is certain that mineral, forest, wildlife, and water resources must be more carefully managed and conserved. After several millennia of unchecked resource use, people are now beginning to act with some restraint and to cooperate in conservation causes. All the various individual and organized efforts cannot be mentioned here, but a few illustrative examples will serve to demonstrate the thrust of these activities.

THE EARTH SUMMIT AND SUSTAINABLE DEVELOPMENT

The 1992 UN Conference on Environment and Development (UNCED) meeting in Rio de Janeiro symbolizes the concern with the environment and the political issues surrounding sustainable development. Popularly dubbed the Earth Summit, the conference, with Canadian diplomat Maurice Strong serving as secretary-general, was attended by 178 countries and 115 heads of state. Some 8,000 journalists covered the proceedings, and 15,000 representatives of NGOs and national citizens' groups flocked to Brazil (Willets, 1996). By its end, the conference produced Agenda 21 (an 800-page document covering 112 topics that constitute a nonbinding blueprint for sustainable development in the twenty-first century) and two treaties (the Biodiversity and the Global Warming Conventions).

Additionally, the conduct of the Earth Summit illustrates the politics of environmental protection. Preliminary negotiations made it clear that environmental issues can be very political (Porter & Brown, 1996). In particular, the North and the South were at odds on many issues. The EDCs objected to and were able to defeat efforts by the LDCs to force the EDCs to set binding timetables to cut down on the use of fossil fuels and to reduce emissions of carbon dioxide and other gases that contribute to global warming.

For its part, the South resisted and was able to defeat restrictions on the use of forest resources proposed by the North (Miller, 1995b). "Forests are clearly a sovereign resource—not like atmosphere and oceans, which are a global commons," said We Lian Ting, Malaysia's chief negotiator. "We cannot allow forests to be taken up in global forums."[1] Instead, the LDCs proposed a statement guaranteeing their "sovereign and inalienable right to use, manage, and develop their forests in accordance with their development needs."

Funding was another issue that split North and South. Many environmental programs are expensive, and Secretary-General Strong estimated that the LDCs would annually need $125 billion for new environmental programs. He proposed an initial EDC commitment of $5 to $10 billion a year for these programs, but the South wanted an even stronger financial commitment. The LDCs wanted to stipulate that the North had caused a disproportionate share of environmental damage and, therefore, should be primarily responsible for financing preservation and reclamation programs. To accomplish this, the LDCs wanted a statement saying that the EDCs would

---

One major step at the international level came in 1994 when the United States, after a decade of opposition, signed the UN's Law of the Sea Treaty. The treaty, which soon thereafter went into effect, gives countries full sovereignty over the seas within 12 miles of their shores and control over fishing rights and oil- and gas-exploration rights within 200 miles of their shores. That should help improve conservation in these coastal zones. Additionally, an International Seabed Authority, with its headquarters in Jamaica, has been established. It will help regulate mining of the seabed in international waters and will receive royalties from those mining operations to help finance ocean-protection programs.

The international community also has begun to act to stem or reverse desertification. Meeting in Paris, some 100 countries signed the Convention on Desertification in 1994. Sri Kamal Nath, India's environment minister, commented that desertification "is as much of a threat to the planet and civil society as war, and we have to combat it with as much vigor."[21] To that end the convention created a "Global Mechanism" to coordinate efforts and to urge countries to channel money through the Global Environmental Facility (see the box, The Earth Summit and Sustainable Development) to meet the $10 to $20 billion that the UN estimates is needed during the next two decades for land preservation and reclamation projects.

Progress is also being made in the preservation of forest and wildlife resources. Membership in environmental groups has grown dramatically. In several European countries and in the European Parliament, Green parties have become viable political forces, and in 1998 one of them became part of the governing coalition of Chancellor Gerhard Schröder in Germany. The growing interest in flora and fauna is also increasing

commit to raising their foreign aid to 0.7 percent of each EDC's GDP. This would have increased aid for 1992 by about $60 billion. The North rejected these ideas. "We do not have an open pocketbook," President George Bush observed.[2] In the end, EDCs committed to the theory of added funding, but, after a two-year delay, agreed to provide just $2 billion in extra aid over three years to LDCs for environmental improvement. The funds are channeled through the Global Environmental Facility (GEF), which is jointly administered by the UN and the World Bank. As of mid-1996, the GEF had extended about $1.2 billion in aid to 186 environmental projects in 90 countries.

In the end, 153 countries signed both the Biodiversity and the Global Warming Conventions, and other countries signed one or the other (Swanson, 1999). Even though neither treaty created legally binding mandates, President Bush attached a reservation to his signature of the Global Warming Convention, saying that the United States would not be bound by the timetables for reducing greenhouse gas emissions. He also refused to sign the Biodiversity Convention on the grounds that it did not protect intellectual property rights in biotechnology. Among other critics, India's environment minister, Kamal Nath, quipped that the only biodiversity that interested the U.S. administration was the political survival "of bushes and quails."[3] Less than a year later, a new U.S. president, Bill Clinton, marked the annual Earth Day, April 21, by signing the biodiversity pact and rescinding the U.S. reservation to the timetables in the Global Warming Convention.

Was the Earth Summit a success? Norway's prime minister observed, "We owe the world to be frank about what we have achieved in Rio." That is, she said, "progress in many fields, too little progress in most fields, and no progress at all in some fields."[4] The important point is that the Earth Summit was a step forward. Not long ago, no one paid any attention to the environment, much less did anything about it. In June 1992 representatives of almost every country on Earth gathered to affirm their support of sustainable development. Principles were established on many issues and a few commitments were made. Even though it was limited, progress was made. Moreover, the 1992 meeting set in progress a process that may lead to other successes. The GEF is receiving and distributing funds. These are limited, but they are greater than the zero that existed before 1992. The signatories of the Global Warming Convention met in Berlin in 1995 and again in Japan in 1997. This latter meeting and its impact are discussed later in the chapter in the box, To Kyoto and Beyond.

the so-called ecotourist trade, and many countries are beginning to realize that they can derive more economic benefit from tourists shooting pictures than from hunters shooting guns or loggers wielding chain saws.

National and international efforts are also being taken in other areas. A 64 percent decline between the mid-1980s and the mid-1990s in the catch of demersal fish (such as cod, flounder, and haddock) in the northwest Atlantic prompted both Canada and the United States to limit severely or temporarily ban catches in rich fishing grounds such as the Grand Banks and the Georges Bank off their North Atlantic coasts. Canada has also reached an agreement with the European Union to regulate fishing in and near these rich fisheries. On an even broader scale, 99 countries, including all the major fishing countries, agreed in 1995 to an international treaty that will regulate the catch of all the species of fish (such as cod, pollock, tuna, and swordfish) that migrate between national and international waters. "The freedom to fish on the high seas no longer exists as it once did. It is no longer a free-for-all situation," explained the elated chairman of the conference, Satya Nandan of Fiji.[22]

At the global level, the International Whaling Commission (IWC) regulates whaling, finally banning it in 1986 except for the taking by Japan and others of about 130 minke whales annually for (dubious, some say) scientific purposes. Since then, Japan has unilaterally increased its catch to about 400 minkes, and announced that in 2000 it would also kill 50 Bryde's whales and 10 sperm whales, again supposedly for scientific research. Norway in 1993 also resumed commercial whaling in defiance of the IWC ban. That year Norway allowed its whalers to harpoon 100 minke whales, and that number was increased to 671 for 1998. Iceland, which had quit the IWC in opposition to the ban, takes 200 minkes annually. At current prices (in Norway), each minke, which weighs about 7 tons, brings about $6,000, making minke whaling a $7.6 million industry.

The controversy over whaling touches on one of the difficulties of environmentalism, which is distinguishing conservation as such from the emotional opposition of many people to killing whales or other creatures, especially those that have captured the public's sympathy. To some people, whaling is abhorrent. A spokesperson from Campaign Whale, an international NGO, declared at the 1998 meeting of the IWC that "it is time to end this obscene industry once and for all."[23]

From another perspective, the scientific committee that advises the IWC has concluded that the substantial number (perhaps 900,000) of minke whales means that the species can tolerate controlled hunting. This evidence is cited by Iceland, Norway, and Japan in support of their decisions to allow whaling. "We cannot allow uninformed sentiment to decide on the controlled use of our natural resources," Norway's prime minister argued.[24] Whaling countries also believe that the international pressure involves a degree of cultural oppression. "Americans are a bunch of culinary imperialists," declared a Tokyo restauranteur who serves whale. "Telling the Japanese not to hunt whales is like telling the British to stop having their afternoon tea or denying French people their pâté. This is how you start a war."[25]

The increasing efforts at the international level to protect global wildlife is represented by this giant sculpture outside the pavilion of the World Wildlife Fund at EXPO 2000, which opened in June 2000 in Hanover, Germany.

For antiwhaling advocates, the hunting of the minke is an ill omen for other whale species, and their foreboding has been increased by Japan's taking of Bryde's and sperm whales in 2000. Environmentalists were also alarmed when Russia in 1999 killed 26 beluga whales, the first taken since the 1960s, and sold them to Japan. Moreover, under international rules indigenous peoples in several countries are allowed to hunt whales. Russia, for example, permits the Chukotka people of Siberia to annually kill up to 105 gray whales in the Bering Sea. To make matters even worse, from an environmentalist's point of view, some of the whale meat is then fed to caged foxes, which are later slaughtered for their pelts. The United States also allows whaling by its indigenous people. The Makah of Washington State are permitted to take up to 5 gray whales a year, and the Inuits of Alaska are permitted about 200 bowhead whales a year.

It is important to note, whatever one's view of whaling, that the overall numbers of most whale species and other marine mammals are recovering. For one, the Pacific gray whale population has doubled since conservation began, and it is no longer on the U.S. endangered species list. Among other marine mammals, the world's walrus population has quintupled to 280,000; Galapagos and Antarctic fur seals, both once at the edge of extinction, now have viable populations.

The world's increasing list of endangered species is also now gaining some relief through the Convention on the International Trade in Endangered Species (CITES). Elephants were added in 1989 to the CITES list of endangered species, and 87 countries meeting in Geneva banned the trade in ivory and elephant parts. This agreement did not end the ivory trade, but, in conjunction with individual bans on importation imposed by most EDCs and many other countries, it dropped ivory prices to about $6 a pound, thereby substantially undercutting the economic incentive to poach elephants for ivory. Indeed, for elephants, the protection was so successful that herds have increased substantially in several African countries. That growth, the competition of elephants with farmers, and the gain that could be reaped from selling stockpiled tusks and licensing elephant hunters led in 1997 to an agreement at the CITES meeting in Johannesburg, South Africa, to allow Botswana, Namibia, and Zimbabwe to sell $30 million worth of their stockpiled ivory to Japan. Even though the ivory came from either legal kills to prevent overpopulation or from confiscations from poachers and would be used in the main for conservation programs, the proposal was highly controversial at CITES. The United States, France, and some other countries opposed the sale. Japan, Switzerland, and others favored it and accused opponents of trying paternally to tell Africans how to manage conservation. "It's difficult for people [outside Africa] to believe that there's any need to kill elephants," one observer at a CITES conference commented. "But they don't have to grow their food in elephant country."[26] In the end, the initial proposal to sell 150 tons was reduced to 60 tons, and the sale was limited to a one-time event. The ban on elephant products remained in place, and new measures were taken to protect tigers, sharks, and some other species that are endangered or under severe pressure.

One of the themes of this book is the role that you as an individual can play on the world stage, and the protection of marine mammals provides one more example of that. Public protest has substantially improved whale conservation. The 1993 movie *Free Willy* flashed a phone number during the closing credits that people could call to learn more about protecting whales. Some 40,000 calls poured in during the first weekend alone. Norway's whaling industry pressured Oslo to ignore the IWC, but other Norwegian industries mounted a countercampaign because of their worry about consumer backlash in other countries. Royal Viking and Norwegian Cruise lines have protested whaling, and the managing director of a Norwegian sporting goods company frets that foreign shops "tell us straight out that they dare not sell Norwegian goods."[27] Such counterpressures have not ended Norwegian whaling, but they may well play a role in keeping it restrained. The bottle-nosed dolphin is also being assisted by consumer concern. Public pressure, which the industry refers to as the "Flipper" factor (after the 1960s TV series), forced U.S. tuna canners to demand that suppliers use dolphin-safe methods of netting to save dolphins. That was followed in 1990 by a U.S. law banning the importation of tuna caught without dolphin-safe methods. The result is that the number of dolphins killed in the eastern Pacific alone dropped from 133,000 in 1986 to just over 3,000 in 1995. The Inter-American Tropical Tuna Commission sponsors a program in which a monitor is onboard all large tuna vessels.

As the U.S. tuna legislation indicates, governments are also becoming more committed to fisheries protection. Many countries have extended their coastal territorial zones and regulate fishing within them. Resource conservation and environmental cooperation are now regular topics between national leaders. Governments are also more willing to pressure other governments to end damaging practices. In 1992 Japan was forced by the condemnation of many countries, based on the "Flipper factor" and the threat of sanctions, to end the use of huge drift nets that trap and kill everything they ensnare. Threats can also become action. In 1994 the United States imposed trade sanctions on Taiwan in retaliation for its refusal to halt the sale of tiger bones and rhinoceros horns. The sanctions were limited, but they were also, as President Clinton noted, "the first time any country has acted on the international call for trade sanctions to protect endangered species."[28]

Faced with adverse public opinion and economic boycotts, known in the tuna canning industry as the "Flipper factor," Starkist and all other major U.S. tuna canners now display logos, such as the one above, to assure their consumers that the tuna are not taken using nets that kill dolphins.

ENVIRONMENTAL ISSUES

The state of the biosphere is related to many of the economic and resource issues we have been examining. Like the concerns over those issues, international awareness and

Although water pollution control has made some progress, the toxic wastes and other pollutants that pour into the Earth's water continue to wreak havoc. These fish were killed when a dam burst near Seville, Spain, dumping 5 million cubic meters of pollutants into the Guadalquivir River.

activity are relatively recent and are still in their early stages. Several concerns that have an environmental impact, such as desertification, deforestation, and biodiversity loss, have already been discussed. The next sections will look at ground pollution, water pollution, air pollution, global warming, and ozone layer depletion.

Ground Pollution

The pollution of the land is a significant problem, but the territorial dominance of states renders this issue primarily domestic and, therefore, outside the realm of international action. Exporting solid waste for disposal does, however, have an international impact. With their disposal sites brimming and frequently dangerous, EDCs annually ship millions of tons of hazardous wastes to LDCs. Financial considerations have persuaded some countries to accept these toxic deliveries. The practice is widely condemned on the grounds that, as one Nigerian diplomat put it, "international dumping is the equivalent of declaring war on the people of a country."[29] Nevertheless, a UN investigation has found that "the volume of transboundary movements of toxic wastes has not diminished." Even more alarmingly, the report went on to warn, "The wastes are sent to poor countries lacking the infrastructure for appropriate treatment. They are usually dumped in overpopulated areas in poor regions or near towns, posing great risks to the environment and to the life and health of the poorest populations and those least able to protect themselves."[30] A closely associated international aspect of ground pollution is that it is often caused by waste disposal by multinational corporations (MNCs), which may set up operations in LDCs because they have fewer environmental regulations.

Water Pollution

There are two water environments: the marine (saltwater) environment and the freshwater environment. Water pollution is damaging both.

Marine pollution has multiple sources. Spillage from shipping, ocean waste dumping, offshore mining, and oil and gas drilling activity account for 23 percent of the pollutants that are introduced into the oceans, seas, and other international waterways. Petroleum is a particular danger. Of the 940 million gallons of petroleum discharged each year into the marine environment, almost half comes from transportation spillage. Municipal and industrial waste discharges account for another 36 percent of the total. Offshore drilling is a rising threat, with the production of petroleum from marine drilling steadily rising.

Another 44 percent of the marine pollution is carried by the rivers, which serve as highways that carry human sewage, industrial waste, pesticide and fertilizer runoff, petroleum spillage, and other pollutants into the seas. One of the worst sources are fertilizers, and their global use has grown from about 40 million metric tons a year in 1960 to some 156 million metric tons annually in the late 1990s. Another major source is the exploding world population, which creates ever more intestinal waste. Many coastal cities are not served by sewage treatment facilities. Sewage is the major polluter of the Mediterranean and Caribbean Seas and the ocean regions off East Africa and Southeast Asia. Industrial waste is also common.

Of these pollutants, the influx of excess nitrogen into the marine system is especially damaging. Human activities, such as using fertilizers and burning fossil fuels, add about 210 million metric tons to the 140 million metric tons generated by natural processes. Excess nitrogen stimulates eutrophication, the rapid growth of algae and other aquatic plants. When these plants die in their natural cycle, the decay process strips the water of its dissolved oxygen, thereby making it less and less inhabitable for aquatic plants, fish, and other marine life. To make matters worse, some algae blooms are toxic, and take a heavy toll on fish, birds, and marine mammals. The Baltic Sea, Black Sea, the Caribbean, Mediterranean Sea, and other partly enclosed seas have been heavily afflicted with eutrophication, and even ocean areas such as the northeast and northwest coasts of the United States have seen a significant increase in the number of algae blooms in the last quarter century. Inasmuch as 99 percent of all commercial fishing is done within 200 miles of continental coasts, such pollution is especially damaging to fishing grounds.

Freshwater pollution of lakes and rivers is an international, as well as a domestic, issue. The discharge of pollutants into lakes and rivers that form international boundaries (the Great Lakes, the Rio Grande) or that flow between countries (the Rhine River) is a source of discord. Freshwater pollution is also caused by acid rain and other contaminants that drift across borders.

Air Pollution

The world's air currents ignore national boundaries, making air pollution a major international concern (Soroos, 1997). To illustrate the many sources of, and problems associated with, air pollution, we will explore the acid rain issue.

Acid rain is caused by air pollutants that contaminate water resources and attack forests through rainfall. Sulfur dioxide (SO_2) and nitric acids from the burning of fossil fuels and from smelting and other industrial processes are the major deleterious components of acid rain. The damage done by acid rain has followed industrialization. The United States, Canada, and Europe were the first to suffer. Especially in the northern part of the United States and in Canada there has been extensive damage to trees, and many lakes have become so acidified that most of the fish have been killed.

Europe has also suffered extensive damage. About a quarter of the continent's trees have sustained moderate to severe defoliation. The annual value of the lost lumber harvest to Europe alone is an estimated $23 billion. The tourist industry in once verdant forests around the world is also in danger, imperiling jobs. The death of trees and their

Many of the world's cities with the worst air pollution are in the less developed countries. Mexico City's air quality is abysmal, making the Mexican flag only hazily visible as it flies over the capital city.

stabilizing root systems increases soil erosion, resulting in the silting-up of lakes and rivers. The list of negative consequences could go on, but that is not necessary to make the point that acid rain is environmentally and economically devastating.

The good news is that pollution control in the EDCs has substantially reduced new air pollution. Annual EDC sulfur dioxide emissions, for instance, have declined from almost 60 million tons in 1960 to about 35 million tons in 1995. The bad news is that the improvement in the EDCs is being more than offset by spiraling levels of air pollution in the LDCs. This is particularly true in Asia. There, rapid industrialization combined with the financial inability to spend the tens of billions of dollars needed to control SO_2 emissions is expected to more than triple annual SO_2 emissions from 34 million tons in 1990 to about 115 million tons in 2020.

Air pollution from sulfur dioxide, nitrogen dioxide, and suspended particles (such as dust and soot) cause about 500,000 deaths a year according to the World Health Organization. The majority of those are in Asia, where most of the major cities exceed WHO guidelines for suspended particles. Bangkok's air pollution is 200 percent of the WHO median standard, Shanghai's is 246 percent, and Beijing's 370 percent of the standard. The people of the industrial city of Taiyuan southwest of Beijing daily gasp in air that is 568 percent dirtier than what WHO thinks is healthy.

Global Warming

Many scientists believe that we are experiencing a gradual pattern of global warming. The reason, according to these scientists, is the *greenhouse effect*, which is caused by carbon dioxide CO_2 from fossil fuel burning and from discharges of other chemical gases. The CO_2 accumulates in the upper atmosphere and creates a blanket effect, trapping heat and preventing the nightly cooling of the Earth. Other gases, especially methane and chlorofluorocarbons (CFCs), also contribute heavily to creating the thermal blanket.

There is controversy about the existence, causes, and impact of the greenhouse effect. We will begin with a brief synopsis of what is known and what is in dispute. Then we will turn to the key issue: What to do.

Global Warming: What We Know Two things are known for sure. First, both global emissions of CO_2 and other gases and the level of these gases in the atmosphere have increased. Second, the Earth is getting warmer.

This rise in global emissions is associated with the industrial revolution and the surge in the world population. For example, global CO_2 emissions have risen 278 percent since 1950. Now more than 26 billion tons of CO_2 are discharged annually, and they are joined by 270 million tons of methane and 400,000 tons of CFCs. Since these gases linger in the atmosphere for 50 to 200 years, the cumulative effect is also worth considering. Scientists estimate that at the beginning of the industrial revolution in the mid-1700s there were about 55 million tons of CO_2 in the atmosphere. Since then, more than an additional 932 billion tons have been discharged, and a great deal of that CO_2 remains trapped in the atmosphere. About 80 percent of these emissions come from the burning of coal, gas, petroleum, and other fossil fuels during industrial

Did You Know That:

The first warning about global warming was issued in 1896 by Swedish chemist Svante Ahrrenius, who wrote that "we are evaporating our coal mines into the air."

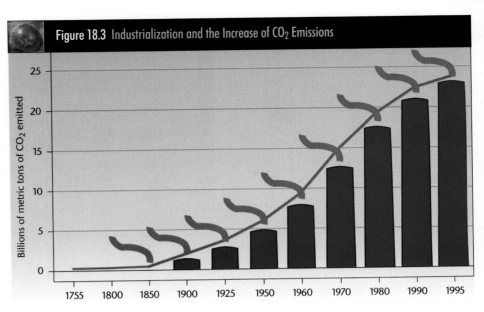

Figure 18.3 Industrialization and the Increase of CO_2 Emissions

Data source: World Resources Institute (1998). These emissions represent about 80 percent of all CO_2 emissions.

Since the industrial revolution began in Great Britain in the mid-1700s, the discharge of carbon dioxide (CO_2) into the air by the industrial burning of coal, gas, oil, and other fossil fuels has rapidly increased. The majority of scientists who study this believe that these emissions are creating a global warming effect that is significantly altering the Earth's climate.

activity. This connection between industrialization and CO_2 emissions is evident in Figure 18.3.

Deforestation also contributes to increased levels of CO_2 in the atmosphere. By destroying a multitude of trees, which are nature's method of converting CO_2 into oxygen, humans over the centuries have added more than 4.1 billion tons of CO_2. Some of that is CO_2 that would have otherwise been absorbed by the vanished trees; some of it is CO_2 discharged into the atmosphere by burning the trees and underbrush to clear the land. A third certainty is that emissions and deforestation have caused atmospheric CO_2 concentrations to rise, at first slowly, then more rapidly, from 277 parts per million (ppm) in 1750, to 280 ppm in 1850, 315 ppm in 1958, and 360 ppm in 1998. During the 1990s, the average annual rate of increase of CO_2 concentrations was 1.2 ppm, with each added 1 ppm the result of retaining an additional 2.13 billion tons of CO_2 in the atmosphere. The problem is discussed further in the box, Bad Math and Sustainable Development.

There is also no doubt that the temperature is rising. Scientists estimate that over the last century the Earth's average temperature rose 0.5°C/1.1°F. In fact, 1998 was the warmest year in recorded history. Moreover, that year and 1981, 1983, 1987, 1988, 1990, 1995, 1996, 1997, and 1999 were the ten warmest years since global record keeping began in 1856.

Global Warming: What Is in Dispute Two things about global warming are controversial. One is whether global warming is caused by humans or is a natural phenomenon. As one atmospheric scientist accurately notes, "I don't think we're arguing over whether there's any global warming. The question is, What is the cause of it?"[31] The second issue is whether global warming will have dire consequences or an impact that will in some cases be beneficial and in other cases can be addressed using modern technology.

Environmental pessimists contend that humans are causing global warming. A report of the UN–sponsored Intergovernmental Panel on Climatic Change (IPCC) argued that the buildup of CO_2 and the climatic changes over the last few decades are

BAD MATH AND SUSTAINABLE DEVELOPMENT

The rapid global increase in the number of gasoline-powered vehicles and the rapid decrease in the world's number of trees add to the buildup of carbon dioxide (CO_2) in the atmosphere. As a mathematical equation, this environmental formula might be written as (+vehicles) + (−trees) = + CO_2. The problem with this equation is, many scientists worry, that this "bad math" is contributing to global warming.

The elements of the equation are not complex. The number of vehicles in the world has risen from about 70 million in 1945 to about 650 million. Analysts predict that there will be one billion vehicles on the world's roads in 2025. Most of this increase will come as the LDCs improve their standard of living. There are in the United States about 750 vehicles for every 1,000 people. By contrast, for every 1,000 people, China has only eight vehicles and India just seven. If the people of China and India were today as well-off as the average American, there would be yet another 1.6 billion cars (+246 percent) on the road. The Chinese and Indians are, of course, a long way from the American standard of living, but the future may hold a car—or several cars—in every Chinese and Indian driveway and garage.

Even the 650 million vehicles being driven today emit an immense amount of CO_2. According to the U.S. Environmental Protection Agency (EPA), a small, fuel-efficient Geo Metro emits 9,200 pounds of CO_2 a year (based on 15,000 miles). A Ford F-150 pickup truck emits 18,500 pounds of CO_2, and a Dodge Durango, one of the popular sport utility vehicles, discharges 21,100 pounds of CO_2 annually.

Trees are another part of the equation. They are the environmental antithesis of vehicles in that they convert CO_2 to oxygen. Unfortunately for the atmosphere, the number of trees have been decreasing as vehicles have been increasing. As noted earlier in this chapter, the forests that remain today are only about half the size of the forests that once were. Inasmuch as a large tree can absorb and convert up to 48 pounds of CO_2 into oxygen annually, the loss of billions of trees has vastly diminished the ability of the Earth to cleanse itself of excess CO_2.

How to balance the equation, that is, how to achieve sustainable development, is complex. Yet there may be some relatively simple guidelines available by plugging numbers into the equation. To wit, in terms of CO_2 conversion to oxygen per tree, 1 Geo Metro = 200 trees. Similarly, 1 Ford F-150 = 385 trees, and 1 Dodge Durango = 440 trees. Sustainable development, then, requires less vehicles (or vehicles that are less polluting), or more trees, or some combination thereof. The current formula of more vehicles and less trees is likely to lead to the wrong answer. An equation such as (−vehicles) + (+less polluting vehicles) + (+trees) will yield a better result.

"unlikely to be entirely due to natural causes." Instead, the report concluded, "A pattern of climatic response to human activities is identifiable in the climatological record."[32]

Environmental pessimists are also alarmed about the impact of global warming. The UN–sponsored Intergovernmental Panel on Climatic Change (IPCC) concluded that, given current trends, the world's average temperature could increase 1°F to 6°F by the year 2100. For comparison, the temperature increase since the last ice age is estimated to be 5°F to 9°F. The pessimists believe that rainfall, wind currents, and other climatic patterns will be dramatically, and sometimes dangerously, altered. The polar ice caps will melt more quickly, and sea levels will rise. There is some evidence that the process has already begun in earnest. A report issued in 1999 by the Goddard Space Science Institute estimated that the Arctic ice cover had thinned by 45 percent over the previous 40-year period, with the size of the ice cover shrinking by about 14,000 square miles, an area larger than Delaware and Maryland combined.

The result of such melting, the IPCC report estimated, is that up to 118 million people could be displaced by rising seas over the next century. Satellite-generated sea measurements indicate, one scientist reported, that "the mean annual rise in sea level will probably be something like one or two millimeters a year."[33] This is a small annual rise, but over time it can be significant. The sea level particularly affects island countries, 37 of which have formed the Alliance of Small Island States. The question, President

Maumoon Abdul Gayoom of the Maldives, an Indian Ocean island country, told the world leaders gathered at the UN Millennium Summit in September 2000 is, "When the UN meets [in 2100] to usher in yet another century, will the Maldives and other low-lying nations be represented here?" Noticing that his five-minute time limit had elapsed, President Gayoom finished with the thought, "My time at the podium is up. But I pray that that of my country is not."[34]

Violent weather caused by rapid evaporation, the buildup of atmospheric heat, and other factors that would create higher winds also worries the pessimists. The head of the IPCC notes that the 1980s and early 1990s were remarkable for their "frequency and intensity of extremes of weather and climate."[35] Insurance industry data shows, for example, that the number of catastrophic windstorms in the world increased from 8 in the 1960s, to 14 in the 1970s, to 29 in the 1980s. Moreover, the scientist added, floods and droughts have increased as well. If anything, the weather turned even worse in many parts of the world during 1997–1998 as the strongest El Niño in history caused torrential rains and floods in some areas, spawned tornadoes in others, and reduced rainfall to near arid levels in yet other areas. That was followed in 1999 and 2000 by La Niña, which also has its perils. The resulting atmospheric conditions, led the U.S. National Oceanic and Atmospheric Administration to predict "strong and more lasting" hurricanes. Pointing out the obvious danger, the head of the U.S. Federal Emergency Management Agency, noted, "Fifty to 58 percent of the [U.S.] population is on the eastern coastline. That's an awful lot of people at higher risk."[36]

Did You Know That:

La Niña is marked by unusually cold water in the mid-Pacific; El Niño is marked by unusually warm water in the same region. The term El Niño originated with South American fishermen who noticed that unusually warm water would appear some years near Christmas. This led to the name, which means "little boy" and refers to the Christ child. Since La Niña is something of the opposite of El Niño, that name soon came into use.

Adding to the possible woes, the UN has warned that global warming "could have a wide range of impacts on human health, most of which would be adverse."[37] Scientists predict, for example, that warming could increase the number and range of mosquitoes, with a resulting annual increase of 80 million malaria cases. Cholera, dengue fever, and other hemorrhagic diseases associated with warm climates could also spread northward and southward.

Environmental optimists treat the pessimists as alarmists. First, the optimists point out, the Earth has natural warming and cooling trends, and the optimists believe that a good part of the observed temperature rise is due to this natural cycle, rather than human activity. They note that the Earth cooled somewhat in the 1950s and 1960s, and some predict that the cooling trend will resume over the next few decades. Other environmental optimists do not believe that increases will be huge, either because they will not occur in any significant way or because offsetting factors, such as increased cloudiness, will ease the effect. One scientist labels CO_2 "an unlikely candidate for causing any significant worldwide temperature change."[38] And only slightly less optimistically, another scientist comments, "The prospects for having a modest climate impact instead of a disastrous one are quite good."[39]

Optimists also down play the damage from global warming. "It should be pretty clear," says one, "that warming to date didn't demonstrably dent health and welfare very much." There is no reason, he added, "to expect a sudden [greater danger] in the next 50 years."[40] Moreover, the optimists predict that some could benefit and most could adapt to the changes brought on by global warming (Moore, 1998). Drought in the lower and middle latitudes would ruin some present agricultural areas, the logic goes, but new ones would be created and would prosper at higher latitudes. Farmers in colder regions might have their growing seasons and bounty increased. Moreover, a U.S. National Academy of Science study concluded that while global warming was occurring, people could adapt and that "we mustn't get into the state of mind that... [leads us to] think the world is going to vaporize."[41]

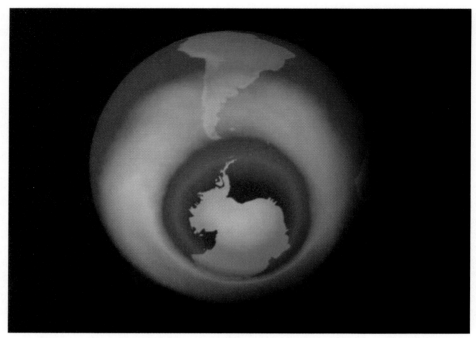

The attack on the ozone layer by chemicals that humans discharge is documented in this NASA image. The land mass toward the bottom of the photograph is Antarctica. It is clearly visible because of the hole that appears each year on the largely depleted ozone layer over that continent. South America, to the north, is less visible because it is still partly shielded.

Global Warming: What to Do The key issue in the global warming debate is what to do. Economic cost is one factor. Those who recommend caution in responding to demands that global warming be halted also point out that significantly reducing CO_2 emissions will not be easy. It might well require substantial lifestyle changes in the industrialized countries. "To stabilize carbon dioxide concentrations at even twice today's levels... over the next 100 years can be attained only [if] emissions eventually drop substantially below the 1990 levels," the IPCC has calculated.[42] To do that "will require a degree of bureaucratic control over economic affairs previously unknown in the West," predict two scholars who oppose such a course.[43] Costs would also be enormous. The Union of Concerned Scientists, for instance, has concluded that a program to cut CO_2 emissions by 70 percent over a 40-year period would cost the U.S. economy $2.7 trillion. The organization argues, however, that the loss would be more than offset by a $5 trillion savings in fuel costs. Additionally, the economy would be stimulated by programs to create and provide alternative, environmentally safe technologies.

In the end, what can be said for certain, then, is that climatic warming is occurring, but, in the words of one scientist, "we have no means of knowing, actually" how much, if any, of that is due to atmospheric emissions.[44] Do you bet trillions in economic costs that emissions-driven global warming is occurring, or do you bet the atmosphere that it is not? Given the fact that CO_2 stays in the atmosphere for centuries and that, if it is having a climatic effect, it will take several lifetimes to begin to reverse significantly, the U.S. National Research recommends betting the money. "Despite the great uncertainties," it counsels, "greenhouse warming is a potential threat sufficient to justify action now."[45]

Ozone Layer Depletion

In contrast to the debate over global warming, there is little doubt about the depletion of the ozone layer and the damage that it causes. Atmospheric ozone (O_3) absorbs ultraviolet (UV) rays from the sun, and, without the ozone layer 10 to 30 miles above the planet, human life could not exist. The ozone layer is being attacked by the emission of chlorofluorocarbons (CFCs), a chemical group that gasifies at low temperatures, releasing chlorine atoms. These attack ozone and turn it into atmospheric oxygen (O_2), which does not block ultraviolet rays. Each chlorine atom can repeat this transformation up to 100,000 times.

Because of their low gasification point, CFCs are good refrigerants and insulators and are therefore used in refrigerators and air-conditioners and in products such as styrofoam. CFCs are also found in many spray can propellants, fire extinguishers, and industrial solvents. Some 400,000 metric tons are spewed into the atmosphere annually. The most dramatic depletion, according to a report by the World Meteorological Organization, is occurring over Antarctica, where a 3.86 million-square-mile hole—about the size of Europe and with as much as a 70 percent depletion of atmospheric O_3—occurs annually. Ozone levels over the rest of the world have declined less, but they are still down about 10 percent since the 1950s.

Emissions of CFCs create several problems. One is that they add to the greenhouse effect, as noted above. More to the point here, the thinning of the ozone layer increases the penetration through the atmosphere of ultraviolet-B (UV-B) rays, which cause cancers and other mutations in life forms below. Scientists estimate that each 1 percent decrease in the ozone layer will increase UV-B penetration 1.3 percent. This can increase the rate of various types of skin cancer from 1 to 3 percent. The impact of this on Americans was noted in chapter 1. Australia and New Zealand have measured temporary increases in UV-B radiation of as much as 20 percent, and light-skinned Australians have the world's highest skin cancer rate. Another possible deleterious effect of increased UV-B bombardment came to light when a study of the water surrounding Antarctica found evidence of a 6 to 12 percent decline in plankton organisms during the period of the annual ozone hole. Such losses at the bottom of the food chain could restrict the nutrition and health of fish and eventually humans farther up the food chain. Also, scientists from Oregon State University, studying the inexplicably rapid drop in the number of frogs around the world, have concluded that UV-B radiation may be killing the eggs before they hatch into mosquito larvae–consuming tadpoles.

Environmental Protection: The International Response

Like many of the other issues discussed in this chapter, environmental problems have been slowly growing for centuries. They have accelerated rapidly in this century, however, and in some cases they have reached hypervelocity growth rates. Only recently has widespread public and governmental concern been sparked. The result is that programs are just beginning. Most of the work that has been done has had a national focus, and there have been many advances. In a great part of the developed world, where the problems were most acute and where the resources to fund programs were available, water is cleaner, acid rain is being curbed, trees are being planted, toxic wastes are being dealt with better, recycling is under way, and a host of other positive programs have stemmed and have sometimes even reversed the flood tide of pollution. Because many forms of pollution spread internationally, the national programs have been beneficial.

There has also been progress at the international level (Meyer, Frank, & Tuma, 1997; Caldwell, 1996). There are many IGOs and NGOs that focus on one or more environmental programs. The UN has been involved in a number of environmental efforts. These began with the 1972 Conference on the Human Environment in Stockholm, which led to the establishment of the United Nations Environmental Programme (UNEP). The work of the many IGOs that are concerned with preserving and enhancing the biosphere is supplemented by a vast host of NGOs dedicated to the same

(continued on page 552)

TO KYOTO AND BEYOND

The Earth Summit in Rio de Janeiro laid out a hopeful path. The economically developed countries (EDCs) that signed the Global Warming Convention agreed to voluntarily stabilize emissions at their 1990s levels by the year 2000. They also resolved to reconvene in Japan after five years to review their progress in restraining the emission of carbon dioxide (CO_2) and other gases that most scientists believe are contributing to global warming.

Like many paths paved with good intentions, the journey to Kyoto did not fulfill its promise. Many of the EDCs had made no progress toward meeting the goals set in 1992. Also, many of the economically less developed countries (LDCs) had generated increasing levels of greenhouse gases. As if to underline this reality, while the delegations from 166 countries gathered in Kyoto in December 1997, the worst El Niño of the century—some say in history—was causing weather that deluged some areas of the world, caused droughts in others, and spawned an unusual rash of typhoons and other violent weather.

The proposals at Kyoto about how to halt global warming were as varied as the types of weather associated with El Niño. The Americans advocated cutting average emissions levels back to 1990 levels by 2012. The Europeans outdid the Americans by advocating slashing emissions to 15 percent below 1990 levels by 2010. The LDCs said nothing about their levels, but proposed that by 2020 the EDCs cut emissions to 35 percent below 1990 levels.

The EDCs did not expect the LDCs to meet the same stringent targets as the EDCs, but did want some upper limits on future emissions. As President Clinton put the U.S. position, there had to be "meaningful participation by key developing nations."[1] To this, Mark Mwandosya of Tanzania, who headed the LDC caucus in Kyoto, rejoined, "Very many of us are struggling to attain a decent standard of living for our people. Any yet we are constantly told that we must share in the effort to reduce emissions so that industrialized countries can continue to enjoy the benefits of their wasteful lifestyle."[2]

The negotiations at Kyoto were intense as then Vice President Al Gore and other diplomats tried to balance the pressure to address the environment with their own country's economic interests. Cost estimates vary widely, with projections of the funds needed globally to stabilize CO_2 concentrations in the atmosphere ranging from $3 trillion to $10 trillion. The LDCs wanted promises of massive aid to help them stem pollution; the EDCs were reluctant to make specific commitments.

Diplomats also had to be wary of the willingness of citizens and interest groups in their respective countries to support mandatory emissions limits and their associated costs. It is easy to be in favor of protecting the environment. Popular support declines, however as the cost goes up. One poll found that when asked, "Would you be willing to invest in new appliances and insulation to cut household emissions of greenhouse gases?" a majority of Americans said they already were or would. Only 10 percent answered with a flat "no." But paying higher taxes on gasoline and heating oil was another matter. Only 2 percent of Americans were willing to do that.[3]

Almost inevitably, the environmental and economic cross-pressures led to a compromise. The treaty concluded in Kyoto stipulates that the EDCs must reduce greenhouse gas emissions by 6 to 8 percent (depending on current emissions) below their respective 1990 levels by 2012. The Kyoto Treaty also allows the EDCs to trade emissions quotas among themselves. If, say, the United States fails to meet its goal, it can buy tons of emissions quotas from an EDC that has more than met its goal. To the disappointment of strong environmentalists, no sanctions for failure to meet standards were set. Furthermore, the LDCs were exempted from binding standards. The negotiators decided that the treaty will go into effect when ratified by at least 55 countries representing at least 55 percent of the world's emissions of greenhouse gases.

Supporters greeted the compromise with faint praise. "This is a modest step forward in what will be a long-term battle to protect the Earth's climate system," said a representative of the Union of Concerned Scientists.[4] Scientists also pointed out that even if fully implemented the treaty would not stop global warming. First, even though in 2012 the EDCs will produce 30 percent less than they would have without restraints, the emissions will still add green-house gases to the atmosphere faster than the Earth can eliminate them. Second, LDC emissions will continue to go up. Therefore, the Kyoto limits will only slow the increase, not reverse the tide.

Other observers were caustic in their denunciations. An environmentalist charged that the treaty's lack of sanctions and limited cutbacks "plays into the hands [of industry]." From the opposite perspective, a representative of a U.S. business lobbying group denounced the treaty as "unilateral economic disarmament [by the EDCs]. It is a terrible deal, and the president should not sign it." The leaders of the Republican-controlled U.S. Congress also rushed to denounce the treaty. The Senate majority leader declared that Congress "will not ratify a flawed treaty."[5] The Speaker of the House called the treaty an "outrage" that would cripple the U.S. economy.[6] President Clinton rejoined that "every time we've tried to improve the American environment in the last 25 or 30 years, somebody has predicted that it would wreck the economy." To the contrary, the president went on, "the air is [now] cleaner, the food supply is safer, there are fewer toxic waste dumps. And the last time I checked, we had the lowest unemployment rate in 20 years. So don't believe the skeptics."[7]

Perhaps, but given the uproar, Vice President Gore left Kyoto without signing the treaty. President Clinton voiced support of the treaty. Even relatively friendly senators were cautious about the prospects of the treaty. John Kerry indicated that he "would counsel the president to go very slowly as to ratification."[8] Clinton seemed to take that advice. He demonstrated how politically sensitive the treaty was and also his lack of commitment to it in the last years of his presidency, by declining to sign it himself and instead relegating the task to a relatively obscure diplomat, Peter Burleigh, acting U.S. ambassador to the United Nations. Moreover, Clinton delayed sending the treaty to the Senate for ratification. The White House took the position that it would not submit the treaty unless the LDCs participated more fully in restraining emissions, but the delay was also convenient to mute the issue in the 2000 presidential election. In that campaign, Democratic candidate Al Gore called the Kyoto treaty a "historic step toward meeting this global challenge," one which "sets strong, realistic targets for reducing emissions." He went on to hedge his support, however, calling the treaty "a work in progress," and declaring, "We must negotiate clear rules for... meaningful participation by key developing countries." Republican candidate George W. Bush took much the same stance, albeit more candidly. "I oppose the Kyoto [treaty]," he told reporters; "it is ineffective, inadequate, and unfair to America because it exempts 80 percent of the world, including major population centers such as China and India, from compliance."[9] There the matter rested as the new U.S. administration took office in January 2001, caught between opposing domestic forces within the United States and other countries and the views and needs of the EDCs and LDCs.

Whatever the eventual fate of the treaty, a few things are clear. One is that greenhouse gas concentrations continue to mount in the atmosphere. Second, the Earth's temperature is rising, the oceans are rising, and global weather appears to be getting more volatile. Many scientists attribute these changes to greenhouse gases. Third, the costs of halting, much less reversing, the buildup of greenhouse cases will be in the trillions of dollars and, a bit less surely, lifestyle changes may be necessary. It is hard to envision, for instance, how the current American love affair with gas-guzzling sport utility vehicles can co-exist with reducing U.S. emissions to below 1990 levels. Fourth, it is very unlikely that progress can be made in stabilizing or reducing greenhouse gas emissions without LDC participation. Yet, while it is easy to criticize their exemption from the Kyoto agreement, one must also answer the question posed by Malawi's minister of environment: "How can we devote our precious [financial] resources towards reducing emissions when we are struggling every day just to feed, clothe, and house our citizens?"[10]

What is also clear is that the path beyond Kyoto goes somewhere, whatever the decisions in the world's capitals are. One road, which involves taking strong measures to reduce greenhouse emissions will, even by optimistic estimates, be costly and may well alter lifestyles. The alternative path involves no decisions or only superficial gestures. The destination of that path evokes the ancient Chinese adage that tells us, "If you continue on the road you are on you will get to where it leads."

purpose (Haas & McCabe, 1996; Wapner, 1996). It is also increasingly common for trade treaties, such as the North American Free Trade Agreement and other international pacts to include environmental protection clauses (Audley, 1997). Additionally, there are countless local organizations and even individuals involved in international environmental activism (Lipschutz & Mayer, 1996).

Protecting the Ozone Layer Among its other accomplishments, the UNEP sponsored a 1987 conference in Montreal to discuss protection of the ozone layer. There, 46 countries agreed to reduce their CFC production and consumption by 50 percent before the end of the century. Subsequent amendments to the Montreal Convention at quadrennial conferences, the last of which was held in Vienna in 1995, resulted in multilateral treaties requiring a complete phaseout of CFC production by EDCs by 1996 and LDCs by 2010. Also, at Vienna, more than 100 countries also agreed to phase out production and use by EDCs of the pesticide methyl bromide, which also weakens the ozone layer, by 2010.

As a result, there is relatively good news on ozone depletion. The annual global production of CFCs has dropped more than 70 percent from 1.1 million tons in 1986 to about 225,000 tons. The annual buildup of CFC concentrations has slowed from 5 percent in the 1980s to a current 1 percent, and scientists now estimate that CFC concentrations will begin to decrease after the year 2000. The Montreal Convention and its amendments are "a beautiful case study of environmental action," one scientist exults.[46] Furthermore, because ozone replenishes itself fairly rapidly, it is, one scientist says, "a renewable resource."[47] This means that by about the year 2020 the ozone level will have increased to about the concentration it was in 1979. "The ozone problem will correct itself," another scientist comments, "if we stick to what we plan" as far as eliminating CFC production and use.[48]

There may be a couple of sticking points to the plan. The most important of these has to do with sustainable development and the economic advancement of the LDCs. The substitutes for CFCs in refrigerants and other products are expensive, and the estimates of phasing out CFCs worldwide range up to $40 billion. Therefore LDCs will be hard-pressed to industrialize and provide their citizens with a better standard of living while simultaneously abandoning the production and use of CFCs. For example, refrigerators, which not long ago were rare in China, are becoming more and more commonplace, and, as one researcher put it, "simply allowing every Chinese family to have a refrigerator… will swamp" efforts in the developed countries to limit CFCs.[49] Representatives of LDCs resist having to give up their progress, especially without help from the EDCs to develop the often more expensive alternative technologies. As a former environment minister of India asked, "Is it fair that the industrialized countries who are responsible for the ozone depletion should arm-twist the poorer nations into bearing the cost of their mistakes?"[50]

Easing Global Warming Progress on dealing with global warming has been more limited. The reduction of CFCs will have a positive impact because of their role in global warming. The significant reduction of CO_2 discharges will be more difficult. There is increased recognition of the need to act, however, and a UNEP–sponsored World Climate Conference convened in Geneva in 1990 with the CO_2 problem as a major focus. At that meeting of 130 countries, most EDCs pledged to stabilize or reduce greenhouse gas emissions by the year 2000. The United States, however, declined to join in because of concern about the cost and the negative domestic economic impact. The global effort to reduce greenhouse gas emissions was reconfirmed in the Global Warming Convention signed at the 1992 Earth Summit. Further progress occurred when President Clinton agreed to drop the U.S. reservation to that treaty's suggested timetables for reducing emissions.

Progress on that treaty will, however, be difficult to put into effect. The next major effort to give practical application to the goal of easing the threat of global warming came in Kyoto, Japan, in 1997. The events leading up to the conference, its outcome, and the implications are related in the box, To Kyoto and Beyond, on pages 548–549.

Addressing Other Environmental Concerns There has also been progress on a range of other environmental concerns, such as international dumping. The 1989 Convention on the Control of Transboundary Movements of Hazardous Wastes and Their Disposal (the Basel Convention), signed by 105 countries in Switzerland, limits such activity. In 1991 almost all African states signed the Bamako Convention in Mali banning the transboundary trade in hazardous wastes on their continent. The limits in the Basel Convention were stiffened further in reaction to the continued export of hazardous wastes under the guise of declaring that the materials were meant for recycling or as foreign aid in the form of recoverable materials. Great Britain alone exported 105,000 tons of such toxic foreign aid in 1993 to 65 LDCs, a practice that one British opposition leader called the "immoral... dumping of our environmental problems in someone else's backyard."[51] As of January 1, 1998, all such shipments for recycling and recovery purposes were banned.

Marine pollution has also been on the international agenda for some time, and progress has been made. One of the first multilateral efforts was the International Convention for the Prevention of Pollution from Ships. More recently, 43 countries, including the world's largest industrial countries, agreed in 1990 to a global ban on dumping industrial wastes in the oceans. It went into effect in 1995. The countries also agreed not to dispose of nuclear waste in the oceans. These efforts make a difference. For example, there were 93 marine spills in 1979 that dumped 608,000 tons of oil into the world's oceans and seas; in 1999 there were only 23 spills and 24,000 tons of oil discharged.

After reading this chapter and the ones on international law, international organization, arms control, and economic cooperation, it is easy to be discouraged. The problems are immense and complex; barriers to cooperation are formidable; failure to find solutions carries potentially dire consequences. And sometimes when you begin to think that you are making progress, as the world has in recent years, a setback occurs. Still, the world must and does continue to try to preserve and improve the condition of the Earth and its people. It is true that the current level of cooperation, when compared with the problems, seems woefully inadequate, but that does not mean that we should despair.

The message here is to avoid the extremes of either unguarded optimism or hopeless pessimism. It is equally unwise to take the rosy "It's darkest before the dawn" approach or the gloom-and-doom approach represented by comedian Eddie Murphy's observation that "Sometimes it's darkest before the light goes out completely."

Don't sell the early efforts that we have discussed in this chapter and elsewhere too short. It is only during this century, and really since World War II, that the need to cooperate has penetrated our consciousness and our conscience. The intervening years have been a microsecond in human history. In that sense, much has been done. Yet, much remains to be done to secure the future, and the microseconds keep ticking by.

This book began its discussion of the alternative nationalist and internationalist approaches to world politics by using Robert Frost's poem about two roads diverging in a wood. The choice of which one to take is yours and that of the rest of humankind. Your present and, more important, your future will be determined by which road you follow. It will be hard to turn back. So, as Shakespeare tells us in *King Richard III*, "Go, tread the path that thou shalt ne'er return."

Less developed countries are becoming more adamant about not accepting toxic wastes from industrialized countries. At the same time these latter countries are closing their own dumps. The question is, Where will the oil-soaked rags, the soiled Pampers, and the rest of humanity's waste products go?

CHAPTER SUMMARY

1. This chapter deals with ecological concerns and cooperation. Self-interest, some people would say self-survival, compels us to attend to issues concerning the world's expanding population, the depletion of natural resources, the increase of chemical discharges into the environment, and the impact of these trends on the global biosphere.

2. A key concept and goal is sustainable development. The question is how to continue to develop industrially and otherwise while simultaneously protecting the environment. Given the justifiable determination of the LDCs to develop economically, the potential for accelerated resource depletion and pollution production is very high.

3. There is a wide range of views about how great the environmental threats are and what can and should be done to address them.

4. Population is a significant problem facing the world, with the global population surpassing the 6 billion mark. The 1994 UN Conference on Population and Development in Cairo marked the latest step in the effort to control population and the associated attempts to improve women's reproductive and other rights. There are also numerous international organizations, such as the United Nations Population Fund, working in the area. The most effective way to control population is to improve the educational and economic status of women and to make contraceptive services widely available.

5. Increasing population and industrialization have rapidly increased the use of a wide range of natural resources. It is possible, using known resources and current use rates, to project that petroleum, natural gas, and a variety of minerals will be totally depleted within the coming century. The world's forests, its supply of fresh water, and its wildlife are also under population and industrialization pressure. There are many international governmental nongovernmental organizations and efforts, symbolized by the 1992 Earth Summit, to address these problems.

6. Population growth and industrialization are also responsible for mounting ground pollution, water pollution, air pollution, global warming, and ozone layer depletion due to atmospheric pollution. Other areas, such as reducing CO_2 emissions, have only just begun and are difficult because of their cost.

7. The efforts at international cooperation in the areas discussed in this chapter return us to the question of standards of judgment. It is easy to view the vast extent of the problems facing the globe, to measure the limited effort being made to resolve them, and to dismiss the entire subject of international cooperation as superficial. It is true that not nearly enough is being done. But it is also true that only a very few decades ago nothing was being done. From that zero base, the progress made since World War II is encouraging. The only question is whether or not we will continue to expand our efforts and whether or not we will do enough, soon enough.

An Epilogue to the Text/ A Prologue to the Future

Where I did begin, there I shall end.

Shakespeare, *Julius Caesar*

So here it is some months later, and we are at the end of this book and this course. Finals await, and then, praise be, vacation. That well-deserved break from your academic labors brings you to an implicit point of decision about what to do with this text, the other course readings, and the knowledge you have gained from your instructor. One option is to sell what books you can back to the bookstore and forget the rest. I can remember from my undergraduate days how attractive an idea that sometimes seems.

But then, again, is that really the best option? Probably not. We began our semester's journey with the idea that we are all inescapably part of the world drama. There may be times when we want to shout, "Stop the world, I want to get off," but we cannot. We have also seen that we are both audience and actors in the global play's progress. At the very least, we are all touched by the action in ways that range from the foreign designer jeans that we wear to, potentially, our atomized end.

We can leave it at that, shrug our shoulders, and complain and mumble at the forces that buffet us. But we also can do more than that. We do not have to be just passive victims. We can, if we want and if we try, help write the script. The plot is ongoing and improvisational. The final scene is yet unwritten. We are not even sure when it will occur. It could be well into the far distant future—or it could be tomorrow. This, more than any particular point of information, is the most important message. You are not helpless, and you owe it to yourself and your fellow humans to take an active role in your life and in the world's tomorrows.

The world is beset by great problems. War continues to kill without cessation. A billion-dollar diet industry prospers in many countries of the North due to the fact that many of its citizens are overweight, while in the South, infants and the elderly starve to death in the dry dust. As if localized malnutrition were too slow and selective, we globally attack our environment with the waste products of our progress, and the human population tide threatens to overwhelm the Earth's ability to sustain the people who live on it. Of even more immediate peril, an expanse of nuclear mushroom clouds could instantly terminate our biosphere's more evolutionary decay.

To face these problems, we have, at best, a primitive political system. Sovereignty strengthens nationalities but divides the world. Frontier justice is the rule. As in a grade-B western, most of the actors carry guns on their hips and sometimes shoot it out. The law is weak, and the marshals have more authority in theory than in practice.

There are few anymore who really try to defend the system of assertive sovereignty as adequate for the future. Clearly, it is not. What is less certain is what to do next and how to do it. Cooperation, humanitarianism, enlightenment, and other such words provide easy answers, but they are vague goals. Real answers are difficult to come by. They may involve tough choices; we may be asked to give up some things now so that they will not be taken later, to curb our lifestyle, to risk arms control in the hope of avoiding nuclear war, and to think of the world in terms of "we."

At every step there will be those who urge caution, who counsel self-preservation first, who see the world as a lifeboat. Maybe they will be right—but probably not. We *have* begun to move toward a more rational order. The last five chapters clearly show this. But they also show how limited and fragile this progress has been. This is where you come in. Your job is to work to make the world the place you want it to be. It is your job to consider the problems, to ponder possible solutions, to reach informed opinions, and to act on your convictions. Think? Yes, of course. But also DO!! That is what is really important.

We began this study with the thought from Shakespeare's *Henry V* that "the world [is] familiar to us and [yet] unknown." My hope is that this text and the course you have just about completed have made the world more familiar, less unknown to you. What you do with what you have learned is now the issue. Will you treat this moment as an end? Or is it a beginning? Heed, if you will, the counsel of Shakespeare's King Lear:

Be governed by your knowledge and proceed.

EXPLANATORY NOTES

Page 42. Some matters of terminology: EDC/LDC. The use of the acronym EDC for economically developed country is not common in the literature. I am using "economically developed" here instead of simply "developed" in order to stress the economic factor and to avoid the all-too-common stereotype of the countries of the South as culturally or otherwise inferior. Indeed, the designation LDC, or less developed country, is misleading in the same way. Less economically developed country (LEDC) would be preferable, and politically and economically disadvantaged country (PEDC) would be better still, because these terms would recognize that the countries are in a relatively weak international political and economic position. The acronym LDC, however, is so common that I will continue to use it. The South is also referred to frequently as the Third World, although this term is rapidly becoming outmoded. It has been used somewhat inconsistently, but it generally has meant LDCs, especially those not aligned with either of the two superpowers in the East-West Axis. It may seem odd to refer to Third World countries when we do not refer to Second World ones, but the term has been useful to designate those countries that are not only politically and economically disadvantaged but that have invariably suffered through or are still undergoing a direct or an indirect colonial experience. It would be reasonable therefore to classify many of the former Soviet republics as Third World countries. Poor, mostly Muslim Uzbekistan, for example, was until recently something of a colony of the Russian-dominated Soviet state. The point is that such countries, many of which have had unfortunate experiences with politically and militarily powerful EDCs, share similar views of EDCs and their alleged role in causing and maintaining the LDCs' unjust economic and politically disadvantaged status. Finally, some analysts have used the words "core" and "periphery" to designate, respectively, those countries with power as being at the center of the political system and those without much power on the margins. These nuances need not concern us here. Therefore, the terms North, EDC, developed country, and core country all mean about the same thing; as do South, LDC, Third World, and periphery country.

Page 88. Names in non-Western Cultures. Names in many parts of the world do not follow the format familiar to Americans, Canadians, and others whose names are most likely to follow the European tradition of a first (given) name followed by a family name (surname). In China, the Koreas, Vietnam, and many other countries in Asia, the custom is to place the surname first, followed by the given name. Thus, Zhu Rongji would be addressed formally as Premier Zhu. Given the greater formality followed in China (and most of the rest of the world) compared to the United States, only Zhu's family and very close friends would call him Rongji. Japan presents something of a twist on this practice. Like most other North and East Asian people, the Japanese in their own usage place the surname first. But the very externally oriented Japanese have long practiced putting the given name first in all communications with the outside world. Thus internally in Japanese characters, the Japanese would refer to their prime minister as Mori (surname) Yoshiro (given name). Externally in English or other languages, he would be designated Yoshiro Mori. There are also countries in which only one name is used. Najibullah is the entire name of the Soviet-backed president of Afghanistan overthrown by U.S.–backed rebels in 1992. In somewhat the same way, the familiar name of President Saddam Hussein of Iraq creates some confusion. Originally, he was given his father's name (Hussein) coupled with what could be construed as a surname, al-Takrit, after the Takrit region of his home in Iraq. The designation "Saddam" is not a name as such. Rather it is an adopted political appellation meaning "one who confronts." In this way, he is President Hussein, but his familiar name is also Hussein. Finally, Spanish-heritage surnames often have longer and shorter versions that relate to family and origin. The full name of the Mexican president elected in 2000 is Vicente Fox Quesada, who succeeded President Ernesto Zedillo Ponce de León. After the first long form, they would be referred to as Presidents Fox and Zedillo. In the same way, former Costa Rican president and 1987 Nobel Peace Prize winner Oscar Arias Sanchez is President Arias.

Page 88. The Spelling and Pronunciation of Chinese. The Chinese language does not have an alphabet. It uses many thousands of characters that mean whole words or can be combined to form new words. Many of the characters also have varying meanings, depending on the way they are pronounced. In written Chinese, this is indicated by accent marks. Unlike Western languages, though, the accent marks indicate tone rather than stress. Words can have an even, high tone, go up, go down, or start in a low tone and trail off. This accounts for the "sing-song" impression that Westerners have of spoken Chinese. Because of its characters, very non-Western pronunciation, and other factors, translating Chinese into English has always been tricky. For many years the English Wade-Giles system of 1859 was used; in 1979 China adopted their own Pinyin (meaning "phonetic") system of romanization. By this, Mao Tse-tung became Mao Zedong; Chou En-lai became Zhou Enlai, Teng Hsiao-ping became Deng Xiaoping. For places, Beijing replaced Peking; Guangzhou replaced Canton; and Chongqing replaced Chungking. Except to maintain accuracy in a few historical references, Pinyin is used in this text. To detail pronunciation would take a great deal of space indeed. Just a few and only approximate guides are to pronounce *eng* as *ung*, *ian* as *en*, *ie* as *yeah*, *q* as *ch*, *ou* as in *bone*, *ua* as *ooa*, *uan* as *won*, *uai* as *why*, *uang* as *wong*, *ue* as *we*, *ui* as *way*, *un* as *oo*, *uo* as *woa*, *x* as *sh*, and *z* as *ds*.

Page 333. The Conditions for Military Success. Elements for success are those of George, Hall, and Simons (1971), which include (1) strong U.S. determination, (2) a less determined opponent, (3) clear U.S. goals, (4) a sense of urgency to accomplish these goals, (5) adequate domestic political support, (6) usable military options, (7) fear of U.S. escalation by the opponent, and (8) clarity concerning terms of the peaceful settlement. Other elements of success have been provided by Blechman and Kaplan (1978) and include (1) the opponent finds the threat credible,

(2) the opponent is not yet fully committed to a course of action, (3) the goal is maintaining the authority of a particular regime abroad, (4) force is used to offset force by an opponent, (5) the goal is to have an opponent continue current behavior, that is, to deter a change in behavior, (6) the action is consistent with prior policy, (7) there has been previous U.S. action in the area, (8) U.S. involvement begins early in the crisis, (9) military action is taken rather than threatened, and (10) strategic forces become involved, thus signaling seriousness of purpose. Caspar Weinberger's six criteria included (1) vital U.S. interests must be at stake, (2) there must be a clear intention of winning, (3) political and military objectives must be clearly defined, (4) sufficient military force must be employed to gain the objective, (5) there must be reasonable congressional and public support, and (6) combat should be a last resort. General Colin Powell's comments, made during a press interview, were not as easily enumerated as Weinberger's, but they generally agreed with the criteria of the then–secretary of defense. Powell's views can be found in the *New York Times*, September 29, 1992, p. A1.

Page 89. **Economics: Technical Terms and Sources.** The terms *gross national product* (GNP) and *gross domestic product* (GDP) are similar but not interchangeable. GNP measures the sum of all goods and services produced by a country's nationals whether they are in the country or abroad. Thus GNP includes data such as the profits of a country's MNCs. By the same logic, GNP does not include profits from production in one's country by foreign MNCs. GDP includes only income within a country (by both nationals and foreigners) and excludes foreign earnings of a country's nationals. The fact that some countries report only GNP and others report only GDP creates slight statistical comparison anomalies.

The most recent change in calculating a country's production of wealth is the addition of "purchasing power parity" (PPP) to the calculation. Because GDP or GNP is expressed in a single currency, usually the U.S. dollar, it does not fully account for the difference in prices for similar goods and services in different countries. Some countries are more expensive than the United States. Refer to the box GNP-PPP on page 397 for a complete explanation of GNP-PPP. There is certainly value to PPP adjustments, but this book uses unadjusted figures. Using both adjusted and unadjusted figures would created more confusion than clarity, and the reason for using the unadjusted GDP/GNP is that since many of the industrial and technological products that LDCs wish to acquire come from abroad, the cost to the LDC is not affected by PPP. A U.S. tractor that costs $50,000, costs $50,000 whether you buy it in the United States or Kenya. Therefore, PPP masks the gap in international purchasing power between LDCs and EDCs and inflates the economic position of LDCs compared to EDCs in the world economy.

All monetary values in this book are in current U.S. dollars (US$), unless otherwise noted. There are two ways to express monetary values. One is in current dollars, which means the value of the dollar in the year reported. Because of inflation, using current dollars means that, for example, the percentage increase in *value* of exports will rise faster than the percentage increase in the *volume* of exports over any period. The second way to express monetary value is in *real dollars*, or uninflated dollars. This means that the currency is reported in terms of what it would have been worth in a stated year. In this book, monetary value is in current U.S. dollars except where noted. Therefore, you could say either that a car in 2000 cost $15,395 or that (assuming a 4 percent inflation rate) it cost $10,000 in real 1989 dol-

lars. Note that you figure inflation by compounding the rate, that is, multiplying $10,000 by 1.04 x 1.04 x 1.04.... The number 100 is used as a baseline in many of the figures in this and other chapters. It is used to show relative change. This number is an abstraction and has no value as such. It simply allows comparisons of later growth or decline. It is used instead of zero to avoid pluses and minuses before subsequent data. For example, if you earned $5,000 in 1989 and a friend earned $7,000, and you wished to compare later earning growth, you would make 1989 earnings for both of you equal to 100. Then, if in 2000 you earned $8,000, but your friend earned only $4,000 (using increments of 10 to equal each $1,000), your earnings would be expressed as 130 and your friend's earnings would be 70. You may find that the data, such as trade expressed in dollars, used in this book for any given year or period varies somewhat from what is cited by another source. Most of the data is based on extensive compilations and complex calculations completed by the sources cited or by the author. But the reporting organizations, such as the U.S. government, the United Nations, the IMF, the World Bank, and GATT all use slightly different assumptions and inputs in calculating their final figures. Most of the major sources used herein include careful discussion of exactly how they arrive at their conclusions. You may refer to these if you wish a detailed explanation of their methodologies. The key, then, usually is not to focus too much on specific numbers, especially if they come from different sources. Rather it is best to concentrate on patterns, such as the rate of growth or decline of trade over a period of years. Unless specifically noted, this chapter relies on the following sources for financial, trade, and other economic data: International Monetary Fund (1999–2000), *Direction of Trade Statistics*, Washington, DC; IMF (2000), *International Financial Statistics*; IMF (2000), *World Economic Outlook*; IMF (2000), *IMF Survey*; U.S. Central Intelligence Agency (CIA) (1999), *The World Factbook, 1999–2000*; (U.S.) Bureau of the Census and U.S. Economics and Statistics Administration (2000), *Statistical Abstract of the United States, 2000*; *World Almanac, 2000*; World Bank (2000), *World Development Report, 2000*; World Resources Institute (2000), *World Resources, 1999–2000*. In addition to these sources, four newspapers—the *Financial Times* (London), the *Hartford Courant* (Hartford, Connecticut), the *New York Times* (New York), and the *Wall Street Journal* (New York)—were used as sources herein. Several further comments on these sources are appropriate. One is that many are periodic publications. The most current year used is shown, but historical data may also be drawn from various issues in the current or earlier years. Second, some sources of historical data are not shown because of the sheer mounting volume of citation that would be necessary through multiple editions of this study. Where it is not cited herein, historical data sources are cited in earlier editions of *International Politics on the World Stage*. Third, full bibliographic citations for most of the sources listed here can be found in this volume's bibliography.

Page 409. **How Exchange Rates Work.** To begin to understand the mysteries of how exchange rates work and the impact of their fluctuation, consider the following two scenarios: the first with the dollar ($) equal to the post–World War II high of 258 yen (¥), which was the case in early 1985; and the second with the dollar equal to the current value of ¥108. For illustration, assume that one automobile costs ¥3,096,000 to manufacture in Japan and another costs $18,000 to build in Detroit. Let us further suppose that an average Japanese worker makes ¥1,806 an hour; an

American makes $10 an hour. Manufacturing costs and wages are not directly affected by exchange rates and, therefore, remain constant.

Automobile Imports at a ¥258 = $1 Exchange Rate

- At ¥258 to the dollar, the equivalent cost is $12,000 for the Japanese car (¥3,096,000 ÷ ¥258) and ¥4,644,000 for the U.S. car ($18,000 × ¥258).
- It will take the Japanese worker earning ¥1,806 ($7) an hour a total of 1,714 work hours (¥3,096,00 ÷ ¥1,806) to buy the Japanese car and 2,571 work hours (¥4,644,000 ÷ ¥1,806) to buy the U.S. car. The Japanese worker will probably buy the Japanese car.
- It will take the American worker earning $10 (¥2,580) an hour a total of 1,200 work hours (¥3,096,000 ÷ ¥2,580) to buy the Japanese car and 1,800 work hours ($18,000 ÷ $10) to buy the U.S. car. The American worker will probably buy the Japanese car.
- With both the Japanese and the American worker buying Japanese cars, Japanese automobile exports to the United States will rise and U.S. exports to Japan will decline.

• Automobile Imports at a ¥108 = $1 Exchange Rate

- At ¥108 per dollar, the equivalent cost is $28,667 for the Japanese car (¥3,096,000 × ¥108) and ¥1,944,000 for the U.S. car ($18,000 ÷ ¥108).
- It will take the Japanese worker earning ¥1,806 ($17) an hour a total of 1,714 work hours (¥3,096,000 ÷ ¥1,806) to buy the Japanese car and 1,076 work hours (¥1,944,000 ÷ ¥1,806) to buy the U.S. car. The Japanese worker will probably buy the U.S. car.
- It will take the American worker earning $10 (¥1,080) an hour a total of 2,867 work hours (¥3,096,000 ÷ ¥1,080) to buy the Japanese car and 1,800 work hours ($18,000 ÷ $10) to buy the U.S. car. The American worker will probably buy the U.S. car.
- With both the Japanese and the American worker buying U.S. cars, exports from Japan will decline and U.S. exports will rise.

ENDNOTES

CHAPTER 1

1. *New York Times*, December 28, 1997, p. A10.
2. *New York Times*, November 28, 1997, p. A28.
3. Korb is quoted in Anthony Lewis, "The Defense Anomaly," *New York Times*, January 22, 1996, p. A15.
4. *Hartford Courant*, June 9, 1996, p. A2.
5. *Time*, March 18, 1996, p. 79. The analyst was J. P. Myers, director of the W. Alton Jones Foundation and coauthor of *Our Stolen Future* (New York: Dutton, 1996).
6. *Hartford Courant*, May 18, 1992, p. A5.
7. *American Enterprise*, March/April, 1991, p. 87.
8. *New York Times*, November 28, 1995, p. A14.
9. *New York Times*, October 6, 1995, p. B10.
10. *Time*, April 13, 1992, p. 28.
11. *New York Times*, March 9, 2000.

BOX, "CINDY BEAUDOIN," P. 10

1. *Hartford Courant*, May 24, 1992.

BOX, "MAKING A DIFFERENCE," P. 12

1. Interview with Lori Wallach, *Foreign Policy*, Spring 2000, on the Foreign Policy Web site at: http://www.foreignpolicy.com/articles.
2. *New York Times*, October 11, 1997, p. A1.
3. *Hartford Courant*, October 17, 1992, p. A1.
4. *New York Times*, March 7, 1998, p. A9.

CHAPTER 2

1. *San Diego Union Tribune*, April 22, 1996.
2. *New York Times*, March 6, 1992, p. D2. The scholar is Shafigul Islam at the U.S.-based Council of Foreign Relations.
3. *New York Times*, February 17, 1998, p. A1.
4. *Hartford Courant*, September 5, 1995, p. A1.
5. *New York Times*, April 17, 1996, p. A23. Clinton recalled the conversation to columnist Thomas L. Friedman, as related in his column "Gardening with Beijing."
6. *New York Times*, March 16, 1998, p. A6.
7. *Time*, June 1, 1992, p. 43.

BOX, "THE 6 BILLIONTH BABY," P. 44

1. Carol Bellamy, "The Progress of Nations 1999: The Roll of the Dice," UNICEF, at: http://www.unfpa.org/modules/6billion/facts.htm.

CHAPTER 3

1. *New York Times*, October 6, 1995, p. B10.
2. *New York Times*, December 2, 1991, p. A9.
3. *New York Times*, September 11, 1995, p. A9.
4. *Hartford Courant*, September 10, 1995, p. A7.
5. *New York Times*, February 15, 1999.
6. *New York Times*, February 15, 1999.
7. *Christian Science Monitor*, February 29, 1990, p. 29.
8. Princeton Survey Research/Pew Survey, October 1999 found on the Public Agenda Online Web site at: http://www.publicagenda.org/issues/pcc_detail.cfm?issue_type=americas_global_role&list=5.
9. Gallup Poll, May 1999, found on the Public Agenda Online Web site at: http://www.publicagenda.org/issues/nation_divided_detail.cfm?issue_type=americas_global_role&list=5.
10. *Time*, November 16, 1992, p. 78.
11. *Hartford Courant*, May 20, 1996, p. B5.
12. Haass's quote is taken from Gaddis Smith, "Saddle Up," a review of Haass's book in the *New York Times Review of Books*, August 3, 1997, p. 20.
13. *Hartford Courant*, September 1, 1995, p. A1.
14. *Time*, November 27, 1995, p. 4.
15. *New York Times*, March 17, 1996, p. D1.
16. *New York Times*, February 12, 1995, p. E5.
17. *New York Times*, February 15, 1999.
18. The quotes from Michael Williams of the International Institute for Strategic Studies in London and David Owen are both from the *Hartford Courant*, December 15, 1995, p. A1.
19. *New York Times*, May 27, 1994, p. A8.
20. *New York Times*, May 5, 1994, p. A11.
21. *Congressional Quarterly Weekly Report*, September 1, 1990, p. 2778.
22. *Time*, September 12, 1991, p. 53.

BOX, "THE NEW NATO MARCHES EAST," PP. 56–57

1. Lord Robertson of Port Ellen, "Kosovo One Year On: Achievement and Challenge," on the NATO Web site at: http://www.nato.int/.
2. The Washington Summit, Fact Sheets: "NATO Summit: NATO's Newest Members," on the U.S. White House Web site at: http://www.whitehouse.gov/WH/New/NATO/fact1.html.
3. *New York Times*, March 14, 1998, p. A4.

BOX, "BALANCE OF POWER," P. 64

1. From Kissinger's 1994 book, Diplomacy, quoted in *Newsweek*, April 11, 1994, p. 42.

BOX, "JAPAN: A RISING SUN?" PP. 66–67

1. *New York Times*, July 26, 1998, p. A12.
2. CNN.com, *Asia Now*, April 17, 2000, Vol. 155 No. 15, CNN Web site at: http://www.cnn.com/ASIANOW/time/magazine/2000/0417/japan.profile.html.
3. *Asahi Shimbun* Poll, April 1997, on the Kanzaki Web site at: http://www.kanzaki.com/jpoll/poll.html#P970426.
4. *Newsweek*, November 22, 1993, p. 38.
5. *Asahi Shimbun* Poll, March 1997, on the Kanzaki Web site at: http://www.kanzaki.com/jpoll/poll.html#P970317.
6. *New York Times*, April 11, 2000.
7. *Washington Post*, March 2, 2000.
8. *New York Times*, June 10, 1992, p. A7.
9. *New York Times*, April 21, 1996, p. E5.

10. *Hartford Courant*, January 6, 1992, p. 49.

CHAPTER 4

1. *New York Times*, November 9, 1999.
2. The 2:1 ratio was of those respondents with an opinion. The survey and the quote by Shi Tianchen at Duke University are from the *Far Eastern Economic Review*, December 7, 1995, excerpted in the *World Press Review*, March 1966, p. 16.
3. "A Roper Center Review of Public Opinion in the Gulf Crisis" (Roper Center for Public Opinion Research: The University of Connecticut, January 24, 1991).
4. Gallup Poll surveys of February 19, 1999, and April 6, 1999, provided by the Roper Center, University of Connecticut.
5. John F. Smith, chairman of General Motors, quoted in the *New York Times*, June 9, 1996, p. F1.
6. BBC News on the Internet, "World: Asia-Pacific Tension Rises over Spratly Islands," February 13, 1999, at: http://news.bbc.co.uk/hi/english/world/asia-pacific/newsid_278000/278359.stm.
7. Kent E. Calder of Princeton University, quoted in the *New York Times*, May 29, 1996, p. A6.
8. Henry A. Kissinger, "China: The Deadlock Can Be Broken," *Washington Post*, March 28, 1994, quoted in "U.S.-China Trade," *CQ Researcher*, Vol. 4. No. 14 (April 15, 1994), p. 319.
9. *U.S. News & World Report*, February 8, 1993, p. 39.
10. All quotes are from the *Foreign Eastern Economic Review*, excerpted in the *World Press Review*, March, 1996, pp. 12, 14.
11. *Time*, March 25, 1995, p. 39.
12. *Washington Post*, November 9, 1999.
13. *New York Times*, September 17, 1995, p. A26.
14. *Washington Post*, April 29, 2000.
15. CNN news item, "Shelton: British General Refused Order from NATO Commander in Kosovo," September 9, 1999, found at the CNN.Com Web site at: http://www.cnn.com/US/9909/09/shelton.nato/.
16. *Hartford Courant*, October 17, 1997, p. A12. The conversation was on a tape of Nixon's conversations released in 1997.
17. Representative Jim Leach, quoted in the *New York Times*, September 26, 1993, p. A12.
18. *New York Times*, October 31, 1995, p. A3.
19. *Washington Post*, February 21, 2000.
20. *Washington Post*, April 21, 2000.
21. *Hartford Courant*, November 25, 1999, p. A28.
22. *New York Times*, April 18, 2000.
23. Associated Press, November 24, 1998, on Nando Media Web site at: http://www.nando.com/.
24. National Farmers Union Submission to the Standing Committee on Foreign Affairs and International Trade on the effects of the WTO and FTAA negotiations on farmers' orderly marketing agencies, safety nets, and agricultural programs, April 27, 1999, NFU Web site at: http://www.nfu.ca/.
25. *New York Times*, January 12, 1998, p. D1.
26. Princeton Survey Research/*Newsweek* survey, October 1999, on the Public Agenda Online Web site at: http://www.publicagenda.org/.
27. James A. Baker III, *The Politics of Diplomacy: Revolution, War and Peace, 1989–1992* (New York: G. P. Putnam's Sons, 1995), quoted in Philip Taubman, "The Man in the Middle," *New York Times Book Review*, October 29, 1995, p. 9.

BOX, "TAIWAN: TO BE OR NOT TO BE," PP. 92–93

1. *New York Times*, June 26, 1994, p. A8.
2. *New York Times*, July 14, 1999.
3. *New York Times*, August 23, 1995, p. A12.
4. *New York Times*, February 22, 2000.
5. *New York Times*, March 6, 2000.
6. *New York Times*, January 31, 1996, p. A2.

BOX, "THE POWER OF THE PURSE: INTEREST GROUPS AND U.S. RELATIONS WITH CHINA," PP. 102–103

1. *New York Times*, May 25, 2000.
2. *New York Times*, April 21, 2000.
3. *New York Times*, May 2, 2000.
4. *New York Times*, April 21, 2000.
5. *New York Times*, May 25, 2000.
6. *New York Times*, April 13, 2000.
7. *New York Times*, May 25, 2000.

CHAPTER 5

1. Interview of Robert McNamara, circa 1997, as part of the CNN "Cold War Experience" series at: http://cnn.com/SPECIALS/cold.war/episodes/11/interviews/mcnamara/.
2. *New York Times*, July 11, 1996, p. A13.
3. *Hartford Courant*, June 18, 1998, p. A13.
4. *New York Times*, June 1, 1998, p. S3.
5. *Hartford Courant*, June 18, 1998, p. A13.
6. *South China Morning Post*, September 16, 1996, p. 1.
7. The adviser was Arthur Goldberg, and the quote is from Robert Dallek, *Flawed Giant: Lyndon Johnson and His Times, 1961–1973* (New York: Oxford University Press, 1998) as reproduced in a review of the book, Sean Wilentz, "Lone Starr Setting," *New York Times Book Review*, April 12, 1998, p. 6.
8. *Hartford Courant*, February 4, 1990, p. C4.
9. *New York Times*, October 2, 1993, p. A8.
10. The psychiatrist is Fritz C. Redlich, professor emeritus at UCLA and former dean of the Yale School of Medicine. His comments are in the *Hartford Courant*, March 22, 1992, p. A2.
11. *New York Times*, June 17, 1991, p. A10.
12. *New York Times*, January 8, 1997, p. A3.
13. *U.S. News & World Report*, February 8, 1993, p. 39.
14. *New York Times*, November 19, 1997, p. A14.
15. *Time*, November 30, 1987, p. 18.

BOX, "FRUSTRATION–AGGRESSION ANALYSIS AND THE RISE OF VLADIMIR PUTIN," PP. 112–113

1. *New York Times*, June 8, 1994, p. A16.
2. *New York Times*, March 28, 2000.
3. *Time*, May 27, 1996, p. 51.
4. *New York Times*, August 11, 1999.
5. *Washington Post*, March 11, 2000.
6. *New York Times*, January 11, 2000.
7. *Washington Post*, January 3, 2000.
8. *Washington Post*, January 3, 2000.
9. *Washington Post*, May 13, 2000.
10. *New York Times*, March 11, 2000.

CHAPTER 6

1. *New York Times*, October 6, 1995, p. B10.

2. *New York Times*, June 8, 1994, p. A16.
3. From "Patrie" in *Dictionnaire Philosophique*, 1764.
4. *New York Times*, August 2, 1994, p. C1. The anthropologist was Eugene Hammel.
5. *New York Times*, April 10, 1994, p. E1.
6. *New York Times*, May 25, 2000.
7. *Time*, March 12, 1990, p. 50.
8. *Christian Science Monitor*, May 8, 2000.
9. Eko Research Associates Polls, November 1995 and November 1999, on the company Web site at: http://www.ekos.com/press/dec14/sld003.htm.
10. *Hartford Courant*, March 12, 2000.
11. *Hartford Courant*, April 8, 1994, p. A8.
12. *New York Times*, May 11, 1998, p. A6.
13. *New York Times*, February 25, 1994, p. A6.
14. Wilson's speech to Congress was on February 11, 1918.
15. Both quotes are from the *New York Times*, December 10, 1995, p. A3.

BOX, "THE CHECHENS: DEATH OR FREEDOM," P. 140

1. Quoted on the Web site of Consortiumnews.com, February 7, 2000, at: http://www.consortiumnews.com.
2. Solzhenitsyn is quoted in Edward Kline, "ASF Chechnya Brief," on the Web site of the Andrei Sakharov Foundation at: http://www.wdn.com/asf/.

BOX, "PALESTINIANS: A NATION WITHOUT A STATE," PP. 148–149

1. *New York Times*, September 14, 1993, p. A1.
2. *New York Times*, November 7, 1995, p. A1.
3. *New York Times*, June 3, 1996, p. A8.
4. *New York Times*, May 18, 1999.
5. *New York Times*, August 7, 2000.
6. *New York Times*, July 9, 1999.
7. Mohamed Heikal, *Secret Channels: The Inside Story of Arab-Israeli Peace Negotiations* (London: HarperCollins, 1996), quoted in Judith Miller, "After the Handshake," a review in the *New York Times Book Review*, August 10, 1997, p. 7.
8. *New York Times*, May 30, 2000.
9. *Newsweek*, May 18, 1998, p. 43.

"DID YOU KNOW THAT," P. 151

1. *New York Times*, July 23, 1996, p. A10.

CHAPTER 7

1. Terry Eagleton, "When Revolution Was Reasonable," a review of *Tom Paine: A Political Life* (London: Bloomsbury, 1995) in the *Manchester Guardian Weekly*, April 30, 1995, p. 12.
2. Pauline Maier, "No Sunshine Patriot." A review of *Tom Paine: A Political Life* (Boston: Little, Brown, 1995) in the *New York Times Book Review*, March 12, 1995, 1—*et. seq.*
3. *New York Times*, June 4, 1996, p. C1.
4. *New York Times*, January 26, 2000.
5. *Time*, June 15, 1996, p. 54.
6. *Hartford Courant*, September 10, 1995, p. A7.
7. *New York Times*, March 8, 1998, p. A15. The scholar was Charlotte Bunch, executive director, Center for Women's Global Leadership, Rutgers University.
8. *New York Times*, June 13, 2000.

9. *Daily Star*, June 12, 2000, the paper's Web site at: http://dailystar.com.lb/features/12_06_00.htm.
10. *New York Times*, June 13, 2000.
11. *Hartford Courant*, July 10, 1992, p A1.
12. *New York Times*, March 5, 1995, p. A10.
13. Colin Powell, *My American Journey* (New York, Random House, 1995), excerpted in *Time*, September 18, 1995, p. 69, and quoted in the *New York Times*, September 17, 1995, p. A26.
14. *Time*, October 31, 1994, p. 20.
15. Survey in the *New York Times*, June 7, 2000.
16. "Women 2000," final unedited document at: http://www.un.org/womenwatch/daw/followup/reports.htm.
17. *New York Times*, September 16, 1995, p. A5.
18. *New York Times*, January 28, 1998.
19. *New York Times*, April 10, 1995, p. A1.
20. *New York Times*, April 10, 1995, p. A1.
21. *New York Times*, August 24, 1994, p. E5.
22. *Newsweek*, June 10, 1994, p. 82.
23. *New York Times*, June 15, 1994, p. A1.
24. *Christian Science Monitor*, June 16, 2000.
25. *New York Times*, June 9, 1996, p. E5.
26. Former Syrian prime minister Maaruf al-Dawalibi, quoted in the *New York Times*, June 2, 1993, p. A3.
27. *Time*, October 2, 1990, p. 55.
28. *New York Times*, February 27, 1998, p. A8.
29. Sheik Abdalah bin Biyah, a member of the Supreme Council of Mosques and a professor of theology at King Abdelziz University in Jidda, Saudi Arabia, quoted in the *New York Times*, June 2, 1993, p. A3.
30. Mohammed Said al-Ashmawi, a justice on Egypt's Supreme Court, quoted in the *New York Times*, June 2, 1993, p. A3.
31. The columns by Thomas L. Friedman and the quote by Fukuyama are from the *New York Times*, December 8, 1996, p. E15, and December 11, 1996, p. A27.
32. *New York Times*, April 14, 1996, p. D1.
33. *Washington Post*, January 29, 2000.
34. *New York Times*, October 21, 1994, p. A4.
35. *Hartford Courant*, September 19, 1999.
36. *Sydney Morning Herald*, November 30, 1999, on the SMH Web site at: http://www.smh.com.au/news/9911/30/world/world9.html.
37. *Hartford Courant*, March 7, 1996, p. E4.
38. *New York Times*, March 15, 1994, p. A1.
39. *New York Times*, July 11, 1992, p. A3.
40. *Hartford Courant*, April 2, 2000.
41. Originally in *Time,* December 8, 1967, and found at Quotations Home Page at: http://www.geocities.com/~spanoudi/quote.html.
42. *New York Times*, May 23, 2000.
43. *New York Times*, April 14, 1996, p. D1.
44. *Manchester Guardian Weekly*, August 13, 1995, p. 18.
45. *New York Times*, February 2, 1996, p. A7.
46. *New York Times*, November 25, 1995, p. A4.
47. Richard M. Nixon, *Beyond Peace* (New York: Random House, 1994), excerpted in *Time*, May 2, 1994, p. 33.
48. Both quotes are from the *New York Times*, August 3, 1992, p. A9.
49. *New York Times*, January 23, 1996, p. A7.
50. *New York Times*, October 21, 1993, p. A1.
51. David Shenk of the Columbia University Freedom Forum Media Studies Center, quoted in the *New York Times*, April 14, 1996, p. D1.

52. *New York Times*, June 4, 1996, p. C1.
53. The scholar was political theorist Michael Sandel of Harvard University, quoted in the *New York Times*, March 18, 1996, p. A21.

BOX, "AND NEVER THE TWAIN SHALL MEET: UNTIL NOW," P. 181

1. *New York Times*, April 24, 1992, p. A4.
2. *New York Times*, February 24, 1996, p. D7.

BOX, "HINDUTVA AND THE BOMB," P. 184

1. *Newsweek*, June 8, 1998, p. 25.
2. *New York Times*, February 16, 1998.
3. *New York Times*, May 16, 1998, p. A1.
4. *New York Times*, May 16, 1998, p. A5.
5. *New York Times*, May 16, 1998, p. A5.
6. *New York Times*, May 5, 1998, p. A6.
7. *New York Times*, May 13, 1998, p. A14.

CHAPTER 8

1. BBC News, 2/2/2000 at: http://news.bbc.co.uk/hi/english/world/europe/newsid_628000/628282.stm.
2. *New York Times*, February 2, 2000.
3. *New York Times*, February 2, 2000.
4. *Washington Post*, May 2, 2000.
5. *New York Times*, February 26, 1992, p. A6.
6. Anti-Defamation League (ADL) Web site at: http://www.adl.org/backgrounders/joerg_haider.html.
7. *Le Monde*, May 1998 at: http://www.monde-diplomatique.fr/en/1998/05/08igou.
8. Front National Web site at: http://www.fnjeunesse.com/english.htm.
9. BBC Web site at: http://news.bbc.co.uk/low/english/world/europe/newsid_484000/484051.stm.
10. Romir Research Group Web site at: http://www.romir.ru/eng/default.htm.
11. *Hartford Courant*, February 25, 1994, p. A4.
12. *Newsweek*, June 6, 1994, p. 37.
13. *New York Times*, September 19, 1994, p. A10.
14. *Newsweek*, September 19, 1994, p. 37.
15. Ambassador David Scheffer, July 23, 1998, U.S. State Department Web site at: http://www.state.gov/www/policy_remarks/1998/980723_scheffer_icc.html.
16. *New York Times*, October 7, 1994, p. A1.
17. CNN.com, April 30, 2000 at: http://www.cnn.com/2000/HEALTH/AIDS/04/30/aids.threat.03/index.html.
18. CNN.com, April 20, 2000, at: http://www.cnn.com/2000/HEALTH/04/26/emerging.infections/index.html.

BOX, "THE DALAI LAMA IN DHARAMSALA," PP. 194–195

1. *New York Times*, March 6, 1996, p. A8.
2. *Newsweek*, May 11, 1998, p. 64.
3. *New York Times*, March 6, 1996, p. A8.
4. *New York Times*, July 28, 1996, p. A11.
5. *Manchester Guardian Weekly*, July 23, 1995, p. 7.
6. *Manchester Guardian Weekly*, July 23, 1995, p. 7.
7. Speech of the Dalai Lama to the German Bundestag, June 19, 1995, in the *Tibetan Bulletin*, July–August 1995, p. 20.
8. *New York Times*, June 28, 1998, p. A6.
9. *New York Times*, June 28, 1998, p. A6.
10. *New York Times*, June 29, 1998, p. A1.
11. *New York Times*, March 6, 1996, p. A8.
12. *New York Times*, July 2, 1999.
13. *Hartford Courant*, April 30, 1998, p. A21.

CHAPTER 9

1. *New York Times*, September 7, 1992, p. A5.
2. Churchill made the widely quoted statement on June 26, 1954, while visiting the United States. Various papers printed it the next day.
3. Address to the General Assembly, July 16, 1997, UN Doc. SG/SM/6284/Rev.2.
4. *Manchester Guardian Weekly*, July 27, 1997, p. 4.
5. "Citizen's Guide: A New Treaty for Europe" at: http://europa.eu.int/en/agenda/igc-home/intro/preface/en.htm.
6. Both quotes are from the *New York Times*, July 16, 1995, p. A1.
7. *New York Times*, June 28, 2000.
8. Indications of public opinion in this section, unless otherwise noted, are drawn from *Eurobarometer* 52, April 2000, on the Web at: http://europa.eu.int/comm/dg10/epo/eb/eb52/eb52.html.
9. ABC News/*Washington Post* Poll. March 30–April 2, 2000, on the Web at: http://www.pollingreport.com/institut.htm#Federal.
10. *New York Times*, January 14, 2000.
11. *New York Times*, June 28, 2000.
12. *World Opinion Update*, March 1997, p. 33.
13. Speech by Joschka Fischer at the Humboldt University in Berlin, May 12, 2000, on the Web at: http://www.auswaertiges-amt.de/6_archiv/2/r/r000512b.htm.
14. *Wall Street Journal Europe*, May 5, 2000, on the Web at: http://www.nejtillemu.com/chevenement.htm.
15. Address to the Council on Foreign Relations, New York, April 22, 1997, UN document SG/SM/6218.
16. *New York Times*, July 8, 1998, p. A1.
17. Prime Minister Morihior Hosokawa, quoted in the *New York Times*, September 26, 1993, p. A16.
18. Foreign Minister Klaus Kinkel, quoted in the *New York Times*, September 30, 1993.
19. Sharad Pawar, quoted in the *New York Times*, November 15, 1995, p. A9.
20. President Chandrika Bandaranaike Kumaratunga of Sri Lanka and President Frederick J. T. Chiluba of Zambia, both quoted in the *New York Times*, October 23, 1995, p. A8.
21. UN Press Release GA/9692, December 20, 1999.
22. Ambassador Francisco Paolo Fulci, quoted in the *New York Times*, November 15, 1995, p. A9.
23. *New York Times*, October 23, 1995, p. A8.
24. *New York Times*, March 6, 1995, p. A6.
25. Address to commencement at the Massachusetts Institute of Technology, Cambridge, June 5, 1997. UN Document SG/SM/6247.
26. James Traub, "Kofi Annan's Next Test," *New York Times Magazine*, March 29, 1998, p. 49.
27. Address to the Council on Foreign Relations, New York, January 19, 1999, UN document SG/SM/6865.
28. James Traub, "Kofi Annan's Next Test," *New York Times Magazine*, March 29, 1998, p. 80.
29. *New York Times*, September 12, 1995, p. A1.
30. *Time*, October 30, 1995, p. 74.
31. *New York Times*, December 16, 1996, p. A8.

32. James Traub, "Kofi Annan's Next Test," *New York Times Magazine*, March 29, 1998, p. 49.
33. Address to "Empower America," Washington, D.C., October 16, 1998, UN Document SG/SM/6754.
34. *New York Times*, November 6, 1994, p. A11.
35. *Time*, October 30, 1995, p. 74.
36. *New York Times*, July 17, 1997, p. A1.
37. Gallup International Millennium Survey, on the Web at: http://www.gallup-international.com/survey8.htm.
38. Address at Princeton University, November 24, 1997, UN document SG/SM/6404.
39. *New York Times*, January 8, 1997, p. A3.
40. *New York Times*, September 18, 1994, p. A16.
41. Kofi Annan, "The Unpaid Bill That's Crippling the UN," an op-ed piece, *New York Times*, March 9, 1998, p. A19.
42. Hammarskjöld's widely quoted statement is attributed to the *New York Times*, June 27, 1955.

BOX, "WHEN IS A BANANA A BANANA?" P. 233

1. *New York Times*, October 6, 1994, p. A16.

BOX, "MUCH ADO ABOUT SOMETHING," PP. 240–241

1. *Time*, December 2, 1991, p. 28.
2. *New York Times*, June 27, 1996, p. A8.
3. Dawn Internet News, March 15, 2000, at: http://www.dawn.com/2000/03/15/int1.htm.
4. *New York Times*, December 18, 1996, p. A1.
5. *Hartford Courant*, November 11, 1999.
6. *New York Times*, December 18, 1996, p. A1.

CHAPTER 10

1. Churchill told this story in a speech on October 24, 1928, and it can be found, among other places, in Robert Rhodes James, ed., *Winston S. Churchill: His Complete Speeches: 1897–1963, Vol. 5* (1974), p. 5421.
2. *New York Times*, March 7, 1996, p. A10.
3. *New York Times*, February 24, 1998, p. A1.
4. "Education at a Glance: OECD Indicators, 1998," reported in the *New York Times*, November 24, 1998.
5. *New York Times*, February 25, 1998, p. B10.
6. Andrei Memin, president of the Public Health Association, quoted in the *Hartford Courant*, November 24, 1995, p. A27.
7. *New York Times*, May 10, 1996, p. A10.
8. *New York Times*, June 8, 1997, p. E1.
9. *Washington Post*, July 9, 2000.
10. *Time*, July 15, 1996, p. 54.
11. *Time*, April 11, 1994, p. A10.
12. *Time*, June 13, 1994, p. 32.
13. *New York Times*, May 29, 1994, p. A1.
14. *Washington Post*, April 13, 1990, p. A7.
15. *New York Times*, August 28, 1994, p. E7.
16. *New York Times*, April 9, 1998, p. A4.
17. *Time*, July 31, 1989, p. 17.
18. Cohen news conference on January 31, 1998, taken from the Web at: http://www.fas.org/ news/iraq/1998/01/index.html.
19. *New York Times*, June 30, 1995, p. D5.
20. *New York Times*, July 10, 2000.
21. The quote is Ambassador J. Stapleton Roy's recollection of what Jiang said, *New York Times*, July 3, 1995, p. E3.

22. *Washington Post*, April 1, 2000.
23. *New York Times*, February 27, 2000.
24. *New York Times*, March 7, 1996, p. A1.
25. *New York Times*, April 19, 2000.
26. *New York Times*, February 27, 2000.
27. *New York Times*, May 6, 1994, p. A6.
28. *New York Times*, March 3, 1998, p. E3.
29. *Hartford Courant*, September 1, 1993, p. A1.
30. *New York Times*, September 14, 1994, p. A1.
31. *New York Times*, June 15, 2000.
32. *Time*, April 9, 1990, p. 39.
33. *New York Times*, October 30, 1997, p. A1.
34. *Washington Post*, April 13, 1990, p. A7.
35. *New York Times*, February 3, 1996, p. A11.
36. *New York Times*, June 30, 1998, p. A9.
37. *New York Times*, February 2, 1996, p. A1.
38. *Hartford Courant*, September 18, 1994, p. A4.
39. *Hartford Courant*, October 14, 1994, p. A9.
40. Statement of November 1993 in *Time*, April 11, 1994, p. 58.
41. Secretary of Defense William Perry, quoted in *Time*, April 11, 1994, p. 58.
42. *Time*, October 31, 1994, p. 35.
43. *New York Times*, April 3, 1994, p. A1.
44. *New York Times Magazine*, March 29, 1998, p. 50.
45. *New York Times*, June 6, 1998, p. A1.
46. *New York Times*, March 6, 2000.
47. *New York Times*, February 27, 2000.
48. *Washington Post*, April 1, 2000.
49. *Hartford Courant*, March 17, 1994, p. A6.
50. *Time*, June 13, 1994, p. 32.
51. *New York Times*, March 17, 1994, p. A10.
52. *New York Times*, February 25, 1998, p. A1.
53. *Christian Science Monitor*, October 15, 1990, p. 18.
54. *New York Times*, October 4, 1994, p. A1. The official was Assistant Secretary of Defense Joseph Nye.
55. *USA Today*, March 11, 1996, p. A7.
56. *New York Times*, January 10, 1998, p. A6.
57. *New York Times*, March 11, 2000.
58. *New York Times*, April 19, 2000.
59. *New York Times*, April 30, 1988, p. 31.
60. *New York Times*, March 16, 1995, p. A5.
61. *New York Times*, March 16, 1995, p. A5. Some words added to smooth out the poor translation quoted in the *Times*.
62. Vice Admiral Archie Ray Clemins, quoted in the *New York Times*, March 17, 1996, p. D1.
63. *Washington Post*, February 25, 2000.
64. *New York Times*, June 6, 1998, p. A1.
65. *New York Times*, August 19, 1995, p. A1.
66. *New York Times*, March 1, 2000.
67. *New York Times*, March 11, 2000.
68. Chief of Staff Leon Panetta, quoted in the *New York Times*, March 18, 1996, p. A3.

BOX, "COME ABROAD TO SEE THE WORLD," PP. 276–277

1. *New York Times*, June 28, 1998.
2. *New York Times*, August 4, 1998.
3. Quoted in the *Christian Science Monitor*, November 21, 1997.
4. Representative Larry Craig, October 5, 1998, *Congressional Record*, p. S11405.
5. U.S. General Accounting Office report GAO/NSAID-99-164 (Presidential Travel).

6. Charles Jones, quoted in the *Christian Science Monitor*, November 21, 1997.
7. *Time*, October 31, 1994, p. 36.

CHAPTER 11

1. *New York Times*, August 12, 1990, p. A10.
2. European Court of Justice Case C-285/98, January 11, 2000, paragraph 29.
3. *New York Times*, November 12, 1997, p. A7.
4. *New York Times*, January 14, 2000.
5. *New York Times*, August 4, 1998, p. A4.
6. International Court of Justice Press Communiqué, 2000/10, March 23, 2000, available at: http://www.icj-cij.org/icjw-ww/idocket/iNH/iNHframe.htm.
7. *New York Times*, July 9, 1996, p. A6.
8. Fernando García, "Amendments to Foreign Investment Law Simplify Investment in Mexico," National Law Center for Inter-American Free Trade on the Web at: http://www.natlaw.com/pubs/spmxfinumber1.htm.
9. *New York Times*, May 5, 1994, p. A11.
10. U.S. Department of State, "1999 Country Reports on Human Rights Practices: China," February 25, 2000, available at: http://www.state.gov/www/global/human_rights/1999_hrp_report/china.html.
11. *Newsweek*, November 29, 1993, p. 47.
12. *New York Times*, March 5, 1997, p. A8.
13. *Hartford Courant*, October 23, 1997, p. A9.
14. *Hartford Courant*, May 1, 1998, p. A15.
15. Address at the University of Tehran on Human Rights Day, December 10, 1997, UN document SG/SM/6419.
16. Address at Ditchley Park, United Kingdom, June 26, 1998, UN document SG/SM/6313.
17. *New York Times*, December 6, 1999.
18. *New York Times*, January 24, 1990, p. A1.
19. *New York Times*, March 3, 2000.
20. *New York Times*, February 4, 2000.
21. *Time*, June 27, 1994, p. 15.
22. Taken from the Web at: http://worldnews.miningo.com/msub.12.htm.
23. *New York Times*, December 15, 1999.
24. CNN, June 1, 2000, at: http://www.cnn.com/2000/LAW/06/01/tanzania.rwandatribun.ap/.
25. Remarks by President Bill Clinton, University of Connecticut, October 15, 1995, available at: http://www.pub.whitehouse.gov/uri-res/I2R?urn:pdi://oma.eop.gov.us/1995/10/17/10.text.1.
26. *New York Times*, June 16, 1998, p. A6.
27. *New York Times*, August 13, 1997, p. A10.
28. *New York Times*, June 10, 1998, p. A9.
29. *New York Times*, June 10, 1998, p. A6, and June 15, 1998, p. A8, respectively.
30. Annan speech was found on the Web at: http://un.org/icc/.
31. *New York Times*, July 22, 2000.
32. *New York Times*, April 7, 1998, p. A17.
33. *New York Times*, April 18, 1992, p. A9.
34. Kennedy's remark was on June 24, 1963, and can be found in the *Public Papers of the President of the United States: John F. Kennedy, 1963*.

BOX, "CORRUPTION AND INTERNATIONAL LAW," P. 294

1. *New York Times*, August 13, 1997, p. A3.

2. *Hartford Courant*, September 21, 1997, p. D1.

CHAPTER 12

1. *Time*, January 28, 1991, p. 33.
2. *New York Times*, March 1, 2000.
3. Pierre Lellouche, quoted in the *New York Times*, February 23, 1996, p. A3.
4. *Hartford Courant*, June 29, 1997, p. A2.
5. *New York Times*, August 23, 1997, p. A5.
6. *Newsweek*, July 13, 1998, p. 59.
7. *New York Times*, July 28, 1997, p. A1.
8. *Time*, September 9, 1996, p. 17.
9. *Time*, July 15, 1996, p. 54.
10. Richard Haas, quoted in *Time*, November 27, 1995, p. 49.
11. *Newsweek*, November 26, 1994, p. 36.
12. *Time*, October 1, 1990, p. 54.
13. *Wall Street Journal*, April 30, 1991, p. A1.
14. *Time*, May 16, 1994, p. 47.
15. Jacob Heilbrunn and Michael Lind, "The Third American Empire," an op-ed piece in the *New York Times*, January 2, 1996, p. A15.
16. The diplomat was Charles H. Thomas II, former U.S envoy to Bosnia, quoted in the *New York Times*, November 29, 1995, p. E2.
17. *New York Times*, February 21, 1998, p. A1.
18. Gary W. Gallagher, "At War with Himself," a review of Michael Fellman, *Citizen Sherman: A Life of William Tecumseh Sherman* (New York: Random House, 1995) in the *New York Times Review of Books*, October 22, 1995, p. 24.
19. *Hartford Courant*, February 17, 1992, p. A3.
20. *New York Times*, June 17, 1998, p. A5.
21. *New York Times*, May 5, 1998, p. A18.
22. All quotes are from *Newsweek*, August 13, 1995, pp. 44–46.
23. *Hartford Courant*, November 16, 1994, p. F6.
24. *New York Times*, February 13, 1994, p. A12. The official was Vladimir Diouhy, Czech minister of industry and trade.
25. *New York Times*, August 23, 1998, p. WK5.
26. *Oklahoma Daily*, August 25, 1998.
27. *Hartford Courant*, March 12, 1999.
28. *World Press Review*, September 1996, p. 42.
29. *New York Times*, March 21, 1996, p. A12.
30. *New York Times*, April 26, 1997, p. A1. The expert was Dr. William A. Haseltine.
31. *Congressional Record*, January 23, 1990, p. S12.
32. Elizabeth A. Fenn, "Biological Warfare, Circa 1750," an op-ed piece in the *New York Times*, April 11, 1998, p. A11.
33. *Hartford Courant*, September 15, 1992, p. A10.
34. *Hartford Courant*, April 2, 2000. The expert was Alan Zellicoff of Sandia National Laboratories.
35. *New York Times*, February 25, 1996, p. A8.
36. *Time*, May 19, 1997, p. 47.
37. Colonel General Lev Rokhlin, quoted in *Time*, June 3, 1996, p. 48.
38. Quoted in John Newhouse, "13 Days That Almost Shook the World," *New York Times Book Review*, July 27, 1997, p. 10.
39. *New York Times*, October 5, 1997, p. WK7.
40. George Rathjens of MIT, quoted in the *New York Times*, January 23, 1990, p. C8.
41. This description is based on a 1979 report by the U.S. Office of Technology Assessment.

BOX, "WAR IS HELL!" P. 321

1. All quotes are from the *New York Times*, November 12, 1996, p. A1.

BOX, "THE KILLING FIELDS," PP. 338–339

1. *New York Times*, May 11, 1996, p. A4.
2. *New York Times*, October 5, 1995, p. E3.
3. U.S. Department of State, "Hidden Killers: The Global Landmine Crisis, September 1998, on the Web at: http://www.state.gov/www/global/arms/rpt_9809_demine_toc.html.
4. Senator Patrick Leahy, quoted in the *New York Times*, October 5, 1995, p. E3.
5. Both quotes are from the *New York Times*, May 7, 1996, p. A10.
6. *New York Times*, June 17, 1997, p. A10.
7. *New York Times*, September 4, 1997, p. A10.

BOX, "THE FLYING GARBAGE CAN," PP. 352–353

1. "Executive Summary of the [Rumsfeld] Commission to Assess the Ballistic Missile Threat to the United States," available on the Web at: ftp://fedbbs.access.gpo.gov/gpo_bbs/cia/bmt.htm.
2. *Washington Post*, January 17, 2000.
3. *Washington Post*, September 3, 2000.
4. *New York Times*, April 26, 2000.
5. *New York Times*, May 11, 2000.
6. *New York Times*, August 9, 2000.

CHAPTER 13

1. *Labor*, September 6, 1947.
2. *Washington Post*, July 2, 2000.
3. *Arms Control Today*, May 2000, Arms Control Association Web site at: http://www.armscontrol.org/ACT/may00/ru1ma00.htm.
4. *New York Times*, August 24, 1991, p. A9.
5. *New York Times*, May 12, 1996, p. A1.
6. *Washington Post National Weekly Edition*, May 22–28, 1995, p. 18.
7. *New York Times*, May 22, 2000.
8. *New York Times*, September 25, 1996, p. A1.
9. *New York Times*, October 14, 1999.
10. *Hartford Courant*, July 7, 1992, p. A6.
11. Ivan Eland, "Tilting at Windmills: Post–Cold War Military Threats to U.S. Security," Cato Institute, February 1999, available through the Columbia Working Papers on the Web at: http://wwwc.cc.columbia.edu/sec/dlc/ciao/wpsfrm.html.
12. U.S. Congress, Senate, Committee on Armed Services, *Current and Projected National Security Threats*, Hearings, February 2, 1999.
13. *New York Times*, September 12, 1996, p. A9.
14. *Newsweek*, May 25, 1998, p. 32B.
15. *New York Times*, May 31, 1998, p. A1.
16. *New York Times*, September 13, 1996, p. A1.
17. *New York Times*, April 11, 2000.
18. Organization for Security and Cooperation in Europe Web site at: http://www.osce.org/field_activities/field_activities.htm.
19. *New York Times*, December 20, 1995, p. A9.
20. *New York Times*, January 31, 1992, p. A9.
21. *New York Times*, May 10, 2000. The analyst was J. Stephen Morrison, the director of Africa programs at the Center for Strategic and International Studies in Washington.
22. *New York Times*, August 8, 2000. The analyst was Stephen Dimoff of the United Nations Association.
23. *New York Times*, January 6, 1995, p. A3.
24. *New York Times*, June 14, 2000.
25. *New York Times*, May 4, 1997, p. 12.
26. *New York Times*, October 3, 1999.

BOX, "CHAINED TO THE NUCLEAR ROCK," PP. 370–371

1. *New York Times*, September 7, 1995, p. A9.
2. The Keating and Takemura quotes are from *Time*, September 18, 1995, p. 85.
3. *New York Times*, May 16, 1998, p. A5.
4. *Newsweek*, May 25, 1998, p. 32C.
5. *Newsweek*, May 25, 1998, p. 32B.
6. *New York Times*, May 16, 1998, p. A15.
7. *New York Times*, May 17, 1998, p. WK2. The scholar was Joseph Cirincione, director of the Nonproliferation Project of the Carnegie Endowment.
8. *New York Times*, May 29, 1998, p. A1.
9. *New York Times*, July 26, 1998, p. A3.
10. *New York Times*, May 17, 1998, p. WK2.
11. *New York Times*, July 26, 1998, p. A3.
12. *New York Times*, July 12, 1998, p. WK18. The expert was Joseph Cirincione, director of the Nonproliferation Project of the Carnegie Endowment.
13. *New York Times*, August 8, 2000.
14. CNN, March 20, 2000 on the Web at: http://www.cnn.com/2000/ASIANOW/south/03/19/india.pakistan.02/.

CHAPTER 14

1. U.S. Congress, House of Representatives., Hearings before the Subcommittee on Trade of the Committee on Ways and Means, May 7, 1998. Michael Ranneberger was the official.
2. Quoted in Michael Lind, "Why Buy American?" a review of Alfred E. Eckes Jr., *U.S. Foreign Trade Policy since 1776* (Chapel Hill: University of North Carolina Press, 1995), in the *New York Times Book Review*, October 29, 1995, p. 42.
3. *New York Times*, April 16, 1992, p. A1.
4. Emerson Kapaz of São Paulo, quoted in the *Wall Street Journal*, June 21, 1991, p. A11.
5. Catherine L. Mann, "Is the U.S. Current Account Deficit Sustainable?" *Finance & Development* (a quarterly magazine of the IMF), March 2000, 37/1, on the IMF Web site at: http://www.imf.org/external/pubs/ft/fandd/2000/03/mann.htm.

BOX, "GNP-PPP: THE BIG MAC STANDARD," P. 397

1. *The Economist*, April 3, 1999, p. 66.

CHAPTER 15

1. *New York Times*, March 9, 1998, p. A1.
2. *New York Times*, May 29, 1992, p. A3.
3. Economist Gary C. Hufbauer, quoted in the *New York Times*, September 11, 1996, p. D1.
4. Stanley Roth of the National Security Council staff, quoted in the *New York Times*, February 21, 1996, p. A9.
5. *New York Times*, June 9, 1996, p. F1.
6. *New York Times*, October 23, 1995, p. A8.

7. *Hartford Courant*, July 23, 2000.
8. *New York Times*, April 4, 1991, p. A6.
9. *New York Times*, March 2, 1997, p. A39.
10. *New York Times*, April 7, 1996, p. E5.
11. BBC News, February 12, 2000, on the Web at: http://news2.thls.bbc.co.uk.
12. *Time*, September 19, 1995, p. 92.
13. *New York Times*, July 28, 1992, p. A1.
14. *New York Times*, June 25, 1996, p. A1.
15. Klaus Schwab, director of the Davos Forum, quoted in Thomas L. Friedman, "Revolt of the Wannabes," a column in the *New York Times*, February 7, 1996, p. A19.
16. *New York Times*, October 12, 1996, p. A1.
17. Speech of January 29, 2000, on the White House Web site at: http://www.pub.whitehouse.gov/uri-res/I2R?urn:pdi://oma.eop.gov.us/2000/1/31/13.text.1.
18. *New York Times*, February 1, 1999.
19. Data supplied by economist Gary Hufbauer and Kimberly Elliott to the *New York Times*, November 12, 1993, p. D1.
20. *New York Times*, November 12, 1993, p. D1.
21. *New York Times*, May 28, 1998, p. A10.
22. *New York Times*, November 2, 1996.
23. Representative Joseph Gaydos in the *Congressional Record*, April 13, 1988, p. A1613.
24. *New York Times*, October 30, 1996, p. A1.
25. *New York Times*, February 1, 1999.

CHAPTER 16

1. *Hartford Courant*, March 12, 1995, p. A1.
2. ILO report, "Child Labour Today: Facts and Figures, Geneva, June 10, 1996," taken from the Web at: http://www.ilo.org.
3. *New York Times*, September 7, 2000.
4. *New York Times*, October 24, 1995, p. A10.
5. The newspaper quoted is the *New York Times*, and that quote and the U.S. reservation are from the *New York Times*, November 18, 1996, p. A3.
6. UNIDO press release (IDO/1658), December 9, 1996, taken from the Web.
7. Web site for UNCTAD's tenth meeting at: http://www.unctad-10.org/index_en.htm.
8. Web site for UNCTAD's tenth meeting at: http://www.unctad-10.org/index_en.htm.
9. John Kirton of the University of Toronto's G-7 Research Group, "What Is the G-7?" document on the Web on November 10, 1996, at: http://unl1.library.utoronto.ca/www/g7/what_is_g7.html.
10. *Hartford Courant*, July 23, 2000. The two scholars were William Anhhtholis and Daniel Benjamin.
11. The Sutherland quote is from the *Hartford Courant*, April 16, 1994, p. A1.
12. The Clinton quote, made at the end of negotiations, is from the *Hartford Courant*, December 16, 1993, p. D8.
13. *New York Times*, December 16, 1993, p. D8.
14. *New York Times*, November 23, 1994, p. A18.
15. Introduction to a pamphlet, "The WTO: 5 Years of Reasons to Resist Corporate Globalization," by Lori Wallach and Michelle Sforza, on the Web at: http://www.citizen.org/Press/pr-wto4.htm.
16. *New York Times*, April 7, 1998, p. D1.
17. *New York Times*, February 21, 1997, p. A1.
18. Speech by President Bill Clinton at the WTO meeting in Seattle, Washington, December 1, 1999, on the U.S. State Department Web site at: http://usinfo.state.gov/topical/econ/wto99/pp1201l.htm#reform.
19. Associated Press photo APA4141750 (2GRSM), December 1, 1999, on the AP proprietary Web site at: http://photoarchive.ap.org.
20. *New York Times*, September 16, 1998, p. C6.
21. Devendra Raj Panday, " Can Aid Conditionality Help Governance Reform in Needy Countries?" Development Forum, on the World Bank Web site at: http://www.worldbank.org/devforum/speaker_panday.html.
22. *New York Times*, February 17, 1998, p. A1.
23. *Hartford Courant*, December 12, 1997, p. A11.
24. *New York Times*, February 12, 1998, p. D2.
25. *Hartford Courant*, February 24, 1993, p. A8.
26. *New York Times*, February 21, 2000.
27. *New York Times*, November 11, 1995, p. A37.
28. *New York Times*, June 20, 1994, p. A1.
29. *New York Times*, April 18, 2000.
30. *New York Times*, August 8, 1993, p. A1.
31. *New York Times*, May 3, 1998, p. A15.
32. "Scenario for Changeover to the Single Currency," taken from the Web in November 1996 at: http://europa.eu.int/en/agenda/emu/enscsc.html.
33. *Hartford Courant*, November 1, 1992, p. F7.
34. *New York Times*, December 8, 1994, p. A14.
35. *New York Times*, December 12, 1994, p. A8.
36. *New York Times*, December 11, 1994, p. A1.
37. Both quotes are from the *New York Times*, December 12, 1994, p. A8.
38. The analyst was Phillip Hughes, chairman of the Council of the Americas, quoted in the *New York Times*, March 24, 1996, p. A13.
39. *New York Times*, September 18, 1997, p. A7.
40. *New York Times*, April 19, 1998, p. A10.
41. All quotes are from the *New York Times*, November 19, 1993, p. A1.
42. *New York Times*, August 23, 1992, p. F5.
43. Jans Kerkhofs of Louvain University, quoted in *Time*, December 9, 1991, p. 40.
44. *New York Times*, December 12, 1994, p. A8.
45. *New York Times*, January 29, 1992, p. D2.

CHAPTER 17

1. Both quotes, the second by Robert Repetto of the World Resources Institute, are from the *New York Times*, September 19, 1995, p. C1.
2. Paul Portney of Resources for the Future, quoted in the *New York Times*, September 19, 1995, p. C1.
3. *New York Times*, February 28, 1996, p. A3.
4. Final document of the World Food Summit, November 17, 1996, taken from the World Wide Web at: http://www.fao.org/wfs/final/rd-e.htm.
5. CNN news item, November 13, 1996, taken from the World Wide Web.
6. Final document of the World Food Summit, November 17, 1996, taken from the World Wide Web at: http://www.fao.org/wfs/final/rd-e.htm.
7. *Hartford Courant*, December 17, 1992, p. A1.
8. *Hartford Courant*, September 30, 1994, p. A8.
9. *New York Times*, November 28, 1996, p. A10.
10. CNN news report of October 18, 1995, taken from the World Wide Web.

11. The quotes are from an interview of Goldhagen, not from his book, and are found in the *New York Times*, April 1, 1996, p. C11.
12. *New York Times*, February 3, 1994, p. A12.
13. *Hartford Courant*, December 13, 1991, p. A1.
14. *Hartford Courant*, December 17, 1992, p. A1.
15. The previous two quotes are from the *New York Times*, December 13, 1991, p. A13.
16. *New York Times*, August 20, 1998, p. A11.
17. *New York Times*, August 29, 1997, p. A4.
18. *New York Times*, August 29, 1997, p. A4.
19. *New York Times*, October 9, 1996, p. A8.
20. Toronto *Globe and Mail*, August 26, 1996, reproduced in the *World Press Review*, November 1996, p. 10.
21. Quoted in Adrian Karatnycky, "The Real Zyuganov," an op-ed piece in the *New York Times*, March 5, 1996, p. A23.
22. The poll, commissioned by the American Jewish Committee, was reported in the *Hartford Courant*, March 30, 1994, p. A11.
23. *New York Times*, March 31, 1996, p. A8.
24. *New York Times*, December 10, 1993, p. A11.
25. *Hartford Courant*, July 7, 1993, p. A1.
26. CNN News, August 31, 2000, on the Web at: http://www.cnn.com/2000/WORLD/europe/08/31/germany.schroeder/index.html.
27. Le Pen is quoted in Timothy Christenfeld, "Wretched Refuse Is Just the Start," *New York Times*, March 10, 1996, p. A15.
28. *Newsweek*, August 9, 1993, p. 11.
29. Priscilla Labovitz, "Immigration—Just the Fact," in the *New York Times*, March 25, 1996, p. A15.
30. *New York Times*, March 11, 1995, p. A5.
31. *New York Times*, March 4, 1998, p. A1.
32. *New York Times*, December 29, 1997, p. A3.
33. *Hartford Courant*, December 12, 1996, p. A8.
34. Report on the World Congress against Commercial Sexual Exploitation of Children, taken in December 1996 from the UNICEF Web site at: http://www.childhub.ch/webpub/csechome/.

BOX, "ASYLUM," PP. 500–501.

1. *New York Times*, April 15, 1996.
2. *New York Times*, September 11, 1996, p. B7.
3. *New York Times*, September 11, 1996, p. B7.
4. *New York Times*, September 11, 1996, p. B7.
5. *New York Times*, August 8, 1996, p. A3.
6. Both quotes are from the *New York Times*, September 11, 1996, p. B7.
7. *New York Times*, April 15, 1996, p. A1.
8. *New York Times*, June 14, 1996, p. A1.
9. *New York Times*, September 11, 1996, p. B7.
10. UNFPA press release, September 18, 1997, on the UNFPA Web site at: http://www.unfpa.org/news/pressroom/1997/dirie.htm.

BOX, "THE ROAD TO BEIJING AND BEYOND," P. 509

1. *New York Times*, June 28, 1996, p. A1.
2. *New York Times*, May 12, 1996, p. A3.

CHAPTER 18

1. The *State of the World* series is written and edited by Lester R. Brown and a shifting group of other analysts. Each annual edition also carries the appropriate year as part of the title. The series is published by W. W. Norton in New York and sponsored by the Worldwatch Institute, which Brown heads.
2. *New York Times*, May 20, 1997, p. C1.
3. *New York Times*, May 20, 1997, p. C1.
4. Theodore Roszak, "Green Guilt and Ecological Overload," an op-ed piece published in the *New York Times*, June 9, 1992, p. A27. Roszak is on the faculty of California State University, Hayward.
5. *New York Times*, November 29, 1995, p. A1.
6. *Time*, December 12, 1990, p. 48.
7. *Time*, June 1, 1992, p. 42.
8. *New York Times*, April 30, 1992, p. A12.
9. *New York Times*, December 31, 1997, p. A6.
10. Representative Christopher Smith and Nafis Sadik are both quoted in the *New York Times*, February 16, 1996.
11. *Time*, September 5, 1994, p. 52.
12. The Pakistani delegate, Said Khawar Mumtaz of Punjab University, and the Chinese delegate, Wang Jiaxaing of Beijing Foreign Studies University, were quoted in the *New York Times*, September 2, 1994, p. A3.
13. *New York Times*, August 31, 1994, p. A9.
14. *New York Times*, September 4, 1994, p. A1.
15. *New York Times*, September 6, 1994, p. A1.
16. Richard C. Duncan and Walter Youngquist, "The World Petroleum Life-Cycle," presented at the Petroleum Technology Transfer Council Workshop "OPEC Oil Pricing and Independent Oil Producers," hosted by the Petroleum Engineering Program, University of Southern California, Los Angeles, October 22, 1998.
17. All quotes are from the *New York Times*, September 4, 1995, p. A2.
18. *New York Times*, December 12, 1993, p. A5.
19. Julian Simon, "Environmentalists May Cause the Truth to Become Extinct," an op-ed piece in the *Hartford Courant*, June 15, 1992, p. C11.
20. *New York Times*, August 23, 1998, p. A19.
21. *New York Times*, October 10, 1994, p. A4.
22. *Hartford Courant*, August 4, 1995, p. A9.
23. *New York Times*, May 17, 1998, p. A1.
24. The quote of the Icelander and Norway's prime minister are both from *Time*, August 2, 1993, p. 45.
25. *New York Times*, August 9, 2000.
26. *Hartford Courant*, November 10, 1994, p. A1. The observer was Perran Ross of the Florida Museum of Natural History in Gainesville.
27. *Time*, May 24, 1993, p. 57.
28. *New York Times*, April 12, 1994, p. D1.
29. *Time*, January 2, 1989, p. 47.
30. UN Human Rights Commission, Document E/CN.4/1998/10. "Adverse Effects of the Illicit Movement and Dumping of Toxic and Dangerous Products and Wastes on the Enjoyment of Human Rights," January 20, 1998. On the Web at: http://www.hri.ca/fortherecord1998/documentation/commission/e-cn4-1998-10.htm#Introduction.
31. *New York Times*, February 29, 2000.
32. *New York Times*, September 10, 1995, p. A1.
33. *New York Times*, December 20, 1994, p. C4. The scientist was R. Steven Nerem of NASA.
34. *New York Times*, September 6, 2000.
35. *New York Times*, May 24, 1994, p. C1. The IPCC head is

John Houghton.

36. *Hartford Courant*, May 11, 2000.

37. *New York Times*, July 8, 1996, p. A2.

38. *New York Times*, September 14, 1993, p. C1. The scientist was Dixy Lee Ray, author of a 1993 book, *Environmental Overkill: Whatever Happened to Common Sense?*

39. *New York Times*, August 19, 2000.

40. *New York Times*, February 29, 2000.

41. *Hartford Courant*, September 22, 1991, p. A1. Statement by Paul Waggoner, who headed the academy's study panel.

42. *Hartford Courant*, September 16, 1994, p. A8.

43. *New York Times*, September 14, 1993. The scholars are Ben W. Bolch and Harold Lyons of Rhodes College, authors of *Apocalypse Not: Science, Economics and Environmentalism.*

44. *New York Times*, May 24, 1994. This scientist was John Houghton, head of the IPCC and author of *Global Warming: The Complete Briefing.*

45. *New York Times*, September 14, 1993, p. C1.

46. *Hartford Courant*, August 26, 1993, p. A3. The scientist was James W. Wilkins of the U.S. National Oceanic and Atmospheric Administration.

47. *The Washington Post National Weekly Edition*, April 26–May 2, 1993, p. 6. The scientist was Richard Stolarski of NASA.

48. *Hartford Courant*, December 16, 1994, p. A6. The scientist was Mark Schoeberl of NASA.

49. *New York Times*, December 18, 1990, p. C1.

50. *New York Times*, December 18, 1990, p. C1.

51. *Manchester Guardian Weekly*, March 20, 1994, p. 10. The opposition leader was Chris Smith, environment spokesman for the Labour Party.

BOX, "THE EARTH SUMMIT AND SUSTAINABLE DEVELOPMENT," PP. 538–539

1. *New York Times*, June 12, 1992, p. A9.
2. *Hartford Courant*, June 8, 1992, p. A2.
3. *Hartford Courant*, June 15, 1992, p. A1.
4. *Hartford Courant*, June 15, 1992, p. A1.

BOX, "TO KYOTO AND BEYOND," PP. 550–551

1. *New York Times*, December 12, 1997, p. A1.
2. *New York Times*, November 20, 1997, p. A7.
3. *New York Times*, November 28, 1997, p. A36.
4. *Hartford Courant*, December 11, 1997, p. A1.
5. *Hartford Courant*, December 11, 1997, p. A1.
6. *New York Times*, December 12, 1997, p. A1.
7. *New York Times*, December 12, 1997, p. A1.
8. *Hartford Courant*, December 11, 1997, p. A1.
9. *New York Times*, December 13, 1997, p. A7.

Glossary

Actors (international) Individuals or organizations that play a direct role in the conduct of world politics. 27

Adjudication The legal process of deciding an issue through the courts. 298

Adversarial diplomacy A negotiation situation where two or more countries' interests clash, but when there is little or no chance of armed conflict. 270

Amorality The philosophy that altruistic acts are unwise and even dangerous, or that morality should never be the absolute guide of human actions, particularly in regard to international law. 314

Anarchical political system An anarchical system is one in which there is no central authority to make rules, to enforce rules, or to resolve disputes about the actors in the political system. Many people believe that a system without central authority is inevitably one either of chaos or one in which the powerful prey on the weak. There is, however, an anarchist political philosophy that contends that the natural tendency of people to cooperate has been corrupted by artificial political, economic, or social institutions. Therefore, anarchists believe that the end of these institutions will lead to a cooperative society. Marxism, insofar as it foresees the collapse of the state once capitalism is destroyed and workers live in proletariat harmony, has elements of anarchism. 27

Appeasement policy A policy advocated by the British and French toward the Germans following World War I. The hope was to maintain peace by allowing Hitler to annex the Sudentenland part of Czechoslovakia. 34

Arms control A variety of approaches to the limitation of weapons. Arms control ranges from restricting the future growth in the number, types, or deployment of weapons; through the reduction of weapons; to the elimination of some types of (or even all) weapons on a global or regional basis. 362

Asia Pacific Economic Cooperation (APEC) A regional trade organization founded in 1989 that includes 18 countries. 479

Association of Southeast Asian Nations (ASEAN) A regional organization that emphasizes trade relations, established in 1967; now includes Brunei, Cambodia, Indonesia, Laos, Malaysia, Myanmar (Burma), the Philippines, Singapore, Thailand, and Vietnam. 479

Autarky Economic independence from external sources. 412

Authoritarian government A political system that allows little or no participation in decision making by individuals and groups outside the upper reaches of the government. 82, 201

Authoritarianism A type of restrictive governmental system where people are under the rule of an individual, such as a dictator or king, or a group, such as a party or military junta. 205

Balance of payments A figure that represents the net flow of money into and out of a country due to trade, tourist expenditures, sale of services (such as consulting), foreign aid, profits, and so forth. 410

Balance of power A concept that describes the degree of equilibrium (balance) or disequilibrium (imbalance) of power in the global or regional system. 32, 64

Beijing + 5 Conference A meeting held at the UN in New York City in 2000 to review the progress made since the 1995 fourth World Conference on Women. 167

Bilateral diplomacy Negotiations between two countries. 273

Bilateral (foreign) aid Foreign aid given by one country directly to another. 435

Biopolitics This theory examines the relationship between the physical nature and political behavior of humans. 114

Bipolar system A type of international system with two roughly equal actors or coalitions of actors that divide the international system into two poles. 63

Bretton Woods system The international monetary system that existed from the end of World War II until the early 1970s; named for an international economic conference held in Bretton Woods, New Hampshire, in 1944. 462

Bureaucracy The bulk of the state's administrative structure that continues even when leaders change. 95

Capitalism An economic system based on the private ownership of the means of production and distribution of goods, competition, and profit incentives. 441

Carrying capacity The number of people that an environment, such as Earth, can feed, provide water for, and otherwise sustain. 515

Cartel An international agreement among producers of a commodity that attempts to control the production and pricing of that commodity. 439

Chemical Weapons Convention (CWC) A treaty that was signed and became effective in 1995 under which signatories pledge to eliminate all chemical weapons by the year 2005; to submit to rigorous inspection; to never develop, produce, stockpile, or use chemical weapons; and to never transfer chemical weapons to another country or assist another country to acquire such weapons. 373

Clash of civilizations Samuel P. Huntington's thesis (1996, 1993) that the source of future conflict will be cultural. 183

Coalition diplomacy A negotiation situation where a number of countries have similar interests, which are often in opposition to the interests of one or more other countries. 271

Codify To write down a law in formal language. 295

Coercive diplomacy The use of threats or force as a diplomatic tactic. 284

Coercive power "Hard power" such as military force or economic sanctions. 257

Cognitive decision making Making choices within the limits of what you consciously know. 109

Cold war The confrontation that emerged following World War II between the bipolar superpowers, the Soviet Union and the United States. Although no direct conflict took place between these countries, it was an era of great tensions and global division. 35

Collective security The original theory behind UN peacekeeping. It holds that aggression against one state is aggression against every member and should be defeated by the collective action of all. 379

Communism An ideology originated in the works of Friedrich Engels and Karl Marx that is essentially an economic theory. As such, it is the idea that an oppressed proletariat class of workers would eventually organize and revolt against those who owned the means of production, the bourgeoisie; a political system of government applied in the Soviet Union, China, and elsewhere, wherein the state owns the means of production as a means to expedite Engels and Marx's economic theory. 201

Communitarianism The concept that the welfare of the collective must be valued over any individual rights or liberties. 205

Conditionality A term that refers to the policy of the International Monetary Fund, the World Bank, and some other international financial agencies to attach conditions to their loans and grants. These conditions may require recipient countries to devalue their currencies, to lift controls on prices, to cut their budgets, and to reduce barriers to trade and capital flows. Such conditions are often politically unpopular, may cause at least short-term economic pain, and are construed by critics as interference in recipient countries' sovereignty. 467

Confederation A group of states that willingly enter into an alliance to form a political unit for a common purpose, such as economic security or defense; it is highly interdependent, but has a weak directorate organization thus allowing the individuals states to maintain a fairly high degree of sovereignty. 224

Containment doctrine U.S. policy that sought to contain communism, during the cold war. 35

Council of Ministers The Council of the European Union involved in political decision making. 228

Countries in transition (CITs) Former communist countries such as Russia whose economies are in transition from socialism to capitalism. 395, 458

Crisis situation A circumstance or event that is a surprise to decision makers, that evokes a sense of threat (particularly physical peril), and that must be responded to within a limited amount of time. 86

Cultural imperialism The attempt to impose your own value system on others, including judging others by how closely they conform to your norms. 304

Current dollars The value of the dollar in the year for which it is being reported. Sometimes called inflated dollars. Any currency can be expressed in current value. *See also* real dollars. 389

Debt service The total amount of money due on principal and interest payments for loan repayment. 430

Decision making The process by which humans choose which policy to pursue and which actions to take in support of policy goals. The study of decision making seeks to identify patterns in the way that humans make decisions. This includes gathering information, analyzing information, and making choices. Decision making is a complex process that relates to personality and other human traits, to the sociopolitical setting in which decision makers function, and to the organizational structures involved. 109

Decision-making analysis A means of investigating how countries make policy choices. 81

Democracy/democratic government The most basic concept describes the ideology of a body governed by and for the people; also the type of governmental system a country has, in terms of free and fair elections and levels of participation. 82, 201

Democratic peace theory The assertion that as more countries become democratic, the likelihood that they will enter into conflict with one another decreases. 206

Democratized diplomacy The current trend in diplomacy where diplomats are drawn from a wider segment of society, making them more representative of their nations. 275

Dependencia theory The belief that the industrialized North has created a neocolonial relationship with the South in which the less developed countries are dependent on and disadvantaged by their economic relations with the capitalist industrial countries. 393

Détente A cold war policy involving the United States, the Soviet Union, and China, which sought to open relations among the countries and ease tensions. 36

Deterrence Persuading an opponent not to attack by having enough forces to disable the attack and/or launch a punishing counterattack. 351

Development capital Monies and resources needed by less developed countries to increase their economic growth and diversify their economies. 430

Direct democracy Policy making through a variety of processes, including referendums, by which citizens directly cast ballots on policy issues. 105

Dual-use technology Technology that has peaceful uses but also has military applications. 448

East-West Axis A term used to describe the ideological division between hemispheres following World War II. The East was associated with communism, while the West was associated with democracy. 35

Economic internationalism The belief that international economic relations should and can be conducted cooperatively because the international economy is a non–zero-sum game in which prosperity is available to all. 391

Economic nationalism The belief that the state should use its economic strength to further national interests, and that a state should use its power to build its economic strength. 389

Economic structuralism The belief that economic structure determines politics, as the conduct of world politics is based on the way that the world is organized economically. A radical restructuring of the economic system is required to end the uneven distribution of wealth and power. 392

Economically developed country (EDC) An industrialized country mainly found in the Northern Hemisphere. 42

Elites Those individuals in a political system who exercise disproportionate control of policy either by occupying policy-making positions or by having direct access to and influence over those who do. 105

Environmental optimists Those analysts who predict that the world population will meet its needs while continuing to grow economically through conservation, population restraints, and technological innovation. 547

Environmental pessimists Those analysts who predict environmental and ecological problems, based on current trends in ecology and population pressure. 545

Escalation Increasing the level of fighting. 345

Ethnonational groups An ethnic group that feels alienated from the state in which it resides and that wishes to break away from that state to establish its own autonomous or independent political structure or to combine with its ethnic kin in another state. Many ethnic groups, such as Italian Americans, have no separatist leanings; many nations, such as Americans, are composed of many ethnic groups. 77

Ethology The comparison of animal and human behavior. 114

European Commission A 20-member commission that serves as the bureaucratic organ of the European Union. 228

European Economic Community (EEC) The regional trade and economic organization established in Western Europe by the Treaty of Rome in 1958; also known as the Common Market. 225

European Ombudsman A mediator between government agencies and citizens who bring complaints to the European Union offices. 230

European Parliament The 626-member legislative branch of the European Union. Representation is determined by population of member-countries, and is based on five-year terms. 229

European Union (EU) The Western European regional organization established in 1983 when the Maastricht Treaty went into effect. The EU encompasses the still legally existing European Community (EC). When the EC was formed in 1967, it in turn encompassed three still legally existing regional organizations formed in the 1950s: the European Coal and Steel Community (ECSC), the European Economic Community (EEC), and the European Atomic Energy Community (EURATOM). 225, 472

Eurowhites A term to distinguish the whites of Europe and of Australia, Canada, New Zealand, the United States, and other countries whose cultures were founded on or converted to European culture from other races and ethnic groups, including Caucasian peoples in Latin America, the Middle East, South Asia, and elsewhere. 32

Event data analysis A study of interactions, called events, and subsequent events used to analyze the reactions and counter-reactions of countries. 81

Exchange rate The values of two currencies relative to each other—for example, how many yen equal a dollar or how many lira equal a pound. 408

Fascism An ideology that advocates extreme nationalism, with a heightened sense of national belonging or ethnic identity. 201

Feudal system Medieval political system of smaller units, such as principalities, dukedoms, baronies, ruled by minor royalty. 196

Foreign direct investment (FDI) Buying stock, real estate, and other assets in another country with the aim of gaining a controlling interest in foreign economic enterprises. Different from portfolio investment, which involves investment solely to gain capital appreciation through market fluctuations. 405, 431

Foreign portfolio investment (FPI) Investment in the stocks and the public and private debt instruments (such as bonds) of another country below the level where the stock- or bondholder can exercise control over the policies of the stock-issuing company or the bond-issuing debtor. 405, 431

Fourth World A term used to designate collectively the indigenous (aboriginal, native) people of the countries of the world. 503

Fourth World Conference on Women (WCW) The largest and most widely noted in a series of UN conferences on the status of women. This international meeting took place in Beijing, China, in 1995. 46, 164

Free economic exchange The absence of tariffs and nontariff barriers in trade between countries. 425

Free Trade Area of the Americas (FTAA) The tentative name given by the 34 countries that met in December 1994 at the Summit of the Americas to the proposed Western Hemisphere free trade zone that is projected to come into existence by the year 2005. 476

Frustration-aggression theory   A psychologically based theory that frustrated societies sometimes become collectively aggressive. 111

Functional relations   Relations that include interaction in such usually nonpolitical areas as communication, travel, trade, and finances. 292

Functionalism   International cooperation in specific areas such as communications, trade, travel, health, or environmental protection activity. Often symbolized by the specialized agencies, such as the World Health Organization, associated with the United Nations. 223

Fundamentalism   Religious traditionalism and values incorporated into secular political activities. 173

Gender opinion gap   The difference between males and females along any one of a number of dimensions, including foreign policy preferences. 84

General Agreement on Tariffs and Trade (GATT) The world's primary organization promoting the expansion of free trade. Established in 1947, it has grown to a membership of over 100. 459

General and complete disarmament (GCD)   Total disarmament. 384

Government   A type of governing political body, such as the democratic system in Canada or the authoritarian system in China; also the specific regime in power, such as the government of a particular leader. 53

Gross domestic product (GDP)   A measure of income within a country that excludes foreign earnings. 6, 58

Gross national product (GNP)   A measure of the sum of all goods and services produced by a country's nationals, whether they are in the country or abroad. 43

Group of Eight (G-8)   The seven economically largest, free market countries plus Russia (a member on political issues since 1998). 425, 458

Group of Seven (G-7)   The seven economically largest free market countries: Canada, France, Great Britain, Italy, Japan, the United States, and Germany. 425

Group of 77 (G-77)   The group of 77 countries of the South that cosponsored the Joint Declaration of Developing Countries in 1963 calling for greater equity in North-South trade. This group has come to include more than 120 members and represents the interests of the less developed countries of the South. 438, 457

Groupthink   How an individual's membership in an organization/decision-making group influences his or her thinking and actions. In particular there are tendencies within a group to think alike, to avoid discordancy, and to ignore ideas or information that threaten to disrupt the consensus. 119

Hague system   Name given to the peace conferences held in the Netherlands in 1899 and 1907. This serves as the first example of an international attempt to improve the condition of humanity. 216

Hard currency   Currencies, such as dollars, marks, francs, and yen, that are acceptable in private channels of international economics. 430

Holy Roman Empire   The domination and unification of a political territory in Western and Central Europe that lasted from its inception with Charlemagne in 800 B.C. to 476 B.C., when Rome fell as the hub of the Western world. 196

Horizontal authority structure   A system in which authority is fragmented. The international system has a mostly horizontal authority structure. 51

Hostile diplomacy   A situation where negotiation takes place in an environment where one or more countries are engaged in armed clashes or when there is a substantial possibility that fighting could result. 270

Idealists   Analysts who reject power politics and argue that failure to follow policies based on humanitarianism and international cooperation will result in disaster. 16

Ideological or theological school of law (principles)   A set of related ideas in secular or religious thought, usually founded on identifiable thinkers and their works, that offers a more or less comprehensive picture of reality. 293

Idiosyncratic analysis   An individual-level analysis approach to decision making that assumes that individuals make foreign policy decisions and that different individuals are likely to make different decisions. 121

Imperial overstretch thesis   The idea that attempting to maintain global order through leadership as a hegemon, especially through military power, is detrimental to the hegemon's existence. 327

Imperialism   A term synonymous with colonization, meaning domination by Northern Eurowhites over Southern nonwhites as a means to tap resources to further their own development. 31

Incremental decision making   The tendency of decision makers to treat existing policy as a given and to follow and continue that policy ("policy inertia") or make only marginal changes in the policy. 120

Incremental policy   *See* Incremental decision making.

Individualism   The concept that rights and liberties of the individual are paramount within a society. 205

Individual-level analysis   An analytical approach that emphasizes the role of individuals as either distinct personalities or biological/psychological beings. 23

Industrial revolution   The development of mechanical and industrial production of goods that began in Great Britain in the mid-1700s and then spread through Europe and North America. 30, 197

Interdependence (economic)   The close interrelationship and mutual dependence of two or more domestic economies on each other. 41, 411

Interest group   A private (nongovernmental) association of people who have similar policy views and who pressure the government to adopt those views as policy. 99

Intergovernmental organizations (IGOs) International/transnational actors composed of member-countries. 53, 215

Intermestic The merger of *inter*national and *dom*estic concerns. 4, 87

International Court of Justice (ICJ) The world court, which sits in The Hague with 15 judges and is associated with the United Nations. 299

International Monetary Fund (IMF) The world's primary organization devoted to maintaining monetary stability by helping countries fund balance-of-payment deficits. Established in 1947, it now has 170 members. 462

International political economy (IPE) An approach to the study of international relations that is concerned with the political determinants of international economic relations and also with the economic determinants of international political relations. 389

International system An abstract concept that encompasses global actors, the interactions (especially patterns of interaction) among those actors, and the factors that cause those interactions. The international system is largest of a vast number of overlapping political systems that extend downward in size to micropolitical systems at the local level. *See also* System-level analysis. 26

Investment, foreign *See* Foreign direct investment, Foreign portfolio investment.

Iron triangle An alliance between interest groups, bureaucracies, and legislators that forms a military-industrial-congressional complex. 377

Irredentism A minority population's demand to join its motherland (often an adjoining state), or when the motherland claims the area in which the minority lives. 147

Issue areas Substantive categories of policy that must be considered when evaluating national interest. 87

Jihad "Struggling to spread or defend the faith"; this concept is derived from Arabic and borrowed by Benjamin Barber to describe the internal pressures on states that can contribute to their fragmentation or collapse. 39

Jus ad bellum The Western concept meaning "just cause of war," which provides a moral and legal basis governing causes for war. 306

Jus in bello The Western concept meaning "just conduct of war," which provides a moral and legal basis governing conduct of war. 306

Leader-public opinion gap Differences of opinion between leaders and public, which may have an impact on foreign policy in a democratic country. 84

League of Nations The first, true general international organization. It existed between the end of World War I and the beginning of World War II and was the immediate predecessor of the United Nations. 216

Least developed countries (LLDCs) Those countries in the poorest of economic circumstances. In this book, this includes those countries with a per capita GNP of less than $400 in 1985 dollars. 396

Less developed countries (LDCs) Countries, located mainly in Africa, Asia, and Latin America, with economies that rely heavily on the production of agriculture and raw materials and whose per capita GDP and standard of living are substantially below Western standards. 42

Levels of analysis Different perspectives (system, state, individual) from which international politics can be analyzed. 23

Limited membership council A representative organization body of the UN that grants special status to members who have a greater stake, responsibility, or capacity in a particular area of concern. The UN Security Council is an example. 237

Maastricht Treaty The most significant agreement in the recent history of the European Union (EU). The Maastricht Treaty was signed by leaders of the EU's 12 member-countries in December 1991 and outlines steps toward further political-economic integration. 226

MAD (Mutual Assured Destruction) A situation in which each nuclear superpower has the capability of launching a devastating nuclear second strike even after an enemy has attacked it. The belief that a MAD capacity prevents nuclear war is the basis of deterrence by punishment theory. 353

Majority voting A system used to determine how votes should count. The theory of majoritarianism springs from the concept of sovereign equality and the democratic notion that the will of the majority should prevail. This system has two main components: (1) each member casts one equal vote, and (2) the issue is carried by either a simple majority (50 percent plus one vote) or, in some cases, an extraordinary majority (commonly two-thirds). 237

Marxism The philosophy of Karl Marx that the economic (material) order determines political and social relationships. Thus, history, the current situation, and the future are determined by the economic struggle, termed dialectical materialism. 393

Mass The nonelite element of a political society. The majority of people who do not occupy policy-making positions and who do not have direct access to those who do. 105

McWorld This concept describes the merging of states into an integrated world. Benjamin Barber coined this term to describe how states are becoming more globalized, especially with the growth of economic interdependence. 39

Mediation diplomacy A negotiation situation where a country that is not involved directly as one of the parties tries to help two or more conflicting sides to resolve their differences. 271

Merchandise trade The import and export of tangible

manufactured goods and raw materials. 401

Microstate A country with a small population that cannot economically survive unaided or that is inherently so militarily weak that it is an inviting target for foreign intervention. 152

Missile Technology Control Regime (MTCR) A series of understandings that commits most of the countries capable of producing extended-range missiles to a ban on the export of ballistic missiles and related technology and that also pledges MTCR adherents to bring economic and diplomatic pressure to bear on countries that export missile-applicable technology. 364

Monarchism A political system that is organized, governed, and defined by the idea of the divine right of kings, or the notion that because a person is born into royalty, he or she is meant to rule. 201

Monetary relations The entire scope of international money issues, such as exchange rates, interest rates, loan policies, balance of payments, and regulating institutions (for example, the International Monetary Fund). 407

Moral absolutism A philosophy based on the notion that the ends never justify the means, or that morality should be the absolute guide of human actions, particularly in regard to international law. 314

Moral prudence The idea that there is a middle ground between amorality and moral absolutism that acts as a guide to human actions, particularly in regard to international law. 315

Moral relativism A philosophy that human actions must be placed in context as a means to inform international law. 314

Multilateral diplomacy Negotiations among three or more countries. 274

Multilateral (foreign) aid Foreign aid distributed by international organizations such as the United Nations. 435

Multinational corporations (MNCs) Private enterprises that have production subsidiaries or branches in more than one country. 58, 406

Multinational states Countries in which there are two or more significant nationalities. 145

Multipolar system A world political system in which power primarily is held by four or more international actors. 32, 64

Multistate nationalities Nations whose members overlap the borders of two or more states. 146

Munich analogy A belief among post–World War II leaders, particularly Americans, that aggression must always be met firmly and that appeasement will only encourage an aggressor. Named for the concessions made to Hitler by Great Britain and France at Munich during the 1938 Czechoslovakian crisis. 124

Munich Conference A meeting between France, Germany, Great Britain, and Italy in 1938, during which France and Great Britain, unwilling to confront Hitler, acquiesced with Germany's decision to annex the Sudetenland (part of Czechoslovakia). This appeasement of Germany became synonymous with a lack of political will. 34

Nation A group of culturally and historically similar people who feel a communal bond and who feel they should govern themselves to at least some degree. 53, 132

National technical means (NTM) An arms control verification technique that involves using satellites, seismic measuring devices, and other equipment to identify, locate, and monitor the manufacturing, testing, or deployment of weapons or delivery vehicles, or other aspects of treaty compliance. 375

Nationalism The belief that the nation is the ultimate basis of political loyalty and that nations should have self-governing states. *See also* Nation-state. 134

Nation-state A politically organized territory that recognizes no higher law, and whose population politically identifies with that entity. *See also* State. 133

Naturalist school of law Those who believe that law springs from the rights and obligations that humans have by nature. 293

Nature versus nurture debate A dispute regarding whether gender differences are the result of biological factors or socialization factors. 117

Neocolonialism The notion that EDCs continue to control and exploit LDCs through indirect means, such as economic dominance and co-opting the local elite. 393

Neofunctionalism The top-down approach to solving world problems. 224

New International Economic Order (NIEO) A term that refers to the goals and demands of the South for basic reforms in the international economic system. 438

Newly industrializing countries (NICs) Less developed countries whose economies and whose trade now include significant amounts of manufactured products. As a result, these countries have a per capita GDP significantly higher than the average per capita GDP for less developed countries. 43, 395

Nongovernmental organizations (NGOs) International/transnational organizations with private memberships. 55, 215

Non–status quo situations Circumstances or events that depart from the existing norm and that portend innovative policy that significantly changes established policy direction. 87

Nontariff barrier (NTB) A nonmonetary restriction on trade, such as quotas, technical specifications, or unnecessarily lengthy quarantine and inspection procedures. 442

Norms A principle of right action that is binding on members of a group and that serves to regulate the behavior of the members of that group. The word is based on the Latin *norma*, which means a carpenter's square or an accurate measure. Norms are based on custom and usage and may also become part of formal law. Norms are recognized in international law under the principle of *jus cogens* (just thought), which states that a standard of behavior accepted by the world community should not be violated by the actions of a state or group of states. In domestic systems, "common law" is equivalent to norms in the international system. 75

North American Free Trade Agreement (NAFTA)   An economic agreement among Canada, Mexico, and the United States that went into effect on January 1, 1994. It will eliminate most trade barriers by 2009 and will also eliminate or reduce restrictions on foreign investments and other financial transactions among the NAFTA countries. 474

North-South Axis   The growing tension between the few economically developed countries (North) and the many economically deprived countries (South). The South is demanding that the North cease economic and political domination and redistribute part of its wealth. 32

NUT (Nuclear Utilization Theory)   The belief that because nuclear war might occur, countries must be ready to fight, survive, and win a nuclear war. NUT advocates believe this posture will limit the damage if nuclear war occurs and also make nuclear war less likely by creating retaliatory options that are more credible than massive retaliation. 353

Objective power   Assets a country objectively possesses and has the will and capacity to use. 257

On-site inspection (OSI)   An arms control verification technique that involves stationing your or a neutral country's personnel in another country to monitor weapons or delivery vehicle manufacturing, testing, deployment, or other aspects of treaty compliance. 375

Open diplomacy   The public conduct of negotiations and the publication of agreements. 275

Operational code   A perceptual phenomenon that describes how an individual acts and responds when faced with specific types of situations. 128

Operational reality   The process by which what is perceived, whether that perception is accurate or not, assumes a level of reality in the mind of the beholder and becomes the basis for making an operational decision (a decision about what to do). 127

Organization for Economic Cooperation and Development (OECD)   An organization that has existed since 1948 (and since 1960 under its present name) to facilitate the exchange of information and otherwise to promote cooperation among the economically developed countries. In recent years, the OECD has begun to accept as members a few newly industrializing and former communist countries in transition. 458

Organization for Security and Cooperation in Europe (OSCE)   Series of conferences among 34 NATO, former Soviet bloc, and neutral European countries that led to permanent organization. Established by the 1976 Helsinki Accords. 378

Organizational behavior   An individual-level analysis approach to decision making that assumes that group dynamics, group interaction, and group and organization structure influence how decisions are made. 118

Pacificism   A bottom-up approach to avoidance of war based on the belief that it is wrong to kill. 385

Pacta sunt servanda   Translates as "treaties are to be served/carried out" and means that agreements between states are binding. 295

Parliamentary diplomacy   Debate and voting in international organizations to settle diplomatic issues. 274

Peacekeeping   The use of military means by an international organization such as the United Nations to prevent fighting, usually by acting as a buffer between combatants. The international force is neutral between the combatants and must have been invited to be present by at least one of the combatants. *See also* Collective security. 380

Peacemaking   The restoration of peace through, if necessary, the use of offensive military force to make one or all sides of a conflict cease their violent behavior. 381

Perceptions   The factors that create a decision maker's images of reality. 126

Persuasive power   "Soft power" such as moral authority or technological excellence. 257

Plenary representative body   An assembly, such as the UN's General Assembly, that consists of all members of the main organization. 236

Pole   An actor that generally has been either (1) a single country or empire or (2) a group of countries that form an alliance or a bloc. 60

Political culture   A concept that refers to a society's general, long-held, and fundamental practices and attitudes. These are based on a country's historical experience and on the values (norms) of its citizens. These attitudes are often an important part of the internal setting in which national leaders make foreign policy. 88

Political executives   Those officials, usually but not always in the executive branch of a government, who are at the center of foreign policy making and whose tenures are variable and dependent on the political contest for power. 95

Politics of identity   A view that national identity will be less important in the future than other subnational identities. 78

Popular sovereignty   A political doctrine that holds that sovereign political authority resides with the citizens of a state. According to this doctrine, the citizenry grant a certain amount of authority to the state, its government, and, especially, its specific political leaders (such as monarchs, presidents, and prime ministers), but do not surrender ultimate sovereignty. 27, 136

Positivist school of law   Those who believe that law reflects society and the way that people want the society to operate. 293

Postindustrial economy   A term used to describe economies that have entered a period where the use of robotics and other techniques requires using fewer and fewer workers to produce more and more manufactured goods, thus resulting in downsizing; these economies are based on services and information technologies rather than on industrial production. 424

Postinternationalism   A concept that extends from postmodernism and holds that in a turbulent world, people have begun to change their political identity and may give much greater weight to subnational political identities, such as ethnic group, or transnational political identities, such as gender. 160

Postmodernism   This theory holds that reality does not exist as such. Rather, reality is created by how we think and our discourse (writing, talking). As applied to world politics, postmodernism is the belief that we have become trapped by stale ways of conceiving of how we organize and conduct ourselves. Postmodernists wish, therefore, to "deconstruct" discourse. 160

Power   The totality of a country's international capabilities. Power is based on multiple resources, which alone or in concert allow one country to have its interests prevail in the international system. Power is especially important in enabling one state to achieve its goals when it clashes with the goals and wills of other international actors. 256

Power to defeat   The ability to overcome in a traditional military sense—that is, to overcome enemy armies and capture and hold territory. 333

Power to hurt   The ability to inflict pain outside the immediate battle area; sometimes called coercive violence. It is often used against civilians and is a particular hallmark of terrorism and nuclear warfare. 333

President of the Commission   Comparable to being president of the European Union (EU), this person is the director of the 20-member European Commission, the policy-making bureaucratic organ of the EU. 228

Primary products   Agricultural products and raw materials, such as minerals. 393

Procedural democracy   A form of democracy that is defined by whether or not particular procedures are followed, such as free and fair elections or following a set of laws or a constitution. 205

Protectionism   The use of tariffs and nontariff barriers to restrict the flow of imports into one's country. 425

Protestant Reformation   The religious movement initiated by Martin Luther in Germany in 1517 that rejected the Catholic Church as the necessary intermediary between people and God. 198

Public diplomacy   A process of creating an overall international image that enhances your ability to achieve diplomatic success. 279

Real dollars   The value of dollars expressed in terms of a base year. This is determined by taking current value and subtracting the amount of inflation between the base year and the year being reported. Sometimes called uninflated dollars. Any currency can be valued in real terms. *See also* Current dollars. 389

Realists   Analysts who believe that countries operate in their own self-interests and that politics is a struggle for power. 16

Realpolitik   Operating according to the belief that politics is based on the pursuit, possession, and application of power. 34

Regime   A complex of norms, treaties, international organizations, and transnational activity that orders an area of activity such as the environment or oceans. 221

Regional government   A possible middle level of governance between the prevalent national governments of today and the world government that some people favor. The regional structure that comes closest to (but still well short of) a regional government is the European Union. 224

Relative power   Power measured in comparison with the power of other international actors. 258

Relativists   A group of people who subscribe to the belief that human rights are the product of cultures. 485

Renaissance   A period of cultural and intellectual rebirth and reform following the Dark Ages from approximately 1350–1650. 198

Role   How an individual's position influences his or her thinking and actions. 118

SALT I   The Strategic Arms Limitation Treaty signed in 1972. 362

SALT II   The Strategic Arms Limitation Treaty signed in 1979 but withdrawn by President Carter from the U.S. Senate before ratification in response to the Soviet invasion of Afghanistan. 362

Secretariat   The administrative organ of the United Nations, headed by the secretary-general. In general, the administrative element of any IGO, headed by a secretary-general. 239

Self-determination   The concept that a people should have the opportunity to map their own destiny. 151

Service economies (trade)   Economies based on the purchase (import) from or sale (export) to another country of intangibles such as architectural fees; insurance premiums; royalties on movies, books, patents, and other intellectual properties; shipping services; advertising fees; and educational programs. 401, 424

Situational power   The power that can be applied, and is reasonable, in a given situation. Not all elements of power can be applied to every situation. 259

Social Darwinism   A social theory that argues it is proper that stronger peoples will prosper and will dominate lesser peoples. 496

Social overstretch thesis   The idea that spending money on altruistic social welfare programs to support the least productive people in society financially drains that economy. 328

Southern Common Market (Mercosur)   A regional organization that emphasizes trade relations, established in 1995 among Argentina, Brazil, Paraguay, and Uruguay, with Chile (1996) and Bolivia (1997) as associate members. 478

Sovereignty The most essential characteristic of an international state. The term strongly implies political independence from any higher authority and also suggests at least theoretical equality. 27, 189

Special drawing rights (SDRs) Reserves held by the International Monetary Fund that the central banks of member countries can draw on to help manage the values of their currencies. SDR value is based on a "market-basket" of currencies, and SDRs are acceptable in transactions between central banks. 464

Sphere of influence A region that a big power claims is of special importance to its national interest and over which the big power exercises special influence. 91

State A political actor that has sovereignty and a number of characteristics, including territory, population, organization, and recognition. 52, 189

State terrorism Terrorism carried out directly by, or encouraged and funded by, an established government of a state (country). 340

State-centric system A system describing the current world system wherein states are the principal actors. 52

State-level analysis An analytical approach that emphasizes the actions of states and the internal (domestic) causes of their policies. 23

Status quo situations Circumstances or events that conform to the existing norm and that are apt to evoke incremental policy decisions that do not significantly change basic policy direction. 87

Strategic Arms Reduction Talks (START I) Treaty I A nuclear weapons treaty signed by the Soviet Union and the United States in 1991 and later re-signed with Belarus, Kazakhstan, Russia, and Ukraine that will limit Russia and the United States to 1,600 delivery vehicles and 6,000 strategic explosive nuclear devices each, with the other three countries destroying their nuclear weapons or transferring them to Russia. 365

Strategic Arms Reduction Talks (START II) Treaty II A nuclear weapons treaty signed by the Soviet Union and the United States in 1993, which establishes nuclear warhead and bomb ceilings of 3,500 for the United States and 2,997 for Russia by the year 2003 and that also eliminates some types of weapons systems. As of February 1997 the treaty had not been ratified by the Russian parliament and, therefore, the treaty is not legally in effect. 366

Subjective power A country's power based on other countries' perception of its current or potential power. 257

Subnational actors Institutions and other elements of a country's political structure, including the political leadership, legislature, bureaucracy, interest groups, political opposition, and the public. 94

Substantive democracy A form of democracy that is defined by whether qualities of democracy, such as equality, justice, or self-rule, are evident. 205

Summit meetings High-level meetings for diplomatic negotiations between national political leaders. 278

Superpower Term used to describe the leader of a system pole in a bipolar system. During the cold war, the Soviet Union and the United States were each leaders of a bipolar system pole. 35

Supranational organization Organization that is founded and operates, at least in part, on the idea that international organizations can or should have authority higher than individual states and that those states should be subordinate to the supranational organization. 55, 223

Sustainable development The ability to continue to improve the quality of life of those in the industrialized countries and, particularly, those in the less developed countries while simultaneously protecting the Earth's biosphere. 46, 515

System-level analysis An analytical approach that emphasizes the importance of the impact of world conditions (economics, technology, power relationships, and so forth) on the actions of states and other international actors. 23, 50

Tariff A tax, usually based on percentage of value, that importers must pay on items purchased abroad; also known as an import tax or import duty. 442

Theocracy A political system that is organized, governed, and defined by spiritual leaders and their religious beliefs. 201

Third World A term once commonly used to designate the countries of Asia, Africa, Latin America, and elsewhere that were economically less developed. The phrase is attributed to French analyst Alfred Sauvy, who in 1952 used *tiers monde* to describe neutral countries in the cold war. By inference, the U.S.–led Western bloc and the Soviet-led Eastern bloc were the other two worlds. But since most of the neutral countries were also relatively poor, the phrase had a double meaning. Sauvy used the older *tiers*, instead of the more modern *troisième*, to allude to the pre-Revolutionary (1789) third estate (*tiers état*), that is, the underprivileged class, the commoners. The nobility and the clergy were the first and second estates. Based on this second meaning, Third World came most commonly to designate the less developed countries of the world, whatever their political orientation. The phrase is less often used since the end of the cold war, although some analysts continue to employ it to designate the less developed countries. 503

Transnational actors Organizations that operate internationally, but whose membership, unlike IGOs, is private. 55

Transnational advocacy networks (TANs) IGOs, NGOs, and national organizations that are based on shared values or common interests and exchange information and services. 55

Transnational corporations (TNCs) Transnational corporations are business enterprises that conduct business beyond just selling a product in more than one country. Countries with factories in several countries are TNCs, as are banks with branches in more than one country. The businesses are also referred to as multinational corporations (MNCs). The two terms are synonymous; TNC is used herein based on UN usage. 58

Transnationalism Extension beyond the borders of a single country; applies to a political movement, issue, organization, or other phenomena. 157

Treaty of Amsterdam (1997) The most recent agreement in a series of treaties that has further integrated the economic and political sectors of the European Union. 227

Treaty of Westphalia (1648) The agreement among European actors that ended the Thirty Years' War. It is significant because it helped to define states as political actors in an international system. 198

Trilateral countries The United States and Canada, Japan, and the Western European countries. 425

Tripolar system A type of international system that describes three roughly equal actors or coalitions of actors that divide the international system into three poles. 63

Two-level game theory The concept that in order to arrive at satisfactory international agreements, a country's diplomats actually have to deal with (at one level) the other country's negotiators and (at the second level) legislators, interest groups, and other domestic forces at home. 95, 272

UN Conference on Population and Development (UNCPD) A UN–sponsored conference that met in Cairo, Egypt, in September 1994 and was attended by delegates from more than 170 countries. The conference called for a program of action to include spending $17 billion annually by the year 2000 on international, national, and local programs to foster family planning and to improve the access of women in such areas as education. 528

UN Conference on Trade and Development (UNCTAD) A UN organization established in 1964 and currently consisting of all UN members plus the Holy See, Switzerland, and Tonga, which holds quadrennial meetings aimed at promoting international trade and economic development. 457

UN Development Programme (UNDP) An agency of the UN established in 1965 to provide technical assistance to stimulate economic and social development in the economically less developed countries. The UNDP has 48 members selected on a rotating basis from the world's regions. 456

UN General Assembly (UNGA) The main representative body of the United Nations, composed of all 188 member-states. 236

UN Industrial Development Organization (UNIDO) A UN specialized agency established in 1967, currently having 165 members, that promotes the industrialization of economically less developed countries. 457

UN Security Council The main peacekeeping organ of the United Nations. The Security Council has 15 members, including 5 permanent members. 237

Unanimity voting A system used to determine how votes should count. In this system, in order for a vote to be valid, all members must agree to the proposed measure. Abstention from a vote may or may not block an agreement. 239

Unipolar system A type of international system that describes a single country with complete global hegemony. 61

United Nations (UN) An international body created with the intention to maintain peace through the cooperation of its member-states. As part of its mission, it addresses human welfare issues such as the environment, human rights, population, and health. It's headquarters are located in New York City, and it was established following World War II to supersede the League of Nations. 216

United Nations Conference on Population and Development (UNCPD) The most recent (1994) world conference held in Cairo, Egypt, that focused on the issue of population control and reproductive health. 528

Universalists A group of people who subscribe to the belief that human rights are derived from sources external to society, such as from a theological, ideological, or natural rights basis. 485

Uruguay Round The eighth, and latest, round of GATT negotiations to reduce tariffs and nontariff barriers to trade. The eighth round was convened in Punta del Este, Uruguay, in 1986 and its resulting agreements were signed in Marrakesh, Morocco, in April 1994. 459

Vertical authority structure A system in which subordinate units answer to higher levels of authority. 51

Veto A negative vote cast in the UN Security Council by one of the five permanent members; has the effect of defeating the issue being voted on. 239

Vietnam analogy An aversion to foreign armed intervention, especially in conflicts in less developed countries involving guerrillas. This attitude is especially common among political leaders and other individuals who were opposed to the U.S. war in Vietnam or who were otherwise influenced by the failed U.S. effort there and the domestic turmoil that resulted. 125

Weapons of mass destruction Generally deemed to be nuclear weapons with a tremendous capability to destroy a population and the planet, but also include some exceptionally devastating conventional arms, such as fuel-air explosives, as well as biological, and chemical weapons. 374

Weapons proliferation   A situation in which countries build up their arms and nuclear arsenal. 362

Weighted voting   A system used to determine how votes should count. In this system, particular votes count more or less depending on what criterion is deemed to be most significant. For instance, population or wealth might be the important defining criterion for a particular vote. In the case of population, a country would receive a particular number of votes based on its population, thus a country with a large population would have more votes than a lesser-populated country. 238

West   Historically, Europe and those countries and regions whose cultures were founded on or converted to European culture. Such countries would include Australia, Canada, New Zealand, and the United States. The majority of the populations in these countries are also "white," in the European, not the larger Caucasian, sense. After World War II, the term West took on two somewhat different but related meanings. One referred to the countries allied with the United States and opposed to the Soviet Union and its allies, called the East. The West also came to mean the industrial democracies, including Japan. *See also* Eurowhites. 30

Westernization of the international system   A number of factors, including scientific and technological advances, contributed to the domination of the West over the international system that was essentially created by the Treaty of Westphalia (1648). 30

World Bank Group   Four associated agencies that grant loans to LDCs for economic development and other financial needs. Two of the agencies, the International Bank for Reconstruction and Development (IBRD) and the International Development Association (IDA), are collectively referred to as the World Bank. The other two agencies are the International Finance Corporation (IFC) and the Multilateral Investment Guarantee Agency (MIGA). 468

World government   The concept of a supranational world authority to which current countries would surrender some or all of their sovereign authority. 224

World Health Organization (WHO)   A UN–affliated organization created in 1946 to address world health issues. 493

World Trade Organization (WTO)   The organization that replaced the General Agreement on Tariffs and Trade (GATT) organization as the body that implements GATT, the treaty. 459

Xenophobia   Fear of others, "they-groups." 141

Zionism   The belief that Jews are a nation and that they should have an independent homeland. 148

ABBREVIATIONS

The following abbreviations are used in the text:

ABM	Anti-Ballistic Missile
APEC	Asia-Pacific Economic Cooperation
APM	Anti-Personnel Mine
ASEAN	Association of Southeast Asian Nations
ATTU	Atlantic to the Urals (region)
BIS	Bank for International Settlement
BMD	Ballistic Missile Defense
BWT	Biological Weapons Treaty
CEDAW	Committee on the Elimination of Discrimination Against Women
CFE	Conventional Forces in Europe (treaty)
CIS	Commonwealth of Independent States
CIT	Country in Transition
CITES	Convention on the International Trade in Endangered Species
CSW	Commission on the State of Women
CTBT	Comprehensive Test Ban Treaty
CWC	Chemical Weapons Convention
EC	European Community
ECB	European Central Bank
ECJ	European Court of Justice
ECOSOC	Economic and Social Council
ECOWAS	Economic Community of West African States
ECSC	European Coal and Steel Community
EDC	Economically Developed Country
EEC	European Economic Community
EMS	European Monetary System
EMU	European Monetary Union
EP	European Parliament
EPA	Environmental Protection Agency
EPP	European People's Party
EU	European Union
EURATOM	European Atomic Energy Community
FAO	Food and Agriculture Organization (United Nations)
FDI	Foreign Direct Investment
FIS	Front for Islamic Salvation
FPI	Foreign Portfolio Investment
FSR	Former Soviet Republic
FTAA	Free Trade Area of the Americas
GATT	General Agreement on Tariffs and Trade
GCD	General and Complete Disarmament
GCP	Gross Corporate Product
GDP	Gross Domestic Product
GEF	Global Environmental Facility
GNP	Gross National Product
GPS	Global Positioning System
HDI	Human Development Index
IAEA	International Atomic Energy Agency
IBRD	International Bank for Reconstruction and Development
ICBM	Intercontinental Ballistic Missile
ICJ	International Court of Justice
IDA	International Development Association
IFAD	International Fund for Agricultural Development
IFC	International Finance Corporation
IFOR	International Force
IGO	Intergovernmental Organization
ILO	International Labor Organization
IMF	International Monetary Fund
INF	Intermediate-Range Nuclear Forces
IOM	International Organization for Migration
IPCC	International Panel on Climatic Change
IPE	International Political Economy
IPPF	International Planned Parenthood Federation
IWC	International Whaling Commission
JCS	Joint Chiefs of Staff
LDC	Less Developed Country
LLDC	Least Developed Country
MAD	Mutual Assured Destruction
MAI	Multilateral Agreement on Investment
MFN	Most-Favored-Nation
MIGA	Multilateral Investment Guarantee Agency

MIRV	Multiple-Independent-Reentry-Vehicle	**SLBM**	Sea-Launched Ballistic Missile
MNC	Multinational Corporation	**SPE**	Socialist Party of Europe
MTCR	Missile Technology Control Regime	**START**	Strategic Arms Reduction Talks
NAFTA	North American Free Trade Association; North American Free Trade Agreement	**TAN**	Transnational Advocacy Network
		THAAD	Theater High Altitude Area Defense
NAM	Non-Aligned Movement	**TI**	Transparency International
NATO	North Atlantic Treaty Organization	**TNC**	Transnational Corporation
NBC	Nuclear-Biological-Chemical	**UN**	United Nations
NGO	Nongovernmental Organization	**UNCED**	United Nations Conference on Environment and Development
NIC	Newly Industrializing Country		
NIEO	New International Economic Order	**UNCHR**	United Nations Commission on Human Rights
NPT	Non-Proliferation Treaty		
NSC	National Security Council	**UNCPD**	United Nations Conference on Population and Development
NTB	Nontariff Barrier		
NTM	National Technical Means	**UNCTAD**	United Nations Council on Trade and Development
NUT	Nuclear Utilization Theory		
OAS	Organization of American States	**UNDHR**	Universal Declaration of Human Rights
OAU	Organization of African Unity	**UNDP**	United Nations Development Programme
ODA	Official Development Aid	**UNEP**	United Nations Environment Program
OECD	Organization for Economic Cooperation and Development	**UNESCO**	United Nations Educational, Scientific, and Cultural Organization
OPEC	Organization of Petroleum Exporting Countries	**UNFPA**	United Nations Population Fund
		UNGA	United Nations General Assembly
OSCE	Organization for Security and Cooperation in Europe	**UNICEF**	United Nations Children's Fund
		UNIDO	United Nations Industrial Development Organization
OSI	On-Site Inspection		
P5	Permanent 5	**UNIFEM**	UN Development Fund for Women
PCIJ	Permanent Court of International Justice	**UNSC**	United Nations Security Council
PLA	People's Liberation Army (China)	**VAT**	Value-Added Tax
PLO	Palestine Liberation Organization	**WEDO**	Women's Environment and Development Organization
PNA	Palestine National Authority		
PNTR	Permanent Normal Trade Relations	**WCHR**	World Conference on Human Rights
SALT	Strategic Arms Limitation Talks	**WCW**	World Conference on Women
SDF	Self-Defense Force (Japan)	**WEU**	Western European Union
SDI	Strategic Defense Initiative	**WFC**	World Food Council
SDR	Special Drawing Right	**WHO**	World Health Organization
SEA	Single European Act	**WTO**	World Trade Organization

REFERENCES

Abbott, Kenneth W., and Duncan Snidal. 1998. "Why States Act through Formal International Organizations." *Journal of Conflict Organization*, 42:3–32.

Ackerman, Peter, and Christopher Kruegler. 1993. *Strategic Nonviolent Conflict: The Dynamics of People Power in the Twentieth Century*. Westport, CT: Praeger.

ADL (Anti-Defamation League). 1999. *Highlights from a September 1999 Anti-Defamation League Survey on Anti-Semitism and Societal Attitudes in Russia*. New York: Martilla Communications Group. Also available at the ADL Website: http://www.adl.org/frames/front_israel.html.

Ahmad, Zakaria Haji, and Baladas Ghoshal. 1999. "The Political Future of ASEAN after the Asian Crisis." *International Affairs*, 75:759–778.

Allulis, Joseph, and Vickie Sullivan, eds. 1996. *Shakespeare's Political Pageant: Essays in Politics and Literature*. Boulder, CO: Rowman & Littlefield.

Alter, Karen J. 1998. "Who Are the 'Masters of the Treaty'?: European Governments and the European Court of Justice." *International Organization*, 52:121–148.

Amadife, Emmanuel N. 1999. *Pre-Theories and Theories of Foreign Policy–Making*. Lanham, MD: University Press of America.

Ambrose, Stephen E. 1991. *Nixon: The Triumph of a Politician, 1962–1972*. New York: Simon & Schuster.

Apodaca, Clair, and Michael Stohl. 1999. "United States Human Rights Policy and Foreign Assistance." *International Studies Quarterly*, 43:185–198.

Archer, Clive. 1983. *International Organizations*. London: Allen & Unwin.

Arend, Anthony Clark, and Robert J. Beck. 1994. *International Law and the Use of Force*. New York: Routledge.

Armstrong, David. 1999. "Law, Justice and the Idea of a World Society." *International Affairs*, 75:563–598.

Astorino-Courtois, Allison. 1998. "Clarifying Decisions: Assessing the Impact of Decision Structures on Foreign Policy Choices during the 1970 Jordanian Civil War." *International Studies Quarterly*, 42:733–754.

Attali, Jacques. 1997. "The Clash of Western Civilization: The Limits of the Market and Democracy." *Foreign Policy*, 107:54–64.

Audley, John J. 1997. *Green Politics and Global Trade: NAFTA and the Future of Environmental Politics*. Washington, DC: Georgetown University Press.

Auerswald, David. P. 1999. "Inward Bound: Domestic Institutions and Military Conflicts." *International Organization*, 53:469–504.

Avant, Deborah. 2000. "From Mercenaries to Citizen Armies: Explaining Change in the Practice of War." *International Organization*, 54: 41–73.

Bacchus, William I. 1997. *The Price of American Foreign Policy: Congress, The Executive, and International Affairs Funding*. University Park: University of Pennsylvania Press.

Bailey, Kathleen C. 1999. "The Comprehensive Test Ban Treaty." *Policy Analysis*, 330 (January 1999):1–31.

Balaam, David N., and Michael Veseth. 1996. *Introduction to International Political Economy*. Upper Saddle River, NJ: Prentice Hall.

Balanzino, Sergio Silvio. 1996. "Adapting the Alliance: Restructuring NATO after the Cold War." In *Annual Editions: World Politics 96/97*, ed. Helen Purkitt. Guilford, CT: Dushkin.

Baldwin, David A. 2000. "The Sanctions Debate and the Logic of Choice." *International Security*, 24/3:80–107.

Barber, Benjamin R. 1995. *Jihad vs. McWorld*. New York: Times Books/Random House.

Barber, Charles T. 1996. "UN Security Council Representation: The First 50 Years and Beyond." Paper presented at the International Studies Association convention, San Diego.

Barber, James David. 1985. *Presidential Character*, 3rd ed. Englewood Cliffs, NJ: Prentice Hall.

Barbieri, Katherine. 1996. "Economic Interdependence: A Path to Peace or a Source of Interstate Conflict." *Journal of Peace Research*, 33:29–49.

Barkey, Karen, and Mark von Hagen, eds. 1997. *After Empire: Multi-Ethnic Societies and Nation-Building*. Boulder, CO: Westview.

Barnett, Michael N., and Martha Finnemore. 1999. "The Politics, Power, and Pathologies of International Organizations." *International Organization*, 53:699–732.

Barrington, Lowell W. 1997. "Nation and 'Nationalism': The Misuse of Key Concepts in Political Science." *PS: Political Science & Politics*, 30:712–724.

Bartlett, David, and Anna Seleny. 1998. "The Political Enforcement of Liberalism: Bargaining, Institutions, and Auto Multinationals in Hungary." *International Studies Quarterly*, 42:319–338.

Barry, James A. 1998. *The Sword of Justice: Ethics and Coercion in International Politics*. Westport, CT: Praeger.

Barzilai, Gad. 1999. "War, Democracy, and Internal Conflict: Israel in a Comparative Perspective." *Comparative Politics*, 31:317–36

Beer, Francis A. 1990. "The Reduction of War and the Creation of Peace." In *A Reader in Peace Studies*, ed. Paul Smoker, Ruth Davies, and Barbara Munske. New York: Pergamon.

Beer, Francis A., and Robert Harriman, eds. 1996. *Post-Realism: The Rhetorical Turn in International Relations*. Ann Arbor: University of Michigan Press.

Beigbeder, Yves. 1999. *Judging War Criminals: The Politics of International Justice*. New York: St. Martin's.

Beiner, Ronald, ed. 1999. *Theorizing Nationalism*. Albany: State University of New York Press.

Beitz, Charles R. 1999. *Political Theory and International Relations*. Princeton: Princeton University Press.

Belgrad, Eric A., and Nitza Nachmias. 1997. *The Politics of International Humanitarian Aid Operations*. Westport, CT: Praeger.

Bellany, Ian. 1997. *The Environment in World Politics: Exploring the Limits*. Lyme, NH: Edward Elgar.

Bennett, D. Scott. 1996. "Security, Bargaining, and the End of Interstate Rivalry." *International Studies Quarterly*, 40:157–184.

Bennett, D. Scott. 1997. "Testing Alternative Models of Alliance

Duration, 1816–1984." *American Journal of Political Science*, 41:846–878.

Bernstein, Richard, and Ross Munro. 1997. "The Coming Conflict with China." *Foreign Affairs*, 76/2:18–32.

Berton, Peter, Hiroshi Kimura, and I. William Zartman. 1999. *International Negotiation: Actors Structure/Process, Values*. New York: St. Martin's.

Best, Geoffrey. 1999. "Peace Conferences and the Century of Total War: The 1899 Hague Conference and What Came After." *International Affairs*, 75:619–634.

Betts, Richard K. 1998. "The New Threat of Mass Destruction." *Foreign Affairs*, 77/1:26–45.

Blanton, Shannon Lindsey. 1996. "Images in Conflict: The Case of Ronald Reagan and El Salvador." *International Studies Quarterly*, 40:23–44.

Blanton, Shannon Lindsey. 1998. "U.S. Arms Transfers and the Promotion of Global Order." Paper presented at the International Studies Association convention, Minneapolis.

Blanton, Shannon Lindsey. 2000. "Promoting Human Rights and Democracy in the Developing World: U.S. Rhetoric versus U.S. Arms Exports." *American Journal of Political Science*, 44:123–133.

Bloomfield, Lincoln P., and Allen Moulton. 1997. *Managing International Conflict: From Theory to Policy*. New York: St. Martin's Press.

Bobrow, Davis B., and Mark A. Boyer. 1998. "International System Stability and American Decline: A Case for Muted Optimism." *International Journal*, 53:285–305.

Bock, Peter, and Nigel Young. 1999. *Pacifism in the Twentieth Century*. Syracuse, NY: Syracuse University Press.

Bohlen, Charles E. 1973. *Witness to History*. New York: W. W. Norton.

Bohman, James. 1999. "International Regimes and Democratic Governance: Political Equality and Influence in Global Institutions." *International Affairs*, 75:499–514.

Bohman, James, and Matthias Lutz-Bachmann, eds. 1997. *Perpetual Peace: Essays on Kant's Cosmopolitan Ideal*. Cambridge, MA: MIT Press.

Bond, Doug. 1992. "Introduction." In *Transforming Struggle: Strategy and the Global Experience of Nonviolent Direct Action*. Cambridge, MA: Program on Nonviolent Sanction in Conflict and Defense, Center for International Affairs, Harvard University.

Bouton, Marshall M. 1998. "India's Problem Is Not Politics." *Foreign Affairs*, 77/3:80–94.

Bova, Russell. 1997. "Democracy and Liberty: The Cultural Connection." *Journal of Democracy*, 8:112–125.

Boyer, Mark A. 1993. *International Cooperation and Public Goods: Opportunities for the Western Alliance*. Baltimore: Johns Hopkins University Press.

Boyer, Mark A. 1996. "Political System and the Logic of Two-Level Games: Moving beyond Democracies in the Study of International Negotiation." Paper presented at the International Studies Association Northeast convention, Boston.

Boyer, Mark A., and John T. Rourke. 1998. "The Costs of NATO Enlargement: The American Debate." In *The Debate on the Costs of NATO-Enlargement to the East,* ed. August Pradetto and Fouzieh Melanie Alamir. Series on "Democracy, Security, Peace" No. 119 (Nomos Verlagsgesell-schaft: Baden-Baden, Germany, 1998), pp. 57–78. The chapter and book titles are translated from their original German.

Bozdogan, Sibel, and Resat Kasaba, eds. 1997. *Rethinking Moder-*

nity and National Identity in Turkey. Seattle: University of Washington Press.

Brandes, Lisa C. O. 1993. "Who Cares? Interest, Concern, and Gender in International Security Policy." Presented at the annual meeting of the International Studies Association, Acapulco, Mexico.

Brawley, Mark. 1996. "Economic Coercion by a Power in Relative Decline: Why Sanctions May Be More Effective as Hegemonic Leadership Ebbs." Paper presented at the International Studies Association convention, San Diego.

Brecher, Jeremy. 1993. "Global Village or Global Pillage." *The Nation*, December 6.

Brecher, Michael, and Jonathan Wilkenfeld. 1997. *A Study of Crisis*. Ann Arbor: University of Michigan Press.

Breuning, Marijke. 1995. "Culture, History, and Role: How the Past Shapes Foreign Policy Now." Paper presented at the International Studies Association convention, Chicago.

Breuning, Marijke. 1996. "Nationalist Parties and Foreign Policy Assistance." Paper presented at the International Studies Association convention, San Diego.

Bright, Chris. 2000. "Anticipating Environmental 'Surprise,'" In *State of the World 2000,* ed. Lester R. Brown, et al. New York: W. W. Norton.

Brooks, Stephen G. 1997. "Dueling Realisms." *International Organization*, 51:445–478.

Brown, Lester, ed. 2000. *State of the World 2000*. New York: W. W. Norton.

Brown, Sarah Graham. 1999. *Sanctioning Saddam: The Politics of Intervention in Iraq*. New York: St. Martin's.

Brown, Seyom. 1988. *New Forces, Old Forces, and the Future of World Politics*. Glenville, IL: Scott, Foresman.

Brown, Seyom. 1992. *International Relations in a Changing Global System*. Boulder, CO: Westview.

Brown, Seyom. 1998. "World Interests and the Changing Dimension of Security." In *World Security: Challenges for a New Century*, 3rd ed., ed. Michael T. Klare and Yogesh Chandran. New York: St. Martin's.

Bueno de Mesquita, Bruce J., and James D. Morrow. 1999. "Sorting through the Wealth of Nations." *International Security*, 24/2:56–73.

Bueno de Mesquita, Bruce J., and Randolph M. Siverson. 1993. "War and the Survival of Political Leaders: A Comparative Analysis." Presented at the annual meeting of the American Political Science Association, Washington, DC.

Bueno de Mesquita, Bruce J., and Randolph M. Siverson. 1995. "War and the Survival of Political Leaders: A Comparative Study of Regime Types and Political Accountability." *American Political Science Review*, 89:841–855.

Bull, Hedley, and Adam Watson. 1982. *The Expansion of International Society*. London: Oxford University Press.

Bunch, Charlotte, and Roxana Carillo. 1998. "Global Violence against Women: The Challenge to Human Rights and Development." In *World Security: Challenges for a New Century*, 3rd ed., ed. Michael T. Klare and Yogesh Chandran. New York: St. Martin's.

Burch, Kurt, and Robert A. Denemark, eds. 1997. *Constituting International Political Economy: International Political Economy Yearbook, vol. 10*. Boulder, CO: Lynne Rienner.

Bureau of the Census. *See* (U.S.) Bureau of the Census.

Burk, Erika. 1994. "Human Rights and Social Issues." In *A Global Agenda: Issues before the 49th General Assembly*, ed. John Tessitore and Susan Woolfson. Lanham, MD: University Press of America.

Burrowes, Robert J. 1996. *The Strategy of Nonviolent Defense*. Albany: State University of New York Press.

Cafruny, Alan W., and Carl Lankowski, eds. 1997. *Europe's Ambiguous Unity: Conflict and Consensus in the Post-Maastricht Era*. Boulder, CO: Lynne Rienner.

Caldwell, Lynton Keith. 1996. *International Environmental Policy: From the Twentieth to the Twenty-First Century*. Durham, NC: Duke University Press.

Cameron, Gavin. 1999. *Nuclear Terrorism: A Threat Assessment for the Twenty-First Century*. New York: St. Martin's.

Caplan, Richard, and John Feffer, eds. 1996. *Europe's New Nationalism: States and Minorities in Conflict*. New York: Oxford University Press.

Caprioli, Mary. 2000. "The Myth of Women's Pacifism." In *Taking Sides: Clashing Views on Controversial Issues in World Politics*, 9th ed., ed. John T. Rourke. Guilford, CT: McGraw-Hill\Dushkin.

Cardús, Salvador, and Joan Estruch. 1995. "Politically Correct Anti-Nationalism." *International Social Science Journal*, 144:347–352.

Carment, David. 1994. "The Ethnic Dimension in World Politics: Theory, Policy, and Early Warning." *Third World Quarterly*, 15:551–579.

Carrington, William J., and Enrica Detragiache. 1999. "How Extensive Is the Brain Drain?" *Finance & Development*, 36/2:108.

Carruthers, Susan L. 1998. "Not like the US? Europeans and the Spread of American Culture." *International Affairs*, 74: 883–892.

Carter, Jimmy. Speech, December 6, 1978. *Department of State Bulletin*, January 1979.

Cashman, Greg. 1999. *What Causes War? An Introduction to Theories of International Conflict*. Lanham, MD: Lexington Books.

Catley-Carlson, Margaret, and Judith A.M. Outlaw. 1998. "Poverty and Population Issues: Clarifying the Connections." *Journal of International Affairs*, 52:233–252.

Cederman, Lars-Erik. 1994. "Emergent Polarity: Analyzing State-Formation and Power Politics." *International Studies Quarterly*, 38:501–533.

Cederman, Lars-Erik. 1997. *Emergent Actors in World Politics: How States and Nations Develop and Dissolve*. Princeton, NJ: Princeton University Press.

Center for Defense Information. *The Defense Monitor*, 28/1 (1999).

Central Intelligence Agency. *See* U.S. (CIA).

Chafetz, Glenn. 1995. "The Political Psychology of the Nuclear Nonproliferation Regime." *Journal of Politics*, 57:743–775.

Chafetz, Glenn, Michael Spirtas, and Benjamin Frankel, eds. 1999. *Origins of National Interests*. Essex, U.K.: Frank Cass.

Chan, Stephen, and Jarrod Weiner, eds. 1998. *Twentieth Century International History*. New York: St. Martin's.

Chase-Dunn, Christopher, and Thomas D. Hall. 1997. *Rise and Demise: Comparing World-Systems*. Boulder, CO: Westview Press.

Chen, Martha Alter. 1995. "Engendering World Conferences: The International Women's Movement and the United Nations." *The Third World Quarterly*, 16:477–495.

China, People's Republic of. 1993. *China's Foreign Policy*. Beijing: New Star Publishers.

Chopra, Jarat. 1995. "Back to the Drawing Board." *Bulletin of the Atomic Scientists*, 51/2 (March/April):29–35.

Christensen, Thomas J., and Jack Snyder. 1997. "Progressive Research on Degenerative Alliances." *American Political Science Review*, 4:919–922.

Chrystal, Jonathan. 1998. "A New Kind of Competition: How American Producers Respond to Incoming Foreign Direct Investment." *International Studies Quarterly*, 42:513–543.

CIA. *See* U.S. (CIA).

Cimbala, Stephen J. 1995. "Deterrence Stability with Smaller Forces: Prospects and Problems." *Journal of Peace Research*, 32:65–78.

Cini, Michelle. 1997. *The European Commission: Leadership, Organization and Culture in the EU Administration*. New York: Manchester University Press.

Cioffi-Revilla, Claudio. 1996. "Origins and Evolution of War and Politics." *International Studies Quarterly*, 40:1–22.

Clapham, Christopher. 1999. "Sovereignty and the Third World State." *Political Studies*, 47:522–537.

Clark, Ann Marie. 1996. "The Contribution of Non-Governmental Organizations to the Creation and Strengthening of International Human Rights Norms." Paper presented at the International Studies Association convention, San Diego.

Clark, Ann Marie, Elisabeth J. Friedman, and Kathryn Hochstetler. 1998. "The Sovereign Limits of Global Civil Society: A Comparison of NGO Participation in UN World Conferences on the Environment, Human Rights, and Women." *World Politics*, 51:1–35.

Cohen, Raymond. 1987. *Theater of Power: The Art of Diplomatic Signaling*. Essex, U.K.: Longman.

Cohen, Raymond. 1996. "Reflection on the New Global Diplomacy: Statecraft 2500 B.C.–A.D. 2000." Paper presented at the International Studies Association convention, San Diego.

Cohen, Stephen D. 2000. *The Making of United States International Economic Policy*, 5th ed. Westport, CT: Praeger.

Conley, Richard S. 1997. "Sovereignty or the Status Quo: The 1995 Pre-Referendum Debate in Québec." *Journal of Commonwealth & Comparative Politics*, 35:67–92.

Constantinou, Costas M. 1996. "Representation of Sovereignty in the Himalayas." Paper presented at the International Studies Association convention, San Diego.

Cooper, Leo. 1999. *Russia and the World: New State-of-Play on the International Stage*. New York: St. Martin's.

Cortell, Andrew P., and James W. Davis Jr. 1996. "How Do International Institutions Matter? The Domestic Impact of International Rules and Norms." *International Studies Quarterly*, 40:451–478.

Cortright, David, and George A. Lopez, eds. 1996. *Economic Sanctions: Panacea or Peacebuilding in a Post–Cold War World?* Boulder, CO: Westview.

Cortright, David, and George A. Lopez. 2000. *The Sanctions Decade: Assessing UN Strategies in the 1990s*. Boulder, CO: Lynne Rienner.

Cox, Robert W., ed. 1997. *The New Realism: Perspectives on Multilateralism and World Order*. New York: St. Martin's.

Craig, Gordon A., and Alexander L. George. 1995. *Force and Statecraft: Diplomatic Problems of Our Time*, 3rd ed. New York: Oxford University Press.

Croft, Stuart. *Strategies of Arms Control: A History and Typology*. New York: St. Martin's.

Crystal, Jonathan. 1998. "A New Kind of Competition: How American Producers Respond to Incoming Foreign Direct Investment." *International Studies Quarterly*, 42:513–544.

Culter, A. Claire, Virginia Haufler, and Tony Porter, eds. 1999. *Private Authority and International Affairs*. Albany: State University of New York Press.

Cusimano, Maryann, ed. 1998. *Beyond Sovereignty: Issues for a Global Agenda.* New York: St. Martin's.

Dassel, Kurt. 1998. "Civilians, Soldiers, and Strife: Domestic Sources of International Aggression." *International Security.* 23:107–140.

Dassel, Kurt, and Eric Reinhardt. 1999. "Domestic Strife and the Initiation of Violence at Home and Abroad." *American Journal of Political Science,* 43:56–85.

Dawisha, Karen. 1997. "Russian Foreign Policy in the Year Abroad and Beyond." In *Annual Editions, World Politics 97/98.* Guilford, CT: Dushkin/McGraw-Hill.

DeCamp, William T. 2000. "The Big Picture: A Moral Analysis of Allied Force in Kosovo." *Marine Corps Gazette,* 84/2:42–44.

Deibert, Ronald. 1997. *Parchment, Printing, and Hypermedia: Communication and World Order Transformation.* New York: Columbia University Press.

DeRouen, Karl R., Jr. 1995. "The Indirect Link: Politics, the Economy, and the Use of Force." *Journal of Conflict Resolution,* 39:671–695.

Dickson, Anna K. 1997. *Development and International Relations: A Critical Introduction.* Cambridge, U.K.: Polity Press.

DiClerico, Robert E. 1979. *The American President.* Englewood Cliffs, NJ: Prentice Hall.

Diehl, Paul F., ed. 1996. *The Politics of Global Governance: International Organizations in an Interdependent World.* Boulder, CO: Lynne Rienner.

Diehl, Paul F., Daniel Druckman, and James Wall. 1998. "International Peacekeeping and Conflict Resolution: A Taxonomic Analysis with Implications." *Journal of Conflict Resolution,* 42:33–55.

Dirie, Waris, with Cathleen Miller. 1998. *Desert Flower: The Extraordinary Journey of a Desert Nomad.* New York: William Morrow.

Downs, Erica Strecker, and Philip C. Saunders. 1999. "Legitimacy and the Limits of Nationalism: China and the Diaoyu Islands." *International Security,* 23/3:114–246.

Doxey, Margaret P. 1996. *International Sanctions in Contemporary Perspective.* New York: St. Martin's.

Drezner, Daniel W. 2000. "Bargaining, Enforcement, and Multilateral Sanctions: When is Cooperation Counterproductive?" *International Organization,* 54:73–102.

Drezner, Daniel W. 1998. "Conflict Expectations and the Paradox of Economic Coercion." *International Studies Quarterly,* 42:709–732.

Drifte, Reinhard. 1999. *Japan's Quest for a Permanent Security Council Seat : A Matter of Pride or Justice?* New York: St. Martin's.

Druckman, Daniel. 1994. "Nationalism, Patriotism and Group Loyalty: A Social Psychological Perspective." *Mershon International Studies Review,* supplement to *International Studies Quarterly,* 38:43–68.

Duchacek, Ivo D. 1975. *Nations and Men.* Hinsdale, IL: Dryden.

Dunn, David H., ed. 1996. *Diplomacy at the Highest Level: The Evolution of International Summitry.* New York: St. Martin's.

Dunn, John. 1995. "Introduction: Crisis of the Nation State." In *Contemporary Crisis of the Nation State,* ed. John Dunn. Oxford, U.K.: Blackwell.

Ebenstein, Alan O., William Ebenstein, and Edwin Fogelman. 1994. *Today's Isms: Socialism, Capitalism, Fascism, and Communism.* Englewood Cliffs, NJ: Prentice Hall.

Ehrenreich, Barbara, and Katha Pollitt, 1999. "Fukuyama's Follies." *Foreign Affairs,* 78/1:118–129.

Eichengreen, Barry. 1996. *Globalizing Capital: A History of the International Monetary System.* Princeton, NJ: Princeton University Press.

Eichengreen, Barry. 1998. "Geography as Destiny." *Foreign Affairs,* 77/2:128–139.

Eide, Asbjorn. 1998. "The Historical Significance of the Universal Declaration." *International Social Science Journal,* 50: 475–498.

El-Agraa, Ali M., ed. 1997. *Economic Integration Worldwide.* New York: St. Martin's.

Eley, Geoff, and Ronald Grigor Suny. 1996. *Becoming National.* New York: Oxford University Press.

Elliott, Kimberly Ann. 1993. "A Look at the Record." *Bulletin of the Atomic Scientists,* November.

Elliot, Kimberly Ann, ed. 1997. *Corruption and the Global Economy.* Washington, DC: Institute for International Economics.

Elliott, Kimberly Ann. 1998. "The Sanctions Glass: Half Full or Completely Empty?" *International Security,* 23:50–65.

Elman, Colin. 1996. "Why Not Neorealist Theories of Foreign Policy?" *Security Studies,* 6:7–53.

Elman, Colin, and Miriam Fendius Elman. 1997. "Diplomatic History and International Relations Theory: Respecting Difference and Cross Boundaries." *International Security,* 22:5–21.

Elman, Colin, and Miriam Fendius Elman. 1997. "Lakatos and Neorealism: A Reply to Vasquez." *American Political Science Review,* 4:923–926.

Enders, Walter, and Todd Sandler. 1999. "Transnational Terrorism in the Post–Cold War Era." *International Studies Quarterly,* 43:145–167.

Engleman, Robert, and Pamela LeRoy. 1995. *Sustaining Water: An Update.* Washington, DC: Population Action International.

Enriquez, Juan. 1999. "Too Many Flags." *Foreign Policy,* 116:30–49.

Esposito, John L., ed. 1997. *Political Islam: Revolution, Radicalism, or Reform?* Boulder, CO: Lynne Rienner.

Etzioni, Amitai. 1993. "The Evils of Self-Determination." *Foreign Policy,* 89:21–35.

Faksh, Mahmud A. 1997. *The Future of Islam in the Middle East: Fundamentalism in Egypt, Algeria, and Saudi Arabia.* Westport, CT: Praeger.

Falk, Richard. 1999. "World Prisms: The Future of Sovereign States and International Order." *Harvard International Review,* 21/3:30–35.

(FAO) Food and Agricultural Organization. 1995. "Forest Resources Assessment 1990: Global Synthesis." *FAO Forestry Paper 124.* Rome: FAO.

Farnen, Russell, ed. 1994. *Nationalism, Ethnicity, and Identity: Cross-National and Comparative Perspectives.* New Brunswick, NJ: Transaction.

Farrell, Robert H. 1998. *The Dying President: Franklin D. Roosevelt, 1944–1945.* Columbia: University of Missouri Press.

Farsoun, Samih. 1997. *Palestine and the Palestinians.* Boulder, CO: Westview.

Feaver, Peter D., and Emerson M. S. Niou. 1996. "Managing Nuclear Proliferation: Condemn, Strike, or Assist?" *International Studies Quarterly,* 40:209–234.

Feld, Werner J. 1979. *International Relations: A Transnational Approach.* New York: Alfred Publishing.

Feldstein, Martin. 1998. "Refocusing the IMF." *Foreign Affairs*, 77/2:46–71.

Felice, William F. 1996. *Taking Suffering Seriously: The Importance of Collective Human Rights.* Albany: State University of New York Press.

Ferguson, Nial, and Laurence J. Kotlikoff. 2000. "The Degeneration of the EMU." *Foreign Affairs*, 79/3:110–212.

Feron, James D. "Signaling Foreign Policy Interests." *Journal of Conflict Resolution*, 41:68–90.

Finn, James, ed. 1997. *Freedom in the World: The Annual Survey of Political and Civil Liberties, 1996–1997.* New York: Freedom House.

Fitzsimons, David M. 1995. "Thomas Paine's New World Order: Idealistic Internationalism in the Ideology of Early American Foreign Relations." *Diplomatic History*, 19:569–582.

Flavin, Christopher. 1996. "Facing up to the Risks of Climate Change." In *State of the World 1996*, ed. Lester R. Brown. New York: W. W. Norton.

Flynn, Gregory, and Henry Farrell. 1999. "Piecing Together the Democratic Peace: The CSCE and the 'Construction' of Security in Post–Cold War Europe." *International Organization*, 53:505–535.

Fordham, Benjamin. 1998. "The Politics of Threat Perception and the Use of Force: A Political Economy Model of U.S. Uses of Force, 1949–1994." *International Studies Quarterly*, 42:567–590.

Fowler, Michael Ross, and Julie Marie Bunck. 1995. *Law, Power, and the Sovereign States: The Evolution and Application of the Concept of Sovereignty.* University Park: University of Pennsylvania Press.

Foyle, Douglas C. 1997. "Public Opinion and Foreign Policy: Elite Beliefs as a Mediating Variable." *International Studies Quarterly*, 41:141–170.

Fozouni, Bahman. 1995. "Confutation of Political Realism." *International Studies Quarterly*, 39:479–510.

Fraser, Arvonne S. 1999. "Becoming Human: The Origins and Development of Women's Human Rights." *Human Rights Quarterly* 21:853–906.

Freedman, Lawrence. 1998. "Military Power and Political Influence." *International Affairs*, 74:36–49.

Freedom House. 1997. *Freedom in the World: The Annual Survey of Political Rights & Civil Liberties, 1996–1997.* New Brunswick, NJ: Transaction.

Frost, Mervyn. 1996. *Ethics in International Relations.* New York: Cambridge University Press.

Fukuyama, Francis. 1989. "The End of History?" *National Interest*, 16:3–18.

Fukuyama, Francis. 1998. "Women and the Evolution of Politics." *Foreign Affairs*, 77/5:24–40.

Fuller, Graham E., and Rend Rahim Francke. 1999. *The Arab Shi'a.* New York: St. Martin's.

Fursenko, Aleksandr, and Timothy Naftali. 1997. *One Hell of a Gamble: Khrushchev, Castro, and Kennedy, 1958–1964.* New York: W. W. Norton.

Gabel, Matthew. 1998. "Public Support for European Integration: An Empirical Test of Five Theories." *Journal of Politics*, 60:333–355.

Gaenslen, Fritz. 1997. "Advancing Cultural Explanations." In *Culture & Foreign Policy*, ed. Valerie M. Hudson. Boulder, CO: Lynne Rienner.

Gallagher, Nancy W., ed. 1998. *Arms Control: New Approaches to Theory and Policy.* Newbury Park, U.K.: Frank Cass.

Galtung, Johan. 1994. *Human Rights in Another Key.* Cambridge, U.K.: Polity Press.

Garrett, Geoffrey, R. Daniel Kelemen, and Heiner Schulz. 1998. "The European Court of Justice, National Governments, and Legal Integration in the European Union." *International Organization*, 52:149–176.

Gartner, Scott Sigmund, and Randolph M. Siverson. 1996. "War Expansion and War Outcome." *Journal of Conflict Resolution*, 40:4–15.

Gartzke, Erik. 1998. "Kant We All Just Get Along? Opportunity, Willingness, and the Origins of the Democratic Peace." *American Journal of Political Science*, 42:1–27.

Gayton, Jeffrey T. 1997. "From Here to Extraterritoriality: The United States Within and Beyond Borders." Paper presented at the International Studies Association convention, Toronto, Canada, March 1997. On the Web at: http://www.polisci.wisc.edu/~jtgayton/papers/.

Geller, Daniel S. 1993. "Power Differentials and War in Rival Dyads." *International Studies Quarterly*, 37:173–193.

Geller, Daniel S., and J. David Singer. 1998. *Nations at War: A Scientific Study of International Conflict.* Cambridge, U.K.: Cambridge University Press.

Gellner, Ernest. 1995. "Introduction." In *Notions of Nationalism*, ed. Sukumar Periwal. Budapest: Central European University Press.

Gelpi, Christopher. 1997. "Democratic Diversions." *International Studies Quarterly*, 41:255–282.

Genest, Marc A. 1994. "Realism and the Problem of Peaceful Change." *Perspectives on Political Science*, 23:70–78.

George, Alexander L. 1994. "Some Guides to Bridging the Gap." *Mershon International Studies Review*, 39:171–172.

Geva, Hehemia, and Alex Mintz, eds. 1997. *Decisionmaking on War and Peace: The Cognitive-Rational Debate.* Boulder, CO: Lynne Rienner.

Gibbs, David N. 1995. "Secrecy and International Relations." *Journal of Peace Research*, 32:213–238.

Gibler, Douglas M., and John A. Vasquez. 1998. "Uncovering the Dangerous Alliances, 1495–1980." *International Studies Quarterly*, 42:785–810.

Gibney, Matthew J. 1999. "Liberal Democratic States and Responsibilities to Refugees." *American Political Science Review*, 93:169–182.

Gilbert, Alan. 1999. *Must Global Politics Constrain Democracy? Great-Power Realism, Democratic Peace, and Democratic Internationalism.* Princeton, NJ:Princeton University Press, 1999.

Gilpin, Robert. 1981. *War and Change in World Politics.* Cambridge, U.K.: Cambridge University Press.

Glad, Betty. 1989. "Personality, Political and Group Process Variables in Foreign Policy Decision Making: Jimmy Carter's Handling of the Iranian Hostage Crisis." *International Political Science Review*, 10:35–61.

Glennon, Michael J. 1999. "The New Interventionism." *Foreign Affairs*, 78/3:2–21.

Gleijeses, Piero. 1995. "The CIA and the Bay of Pigs." *Journal of Latin American Studies*, 27:18–42.

Gochman, Charles S., and Aaron M. Hoffman. 1996. "Peace in the Balance? A Matter of Design." *International Studies Notes*, 21/2 (Spring):20–25.

Goldgeier, James M. 1999. *Not Whether but When: The U.S. Decision to Enlarge NATO.* Washington, DC: Brookings Institution Press.

Goldstein, Melvyn C. 1997. *The Snow Lion and the Dragon: China, Tibet and the Dalai Lama.* Berkeley: University of California Press.

Graebner, Norman, ed. 1964. *Ideas and Diplomacy*. New York: Oxford University Press.

Grant, Rebecca, and Kathleen Newland, eds. 1991. *Gender and International Relations*. Bloomington: Indiana University Press.

Grantham, Bill. 1998. "America the Menace: France's Feud with Hollywood." *World Policy Journal*, 15/2:58–66.

Gray, Colin S. 1994. "Force, Order, and Justice: The Ethics of Realism in Statecraft." *Global Affairs*, 14:1–17.

Green, Michael. 1996. *Arming Japan: Defense Production, Alliance Politics, and the Post-War Search for Autonomy*. Baltimore: Johns Hopkins University Press.

Greenfeld, Liah. 1992. *Nationalism: Five Roads to Modernity*. Cambridge, MA: Harvard University Press.

Greider, William. 1997. *The Manic Logic of Global Capitalism*. New York: Simon & Schuster.

Griffin, Roger, ed. 1995. *Fascism*. New York: Oxford University Press.

Griffiths, Martin. 1995. *Realism, Idealism, and International Politics*. New York: Routledge.

Gruenberg, Leon. 1996. "The IPE of Multinational Corporations." In *Introduction to International Political Economy*, ed. David N. Balaam and Michael Veseth. Upper Saddle River, NJ: Prentice Hall.

Guelke, Adrian. 1998. *The Age of Terrorism and the International Political System*. New York: St Martin's.

Guibernau, Montserrat. 1996. *Nationalisms: The Nation-State and Nationalism in the Twentieth Century*. Cambridge, U.K.: Polity Press.

Gurr, Nadine, and Benjamin Cole. 2000. *The New Face of Terrorism : Threats from Weapons of Mass Destruction*. New York: St. Martin's.

Gurr, Ted Robert. 2000. *Peoples Versus States*. Washington, DC; United States Institute of Peace Press.

Gurr, Ted Robert. 2000a. "Ethnic Warfare on the Wane." *Foreign Affairs*, 79/3:52–64.

Gurr, Ted Robert, and Michael Haxton. 1996. "Minorities Report (1). Ethnopolitical Conflict in the 1990s: Patterns and Trends." Paper presented at the International Studies Association convention, San Diego.

Haas, Michael. 1994. "International Communitarianism." Presented at the annual meeting of the American Political Science Association, Washington, DC.

Haas, Peter M., and David McCabe. 1996. "International Institutions and Social Learning in the Management of Global Environmental Risks." Paper presented at the International Studies Association convention, San Diego.

Hall, John. 1995. "Nationalism, Classified and Explained." In *Notions of Nationalism*, ed. Sukumar Periwal. Budapest: Central European University Press.

Hall, Rodney Bruce. 1999. *National Collective Identity: Social Constructs and International Systems*. New York: Columbia University Press.

Haney, Patrick J., and Walt Vanderbush. 1999. "The Role of Ethnic Interest Groups in U.S. Foreign Policy: The Case of the Cuban American National Foundation." *International Studies Quarterly*, 43:341–361.

Hannum, Hurst. 1999. "The Specter of Secession." *Foreign Affairs*, 77/2:13–19.

Harbour, Frances V. 1998. *Thinking about International Ethics: Moral Theory and Cases from American Foreign Policy*. Boulder, CO: Westview.

Hart, Paul, and Eric K. Stern, eds. 1997. *Beyond Groupthink: Political Group Dynamics and Foreign Policy Making*. Ann Arbor: University of Michigan Press.

Hasenclever, Andreas, and Peter Mayer. 1997. *Theories of International Regimes*. Cambridge, U.K.: Cambridge University Press.

Hashim, Ahmed S. 1998. "The Revolution in Military Affairs Outside the West." *Journal of International Affairs*, 51:431–446.

Hashmi, Sohail H., ed. 1997. *State Sovereignty: Change and Persistence in International Relations*. University Park: Pennsylvania State University Press.

Hawkins, Darren. 1999. "Transnational Activists as Motors for Change." *International Studies Review*, I/1:119–122.

Heberer, Thomas. 1995. "The Tibet Question as a Problem of International Politics." *Aussen Politik*, 46:299–309.

Helleiner, Eric. 1998. "Electronic Money: A Challenge to the Sovereign State?" *Journal of International Affairs*, 51:387–410.

Henderson, Earl Anthony. 1998. "Military Spending and Poverty." *Journal of Politics*, 60/2:503–529.

Henderson, Earl Anthony. 1998a. "The Democratic Peace through the Lens of Culture, 1820–1989." *International Studies Quarterly*, 42/3:461–484.

Herek, Gregory M., Irving L. Janis, and Paul Huth. 1987. "Decision-Making during International Crises: Is the Quality of Progress Related to the Outcome?" *Journal of Conflict Resolution*, 31:203–236.

Hermann, Margaret G. 1998. "One Field, Many Perspectives: Building the Foundations for Dialogue." *International Studies Quarterly*, 42/4:605–620.

Hermann, Margaret G., and Joe D. Hagan. 1998. "International Decision Making: Leadership Matters." *Foreign Policy*, No. 110 (Spring):124–137.

Hermann, Richard K., James F. Voss, Tonya Y. E. Schooler, and Joseph Ciarrochi. 1997. "Images in International Relations: An Experimental Test of Cognitive Schema." *International Studies Quarterly*, 41:403–433.

Higgins, Rosalyn. 1994. *Problems and Process: International Law and How We Use It*. New York: Oxford University Press.

Hirst, Paul, and Grahame Thompson. 1996. *Globalization in Question: The International Economy and the Possibilities of Governance*. Cambridge, U.K.: Polity Press.

Hix, Simon. 1999. *The Political System of the European Union*. New York: St. Martin's.

Hobbes, Heidi H., ed. 2000. *Pondering Postinternationalism: A Paradigm for the Twenty-First Century*. Albany, NY: State University of New York Press.

Hobsbawm, Eric J. 1990. *Nations and Nationalism since 1780: Programme, Myth, Reality*. Cambridge, U.K.: Cambridge University Press.

Hoffmann, Stanley. 1995. "The Crisis of Liberal Internationalism." *Foreign Policy*, 98:159–179.

Hoffmann, Stanley. 1998. *World Disorders: Troubled Peace in the Post–Cold War Era*. Lanham, MD: Rowman & Littlefield.

Holloway, Steven K., and Rodney Tomlinson. 1995. "The New World Order and the General Assembly: Block Realignment at the UN in the Post–Cold War World." *Canadian Journal of Political Science*, 28:227–254.

Holsti, Ole R. 1997. *Public Opinion and American Foreign Policy*. Ann Arbor: University of Michigan Press.

Homer-Dixon, Thomas. 1998. "Environmental Scarcity and Intergroup Conflict." In *World Security: Challenges for a New Century*, 3rd ed., ed. Michael T. Klare and Yogesh Chandran. New York: St. Martin's.

Hoogvelt, Ankie. 1997. *Globalization and the Postcolonial World: The New Political Economy of Development*. Baltimore, MD: Johns Hopkins University Press.

Hook, Steven W. 1996. *Foreign Aid toward the Millennium*. Boulder, CO: Lynne Rienner.

Hopf, Ted. 1991. "Polarity, the Offense-Defense Balance, and War." *American Political Science Review*, 85:475–493.

Hopmann, P. Terrence. 1996. *The Negotiation Process and the Resolution of International Conflicts*. Columbia: University of South Carolina Press.

Hout, Will. 1997. "Globalization and the Quest for Governance." *Mershon International Studies Review*, 41:99–106.

Howard, Michael, George J. Andreopoulos, and Mark R. Shulman, eds. 1994. *The Laws of War*. New Haven, CT: Yale University Press.

Howland, Courtney, ed. 1999. *Religious Fundamentalism and the Human Rights of Women*. New York: St. Martin's.

Hudson, Valerie M., ed. 1997. *Culture and Foreign Policy*. Boulder, CO: Lynne Rienner.

Hufbauer, Gary Clyde, and Jeffrey J. Schott. 1994. *Western Hemisphere Economic Integration*. Washington, DC: Institute for International Economics.

Hughes, Donna M. 2000. "The 'Natasha' Trade: The Transnational Shadow Market of Trafficking in Women." *Journal of International Affairs*, 53:625–652.

Huntington, Samuel. 1993. "The Clash of Civilizations." *Foreign Affairs*, 72(3):56–73.

Huntington, Samuel P. 1996. *The Clash of Civilizations and the Remaking of World Order*. New York: Simon & Schuster.

Huntington, Samuel P. 1999. "The Lonely Superpower." *Foreign Affairs*, 78/2 (March/April 1999):35–49.

Huntley, James Robert. 1998. *Pax Democratica: A Strategy for the Twenty-First Century*. New York: St. Martin's.

Hurd, Ian. 1999. "Legitimacy and Authority in International Politics." *International Organization*, 53:379–408.

Huth, Paul K. 1996. *Standing Your Ground: Territorial Disputes and International Conflict*. Ann Arbor: University of Michigan Press.

Huth, Paul K., Christopher Gelpi, and D. Scott Bennett. 1993. "The Escalation of Great Power Militarized Disputes: Testing Rational Deterrence Theory and Structural Realism." *American Political Science Review*, 87:609–623.

IMF (International Monetary Fund). 1999. *World Economic Outlook*. October 1999. On the IMF Web site at: http://www.imf.org/external/pubs/ft/weo/1999/02/index.htm.

IMF (International Monetary Fund). 1999a. *International Capital Markets*. Washington, DC: IMF.

IMF (International Monetary Fund). 2000. *World Economic Outlook*. May 2000. On the IMF Web site at: http://www.imf.org/external/pubs/ft/weo/2000/01/index.htm.

Iriye, Akira. 1997. *Cultural Internationalism and World Order*. Baltimore, MD: Johns Hopkins University Press.

Ishiyama, John T., and Marijke Breuning. 1998. *Ethnopolitics in the "New" Europe*. Boulder, CO: Lynne Rienner.

Iyer, Pico. 1996. "The Global Village Finally Arrives." In *Annual Editions: Global Issues 96/97*. Guilford, CT: Dushkin/McGraw-Hill.

Jackson, Robert. 1999. "TI Sovereignty in World Politics: A Glance at the Conceptual and Historical Landscape." *Political Studies*, 47:431–56.

James, Alan. 1999. "The Practice of Sovereign Statehood in Contemporary International Society." *Political Studies*, 47: 457–573.

James, Patrick, and Frank Harvey. 1992. "The Most Dangerous Game: Superpower Rivalry in International Crises, 1948–1985." *The Journal of Politics*, 54:25–53.

James, Patrick, and Jean-Sebastain Rioux. 1998. "International Crises and Linkage Politics: The Experiences of the United States, 1953–1994." *Political Research Quarterly*, 51/3: 781–812.

Jaquette, Jane S. 1997. "Women in Power: From Tokenism to Critical Mass." *Foreign Policy*, 108:23–97.

Javeline, Debra. 1999. "Protest and Passivity: How Russians Respond to Not Getting Paid." Davis Center for Russian Studies, Harvard University. Published on the Web at: http://data.fas.harvard.edu/~javeline/draft1.htm.

Jensen, Lloyd. 1982. *Explaining Foreign Policy*. Englewood Cliffs, NJ: Prentice Hall.

Jervis, Robert. 1999. "Realism, Neoliberalism, and Cooperation: Understanding the Debate." *International Security*, 24:42–63.

Jett, Dennis C. 2000. *Why Peacekeeping Fails*. New York: St. Martin's.

Johansen, Robert C. 1994. "Building World Security: The Need for Strengthened International Institutions." In *World Security: Challenges for a New Century*, ed. Michael T. Klare and Daniel C. Thomas. New York: St. Martin's.

Johnson, Bryan T. 1991. "The World Bank: Promoting Stagnation." *The World & I*, February.

Johnson, James Turner. 1997. *The Holy War Idea in Western and Islamic Traditions*. University Park: Pennsylvania State University Press.

Johnston, Alastair I., and Robert S. Ross, eds. *Engaging China: The Management of an Emerging Power*. New York: Routledge.

Jones, Howard. 1988. *The Course of American Diplomacy*, 2nd ed. Chicago: Dorsey.

Jones, R. J. Barry. 1999. "Globalization and Change in the International Political Economy." *International Affairs*, 75/2: 357–369.

Joyner, Christopher C. 2000. "The Reality and Relevance of International Law in the Twenty-First Century." In *The Global Agenda: Issues and Perspectives*, ed. Charles W. Kegley, Jr. and Eugene R. Wittkopf. Boston: McGraw-Hill.

Kaempfer, Willliam H., and Anton D. Lowenberg. 1999. "Unilateral Versus Multilateral International Sanctions: A Public Choice Perspective." *International Studies Quarterly*, 43:37–58.

Kagan, Robert, and Gary Schmitt. 1998. "Now May We Please Defend Ourselves?" *Commentary*, July 1998:21–25.

Kaplan, Robert D. 1994. "The Coming Anarchy." *The Atlantic*, February.

Kaplan, Robert D. 1999. "Was Democracy Just a Moment?" In *Stand: Contending Issue and Opinion, World Politics*, ed., Marc Genest. Boulder, CO: Coursewise Publishing.

Karatnycky, Adrian. 1997. *Freedom in the World: The Annual Survey of Political Rights & Civil Liberties*. New York: Freedom House.

Karl, Terry Lynn. 1999. "The Perils of the Petro-State: Reflections on the Paradox of Plenty." *Journal of International Affairs*, 53:31–51.

Karmel, Solomon. 2000. *China and the People's Liberation Army: Great Power or Struggling Developing State?* New York: St. Martin's.

Katzenstein, Lawrence. 1997. "Change, Myth, and the Reunification of China." In *Culture & Foreign Policy*, ed. Valerie M. Hudson. Boulder, CO: Lynne Rienner.

Kaufman, Stuart J. 1997. "The Fragmentation and Consolidation of International Systems." *International Organization*, 51:755–776.

Keane, John. 1994. "Nations, Nationalism, and Citizens in Europe." *International Social Science Journal*, 140:169–184.

Keating, Michael. 1996. *Nations against the State: The New Politics of Nationalism in Quebec, Catalonia, and Scotland*. New York: St. Martin's.

Keck, Margaret E., and Kathrn Sikkink. 1999. *Activists beyond Borders: Advocacy Network in International Politics*. Ithaca, NY: Cornell University Press.

Kegley, Charles W., Jr., and Gregory A. Raymond. 1999. *How Nations Make Peace*. New York: St. Martin's.

Keller, Edmund J., and Donald Rothchild, eds. 1996. *Africa in the New International Order: Rethinking State Sovereignty and Regional Security*. Boulder, CO: Lynne Rienner.

Keller, William W. 1995. *Arm in Arm: The Political Economy of the Global Arms Trade*. New York: Basic Books.

Keller, William W., and Janne E. Nolan. 1997. "The Arms Trade: Business As Usual?" *Foreign Policy*, 109:113–125.

Kennedy, Paul. 1988. *The Rise and Fall of the Great Powers*. New York: Random House.

Kennedy, Robert F. 1969. *Thirteen Days: A Memoir of the Cuban Missile Crisis*. New York: W. W. Norton.

Kent, Ann. 1999. *China, the United Nations, and Human Rights: The Limits of Compliance*. Philadelphia: University of Pennsylvania Press.

Keohane, Robert O. 1998. "International Institutions: Can Interdependence Work?" *Foreign Policy*, 110:82–96.

Keohane, Robert O., and Lisa L. Martin. 1995. "The Promise of Institutionalist Theory." *International Security*, 20/1:39–51.

Keohane, Robert O., and Joseph S. Nye, Jr. 1999. "Globalization: What's New? What's Not? (And So What?)." *Foreign Policy*, 114:104–119.

Keylor, William. 1996. *The Twentieth Century World*. New York: Oxford University Press.

Kim, Samuel S. 1997. "China as a Great Power." *Current History*, 96:246–251.

Kimura, Masato, and David A. Welch. 1998. "Specifying 'Interests': Japan's Claim to the Northern Territories and Its Implications for International Relations Theory." *International Studies Quarterly*, 42:213–244.

Kissinger, Henry A. 1970. "The Just and the Possible." In *Negotiation and Statecraft: A Selection of Readings*, U.S. Congress, Senate Committee on Government Operations, 91st Cong., 2nd sess.

Kissinger, Henry A. 1979. *The White House Years*. Boston: Little, Brown.

Kissinger, Henry A. 1994. *Diplomacy*. New York: Simon & Schuster.

Klare, Michael T., and Lora Lumpe. 1998. "Fanning the Flames of War: Conventional Arms Transfers in the 1990s." In *World Security: Challenges for a New Century*, 3rd ed., eds. Michael T. Klare and Yogesh Chandrani. New York: St. Martin's.

Klare, Michael T., and Yogesh Chandrani, eds. 1998. *World Security: Challenges for a New Century*, 3rd ed. New York: St. Martin's.

Klotz, Audie. 1997. *Norms in International Relations: The Struggle against Apartheid*. Ithaca, NY: Cornell University Press.

Knutsen, Torbjorn L. 1999. *The Rise and Fall of World Orders*. New York: St. Martin's.

Kocs, Stephen A. 1995. "Territorial Disputes and Interstate War, 1945–1987." *Journal of Politics*, 57:159–175.

Koehn, Peter H., and Olatunde J. B. Ojo. 1999. *Making Aid Work: Innovative Approaches for Africa at the Turn of the Century*. Lanham, MD: University Press of America.

Koll, Steven. 1997. *Americans on Expanding NATO: A Study of U.S. Public Attitudes*. College Park, MD: Center for the Study of Policy Attitudes and Center for International and Security Studies.

Korbin, Stephen. 1996. "The Architecture of Globalization: State Sovereignty in a Networked Global Economy." In *Globalization, Governments and Competition*. Oxford, U.K.: Oxford University Press.

Korey, William. 1998. *NGOs and the Universal Declaration of Human Rights: The Curious Grapevine*. New York: St. Martin's.

Koubi, Vally. 1999. "Military Technology Races." *International Organization*, 53:537–565.

Krasner, Stephen D. 1999. *Sovereignty: Organized Hypocrisy*. Princeton, NJ: Princeton University Press.

Krause, Keith, and W. Andy Knight, eds. 1995. *State, Society, and the UN System: Perspectives on Multilateralism*. Tokyo: United Nations University Press.

Kriesberg, Louis. 1992. *International Conflict Resolution*. New Haven, CT: Yale University Press.

Krosnick, Jon, and Shibley Telhami. 1995. "Public Attitudes toward Israel: A Study of the Attentive and Issue Publics." *International Studies Quarterly*, 39:535–554.

Krugman, Paul. 1998. "America the Boastful." *Foreign Affairs*, 77/3:32–45.

Ku, Charlotte, and Paul F. Diehl. 1998. *International Law: Classic and Contemporary Readings*. Boulder, CO: Lynne Rienner.

Kugler, Jacek, and Douglas Lemke, eds. 1996. *Parity and War: Evaluations and Extensions of the War Ledger*. Ann Arbor: University of Michigan Press.

Kunihiro, Masao. 1997. "The Decline and Fall of Pacifism." *Bulletin of the Atomic Scientists*, 36 (January/February):35–39.

Kurth, James. 1994. "The *Real* Clash." *National Interest*, 37:3–15.

Kuttner, Robert. 1998. "Globalism Bites Back." *American Prospect*, 37 (March-April, 1998):6–8.

Kydd, Andrew. 2000. "Arms Races and Arms Control: Modeling the Hawk Perspective." *American Journal of Political Science*, 44:228–244.

Lackey, Douglas. 1989. *The Ethics of War and Peace*. Englewood Cliffs, NJ: Prentice Hall.

Ladd, Everett C., Jr., and Karlyn H. Bowman. 1996. *Public Opinion in America and Japan*. Washington, DC: AEI Press.

Landau, Alice, and Richard Whitman, eds. 1997. *Rethinking the European Union: Institutions, Interests, and Identities*. New York: St. Martin's.

Lapid, Yosef, and Friedrich Kratochwil. 1996. *The Return of Culture and Identity in IR Theory*. Boulder, CO: Lynne Rienner.

Larsen, Jeffrey A., and Gregory J. Rattray, eds. 1996. *Arms Control: Toward the Twenty-First Century*. Boulder, CO: Lynne Rienner.

Latham, Robert. 1997. *The Liberal Moment: Modernization, Security, and the Making of the Postwar International World*. New York: Columbia University Press.

Lauren, Paul Gordon. 1998. *The Evolution of International Human Rights*. Philadelphia: University of Pennsylvania Press.

Lawrence, Philip K. 1998. *Modernity and War: The Creed of Absolute Violence*. New York: St. Martin's.

Lefebvre, Jeffrey A. 1996. "Middle East Conflicts and Middle Level Power Intervention in the Horn of Africa." *Middle East Journal*, 50:387–404.

Legro, Jeffrey W. 1996. "Culture and Preferences in the International Cooperation Two-Step." *American Political Science Review*, 90:118–137.

Legro, Jeffrey W. 1997. "Which Norms Matter: Revisiting the 'Failure' of Internationalism." *International Organization*, 51:31–63.

Legro, Jeffrey W., and Andrew Moravcsik. 1999. "Is Anybody Still a Realist?" *International Security*, 24/ 2:5–55.

Lemke, Douglas, and Suzanne Warner. 1996. "Power Parity, Commitment to Change, and War." *International Studies Quarterly*, 40:235–260.

Lensu, Maria, and Jan-Sefan Fritz, eds. 1999. *Value Pluralism, Normative Theory, and International Relations*. New York: St. Martin's.

Lepgold, Joseph. 1998. "Is Anyone Listening? International Relations Theory and the Problem of Policy Relevance." *Political Science Quarterly*, 113:43–63.

L'Etang, Hugh. 1970. *The Pathology of Leadership*. New York: Hawthorne Books.

Levi, Werner. 1991. *Contemporary International Law*, 2nd ed. Boulder, CO: Westview.

Lewis, Bernard. 1996. *The Middle East: A Brief History of the Last 2,000 Years*. New York: Scribner.

Li Chien-pin. 1996. "Fear, Greed, or Garage Sale: The Analysis of Defense Spending in East Asia." Paper presented at the International Studies Association convention, San Diego.

Liddle, William, and Saiful Mujani. 2000. "The Triumph of Leadership: Explaining the 1999 Indonesian Vote." Paper presented at the International Political Science Association convention, August 2000, Quebec, Canada.

Lincoln, Edward J. 1998. "Japan's Financial Mess." *Foreign Affairs*, 77/3:57–66.

Lind, Michael. 1994. "In Defense of Liberal Nationalism." *Foreign Affairs*, 73(3):87–99.

Lindsay, James M. 1994. "Congress, Foreign Policy, and the New Institutionalism." *International Studies Quarterly*, 38:281–304.

Linklater, Andrew. 1999. "The Evolving Spheres of International Justice." *International Affairs*, 75:473–482.

Lipschutz, Ronnie D., and Judith Mayer. 1996. *Global Civil Society and Global Environmental Governance: The Politics of Nature from Place to Planet*. Albany: State University of New York.

Litfin, Karen T. 1994. *Ozone Discourses: Science and Politics in Global Environmental Cooperation*. New York: Columbia University Press.

Lopez, George A., Jackie G. Smith, and Ron Pagnucco. 1995. "The Global Tide." *Bulletin of the Atomic Scientists*, 51/6 (July/August):33–39.

Love, Herbert. 1996. "Lessons of Liberia: ECOMOG and Regional Peacekeeping." *International Security*, 21:145–176.

Lugo, Luis E. 1996. *Sovereignty at the Crossroads? Morality and International Politics in the Post–Cold War Era*. Lanham, MD: Rowman & Littlefield.

Lustick, Ian S. 1997. "The Absence of Middle Eastern Great Powers: Political 'Backwardness' in Historical Perspective." *International Organization*, 51:653–684.

Mace, Gordon, and Jean-Philippe Therien, eds. 1996. *Foreign Policy and Regionalism in the Americas*. Boulder, CO: Lynne Rienner.

Macesich, George. 1997. *World Economy at the Crossroads*. Westport, CT: Praeger.

MacIver, Don. 1999. *The Politics of Multinational States*. New York: St. Martin's.

Mahbubani, Kishore. 1994. "The Dangers of Decadence." *Foreign Affairs*, 72/4 (September/October):10–14.

Manning, Robert A. 1998. "The Nuclear Age: The Next Chapter." *Foreign Policy*, 109:70–84.

Mansbach, Richard W. 1996. "Neo-This and Neo-That: Or, 'Play It Sam' (Again and Again)." *Mershon International Studies Review*, 40:90–95.

Mansbach, Richard W., and Edward Rhodes, eds. 2000. *Global Politics in a Changing World*. Boston: Houghton Mifflin.

Mansfield, Edward D., and Helen V. Milner. 1999. "The New Wave of Regionalism." *International Organization*, 53: 589–628.

Mansfield, Edward D., and Rachel Bronson. 1997. "Alliances, Preferential Trading Arrangements, and International Trade." *American Political Science Review*, 91:94–106.

Margulis-Ohnuma, Zachary. 1999. "The Unavoidable Correlative: Extraterritorial Power and the United States Constitution." *Journal of International Law & Politics* 32:147–203.

Maoz, Zeev. 1996. *Domestic Sources of Global Change*. Ann Arbor: University of Michigan Press.

Marshall, Monty G. 1999. *Third World War: System, Process, and Conflict Dynamics*. Lanham, MD: Rowman & Littlefield.

Matheson, Michael J. 1997. "The Opinions of the International Court of Justice on the Threat or Use of Nuclear Weapons." *American Journal of International Law*, 91:417–436.

Mattli, Walter, and Anne-Marie Slaughter. 1998. "Revisiting the European Court of Justice." *International Organization*, 52:177–210.

May, Ernest R. 1994. "The 'Great Man' Theory of Foreign Policy." Review of Henry Kissinger. *Diplomacy*. *New York Times Book Review*, April 3.

May, Greg. 1998. "China and the World." *The World & I* (October):52–57.

Mayall, James. 1999. "Sovereignty, Nationalism, and Self-Determination." *Political Studies*, 47/3:474–502.

Maynes, Charles William. 1998. "The Perils of (and for) an Imperial America." *Foreign Policy*, 111:503–521.

McCormick, John. 1999. *Understanding the European Union*. Boulder, CO: Westview Press.

McKay, David. 1999. "The Political Sustainability of European Monetary Union." *British Journal of Political Science*, 29: 463–486.

McKim, Robert, and Jeff McMahan. 1997. *The Morality of Nationalism*. New York: Oxford University Press.

Mearsheimer, John J. 1995. "The False Promise of International Institutions." *International Security*, 19/3:5–49.

Menon, Rajan. 1997. "The Once and Future Superpower." *Bulletin of the Atomic Scientists*, 36 (January/February):29–34.

Mercer, Jonathan C. 1996. *Reputation and International Politics*. Ithaca, NY: Cornell University Press.

Meunier, Sophie. 2000. "What Single Voice? European Institutions and EU-US Trade Negotiations. *International Organization*, 54/2:103–135.

Meyer, John W., David John Frank, and Nancy Brandon Tuma. 1997. "The Structuring of a World Environmental Regime, 1870–1990." *International Organization*, 51:623–652.

Meyer, Mary K., and Elisabeth Prügel, eds. 1999. *Gender Politics in Global Governance*. Lanham, MD: Rowman & Littlefield.

Midlarsky, Manus. 1999. "Democracy and Islam: Implications for Civilizational Conflict and the Democratic Peace." *International Studies Quarterly*, 42:485–512.

Miller, Benjamin. 1995. *When Opponents Cooperate: Great Power Conflict and Collaboration in World Politics.* Ann Arbor: University of Michigan Press.

Miller, David. 1995. *On Nationality.* Oxford, U.K.: Clarendon Press.

Miller, Marian A. L. 1995. *The Third World in Global Politics.* Boulder, CO: Lynne Rienner.

Milner, Helen V. 1997. *Interests, Institutions, and Information: Domestic Politics and International Relations.* Princeton, NJ: Princeton University Press.

Milner, Helen V. 1998. "International Political Economy: Beyond Hegemonic Stability." *Foreign Policy,* 110:112–123.

Milner, Helen V., and B. Peter Rosendorff. 1997. "Democratic Politics and International Trade Negotiations." *Journal of Conflict Resolution,* 412:117–146.

Mirsky, Georgiy I. 1997. *On Ruins of Empire: Ethnicity and Nationalism in the Former Soviet Union.* Westport, CT: Greenwood.

Mo, Jongryn. 1994. "The Logic of Two-Level Games with Endogenous Domestic Coalitions." *Journal of Conflict Resolution,* 38:402–422.

Mockaitis, Thomas R. 1999. *Peace Operations and Interstate Conflict: The Sword or the Olive Branch.* Westport, CT: Praeger.

Modelski, George, and William R. Thompson. 1998. "The Long and the Short of Global Politics in the Twenty-First Century: An Evolutionary Approach." Paper presented at the International Studies Association convention, Minneapolis.

Moller, Bjorn. 1995. *Dictionary of Alternative Defense.* Boulder, CO: Lynne Rienner.

Moon, Bruce E. 1996. *Dilemmas of International Trade.* Boulder, CO: Westview.

Moore, Gale. 1998. *Climate of Fear: Why We Shouldn't Worry about Global Warming.* Washington, DC: Cato Institute.

Moore, Margaret. 1997. "On National Self-Determination." *Political Studies,* 45:900–915.

Moran, Theodore H. 1990. "The Globalization of America's Defense Industries: Managing the Threat of Foreign Dependence." *International Security,* 15:57–99.

Moravcsik, Andrew. 1997. "Taking Preferences Seriously: A Liberal Theory of International Politics." *International Organization,* 51:513–554.

Moravcsik, Andrew. 2000. "The Origin of Human Rights Regimes: Democratic Delegation in Postwar Europe." *International Organization,* 54:217–252.

Morgan, T. Clifton, and Christopher J. Anderson. 1999. "Domestic Support and Diversionary External Conflict in Great Britain, 1950–1992." *Journal of Politics,* 61:799–814.

Morgenthau, Hans W. 1973, 1986. *Politics among Nations.* New York: Knopf. Morgenthau's text was first published in 1948 and periodically thereafter. Two sources are used herein. One is the fifth edition, published in 1973. The second is an edited abstract drawn from pp. 3–4, 10–12, 14, 27–29, and 31–35 of the third edition, published in 1960. The abstract appears in Vasquez 1986:37–41. Pages cited for Morgenthau 1986 refer to Vasquez's, not Morgenthau's, book.

Morse, Edward L. 1999. "A New Political Economy of Oil?" *Journal of International Affairs,* 53:1–30.

Mortimer, Edward, and Robert Fine. 1999. *People, Nation, and State: The Meaning of Ethnicity and Nationalism.* New York: St. Martin's.

Mott, William H., IV. 1997. *The Economic Basis of Peace: Linkages between Economic Growth and International Conflict.* Westport, CT: Greenwood.

Mower, A. Glenn, Jr. 1997. *The Convention of the Rights of the Child: International Law Support for Children.* Westport, CT: Greenwood.

Murray, A. J. H. 1996. "The Moral Politics of Hans Morgenthau." *The Review of Politics,* 58:81–109.

Murray, Geoffrey. 1998. *China: The Next Superpower: Dilemmas in Change and Continuity.* New York: St. Martins.

Murray, Shoon Kathleen. 1997. *Anchors against Change: American Opinion Leaders' Beliefs after the Cold War.* Ann Arbor: University of Michigan Press.

Musgrave, Thomas D. 1997. *Self Determination and National Minorities.* Oxford, U.K.: Clarendon.

Namkung, Gon. 1998. *Japanese Images of the United States and Other Nations: A Comparative Study of Public Opinion and Foreign Policy.* Doctoral dissertation. Storrs, CT: University of Connecticut.

Nathan, Andrew. 1998. *China's Transition.* New York: Columbia University Press.

Neack, Laura. 1995. "UN Peace-Keeping: In the Interest of Community or Self?" *Journal of Peace Research,* 32:181–196.

Neuman, Stephanie. 1998. *International Relations Theory and the Third World.* New York: St. Martin's.

Neumann, Iver B., and Ole Weaver, eds. 1997. *The Future of International Relations: Masters in the Making.* New York: Routledge.

Nevin, John A. 1996. "War Initiation and Selection by Consequences." *Journal of Peace Research,* 33:99–108.

Noël, Alain, and Jean-Philippe Thérien. 1996. "Political Parties, Domestic Institutions, and Foreign Aid." Paper presented at the International Studies Association convention, San Diego.

Norman, Richard. 1995. *Ethics, Killing, and War.* Cambridge, U.K.: Cambridge University Press.

Nugent, Neill, ed. 1997. *At the Heart of the Union: Studies of the European Commission.* New York: St. Martin's.

Nye, Joseph. 2000. *Understanding International Conflicts,* 3rd ed. New York: Longman.

O'Driscoll, Gerald P., Jr., Kim R. Holmes, and Melanie Kirkpatrick. 2000. *2000 Index of Economic Freedom.* Washington, DC and New York: The Heritage Foundation and the *Wall Street Journal.*

O'Leary, Brendan. 1997. "On the Nature of Nationalism: An Appraisal of Ernest Gellner's Writings on Nationalism." *British Journal of Political Science,* 27:191–222.

Olmer, Lionel H. 1989. "Statement on EC 1992 and the Requirement for U.S. Industry and Government Partnership." *Europe 1992.* Hearings before the U.S. Congress, House of Representatives, Sub-committee on Trade of the Committee on Ways and Means. March 20.

Oneal, John R., and Bruce M. Russett. 1997. "The Classical Liberals Were Right: Democracy, Interdependence, and Conflict, 1950–1985. *International Studies Quarterly,* 41:267–294.

Oneal, John R., and Bruce Russett. 1999. "The Kantian Peace: The Pacific Benefits of Democracy, Interdependence, and International Organizations, 1885–1992." *World Politics,* 52: 1–37.

O'Neill, Barry O. "Power and Satisfaction in the Security Council." In *The Once and Future Security Council,* ed. Bruce Russett. New York: St. Martin's.

Opello, Walter C., Jr., and Stephen Rosow. 1999. *The Nation-State and Global Order: A Historical Introduction to Contemporary Politics.* Boulder, CO: Lynne Rienner.

O'Reilly, Marc J. 1997. "'Following Ike': Explaining Canadian-U.S. Co-operation during the 1956 Suez Crisis." *Journal of Commonwealth & Comparative Studies*, 35/3:75–107.

Orme, John. 1998. "The Utility of Force in a World of Scarcity." *International Security*, 22/3:138–167.

Osiander, Andreas. 1998. "Rereading Early Twentieth-Century IR Theory: Idealism Revisited." *International Studies Quarterly*, 42:409–432.

Osiel, Mark. 1999. *Obeying Orders: Atrocity, Military Discipline, and the Law of War*. New Brunswick, NJ: Transaction.

Ostrom, Charles W., and H. J. Aldrich. 1978. "The Relationship between Size and Stability in the Major Power International System." *American Journal of Political Science*, 22:743–771.

Pace, John P. 1998. "The Development of Human Rights Law in the United Nations, its Control and Monitoring Machine." *International Social Science Journal*, 50:499–512.

Pagden, Anthony. 1998. "The Genesis of 'Governance' and Enlightenment Conceptions of the Cosmopolitan World Order." *International Social Science Journal*, 50:7–16.

Papayoanou, Paul A. 1997. "Economic Interdependence and the Balance of Power." *International Studies Quarterly*, 41:113–140.

Pape, Robert A. 1997. "Why Economic Sanctions Do Not Work." *International Security*, 22:90–136.

Pape, Robert A. 1998. "Why Economic Sanctions Still Do Not Work." *International Security*, 23:66–77.

Parenti, Michael. 1992. "U.S. Intervention: More Foul than Foolish." In *Competing Conceptions of American Foreign Policy*, ed. Stanley J. Michalak, Jr. New York: HarperCollins.

Park, Bert Edward. 1994. *Ailing, Aging, Addicted: Studies of Compromised Leadership*. Lexington, KY: University Press of Kentucky.

Parker, Christopher S. 1999. "New Weapons for Old Problems: Conventional Proliferation and Military Effectiveness in Developing States." *International Security*, 23/4:119–147.

Paterson, Thomas G. J., Garry Clifford, and Kenneth J. Hagen. 2000. *American Foreign Relations: A History. Vol. II: Since 1945*, 5th ed. Boston: Houghton Mifflin.

Pauly, Louis W., and Simon Reich. 1997. "National Structures and Multinational Corporate Behavior: Enduring Differences in the Age of Globalization." *International Organization*, 51:1–30.

Perlmutter, Amos, and Ted G. Carpenter. 1998. "NATO's Expensive Trip East." *Foreign Affairs*, 77 (January):2–6.

Peterson, John, and Elizabeth Bomberg. 1999. *Decision-Making in the European Union*. New York: St. Martin's.

Peterson, M. J. 1997. "The Use of Analogies in Developing Outer Space Law. *International Organization*, 51:245–274.

Peterson, Susan. 1996. *Crisis Bargain and the State: The Domestic Politics of International Conflict*. Ann Arbor: University of Michigan Press.

Pettman, Ralph, ed. 1996. *Understanding International Political Economy, with Readings for the Fatigued*. Boulder, CO: Lynne Rienner.

Phan, Chau T. 1996. "International Nongovernmental Organizations, Global Negotiations, and Global Activist Networks: The Emergence of INGOs as Partners in the Global Governance Process." *International Organization*, 51:591–622.

Philpott, Daniel. 1999. "Westphalia, Authority, and International Society." *Political Studies*, 47/3:566–589.

Pickering, Jeffrey, and William R. Thompson. 1998. "Stability in a Fragmenting World: Interstate Military Force, 1946–1988." *Political Research Quarterly*, 51:241–264.

Piening, Christopher. 1997. *Global Europe: The European Union in World Affairs*. Boulder, CO: Lynne Rienner.

Pierre, Andrew J., ed. 1997. *Cascade of Arms: Managing Conventional Weapons Proliferation*. Washington, DC: Brookings Institution.

Pollins, Brian M. 1996. "Global Political Order, Economic Change, and Armed Conflict: Coevolving Systems and the Use of Force." *American Political Science Review*, 90:103–117.

Porter, Gareth, and Janet Welsh Brown. 1996. *Global Environmental Politics*, 2nd ed. Boulder, CO: Westview.

Poulton, Hugh. 1997. *Top Hat, Grey Wolf and Crescent: Turkish Nationalism and the Turkish Republic*. New York: New York University Press.

Powell, Robert. 1996. "Stability and the Distribution of Power." *World Politics*, 48:239–267.

Powlick, Philip. J. 1995. "The Sources of Public Opinion for American Foreign Policy Officials." *International Studies Quarterly*, 39:427–52.

Powlick, Philip J., and Andrew Z. Katz. 1998. "Defining the American Public Opinion/Foreign Policy Nexus." *Mershon International Studies Review*, 42/1:29–62.

Preston, Christopher. 1998. *Enlargement and Integration in the European Union*. New York: Routledge.

Price, Richard M. 1995. "A Genealogy of the Chemical Weapons Taboo." *International Organization*, 49:73–104.

Price, Richard M. 1998. *The Chemical Weapons Taboo*. Ithaca, NY: Cornell University Press.

Pritchard, Sarah, ed. 1998. *Indigenous Peoples, the United Nations, and Human Rights*. New York: St. Martin's.

Rabkin, Jeremy. 1994. "Threats to U.S. Sovereignty." *Commentary*, 97(3):41–47.

Ratner, Steven R. 1996. *The New UN Peacekeeping: Building Peace in Lands of Conflict after the Cold War*. New York: St. Martin's.

Ratner, Steven R. 1998. "International Law: The Trials of Global Norms." *Foreign Policy*, 110:65–81.

Raustiala, Kal. 1997. "State, NGOs, and International Environmental Institutions." *International Studies Quarterly*, 41:719–770.

Razavi, Shahra. 1999. "Seeing Poverty through a Gender Lens." *International Social Science Journal*, 51:473–483.

Reich, Walter, ed. 1998. *Origins of Terrorism : Psychologies, Ideologies, Theologies, States of Mind*. Princton, N.J.: Woodrow Wilson Center Press.

Renan, Ernest. 1995. "Qu'est-ce Qu'une Nation?" In *Nationalism*, ed. John Hutchinson and Anthony D. Smith. New York: Oxford University Press.

Renshon, Stanley A. 1995. "Character, Judgment, and Political Leadership: Promise, Problems, and Prospects of the Clinton Presidency." In *The Clinton Presidency: Campaigning, Governing, and the Psychology of Leadership*, ed. Stanley Renshon. Boulder, CO: Westview.

Renshon, Stanley A. 2000. "After the Fall: The Clinton Presidency in Psychological Perspective." *Political Science Quarterly*, 115: 41–66.

Reynolds, Andrew. 1999. "Women in the Legislatures and Executives of the World: Knocking at the Highest Glass Ceiling." *World Politics*, 514: 547–569.

Rhein, Wendy. 1998. "The Feminization of Poverty: Unemployment in Russia." *Journal of International Affairs*, 52:351–367.

Rhodes, Carolyn, ed. 1997. *The European Union in the World Community*. Boulder, CO: Lynne Rienner.

Richards, Diana. 1993. "A Chaotic Model of Power Concentration in the International System." *International Studies Quarterly*, 37:55–72.

Richardson, Jeremy, ed. 1997. *European Union: Power and Policy-Making*. New York: Routledge.

Riddell-Dixon, Elizabeth. 1996. "Canada and the Fourth UN Conference on Women: NGO-Government Relations." Paper presented at the International Studies Association convention, San Diego.

Rieff, David. 1996. "An Age of Genocide." *New Republic* (January 29, 1996):27–36.

Rielly, John E. 1995. "The Public Mood at Mid-Decade." *Foreign Policy*, 82:79–96.

Rielly, John E. 1999. "Americans and the World: A Survey at Century's End." *Foreign Policy*, 114:97–113.

Ripley, Brian. 1995. "Cognition, Culture, and Bureaucratic Politics." In *Foreign Policy Analysis*, ed. Laura Neack, Jeane A. K. Hey, and Patrick J. Haney. Englewood Cliffs, NJ: Prentice Hall.

Roberts, Adam. 1996. "From San Francisco to Sarajevo: The UN and the Use of Force." *Survival*, 37/4 (Winter):7–28.

Robertson, Charles L. 1997. *International Politics since World War II: A Short History*. Armonk, NY: M. E. Sharpe.

Rodrik, Dani. 1998. *Has Globalization Gone Too Far?* Washington, DC: Institute for International Economics.

Rogers, J. Phillip. 1987. "The Crisis Bargaining Code Model: A Cognitive Schema Approach to Crisis Decision-Making." Presented at the International Studies Association convention, April, Washington, DC.

Roht-Arriaza, Naomi. 1999. "Establishing a Framework." *Journal of International Affairs*, 52:473–492.

Rose, Gideon. 1998. "Neoclassical Realism and Theories of Foreign Policy." *World Politics*, 51:144–169.

Rosenau, James N. 1990. *Turbulence in World Politics: A Theory of Change and Continuity*. Princeton, NJ: Princeton University Press.

Rosenau, James N. 1997. *Along the Domestic-Foreign Frontier: Exploring Governance in a Turbulent World*. Cambridge, U.K.: Cambridge University Press.

Rosenau, James N. 1998. "The Dynamism of a Turbulent World." In *World Security: Challenges for a New Century*, 3rd ed., ed. Michael T. Klare and Yogesh Chandran. New York: St. Martin's.

Rosenau, James N., and Mary Durfee. 1995. *Thinking Theory Thoroughly*. Boulder, CO: Westview.

Rosenblatt, Lionel, and Larry Thompson. 1998. "The Door of Opportunity: Creating a Permanent Peacekeeping Force." *World Policy Journal*. 15:36–47.

Rothgeb, John M., Jr. 1993. *Defining Power: Influence and Force in the Contemporary International System*. New York: St. Martin's.

Rothkopf, David J. 1998. "Cyberpolitik: The Changing Nature of Power in the Information Age." *Journal of International Affairs*. 51:325–360.

Rourke, John T. 1990. *Making Foreign Policy: United States, Soviet Union, China*. Pacific Grove, CA: Brooks/Cole.

Rourke, John T. 1993. *Presidential Wars and American Democracy: Rally 'Round the Chief*. New York: Paragon.

Rourke, John T. 1994. "United States-China Trade: Economics, Human Rights, and Strategic Issues." *In Depth*, 4/3:135–162.

Rourke, John, and Richard Clark. 1998. "Making U.S. Foreign Policy toward China in the Clinton Administration." In *After the End: Making U.S. Foreign Policy in the Post-Cold War World*, ed. James M. Scott. Durham, N.C.: Duke University Press.

Rourke, John T., Ralph G. Carter, and Mark A. Boyer. 1996. *Making American Foreign Policy*, 2nd ed. Guilford, CT: Brown & Benchmark/Dushkin.

Rourke, John T., Richard P. Hiskes, and Cyrus Ernesto Zirakzadeh. 1992. *Direct Democracy and International Politics*. Boulder, CO: Lynne Rienner.

Rusk, Dean, as told to Richard Rusk. 1990. *As I Saw It*. New York: W. W. Norton.

Russett, Bruce, ed. 1997. *The Once and Future Security Council*. New York: St. Martin's.

Russett, Bruce. 2000. "How Democracy, Interdependence, and International Organizations Create a System for Peace." In *The Global Agenda: Issues and Perspectives*, ed. Charles W. Kegley, Jr. and Eugene R. Wittkopf. Boston: McGraw-Hill.

Ryan, Stephen. 2000. *The United Nations and International Politics*. New York: St. Martin's.

Sachs, Jeffrey. 1998. "International Economics: Unlocking the Mysteries of Globalization." *Foreign Policy*, 110:97–111.

Saideman, Stephen M. 1997. "Explaining the International Relations of Secessionist Conflicts: Vulnerability versus Ethnic Ties." *International Organization*, 51:721–754.

Sanjian, Gregory S. 1998. "Cold War Imperatives and Quarrelsome Clients: Modeling U.S. and USSR Arms Transfers to India and Pakistan." *Journal of Conflict Resolution*, 42:97–127.

Sanjian, Gregory. 1999. "Promoting Stability or Instability? Arms Transfers and Regional Rivalries, 1950–1991." *International Studies Quarterly*, 43:641–670.

Sazanami, Yoko, Shujiro Urata, and Hiroki Kawai. 1994. *Measuring the Costs of Protectionism in Japan*. Washington, DC: Institute for International Economics.

Schampel, James H. 1996. "A Preponderance of Conflict over Peace: A Dialogue with Charles Gochman and Aaron Hoffman." *International Studies Notes*, 21/2 (Spring):26–27.

Schmidt, Brian C. 1997. *The Political Discourse of Anarchy*. Albany: State University of New York Press.

Schmidt, Brian C. 1998. "Lessons from the Past: Reassessing the Interwar Disciplinary History of International Relations." *International Studies Quarterly*, 42:433–460.

Schraeder, Peter J., Steven W. Hook, and Bruce Taylor. 1998. "Clarifying the Foreign Aid Puzzle: A Comparison of American, Japanese, French, and Swedish Aid Flows." *World Politics*, 50:294–324.

Schultz, Kathryn R., and David Isenberg. 1997. "Arms Control and Disarmament." In *A Global Agenda: Issues before the 52nd General Assembly of the United Nations*, ed. John Tessitore and Susan Woolfson. Lanham, MD: Rowman & Littlefield.

Schultz, Kenneth A. 1999. "Do Democratic Institutions Constrain or Inform? Contrasting Two Institutional Perspectives on Democracy and War." *International Organization*, 53:233–266.

Schulzinger, Robert D. 1989. *Henry Kissinger: Doctor of Diplomacy*. New York: Columbia University Press.

Schweller, Randall L. 1997. "New Realist Research on Alliances: Refining, Not Refuting, Waltz's Balancing Proposition." *American Political Science Review*, 4:927–930.

Schweller, Randall L., and David Priess. 1997. "A Tale of Two Realisms: Expanding the Institutions Debate." *Mershon International Studies Review*, 41:1–32.

Schweller, Randall L. 1998. *Deadly Imbalances: Tripolarity and*

Hitler's Strategy of World Conquest. New York: Columbia University Press.

Scott, Catherine V. 1996. *Gender and Development: Rethinking Modernization and Dependency Theory.* Boulder, CO: Lynne Rienner.

Sen, Amartya. 1999. *Development as Freedom.* New York: Alfred A. Knopf.

Setala, Maija. 1999. *Referendums and Democratic Government.* New York: St. Martin's.

Seymour, Michel. 2000 "Quebec and Canada at the Crossroads: A Nation within a Nation." *Nations and Nationalism,* 6:227–256.

Shaheed, Farida. 1999. "Constructing Identities: Culture, Women's Agency and the Muslim World." *International Social Science Journal,* 51:61–75.

Shambaugh, David. 2000. "China's Military Views the World: Ambivalent Security." *International Security,* 24/3:52–79.

Shambaugh, George E., IV. 1996. "Dominance, Dependence, and Political Power: Tethering Technology in the 1980s and Today." *International Studies Quarterly,* 40:559–588.

Shambaugh, George E. 2000. *States, Firms, and Power: Successful Sanctions in United States Foreign Policy.* Albany, NY: State University of New York Press.

Sharp, Paul. 1999. "For Diplomacy: Representation and the Study of International Relations." *International Studies Review,* 1:33–58.

Sherill, Robert. 1979. *Why They Call It Politics.* New York: Harcourt Brace Jovanovich.

Shevchenko, Arkady. 1985. *Breaking with Moscow.* New York: Alfred A. Knopf.

Shikaki, Khalil. 1998. "Peace Now or Hamas Later." *Foreign Affairs,* 77/4:29–43.

Shlaim, Avi. 1999. *The Iron Wall: Israel and the Arab World.* New York: W. W. Norton.

Simmons, Beth A. 1993. "Why Innovate? Founding the Bank for International Settlements." *World Politics,* 45:361–405.

Simmons, Geoff. 1998. *Vietnam Syndrome: Impact on U.S. Foreign Policy.* New York: St. Martin's.

Simon, Julian L. 1994. "More People, Greater Wealth, More Resources, Healthier Environment." In *Taking Sides: Clashing Views on Controversial Issues in World Politics,* 6th ed., ed. John T. Rourke. Guilford, CT: Dushkin.

(SIPRI) Stockholm International Peace Research Institute. Annual Editions. *SIPRI Yearbook.* Oxford, U.K.: Oxford University Press.

Sislin, John. 1994. "Arms as Influence: The Determinants of Successful Influence." *Journal of Conflict Resolution,* 38:665–689.

Smith, Steve. 1984. "Groupthink and the Hostage Rescue Mission. *British Journal of Political Science,* 15:117–126.

Snyder, Robert S. 1999. "The U.S. and Third World Revolultionary States: Understanding the Breakdown in Relations." *International Studies Quarterly,* 43:265–290.

Somit, Albert, and Steven A. Peterson. 1997. *Darwinism, Dominance, Democracy: The Biological Bases of Authoritarianism.* Westport, CT: Greenwood.

Sorensen, George. 1999. "Sovereignty: Change and Continuity in a Fundamental Institution." *Political Studies,* 47:590–609.

Soroos, Marvin S. 1997. *The Endangered Atmosphere: Preserving a Global Commons.* Norman: University of Oklahoma Press.

Spanier, John, and Eric M. Uslaner. 1993. *American Foreign Policy Making and the Democratic Dilemmas,* 6th ed. New York: Macmillan.

Spegele, Roger D. 1996. *Political Realism in International Theory.* Cambridge, U.K.: Cambridge University Press.

Speth, James Gustave. 1998. "Poverty: A Denial of Human Rights." *Journal of International Affairs,* 52:277–292.

Spiers, Edward M. 2000. *Weapons of Mass Destruction: Prospects for Proliferation.* New York: St. Martin's.

Spruyt, Hendrik. 1994. *The Sovereign State and Its Competitors: An Analysis of Systems Change.* Princeton, NJ: Princeton University Press.

Starkey, Brigid, Mark A. Boyer, and Jonathan Wilkenfeld. 1999. *Negotiating a Complex World.* Lanham, MD: Rowman & Littlefield.

Sterling-Folker, Jennifer. 1996. "Realist Environment, Liberal Process, and Domestic-Level Variables." Paper presented at the International Studies Association convention, San Diego.

Sterling-Folker, Jennifer. 1997. "Realist Environment, Liberal Process, and Domestic-Level Variables." *International Studies Quarterly,* 41:1–26.

Stoessinger, John G. 1998. *Why Nations Go to War,* 7th ed. New York: St. Martin's.

Strange, Susan. 1997. *The Retreat of the State: The Diffusion of Power in the World Economy.* New York: Cambridge University Press.

Suu Kyi, Aung San. 1995. "Freedom, Development, and Human Worth." *Journal of Democracy,* 6/2 (April):12–19.

Swanson, Timothy. 1999. "Why Is There a Biodiversity Convention? The International Interest in Centralized Development Planning." *International Affairs,* 75:307–331.

Sylvester, Christine. 1993. "Editor's Introduction: Feminists Write International Relations." *Alternatives,* 18:1–4.

Taber, Charles S. 1989. "Power Capability Indexes in the Third World." In *Power in World Politics,* ed. Richard J. Stoll and Michael D. Ward. Boulder, CO: Lynne Rienner.

Talbott, Strobe. 2000. "Self-Determination in an Interdependent World." *Foreign Policy,* 118 (Spring 2000):152–163.

Tamir, Yael. 1995. "The Enigma of Nationalism." *World Politics,* 47:418–440.

Tammen, Ronald L., et al. 2000. *Power Transitions: Strategies for the Twenty-First Century.* New York: Chatham House/Seven Bridges Press.

Tannenwald, Nina. 1999. "The Nuclear Taboo: The United States and the Normative Basis of Nuclear Non-Use." *International Organization,* 53:433–468.

Taylor, Andrew J., and John T. Rourke. 1995. "Historical Analogies in the Congressional Foreign Policy Process." *Journal of Politics,* 57:460–468.

Taylor, Paul. 1999. "The United Nations in the 1990s: Proactive Cosmopolitanism and the Issue of Sovereignty." *Political Studies,* 47: 538–565.

Taylor, Robert L., and William E. Rosenbach. 1996. *Military Leadership: In Pursuit of Excellence.* Boulder, CO: Westview.

Tehranian, Majid. 1999. *Global Communication and World Politics: Domination, Development, and Discourse.* Boulder, CO: Lynne Rienner.

Thies, Wallace J. 1998. "Deliberate and Inadvertent War in the Post–Cold War World." In *Annual Editions, American Foreign Policy 98/99,* ed. Glenn P. Hastedt. Guilford, CT: Dushkin/McGraw-Hill.

Thompson, James C., Jr. 1989. "Historical Legacies and Bureaucratic Procedures." In *Major Problems in American Foreign Policy, Vol. 2,* ed. Thomas G. Paterson. Lexington, MA: D. C. Heath.

Thompson, Kenneth W. 1994. *Fathers of International Thought: The Legacy of Political Theory*. Baton Rouge: Louisiana State University Press.

Tibi, Bassam. 1997. *Arab Nationalism: Between Islam and the Nation-State*. New York: St. Martin's.

Tickner, J. Ann. 1997. "You Just Don't Understand: Troubled Engagements between Feminists and IR Theorists." *International Studies Quarterly*, 41:611–632.

Trumbore, Peter F. 1998. "Public Opinion as a Domestic Constraint in International Negotiations: Two-Level Games in the Anglo-Irish Peace Process." *International Studies Quarterly*, 42:545–565.

Tucker, Jonathan B. 2000. *Toxic Terror: Assessing Terrorist Use of Chemical and Biological Weapons*. Cambridge, MA: MIT Press.

Turner, Frederick C., and Alejandro L. Corbacho. 2000. "New Roles for the State." *International Social Science Journal*, 163:109–120.

UN, Department of Economic and Social Affairs, Population Division. 1999. *World Population 1998* at: http://www.undp.org/popin/wdtrends/p98/p98.htm.

(UN, UNICEF) United Nations Children's Fund. Annual editions. *State of the World's Children 1998*. New York: Oxford University Press.

(UNDP) United Nations Development Programme. Annual editions. *Human Development Report*. New York: Oxford University Press.

United Nations. *See* (UN).

(U.S.) Bureau of the Census. Annual editions. *Statistical Abstract of the United States*. Washington, DC.

U.S. (CIA) Central Intelligence Agency. Annual editions. *World Fact Book*. Washington: GPO.

Van Dervort, Thomas R. 1997. *International Law and Organization*. Thousand Oaks, CA: Sage.

Vandenbroucke, Lucien. 1991. *Perilous Options: Special Operations in U.S. Foreign Policy*. Unpublished dissertation, The University of Connecticut. A manuscript based on Vandenbroucke's revised dissertation was published in 1993 under the same title by Oxford University Press.

Vasquez, John A. 1995. "Why Do Neighbors Fight? Proximity, Interaction, or Territoriality." *Journal of Peace Research*, 32:277–293.

Vasquez, John A. 1996. "Distinguishing Rivals That Go to War from Those That Do Not: A Quantitative Comparative Case Study of the Two Paths to War." *International Studies Quarterly*, 40:531–558.

Vasquez, John A. 1997. "The Realist Paradigm and Degenerative versus Progressive Research Programs: An Appraisal of Neotraditional Research on Waltz's Balancing Proposition." *American Political Science Review*, 4:899–912.

Vertzberger, Yaakov Y. I. 1994. "Collective Risk Taking: The Decisionmaking Group and Organization." Presented at the annual meeting of the International Studies Association, Washington, DC.

Vertzberger. Yaakov Y. I. 1998. *Risk Taking and Decision Making: Foreign Military Intervention Decisions*. Palo Alto, CA: Stanford University Press.

Vlahos, Michael. 1998. "Entering the Infosphere." *Journal of International Affairs*, 51:497–526.

Voeten, Erik. 2000. "Clashes in the Assembly." *International Organization*, 54:185–216.

Volgy, Thomas J., and Lawrence E. Imwalle. 1995. "Hegemonic and Bipolar Perspective on the New World Order." *American Journal of Political Science*, 39:819–834.

Walker, Stephen G., Mark Schafer, and Michael D. Young. 1998. "Systematic Procedures for Operational Code Analysis: Measuring and Modeling Jimmy Carter's Operational Code." *International Studies Quarterly*, 42:175–189.

Walker, William. 1998. "International Nuclear Relations after the Indian and Pakistani Test Explosions." *International Affairs*, 74:505–528.

Wallace, William. 1999. "The Sharing of Sovereignty: The European Paradox." *Political Studies*, 47:503–521.

Walt, Stephen M. 1996. "Alliances: Balancing and Bandwagoning." In *International Politics*, 4th ed., ed. Robert J. Art and Robert Jervis. New York: HarperCollins.

Walt, Stephen M. 1996a. *Revolution and War*. Ithaca, NY: Cornell University Press.

Walt, Stephen M. 1997. "The Progressive Power of Realism." *American Political Science Review*, 4:931–935.

Walt, Stephen M. 1997a. "Building up New Bogeymen: Review of Huntington's *The Clash of Civilizations and the Remaking of World Order*." Foreign Affairs, 76/3:132–139.

Walt, Stephen M. 1998. "International Relations: One World, Many Theories." *Foreign Policy*, 110:29–47.

Waltz, Kenneth N. 1997. "Evaluating Theories." *American Political Science Review*, 4:913–918.

Wang, Kevin H. 1996. "Presidential Responses to Foreign Policy Crises: Rational Choice and Domestic Politics." *Journal of Conflict Resolution*, 40:68–97.

Wang, Kevin H., and James Lee Ray. 1994. "Beginnings and Winners: The Fate of Initiators of Interstate Wars Involving Great Powers since 1495." *International Studies Quarterly*, 38:139–154.

Wapner, Paul. 1996. *Environmental Activism and World Civic Politics*. Albany: State University of New York.

Wapner, Paul, and Lester Edwin J. Ruiz, eds. 2000. *Principled World Politics: The Challenge of Normative International Relations at the Millennium*. Lanham, MD: Rowman & Littlefield.

Watson, James L. 2000. "China's Big Mac Attack." *Foreign Affairs*, 79/3:120–142.

Weber, Peter. 1994. "Safeguarding the Oceans." In *The State of the World, 1994*, ed. Lester R. Brown et al. New York: W. W. Norton.

Weigel, George. 1995. "Are Human Rights Still Universal?" *Commentary*, 99/2 (February):41–45.

Weiss, Linda. 1998. *The Myth of the Powerless State*. Ithaca, NY: Cornell University Press.

Weller, Marc. 1999. "On the Hazards of Foreign Travel for Dictators and Other International Criminals." *International Affairs*, 75:599–618.

Wesley, Michael. 1997. *Casualties of the New World Order: The Causes of Failure of UN Missions to Civil Wars*. New York: St. Martin's.

Wilcox, Clyde, Lara Hewitt, and Dee Allsop. 1996. "The Gender Gap in Attitudes toward the Gulf War: A Cross-National Perspective." *Journal of Peace Research* 33:67–82.

Wilhelm, Alfred D. 1994. *The Chinese at the Negotiating Table*. Washington, DC: National Defense University Press.

Willets, Peter. 1996. "From Stockholm to Rio and Beyond: The Impact of the Environmental Movement on the United Nations Consultative Arrangements for NGOs." *Review of International Studies*, 22:57–80.

Wohlforth, William C. 1999. "The Stability of a Unipolar World." *International Security*, 24/1:5–41.

Woods, Ngaire. 1995. "Economic Ideas and International Relations: Beyond Rational Neglect." *International Studies*, 39:161–180.

World Almanac and Book of Facts. Annual editions. New York: Funk & Wagnalls.

World Bank. 2000a. *World Development Indicators 2000*. Washington, DC: World Bank.

World Bank. Annual editions. *World Development Report*. New York: Oxford University Press.

World Resources Institute. Annual editions. *World Resources*. New York: Oxford University Press.

Yost, David S. 1999. *NATO Transformed: The Alliance's New Roles in International Security*. Washington, DC: United States Institute of Peace Press.

Yu Bin, ed. 1996. *Dynamics and Dilemma: Mainland, Taiwan, and Hong Kong Relations in a Changing World*. New York: Nova Science.

Yu Quanyu. 1994. "Human Rights: A Comparative Study Between China and the U.S." Presented at the Sino-American Relations Conference, cosponsored by the China Institute of Contemporary International Relations and the Washington Institute for Values in Public Policy, Beijing, China.

Zakaria, Fareed. 1993. "Is Realism Finished?" *National Interest*, 32:21–32.

Zakaria, Fareed. 1996. "Speak Softly, Carry a Veiled Threat." *New York Times Magazine*, February 18.

Zhang, Ming, and Ronald N. Montaperto. 1999. *A Triad of Another Kind*. New York: St. Martin's.

Zielonka, Jan. 1998. *Explaining Euro-Paralysis: Why Europe Is Unable to Act in International Politics*. New York: St. Martin's.

Zolo, Danilo. 1997. Cosmopolis: Prospects for World Government. Cambridge, MA: Blackwell.

Zuckerman, Mortimer B. 1998. "A Second American Century." *Foreign Affairs*, 77/3:13–31.

Zurn, Michael. 1998. "The Rise of International Environmental Politics: A Review of Current Research." *World Politics*, 50:617–649.

INDEX

Page numbers in boldface refer to glossary terms.

security, national, 40, 219, 221, 246–248

self-determination, national, 136, 137, 139–140, 150, **151**–152, 154, 155

Senate, U.S., 366, 369, 373, 375, 376

Senkako Islands, 89, 114–115

Serbia, 56–57, 142, 147, 151, 185, 186, 190, 246, 293, 307

service economies, **424**

service trade, **401**, 404, 413

Sierra Leone, 185, 193, 225, 247, 312, 379, 382, 383

signaling, 255, 281, 285, 286, 288

Singapore, 186, 304, 395

Sinocentrism, 88, 89, 94

situation, policy-making and, 85–87, 104–105, 107

situational power, **259**, 288

Small Boy Unit, 338

smallpox, 343, 346

"smart" bombs, 319, 325

"So Say the Mamas," 117

social Darwinism, **496**–497

social dignity, 483–513

social overstretch theory, **328**–329

social problems, international organization and, 217, 218, 224, 250

Somalia, 7, 40, 98, 185, 193, 327, 338

South Africa, 45, 76, 128, 189–190, 209, 236, 247, 263, 294, 306, 385

South, economic issues in, 423, 426–441, 450, 452, 453, 455, 456

Southeast Asia, China and, 89, 91

Southern Common Market (Mercosur), **478**–479

sovereign equality, 377

sovereignty, **27**, 39, 41, 47, 51, 52, 61, 77, 78, 107, 137, 138, 146, 151–153, 154, 176, **189**–191, 196, 198–200, 210–213, 291, 292, 300, 302, 303, 305, 306, 310, 314, 316, 317, 382–383, 391; China and, 90, 93; feudal system and, 196–197; international organization and, 215, 223, 224, 239; Palestine and, 192–193; Tibet and, 194–195

Soviet Union, 26, 69, 84, 85, 96–97, 112, 114, 128, 138–140, 144, 150, 172, 177, 192, 193, 196, 201, 206, 248, 256, 257, 264, 268, 270, 282, 307, 327, 334, 340, 342, 344–347, 349–350, 355, 363, 365, 369, 371, 393; China and, 36; cold war and, 35–36, 48, 111, 124, 127; collapse of, 36–37, 40, 48, 265; NATO and, 56; polar system and, 63–64; UN and, 235, 242

Spain, 31–32, 64, 138, 151, 196, 198, 199, 202, 226, 228, 244, 260, 310–311

Special Drawing Rights (SDRs), **464**

Sri Lanka, 150, 237, 259, 304–305

Stalin, Josef, 122, 140, 172, 201

standard of living, 26, 33, 43, 45, 75, 321, 403, 406, 409, 411

state, 132, 133, 134, 135, 136, 137, 138, 140, 141, 145–155, 176, 178, **189**–213, 215, 218–221, 223–224, 291, 292, 305–309, 321–322, 393; authority of, 37–40, 48, **52**, 77, 81–107; emergence of, 26–27, 47

state terrorism, **340**–341

state-centric system, **52**, 77, 160, 164, 173, 392, 483

state-level analysis, **23**, 24, 81–107, 320, 321–322

status quo situations, **87**

stoicism, 158–159, 160, 187

Strategic Arms Limitation Talks I (SALT I), **362**, 363, 365

Strategic Arms Limitation Talks II (SALT II), **362**, 363, 365

Strategic Arms Reduction Talks I (START I), 362, 363, 365, 367, 387

Strategic Arms Reduction Talks II (START II), 362, 363, 364, **366**–367, 387

strategetic nuclear conflict, 334, 347–355

subjective power, **257**–258, 259

subnational actors, 86, 87, **94**–107

substantive democracy, **205**, 213

summit meetings, 273, **278**, 279, 280

superpower, **35**, 48, 63, 71, 72, 87, 112, 181, 257, 258, 327, 334, 339, 347, 371

supranational organizations, **55**, 200, **223**–225, 239, 252

substainable development, **46**, 47, 515–554

Sweden, 7, 14, 64, 105, 212, 226, 241, 335

Switzerland, 13–14, 105, 106, 136, 170, 212, 234, 260, 297

Syria, 34, 147, 149, 176, 271, 341, 349, 373

system-level analysis, **23**, 24, 50–79, 81, 320–321

T

Taiwan, 32, 84, 267, 395; China and, 89, 90–93, 267, 270, 272, 280, 281, 284–287; statehood and, 192–193

tariff barriers, 391, 401, 403–404, 420–421, **442**, 444, 450

technology, 26, 30, 33, 94, 325, 333, 399, 401–403; diplomacy and, 274; national power and, 257, 266–268, 288, 416

territoriality, 114, 115, 323, 359

territory, 189, 192, 193, 196, 197, 199–200, 210, 213

terrorism, 89, 149, 306, 307, 329, 334, 340–344

testing, of nuclear weapons, 362, 365, 367, 368, 369, 370, 371, 386

theocracy, 194, **201**, 213

Third World, **503**

Three Gorges Dam, 317–318

Tiananmen Square Massacre, 65, 102, 304

Tibet, 193, 194–195, 201, 280; China and, 57, 90

trade, 137, 160, 165, 173, 211, 212, 219, 220, 291, 292, 297, 316, 390, 391–392, 397, 399–405, 406, 407, 410–412, 420, 425, 426, 430, 432–434, 439, 442–443, 445–447, 450, 453, 454; China and, 20, 287; EU and, 225–226; jobs and, 3–5, 24, 197; states and, 192, 197; U.S. relations with China and, 102–103

transnational actors, 52, **55**–59, 78

transnational advocacy networks (TANs), **55**–58, 164, 167, 170, 187

transnational corporations (TNCs). *See* multinational corporations

transnationalism, **157**–187

transportation, 59, 163–165, 173, 187, 198, 218, 329, 343, 401, 403; national power and, 265–266, 269, 288

travel, 26, 39, 60, 211, 291, 317; diplomacy and, 274, 276–277

Treaty of Amsterdam, **227**, 228, 230

Treaty of Westphalia, 26–27, 32, 47, 198, 200, 210

trilateral countries, **424**

tripolar systems, 61, 62, **63**–64, 66

Turkey, 34, 40, 85, 86, 128, 142, 147, 148, 150, 174, 176, 178, 180, 184

Tutsi, 40, 133, 142, 311–312

two-level game, **95**, **272**, 275

U

Ukraine, 13, 200, 372

unanimity voting, **239**, 252

unemployment, EU and, 231, 429

unipolar systems, 50, 61, 62, 66